Customer Support Information

Plunkett's Real Estate & Construction Industry Almanac 2011

Please register your book immediately...

if you did not purchase it directly from Plunkett Research, Ltd. This will enable us to fulfill your requests for assistance. Also, it will enable us to notify you of future editions.

Your purchase includes access to Book Data and Exports online

As a book purchaser, you can register for free, 1-year, 1-seat online access to the latest data for your book's industry trends, statistics and company profiles. This includes tools to export company data. We are migrating from our former CD-ROMs, for supplemental data and export tools, to the web. Simply send us this registration form, and we will send you a user name and password. In this manner, you will have access to our continual updates during the year. Certain restrictions apply.

_____ YES, please register me as a purchaser of the book.
I did not buy it directly from Plunkett Research, Ltd.

_____ YES, please register me for free online access. I am the actual, original purchaser. (Proof of purchase may be required.)

Customer Name ____

Title____

Organization ____

Address____

City_____________________________State________Zip_____________

Country (if other than USA) _____________________________________

Phone__________________________Fax ___________________________

E-mail ____

Return to: ## Plunkett Research, Ltd.

Attn: Registration
P.O. Drawer 541737, Houston, TX 77254-1737 USA
713.932.0000 · Fax 713.932.7080 · www.plunkettresearch.com
customersupport@plunkettresearch.com

* Purchasers of used books are not eligible to register. Use of online access is subject to the terms of the end user license agreement.

PLUNKETT'S REAL ESTATE & CONSTRUCTION INDUSTRY ALMANAC 2011

The Only Comprehensive Guide to the Real Estate & Construction Industry

Jack W. Plunkett

Published by:
Plunkett Research, Ltd., Houston, Texas
www.plunkettresearch.com

PLUNKETT'S REAL ESTATE & CONSTRUCTION INDUSTRY ALMANAC 2011

Editor and Publisher:
Jack W. Plunkett

Executive Editor and Database Manager:
Martha Burgher Plunkett

Senior Editors and Researchers:
Addie K. FryeWeaver
Christie Manck

Editors, Researchers and Assistants:
Kalonji Bobb
Elizabeth Braddock
Michelle Dotter
Jeremy Faulk
Andrew Olsen
Jill Steinberg
Suzanne Zarosky

Enterprise Accounts Managers:
Emily Hurley
Kelly Burke

Information Technology Manager:
Wenping Guo

E-Commerce Manager:
Alejandra Avila

Video & Graphics Manager:
Geoffrey Trudeau

Special Thanks to:
American Hotel & Lodging Association
National Association of Realtors
National Association of Home Builders
National Bureau of Statistics of China
Real Capital Analytics
U.S. Bureau of Economic Analysis
U.S. Bureau of Labor Statistics
U.S. Census Bureau
U.S. Federal Reserve

Plunkett Research, Ltd.
P. O. Drawer 541737, Houston, Texas 77254, USA
Phone: 713.932.0000 Fax: 713.932.7080 www.plunkettresearch.com

Published by:
Plunkett Research, Ltd.
P. O. Drawer 541737
Houston, Texas 77254-1737

Phone: 713.932.0000
Fax: 713.932.7080
Internet: www.plunkettresearch.com

ISBN13 # 978-1-59392-199-6
(eBook Edition # 978-1-59392-542-0)

Disclaimer of liability
for use and results of use:

PLUNKETT'S
REAL ESTATE & CONSTRUCTION INDUSTRY
ALMANAC 2011

CONTENTS

Continued on the next page

Continued from previous page

A Short Real Estate & Construction Industry Glossary

10-K: An annual report filed by publicly held companies. It provides a comprehensive overview of the company's business and its finances. By law, it must contain specific information and follow a given form, the "Annual Report on Form 10-K." The U.S. Securities and Exchange Commission requires that it be filed within 90 days after fiscal year end. However, these reports are often filed late due to extenuating circumstances. Variations of a 10-K are often filed to indicate amendments and changes. Most publicly held companies also publish an "annual report" that is not on Form 10-K. These annual reports are more informal and are frequently used by a company to enhance its image with customers, investors and industry peers.

Abatement (Property Tax): A decrease in property taxes, due to a problem with the property or to an agreement by taxing authorities to delay taxing the property at full value.

Acceleration Clause: A clause in a contract of debt, such as a mortgage, which causes the entire amount to become due upon the borrower's default.

Accessibility: The degree to which customers can easily get into and out of a shopping center, store or office.

Acre: A measure of land equaling 43,560 square feet.

Adjustable-Rate Mortgage (ARM): A mortgage that changes interest rates periodically to match a specific index.

Adjusted Funds From Operations (AFFO): A measure of cash flow from operations, typically used to gauge REITs. AFFO is the result of subtracting from funds from operations (FFO) certain costs that otherwise would have been capitalized for depreciation, but are actually needed to maintain a property on a day-to-day basis, such as the replacement of carpeting, or leasing expenses such as remodeling allowances.

Air Rights: A sellable right to the air space above a property.

Alt-A: See "Alternative Documentation Mortgage (Alt-A)."

Alternative Documentation Mortgage (Alt-A): An alternative method of documenting a loan file, often referred to as "alt doc" or "Alt-A," that relies on unsubstantiated information provided by the borrower regarding personal income and assets, rather than positive proof such as income tax returns, W2 forms from employers, bank statements and investment account statements.

Amortization Schedule: A printed table showing the principal and interest payments and due dates of the payments owed on a mortgage or loan.

Amortization through Equal Monthly Payments: A repayment method in which the amount borrowed is repaid gradually through regular monthly payments of principal and interest. During the first few years, most of each payment is applied toward the interest owed. During the final years of the loan, payment amounts are applied almost exclusively to the remaining principal.

Anticompetitive Leasing Arrangement: A lease that limits the type and amount of competition a particular retailer faces within a trading area (e.g., a lease that will not allow two supermarkets in one shopping center).

Arbitration: A legal process wherein an impartial third party decides a dispute. This practice is used instead of a standard trial in court.

Assumable Mortgage (Assumable Loan): An existing mortgage that can be assumed by a future purchaser of a piece of real estate.

Atmosphere (Retail Stores): Architecture, layout, signs and displays, color, lighting, music and scents which together create an image of a store in the customer's mind.

Average Daily Rate (ADR): In hotels, room revenue divided by rooms sold.

Baby Boomer: Generally refers to people born in the U.S. and Western Europe from 1946 to 1964. In the U.S., the initial number of Baby Boomers totaled about 78 million. The term evolved to include the children of soldiers and war industry workers who were involved in World War II.

Back-End Ratio: See "Debt-to-Income Ratio (Mortgages)."

Balloon Loan: A loan in which a large payment for the remaining balance is due at the end of the loan.

Balloon Payment: The final principal payment due at the end of a balloon mortgage. Typically, lower monthly payments are provided for under a balloon mortgage, with a substantial final payment due later.

Basis Point: One 100th of 1%.

Below-Market Interest Rate (BMIR): An interest rate that is lower than rates generally charged on similar loans in the marketplace. In real estate, this is typically a subsidized interest rate provided by the Federal Government for low-income housing.

Biennial Payments: Loan payments that are due every other year.

Blanket Mortgage: A mortgage covering at least two pieces of real estate as security for the same mortgage.

Boiler Plate: A standard clause that appears in all similar contracts.

BPO: See "Business Process Outsourcing (BPO)."

BRAC: Base realignment and closure. The process whereby military bases are closed and repurposed into commercial, industrial or other real estate uses.

Branding: A marketing strategy that places a focus on the brand name of a product, service or firm in order to increase the brand's market share, increase sales, establish credibility, improve satisfaction, raise the profile of the firm and increase profits.

BRIC: An acronym representing Brazil, Russia, India and China. The economies of these four countries are seen as some of the fastest growing in the world. A 2003 report by investment bank Goldman Sachs is often credited for popularizing the term; the report suggested that by 2050, BRIC economies will likely outshine those countries which are currently the richest in the world.

B-to-B, or B2B: See "Business-to-Business."

B-to-C, or B2C: See "Business-to-Consumer."

Build-to-Suit: A building created by a landlord specifically for one tenant, designed to suit the tenant's particular needs.

Business Process Outsourcing (BPO): The process of hiring another company to handle business activities. BPO is one of the fastest-growing segments in the offshoring sector. Services include human resources management, billing and purchasing and call centers, as well as many types of customer service or marketing activities, depending on the industry involved. Also, see "Knowledge Process Outsourcing (KPO)."

Business-to-Business: An organization focused on selling products, services or data to commercial customers rather than individual consumers. Also known as B2B.

Business-to-Consumer: An organization focused on selling products, services or data to individual consumers rather than commercial customers. Also known as B2C.

Buy-down (Buydown): With a "temporary" buydown, a lender or homebuilder subsidizes a mortgage by lowering the interest rate during the first few years of the loan. While the payments are initially low, they increase when the subsidy expires. A "permanent" buydown, however, reduces the interest rate over the entire life of the loan.

Buying Power Index (BPI): An index indicating the percentage of total U.S. retail sales occurring in a specific geographic area. Used to forecast demand for new stores and to evaluate the performance of existing stores.

Call Option: 1) A contract giving the holder of an option the right to purchase (and obligating the writer of the option to sell) a specified number of shares of a stock at the given strike price. 2) The right of a lender to demand the outstanding balance of a loan at a given time.

Capital Expenditures: Expenditures to acquire or add to capital assets that will yield benefits over several years.

Capital Gain on Real Estate: The amount of increase in value of a property, other than a primary residence, that is taxable.

Capitalization Rate (Real Estate): A measure of a property's sale price, determined by dividing the annual net income of a property by the purchase price.

Captive Offshoring: Used to describe a company-owned offshore operation. For example, Microsoft owns and operates significant captive offshore research and development centers in China and elsewhere that are offshore from Microsoft's U.S. home base. Also see "Offshoring."

Cash Available for Distribution (CAD): A measure of a REIT's ability to generate cash and to distribute dividends. Also known as FAD (Funds Available for Distribution.)

Caveat Emptor: Latin for "buyer beware." In real estate it is generally incumbent upon the buyer to discover defects with the property unless those defects are known to the seller.

CDO: See "Collateralized Debt Obligation (CDO)."

Central Business District (CBD): The traditional downtown business area of a city or town.

Certificate of Eligibility: The document given to qualified veterans that entitles them to obtain VA-guaranteed loans for homes, businesses and mobile homes. Certificates of eligibility may be obtained by sending Form DD-214 (Separation Paper) to the local VA office with VA form 1880 (request for Certificate of Eligibility).

Certificate of Insurance: A document detailing the insurance coverage provided for a property, asset or business.

Certificate of Occupancy: A document issued by the local government stating that a property is ready for occupancy.

Chattel: An item not attached to the land or buildings in a purchase agreement unless otherwise specified.

CIS: See "Commonwealth of Independent States (CIS)."

Class A Building: The most visible, best-located, most prestigious buildings that rent to tenants at rates above typical buildings in the area.

Class B Building: Typical buildings within a given area, which rent to tenants seeking to pay average rates for the neighborhood. These buildings are well-maintained and well-located but are below the standards of Class A buildings.

Class C Building: Buildings that are maintained and located in a fashion that is satisfactory for tenants seeking to pay rents that are below average for the neighborhood. These buildings have a presence and level of finish that is well below those of Class A or B buildings.

Close-Out Store: A retailer offering low-priced merchandise obtained through liquidations.

Closing: The meeting between the buyer, seller and lender or their agents where the property or asset and funds legally change hands. Also called "settlement."

Closing Costs: Costs associated with the closing of a mortgage, including legal fees, taxes, mortgage application fees and other items.

CMO: See "Collateralized Mortgage Obligation (CMO)."

Collateralized Debt Obligation (CDO): A method of taking a pool of debts, such as mortgages, and selling pieces of that pool to multiple investors. CDOs can also be created for pools of bonds, loans, leases and other types of financial assets.

Collateralized Mortgage Obligation (CMO): A bond that is a debt instrument backed by a pool of underlying mortgages that pass through payments received to the holder of the CMO. A CMO is a popular way to trade large amounts of mortgages at once. The underlying pool may represent thousands of individual mortgages.

Combination Store: A store that combines grocery and drug products in the same building. See "Food/Drug Combo."

Commitment: 1) A promise by a lender to make a loan on specific terms or conditions to a borrower. 2) A promise by an investor to purchase mortgages from a lender with specific terms or conditions. 3) An agreement, often in writing, between a lender and a borrower to loan money at a future date subject to the completion of paperwork or compliance with stated conditions.

Common Area Maintenance (CAM) Assessments: Fees paid to a landlord or property owners association for the maintenance of common areas such as hallways, elevators, exterior lighting, sidewalks or recreational facilities.

Common Areas: Areas shared by tenants or property owners. For example, in a shopping center, the parking lots, sidewalks and hallways are common areas. In a housing development, recreational facilities, greenbelts and hike or bike trails may be common areas.

Commonwealth of Independent States (CIS): An organization consisting of 11 former members of the Soviet Union: Russia, Ukraine, Armenia, Moldova, Georgia, Belarus, Kazakhstan, Uzbekistan, Azerbaijan, Kyrgyzstan and Tajikistan. It was created in 1991. Turkmenistan recently left the Commonwealth as a permanent member, but remained as an associate member. The Commonwealth seeks to coordinate a variety of economic and social policies, including taxation, pricing, customs and economic regulation, as well as to promote the free movement of capital, goods, services and labor.

Community Center: A large shopping center that includes a discount store, specialty department store, super drugstore, home-improvement center and other convenience and shopping goods stores.

Compact Fluorescent Lamp (CFL): A type of light bulb that provides considerable energy savings over traditional incandescent light bulbs.

Condemnation: The claiming of private land by a government for public use or because of code violations. Also see "Eminent Domain."

Condominium: 1) In the travel industry, lodging similar to furnished, private apartments that are available to rent for days or weeks. 2) In real estate, a kind of property ownership in which the owner holds title to an individual unit in a multi-unit dwelling and shares ownership of common areas such as hallways or swimming pools.

Conforming Loan: See "Non-Conforming Loan."

Construction Loan: A short-term interim loan to pay for the construction a building or home. Such loans are usually designed to provide periodic disbursements to the builder as progress with construction is made.

Construction/Permanent Loan: A mortgage loan combining short-term financing of construction with long-term financing of the completed property.

Consumer Price Index (CPI): A measure of the average change in consumer prices over time in a fixed market basket of goods and services, such as food, clothing and housing. The CPI is calculated by the U.S. Federal Government and is considered to be one measure of inflation.

Consumerism: The activities of government, business and independent organizations designed to protect individuals from practices that infringe upon their rights as consumers.

Contract for Deed: A property transaction wherein the seller retains the title to the property until the buyer has paid a certain amount, usually the entire balance owned. This is generally a risky way for a buyer to enter into a purchase.

Convenience Center: A shopping center that typically includes such stores as a convenience store and a dry cleaner.

Convenience Stores: Stores between 3,000 and 8,000 square feet in size providing a limited assortment of merchandise at a convenient location and time (e.g., 7-Eleven). Many also sell gasoline.

Conventional Mortgage: A loan other than a government-financed loan (e.g., a loan that is not a VA mortgage).

Conventional Supermarket: A market that offers a complete line of groceries, meat and produce with a minimum of $2 million in annual revenue, at least 9% of which comes from GM/HBC. Stores typically carry approximately 15,000 items. Many stores offer bakery, deli, banking and other services.

Cooperative (Co-Op): In real estate, a type of multiple ownership in which members of the co-operative own shares in the corporation owning the property. Co-op owners typically have the right to occupy one unit in the co-op building. It is a distinctly different type of ownership from a condominium, wherein each unit's owner takes title to the condominium and then shares ownership of the common areas such as hallways.

Cost Plus Contract: A contract that sets the contractor's compensation as a percentage of the total cost of labor and materials.

Credit Risk: The risk assumed by the lender that the borrower may default on a loan or mortgage. The apparent credit risk is considered when setting an interest rate to be charged.

Customer Relationship Management (CRM): Refers to the automation, via sophisticated software, of business processes involving existing and prospective customers. CRM may cover aspects such as sales (contact management and contact history), marketing (campaign management and telemarketing) and customer service (call center history and field service history). Well known providers of CRM software include Salesforce, which delivers via a Software as a Service model (see "Software as a Service (Saas)"), Microsoft and Siebel, which as been acquired by Oracle.

Debt-to-Income Ratio (Mortgages): Also called the "back-end" ratio, this ratio, expressed as a percentage, is calculated by dividing a borrower's monthly payment obligations on long-term debt (including housing expense) by his or her gross monthly income.

Deed of Trust: In conjunction with a, this instrument is used in many western states to pledge the home or other real estate as security for a loan.

Deferred-Interest Mortgage: A mortgage that defers some of the interest to a later date.

Demographics: The breakdown of the population into statistical categories such as age, income, education and sex.

Department Stores: Very large stores carrying a wide variety and deep assortment while offering considerable customer services (e.g., Dillard's or Saks Fifth Avenue). Stores are organized into separate departments for displaying merchandise. However, the variety of departments has lessened in recent years, and these stores now tend to focus on apparel.

Depreciation: A method of amortizing the cost of an asset in equal dollar amounts over the useful life of an asset. For example, an item with a five-year life would be charged with a certain amount of its cost every year for five years.

Discount Broker: A broker or brokerage firm that executes buy and sell transactions at commission rates lower than a full-service broker or brokerage.

Discount Points (Mortgages): The amount paid either to maintain or to lower the interest rate charged on a mortgage. Each point is equal to 1% of the loan amount. (For example, two points on a $100,000 mortgage would equal $2,000.)

Discount Store: A general merchandise retailer offering a wide variety of merchandise, limited service and low prices (e.g., Target or Kmart).

Discount-Anchored Center: A shopping center that contains one or more discount stores plus smaller retail tenants.

Distributed Power Generation: A method of generating electricity at or near the site where it will be consumed, such as the use of small, local generators or fuel cells to power individual buildings, homes or neighborhoods. Distributed power is thought by many analysts to offer distinct advantages. For example, electricity generated in this manner is not reliant upon the grid for distribution to the end user.

Down Payment: The difference between the purchase price and that portion of the purchase price being financed.

DownREIT: A structure that enables an REIT to acquire properties in exchange for partnership units.

Earnest Money: Good faith money provided to the seller by the potential buyer to show that he or she is serious about purchasing a piece of real estate. This amount can be applied to the purchase at closing, but if the deal does not go through it may be forfeited, or in some cases returned, depending on the terms of the purchase contract.

Easement: A right of way giving persons other than the owner access to a property. A common use is to provide a driveway through one property owner's land for access to an adjacent property.

Echo Boomers: See "Generation Y."

E-Commerce: The use of online, Internet-based sales methods. The phrase is used to describe both business-to-consumer and business-to-business sales.

Eminent Domain: The right of a governmental unit to force an owner to sell his or her property for fair market value for public use. This is the legal basis for the condemnation of private property. For example, if a state needs property for the construction or widening of a highway, it may condemn the needed property under this feature of the law.

Encroachment: An intrusion onto a property. For example, if one property owner erects a fence along his property border and fails to properly stay inside of his property line, a portion of the fence lies on the adjacent property, forming an encroachment.

Encumbrance: Any claim on a title or property that might prevent the owner from passing good title at a sale.

End Caps: Display fixtures located at the end of an aisle. Also, in real estate, the end unit or corner unit in a shopping center.

Enterprise Resource Planning (ERP): An integrated information system that helps manage all aspects of a business, including accounting, ordering and human resources, typically across all locations of a major corporation or organization. ERP is considered to be a critical tool for management of large organizations. Suppliers of ERP tools include SAP and Oracle.

Equal Credit Opportunity Act (ECOA): A federal law that requires lenders to make credit equally available without discrimination based on race, religion, national origin, age, sex, marital status or receipt of income from public assistance programs.

Equity: 1) The net value of the common stockholders' interest in a company as listed on a company's balance sheet. 2) The difference between a company's assets and liabilities (it is possible for a company to have negative equity). 3) The difference between the value of a property and the amount owed on that property. 4) A share of stock.

Equity REIT: A REIT that owns real estate, as opposed to an REIT that specializes in making mortgage loans.

ERP: See "Enterprise Resource Planning (ERP)."

Escrow Account: A mortgage lender's method of accounting for escrow monies received from the borrower. See "Escrow(s)."

Escrow Waiver Fee: A fee paid by a home mortgage borrower who elects to pay insurance and property taxes directly, rather than paying them into an escrow account at the mortgage company. There is a one-time charge by the mortgage company of 0.25% to 0.375% of the loan amount.

Escrow(s): That portion of a borrower's monthly payments held by the lender or servicer to pay for taxes, hazard insurance, mortgage insurance and other items as they become due. Also known as impound(s).

EU: See "European Union (EU)."

EU Competence: The jurisdiction in which the European Union (EU) can take legal action.

European Union (EU): A consolidation of European countries (member states) functioning as one body to facilitate trade. Previously known as the European Community (EC), the EU expanded to include much of Eastern Europe in 2004, raising the total number of member states to 25. In 2002, the EU launched a unified currency, the Euro. See europa.eu.int.

Expense Ratio: The comparison of the cost of operating a property, business or organization to its gross income.

Facilities Management: The management of a company's physical buildings and/or information systems on an outsourced basis.

Factory Outlet Stores: Off-price retail stores owned by manufacturers.

Fair Credit Reporting Act: A consumer protection law that regulates consumer credit report providers. For example, the act sets up procedures for correcting mistakes on an individual's credit record, provides certain restrictions on publishing credit reports and generally governs a consumer's rights.

Fair Market Value (FMV): A term used to indicate the value of a property on the open market.

Fannie Mae: See "Federal National Mortgage Association (FNMA)."

Farmers Home Administration (FmHA): A part of the U.S. Department of Agriculture that provides financing for farmers and residents of rural areas.

Federal Home Loan Bank Board (FHLBB): The agency of the federal government that supervises all federal savings and loan associations and federally insured state-chartered savings and loan associations. The FHLBB also operates the Federal Savings and Loan Insurance Corporation, which insures accounts at federal savings and loan associations and those state-chartered associations that apply and are accepted. In addition, the FHLBB directs the Federal Home Loan Bank System, which provides a flexible credit facility for member savings institutions to promote the availability of home financing. The FHL Banks also own the Federal Home Loan Mortgage Corporation, established in 1970 to promote secondary markets for mortgages.

Federal Home Loan Mortgage Corporation (FHLMC): A U.S. government-sponsored agency that purchases conventional mortgages from lending institutions, thus adding liquidity to the market. Also known as "Freddie Mac."

Federal Housing Administration (FHA): An agency of the U.S. Department of Housing and Urban Development (HUD). The FHA primarily insures housing loans.

Federal National Mortgage Association (FNMA): A major, government-sponsored investor that purchases mortgage loans from mortgage bankers. It is similar to FHLMC. Also known as "Fannie Mae."

Fee Simple: Absolute or sole ownership of a property.

FHA: See "Federal Housing Administration (FHA)."

FHLMC: See "Federal Home Loan Mortgage Corporation (FHLMC)."

First Mortgage: The mortgage that has legal precedence over other mortgage claims, usually, but not always, chronologically first in the history of the property. Also see "Second Mortgage."

Fixed-Rate Mortgage or Loan: A mortgage (or loan) that has an interest rate that does not change over the life of the loan.

FmHA: See "Farmers Home Administration (FmHA)."

FNMA: See "Federal National Mortgage Association (FNMA)."

Food/Drug Combo: A superstore and drug store that share checkout lanes. GM/HBC (General Merchandise/Health and Beauty Care) takes up at least one-third of retail space in the store, and accounts for 15% or more of revenue. Food/drug combos offer pharmacy services.

Forbearance (Mortgages): A temporary reprieve from paying a mortgage, usually granted because of some kind of hardship.

Foreclosure: The process whereby a borrower in default under a mortgage is deprived of his or her interest in a property, which is taken away by the lender via a legal procedure.

Franchise: 1) A contractual agreement between a franchisor (for example, a company or organization owning all rights to a brand, type of business, retail operation, restaurant concept or sports league) and a franchisee (person or organization desiring to license the use of those rights for a specific purpose within a specific region) that allows the franchisee to operate a retail outlet or other type of business using a brand, trade secrets, formulas and format developed and supported by the franchisor. Typically, a franchisee pays an upfront fee and then continuing fees to the franchisor. 2) A generic term used to describe a very well established business or brand.

Franchisee: See "Franchise."

Franchisor: See "Franchise."

Freddie Mac: See "Federal Home Loan Mortgage Corporation (FHLMC)."

Free-Standing Retailer: A location for a retailer that is a building by itself, frequently on a pad site in front of a shopping center.

Front-End Ratio: See "Housing-Expenses-to-Income Ratio."

Full-Service Leasing: A program under which a vehicle or building is leased and the operation and maintenance are included in the lease fee.

GDP: See "Gross Domestic Product (GDP)."

General Merchandise, Apparel, Furniture and Other (GAFO): Usually used in reference to the retail sector, excluding automotive and food stores, and includes general merchandise, department, discount apparel, furniture and miscellaneous specialty stores.

Generation X: A loosely-defined and variously-used term that describes people born in the U.S. and Canada between approximately 1965 and 1980, but other time frames are recited. Generation X is often referred to as a group influential in defining tastes in consumer goods, entertainment and/or political and social matters.

Generation Y: Refers to people born between approximately 1980 and 2000, who number about 50 million in the U.S. They are also known as Echo Boomers, Millenials or the Millenial Generation. These are children of the Baby Boom generation who will be filling the work force as Baby Boomers retire.

Geological Information System (GIS): A computer software system which captures, stores, updates, manipulates, analyzes, and displays all forms of geographically referenced information.

Ginnie Mae: See "Government National Mortgage Association (GNMA)."

Globalization: The increased mobility of goods, services, labor, technology and capital throughout the world. Although globalization is not a new development, its pace has increased with the advent of new technologies, especially in the areas of telecommunications, finance and shipping.

GM/HBC: General Merchandise/Health and Beauty Care.

GNMA: See "Government National Mortgage Association (GNMA)."

Good Faith Estimate: A written estimate of closing costs that a lender must provide for the borrower within three days of submitting a new loan application.

Government National Mortgage Association (GNMA): A government-owned corporation within the U.S. Department of Housing and Urban Development (HUD) that specializes in the purchase of FHA and VA loans. Also known as "Ginnie Mae."

Graduated Payment Mortgage (GPM): A type of flexible-payment mortgage where the payments increase for a specified period of time and then level off. This type of mortgage has negative amortization built into it. For example, a homebuyer who believes that his or her income may increase a few years later may enter into a mortgage that has lower payments in the first five years but substantially higher monthly payments later in the loan.

Gross Domestic Product (GDP): The total value of a nation's output, income and expenditures produced with a nation's physical borders.

Gross Leasable Area (GLA): The total space that is leasable in a property. GLA may include common areas. Also see "Net Leasable Area (NLA)."

Gross National Product (GNP): A country's total output of goods and services from all forms of economic activity measured at market prices for one calendar year. It differs from Gross Domestic Product (GDP) in that GNP includes income from investments made in foreign nations.

Hard-Lines: Durable, non-apparel items, such as furniture, appliances and housewares.

Hectare (ha): A measurement of area equal to 10,000 square meters or 2.471 acres.

Historic District: A zoning classification for neighborhoods of historic value. This classification may limit what changes an owner can make to the property. For example, the colors of exterior paint or types of doors, windows and fences that may be used may be regulated.

Home Equity Loan: A fixed- or adjustable-rate loan obtained for a variety of purposes, secured by the equity in a home. Interest paid is usually tax-deductible. Often used for home improvement or the freeing of equity for investment. Home equity loans are tax-advantaged alternatives to consumer loans whose interest is not tax-deductible, such as auto or boat loans, credit card debt, medical debt and education loans.

Home Improvement Center: A category specialist combining the traditional hardware store and lumberyard (e.g., Home Depot).

Home Inspection: A thorough inspection by a professional that ensures that a property is mechanically and structurally sound. Home inspectors generally are licensed by the states in which they work.

Homeowners' Association: A nonprofit association that manages the common areas of a housing development or condominium project. In addition to owning and maintaining common areas, it may enforce deed restrictions and covenants.

Housing-Expenses-to-Income Ratio: Used in evaluating the income of a potential mortgage borrower. It is calculated by dividing the anticipated housing expense by the gross monthly income of the borrower. Also known as the "front-end" ratio.

HUD: The Department of Housing and Urban Development, a U.S. Government agency. HUD's mission is to increase homeownership, support community development and increase access to affordable housing free from discrimination.

HUD-I Settlement Statement: A form utilized at mortgage closing to itemize the costs associated with purchasing a home. Used universally by mandate of HUD (the U.S. Department of Housing and Urban Development).

Hybrid Mortgage: A type of mortgage that includes some compensation to the lender, such as a portion of income, in addition to the principal and interest on the loan.

Hybrid REIT: A REIT that combines the strategies of both an equity REIT and a mortgage REIT.

Hypermarket: A very large retail store that offers low prices and combines a discount store and a superstore food retailer in one warehouse-like building (e.g., a Wal-Mart Supercenter). These stores may be as large as 200,000 square feet.

Implied Equity Market Cap (REITs): The market value of all outstanding common stock of a company plus the value of all UPREIT partnership units as if they had been converted into stock.

Independent Retailer: A retailer that owns only one or a few retail stores and is not part of a large chain.

Indexed Lease: A rental agreement whereby the rent changes in accordance with a certain index, such as the consumer price index.

Industry Code: A descriptive code assigned to any company in order to group it with firms that operate in similar businesses. Common industry codes include the NAICS (North American Industrial Classification System) and the SIC (Standard Industrial Classification), both of which are standards widely used in America, as well as the International Standard Industrial Classification of all Economic Activities (ISIC), the Standard International Trade Classification established by the United Nations (SITC) and the General Industrial Classification of Economic Activities within the European Communities (NACE).

Infrastructure: 1) The equipment that comprises a system. 2) Public-use assets such as roads, bridges, sewers and other assets necessary for public accommodation and utilities. 3) The underlying base of a system or network.

Initial Public Offering (IPO): A company's first effort to sell its stock to investors (the public). Investors in an up-trending market eagerly seek stocks offered in many IPOs because the stocks of newly public companies that seem to have great promise may appreciate very rapidly in price, reaping great profits for those who were able to get the stock at the first offering. In the United States, IPOs are regulated by the SEC (U.S. Securities Exchange Commission) and by the state-level regulatory agencies of the states in which the IPO shares are offered.

Intellectual Property (IP): The exclusive ownership of original concepts, ideas, designs, engineering plans or other assets that are protected by law. Examples include items covered by trademarks, copyrights and patents. Items such as software, engineering plans, fashion designs and architectural designs, as well as games, books, songs and other entertainment items are among the many things that may be considered to be intellectual property. (Also, see "Patent.")

Interim Loan: A loan that provides proceeds for the construction costs of a project. Often paid out in installments as the work progresses.

Interstate Sales Full Disclosure Act: A law that requires a residential development of 100 or more lots to file a disclosure statement with HUD.

IP: See "Intellectual Property (IP)."

Jumbo Loan: Also known as "non-conforming" loans, mortgage loans over the maximum "conforming" amount as set by FNMA are considered jumbo and are subject to different underwriting criteria. The benchmark loan amount is evaluated on a yearly basis by FNMA and adjusted accordingly. Interest rates on jumbo loans are generally 0.25% higher than their conforming counterparts. Also see "Non-Conforming Loan."

Knowledge Process Outsourcing (KPO): The use of outsourced and/or offshore workers to perform business tasks that require judgment and analysis. Examples include such professional tasks as patent research, legal research, architecture, design, engineering, market research, scientific research, accounting and tax return preparation. Also, see "Business Process Outsourcing (BPO)."

LAC: An acronym for Latin America and the Caribbean.

LDCs: See "Least Developed Countries (LDCs)."

Leased Department: A department in a retail store operated by an outside party. The outside party either pays fixed rent or a percentage of sales to the retailer for the space.

Least Developed Countries (LDCs): Nations determined by the U.N. Economic and Social Council to be the poorest and weakest members of the international community. There are currently 50 LDCs, of which 34 are in Africa, 15 are in Asia Pacific and the remaining one (Haiti) is in Latin America. The top 10 on the LDC list, in descending order from top to 10th, are Afghanistan, Angola, Bangladesh, Benin, Bhutan, Burkina Faso, Burundi, Cambodia, Cape Verde and the Central African Republic. Sixteen of the LDCs are also Landlocked

Least Developed Countries (LLDCs) which present them with additional difficulties often due to the high cost of transporting trade goods. Eleven of the LDCs are Small Island Developing States (SIDS), which are often at risk of extreme weather phenomenon (hurricanes, typhoons, Tsunami); have fragile ecosystems; are often dependent on foreign energy sources; can have high disease rates for HIV/AIDS and malaria; and can have poor market access and trade terms.

Legal Description: A description of a property that fulfills legal requirements and properly identifies the property. A legal description is commonly used in conjunction with a boundary survey. Also see "Survey (Real Estate)."

Lifestyle Center: An open-air, highly landscaped configuration of approximately 50 stores. Generally located near upscale neighborhoods, lifestyle centers offer leasable retail area of 150,000 to 500,000 square feet (typically, at least 50,000 square feet are dedicated to upscale national specialty stores).

Limited-Assortment Store: A small, low-priced grocery store that provides limited service, few or no perishables and generally fewer than 2,000 items.

Loan Application Fee: A lender's fee, usually ranging from $75 to $300, which the buyer must pay when applying for a mortgage.

Loan Origination Fee: A fee charged by the lender for processing a mortgage or loan. The mortgage industry standard is 1% of the loan amount, but if the application is taken over the Internet, it is often reduced to 0.5% or even zero, depending on the lender.

Loan-to-Value Ratio (LTV): An underwriting ratio determined by dividing the sales price or appraised value into the loan amount, expressed as a percentage. For example, with a sales price of $100,000 and a mortgage loan of $80,000, the LTV ratio would be 80%. Loans with an LTV over 80% usually require private mortgage insurance. See "Private Mortgage Insurance (PMI)."

Lock (Lock In): A commitment that a borrower obtains from a lender assuring a particular interest rate for a limited time period, such as 30 days. A lock provides protection to the borrower should interest rates rise between the time the borrower applies for a loan, acquires loan approval and, subsequently, closes the purchase.

LOHAS: Lifestyles of Health and Sustainability. A marketing term that refers to consumers who choose to purchase and/or live with items that are natural, organic, less polluting, etc. Such consumers may also prefer products powered by alternative energy, such as hybrid cars.

Low-E: A coating for windows that can prevent warmth from escaping from the inside of a building during the winter, while preventing solar heat from entering the building during the summer. Significant savings in energy usage can result.

Market Segmentation: The division of a consumer market into specific groups of buyers based on demographic factors.

Market Value: An estimation of how much a property or asset would sell for on the open market.

Marketing: Includes all planning and management activities and expenses associated with the promotion of a product or service. Marketing can encompass advertising, customer surveys, public relations and many other disciplines. Marketing is distinct from selling, which is the process of sell-through to the end user.

Material Breach: The violation of a contract that causes invalidation or some other penalty.

Megapolitan: Massive corridors comprising several million residents across several cities. Examples include the IH35 Corridor anchored by Dallas and Ft. Worth, Texas, and the Atlantic Coast corridor anchored by Miami, Ft. Lauderdale and Boca Raton, Florida.

Mill: One 10th of a penny. Usually used in real estate taxation.

Millenials: See "Generation Y."

Mineral Interests: The rights of ownership to gas, oil or other minerals as they naturally occur at or below a tract of land. Also known as "mineral rights."

Mineral Rights: See "Mineral Interests."

MIP: See "Mortgage Insurance Premium (MIP)."

Mixed-Use Development: A development that has some combination of residential, office, retail and/or industrial space.

Mortgage Banker: An organization that specializes in underwriting mortgage loans. Mortgage bankers typically sell some or all of their loans to investors but may continue to own and/or service them. Also see "Mortgage Broker."

Mortgage Broker: An organization in the business of arranging funding for a borrower. In contrast to a mortgage banker, a broker does not actually loan the money. Brokers usually charge a fee or receive a commission for their services.

Mortgage Insurance Premium (MIP): Insurance purchased by the borrower to insure the lender against loss should he or she default. MIP is paid on government-insured loans (FHA or VA loans) regardless of the LTV (loan-to-value ratio). Should the borrower pay off a government-insured loan in advance of maturity, he or she may be entitled to a small refund of MIP. Also see "Private Mortgage Insurance (PMI)."

Mortgage REIT: A REIT that specializes in making mortgages rather than owning property outright.

Mortgage-Backed Security (MBS): A security that represents ownership of an undivided interest in a group of mortgages. Mortgage bankers often form MBSs in order to sell pools of their mortgages on the secondary market. Also see "Collateralized Debt Obligation (CDO)."

Municipal Utility District (MUD): A political unit, regulated by state authorities, that has been established to own and operate utilities within its boundaries. These utilities typically include water, sewer and/or drainage. MUDs may be inside or outside of city limits. MUDs generally are empowered to sell bonds in order to raise capital with which to install utility pipes and systems. Property owners within a MUD pay regular fees to the MUD for services.

NAICS: North American Industrial Classification System. See "Industry Code."

National Flood Insurance Program (NFIP): A program offered by the Federal Emergency Management Association (FEMA) that provides flood insurance to individual property owners and tenants.

Negative Amortization: Amortization in which the payments made are insufficient to fund complete repayment of the loan at its termination. This usually occurs when the increase in the monthly payment on an adjustable-rate mortgage (ARM) is limited by a pre-set ceiling. The portion of the payment that should be paid is added to the remaining balance owed. The balance owed may increase rather than decrease at various times in the life of the loan.

Neighborhood Center: A shopping center that includes a supermarket, drugstore, home-improvement center or variety store. Neighborhood centers often include small stores, such as apparel, shoe, camera and other shopping goods stores.

Net Leasable Area (NLA): The square footage in a building or property that is leasable excluding common areas, common hallways, common baths, etc. Also, see "Gross Leasable Area (GLA)."

Net Lease: A lease that requires all maintenance expenses, such as heating, insurance and interior repair, to be paid for by the tenant.

New Urbanism: A relatively new term that refers to neighborhood developments that feature shorter blocks, more sidewalks and pedestrian ways, access to convenient mass transit, bicycle paths and conveniently placed open spaces. The intent is to promote walking and social interaction while decreasing automobile traffic. The concept may also include close proximity to stores and offices that may be reached by walking rather than driving.

Non-Conforming Loan: A loan that is not eligible to be purchased by Fannie Mae or Freddie Mac. These loan agencies have specific upper limits on how large a loan they will buy. These limits are adjusted on a regular basis. Also, several other factors regarding the loan must meet guidelines before they are considered to conform. Also see "Jumbo Loan."

Non-Store Retailing: A form of retailing that is not store-based. Non-store retailing can be conducted through vending machines, direct-selling, direct-marketing, party-based selling, catalogs, television programming, telemarketing and Internet-based selling.

OECD: See "Organisation for Economic Co-operation and Development (OECD)."

Office of Interstate Land Sales Registration: The HUD agency that is responsible for implementing the Interstate Sales Full Disclosure Act.

Off-Price Retailer: A retailer that offers an inconsistent assortment of brand-name, fashion-oriented soft goods at low prices.

Offshoring: The rapidly growing tendency among U.S., Japanese and Western European firms to send knowledge-based and manufacturing work overseas. The intent is to take advantage of lower wages and operating costs in such nations as China, India, Hungary and Russia. The choice of a nation for offshore work may be influenced by such factors as language and education of the local workforce, transportation systems or natural resources. For example, China and India are graduating high numbers of skilled engineers and scientists from their universities. Also, some nations are noted for large numbers of workers skilled in the English language, such as the Philippines and India. Also see "Captive Offshoring" and "Outsourcing."

Option ARM: An adjustable rate mortgage that lets the borrower decide how much to pay each month. The borrower may choose between the standard principal and interest amount, or simply pay the interest. Some plans allow the borrower to pay even less, adding the unpaid interest to the total amount due under the note.

Organisation for Economic Co-operation and Development (OECD): A group of more than 30 nations that are strongly committed to the market economy and democracy. Some of the OECD members include Japan, the U.S., Spain, Germany, Australia, Korea, the U.K., Canada and Mexico. Although not members, Estonia, Israel and Russia are invited to member talks; and Brazil, China, India, Indonesia and South Africa have enhanced engagement policies with the OECD. The Organisation provides statistics, as well as social and economic data; and researches social changes, including patterns in evolving fiscal policy, agriculture, technology, trade, the environment and other areas. It publishes over 250 titles annually;

publishes a corporate magazine, the OECD Observer; has radio and TV studios; and has centers in Tokyo, Washington, D.C., Berlin and Mexico City that distributed the Organisation's work and organizes events.

Outsourcing: The hiring of an outside company to perform a task otherwise performed internally by the company, generally with the goal of lowering costs and/or streamlining work flow. Outsourcing contracts are generally several years in length. Companies that hire outsourced services providers often prefer to focus on their core strengths while sending more routine tasks outside for others to perform. Typical outsourced services include the running of human resources departments, telephone call centers and computer departments. When outsourcing is performed overseas, it may be referred to as offshoring. Also see "Offshoring."

Owner Financing: A mortgage transaction whereby the property seller provides some or all of the financing and takes back a mortgage loan at closing.

Pad Site: A location for a free-standing retail building that sits in front of a mall or shopping center.

Participating Mortgage: A mortgage in which the lender is entitled to a share of the income from the property.

Passive Solar: A system in which solar energy (heat from sunlight) alone is used for the transfer of thermal energy. Heat transfer devices that depend on energy other than solar are not used. A good example is a passive solar water heater on the roof of a building.

Pass-Through (Mortgages): See "Collateralized Mortgage Obligation (CMO)."

Patent: An intellectual property right granted by a national government to an inventor to exclude others from making, using, offering for sale, or selling the invention throughout that nation or importing the invention into the nation for a limited time in exchange for public disclosure of the invention when the patent is granted. In addition to national patenting agencies, such as the United States Patent and Trademark Office, and regional organizations such as the European Patent Office, there is a cooperative international patent organization, the World Intellectual Property Organization, or WIPO, established by the United Nations.

Percentage Lease: A lease in which rent payments are based on a store's sales.

Photovoltaic (PV) Cell: An electronic device consisting of layers of semiconductor materials fabricated to form a junction (adjacent layers of materials with different electronic characteristics) and electrical contacts, capable of converting incident light directly into electricity (direct current). Photovoltaic technology works by harnessing the movement of electrons between the layers of a solar cell when the sun strikes the material.

PITI: Principal, interest, taxes and insurance: the elements of a monthly mortgage payment.

Planned Unit Development (PUD): A housing subdivision that contains pre-planned community features, such as parks or adjacent office or retail districts. The common space is owned by a homeowners' association.

Power Shopping Center: A large, open-air shopping center with the majority of space leased to several well-known anchor retail tenants-typically specialty retailers operating large stores that specialize in one type of merchandise. Typical anchor tenants include OfficeMax, Linens 'n Things, Marshall's and Best Buy. Some of these tenants may be on pad sites. Convenient access and parking are emphasized. These centers usually sit on major intersections.

PPP: See "Purchasing Power Parity (PPP) or Point-to-Point Protocol (PPP)."

Prefabricated (Construction): A term for buildings erected onsite from factory-made components, or built entirely offsite and then set down on the property. A mobile home is prefabricated. However, a few manufacturers factory-build certain types of houses and buildings that are not considered in the same class as mobile homes.

Pre-Paid Expenses: At closing of a real estate purchase, monies necessary to create an escrow account. These typically include two month's worth of taxes, hazard insurance, private mortgage insurance and special assessments.

Pre-Paid Interest: The amount of interest paid to cover the period from the closing of a sale until the beginning of the first payment on the mortgage or loan.

Pre-Payment (Prepayment): The unscheduled payment of all or part of the outstanding principal of a loan or mortgage. Pre-payments are typically made, by the borrower, but may also result by foreclosures, condemnations or casualties, such as an insurance settlement resulting from a total loss by fire or flood.

Pre-Payment Penalty (Prepayment Penalty): A penalty found in a promissory note or mortgage, imposed by the lender if the principal of a loan is paid before it is due, thereby reducing the lender's stream of interest earned on the note.

Pre-Payment Privilege: The right to repay the principal of a loan before interest is due.

Pre-Payment Risk: The possibility that the mortgages underlying a mortgage-backed security are repaid faster or more slowly than expected.

Pre-Qualification (Mortgages): The process of determining how much money a prospective property buyer will be eligible to borrow before actually applying for a loan.

Private Mortgage Insurance (PMI): Insurance paid on those loans that are not government-insured when the loan to value ratio is greater than 80%. When you have accumulated 20% of your home's value as equity, your lender may waive PMI at your request. Note that such insurance does not constitute a form of life insurance that pays off the loan in case of death. Also see "Mortgage Insurance Premium (MIP)."

PUD: See "Planned Unit Development (PUD)."

Purchasing Power Parity (PPP): A comparative monetary calculation. PPP is used to attempt to account for differences in local prices in a given country such as Mexico, China or Indonesia, compared to prices for similar items in, for example, America. That is, it's an effort to compare apples to apples. PPP is difficult to compute. For instance, to attempt to evaluate an emerging nation's total GDP on this basis, a value, in American dollars, has to be assigned to all goods and services produced in that country. Analysts use PPP as an educated guess as to how much money someone has to earn, in local currency, to enjoy certain consumer goods or a certain level of lifestyle.

R&D-Flex Building: Industrial-type buildings that are designed to satisfy tenants that require an above-average amount of office space as well as an above-average level of finish that presents a more office-like environment, such as more windows and better landscape. From 30% to 100% of the space in such buildings may be devoted to office or laboratory space, with the balance devoted to light assembly or warehouse space.

Radon: A radioactive gas that may cause health problems. Some state laws require that a property owner disclose any known radon gas conditions. Concerned buyers may include testing for radon in their property inspections.

Real Estate Investment Trust (REIT): Investments that work in a manner very similar to mutual funds in that money from several investors is pooled together to jointly own real estate and/or invest in mortgages. REITs are required to distribute almost all (90%) of their net income annually, directly to shareholders. Many REITs specialize in a specific kind of real estate, such as shopping centers or apartments. Investors generally buy shares in REITs with a two-fold purpose: 1) to earn current income and 2) for long-term capital gains on appreciation in the value of the real estate.

Real Estate Investment Trust Act of 1960: The federal law that established guidelines for establishing REITs.

Real Estate Settlement Procedures Act (RESPA): A federal law that allows consumers to review information on known or estimated settlement costs. A statement of estimated costs must be provided by the lender once after a mortgage application has been completed and once again prior to or at closing.

Refinancing: In mortgages, refinancing is the process of paying off an existing mortgage with a new mortgage, often to attain a certain interest rate or to obtain cash from the transaction by increasing the principal balance.

Regional Center: A shopping center or mall which includes up to three department stores plus shopping or specialty stores rather than convenience stores. Super-regionals are similar but have at least four department stores and at least 1 million square feet of retail space.

Regulation Z: A federal rule that requires a lender to disclose the terms of a loan to the borrower.

REIT Modernization Act of 1999: The federal law that enabled an REIT to own up to 100% of the stock of a taxable subsidiary that provides services to REIT tenants and other customers. The law also changed the minimum distribution requirement from 95% to 90% of a REIT's taxable income.

RESPA: See "Real Estate Settlement Procedures Act (RESPA)."

Retail Chain: A firm that consists of multiple retail units under common ownership and usually has some centralization of decision-making in defining and implementing its strategy.

Return on Investment (ROI): A measure of a company's profitability, expressed in percentage as net profit (after taxes) divided by total dollar investment.

Revenue Per Available Room (REVPAR): A hotel performance measure that divides revenue by the number of available rooms, as opposed to the number of occupied rooms.

Reverse Mortgage: Enables older homeowners (aged 62+) to convert part of the equity in their homes into tax-free income without having to sell the home, give up title, or take on a new monthly mortgage payment. The lender provides either a line of credit, steady monthly payments or one upfront payment to the borrower. In return, the lender receives a right to proceeds upon the eventual sale of the home, typically after the borrower's death. There are no monthly payments to be made by the borrower, and there are no income or health requirements. Sometimes called a reverse annuity mortgage or RAM.

Right of Rescission: The legal right to void or cancel a mortgage contract in such a way as to treat the contract as if it never existed. Right of rescission is not applicable to mortgages made to purchase a home, but may be applicable to other mortgages, such as cash-out refinances.

Robosigning: An illegal practice of signing documents without verifying the information therein. Robosigning was common during the high volume of real estate foreclosures conducted in 2009 and 2010.

R-Value (R Value): A method of measuring the effectiveness of building materials such as insulation. Technically, it is the resistance that a material has to heat flow. The higher the R-Value, the better the insulation provided. It is the inverse of U-Value. See "U-Value (U Value)."

Sales Per Square Foot of Selling Space: Net sales divided by square feet of selling space.

Same-Store Sales: Sales dollars generated only by those stores that have been open more than a year and have historical data to compare this year's sales to the same time-frame last year.

Savings and Loan (S&L, Thrift, Savings Association, Savings Bank): Depository institution historically engaged primarily in accepting consumer savings deposits and in originating and investing in securities and residential mortgage loans; now may offer checking-type deposits and make a wider range of loans. Federally-chartered and federally-insured savings and loans are supervised by the Federal Home Loan Bank Board (FHLBB).

Second Mortgage: A mortgage with collateralization rights that is secondary to a first mortgage. In the event that the borrower defaults, the second mortgage holder may be forced to pay off the first mortgage in order to protect the second mortgage's interests in the property. Second mortgages involve more risks to the mortgage holder and generally are written at higher interest rates. It is also possible to create third or fourth mortgages, etc.

Secondary Market: A market providing for securities to be bought or sold. This market is where the majority of trading occurs. The New York Stock Exchange, all other stock exchanges and the bond markets are secondary markets. In mortgages, large pools of mortgages are bought and sold by major investors in the secondary market.

Securitization: The process of financing a pool of similar assets (such as mortgages, automobile loans, corporate debt instruments or credit card debts) by issuing to investors interests in the funds generated by that pool. Such pools are generally in the range of

$100 million or higher, and may represent the debts of dozens of companies or thousands of consumers. Securitization enables banks and other lenders to have ready markets into which they may sell loans that they generate.

Servicing (Mortgages): The steps and operations necessary to manage a mortgage or pool of mortgages, such as the collection of payments and the disbursement of escrowed funds for taxes and insurance. Servicing also includes following up on delinquent borrowers and foreclosure, if necessary. Servicing companies charge a fee to the investor that owns the loan.

Shared-Appreciation Mortgage: A loan that provides a share of the appreciation of the value of the property to the lender. Such loans are typically written at below-market interest rates.

SIC: Standard Industrial Classification. See "Industry Code."

Smart Buildings: Buildings or homes that have been designed with interconnected electronic sensors and electrical systems which can be controlled by computers. Advantages include the ability to turn appliances and systems on or off remotely or on a set schedule, leading to greatly enhanced energy efficiency.

Soft Goods: Apparel and linens.

Software as a Service (SaaS): Refers to the practice of providing users with software applications that are hosted on remote servers and accessed via the Internet. Excellent examples include the CRM (Customer Relationship Management) software provided in SaaS format by Salesforce. An earlier technology that operated in a similar, but less sophisticated, manner was called ASP or Application Service Provider.

Specialty Department Store: A store with a department store format that focuses on apparel and soft home goods (e.g., Neiman Marcus).

Specialty Store: A store specializing in one category of merchandising, frequently fashion-related.

Straight-Lining (Real Estate): Required by GAAP (Generally Accepted Accounting Principles),

straight-lining averages a tenant's rent payments over the life of a lease.

Strip Center: A small shopping center that includes several adjacent stores located along a major street or highway.

Subprime: A term used to describe mortgages offered to borrowers with less than perfect credit. Subprime rates are generally higher than typical interest rates.

Subsidiary, Wholly-Owned: A company that is wholly controlled by another company through stock ownership.

Super Warehouse: A large, high-volume warehouse store that offers expanded services similar to a superstore, such as a service deli and bakery. These stores typically focus largely on food and drug items, and offer reduced prices on merchandise.

Super-Regionals: See "Regional Center."

Superstore: A large specialty store, usually over 40,000 square feet. Many superstores focus on a particular field of merchandise. For example, BestBuy is a consumer electronics superstore.

Supply Chain: The complete set of suppliers of goods and services required for a company to operate its business. For example, a manufacturer's supply chain may include providers of raw materials, components, custom-made parts and packaging materials.

Survey (Real Estate): A technical drawing that shows the precise legal boundaries of a property. Also known as a boundary survey. Surveys are generally recognized only when they are drawn by licensed professionals known as registered surveyors. Also see "Legal Description."

Sustainable Development: Development that ensures that the use of resources and the environment today does not impair their availability to be used by future generations.

Sweat Equity: In mortgages, sweat equity created by a purchaser performing work on a property being purchased.

Three/Two (3/2) Option: An alternative mortgage plan that enables households whose earnings are no more than 100% of the median income in their regional area to make a 3% down payment with their own funds, coupled with a 2% gift from a relative or a 2% grant or unsecured loan from a nonprofit agency or state or local government program.

Time-share (Timeshare): A type of joint ownership in which a group of owners share a particular piece of property, agreeing to have use of the property only during set days each year. Typically, time-share properties are vacation properties in such areas as beach resorts or ski resorts. They typically are condominium properties in which each condominium is jointly owned by a large group of people. Each owner typically has access to one week's use per year and pays for a proportionate share of the property's upkeep, taxes and insurance as well as management fees.

Title Company: This is a generic term that generally refers to a company that provides services to buyers and sellers by facilitating the closing of a sale. While a title company charges various fees for services in connection with the closing, it makes most of its revenues from commissions received from the sale of title insurance. The title insurance itself is generally provided and guaranteed by a title insurance underwriter.

Title Examination Fee: A standard fee paid to a title company at closing of a real estate purchase. Also see "Title Search."

Title Insurance (Title Policy): Insurance to protect the lender (referred to as a "lender's policy" or "mortgage policy") or the buyer (an "owner's policy") against losses arising from disputes over ownership or unknown liens on a property.

Title Search: A check of property deed records to ensure that the seller is the legal owner of the property and that there are no unknown liens or other claims outstanding.

TND: Traditional Neighborhood Development. See "New Urbanism."

Traditional Neighborhood Development (TND): See "New Urbanism."

Truth-in-Lending Act: A federal law that requires lenders to fully disclose, in writing, the terms and conditions of a mortgage or loan, including the annual percentage rate and other charges.

Umbrella Partnership REIT (UPREIT): A real estate trust in which the partners of existing partnerships and a newly formed REIT become partners in a new entity called the operating partnership. The existing partners contribute property interests and the REIT contributes cash (typically proceeds from a public offering of stock).

Underwriter: The issuer of a publicly-held security, a loan or an insurance policy. Also see "Underwriting."

Underwriting: In lending, the reviewing of a loan file to determine the applicant's ability to meet the loan obligation. In insurance, underwriting is the process of reviewing the risk in a given insurance policy. In securities and investments, underwriting is the process of analyzing a bond or stock offering and then completing the necessary paperwork and regulatory filings necessary to offer the bond or stock for sale.

Universal Design: An approach to residential as well as commercial building design that attempts to accommodate as many people as possible, regardless of physical or mental limitations. For example, design elements may include wider doorways and stepless entries that are easy for the physically challenged to navigate.

Urban Development Action Grant (UDAG): A program under the department of Housing and Urban Development that lends money for redevelopment of urban commercial areas.

Urban Renewal: The process of the revitalization of urban areas, usually through redevelopment or older buildings or neighborhoods sponsored by a government or private organization.

Urban Sprawl: The growth of a city in a way that may be viewed by some as unsightly, crowded, unplanned or unproductive.

Urbanism: See "New Urbanism."

U-Value (U Value): A measure of the amount of heat that is transferred into or out of a building. The lower the U-Value, the higher the insulating value of a window or other building material being rated. It is the reciprocal of an R-Value. See "R-Value (R Value)."

VA Mortgage: A mortgage that is guaranteed by the Veterans Administration, a Federal Government agency that provides benefits to U.S. veterans. VA mortgages tend to be made at below-market interest rates and may feature lower down payments or other benefits for the borrower.

Vacancy Rate: The percentage of units available to rent in a given area or building. For example, if 10 units are unrented in a 100-unit apartment building, then the vacancy rate is 10%.

Value Added Tax (VAT): A tax that imposes a levy on businesses at every stage of manufacturing based on the value it adds to a product. Each business in the supply chain pays its own VAT and is subsequently repaid by the next link down the chain; hence, a VAT is ultimately paid by the consumer, being the last link in the supply chain, making it comparable to a sales tax. Generally, VAT only applies to goods bought for consumption within a given country; export goods are exempt from VAT, and purchasers from other countries taking goods back home may apply for a VAT refund.

Variable-Maturity Mortgage: A long-term loan where the due date of the final payment may be changed when the amount of earlier payments has been altered.

Variable-Rate Mortgage: See "Adjustable-Rate Mortgage (ARM)."

Warehouse Store: A discount retailer offering merchandise in a no-frills environment. These stores often cut costs by reducing services and product variety.

Wholesale Club: A retail store that sells a limited assortment of general merchandise to customers who are members of the club. Memberships are generally fee-based, margins are small and there is little customer service provided to the members. Groceries are often sold in bulk sizes. The largest wholesale club chain is Sam's, owned by Wal-Mart. Costco is Sam's biggest competitor in the U.S.

World Trade Organization (WTO): One of the only globally active international organizations dealing with the trade rules between nations. Its goal is to assist the free flow of trade goods, ensuring a smooth, predictable supply of goods to help raise the quality of life of member citizens. Members form consensus decisions that are then ratified by their respective parliaments. The WTO's conflict resolution process generally emphasizes interpreting existing commitments and agreements, and discovers how to ensure trade policies to conform to those agreements, with the ultimate aim of avoiding military or political conflict.

Wraparound Mortgage: A transaction whereby an old mortgage is included with a new loan. This is different from a second mortgage in that a second mortgage is legally subordinate to a first mortgage. The borrower makes payments on both loans to the holder of the wraparound.

WTO: See "World Trade Organization (WTO)."

ZigBee: May become the ultimate wireless control system for home and office lighting and entertainment systems. The ZigBee Alliance is an association of companies working together to enable reliable, cost-effective, low-power, wirelessly networked monitoring and control products based on an open global standard, 802.15.4 entertainment systems.

INTRODUCTION

PLUNKETT'S REAL ESTATE & CONSTRUCTION INDUSTRY ALMANAC, the eighth edition of our guide to the real estate and construction field, is designed as a general source for researchers of all types.

The data and areas of interest covered are intentionally broad, ranging from the various types of businesses involved in real estate and construction, to the online services and technologies that are changing the real estate and mortgage sectors, to an in-depth look at the major firms (which we call "THE REAL ESTATE AND CONSTRUCTION 400") within the many segments that make up the real estate and construction industry. Our definition of the types of businesses involved in real estate and construction is applied in a liberal sense. Accordingly, this book includes real estate brokerage, investment, development and management firms (both commercial and residential). It also covers companies involved in construction of all types, mortgages, hotels, shopping centers and apartments. In addition, this book covers companies that provide important services to the real estate industry, such as firms that write title insurance or operate industry databases and web sites.

This reference book is designed to be a general source for researchers. It is especially intended to assist with market research, strategic planning, employment searches, contact or prospect list creation and financial research, and as a data resource for executives and students of all types.

PLUNKETT'S REAL ESTATE & CONSTRUCTION INDUSTRY ALMANAC takes a rounded approach for the general reader and presents a complete overview of the real estate and construction field (see "How To Use This Book").

THE REAL ESTATE AND CONSTRUCTION 400 is our unique grouping of the biggest, most successful corporations in all segments of the real estate and construction industry. Tens of thousands of pieces of information, gathered from a wide variety of sources, have been researched and are presented in a unique form that can be easily understood. This section includes thorough indexes to THE REAL ESTATE AND CONSTRUCTION 400, by geography, industry, sales, brand names, subsidiary names and many other topics. (See Chapter 4.)

Especially helpful is the way in which PLUNKETT'S REAL ESTATE & CONSTRUCTION INDUSTRY ALMANAC enables readers who have no business background to readily compare the financial records and growth plans of real estate and construction companies and major industry groups. You'll see the mid-term financial record of each firm, along with the impact of earnings, sales and strategic plans on each company's potential to fuel growth, to serve new markets and to provide investment and employment opportunities.

No other source provides this book's easy-to-understand comparisons of growth, expenditures, technologies, corporations and many other items of great importance to people of all types who may be studying this, one of the largest industry sectors in the world today.

By scanning the data groups and the unique indexes, you can find the best information to fit your personal research needs. The major companies in real estate and construction are profiled and then ranked using several different groups of specific criteria. Which firms are the biggest employers? Which companies earn the most profits? These things and much more are easy to find.

In addition to individual company profiles, a thorough analysis of trends in real estate and construction sectors is provided. These trends include the growth of discount residential brokerage firms, online real estate services and the changing nature of the mortgage industry. This book's job is to help you sort through easy-to-understand summaries of today's trends in a quick and effective manner.

Whatever your purpose for researching the real estate and construction field, you'll find this book to be a valuable guide. Nonetheless, as is true with all resources, this volume has limitations that the reader should be aware of:

- Financial data and other corporate information can change quickly. A book of this type can be no more current than the data that was available as of the time of editing. Consequently, the financial picture, management and ownership of the firm(s) you are studying may have changed since the date of this book. For example, this almanac includes the most up-to-date sales figures and profits available to the editors as of early 2011. That means that we have typically used corporate financial data as of late-2010.

- Corporate mergers, acquisitions and downsizing are occurring at a very rapid rate. Such events may have created significant change, subsequent to the publishing of this book, within a company you are studying.

- Some of the companies in THE REAL ESTATE AND CONSTRUCTION 400 are so large in scope, and in variety of business endeavors conducted within a parent organization, that we have been unable to completely list all subsidiaries, affiliations, divisions and activities within a firm's corporate structure.

- This volume is intended to be a general guide to a vast industry. That means that researchers should look to this book for an overview and, when conducting in-depth research, should contact the specific corporations or industry associations in question for the very latest changes and data. Where possible, we have listed contact names, toll-free telephone numbers and Internet site addresses for the companies, government agencies and industry associations involved so that the reader may get further details without unnecessary delay.

- Tables of industry data and statistics used in this book include the latest numbers available at the time of printing, generally through 2010. In a few cases, the only complete data available was for earlier years.

- We have used exhaustive efforts to locate and fairly present accurate and complete data. However, when using this book or any other source for business and industry information, the reader should use caution and diligence by conducting further research where it seems appropriate. We wish you success in your endeavors, and we trust that your experience with this book will be both satisfactory and productive.

Jack W. Plunkett
Houston, Texas
May 2011

HOW TO USE THIS BOOK

The two primary sections of this book are devoted first to the real estate and construction industry as a whole and then to the "Individual Data Listings" for THE REAL ESTATE 400. If time permits, you should begin your research in the front chapters of this book. Also, you will find lengthy indexes in Chapter 4 and in the back of the book.

THE REAL ESTATE AND CONSTRUCTION INDUSTRY

Glossary: A short list of real estate and construction industry terms.

Chapter 1: Major Trends Affecting the Real Estate and Construction Industry. This chapter presents an encapsulated view of the major trends that are creating rapid changes in the real estate and construction industry today.

Chapter 2: Real Estate and Construction Industry Statistics. This chapter presents in-depth statistics ranging from an industry overview to new and existing home sales, mortgage statistics, apartment vacancies and much more.

Chapter 3: Important Real Estate and Construction Industry Contacts – Addresses, Telephone Numbers and Internet Sites. This chapter covers contacts for important government agencies, industry organizations and trade groups. Included are numerous important Internet sites.

THE REAL ESTATE 400

Chapter 4: THE REAL ESTATE 400: Who They Are and How They Were Chosen. The companies compared in this book were carefully selected from the real estate and construction industry, largely in the United States. 114 of the firms are based outside the U.S. For a complete description, see THE REAL ESTATE 400 indexes in this chapter.

   Individual Data Listings:
   Look at one of the companies in THE REAL ESTATE 400's Individual Data Listings. You'll find the following information fields:
   Company Name:
   The company profiles are in alphabetical order by company name. If you don't find the company you are seeking, it may be a subsidiary or division of one of the firms covered in this book. Try looking it up in the Index by Subsidiaries, Brand Names and Selected Affiliations in the back of the book.

Ranks:

Industry Group Code: An NAIC code used to group companies within like segments. (See Chapter 4 for a list of codes.)

Ranks Within This Company's Industry Group: Ranks, within this firm's segment only, for annual sales and annual profits, with 1 being the highest rank.

Business Activities:

A grid arranged into six major industry categories and several sub-categories. A "Y" indicates that the firm operates within the sub-category. A complete Index by Industry is included in the beginning of Chapter 4.

Types of Business:

A listing of the primary types of business specialties conducted by the firm.

Brands/Divisions/Affiliations:

Major brand names, operating divisions or subsidiaries of the firm, as well as major corporate affiliations—such as another firm that owns a significant portion of the company's stock. A complete Index by Subsidiaries, Brand Names and Selected Affiliations is in the back of the book.

Contacts:

The names and titles up to 27 top officers of the company are listed, including human resources contacts.

Address:

The firm's full headquarters address, the headquarters telephone, plus toll-free and fax numbers where available. Also provided is the World Wide Web site address.

Financials:

Annual Sales (2010 or the latest fiscal year available to the editors, plus up to four previous years): These are stated in thousands of dollars (add three zeros if you want the full number). This figure represents consolidated worldwide sales from all operations. 2010 figures may be estimates.

Annual Profits (2010 or the latest fiscal year available to the editors, plus up to four previous years): These are stated in thousands of dollars (add three zeros if you want the full number). This figure represents consolidated, after-tax net profit from all operations. 2010 figures may be estimates.

Stock Ticker, International Exchange, Parent Company: When available, the unique stock market symbol used to identify this firm's common stock for trading and tracking purposes is indicated. Where appropriate, this field may contain "private" or "subsidiary" rather than a ticker symbol. If the firm is a publicly-held company headquartered outside of the U.S., its international ticker and exchange are given. If the firm is a subsidiary, its parent company is listed.

Total Number of Employees: The approximate total number of employees, worldwide, as of the end of 2010 (or the latest data available to the editors).

Apparent Salaries/Benefits:

(The following descriptions generally apply to U.S. employers only.) A "Y" in appropriate fields indicates "Yes."

Due to wide variations in the manner in which corporations report benefits to the U.S. Government's regulatory bodies, not all plans will have been uncovered or correctly evaluated during our effort to research this data. Also, the availability to employees of such plans will vary according to the qualifications that employees must meet to become eligible. For example, some benefit plans may be available only to salaried workers—others only to employees who work more than 1,000 hours yearly. Benefits that are available to employees of the main or parent company may not be available to employees of the subsidiaries. In addition, employers frequently alter the nature and terms of plans offered.

NOTE: Generally, employees covered by wealth-building benefit plans do not *fully* own ("vest in") funds contributed on their behalf by the employer until as many as five years of service with that employer have passed. All pension plans are voluntary—that is, employers are not obligated to offer pensions.

Pension Plan: The firm offers a pension plan to qualified employees. In this case, in order for a "Y" to appear, the editors believe that the employer offers a defined benefit or cash balance pension plan (see discussions below).The type and generosity of these plans vary widely from firm to firm. Caution: Some employers refer to plans as "pension" or "retirement" plans when they are actually 401(k) savings plans that require a contribution by the employee.

- Defined Benefit Pension Plans: Pension plans that do not require a contribution from the employee are infrequently offered. However, a few companies, particularly larger employers in high-profit-margin industries, offer defined benefit pension plans where the employee is guaranteed to receive a set pension benefit upon retirement. The amount of the benefit is determined by the years of service with the company and the employee's salary during the later years of employment. The longer a person works for the employer, the higher the retirement benefit. These defined benefit plans are funded entirely by the employer. The benefits, up to a reasonable limit, are guaranteed by the Federal Government's Pension Benefit Guaranty Corporation. These plans are not portable—if you leave the company, you cannot transfer your benefits into a different plan. Instead, upon retirement you will receive the benefits that vested during your service with the company. If your employer offers a pension plan, it must give you a summary plan description within 90 days of the date you join the plan. You can also request a summary annual report of the plan, and once every 12 months you may request an individual benefit statement accounting of your interest in the plan.

- Defined Contribution Plans: These are quite different. They do not guarantee a certain amount of pension benefit. Instead, they set out circumstances under which the employer will make a contribution to a plan on your behalf. The most common example is the 401(k) savings plan. Pension benefits are not guaranteed under these plans.

- Cash Balance Pension Plans: These plans were recently invented. These are hybrid plans—part defined benefit and part defined contribution. Many employers have converted their older defined benefit plans into cash balance plans. The employer makes deposits (or credits a given amount of money) on the employee's behalf, usually based on a percentage of pay. Employee accounts grow based on a predetermined interest benchmark, such as the interest rate on Treasury Bonds. There are some advantages to these plans, particularly for younger workers: a) The benefits, up to a reasonable limit, are guaranteed by the Pension Benefit Guaranty Corporation. b) Benefits are portable—they can be moved to another plan when the employee changes companies. c) Younger workers and those who spend a shorter number of years with an employer may receive higher benefits than they would under a traditional defined benefit plan.

ESOP Stock Plan (Employees' Stock Ownership Plan): This type of plan is in wide use. Typically, the plan borrows money from a bank and uses those funds to purchase a large block of the corporation's stock. The corporation makes contributions to the plan over a period of time, and the stock purchase loan is eventually paid off. The value of the plan grows significantly as long as the market price of the stock holds up. Qualified employees are allocated a share of the plan based on their length of service and their level of salary. Under federal regulations, participants in ESOPs are allowed to diversify their account holdings in set percentages that rise as the employee ages and gains years of service with the company. In this manner, not all of the employee's assets are tied up in the employer's stock.

Savings Plan, 401(k): Under this type of plan, employees make a tax-deferred deposit into an account. In the best plans, the company makes annual matching donations to the employees' accounts, typically in some proportion to deposits made by the employees themselves. A good plan will match one-half of employee deposits of up to 6% of wages. For example, an employee earning $30,000 yearly might deposit $1,800 (6%) into the plan. The company will match one-half of the employee's deposit, or $900. The plan grows on a tax-deferred basis, similar to an IRA. A very generous plan will match 100% of employee deposits. However, some plans do not call for the employer to make a matching deposit at all. Other plans call for a matching contribution to be made at the discretion of the firm's board of directors. Actual terms of these plans vary widely from firm to firm. Generally, these savings plans allow employees to deposit as much as 15% of salary into the plan on a tax-deferred basis. However, the portion that the company uses to calculate its matching deposit is generally limited to a maximum of 6%. Employees should take care to diversify the holdings in their 401(k) accounts, and most people should seek professional guidance or investment management for their accounts.

Stock Purchase Plan: Qualified employees may purchase the company's common stock at a price below its market value under a specific plan. Typically, the employee is limited to investing a small percentage of wages in this plan. The discount may range from 5 to 15%. Some of these plans allow for deposits to be made through regular monthly payroll deductions. However, new accounting rules for corporations, along with other factors, are leading many companies to curtail these plans—dropping the discount allowed, cutting the maximum yearly stock purchase or otherwise making the plans less generous or appealing.

Profit Sharing: Qualified employees are awarded an annual amount equal to some portion of a company's profits. In a very generous plan, the pool of money awarded to employees would be 15% of profits. Typically, this money is deposited into a long-term retirement account. Caution: Some employers refer to plans as "profit sharing" when they are actually 401(k) savings plans. True profit sharing plans are rarely offered.

Highest Executive Salary: The highest executive salary paid, typically a 2010 amount (or the latest year available to the editors) and typically paid to the Chief Executive Officer.

Highest Executive Bonus: The apparent bonus, if any, paid to the above person.

Second Highest Executive Salary: The next-highest executive salary paid, typically a 2010 amount (or the latest year available to the editors) and typically paid to the President or Chief Operating Officer.

Second Highest Executive Bonus: The apparent bonus, if any, paid to the above person.

Other Thoughts:

Apparent Women Officers or Directors: It is difficult to obtain this information on an exact basis, and employers generally do not disclose the data in a public way. However, we have indicated what our best efforts reveal to be the apparent number of women who either are in the posts of corporate officers or sit on the board of directors. There is a wide variance from company to company.

Hot Spot for Advancement for Women/Minorities: A "Y" in appropriate fields indicates "Yes." These are firms that appear either to have posted a substantial number of women and/or minorities to high posts or that appear to have a good record of going out of their way to recruit, train, promote and retain women or minorities. (See the Index of Hot Spots For Women and Minorities in the back of the book.) This information may change frequently and can be difficult to obtain and verify. Consequently, the reader should use caution and conduct further investigation where appropriate.

Growth Plans/ Special Features:

Listed here are observations regarding the firm's strategy, hiring plans, plans for growth and product development, along with general information regarding a company's business and prospects.

Locations:

A "Y" in the appropriate field indicates "Yes."

Primary locations outside of the headquarters, categorized by regions of the United States and by international locations. A complete index by locations is also in the front of this chapter.

Chapter 1

MAJOR TRENDS AFFECTING THE REAL ESTATE & CONSTRUCTION INDUSTRY

Major Trends Affecting the Real Estate and Construction Industry:

1) Introduction to the Real Estate and Construction Industry
2) U.S. Foreclosures Reach Record Numbers
3) Online Competition Changes the Mortgage Industry
4) U.S. Home Sales Rebound Slightly
5) Real Estate Goes Online
6) Internet-Based Home Sales and Cheap Commissions Rock Residential Brokers
7) Homes and Commercial Buildings Seek Green Certification
8) Prefabricated Housing Causes a Stir
9) Baby Boomers Become a Strong Influence in the Housing Market/Universal Design Catches On
10) Commercial Construction Begins a Revival
11) Commercial Mortgage Defaults and Foreclosures Rise
12) Real Estate Markets in China and India Heat Up
13) Mixed-Use Developments Go Vertical
14) Retail Sales Begin to Rebound but Shopping Center Leasing Remains Problematic
15) Lifestyle Centers and Super-Regional Malls Falter
16) Malls Morph to Stay Afloat
17) Apartment House Occupancy Rates Rise
18) Hotel Operators Challenged/Pod Rooms Grow in Popularity
19) New Urbanism and Traditional Neighborhood Development are Retro Trends
20) Megapolitans Will Define America of the Future/Mega-Regions Defined Internationally
21) Remodeling Rebounds/Home Sizes Shrink

1)   Introduction to the Real Estate and Construction Industry

After a dismal crash during 2007-09, real estate had improved to a small extent in some markets in the U.S. by early 2011, although prices remained at depressed levels. Meanwhile, real estate had enjoyed a significant boom in China, Canada and a few other select spots during 2010 and into early 2011.

During most of the 2001–07 period, easy availability of development loans and mortgages, low interest rates, eager investors and unbridled optimism caused massive new developments of homes, shopping centers and office buildings to sprout on a global basis. The effect was widespread. For example, large portions of the economies of Ireland and Spain were driven by real estate speculation and investment. China, Australia and India saw significant real estate booms, as did Dubai. By 2007, however, the global boom in real estate was unwinding, and in many cases markets were crashing.

"Subprime" mortgages issued to home buyers with poor credit and little income plummeted in value, particularly in the U.S. and Europe, and what began as a real estate crash unleashed a global financial nightmare and a daunting recession.

Many of the resulting problems have been resolved, in some cases through massive bankruptcies of mortgage firms, banks and construction companies. However, in the United States and parts of Europe, the market for houses remains very low. Part of the problem is an enormous number of houses that are either going through the foreclosure process, or are already bank-owned and on the market at modest prices.

In the U.S., home sales volume had picked up slightly by 2010, but remained far below pre-recession levels. For 2009, the National Association of Realtors (NAR) reported 4.91 million existing homes sold. For 2010, the number grew to 5.14 million. While the median sales price for these homes was $172,900 in 2009, it fell to $156,100 in 2010.

In total, the real estate and construction sectors, including the many professions and fields associated with them, make up one of the larger components of the global economy. As of 2010, the U.S. Bureau of Labor estimated that 5.5 million Americans were employed in the construction industry, down from 6.0 million in 2009, 7.2 million in 2008 and 7.6 million in 2007. The agency also estimated that 1.4 million Americans were employed in the real estate industry as of 2010, unchanged from 2009 and down slightly from 2008.

There was $13.8 trillion in outstanding mortgage debt in America at year-end 2010, down from $14.3 trillion one year earlier, including $10.5 trillion in home mortgages (down from $10.8 trillion in 2009). However, many home mortgages remained in arrears as 2011 began, and mortgage owners will continue to suffer write-downs to some degree. During 2010, banks foreclosed on 1.05 million U.S. homes, according to RealtyTrac, up from 918,000 in 2009.

About $814.5 billion in new American construction was put in place during 2010, according to the U.S. Bureau of the Census. Sales of newly-built, single-family homes plummeted to about 323,000 in 2010, from 374,000 in 2009 and 485,000 in 2008 (according to the U.S. Bureau of the Census). These numbers are an immense reduction from the 1.05 million sold in 2006. As of April 2011, the Mortgage Bankers Association (MBA) forecast America's new single-family housing starts to total only 458,000 for 2011, growing to 648,000 in 2012.

Clearly, homebuilders have been suffering. For example, Pulte Homes, Inc., one of the world's largest builders of new homes, saw its revenues soar from $8.8 billion in 2003 to $14.5 billion at its peak in 2005. In 2007-08 the bottom fell out. Pulte's revenues dropped to $9.1 billion in 2007, with a net loss of $2.2 billion. Revenues dropped even further in 2008 to $6.1 billion, with a net loss recorded for the year of $1.4 billion. Now renamed PulteGroup after a merger with Centex, business remains dull. PulteGroup's 2009 revenues were only $3.9 billion and large losses continued. In 2010, revenues improved to $4.4 billion, but the company continued to post losses ($1.1 billion for the year).

On the opposite end of the spectrum, luxury home builder Toll Brothers saw sales rocket from $2.7 billion in 2003 to $6.1 billion at its peak in 2006. Buyers of these expensive homes (averaging about $688,000 during the boom) found it incredibly easy to get a mortgage, often a mortgage that they couldn't afford in the long run. For 2009, Toll Brothers' revenues were only $1.7 billion and the firm recorded a $755 million loss. In 2010, revenues fell further to $1.5 billion, but losses were reduced (totaling $3.3 million for the year).

Many owners of retail centers and malls were hit hard by the recent recession. General Growth Properties, Inc., America's second largest mall operator, filed bankruptcy in early 2009. The company had been unable to refinance its massive mortgages as they came due. At $27.3 billion, this was the largest bankruptcy in U.S. real estate history.

Retail centers in the U.S. were seriously overbuilt during the boom, through 2007. The end result of the glut of mall and shopping center space was a retail space shakeout. Reis, Inc. reported that the vacancy rate at U.S. neighborhood and community shopping centers in the U.S. rose to 10.9% in mid-2010, up from 10.0% a year earlier. The highest vacancy rate on record was 11.1% in 1990. As for regional and super-regional malls, vacancies hovered close to a 10-year high, reaching 9% in mid-2010 compared to 8.4% a year earlier. The third quarter of 2010 showed a slight improvement, with vacancy rates dropping to 8.8%. Large numbers of retail store chains took bankruptcy during the recession, and many others have either curtailed expansion plans, or are opening much smaller stores than in the past.

U.S. apartment house occupancy rates increased during 2010. Apartment house operators are enjoying brisk business in general.

Office building occupancy rates in the U.S. have been low in many markets, and rents are depressed.

This will improve significantly when economic growth resumes in earnest.

Commercial construction spending was at record levels for several years. Private sector (non-governmental), non-residential construction put in place in the U.S. reached $266.6 billion in 2010, according to figures compiled by the U.S. Census Bureau. Private, residential construction put in place was $241.7 billion. Commercial public sector (for government), construction totaled $306.3 billion during 2010.

Over the long term on a global basis, there will be continuing demand from the health care sector for new or remodeled properties as the percentage of the population over age 65 continues to grow, increasing demand for medical care and assisted living centers. Another growing trend in construction in major economies is to incorporate a higher number of energy conservation technologies in new buildings. This is true in both residential and commercial construction. Several "green" building certification plans are now in place, so that architects and builders may seek to attain certain energy conservation and eco-friendly standards.

2)   U.S. Foreclosures Reach Record Numbers

For all of 2010, banks foreclosed on 1.05 million U.S. homes, according to RealtyTrac, up from 918,000 in 2009. There were slightly more than 100,000 in 2005. Foreclosure filings, which include default notices, auctions and repossessions, numbered 2.9 million for 2010. The five states that were hardest hit (and accounted for more than 50% of all foreclosures) were California, Florida, Arizona, Illinois and Michigan.

Just when lenders and homebuyers appeared to be emerging somewhat from the subprime mortgage debacle of 2008 and 2009, a new crisis emerged in the autumn of 2010. An epidemic of improperly documented foreclosures came to light causing a number of banks, including Bank of America, JPMorgan Chase, Wells Fargo and Citigroup to temporarily halt foreclosure activity in a number of states. Attorneys general in all 50 states announced plans to conduct inquiries into foreclosure abuses. With so many foreclosures to process, some foreclosures were subject to "robo-signing," a practice in which bank officers sign off on mortgage documents without true knowledge of the facts therein. Notaries could also be implicated should their signatures and seals be found on fraudulent documents.

Government programs that were intended to reduce foreclosures by negotiating lowered house payments or mortgage balance reductions have generally been unsuccessful. In March 2009, as a $75 billion part of the government's $787 billion economic stimulus package, a foreclosure-prevention plan was announced by the federal government. As of late 2010, fewer than 500,000 loans had been modified, far below the program's goal of 3 million to 4 million.

3)   Online Competition Changes the Mortgage Industry

Despite the difficulties facing the mortgage market, online mortgage sites continue to offer financing to qualified borrowers. The Internet created a much more competitive landscape for home mortgages. Sites ranging from Ditech.com to LendingTree set low origination fees and make it simple to complete applications online, while the Internet itself makes it much simpler for consumers to compare interest rates and mortgage options. Since first starting up several years ago, LendingTree claimed to have closed $214 billion in total transactions by early 2011. Ditech offers, in addition to low origination fees, the ability to apply for and process loans online and 24/7 availability of customer service staff. Bank of America, after acquiring the nation's largest mortgage broker, Countrywide, in 2008, offers low-fee home loans with online service. At Bank of America's user-friendly web site, prospective borrowers can apply online, view a breakdown of proposed fees, compare mortgage options and check the status of a loan in progress.

Mortgage competition online is really part of a much larger, global trend: fierce competition among financial services providers of all types. Firms throughout the consumer financial sector, from banks to insurance companies to stock brokerages, are fiercely battling to attract, retain and cross-market new services to consumers

Total home mortgage originations (which include loans for new purchases as well as refinancings) reached $3.81 trillion in America in 2003, during a low-interest-rate environment and a booming U.S. housing market. Experts at the Mortgage Bankers Association reported $1.99 trillion in home loans originated during 2009, and an abrupt drop in 2010 to $1.50 trillion. Their forecast for 2011 drops to $995 billion, with 2012 forecast to remain below the $1 trillion mark.

Internet Research Tip: Online Mortgage Tools
For mortgage loan and loan provider advice, see
1) www.mtgprofessor.com, a site run by Jack M. Guttentag, Professor of Finance Emeritus at the Wharton School of the University of Pennsylvania.
2) www.myfico.com, a site operated by the credit analysis firm Fair Isaac Corp.
3) www.bankrate.com, a site that provides financial rate information.
4) www.hsh.com, a site run by financial publisher HSH Associates.

SPOTLIGHT: Reverse Mortgages
Reverse mortgages are U.S. federally-insured loans that allow older homeowners (age 62 and up) to take money out of their home equities without selling their homes. In this manner, they are enabled to continue to live in their homes, hopefully for the rest of their lives. Generally, no payment is due as long as the borrower remains in the house. These mortgages enable seniors to supplement retirement savings, which has been especially critical due to crushing losses on the stock market during the global economic crisis. In February 2009, Congress raised the maximum value that seniors can borrow against from $417,000 to $625,500; and capped mortgage origination fees at 2% on the first $200,000 and 1% on any amount over that. Fees are not to exceed $6,000. These measures recently were extended by Congress through fiscal 2011.

---

4) U.S. Home Sales Rebound Slightly

According to the National Association of Realtors (NAR), sales of existing homes fell from 4.91 million units in 2008 to 4.69 million in 2009. For 2010, the association estimated 5.14 million sold.

In response to crashing demand in recent years, home prices fell significantly. NAR reported a drop in median existing U.S. home prices to $218,900 for 2007 (from the 2006 level of $221,900), the first annual fall since the Great Depression. Prices fell further in 2008 to $198,100, $165,400 in 2009, and only $156,100 in 2010.

The Standard & Poor's/Case-Shiller Home Price Index fell 3.3% in February 2011 compared to February 2010 in a study of 20 major American cities. Washington D.C. remained the only city showing positive change over the period (up 2.7%), while the biggest drop was in Phoenix, (down 8.4%).

Falling home values force some homeowners to put their homes on the market for asking prices that are lower than the value of their mortgages. These are typically homeowners who do not have the financial resources to keep their homes, due to rising adjustable mortgage payments or other factors. That is, they may be facing foreclosure. However, in a growing number of these cases, lenders are agreeing to accept a mortgage payoff that is less than face value. This is called a "short sale." Foreclosures can be terribly expensive to lenders. Also, values of nearby homes can drop as a ripple effect takes hold.

Nonetheless, many housing markets in the U.S. will hit bottom and begin to post growth in unit sales. (Eventually, median prices will rise as well, but it remains to be seen how long this will take.) Positive factors supporting this trend in America include:

- Low prices for both new and existing homes will encourage buyers, including the fact that builders are cutting new home sizes and features in order to offer lower prices.
- A growing number of individual investors are snapping up homes at bargain rates.
- There are historically low numbers of new homes under construction.
- There are also an increasing number of markets in which it is cheaper to own than to rent, thanks to low home prices and low mortgage interest rates
- There is pent-up homebuyer demand in general.
- There has been a rebound in consumer wealth thanks to a large, recent boost in stock market values.

(Significant, remaining negative factors include high unemployment rates and job insecurity in general.)

A recent study by Deutsche Bank found that U.S. homeowners spend only 9.8% of their incomes on after-tax mortgage payments (including taxes and insurance payments). In 2007, during the peak of the real estate market bubble, Americans were paying 17.2% of their incomes.

The U.S. government is helping further, on the low to mid end of the market, by encouraging FHA to make large quantities of mortgages with very small down payments. These loans come with strict income requirements. Buyers must submit proof of income and document employment history with two years of pay stubs and W-2 forms. Borrowers are typically limited to amounts that are about 31% of their income, or 43% when other debt is taken into account. In addition, down payments of at least 3.5% are required. The FHA's market share of home purchase financing has increased substantially. (While the FHA programs may boost demand and borrowing, they also can lead to defaults by those buyers who fall behind financially and feel little regret at walking away from their very small home equities.)

In the past, real estate loans in the U.S. often stayed in the hands of federally insured lenders (such as savings associations and banks), but this changed dramatically when massive, securitized pools of mortgages became popular investments, snapped up by private investment funds, pension funds and other major accounts. Billions of dollars of these loans are held on the books of investment banks and commercial banks. By early 2007, more than one-half of all mortgages were owned in securitized pools. Sadly, this trend continued to balloon until the real estate speculation bubble burst, taking major mortgage holder and investment bank Bear Stearns down with it in early 2008. Managers of these mortgage pools are attempting to stem the tide of their losses, in some cases by agreeing to short sales. In other cases, managers are offering better terms, such as lower monthly payments, to homeowners in trouble.

Sales of newly-built, single-family homes plummeted to about 374,000 in 2009 from 485,000 in 2008 (according to the U.S. Bureau of the Census). For 2010, the total was 323,000 new homes sold. These numbers are an immense reduction from the 1.05 million sold in 2006.

Clearly, homebuilders have been suffering. For example, Pulte Homes, Inc., one of the world's largest builders of new homes, saw its revenues soar from $8.8 billion in 2003 to $14.5 billion at its peak in 2005. In 2007-08 the bottom fell out. Pulte's revenues dropped to $9.1 billion in 2007, with a net loss of $2.2 billion. Revenues dropped even further in 2008 to $6.1 billion, with a net loss recorded for the year of $1.4 billion. Now renamed PulteGroup after a merger with Centex, business remains dull. PulteGroup's 2009 revenues were only $3.9 billion and large losses continued. In 2010, revenues improved ($4.4 billion), but the company continued to post losses ($1.1 billion).

On the opposite end of the spectrum, luxury home builder Toll Brothers saw sales rocket from $2.7 billion in 2003 to $6.1 billion at its peak in 2006. Buyers of these expensive homes (averaging about $688,000 during the boom) found it incredibly easy to get a mortgage, often a mortgage that they couldn't afford in the long run. For 2009, Toll Brothers' revenues were only $1.7 billion and the firm recorded a $755 million loss. In 2010, revenues fell further to $1.5 billion, but losses were cut ($3.3 million).

In the U.S., during 2009, only 441,100 single family homes were started, according to the Census Bureau, increasing to 446,600 in 2010.

5)   Real Estate Goes Online

According to a National Association of Realtors (NAR) survey, a large majority of homebuyers go online to research the market before purchasing. Among the busiest sites are Realtor.com, Move.com, HomeGain.com, ZipRealty.com and Yahoo! Real Estate, along with the sites operated by RE/MAX and Coldwell Banker.

Sites such as HomeGain, ZipRealty and Move.com provide home listings as well as tools for calculating mortgages and researching schools in different neighborhoods. The sites make money by selling advertising, selling customer leads to real estate agents and placing home listings on their sites. Move.com, formerly Homestore, is among the most popular. It collaborates with the NAR to operate Realtor.com.

Home finance is also a hot Internet area. A large percent of homebuyers apply for mortgage pre-approval before deciding upon a house. Many of those buyers make their applications online. Sites such as LendingTree and E-Loan, Inc. make applying for a mortgage online simple and competitive, because they maintain relationships with a wide variety of lending institutions and can offer several options.

LendingTree, for example, sends each mortgage application to up to five different lenders. In return, the lenders offer competing interest rates, closing costs and terms. LendingTree earns an average of $500 at each loan's closing. The site also generates revenue through matching potential homebuyers with Realtors, taking a healthy fee from the Realtor.

Even eBay is having success selling real estate online. It's doing a significant volume of business auctioning houses, land, commercial property and time-share interests.

Zillow, www.zillow.com , is an extremely popular site launched in 2005. It provides online access to aerial home photos, and enables users to estimate home values based on a variety of factors, using a proprietary algorithm.

<table>
<tr><td>

Internet Research Tip: Public Real Estate Data
For home value estimates, recent sales activity, tax information, title history and more, see:

Coldwell Banker's Home Value Estimation
       www.coldwellbanker.com/real_estate/learn
Property Shark   www.propertyshark.com
RealEstateABC   www.realestateabc.com
Zillow   www.zillow.com

</td></tr>
</table>

Online listings are typically generated by Multiple Listing Services (MLS), which are run by groups of Realtors. The services feed information about homes for sale to brokers' web sites and national real estate sites, as well as sites representing a geographic area (most cities have real estate sites such as www.har.com which is operated by the Houston Association of Realtors in Houston, Texas). Most prospective buyers hope to see all available listings on these sites, as opposed to listings for a particular Realtor.

Savvy real estate agents are utilizing web sites such as YouTube and Facebook, blogs and text messages to reach younger, first time buyers. Some realty firms are hiring agents in their 20's to help reach this market.

6) Internet-Based Home Sales and Cheap Commissions Rock Residential Brokers

From around 2004 through 2007, residential real estate agents enjoyed a golden age. (In fact, making money by brokering real estate looked so easy that membership in the National Association of Realtors grew from about 750,000 in 2000 to more than 1,300,000 in 2007.) Meanwhile, the amount of time or effort necessary to sell a house declined significantly in many markets before the real estate bubble burst, as eager buyers snapped up houses as soon as they came on the market. Many residential agents had been earning huge sums—sellers were paying ever-larger fees as home prices escalated.

However, the real estate broker as an intermediary is increasingly facing intense competition from Internet sites that connect buyers and sellers directly. A good analogy can be found in the travel agent industry, in which travel consumers have turned to the Internet for a vast portion of their purchases and information needs, and travel agents have been forced to downsize or become providers of new enhanced services and value-added packages.

The days of 6% commissions for real estate brokers are under pressure thanks to maverick real estate brokers such as Foxtons (www.foxtons.co.uk)

and ZipRealty (www.ziprealty.com). Instead of the usual 6% commission, these upstart brokers' fees are as little as 3% and up to 5% of the selling price. They are able to cut costs by capitalizing on the power of the Internet to advertise homes for sale, listing homes with accompanying photographs and virtual tours, but not always including services such as conducting in-person showings and open houses or negotiating prices.

ZipRealty offers sellers a reduced commission structure that is about 5% of the sales price, compared to standard commissions of 6% elsewhere. At the same time, it attracts buyers with rebates of up to 20% of its commissions. For example, the seller of a $200,000 home might save $2,000 in commissions. When ZipRealty represents a buyer of a $200,000 home listed by another real estate firm, the buyer might receive a rebate of $1,200, assuming ZipRealty earns a co-brokerage commission of 3%. (ZipRealty's 3% commission would be $6,000 in this case, and the buyer would receive 20% of that amount, or $1,200.) Certain restrictions apply.

Competing against the extremely well-entrenched Realtors group is difficult at best. Discount brokerage Foxtons, which originated in the U.K., at one time charged sellers as little as 2% for listing their homes, provided the sellers did the showings and other tasks themselves. In 2000, Foxtons opened operations in the U.S., focused on the New York City area. In May 2007, before the current housing slump had gained much momentum in the U.K., Foxtons was acquired by a private equity firm for about $770 million. The acquisition excluded the U.S. operations. By September 2007, the U.S. unit filed for bankruptcy, despite the fact that it had listed about 4,400 homes for sale at the time. As of 2011, Foxtons continues to operate in London and Surrey in the U.K.

Another discount alternative for sellers is to pay a flat fee (usually around $500) to a discount broker to list their home in MLS. Sellers then do the showing and negotiating themselves.

Some online home-selling sites regularly mine MLS listings and then post those listings on their own sites. In order to have access to MLS data, a broker employed by the site must be a member of the local Realtors organization. Some online sites have been known to hire a member Realtor to feed MLS data to them. Disputes frequently break out between local boards of Realtors and such sites as to whether MLS data is proprietary.

Traditional brokers argue that in a declining home market, their services are more valuable. The

National Association of Realtors (NAR) has spent millions on television and radio campaigns that highlight the benefits of using a Realtor and the difficulties homeowners face when selling on their own. Traditional brokers are also adding services to their portfolios. Full-service brokerage firm Real Living, Inc., for example, enhanced its web site (www.realliving.com) to enable sellers to see how many people have viewed their homes.

7) Homes and Commercial Buildings Seek Green Certification

In a growing trend, many homebuilders across the U.S. are constructing homes in accordance with the National Association of Home Builders' (NAHB) "green" specifications. These specifications require resource-efficient design, construction and operation, focusing on environmentally friendly materials. Today's much higher energy costs are spurring this trend. In addition, local building codes in many cities, such as Houston, are requiring that greater energy efficiency be incorporated in plans before a building permit can be issued.

There are several advantages to building along eco-sensitive lines. Lower operating costs are incurred because buildings built with highly energy-efficient components have superior insulation and require less heating and/or cooling. These practices include using oriented strand board instead of plywood; vinyl and fiber-cement sidings instead of wood products; and insulated foundations, windows and doors. Low-maintenance landscaping demands less water and weeding. Heating and cooling equipment with greater efficiency is being installed, as well as dishwashers, refrigerators and washing machines that use between 40% and 70% less energy than their 1970s counterparts. Wastewater heat recovery systems use hot wastewater to heat incoming water. Even toilets are more efficient than before. Current models use a mere 1.28 gallons of water per flush, as opposed to four gallons in the 70s.

The main disadvantage is that this kind of building is often more expensive than traditional construction methods. Added building costs often reach 10% to 15% and more per home; however, some homebuyers are willing to pay the increased price for future savings on utilities and maintenance. As energy prices increased over the last decade, builders became more amenable to constructing homes with energy-savings measures. In addition, some consumers are inclined to spend more when they feel they are buying environmentally friendly products, including homes. (Marketing analysts refer to this segment as "LOHAS," a term that stands for "Lifestyles of Health and Sustainability." It refers to consumers who choose to purchase items that are natural, organic, less polluting and so forth. Such consumers may also prefer products powered by alternative energy, such as hybrid cars.)

The U.S. government and all 50 states offer tax incentives in varying amounts to builders using solar technology. A handful of "zero-energy homes" that produce as much electricity as they use are being built (see www.zeroenergy.com.) By installing photovoltaic panels or other renewable sources to generate electricity, and using improved insulation and energy-efficient appliances and lighting, the zero-energy goal may be achieved, at least in sunny climates such as those in the American West and Southwest.

In the commercial sector, businesses may have several reasons to build greener, more energy-efficient buildings. To begin with, long-term operating costs will be lower, which will likely more than offset higher construction costs. Next, many companies see great public relations benefit in the ability to state that their new factory or headquarters building is environmentally friendly. Many office buildings, both public and private, are featuring alternative energy systems, ultra-high-efficiency heating and cooling, or high-efficiency lighting. In California, many public structures are incorporating solar power generation.

Even building maintenance is getting involved— building owners are finding that they can save huge amounts of money by scheduling janitorial service during the day, instead of the usual after-hours, after-dark schedule. In this manner, there is no need to leave lighting, heating or cooling running late at night for the cleaning crews.

An exemplary green office building is Bank of America Tower (formerly One Bryant Park), a 54-story skyscraper on the Avenue of the Americas in New York City. Completed in 2009, the $1.2-billion project is constructed largely of recycled and recyclable materials. Rainwater and wastewater is collected and reused, and a lighting and dimming system reduces electrical light levels when daylight is available. The building supplies about 70% of its own energy needs with an on-site natural gas burning power plant. It was the first skyscraper to rate platinum certification by adhering to the Leadership in Energy and Environmental Design (LEED) standards, set by the U.S. Green Building Council in 2000 (see www.usgbc.org).

The Pearl River Tower, a 71-story skyscraper set to open in 2011 in Guangzhou, China, may be the first major zero-energy building, or may at least come close. Designed by Chicago architecture firm SOM, the tower is planned to be 58% more energy efficient than traditional skyscrapers by using solar roof panels, novel wind turbines embedded in four openings spaced throughout the tower and walls with eight-inch air gaps that trap heat which then rises to power heat exchangers for use in cooling systems. The building encompasses about 2.3 million square feet of floor space.

A growing number of buildings are being retrofitted to use energy more efficiently. One example is the initiative underway at Citigroup, Inc. The banking firm is turning off lobby escalators, incorporating more natural light and using recycled materials in dozens of its properties around the world. Citigroup says it can save as much as $1 per square foot per year by making its offices more efficient. Elsewhere, Google, Inc. installed a solar rooftop at its California headquarters as early as 2007, and retail chains such as Wal-Mart and Kohl's are installing solar panels on their California stores. In Wal-Mart's case, it had 31 solar installations in California and Hawaii by mid-2010, and had an additional 20 to 30 sites in California and Arizona planned.

The Environmental Protection Agency (EPA) sponsored a contest in 2010, challenging commercial buildings to cut energy use over a 12-month period. The winner was the Morrison Residence Hall at the University of North Carolina-Chapel Hill. The hall cut its energy consumption by approximately 36% and saved more than $250,000 on its energy bills. Green initiatives during the year included expanding a solar-powered hot water system, upgrading lighting and convincing students to cut down on hot water use.

Sports stadiums are also going green in a big way. Lincoln National Field, the home of the Philadelphia Eagles, announced in late 2010 plans to install 2,500 solar panels, 80 wind turbines (each measuring 20 feet high) and a natural gas and biodiesel-burning generator. The field is contracting with Florida-based Solar Blue, which will spend $30 million to install the equipment. In return, the Eagles will pay Solar Blue fixed amounts for energy with increases of 3% per year for a period of 20 years. Solar Blue is free to sell excess energy created in the stadium to the local utility. Staples Center in Los Angeles and New Meadowlands Stadium in New York also have significant green initiatives underway.

LEED standards have been adopted by companies such as Ford, Pfizer, Nestlé and Toyota, which have all built LEED-certified structures in the U.S. In addition, the standards have been adopted by 25 states and 48 cities for government-funded projects, including New York, Los Angeles and Chicago. Industry analysts estimate the value of government-financed construction projects at $200 billion per year. One of the world's largest green complexes is the campus of King Abdullah University of Science and Technology (KAUST) in Saudi Arabia. The campus spans more than 118 million square feet of classrooms, laboratories and a coral reef ecosystem, and features more than 13,500 square feet of solar thermal panels and upwards of 54,300 square feet of photovoltaic arrays.

LEED is not without competition. Another green verification program called Green Globes is backed by the Green Building Initiative in the U.S. Green Building Initiative is a group led by a former timber company executive and funded by several timber and wood products firms. Several U.S. states have adopted Green Globes guidelines instead of those supported by LEED for government-subsidized building projects. In Canada, a version of Green Globes for existing buildings is overseen by the Building Owners and Managers Association of Canada (BOMA Canada) under the brand "BOMA Best." Green Globes is more wood friendly than LEED, which is not surprising considering the involvement of the timber industry. It promotes the use of wood and wood products in construction with fewer restrictions than LEED, which approves of wood if it comes from timber grown under sustainable forestry practices approved by the Forest Stewardship Council, an international accrediting group.

In a similar vein, the Environmental Protection Agency (EPA) established WaterSense, a voluntary public-private partnership program to promote water-efficient products and services; and EnergyStar, a program that promotes energy efficiency. WaterSense certifies low-flow toilets that use a mere 1.28 gallons per flush, creates standards for bathroom-sink faucets that flow at no more than 1.5 gallons per minute and offers a certification program for irrigation companies that use water-efficient practices. EnergyStar homes are at least 15% more efficient than homes built to the 2004 U.S. residential code.

Retail giant Wal-Mart has been pursuing an aggressive policy to reduce energy use in its stores. The company is investing $500 million to reduce greenhouse gas emissions from its stores and distribution centers by 20% through 2012. The firm also pledged to increase the fuel efficiency of its trucking fleet by 25% by the year 2008, and up to 50% by 2015.

Dow Chemical has invested $100 million (plus a $10 million grant from the Department of Energy) in researching new plastic photovoltaic roof panels using thin-film solar cells. Prototypes of the product, called Powerhouse, were tested in early 2010 with a goal of commercial release of the product sometime in 2011. Dow has not published pricing, but observers estimate that Powerhouse (or products like it) would cost a homeowner about $10,000 after subsidies and tax rebates for approximately 1,000 square feet of roofing material. This compares to about $5,000 for traditional asphalt shingles. Dow projects the value of the solar shingles market could reach $5 billion by 2015.

Internet Research Tip: Green Buildings

For a look at government-sponsored projects in green commercial buildings, see:

1) Rebuilding America, www.energyfuturecoalition.org/What-Were-Doing/Energy-Efficiency/Rebuilding-America

2) U.S. Green Building Council, www.usgbc.org

In Europe, the EU has mandated that member states revisit building codes every five years and create standards of energy efficiency. Buildings are also required to submit an energy certificate that can be shown to prospective buyers and renters. Elsewhere, nations such as Japan that are focused on becoming much more energy-efficient are emphasizing the use of green methods in new construction.

8)   Prefabricated Housing Causes a Stir

In this increasingly high-tech era, it's interesting to note that homebuilding is one of the last industries to remain focused on manufacturing by hand. For several decades, entrepreneurs have attempted to commercialize various kinds of prefabricated housing. For example, HUD (the U.S. Department of Housing and Urban Development) pushed a well-funded program in the late 1960s that sought to encourage lower-priced, high-quality housing through factory fabrication in materials that included steel as well as wood. Nonetheless, until recently, the market for prefabricated housing was tiny, and most homes are still constructed on-site by hand.

Enter "panelization," the practice of building and assembling elements such as foundations, walls and staircases off-site at a factory and then trucking them to a home site for assembly. PulteGroup, one of the largest homebuilders in the U.S., is embracing the practice, as are many major builders across the nation. It is estimated that more than 10% of new homes constructed in the past decade have some panelized elements. The trend is not entirely new; as the Sears catalog sold home kits as early as 1908 (these now historic homes are considered highly desirable today). Post-World War II, William J. Levitt introduced modular housing to lukewarm response, which petered out once the housing boom subsided.

Today's panelization is more far-reaching than Levitt's practice, which merely assembled basic framing off-site. The quality of panelized flooring, walls and staircases has risen remarkably thanks to new techniques, and building these elements at a factory offers many advantages to working on-site. A foundation can be poured and cured indoors, thereby eliminating the need to wait for good weather at the home site. Substantial savings in construction time are a plus, and panelization also addresses the problem of the scarcity of skilled laborers in many areas. Homebuilders who have embraced at least some aspect of the prefab component trend include PulteGroup, Toll Brothers, Inc. and Beazer Homes USA, Inc.

SPOTLIGHT: Resolution: 4 Architecture

Bucking a long-term, widely held distaste for prefabricated housing, a maverick firm called Resolution: 4 Architecture (www.re4a.com) is promoting manufactured, modular housing. Starting at around $200,000, modules can be manufactured in a factory and assembled into a completed house in one of several dozen designs.

The company won a competition sponsored by *Dwell*, a home design magazine, to design a house near Chapel Hill, North Carolina. In addition, the firm has designed a beach house in Ventura, California, a vacation home in East Hampton, New York and a 1,725-square-foot suburban home in Long Island, New York. Contemporary and hip in design, the homes generally appeal to young, cost-conscious homebuyers with cutting-edge tastes.

9)   Baby Boomers Become a Strong Influence in the Housing Market/Universal Design Catches On

Americans aged 55 years or older are the fastest-growing segment of the population. 2006 marked the year that the first Baby Boomers turned 60. The term "Baby Boomer," generally referring to people born from 1946 to 1964, has evolved to include the children of soldiers and war industry workers who were involved in World War II. When those veterans and workers returned to civilian life, they started or added to families in large numbers. As a result, the Baby Boom generation is one of the largest demographic segments in the U.S. According to MetLife, Baby Boomers make up about 27% of the U.S. population. As of early 2010, there were about 76 million surviving Baby Boomers. In 2011, millions are beginning to turn traditional retirement age (65), resulting in extremely rapid growth in the senior portion of the population.

The real estate industry is quickly evolving to meet the needs and tastes of the people in this rapidly growing population segment. Housing options that cater to aging homeowners include retirement communities (also referred to as "independent living"), continuing care (which provides a broad spectrum of living options from independent living to nursing homes), assisted living (which offers assistance in daily tasks such as shopping, cleaning, etc. but does not provide onsite medical care) and communities that provide medical care for specific conditions such as Alzheimer's disease.

Another trend in senior housing is cooperative or communal living, in which private dwellings are grouped around a communal area or "common house" which usually contains a living room, kitchen and dining area for group dinners. Some communities of this type also include housing for on-site medical caregivers. Watch for growth in all senior living real estate in the coming years as more Baby Boomers reach retirement age.

SPOTLIGHT: Universal Design

Universal design (UD) creates living spaces that are comfortably livable for the largest variety of people, including those who are older or dealing with physical challenges. As many homeowners age, they look for a house with elements such as wide, stepless doorways, sturdy hand rails, automatic faucets and stacked closets that can be converted to elevators. The Center for Universal Design promotes UD throughout the U.S. Located at North Carolina State University in Raleigh, North Carolina, the center conducts research and collaborates with builders and manufacturers. For more information, see www.design.ncsu.edu/cud.

---

10)   Commercial Construction Begins a Revival

The global recession of 2008-09 hit commercial real estate, especially in the U.S., in the form of increased vacancy rates, lower property values and delinquent commercial mortgages. The office space vacancy rate in 2006, before the global recession, was 12.1%. 2010 saw vacancy rates rise to 17.2%, according to research firm Reis, Inc. Part of the reason for the rising vacancy rates is that many tenants either maintained or cut staff numbers in response to lower revenues. Also, consolidations of the business locations of tenants due to mergers, and a long list of major bankruptcies, particularly in retailing and financial services, put downward pressure on commercial property rentals. However, lease prices were firming as of the first quarter of 2010, indicating the beginning of a recovery.

Through 2005 and 2006, there was a tremendous construction market in such sectors as office buildings, hotels, hospitals, shopping centers and state and local government projects. These commercial projects remained a strong, positive influence on the construction market through much of 2007. However, by the end of 2007, demand slowed in some sectors, and it was vastly harder to obtain financial backing for speculative commercial projects.

Commercial construction spending had been at record levels. Private sector (non-governmental), non-residential construction put in place in the U.S. reached $298 billion in 2006, growing to $357 billion in 2007 and $410 billion in 2008, according to figures compiled by the U.S. Census Bureau. However, spending fell in 2009 to $367 billion and $266.6 billion in 2010.

In the U.S., commercial public sector (for government), non-residential construction was $249 billion in 2006, growing to $282 billion in 2007 and

$299 billion in 2008. The $787 billion economic stimulus package passed by the federal government in early 2009 gave a big boost to spending on buildings and infrastructure for higher education, transportation (including highways), research laboratories and renewable energy. Total non-residential public construction spending was $308 billion in 2009 and $306.3 billion in 2010.

In early 2011, the commercial construction horizon began to brighten as lenders once again invested in new projects. J.P. Morgan Chase & Co., for example, wrote as many construction loans in the first six weeks of 2011 as it did during the whole of 2010. The Mortgage Brokers Association (MBA) reported that commercial and multifamily mortgage origination volumes rose by 44% in 2010 over 2009 to reach $118.8 billion.

A number of projects that stood uncompleted during the recession are once again under construction. They include the Streets of Buckhead multiuse development in Atlanta, Georgia, which includes shops, office space and residential units; and the 1,100 room Revel casino hotel in Atlantic City, New Jersey. This is just a beginning of a rebound, however. Thousands of unfinished projects remain spread across the U.S. as of early 2011.

For the mid term, construction spending for certain sectors will remain slow, due to high unemployment, changes in consumer spending habits, difficulties in the banking and automobile industries, and a close scrutiny by corporations on their budgets for office and factory space. This slowdown will affect retail space, restaurant buildings, non-government office buildings, manufacturing/ warehouse space, automobile dealers, entertainment facilities and hotels/motels in particular.

Another potential snag in commercial property is the establishment of new accounting rules established by the Financial Accounting Standards Board in the U.S. and the International Accounting Standards Board elsewhere. Working together, the two boards created a new generally accepted accounting principles (GAAP) standard to be completed in 2011 and take effect in 2013. The standard requires companies to include property leases as assets and liabilities on their balance sheets. Rent owed for the remaining term of a lease must be logged as a liability while the right to use leased space must be recorded as an asset. It is estimated that the new standard will result in public companies putting an estimated $1.3 trillion in leases on their balance sheets, according to the Securities and Exchange Commission (SEC). Private companies could push the estimate as high as $2 trillion. The result may be that more companies will choose to buy office space, driving down demand for leased space. The new standard may also encourage tenants to shorten lease lengths.

11)   Commercial Mortgage Defaults and Foreclosures Rise

Commercial mortgage delinquencies and foreclosures will rise over the short-term, and funding for speculative commercial projects remains extremely difficult to obtain. Write-offs on those loans are running at extremely high rates. These loans cover both completed buildings and commercial projects under construction, many of which are now rusting away in uncompleted states. As of the end of 2010, commercial real estate debt totaled about $2.3 trillion, according to the U.S. Federal Reserve. A recent panel of representatives from the Federal Reserve, U.S. Treasury Department and the Office of the Comptroller of the Currency (OCC) reported that from 2010 through 2014, about $1.4 trillion in commercial real estate loans will come due, with almost 50% of those loans worth more than the value of the properties concerned. The 30+ day delinquency rate on securitized loans backed by commercial properties such as office buildings, hotels and retail stores reached 8.95% in the fourth quarter of 2010, up from 8.58% in the third quarter of the year, according to the Mortgage Bankers Association. For the fourth quarter of 2009 the delinquency rate was only 5.70%.

There are two big issues here: The first is the fact that commercial property values, in many cases, are now far below the amount of the mortgages secured by them. During the 2003-07 era of easy money and soaring property prices, many real estate investors overpaid dramatically for office buildings, hotels and shopping centers. Today, their investments are "underwater," and their equities are wiped out.

The second issue that is devastating commercial properties, and therefore threatening the mortgages against them, is that rental incomes have fallen significantly in many cities. In some cases, tenants are unable to pay their rents or have taken bankruptcy. At the same time, vacancy rates are high, and it is very difficult to obtain tenants. When new leases are written, it is often at rental prices that are much lower than those of a few years ago. This situation will improve as the economic recovery takes hold, but it will remain a significant problem at least through 2011.

In the U.S., an October 2009 guideline issued by federal bank regulators will allow banks to maintain property loans on their books as "performing," even though the market value of the underlying real estate has fallen to less than the mortgage amount. This is an attempt by regulators to encourage bankers to do "work outs," on such loans, rather than filing foreclosures. As of 2010, work outs were very common. Developers or property owners pay a bit of interest to the bank, if they can, and then promise to take all possible steps to improve the financial outlook of their properties. In many cases, lenders restructure these loans, trade some of their debt for equity, or agree to write down the amount of the loan if the buildings' owners will inject new capital of their own into the project.

The most glaring example of troubled real estate financing may be giant mall owner General Growth Properties, which filed for bankruptcy protection in 2008 due to its inability to pay mortgages on hundreds of properties in a timely manner. However, there are myriad other examples, including the October 2009 bankruptcy of major commercial lender Capmark Financial Group and the September 2009 seizure of Chicago-based Corus Bank by the FDIC. Capmark Financial, based in Horsham, Pennsylvania, was one of the world's largest commercial lending companies, with $9.53 billion in assets. Corus Bank, based in Chicago, was one of the world's largest lenders to condominium developers. It had $7 billion in assets at one time, but was shut down in late 2009 by the Office of the Comptroller of the Currency with the FDIC named as receiver. MB Financial Bank of Chicago assumed all deposits and about $3 billion in assets.

The problem is not limited to the United States. During the recent boom, commercial property prices skyrocketed and lending was very easy to obtain. As a result, commercial loans are in trouble to some extent in many markets worldwide. Newly developed shopping centers, office buildings and resorts have been particularly hard hit by the economic downturn. Morgan Stanley's real estate funds business, called Msref, was projected to lose as much as $5.4 billion on its commercial real estate investments, especially in properties outside the U.S. In Japan, for example, Msref's VI fund had $3.17 billion in equity with a projected return of only $320 million. In Europe, the fund had $3.14 billion in equity with a projected return of only $630 million.

12)   Real Estate Markets in China and India Heat Up

After the global economic crisis wreaked havoc on the real estate markets in China and India in 2008 and early 2009, prices in major cities escalated almost exponentially from late 2009 and into 2010. For example, in Shanghai, analysts estimated that prices per square foot for luxury residential real estate rose 54% through September 2009 to $500 per square foot. In the month of November 2009 alone, prices for homes in 70 major Chinese cities jumped 5.7%, while housing starts across China skyrocketed 194%. Obviously, speculators are playing a major role in driving up these prices. Total outstanding property loans in 2010 rose by 27.5% over 2009. Construction in China especially is booming. Barclays Capital reported that more than 40% of the world's skyscrapers due to be completed between 2011 and 2017 will be in China.

Leading up to the financial crisis, China had become the capital of offshored manufacturing. The Chinese government constructed a series of high-technology parks in addition to millions of square feet of new manufacturing space. Global manufacturing needs for everything from running shoes to telecommunications equipment are being met by factories in China. A growing number of Chinese entrepreneurs and investors have become truly wealthy. Meanwhile, wages for factory workers and managers are rising rapidly.

Companies like Microsoft hired large numbers of engineers for research and development in China, as did leading biopharmaceutical firms and a wide variety of other tech industry leaders. At the same time, the escalating number of commercial and leisure visitors to China created a boom in hotels, and the overall hot business climate fueled the need for millions of square feet in new office and shopping center space. China's economic growth remained very robust as of early 2011. However, it remains to be seen whether actual demand will catch up to very large recent growth in the square footage of newly-built offices, malls and residential condominiums.

The boom in China has many analysts concerned about inflation with regard to home prices. The Chinese government instituted measures starting in April 2010 to reverse spiraling prices. Among the measures is raising the minimum down payment for first-time buyers from 20% of the home's value to 30% and refusing mortgages for people buying a third or subsequent home. Year-over-year price growth in December 2009 compared to the same month in 2010 was 6.4%, only slightly higher than China's overall inflation rate.

Meanwhile, India is enjoying a boom focused on low-income housing that began in 2009. India has become the global capital of business process outsourcing (BPO). While millions of Indians are enjoying a new life in the middle class as managers in call centers and as professionals in commercial complexes, lower income workers are leaving the remote villages and finding employment as drivers, factory staff and tailors. Some of these workers earn enough to afford newly built, low-cost housing. Two government owned banks, the National Bank for Agriculture and Rural Development and the National Housing Bank are backing mortgage companies to service higher-risk loans, provided that the buyer can put down a minimum of a quarter of the value of the home and provide proof of income.

A growing number of builders are rushing to meet the demand. For example, Matheran Realty built flats in the town of Karjat, about 56 miles east of Mumbai, that start at about $4,500. Indian conglomerate Tata has likewise been constructing large numbers of new homes.

13) Mixed Use Developments Go Vertical

Mixing office, retail, residential and entertainment space in one location is an idea on the rise, literally. For example, take the Time Warner Center in New York City. The 80-story, $1.7-billion building houses a 2.8-million-square-foot combination of condominiums, office space, a Mandarin Oriental hotel, CNN television studios, performance space, restaurants and retail space that includes a Whole Foods Market. It's a stupendous urban version of mixed-use developments that have cropped up in suburbs across the U.S. since the early 90s.

These spaces often outperform standard suburban real estate in office and retail lease rates, residential rents, retail sales, hotel room occupancy rates and property values, both on-site and in surrounding areas (according to a study by Charles Lockwood, a real estate historian and author). Many retailers in the Time Warner Center reported sales as high as 70% to 80% above their initial projections, before the current economic crisis. All this multi-use bounty comes at a price, however, since building these 24/7 communities costs more. Design is more complex because retail needs are often at odds with residential needs. Restaurants have different logistical requirements than office space. It's also difficult to find the right mix of high- and low-end retail tenants.

Residents need groceries and dry cleaning far more often than luxury jewelry or clothing, making the right mix of tenants a top priority for developers. Nonetheless, in close-in urban areas or highly desirable waterfront or scenic locations, the extremely high cost of land often dictates dense, vertical mixed use development.

The vertical trend is expected to dominate built-out suburban cities with set boundaries over the mid-term and beyond. Michael Beyard at the Urban Land Institute projects that vertical, multi-use expansion of aging strip malls that are on prime land will promote significant reinvestment and tax base expansion.

Another twist to the vertical trend is to build "live, work, play" communities around sports arenas. Take the 75-acre Victory Park project in Dallas, Texas, for example (www.victorypark.com). Built around the American Airlines Center, home of the NBA Mavericks, Victory Park currently boasts the W Dallas Victory Hotel and Residences, The House (a 28-story condominium high-rise) and two apartment complexes, Cirque and The Vista. Developed by Hillwood and partly owned by Hicks Holding LLC, the multi-billion dollar project is expected to include large amounts of office, hotel, residential and retail space when complete.

A number of vertical developments are cropping up around light rail line terminals such as the new project in Carrollton, Texas near Dallas. The city approved a $38 million mixed-use development next to a commuter rail station that links Carrollton with Dallas. Commuters using rail are likely to look for housing, shopping and entertainment venues close to stations. Many communities are using funds from bonds and government subsidies to build new developments. Examples of recent developments include the $1 billion revitalization of Union Station in Denver, Colorado and a $2.3 billion ($1.5 billion from private investors and $800 million in municipal, county, state and federal funds) redevelopment of central Columbus, Ohio.

14) Retail Sales Begin to Rebound but Shopping Center Leasing Remains Problematic

Many major chain store companies cut expansion plans for 2009 and beyond, as revenues per store were generally disappointing compared to the boom years that ended in 2007. Some chains that continue to expand are doing so with new formats that utilize less square footage and lower inventories. Store managers in malls found themselves facing light traffic and devastating losses in 2008 and into 2009. By early 2010, however, savvy retailers had learned to operate with lower overhead and lean inventories, while retail sales had finally begun to show positive growth that will help mall owners and retailers alike.

Retail industry analysts generally consider mall sales per square foot of $250 per year or less as an indicator of potential failure. As of late 2010, Green Street Advisors, Inc. listed 95 troubled malls on its analysis of 1,000 enclosed U.S. malls.

Macy's closed 11 stores across the U.S. in 2009 and another five in 2010. Worse still, a growing number of chains filed for bankruptcy over the past few years, including Sharper Image (high-end gifts), Domain, Inc. (furniture), Fortunoff (jewelry) Circuit City (electronics), Linens 'n Things (housewares) and Blockbuster (movie rentals and sales). More announcements of closings, retrenching and bankruptcy occurred throughout 2009, such as the June closing of Century Plaza Mall in Birmingham, Alabama. A leading trade group, the International Council of Shopping Centers (ICSC), reported that 5,170 American general merchandise, apparel, furniture and other stores announced closings in 2010.

According to Reis, Inc., occupied space in U.S. shopping centers and malls dropped a net 24.1 million square feel during all of 2009. The overall vacancy rate for malls and shopping centers in the top 80 U.S. markets in the first quarter of 2011 rose to 9.1%, the highest level in 11 years.

The net effect of these store closings is hard on suppliers, employees and mall owners alike. Firms that own and operate malls and shopping centers are scrambling to find replacements for empty spaces. Meanwhile, landlords' rental income is falling. According to Reis, mall lease prices were $38.79 per square foot in the fourth quarter of 2010, 3% lower than a year earlier, while shopping center lease rates remained flat at $16.56, compared to a year earlier.

Of particular difficulty for landlords is the task of finding tenants for empty "big boxes" and department store sites, for example when a department store abandons perhaps 200,000-square feet under one roof due to consolidation and store closings. Owners are having a tough time finding tenants for such large volumes of space. A recent survey by Colliers International covered 233 of the 1,259 stores closed by four national big-box retailers in 2008 and 2009. Of those 233, 51% remained vacant as of April 2011. The remaining 49% were leased for rents averaging 17.9% less than those paid by the previous tenants.

In some cases, cutting the boxes into smaller spaces is a viable option. Paradise Development Co., a Las Vegas owner and property developer, split a former large store into two 25,000 square-foot spaces now leased by Copeland's Sporting Goods and Barnes & Noble. In a similar circumstance, the developer split a defunct Home Place store into a 30,000-square-foot Bed, Bath & Beyond and a 20,000-square-foot DSW Shoes discount store. Both projects cost a cool $2 million to renovate. Faced with tens of thousands of empty square feet in large spaces, many developers are biting the bullet and following suit.

Meanwhile, as some major chains have closed stores, mall operators are looking for new categories of niche tenants. For example, day spas or medical spas are becoming commonplace in malls, where clients can receive a botox shot or laser-based removal of unwanted hair. Mall owners are now more likely to consider incorporating nightclubs or additional food and drink venues in their empty spaces. In addition, rental agents are actively seeking unique locally-owned stores to expand into mall spaces when national chain store tenants vacate.

15) Lifestyle Centers and Super-Regional Malls Falter

Super-regional centers (that is, shopping centers or malls which include at least three department stores and at least 800,000 square feet of retail space) were favored in new construction up until 2008. New malls have been slightly smaller than those of the past, averaging 1,060,000 square feet between 2008 and 2009, compared to an average of 1,148,000 square feet from 1997 through 1999. Malls like these can cost more than $200 per square foot to build, making the new properties' investments in the range of $150 million to $250 million each.

Other types of shopping center properties, such as power centers and lifestyle centers, had been developing rapidly in recent years, in many cases robbing traffic from traditional malls. A "power center" is typically an open-air complex of category-dominant anchors such as category-killers, home improvement stores, discount stores and warehouse clubs. A "lifestyle center" is an open-air, highly landscaped configuration of approximately 50+ stores. Generally located near upscale neighborhoods, lifestyle centers offer leasable retail area of 150,000 to 500,000 square feet, with at least 50,000 square feet of space typically dedicated to upscale national specialty stores such as Williams-Sonoma.

There are also hybrid centers, and value-oriented centers. Hybrids have some of the features of enclosed malls and lifestyle centers. That is, they have both open-air sections and enclosed sections. Value-oriented centers are built on formats that emphasize discounted prices. These include outlet malls. Many new value-oriented centers feature significant entertainment segments.

Real estate research firm CoStar Group reported that in 2010, developers were expected to open 18 million square feet of new stores in the 54 largest markets. For 2011, only 20 million square feet of new space is projected.

The end result of the glut of mall space was a retail space shakeout. Reis, Inc. reported that the vacancy rate at U.S. neighborhood and community shopping centers in the U.S. rose to 10.9% in mid-2010, up from 10.0% a year earlier. The highest vacancy rate on record was 11.1% in 1990. As for regional and super-regional malls, vacancies hovered close to a 10-year high, reaching 9% in mid-2010 compared to 8.4% a year earlier. The third quarter of 2010 showed a slight improvement, with vacancy rates dropping to 8.8%.

General Growth Properties, Inc., owner of some of the most admired retail centers in America, including Boston's Faneuil Hall, the Ala Moana Center in Honolulu, Fashion Show in Las Vegas and the South Street Seaport in Manhattan, filed bankruptcy in early 2009. The company had been unable to refinance its massive mortgages as they came due. These loans were the result of an acquisitions binge that drove General Growth to become America's second-largest mall owner. At $27.3 billion, this was one of the largest bankruptcies in U.S. real estate history. In early 2010, Simon Property Group attempted to acquire General Growth with a $10 billion offer which was rejected. In April 2010, Simon Property altered its offer to a $2.5 billion investment for voting rights of about 20%. The bid ultimately failed, and General Growth emerged from bankruptcy in late 2010 after completing a financial restructuring.

Shopping mall performance in recent years was sharply delineated by economic scale. Low-end malls showed weak sales per square foot while high-end malls were the most successful. Malls catering to wealthier customers also cost more to build and operate, and are able to charge higher rental rates. For example, Taubman Centers, Inc., a luxury shopping center developer that owns 25 malls in 12 states, reported average sales per square foot of mall space of $550 in 2007, a figure much higher than typical malls, which often report average sales in the $350 range. Taubman Center's sales per square foot for 2010 were $564, up 12.4% from 2009.

Retailers who are successfully weathering the storm tend to be discount stores and outlets where low prices can still attract shoppers. Simon Property Group, which owns, develops and manages major shopping centers throughout the U.S. and Puerto Rico, reported that year-to-year growth in comparable sales per square foot was stronger at outlet centers than at traditional high-end malls as of early 2008. Overall, Simon Property regional mall comparable sales per square foot fell 11.2% for the 12 month period ending in September 2009 to $438, down from $493 per square foot for 2008 (rolling 12 month comparable sales per square foot for mall stores, less than 10,000 square feet in regional malls and all owned gross leasable area in premium outlets). However, sales per square foot improved in 2010, reaching $494 in the fourth quarter, compared to $452 in fourth quarter 2009. Average rents per square foot reached $38.87, up from $38.47 for the fourth quarter in 2010. Simon also managed to open a 100% leased, 62,000 square-foot expansion of Toki Premium Outlets in Toki, Japan (the company has a 40% stake in the center) and began construction on two projects, the 175,000-square-foot Johor Premium Outlets in Johor, Malaysia (50% owned by Simon) and the 380,000-square-foot Merrimack Premium Outlets in Merrimack, New Hampshire (fully owned by Simon).

A number of retail chains, including Bloomingdale's, Nike and teen apparel company Anchor Blue are experimenting with downsizing. Bloomingdale's latest store in Santa Monica, California, for example, is about one-eighth the size of its New York flagship store at just 105,000 square feet. The chain is gambling that shoppers are overwhelmed in larger stores that have greater volumes of merchandise from which to choose. Smaller spaces with few items could prove a cozier alternative, making shoppers more comfortable and therefore (hopefully) spending more. The new Bloomingdale's store creatively utilizes its pared-down spaces by dropping dressing rooms when needed from recessed areas in the ceiling. The pod-like "rooms" look like Japanese lanterns. The new 22,000-square-foot Nike store (compared to typical Nike-towns which are 50,000 square feet) in Santa Monica also uses flexible layout designs with cash registers mounted on moveable counters and interchangeable hardware fixtures that can be moved about at will. Anchor Blue closed off half the space in one of its stores in Santa Ana, California, leaving a streamlined area where foot traffic increased 7% and sales grew 23% in a year. Smaller spaces translate to lower rents, less inventory and fewer employees which further enhance the bottom line.

SPOTLIGHT: Mall of America

The largest mall in the U.S. is the Mall of America (www.mallofamerica.com), located in Bloomington, Minnesota. First opened in 1992, it contains 4.2 million square feet of gross building area (2.5 million leasable) and is visited by an average of 110,000 people daily (or 40 million people per year). Entertainment is everywhere in this mall: 14 movie screens, a comedy club, night clubs, a 1.2-million gallon walk-through aquarium, a seven-acre amusement park, the NASCAR Silicon Motor Speedway, LEGO building center, A.C.E.S. Flight Simulation and over 520 specialty shops. Total employment in the center ranges from 11,000 in normal times and up to 13,000 during holiday and summer seasons.

(Not everyone comes here just to shop: the Mall of America reports that more than 5,500 couples have exchanged wedding vows in the Mall's "Chapel of Love" wedding chapel, and the mall's mall-walking list, the "Walksport Mall Stars!" has registered more than 4,000 people.)

With the addition of a 306,000-square-foot Ikea home furnishings store, the mall enters its newest phase of construction. Shoppers from far and wide visit Bloomington and stay several days specifically to shop this mammoth mall. International visitors are common. Overall, visitors from outside the mall's 150-mile radius hover at around 35%.

The Ikea store, while not directly connected to the original mall, is part of a 42-acre new Phase II development just north of the original site. Tentative plans for new tenants include several hotels, an office building, a spa and entertainment attractions, which may include a performing arts theater. In 2009, the Mayo Clinic signed a letter of intent to be part of the expansion. The Phase II mixed-use complex is zoned for up to 5.6 million square feet of new development.

---

16)   Malls Morph to Stay Afloat

The days of the dull, old-fashioned enclosed mall are numbered. Anchor tenants such as major department stores are moving or going out of business, leaving mall owners with echoing empty spaces of painfully high square footage. An estimated one-third of the malls in the U.S. are obsolete or soon to become so. Malls are forced to adjust in order to stay in business.

One way to attract customers is to raise the roof—literally tear off the connecting roofs between stores to create an open-air environment. Parking garages are coming down as well so shoppers can park directly by the entrance of their favorite stores. Department store chains such as J.C. Penney and Macy's opened freestanding stores at mall sites. Typically built to have a single floor, the stand-alone locations have plenty of close-in parking, and offer shopping carts and centralized checkout stands for convenience.

For example, Bella Terra in Huntington Beach, California was an enclosed shopping mall built in 1966. Builder J.H. Snyder Company spent $170 million to tear off the roof and knock down walls, transforming the mall into an open-air lifestyle center with 74 shops and restaurants and a 4,000-seat, 20-screen cinema megaplex. The rebuilt center features Italian architecture and design accents. The Santa Monica Place mall underwent a two-year, $265 million renovation, reopening in late 2010. The mall, formerly an enclosed, three-story structure built in the 1980s, now has roof-free spaces between stores which converge on a central, open-air plaza

Some operators of enclosed malls are scrambling to find alternative tenants to fill empty spaces. Wal-Mart, for example, opened a two-story store in a mall in a suburb of New York City and a three-story location in a Los Angeles mall formerly occupied by a Macy's department store. The pluses for Wal-Mart in these locations are access to mall shoppers without having to acquire real estate that is scarce in congested areas, as well as favorable leases with mall owners who are anxious to fill large amounts of space. On the other hand, Wal-Mart faces increased security and logistics costs and the difficulty of having to switch from a single-floor sprawl to multi-story confusion. Costco is also experimenting with former department-store spaces, announcing in late 2010 that it plans to open three mall-based stores in the near- to mid-term.

Internet Research Tip: Shopping Centers
For up-to-the-minute facts and figures about shopping centers of all types, visit the International Council of Shopping Centers, www.icsc.org.

---

17)   Apartment House Occupancy Rates Rise

In 2009, apartment owners saw vacancy rate rise along with unemployment rates. According to real estate research company Reis, Inc., the top 79 U.S. rental markets saw vacancy rates hit 8% in 2009. The rise occurred despite the fact that landlords reduced asking rents (which include concessions) by 3% overall in 2009.

Today, occupancy in U.S. apartment houses is showing improvement. For the fourth quarter of 2010, occupancy reached 93.5%, up from 91.8% in fourth quarter 2009, according to MPF Research (a subsidiary of RealPage, Inc.).

Landlords continue to offer enticements to sign or renew leases, including new carpet and paint, a free month's rent and gift cards from local retailers such as Starbucks. Rents throughout the U.S. fell during the economic recession by as much as 3% in 2009 according to Reis. MPF Research reported that rents increased slightly in 2010, reaching an average of $1,029 per month. The research firm expects rents to rise further in 2011, up as much as 5.1%. Major apartment complex owners and operators are reporting that renters are staying longer. The average stay in 2009 was 14 months, but in 2010, renters are leasing for 19 months.

Internet Research Tip: Apartments

Find out everything you ever wanted to know about apartments at the web site of the highly regarded National Apartment Association, www.naahq.org. Particularly useful are its archive of historical statistics and its commentary on the rental market.

---

18) Hotel Operators Challenged/Pod Rooms Grow in Popularity

With some signs of an economic recovery, the hotel industry has been enjoying a rebound. For example, for 2010, global hotel giant Marriott reported the arrival of increasing numbers of business and leisure travelers. Its occupancy increased by 4.1% worldwide during the year to reach 68.7%. Good news such as this is very welcome in this industry, particularly in light of the many foreclosures of major hotel and resort properties during the recent recession.

Marriott reported that its revpar (revenue per available room) on a global basis was up 6.3% for 2010, compared to 2009 (on a company-operated, worldwide hotel basis, adjusted for the effects of inflation). While revpar remained well below 2008 levels, Marriott continued to see strengthening in properties in Asia, Europe, the Caribbean, Latin America, and in its luxury properties around the world. Hotels in Asia particularly benefitted from strong economic growth in that region.

The economic slowdown was especially tough for a number of hotel companies that were in the midst of expansion. According to Lodging Econometrics (LE), there were about 6,000 new hotels under construction in the U.S. as of mid-2008,

totaling about 800,000 rooms. Still more projects that were on the drawing board were scrapped due to lack of financing. In 2009, 1,301 hotels with 146,929 rooms opened compared to 1,345 hotels with 154,667 rooms in 2008. In 2010, the picture was far grimmer, with 635 new hotels and 70,849 rooms opened. LE forecasts 446 hotels and 46,343 rooms to open in 2011 (up 0.9% from 2010), and 487 hotels and 48,860 rooms to open in 2012.

Many major hotel chains cut back on their growth plans. Hyatt, for example, planned to open 80 hotels in 2008, but scaled back to 64. Their openings continued to be low in 2009 and 2010, with 19 and 22 respectively planned. The bright spots in hotel construction and expansion were in China and India. Hotel construction remains robust there. In China, Marriott opened 10 properties while Starwood Hotels & Resorts opened approximately 30 newly built properties in 2010.

Another interesting trend in hotel openings is for Asian luxury hotels to open properties in Europe. Throughout 2010 and into 2011, European locations for hotels under brands including Raffles Hotels & Resorts, Shangri-La Hotels and Resorts and Meritus Hotels & Resorts are opening. For example, Shangri-La is opening projects in Vienna, London and Moscow.

As hoteliers faced falling occupancy rates, many dropped prices significantly. Growing numbers of hotels are attempting to create compelling package offerings at great prices in order to drive business. For example, room packages may include breakfast, spa credits, dinners in luxury on-site restaurants or other perks. Members of the loyalty reward programs of major hotel chains receive a continual stream of emails offering last minute discounts, resort travel packages or deep discounts on weekend rates. Hotels in Las Vegas are being particularly aggressive, and some owners are finding this strategy successful. The Wynn resort in Las Vegas opened its massive new ultra-luxury wing "Encore" in late 2008, just in time for the economic bust. The owners decided to use bargain pricing to drive up occupancy with good results. In their case, a relatively full hotel at lower rates was preferable to empty rooms. The opening of large numbers of hotel rooms at Las Vegas' massive new City Center in 2010 forced hoteliers to continue to rely on deep discounts and package deals.

Corporate and business travel destinations were especially hard hit. Major corporations cancelled or downsized meetings, while many firms instructed employees to curtail travel to visit clients and trips to conferences or conventions. The fall off in luxury retreats and meetings by hedge funds, investment banks and other financial industry companies was also a serious blow to the hotel and resort sector. However, the industry was seeing a rebound in business travel in 2010, with the more expensive luxury hotels recovering more quickly than lower priced hotels. In general, room rates were on the rise along with occupancy rates as of early 2011.

Faced with tight travel budgets during the recession of 2008 and 2009, hotels responded with new, cost effective room alternatives, especially in Europe and Japan. Busy travelers can now book tiny rooms or "pods" that typically measure about 100 square feet (some as small as 65 square feet) in size for the night or just a few hours to rest and freshen up. (In contrast, a more traditional motel is about 300 square feet, and luxury hotel rooms are 450 to 600 square feet.) Rooms generally have a small bed, flat screen TV and tiny bathrooms (some offered shared bathrooms), and windows, if there are any, may open onto a corridor instead of outside. Examples of hotels offering pods are Yotel at London's Heathrow Airport (about $105 per night for a 117 square foot "premium cabin"), Pod Hotel in New York (about $139 per night for 91.5 square feet) and EasyHotel in Zurich (about $71 per night for 104 square feet).

The pod business model is similar to discount airlines in that only the basics are available and low prices are of supreme importance. Pod hotels do not generally offer perks such as fitness facilities, meeting rooms or lavish room service (some do not offer food of any kind). Yet, the services they do offer can be top of the line such as plasma TV screens and high-thread-count sheets. In addition to business travelers, the rooms attract vacationers looking for good deals in locations near major tourist attractions.

On the other end of the scale, a big trend in luxury hotels was the construction of adjacent condominiums. However, as the real estate bubble burst in 2008, owners of many of these properties saw their unit values plummet, and many developers ran into financial difficulty. Some of the residential units were selling for almost $2,000 per square foot before the crash. Of course, the condos make initial profits for the developers, when they are sold. Equally important, the condo owners pay hefty monthly common area fees to help defray the costs of luxurious lobbies, swimming pools, landscape and a high level of personal service. The economic crisis weakened the luxury condominium market as it did in all other real estate sectors.

19) New Urbanism and Traditional Neighborhood Developments are Retro Trends

New Urbanism, or traditional neighborhood development (TND) represent a strong trend among developers in many parts of America. TND is an attempt to create an old-fashioned aura in a newly built neighborhood. Typical elements include small lots, front porches and other features that encourage being outdoors, meeting your neighbors and walking or cycling (rather than driving) through the neighborhood. The architecture is frequently pre-1940s in style, and easy-to-walk-to retail spaces are often incorporated, sometimes in a town-center style. Also, live-work buildings are frequently placed in special parts of the neighborhood, encouraging entrepreneurs or professionals to work downstairs and live upstairs.

The most noted TND is a community in Florida called Seaside, www.seasidefl.com, which has been in place for more than a decade. Many other TNDs are attempting to emulate Seaside's success, which is based partly on its beachfront location, a tried-and-true draw for the retiree crowd and vacationers looking for something different from life back home.

TNDs are not necessarily instant successes, and they may not be suitable for development in many areas. To begin with, while many developers like the concept because municipal governments are likely to approve smaller lots in higher density arrangements, some elements of TNDs are more expensive to build, such as period streetlights, cobblestone streets or dense landscape. Also, the retail space offered in town-center sections of TNDs is often difficult to rent, resulting in costly high vacancy rates and unsightly empty storefronts. These high costs were especially problematic in the recent economic crisis, and caused new projects to be delayed or shelved altogether.

20) Megapolitans Will Define America of the Future/Mega-Regions Defined Internationally

The Metropolitan Institute (MI) at Virginia Tech University has done extensive research into what it calls "megapolitans;" that is, regional concentrations of population totaling 10 million people (now or by 2040) that comprise two or more contiguous metropolitan areas and feature other selected characteristics.

MI finds that 10 megapolitan areas exist within the U.S. today, comprising less than 20% of all land area in the lower 48 states, but holding almost 200 million people, about 66% of total U.S. population. By 2040, MI projects that these 10 areas will add 83 million additional residents and will attract more than 75% of all private real estate development investments from 2003 to 2040, or about $33 trillion.

MI lists the 10 megapolitans as 1) Cascadia in the Seattle/Portland area of the Pacific Northwest; 2) NorCal in Northern California; 3) Southland in Southern California; 4) Valley of the Sun in the Phoenix/Tucson area; 5) I-35 Corridor stretching from Dallas-Ft. Worth through central Oklahoma and parts of Kansas; 6) Gulf Coast comprising the coastal areas of Texas, Louisiana, Mississippi and Alabama; 7) Peninsula comprising all of Southern and Central Florida; 8) Piedmont in Central Georgia, the Carolinas, and nearby metro areas; 9) Northeast in the Northeast Corridor of the U.S.; and 10) Midwest in Chicago and the surrounding Midwestern metro areas.

Growth of these megapolitans can create unique new problems. For example, a migration of millions of people from suburban living in large homes to urban living on smaller lots could leave a surplus of as many as 22 million large-lot homes (built on at least one-sixth of an acre) in suburban areas by 2025 according to one estimate. Some analysts project that aging Baby Boomers will desire smaller, urban homes as they age, homes that are easier to care for and less expensive to operate than suburban houses on large lots.

The high gasoline prices of 2008 and again in early 2011 added fuel to the megapolitan fire. Dense population areas where people live and work close together foster the use of bicycles, public transportation and walking to get from place to place.

On the other hand, there is the possibility that urban living may not appeal to such a vast swath of the population. Advanced communication technologies centered on the Internet will continue to evolve quickly, making it ever more effective to work remotely while collaborating with associates, customers and suppliers who are far away. People will be able to use advances in communications to stay in touch with far-flung family and friends. This will encourage many people to live in communities with smaller populations that offer better recreation, cleaner air, lower crime, better weather and/or better public education than they would find in major cities. This could cause large numbers of knowledge workers to relocate to cities such as Boise, Idaho or the Spokane, Washington area. Communities that are even more rural, such as Taos, New Mexico; Grand Junction, Colorado or College Station, Texas could find an influx of knowledge workers who realize that they can live nearly anywhere that suits their unique individual tastes and budgets, as long as they have very fast Internet access and reasonable proximity to a major airport.

On a global scale, the Martin Prosperity Institute at the University of Toronto defines 40 mega-regions around the world that collectively power the global economy. While home to one-fifth of the world's population, these mega-regions produce two-thirds of global economic output and more than 85% of global innovation. Major mega-regions include Greater Tokyo (55 million people and $2.5 trillion in economic activity) and the 500-mile Boston-Washington corridor (54 million people and $2.2 trillion in output). Other regions of note include Chicago to Pittsburgh, Los Angeles to San Diego and the areas around global centers such as Amsterdam, London and Bangalore and Mumbai.

21)   Remodeling Rebounds/Home Sizes Shrink

Home remodeling in the U.S. hit its peak in 2007 at $575.3 billion, according to the Joint Center for Housing Studies of Harvard University. By 2009, it had fallen to $458.3 billion. One result was declining profits at building center giants Home Depot and Lowe's. For example, at Home Depot net sales for the fiscal year ending February 3, 2008 were down by 2.1%, or $1.6 billion, to $77.3 billion, while net profits were off 23.7% to $4.4 billion. The fiscal year ending January 31, 2009 was significantly worse, with revenues decreasing to $71.2 billion and profits plummeting to $2.2 billion, a decrease of 48.6%. For 2010, Home Depot's revenues fell further to $66.2 billion, while profits rose slightly to $2.6 million.

However, there appears to be a glow on the remodeling horizon. Harvard researchers saw improvement in home remodeling in 2010, with $463.4 billion spent. First quarter spending in 2011 was a healthy $122.8 billion, with a total of $491.5 billion forecast for the entire year. Many homeowners are remodeling in order to increase energy efficiency, while others hope to capitalize on tax credits for new appliances and other energy saving improvements.

> **Important trends in remodeling:**
> - Consumers are in do-it-yourself mode to reduce costs. One interesting result is that the short-term rental of construction tools and equipment is soaring.
> - Financing for remodeling via home equity loans is much harder to obtain.
> - Projects are smaller and less expensive.
> - There is a growing focus on green, energy-efficient remodeling projects.
> - Federal and state government incentives, such as tax credits, will fuel investments in home solar projects, weather stripping, insulation and energy-efficient appliances and windows.
> - As America's 76 million surviving Baby Boomers age, investments in remodeling for easier access for the aged will boom. Features such as wider doors for wheelchair access, firm handholds in bathrooms and better kitchen accessibility will be a focus. "Universal Design," a concept that focuses on ease of use by residents of limited physical ability, will grow.
>
> *Source: Plunkett Research, Ltd.*

The size of the median new home in the U.S. grew steadily for several years, reaching 2,277 square feet in 2007, up from 1,940 in 1994. That trend was broken in 2008. Concerned about purchase price and energy expenses, American consumers are now looking for smaller homes. According to the U.S. Census Bureau, the median house started during the first quarter of 2009 was 2,065 square feet. In 2010, the figure rose slightly to 2,152 square feet. In addition to smaller size overall, consumers are willing to accept fewer luxuries, such as only one fireplace instead of two, in order to save money. However, consumers are not willing to skimp on energy efficiency in their appliances, insulation and air conditioning systems. Energy efficiency is a high priority.

Chapter 2

REAL ESTATE & CONSTRUCTION INDUSTRY STATISTICS

CONTENTS:

Real Estate & Construction Industry Overview

	Quantity	Unit	Date	Source
Existing Home Sales, 2009, U.S.[1]	4.91	Million	2009	NAR
Existing Home Sales, 2010, U.S.	5.14	Million	2010[2]	NAR
New Single Family Home Sales, U.S.	323	Thousand	2010	Census
New Single Family Homes For Sale, U.S., End of Period	188	Thousand	2010	Census
Single & Multi-family Home Housing Starts (Private), U.S.	587	Thousand	2010	Census
Median Sales Price of New Single-Family Houses Sold, U.S.	221,900	US$	2010	Census
Average Sales Price of New Single-Family Houses Sold, U.S.	271,600	US$	2010	Census
Median Existing Home Sales Price, 2009, U.S.	172,900	US$	2010	NAR
Median Existing Home Sales Price, 2010, U.S.	156,100	US$	2011[2]	NAR
Size of Median Newly Built Single Family Home, U.S.	2,152	Sq. Ft.	2010	Census
Placements of New Manufactured Homes, U.S.	49,400	Units	2010	Census
Real Estate Sales Volume Worldwide: Last 6 Months	462.2	Bil. US$	Apr. 2011	RCA
U.S.	110.9	Bil. US$	Apr. 2011	RCA
U.K.	35.1	Bil. US$	Apr. 2011	RCA
Canada	9.3	Bil. US$	Apr. 2011	RCA
Value of U.S. Construction Put into Place	814.5	Bil. US$	2010	Census
Private	508.2	Bil. US$	2010	Census
Residential	241.7	Bil. US$	2010	Census
Non-Residential	266.6	Bil. US$	2010	Census
Public	306.3	Bil. US$	2010	Census
State & Local	275.5	Bil. US$	2010	Census
Federal	30.8	Bil. US$	2010	Census
Average 1-Year Adjustable Rate Mortgage	3.25	%	Apr. 2011	Freddie Mac
Average 15-Year Fixed-Rate Mortgage	4.13	%	Apr. 2011	Freddie Mac
Average 30-Year Fixed-Rate Mortgage	4.91	%	Apr. 2011	Freddie Mac
Total Outstanding Mortgage Debt, U.S.	13.8	Tril. US$	Q4 2010	Federal Reserve
Home Mortgage Debt, U.S.	10.5	Tril. US$	Q4 2010	Federal Reserve
Commercial Mortgage Debt, U.S.	2.3	Tril. US$	Q4 2010	Federal Reserve
Homeownership Rate (% of Households), U.S.	66.5	%	Q4 2010	Census
Gross Real Estate Vacancy Rate, U.S.	14.1	%	Q4 2010	Census
Estimated Construction Industry Employment (NAICS 23), U.S.	5.5	Million	2010	BLS
Estimated Real Estate Industry Employment (NAICS 531), U.S.	1.4	Million	2010	BLS
Hotel Industry Revenue, U.S.	127.2	Bil. US$	2009	AH&LA

[1] Existing home sales of single-family homes and condo/coops. [2] Estimate as of February 2011.

NAR = National Association of Realtors
RCA = Real Capital Analytics
BLS = U.S. Bureau of Labor Statistics

Census = U.S. Census Bureau
BEA = Bureau of Economic Analysis
AH&LA = American Hotel & Lodging Association

Value of U.S. Private Construction Put in Place: 2004-2010

(In Millions of US$)

Type of Construction	2004	2005	2006	2007	2008	2009	2010
Total Private Construction	771,173	869,976	911,837	863,278	758,827	592,326	508,240
Residential	532,900	611,899	613,731	493,246	350,257	245,621	241,690
New single family	377,557	433,510	415,997	305,184	185,776	105,336	112,726
New multi-family	39,944	47,297	52,803	48,959	44,338	28,246	14,022
Improvements	115,399	131,092	144,931	139,103	120,144	112,038	114,942
Nonresidential	238,273	258,077	298,105	370,032	408,569	346,705	266,550
Lodging	11,982	12,666	17,624	27,481	35,364	25,350	11,014
Office	32,879	37,276	45,680	53,815	55,502	37,904	24,408
General	28,679	32,962	41,085	48,945	50,137	33,861	22,154
Financial	4,186	4,285	4,542	4,785	5,054	3,822	2,215
Commercial	63,195	66,584	73,368	85,858	82,654	51,286	37,998
Automotive	5,235	5,614	5,528	6,281	5,640	4,487	3,392
Sales	2,443	2,834	2,285	2,571	2,430	1,513	1,305
Service/parts	1,978	1,805	2,184	2,356	1,843	2,052	1,544
Parking	814	975	1,059	1,354	1,367	923	543
Food/beverage	8,232	7,795	7,442	8,046	8,029	4,869	4,525
Food	3,590	3,128	2,752	2,779	3,124	1,989	2,010
Dining/drinking	3,937	4,078	3,780	3,957	3,976	2,221	1,913
Fast food	705	590	910	1,310	930	660	602
Multi-retail	18,828	22,750	29,218	34,751	31,963	18,655	13,071
General merchandise	6,416	6,740	5,699	7,572	4,373	4,028	4,153
Shopping center	9,256	12,462	18,417	22,197	22,780	11,614	6,866
Shopping mall	2,138	2,631	3,616	4,000	4,045	2,235	1,371
Other commercial	13,341	11,744	10,874	13,580	12,087	6,439	4,179
Drug store	1,427	1,315	1,238	1,500	1,967	1,920	1,066
Building supply store	2,521	2,416	2,594	3,507	2,539	1,142	800
Other stores	8,229	7,075	6,135	7,744	6,552	2,594	1,680
Warehouse	12,074	12,827	14,491	16,909	16,707	9,607	5,485
General commercial	10,830	11,468	13,493	15,641	15,482	8,621	5,018
Mini-storage	1,141	1,311	979	1,218	1,125	908	455
Farm	5,485	5,854	5,817	6,292	8,227	7,230	7,346
Health Care	26,272	28,495	32,016	35,588	38,437	35,651	30,758
Hospital	16,147	18,250	21,914	24,532	25,571	24,992	22,690
Medical building	7,615	8,031	7,165	7,981	9,242	7,562	5,309
Special care	2,510	2,213	2,937	3,074	3,625	3,097	2,760
Educational	12,701	12,788	13,839	16,691	18,624	16,800	13,599
Preschool	674	516	487	704	746	723	437
Primary/secondary	3,202	2,718	3,240	3,968	3,919	3,381	2,376
Higher education	6,496	6,946	7,611	9,424	11,587	10,739	8,612
Instructional	3,200	3,556	3,501	4,219	5,463	6,191	5,288
Dormitory	1,669	1,537	2,065	2,900	3,791	2,472	1,624
Sports/recreation	739	821	858	771	841	815	821
Other educational	1,998	2,294	2,090	2,167	1,965	1,634	1,842
Gallery/museum	1,335	1,745	1,697	1,939	1,708	1,382	1,670

(Continued on next page)

Value of U.S. Private Construction Put in Place: 2004-2010 (cont.)

(In Millions of US$)

Type of Construction	2004	2005	2006	2007	2008	2009	2010
Religious	8,153	7,715	7,740	7,522	7,197	6,190	5,260
House of worship	6,015	5,992	6,262	6,270	5,884	5,037	4,257
Other religious	2,138	1,723	1,478	1,252	1,313	1,154	1,003
Auxiliary building	1,258	1,251	1,219	1,099	1,122	1,025	769
Public Safety	289	408	419	595	623	486	234
Amusement & Recreation	8,432	7,507	9,326	10,193	10,508	7,817	6,288
Theme/amusement park	198	200	417	522	324	269	262
Sports	900	807	959	1,902	2,280	1,601	1,721
Fitness	1,141	1,425	2,028	1,945	2,051	1,751	1,184
Performance/meeting center	1,054	1,072	737	823	1,102	781	581
Social center	2,594	1,626	1,538	1,602	1,552	1,011	771
Movie theater/studio	1,218	1,248	1,309	1,159	601	321	371
Transportation	6,841	7,124	8,654	9,009	9,934	8,983	8,466
Air	869	748	719	732	776	531	273
Land	5,800	6,214	7,764	8,008	9,020	8,375	8,071
Railroad	5,392	5,816	7,313	7,423	8,378	7,898	7,496
Communication	15,468	18,846	22,187	27,488	26,343	19,713	17,945
Power	27,603	29,210	33,654	54,115	69,242	77,622	71,375
Electric	20,928	22,678	26,295	41,460	52,799	60,807	56,653
Gas	5,096	5,239	5,528	7,876	10,560	11,928	10,302
Oil	1,579	1,293	1,831	4,779	5,883	4,887	4,420
Sewage & Waste Disposal	331	240	305	408	665	488	410
Water Supply	405	326	477	516	466	295	528
Manufacturing	23,219	28,413	32,264	40,215	52,754	57,976	38,105
Food/beverage/tobacco	3,094	4,446	4,330	3,794	4,514	3,291	3,578
Textile/apparel/leather & allied	185	396	133	35	260	283	527
Wood	475	933	1,350	702	352	416	317
Paper	540	442	515	450	577	519	550
Print/publishing	642	739	670	236	243	172	54
Petroleum/coal	1,181	734	1,650	5,061	14,724	24,743	10,030
Chemical	5,406	6,263	8,484	13,279	12,576	9,811	7,690
Plastic/rubber	919	834	812	974	1,035	584	575
Nonmetallic mineral	880	1,105	2,388	3,417	2,838	1,868	831
Primary metal	305	793	1,327	1,558	3,329	4,573	4,880
Fabricated metal	584	664	517	931	1,474	1,493	1,058
Machinery	633	872	862	489	917	1,083	944
Computer/electronic/electrical	2,779	4,039	4,001	2,556	2,129	3,756	4,565
Transportation equipment	2,562	3,518	2,422	3,218	4,537	3,642	1,957
Furniture	214	91	111	160	34	(S)	(S)
Miscellaneous	2,821	2,545	2,693	3,356	3,215	1,743	551

Notes: Details may not add to totals since all types of construction are not shown separately. Total private construction includes the following categories of construction not shown: highway and street, and conservation and development.
S = Estimate does not meet publication standards.

Source: U.S. Census Bureau
Plunkett Research,® Ltd.
www.plunkettresearch.com

Value of U.S. Public Construction Put in Place: 2004-2010

(In Millions of US$)

Type of Construction	2004	2005	2006	2007	2008	2009	2010
Total Public Construction[1]	**220,183**	**234,160**	**255,385**	**289,073**	**308,738**	**315,459**	**306,293**
Residential	5,508	5,608	6,083	7,222	7,489	7,956	9,779
Nonresidential	214,675	228,552	249,303	281,852	301,249	307,502	296,513
Office	9,525	8,487	8,507	11,445	13,061	14,812	13,107
Commercial	3,862	3,658	3,345	3,827	3,558	3,756	2,869
Health care	5,912	5,935	6,456	8,179	8,464	9,460	9,443
Educational	61,549	66,899	71,089	80,068	86,267	86,107	74,340
Public safety	6,730	6,906	7,350	9,606	12,460	13,613	11,538
Amusement & recreation	8,263	7,728	9,707	11,019	11,320	11,084	10,714
Transportation	18,219	17,928	19,310	22,868	25,537	29,476	30,983
Power	8,035	9,161	8,590	11,940	11,833	11,784	12,256
Highway and street	58,294	63,790	71,567	76,248	81,161	81,915	83,323
Sewage & waste disposal	17,598	19,627	22,881	24,464	25,031	23,922	25,121
Water supply	12,215	13,703	14,483	15,282	16,286	15,266	14,874
Conservation & development	3,869	4,322	5,047	5,155	5,179	5,593	6,775
Total State & Local Construction[1]	**201,841**	**216,860**	**237,831**	**268,494**	**285,007**	**287,145**	**275,493**
Residential	4,110	4,047	4,349	5,094	4,894	5,756	7,407
Nonresidential	197,731	212,813	233,482	263,399	280,113	281,389	268,086
Office	6,024	5,211	5,588	7,249	8,515	9,382	8,205
Commercial	1,979	1,882	1,567	1,777	1,965	2,148	1,555
Health care	5,025	5,059	5,615	7,028	7,010	6,819	6,077
Educational	59,741	65,750	69,790	78,376	84,489	83,495	71,101
Public safety	5,477	6,013	6,608	8,423	9,666	9,426	7,594
Amusement & recreation	7,794	7,340	9,444	10,670	10,872	10,638	9,826
Transportation	16,440	16,256	17,695	21,144	23,230	27,267	29,089
Power	7,044	8,320	7,766	11,449	10,992	10,776	11,172
Highway & street	57,351	63,157	71,032	75,455	80,424	81,081	82,185
Sewage & waste disposal	17,084	18,336	21,524	23,323	24,102	23,229	24,132
Water supply	11,977	13,483	14,299	15,029	16,017	14,971	14,598
Conservation & development	1,466	1,752	2,000	2,198	2,251	1,987	2,014
Total Federal Construction[2]	**18,342**	**17,300**	**17,555**	**20,580**	**23,731**	**28,314**	**30,800**
Residential	1,398	1,561	1,734	2,127	2,595	2,201	2,372
Nonresidential	16,944	15,739	15,821	18,452	21,136	26,113	28,427
Office	3,500	3,275	2,919	4,195	4,546	5,430	4,902
Commercial	1,882	1,776	1,778	2,049	1,593	1,608	1,314
Health care	887	877	842	1,150	1,454	2,640	3,366
Educational	1,808	1,149	1,299	1,691	1,778	2,612	3,239
Public safety	1,253	893	741	1,183	2,793	4,187	3,944
Amusement & recreation	469	388	263	349	448	446	888
Transportation	1,779	1,672	1,615	1,724	2,307	2,209	1,894
Power	990	842	824	491	841	1,008	1,084
Highway & street	943	633	536	792	737	834	1,138
Conservation & development	2,403	2,570	3,047	2,957	2,928	3,606	4,761

NA = Not applicable.

[1] Includes the following categories of construction not shown separately: lodging, religious, communication and manufacturing.

[2] Includes the following categories of federal construction not shown separately: lodging, religious, communication, sewage and waste disposal, water supply, and manufacturing.

Source: U.S. Census Bureau

Plunkett Research,® Ltd.

www.plunkettresearch.com

Estimates of the Total Housing Inventory for the U.S.: 2009-2010

(In Thousands of Units)

Type of Housing	2009 Estimate	2010 Estimate	90-Percent Confidence Interval (+/-)*		2010 Percent of Total
			of 2010 Estimate	of Difference	
All housing units	129,944	130,599	(X)	(X)	100
Occupied	111,159	111,860	230	213	85.7
Owner occupied	74,892	74,791	565	481	57.3
Renter occupied	36,267	37,069	491	433	28.4
Vacant	18,785	18,739	300	274	14.3
Year-round vacant	14,121	14,294	313	285	10.9
For rent	4,386	4,284	145	151	3.3
For sale only	2,016	1,983	75	86	1.5
Rented or sold, awaiting occupancy	992	908	44	58	0.7
Held off market	6,726	7,120	231	209	5.5
For occasional use	2,064	2,241	132	119	1.7
Temporarily occupied by persons with usual residence elsewhere	1,185	1,254	99	90	1.0
For other reasons	3,478	3,625	167	152	2.8
Seasonal vacant	4,665	4,444	208	197	3.4

Estimates may not add to total due to rounding.

* A 90-percent confidence interval is a measure of an estimate's reliability. The larger the confidence interval is, in relation to the size of the estimate, the less reliable the estimate.

X = Not applicable. Because the number of housing units is set equal to an independent national measure, there is no sampling error, and hence no confidence interval.

Source: U.S. Census Bureau
Plunkett Research,® Ltd.
www.plunkettresearch.com

Assets & Liabilities, U.S. Agency- & Government Sponsored Enterprise (GSE)-Backed Securities by Holder: 2006-2010

(In Billions of US$; Amounts Outstanding End of Period, Not Seasonally Adjusted)

Assets & Liabilities	2006	2007	2008	2009				2010			
				Q1	Q2	Q3	Q4	Q1	Q2	Q3	Q4
Total liabilities	**6,492.4**	**7,397.7**	**8,166.7**	**8,182.8**	**8,141.1**	**8,121.3**	**8,106.5**	**7,633.2**	**7,631.1**	**7,593.5**	**7,569.3**
Budget agencies	23.5	23.1	23.3	22.5	22.3	23.2	23.5	23.6	23.9	24.0	24.2
Government-sponsored enterprises	2,627.8	2,910.2	3,181.9	3,118.3	2,948.1	2,800.5	2,706.6	6,602.7	6,535.6	6,448.8	6,378.8
Agency- & GSE-backed mortgage pools	3,841.1	4,464.4	4,961.4	5,042.0	5,170.7	5,297.5	5,376.4	1,006.9	1,071.6	1,120.7	1,166.3
Total assets	**6,492.4**	**7,397.7**	**8,166.7**	**8,182.8**	**8,141.1**	**8,121.3**	**8,106.5**	**7,633.2**	**7,631.1**	**7,593.5**	**7,569.3**
Household sector	403.6	669.0	711.4	499.5	202.1	201.6	82.6	9.9	14.8	39.6	77.9
Nonfinancial corporate business	15.2	12.8	10.2	6.2	11.4	11.1	11.7	13.7	14.5	14.3	14.4
State and local governments	439.9	458.7	451.1	452.0	444.5	440.0	436.1	441.1	432.1	438.8	449.4
Federal government	0.0	0.0	54.4	111.4	164.7	195.6	225.5	225.5	225.5	225.5	225.5
Rest of the world	1,263.6	1,582.4	1,406.9	1,338.1	1,316.5	1,262.6	1,188.6	1,177.1	1,215.8	1,201.9	1,185.9
Monetary authority	0.0	0.0	19.7	287.0	559.1	823.5	1,068.3	1,237.7	1,282.9	1,232.6	1,139.6
Commercial banking	1,135.6	1,022.3	1,169.4	1,175.4	1,221.3	1,185.8	1,276.9	1,269.3	1,261.6	1,316.2	1,354.0
U.S.-chartered commercial banks	1,040.3	928.9	1,068.7	1,085.4	1,136.8	1,106.5	1,200.0	1,196.9	1,192.9	1,242.9	1,292.8
Foreign banking offices in the U.S.	55.1	57.1	50.5	45.6	38.7	35.2	32.1	31.4	30.4	30.2	27.3
Bank holding companies	11.2	9.9	25.8	21.6	22.4	22.3	24.3	22.6	22.1	30.1	21.1
Banks in U.S.-affiliated areas	29.0	26.3	24.4	22.8	23.5	21.8	20.5	18.4	16.2	13.0	12.8
Savings institutions	177.0	177.4	173.8	175.9	187.6	197.4	201.6	209.9	206.5	209.1	221.9
Credit unions	72.5	68.4	82.9	91.9	100.7	105.2	110.8	123.5	133.6	136.3	148.0
Property-casualty insurance companies	122.0	125.8	114.3	113.8	114.5	115.2	116.2	113.8	112.2	110.4	109.4
Life insurance companies	377.4	382.9	366.2	363.3	367.2	368.2	371.9	369.6	365.0	357.9	357.0
Private pension funds	268.6	296.8	318.1	310.6	294.4	278.8	269.1	259.6	210.9	170.2	170.9
State and local government retirement funds	307.8	331.1	337.5	329.7	319.0	311.2	306.9	301.0	292.3	285.1	285.5
Federal government retirement funds	4.7	5.0	5.1	5.0	5.0	5.4	5.6	5.8	6.0	6.6	6.3
Money market mutual funds	131.4	235.9	756.2	776.3	741.5	635.2	543.0	465.1	450.3	415.3	402.8
Mutual funds	499.1	565.4	592.7	588.1	616.9	635.1	639.1	684.3	710.7	760.8	786.7
Government-sponsored enterprises	714.0	702.9	910.0	954.0	949.0	919.4	924.5	417.0	387.7	375.1	368.4
ABS Issuers	356.7	381.9	353.8	290.9	251.7	191.0	125.8	90.0	53.1	28.3	17.7
REITs	65.4	88.9	90.5	91.7	96.8	97.5	91.4	91.8	93.8	96.1	98.3
Brokers & dealers	138.0	290.2	242.6	222.0	177.2	141.6	110.9	127.5	161.9	173.5	149.8

Notes: Agency- and GSE-backed securities include: issues of federal budget agencies such as those for the TVA; issues of government sponsored enterprises such as FNMA and FHLB; and agency- and GSE-backed mortgage pool securities issued by GNMA, FNMA, FHLMC, and the Farmers Home Administration. Only the budget agency issues are considered officially to be part of the total debt of the federal government.

ABS = Asset-Backed Security. REIT = Real Estate Investment Trust.

Source: U.S. Federal Reserve
Plunkett Research,® Ltd.
www.plunkettresearch.com

Commercial, Residential & Farm Mortgages by Holder, U.S.: 2006-2010

(In Billions of US$; Amounts Outstanding End of Period, Not Seasonally Adjusted)

Holder	2006	2007	2008	2009				2010			
				Q1	Q2	Q3	Q4	Q1	Q2	Q3	Q4
Total mortgages	**13,462.5**	**14,515.6**	**14,605.5**	**14,602.4**	**14,546.5**	**14,436.0**	**14,315.9**	**14,169.1**	**14,053.9**	**13,935.0**	**13,832.8**
Home	10,455.6	11,167.2	11,069.1	11,063.7	11,011.8	10,924.4	10,859.2	10,746.3	10,683.4	10,607.3	10,546.5
Multi-family residential	707.5	786.8	837.3	845.0	852.3	855.3	848.5	847.9	842.4	843.1	841.2
Commercial	2,191.3	2,448.9	2,565.4	2,559.9	2,548.3	2,522.1	2,473.7	2,440.9	2,394.7	2,351.9	2,312.5
Farm	108.0	112.7	133.6	133.8	134.0	134.3	134.5	134.0	133.4	132.8	132.6
Total liabilities	**13,462.5**	**14,515.6**	**14,605.5**	**14,602.4**	**14,546.5**	**14,436.0**	**14,315.9**	**14,169.1**	**14,053.9**	**13,935.0**	**13,832.8**
Household sector	10,079.3	10,780.0	10,707.0	10,711.2	10,671.8	10,602.4	10,542.3	10,446.9	10,389.1	10,312.3	10,249.6
Nonfinancial business	3,231.1	3,578.8	3,735.0	3,726.3	3,707.4	3,666.8	3,606.7	3,555.1	3,497.3	3,454.4	3,414.3
Corporate	834.2	873.0	837.3	833.0	829.4	816.9	798.1	777.0	761.6	748.4	731.2
Nonfarm noncorporate	2,288.9	2,593.1	2,764.0	2,759.5	2,743.9	2,715.6	2,674.0	2,644.2	2,602.3	2,573.2	2,550.4
Farm	108.0	112.7	133.6	133.8	134.0	134.3	134.5	134.0	133.4	132.8	132.6
Federal government	0.0	0.0	0.0	0.0	0.0	0.0	0.0	0.0	0.0	0.0	0.0
REITs	152.1	156.7	163.5	164.9	167.3	166.9	166.9	167.1	167.6	168.3	169.0
Total assets	**13,462.5**	**14,515.6**	**14,605.5**	**14,602.4**	**14,546.5**	**14,436.0**	**14,315.9**	**14,169.1**	**14,053.9**	**13,935.0**	**13,832.8**
Household sector	122.1	109.8	111.8	109.9	107.7	105.1	102.5	101.0	97.7	94.8	92.3
Nonfinancial corporate business	59.8	41.4	33.6	31.7	29.8	27.9	25.9	24.0	22.1	20.1	18.2
Nonfarm noncorporate business	34.6	42.1	39.1	38.5	37.7	36.9	36.1	35.6	35.0	34.6	34.4
State & local governments	166.4	172.8	169.7	170.0	172.8	176.7	179.0	182.8	181.2	182.8	184.5
Federal government	80.3	82.4	95.8	96.7	102.2	110.0	108.4	107.1	108.4	106.6	106.6
Commercial banking	3,403.1	3,644.4	3,841.4	3,853.3	3,897.6	3,795.4	3,818.7	3,761.3	3,706.8	3,674.4	3,651.2
Savings institutions*	1,076.8	1,094.0	860.6	849.8	752.2	725.8	633.3	629.3	619.3	617.8	614.9
Credit unions	249.7	281.5	314.7	316.3	319.0	317.7	317.9	320.1	322.6	324.4	319.0
Property-casualty insurance companies	3.5	4.8	5.0	5.0	5.0	4.8	4.4	4.3	4.2	4.2	4.1
Life insurance companies	303.8	326.2	342.4	338.6	335.0	332.4	326.1	321.4	317.9	318.2	318.0
Private pension funds	9.5	10.2	11.1	11.6	12.1	12.8	13.6	14.6	15.7	15.2	15.1
State & local government retirement funds	14.4	9.7	9.4	9.4	9.4	9.4	9.3	9.4	9.3	9.4	9.3
Government-sponsored enterprises*	607.2	643.1	701.4	725.9	713.2	710.5	707.7	5,104.4	5,084.4	5,035.8	5,019.9
Agency- & GSE-backed mortgage pools	3,841.1	4,464.4	4,961.4	5,042.0	5,170.7	5,297.5	5,376.4	1,006.9	1,071.6	1,120.7	1,166.3
ABS issuers	2,760.0	2,935.7	2,584.2	2,492.2	2,386.3	2,294.2	2,199.9	2,102.8	2,030.7	1,961.6	1,887.3
Finance companies	594.4	531.9	447.9	440.2	426.8	415.6	397.4	386.9	371.1	361.2	340.5
REITs	135.8	121.3	75.9	71.5	68.9	63.5	59.2	57.4	55.7	53.2	51.3

* FHLB loans to savings institutions are included in other loans and advances.

REIT = Real Estate Investment Trust. GSE = Government Sponsored Enterprise. ABS = Asset Backed Security.

Source: U.S. Federal Reserve

Plunkett Research,® Ltd.

www.plunkettresearch.com

Home Mortgages by Holder, U.S.: 2006-2010

(In Billions of US$; Amounts Outstanding End of Period; Not Seasonally Adjusted)

Holder	2006	2007	2008	2009				2010			
				Q1	Q2	Q3	Q4	Q1	Q2	Q3	Q4
Total liabilities	**10,455.6**	**11,167.2**	**11,069.1**	**11,063.7**	**11,011.8**	**10,924.4**	**10,859.2**	**10,746.3**	**10,683.4**	**10,607.3**	**10,546.5**
Household sector	9,865.0	10,539.9	10,495.5	10,500.2	10,461.9	10,395.1	10,339.8	10,240.8	10,192.5	10,125.0	10,069.6
Nonfinancial corporate business	39.4	42.2	32.7	30.0	26.8	23.3	20.3	18.4	15.9	14.8	13.6
Nonfarm noncorporate business	551.2	585.1	540.9	533.4	523.0	506.0	499.1	487.1	475.0	467.5	463.3
Total assets	**10,455.6**	**11,167.2**	**11,069.1**	**11,063.7**	**11,011.8**	**10,924.4**	**10,859.2**	**10,746.3**	**10,683.4**	**10,607.3**	**10,546.5**
Household sector	102.9	90.8	91.2	89.2	87.2	85.2	83.2	81.2	79.2	77.2	75.2
Nonfinancial corporate business	35.9	25.0	20.2	19.0	17.9	16.7	15.5	14.4	13.2	12.1	10.9
Nonfarm noncorporate business	12.7	15.4	14.3	14.1	13.8	13.5	13.2	13.0	12.8	12.7	12.6
State & local governments	84.9	88.5	87.0	87.2	88.7	90.7	91.9	93.8	93.0	93.6	94.1
Federal government	13.3	13.7	16.4	16.4	18.9	22.8	22.1	23.2	23.9	23.6	23.9
Commercial banking	2,082.1	2,210.5	2,248.1	2,253.1	2,300.3	2,212.6	2,261.3	2,222.6	2,198.6	2,196.6	2,207.0
Savings institutions	867.8	879.0	666.3	654.9	556.6	534.5	448.6	444.5	438.7	437.0	430.5
Credit unions	249.7	281.5	314.7	316.3	319.0	317.7	317.9	320.1	322.6	324.4	319.0
Life insurance companies	10.3	9.4	8.8	8.7	8.6	8.5	5.6	5.4	5.2	5.3	5.4
Private pension funds	1.3	1.2	1.3	1.7	1.8	1.9	2.0	2.1	2.1	2.1	2.1
State & local government retirement funds	5.2	3.5	3.4	3.4	3.4	3.4	3.3	3.4	3.4	3.4	3.4
Government-sponsored enterprises	457.6	447.9	455.9	472.9	455.6	448.6	444.1	4,795.7	4,776.3	4,725.7	4,705.0
Federally related mortgage pools	3,749.1	4,371.8	4,864.0	4,943.5	5,068.6	5,192.1	5,266.5	942.3	1,004.6	1,051.0	1,094.5
ABS issuers	2,140.8	2,177.2	1,865.4	1,781.2	1,682.5	1,599.6	1,528.6	1,442.3	1,383.6	1,326.0	1,266.4
Finance companies	538.1	472.7	375.4	368.4	356.1	345.1	327.7	317.0	303.3	295.3	276.9
REITs	103.7	79.2	36.7	33.7	32.8	31.5	27.5	25.4	22.8	21.4	19.7
Memo:											
Home equity loans included above[2]	1,066.1	1,130.9	1,114.3	1,096.5	1,074.7	1,051.4	1,032.1	1,013.4	995.6	975.4	948.9
Commercial banking	653.6	692.3	776.1	769.7	781.2	766.8	761.7	751.5	741.3	726.9	709.6
Savings institutions	137.6	180.5	119.5	116.0	90.0	87.9	80.0	78.4	76.6	75.5	74.0
Credit unions	86.9	94.1	98.7	97.0	96.1	95.0	94.6	92.7	91.8	90.3	88.0
ABS issuers	80.4	69.5	45.0	40.2	36.1	32.7	30.3	27.4	25.3	23.7	22.0
Finance companies	107.6	94.5	75.1	73.7	71.2	69.0	65.5	63.4	60.7	59.1	55.4

[1] Mortgages on 1-4 family properties. [2] Loans made under home equity lines of credit and home equity loans secured by junior liens. Excludes home equity loans held by individuals. REIT = Real Estate Investment Trust. ABS = Asset Backed Security.
Source: U.S. Federal Reserve
Plunkett Research,® Ltd.
www.plunkettresearch.com

New Privately-Owned Housing Starts, U.S.: 1980-2010

(In Thousands)

Year	Single Unit	2-4 Units	5+ Units	Total
1980	852.2	109.5	330.5	1,292.2
1981	705.4	91.2	287.7	1,084.2
1982	662.6	80.1	319.6	1,062.2
1983	1,067.6	113.5	522.0	1,703.0
1984	1,084.2	121.4	543.9	1,749.5
1985	1,072.4	93.5	576.0	1,741.8
1986	1,179.4	84.0	542.0	1,805.4
1987	1,146.4	65.1	408.7	1,620.5
1988	1,081.3	58.7	348.0	1,488.1
1989	1,003.3	55.3	317.6	1,376.1
1990	894.8	37.6	260.4	1,192.7
1991	840.4	35.6	137.9	1,013.9
1992	1,029.9	30.9	139.0	1,199.7
1993	1,125.7	29.4	132.6	1,287.6
1994	1,198.4	35.2	223.5	1,457.0
1995	1,076.2	33.8	244.1	1,354.1
1996	1,160.9	45.3	270.8	1,476.8
1997	1,133.7	44.5	295.8	1,474.0
1998	1,271.4	42.6	302.9	1,616.9
1999	1,302.4	31.9	306.6	1,640.9
2000	1,230.9	38.7	299.1	1,568.7
2001	1,273.3	36.6	292.8	1,602.7
2002	1,358.6	38.5	307.9	1,704.9
2003	1,499.0	33.5	315.2	1,847.7
2004	1,610.5	42.3	303.0	1,955.8
2005	1,715.8	41.1	311.4	2,068.3
2006	1,465.4	42.7	292.8	1,800.9
2007	1,046.0	31.7	277.3	1,355.0
2008	622.0	17.5	266.0	905.5
2009	445.1	11.6	97.3	554.0
2010	471.2	11.4	104.3	586.9

Note: Single-family estimates prior to 1999 include an upward adjustment of 3.3 percent made to account for structures started in permit-issuing areas without permit authorization.

Source: U.S. Census Bureau

Plunkett Research,® Ltd.

www.plunkettresearch.com

Homeownership Rates by Region, U.S.: 1995-2010

(Percent of All Households)

Area	1995	2000	2004	2005	2006	2007	2008	2009	2010
United States	**64.7**	**67.4**	**69.0**	**68.9**	**68.8**	**68.1**	**67.8**	**67.4**	**66.9**
Inside Metropolitan Areas[1]	62.7	65.5	67.3	67.4	67.4	66.8	66.4	65.9	65.4
In Central Cities	49.5	51.4	53.1	54.2	54.3	53.6	53.2	52.8	52.1
Not in Central Cities[1] (suburbs)	71.2	74.0	75.7	76.4	76.1	75.5	75.1	74.6	74.0
Outside Metropolitan Areas[1]	72.7	75.2	76.3	76.3	75.9	75.1	75.2	74.7	74.5
Northeast	62.0	63.4	65.0	65.2	65.2	65.0	64.6	64.0	64.1
Midwest	69.2	72.6	73.8	73.1	72.7	71.9	71.7	71.0	70.8
South	66.7	69.6	70.9	70.8	70.5	70.1	69.9	69.6	69.0
West	59.2	61.7	64.2	64.4	64.7	63.5	63.0	62.6	61.4

[1] Approximately every 10 years, metropolitan/nonmetropolitan area definitions are redefined by the Office of Management and Budget. Therefore metropolitan/nonmetropolitan data for 1986 to 1994, 1995 to 2004, and 2005 and later are not comparable to each other.

Source: U.S. Census Bureau

Plunkett Research,® Ltd.

www.plunkettresearch.com

Homeownership Rates by Race
& Ethnicity of Householder, U.S.: 2003-2010

(Percent of All Households)

	2003	2004	2005	2006	2007	2008	2009	2010
U.S. Total	**68.3**	**69.0**	**68.9**	**68.8**	**68.1**	**67.8**	**67.4**	**66.9**
White Alone, Total	72.1	72.8	72.7	72.6	72.0	71.7	71.4	71.0
Non-Hispanic White	75.4	76.0	75.8	75.8	75.2	75.0	74.8	74.4
Black, Total	48.1	49.1	48.2	47.9	47.2	47.4	46.2	45.4
All Other Races, Total*	56.0	58.6	59.2	59.9	59.2	58.5	57.8	57.0
American Indian or Alaskan Native	54.3	55.6	58.2	58.2	56.9	56.5	56.2	52.3
Asian or Native Hawaiian/Pacific Islander	56.3	59.8	60.1	60.8	60.0	59.5	59.3	58.9
Hispanic or Latino	46.7	48.1	49.5	49.7	49.7	49.1	48.4	47.5
Non-Hispanic	70.8	71.5	71.2	71.2	70.5	70.3	69.8	69.4

Notes: Beginning in 1996 to 2002, those answering 'other' for race were allocated to one of the 4 race categories-- White, Black, American Indian, Aleut, or Eskimo (one category), or Asian or Native Hawaiian.

* Asian, Native Hawaiian or other Pacific Islander, American Indian or Alaska Native (only one race reported) and Two or more races.

Source: U.S. Census Bureau
Plunkett Research,® Ltd.
www.plunkettresearch.com

Homeownership Rates by Age of Householder, U.S.: Selected Years, 1985-2010

(In Percentage of Households)

Age Range	1985	1990	1995	2000	2009	2010
United States, Total	**63.9**	**63.9**	**64.7**	**67.4**	**67.4**	**66.9**
Less than 25 years	17.2	15.7	15.9	21.7	23.3	22.8
25 to 29 years	37.7	35.2	34.4	38.1	37.7	36.8
30 to 34 years	54.0	51.8	53.1	54.6	52.5	51.6
35 to 39 years	65.4	63.0	62.1	65.0	63.4	61.9
40 to 44 years	71.4	69.8	68.6	70.6	68.7	67.9
45 to 49 years	74.3	73.9	73.7	74.7	72.3	72.0
50 to 54 years	77.5	76.8	77.0	78.5	76.5	75.0
55 to 59years	79.2	78.8	78.8	80.4	78.6	77.7
60 to 64 years	79.9	79.8	80.3	80.3	80.6	80.4
65 to 69 years	79.5	80.0	81.0	83.0	82.0	81.6
70 to 74 years	76.8	78.4	80.9	82.6	81.9	82.4
75 years and over	69.8	72.3	74.6	77.7	78.9	78.9
Less than 35 years	39.9	38.5	38.6	40.8	39.7	39.1
35 to 44 years	68.1	66.3	65.2	67.9	66.2	65.0
45 to 54 years	75.9	75.2	75.2	76.5	74.4	73.5
55 to 64 years	79.5	79.3	79.5	80.3	79.5	79.0
65 years and over	74.8	76.3	78.1	80.4	80.5	80.5

Source: U.S. Census Bureau
Plunkett Research,® Ltd.
www.plunkettresearch.com

Median & Average Sales Price of New Single Family Homes by Region, U.S.: 1985-2010

(In US$)

Period	Median sales price					Average sales price				
	U.S.	Northeast	Midwest	South	West	U.S.	Northeast	Midwest	South	West
1985	84,300	103,300	80,300	75,000	92,600	100,800	121,900	95,400	88,900	111,800
1986	92,000	125,000	88,300	80,200	95,700	111,900	151,300	102,600	95,300	116,100
1987	104,500	140,000	95,000	88,000	111,000	127,200	170,900	115,500	106,600	134,600
1988	112,500	149,000	101,600	92,000	126,500	138,300	179,300	123,700	114,800	155,700
1989	120,000	159,600	108,800	96,400	139,000	148,800	188,600	130,600	123,100	173,900
1990	122,900	159,000	107,900	99,000	147,500	149,800	190,500	133,000	123,500	180,600
1991	120,000	155,900	110,000	100,000	141,100	147,200	188,800	134,500	123,000	176,400
1992	121,500	169,000	115,600	105,500	130,400	144,100	194,900	136,400	126,900	157,800
1993	126,500	162,600	125,000	115,000	135,000	147,700	183,600	143,100	133,600	161,900
1994	130,000	169,000	132,900	116,900	140,400	154,500	200,500	152,700	136,800	168,900
1995	133,900	180,000	134,000	124,500	141,000	158,700	216,600	157,200	142,000	169,800
1996	140,000	186,900	137,500	125,000	153,900	166,400	226,800	158,100	143,100	185,900
1997	146,000	190,000	149,900	129,600	160,000	176,200	234,100	173,000	151,400	198,200
1998	152,500	200,000	157,500	135,800	163,500	181,900	240,100	179,200	159,700	200,500
1999	161,000	210,500	164,000	145,900	173,700	195,600	247,900	186,800	173,000	221,700
2000	169,000	227,400	169,700	148,000	196,400	207,000	274,800	199,300	179,000	238,900
2001	175,200	246,400	172,600	155,400	213,600	213,200	294,300	201,300	185,700	250,000
2002	187,600	264,300	178,000	163,400	238,500	228,700	301,300	209,800	197,500	276,500
2003	195,000	264,500	184,300	168,100	260,900	246,300	315,700	218,200	208,900	306,800
2004	221,000	315,800	205,000	181,100	283,100	274,500	366,100	240,800	232,800	340,000
2005	240,900	343,800	216,900	197,300	332,600	297,000	397,000	249,800	249,200	388,700
2006	246,500	346,000	213,500	208,200	337,700	305,900	428,300	257,100	257,700	405,900
2007	247,900	320,200	208,600	217,700	330,900	313,600	437,700	256,800	269,800	403,700
2008	232,100	343,600	198,900	203,700	294,800	292,600	475,500	250,000	253,400	361,500
2009	216,700	302,500	189,200	194,800	263,700	270,900	411,300	227,700	241,200	321,600
2010	221,900	335,500	197,600	196,000	259,700	271,600	418,400	230,600	242,800	315,700

Source: U.S. Census Bureau

Plunkett Research,® Ltd.

www.plunkettresearch.com

New Single Family Homes Sold by Region, U.S.: 1985-2010

(Not Seasonally Adjusted; In Thousands)

Period	U.S.	Northeast	Midwest	South	West
1985	688	112	82	323	171
1986	750	136	96	322	196
1987	671	117	97	271	186
1988	676	101	97	276	202
1989	650	86	102	260	202
1990	534	71	89	225	149
1991	509	57	93	215	144
1992	610	65	116	259	170
1993	666	60	123	295	188
1994	670	61	123	295	191
1995	667	55	125	300	187
1996	757	74	137	337	209
1997	804	78	140	363	223
1998	886	81	164	398	243
1999	880	76	168	395	242
2000	877	71	155	406	244
2001	908	66	164	439	239
2002	973	65	185	450	273
2003	1,086	79	189	511	307
2004	1,203	83	210	562	348
2005	1,283	81	205	638	358
2006	1,051	63	161	559	267
2007	776	65	118	411	181
2008	485	35	70	266	114
2009	375	31	54	202	87
2010	323	31	45	174	74

Note: Components may not add to total because of rounding. Estimates prior to 1999 include an upward adjustment of 3.3 percent made to account for houses sold in permit-issuing areas that will never have a permit authorization.

Source: U.S. Census Bureau

Plunkett Research,® Ltd.

www.plunkettresearch.com

New Single Family Homes Sold by Type of Financing, U.S.: 1988-2010

(In Thousands)

Period	Total Sold	Type of Financing				
		Conventional*	FHA Insured	VA Guaranteed	Rural Housing Service	Cash
1988	676	437	127	44	6	62
1989	650	416	118	44	14	58
1990	534	337	105	33	10	50
1991	509	329	92	36	9	43
1992	610	428	86	48	7	41
1993	666	476	92	55	6	37
1994	670	490	78	51	9	41
1995	667	490	79	50	9	39
1996	757	570	89	51	9	38
1997	804	616	90	47	6	46
1998	886	693	90	46	9	48
1999	880	689	106	37	6	41
2000	877	695	108	30	4	40
2001	908	726	106	35	2	39
2002	973	788	106	34	4	42
2003	1,086	911	94	36	4	41
2004	1,203	1,047	77	28	6	46
2005	1,283	1,151	51	28	1	52
2006	1,051	949	38	25	1	38
2007	776	695	28	24	2	30
2008	485	358	77	27	NA	23
2009	375	234	92	32	NA	17
2010	321	187	81	35	NA	18

* Includes houses reporting other types of financing. Beginning in 2005, also includes Rural Housing Service.

Note: Estimates prior to 1999 include an upward adjustment of 3.3 percent made to account for houses sold in permit-issuing areas that will never have a permit authorization.

Source: U.S. Census Bureau

Plunkett Research,® Ltd.

www.plunkettresearch.com

New Single Family Homes for Sale at End of Period, by Region, U.S.: 1985-2010

(Not Seasonally Adjusted; In Thousands)

Period	U.S.	Northeast	Midwest	South	West
1985	350	66	34	172	79
1986	361	88	32	153	87
1987	370	103	39	149	79
1988	371	112	43	133	82
1989	366	108	41	123	93
1990	321	77	42	105	97
1991	284	62	41	97	83
1992	267	48	41	104	74
1993	295	53	48	121	73
1994	340	55	63	140	82
1995	374	62	69	158	86
1996	326	38	67	146	74
1997	287	26	65	127	69
1998	300	28	63	142	68
1999	315	28	64	153	70
2000	301	28	65	146	62
2001	310	28	70	142	69
2002	344	36	77	161	70
2003	377	29	97	172	79
2004	431	30	111	200	91
2005	515	47	109	249	109
2006	537	54	97	267	119
2007	496	48	79	248	121
2008	352	37	57	175	83
2009	232	27	38	118	48
2010	188	22	27	98	41

Note: Components may not add to total because of rounding. Estimates prior to 1999 include an upward adjustment of 3.3 percent made to account for houses for sale in permit-issuing areas that will never have a permit authorization.

Source: U.S. Census Bureau

Plunkett Research,® Ltd.

www.plunkettresearch.com

Placements of New Manufactured Homes, U.S.: 1995-2010

(In Thousands)

Year	Total*	Single Units	Double-Wide
1995	319.4	163.0	152.1
1996	337.7	163.4	168.9
1997	336.3	144.0	186.2
1998	373.7	149.6	218.1
1999	338.3	122.5	213.0
2000	280.9	88.3	190.3
2001	196.2	53.3	139.3
2002	174.3	41.1	128.7
2003	139.8	29.4	106.0
2004	124.4	28.2	91.7
2005	122.9	28.7	89.4
2006	112.4	28.9	79.2
2007	94.8	28.6	63.1
2008	80.5	27.8	50.8
2009	52.2	19.2	31.9
2010	49.5	19.0	29.8

* Includes manufactured homes with more than two sections.

Source: U.S. Census Bureau
Plunkett Research,® Ltd.
www.plunkettresearch.com

Price Deflator (Fisher) Index of New One-Family Houses Under Construction, U.S.: 1975-February 2011

(2005 = 100)

Year	Annual		Monthly											
	Ann. Index	% Chg.	Jan	Feb	Mar	Apr	May	Jun	Jul	Aug	Sep	Oct	Nov	Dec
1975	22.9	8.5%	22.3	22.3	22.3	22.6	22.9	23.1	23.1	22.9	23.1	23.2	23.4	23.6
1976	24.4	6.6%	23.4	23.4	23.5	23.9	24.3	24.5	24.7	24.6	24.6	24.8	25.0	25.2
1977	27.0	10.7%	25.6	25.7	25.8	26.0	26.4	26.9	27.2	27.6	27.8	28.0	28.2	28.5
1978	30.6	13.3%	28.9	29.2	29.6	30.0	30.2	30.6	30.9	31.2	31.4	31.7	32.0	32.2
1979	34.3	12.1%	32.4	32.5	32.8	33.2	33.8	34.4	34.8	35.2	35.4	35.6	35.8	36.1
1980	37.9	10.5%	36.5	36.7	37.0	37.3	37.4	37.7	38.0	38.1	38.5	38.9	39.3	39.5
1981	40.5	6.9%	39.8	40.1	40.1	40.3	40.4	40.5	40.7	40.7	40.8	40.9	41.1	41.0
1982	41.7	3.0%	41.3	41.3	41.5	41.5	41.7	41.7	41.7	42.0	42.3	42.1	42.1	42.2
1983	42.9	2.9%	42.5	42.7	42.8	42.6	42.5	42.6	42.7	42.8	42.9	43.3	43.3	43.4
1984	44.5	3.7%	43.8	44.1	44.2	44.1	44.1	44.2	44.4	44.8	45.0	45.0	45.0	45.0
1985	45.4	2.0%	45.2	45.3	45.5	45.2	45.0	45.0	45.0	45.2	45.4	45.7	45.9	46.1
1986	47.4	4.4%	46.5	46.6	46.7	46.8	47.0	47.3	47.6	47.6	47.8	48.2	48.6	48.8
1987	49.6	4.6%	49.2	49.2	49.2	49.3	49.4	49.5	49.7	49.8	49.8	50.0	50.2	50.6
1988	51.6	4.0%	51.2	51.4	51.4	51.3	51.4	51.4	51.4	51.6	51.8	51.9	52.2	52.3
1989	53.7	4.1%	52.6	53.0	53.0	53.4	53.7	53.7	53.9	53.8	53.9	54.1	54.1	54.5
1990	55.4	3.2%	55.0	55.0	55.1	55.1	55.1	55.4	55.8	55.8	55.7	55.7	55.8	55.7
1991	55.9	0.9%	55.8	55.7	55.4	55.4	55.5	55.8	56.0	56.2	56.3	56.2	56.1	56.1
1992	57.0	2.0%	56.4	56.5	56.5	56.6	56.5	56.7	56.9	57.0	57.2	57.7	58.0	58.3
1993	59.8	4.9%	58.7	58.9	59.0	59.1	59.3	59.7	59.9	60.1	60.3	60.5	60.9	61.1
1994	62.5	4.5%	61.3	61.5	61.5	61.5	61.7	62.1	62.3	62.7	63.1	63.4	63.8	64.4
1995	65.2	4.3%	64.6	64.8	64.8	64.9	65.0	65.2	65.1	65.4	65.6	65.6	65.6	65.6
1996	66.4	1.8%	65.6	65.8	65.7	65.6	65.8	66.2	66.6	66.8	66.8	67.0	67.1	67.3
1997	68.4	3.0%	67.6	67.6	67.6	67.8	67.8	68.1	68.4	68.6	69.0	69.2	69.3	69.3
1998	70.2	2.6%	69.4	69.2	69.2	69.4	69.5	70.0	70.3	70.4	70.4	70.8	71.2	71.6
1999	73.3	4.4%	72.0	72.1	72.3	72.7	73.0	73.3	73.6	73.6	73.7	73.9	74.3	74.6
2000	76.7	4.6%	75.5	75.8	76.0	76.2	76.4	76.7	76.9	76.9	77.1	77.2	77.3	77.7
2001	80.2	4.6%	78.2	78.4	78.6	79.1	79.7	80.2	80.8	81.6	81.6	82.1	82.1	81.8
2002	82.1	2.4%	81.2	81.4	81.7	81.8	82.1	82.2	82.1	81.8	82.3	82.9	82.6	83.2
2003	86.1	4.9%	84.1	84.6	85.1	85.3	85.3	85.4	85.4	86.1	86.8	87.4	88.1	88.5
2004	93.0	8.0%	89.1	89.4	90.3	91.1	92.2	92.8	93.4	93.9	94.4	94.9	95.6	96.3
2005	100.0	7.5%	96.5	96.3	96.9	97.2	98.3	99.3	100.7	100.8	101.3	101.9	102.8	104.1
2006	106.2	6.2%	104.5	104.7	105.7	105.9	106.1	106.1	105.6	105.9	107.0	107.4	107.5	107.8
2007	107.2	0.9%	107.8	107.9	108.2	107.9	106.9	106.5	106.7	107.0	107.2	107.2	106.7	106.4
2008	104.1	-2.9%	105.8	105.5	105.2	104.8	105.2	104.0	104.1	103.4	102.6	102.2	102.2	102.6
2009	99.5	-4.4%	102.4	101.8	101.8	100.8	99.3	98.4	98.0	97.9	98.3	98.6	99.0	99.5
2010	98.0	-1.5%	99.5	98.8	98.0	97.3	97.1	97.4	97.8	97.7	97.5	98.1	98.4	98.8
2011	--	--	98.8	98.6	--	--	--	--	--	--	--	--	--	--

Fisher Ideal Index (Price Deflator): This index helps answers the question, "What is the (unbiased) value of today's homes being constructed in constant dollars?" In doing this it attempts to eliminate two kinds of problems associated with two other indexes: the tendency to overstate inflation (Laspeyres); and the tendency to understate inflation (Paasche). The Fisher Ideal index is the geometric average of a Laspeyres and Paasche indexes for the same time period. The geometric average is calculated by multiplying the Laspeyres index by the Paasche index and then taking the square root of the result. The biases associated with each component index are minimized by calculating the geometric average.

Source: U.S. Census Bureau

Plunkett Research,® Ltd.

www.plunkettresearch.com

Constant Quality (Laspeyres) Price Index of New One-Family Houses Under Construction, U.S.: 1970-2010

(2005 = 100)

Year	Annual		Monthly											
	Ann. Index	% Chg.	Jan	Feb	Mar	Apr	May	Jun	Jul	Aug	Sep	Oct	Nov	Dec
1970	15.9	2.7%	15.6	15.6	15.7	16.1	16.3	16.7	16.0	15.6	15.5	15.6	15.8	16.0
1971	16.8	5.6%	15.9	16.4	16.5	16.6	16.6	16.7	16.7	17.2	17.1	17.2	17.3	17.5
1972	18.0	6.9%	17.6	17.6	17.6	17.6	17.6	17.7	17.9	18.0	18.2	18.5	18.7	18.9
1973	19.8	9.9%	18.9	18.9	19.1	19.3	19.5	19.6	19.9	20.2	20.4	20.5	20.6	20.6
1974	21.8	10.1%	20.8	20.9	21.4	21.1	21.3	21.8	22.0	22.0	22.1	22.4	22.6	22.8
1975	23.7	8.8%	23.1	23.1	23.1	23.3	23.7	23.8	23.8	23.7	23.9	24.0	24.2	24.4
1976	25.2	6.4%	24.2	24.2	24.3	24.6	25.1	25.4	25.5	25.5	25.5	25.7	25.9	26.1
1977	28.2	12.0%	26.6	26.8	27.0	27.2	27.6	27.9	28.3	28.5	28.7	29.0	29.3	29.7
1978	31.7	12.4%	30.0	30.3	30.5	30.8	31.2	31.3	31.6	32.0	32.5	32.9	33.3	33.6
1979	35.7	12.8%	33.9	34.2	34.4	34.8	35.2	35.7	36.2	36.5	36.8	37.0	37.3	37.6
1980	39.8	11.3%	38.1	38.4	38.6	39.0	39.2	39.6	40.1	40.3	40.5	40.7	41.0	41.3
1981	42.6	7.1%	41.6	41.9	42.0	42.3	42.6	42.7	42.7	42.8	43.0	43.2	43.5	43.5
1982	43.4	1.9%	43.4	43.4	43.5	43.6	43.5	43.4	43.2	43.4	43.6	43.5	43.7	43.7
1983	44.7	2.8%	44.0	44.1	44.0	44.0	44.3	44.4	44.6	44.7	44.9	45.2	45.4	45.6
1984	46.7	4.6%	45.8	46.0	46.1	46.1	46.2	46.5	46.5	46.9	47.3	47.5	47.6	47.5
1985	47.9	2.5%	47.7	47.5	47.6	47.5	47.4	47.5	47.6	47.8	48.0	48.2	48.4	48.8
1986	50.4	5.2%	49.1	49.2	49.3	49.5	49.8	50.2	50.4	50.6	50.8	51.1	51.5	51.8
1987	52.7	4.6%	52.1	52.1	52.2	52.4	52.4	52.6	52.7	52.8	52.8	53.0	53.3	53.7
1988	54.5	3.5%	54.1	54.3	54.1	54.1	54.3	54.3	54.3	54.5	54.8	54.9	55.2	55.2
1989	56.4	3.4%	55.4	55.6	55.8	56.1	56.3	56.3	56.5	56.6	56.8	56.8	56.8	57.0
1990	58.0	2.9%	57.2	57.4	57.5	57.6	57.6	57.9	58.2	58.2	58.2	58.1	58.5	58.5
1991	58.2	0.2%	58.5	58.4	58.0	57.9	58.0	58.3	58.4	58.5	58.6	58.3	58.2	58.1
1992	58.9	1.2%	58.4	58.4	58.4	58.5	58.4	58.5	58.5	58.7	58.9	59.4	59.7	60.0
1993	61.8	4.9%	60.4	60.7	60.8	60.9	61.1	61.4	61.8	61.9	62.1	62.5	63.0	63.2
1994	64.6	4.6%	63.3	63.5	63.5	63.5	63.8	64.2	64.4	64.7	65.1	65.5	66.0	66.7
1995	67.3	4.3%	67.0	67.0	67.0	67.0	67.2	67.3	67.2	67.4	67.6	67.7	67.6	67.6
1996	68.6	1.9%	67.9	67.9	67.9	67.7	67.9	68.3	68.8	69.0	69.0	69.2	69.3	69.4
1997	70.6	2.9%	69.8	69.8	69.8	70.0	70.1	70.3	70.6	70.7	71.2	71.4	71.6	71.6
1998	72.5	2.6%	71.6	71.4	71.4	71.7	71.8	72.4	72.7	72.7	72.7	73.0	73.5	74.0
1999	72.7	0.3%	71.3	71.4	71.7	72.0	72.4	72.7	73.0	73.2	73.2	73.4	73.5	73.8
2000	75.9	4.4%	74.7	75.0	75.2	75.3	75.5	75.9	76.0	76.1	76.4	76.5	76.7	77.1
2001	79.7	5.0%	77.7	78.0	78.2	78.6	79.2	79.6	80.0	80.8	81.0	81.5	81.5	81.2
2002	81.7	2.5%	80.6	80.9	81.2	81.4	81.7	81.9	81.7	81.4	81.8	82.3	81.9	82.6
2003	85.9	5.1%	83.7	84.5	85.0	85.3	85.2	85.3	85.1	85.9	86.5	87.1	87.8	88.4
2004	93.1	8.4%	88.9	89.4	90.5	91.4	92.5	93.0	93.6	94.1	94.5	95.1	95.7	96.5
2005	100.0	7.4%	96.7	96.4	96.9	97.1	98.3	99.3	100.7	100.8	101.2	101.8	102.8	104.0
2006	106.0	6.0%	104.4	104.7	105.6	105.7	105.9	105.8	105.4	105.9	106.9	107.3	107.5	107.8
2007	107.0	0.9%	107.9	108.1	108.4	108.0	106.8	106.3	106.4	106.6	106.7	106.7	106.2	105.8
2008	103.3	-3.5%	105.1	104.9	104.5	103.8	104.1	103.0	103.3	102.7	101.8	101.4	101.6	102.0
2009	98.1	-5.0%	101.7	100.8	100.5	99.2	97.7	96.9	96.7	96.6	96.9	97.2	97.5	97.9
2010	96.4	-1.7%	97.8	97.2	96.4	95.7	95.6	95.9	96.4	96.4	96.0	96.6	96.7	97.0

Notes: Laspeyres Price Index (Constant Quality). This index answers the question, "How much is the sales price today for the same quality house as in the base year?" The base year we are now using is 2005; its index value is set to 100.0. Quality includes not only the physical size and amenities of the house, but also its geographic location. A hypothetical calculation is made in which the base year kind of house is held constant over time while its selling price is calculated in current dollars.

Source: U.S. Census Bureau

Plunkett Research,® Ltd.

www.plunkettresearch.com

Rental & Homeowner Vacancy Rates by Area, U.S.: 1995-2010

(Percentage of Rental Units; End of Year)

Area	1995	2000	2004	2005	2006	2007	2008	2009	2010
United States	**7.6**	**8.0**	**10.2**	**9.8**	**9.7**	**9.7**	**10.0**	**10.6**	**10.2**
Inside Metropolitan Areas	7.6	7.7	10.2	9.7	9.7	9.8	10.0	10.7	10.3
In Principal Cities[1]	8.4	8.2	10.8	10.0	10.0	10.0	10.2	11.1	10.7
Outside Principal Cities[1] (suburbs)	6.6	7.2	9.5	9.4	9.3	9.6	9.7	10.2	9.8
Outside Metropolitan Areas	7.9	9.5	10.2	10.5	10.0	9.3	10.4	10.4	9.9
Northeast	7.2	5.6	7.3	6.5	7.1	7.0	6.9	7.2	7.6
Midwest	7.2	8.8	12.2	12.6	12.4	11.5	10.8	10.7	10.8
South	8.3	10.5	12.6	11.8	11.6	12.3	13.0	13.6	12.7
West	7.5	5.8	7.5	7.3	6.8	6.7	7.5	9.0	8.2

[1] Approximately every 10 years, metropolitan/nonmetropolitan area definitions are redefined by the Office of Management and Budget. Therefore metropolitan/nonmetropolitan data prior to 1986, 1986 to 1994, 1995 to 2004, and 2005 and later are not comparable to each other.

Source: U.S. Census Bureau

Plunkett Research,® Ltd.

www.plunkettresearch.com

U.S. Construction Industry Employment: 2005-2010

(In Thousands; Not Seasonally Adjusted)

NAICS Code	Industry Type	2005	2006	2007	2008	2009	2010
23	**Construction**	**7,336.0**	**7,691.0**	**7,630.0**	**7,162.0**	**6,016.0**	**5,526.0**
236	Construction of buildings	1,711.9	1,804.9	1,774.2	1,641.7	1,357.2	1,231.6
2361	Residential building	960.3	1,008.8	949.0	816.1	638.1	571.6
236115	New single-family general contractors	601.3	618.2	567.2	466.8	339.2	291.9
236116	New multifamily general contractors	31.1	32.8	30.9	29.2	24.5	21.3
236118	Residential remodelers	288.7	310.2	305.8	284.1	248.1	235.6
2362	Nonresidential building	751.5	796.1	825.2	825.6	719.1	660.0
23621	Industrial building	167.5	178.6	186.6	186.4	165.2	156.8
23622	Commercial building	584.0	617.5	638.7	639.2	553.9	503.2
237	**Heavy & civil engineering construction**	**951.2**	**985.1**	**1,005.4**	**964.5**	**851.3**	**828.6**
2371	Utility system construction	403.0	430.0	452.8	447.8	397.8	390.1
23711	Water & sewer system construction	199.6	209.8	209.1	192.7	163.9	156.5
23712	Oil & gas pipeline construction	70.5	84.3	99.6	109.1	100.7	94.2
23713	Power & communication system construction	132.9	135.9	144.0	146.1	133.2	139.4
2372	Land subdivision	91.8	95.7	93.2	79.6	60.9	52.0
2373	Highway, street & bridge construction	350.8	348.3	344.5	327.3	291.3	289.0
2379	Other heavy construction	105.7	111.2	115.0	109.8	101.2	97.5
238	**Specialty trade contractors**	**4,673.1**	**4,901.1**	**4,850.2**	**4,555.8**	**3,807.9**	**3,465.5**
238 pt.1	Residential specialty trade contractors	2,302.2	2,396.8	2,277.1	1,999.2	1,610.8	1,466.6
238 pt.2	Nonresidential specialty trade contractors	2,370.9	2,504.4	2,573.0	2,556.7	2,197.2	1,998.8
2381	Building foundation & exterior contractors	1,083.4	1,133.2	1,080.2	979.1	779.0	690.3
2381 pt.1	Res. building foundation & ext. contractors	604.8	622.6	560.6	465.7	353.8	316.1
2381 pt.2	Nonres. building foundation & ext. contractors	478.6	510.6	519.7	513.4	425.2	374.2
23811	Poured concrete structure contractors	230.6	250.4	241.0	220.5	168.2	148.7
23812	Steel and precast concrete contractors	87.9	97.4	101.6	101.2	77.5	67.3
23813	Framing contractors	174.6	164.1	134.3	98.1	66.7	55.6
23814	Masonry contractors	240.6	256.4	240.6	212.6	161.3	131.9
23815	Glass and glazing contractors	55.6	59.2	64.0	64.5	59.3	47.4
23816	Roofing contractors	203.3	204.5	197.7	191.4	170.9	169.2
23817	Siding contractors	46.1	48.8	47.1	40.9	33.8	31.8
23819	Other building exterior contractors	44.7	52.2	54.0	50.1	41.4	38.4
2382	Building equipment contractors	1,116.4	1,177.0	1,229.8	1,246.8	1,098.5	1,013.6
2382 pt.1	Residential building equipment contractors	1,918.1	2,012.8	2,057.0	2,019.9	1,758.2	1,633.4
2382 pt.2	Nonresidential building equipment contractors	801.7	835.8	827.2	773.1	659.7	619.7
23821	Electrical contractors	868.9	904.2	925.9	906.0	788.3	723.2
23822	Plumbing and HVAC contractors	936.1	987.4	1,003.3	982.0	847.0	794.0
23829	Other building equipment contractors	113.2	121.2	127.9	131.9	123.0	116.1
2383	Building finishing contractors	991.6	1,030.3	1,002.8	899.8	722.3	629.4
2383 pt.1	Residential building finishing contractors	596.4	617.3	580.6	491.9	382.3	325.8
2383 pt.2	Nonresidential building finishing contractors	395.3	413.1	422.2	407.9	340.0	303.6
23831	Drywall & insulation contractors	359.4	372.3	352.4	309.3	240.1	199.9
23832	Painting & wall covering contractors	240.0	245.2	241.4	220.6	180.5	160.9
23833	Flooring contractors	84.8	85.7	86.8	79.2	65.9	59.4
23834	Tile & terrazzo contractors	72.6	78.3	73.8	61.9	49.2	41.3
23835	Finish carpentry contractors	167.3	176.5	174.8	156.2	121.1	108.1
23839	Other building finishing contractors	67.5	72.4	73.6	72.8	65.5	59.8
2389	Other specialty trade contractors	680.0	724.9	710.2	657.0	548.4	512.4
2389 pt.1	Other residential trade contractors	299.4	321.2	308.8	268.4	214.9	205.0
2389 pt.2	Other nonresidential trade contractors	380.6	403.7	401.3	388.6	333.5	307.4
23891	Site preparation contractors	357.2	383.7	377.1	347.3	282.7	265.2
23899	All other specialty trade contractors	322.7	341.2	333.1	309.7	265.7	247.2

Source: U.S. Bureau of Labor Statistics

Miscellaneous Real Estate & Construction Industry Employment, U.S.: 2005-2010

(In Thousands; Not Seasonally Adjusted)

NAICS Code	Industry Type	2005	2006	2007	2008	2009	2010
Manufacturing							
321991	Manufactured & mobile homes	46.4	48.4	40.1	33.5	21.1	19.7
3271	Clay products & refractories	61.9	60.5	57.0	52.0	43.6	40.4
3273	Cement & concrete products	240.1	248.3	242.2	220.3	184.9	171.8
3323	Architectural & structural metals	397.9	411.6	417.2	405.9	344.7	320.2
33231	Plate work & fabricated structural products	170.9	179.8	186.1	188.8	158.8	145.6
332312	Fabricated structural metal products	91.1	95.1	99.1	99.9	87.3	76.3
332313	Plate work	79.9	84.8	87.1	88.9	71.5	69.3
33232	Ornamental & architectural metal products	227.0	231.8	231.0	217.0	185.8	174.6
332321	Metal windows & doors	84.3	81.4	76.5	67.6	56.0	50.5
332322	Sheet metal work	103.4	108.7	112.4	107.7	93.8	91.7
332323	Ornamental & architectural metal work	39.3	41.8	42.1	41.8	36.0	32.4
33312	Construction machinery	71.4	77.7	78.9	82.3	66.6	62.1
Financial Activities							
522292	Real estate credit	349.0	351.4	292.2	225.8	200.0	199.4
52231	Mortgage & nonmortgage loan brokers	140.8	144.9	121.3	82.5	66.2	61.1
531	Real estate	1,460.8	1,499.0	1,500.4	1,485.0	1,420.2	1,395.5
5311	Lessors of real estate	603.4	602.4	599.3	596.2	575.9	565.2
53111	Lessors of residential buildings	374.8	371.8	365.5	365.4	353.8	348.4
53112	Lessors of nonresidential buildings	147.7	147.5	149.5	147.7	139.7	133.5
53113	Miniwarehouse & self-storage unit operators	38.7	42.0	43.6	43.7	43.4	43.8
53119	Lessors of other real estate property	42.2	41.2	40.7	39.4	39.0	39.6
5312	Offices of real estate agents & brokers	355.8	374.6	368.3	343.3	304.9	283.9
5313	Activities related to real estate	501.6	521.9	532.9	545.5	539.3	546.4
53131	Real estate property managers	421.8	438.0	451.9	468.8	468.1	473.3
531311	Residential property managers	300.2	310.6	321.8	334.1	335.7	338.3
531312	Nonresidential property managers	121.6	127.4	130.1	134.8	132.4	135.0
53132	Offices of real estate appraisers	41.9	41.8	41.4	37.9	35.1	35.8
53139	Other activities related to real estate	37.9	42.1	39.6	38.8	36.1	37.3
Professional & Business Services							
54131	Architectural services	193.1	205.1	214.1	213.1	176.6	156.3
54132	Landscape architectural services	42.1	45.1	43.7	41.5	33.7	29.4
54134	Engineering & drafting services	839.0	886.5	921.3	940.5	891.8	869.8
54137	Building inspection, surveying & mapping svcs.	95.5	101.9	102.6	94.6	78.4	74.6
Leisure & Hospitality							
7211,3	Traveler accommodations & other longer-term	1,765.4	1,778.0	1,812.4	1,815.0	1,707.5	1,702.0
72111	Hotels & motels, except casino hotels	1,443.9	1,458.6	1,493.9	1,501.1	1,411.7	1,409.5
72112	Casino hotels	286.3	283.6	281.8	275.6	259.6	256.7

Source: U.S. Bureau of Labor Statistics

Plunkett Research,® Ltd.

www.plunkettresearch.com

Chapter 3

IMPORTANT REAL ESTATE & CONSTRUCTION INDUSTRY CONTACTS

Addresses, Telephone Numbers and Internet Sites

Contents:

I.   Affordable Housing Associations

National Community Reinvestment Coalition (NCRC)
727 15th St. NW, Ste. 900
Washington, DC 20005 US
Phone: 202-628-8866
Fax: 202-628-9800
E-mail Address: *jvantol@ncrc.org*
Web Address: www.ncrc.org
The National Community Reinvestment Coalition
(NCRC) is a national nonprofit 501(c)3 organization
with 640 dues-paying chapters located in every state
in America. NCRC was founded in 1990 to unite

efforts around the nation to increase the flow of
private capital into traditionally underserved
communities, with a focus on affordable mortgages
and loans for housing and small businesses in low
income neighborhoods.

II. Alternative Energy-General

Alliance to Save Energy (ASE)
1850 M St. NW, Ste. 600
Washington, DC 20036 US
Phone: 202-857-0666
Fax: 202-331-9588
E-mail Address: *info@ase.org*
Web Address: www.ase.org
The Alliance to Save Energy (ASE) promotes
energy-efficiency worldwide to achieve a healthier
economy, a cleaner environment and energy security.

**American Council for an Energy-Efficient
Economy (ACEEE)**
529 14th St. NW, Ste. 600
Washington, DC 20045-1000 US
Phone: 202-507-4000
Fax: 202-429-2248
E-mail Address: *info@aceee.org*
Web Address: www.aceee.org
The American Council for an Energy-Efficient
Economy (ACEEE) is a nonprofit organization
dedicated to advancing energy-efficiency as a means
of promoting both economic prosperity and
environmental protection.

**Center for Energy Efficiency and Renewable
Technologies (CEERT)**
1100 11th St., Ste. 311
Sacramento, CA 95814 US
Phone: 916-442-7785
Fax: 916-447-2940
Toll Free: 877-758-4462
E-mail Address: *info@ceert.org*
Web Address: www.ceert.org
The Center for Energy Efficiency and Renewable
Technologies (CEERT) provides technical support to
environmental advocates and clean technology
developers.

III.   Careers-First Time Jobs/New Grads

Black Collegian Online (The)
140 Carondelet St.
New Orleans, LA 70130 US

Phone: 504-523-0154
Web Address: www.black-collegian.com
The Black Collegian Online features listings for job
and internship opportunities, as well as other tools for
students of color; it is the web site of The Black
Collegian Magazine, published by IMDiversity, Inc.
The site includes a list of the top 100 minority
corporate employers and an assessment of job
opportunities.

CollegeGrad.com, Inc.
234 E. College Ave., Ste. 200
State College, PA 16801 US
Phone: 262-375-6700
Toll Free: 1-800-991-4642
Web Address: www.collegegrad.com
CollegeGrad.com, Inc. offers in-depth resources for
college students and recent grads seeking entry-level
jobs.

Job Web
62 Highland Ave.
c/o Nat'l Association of Colleges & Employers
(NACE)
Bethlehem, PA 18017-9085 US
Phone: 610-868-1421
Fax: 610-868-0208
Toll Free: 800-544-5272
E-mail Address: *editors@jobweb.com*
Web Address: www.jobweb.com
Job Web, owned and sponsored by National
Association of Colleges and Employers (NACE),
displays job openings and employer descriptions. The
site also offers a database of career fairs, searchable
by state or keyword, with contact information.

MBAjobs.net
Fax: 413-556-8849
E-mail Address: *contact@mbajobs.net*
Web Address: www.mbajobs.net
MBAjobs.net is a unique international service for
MBA students and graduates, employers, recruiters
and business schools. The MBAjobs.net service is
provided by WebInfoCo.

MonsterTRAK
11845 W. Olympic Blvd., Ste. 500
Los Angeles, CA 90064 US
Toll Free: 800-999-8725
E-mail Address: *trakstudent@monster.com*
Web Address: www.college.monster.com

MonsterTRAK provides information about internships and entry-level jobs.

National Association of Colleges and Employers (NACE)
62 Highland Ave.
Bethlehem, PA 18017-9085 US
Phone: 610-868-1421
Fax: 610-868-0208
Toll Free: 800-544-5272
E-mail Address: *mcollins@naceweb.org*
Web Address: www.naceweb.org
The National Association of Colleges and Employers (NACE) is a premier U.S. organization representing college placement offices and corporate recruiters who focus on hiring new grads.

IV. Careers-General Job Listings

Career Exposure, Inc.
805 SW Broadway, Ste. 2250
Portland, OR 97205 US
Phone: 503-221-7779
Fax: 503-221-7780
E-mail Address: *lisam@mackenzie-marketing.com*
Web Address: www.careerexposure.com
Career Exposure, Inc. is an online career center and job placement service, with resources for employers, recruiters and job seekers.

CareerBuilder, Inc.
200 N. LaSalle St., Ste. 1100
Chicago, IL 60601 US
Phone: 773-527-3600
Toll Free: 800-638-4212
Web Address: www.careerbuilder.com
CareerBuilder, Inc. focuses on the needs of companies and also provides a database of job openings. The site has 1.5 million jobs posted by 300,000 employers, and receives an average 23 million unique visitors monthly. The company also operates online career centers for 150 newspapers, 1,000 partners and other online portals such as America Online. Resumes are sent directly to the company, and applicants can set up a special e-mail account for job-seeking purposes. CareerBuilder is primarily a joint venture between three newspaper giants: The McClatchy Company (which recently acquired former partner Knight Ridder), Gannett Co., Inc. and Tribune Company. In 2007, Microsoft acquired a minority interest in CareerBuilder, allowing the site to ally itself with MSN.

CareerOneStop
Toll Free: 877-348-0502
E-mail Address: *info@careeronestop.org*
Web Address: www.careeronestop.org
CareerOneStop is operated by the employment commissions of various state agencies. It contains job listings in both the private sector and in government. CareerOneStop is sponsored by the U.S. Department of Labor. It includes a wide variety of useful career resources and workforce information.

HotJobs
45 W. 18th St., Fl. 6
New York, NY 10011 US
Phone: 646-351-5300
Web Address: www.hotjobs.yahoo.com
HotJobs, designed for experienced professionals, employers and job seekers, is a Monster-owned site that provides company profiles, a resume posting service and a resume workshop. The site allows posters to block resumes from being viewed by certain companies and provides a notification service of new jobs.

JobCentral
9002 N. Purdue Rd., Quad III, Ste. 100
c/o DirectEmployers Association, Inc.
Indianapolis, IN 46268 US
Phone: 317-874-9000
Fax: 317-874-9100
Toll Free: 866-268-6206
E-mail Address: *info@jobcentral.com*
Web Address: www.jobcentral.com
JobCentral, operated by the nonprofit DirectEmployers Association, Inc., links users directly to hundreds of thousands of job opportunities posted on the sites of participating employers, thus bypassing the usual job search sites. This saves employers money and allows job seekers to access many more job opportunities.

LaborMarketInfo
800 Capitol Mall, MIC 83
c/o Employment Dev. Dept., Labor Market Info. Div.
Sacramento, CA 95814 US
Phone: 916-262-2162
Fax: 916-262-2352
Toll Free: 800-480-3287
Web Address: www.labormarketinfo.edd.ca.gov
LaborMarketInfo, formerly the California Cooperative Occupational Information System, is geared to providing job seekers and employers a wide range of resources, namely the ability to find, access

and use labor market information and services. It provides demographical statistics for employment on both a local and regional level, as well as career searching tools for California residents. The web site is sponsored by California's Employment Development Office.

Recruiters Online Network
947 Essex Ln.
Medina, OH 44256 US
Phone: 888-364-4667
Fax: 888-237-8686
E-mail Address: *info@recruitersonline.com*
Web Address: www.recruitersonline.com
The Recruiters Online Network provides job postings from thousands of recruiters, Careers Online Magazine, a resume database, as well as other career resources.

True Careers, Inc.
Web Address: www.truecareers.com
True Careers, Inc. offers job listings and provides an array of career resources. The company also offers a search of over 2 million scholarships. It is partnered with CareerBuilder.com, which powers its career information and resume posting functions.

USAJOBS
1900 E St. NW
Washington, DC 20415 US
Phone: 202-606-1800
Web Address: usajobs.opm.gov
USAJOBS, a program of the U.S. Office of Personnel Management, is the official job site for the U.S. Federal Government. It provides a comprehensive list of U.S. government jobs, allowing users to search for employment by location; agency; type of work, using the Federal Government's numerical identification code, the General Schedule (GS) Series; or by senior executive positions. It also has a special veterans' employment section; an information center, offering resume and interview tips and other useful information such as hiring trends and a glossary of Federal terms; and allows users to create a profile and post a resume.

Wall Street Journal - CareerJournal
200 Liberty St.
New York, NY 10281 US
Phone: 212-416-2000
Toll Free: 800-568-7625
E-mail Address: *onelinejournal@wsj.com*
Web Address: cj.careercast.com/careers/jobsearch

The Wall Street Journal's CareerJournal, an executive career site, features a job database with thousands of available positions; career news and employment related articles; and advice regarding resume writing, interviews, networking, office life and job hunting.

V.   Careers-Job Reference Tools

NewsVoyager
4401 Wilson Blvd., Ste. 900
Arlington, VA 22203-1867 US
Phone: 571-366-1000
Fax: 571-366-1195
E-mail Address: *sally.clarke@naa.org*
Web Address: www.newsvoyager.com
NewsVoyager, a service of the Newspaper Association of America (NAA), links individuals to local, national and international newspapers. Job seekers can search through thousands of classified sections.

Vault.com, Inc.
75 Varick St., Fl. 8
New York, NY 10013 US
Phone: 212-366-4212
E-mail Address: *feedback@staff.vault.com*
Web Address: www.vault.com
Vault.com, Inc. is a comprehensive career web site for employers and employees, with job postings and valuable information on a wide variety of industries. Vault gears many of its features toward MBAs. The site has been recognized by Forbes and Fortune Magazines.

VI.   Construction Industry Resources & Associations

American Concrete Institute (ACI)
38800 Country Club Dr.
Farmington Hills, MI 48331 US
Phone: 248-848-3700
Fax: 248-848-3701
E-mail Address: *BKStore@concrete.org*
Web Address: www.concrete.org
The American Concrete Institute (ACI) is a professional organization that provides information on the use of concrete for structures and facilities.

American Society of Professional Estimators (ASPE)
2525 Perimeter Place Dr., Ste. 103
Nashville, TN 37214 US

Phone: 615-316-9200
Fax: 615-316-9800
Toll Free: 888-378-6273
E-mail Address: *info@aspenational.com*
Web Address: www.aspenational.org
The American Society of Professional Estimators
(ASPE) serves construction estimators by providing
education, fellowships and opportunities for
professional development.

American Subcontractors Association (ASA)
1004 Duke St.
Alexandria, VA 22314-3588 US
Phone: 703-684-3450
Fax: 703-836-3482
E-mail Address: *ASAoffice@asa-hq.com*
Web Address: www.asaonline.com
The American Subcontractors Association (ASA) is
an association of professional construction
contractors and suppliers.

Associated Builders and Contractors (ABC)
4250 N. Fairfax Dr., Fl. 9
Arlington, VA 22203-1607 US
Phone: 703-812-2000
E-mail Address: *gotquestions@abc.org*
Web Address: www.abc.org
Associated Builders and Contractors (ABC) is a
national trade association representing more than
23,000 merit shop contractors, subcontractors,
material suppliers and related firms in 80 chapters
across the United States.

Associated General Contractors of America (The, AGC)
2300 Wilson Blvd., Ste. 400
Arlington, VA 22201 US
Phone: 703-548-3118
Fax: 703-548-3119
Toll Free: 800-242-1767
Web Address: www.agc.org
The Associated General Contractors of America
(AGC) is a membership organization dedicated to
furthering the agenda of commercial construction
contractors, improving job site safety, expanding the
use of cutting edge technologies and techniques and
strengthening the dialogue between contractors and
owners.

Bookworkz-The Construction Industry Bookstore
P.O. Box 948
Valrico, FL 33595-0948 US
Phone: 813-662-6793

Fax: 888-533-5680
Toll Free: 800-997-2922
E-mail Address: *books@bookworkz.com*
Web Address: www.bookworkz.com
The Bookworkz web site offers users the opportunity
to browse and purchase from thousands of
construction, engineering and architectural titles.

Canadian Construction Association (CCA)
75 Albert St., Ste. 400
Ottawa, ON K1P 5E7 Canada
Phone: 613-236-9455
Fax: 613-236-9526
E-mail Address: *cca@cca-acc.com*
Web Address: www.cca-acc.com
The Canadian Construction Association (CCA), or, in
French, the Association canadienne de la construction
(ACC), is a Canadian organization devoted to setting
standards for construction industry practices and
labor issues nationwide.

Canadian Wood Council (The) (CWC)
99 Bank St., Ste. 400
Ottawa, ON K1P 6B9 Canada
Phone: 613-747-5544
Fax: 613-747-6264
Toll Free: 800-463-5091
E-mail Address: *info@cwc.ca*
Web Address: www.cwc.ca
The CWC is the Canadian national association of
manufacturers of wood products that are used in
construction.

Certified Aging in Place Specialist (CAPS)
1201 15th St. NW
National Association of Home Builders
Washington, DC 20005 US
Phone: 202-266-8200 x0
Fax: 202-266-8400
Toll Free: 800-368-5242
Web Address:
www.nahb.org/category.aspx?sectionID=686
The Certified Aging in Place Specialist (CAPS)
designation program teaches the technical, business
management and customer service skills necessary to
make residential environments capable of housing
people as they age. It is offered by the National
Association of Home Builders (NAHB)

Construction Industry Institute (CII)
3925 W. Braker Ln.
Austin, TX 78759-5316 US
Phone: 512-232-3000

Fax: 512-499-8101
E-mail Address: *wcrew@mail.utexas.edu*
Web Address: www.construction-institute.org
The Construction Industry Institute (CII) is a
consortium of leading owners, contractors and
suppliers who work with academia to find better
ways to plan and execute capital construction
programs.

Contractors Group (The)
555 NW Fairhaven Dr.
c/o Diane Dennis Enterprises
Oak Harbor, WA 98277 US
Fax: 866-480-7105
E-mail Address: *diane@TheContractorsGroup.com*
Web Address: www.thecontractorsgroup.com
The Contractors Group offers free editable
construction forms, tutorials, forums and related
links. It was founded, and is still run by Diane
Dennis Enterprises.

McGraw-Hill Construction Sweets Network
The McGraw-Hill Companies
P.O. Box 182604
Columbus, OH 43272 US
Phone: 212-904-4376
Toll Free: 800-393-6343
E-mail Address: *kathy_malangone@mcgraw-
hill.com*
Web Address: products.construction.com
The McGraw-Hill Construction Sweets Network online resource offers access to product and
manufacturer information quickly and easily through
a searchable database. Its design facilitates design
specifications and document creation with
downloadable, insertable product information. The
service also offers access to the latest green products,
trends, developments and innovations. The service is
part of McGraw-Hill Construction, which is itself
part of The McGraw-Hill Companies, Inc.

**Metal Building Manufacturers Association
(MBMA)**
1300 Sumner Ave.
Cleveland, OH 44115-2851 US
Phone: 216-241-7333
Fax: 216-241-0105
E-mail Address: *mbma@mbma.com*
Web Address: www.mbma.com
The Metal Building Manufacturers Association
(MBMA) promotes the design and construction of
metal building and metal roofing systems in the low-

rise, non-residential building and roofing
marketplace.

National Asphalt Pavement Association (NAPA)
5100 Forbes Blvd.
Lanham, MD 20706 US
Phone: 301-731-4748
Fax: 301-731-4621
Toll Free: 888-468-6499
Web Address: www.hotmix.org
The National Asphalt Pavement Association is the
only trade association that exclusively represents the
interests of the hot-mix asphalt producer/contractor
on the national level with Congress, government
agencies, and other national trade and business
organizations. NAPA supports an active research
program designed to improve the quality of HMA
pavements and paving techniques used in the
construction of roads, streets, highways, parking lots,
airports, and environmental and recreational
facilities. The association provides technical,
educational, and marketing materials and information
to its members; supplies product information to users
and specifiers of paving materials; and conducts
training courses. The association, which counts
nearly 1,200 companies as its members, was founded
in 1955.

National Association of Home Builders (NAHB)
1201 15th St. NW
Washington, DC 20005 US
Phone: 202-266-8200
Fax: 202-266-8400
Toll Free: 800-368-5242
E-mail Address: *cdouglas@nahb.com*
Web Address: www.nahb.org
The National Association of Home Builders (NAHB)
exists to represent the building industry by serving its
members and affiliated state and local builders
associations.

**National Association of Women in Construction
(NAWIC)**
327 S. Adams St.
Fort Worth, TX 76104 US
Phone: 817-877-5551
Fax: 817-877-0324
Toll Free: 800-552-3506
E-mail Address: *nawic@nawic.org*
Web Address: www.nawic.org
The National Association of Women in Construction
(NAWIC) is an association to promote the
advancement of women in the construction industry.

Precast/Prestressed Concrete Institute
209 W. Jackson Blvd., Ste. 500
Chicago, IL 60606 US
Phone: 312-786-0300
Fax: 312-786-0353
E-mail Address: *info@pci.org*
Web Address: www.pci.org
The Precast/Prestressed Concrete Institute (PCI) is an organization dedicated to the precast and prestressed concrete industry and includes a staff of technical and marketing specialists.

Public Works and Government Services Canada (PWGSC)
16A1, 102 Corporate Communications
Portage III
Gatineau, Quebec K1A 0S5 Canada
Fax: 819-956-9062
Toll Free: 800-622-6232
E-mail Address: *questions@pwgsc.gc.ca*
Web Address: www.pwgsc.gc.ca
Public Works and Government Services Canada (PWGSC) is a government agency that performs the following functions for all 106 Canadian federal departments: purchases goods and services; provides office accommodations for public servants; manages national heritage properties; oversees public construction; and offers information technology, telecommunications, translation, banking and auditing services to the government.

Singapore Contractors Association Ltd. (SCAL)
Construction House
Bukit Merah Ln. 2
159760 Singapore
Phone: 65-6278-9577
Fax: 65-6273-3977
E-mail Address: *enquiry@scal.com.sg*
Web Address: www.scal.com.sg
The Singapore Contractors Association (SCAL) has a membership of more than 2000 members under her wing, making it a representative of the construction industry in Singapore.

SmartMaket Report
Toll Free: 800-393-6343
Web Address: www.construction.com/SmartMarket
The SmartMarket Report series from McGraw-Hill Construction provides current, relevant intelligence about specific markets that offer significant opportunities for design and construction firms. The information is managed in the McGraw-Hill Construction statistical database, which has tracked the activity of over a million owners, designers, builders and supplier and the data of tens of millions of new, addition and renovation projects throughout the U.S. and Canada since 1967.

> **VII. Construction Resources-Energy Efficient Buildings**

EERE Rebuild America
1000 Independence Ave. SW
Mail Stop EE-1
Washington, DC 20585 US
Phone: 202-586-5463
Toll Free: 877-337-3463
Web Address:
www.eere.energy.gov/buildings/program_areas/rebuild.html
The Building Technologies Program of the Office of Energy Efficiency and Renewable Energy (EERE), a division of the U.S. Department of Energy, operates Rebuild America, which is a network of hundreds of community-based partnerships that are focused on increasing the number of energy-efficient buildings in the nation.

Efficient Windows Collaborative (EWC)
1850 M St. NW, Ste. 600
Nils Petermann,Alliance to Save Energy
Washington, DC 20036 US
Phone: 202-530-2254
Fax: 202-331-9588
E-mail Address: *ewc@ase.org*
Web Address: www.efficientwindows.org
The Efficient Windows Collaborative (EWC) web site provides unbiased information on the benefits of energy-efficient windows, descriptions of how they work and recommendations for their selection and use. The web site is sponsored by the U.S. Department of Energy's Windows and Glazings Program and the participation of industry members.

Green Building Initiative (GBI)
2104 SE Morrison
Portland, OR 97214 US
Fax: 503-961-8991
Toll Free: 877-424-4241
E-mail Address: *info@thegbi.org*
Web Address: www.thegbi.org
The Green Building Initiative (GBI) is a nonprofit network of building industry leaders committed to bringing green to mainstream residential and commercial construction. The GBI believes in building approaches that are environmentally

progressive, but also practical and affordable for builders to implement.

GreenSource
2 Penn Plz.
New York, NY 10121-2298 US
Phone: 717-399-8900
Toll Free: 800-360-5549
E-mail Address: *greensourcemag@mcgraw-hill.com*
Web Address: www.greensource.construction.com
GreenSource is McGraw-Hill Construction's on-line directory of information on sustainable design, practice and products. It includes information from GreenSource, Architectural Record and Engineering News-Record magazines for architects, engineers, contractors and consumers. It also offers Internet-only exclusives.

Sustainable Buildings Industry Council (SBIC)
1112 16th St. NW, Ste. 240
Washington, DC 20036 US
Phone: 202-628-7400
Fax: 202-393-5043
E-mail Address: *sbic@sbicouncil.com*
Web Address: www.sbicouncil.org
The Sustainable Buildings Industry Council (SBIC) is an independent, nonprofit organization that concentrates on providing information on energy conservation in regards to building construction.

U.S. Green Building Council (USGBC)
1800 Massachusetts Ave. NW, Ste. 300
Washington, DC 20036 US
Phone: 202-742-3792
Fax: 202-828-5110
Toll Free: 800-795-1747
E-mail Address: *info@usgbc.org*
Web Address: www.usgbc.org
The United States Green Building Council (USGBC) is a coalition of building industry leaders working to promote environmentally responsible commercial and residential structures.

VIII.   Corporate Information Resources

bizjournals.com
120 W. Morehead St., Ste. 400
Charlotte, NC 28202 US
Web Address: www.bizjournals.com
Bizjournals.com is the online media division of American City Business Journals, the publisher of dozens of leading city business journals nationwide.

It provides access to research into the latest news regarding companies small and large.

Business Wire
44 Montgomery St., Fl. 39
San Francisco, CA 94104 US
Phone: 415-986-4422
Fax: 415-788-5335
Toll Free: 800-227-0845
Web Address: www.businesswire.com
Business Wire offers news releases, industry- and company-specific news, top headlines, conference calls, IPOs on the Internet, media services and access to tradeshownews.com and BW Connect On-line through its informative and continuously updated web site.

Edgar Online, Inc.
50 Washington St., Fl. 11
Norwalk, CT 06854 US
Phone: 203-852-5666
Fax: 203-852-5667
Toll Free: 800-416-6651
Web Address: www.edgar-online.com
Edgar Online, Inc. is a gateway and search tool for viewing corporate documents, such as annual reports on Form 10-K, filed with the U.S. Securities and Exchange Commission.

PR Newswire Association LLC
810 7th Ave., Fl. 32
New York, NY 10019 US
Phone: 201-360-6700
Toll Free: 800-832-5522
E-mail Address: *information@prnewswire.com*
Web Address: www.prnewswire.com
PR Newswire Association LLC provides comprehensive communications services for public relations and investor relations professionals ranging from information distribution and market intelligence to the creation of online multimedia content and investor relations web sites. Users can also view recent corporate press releases. The Association is owned by United Business Media plc.

IX.   Design & Architectural Associations

American Institute of Architects (The) (AIA)
1735 New York Ave. NW
Washington, DC 20006-5292 US
Phone: 202-626-7300
Fax: 202-626-7547
Toll Free: 800-242-3837

E-mail Address: *infocentral@aia.org*
Web Address: www.aia.org
The American Institute of Architects (AIA) is a
professional trade group for architects in the United
States.

American Institute of Building Design (AIBD)
7059 Blair Rd. NW, Ste. 201
Washington, DC 20012 US
Fax: 202-249-2473
Toll Free: 800-366-2423
E-mail Address: *Info@AIBD.org*
Web Address: www.aibd.org
The American Institute of Building Design (AIBD) is
a nonprofit professional organization dedicated to the
development, recognition and enhancement of the
profession of building design.

Center for Universal Design (The) (CUD)
College of Design, North Carolina State University
Campus Box 8613
Raleigh, NC 27695-8613 US
Phone: 919-515-3082
Fax: 919-515-8951
Toll Free: 800-647-6777
E-mail Address: *cud@ncsu.edu*
Web Address: www.design.ncsu.edu/cud
The Center for Universal Design (CUD) is a national
information, technical assistance and research center
that evaluates, develops and promotes products and
environments so that they can be used by all people,
regardless of physical or mental limitations.

**National Council of Architectural Registration
Board (NCARB)**
1801 K St. NW, Ste. 1100K
Washington, DC 20006-1310 US
Phone: 202-783-6500
Fax: 202-783-0290
E-mail Address: *customerservice@ncarb.org*
Web Address: www.ncarb.org
The National Council of Architectural Registration
Board (NCARB) is a nonprofit federation of
architectural licensing boards in the U.S. that
provides state registration requirements, information
on the Intern Development Program (IDP) and
Architect Registration Examination (ARE)
certification, continuing education and an architect
database.

Royal Architectural Institute of Canada (RAIC)
330-55 Rue Murray St.
Ottawa, Ontario K1N 5M3 Canada

Phone: 613-241-3600
Fax: 613-241-5750
E-mail Address: *info@raic.org*
Web Address: www.raic.org
The Royal Architectural Institute of Canada (RAIC)
is a voluntary national association representing
professional architects, and faculty and graduates of
accredited Canadian Schools of Architecture.

Royal Institute of British Architects (RIBA)
66 Portland Pl.
London, W1B 1AD UK
Phone: 44-20-7580-5533
Fax: 44-20-7255-1541
E-mail Address: *info@inst.riba.org*
Web Address: www.riba.org
The Royal Institute of British Architects (RIBA) is a
professional association of architects in the United
Kingdom, which also offers lectures, exhibitions and
events, community architecture projects and
community architecture schemes.

Singapore Institute of Architects (SIA)
79B Neil Rd.
088904 Singapore
Phone: 65-6226-2668
Fax: 65-6226-2663
E-mail Address: *info@sia.org.sg*
Web Address: www.sia.org.sg
The Singapore Institute of Architects (SIA) is the
national organization representing architects in
Singapore.

The Architectural Society of China (ASC)
No. 9 Sanlihe Rd.
Beijing, 100835 China
Phone: 86-10-88082224
Fax: 86-10-88082223
Web Address: www.chinaasc.org
The Architectural Society of China (ASC) represents
professional architects in China.

X.   Economic Data & Research

**(Japan) Statistics Bureau, Director-General for
Policy Planning**
19-1 Wakamatsu-cho
Shinjuku-ku
Tokyo, 162-8668 Japan
Phone: 81-3-5273-2020
Web Address: www.stat.go.jp/english
The Statistics Bureau and the Director-General for
Policy Planning of Japan play the central role in the

official statistical system in producing and disseminating basic official statistics, and coordinating statistical work under the Statistics Act and other legislation.

Economic and Social Research Council (ESRC)
Polaris House
North Star Avenue
Swindon, SN2 1UJ UK
Phone: 01793 413000
Fax: 01793 413001
Web Address: www.esrc.ac.uk
The Economic and Social Research Council (ESRC) funds research and training in social and economic issues. It is an independent organization, established by Royal Charter. The group focuses on six research areas: economic affairs, education and human development, environment and planning, government and law, industry and employment and social affairs.

Eurostat
Phone: 32-2-299-9696
Toll Free: 80-0-6789-1011
Web Address: www.epp.eurostat.ec.europa.eu
Eurostat is the European Union's service that publishes a wide variety of comprehensive statistics on European industries, populations, trade, agriculture, technology, environment and other matters.

India Brand Equity Foundation (IBEF)
249-F Sector 18
Udyog Vihar Phase IV
Gurgaon, Haryana 122015 India
Phone: 91-124-4014060
Fax: 91-124-4013873
E-mail Address: *ceo@ibef.org*
Web Address: www.ibef.org
India Brand Equity Foundation (IBEF) is a public-private partnership between the Ministry of Commerce and Industry, Government of India, and the Confederation of Indian Industry. The Foundation's primary objective is to build positive economic perceptions of India globally. It aims to effectively present the India business perspective and leverage business partnerships in a globalizing market-place.

National Bureau of Statistics (China)
57, Yuetan Nanjie, Sanlihe
Xicheng District
Beijing, 100826 China
Fax: 86-10-68782000

E-mail Address: *info@stats.gov.cn*
Web Address: www.stats.gov.cn/english
The National Bureau of Statistics of China provides statistics and economic data regarding China's economic and social issues.

Organization for Economic Co-operation and Development (OECD)
2 rue André Pascal
Cedex 16
Paris, F-75775 France
Phone: 33-145-24-8200
Fax: 33-145-24-8500
Web Address: www.oecd.org
The Organization for Economic Co-operation and Development (OECD) publishes detailed economic, government, population, social and trade statistics on a country-by-country basis for over 30 nations representing the world's largest economies. Sectors covered range from industry, labor, technology and patents, to health care, environment and globalization.

Statistics Canada
150 Tunney's Pasture Driveway
Ottawa, ON K1A 0T6 Canada
Phone: 613-951-8116
Fax: 613-951-0581
Toll Free: 800-263-1136
Web Address: www.statcan.gc.ca
A complete portal to Canadian economic data and statistics.

The Centre for European Economic Research (ZEW)
Wirtschaftsforschung GmbH
Postfach 10 34 43
Mannheim, D-68034 Germany
Phone: 49(0)621-1235-01
Fax: 49(0)621-1235-224
E-mail Address: *info@zew.de*
Web Address: www.zew.de/en
Zentrum fur Europaische, The Centre for European Economic Research (ZEW), distinguishes itself in the analyses of internationally comparative data in the European context and in the creation of databases which are important as a basis for scientific research. The institute maintains a special library relevant to economic research and provides external parties with selected data for the purpose of scientific research. ZEW also offers public events and seminars concentrating on banking, business and other economic-political topics.

XI. Engineering, Research & Scientific Associations

American National Standards Institute (ANSI)
1819 L St. NW, Fl. 6
Washington, DC 20036 US
Phone: 202-293-8020
Fax: 202-293-9287
E-mail Address: *info@ansi.org*
Web Address: www.ansi.org
The American National Standards Institute (ANSI) is a private, nonprofit organization that administers and coordinates the U.S. voluntary standardization and conformity assessment system. Its mission is to enhance both the global competitiveness of U.S. business and the quality of life by promoting and facilitating voluntary consensus standards and conformity assessment systems and safeguarding their integrity.

American Society of Civil Engineers (ASCE)
1801 Alexander Bell Dr.
Reston, VA 20191-4400 US
Phone: 703-295-6300
Fax: 703-295-6222
Toll Free: 800-548-2723
Web Address: www.asce.org
The American Society of Civil Engineers (ASCE) is a leading professional organization serving civil engineers. It ensures safer buildings, water systems and other civil engineering works by developing technical codes and standards.

Association for Facilities Engineering (AFE)
12100 Sunset Hills Rd., Ste. 130
Reston, VA 20190 US
Phone: 703-234-4066
E-mail Address: *info@afe.org*
Web Address: www.afe.org
The Association for Facilities Engineering (AFE) provides education, certification, technical information and other relevant resources for plant and facility engineering, operations and maintenance professionals worldwide.

China Academy of Building Research (CABR)
30 Bei San Huan Dong Lu
Beijing, 100013 China
Phone: 010-84272233
Fax: 010-84281369
E-mail Address: *office@cabr.com.cn*
Web Address: www.cabr.cn

CABR is responsible for the development and management of the major engineering construction and product standards of China and is also the largest comprehensive research and development institute in the building industry in China. Some related institutes include Institute of Earthquake Engineering, Institute of Building Fire Research, Institute of Building Environment and Energy Efficiency (Building Physics), Institute of Foundation Engineering as well as many others.

Chinese Association of Earthquake Engineering (CAEE)
No. 29 Xuefu Rd. Harbin
Heilongjiang, 150080 China
Phone: 86-45186652663
Fax: 86-45186664755
Web Address: www.caee.org.cn
Chinese Association of Earthquake Engineering (CAEE) promotes the field of earthquake engineering and the research in seismic activity and earthquake sciences.

Civil Engineering Forum for Innovation (CEFI)
1801 Alexander Bell Dr.
American Society of Civil Engineers
Reston, VA 20191-4400 US
Phone: 703-295-6314
Fax: 703-295-6015
E-mail Address: *mdalton@asce.org*
Web Address: content.asce.org/cefi
The Civil Engineering Forum for Innovation (CEFI) is an independent nonprofit organization established by the American Society of Civil Engineers (ASCE) to strengthen the civil engineering profession and industry through technical innovation and public policy.

Earthquake Engineering Research Institute (EERI)
499 14th St., Ste. 320
Oakland, CA 94612-1934 US
Phone: 510-451-0905
Fax: 510-451-5411
E-mail Address: *eeri@eeri.org*
Web Address: www.eeri.org
The Earthquake Engineering Research Institute (EERI) is a national nonprofit technical organization of engineers, geoscientists, architects, planners, public officials and social scientists aimed at reducing earthquake risk by advancing the science and practice of earthquake engineering.

Illuminating Engineering Society of North America (IESNA)
120 Wall St., Fl. 17
New York, NY 10005 US
Phone: 212-248-5000
Fax: 212-248-5017
E-mail Address: *iesna@iesna.org*
Web Address: www.iesna.org
A recognized authority on lighting in North America, the Illuminating Engineering Society of North America (IESNA) establishes scientific lighting recommendations. Members include engineers, architects, designers, educators, students, manufacturers and scientists.

Institute for Research in Construction (IRC)
1200 Montreal Rd., Bldg. M-24
National Research Council of Canada
Ottawa, ON K1A 0R6 Canada
Phone: 613-993-2607
Fax: 613-952-7673
E-mail Address: *irc.client-services@nrc-cnrc.gc.ca*
Web Address: irc.nrc-cnrc.gc.ca
The Institute for Research in Construction (IRC) provides research, building code development and materials evaluation services. The IRC is Canada's construction technology center and a division of the National Research Council.

Institute of Structural Engineers (IStructE)
11 Upper Belgrave St.
London, SW1X 8BH UK
Phone: 44-(0)20-7235-4535
Fax: 44-(0)20-7235-4294
Web Address: www.istructe.org.uk
The Institute of Structural Engineers (IStructE) is a professional organization, headquartered in the U.K., that sets and maintains standards for professional structural engineers.

National Academy of Building Inspection Engineers (NABIE)
P.O. Box 522158
Salt Lake City, UT 84152 US
Fax: 801-943-3689
Toll Free: 800-294-7729
E-mail Address: *director@nabie.org*
Web Address: www.nabie.org
The National Academy of Building Inspection Engineers (NABIE) is a chartered affinity group of the National Society of Professional Engineers. NABIE accepts only state-licensed engineers and

architects as members in its building inspection association.

National Society of Professional Engineers (NSPE)
1420 King St.
Alexandria, VA 22314-2794 US
Phone: 703-684-2800
Fax: 703-836-4875
Toll Free: 888-285-6773
E-mail Address: *memserv@nspe.org*
Web Address: www.nspe.org
The National Society of Professional Engineers (NSPE) represents individual engineering professionals and licensed engineers across all disciplines. NSPE serves approximately 45,000 members and has more than 500 chapters.

World Federation of Engineering Organizations
Maison de l'UNESCO 1
rue Miollis
Paris, Cedex 15 F-75732 France
Phone: 33-1-45-68-48-46
Fax: 33-1-45-68-48-65
E-mail Address: *tl.fmoi@unesco.org*
Web Address: www.wfeo.org
World Federation of Engineering Organizations (WFEO) is an international non-governmental organization that represents major engineering professional societies in over 90 nations. It has several standing committees including engineering and the environment, technology, communications, capacity building, education, energy and women in engineering.

XII. Environmental & Ecological Organizations

Global Footprint Network
312 Clay St., Ste. 300
Oakland, CA 94607-3510 US
Phone: 510-839-8879
Fax: 510-251-2410
E-mail Address: *info@footprintnetwork.org*
Web Address: www.footprintnetwork.org
Global Footprint Network publishes regional studies of human demands on the ecology which it calls an Ecological Footprint. The Footprint takes into consideration human use of land, water and other resources to fill needs for housing, agriculture, energy and more, along with nature's ability to fulfill those demands. The organization's analysis creates a scale by which one nation may compare its footprint against that of others.

XIII.   Financial Industry Resources

SNL Financial
1 SNL Plz.
P.O. Box 2124
Charlottesville, VA 22902 US
Phone: 434-977-1600
Fax: 434-977-4466
Toll Free: 866-296-3743
E-mail Address: *support@snl.com*
Web Address: www.snl.com
SNL Financial provides industry-specific research
and statistics in the banking, financial services,
insurance, real estate and energy sectors.

XIV. Forest Products Associations

Canadian Lumbermen's Association (CLA)
30 Concourse Gate, Ste. 200
Ottawa, ON K2E 7V7 Canada
Phone: 613-233-6205
Fax: 613-233-1929
Web Address: www.canadianlumbermen.com
The CLA represents the interests of Canadian lumber
manufacturers and various supporting industries as
well.

XV.   Home Values Online

Trulia
208 Utah St., Ste. 310
San Francisco, CA 94103 US
E-mail Address: *customerservice@trulia.com*
Web Address: www.trulia.com
An excellent site for finding price trends for specific
properties. The site includes many tools for buyers,
sellers and real estate professionals. Trulia Voices,
one of the largest real estate communities on the web,
allows home buyers, sellers, agents and real estate
enthusiasts to ask questions, receive advice and blog
on topics such as the buying and selling process,
foreclosures, refinancing and more.

Zillow
999 Third Ave., Ste. 4600
Seattle, WA 98104 US
Phone: 206-470-7167
E-mail Address: *press@zillow.com*
Web Address: www.zillow.com
Zillow is an extremely popular site launched in 2005.
It provides online access to aerial home photos, and
enables users to estimate home values based on a
variety of factors, using a proprietary algorithm.

XVI.   Industry Research/Market Research

Forrester Research
400 Technology Sq.
Cambridge, MA 02139 US
Phone: 617-613-6000
Fax: 617-613-5200
Toll Free: 866-367-7378
Web Address: www.forrester.com
Forrester Research identifies and analyzes emerging
trends in technology and their impact on business.
Among the firm's specialties are the financial
services, retail, health care, entertainment,
automotive and information technology industries.

MarketResearch.com
11200 Rockville Pike, Ste. 504
Rockville, MD 20852 US
Phone: 240-747-3000
Fax: 240-747-3004
Toll Free: 800-298-5699
E-mail Address:
customerservice@marketresearch.com
Web Address: www.marketresearch.com
MarketResearch.com is a leading broker for
professional market research and industry analysis.
Users are able to search the company's database of
research publications including data on global
industries, companies, products and trends.

Plunkett Research, Ltd.
P.O. Drawer 541737
Houston, TX 77254-1737 US
Phone: 713-932-0000
Fax: 713-932-7080
E-mail Address:
customersupport@plunkettresearch.com
Web Address: www.plunkettresearch.com
Plunkett Research, Ltd. is a leading provider of
market research, industry trends analysis and
business statistics. Since 1985, it has served clients
worldwide, including corporations, universities,
libraries, consultants and government agencies. At
the firm's web site, visitors can view product
information and pricing and access a great deal of
basic market information on industries such as
financial services, infotech, e-commerce, health care
and biotech.

STR Global (Smith Travel Research)
735 East Main Street
Hendersonville, TN 37075 US
Phone: 615 824 8664
Fax: 615 824 3848
E-mail Address: *info@smithtravelresearch.com*
Web Address: www.strglobal.com
In 2008, STR brought together Deloitte's
HotelBenchmark and The Bench to form STR
Global. STR Global offers monthly, weekly, and
daily STAR benchmarking reports to more than
38,000 hotel clients, representing nearly 5 million
rooms worldwide. STR Global and STR are now the
world's foremost sources of hotel performance trends
and will offer the definitive global hotel database and
development pipeline. STR is headquartered in
Hendersonville, TN, and STR Global is based in
London, with a satellite office in Singapore.
www.strglobal.com now combines the websites of
HotelBenchmark, Smith Travel Research and The
Bench.

XVII. Long Term Care, Assisted Living Associations

Assisted Living Federation of America (ALFA)
1650 King St., Ste. 602
Alexandria, VA 22314-2747 US
Phone: 703-894-1805
Fax: 703-894-1831
E-mail Address: *info@alfa.org*
Web Address: www.alfa.org
The Assisted Living Federation of America (ALFA)
represents for-profit and nonprofit providers of
assisted living, continuing care retirement
communities, independent living and other forms of
housing and services.

**National Investment Center for the Seniors
Housing & Care Industry (NIC)**
1997 Annapolis Exchange Parkway, Ste. 110
Annapolis, MD 21401 US
Phone: 410-267-0504
Fax: 410-268-4620
Web Address: www.nic.org
NIC serves as a resource to lenders, investors,
developers/operators, and others interested in
meeting the housing and healthcare needs of
America's seniors. NIC serves the entire industry as
an objective purveyor of information: NIC's research
and educational efforts are neither association-driven
nor company-oriented. As an impartial observer and
unbiased source, NIC has become the primary link

between the financial markets and seniors housing
developers/operators, connecting each side through
relevant research and practical information.

XVIII. MBA Resources

MBA Depot
Phone: 512-499-8728
Web Address: www.mbadepot.com
MBA Depot is an online community for MBA
professionals.

XIX. Mortgage Industry Associations

Association of Mortgage Investors (AMI)
900 19th St. NW, Ste. 800
Washington, DC 20006 US
Phone: 202-327-8100
Fax: 202-327-8101
E-mail Address: *info@the-ami.org*
Web Address: www.the-ami.org
The Association of Mortgage Investors (AMI) is an
agency formed to help homeowners avoid
foreclosure. It represents private investors, public
and private pension funds and endowments with
interests in mortgage securities.

Council of Mortgage Lenders
Bush House, N. W. Wing
Aldwych
London, WC2B 4PJ UK
Phone: 44-845-373-6771
Fax: 44-845-373-6778
E-mail Address: *info@cml.org.uk*
Web Address: www.cml.org.uk
The Council of Mortgage Lenders is a trade
organization whose members account for
approximately 98% of U.K. mortgage lending
industry.

Mortgage Bankers Association (MBA)
1331 L St. NW
Washington, DC 20005 US
Phone: 202-557-2700
Web Address: www.mbaa.org
The Mortgage Bankers Association (MBA) serves
the real estate finance industry by representing its
legislative and regulatory interests before Congress
and federal agencies; providing educational
programs, periodicals and publications; and
supporting its business interests with research
initiatives, products and services.

National Association of Professional Mortgage Women (NAPMW)
130 E. John Carpenter Fwy.
Irving, TX 75062 US
Fax: 469-524-5121
Toll Free: 800-827-3034
E-mail Address: *info@napmw.org*
Web Address: www.napmw.org
The National Association of Professional Mortgage Women (NAPMW) is an association for women in the banking and mortgage industry.

National Reverse Mortgage Lenders Association (NRMLA)
1400 16th St. NW, Ste. 420
Washington, DC 20036 US
Phone: 202-939-1760
Fax: 202-265-4435
E-mail Address: *dhicks@dworbell.com*
Web Address: www.nrmlaonline.org
The National Reverse Mortgage Lenders Association (NRMLA) was established in 1997 to provide consumer education, industry events and information, and public policy initiatives for the reverse mortgage industry.

XX. Mortgage Industry Resources

---

1 Mortgage Loan Calculators
Web Address: www.1mortgageloancalculators.com
1 Mortgage Loan Calculators is a web site that allows users to determine their mortgage eligibility through various mortgage calculators and comparative data.

Canadian Association of Accredited Mortgage Professionals
2235 Sheppard Ave. East, Ste. 1401
Toronto, ON M2J 5B5 Canada
Phone: 416.385.2333
Fax: 416-385-1177
Toll Free: 888-442-4625
E-mail Address: *info@caamp.org*
Web Address: www.caamp.org
The Canadian Association of Accredited Mortgage Professionals, founded in 1994, includes members from all segments of Canada's mortgage industry. It offers professional development and networking through regional and national events as well as sponsoring industry-related research and publications. The group launched the Accredited Mortgage Professional (AMP) designation in Canada in 2004, and it also advocates for the mortgage

industry through ongoing government and regulatory lobbying, media outreach and other activities.

E-Loan
6230 Stoneridge Mall Rd.
Pleasanton, CA 94588 US
Phone: 925-847-6200
Fax: 925-847-0831
Toll Free: 888-533-5333
Web Address: www.eloan.com
E-Loan provides information on a large variety of loan types, debt consolidation, refinancing, home equity and mortgage management. Additionally, the companies website offers several loan calculators and free credit reports.

Fannie Mae
3900 Wisconsin Ave. NW
Washington, DC 20016-2892 US
Phone: 202-752-7000
Toll Free: 800-732-6643
E-mail Address: *headquarters@fanniemae.com*
Web Address: www.fanniemae.com
Fannie Mae is one of the world's largest non-bank financial services companies and one of the nation's largest sources of financing for home mortgages. It operates under special sanction by the U.S. Congress. It's purpose is to provide liquidity in the national mortgage market.

Federal Agricultural Mortgage Corporation
1133 21st St. NW, Ste. 600
Washington, DC 20036 US
Fax: 202-872-7713
Toll Free: 800-879-3276
Web Address: www.farmermac.com
Federal Agricultural Mortgage Corporation, known as Farmer Mac, is America's secondary market for agricultural real estate and rural housing mortgage loans. Congress created Farmer Mac in 1988 to improve the availability of mortgage credit to America's farmers, ranchers and rural homeowners, businesses and communities.

Federal Citizen Information Center (FCIC)
Dept. WWW
Pueblo, CO 81009 US
Fax: 719-948-9724
Toll Free: 888-878-3256
Web Address: www.pueblo.gsa.gov
The Federal Citizen Information Center (FCIC) offers information and resources for consumers on topics such as cars, children, education, housing,

small businesses and more, as well as current consumer news.

Federal Home Loan Mortgage Corporation (Freddie Mac)
8200 Jones Branch Dr.
McLean, VA 22102-3110 US
Phone: 703-903-2000
E-mail Address: *corprel@freddiemac.com*
Web Address: www.freddiemac.com
The Federal Home Loan Mortgage Corporation (Freddie Mac) operates under special sanction by the U.S. Congress. Its purpose is to provide liquidity in the national mortgage market.

Government National Mortgage Association (Ginnie Mae)
451 7th St. SW
Rm. B-133
Washington, DC 20410-9000 US
Phone: 202-708-1535
Toll Free: 888-446-6434
E-mail Address: *ginniemae.helpdesk@lmco.com*
Web Address: www.ginniemae.gov
The Government National Mortgage Association (Ginnie Mae) is a Federal Government enterprise that provides mortgages to low-income families.

Homepath
3900 Wisconsin Ave. NW
c/o Fannie Mae
Washington, DC 20016-2892 US
Phone: 202-752-7000
Toll Free: 800-732-6643
E-mail Address: *resource_center@fanniemae.com*
Web Address:
www.fanniemae.com/homebuyers/homepath
Homepath, powered by Fannie Mae, helps users find a home, get the most out of their current home, find lenders and other services that will assist in the purchase of a home and help customers avoid mortgage fraud.

LendingTree, LLC
11115 Rushmore Dr.
Charlotte, NC 28277 US
Toll Free: 800-555-8733
Web Address: www.lendingtree.com
LendingTree, LLC serves as an online loan center that connects borrowers to a nationwide network of lenders with exceptional speed and efficiency. LendingTree's simple online forms allow borrowers to provide required information in a matter of

minutes. Additionally, the site's network of some of the most respected financial institutions in the United States allows for quick loan offers, often in less than 48 hours.

Mortgage 101
909 N. Sepulveda Blvd., Fl. 11
El Segundo, CA 90245 US
Toll Free: 888-265-1110
Web Address: www.mortgage101.com
Mortgage 101 lets users find information on rates and local companies, as well as apply for financing. It also offers various calculators concerning refinancing, renting or buying and how much home can be afforded based on monthly mortgage payments. Mortgage 101 is a division of Internet Brands, Inc.

Mortgage.com
Toll Free: 866-422-9432
Web Address: www.mortgage.com
Mortgage.com provides customers with rate quotes and with mortgages, home buying, refinancing and debt consolidation; it is powered by Citigroup, Inc.

Mortgage-calc.com
11760 US Hwy. 1, Ste. 500
North Palm Beach, FL 33408 US
Phone: 561-630-2400
Fax: 561-625-4540
E-mail Address: *webmaster@mortgage-calc.com*
Web Address: www.mortgage-calc.com
Mortgage-calc.com is a web site with a multitude of calculators for home mortgage, amortization, mortgage refinance, home equity loans and debt consolidation.

ReverseMortgage.org
E-mail Address: *dhicks@nrmlaonline.org*
Web Address: www.reversemortgage.org
ReverseMortgage.org is a web site that is maintained by the National Reverse Mortgage Lenders Association. ReverseMortgage.org offers excellent information to consumers who want to learn more about how reverse mortgages work.

XXI.   Property Tax Professionals Associations

International Association of Assessing Officers (IAAO)
314 West 10th St.
Kansas City, MO 64105-1616 US
Phone: 816-701-8100

Fax: 816-701-8149
Toll Free: 800-616-4226
E-mail Address: *daniels@iaao.org*
Web Address: www.iaao.org
The International Association of Assessing Officers (IAAO) is an association of professionals in the field of property assessment and taxation.

XXII. Real Estate Industry Associations

Affordable Housing Tax Credit Coalition
1900 K St. NW, Ste. 1200
Washington, DC 20006-1109 US
Phone: 202-419-2025
Fax: 202-828-3738
E-mail Address: *info@taxcreditcoalition.org*
Web Address: www.taxcreditcoalition.org
The Affordable Housing Tax Credit Coalition is a nonprofit organization of individuals and groups involved in providing affordable housing under the low-income housing tax credit program.

American Escrow Association (AEA)
211 N. Union St., Ste. 100
Alexandria, VA 22314 US
Phone: 703-519-1240
E-mail Address: *hq@a-e-a.org*
Web Address: www.a-e-a.org
The American Escrow Association (AEA) is a national trade association of settlement and escrow industry professionals.

American Institute of Inspectors
P.O. Box 248
Lower Lake, CA 95457 US
Fax: 707-277-7852
Toll Free: 800-877-4770
E-mail Address: *execdir@inspection.org*
Web Address: www.inspection.org
The American Institute of Inspectors is a nonprofit association for residential and commercial building inspectors across North America.

American Investors in Real Estate Online (AIREO)
1824 Sylvan Ave.
Dallas, TX 75208 US
Phone: 214-745-8900
Fax: 214-745-8922
Web Address: www.aireo.com
American Investors in Real Estate Online (AIREO) is a nonprofit organization of real estate investors and professionals dedicated to learning and sharing successful investment techniques.

American Property Tax Counsel (APTC)
77 W. Washington St., Ste. 900
Chicago, IL 60602 US
Toll Free: 877-829-2782
E-mail Address: *bulletin@aptcnet.com*
Web Address: www.aptcnet.com
The American Property Tax Counsel (APTC) is a professional association of property and tax attorneys.

American Society of Appraisers
555 Herndon Pkwy., Ste. 125
Herndon, VA 20170 US
Phone: 703-478-2228
Fax: 703-742-8471
E-mail Address: *asainfo@appraisers.org*
Web Address: www.appraisers.org
The American Society of Appraisers is an organization that provides education and accreditation for appraisers, plus an appraiser locator and electronic recruitment resource for employers and job seekers.

Association of Foreign Investors in Real Estate (AFIRE)
1300 Pennsylvania Ave. NW
Ronald Reagan Bldg.
Washington, DC 20004 US
Phone: 202-312-1400
Fax: 202-312-1401
E-mail Address: *afireinfo@afire.org*
Web Address: www.afire.org
The Association of Foreign Investors in Real Estate (AFIRE) is the only not-for-profit association for the foreign real estate investment community, with more than 180 members representing 21 countries.

Building Owners and Managers Association (BOMA) International
1101 15th St. NW, Ste. 800
Washington, DC 20005 US
Phone: 202-408-2662
Fax: 202-326-6377
E-mail Address: *info@boma.org*
Web Address: www.boma.org
The Building Owners and Managers Association (BOMA) International is a premier network 92 local associations in the U.S. as well as 12 affiliates in 11 other countries, representing more than 16,500 commercial real estate professionals.

Canadian Real Estate Association
200 Catherine St., 6th Fl.
Ottawa, ON K2P 2K9 Canada
Phone: 613-237-7111
Fax: 613-234-2567
E-mail Address: *info@crea.ca*
Web Address: www.crea.ca
The Canadian Real Estate Association (CREA) is
among Canada's largest single-industry trade
organizations. It represents more than 96,000 real
estate agents and salespeople. The organization owns
the "Realtor" trademark in Canada and operates
several industry websites, including Realtor.ca;
HowRealtorsHelp.ca; and ICX.ca, a commercial real
estate web site. CREA monitors public policy and
maintains active relationships with Canadian
government offices in order to represent and promote
the work of its members. It also sponsors industry
research and professional development activities for
its membership.

**Certified Commercial Investment Member
Institute (CCIM)**
430 N. Michigan Ave., Ste. 800
Chicago, IL 60611-4092 US
Phone: 312-321-4460
Fax: 312-321-4530
Toll Free: 800-621-7027
E-mail Address: *info@ccim.com*
Web Address: www.ccim.com
The Certified Commercial Investment Member
Institute (CCIM) is an organization that provides
accreditation for certified commercial investment
members.

Certified New Home Specialist
2222 Colony Plz.
Dennis Walsh & Associates, Inc.
Newport Beach, CA 92660 US
Phone: 949-706-3500
Toll Free: 800-428-1122
E-mail Address: *info@sellnewhomes.com*
Web Address: www.sellnewhomes.com
The Certified New Home Specialist web site offers
certification as a New Home Specialist, an
accreditation endorsed by GMAC, Coldwell Banker,
ERA Real Estate and Prudential Real Estate. The
web site is offered by Dennis Walsh & Associates,
Inc.

China Commercial Real Estate Association
No. 3 Shijingshan Rd., Yuquan Mansion, Rm. 513
Beijing, 100049 China

Phone: 86-10-88255833
Fax: 86-10-88255149
E-mail Address: *ccreu@163.com*
Web Address: www.ccreu.com.cn
The China Commercial Real Estate Association
(CCREA) primary members are commercial real
estate development enterprises, retailers, chain store
companies, commercial consultant companies,
designing companies, funds companies, devices
suppliers and professionals.

**Commercial Real Estate Women Network
(CREW Network)**
1201 Wakarusa Dr., Ste. C3
Lawrence, KS 66049-3803 US
Phone: 785-832-1808
Fax: 785-832-1551
E-mail Address: *denisek@crewnetwork.org*
Web Address: www.crewnetwork.org
The Commercial Real Estate Women Network
(CREW Network) is a national association of women
in the commercial real estate industry.

Community Associations Institute (CAI)
225 Reinekers Ln., Ste. 300
Alexandria, VA 22314 US
Phone: 703-548-8600
Fax: 703-684-1581
Toll Free: 888-224-4321
Web Address: www.caionline.org
The Community Associations Institute (CAI) is an
association of condominium, cooperative and
homeowner associations.

**Confederation of Real Estate Developer's
Associations of India**
105 Ansal Bhawan
16 Kasturba Gandhi Marg
New Delhi, 110 001 India
Phone: 91-11-4152 0549
Fax: 91-11-4152 0548
E-mail Address: *info@credai.org*
Web Address: www.cbec.gov.in
Confederation of Real Estate Developer's
Associations of India (CREDAI) is the apex body of
the organized real estate developers/builders across
India.

**Council of International Restaurant Real Estate
Brokers (CIRB)**
8350 N. Central Expy., Ste. 1300
Dallas, TX 75206 US
Fax: 866-247-2329

Toll Free: 866-247-2123
E-mail Address: *cirbhq@cirb.net*
Web Address: www.cirb.net
The Council of International Restaurant Real Estate
Brokers (CIRB) is the only international network of
independent real estate brokers who specialize solely
in restaurant and related real estate.

Council of Residential Specialists (CRS)
430 N. Michigan Ave., Fl. 3
Chicago, IL 60611 US
Fax: 312-329-8882
Toll Free: 800-462-8841
Web Address: www.crs.com
The Council of Residential Specialists (CRS) is an
association of realtors providing training for the
Certified Residential Specialist designation.

Counselors of Real Estate (CRE)
430 N. Michigan Ave.
Chicago, Il 60611 US
Phone: 312-329-8427
E-mail Address: *pcoady@cre.org*
Web Address: www.cre.org
The Counselors of Real Estate (CRE) is an
international group of high-profile professionals,
including members of prominent real estate,
financial, legal and accounting firms as well as
leaders in government and academia, who provide
objective advice on complex real property situations
and land-related matters.

European Public Real Estate Association (EPRA)
Schiphol Blvd. 283
Schiphol Airport
1118 BH The Netherlands
Phone: 31-20-405-3830
Fax: 31-20-405-3840
E-mail Address: *info@epra.com*
Web Address: www.epra.com
The European Public Real Estate Association
(EPRA) is a trade association of European real estate
companies.

Foundation of Real Estate Appraisers (FREA)
4907 Morena Blvd., Ste. 1415
San Diego, CA 92117 US
Fax: 858-273-8206
Toll Free: 800-882-4410
E-mail Address: *info@frea.com*
Web Address: www.frea.com
The Foundation of Real Estate Appraisers (FREA) is
an organization of appraisers, home inspectors and

environmental site assessors offering errors and
omissions insurance, continuing education and other
benefits.

Hong Kong Institute of Surveyors (HKIS)
1 Connaught Pl.
8/F Jardine House, Ste. 801
Hong Kong, Hong Kong China
Phone: 852-2526-3679
Fax: 852-2868-4612
Web Address: www.hkis.org.hk
The Hong Kong Institute of Surveyors (HKIS) is the
professional organization representing the surveying
industry and surveying professionals in Hong Kong.

India Institute of Real Estate
Orchard Dr. Pai Marg, Nachiket Pk.
Baner, Ste. 400
Pune, 411 045 India
Phone: 9890238936
E-mail Address: *support@iire.co.in*
Web Address: www.iire.co.in
The India Institute of Real Estate is a nonprofit
organization supporting the real estate industry. The
organization provides accreditation and certifications
pertaining to the real estate practice in India.

**Institute for Responsible Housing Preservation
(IRHP)**
401 9th St. NW, Ste. 900
Washington, DC 20004 US
Phone: 202-585-8739
Fax: 202-585-8080
E-mail Address: *info@HousingPreservation.org*
Web Address: www.housingpreservation.org
The Institute for Responsible Housing Preservation
(IRHP) is a nonprofit association of owners and
managers of Section 221(d)(3) and Section 236
projects participating in HUD preservation programs.

Institute of Housing Management (IHM)
2175 Sheppard Ave. E., Ste. 310
Toronto, ON M2J 1W8 Canada
Phone: 416-493-7382
Fax: 416-491-1670
Toll Free: 866-212-4377
E-mail Address: *ihm@taylorenterprises.com*
Web Address: www.ihm-canada.com
The Institute of Housing Management (IHM) is a
Canadian organization of property management
professionals.

Institute of Real Estate Management (IREM)
430 N. Michigan Ave.
Chicago, IL 60611 US
Fax: 800-338-4736
Toll Free: 800-837-0706
E-mail Address: *custserv@irem.org*
Web Address: www.irem.org
The Institute of Real Estate Management (IREM)
seeks to educate real estate managers, certify their
competence and professionalism, serve as an
advocate on issues affecting the real estate
management industry and enhance its members'
professional competence so they can better identify
and meet the needs of those who use their services.

**International Association of Certified Home
Inspectors (InterNACHI)**
1750 30th St.
Boulder, CO 80301 US
Phone: 303-502-6214
Fax: 650-429-2057
Toll Free: 877-346-3467
E-mail Address: *fastreply@nachi.org*
Web Address: www.nachi.org
The International Association of Certified Home
Inspectors (InterNACHI) is a nonprofit organization
designed to help home inspectors to achieve financial
success and remain highly educated. The
organizations web site provides free course material
for home inspectors and online tools to help
consumers find a qualified professional, mainly in the
U.S. and Canada.

International Business Broker Association (IBBA)
401 N. Michigan Ave., Ste. 2200
Chicago, IL 60611-4267 US
Phone: 312-673-4097
Fax: 312-673-6599
Toll Free: 888-686-4222
E-mail Address: *admin@ibba.org*
Web Address: www.ibba.org
The International Business Broker Association
(IBBA) is the largest international nonprofit
association operating exclusively for the benefit of
people and firms engaged in the various aspects of
business brokerage and mergers and acquisitions.

**International Facility Management Association
(IFMA)**
1 E. Greenway Plz., Ste. 1100
Houston, TX 77046-0194 US
Phone: 713-623-4362
Fax: 713-623-6124

E-mail Address: *ifma@ifma.org*
Web Address: www.ifma.org
The International Facility Management Association
(IFMA) is a trade association of facilities managers.
IFMA certifies facility managers, provides
educational programs, conducts research, recognizes
facility management degree and certificate programs
and produces World Workplace, a facility
management-related conference and exposition.

International Real Estate Institute (IREI)
1224 N. Nokomis NE
Alexandria, MN 56308 US
Phone: 320-763-4648
Fax: 320-763-9290
E-mail Address: *info@irei-assoc.org*
Web Address: irei-assoc.org
The International Real Estate Institute (IREI) is one
of the largest international real estate associations in
the world, with members in over more cities than any
other organization.

International Society of Appraisers (ISA)
1131 SW 7th St., Ste. 105
Renton, WA 98057-1215 US
Phone: 206-241-0359
Fax: 206-241-0436
E-mail Address: *isa@isa-appraisers.org*
Web Address: www.isa-appraisers.org
The International Society of Appraisers (ISA) is a
nonprofit association that provides education and
organizational support to its members and serves the
public by producing highly qualified and ethical
appraisers who are recognized authorities in
professional personal property appraising.

National Apartment Association (NAA)
4300 Wilson Blvd., Ste. 400
Arlington, VA 22203 US
Phone: 703-518-6141
Fax: 703-248-9440
E-mail Address: *webmaster@naahq.org*
Web Address: www.naahq.org
The National Apartment Association (NAA) is a
national federation of state and local apartment
associations designed to serve the interests of
multifamily housing owners, managers, developers
and suppliers.

**National Association of Hispanic Real Estate
Professionals (NAHREP)**
1150 17th St. NW, Ste. 504
Washington, DC 20036 US

Fax: 202-955-1066
Toll Free: 800-964-5373
Web Address: www.nahrep.org
The National Association of Hispanic Real Estate
Professionals (NAHREP) is an organization that
serves real estate agents, brokers, loan officers,
mortgage brokers, title officers, escrow officers,
appraisers and insurance agents from diverse cultural
backgrounds, as membership is not limited to
professionals of Hispanic descent.

National Association of Home Inspectors (NAHI)
4248 Park Glen Rd.
Minneapolis, MN 55416 US
Phone: 952-928-4641
Fax: 952-929-1318
Toll Free: 800-448-3942
E-mail Address: *info@nahi.org*
Web Address: www.nahi.org
The National Association of Home Inspectors
(NAHI) is a nonprofit association that exists to
promote and develop the home inspection industry.

**National Association of Housing and
Redevelopment Officials (NAHRO)**
630 Eye St. NW
Washington, DC 20001 US
Phone: 202-289-3500
Fax: 202-289-8181
Toll Free: 877-866-2476
E-mail Address: *nahro@nahro.org*
Web Address: www.nahro.org
The National Association of Housing and
Redevelopment Officials (NAHRO) is an association
of professionals in affordable housing and
community redevelopment. Its members administer
Hud programs such as Public Housing, Section 8,
CDBG and HOME.

**National Association of Independent Fee
Appraisers (NAIFA)**
401 N. Michigan Ave., Ste. 2200
Chicago, IL 60611 US
Phone: 312-321-6830
Fax: 312-673-6652
E-mail Address: *info@naifa.com*
Web Address: www.naifa.com
The National Association of Independent Fee
Appraisers (NAIFA) offers education, professional
designations, an online appraiser directory and other
services for appraisers and the public.

**National Association of Industrial and Office
Properties (NAIOP)**
2201 Cooperative Way, Fl. 3
Herndon, VA 20171-3034 US
Phone: 703-904-7100
Fax: 703-904-7942
E-mail Address: *hamilton@naiop.org*
Web Address: www.naiop.org
The National Association of Industrial and Office
Properties (NAIOP) is a trade association of
commercial real estate professionals.

**National Association of Mold Professionals
(NAMP)**
3250 Old Farm Ln., Ste. 1
Walled Lake, MI 48390 US
Phone: 248-669-5673
E-mail Address: *info@moldpro.org*
Web Address: www.moldpro.org
The National Association of Mold Professionals
(NAMP) is a nonprofit organization that was
established with the goal of developing and
promoting the mold inspection and remediation
industry.

**National Association of Real Estate Brokers
(NAREB)**
9831 Greenbelt Rd., Ste. 309
Lanham, MD 20706 US
Phone: 301-552-9340
Fax: 301-552-9216
E-mail Address: *NAREB3@comcast.net*
Web Address: www.nareb.com
The National Association of Real Estate Brokers
(NAREB) is a national trade organization dedicated
to bringing together the nation's minority
professionals in the real estate industry.

**National Association of Real Estate Companies
(NAREC)**
216 W. Jackson Blvd., Ste. 625
Chicago, IL 60606 US
Phone: 312-263-1755
Fax: 312-750-1203
E-mail Address: *info@narec.org*
Web Address: www.narec.org
The National Association of Real Estate Companies
(NAREC) is composed of representatives of publicly
and privately owned real estate companies,
significant subsidiaries of publicly owned companies
and public accounting firms.

National Association of Real Estate Investment Trusts (NAREIT)
1875 I St. NW, Ste. 600
Washington, DC 20006 US
Phone: 202-739-9400
Fax: 202-739-9401
Toll Free: 800-362-7348
E-mail Address: *info@nareit.org*
Web Address: www.nareit.org
The National Association of Real Estate Investment
Trusts (NAREIT) is the representative to
governmental policymakers for U.S. Real Estate
Investment Trusts (REITs) and publicly traded real
estate companies worldwide.

National Association of Real Estate Property Managers (NARPM)
638 Independence Pkwy., Ste. 100
Chesapeake, VA 23320 US
Fax: 866-466-2776
Toll Free: 800-782-3452
E-mail Address: *info@narpm.org*
Web Address: www.narpm.org
National Association of Real Estate Property
Managers (NARPM) is an association of real estate
management professionals that specializes in single-
family and small residential properties.

National Association of Real-Estate Inspection & Evaluation Services (NARIES)
P.O. Box 532
Edmonds, WA 98020 US
Phone: 206-778-1296
Toll Free: 800-583-5821
E-mail Address: *crmsnsky@verizon.net*
Web Address: www.naries.org
The National Association of Real-Estate Inspection
& Evaluation Services (NARIES) is an association
dedicated to the education of consumers hiring
building and home inspectors, appraisers, real-estate
professionals, architects, engineers and building
officials.

National Association of Realtors (NAR)
430 N. Michigan Ave.
Chicago, IL 60611-4087 US
Phone: 202-383-1176
Toll Free: 800-874-6500
E-mail Address: *lsalvant@realtors.org*
Web Address: www.realtor.org
The National Association of Realtors (NAR) is
composed of realtors involved in residential and
commercial real estate as brokers, salespeople,

property managers, appraisers and counselors and in
other areas of the industry. NAR also sponsors
Realtor.com, operated by Move, Inc.

National Council of Real Estate Investment Fiduciaries (NCREIF)
180 N. Stetson Ave.
2 Prudential Plz.
Chicago, IL 60601 US
Phone: 312-819-5890
Fax: 312-819-5891
E-mail Address: *dpoutasse@ncreif.org*
Web Address: www.ncreif.com
The National Council of Real Estate Investment
Fiduciaries (NCREIF) is an association of
institutional real estate professionals such as
investment managers, plan sponsors, academicians,
consultants, appraisers, CPAs and other service
providers who have a significant involvement in
pension fund real estate investments.

National Multi Housing Council (NMHC)
1850 M St. NW, Ste. 540
Washington, DC 20036-5803 US
Phone: 202-974-2300
Fax: 202-775-0112
E-mail Address: *info@nmhc.org*
Web Address: www.nmhc.org
The National Multi Housing Council (NMHC) is a
trade association representing apartment owners,
managers, developers, lenders and service providers.

Pension Real Estate Association (PREA)
100 Pearl St., Fl. 13
Hartford, CT 06103 US
Phone: 860-692-6341
Fax: 860-692-6351
E-mail Address: *prea@prea.org*
Web Address: www.prea.org
The Pension Real Estate Association (PREA) is a
nonprofit organization whose members are engaged
in the investment of tax-exempt pension and
endowment funds into real estate assets.

Property Management Association (PMA)
7900 Wisconsin Ave., Ste. 305
Bethesda, MD 20814 US
Phone: 301-657-9200
Fax: 301-907-9326
E-mail Address: *info@pma-dc.org*
Web Address: www.pma-dc.org
The Property Management Association (PMA) is a
real estate management organization that promotes

the knowledge and practical education of the industry through monthly meetings, seminars and publications.

Real Estate Developers' Association of Singapore (REDAS)
190 Clemenceau Ave.
07-01 Singapore Shopping Ctr.
Singapore
Phone: 65-6336-6655
Fax: 65-6337-2217
E-mail Address: *enquiry@redas.com*
Web Address: www.redas.com.sg
Real Estate Developers' Association of Singapore's (REDAS) website, Redas.com, is an information center as well as an electronic marketplace that offers a broad array of services and resources including but not limited to property search engines, market trends, policy updates, on-line purchases of products and services, business message exchange, and links to other trade associations, professional bodies, government agencies and statutory boards in Singapore and the region.

Real Estate Institute of Canada (REIC)
5407 Eglinton Ave. W., Ste. 208
Toronto, ON M9C 5K6 Canada
Phone: 416-695-9000
Fax: 416-695-7230
Toll Free: 800-542-7342
E-mail Address: *infocentral@reic.com*
Web Address: www.reic.ca
The Real Estate Institute of Canada (REIC) is an association of professionals dedicated to establishing, maintaining, promoting and advancing high standards of practice through education, certification and accreditation.

Realtors Land Institute (RLI)
430 N. Michigan Ave.
Chicago, IL 60611 US
Fax: 312-329-8633
Toll Free: 800-441-5263
E-mail Address: *rli@realtors.org*
Web Address: www.rliland.com
Realtors Land Institute (RLI) serves professionals specializing in land brokerage. The web site includes membership benefits, land listings and state chapters.

Research Institute for Housing America
1919 Pennsylvania Ave. NW
Mortgage Bankers Association
Washington, DC 20006 US

Phone: 202-557-2700
E-mail Address: *info@mortgagebankers.org*
Web Address: www.housingamerica.org
The Research Institute for Housing America of the Mortgage Bankers Association is a 501(c)(3) trust fund. Its chief purpose is to encourage and aid - through grants and sponsored research to distinguished scholars, educational institutions, research facilities, and government organizations - the pursuit of knowledge of mortgage markets and real estate finance. Excellent research papers on various housing issues are available on its web site.

Royal Institution of Chartered Surveyors
RICS Contact Ctr.
Surveyor Ct., Westwood Way
Coventry, CV4 8JE UK
Phone: 44-870-333-1600
Fax: 44-20-7-334-3811
E-mail Address: *contactrics@rics.org*
Web Address: www.rics.org
The Royal Institution of Chartered Surveyors (RICS) is a U.K.-based trade organization representing 140,000 members operating in 146 countries; it has offices around the globe, on every continent.

Society of Industrial and Office Realtors (SIOR)
1201 New York Ave. NW, Ste. 350
Washington, DC 20005-6126 US
Phone: 202-449-8200
Fax: 202-216-9325
E-mail Address: *admin@sior.com*
Web Address: www.sior.com
The Society of Industrial and Office Realtors (SIOR) provides support for industrial and office real estate specialists holding the SIOR designation.

Surveyors and Valuers Accreditation Association (SAVA)
SAVA, National Energy Ctr.
Davy Ave.
Milton Keynes, Surrey MK5 8NA UK
Phone: 44-1908-672787
Fax: 44-1908-662296
E-mail Address: *info@sava.org.uk*
Web Address: www.sava.org.uk
The Surveyors and Valuers Accreditation Association (SAVA) sets surveying standards for the Royal Institution of Chartered Surveyors.

TriState REALTORS Commercial Alliance
555 E. North Ln., Ste. 6125
Conshohocken, PA 19428-4425 US

Phone: 610-238-9950
Fax: 610-238-9959
E-mail Address: *tristate@tristaterca.com*
Web Address: www.tristaterca.com
The TriState REALTORS Commercial Alliance is an
association of commercial real estate professionals in
Pennsylvania, New Jersey and Delaware.

Women's Council of Realtors (WCR)

430 N. Michigan Ave.
Chicago, IL 60611 US
Toll Free: 800-245-8512
E-mail Address: *wcr@wcr.org*
Web Address: www.wcr.org
The Women's Council of Realtors (WCR) is a
community of female real estate professionals.

XXIII.   Real Estate Industry Resources

CoStar Group

2 Bethesda Metro Ctr., Fl. 10
Bethesda, MD 20814-5388 US
Phone: 301-215-8300
Fax: 800-613-1301
Toll Free: 800-204-5960
E-mail Address: *info@costar.com*
Web Address: www.costar.com
CoStar Group operates a web site with extensive
resources for brokers, owners and users of
commercial real estate space. The group operates a
listings database that allows users to analyze market
trends, research property history and compare local
rental rates for commercial real estate.

Joint Center for Housing Studies--Harvard University

1033 Massachusetts Avenue, Fl. 5
Cambridge, MA 02138 US
Phone: 617-495-7908
Fax: 617-496-9957
Web Address: www.jchs.harvard.edu
The Joint Center for Housing Studies is Harvard
University's unit for information and research on
housing in the United States. JCHS analyzes the
relationships between housing markets and
economic, demographic, and social trends. It
publishes several excellent reports each year.

Marcus & Millichap Real Estate Investment Services, Inc.

16830 Ventura Blvd., Ste. 352
Encino, CA 91436 US
Phone: 818-907-0600

Fax: 818-501-8230
Web Address: www.marcusmillichap.com
Marcus & Millichap Real Estate Investment Services,
Inc., a national investment real estate brokerage firm,
offers in-depth reports on various commercial
property and apartment sectors, by city and on a
nationwide basis. Users can register to receive its e-
mail reports.

Metropolitan Institute at Virginia Tech (MI)

1021 Prince St., Ste. 100
Alexandria, VA 22314 US
Phone: 703-706-8100
Fax: 703-518-8009
E-mail Address: *mivt@vt.edu*
Web Address: www.mi.vt.edu
The Metropolitan Institute at Virginia Tech (MI)
conducts basic and applied research on national and
international development patterns, focusing on key
forces shaping metropolitan growth such as
demographics, environment, technology, design,
transportation, and governance. MI publishes several
excellent white papers and reports yearly.

MSN Real Estate

1 Microsoft Way
Microsoft Corporation
Redmond, WA 98052-6399 US
Toll Free: 800-642-7676
Web Address: realestate.msn.com
MSN Real Estate features advice, links and services
for buying and selling houses and managing and
maintaining residential property.

Real Estate Industry Resources
Real Estate Library

200 SW Shining Mist
Depoe Bay, OR 97345 US
Phone: 541-765-3090
E-mail Address: *admin@relibrary.com*
Web Address: www.relibrary.com
The Real Estate Library contains resources such as
mortgage loan assistance, online real estate courses
for certification, real estate web design walkthroughs
and other useful tools for buyers, sellers, home
owners and real estate professionals.

REITNet

Web Address: www.reitnet.com
REITNet is a web site that offers a number of articles
and glossaries for anyone researching or investing in
real estate investment trusts (REITs). The
REITNet.com domain is currently up for sale.

RentLaw.com
Phone: 732-539-2914
E-mail Address: *info@rentlaw.com*
Web Address: www.rentlaw.com
RentLaw.com provides landlords, tenants, investors, lawyers, agent associations and homeowners with extensive information regarding landlord-tenant laws and legal advice.

XXIV.   RealtyTrac

Real Estate Industry Resources
One Venture Plaza
Suite 300
Irvine, CA 92618 US
Fax: 949-861-9413
Toll Free: 877-888-8722
E-mail Address: *support@realtytrac.com*
Web Address: www.realtytrac.com
RealtyTrac offers comprehensive online data and listings regarding properties in the U.S. that in foreclosure.

XXV.   Remodeling Industry Associations

National Association of the Remodeling Industry (NARI)
780 Lee St., Ste. 200
Des Plaines, IL 60016 US
Phone: 847-298-9200
Fax: 847-298-9225
Toll Free: 800-298-6274
E-mail Address: *info@nari.org*
Web Address: www.nari.org
The National Association of the Remodeling Industry (NARI) provides certifications, education and support to professionals working in the remodeling industry, along with support to consumers.

National Kitchen & Bath Association (NKBA)
687 Willow Grove St.
Hackettstown, NJ 07840 US
Fax: 908-852-1695
Toll Free: 800-843-6522
E-mail Address: *feedback@nkba.org*
Web Address: www.nkba.org
The National Kitchen & Bath Association (NKBA) is a premier resource for kitchen and bath remodelers, designers, planners and consumers. It offers courses and certifications for professionals in design, installation and education. It is the owner of the

Kitchen/Bath Industry Show & Conference each year and it sponsors annual design competitions.

XXVI.   Science Parks

International Association of Science Parks (IASP)
29590 Campanillas
Malaga,   Spain
Phone: 34 95 202 83 03
Fax: 34 95 202 04 64
E-mail Address: *iasp@iasp.ws*
Web Address: www.iasp.ws
The IASP is a worldwide network of science and technology parks. It enjoys Special Consultative status with the Economic and Social Council of the United Nations. Its 350 members represent science parks in 72 nations. It is also a founding member of the World Alliance for Innovation WAINOVA. World headquarters are in Spain, with an additional office in the Tsinghua University Science Park, Beijing, China.

XXVII. Shopping Center Directories

Chain Store Guide (CSG)
3922 Coconut Palm Dr.
Tampa, FL 33619 US
Fax: 813-627-6883
Toll Free: 800-778-9794
E-mail Address: *info@csgis.com*
Web Address: www.csgis.com
The Chain Store Guide (CSG) is a provider of comprehensive retail and foodservice intelligence. The CSG database contains over 200,000 retailers, foodservice operators, distributors and wholesalers in the U.S. and Canada.

National Research Bureau (NRB)
2 Bethesda Metro Ctr., Fl. 10
Bethesda, MD 20814-5388 US
Phone: 301-215-8300
Fax: 800-613-1301
Toll Free: 800-204-5960
E-mail Address: *info@costar.com*
Web Address: www.nrbonline.com
CoStar Group, publishes The Shopping Center Information Products database, which contains approximately 41,000 U.S. shopping centers; Shopping Center Directory; the Shopping Center Directions Newsletter and Real Estate America.

The Directory of Major Malls, Inc.
20 N. Broadway
P.O. Box 837
Nyack, NY 10960 US
Phone: 845-348-7000
Fax: 845-348-7011
Toll Free: 800-898-6255
Web Address: www.directoryofmajormalls.com
The Directory of Major Malls, Inc. offers information
on centers that have above 250,000 square feet of
gross leaseable area (GLA). Information includes
location, GLA, household income, area population
and design of various centers.

Value Retail News
29399 US Hwy. 19 N, Ste. 370
Clearwater, FL 33761-2137 US
Phone: 727-781-7557
Fax: 727-781-9717
E-mail Address: *lhumphers@icsc.org*
Web Address: www.valueretailnews.com
Value Retail News, a division of the International
Council of Shopping Centers, publishes several
directories, including the Outlet Project Directory, a
listing of factory outlet information; and the Value
Retail Directory, which provides factory outlet tenant
data.

XXVIII.   Shopping Center Resources

ChainLinks Retail Advisors
2 Ravinia Dr., Ste. 1550
Atlanta, GA 30346 US
Phone: 678-336-8960
Fax: 678-336-8965
Toll Free: 800-394-3701
Web Address: www.chainlinks.com
ChainLinks is a major retail-only, full-service real
estate broker in the United States and Canada.

CoreNet Global
260 Peachtree St. NW, Ste. 1500
Atlanta, GA 30303 US
Phone: 404-589-3200
Fax: 404-589-3201
Toll Free: 800-726-8111
E-mail Address: *sguree@corenetglobal.org*
Web Address: www2.corenetglobal.org
CoreNet Global is an organization for business
leaders engaged in the strategic management of real
estate for major corporations worldwide.

International Council of Shopping Centers (ICSC)
1221 Ave. of the Americas, Fl. 41
New York, NY 10020-1099 US
Phone: 646-728-3800
Fax: 732 694 1800
E-mail Address: *icsc@icsc.org*
Web Address: www.icsc.org
The International Council of Shopping Centers
(ICSC) is the global trade association of the shopping
center industry, and includes shopping center owners,
developers, managers, marketing specialists,
investors, lenders and retailers. ICSC's 70,000
members reach to over 80 countries and the
organization links with more than 25 national and
regional shopping center councils throughout the
world.

Retail Traffic Online
249 W. 17th St.
New York, NY 10011 US
Phone: 212-204-4200
Fax: 914-514-9050
E-mail Address: *david.bodamer@penton.com*
Web Address: www.retailtrafficmag.com
RetailTraffic Online serves as the web site for the
Retail Traffic magazine. The site offers retail news,
store expansion plans, financial news, research tools
and much more.

XXIX.   Spa Industry Associations

International Spa Association (ISPA)
2365 Harrodsburg Rd., Ste. A325
Lexington, KY 40504 US
Phone: 859-226-4326
Fax: 859-226-4445
Toll Free: 888-651-4772
E-mail Address: *ispa@ispastaff.com*
Web Address: www.experienceispa.com
The International Spa Association (ISPA) is
recognized worldwide as one of the leading
professional organizations and voices of the spa
industry. It provides educational and networking
opportunities, promotes the value of the spa
experience and speaks as the authoritative voice to
foster professionalism and growth. ISPA represents
more than 3,000 health and wellness facilities and
providers in 75 countries.

XXX.   Telecommunications Industry Associations

FTTH Council (Fiber to the Home Council)
P. O. Box 21071
Spokane, WA 99201 US
Phone: 503-635-3114
E-mail Address: *info@ftthcouncil.org*
Web Address: www.ftthcouncil.org
The Fiber-to-the-Home (FTTH) Council is a nonprofit organization established in 2001 to educate the public on the opportunities and benefits of FTTH solutions. Its website is an excellent resource for statistics, general reference and trends in the delivery of fiber optic cable directly to the home and office.

XXXI.   Travel-Local Transportation, Bus & Car Rental

American Public Transportation Association (APTA)
1666 K St. NW
Washington, DC 20006 US
Phone: 202-496-4800
Fax: 202-496-4321
Web Address: www.apta.com
APTA is a nonprofit international association of more than 1,500 member organizations including public transportation systems; planning, design, construction and finance firms; product and service providers; academic institutions; and state associations and departments of transportation. APTA members serve more than 90 percent of persons using public transportation in the United States and Canada.

XXXII.   U.S. Government Agencies

Bureau of Economic Analysis (BEA)
1441 L St. NW
Washington, DC 20230 US
Phone: 202-606-9900
E-mail Address: *customerservice@bea.gov*
Web Address: www.bea.gov
The Bureau of Economic Analysis (BEA), an agency of the U.S. Department of Commerce, is the nation's economic accountant, preparing estimates that illuminate key national, international and regional aspects of the U.S. economy.

Bureau of Labor Statistics (BLS)
2 Massachusetts Ave. NE
Washington, DC 20212-0001 US
Phone: 202-691-5200
Web Address: stats.bls.gov
The Bureau of Labor Statistics (BLS) is the principal fact-finding agency for the Federal Government in the field of labor economics and statistics. It is an independent national statistical agency that collects, processes, analyzes and disseminates statistical data to the American public, U.S. Congress, other federal agencies, state and local governments, business and labor. The BLS also serves as a statistical resource to the Department of Labor.

Department of Housing and Urban Development (HUD)
451 7th St. SW
Washington, DC 20410 US
Phone: 202-708-1112
E-mail Address: *Helen.A.Savoye@hud.gov*
Web Address: www.hud.gov
The Department of Housing and Urban Development, commonly known as HUD, is a Federal Government agency involved in increasing homeownership, supporting community development and increasing access to affordable housing free from discrimination.

Energy Efficiency and Renewable Energy (EERE)
1000 Independence Ave. SW
Mail Stop EE-1
Washington, DC 20585 US
Phone: 202-586-4403
Toll Free: 877-337-3463
Web Address: www.eere.energy.gov
The Energy Efficiency and Renewable Energy (EERE), an office of the U.S. Department of Energy, provides information on bioenergy, geothermal, hydrogen, hydropower, tidal, hydropower, solar, wind and energy conservation methods. The Office also works with U.S. industries to advance the development of various alternative energy technologies.

Federal Housing Administration (FHA)
451 7th Street S.W.
Washington, DC 20410 US
Toll Free: 800-225-5342
Web Address: www.fha.gov
The Federal Housing Administration, generally known as FHA, is the largest government insurer of mortgages in the world, insuring over 35 million properties since its inception in 1934. A part of the United States Department of Housing and Urban Development (HUD), FHA provides mortgage

insurance on single-family, multifamily, manufactured homes and hospital loans made by FHA-approved lenders throughout the United States and its territories.

Office of Federal Housing Enterprise Oversight (OFHEO)

1700 G St. NW, Fl. 4
Washington, DC 02552 US
Phone: 202-414-3800
Fax: 202-414-3823
E-mail Address: *fhfainfo@fhfa.gov*
Web Address: www.ofheo.gov
The Office of Federal Housing Enterprise Oversight (OFHEO) publishes a housing price index along with many other very useful statistics about America's housing and mortgage sectors.

U.S. Census Bureau

4600 Silver Hill Rd.
Washington, DC 20233-8800 US
Phone: 301-763-4636
Fax: 301-457-3670
Toll Free: 800-923-8282
E-mail Address: *pio@census.gov*
Web Address: www.census.gov
The U.S. Census Bureau is the official collector of data about the people and economy of the U.S. Founded in 1790, it provides official social, demographic and economic information.

U.S. Department of Commerce (DOC)

1401 Constitution Ave. NW
Washington, DC 20230 US
Phone: 202-482-2000
E-mail Address: *cgutierrez@doc.gov*
Web Address: www.commerce.gov
The U.S. Department of Commerce (DOC) regulates trade and provides valuable economic analysis of the economy.

U.S. Department of Labor (DOL)

200 Constitution Ave. NW
Frances Perkins Bldg.
Washington, DC 20210 US
Toll Free: 866-487-2365
Web Address: www.dol.gov
The U.S. Department of Labor (DOL) is the government agency responsible for labor regulations. This site provides tools to help citizens find out whether companies are complying with family and medical-leave requirements.

U.S. Securities and Exchange Commission (SEC)

100 F St. NE
Washington, DC 20549 US
Phone: 202-551-6000
Toll Free: 888-732-6585
E-mail Address: *publicinfo@sec.gov*
Web Address: www.sec.gov
The U.S. Securities and Exchange Commission (SEC) is a nonpartisan, quasi-judicial regulatory agency responsible for administering federal securities laws. These laws are designed to protect investors in securities markets and ensure that they have access to disclosure of all material information concerning publicly traded securities. Visitors to the web site can access the EDGAR database of corporate financial and business information.

Chapter 4

THE REAL ESTATE 400:
WHO THEY ARE AND HOW THEY WERE CHOSEN

Includes Indexes by Company Name, Industry & Location, And a Complete Table of Sales, Profits and Ranks

The companies chosen to be listed in PLUNKETT'S REAL ESTATE & CONSTRUCTION INDUSTRY ALMANAC comprise a unique list. THE REAL ESTATE 400 (the actual count is 431 companies) were chosen specifically for their dominance in the many facets of the real estate and construction industry in which they operate. Complete information about each firm can be found in the "Individual Profiles," beginning at the end of this chapter. These profiles are in alphabetical order by company name.

THE REAL ESTATE 400 companies are from all parts of the United States, Asia, Canada, Europe and beyond. Essentially, THE REAL ESTATE 400 includes companies that are deeply involved in the services, trends and technologies that keep the entire industry forging ahead.

Simply stated, THE REAL ESTATE 400 contains the largest, most successful, fastest growing firms in real estate, construction and related industries in the world. To be included in our list, the firms had to meet the following criteria:

1) Generally, these are corporations based in the U.S., however, the headquarters of 114 firms are located in other nations.

2) Prominence, or a significant presence, in real estate, construction and supporting fields. (See the following Industry Codes section for a complete list of types of businesses that are covered).

3) The companies in THE REAL ESTATE 400 do not have to be exclusively in the real estate and construction field.

4) Financial data and vital statistics must have been available to the editors of this book, either directly from the company being written about or from outside sources deemed reliable and accurate by the editors. A small number of companies that we would like to have included are not listed because of a lack of sufficient, objective data.

INDUSTRY LIST, WITH CODES

**This book refers to the following list of unique
industry codes, based on the 2007 NAIC code
system (NAIC is used by many analysts as a
replacement for older SIC codes because NAIC is
more specific to today's industry sectors, see
www.census.gov/NAICS). Companies profiled in
this book are given a primary NAIC code,
reflecting the main line of business of each firm.**

Automotive

Automotive Manufacturing
3363 — Automobile Parts Manufacturing

Entertainment

Hotels & Accommodations
721110 — Hotels/Resorts/Motels
721120 — Casino Resorts

Financial Services

Banking, Credit & Finance
522220 — Financing--Business
522291 — Finance--Consumer
522310 — Mortgages
522310E — Mortgages, Online
522320 — Payment & Transaction Processing Services

Stocks & Investments
523910 — Venture Capital/Private Equity Investments
523920 — Investment Management/Mutual
Funds/Pension Funds

Insurance
524126 — Insurance--Property & Casualty, Specialty,
Surety
524127 — Insurance-Title (Real Estate)

Health Care

Nursing
623110 — Long-Term Health Care & Assisted Living

InfoTech

Software
511210 — Computer Software, Publisher
511210A — Computer Software, Supply Chain &
Logistics
511210H — Computer Software, Business Management
& ERP
511210J — Computer Software, Data Base & File
Management

Internet

519130 — Internet Publishing & Web Search Portals

Manufacturing

Manufactured Housing
321991 — Housing (Mobile Homes), Manufactured

Paper Products/Forest Products
322 — Forest Products/Paper, Manufacturing

Construction
326199 — Building Products & Construction Materials
in Plastic, Manufacturing

Nonmetallic Minerals/Rock/Aggregate
327 — Nonmetallic Mineral, Rock & Aggregate
Manufacturing

Fabricated Metals
332311 — Prefabricated Metal Building & Component
Manufacturing

Machinery & Manufacturing Equipment
333 — Machinery, Manufacturing

Real Estate

Real Estate
525990 — Real Estate Investment Trusts - Mortgage
531110 — Real Estate Investment Trusts - Residential
531120 — Real Estate Investment Trusts -
Nonresidential

Retailing

Building Materials & Garden Supplies Stores
444110 — Home Centers, Retail
444130 — Building Materials/Hardware Stores

Services

Construction

23	Construction Services
2361	Construction, Residential
237	Construction, Heavy & Civil Engineering
238210	Electric Contractors
238220	Plumbing, Heating & Air Conditioning Contractors
2389	Construction--Other Special Trade Contractors

Real Estate

5311	Real Estate Operations & Development-- General
531210	Real Estate Brokerage

Consulting & Professional Services

541310	Architectural Services
541330	Engineering Services

Personnel, Administrative & Support Services

561210	Facilities Support Services
561720	Janitorial Services

Travel Agencies

561599	Time Share Arrangements & Management

Transportation

Transportation-Manufacturing of Equipment

3366	Ship Manufacturing

Ships

483111	Shipping-Deep Sea

Truck

4885	Freight Forwarding & Support Services
532120	Trucks, Rental/Leasing

Wholesale Distribution-Other

Distribution-Durable Goods

4233	Lumber & Construction Materials, Wholesale Distribution

INDEX OF RANKINGS WITHIN INDUSTRY GROUPS

Company	Industry Code	2009 Sales (U.S. $ thousands)	Sales Rank	2009 Profits (U.S. $ thousands)	Profits Rank
Architectural Services					
SIEMENS BUILDING TECHNOLOGIES	541310				
Automobile Parts Manufacturing					
GEORG FISCHER LTD	3363	3,916,960	2	122,720	2
JOHNSON CONTROLS INC	3363	34,305,000	1	1,491,000	1
Building Materials/Hardware Stores					
84 LUMBER COMPANY	444130				
BUILDING MATERIALS HOLDING	444130				
FERGUSON ENTERPRISES INC	444130				
PACIFIC COAST BUILDING PRODUCTS INC	444130				
PLUM CREEK TIMBER CO INC	444130	1,190,000	1	213,000	1
STOCK BUILDING SUPPLY INC	444130				
TRUE HOME VALUE INC	444130				
Building Products & Construction Materials in Plastic, Manufacturing					
ROYAL GROUP INC	326199				
TRACO	326199				
Casino Resorts					
AMERICAN CASINO & ENTERTAINMENT PROPERTIES INC	721120				
AMERISTAR CASINOS INC	721120	1,491,850	6	8,630	4
BOYD GAMING CORP	721120	2,494,724	5	183,938	2
CAESARS ENTERTAINMENT CORPORATION	721120	8,818,600	1	-823,300	7
KERZNER INTERNATIONAL HOLDINGS LIMITED	721120				
LAS VEGAS SANDS CORP (THE VENETIAN)	721120	7,317,937	2	781,603	1
MGM RESORTS INTERNATIONAL	721120	6,019,233	3	-1,437,397	8
RIO PROPERTIES INC	721120				
RIVIERA HOLDINGS CORP	721120	119,156	8	-20,837	5
SANDS REGENT	721120				
SOCIETE DES BAINS DE MER ET DU CERCLE DES ETRANGERS A MONACO	721120				
STATION CASINOS INC	721120				
TRUMP ENTERTAINMENT RESORTS INC	721120	710,570	7	-60,804	6
WYNN RESORTS LIMITED	721120	4,184,698	4	160,127	3
Computer Software Publisher					
LENDER PROCESSING SERVICES INC	511210	2,456,335	1	302,344	1
Computer Software, Business Management & ERP					
REALPAGE INC	511210H	188,274	1	67	1
Computer Software, Data Base & File Management					
REIS INC	511210J	27,576	1	668	1
Construction Services					
CHINA COMMUNICATIONS CONSTRUCTION COMPANY LTD	23	41,830,500	1	1,512,730	1
SAMWHAN CORPORATION	23				
YIT CORPORATION	23	5,701,910	2	339,570	2

Company	Industry Code	2009 Sales (U.S. $ thousands)	Sales Rank	2009 Profits (U.S. $ thousands)	Profits Rank
Construction, Heavy & Civil Engineering					
ACCIONA SA	237	9,371,870	14	230,820	17
ACS ACTIVIDADES DE CONSTRUCCION Y SERVICIOS	237	22,296,400	5	1,898,350	3
AECOM TECHNOLOGY CORP	237	6,545,791	20	249,344	15
AECON GROUP INC	237	2,871,780	24	28,550	25
AMEC PLC	237	4,830,070	21	378,140	12
BALFOUR BEATTY PLC	237	17,143,400	10	549,710	7
BECHTEL GROUP INC	237	32,500,000	3		
BLACK & VEATCH HOLDING CO	237				
BOUYGUES SA	237	45,123,600	2	1,547,710	5
BURNS & MCDONNELL	237				
CAMP DRESSER & MCKEE INC	237				
CHICAGO BRIDGE & IRON COMPANY NV	237	3,642,318	22	204,559	18
DAELIM INDUSTRIAL CO LTD	237	7,086,410	16	325,610	14
DESARROLLADORA HOMEX SAB DE CV	237	1,696,580	28	132,730	20
DOOSAN HEAVY INDUSTRY & CONSTRUCTION CO	237	18,912,600	8	-18,450	29
EMPRESAS ICA SA DE CV	237	2,364,000	26	68,000	24
FLUOR CORP	237	20,849,300	7	441,100	9
FOMENTO DE CONSTRUCCIONES Y CONTRATAS SA (FCC)	237	16,939,300	11	421,310	10
GRANITE CONSTRUCTION INC	237	1,762,965	27	-62,448	30
GRUPO ACS	237	21,514,800	6	1,836,730	4
GRUPO FERROVIAL SA	237	17,714,200	9	3,148,640	1
GS ENGINEERING & CONSTRUCTION CORP	237	7,669,380	15	370,010	13
HDR INC	237				
HOCHTIEF AG	237	29,120,500	4	416,020	11
HYUNDAI ENGINEERING & CONSTRUCTION COMPANY LTD	237	10,274,800	12	476,880	8
IMPREGILO SPA	237	2,790,090	25	185,480	19
JACOBS ENGINEERING GROUP	237	9,915,517	13	245,974	16
KUMHO INDUSTRIAL CO LTD	237	7,004,810	17	93,310	22
LAYNE CHRISTENSEN CO	237	866,417	29	1,365	28
LOUIS BERGER GROUP INC	237				
MATRIX SERVICE COMPANY	237	550,814	30	4,876	27
MEADOW VALLEY CORP	237				
MWH GLOBAL INC	237				
ODEBRECHT SA	237				
PARSONS BRINCKERHOFF INC	237				
PCL CONSTRUCTION GROUP	237				
RAILWORKS CORP	237				
SEMBCORP INDUSTRIES LTD	237	6,886,630	19	623,130	6
SHAW GROUP INC	237	7,000,800	18	92,700	23
STERLING CONSTRUCTION CO	237	459,893	31	26,224	26
TDINDUSTRIES	237				
TUTOR PERINI CORPORATION	237	3,199,210	23	103,500	21
VINCI	237	47,566,100	1	2,484,410	2

Company	Industry Code	2009 Sales (U.S. $ thousands)	Sales Rank	2009 Profits (U.S. $ thousands)	Profits Rank
Construction, Residential					
AVATAR HOLDINGS INC	2361	59,138	17	-35,682	12
BEAZER HOMES USA INC	2361	1,009,841	11	-34,049	11
BROOKFIELD HOMES CORP	2361	339,000	16	3,000	6
CAPITAL PACIFIC HOLDINGS INC	2361				
CENTEX CORP	2361				
CYRELA BRAZIL REALTY SA EMPREENDIMENTOS E PARTICIPACOES	2361	3,117,490	4	382,630	1
CYRELA BRAZIL REALTY SA EMPREENDIMENTOS E PARTICIPACOES	2361				
DR HORTON INC	2361	4,309,700	3	245,100	2
HOVNANIAN ENTERPRISES INC	2361	1,371,842	9	2,588	7
KB HOME	2361	1,589,996	7	-69,368	14
LENNAR CORPORATION	2361	3,074,022	5	95,261	4
M/I HOMES INC	2361	616,377	15	-26,269	10
MDC HOLDINGS INC	2361	958,655	12	-64,770	13
MERITAGE HOMES CORP	2361	941,656	13	7,150	5
NVR INC	2361	2,980,758	6	206,005	3
ORLEANS HOMEBUILDERS INC	2361				
PULTEGROUP INC	2361	4,447,627	2	-1,096,729	17
RYLAND GROUP INC	2361	1,063,892	10	-85,139	15
SEKISUI HOUSE LTD	2361	16,511,100	1	-357,230	16
STANDARD PACIFIC CORP	2361	912,418	14	-11,724	9
TECHNICAL OLYMPIC USA INC	2361				
TOLL BROTHERS INC	2361	1,494,771	8	-3,374	8
WCI COMMUNITIES INC	2361				
WILLIAM LYON HOMES INC	2361				
Construction--Other Special Trade Contractors					
ACERGY SA	2389	2,369,000	1	313,000	1
ANTHONY & SYLVAN POOLS	2389				
INSITUFORM TECHNOLOGIES	2389	914,975	2	60,462	2
ORION MARINE GROUP INC	2389	353,135	3	21,882	3
SCHUFF INTERNATIONAL INC	2389	287,566	4	1,280	4
Electric Contractors					
EMCOR GROUP INC	238210	5,121,285	1	-86,691	2
INTEGRATED ELECTRICAL SERVICES	238210	460,633	2	-32,147	1
Engineering Services					
AMEY PLC	541330				
ARCADIS NV	541330	2,919,410	4	114,270	4
CH2M HILL COMPANIES LTD	541330	5,422,801	2	93,695	5
CHIYODA CORPORATION	541330	3,693,520	3	34,850	7
ENGLOBAL CORP	541330	320,615	8	-11,752	8
MCDERMOTT INTERNATIONAL	541330	2,403,743	5	201,666	2
SKIDMORE OWINGS & MERRILL	541330				
STV GROUP INC	541330				
TREVI-FINANZIARIA INDUSTRIALE SPA (TREVI GROUP)	541330	1,318,780	7	67,070	6
URS CORPORATION	541330	9,177,051	1	287,889	1

Company	Industry Code	2009 Sales (U.S. $ thousands)	Sales Rank	2009 Profits (U.S. $ thousands)	Profits Rank
WS ATKINS PLC	541330	2,314,280	6	181,490	3
Facilities Support Services					
ABERTIS INFRAESTRUCTURAS	561210	5,638,690	1	913,350	1
Financing--Business					
ALLY FINANCIAL INC	522220	11,447,000	2	1,075,000	2
GENERAL ELECTRIC CO (GE)	522220	150,211,000	1	11,644,000	1
Financing--Consumer					
GE CAPITAL	522291	47,040,000	1	3,265,000	1
ORIGEN FINANCIAL INC	522291	71,641	2	-16,594	2
Forest Products/Paper, Manufacturing					
BOISE CASCADE CORP	322	2,240,591	1	-6,101	1
Freight Forwarding & Support Services					
ORIENT OVERSEAS (INTERNATIONAL) LTD	4885	6,033,400	1	1,866,800	1
Home Centers, Retail					
HOME DEPOT INC	444110	66,176,000	1	2,661,000	1
LOWE'S COMPANIES INC	444110	47,220,000	2	1,783,000	2
Hotels/Resorts/Motels					
ACCOR NORTH AMERICA	721110				
ACCOR SA	721110	8,668,380	2	5,246,500	1
AMAN RESORTS	721110				
AMERICA'S BEST FRANCHISING	721110				
BANYAN TREE HOLDINGS LTD	721110	248,240	25	24,400	18
BARCELO CRESTLINE CORP	721110				
BEST WESTERN INTERNATIONAL INC	721110				
CARLSON HOTELS WORLDWIDE	721110				
CHINA LODGING GROUP LTD	721110	263,408	24	33,606	17
CHOICE HOTELS INTERNATIONAL INC	721110	596,076	17	107,441	11
CLUB MEDITERRANEE SA	721110	1,947,030	6	-23,320	23
DAYS INN WORLDWIDE INC	721110				
DOYLE COLLECTION	721110				
FAIRMONT RAFFLES HOTELS INTERNATIONAL INC	721110				
FOUR SEASONS HOTELS INC	721110				
GAYLORD ENTERTAINMENT CO	721110	769,961	14	-89,128	27
GOLDEN TULIP HOSPITALITY GROUP	721110				
GROUPE DU LOUVRE	721110				
GUOMAN HOTELS LIMITED	721110				
HILTON HOTELS CORP	721110				
HOME INNS & HOTELS MANAGEMENT INC	721110	450,912	20	55,545	15
HONGKONG AND SHANGHAI HOTELS LTD	721110	605,600	16	387,010	4
HOTEL PROPERTIES LTD	721110	357,860	23	113,570	9
HOWARD JOHNSON INTERNATIONAL INC	721110				
HVM LLC	721110				
HYATT HOTELS CORPORATION	721110	3,527,000	5	66,000	14
INDIAN HOTELS COMPANY LTD	721110				
INTERCONTINENTAL HOTELS GROUP PLC	721110	1,628,000	9	280,000	7
INTERSTATE HOTELS & RESORTS INC	721110				
INTOWN SUITES MANAGEMENT	721110				

Company	Industry Code	2009 Sales (U.S. $ thousands)	Sales Rank	2009 Profits (U.S. $ thousands)	Profits Rank
JAMESON INN INC	721110				
JANUS HOTELS AND RESORTS	721110				
JOHN Q HAMMONS HOTELS	721110				
JOIE DE VIVRE HOSPITALITY	721110				
KIMPTON HOTEL & RESTAURANT GROUP LLC	721110				
LODGIAN INC	721110				
LOEWS HOTELS HOLDING	721110				
LQ MANAGEMENT LLC	721110				
MANDARIN ORIENTAL INTERNATIONAL LTD	721110	513,200	19	41,400	16
MARCUS CORPORATION	721110	379,069	22	16,115	19
MARRIOTT INTERNATIONAL INC	721110	11,691,000	1	458,000	3
MERITUS HOTELS & RESORTS	721110				
MILLENNIUM & COPTHORNE HOTELS PLC	721110	1,225,410	11	158,510	8
MORGANS HOTEL GROUP CO	721110	236,370	26	-83,648	26
NH HOTELES SA	721110	1,883,620	7	-60,650	24
OAKWOOD WORLDWIDE	721110				
OBEROI GROUP (EIH LTD)	721110				
ORIENT-EXPRESS HOTELS LTD	721110	571,942	18	-62,759	25
QMH UK LTD	721110				
RAMADA WORLDWIDE INC	721110				
RED LION HOTELS CORP	721110	163,494	27	-8,619	22
RESORTQUEST INTERNATIONAL INC	721110				
REZIDOR HOTEL GROUP AB	721110	1,153,780	12	-3,670	21
RITZ-CARLTON HOTEL COMPANY LLC	721110				
ROSEWOOD HOTELS & RESORTS LLC	721110				
SCANDIC HOTELS AB	721110	1,107,670	13	90,750	12
SHANGRI-LA ASIA LTD	721110	1,575,100	10	287,100	6
SHUN TAK HOLDINGS LIMITED	721110	411,370	21	109,820	10
SOL MELIA SA	721110	1,853,750	8	74,260	13
SONESTA INTERNATIONAL HOTELS CORP	721110	71,544	28	-2,024	20
STARWOOD CAPITAL GROUP GLOBAL LLC	721110				
STARWOOD HOTELS & RESORTS WORLDWIDE INC	721110	5,071,000	3	477,000	2
STRATEGIC HOTELS & RESORTS INC	721110	686,293	15	-230,800	28
SUNBURST HOSPITALITY CORP	721110				
SUPER 8 MOTELS INC	721110				
THARALDSON ENTERPRISES	721110				
TRT HOLDINGS	721110				
WYNDHAM WORLDWIDE	721110	3,851,000	4	379,000	5
XANTERRA PARKS AND RESORTS	721110				
Housing (Mobile Homes), Manufactured					
CHAMPION ENTERPRISES INC	321991				
CLAYTON HOMES INC	321991				
DREW INDUSTRIES INC	321991	572,755	1	28,034	1
FAIRMONT HOMES INC	321991				
HORTON HOMES INC	321991				
MODTECH HOLDINGS INC	321991				

Company	Industry Code	2009 Sales (U.S. $ thousands)	Sales Rank	2009 Profits (U.S. $ thousands)	Profits Rank
PALM HARBOR HOMES INC	321991	298,371	2	-51,132	2
SOUTHERN ENERGY HOMES	321991				
Insurance--Property & Casualty, Specialty, Surety					
PMI GROUP INC	524126	641,118	1	-773,028	1
RADIAN GROUP INC	524126	417,500	2	-1,805,900	2
Insurance--Title (Real Estate)					
FIDELITY NATIONAL FINANCIAL	524127	5,740,300	1	370,100	1
FIRST AMERICAN FINANCIAL CORPORATION	524127	3,906,612	2	128,956	2
INVESTORS TITLE COMPANY	524127	71,309	4	6,373	3
STEWART INFORMATION SERVICES CORP	524127	1,672,400	3	-12,582	4
Internet Publishing & Web Search Portals					
COSTAR GROUP INC	519130	226,260	1	13,289	1
MOVE INC	519130	197,503	2	-15,472	2
Investment Management/Mutual Funds/Pension Funds					
TRINITY LTD	523920				
Janitorial Services					
SERVICEMASTER COMPANY	561720	3,365,902	1	-14,559	1
Long-Term Health Care & Assisted Living					
ADVOCAT INC	623110	290,130	5	3,849	4
ATRIA SENIOR LIVING GROUP	623110				
BROOKDALE SENIOR LIVING	623110	2,213,264	1	-48,901	5
CAPITAL SENIOR LIVING CORP	623110	211,929	6	4,254	3
EMERITUS CORP	623110	1,007,065	4	-57,842	6
ERICKSON RETIREMENT COMMUNITIES	623110				
EXTENDICARE REAL ESTATE INVESTMENT TRUST	623110	2,177,380	2	54,410	2
MANOR CARE INC	623110				
SUNRISE SENIOR LIVING	623110	1,406,701	3	100,826	1
Lumber & Construction Materials, Wholesale Distribution					
CEMEX INC	4233				
CEMEX SAB DE CV	4233	14,069,000	2	856,000	1
FIVE STAR PRODUCTS INC	4233				
LB FOSTER COMPANY	4233	475,050	3	20,492	2
WOLSELEY PLC	4233	22,003,900	1	-566,640	3
Machinery, Manufacturing					
HYUNDAI ELEVATOR CO LTD	333	629,660	1	27,500	1
Mortgages					
BANK OF AMERICA HOME LOANS	522310				
CAPMARK FINANCIAL GROUP	522310				
CITIMORTGAGE INC	522310				
FANNIE MAE	522310	17,493,000	1	-14,018,000	5
FEDERAL AGRICULTURAL MORTGAGE CORP (FARMER MAC)	522310	94,150	4	22,080	1
FIRST MORTGAGE CORP	522310				
FIRSTCITY FINANCIAL CORP	522310	85,564	5	12,503	2
FREDDIE MAC	522310	0		-14,025,000	6
GE CAPITAL REAL ESTATE	522310	3,744,000	2	-1,741,000	4
MUNICIPAL MORTGAGE & EQUITY	522310	107,677	3	-28,709	3

Company	Industry Code	2009 Sales (U.S. $ thousands)	Sales Rank	2009 Profits (U.S. $ thousands)	Profits Rank
Mortgages--Online					
DITECH.COM	522310E				
E-LOAN INC	522310E				
LENDINGTREE LLC	522310E				
Nonmetallic Mineral, Rock & Aggregate Manufacturing					
CRH PLC	327	24,505,400	1	626,440	1
Payment & Transaction Processing Services					
FIDELITY NATIONAL INFORMATION SERVICES INC	522320	5,269,500	1	404,500	1
Plumbing, Heating & Air Conditioning Contractors					
COMFORT SYSTEMS USA INC	238220	1,108,282	1	14,740	1
Prefabricated Metal Building & Component Manufacturing					
BUTLER MANUFACTURING CO	332311				
NCI BUILDING SYSTEMS INC	332311	870,526	1	-26,877	1
SKYLINE CORPORATION	332311	136,230	2	-28,993	2
Real Estate Brokerage					
CB RICHARD ELLIS GROUP INC (CBRE)	531210	5,115,316	1	156,009	1
CENTURY 21 REAL ESTATE LLC	531210				
CHRISTIES INTERNATIONAL REAL ESTATE	531210				
COLDWELL BANKER REAL ESTATE LLC	531210				
COLLIERS INTERNATIONAL PROPERTY CONSULTANTS INC	531210				
CORE NETWORK	531210				
CUSHMAN & WAKEFIELD INC	531210				
GRUBB & ELLIS CO	531210	575,457	2	-66,780	3
HOMESERVICES OF AMERICA	531210				
NAI GLOBAL INC	531210				
NRT LLC	531210				
PRUDENTIAL REAL ESTATE AFFILIATES INC	531210				
RE/MAX INTERNATIONAL INC	531210				
ZIPREALTY INC	531210	118,696	3	-15,550	2
Real Estate Investment Trusts - Mortgage					
DYNEX CAPITAL INC	525990	54,024	3	29,472	2
IMPAC MORTGAGE HOLDINGS	525990	1,048,614	1	10,294	3
MFA FINANCIAL INC	525990	390,953	2	269,762	1
Real Estate Investment Trusts - Nonresidential					
ALEXANDRIA REAL ESTATE EQUITIES INC	531120	487,303	35	139,022	15
AMLI RESIDENTIAL PROPERTIES TRUST	531120				
ANDERSON-TULLY LUMBER CO	531120				
ANNALY CAPITAL MANAGEMENT	531120	2,683,134	6	1,267,280	3
APARTMENT INVESTMENT AND MANAGEMENT CO	531120	1,144,934	12	-89,624	58
ARC GROUP OF COMPANIES	531120				
ARDEN REALTY INC	531120				
BOSTON PROPERTIES INC	531120	1,550,804	8	190,327	12
BRANDYWINE REALTY TRUST	531120	566,897	31	-17,606	53
CAMDEN PROPERTY TRUST	531120	610,404	28	23,216	39
CAPITAL AUTOMOTIVE REIT	531120				

Company	Industry Code	2009 Sales (U.S. $ thousands)	Sales Rank	2009 Profits (U.S. $ thousands)	Profits Rank
CBL & ASSOCIATES PROPERTIES INC	531120	1,071,804	15	98,170	24
CENTRO NP LLC	531120				
CNL FINANCIAL GROUP INC	531120				
COMMONWEALTH REIT	531120	793,370	20	135,409	16
CORPORATE OFFICE PROPERTIES TRUST	531120	564,475	32	45,504	34
CRESCENT REAL ESTATE EQUITIES LP	531120				
DCT INDUSTRIAL TRUST INC	531120	239,417	55	-37,830	55
DIVIDEND CAPITAL GROUP LLC	531120				
DUKE REALTY CORP	531120	1,393,603	10	65,262	30
EASTGROUP PROPERTIES INC	531120	173,126	57	18,755	42
ENTERTAINMENT PROPERTIES TRUST	531120	313,064	44	84,668	25
EQUITY OFFICE PROPERTIES TRUST	531120				
EQUITY ONE INC	531120	271,172	50	81,375	26
FEDERAL REALTY INVESTMENT TRUST	531120	544,674	34	122,249	20
FELCOR LODGING TRUST INC	531120	928,311	17	-225,837	60
FELCOR LODGING TRUST INC	531120	351,838	40	-222,619	59
GENERAL GROWTH PROPERTIES INC	531120	2,823,486	4	-1,439,974	62
GLENBOROUGH LLC	531120				
GLIMCHER REALTY TRUST	531120	274,772	49	5,853	46
GRUBB & ELLIS REALTY INVESTORS LLC	531120				
HCP INC	531120	1,255,134	11	344,395	9
HEALTH CARE REIT INC	531120	680,530	24	128,884	19
HEALTHCARE REALTY TRUST	531120	258,394	52	8,247	45
HIGHWOODS PROPERTIES INC	531120	463,321	37	72,303	28
HOSPITALITY PROPERTIES TRUST	531120	1,085,488	14	21,351	40
HOST HOTELS & RESORTS LP	531120	4,437,000	1	132,000	17
INLAND AMERICAN REAL ESTATE TRUST INC	531120				
INLAND REAL ESTATE CORP	531120	167,029	58	43	49
INNKEEPERS USA TRUST	531120				
ISTAR FINANCIAL INC	531120	575,251	30	80,206	27
KILROY REALTY CORPORATION	531120	301,980	45	19,886	41
KIMCO REALTY CORP	531120	849,549	19	2,377	47
LASALLE HOTEL PROPERTIES	531120	600,357	29	1,770	48
LEXINGTON REALTY TRUST	531120	342,855	42	-37,410	54
LIBERTY PROPERTY TRUST	531120	746,830	23	153,375	13
LILLIBRIDGE HEALTHCARE REAL ESTATE TRUST	531120				
LINK REAL ESTATE INVESTMENT TRUST	531120	642,010	27	1,333,300	2
MACERICH COMPANY	531120	758,559	22	28,420	38
MACK-CALI REALTY CORP	531120	787,480	21	52,900	32
MISSION WEST PROPERTIES INC	531120	99,428	60	8,473	44
NATIONAL HEALTH INVESTORS INC	531120	78,396	62	69,421	29
NATIONWIDE HEALTH PROPERTIES INC	531120	439,251	39	142,123	14
NEWCASTLE INVESTMENT	531120	300,272	46	621,662	8
OMEGA HEALTHCARE INVESTORS INC	531120	258,321	53	58,436	31
PARKWAY PROPERTIES INC	531120	256,263	54	-2,618	50
PENNSYLVANIA REIT	531120	455,641	38	-54,363	56
PRIME GROUP REALTY TRUST	531120				

Company	Industry Code	2009 Sales (U.S. $ thousands)	Sales Rank	2009 Profits (U.S. $ thousands)	Profits Rank
PRIME RETAIL INC	531120				
PROLOGIS	531120	909,000	18	-1,270,000	61
PS BUSINESS PARKS INC	531120	279,089	47	102,022	23
PUBLIC STORAGE INC	531120	1,513,324	9	696,114	6
REALTY INCOME CORP	531120	345,009	41	130,784	18
REGENCY CENTERS CORP	531120	486,806	36	16,199	43
RXR REALTY	531120				
SENIOR HOUSING PROPERTIES	531120	339,009	43	116,485	21
SIMON PROPERTY GROUP INC	531120	3,957,630	3	753,514	5
SL GREEN REALTY CORP	531120	1,101,246	13	270,826	10
SOVRAN SELF STORAGE INC	531120	192,072	56	40,642	35
SUN COMMUNITIES INC	531120	263,140	51	-2,883	51
SUNSTONE HOTEL INVESTORS	531120	643,090	26	38,542	36
SUPERTEL HOSPITALITY INC	531120	84,114	61	-10,585	52
TANGER FACTORY OUTLET CENTERS INC	531120	276,303	48	38,244	37
TAUBMAN CENTERS INC	531120	654,558	25	102,327	22
TRANSCONTINENTAL REALTY INVESTORS INC	531120	129,862	59	-67,098	57
UNIBAIL-RODAMCO	531120	2,224,290	7	3,242,400	1
VENTAS INC	531120	1,016,867	16	246,729	11
VORNADO REALTY TRUST	531120	2,779,727	5	647,883	7
WEINGARTEN REALTY INVESTORS	531120	554,667	33	51,238	33
WELLS REAL ESTATE FUNDS	531120				
WESTFIELD GROUP	531120	3,967,570	2	1,214,880	4
Real Estate Investment Trusts - Residential					
ARCHSTONE TRUST	531110				
ASSOCIATED ESTATES REALTY CORPORATION	531110	153,715	17	-8,585	13
AVALONBAY COMMUNITIES INC	531110	895,266	2	175,331	2
BOARDWALK REAL ESTATE INVESTMENT TRUST	531110	436,580	7	75,260	4
BRE PROPERTIES INC	531110	341,973	11	54,835	5
CAPREIT INC	531110				
CAPSTEAD MORTGAGE CORP	531110	199,778	16	126,896	3
COLONIAL PROPERTIES TRUST	531110	367,009	10	-38,543	15
COMMUNITY DEVELOPMENT TRUST	531110				
COUSINS PROPERTIES INC	531110	228,506	15	-12,033	14
DEVELOPERS DIVERSIFIED REALTY CORP	531110	803,069	3	-209,358	17
EQUITY LIFESTYLE PROPERTIES INC	531110	511,361	6	38,354	7
EQUITY RESIDENTIAL	531110	1,995,519	1	295,983	1
ESSEX PROPERTY TRUST INC	531110	415,732	8	50,782	6
GABLES RESIDENTIAL TRUST	531110				
HOME PROPERTIES INC	531110	516,579	5	26,318	10
HOMETOWN AMERICA LLC	531110				
INVESTORS REAL ESTATE TRUST	531110	242,775	14	4,585	11
LIGHTSTONE GROUP LLC	531110				
MID-AMERICA APARTMENT COMMUNITIES INC	531110	401,549	9	29,761	9

Company	Industry Code	2009 Sales (U.S. $ thousands)	Sales Rank	2009 Profits (U.S. $ thousands)	Profits Rank
POST PROPERTIES INC	531110	285,138	13	-6,991	12
SAWYER REALTY HOLDINGS	531110				
TRANSWESTERN INVESTMENT CO LLC	531110				
UDR INC	531110	632,249	4	-112,362	16
WASHINGTON REAL ESTATE INVESTMENT TRUST	531110	297,977	12	37,559	8
Real Estate Rental, Leasing, Development & Management					
ABM INDUSTRIES INC	5311	3,495,747	8	64,121	22
AMB PROPERTY CORPORATION	5311	633,500	24	27,119	25
AMERICAN CAMPUS COMMUNITIES INC	5311	344,991	27	16,210	26
AMERICAN REALTY INVESTORS	5311	157,030	30	-106,195	30
BROOKFIELD ASSET MANAGEMENT INC	5311	13,623,000	1	1,454,000	9
CENTRO PROPERTIES GROUP	5311				
CHINA OVERSEAS LAND & INVESTMENT LIMITED	5311	5,703,100	4	1,592,430	8
CHINA STATE CONSTRUCTION ENGINEERING CORP	5311				
CHINESE ESTATES HOLDINGS	5311	351,040	26	-1,140,050	32
COLONY CAPITAL LLC	5311				
CREST NICHOLSON PLC	5311				
DLF LIMITED	5311	1,751,680	15	383,730	17
EMAAR PROPERTIES PJSC	5311	3,307,550	11	666,450	14
EVERGRANDE REAL ESTATE GROUP	5311	7,024,780	3	1,163,930	10
FIRSTSERVICE CORPORATION	5311	1,986,271	14	47,900	23
FOREST CITY ENTERPRISES	5311	820,645	22	-58,541	28
GAFISA SA	5311				
HANG LUNG GROUP LTD	5311	1,657,780	16	1,595,900	7
HANG LUNG PROPERTIES LTD	5311	1,572,610	18	2,863,450	3
HENDERSON LAND DEVELOPMENT COMPANY LTD	5311	912,460	21	2,035,400	5
HINES INTERESTS LP	5311				
HONGKONG LAND HOLDINGS	5311	1,340,600	19	4,739,400	1
HUTCHISON WHAMPOA PROPERTIES LTD	5311				
HYPO REAL ESTATE HOLDING AG (HYPO BANK)	5311				
HYSAN DEVELOPMENT CO LTD	5311	226,960	29	494,570	16
ICAHN ENTERPRISES LP	5311	7,934,000	2	743,000	12
INDUSTRIAL DEVELOPMENTS INTERNATIONAL INC	5311				
JOHN LAING PLC	5311				
JONES LANG LASALLE INC	5311	2,925,613	13	154,439	19
LBA REALTY LLC	5311				
MAX PROPERTY GROUP PLC	5311				
MPG OFFICE TRUST INC	5311	406,896	25	-197,938	31
MRV ENGENHARIA E PARTICIPACOES SA	5311				
NEW WORLD DEVELOPMENT COMPANY LIMITED	5311	3,888,470	7	1,912,150	6
NEWHALL LAND & FARMING COMPANY	5311				

Company	Industry Code	2009 Sales (U.S. $ thousands)	Sales Rank	2009 Profits (U.S. $ thousands)	Profits Rank
PDG REALTY SA EMPREENDIMENTOS E PARTICIPACOES	5311	3,338,850	10	504,100	15
REALOGY CORPORATION	5311	4,090,000	6	-99,000	29
RELATED GROUP	5311				
ROSSI RESIDENCIAL SA	5311	1,593,390	17	223,320	18
SAHA PATHANA INTER-HOLDING	5311	101,900	31	34,010	24
SHIMAO PROPERTY HOLDINGS	5311	3,345,490	9	717,250	13
SINO LAND COMPANY LIMITED	5311	990,760	20	784,290	11
ST JOE COMPANY	5311	99,540	32	-35,864	27
SUN HUNG KAI PROPERTIES	5311	4,262,690	5	3,599,370	2
TRAMMELL CROW COMPANY	5311				
TRANSWESTERN COMMERCIAL SERVICES	5311				
TRIPLE FIVE GROUP	5311				
TRUMP ORGANIZATION	5311				
UNITECH LIMITED	5311	673,260	23	150,730	20
WATSON LAND COMPANY	5311				
WHARF (HOLDINGS) LIMITED, THE	5311				
WHEELOCK AND CO LTD	5311	3,112,860	12	2,599,070	4
WP CAREY & CO LLC	5311	273,910	28	73,972	21
Ship Manufacturing					
HANJIN HEAVY INDUSTRIES CO	3366	3,925,870	1	4,460	1
Shipping-Deep Sea					
SWIRE PACIFIC LTD	483111	3,758,310	1	4,923,220	1
Time Share Arrangements & Management					
BLUEGREEN CORPORATION	561599	365,677	1	-43,966	1
DIAMOND RESORTS HOLDINGS	561599				
WORLDMARK BY WYNDHAM	561599				
WYNDHAM VACATION OWNERSHIP	561599				
Trucks, Rental/Leasing					
AMERCO	532120	2,002,005	1	65,623	1
Venture Capital/Private Equity Investments					
ESSAR GROUP LTD	523910				

ALPHABETICAL INDEX

DAELIM INDUSTRIAL CO LTD
DAYS INN WORLDWIDE INC
DCT INDUSTRIAL TRUST INC
DESARROLLADORA HOMEX SAB DE CV
DEVELOPERS DIVERSIFIED REALTY CORP
DIAMOND RESORTS HOLDINGS LLC
DITECH.COM
DIVIDEND CAPITAL GROUP LLC
DLF LIMITED
DOMINION HOMES INC
DOOSAN HEAVY INDUSTRY & CONSTRUCTION CO
DOYLE COLLECTION (THE)
DR HORTON INC
DREW INDUSTRIES INC
DUKE REALTY CORP
DYNEX CAPITAL INC
EASTGROUP PROPERTIES INC
E-LOAN INC
EMAAR PROPERTIES PJSC
EMCOR GROUP INC
EMERITUS CORP
EMPRESAS ICA SA DE CV
ENGLOBAL CORP
ENTERTAINMENT PROPERTIES TRUST
EQUITY LIFESTYLE PROPERTIES INC
EQUITY OFFICE PROPERTIES TRUST
EQUITY ONE INC
EQUITY RESIDENTIAL
ERICKSON RETIREMENT COMMUNITIES
ESSAR GROUP LTD
ESSEX PROPERTY TRUST INC
EVERGRANDE REAL ESTATE GROUP
EXTENDICARE REAL ESTATE INVESTMENT TRUST
FAIRMONT HOMES INC
FAIRMONT RAFFLES HOTELS INTERNATIONAL INC
FANNIE MAE
FEDERAL AGRICULTURAL MORTGAGE CORP (FARMER MAC)
FEDERAL REALTY INVESTMENT TRUST
FELCOR LODGING TRUST INC
FERGUSON ENTERPRISES INC
FIDELITY NATIONAL FINANCIAL INC
FIDELITY NATIONAL INFORMATION SERVICES INC
FIRST AMERICAN FINANCIAL CORPORATION
FIRST INDUSTRIAL REALTY TRUST INC
FIRST MORTGAGE CORP
FIRSTCITY FINANCIAL CORP
FIRSTSERVICE CORPORATION
FIVE STAR PRODUCTS INC
FLUOR CORP
FOMENTO DE CONSTRUCCIONES Y CONTRATAS SA (FCC)
FOREST CITY ENTERPRISES INC
FOUR SEASONS HOTELS INC

FREDDIE MAC
GABLES RESIDENTIAL TRUST
GAFISA SA
GAYLORD ENTERTAINMENT CO
GE CAPITAL
GE CAPITAL REAL ESTATE
GENERAL ELECTRIC CO (GE)
GENERAL GROWTH PROPERTIES INC
GEORG FISCHER LTD
GLENBOROUGH LLC
GLIMCHER REALTY TRUST
GOLDEN TULIP HOSPITALITY GROUP
GRANITE CONSTRUCTION INC
GROUPE DU LOUVRE
GRUBB & ELLIS CO
GRUBB & ELLIS REALTY INVESTORS LLC
GRUPO ACS
GRUPO FERROVIAL SA
GS ENGINEERING & CONSTRUCTION CORP
GUOMAN HOTELS LIMITED
HANG LUNG GROUP LTD
HANG LUNG PROPERTIES LIMITED
HANJIN HEAVY INDUSTRIES CO LTD
HCP INC
HDR INC
HEALTH CARE REIT INC
HEALTHCARE REALTY TRUST INC
HENDERSON LAND DEVELOPMENT COMPANY LIMITED
HIGHWOODS PROPERTIES INC
HILTON HOTELS CORP
HINES INTERESTS LP
HOCHTIEF AG
HOME DEPOT INC
HOME INNS & HOTELS MANAGEMENT INC
HOME PROPERTIES INC
HOMESERVICES OF AMERICA INC
HOMETOWN AMERICA LLC
HONGKONG AND SHANGHAI HOTELS LTD
HONGKONG LAND HOLDINGS LTD
HORTON HOMES INC
HOSPITALITY PROPERTIES TRUST
HOST HOTELS & RESORTS LP
HOTEL PROPERTIES LTD
HOVNANIAN ENTERPRISES INC
HOWARD JOHNSON INTERNATIONAL INC
HUTCHISON WHAMPOA PROPERTIES LTD
HVM LLC
HYATT HOTELS CORPORATION
HYPO REAL ESTATE HOLDING AG (HYPO BANK)
HYSAN DEVELOPMENT CO LTD
HYUNDAI ELEVATOR CO LTD
HYUNDAI ENGINEERING & CONSTRUCTION COMPANY LTD
ICAHN ENTERPRISES LP
IMPAC MORTGAGE HOLDINGS INC
IMPREGILO SPA
INDIAN HOTELS COMPANY LIMITED (THE)

INDUSTRIAL DEVELOPMENTS INTERNATIONAL INC
INLAND AMERICAN REAL ESTATE TRUST INC
INLAND REAL ESTATE CORPORATION
INNKEEPERS USA TRUST
INSITUFORM TECHNOLOGIES
INTEGRATED ELECTRICAL SERVICES
INTERCONTINENTAL HOTELS GROUP PLC
INTERSTATE HOTELS & RESORTS INC
INTOWN SUITES MANAGEMENT INC
INVESTORS REAL ESTATE TRUST
INVESTORS TITLE COMPANY
ISTAR FINANCIAL INC
JACOBS ENGINEERING GROUP INC
JAMESON INN INC
JANUS HOTELS AND RESORTS INC
JOHN LAING PLC
JOHN Q HAMMONS HOTELS LLC
JOHNSON CONTROLS INC
JOIE DE VIVRE HOSPITALITY
JONES LANG LASALLE INC
KB HOME
KERZNER INTERNATIONAL HOLDINGS LIMITED
KILROY REALTY CORPORATION
KIMCO REALTY CORP
KIMPTON HOTEL & RESTAURANT GROUP LLC
KUMHO INDUSTRIAL CO LTD
LAS VEGAS SANDS CORP (THE VENETIAN)
LASALLE HOTEL PROPERTIES
LAYNE CHRISTENSEN COMPANY
LB FOSTER COMPANY
LBA REALTY LLC
LENDER PROCESSING SERVICES INC
LENDINGTREE LLC
LENNAR CORPORATION
LEXINGTON REALTY TRUST
LIBERTY PROPERTY TRUST
LIGHTSTONE GROUP LLC (THE)
LILLIBRIDGE HEALTHCARE REAL ESTATE TRUST
LINK REAL ESTATE INVESTMENT TRUST (THE)
LODGIAN INC
LOEWS HOTELS HOLDING CORPORATION
LOUIS BERGER GROUP INC (THE)
LOWE'S COMPANIES INC
LQ MANAGEMENT LLC
M/I HOMES INC
MACERICH COMPANY (THE)
MACK-CALI REALTY CORP
MANDARIN ORIENTAL INTERNATIONAL LTD
MANOR CARE INC
MARCUS CORPORATION (THE)
MARRIOTT INTERNATIONAL INC
MATRIX SERVICE COMPANY
MAX PROPERTY GROUP PLC
MCDERMOTT INTERNATIONAL INC
MDC HOLDINGS INC
MEADOW VALLEY CORPORATION
MERITAGE HOMES CORP

MERITUS HOTELS & RESORTS INC
MFA FINANCIAL INC
MGM RESORTS INTERNATIONAL
MID-AMERICA APARTMENT COMMUNITIES INC
MILLENNIUM & COPTHORNE HOTELS PLC
MISSION WEST PROPERTIES INC
MODTECH HOLDINGS INC
MORGANS HOTEL GROUP CO
MOVE INC
MPG OFFICE TRUST INC
MRV ENGENHARIA E PARTICIPACOES SA
MUNICIPAL MORTGAGE & EQUITY
MWH GLOBAL INC
NAI GLOBAL INC
NATIONAL HEALTH INVESTORS INC
NATIONWIDE HEALTH PROPERTIES INC
NCI BUILDING SYSTEMS INC
NEW WORLD DEVELOPMENT COMPANY LIMITED
NEWCASTLE INVESTMENT CORP
NEWHALL LAND & FARMING COMPANY
NH HOTELES SA
NRT LLC
NVR INC
OAKWOOD WORLDWIDE
OBEROI GROUP (EIH LTD)
ODEBRECHT SA
OMEGA HEALTHCARE INVESTORS INC
ORIENT OVERSEAS (INTERNATIONAL) LTD
ORIENT-EXPRESS HOTELS LTD
ORIGEN FINANCIAL INC
ORION MARINE GROUP INC
ORLEANS HOMEBUILDERS INC
PACIFIC COAST BUILDING PRODUCTS INC
PALM HARBOR HOMES INC
PARKWAY PROPERTIES INC
PARSONS BRINCKERHOFF INC
PCL CONSTRUCTION GROUP INC
PDG REALTY SA EMPREENDIMENTOS E PARTICIPACOES
PENNSYLVANIA REIT
PLUM CREEK TIMBER CO INC
PMI GROUP INC (THE)
POST PROPERTIES INC
PRIME GROUP REALTY TRUST
PRIME RETAIL INC
PROLOGIS
PRUDENTIAL REAL ESTATE AFFILIATES INC
PS BUSINESS PARKS INC
PUBLIC STORAGE INC
PULTEGROUP INC
QMH UK LTD
RADIAN GROUP INC
RAILWORKS CORP
RAMADA WORLDWIDE INC
RE/MAX INTERNATIONAL INC
REALOGY CORPORATION
REALPAGE INC
REALTY INCOME CORP

RED LION HOTELS CORPORATION
REGENCY CENTERS CORP
REIS INC
RELATED GROUP (THE)
RESORTQUEST INTERNATIONAL INC
REZIDOR HOTEL GROUP AB
RIO PROPERTIES INC
RITZ-CARLTON HOTEL COMPANY LLC (THE)
RIVIERA HOLDINGS CORP
ROSEWOOD HOTELS & RESORTS LLC
ROSSI RESIDENCIAL SA
ROYAL GROUP INC
RXR REALTY
RYLAND GROUP INC (THE)
SAHA PATHANA INTER-HOLDING PCL
SAMWHAN CORPORATION
SANDS REGENT
SAWYER REALTY HOLDINGS LLC
SCANDIC HOTELS AB
SCHUFF INTERNATIONAL INC
SEKISUI HOUSE LTD
SEMBCORP INDUSTRIES LTD
SENIOR HOUSING PROPERTIES
SERVICEMASTER COMPANY (THE)
SHANGRI-LA ASIA LTD
SHAW GROUP INC (THE)
SHIMAO PROPERTY HOLDINGS LTD
SHUN TAK HOLDINGS LIMITED
SIEMENS BUILDING TECHNOLOGIES
SIMON PROPERTY GROUP INC
SINO LAND COMPANY LIMITED
SKIDMORE OWINGS & MERRILL LLP
SKYLINE CORPORATION
SL GREEN REALTY CORP
SOCIETE DES BAINS DE MER ET DU CERCLE DES
ETRANGERS A MONACO
SOL MELIA SA
SONESTA INTERNATIONAL HOTELS CORP
SOUTHERN ENERGY HOMES INC
SOVRAN SELF STORAGE INC
ST JOE COMPANY (THE)
STANDARD PACIFIC CORP
STARWOOD CAPITAL GROUP GLOBAL LLC
STARWOOD HOTELS & RESORTS WORLDWIDE
INC
STATION CASINOS INC
STERLING CONSTRUCTION COMPANY
STEWART INFORMATION SERVICES CORP
STOCK BUILDING SUPPLY INC
STRATEGIC HOTELS & RESORTS INC
STV GROUP INC
SUN COMMUNITIES INC
SUN HUNG KAI PROPERTIES
SUNBURST HOSPITALITY CORPORATION
SUNRISE SENIOR LIVING
SUNSTONE HOTEL INVESTORS INC
SUPER 8 MOTELS INC
SUPERTEL HOSPITALITY INC

SWIRE PACIFIC LTD
TANGER FACTORY OUTLET CENTERS INC
TAUBMAN CENTERS INC
TDINDUSTRIES
TECHNICAL OLYMPIC USA INC
THARALDSON ENTERPRISES INC
TOLL BROTHERS INC
TRACO
TRAMMELL CROW COMPANY
TRANSCONTINENTAL REALTY INVESTORS INC
TRANSWESTERN COMMERCIAL SERVICES
TRANSWESTERN INVESTMENT CO LLC
TREVI-FINANZIARIA INDUSTRIALE SPA (TREVI
GROUP)
TRINITY LTD
TRIPLE FIVE GROUP
TRT HOLDINGS
TRUE HOME VALUE INC
TRUMP ENTERTAINMENT RESORTS INC
TRUMP ORGANIZATION (THE)
TUTOR PERINI CORPORATION
UDR INC
UNIBAIL-RODAMCO
UNITECH LIMITED
URS CORPORATION
VENTAS INC
VINCI
VORNADO REALTY TRUST
WASHINGTON REAL ESTATE INVESTMENT TRUST
WATSON LAND COMPANY
WCI COMMUNITIES INC
WEINGARTEN REALTY INVESTORS
WELLS REAL ESTATE FUNDS INC
WESTFIELD GROUP (THE)
WHARF (HOLDINGS) LIMITED, THE
WHEELOCK AND COMPANY LIMITED
WILLIAM LYON HOMES INC
WOLSELEY PLC
WORLDMARK BY WYNDHAM INC
WP CAREY & CO LLC
WS ATKINS PLC
WYNDHAM VACATION OWNERSHIP
WYNDHAM WORLDWIDE
WYNN RESORTS LIMITED
XANTERRA PARKS AND RESORTS
YIT CORPORATION
ZIPREALTY INC

INDEX OF U.S. HEADQUARTERS LOCATION BY STATE

To help you locate members of the firms geographically, the city and state of the headquarters of each company are in the following index.

LENNAR CORPORATION; Miami
REGENCY CENTERS CORP; Jacksonville
RELATED GROUP (THE); Miami
RESORTQUEST INTERNATIONAL INC; Fort Walton
Beach
ST JOE COMPANY (THE); WaterSound
TECHNICAL OLYMPIC USA INC; Hollywood
WCI COMMUNITIES INC; Bonita Springs
WYNDHAM VACATION OWNERSHIP; Orlando

GEORGIA
AMERICA'S BEST FRANCHISING INC; Atlanta
BEAZER HOMES USA INC; Atlanta
COUSINS PROPERTIES INC; Atlanta
GABLES RESIDENTIAL TRUST; Atlanta
HOME DEPOT INC; Atlanta
HORTON HOMES INC; Eatonton
INDUSTRIAL DEVELOPMENTS INTERNATIONAL
INC; Atlanta
INTOWN SUITES MANAGEMENT INC; Atlanta
JAMESON INN INC; Smyrna
LODGIAN INC; Atlanta
POST PROPERTIES INC; Atlanta
WELLS REAL ESTATE FUNDS INC; Norcross

IDAHO
BOISE CASCADE CORP; Boise
BUILDING MATERIALS HOLDING CORP; Boise

ILLINOIS
AMLI RESIDENTIAL PROPERTIES TRUST; Chicago
EQUITY LIFESTYLE PROPERTIES INC; Chicago
EQUITY OFFICE PROPERTIES TRUST; Chicago
EQUITY RESIDENTIAL; Chicago
FIRST INDUSTRIAL REALTY TRUST INC; Chicago
GENERAL GROWTH PROPERTIES INC; Chicago
HOMETOWN AMERICA LLC; Chicago
HYATT HOTELS CORPORATION; Chicago
INLAND AMERICAN REAL ESTATE TRUST INC;
Oak Brook
INLAND REAL ESTATE CORPORATION; Oak Brook
JONES LANG LASALLE INC; Chicago
LILLIBRIDGE HEALTHCARE REAL ESTATE TRUST;
Chicago
PRIME GROUP REALTY TRUST; Chicago
SKIDMORE OWINGS & MERRILL LLP; Chicago
STRATEGIC HOTELS & RESORTS INC; Chicago
TRANSWESTERN INVESTMENT CO LLC; Chicago
VENTAS INC; Chicago

INDIANA
DUKE REALTY CORP; Indianapolis
FAIRMONT HOMES INC; Nappanee
SIMON PROPERTY GROUP INC; Indianapolis
SKYLINE CORPORATION; Elkhart

KANSAS
BLACK & VEATCH HOLDING COMPANY; Overland
Park
LAYNE CHRISTENSEN COMPANY; Mission Woods

KENTUCKY
ATRIA SENIOR LIVING GROUP; Louisville
TRUE HOME VALUE INC; Louisville

LOUISIANA
SHAW GROUP INC (THE); Baton Rouge

MARYLAND
CAPREIT INC; Rockville
CHOICE HOTELS INTERNATIONAL INC; Silver
Spring
CORPORATE OFFICE PROPERTIES TRUST; Columbia
ERICKSON RETIREMENT COMMUNITIES;
Catonsville
FEDERAL REALTY INVESTMENT TRUST; Rockville
HOST HOTELS & RESORTS LP; Bethesda
LASALLE HOTEL PROPERTIES; Bethesda
MARRIOTT INTERNATIONAL INC; Bethesda
MUNICIPAL MORTGAGE & EQUITY; Baltimore
OMEGA HEALTHCARE INVESTORS INC; Hunt Valley
PRIME RETAIL INC; Baltimore
RITZ-CARLTON HOTEL COMPANY LLC (THE);
Chevy Chase
SAWYER REALTY HOLDINGS LLC; College Park
SUNBURST HOSPITALITY CORPORATION; Silver
Spring
WASHINGTON REAL ESTATE INVESTMENT
TRUST; Rockville

MASSACHUSETTS
BOSTON PROPERTIES INC; Boston
CAMP DRESSER & MCKEE INC; Cambridge
COMMONWEALTH REIT; Newton
HOSPITALITY PROPERTIES TRUST; Newton
SENIOR HOUSING PROPERTIES; Newton
SONESTA INTERNATIONAL HOTELS CORP; Boston

MICHIGAN
ALLY FINANCIAL INC; Detroit
CHAMPION ENTERPRISES INC; Troy
ORIGEN FINANCIAL INC; Southfield
PULTEGROUP INC; Bloomfield Hills
SUN COMMUNITIES INC; Southfield
TAUBMAN CENTERS INC; Bloomfield Hills

MINNESOTA
CARLSON HOTELS WORLDWIDE; Minnetonka
HOMESERVICES OF AMERICA INC; Minneapolis

MISSISSIPPI
ANDERSON-TULLY LUMBER COMPANY; Vicksburg
EASTGROUP PROPERTIES INC; Jackson

PARKWAY PROPERTIES INC; Jackson

MISSOURI
BURNS & MCDONNELL; Kansas City
BUTLER MANUFACTURING CO; Kansas City
CITIMORTGAGE INC; O'Fallon
ENTERTAINMENT PROPERTIES TRUST; Kansas City
INSITUFORM TECHNOLOGIES; Chesterfield
JOHN Q HAMMONS HOTELS LLC; Springfield

NEBRASKA
HDR INC; Omaha
SUPERTEL HOSPITALITY INC; Norfolk

NEVADA
AMERCO; Reno
AMERICAN CASINO & ENTERTAINMENT PROPERTIES INC; Las Vegas
AMERISTAR CASINOS INC; Las Vegas
BOYD GAMING CORP; Las Vegas
CAESARS ENTERTAINMENT CORPORATION; Las Vegas
DIAMOND RESORTS HOLDINGS LLC; Las Vegas
LAS VEGAS SANDS CORP (THE VENETIAN); Las Vegas
MGM RESORTS INTERNATIONAL; Las Vegas
RIO PROPERTIES INC; Las Vegas
RIVIERA HOLDINGS CORP; Las Vegas
SANDS REGENT; Reno
STATION CASINOS INC; Las Vegas
WYNN RESORTS LIMITED; Las Vegas

NEW JERSEY
ANTHONY & SYLVAN POOLS; Mays landing
ARC GROUP OF COMPANIES (THE); Clifton
CENTURY 21 REAL ESTATE LLC; Parsippany
COLDWELL BANKER REAL ESTATE LLC; Parsippany
DAYS INN WORLDWIDE INC; Parsippany
HOVNANIAN ENTERPRISES INC; Red Bank
HOWARD JOHNSON INTERNATIONAL INC; Parsippany
LOUIS BERGER GROUP INC (THE); Morristown
MACK-CALI REALTY CORP; Edison
NAI GLOBAL INC; Princeton
NRT LLC; Parsippany
RAMADA WORLDWIDE INC; Parsippany
REALOGY CORPORATION; Parsippany
SUPER 8 MOTELS INC; Parsippany
TRUMP ENTERTAINMENT RESORTS INC; Atlantic City
WYNDHAM WORLDWIDE; Parsippany

NEW YORK
ABM INDUSTRIES INC; New York
ANNALY CAPITAL MANAGEMENT INC; New York
CENTRO NP LLC; New York
CHRISTIES INTERNATIONAL REAL ESTATE; New York
COMMUNITY DEVELOPMENT TRUST; New York
CUSHMAN & WAKEFIELD INC; New York
DREW INDUSTRIES INC; White Plains
HOME PROPERTIES INC; Rochester
ICAHN ENTERPRISES LP; New York
ISTAR FINANCIAL INC; New York
KIMCO REALTY CORP; New Hyde Park
LEXINGTON REALTY TRUST; New York
LIGHTSTONE GROUP LLC (THE); New York
LOEWS HOTELS HOLDING CORPORATION; New York
MFA FINANCIAL INC; New York
MORGANS HOTEL GROUP CO; New York
NEWCASTLE INVESTMENT CORP; New York
PARSONS BRINCKERHOFF INC; New York
RAILWORKS CORP; New York
REIS INC; New York
RXR REALTY; Uniondale
SL GREEN REALTY CORP; New York
SOVRAN SELF STORAGE INC; Williamsville
STARWOOD HOTELS & RESORTS WORLDWIDE INC; White Plains
TRUMP ORGANIZATION (THE); New York
VORNADO REALTY TRUST; New York
WP CAREY & CO LLC; New York

NORTH CAROLINA
HIGHWOODS PROPERTIES INC; Raleigh
INVESTORS TITLE COMPANY; Chapel Hill
LENDINGTREE LLC; Charlotte
LOWE'S COMPANIES INC; Mooresville
STOCK BUILDING SUPPLY INC; Raleigh
TANGER FACTORY OUTLET CENTERS INC; Greensboro

NORTH DAKOTA
INVESTORS REAL ESTATE TRUST; Minot
THARALDSON ENTERPRISES INC; Fargo

OHIO
ASSOCIATED ESTATES REALTY CORPORATION; Richmond Heights
DEVELOPERS DIVERSIFIED REALTY CORP; Beachwood
DOMINION HOMES INC; Dublin
FOREST CITY ENTERPRISES INC; Cleveland
GLIMCHER REALTY TRUST; Columbus
HEALTH CARE REIT INC; Toledo
M/I HOMES INC; Columbus
MANOR CARE INC; Toledo

OKLAHOMA
MATRIX SERVICE COMPANY; Tulsa

PENNSYLVANIA
84 LUMBER COMPANY; Eighty Four

BRANDYWINE REALTY TRUST; Radnor
CAPMARK FINANCIAL GROUP INC; Horsham
DITECH.COM; Ft. Washington
LB FOSTER COMPANY; Pittsburgh
LIBERTY PROPERTY TRUST; Malvern
ORLEANS HOMEBUILDERS INC; Bensalem
PENNSYLVANIA REIT; Philadelphia
RADIAN GROUP INC; Philadelphia
STV GROUP INC; Douglassville
TOLL BROTHERS INC; Horsham
TRACO; Cranberry Township

SOUTH CAROLINA
HVM LLC; Spartanburg

TENNESSEE
ADVOCAT INC; Brentwood
BROOKDALE SENIOR LIVING INC; Brentwood
CBL & ASSOCIATES PROPERTIES INC; Chattanooga
CLAYTON HOMES INC; Maryville
GAYLORD ENTERTAINMENT CO; Nashville
HEALTHCARE REALTY TRUST INC; Nashville
MID-AMERICA APARTMENT COMMUNITIES INC;
Memphis
NATIONAL HEALTH INVESTORS INC; Murfreesboro
SERVICEMASTER COMPANY (THE); Memphis

TEXAS
ACCOR NORTH AMERICA; Carrollton
AMERICAN CAMPUS COMMUNITIES INC; Austin
AMERICAN REALTY INVESTORS INC; Dallas
CAMDEN PROPERTY TRUST; Houston
CAPITAL SENIOR LIVING CORP; Dallas
CAPSTEAD MORTGAGE CORPORATION; Dallas
CEMEX INC; Houston
CENTEX CORP; Dallas
COMFORT SYSTEMS USA INC; Houston
CORE NETWORK (THE); Dallas
CRESCENT REAL ESTATE EQUITIES LP; Fort Worth
DR HORTON INC; Fort Worth
ENGLOBAL CORP; Houston
FELCOR LODGING TRUST INC; Irving
FIRSTCITY FINANCIAL CORP; Waco
FLUOR CORP; Irving
HINES INTERESTS LP; Houston
INTEGRATED ELECTRICAL SERVICES; Houston
LQ MANAGEMENT LLC; Irving
MCDERMOTT INTERNATIONAL INC; Houston
NCI BUILDING SYSTEMS INC; Houston
ORION MARINE GROUP INC; Houston
PALM HARBOR HOMES INC; Addison
REALPAGE INC; Carrollton
ROSEWOOD HOTELS & RESORTS LLC; Dallas
STERLING CONSTRUCTION COMPANY; Houston
STEWART INFORMATION SERVICES CORP; Houston
TDINDUSTRIES; Dallas
TRAMMELL CROW COMPANY; Dallas

TRANSCONTINENTAL REALTY INVESTORS INC;
Dallas
TRANSWESTERN COMMERCIAL SERVICES;
Houston
TRT HOLDINGS; Irving
WEINGARTEN REALTY INVESTORS; Houston

VIRGINIA
AVALONBAY COMMUNITIES INC; Alexandria
BARCELO CRESTLINE CORPORATION; Fairfax
BROOKFIELD HOMES CORP; Fairfax
CAPITAL AUTOMOTIVE REIT; McLean
DYNEX CAPITAL INC; Glen Allen
FERGUSON ENTERPRISES INC; Newport News
FREDDIE MAC; McLean
HILTON HOTELS CORP; McLean
INTERSTATE HOTELS & RESORTS INC; Arlington
NVR INC; Reston
SUNRISE SENIOR LIVING; McLean

WASHINGTON
COLLIERS INTERNATIONAL PROPERTY
CONSULTANTS INC; Seattle
EMERITUS CORP; Seattle
PLUM CREEK TIMBER CO INC; Seattle
RED LION HOTELS CORPORATION; Spokane
WORLDMARK BY WYNDHAM INC; Redmond

WISCONSIN
JOHNSON CONTROLS INC; Milwaukee
MARCUS CORPORATION (THE); Milwaukee

INDEX OF NON-U.S. HEADQUARTERS LOCATION BY COUNTRY

ITALY
IMPREGILO SPA; Milan
TREVI-FINANZIARIA INDUSTRIALE SPA (TREVI
GROUP); Cesena

JAPAN
CHIYODA CORPORATION; Yokohama
SEKISUI HOUSE LTD; Osaka

KOREA
DAELIM INDUSTRIAL CO LTD; Seoul
DOOSAN HEAVY INDUSTRY & CONSTRUCTION
CO; Changwon
GS ENGINEERING & CONSTRUCTION CORP; Seoul
HANJIN HEAVY INDUSTRIES CO LTD; Busan
HYUNDAI ELEVATOR CO LTD; Gyeonggi-do
HYUNDAI ENGINEERING & CONSTRUCTION
COMPANY LTD; Seoul
KUMHO INDUSTRIAL CO LTD; Seoul
SAMWHAN CORPORATION; Seoul

MEXICO
CEMEX SAB DE CV; San Pedro Garza Garcia
DESARROLLADORA HOMEX SAB DE CV; Sinaloa
EMPRESAS ICA SA DE CV; Mexico City

MONACO
SOCIETE DES BAINS DE MER ET DU CERCLE DES
ETRANGERS A MONACO; Monaco

SINGAPORE
AMAN RESORTS; Singapore
BANYAN TREE HOLDINGS LIMITED; Singapore
HOTEL PROPERTIES LTD; Singapore
MERITUS HOTELS & RESORTS INC; Singapore
SEMBCORP INDUSTRIES LTD; Singapore

SPAIN
ABERTIS INFRAESTRUCTURAS SA; Barcelona
ACCIONA SA; Alcobendas
ACS ACTIVIDADES DE CONSTRUCCION Y
SERVICIOS SA; Madrid
FOMENTO DE CONSTRUCCIONES Y CONTRATAS
SA (FCC); Madrid
GRUPO ACS; Madrid
GRUPO FERROVIAL SA; Madrid
NH HOTELES SA; Madrid
SOL MELIA SA; Palma de Mallorca

SWEDEN
SCANDIC HOTELS AB; Stockholm

SWITZERLAND
GEORG FISCHER LTD; Schaffhausen
SIEMENS BUILDING TECHNOLOGIES; Zug
WOLSELEY PLC; Zug

THAILAND
SAHA PATHANA INTER-HOLDING PCL; Bangkok

THE NETHERLANDS
ARCADIS NV; Amsterdam
CHICAGO BRIDGE & IRON COMPANY NV; The
Hague

UNITED ARAB EMIRATES
EMAAR PROPERTIES PJSC; Dubai

UNITED KINGDOM
ACERGY SA; London
AMEC PLC; London
AMEY PLC; Oxford
BALFOUR BEATTY PLC; London
CREST NICHOLSON PLC; Chertsey
CRH PLC; Dublin
DOYLE COLLECTION (THE); Dublin
GUOMAN HOTELS LIMITED; Uxbridge
INTERCONTINENTAL HOTELS GROUP PLC; Denham
JOHN LAING PLC; London
MILLENNIUM & COPTHORNE HOTELS PLC; London
QMH UK LTD; Romford
WS ATKINS PLC; Epsom

INDEX BY REGIONS OF THE U.S.
WHERE THE FIRMS HAVE LOCATIONS

FAIRMONT RAFFLES HOTELS INTERNATIONAL INC
FEDERAL REALTY INVESTMENT TRUST
FELCOR LODGING TRUST INC
FERGUSON ENTERPRISES INC
FIDELITY NATIONAL FINANCIAL INC
FIDELITY NATIONAL INFORMATION SERVICES INC
FIRST AMERICAN FINANCIAL CORPORATION
FIRST INDUSTRIAL REALTY TRUST INC
FIRST MORTGAGE CORP
FIRSTCITY FINANCIAL CORP
FIRSTSERVICE CORPORATION
FIVE STAR PRODUCTS INC
FLUOR CORP
FOREST CITY ENTERPRISES INC
FOUR SEASONS HOTELS INC
GABLES RESIDENTIAL TRUST
GE CAPITAL
GE CAPITAL REAL ESTATE
GENERAL ELECTRIC CO (GE)
GENERAL GROWTH PROPERTIES INC
GEORG FISCHER LTD
GLENBOROUGH LLC
GLIMCHER REALTY TRUST
GRANITE CONSTRUCTION INC
GRUBB & ELLIS CO
GRUBB & ELLIS REALTY INVESTORS LLC
HCP INC
HDR INC
HEALTH CARE REIT INC
HEALTHCARE REALTY TRUST INC
HILTON HOTELS CORP
HINES INTERESTS LP
HOCHTIEF AG
HOME DEPOT INC
HOMESERVICES OF AMERICA INC
HOMETOWN AMERICA LLC
HONGKONG AND SHANGHAI HOTELS LTD
HOSPITALITY PROPERTIES TRUST
HOST HOTELS & RESORTS LP
HOVNANIAN ENTERPRISES INC
HOWARD JOHNSON INTERNATIONAL INC
HVM LLC
HYATT HOTELS CORPORATION
HYUNDAI ELEVATOR CO LTD
ICAHN ENTERPRISES LP
IMPAC MORTGAGE HOLDINGS INC
INDIAN HOTELS COMPANY LIMITED (THE)
INDUSTRIAL DEVELOPMENTS INTERNATIONAL INC
INNKEEPERS USA TRUST
INSITUFORM TECHNOLOGIES
INTEGRATED ELECTRICAL SERVICES
INTERCONTINENTAL HOTELS GROUP PLC
INTERSTATE HOTELS & RESORTS INC
INTOWN SUITES MANAGEMENT INC
INVESTORS REAL ESTATE TRUST
ISTAR FINANCIAL INC
JACOBS ENGINEERING GROUP INC
JOHN Q HAMMONS HOTELS LLC
JOHNSON CONTROLS INC
JOIE DE VIVRE HOSPITALITY
JONES LANG LASALLE INC
KB HOME
KILROY REALTY CORPORATION
KIMCO REALTY CORP
KIMPTON HOTEL & RESTAURANT GROUP LLC
LAS VEGAS SANDS CORP (THE VENETIAN)
LASALLE HOTEL PROPERTIES
LAYNE CHRISTENSEN COMPANY
LB FOSTER COMPANY
LBA REALTY LLC
LENDER PROCESSING SERVICES INC
LENDINGTREE LLC
LENNAR CORPORATION
LEXINGTON REALTY TRUST
LODGIAN INC
LOEWS HOTELS HOLDING CORPORATION
LOUIS BERGER GROUP INC (THE)
LOWE'S COMPANIES INC
LQ MANAGEMENT LLC
MACERICH COMPANY (THE)
MANDARIN ORIENTAL INTERNATIONAL LTD
MANOR CARE INC
MARCUS CORPORATION (THE)
MARRIOTT INTERNATIONAL INC
MATRIX SERVICE COMPANY
MCDERMOTT INTERNATIONAL INC
MDC HOLDINGS INC
MEADOW VALLEY CORPORATION
MERITAGE HOMES CORP
MGM RESORTS INTERNATIONAL
MILLENNIUM & COPTHORNE HOTELS PLC
MISSION WEST PROPERTIES INC
MODTECH HOLDINGS INC
MORGANS HOTEL GROUP CO
MOVE INC
MPG OFFICE TRUST INC
MUNICIPAL MORTGAGE & EQUITY
MWH GLOBAL INC
NAI GLOBAL INC
NATIONAL HEALTH INVESTORS INC
NATIONWIDE HEALTH PROPERTIES INC
NCI BUILDING SYSTEMS INC
NEWHALL LAND & FARMING COMPANY
NRT LLC
OAKWOOD WORLDWIDE
OMEGA HEALTHCARE INVESTORS INC
ORIENT OVERSEAS (INTERNATIONAL) LTD
ORIENT-EXPRESS HOTELS LTD
PACIFIC COAST BUILDING PRODUCTS INC
PALM HARBOR HOMES INC
PARSONS BRINCKERHOFF INC
PCL CONSTRUCTION GROUP INC
PLUM CREEK TIMBER CO INC

PMI GROUP INC (THE)
PRIME RETAIL INC
PROLOGIS
PRUDENTIAL REAL ESTATE AFFILIATES INC
PS BUSINESS PARKS INC
PUBLIC STORAGE INC
PULTEGROUP INC
RADIAN GROUP INC
RAILWORKS CORP
RAMADA WORLDWIDE INC
RE/MAX INTERNATIONAL INC
REALOGY CORPORATION
REALPAGE INC
REALTY INCOME CORP
RED LION HOTELS CORPORATION
REGENCY CENTERS CORP
RELATED GROUP (THE)
RESORTQUEST INTERNATIONAL INC
RIO PROPERTIES INC
RITZ-CARLTON HOTEL COMPANY LLC (THE)
RIVIERA HOLDINGS CORP
ROSEWOOD HOTELS & RESORTS LLC
ROYAL GROUP INC
RYLAND GROUP INC (THE)
SAMWHAN CORPORATION
SANDS REGENT
SCHUFF INTERNATIONAL INC
SENIOR HOUSING PROPERTIES
SERVICEMASTER COMPANY (THE)
SHANGRI-LA ASIA LTD
SHAW GROUP INC (THE)
SIEMENS BUILDING TECHNOLOGIES
SIMON PROPERTY GROUP INC
SKIDMORE OWINGS & MERRILL LLP
SKYLINE CORPORATION
STANDARD PACIFIC CORP
STARWOOD CAPITAL GROUP GLOBAL LLC
STARWOOD HOTELS & RESORTS WORLDWIDE
INC
STATION CASINOS INC
STERLING CONSTRUCTION COMPANY
STEWART INFORMATION SERVICES CORP
STOCK BUILDING SUPPLY INC
STRATEGIC HOTELS & RESORTS INC
STV GROUP INC
SUN COMMUNITIES INC
SUNBURST HOSPITALITY CORPORATION
SUNRISE SENIOR LIVING
SUNSTONE HOTEL INVESTORS INC
SUPER 8 MOTELS INC
SUPERTEL HOSPITALITY INC
SWIRE PACIFIC LTD
TANGER FACTORY OUTLET CENTERS INC
TAUBMAN CENTERS INC
TECHNICAL OLYMPIC USA INC
THARALDSON ENTERPRISES INC
TOLL BROTHERS INC
TRAMMELL CROW COMPANY

TRANSCONTINENTAL REALTY INVESTORS INC
TRANSWESTERN COMMERCIAL SERVICES
TRANSWESTERN INVESTMENT CO LLC
TREVI-FINANZIARIA INDUSTRIALE SPA (TREVI
GROUP)
TRIPLE FIVE GROUP
TRT HOLDINGS
TRUMP ORGANIZATION (THE)
TUTOR PERINI CORPORATION
UDR INC
URS CORPORATION
VENTAS INC
VINCI
VORNADO REALTY TRUST
WATSON LAND COMPANY
WEINGARTEN REALTY INVESTORS
WELLS REAL ESTATE FUNDS INC
WESTFIELD GROUP (THE)
WILLIAM LYON HOMES INC
WOLSELEY PLC
WORLDMARK BY WYNDHAM INC
WP CAREY & CO LLC
WS ATKINS PLC
WYNDHAM VACATION OWNERSHIP
WYNDHAM WORLDWIDE
WYNN RESORTS LIMITED
XANTERRA PARKS AND RESORTS
ZIPREALTY INC

SOUTHWEST
84 LUMBER COMPANY
ABERTIS INFRAESTRUCTURAS SA
ABM INDUSTRIES INC
ACCOR NORTH AMERICA
ACCOR SA
ACERGY SA
ADVOCAT INC
AECOM TECHNOLOGY CORPORATION
ALLY FINANCIAL INC
AMB PROPERTY CORPORATION
AMEC PLC
AMERCO
AMERICAN CAMPUS COMMUNITIES INC
AMERICAN REALTY INVESTORS INC
AMERICA'S BEST FRANCHISING INC
AMLI RESIDENTIAL PROPERTIES TRUST
ANTHONY & SYLVAN POOLS
APARTMENT INVESTMENT AND MANAGEMENT
CO
ARC GROUP OF COMPANIES (THE)
ARCADIS NV
ARCHSTONE TRUST
ARDEN REALTY INC
ASSOCIATED ESTATES REALTY CORPORATION
ATRIA SENIOR LIVING GROUP
AVATAR HOLDINGS INC
BALFOUR BEATTY PLC
BANK OF AMERICA HOME LOANS

BARCELO CRESTLINE CORPORATION
BEAZER HOMES USA INC
BECHTEL GROUP INC
BEST WESTERN INTERNATIONAL INC
BLACK & VEATCH HOLDING COMPANY
BLUEGREEN CORPORATION
BOISE CASCADE CORP
BRANDYWINE REALTY TRUST
BROOKDALE SENIOR LIVING INC
BROOKFIELD ASSET MANAGEMENT INC
BUILDING MATERIALS HOLDING CORP
BURNS & MCDONNELL
BUTLER MANUFACTURING CO
CAESARS ENTERTAINMENT CORPORATION
CAMDEN PROPERTY TRUST
CAMP DRESSER & MCKEE INC
CAPITAL AUTOMOTIVE REIT
CAPITAL PACIFIC HOLDINGS INC
CAPITAL SENIOR LIVING CORP
CAPREIT INC
CAPSTEAD MORTGAGE CORPORATION
CARLSON HOTELS WORLDWIDE
CB RICHARD ELLIS GROUP INC (CBRE)
CBL & ASSOCIATES PROPERTIES INC
CEMEX INC
CEMEX SAB DE CV
CENTEX CORP
CENTRO NP LLC
CENTRO PROPERTIES GROUP
CENTURY 21 REAL ESTATE LLC
CH2M HILL COMPANIES LTD
CHAMPION ENTERPRISES INC
CHICAGO BRIDGE & IRON COMPANY NV
CHOICE HOTELS INTERNATIONAL INC
CHRISTIES INTERNATIONAL REAL ESTATE
CLAYTON HOMES INC
CNL FINANCIAL GROUP INC
COLDWELL BANKER REAL ESTATE LLC
COLLIERS INTERNATIONAL PROPERTY
CONSULTANTS INC
COLONIAL PROPERTIES TRUST
COMFORT SYSTEMS USA INC
COMMONWEALTH REIT
CORE NETWORK (THE)
CORPORATE OFFICE PROPERTIES TRUST
COSTAR GROUP INC
COUSINS PROPERTIES INC
CRESCENT REAL ESTATE EQUITIES LP
CRH PLC
CUSHMAN & WAKEFIELD INC
DAELIM INDUSTRIAL CO LTD
DAYS INN WORLDWIDE INC
DCT INDUSTRIAL TRUST INC
DEVELOPERS DIVERSIFIED REALTY CORP
DIAMOND RESORTS HOLDINGS LLC
DITECH.COM
DOOSAN HEAVY INDUSTRY & CONSTRUCTION
CO

DR HORTON INC
DREW INDUSTRIES INC
DUKE REALTY CORP
EASTGROUP PROPERTIES INC
EMCOR GROUP INC
EMERITUS CORP
ENGLOBAL CORP
ENTERTAINMENT PROPERTIES TRUST
EQUITY LIFESTYLE PROPERTIES INC
EQUITY OFFICE PROPERTIES TRUST
EQUITY RESIDENTIAL
ERICKSON RETIREMENT COMMUNITIES
ESSAR GROUP LTD
FAIRMONT RAFFLES HOTELS INTERNATIONAL
INC
FEDERAL REALTY INVESTMENT TRUST
FELCOR LODGING TRUST INC
FERGUSON ENTERPRISES INC
FIDELITY NATIONAL FINANCIAL INC
FIDELITY NATIONAL INFORMATION SERVICES
INC
FIRST AMERICAN FINANCIAL CORPORATION
FIRST INDUSTRIAL REALTY TRUST INC
FIRSTCITY FINANCIAL CORP
FIRSTSERVICE CORPORATION
FIVE STAR PRODUCTS INC
FLUOR CORP
FOREST CITY ENTERPRISES INC
FOUR SEASONS HOTELS INC
GABLES RESIDENTIAL TRUST
GAYLORD ENTERTAINMENT CO
GE CAPITAL
GE CAPITAL REAL ESTATE
GENERAL ELECTRIC CO (GE)
GENERAL GROWTH PROPERTIES INC
GLIMCHER REALTY TRUST
GRANITE CONSTRUCTION INC
GRUBB & ELLIS CO
GRUBB & ELLIS REALTY INVESTORS LLC
GRUPO FERROVIAL SA
HDR INC
HEALTH CARE REIT INC
HEALTHCARE REALTY TRUST INC
HILTON HOTELS CORP
HINES INTERESTS LP
HOCHTIEF AG
HOME DEPOT INC
HOMESERVICES OF AMERICA INC
HOMETOWN AMERICA LLC
HOSPITALITY PROPERTIES TRUST
HOST HOTELS & RESORTS LP
HOVNANIAN ENTERPRISES INC
HOWARD JOHNSON INTERNATIONAL INC
HVM LLC
HYATT HOTELS CORPORATION
ICAHN ENTERPRISES LP
INDUSTRIAL DEVELOPMENTS INTERNATIONAL
INC

INLAND AMERICAN REAL ESTATE TRUST INC
INNKEEPERS USA TRUST
INSITUFORM TECHNOLOGIES
INTEGRATED ELECTRICAL SERVICES
INTERCONTINENTAL HOTELS GROUP PLC
INTERSTATE HOTELS & RESORTS INC
INTOWN SUITES MANAGEMENT INC
ISTAR FINANCIAL INC
JACOBS ENGINEERING GROUP INC
JANUS HOTELS AND RESORTS INC
JOHN Q HAMMONS HOTELS LLC
JOHNSON CONTROLS INC
JONES LANG LASALLE INC
KB HOME
KIMCO REALTY CORP
KIMPTON HOTEL & RESTAURANT GROUP LLC
LASALLE HOTEL PROPERTIES
LAYNE CHRISTENSEN COMPANY
LB FOSTER COMPANY
LBA REALTY LLC
LENDER PROCESSING SERVICES INC
LENNAR CORPORATION
LEXINGTON REALTY TRUST
LIBERTY PROPERTY TRUST
LIGHTSTONE GROUP LLC (THE)
LILLIBRIDGE HEALTHCARE REAL ESTATE TRUST
LODGIAN INC
LOEWS HOTELS HOLDING CORPORATION
LOUIS BERGER GROUP INC (THE)
LOWE'S COMPANIES INC
LQ MANAGEMENT LLC
M/I HOMES INC
MACERICH COMPANY (THE)
MANOR CARE INC
MARCUS CORPORATION (THE)
MARRIOTT INTERNATIONAL INC
MATRIX SERVICE COMPANY
MCDERMOTT INTERNATIONAL INC
MDC HOLDINGS INC
MEADOW VALLEY CORPORATION
MERITAGE HOMES CORP
MID-AMERICA APARTMENT COMMUNITIES INC
MILLENNIUM & COPTHORNE HOTELS PLC
MOVE INC
MUNICIPAL MORTGAGE & EQUITY
MWH GLOBAL INC
NAI GLOBAL INC
NATIONAL HEALTH INVESTORS INC
NATIONWIDE HEALTH PROPERTIES INC
NCI BUILDING SYSTEMS INC
NH HOTELES SA
NRT LLC
OAKWOOD WORLDWIDE
OMEGA HEALTHCARE INVESTORS INC
ORION MARINE GROUP INC
PALM HARBOR HOMES INC
PARKWAY PROPERTIES INC
PARSONS BRINCKERHOFF INC
PCL CONSTRUCTION GROUP INC
PLUM CREEK TIMBER CO INC
PMI GROUP INC (THE)
POST PROPERTIES INC
PRIME RETAIL INC
PROLOGIS
PRUDENTIAL REAL ESTATE AFFILIATES INC
PS BUSINESS PARKS INC
PUBLIC STORAGE INC
PULTEGROUP INC
RADIAN GROUP INC
RAILWORKS CORP
RAMADA WORLDWIDE INC
RE/MAX INTERNATIONAL INC
REALOGY CORPORATION
REALPAGE INC
REALTY INCOME CORP
REGENCY CENTERS CORP
RITZ-CARLTON HOTEL COMPANY LLC (THE)
ROSEWOOD HOTELS & RESORTS LLC
ROYAL GROUP INC
RYLAND GROUP INC (THE)
SCHUFF INTERNATIONAL INC
SENIOR HOUSING PROPERTIES
SERVICEMASTER COMPANY (THE)
SHAW GROUP INC (THE)
SIEMENS BUILDING TECHNOLOGIES
SIMON PROPERTY GROUP INC
SKYLINE CORPORATION
SONESTA INTERNATIONAL HOTELS CORP
SOUTHERN ENERGY HOMES INC
SOVRAN SELF STORAGE INC
STANDARD PACIFIC CORP
STARWOOD HOTELS & RESORTS WORLDWIDE INC
STATION CASINOS INC
STERLING CONSTRUCTION COMPANY
STEWART INFORMATION SERVICES CORP
STOCK BUILDING SUPPLY INC
STRATEGIC HOTELS & RESORTS INC
STV GROUP INC
SUN COMMUNITIES INC
SUNBURST HOSPITALITY CORPORATION
SUNRISE SENIOR LIVING
SUNSTONE HOTEL INVESTORS INC
SUPER 8 MOTELS INC
SWIRE PACIFIC LTD
TANGER FACTORY OUTLET CENTERS INC
TAUBMAN CENTERS INC
TDINDUSTRIES
TECHNICAL OLYMPIC USA INC
THARALDSON ENTERPRISES INC
TOLL BROTHERS INC
TRAMMELL CROW COMPANY
TRANSCONTINENTAL REALTY INVESTORS INC
TRANSWESTERN COMMERCIAL SERVICES
TREVI-FINANZIARIA INDUSTRIALE SPA (TREVI GROUP)

TRIPLE FIVE GROUP
TRT HOLDINGS
TRUE HOME VALUE INC
UDR INC
URS CORPORATION
VENTAS INC
VINCI
VORNADO REALTY TRUST
WEINGARTEN REALTY INVESTORS
WELLS REAL ESTATE FUNDS INC
WILLIAM LYON HOMES INC
WOLSELEY PLC
WORLDMARK BY WYNDHAM INC
WP CAREY & CO LLC
WS ATKINS PLC
WYNDHAM VACATION OWNERSHIP
WYNDHAM WORLDWIDE
XANTERRA PARKS AND RESORTS
ZIPREALTY INC

MIDWEST
84 LUMBER COMPANY
ABM INDUSTRIES INC
ACCIONA SA
ACCOR NORTH AMERICA
ACCOR SA
ADVOCAT INC
AECOM TECHNOLOGY CORPORATION
ALLY FINANCIAL INC
AMB PROPERTY CORPORATION
AMEC PLC
AMERCO
AMERICAN CAMPUS COMMUNITIES INC
AMERICAN REALTY INVESTORS INC
AMERICA'S BEST FRANCHISING INC
AMERISTAR CASINOS INC
AMLI RESIDENTIAL PROPERTIES TRUST
APARTMENT INVESTMENT AND MANAGEMENT CO
ARC GROUP OF COMPANIES (THE)
ARCADIS NV
ARDEN REALTY INC
ASSOCIATED ESTATES REALTY CORPORATION
ATRIA SENIOR LIVING GROUP
AVALONBAY COMMUNITIES INC
BANK OF AMERICA HOME LOANS
BARCELO CRESTLINE CORPORATION
BEAZER HOMES USA INC
BECHTEL GROUP INC
BEST WESTERN INTERNATIONAL INC
BLACK & VEATCH HOLDING COMPANY
BLUEGREEN CORPORATION
BOISE CASCADE CORP
BOUYGUES SA
BOYD GAMING CORP
BROOKDALE SENIOR LIVING INC
BROOKFIELD ASSET MANAGEMENT INC
BUILDING MATERIALS HOLDING CORP

BURNS & MCDONNELL
BUTLER MANUFACTURING CO
CAESARS ENTERTAINMENT CORPORATION
CAMDEN PROPERTY TRUST
CAMP DRESSER & MCKEE INC
CAPITAL AUTOMOTIVE REIT
CAPITAL SENIOR LIVING CORP
CAPMARK FINANCIAL GROUP INC
CAPREIT INC
CARLSON HOTELS WORLDWIDE
CB RICHARD ELLIS GROUP INC (CBRE)
CBL & ASSOCIATES PROPERTIES INC
CEMEX INC
CEMEX SAB DE CV
CENTEX CORP
CENTRO NP LLC
CENTRO PROPERTIES GROUP
CENTURY 21 REAL ESTATE LLC
CH2M HILL COMPANIES LTD
CHAMPION ENTERPRISES INC
CHICAGO BRIDGE & IRON COMPANY NV
CHOICE HOTELS INTERNATIONAL INC
CHRISTIES INTERNATIONAL REAL ESTATE
CITIMORTGAGE INC
CLAYTON HOMES INC
CNL FINANCIAL GROUP INC
COLDWELL BANKER REAL ESTATE LLC
COLLIERS INTERNATIONAL PROPERTY CONSULTANTS INC
COMFORT SYSTEMS USA INC
COMMONWEALTH REIT
CORE NETWORK (THE)
COSTAR GROUP INC
CRH PLC
CUSHMAN & WAKEFIELD INC
DAYS INN WORLDWIDE INC
DCT INDUSTRIAL TRUST INC
DEVELOPERS DIVERSIFIED REALTY CORP
DIAMOND RESORTS HOLDINGS LLC
DOMINION HOMES INC
DR HORTON INC
DREW INDUSTRIES INC
DUKE REALTY CORP
EMCOR GROUP INC
EMERITUS CORP
ENGLOBAL CORP
ENTERTAINMENT PROPERTIES TRUST
EQUITY LIFESTYLE PROPERTIES INC
EQUITY OFFICE PROPERTIES TRUST
EQUITY RESIDENTIAL
ERICKSON RETIREMENT COMMUNITIES
EXTENDICARE REAL ESTATE INVESTMENT TRUST
FAIRMONT HOMES INC
FAIRMONT RAFFLES HOTELS INTERNATIONAL INC
FANNIE MAE

FEDERAL AGRICULTURAL MORTGAGE CORP (FARMER MAC)
FEDERAL REALTY INVESTMENT TRUST
FELCOR LODGING TRUST INC
FERGUSON ENTERPRISES INC
FIDELITY NATIONAL FINANCIAL INC
FIDELITY NATIONAL INFORMATION SERVICES INC
FIRST AMERICAN FINANCIAL CORPORATION
FIRST INDUSTRIAL REALTY TRUST INC
FIRSTSERVICE CORPORATION
FIVE STAR PRODUCTS INC
FLUOR CORP
FOREST CITY ENTERPRISES INC
FOUR SEASONS HOTELS INC
GABLES RESIDENTIAL TRUST
GE CAPITAL
GE CAPITAL REAL ESTATE
GENERAL ELECTRIC CO (GE)
GENERAL GROWTH PROPERTIES INC
GLIMCHER REALTY TRUST
GRANITE CONSTRUCTION INC
GRUBB & ELLIS CO
GRUBB & ELLIS REALTY INVESTORS LLC
GRUPO FERROVIAL SA
HDR INC
HEALTH CARE REIT INC
HEALTHCARE REALTY TRUST INC
HIGHWOODS PROPERTIES INC
HILTON HOTELS CORP
HINES INTERESTS LP
HOCHTIEF AG
HOME DEPOT INC
HOME PROPERTIES INC
HOMESERVICES OF AMERICA INC
HOMETOWN AMERICA LLC
HONGKONG AND SHANGHAI HOTELS LTD
HOSPITALITY PROPERTIES TRUST
HOST HOTELS & RESORTS LP
HOVNANIAN ENTERPRISES INC
HOWARD JOHNSON INTERNATIONAL INC
HVM LLC
HYATT HOTELS CORPORATION
ICAHN ENTERPRISES LP
INDUSTRIAL DEVELOPMENTS INTERNATIONAL INC
INLAND AMERICAN REAL ESTATE TRUST INC
INLAND REAL ESTATE CORPORATION
INNKEEPERS USA TRUST
INSITUFORM TECHNOLOGIES
INTEGRATED ELECTRICAL SERVICES
INTERCONTINENTAL HOTELS GROUP PLC
INTERSTATE HOTELS & RESORTS INC
INTOWN SUITES MANAGEMENT INC
INVESTORS REAL ESTATE TRUST
INVESTORS TITLE COMPANY
ISTAR FINANCIAL INC
JACOBS ENGINEERING GROUP INC
JAMESON INN INC
JANUS HOTELS AND RESORTS INC
JOHN Q HAMMONS HOTELS LLC
JOHNSON CONTROLS INC
JONES LANG LASALLE INC
KB HOME
KIMCO REALTY CORP
KIMPTON HOTEL & RESTAURANT GROUP LLC
LASALLE HOTEL PROPERTIES
LAYNE CHRISTENSEN COMPANY
LB FOSTER COMPANY
LENDER PROCESSING SERVICES INC
LENNAR CORPORATION
LEXINGTON REALTY TRUST
LIBERTY PROPERTY TRUST
LIGHTSTONE GROUP LLC (THE)
LILLIBRIDGE HEALTHCARE REAL ESTATE TRUST
LODGIAN INC
LOUIS BERGER GROUP INC (THE)
LOWE'S COMPANIES INC
LQ MANAGEMENT LLC
M/I HOMES INC
MACERICH COMPANY (THE)
MANOR CARE INC
MARCUS CORPORATION (THE)
MARRIOTT INTERNATIONAL INC
MATRIX SERVICE COMPANY
MCDERMOTT INTERNATIONAL INC
MGM RESORTS INTERNATIONAL
MID-AMERICA APARTMENT COMMUNITIES INC
MILLENNIUM & COPTHORNE HOTELS PLC
MUNICIPAL MORTGAGE & EQUITY
MWH GLOBAL INC
NAI GLOBAL INC
NATIONAL HEALTH INVESTORS INC
NATIONWIDE HEALTH PROPERTIES INC
NCI BUILDING SYSTEMS INC
NRT LLC
NVR INC
OAKWOOD WORLDWIDE
OMEGA HEALTHCARE INVESTORS INC
ORIGEN FINANCIAL INC
ORLEANS HOMEBUILDERS INC
PALM HARBOR HOMES INC
PARKWAY PROPERTIES INC
PARSONS BRINCKERHOFF INC
PCL CONSTRUCTION GROUP INC
PENNSYLVANIA REIT
PLUM CREEK TIMBER CO INC
PMI GROUP INC (THE)
PRIME GROUP REALTY TRUST
PRIME RETAIL INC
PROLOGIS
PRUDENTIAL REAL ESTATE AFFILIATES INC
PUBLIC STORAGE INC
PULTEGROUP INC
RADIAN GROUP INC
RAILWORKS CORP

RAMADA WORLDWIDE INC
RE/MAX INTERNATIONAL INC
REALOGY CORPORATION
REALTY INCOME CORP
REGENCY CENTERS CORP
RITZ-CARLTON HOTEL COMPANY LLC (THE)
ROSEWOOD HOTELS & RESORTS LLC
ROYAL GROUP INC
RYLAND GROUP INC (THE)
SANDS REGENT
SCHUFF INTERNATIONAL INC
SENIOR HOUSING PROPERTIES
SERVICEMASTER COMPANY (THE)
SHAW GROUP INC (THE)
SIEMENS BUILDING TECHNOLOGIES
SIMON PROPERTY GROUP INC
SKIDMORE OWINGS & MERRILL LLP
SKYLINE CORPORATION
SOUTHERN ENERGY HOMES INC
SOVRAN SELF STORAGE INC
STARWOOD HOTELS & RESORTS WORLDWIDE
INC
STEWART INFORMATION SERVICES CORP
STOCK BUILDING SUPPLY INC
STRATEGIC HOTELS & RESORTS INC
STV GROUP INC
SUN COMMUNITIES INC
SUNBURST HOSPITALITY CORPORATION
SUNRISE SENIOR LIVING
SUNSTONE HOTEL INVESTORS INC
SUPER 8 MOTELS INC
SUPERTEL HOSPITALITY INC
SWIRE PACIFIC LTD
TANGER FACTORY OUTLET CENTERS INC
TAUBMAN CENTERS INC
THARALDSON ENTERPRISES INC
TOLL BROTHERS INC
TRACO
TRAMMELL CROW COMPANY
TRANSCONTINENTAL REALTY INVESTORS INC
TRANSWESTERN COMMERCIAL SERVICES
TRANSWESTERN INVESTMENT CO LLC
TRIPLE FIVE GROUP
TRT HOLDINGS
TRUE HOME VALUE INC
TRUMP ORGANIZATION (THE)
URS CORPORATION
VENTAS INC
VINCI
VORNADO REALTY TRUST
WELLS REAL ESTATE FUNDS INC
WESTFIELD GROUP (THE)
WOLSELEY PLC
WORLDMARK BY WYNDHAM INC
WS ATKINS PLC
WYNDHAM VACATION OWNERSHIP
WYNDHAM WORLDWIDE
XANTERRA PARKS AND RESORTS

ZIPREALTY INC

SOUTHEAST
84 LUMBER COMPANY
ABERTIS INFRAESTRUCTURAS SA
ABM INDUSTRIES INC
ACCOR NORTH AMERICA
ACCOR SA
ADVOCAT INC
AECOM TECHNOLOGY CORPORATION
ALLY FINANCIAL INC
AMB PROPERTY CORPORATION
AMEC PLC
AMERCO
AMERICAN CAMPUS COMMUNITIES INC
AMERICAN REALTY INVESTORS INC
AMERICA'S BEST FRANCHISING INC
AMERISTAR CASINOS INC
AMLI RESIDENTIAL PROPERTIES TRUST
ANDERSON-TULLY LUMBER COMPANY
APARTMENT INVESTMENT AND MANAGEMENT
CO
ARC GROUP OF COMPANIES (THE)
ARCADIS NV
ARCHSTONE TRUST
ASSOCIATED ESTATES REALTY CORPORATION
ATRIA SENIOR LIVING GROUP
AVATAR HOLDINGS INC
BALFOUR BEATTY PLC
BANK OF AMERICA HOME LOANS
BARCELO CRESTLINE CORPORATION
BEAZER HOMES USA INC
BECHTEL GROUP INC
BEST WESTERN INTERNATIONAL INC
BLACK & VEATCH HOLDING COMPANY
BLUEGREEN CORPORATION
BOISE CASCADE CORP
BOUYGUES SA
BOYD GAMING CORP
BROOKDALE SENIOR LIVING INC
BROOKFIELD ASSET MANAGEMENT INC
BUILDING MATERIALS HOLDING CORP
BURNS & MCDONNELL
BUTLER MANUFACTURING CO
CAESARS ENTERTAINMENT CORPORATION
CAMDEN PROPERTY TRUST
CAMP DRESSER & MCKEE INC
CAPITAL AUTOMOTIVE REIT
CAPITAL SENIOR LIVING CORP
CAPMARK FINANCIAL GROUP INC
CAPREIT INC
CARLSON HOTELS WORLDWIDE
CB RICHARD ELLIS GROUP INC (CBRE)
CBL & ASSOCIATES PROPERTIES INC
CEMEX INC
CEMEX SAB DE CV
CENTEX CORP
CENTRO NP LLC

CENTRO PROPERTIES GROUP
CENTURY 21 REAL ESTATE LLC
CH2M HILL COMPANIES LTD
CHAMPION ENTERPRISES INC
CHICAGO BRIDGE & IRON COMPANY NV
CHOICE HOTELS INTERNATIONAL INC
CHRISTIES INTERNATIONAL REAL ESTATE
CLAYTON HOMES INC
CLUB MEDITERRANEE SA
CNL FINANCIAL GROUP INC
COLDWELL BANKER REAL ESTATE LLC
COLLIERS INTERNATIONAL PROPERTY
CONSULTANTS INC
COLONIAL PROPERTIES TRUST
COMFORT SYSTEMS USA INC
COMMONWEALTH REIT
COMMUNITY DEVELOPMENT TRUST
CORE NETWORK (THE)
CORPORATE OFFICE PROPERTIES TRUST
COSTAR GROUP INC
COUSINS PROPERTIES INC
CRH PLC
CUSHMAN & WAKEFIELD INC
DAYS INN WORLDWIDE INC
DCT INDUSTRIAL TRUST INC
DEVELOPERS DIVERSIFIED REALTY CORP
DIAMOND RESORTS HOLDINGS LLC
DOOSAN HEAVY INDUSTRY & CONSTRUCTION
CO
DR HORTON INC
DREW INDUSTRIES INC
DUKE REALTY CORP
EASTGROUP PROPERTIES INC
EMCOR GROUP INC
EMERITUS CORP
ENGLOBAL CORP
ENTERTAINMENT PROPERTIES TRUST
EQUITY LIFESTYLE PROPERTIES INC
EQUITY OFFICE PROPERTIES TRUST
EQUITY ONE INC
EQUITY RESIDENTIAL
ERICKSON RETIREMENT COMMUNITIES
FAIRMONT RAFFLES HOTELS INTERNATIONAL
INC
FANNIE MAE
FEDERAL REALTY INVESTMENT TRUST
FELCOR LODGING TRUST INC
FERGUSON ENTERPRISES INC
FIDELITY NATIONAL FINANCIAL INC
FIDELITY NATIONAL INFORMATION SERVICES
INC
FIRST AMERICAN FINANCIAL CORPORATION
FIRST INDUSTRIAL REALTY TRUST INC
FIRSTSERVICE CORPORATION
FLUOR CORP
FOMENTO DE CONSTRUCCIONES Y CONTRATAS
SA (FCC)
FOUR SEASONS HOTELS INC
GABLES RESIDENTIAL TRUST
GAYLORD ENTERTAINMENT CO
GE CAPITAL
GE CAPITAL REAL ESTATE
GENERAL ELECTRIC CO (GE)
GENERAL GROWTH PROPERTIES INC
GEORG FISCHER LTD
GLENBOROUGH LLC
GLIMCHER REALTY TRUST
GRANITE CONSTRUCTION INC
GRUBB & ELLIS CO
GRUBB & ELLIS REALTY INVESTORS LLC
HCP INC
HDR INC
HEALTH CARE REIT INC
HEALTHCARE REALTY TRUST INC
HIGHWOODS PROPERTIES INC
HILTON HOTELS CORP
HINES INTERESTS LP
HOCHTIEF AG
HOME DEPOT INC
HOME PROPERTIES INC
HOMESERVICES OF AMERICA INC
HOMETOWN AMERICA LLC
HORTON HOMES INC
HOSPITALITY PROPERTIES TRUST
HOST HOTELS & RESORTS LP
HOVNANIAN ENTERPRISES INC
HOWARD JOHNSON INTERNATIONAL INC
HVM LLC
HYATT HOTELS CORPORATION
ICAHN ENTERPRISES LP
INDUSTRIAL DEVELOPMENTS INTERNATIONAL
INC
INLAND REAL ESTATE CORPORATION
INNKEEPERS USA TRUST
INSITUFORM TECHNOLOGIES
INTEGRATED ELECTRICAL SERVICES
INTERCONTINENTAL HOTELS GROUP PLC
INTERSTATE HOTELS & RESORTS INC
INTOWN SUITES MANAGEMENT INC
ISTAR FINANCIAL INC
JACOBS ENGINEERING GROUP INC
JAMESON INN INC
JANUS HOTELS AND RESORTS INC
JOHN Q HAMMONS HOTELS LLC
JOHNSON CONTROLS INC
JONES LANG LASALLE INC
KB HOME
KIMCO REALTY CORP
KIMPTON HOTEL & RESTAURANT GROUP LLC
LAYNE CHRISTENSEN COMPANY
LB FOSTER COMPANY
LENDER PROCESSING SERVICES INC
LENNAR CORPORATION
LEXINGTON REALTY TRUST
LIBERTY PROPERTY TRUST
LIGHTSTONE GROUP LLC (THE)

LODGIAN INC
LOEWS HOTELS HOLDING CORPORATION
LOUIS BERGER GROUP INC (THE)
LOWE'S COMPANIES INC
LQ MANAGEMENT LLC
M/I HOMES INC
MACERICH COMPANY (THE)
MANDARIN ORIENTAL INTERNATIONAL LTD
MANOR CARE INC
MARRIOTT INTERNATIONAL INC
MCDERMOTT INTERNATIONAL INC
MDC HOLDINGS INC
MERITAGE HOMES CORP
MGM RESORTS INTERNATIONAL
MID-AMERICA APARTMENT COMMUNITIES INC
MILLENNIUM & COPTHORNE HOTELS PLC
MORGANS HOTEL GROUP CO
MUNICIPAL MORTGAGE & EQUITY
MWH GLOBAL INC
NAI GLOBAL INC
NATIONAL HEALTH INVESTORS INC
NATIONWIDE HEALTH PROPERTIES INC
NCI BUILDING SYSTEMS INC
NH HOTELES SA
NRT LLC
NVR INC
OAKWOOD WORLDWIDE
OMEGA HEALTHCARE INVESTORS INC
ORIENT OVERSEAS (INTERNATIONAL) LTD
ORION MARINE GROUP INC
ORLEANS HOMEBUILDERS INC
PALM HARBOR HOMES INC
PARKWAY PROPERTIES INC
PARSONS BRINCKERHOFF INC
PCL CONSTRUCTION GROUP INC
PENNSYLVANIA REIT
PLUM CREEK TIMBER CO INC
PMI GROUP INC (THE)
POST PROPERTIES INC
PRIME RETAIL INC
PROLOGIS
PRUDENTIAL REAL ESTATE AFFILIATES INC
PS BUSINESS PARKS INC
PUBLIC STORAGE INC
PULTEGROUP INC
RADIAN GROUP INC
RAILWORKS CORP
RAMADA WORLDWIDE INC
RE/MAX INTERNATIONAL INC
REALOGY CORPORATION
REALTY INCOME CORP
REGENCY CENTERS CORP
RELATED GROUP (THE)
RESORTQUEST INTERNATIONAL INC
RITZ-CARLTON HOTEL COMPANY LLC (THE)
ROSEWOOD HOTELS & RESORTS LLC
ROYAL GROUP INC
RYLAND GROUP INC (THE)

SCHUFF INTERNATIONAL INC
SENIOR HOUSING PROPERTIES
SERVICEMASTER COMPANY (THE)
SHAW GROUP INC (THE)
SIEMENS BUILDING TECHNOLOGIES
SIMON PROPERTY GROUP INC
SKYLINE CORPORATION
SOL MELIA SA
SONESTA INTERNATIONAL HOTELS CORP
SOUTHERN ENERGY HOMES INC
SOVRAN SELF STORAGE INC
ST JOE COMPANY (THE)
STANDARD PACIFIC CORP
STARWOOD CAPITAL GROUP GLOBAL LLC
STARWOOD HOTELS & RESORTS WORLDWIDE
INC
STEWART INFORMATION SERVICES CORP
STOCK BUILDING SUPPLY INC
STRATEGIC HOTELS & RESORTS INC
STV GROUP INC
SUN COMMUNITIES INC
SUNBURST HOSPITALITY CORPORATION
SUNRISE SENIOR LIVING
SUNSTONE HOTEL INVESTORS INC
SUPER 8 MOTELS INC
SUPERTEL HOSPITALITY INC
TANGER FACTORY OUTLET CENTERS INC
TAUBMAN CENTERS INC
TECHNICAL OLYMPIC USA INC
THARALDSON ENTERPRISES INC
TOLL BROTHERS INC
TRAMMELL CROW COMPANY
TRANSCONTINENTAL REALTY INVESTORS INC
TRANSWESTERN COMMERCIAL SERVICES
TREVI-FINANZIARIA INDUSTRIALE SPA (TREVI
GROUP)
TRIPLE FIVE GROUP
TRT HOLDINGS
TRUE HOME VALUE INC
TRUMP ORGANIZATION (THE)
TUTOR PERINI CORPORATION
UDR INC
URS CORPORATION
VENTAS INC
VINCI
VORNADO REALTY TRUST
WCI COMMUNITIES INC
WEINGARTEN REALTY INVESTORS
WELLS REAL ESTATE FUNDS INC
WESTFIELD GROUP (THE)
WOLSELEY PLC
WORLDMARK BY WYNDHAM INC
WS ATKINS PLC
WYNDHAM VACATION OWNERSHIP
WYNDHAM WORLDWIDE
ZIPREALTY INC

NORTHEAST
84 LUMBER COMPANY
ABM INDUSTRIES INC
ACCOR NORTH AMERICA
ACCOR SA
ACS ACTIVIDADES DE CONSTRUCCION Y
SERVICIOS SA
ADVOCAT INC
AECOM TECHNOLOGY CORPORATION
ALEXANDRIA REAL ESTATE EQUITIES INC
ALLY FINANCIAL INC
AMB PROPERTY CORPORATION
AMEC PLC
AMERCO
AMERICAN CAMPUS COMMUNITIES INC
AMERICAN REALTY INVESTORS INC
AMERICA'S BEST FRANCHISING INC
AMLI RESIDENTIAL PROPERTIES TRUST
ANNALY CAPITAL MANAGEMENT INC
ANTHONY & SYLVAN POOLS
APARTMENT INVESTMENT AND MANAGEMENT
CO
ARC GROUP OF COMPANIES (THE)
ARCADIS NV
ARCHSTONE TRUST
ASSOCIATED ESTATES REALTY CORPORATION
ATRIA SENIOR LIVING GROUP
AVALONBAY COMMUNITIES INC
BANK OF AMERICA HOME LOANS
BARCELO CRESTLINE CORPORATION
BEAZER HOMES USA INC
BECHTEL GROUP INC
BEST WESTERN INTERNATIONAL INC
BLACK & VEATCH HOLDING COMPANY
BLUEGREEN CORPORATION
BOISE CASCADE CORP
BOSTON PROPERTIES INC
BOUYGUES SA
BOYD GAMING CORP
BRANDYWINE REALTY TRUST
BROOKDALE SENIOR LIVING INC
BROOKFIELD ASSET MANAGEMENT INC
BROOKFIELD HOMES CORP
BUILDING MATERIALS HOLDING CORP
BURNS & MCDONNELL
BUTLER MANUFACTURING CO
CAESARS ENTERTAINMENT CORPORATION
CAMDEN PROPERTY TRUST
CAMP DRESSER & MCKEE INC
CAPITAL AUTOMOTIVE REIT
CAPITAL SENIOR LIVING CORP
CAPMARK FINANCIAL GROUP INC
CAPREIT INC
CARLSON HOTELS WORLDWIDE
CB RICHARD ELLIS GROUP INC (CBRE)
CBL & ASSOCIATES PROPERTIES INC
CEMEX INC
CEMEX SAB DE CV

CENTEX CORP
CENTRO NP LLC
CENTRO PROPERTIES GROUP
CENTURY 21 REAL ESTATE LLC
CH2M HILL COMPANIES LTD
CHAMPION ENTERPRISES INC
CHICAGO BRIDGE & IRON COMPANY NV
CHINA STATE CONSTRUCTION ENGINEERING
CORP
CHOICE HOTELS INTERNATIONAL INC
CHRISTIES INTERNATIONAL REAL ESTATE
CLAYTON HOMES INC
CNL FINANCIAL GROUP INC
COLDWELL BANKER REAL ESTATE LLC
COLLIERS INTERNATIONAL PROPERTY
CONSULTANTS INC
COLONIAL PROPERTIES TRUST
COLONY CAPITAL LLC
COMFORT SYSTEMS USA INC
COMMONWEALTH REIT
COMMUNITY DEVELOPMENT TRUST
CORE NETWORK (THE)
CORPORATE OFFICE PROPERTIES TRUST
COSTAR GROUP INC
COUSINS PROPERTIES INC
CRH PLC
CUSHMAN & WAKEFIELD INC
DAYS INN WORLDWIDE INC
DCT INDUSTRIAL TRUST INC
DEVELOPERS DIVERSIFIED REALTY CORP
DIAMOND RESORTS HOLDINGS LLC
DOOSAN HEAVY INDUSTRY & CONSTRUCTION
CO
DOYLE COLLECTION (THE)
DR HORTON INC
DREW INDUSTRIES INC
DUKE REALTY CORP
DYNEX CAPITAL INC
EASTGROUP PROPERTIES INC
EMCOR GROUP INC
EMERITUS CORP
ENGLOBAL CORP
ENTERTAINMENT PROPERTIES TRUST
EQUITY LIFESTYLE PROPERTIES INC
EQUITY OFFICE PROPERTIES TRUST
EQUITY ONE INC
EQUITY RESIDENTIAL
ERICKSON RETIREMENT COMMUNITIES
ESSAR GROUP LTD
EXTENDICARE REAL ESTATE INVESTMENT
TRUST
FAIRMONT RAFFLES HOTELS INTERNATIONAL
INC
FANNIE MAE
FEDERAL AGRICULTURAL MORTGAGE CORP
(FARMER MAC)
FEDERAL REALTY INVESTMENT TRUST
FELCOR LODGING TRUST INC

FERGUSON ENTERPRISES INC
FIDELITY NATIONAL FINANCIAL INC
FIDELITY NATIONAL INFORMATION SERVICES
INC
FIRST AMERICAN FINANCIAL CORPORATION
FIRST INDUSTRIAL REALTY TRUST INC
FIRSTSERVICE CORPORATION
FIVE STAR PRODUCTS INC
FLUOR CORP
FOMENTO DE CONSTRUCCIONES Y CONTRATAS
SA (FCC)
FOREST CITY ENTERPRISES INC
FOUR SEASONS HOTELS INC
FREDDIE MAC
GABLES RESIDENTIAL TRUST
GAYLORD ENTERTAINMENT CO
GE CAPITAL
GE CAPITAL REAL ESTATE
GENERAL ELECTRIC CO (GE)
GENERAL GROWTH PROPERTIES INC
GLENBOROUGH LLC
GLIMCHER REALTY TRUST
GOLDEN TULIP HOSPITALITY GROUP
GRANITE CONSTRUCTION INC
GRUBB & ELLIS CO
HDR INC
HEALTH CARE REIT INC
HEALTHCARE REALTY TRUST INC
HIGHWOODS PROPERTIES INC
HILTON HOTELS CORP
HINES INTERESTS LP
HOCHTIEF AG
HOME DEPOT INC
HOME PROPERTIES INC
HOMESERVICES OF AMERICA INC
HOMETOWN AMERICA LLC
HONGKONG AND SHANGHAI HOTELS LTD
HORTON HOMES INC
HOSPITALITY PROPERTIES TRUST
HOST HOTELS & RESORTS LP
HOVNANIAN ENTERPRISES INC
HOWARD JOHNSON INTERNATIONAL INC
HVM LLC
HYATT HOTELS CORPORATION
HYPO REAL ESTATE HOLDING AG (HYPO BANK)
HYUNDAI ENGINEERING & CONSTRUCTION
COMPANY LTD
ICAHN ENTERPRISES LP
INDIAN HOTELS COMPANY LIMITED (THE)
INDUSTRIAL DEVELOPMENTS INTERNATIONAL
INC
INLAND AMERICAN REAL ESTATE TRUST INC
INNKEEPERS USA TRUST
INSITUFORM TECHNOLOGIES
INTEGRATED ELECTRICAL SERVICES
INTERCONTINENTAL HOTELS GROUP PLC
INTERSTATE HOTELS & RESORTS INC
INTOWN SUITES MANAGEMENT INC

INVESTORS TITLE COMPANY
ISTAR FINANCIAL INC
JACOBS ENGINEERING GROUP INC
JAMESON INN INC
JANUS HOTELS AND RESORTS INC
JOHN Q HAMMONS HOTELS LLC
JOHNSON CONTROLS INC
JONES LANG LASALLE INC
KB HOME
KERZNER INTERNATIONAL HOLDINGS LIMITED
KIMCO REALTY CORP
KIMPTON HOTEL & RESTAURANT GROUP LLC
LAS VEGAS SANDS CORP (THE VENETIAN)
LASALLE HOTEL PROPERTIES
LAYNE CHRISTENSEN COMPANY
LB FOSTER COMPANY
LENDER PROCESSING SERVICES INC
LENDINGTREE LLC
LENNAR CORPORATION
LEXINGTON REALTY TRUST
LIBERTY PROPERTY TRUST
LIGHTSTONE GROUP LLC (THE)
LODGIAN INC
LOEWS HOTELS HOLDING CORPORATION
LOUIS BERGER GROUP INC (THE)
LOWE'S COMPANIES INC
LQ MANAGEMENT LLC
M/I HOMES INC
MACERICH COMPANY (THE)
MACK-CALI REALTY CORP
MANDARIN ORIENTAL INTERNATIONAL LTD
MANOR CARE INC
MARRIOTT INTERNATIONAL INC
MATRIX SERVICE COMPANY
MCDERMOTT INTERNATIONAL INC
MDC HOLDINGS INC
MERITUS HOTELS & RESORTS INC
MFA FINANCIAL INC
MID-AMERICA APARTMENT COMMUNITIES INC
MILLENNIUM & COPTHORNE HOTELS PLC
MORGANS HOTEL GROUP CO
MOVE INC
MUNICIPAL MORTGAGE & EQUITY
MWH GLOBAL INC
NAI GLOBAL INC
NATIONAL HEALTH INVESTORS INC
NATIONWIDE HEALTH PROPERTIES INC
NCI BUILDING SYSTEMS INC
NEWCASTLE INVESTMENT CORP
NH HOTELES SA
NRT LLC
NVR INC
OAKWOOD WORLDWIDE
OMEGA HEALTHCARE INVESTORS INC
ORIENT OVERSEAS (INTERNATIONAL) LTD
ORIENT-EXPRESS HOTELS LTD
ORION MARINE GROUP INC
ORLEANS HOMEBUILDERS INC

PALM HARBOR HOMES INC
PARKWAY PROPERTIES INC
PARSONS BRINCKERHOFF INC
PENNSYLVANIA REIT
PLUM CREEK TIMBER CO INC
PMI GROUP INC (THE)
POST PROPERTIES INC
PRIME RETAIL INC
PROLOGIS
PRUDENTIAL REAL ESTATE AFFILIATES INC
PS BUSINESS PARKS INC
PUBLIC STORAGE INC
PULTEGROUP INC
RADIAN GROUP INC
RAILWORKS CORP
RAMADA WORLDWIDE INC
RE/MAX INTERNATIONAL INC
REALOGY CORPORATION
REALPAGE INC
REALTY INCOME CORP
REGENCY CENTERS CORP
REIS INC
RESORTQUEST INTERNATIONAL INC
RITZ-CARLTON HOTEL COMPANY LLC (THE)
ROSEWOOD HOTELS & RESORTS LLC
ROYAL GROUP INC
RXR REALTY
RYLAND GROUP INC (THE)
SAWYER REALTY HOLDINGS LLC
SENIOR HOUSING PROPERTIES
SERVICEMASTER COMPANY (THE)
SHANGRI-LA ASIA LTD
SHAW GROUP INC (THE)
SIEMENS BUILDING TECHNOLOGIES
SIMON PROPERTY GROUP INC
SKIDMORE OWINGS & MERRILL LLP
SKYLINE CORPORATION
SL GREEN REALTY CORP
SOL MELIA SA
SONESTA INTERNATIONAL HOTELS CORP
SOUTHERN ENERGY HOMES INC
SOVRAN SELF STORAGE INC
STANDARD PACIFIC CORP
STARWOOD CAPITAL GROUP GLOBAL LLC
STARWOOD HOTELS & RESORTS WORLDWIDE
INC
STEWART INFORMATION SERVICES CORP
STOCK BUILDING SUPPLY INC
STRATEGIC HOTELS & RESORTS INC
STV GROUP INC
SUN COMMUNITIES INC
SUNBURST HOSPITALITY CORPORATION
SUNRISE SENIOR LIVING
SUNSTONE HOTEL INVESTORS INC
SUPER 8 MOTELS INC
SUPERTEL HOSPITALITY INC
SWIRE PACIFIC LTD
TANGER FACTORY OUTLET CENTERS INC

TAUBMAN CENTERS INC
TECHNICAL OLYMPIC USA INC
THARALDSON ENTERPRISES INC
TOLL BROTHERS INC
TRACO
TRAMMELL CROW COMPANY
TRANSCONTINENTAL REALTY INVESTORS INC
TRANSWESTERN COMMERCIAL SERVICES
TRANSWESTERN INVESTMENT CO LLC
TREVI-FINANZIARIA INDUSTRIALE SPA (TREVI
GROUP)
TRIPLE FIVE GROUP
TRT HOLDINGS
TRUE HOME VALUE INC
TRUMP ENTERTAINMENT RESORTS INC
TRUMP ORGANIZATION (THE)
TUTOR PERINI CORPORATION
UDR INC
URS CORPORATION
VENTAS INC
VINCI
VORNADO REALTY TRUST
WASHINGTON REAL ESTATE INVESTMENT TRUST
WCI COMMUNITIES INC
WEINGARTEN REALTY INVESTORS
WELLS REAL ESTATE FUNDS INC
WESTFIELD GROUP (THE)
WOLSELEY PLC
WP CAREY & CO LLC
WS ATKINS PLC
WYNDHAM VACATION OWNERSHIP
WYNDHAM WORLDWIDE
ZIPREALTY INC

INDEX OF FIRMS WITH INTERNATIONAL OPERATIONS

GOLDEN TULIP HOSPITALITY GROUP
GROUPE DU LOUVRE
GRUBB & ELLIS CO
GRUPO ACS
GRUPO FERROVIAL SA
GS ENGINEERING & CONSTRUCTION CORP
GUOMAN HOTELS LIMITED
HANG LUNG GROUP LTD
HANG LUNG PROPERTIES LIMITED
HANJIN HEAVY INDUSTRIES CO LTD
HDR INC
HENDERSON LAND DEVELOPMENT COMPANY
LIMITED
HILTON HOTELS CORP
HINES INTERESTS LP
HOCHTIEF AG
HOME DEPOT INC
HOME INNS & HOTELS MANAGEMENT INC
HONGKONG AND SHANGHAI HOTELS LTD
HONGKONG LAND HOLDINGS LTD
HOSPITALITY PROPERTIES TRUST
HOST HOTELS & RESORTS LP
HOTEL PROPERTIES LTD
HOWARD JOHNSON INTERNATIONAL INC
HUTCHISON WHAMPOA PROPERTIES LTD
HVM LLC
HYATT HOTELS CORPORATION
HYPO REAL ESTATE HOLDING AG (HYPO BANK)
HYSAN DEVELOPMENT CO LTD
HYUNDAI ELEVATOR CO LTD
HYUNDAI ENGINEERING & CONSTRUCTION
COMPANY LTD
ICAHN ENTERPRISES LP
IMPREGILO SPA
INDIAN HOTELS COMPANY LIMITED (THE)
INSITUFORM TECHNOLOGIES
INTERCONTINENTAL HOTELS GROUP PLC
INTERSTATE HOTELS & RESORTS INC
JACOBS ENGINEERING GROUP INC
JOHN LAING PLC
JOHNSON CONTROLS INC
JONES LANG LASALLE INC
KERZNER INTERNATIONAL HOLDINGS LIMITED
KIMCO REALTY CORP
KUMHO INDUSTRIAL CO LTD
LAS VEGAS SANDS CORP (THE VENETIAN)
LAYNE CHRISTENSEN COMPANY
LEXINGTON REALTY TRUST
LIBERTY PROPERTY TRUST
LINK REAL ESTATE INVESTMENT TRUST (THE)
LOEWS HOTELS HOLDING CORPORATION
LOUIS BERGER GROUP INC (THE)
LOWE'S COMPANIES INC
LQ MANAGEMENT LLC
MANDARIN ORIENTAL INTERNATIONAL LTD
MARRIOTT INTERNATIONAL INC
MATRIX SERVICE COMPANY
MAX PROPERTY GROUP PLC

MCDERMOTT INTERNATIONAL INC
MERITUS HOTELS & RESORTS INC
MGM RESORTS INTERNATIONAL
MILLENNIUM & COPTHORNE HOTELS PLC
MORGANS HOTEL GROUP CO
MOVE INC
MRV ENGENHARIA E PARTICIPACOES SA
MWH GLOBAL INC
NAI GLOBAL INC
NCI BUILDING SYSTEMS INC
NEW WORLD DEVELOPMENT COMPANY LIMITED
NEWCASTLE INVESTMENT CORP
NH HOTELES SA
NRT LLC
OAKWOOD WORLDWIDE
OBEROI GROUP (EIH LTD)
ODEBRECHT SA
ORIENT OVERSEAS (INTERNATIONAL) LTD
ORIENT-EXPRESS HOTELS LTD
PACIFIC COAST BUILDING PRODUCTS INC
PARSONS BRINCKERHOFF INC
PCL CONSTRUCTION GROUP INC
PDG REALTY SA EMPREENDIMENTOS E
PARTICIPACOES
PMI GROUP INC (THE)
PROLOGIS
PRUDENTIAL REAL ESTATE AFFILIATES INC
QMH UK LTD
RADIAN GROUP INC
RAILWORKS CORP
RAMADA WORLDWIDE INC
RE/MAX INTERNATIONAL INC
REALOGY CORPORATION
REALPAGE INC
RED LION HOTELS CORPORATION
RESORTQUEST INTERNATIONAL INC
REZIDOR HOTEL GROUP AB
RITZ-CARLTON HOTEL COMPANY LLC (THE)
ROSEWOOD HOTELS & RESORTS LLC
ROSSI RESIDENCIAL SA
ROYAL GROUP INC
SAHA PATHANA INTER-HOLDING PCL
SAMWHAN CORPORATION
SCANDIC HOTELS AB
SEKISUI HOUSE LTD
SEMBCORP INDUSTRIES LTD
SENIOR HOUSING PROPERTIES
SERVICEMASTER COMPANY (THE)
SHANGRI-LA ASIA LTD
SHAW GROUP INC (THE)
SHIMAO PROPERTY HOLDINGS LTD
SHUN TAK HOLDINGS LIMITED
SIEMENS BUILDING TECHNOLOGIES
SIMON PROPERTY GROUP INC
SINO LAND COMPANY LIMITED
SKIDMORE OWINGS & MERRILL LLP
SOCIETE DES BAINS DE MER ET DU CERCLE DES
ETRANGERS A MONACO

SOL MELIA SA
SONESTA INTERNATIONAL HOTELS CORP
STARWOOD CAPITAL GROUP GLOBAL LLC
STARWOOD HOTELS & RESORTS WORLDWIDE
INC
STEWART INFORMATION SERVICES CORP
STRATEGIC HOTELS & RESORTS INC
STV GROUP INC
SUN HUNG KAI PROPERTIES
SUNRISE SENIOR LIVING
SUPER 8 MOTELS INC
SWIRE PACIFIC LTD
TAUBMAN CENTERS INC
TRAMMELL CROW COMPANY
TRANSCONTINENTAL REALTY INVESTORS INC
TREVI-FINANZIARIA INDUSTRIALE SPA (TREVI
GROUP)
TRINITY LTD
TRIPLE FIVE GROUP
TRT HOLDINGS
TRUMP ORGANIZATION (THE)
TUTOR PERINI CORPORATION
UNIBAIL-RODAMCO
UNITECH LIMITED
URS CORPORATION
VINCI
VORNADO REALTY TRUST
WESTFIELD GROUP (THE)
WHARF (HOLDINGS) LIMITED, THE
WHEELOCK AND COMPANY LIMITED
WOLSELEY PLC
WORLDMARK BY WYNDHAM INC
WP CAREY & CO LLC
WS ATKINS PLC
WYNDHAM VACATION OWNERSHIP
WYNDHAM WORLDWIDE
WYNN RESORTS LIMITED
YIT CORPORATION

Individual Profiles
On Each Of
THE REAL ESTATE 400

84 LUMBER COMPANY

www.84lumber.com

Industry Group Code: 444130 Ranks within this company's industry group: Sales: Profits:

Properties:	Financial Services:	Construction/Development:		Investments:	Specialty Services:	Brokerage:
Apartments:	Mortgages:	Commercial Construction:		REIT:	Property Management:	Commercial Sales:
Malls/Shopping:	Title Insurance:	Residential Construction:			Online Services:	Residential Sales:
Offices:	Property Insurance:	Land Development:			Software/IT:	Specialty:
Hotels/Motels:		Support Services:	Y		Consulting:	
Industrial/Warehouses:		Design/Engineering:	Y			
Other:						

TYPES OF BUSINESS:

Hardware Stores
Building Materials
Construction Financing
Builder's Insurance
Travel Agency

BRANDS/DIVISIONS/AFFILIATES:

Affordable Collection
Oaks Collection
Builder Lending Program
Maggie's Management LLC
84 Travel
84 Components
84 Lumber Credit Card
84 Lumber Contractor Card

CONTACTS: Note: Officers with more than one job title may be intentionally listed here more than once.

Joseph A. Hardy III, CEO
Frank Cicero, COO
Maggie H. Magerko, Pres./Owner
Paul Lentz, CFO
Jeff Nobers, VP-Mktg.
Dan Wallach, Exec. VP-Strategic Initiatives
Jeff Nobers, VP-Corp. Comm.

Phone: 724-228-8820	Fax: 724-228-8058
Toll-Free:	
Address: 1019 Rte. 519, Eighty Four, PA 15330 US	

GROWTH PLANS/SPECIAL FEATURES:

84 Lumber Company is a supplier of building materials, supplies and expertise to professional contractors, remodelers and individuals. The company operates approximately 281 locations nationwide, including six component manufacturing facilities. 84 Lumber has store locations in 35 states, which offer lumber, plywood, insulation, trim, molding, flooring, siding, drywall, trusses, roofing, skylights, engineered lumber, hardware, doors and windows. In addition to its retail store operations, 84 Lumber offers a variety of good and services. 84 Components is the company's manufacturing division, which builds metal plate connected roof and floor trusses and wall panels. 84 Lumber Travel is a full-service accredited travel agency offering no-fee service to professional contractors and other 84 Lumber's customers. The firm offers builder's risk, general liability, workers compensation, commercial auto and personal insurance through Maggie's Management, LLC. The 84 Lumber Credit Card and the 84 Lumber Contractor Card are available to general customers and contractors respectively. The firm offers installed services that include framing, roofing, insulation, windows, doors, trip and siding. 84 Lumber also sells entire home packages such as the Affordable Collection, which contains plans for easy-to-build homes from 500 square feet up to 2,851 square feet; and the Oaks Collection, which includes more elaborate designs in sizes up to 4,963 square feet. In addition, 84 Lumber has an affiliation with Nelson Design Group, an online provider of over 900 house plans. In September 2010, the firm re-opened a store location in Milton, Florida. In May 2011, 84 Lumber closed down 10 stores in eight states.

The company offers its employees life, disability, medical, mental and dental insurance; a 401(K) plan; a profit sharing plan; and training and development programs.

FINANCIALS: Sales and profits are in thousands of dollars—add 000 to get the full amount. 2010 Note: Financial information for 2010 was not available for all companies at press time.

2010 Sales: $	2010 Profits: $	U.S. Stock Ticker: Private
2009 Sales: $	2009 Profits: $	Int'l Ticker: Int'l Exchange:
2008 Sales: $2,100,000	2008 Profits: $	Employees: 4,500
2007 Sales: $3,100,000	2007 Profits: $	Fiscal Year Ends: 12/31
2006 Sales: $3,920,000	2006 Profits: $	Parent Company:

SALARIES/BENEFITS:

Pension Plan:	ESOP Stock Plan:	Profit Sharing: Y	Top Exec. Salary: $	Bonus: $
Savings Plan: Y	Stock Purch. Plan:		Second Exec. Salary: $	Bonus: $

OTHER THOUGHTS:

Apparent Women Officers or Directors: 1
Hot Spot for Advancement for Women/Minorities:

LOCATIONS: ("Y" = Yes)

West:	Southwest:	Midwest:	Southeast:	Northeast:	International:
Y	Y	Y	Y	Y	

ABERTIS INFRAESTRUCTURAS SA   www.abertis.com

Industry Group Code: 561210 Ranks within this company's industry group: Sales: 1   Profits: 1

Properties:	Financial Services:	Construction/Development:	Investments:	Specialty Services:		Brokerage:
Apartments:	Mortgages:	Commercial Construction:	REIT:	Property Management:	Y	Commercial Sales:
Malls/Shopping:	Title Insurance:	Residential Construction:		Online Services:		Residential Sales:
Offices:	Property Insurance:	Land Development:		Software/IT:		Specialty:
Hotels/Motels:		Support Services:		Consulting:		
Industrial/Warehouses:		Design/Engineering:				
Other: Y						

TYPES OF BUSINESS:

Transport & Communications
Logistics Services
TV & Radio Broadcasting
Airport Operations
Parking Facilities Management
Motorway Construction & Management
Warehouses
Heavy Construction

BRANDS/DIVISIONS/AFFILIATES:

Saba
Tradia
Retevision
Abertis Logistica
Abertis Telecom

CONTACTS: *Note: Officers with more than one job title may be intentionally listed here more than once.*

Salvador Alemany Mas, CEO
Josep Martinez Vila, Dir.-Oper.
Francisco Jose Aljaro Navarro, CFO
Joan Rafel Herrero, Dir.-Personnel & Organization
Juan A. Margenat Padros, Sec.
David Diaz Almazan, Dir.-Corp. Dev.
Antoni Brunet Mauri, Dir.-Corp. Comm.
Jose Aljaro Navarro, Managing Dir.-Finance
Luis Jimenez Arrebola, Dir.-Corp. Security
Sergi Loughney Castells, Dir.-Institutional Rel.
Tobias Martinez Gimeno, Managing Dir.-Abertis Telecom
Salvador Alemany Mas, Chmn.
Jordi Graells Ferrandez, Managing Dir.-Toll Roads North America & Int'l

Phone: 34-932-305-000	Fax: 34-932-305-001
Toll-Free:	
Address: 12-20 Parc Logistic Ave., Barcelona, 08040 Spain	

GROWTH PLANS/SPECIAL FEATURES:

Abertis Infraestructuras S.A. is a private transport and communications infrastructure management company based in Barcelona and is a leading Spain-based operator of motorways and car parks. The company, which is active in 18 countries in Europe, North America, South America, Africa and the Caribbean, also offers logistics parks, telecommunications infrastructure and airport operation services. It organizes its business activities into five units: toll roads, telecommunications infrastructures, airports, car parks and logistic parks. The toll roads division operates 2,333 miles of toll roads in France, Spain, Chile, Argentina and Puerto Rico. Through its concessions in Latin America and Europe, the division also has a share in an additional 3,464 miles. Abertis Telecom, the company's telecommunications division, consists of two companies, Tradia and Retevision. Tradia's activities include provision of radio and TV signal broadcasting services and the renting of space for telecommunications operators. Retevision, which provides national coverage with its analog and digital network, focuses on audiovisual signal transportation and broadcasting. The airports division operates in 29 airports in Europe and Latin America, as well as the U.S. The division also provides airport-related consulting services. The company's car park division is headed by Saba and manages facilities in over 77 municipalities in Spain, Italy, Portugal, Chile, France, Morocco and Andorra. The company's logistic parks activities, headed by Abertis Logistica, consist of warehouses and offices in Spain and abroad.

FINANCIALS: Sales and profits are in thousands of dollars—add 000 to get the full amount. 2010 Note: Financial information for 2010 was not available for all companies at press time.

2010 Sales: $5,638,690	2010 Profits: $913,350	**U.S. Stock Ticker: ABE**
2009 Sales: $5,252,880	2009 Profits: $889,560	**Int'l Ticker: ABE** Int'l Exchange: Madrid-MCE
2008 Sales: $4,883,650	2008 Profits: $820,360	Employees: 11,894
2007 Sales: $4,805,330	2007 Profits: $905,310	Fiscal Year Ends: 12/31
2006 Sales: $4,880,810	2006 Profits: $775,660	Parent Company:

SALARIES/BENEFITS:

Pension Plan:	ESOP Stock Plan:	Profit Sharing:	Top Exec. Salary: $	Bonus: $
Savings Plan:	Stock Purch. Plan:		Second Exec. Salary: $	Bonus: $

OTHER THOUGHTS:

Apparent Women Officers or Directors: 2
Hot Spot for Advancement for Women/Minorities:

LOCATIONS: ("Y" = Yes)

West:	Southwest:	Midwest:	Southeast:	Northeast:	International:
	Y		Y		Y

ABM INDUSTRIES INC

www.abm.com

Industry Group Code: 5311 Ranks within this company's industry group: Sales: 8 Profits: 22

Properties:	Financial Services:	Construction/Development:		Investments:	Specialty Services:		Brokerage:
Apartments:	Mortgages:	Commercial Construction:		REIT:	Property Management:	Y	Commercial Sales:
Malls/Shopping:	Title Insurance:	Residential Construction:			Online Services:		Residential Sales:
Offices:	Property Insurance:	Land Development:			Software/IT:		Specialty:
Hotels/Motels:		Support Services:	Y		Consulting:		
Industrial/Warehouses:		Design/Engineering:					
Other:							

TYPES OF BUSINESS:

Janitorial Services
Parking Facilities
Maintenance Personnel
Security Services
Lighting Services
Billing & Accounting Services
Supplier Management
Call Center Services

BRANDS/DIVISIONS/AFFILIATES:

ABM Janitorial Services
ABM Security Services
Security Services of America
Silverhawk Security Specialists
Elite Protection Services
ABM Engineering Services
DHI HOLDINGS, Inc.
Linc Group, LLC (The)

CONTACTS: *Note: Officers with more than one job title may be intentionally listed here more than once.*

Henrik C. Slipsager, CEO
Henrik C. Slipsager, Pres.
James Lusk, CFO/Exec. VP
Erin M. Andre, Sr. VP-Human Resources
Tracy K. Price, Exec. VP/Pres., Eng.
Sarah Hlavinka McConnell, General Counsel/Sr. VP/Corp. Sec.
Tony Mitchell, VP-Corp. Comm.
David L. Farwell, Sr. VP-Investor Rel.
Dean Chin, Chief Acct. Officer/Controller/Sr. VP
James P. McClure, Exec. VP/Pres., ABM Janitorial Svcs.
Steven M. Zaccagnini, Exec. VP/Pres., ABM Facility Svcs.
Maryellen C. Herringer, Chmn.

Phone: 212-297-0200	Fax: 415-733-7333
Toll-Free:	
Address: 551 5th Ave., Ste. 300, New York, NY 10176 US	

GROWTH PLANS/SPECIAL FEATURES:

ABM Industries, Inc. is one of the country's largest facility services providers. Founded in California in 1909 as a one-man window cleaning business, today the firm provides janitorial, parking, engineering, security, and mechanical services to commercial, industrial, institutional and retail facilities throughout the U.S., Puerto Rico and Canada. ABM operates through a number of subsidiaries, which are grouped into four segments: janitorial, parking, security and engineering. The company's janitorial services, operated through ABM Janitorial Services, include floor cleaning and finishing; window washing; furniture polishing; and carpet cleaning and dusting. Through Ampco System Parking, the company provides parking and shuttle transportation services in 38 states and Washington D.C. It currently manages more than 1,800 parking operations and offers parking management services to facilities such as airports, universities, office buildings, hotels, retail centers, hospitals and shopping malls. ABM's security services subsidiaries include ABM Security Services, Security Services of America, Silverhawk Security Specialists and Elite Protection Services. Security services offered by these subsidiaries include security officers; investigative services; electronic monitoring of fire, life safety systems and access control devices; and security consulting. ABM Engineering Services is the company's primary engineering subsidiary, offering on-site engineers to operate and maintain mechanical, electrical and plumbing systems at such facilities as high-rise office buildings, schools, computer centers, shopping malls, manufacturing facilities, museums and universities. The engineering segment also provides facility services through ABM Facility Services, which provides streamlined, centralized control and coordination of multiple facility service needs. In addition, this segment also provides an energy management service, which helps clients identify and amend drains on energy efficiency. The company also provides landscaping and golf services through its subsidiary OneSource. In June 2010, ABM Janitorial Services acquired janitorial services firm Diversco, Inc. from DHI HOLDINGS, Inc. In December 2010, the firm acquired The Linc Group, LLC for $300 million.

FINANCIALS: Sales and profits are in thousands of dollars—add 000 to get the full amount. 2010 Note: Financial information for 2010 was not available for all companies at press time.

2010 Sales: $3,495,747	2010 Profits: $64,121	**U.S. Stock Ticker: ABM**
2009 Sales: $3,481,823	2009 Profits: $54,293	**Int'l Ticker:** Int'l Exchange:
2008 Sales: $3,623,590	2008 Profits: $45,434	Employees: 96,000
2007 Sales: $2,706,105	2007 Profits: $52,440	Fiscal Year Ends: 10/31
2006 Sales: $2,579,351	2006 Profits: $93,205	Parent Company:

SALARIES/BENEFITS:

Pension Plan:	ESOP Stock Plan:	Profit Sharing:	Top Exec. Salary: $805,000	Bonus: $1,008,000
Savings Plan: Y	Stock Purch. Plan: Y		Second Exec. Salary: $576,250	Bonus: $270,833

OTHER THOUGHTS:

Apparent Women Officers or Directors: 4
Hot Spot for Advancement for Women/Minorities: Y

LOCATIONS: ("Y" = Yes)

West:	Southwest:	Midwest:	Southeast:	Northeast:	International:
Y	Y	Y	Y	Y	Y

ACCIONA SA

www.acciona.es

Industry Group Code: 237 Ranks within this company's industry group: Sales: 14   Profits: 17

Properties:	Financial Services:	Construction/Development:		Investments:	Specialty Services:	Brokerage:
Apartments:	Mortgages:	Commercial Construction:	Y	REIT:	Property Management:	Commercial Sales:
Malls/Shopping:	Title Insurance:	Residential Construction:			Online Services:	Residential Sales:
Offices:	Property Insurance:	Land Development:			Software/IT:	Specialty:
Hotels/Motels:		Support Services:	Y		Consulting:	
Industrial/Warehouses:		Design/Engineering:				
Other:						

TYPES OF BUSINESS:

Heavy Construction
Infrastructure Services
Road Concessions
Logistics Services
Airport Services
Passenger Ferries
Urban & Environmental Services
Alternative Energy Installation

BRANDS/DIVISIONS/AFFILIATES:

Acciona Infraestructuras SA
Acciona Agua
Acciona Facility Services
Acciona Environmental Services
Acciona Urban Services
Acciona Logistics
Acciona Airport Services
Acciona TrasMediterranea

CONTACTS: *Note: Officers with more than one job title may be intentionally listed here more than once.*

Juan Gallardo, CFO
Jorge Vega-Penichet, General Counsel/Corp. Sec.
Juan Muro-Lara, Head-Corp. Dev.
Pio Cabanillas, Chief Comm. Officer
Juan Muro-Lara, Head-Investor Rel.
Juan Ignacio Entrecanales Franco, Vice Chmn.
Pedro Martinez, Pres., Infrastructure Div.
Luis Castilla, Pres., Water Div.
Alfonso Callejo, Chief Corp. Resources Officer
Jose Manuel Entrecanales Domecq, Chmn.
Frank Gelardin, Head-Int'l

Phone: 34-91-663-28-50	Fax: 34-91-663-28-51
Toll-Free:	
Address: Ave. De Europa, 18, Parque Empresarial La Moreleja, Alcobendas, 28108 Spain	

GROWTH PLANS/SPECIAL FEATURES:

Acciona S.A. develops and manages infrastructure and related projects in Spain and internationally. The company has six primary divisions: Infrastructure; Real Estate; Energy; Water; Environmental & Urban Services; and Logistics & Transport Services. The infrastructure division includes Acciona Infrastructure SA, a leading construction and civil engineering group formed in 1850. The firm builds roads, bridges, railways, dams, canals, sewer systems, hospitals, seaports and airports, industrial facilities and municipal buildings. The real estate division is involved in property management, car park operations, apartments, shopping centers, office buildings, university campus accommodations and general real estate development. The division is currently involved in developing residential housing projects in Spain, Portugal, Mexico and Poland. The energy division is focused on the development of renewable energy facilities, primarily through the installation of wind farms and solar arrays. The water division is involved in the engineering, construction and management of drinking water plants, sewage treatment plants and reverse-osmosis desalination plants. Subsidiary Acciona Agua is involved in the building of water treatment plans and desalination plants in 20 countries, serving more than 50 million people. The environmental and urban services division offers street cleaning, municipal solid waste collection, park design and maintenance and facility management services through subsidiaries Acciona Facility Services, Acciona Environmental Services and Acciona Urban Services. The logistics and transport services division encompasses subsidiaries such as Acciona Logistics; Acciona Rail Services; Acciona Airport Services; Acciona Forwarding, a provider of logistic services, Acciona Interpress, a magazine and press distribution firm; and Acciona TrasMediterranea, a passenger ferry and cargo shipping firm. The company is active in over 30 countries across Europe, North and South America, Africa, the Middle East and Asia.

FINANCIALS: Sales and profits are in thousands of dollars—add 000 to get the full amount. 2010 Note: Financial information for 2010 was not available for all companies at press time.

2010 Sales: $9,371,870	2010 Profits: $230,820	U.S. Stock Ticker: ACXIF.PK
2009 Sales: $10,374,100	2009 Profits: $1,720,540	Int'l Ticker: ANA Int'l Exchange: Madrid-MCE
2008 Sales: $17,094,300	2008 Profits: $626,280	Employees:
2007 Sales: $10,734,400	2007 Profits: $1,282,240	Fiscal Year Ends: 12/31
2006 Sales: $7,418,400	2006 Profits: $452,500	Parent Company:

SALARIES/BENEFITS:

Pension Plan:	ESOP Stock Plan:	Profit Sharing:	Top Exec. Salary: $	Bonus: $
Savings Plan:	Stock Purch. Plan:		Second Exec. Salary: $	Bonus: $

OTHER THOUGHTS:

Apparent Women Officers or Directors: 2
Hot Spot for Advancement for Women/Minorities:

LOCATIONS: ("Y" = Yes)

West:	Southwest:	Midwest:	Southeast:	Northeast:	International:
Y		Y			Y

ACCOR NORTH AMERICA

www.accor-na.com

Industry Group Code: 721110 Ranks within this company's industry group: Sales: Profits:

Properties:	Financial Services:	Construction/Development:	Investments:	Specialty Services:	Brokerage:
Apartments:	Mortgages:	Commercial Construction:	REIT:	Property Management:	Commercial Sales:
Malls/Shopping:	Title Insurance:	Residential Construction:		Online Services:	Residential Sales:
Offices:	Property Insurance:	Land Development:		Software/IT:	Specialty:
Hotels/Motels: Y		Support Services:		Consulting:	
Industrial/Warehouses:		Design/Engineering:			
Other:					

TYPES OF BUSINESS:

Hotels

BRANDS/DIVISIONS/AFFILIATES:

Accor SA
Accor Economy Lodging
Motel 6
Studio 6
Sofitel
Novotel
Ibis

CONTACTS: *Note: Officers with more than one job title may be intentionally listed here more than once.*

Didier Bosc, CFO-Motel 6 & Studio 6
Loic Samson, Dir.-Accor Bus. & Leisure IT
John Henrich, Sr. Counsel
Sunny Bhanot, Sr. Dr. Franchise Oper.
Laura Rojo-Eddy, Dir.-Corp. Comm.
James Amorosia, Pres./COO-Motel 6 & Studio 6
Oliver Poirot, CEO-Motel 6 & Studio 6
Dave Redmond, Dir.-Oper. Support
Gaeten Mony, Dir.-Franchise Dev. Support
Bernard Rudler, Exec. VP-Int'l Dev.
Bernard Rudler, Exec. VP-Franchising & Procurement

Phone: 972-360-9000	Fax: 972-716-6590
Toll-Free:	
Address: 4001 International Parkway, Carrollton, TX 75007 US	

GROWTH PLANS/SPECIAL FEATURES:

Accor North America, a subsidiary of French hotel and human resources conglomerate Accor SA, operates more than 1,100 hotels with approximately 112,000 rooms across the U.S., Canada and Mexico. The firm's North American hotel chains include 10 Sofitel hotels, a French luxury brand that incorporates the local culture into its decor. It offers visitors first-rate accommodations with upscale restaurants, complete business facilities, fitness centers, fine art and antiques. The Novotel Chain is another of the company's more upscale offerings that consists of a relaxed modern decor that makes it accessible to both business and leisure travelers. Novotel properties offer rooms with sitting/working areas, mid-scale restaurants and pools and golf course privileges, with six locations in the U.S. and Canada. The company's Accor Economy Lodging properties brand names include Motel 6, which offers visitors only the essentials at one of the lowest prices for a national chain, with some locations offering free Wi-Fi Internet access, swimming pools and guest laundry facilities. The firm operates more than 1,000 Motel 6 locations in the U.S. and Canada. Studio 6 hotels offer extended stay lodging at fiscally convenient prices, with 50 North American locations in the central business districts of major metropolitan areas. Ibis is the company's international economy hotel that has seven locations in Mexico. It offers visitors 24/7 hotel services, an en-suite bedroom and on-site food and beverage locations. Accor incorporates a green policy into all of its chains that consists of water-saving shower heads and faucet aerators, Energy Star program participation, power-reducing heating and cooling systems, recycled paper and soy ink for its directories, energy efficient fluorescent lighting and the use of green Ecolab products for laundry and cleaning.

FINANCIALS: Sales and profits are in thousands of dollars—add 000 to get the full amount. 2010 Note: Financial information for 2010 was not available for all companies at press time.

2010 Sales: $	2010 Profits: $	U.S. Stock Ticker: Subsidiary
2009 Sales: $	2009 Profits: $	Int'l Ticker: Int'l Exchange:
2008 Sales: $	2008 Profits: $	Employees:
2007 Sales: $	2007 Profits: $	Fiscal Year Ends: 12/31
2006 Sales: $	2006 Profits: $	Parent Company: ACCOR SA

SALARIES/BENEFITS:

Pension Plan:	ESOP Stock Plan:	Profit Sharing:	Top Exec. Salary: $	Bonus: $
Savings Plan:	Stock Purch. Plan:		Second Exec. Salary: $	Bonus: $

OTHER THOUGHTS:

Apparent Women Officers or Directors: 1
Hot Spot for Advancement for Women/Minorities:

LOCATIONS: ("Y" = Yes)

West:	Southwest:	Midwest:	Southeast:	Northeast:	International:
Y	Y	Y	Y	Y	Y

ACCOR SA

www.accor.com

Industry Group Code: 721110 Ranks within this company's industry group: Sales: 2   Profits: 1

Properties:		Financial Services:	Construction/Development:	Investments:	Specialty Services:		Brokerage:
Apartments:	Y	Mortgages:	Commercial Construction:	REIT:	Property Management:	Y	Commercial Sales:
Malls/Shopping:		Title Insurance:	Residential Construction:		Online Services:		Residential Sales:
Offices:		Property Insurance:	Land Development:		Software/IT:		Specialty:
Hotels/Motels:	Y		Support Services:		Consulting:		
Industrial/Warehouses:			Design/Engineering:				
Other:							

TYPES OF BUSINESS:

Hotels

BRANDS/DIVISIONS/AFFILIATES:

Motel6
Etap
Formule 1
Novotel
Sofitel
Studio6
MGallery
Pullman

CONTACTS: *Note: Officers with more than one job title may be intentionally listed here more than once.*

Gilles Pelisson, CEO
Jacques Stern, CFO
Jean-Luc Chretien, Exec. VP-Mktg.
Patrick Ollivier, Exec. VP-Human Resources
Pascal Quint, Corp. Sec.
Jacques Stern, Sr. Exec. VP-Finance
Michael Issenberg, COO-Asia Pacific
Michael Flaxman, COO-Americas
Jacques Stern, Sr. Exec. VP-Svcs.
Yann Caillere, COO-EMEA
Gilles Pelisson, Chmn.
Serge Ragozin, COO-Worldwide
Jean-Luc Chretien, Exec. VP-Dist.

Phone: 33-0169-36-8080	Fax: 33-0169-36-7900
Toll-Free:	
Address: 2 rue de la Mare-Neuve, Evry Cedex, 91021 France	

GROWTH PLANS/SPECIAL FEATURES:

Accor SA is one of the largest hot operators, with locations around the world. Hotel operations accounted for 96% of 2010 revenue, while other business accounted for the remaining 4%. The company derives its profits primarily from France, which alone accounts for 34% of business; with 39% coming from the rest of Europe, 10% from North America, 5% from Latin America and 12% from the rest of the world. Accor has 4,229 hotels in about 100 countries worldwide. Its Motel6 locations, which are all located in the U.S. and Canada, offer standardized budget accommodations. Studio6, a similar brand, provides extended-stay amenities such as kitchen appliances, laundry and housekeeping. Etap offers budget accommodations throughout Europe with services such as wireless Internet access, snacks and an all-you-can-eat breakfast. The HotelF1 and Formule 1 brands are similar to Etap, but are offered in South Africa, Australia, Brazil, Indonesia and Japan. Accor's economy offerings include Ibis and All Seasons, which provide higher quality lodgings at modest prices. These brands can be found in Europe, Australia, Asia and Africa. The company's midscale hotels include Novotel, Suite Novotel and Mercure, and primarily cater to travelers in international cities or vacation locations. Extended stay capabilities are available through the Adagio brand. The firm's upscale hotels include Pullman, MGallery, Grand Mercure Apartments and Thalassa Sea & Spa. Brands in this category are primarily used by tourists in destination cities. Accor's premier luxury brands, Sofitel and Lenotre, provide guests with gourmet cuisine, specialized treatment and high quality sleeping amenities. In June 2010, the company announced plans to open a new luxury Sofitel hotel in Shanghai, China in 2011. In July 2010, the company demerged its services business into an independent entity known as Edenred.

FINANCIALS: Sales and profits are in thousands of dollars—add 000 to get the full amount. 2010 Note: Financial information for 2010 was not available for all companies at press time.

		U.S. Stock Ticker:
2010 Sales: $8,668,380	2010 Profits: $5,246,500	Int'l Ticker: AC Int'l Exchange: Paris-Euronext
2009 Sales: $9,351,450	2009 Profits: $-373,260	Employees: 65,170
2008 Sales: $10,730,100	2008 Profits: $810,800	Fiscal Year Ends: 12/31
2007 Sales: $11,951,184	2007 Profits: $1,299,596	Parent Company:
2006 Sales: $11,194,761	2006 Profits: $737,291	

SALARIES/BENEFITS:

Pension Plan:	ESOP Stock Plan:	Profit Sharing:	Top Exec. Salary: $	Bonus: $
Savings Plan:	Stock Purch. Plan:		Second Exec. Salary: $	Bonus: $

OTHER THOUGHTS:

Apparent Women Officers or Directors:
Hot Spot for Advancement for Women/Minorities:

LOCATIONS: ("Y" = Yes)

West:	Southwest:	Midwest:	Southeast:	Northeast:	International:
Y	Y	Y	Y	Y	Y

ACERGY SA

www.acergy-group.com

Industry Group Code: 2389 Ranks within this company's industry group: Sales: 1 Profits: 1

Properties:	Financial Services:	Construction/Development:		Investments:	Specialty Services:	Brokerage:
Apartments:	Mortgages:	Commercial Construction:		REIT:	Property Management:	Commercial Sales:
Malls/Shopping:	Title Insurance:	Residential Construction:			Online Services:	Residential Sales:
Offices:	Property Insurance:	Land Development:			Software/IT:	Specialty:
Hotels/Motels:		Support Services:	Y		Consulting:	
Industrial/Warehouses:		Design/Engineering:	Y			
Other:						

TYPES OF BUSINESS:

Offshore Platform Construction
Pipeline Construction
Offshore Support Services
Design Services
Oil Field Services

BRANDS/DIVISIONS/AFFILIATES:

NKT Flexibles
Seaway Heavy Lifting
Sapura-Acergy
Sonamet
Stanislav Yudin
Acergy M.S. Limited
Subsea 7, Inc.

CONTACTS: *Note: Officers with more than one job title may be intentionally listed here more than once.*

Jean Cahuzac, CEO
Bruno Chabas, COO
Simon Crowe, CFO
Mark Preece, VP-Mktg. & Bus. Dev.
Keith Tipson, Sr. VP-Human Resources
Allen Leatt, CTO
Allen Leatt, Sr. VP-Eng.
Johan Rasmussen, General Counsel/Sr. VP
Jean-Luc Laloe, Sr. VP-Corp. Dev.
Karen Menzel, Group Mgr.-Investor Rel.
Andy Culwell, VP-Health, Safety, Environment & Quality
Gael Cailleaux, VP-Offshore Resources
Olivier Carre, Sr. VP-Territory II
Oyvind Mikaelsen, Sr. VP-Territory I
Peter Mason, Chmn.

Phone: 44--8210-5500	Fax: 44-8210-5501
Toll-Free:	
Address: 200 Hammersmith Rd., London, W6 7DL UK	

GROWTH PLANS/SPECIAL FEATURES:

Acergy S.A., formerly Stolt Offshore S.A., is a U.K.-based company that offers contract seabed-to-surface engineering and construction for the offshore oil and gas production industry throughout the world. The company provides products and services from flowline and pipeline construction to subsea wells, umbilicals, risers and fixed or floating platforms. Acergy manages its marine assets through a global asset organization based in Aberdeen, U.K. and operates in two territories: Territory I is composed of the Northern European, Canadian, Southeast Asian and Middle Eastern operations; and Territory II, which includes activities in Africa, the Mediterranean, North America and Mexico and South America. Territory II represented 61% of the firm's revenue in 2009. The majority of the firm's activities fall into the areas of engineering, procurement, installation, and commissioning (EPIC) project delivery. Within the restraints of these activities, the company can be further branched into several additional types including deepwater operations; inspection, maintenance and repair; and conventional field development. The deepwater division provides design, installation and commissioning of subsea infrastructure, umbilical, riser and flowline systems. Inspection, maintenance and repair services includes both diver and remotely operated vehicle inspection as well as maintenance and repair services that keep oil and gas fields producing at a desired level. The conventional field development division focuses on hydrocarbon extraction and field development problems. In September 2010, Acergy received anti-trust clearance from the U.S. Federal Trade Commission and the Norwegian Competition Authority in regards to its proposed merger transaction with Subsea 7, Inc.

FINANCIALS: Sales and profits are in thousands of dollars—add 000 to get the full amount. 2010 Note: Financial information for 2010 was not available for all companies at press time.

2010 Sales: $2,369,000	2010 Profits: $313,000	**U.S. Stock Ticker: ACGY**
2009 Sales: $2,208,800	2009 Profits: $265,700	**Int'l Ticker: ACY** Int'l Exchange: Oslo-OBX
2008 Sales: $2,522,400	2008 Profits: $307,200	Employees: 6,385
2007 Sales: $2,406,300	2007 Profits: $134,500	Fiscal Year Ends: 11/30
2006 Sales: $2,124,200	2006 Profits: $236,700	Parent Company:

SALARIES/BENEFITS:

Pension Plan:	ESOP Stock Plan:	Profit Sharing:	Top Exec. Salary: $2,100,000	Bonus: $
Savings Plan:	Stock Purch. Plan:		Second Exec. Salary: $111,499	Bonus: $

OTHER THOUGHTS:

Apparent Women Officers or Directors: 1
Hot Spot for Advancement for Women/Minorities:

LOCATIONS: ("Y" = Yes)

West:	Southwest:	Midwest:	Southeast:	Northeast:	International:
	Y				Y

ACS ACTIVIDADES DE CONSTRUCCION Y SERVICIOS SA

www.grupoacs.com

Industry Group Code: 237 Ranks within this company's industry group: Sales: 5   Profits: 3

Properties:	Financial Services:	Construction/Development:		Investments:	Specialty Services:	Brokerage:
Apartments:	Mortgages:	Commercial Construction:		REIT:	Property Management:	Commercial Sales:
Malls/Shopping:	Title Insurance:	Residential Construction:			Online Services:	Residential Sales:
Offices:	Property Insurance:	Land Development:			Software/IT:	Specialty:
Hotels/Motels:		Support Services:	Y		Consulting:	
Industrial/Warehouses:		Design/Engineering:				
Other:						

TYPES OF BUSINESS:

Construction Services

BRANDS/DIVISIONS/AFFILIATES:

Dragados SA
Vias Y Construcciones SA
Dravo S.A.
Iridium Concesiones de Infraestructuras SA
Dragados SPL
Cobra Gestion de Infraestructuras SA
Abertis Infraestructuras SA
John Picone Inc

CONTACTS: *Note: Officers with more than one job title may be intentionally listed here more than once.*

Florentino Perez Rodriguez, CEO
Jose Luis del Valle Perez, Sec. Gen.
Eugenio Llorente Gomez, CEO-Cobra Group
Marcelino Fernandez Verdes, CEO-Dragados
Antonio Garcia Ferrer, Exec. Vice Chmn.
Angel Garcia Altozano, Corp. Gen. Mgr.
Florentino Perez Rodriguez, Exec. Chmn.

Phone: 34-91-3439200	Fax: 34-91-3439456
Toll-Free:	
Address: Avenida Pio XII 102, Madrid, 28036 Spain	

GROWTH PLANS/SPECIAL FEATURES:

ACS Actividades de Construccion Y Servicios S.A. is a Spanish-based construction group. The company and its subsidiaries are involved in four operating areas: construction (civil works, residential and non-residential building); concessions; environmental and facility management; and industrial services. The group's primary construction subsidiaries include Dragados S.A., a general-purpose contracting firm; Vias Y Construcciones S.A., a builder of railways; Drace Medio Ambiente water and waste treatment plant specialists; Flota Proyectos Singulares maritime and port specialists; Seis modular and pre-fabricated construction; Dravo S.A. dredging and beach reconstruction specialists; Geocisa foundation and land engineering; Tecsa specialized railway projects; Dycvensa civil works in Venezuela; Dycasa roadway construction in Argentina; Cogesa real-estate; Pol-Aqua civil works in Poland; Pulice roads and highways; and John Picone tunnels and infrastructure in the U.S. The firm has been involved in several major civil works and building projects, many of which are in Spain. The concessions division, through Iridium Concesiones de Infraestructuras, S.A., is involved in project identification, financing, and all activities related. The environmental segment, which includes Urbaser S.A.; Dragados S.P.L.; and Clece S.A., works to deal with waste handling and transportation management. The industrial services segment, through Cobra Gestion de Infraestructuras, S.A. and Dragados Industrial, builds, operates and maintains industrial and energy infrastructure. The company also invests in the infrastructure and energy sectors through its Abertis, Iberdrola, Hochtief subsidiaries. The company is active in over 40 countries worldwide.

FINANCIALS: Sales and profits are in thousands of dollars—add 000 to get the full amount. 2010 Note: Financial information for 2010 was not available for all companies at press time.

2010 Sales: $22,296,400	2010 Profits: $1,898,350	**U.S. Stock Ticker:**
2009 Sales: $21,045,400	2009 Profits: $2,607,980	**Int'l Ticker: ACS** Int'l Exchange: Madrid-MCE
2008 Sales: $20,786,400	2008 Profits: $2,412,200	Employees:
2007 Sales: $20,917,300	2007 Profits: $2,072,890	Fiscal Year Ends: 12/31
2006 Sales: $	2006 Profits: $	Parent Company:

SALARIES/BENEFITS:

Pension Plan:	ESOP Stock Plan:	Profit Sharing:	Top Exec. Salary: $	Bonus: $
Savings Plan:	Stock Purch. Plan:		Second Exec. Salary: $	Bonus: $

OTHER THOUGHTS:

Apparent Women Officers or Directors:
Hot Spot for Advancement for Women/Minorities:

LOCATIONS: ("Y" = Yes)

West:	Southwest:	Midwest:	Southeast:	Northeast:	International:
				Y	Y

ADVOCAT INC

www.advocat-inc.com

Industry Group Code: 623110 Ranks within this company's industry group: Sales: 5 Profits: 4

Properties:	Financial Services:	Construction/Development:	Investments:	Specialty Services:	Brokerage:
Apartments:	Mortgages:	Commercial Construction:	REIT:	Property Management:	Commercial Sales:
Malls/Shopping:	Title Insurance:	Residential Construction:		Online Services:	Residential Sales:
Offices:	Property Insurance:	Land Development:		Software/IT:	Specialty:
Hotels/Motels:		Support Services:		Consulting:	
Industrial/Warehouses:		Design/Engineering:			
Other: Y					

TYPES OF BUSINESS:

Nursing Homes
Assisted Living Facilities

BRANDS/DIVISIONS/AFFILIATES:

CONTACTS: *Note: Officers with more than one job title may be intentionally listed here more than once.*

William R. Council, III, CEO
Kelly J. Gill, COO/Exec. VP
William R. Council, III, Pres.
L. Glynn Riddle, Jr., CFO/Exec. VP
David Houghton, CIO
Raymond L. Tyler, Sr. VP-Nursing Home Oper.
Wallace E. Olson, Chmn.

Phone: 615-771-7575	**Fax:** 615-771-7409
Toll-Free:	
Address: 1621 Galleria Blvd., Brentwood, TN 37027 US	

GROWTH PLANS/SPECIAL FEATURES:

Advocat, Inc. provides long-term care services to nursing home patients and residents of assisted living facilities in eight states, primarily in the Southeast. The company's operations consist of 46 nursing homes containing approximately 5,364 licensed nursing beds. Facilities are located in the states of Alabama, Arkansas, Florida, Kentucky, Ohio, Tennessee, Texas and West Virginia. The firm's nursing centers provide traditional nursing and social services usually provided in long-term care facilities, including skilled nursing health care services such as medication dispensing and plan of care development for each resident; nutrition services; recreational therapy; social services; and housekeeping and laundry services. Additionally, Advocat offers a variety of rehabilitative, nutritional, respiratory and other specialized ancillary services. These specialty services include rehabilitation therapy services, such as audiology, speech, occupational and physical therapies, which are provided through licensed therapists and registered nurses; and the provision of medical supplies, nutritional support, infusion therapies, and related clinical services. The majority of these services are provided using internal resources and clinicians. Many of its nursing centers include specialty sub-units designed to meet the needs of special care patients, including 19 facilities equipped with Life Steps units for patients requiring short-term rehabilitation following an incident such as a stroke, joint replacement or bone fracture; and 22 facilities with Lighthouse units for advanced care for patients suffering from dementia related disorders. Other specialty care services include one adult day care facility and specialty programming for bariatric patients - generally, patients weighing more than 350 pounds.

FINANCIALS: Sales and profits are in thousands of dollars—add 000 to get the full amount. 2010 Note: Financial information for 2010 was not available for all companies at press time.

2010 Sales: $290,130	2010 Profits: $3,849	**U.S. Stock Ticker:** AVCA
2009 Sales: $276,979	2009 Profits: $2,601	**Int'l Ticker:** **Int'l Exchange:**
2008 Sales: $263,837	2008 Profits: $5,735	**Employees:** 5,600
2007 Sales: $243,907	2007 Profits: $9,387	**Fiscal Year Ends:** 12/31
2006 Sales: $214,653	2006 Profits: $22,395	**Parent Company:**

SALARIES/BENEFITS:

Pension Plan:	ESOP Stock Plan:	Profit Sharing:	Top Exec. Salary: $442,000	Bonus: $47,000
Savings Plan: Y	Stock Purch. Plan:		Second Exec. Salary: $264,000	Bonus: $17,000

OTHER THOUGHTS:

Apparent Women Officers or Directors:
Hot Spot for Advancement for Women/Minorities:

LOCATIONS: ("Y" = Yes)

West:	Southwest:	Midwest:	Southeast:	Northeast:	International:
	Y	Y	Y	Y	

AECOM TECHNOLOGY CORPORATION

www.aecom.com

Industry Group Code: 237 Ranks within this company's industry group: Sales: 20 Profits: 15

Properties:	Financial Services:	Construction/Development:		Investments:	Specialty Services:	Brokerage:
Apartments:	Mortgages:	Commercial Construction:		REIT:	Property Management:	Commercial Sales:
Malls/Shopping:	Title Insurance:	Residential Construction:			Online Services:	Residential Sales:
Offices:	Property Insurance:	Land Development:	Y		Software/IT:	Specialty:
Hotels/Motels:		Support Services:			Consulting:	
Industrial/Warehouses:		Design/Engineering:	Y			
Other:						

TYPES OF BUSINESS:

Engineering & Design Services
Transportation Projects
Environmental Projects
Power & Mining Support
Consulting
Economic Development Consulting

BRANDS/DIVISIONS/AFFILIATES:

AGS
CTE
DMJM Aviation
Faber Maunsell
Tishman Construction Corp.
McNeil Technologies, Inc.
Davis Langdon
RSW Inc

CONTACTS: *Note: Officers with more than one job title may be intentionally listed here more than once.*

John M. Dionisio, CEO
John M. Dionisio, Pres.
Michael S. Burke, CFO/Sr. VP
Ian R. MacLeod, Sr. VP-Human Resources
Raul Cruz, CIO/Sr. VP
James T. Walsh, CTO/Sr. VP
Nancy Laben, General Counsel/Sr. VP-Legal
Bob Pell, Sr. VP-Oper./Chief Integration Officer
Alan P. Krusi, Exec. VP-Corp. Dev.
Paul J. Gennaro, Jr., Chief Comm. Officer
Eric Chen, Sr. VP-Finance
Glenn R. Robson, Chief Strategy Officer/Sr. VP-Finance
Gary Lawrence, Chief Sustainability Officer/VP
Robert Andrews, Global Managing Dir.-Water
Luc Benoit, Global Managing Dir.-Energy
Richard G. Newman, Chmn.
Dickson Lo, CEO-Asia

Phone: 213-593-8000	Fax: 213-593-8730
Toll-Free:	
Address: 555 S. Flower St., Ste. 3700, Los Angeles, CA 90071-2300 US	

GROWTH PLANS/SPECIAL FEATURES:

AECOM Technology Corporation is a global engineering and design company engaged in facility, transportation, environment and specialty engineering projects for corporate, institutional and government clients. Its operations are divided into two segments: Professional Technical Services (PTS) and Management Support Services (MSS). The PTS segment provides planning; consulting; architectural and engineering design; and program and construction management services to clients in the transportation, facilities, energy, water and government markets. Transportation services include feasibility studies, planning, design, engineering, construction management and asset management for transit and rail, highway, bridge, port, harbor and airport projects. The firm's facility design and construction projects encompass land development assignments and a wide variety of building projects. For the energy sector, it offers design, construction management and commissioning services. AECOM offers water resource, wastewater, wet weather, hazardous waste management and other environmental engineering services. The MSS segment provides program and facilities management and maintenance, training, logistics, consulting, technical assistance and systems integration services, primarily for agencies of the U.S. government. The company operates largely through a network of subsidiaries, including AGS, AECOM's government services arm; CTE, an infrastructure engineering firm; DMJM Aviation, the firm's flagship aviation design and construction management company; Faber Maunsell, a European engineering consultancy firm; Metcalf & Eddy, an environmental engineering group; Hayes, Seay, Mattern & Mattern, Inc., an architectural and engineering firm; and PADCO, a firm that promotes sustainable economic development in more than 100 countries. In July 2010, the firm acquired Tishman Construction Corp. In August 2010, it acquired McNeil Technologies, Inc. In November 2010, AECOM acquired Davis Langdon and RSW Inc.

The company offers its employees medical, dental and life insurance; a stock purchase program with company match; a 401(k) and Roth IRA; and a merit based scholarship program for the children of employees.

FINANCIALS: Sales and profits are in thousands of dollars—add 000 to get the full amount. 2010 Note: Financial information for 2010 was not available for all companies at press time.

2010 Sales: $6,545,791	2010 Profits: $249,344	**U.S. Stock Ticker: ACM**
2009 Sales: $6,119,465	2009 Profits: $189,696	**Int'l Ticker:** Int'l Exchange:
2008 Sales: $5,194,482	2008 Profits: $147,226	Employees: 48,100
2007 Sales: $4,237,270	2007 Profits: $100,297	Fiscal Year Ends: 9/30
2006 Sales: $3,421,492	2006 Profits: $53,686	Parent Company:

SALARIES/BENEFITS:

Pension Plan: Y	ESOP Stock Plan:	Profit Sharing:	Top Exec. Salary: $997,506	Bonus: $3,000,000
Savings Plan: Y	Stock Purch. Plan: Y		Second Exec. Salary: $650,021	Bonus: $1,000,000

OTHER THOUGHTS:

Apparent Women Officers or Directors: 4
Hot Spot for Advancement for Women/Minorities: Y

LOCATIONS: ("Y" = Yes)

West:	Southwest:	Midwest:	Southeast:	Northeast:	International:
Y	Y	Y	Y	Y	Y

AECON GROUP INC

www.aecon.com

Industry Group Code: 237 Ranks within this company's industry group: Sales: 24   Profits: 25

Properties:	Financial Services:	Construction/Development:		Investments:	Specialty Services:	Brokerage:
Apartments:	Mortgages:	Commercial Construction:	Y	REIT:	Property Management:	Commercial Sales:
Malls/Shopping:	Title Insurance:	Residential Construction:			Online Services:	Residential Sales:
Offices:	Property Insurance:	Land Development:			Software/IT:	Specialty:
Hotels/Motels:		Support Services:	Y		Consulting:	
Industrial/Warehouses:		Design/Engineering:	Y			
Other:						

TYPES OF BUSINESS:

Construction
Infrastructure Development
Utility Systems
Steam Power Generation
Renovation

BRANDS/DIVISIONS/AFFILIATES:

Aecon Concessions
Aecon Buildings
Aecon Civil & Utilities
Lockerbie & Hole, Inc.
Aecon Atlantic
Group Aecon Quebec Ltee.
Innovative Steam Technologies, Inc.
South Rock, Ltd.

CONTACTS: *Note: Officers with more than one job title may be intentionally listed here more than once.*

John M. Beck, CEO
Scott C. Balfour, Pres.
David Smales, CFO/Exec. VP
Mitch Patten, VP-Human Resources
Bruce Fleming, CIO/VP
L. Brian Swartz, Sr. VP-Legal Svcs.
Mitch Patten, Sr. VP-Corp. Affairs
Gerard A. Kelly, Sr. VP-Finance
Terrance L. McKibbon, CEO-Aecon Infrastructure
Paul P. Koenderman, Exec. VP/CEO-Aecon Industrial Group
Steven Nackan, Pres., Aecon Concessions
Frank Ross, Pres., Aecon Buildings
John M. Beck, Chmn.

Phone: 416-293-7004	Fax: 416-754-8736
Toll-Free: 877-232-2677	
Address: 20 Carlson Ct., Ste. 800, Toronto, ON M9W 7K6 Canada	

GROWTH PLANS/SPECIAL FEATURES:

Aecon Group, Inc. is one of Canada's largest construction and infrastructure development companies. The firm operates in four principal segments: Buildings, Infrastructure, Industrial and Concessions. The Buildings segment provides construction and construction management, retrofit and renovation, design build, general contracting and green construction services for commercial office buildings, institutional and educational facilities, retail facilities, multi-unit residential properties, industrial buildings and high technology, health care, environment, hospitality, government and aviation buildings. The Infrastructure segment, through its various business units, provides all aspects of the construction of both public and private infrastructure, including roads, highways, bridges, airport facilities, dams, tunnels, marine facilities, transit systems and power projects. This segment also offers design, project management and construction management services; and utility infrastructure services for gas projects, hydro distribution networks, telecommunication networks, water mains and sewers. The Industrial segment encompasses all of Aecon Group's industrial construction and manufacturing activities, including platform construction and assembly, as well as installation and maintenance for specialized industrial systems and equipment. Activities within the Concessions segment include the development, financing and operation of infrastructure projects by way of build-operate-transfer and other public-private partnership contract structures. In March 2010, the company acquired GCCL Contracting Ltd., an Ontario-based asphalt, paving and construction company. In August 2010, the firm acquired the assets of Cow Harbour Construction Ltd. and will roll that business into a new division within the Infrastructure segment called Aecon Mining. In September 2010, the company announced the restructuring of its Buildings division, such that it will now form part of the expanded Infrastructure Group while still operating as a separate business unit.

Aecon Group offers its employees medical, dental, life insurance and disability plans; an employee stock purchase program; group home and auto insurance; and an employee assistance program.

FINANCIALS: Sales and profits are in thousands of dollars—add 000 to get the full amount. 2010 Note: Financial information for 2010 was not available for all companies at press time.

2010 Sales: $2,871,780	2010 Profits: $28,550	**U.S. Stock Ticker:**
2009 Sales: $2,196,360	2009 Profits: $43,130	**Int'l Ticker: ARE** Int'l Exchange: Toronto-TSX
2008 Sales: $1,492,630	2008 Profits: $47,160	Employees:
2007 Sales: $1,187,260	2007 Profits: $38,410	Fiscal Year Ends: 12/31
2006 Sales: $1,091,000	2006 Profits: $11,300	Parent Company:

SALARIES/BENEFITS:

Pension Plan: Y	ESOP Stock Plan:	Profit Sharing:	Top Exec. Salary: $489,770	Bonus: $946,894
Savings Plan: Y	Stock Purch. Plan: Y		Second Exec. Salary: $431,781	Bonus: $834,782

OTHER THOUGHTS:

Apparent Women Officers or Directors:
Hot Spot for Advancement for Women/Minorities:

LOCATIONS: ("Y" = Yes)

West:	Southwest:	Midwest:	Southeast:	Northeast:	International:
Y					Y

ALEXANDRIA REAL ESTATE EQUITIES INC

www.labspace.com

Industry Group Code: 531120 Ranks within this company's industry group: Sales: 35   Profits: 15

Properties:		Financial Services:	Construction/Development:	Investments:	Specialty Services:		Brokerage:
Apartments:		Mortgages:	Commercial Construction:	REIT: Y	Property Management: Y		Commercial Sales:
Malls/Shopping: Y		Title Insurance:	Residential Construction:		Online Services:		Residential Sales:
Offices: Y		Property Insurance:	Land Development:		Software/IT:		Specialty:
Hotels/Motels:			Support Services:		Consulting:		
Industrial/Warehouses:			Design/Engineering:				
Other: Y							

TYPES OF BUSINESS:

Real Estate Investment Trust
Scientific Properties
Office & Laboratory Space
Property Development

BRANDS/DIVISIONS/AFFILIATES:

CONTACTS: *Note: Officers with more than one job title may be intentionally listed here more than once.*

Joel S. Marcus, CEO
Joel S. Marcus, Pres.
Dean A. Shigenaga, CFO
Joel S. Marcus, Chmn.

Phone: 626-578-0777	**Fax:** 626-578-0896
Toll-Free:	
Address: 385 E. Colorado Blvd., Ste. 299, Pasadena, CA 91101 US	

GROWTH PLANS/SPECIAL FEATURES:

Alexandria Real Estate Equities, Inc. is a real estate investment trust (REIT) that owns, acquires, operates, manages, expands and redevelops scientific properties containing a mixture of office and laboratory space. Alexandria's portfolio currently consists of 167 properties, 163 in ten U.S. states and four in Canada, comprising approximately 13.7 million rentable square feet of office/laboratory space. The company's portfolio also includes five land parcels with 475,000 rentable square feet undergoing ground-up development and an imbedded pipeline for future ground-up development, approximating 12.7 million developable square feet. The firm focuses its activities principally in the life science markets of California (in the San Diego and San Francisco Bay areas); Seattle; suburban Washington, D.C. (both in Maryland and Virginia); greater Boston; New Jersey; New York City; suburban Philadelphia; and the Southeast, as well as certain parts of Canada. The company's goal is to acquire high-quality life science facilities that it can then expand or to redevelop existing office, warehouse or vacant space into generic laboratory space. Its properties are leased principally to tenants in a broad spectrum of sectors within the life science industry, such as institutional (universities and independent not-for-profit institutions), pharmaceutical, biopharmaceutical, medical device, life science product, service and translational entities, as well as government agencies. Some of its tenants include Eli Lilly and Company; ZymoGenetics; GlaxoSmithKline; the Massachusetts Institute of Technology; Theravance; Genentech; Quest Diagnostics, Inc.; Johnson & Johnson; and the U.S. government.

FINANCIALS: Sales and profits are in thousands of dollars—add 000 to get the full amount. 2010 Note: Financial information for 2010 was not available for all companies at press time.

2010 Sales: $487,303	2010 Profits: $139,022	**U.S. Stock Ticker: ARE**
2009 Sales: $483,172	2009 Profits: $141,648	**Int'l Ticker:** Int'l Exchange:
2008 Sales: $455,234	2008 Profits: $120,097	Employees: 151
2007 Sales: $388,339	2007 Profits: $89,980	Fiscal Year Ends: 12/31
2006 Sales: $302,061	2006 Profits: $73,416	Parent Company:

SALARIES/BENEFITS:

Pension Plan:	ESOP Stock Plan:	Profit Sharing:	Top Exec. Salary: $500,000	Bonus: $392,500
Savings Plan:	Stock Purch. Plan:		Second Exec. Salary: $305,000	Bonus: $152,500

OTHER THOUGHTS:

Apparent Women Officers or Directors:
Hot Spot for Advancement for Women/Minorities:

LOCATIONS: ("Y" = Yes)

West:	Southwest:	Midwest:	Southeast:	Northeast:	International:
Y				Y	Y

ALLY FINANCIAL INC

www.ally.com

Industry Group Code: 522220 Ranks within this company's industry group: Sales: 2   Profits: 2

Properties:	Financial Services:		Construction/Development:	Investments:	Specialty Services:	Brokerage:
Apartments:	Mortgages:	Y	Commercial Construction:	REIT:	Property Management:	Commercial Sales:
Malls/Shopping:	Title Insurance:		Residential Construction:		Online Services:	Residential Sales:
Offices:	Property Insurance:	Y	Land Development:		Software/IT:	Specialty:
Hotels/Motels:			Support Services:		Consulting:	
Industrial/Warehouses:			Design/Engineering:			
Other:						

TYPES OF BUSINESS:

Automobile Financing
Mortgage Banking
Insurance
Commercial Mortgages
Residential Mortgages

BRANDS/DIVISIONS/AFFILIATES:

GMAC Inc
ResMor Trust
Residential Capital LLC (ResCap)
Ally Bank

CONTACTS: Note: Officers with more than one job title may be intentionally listed here more than once.

Michael A. Carpenter, CEO
William F. Muir, Pres.
James G. Mackey, Interim CFO
Sanjay Gupta, Chief Mktg. Officer
James Duffy, Chief Human Resources Officer
Barbara A. Yastine, Chief Admin. Officer
William B. Solomon, Jr., General Counsel
Gina Proia, Chief Comm. Officer
Jeffrey Brown, Treas.
Michele E. Lieber, Chief Public Policy Officer
William (Bill) Hall, Jr., Pres./CEO-Ally Commercial Finance LLC
Thomas Marano, CEO-Mortgage Oper./Capital Finance
Corey Pinkston, Head-Corp. Debt & Equity
Franklin W. Hobbs, Chmn.

Phone:	Fax: 815-282-6156
Toll-Free: 866-710-4623	
Address: 200 Renaissance Ctr., P.O. Box 200, Detroit, MI 48265-2000 US	

GROWTH PLANS/SPECIAL FEATURES:

Ally Financial, Inc., formerly GMAC, Inc., is a global financial services company providing automotive finance and residential mortgage services in roughly 37 countries. Ally operates in three primary business lines: Global Automotive Services; Mortgage; and Corporate and Other. The Global Automotive Services division offers over 18,000 dealers globally a wide range of financial services and insurance products, including new and used vehicle inventory financing, inventory insurance, working capital and capital improvement loans and vehicle remarketing services; and consumer and commercial insurance products. The Mortgage business division is divided between the firm's origination and servicing operations and its legacy portfolio operations. The former segment's operations consist of the origination of conforming and government-insured residential mortgage loans in the U.S. and the origination and purchase government-insured residential mortgage loans in Canada. Ally originates and purchases about 300,000 loans annually. Loan origination is conducted through Ally Bank in the U.S. and in ResMor Trust in Canada. The company's legacy portfolio operations relate to loans originated before 2009. The Corporate and other business division consists of Ally's commercial finance group, which provides senior secured commercial lending products to small and medium sized businesses. The U.S. Treasury department owns roughly 75% of Ally. In recent years, the U.S. federal government injected a total of $14.5 billion into GMAC in efforts to keep the firm afloat. Following GM's bankruptcy filing, the company announced that it would not be seeking bankruptcy protection. In March 2010, the firm sold its U.S. consumer property and casualty insurance business. In May 2010, the firm changed its name to Ally Financial, Inc. In October 2010, subsidiary Residential Capital LLC sold its European mortgage assets and operations.

Ally offers its employees health, dental, vision, life and disability insurance; tuition reimbursement; adoption assistance; non-smokers' discounts and smoking cessation programs; and a 401(k) plan.

FINANCIALS: Sales and profits are in thousands of dollars—add 000 to get the full amount. 2010 Note: Financial information for 2010 was not available for all companies at press time.

2010 Sales: $11,447,000	2010 Profits: $1,075,000	**U.S. Stock Ticker: Private**
2009 Sales: $13,444,000	2009 Profits: $-10,298,000	**Int'l Ticker:** Int'l Exchange:
2008 Sales: $18,395,000	2008 Profits: $1,868,000	Employees: 22,700
2007 Sales: $21,187,000	2007 Profits: $-2,332,000	Fiscal Year Ends: 12/31
2006 Sales: $23,103,000	2006 Profits: $2,125,000	Parent Company:

SALARIES/BENEFITS:

Pension Plan:	ESOP Stock Plan:	Profit Sharing:	Top Exec. Salary: $	Bonus: $
Savings Plan: Y	Stock Purch. Plan:		Second Exec. Salary: $	Bonus: $

OTHER THOUGHTS:

Apparent Women Officers or Directors: 4
Hot Spot for Advancement for Women/Minorities: Y

LOCATIONS: ("Y" = Yes)

West:	Southwest:	Midwest:	Southeast:	Northeast:	International:
Y	Y	Y	Y	Y	Y

AMAN RESORTS

www.amanresorts.com

Industry Group Code: 721110 Ranks within this company's industry group: Sales: Profits:

Properties:		Financial Services:	Construction/Development:	Investments:	Specialty Services:	Brokerage:
Apartments:		Mortgages:	Commercial Construction:	REIT:	Property Management:	Commercial Sales:
Malls/Shopping:		Title Insurance:	Residential Construction:		Online Services:	Residential Sales:
Offices:		Property Insurance:	Land Development:		Software/IT:	Specialty:
Hotels/Motels:	Y		Support Services:		Consulting:	
Industrial/Warehouses:			Design/Engineering:			
Other:						

TYPES OF BUSINESS:

Hotels & Resorts

BRANDS/DIVISIONS/AFFILIATES:

DLF Limited
Aman-i-Khas
Amandari
Amankora
Amansara
Le Melezin
Amangani
Aman at Summer Palace

CONTACTS: *Note: Officers with more than one job title may be intentionally listed here more than once.*

K. P. Singh, Exec. Chmn.-DLF Limited

Phone: 65-6883-2555	Fax: 65-6883-0555
Toll-Free: 800-477-9780	
Address: 1 Orchard Spring Ln., #05-01 Tourism Ct., Singapore, 247729 Singapore	

GROWTH PLANS/SPECIAL FEATURES:

Aman Resorts (also known as Amanresorts), majority-owned by DLF Limited, owns and operates luxury resorts. The company name derives from the Sanskrit word aman, meaning peace. Since opening its first location, the Amanpuri (meaning place of peace) in Phuket, Thailand in 1988, the firm has expanded to operating 24 resorts in 15 countries, mostly in and around Southeast Asia. These resorts are small, ranging from 10 luxurious, air-conditioned tents at the Aman-i-Khas, located near a wildlife sanctuary in Ranthambhore, India, to the 70 pavilions and villas in Amanpuri. In total, the firm offers more than 800 private rooms, suites, villas, tents, bungalows and pavilions, with an average size of 40 rooms per resort. Besides those listed above, its other resorts include Amandari, Amankila, Amanusa, Amanwana and Amanjiwo, all located in Indonesia. Amankora is spread across five towns in Bhutan; Amansara is in Cambodia; and Amanpulo is in the Philippines. Hotel Bora Bora in French Polynesia is currently closed for renovations. Amanbagh and Aman New Delhi comprise its other Indian locations. Amangalla and Amanwella are in Sri Lanka. Amanjena is in Marrakech, Morocco. Amanyara is located in Turks and Caicos, in the Caribbean. Le Melezin is in Courcheval, France, while Amangani is in Wyoming, near the Grand Tetons and Yellowstone. Another U.S. property, Amangiri, is a small 34 suite resort in Southern Utah. The firm also recently opened an Aman Spa in The Connaught Hotel in Mayfair, London. The company sources the decor for its resorts locally, in order to reflect the natural surroundings and local cultures. In early 2010, the Amanfayun resort, featuring a spa, tea house and restaurants, modeled after an ancient Chinese village, was opened in China near Hangzhou.

FINANCIALS: Sales and profits are in thousands of dollars—add 000 to get the full amount. 2010 Note: Financial information for 2010 was not available for all companies at press time.

2010 Sales: $	2010 Profits: $	U.S. Stock Ticker: Subsidiary
2009 Sales: $	2009 Profits: $	Int'l Ticker: Int'l Exchange:
2008 Sales: $	2008 Profits: $	Employees:
2007 Sales: $	2007 Profits: $	Fiscal Year Ends:
2006 Sales: $	2006 Profits: $	Parent Company: DLF LIMITED

SALARIES/BENEFITS:

Pension Plan:	ESOP Stock Plan:	Profit Sharing:	Top Exec. Salary: $	Bonus: $
Savings Plan:	Stock Purch. Plan:		Second Exec. Salary: $	Bonus: $

OTHER THOUGHTS:

Apparent Women Officers or Directors:
Hot Spot for Advancement for Women/Minorities:

LOCATIONS: ("Y" = Yes)

West:	Southwest:	Midwest:	Southeast:	Northeast:	International:
Y					Y

AMB PROPERTY CORPORATION

www.amb.com

Industry Group Code: 5311 Ranks within this company's industry group: Sales: 24   Profits: 25

Properties:		Financial Services:	Construction/Development:	Investments:	Specialty Services:		Brokerage:
Apartments:		Mortgages:	Commercial Construction:	REIT: Y	Property Management: Y		Commercial Sales:
Malls/Shopping:		Title Insurance:	Residential Construction:		Online Services:		Residential Sales:
Offices:		Property Insurance:	Land Development:		Software/IT:		Specialty:
Hotels/Motels:			Support Services:		Consulting:		
Industrial/Warehouses:	Y		Design/Engineering:				
Other:							

TYPES OF BUSINESS:

Real Estate Operations- Industrial
Port Facilities
Distribution Centers

BRANDS/DIVISIONS/AFFILIATES:

AMB Capital Partners LLC
AMB Property LP
AMB Industrial Business Indicator
AMB Mexico Fondo Logistico
AMB Brazil Logistics Partners Fund I LP
ProLogis

CONTACTS: *Note: Officers with more than one job title may be intentionally listed here more than once.*

Hamid R. Moghadam, CEO
Thomas S. Olinger, CFO
Tracy A. Ward, VP-Corp. Comm.
Tracy A. Ward, VP-Investor Rel.
Eugene F. Reilly, Pres., The Americas
Guy F. Jaquier, Pres., Private Capital
Maria Salazar Lukens, Dir.-Investor Rel.
Hamid R. Moghadam, Chmn.
Guy F. Jaquier, Pres., Europe & Asia

Phone: 415-394-9000	Fax: 415-394-9001
Toll-Free:	
Address: Pier 1, Bay 1, San Francisco, CA 94111 US	

GROWTH PLANS/SPECIAL FEATURES:

AMB Property Corporation is a global owner, acquirer, developer and operator of industrial distribution properties, such as logistics facilities, centers or warehouses; distribution facilities, centers or warehouses, throughout North America, Europe and Asia. The company's portfolio of owned and managed properties and renovation and development projects spans 158.4 million square feet in 49 markets within 15 countries. Through its primary operating subsidiary company, AMB Property, L.P., AMB invests in high-throughput distribution centers that have a variety of characteristics allowing for the rapid point-to-point transport of goods, including numerous dock doors, shallower building depths, fewer columns, large truck courts and more space for trailer parking. These facilities function best when located in convenient proximity to transportation infrastructure such as major airports and seaports. Target customer sectors include freight forwarders, third-party logistics companies, integrators, retailers, consumer products, airlines and cargo handlers. The firm's AMB Capital Partners LLC subsidiary co-invests with private capital sources instead of shareholder investments. Recently, the company launched the AMB Industrial Business Indicator (AMB IBI), a diffusion index that combines information from customers with economic variables to study business activity in the industrial real estate market. In August 2010, the firm announced the creation of AMB Mexico Fondo Logistico, a co-investment venture for the development, acquisition and operation of industrial distribution facilities in Mexico. In December 2010, the company launched AMB Brazil Logistics Partners Fund I, L.P., for the development and management of logistics properties in Brazil. In January 2011, AMB agreed to merge with ProLogis, a distribution facilities provider, with AMB as the surviving company. Following the merger, AMB would be renamed ProLogis.

Employees are offered medical, dental and vision insurance; flexible spending accounts; life insurance; disability coverage; a retirement plan; a bonus program; wellness programs; education reimbursement; a stock option plan; and an employee assistance program.

FINANCIALS: Sales and profits are in thousands of dollars—add 000 to get the full amount. 2010 Note: Financial information for 2010 was not available for all companies at press time.

2010 Sales: $633,500	2010 Profits: $27,119	**U.S. Stock Ticker:** AMB
2009 Sales: $618,424	2009 Profits: $-43,001	**Int'l Ticker:** Int'l Exchange:
2008 Sales: $693,842	2008 Profits: $-49,310	Employees:
2007 Sales: $650,886	2007 Profits: $314,260	Fiscal Year Ends: 12/31
2006 Sales: $712,391	2006 Profits: $224,072	Parent Company:

SALARIES/BENEFITS:

Pension Plan: Y	ESOP Stock Plan:	Profit Sharing:	Top Exec. Salary: $613,250	Bonus: $1,200,000
Savings Plan:	Stock Purch. Plan:		Second Exec. Salary: $390,250	Bonus: $530,000

OTHER THOUGHTS:

Apparent Women Officers or Directors: 3
Hot Spot for Advancement for Women/Minorities: Y

LOCATIONS: ("Y" = Yes)

West:	Southwest:	Midwest:	Southeast:	Northeast:	International:
Y	Y	Y	Y	Y	Y

AMEC PLC

www.amec.com

Industry Group Code: 237 Ranks within this company's industry group: Sales: 21   Profits: 12

Properties:	Financial Services:	Construction/Development:		Investments:	Specialty Services:	Brokerage:
Apartments:	Mortgages:	Commercial Construction:		REIT:	Property Management:	Commercial Sales:
Malls/Shopping:	Title Insurance:	Residential Construction:			Online Services:	Residential Sales:
Offices:	Property Insurance:	Land Development:			Software/IT:	Specialty:
Hotels/Motels:		Support Services:	Y		Consulting:	
Industrial/Warehouses:		Design/Engineering:	Y			
Other:						

TYPES OF BUSINESS:

Architectural & Engineering Services
Commercial & Heavy Construction
Environmental Services
Nuclear Power Services
Renewable Energy Services
Support & Maintenance Services
Consulting
Mining

BRANDS/DIVISIONS/AFFILIATES:

Entec Holdings Ltd
SZPE AMEC
Zektingroup
BCI Engineers and Scientists, Inc.
qedi

CONTACTS: Note: Officers with more than one job title may be intentionally listed here more than once.

Samir Brikho, CEO
Neil Bruce, COO
Ian McHoul, CFO
Keith Bradford, Dir.-Human Resources
Eleanor Evans, General Counsel
Francois-Philippe Champagne, Dir.-Strategic Dev.
Sue Scholes, Dir.-Comm.
Sue Scholes, Dir.-Investor Rel.
Hisham Mahmoud, Pres., Earth & Environmental Div.
Tony Cruddas, Pres., Growth Regions
John Pearson, Managing Dir.-Natural Resources
Jock Green-Armytage, Chmn.

Phone: 44-20-7539-5800	Fax: 44-20-7539-5900
Toll-Free:	
Address: 76 - 78 Old St., London, EC1V 9RU UK	

GROWTH PLANS/SPECIAL FEATURES:

AMEC plc, headquartered in London, is a global engineering and construction management firm with operations in more than 40 countries worldwide. Its operations are divided into three primary segments: Natural Resources; Power & Process; and Earth & Environmental. The Natural Resources segment focuses on the oil and gas, oil sands and mining industries. Services include design, delivery, commissioning and decommissioning of oil and gas facilities, surface mining and oil sands engineering services, as well as minerals and metals mining consultancy, design and project management. The Power & Process segment is concerned with power transmission and distribution, nuclear power, renewables, bio-process energy and conventional power delivery. The company's nuclear service areas include new build, the licensing, regulatory and project support; reactor support, life time extension and asset performance improvement; clean up, specialist decommissioning and waste management services; and nuclear defense, engineering and technical services. The power and utilities sector includes engineering; project management; risk and reputation management; environmental impact assessments and sustainable solutions, for the Americas and Europe; and a Power Training School. The Earth & Environmental segment is organized into federal government, mining, oil and gas, transportation and water units. Environmental services include consultancy and engineering, as well as specialty services such as environmental assessment, materials testing, specialty water services and clean-up. One of the company's most recently acquired subsidiaries is Entec Holdings Ltd., an environmental and engineering consultancy based in the U.K. In August 2010, the company formed a joint venture in China with Shanghai ZonePetrochemical Engineering Co., Ltd called SZPE AMEC. In 2011, the firm agreed to acquire Australian engineering consulting company, Zektingroup. Also in 2011, the AMEC acquired U.S. engineering consulting company, BCI Engineers and Scientists, Inc.; and qedi, a provider of completion and commissioning services for projects in the oil and gas market.

FINANCIALS: Sales and profits are in thousands of dollars—add 000 to get the full amount. 2010 Note: Financial information for 2010 was not available for all companies at press time.

2010 Sales: $4,830,070	2010 Profits: $378,140	**U.S. Stock Ticker:**
2009 Sales: $3,865,270	2009 Profits: $261,380	**Int'l Ticker: AMEC** Int'l Exchange: London-LSE
2008 Sales: $3,823,620	2008 Profits: $291,940	Employees: 22,000
2007 Sales: $3,456,570	2007 Profits: $505,240	Fiscal Year Ends: 12/31
2006 Sales: $3,112,410	2006 Profits: $321,569	Parent Company:

SALARIES/BENEFITS:

Pension Plan:	ESOP Stock Plan:	Profit Sharing:	Top Exec. Salary: $	Bonus: $
Savings Plan:	Stock Purch. Plan:		Second Exec. Salary: $	Bonus: $

OTHER THOUGHTS:

Apparent Women Officers or Directors: 2
Hot Spot for Advancement for Women/Minorities:

LOCATIONS: ("Y" = Yes)

West:	Southwest:	Midwest:	Southeast:	Northeast:	International:
Y	Y	Y	Y	Y	Y

AMERCO

www.amerco.com

Industry Group Code: 532120 Ranks within this company's industry group: Sales: 1   Profits: 1

Properties:		Financial Services:		Construction/Development:	Investments:	Specialty Services:	Brokerage:	
Apartments:		Mortgages:		Commercial Construction:	REIT:	Property Management:	Commercial Sales:	Y
Malls/Shopping:	Y	Title Insurance:		Residential Construction:		Online Services:	Residential Sales:	
Offices:	Y	Property Insurance:	Y	Land Development:		Software/IT:	Specialty:	
Hotels/Motels:				Support Services:		Consulting:		
Industrial/Warehouses:	Y			Design/Engineering:				
Other:	Y							

TYPES OF BUSINESS:

Truck Rental & Leasing Services
Moving & Storage Services & Supplies
Property & Casualty Insurance
Life Insurance
Annuities
Self-Storage Properties

BRANDS/DIVISIONS/AFFILIATES:

U-Haul International, Inc.
Republic Western Insurance Company
Oxford Life Insurance Company
Amerco Real Estate Company
Safemove
Safetow
Safestor

CONTACTS: *Note: Officers with more than one job title may be intentionally listed here more than once.*

Edward J. Shoen, Pres.
Laurence J. De Respino, General Counsel
Jennifer Flachman, Dir.-Investor Rel.
Jason A. Berg, Principal Acct. Officer
Gary B. Horton, Treas.
Edward J. Shoen, CEO/Chmn.-U-Haul
Carlos Vizcarra, Pres., Amerco Real Estate Co.
John C. Taylor, Pres., U-Haul
Edward J. Shoen, Chmn.

Phone: 775-688-6300	Fax: 775-688-6338
Toll-Free:	
Address: 1325 Airmotive Way, Ste. 100, Reno, NV 89502 US	

GROWTH PLANS/SPECIAL FEATURES:

AMERCO is a holding company. The firm operates through subsidiaries U-Haul International, Inc.; Amerco Real Estate Company; Republic Western Insurance Company; and Oxford Life Insurance Company. Accordingly, the firm has three reportable business segments: moving and storage; property and casualty insurance; and life insurance. The moving and storage segment consists of U-Haul, with its rental equipment fleet of trucks, trailers and tow dollies being offered by approximately 14,900 independent dealers. It also provides furniture pads, utility dollies and hand trucks; sells a wide selection of other moving supplies; and offers protection packages for moving and storage. U-Haul owns more than 98,000 trucks, 77,000 trailers and 34,000 towing devices. The firm's Emove.com and Uhaul.com online reservation portals are significant drivers of U-Haul's rental transaction volume. The company also offers moving and storage protection packages such as Safemove and Safetow, providing moving and towing customers a damage waiver; cargo protection; and medical and life coverage. Additionally, Safestor protects storage customers from loss on their goods in storage. Amerco Real Estate Company markets commercial properties available for sale or lease. The property and casualty insurance business consists of Republic Western Insurance Company's business activities, which includes coverage for U-Haul customers, independent dealers, fleet owners and employees of AMERCO. The life insurance operating segment consists of Oxford Life Insurance Company, which offers annuities, credit life and disability, critical illness insurance, single premium whole life, group life and disability coverage as well as Medicare supplement insurance. Oxford also administers self-insured group health and dental plans for AMERCO.

Employees are offered medical, dental and vision insurance; life and AD&D insurance; disability coverage; a 401(k) plan; and an employee stock ownership plan.

FINANCIALS: Sales and profits are in thousands of dollars—add 000 to get the full amount. 2010 Note: Financial information for 2010 was not available for all companies at press time.

2010 Sales: $2,002,005	2010 Profits: $65,623	**U.S. Stock Ticker:** UHAL
2009 Sales: $1,992,266	2009 Profits: $13,410	**Int'l Ticker:** Int'l Exchange:
2008 Sales: $2,049,174	2008 Profits: $67,784	Employees: 17,600
2007 Sales: $2,069,298	2007 Profits: $90,553	Fiscal Year Ends: 3/31
2006 Sales: $2,087,525	2006 Profits: $121,154	Parent Company:

SALARIES/BENEFITS:

Pension Plan:	ESOP Stock Plan: Y	Profit Sharing:	Top Exec. Salary: $675,004	Bonus: $
Savings Plan: Y	Stock Purch. Plan:		Second Exec. Salary: $623,077	Bonus: $

OTHER THOUGHTS:

Apparent Women Officers or Directors: 2
Hot Spot for Advancement for Women/Minorities:

LOCATIONS: ("Y" = Yes)

West:	Southwest:	Midwest:	Southeast:	Northeast:	International:
Y	Y	Y	Y	Y	Y

AMERICAN CAMPUS COMMUNITIES INC

americancampus.com

Industry Group Code: 5311 Ranks within this company's industry group: Sales: 27   Profits: 26

Properties:		Financial Services:		Construction/Development:		Investments:		Specialty Services:		Brokerage:	
Apartments:	Y	Mortgages:		Commercial Construction:		REIT:	Y	Property Management:	Y	Commercial Sales:	
Malls/Shopping:		Title Insurance:		Residential Construction:	Y			Online Services:		Residential Sales:	
Offices:		Property Insurance:		Land Development:				Software/IT:		Specialty:	
Hotels/Motels:				Support Services:	Y			Consulting:			
Industrial/Warehouses:				Design/Engineering:							
Other:	Y										

TYPES OF BUSINESS:

Student Housing Development

BRANDS/DIVISIONS/AFFILIATES:

American Campus Communities Operating Partnership
American Campus Equity

CONTACTS: *Note: Officers with more than one job title may be intentionally listed here more than once.*

William C. Bayless, Jr., CEO
Greg A. Dowell, COO/Sr. Exec. VP
William C. Bayless, Jr., Pres.
Jonathan A. Graf, CFO/Exec. VP/Treas.
Jorge de Cardenas, Sr. VP-IT
Kim K. Voss, Sr. VP/Controller
James C. Hopke Jr., Exec. VP-Project Mgmt. & Construction
James E. Wilhelm III, Exec. VP-Public & Private Transactions
Clint Braun, Sr. VP-Construction Mgmt.
Steve Crawford, Sr. VP-Mgmt. Svcs.
R.D. Burck, Chmn.

Phone: 512-732-1000	Fax: 517-732-2450
Toll-Free:	
Address: 805 Las Cimas Pkwy., Ste. 400, Austin, TX 78746 US	

GROWTH PLANS/SPECIAL FEATURES:

American Campus Communities, Inc. (ACC) is a real estate investment trust (REIT) with expertise in the acquisition, design, financing, development, construction management, leasing and management of student housing properties. The company, operating primarily via subsidiary American Campus Communities Operating Partnership LP, is one of the largest owners, managers and developers of student housing properties in the U.S. in terms of beds owned, developed, and under management. ACC's property portfolio consists of 104 student housing properties with approximately 65,000 beds and 20,800 apartment units. The company operates in four segments: wholly-owned properties, on-campus participating properties, development services and property management services. The wholly-owned property segment consists of all properties in proximity to college campuses; these include 96 wholly-owned complexes in 27 states, as well as four properties operated under a ground/facility lease through American Campus Equity. The on-campus participating segment consists of facilities leased from universities that are managed by the company. The development services segment provides consulting services, through the company's subsidiaries, to colleges and universities for all stages of property construction. The property management segment is conducted primarily through subsidiaries for college or university clients and includes all aspect of facility maintenance and administration. ACC provides property management services to 37 properties. ACC's communities contain modern housing units and are supported by a resident assistant system and other student-oriented programming, with many offering resort-style amenities.

FINANCIALS: Sales and profits are in thousands of dollars—add 000 to get the full amount. 2010 Note: Financial information for 2010 was not available for all companies at press time.

2010 Sales: $344,991	2010 Profits: $16,210	**U.S. Stock Ticker: ACC**	
2009 Sales: $304,946	2009 Profits: $-12,840	**Int'l Ticker:** Int'l Exchange:	
2008 Sales: $233,579	2008 Profits: $-13,055	Employees: 2,334	
2007 Sales: $147,135	2007 Profits: $-1,686	Fiscal Year Ends: 12/31	
2006 Sales: $118,953	2006 Profits: $1,662	Parent Company:	

SALARIES/BENEFITS:

Pension Plan:	ESOP Stock Plan:	Profit Sharing:	Top Exec. Salary: $352,000	Bonus: $496,232
Savings Plan:	Stock Purch. Plan:		Second Exec. Salary: $312,125	Bonus: $300,000

OTHER THOUGHTS:

Apparent Women Officers or Directors: 3
Hot Spot for Advancement for Women/Minorities: Y

LOCATIONS: ("Y" = Yes)

West:	Southwest:	Midwest:	Southeast:	Northeast:	International:
Y	Y	Y	Y	Y	Y

AMERICAN CASINO & ENTERTAINMENT PROPERTIES INC

www.stratospherehotel.com

Industry Group Code: 721120 Ranks within this company's industry group: Sales: Profits:

Properties:		Financial Services:	Construction/Development:	Investments:	Specialty Services:	Brokerage:
Apartments:		Mortgages:	Commercial Construction:	REIT:	Property Management:	Commercial Sales:
Malls/Shopping:	Y	Title Insurance:	Residential Construction:		Online Services:	Residential Sales:
Offices:		Property Insurance:	Land Development:		Software/IT:	Specialty:
Hotels/Motels:	Y		Support Services:		Consulting:	
Industrial/Warehouses:			Design/Engineering:			
Other:	Y					

TYPES OF BUSINESS:

Casino Hotel Properties
Retail Outlets
Restaurants
Recreational Vehicle Park

BRANDS/DIVISIONS/AFFILIATES:

Stratosphere Casino Hotel & Tower
Arizona Charlie's Decatur
Arizona Charlie's Boulder
Aquarius Casino Resort
Whitehall Street Real Estate Fund
Goldman Sachs Group

CONTACTS: Note: Officers with more than one job title may be intentionally listed here more than once.

Frank V. Riolo, CEO
Arthur Keith, Pres.
Ned Martin, CFO/Treas.
Rachel Hunt, Assistant VP-Mktg., Stratosphere
Phyllis A. Gilland, General Counsel/Sec./VP
David Grolman, VP-Hotel Oper.
Steve Klein, Controller-Casino
Steve Mann, VP-Table Games, Stratosphere
Ronald P. Lurie, Exec. VP/Gen. Mgr.-Arizona Charlie's Decatur
Mark Majetich, Sr. VP/Gen. Mgr.-Arizona Charlie's Boulder
Paul Hobson, Sr. VP/Gen. Mgr.-Aquarius Casino Resort

Phone: 702-380-7632	Fax: 702-383-4734
Toll-Free:	
Address: 2000 S. Las Vegas Blvd., Las Vegas, NV 89104 US	

GROWTH PLANS/SPECIAL FEATURES:

American Casino & Entertainment Properties LLC (ACEP) is a holding company that owns and operates gaming and entertainment properties throughout Nevada. The company is owned by the Whitehall Street Real Estate Fund, which is an affiliate of the Goldman Sachs Group. ACEP operates four entertainment properties: Stratosphere Tower Hotel & Casino, a mixed-use resort destination on the Las Vegas Strip; Arizona Charlie's Decatur and Arizona Charlie's Boulder, two casinos also located in Las Vegas; and the Aquarius Casino Resort in Laughlin, Nevada, south of Las Vegas. The Stratosphere is the firm's flagship property, featuring 2,444 hotel rooms, 80,000 square feet of casino space and 150,000 square feet of retail space, as well as a revolving restaurant, a roller coaster and the Stratosphere Tower, the tallest freestanding observation tower in the U.S. The Arizona Charlie's Decatur and Arizona Charlie's Boulder are off-Strip full-service casinos and restaurants featuring slot machines, game tables, poker lounges and various other gaming features. Arizona Charlie's Boulder also features a recreational vehicle (RV) park offering amenities such as game and exercise rooms, a swimming pool and shower and laundry facilities. The Aquarius Casino Resort features a 57,070-square-foot casino and 1,907 hotel rooms, including 90 suites, along with seven restaurants. The Aquarius also maintains 35,000 square feet of rentable meeting space, indoor and outdoor entertainment facilities and a wedding chapel.

FINANCIALS: Sales and profits are in thousands of dollars—add 000 to get the full amount. 2010 Note: Financial information for 2010 was not available for all companies at press time.

2010 Sales: $	2010 Profits: $	U.S. Stock Ticker: Private
2009 Sales: $	2009 Profits: $	Int'l Ticker: Int'l Exchange:
2008 Sales: $	2008 Profits: $	Employees:
2007 Sales: $182,900	2007 Profits: $	Fiscal Year Ends: 12/31
2006 Sales: $	2006 Profits: $	Parent Company: WHITEHALL STREET REAL ESTATE FUND

SALARIES/BENEFITS:

Pension Plan:	ESOP Stock Plan:	Profit Sharing:	Top Exec. Salary: $	Bonus: $
Savings Plan:	Stock Purch. Plan:		Second Exec. Salary: $	Bonus: $

OTHER THOUGHTS:

Apparent Women Officers or Directors: 2
Hot Spot for Advancement for Women/Minorities:

LOCATIONS: ("Y" = Yes)

West:	Southwest:	Midwest:	Southeast:	Northeast:	International:
Y					

AMERICAN REALTY INVESTORS INC

www.amrealtytrust.com

Industry Group Code: 5311 Ranks within this company's industry group: Sales: 30   Profits: 30

Properties:		Financial Services:	Construction/Development:		Investments:		Specialty Services:		Brokerage:
Apartments:	Y	Mortgages:	Commercial Construction:		REIT:	Y	Property Management:	Y	Commercial Sales:
Malls/Shopping:	Y	Title Insurance:	Residential Construction:				Online Services:		Residential Sales:
Offices:	Y	Property Insurance:	Land Development:	Y			Software/IT:		Specialty:
Hotels/Motels:	Y		Support Services:				Consulting:		
Industrial/Warehouses:	Y		Design/Engineering:						
Other:	Y								

TYPES OF BUSINESS:

Real Estate Development & Management
Real Estate Investments
Apartments
Land
Commercial/Office Property
Hotels

BRANDS/DIVISIONS/AFFILIATES:

Transcontinental Realty Investors Inc
HarmInvest GmbH Berlin

CONTACTS: *Note: Officers with more than one job title may be intentionally listed here more than once.*

Daniel J. Moos, COO
Daniel J. Moos, Pres.
Gene S. Bertcher, CFO/Exec. VP
Henry A. Butler, Chmn.

Phone: 469-522-4200	Fax: 469-522-4299
Toll-Free: 800-400-6407	
Address: 1800 Valley View Ln., Ste. 300, Dallas, TX 75234 US	

GROWTH PLANS/SPECIAL FEATURES:

American Realty Investors (ARI), Inc. owns, develops and manages residential and commercial real estate throughout the U.S. Its investments include apartments, commercial/office buildings, hotels, parcels of land and other equity ownership interests. The company develops residential complexes through third party agreements, in which it contributes land and in some cases cash support. ARI owns 61 residential apartment communities with a total of 11,942 units. It currently has several units under construction, including a 224 unit complex in Garland, Texas and a 240 unit complex in Gautier, Mississippi. The firm's commercial portfolio consists of 32 properties totaling more than 5.7 million square feet of rentable space that include 21 office buildings, six industrial facilities, four retail properties and 344,975 square feet of trade show and exhibit hall. Additionally, it owns five hotels (four in California and one in Colorado) with a combined total of 808 rooms. ARI generates revenue through its income producing properties, third party development strategies and land acquisitions in high growth suburban markets. The firm also buys large tracts of underdeveloped or partially developed land in areas that are or will be likely growth communities; these tracts of land are located primarily in suburban communities. It uses the purchased land for its own developments or sells it for a profit to other developers. Current development projects of this nature include a joint venture with HarmInvest GmbH Berlin to develop a decommissioned navel base into a family resort in Schleswig-Holstein, Germany. Through majority-owned subsidiary Transcontinental Realty Investors, Inc. (TRI), ARI invests in under-valued properties. TRI currently holds 6,813 acres for development, with a total of 14 projects under construction.

FINANCIALS: Sales and profits are in thousands of dollars—add 000 to get the full amount. 2010 Note: Financial information for 2010 was not available for all companies at press time.

2010 Sales: $157,030	2010 Profits: $-106,195	**U.S. Stock Ticker: ARL**
2009 Sales: $161,863	2009 Profits: $-82,659	**Int'l Ticker:** Int'l Exchange:
2008 Sales: $150,645	2008 Profits: $26,969	Employees:
2007 Sales: $164,622	2007 Profits: $26,562	Fiscal Year Ends: 12/31
2006 Sales: $142,138	2006 Profits: $13,066	Parent Company:

SALARIES/BENEFITS:

Pension Plan:	ESOP Stock Plan:	Profit Sharing:	Top Exec. Salary: $	Bonus: $
Savings Plan:	Stock Purch. Plan:		Second Exec. Salary: $	Bonus: $

OTHER THOUGHTS:

Apparent Women Officers or Directors:
Hot Spot for Advancement for Women/Minorities:

LOCATIONS: ("Y" = Yes)

West:	Southwest:	Midwest:	Southeast:	Northeast:	International:
Y	Y	Y	Y	Y	Y

AMERICA'S BEST FRANCHISING INC

www.abestfranchise.com

Industry Group Code: 721110 Ranks within this company's industry group: Sales: Profits:

Properties:	Financial Services:	Construction/Development:	Investments:	Specialty Services:		Brokerage:
Apartments:	Mortgages:	Commercial Construction:	REIT:	Property Management:	Y	Commercial Sales:
Malls/Shopping:	Title Insurance:	Residential Construction:		Online Services:	Y	Residential Sales:
Offices:	Property Insurance:	Land Development:		Software/IT:		Specialty:
Hotels/Motels: Y		Support Services:		Consulting:		
Industrial/Warehouses:		Design/Engineering:				
Other:						

TYPES OF BUSINESS:

Hotels
Hospitality Services
Hotel Franchising
Hotel Management
Back Office Services

BRANDS/DIVISIONS/AFFILIATES:

America's Best Hotels Services, Inc.
America's Best Inns & Suites
Country Hearth Inn
EverGreen Rooms
3 Palms Hotels & Resorts

CONTACTS: *Note: Officers with more than one job title may be intentionally listed here more than once.*

Douglas C. Collins, CEO
Douglas C. Collins, Pres.
Chris Elbers, VP-Franchise Oper.
Douglas C. Collins, Chmn.

Phone: 770-393-2662	**Fax:** 770-393-2480
Toll-Free: 800-432-7992	
Address: 50 Glenlake Pkwy., Ste. 350, Atlanta, GA 30328 US	

GROWTH PLANS/SPECIAL FEATURES:

America's Best Franchising, Inc. is a holding and franchising company for mid-priced hotels, hotel loan portfolios and other hospitality-related assets. The company franchises consist of America's Best Inns & Suites, which is geared toward the business traveler; Country Hearth Inns & Suites, which strives to combine the intimate atmosphere of a bed-and-breakfast with all the conveniences of a contemporary hotel. Other Hotels include the Vagabond Inn, which offers California ranch style accommodations and the Vagabond Inn Executive, which offers the same California ranch style accommodations with extra services geared towards business travelers, such as high speed Internet and free incoming fax documents. Budgetel Inns & Suites is marketed towards leisure travelers that include seniors, families, tour groups, with most locations offering free parking and liberal pet policies. The company's more upscale offering is the 3 Palms Hotels & Resorts that has six locations located in proximity to major family oriented attractions, and offers a condo-hotel style brand. The 3 Palms amenities include guest spa packages, pillow top mattresses, guest laundry, golf packages, shuttle and valet service. Each of the hotel chains possesses different special services, such as the EverGreen Room accommodations, which offers rooms designed to support allergen- and irritant-free air, water and mattresses. America's Best and Country Hearth lines offers visitors the EcoRooms opinion, which offers energy efficient, water efficient, waste-reducing and biodegradable products; this is similar to the Green Suites Certification offered by the 3 Palms. The company operates over 200 hotels under its various brands that are located throughout the U.S. Additionally, the firm formed America's Best Hotel Services, Inc., a company intended to provide hospitality and back office services to independent hotels, other franchisors and emerging brands. In January 2011, the firm announced plans to expand its 3 Palms Hotels and Resorts into India.

FINANCIALS: Sales and profits are in thousands of dollars—add 000 to get the full amount. 2010 Note: Financial information for 2010 was not available for all companies at press time.

2010 Sales: $	2010 Profits: $	**U.S. Stock Ticker: Private**
2009 Sales: $	2009 Profits: $	**Int'l Ticker:** Int'l Exchange:
2008 Sales: $	2008 Profits: $	Employees:
2007 Sales: $	2007 Profits: $	Fiscal Year Ends: 12/31
2006 Sales: $	2006 Profits: $	Parent Company:

SALARIES/BENEFITS:

Pension Plan:	ESOP Stock Plan:	Profit Sharing:	Top Exec. Salary: $	Bonus: $
Savings Plan:	Stock Purch. Plan:		Second Exec. Salary: $	Bonus: $

OTHER THOUGHTS:

Apparent Women Officers or Directors:
Hot Spot for Advancement for Women/Minorities:

LOCATIONS: ("Y" = Yes)

West:	Southwest:	Midwest:	Southeast:	Northeast:	International:
Y	Y	Y	Y	Y	Y

AMERISTAR CASINOS INC

www.ameristarcasinos.com

Industry Group Code: 721120 Ranks within this company's industry group: Sales: 6 Profits: 4

Properties:		Financial Services:	Construction/Development:	Investments:	Specialty Services:	Brokerage:
Apartments:		Mortgages:	Commercial Construction:	REIT:	Property Management:	Commercial Sales:
Malls/Shopping:		Title Insurance:	Residential Construction:		Online Services:	Residential Sales:
Offices:		Property Insurance:	Land Development:		Software/IT:	Specialty:
Hotels/Motels:	Y		Support Services:		Consulting:	
Industrial/Warehouses:			Design/Engineering:			
Other:	Y					

TYPES OF BUSINESS:

Casino Resorts
Casino Management

BRANDS/DIVISIONS/AFFILIATES:

Cactus Pete's Resort Casino
Ameristar Kansas City
Ameristar St. Charles
Ameristar Council Bluffs
Ameristar Vicksburg
Horseshu Hotel & Casino
Ameristar Black Hawk
Ameristar Casino Hotel East Chicago

CONTACTS: *Note: Officers with more than one job title may be intentionally listed here more than once.*

Gordon R. Kanofsky, CEO
Larry A. Hodges, COO
Larry A. Hodges, Pres.
Thomas M. Steinbauer, CFO/Sr. VP-Finance/Treas./Sec.
Sheleen Quish, Sr. VP-Human Resources
Sheleen Quish, Sr. VP-IT
Peter C. Walsh, Chief Admin. Officer
Peter C. Walsh, General Counsel/Sr. VP
Roxann M. Kinkade, Dir.-External Comm.
Heather Rollo, Sr. VP-Acct.
George Stadler, Sr. VP/Gen. Mgr.-Ameristar Casino Vicksburg
Andrew Hamblen, Sr. VP/Gen. Mgr.-Ameristar Casino Black Hawk
Montgomery Terhune, Sr. VP/Gen. Mgr.-Ameristar Council Bluffs
Ray H. Neilsen, Chmn.

Phone: 702-567-7000	Fax: 702-369-8860
Toll-Free:	
Address: 3773 Howard Hughes Pkwy., Ste. 490S, Las Vegas, NV 89169 US	

GROWTH PLANS/SPECIAL FEATURES:

Ameristar Casinos, Inc. (ASCA) is a gaming and entertainment company that develops, owns and operates eight casino facilities. Its properties include Ameristar St. Charles and Ameristar Kansas City in Missouri; Ameristar Council Bluffs in southwestern Iowa; Ameristar Vicksburg in Mississippi; Ameristar Black Hawk in Denver, Colorado; Ameristar Casino Hotel East Chicago; and Cactus Pete's Resort Casino and Horseshu Hotel and Casino, both near the Idaho boarder in Jackpot, Nevada. The casinos typically offer slot machines and a variety of table games, including blackjack, craps, roulette, baccarat and numerous live poker variations such as Texas Hold 'Em and Pai Gow. In addition, some locations offer sports book wagering. Ameristar is a leader in the casino industry in the implementation of cashless slot technology and new-generation multi-coin slot machines. The casinos also offer a variety of casual dining and upscale restaurants; sports bars; and private clubs for Star Awards members. Ameristar St. Charles offers two ballrooms for its guests, five meeting rooms and an executive board room. Ameristar Kansas City features an 18-screen movie theater, a 4,280 square foot arcade and an activity center named Kids Quest. Ameristar Vicksburg is a permanently docked riverboat casino located on the Mississippi River, while Ameristar Council Bluffs offers a cruising riverboat casino that travels down the Missouri River, as well as landside amenities such as the Ameristar Hotel and Main Street Pavilion. Cactus Pete's features an outdoor amphitheater, arcades, an 18-hole golf course and tennis courts. The East Chicago property is a 56,000 square foot complex that features a 550-seat ballroom and a nearly 2,000 space parking garage.

Employees are offered medical, dental and vision insurance; a 401(k) plan; life insurance, additional voluntary life insurance and supplemental life insurance for spouses and children; disability insurance; flexible spending accounts; an employee assistance program; and tuition reimbursement.

FINANCIALS: Sales and profits are in thousands of dollars—add 000 to get the full amount. 2010 Note: Financial information for 2010 was not available for all companies at press time.

2010 Sales: $1,491,850	2010 Profits: $8,630	U.S. Stock Ticker: ASCA
2009 Sales: $1,489,634	2009 Profits: $-4,667	Int'l Ticker: Int'l Exchange:
2008 Sales: $1,548,308	2008 Profits: $-130,672	Employees: 7,625
2007 Sales: $1,080,523	2007 Profits: $69,433	Fiscal Year Ends: 12/31
2006 Sales: $1,000,298	2006 Profits: $59,565	Parent Company:

SALARIES/BENEFITS:

Pension Plan:	ESOP Stock Plan:	Profit Sharing:	Top Exec. Salary: $750,000	Bonus: $900,000
Savings Plan: Y	Stock Purch. Plan:		Second Exec. Salary: $575,000	Bonus: $690,000

OTHER THOUGHTS:

Apparent Women Officers or Directors: 3
Hot Spot for Advancement for Women/Minorities: Y

LOCATIONS: ("Y" = Yes)

West:	Southwest:	Midwest:	Southeast:	Northeast:	International:
Y		Y	Y		

AMEY PLC

www.amey.co.uk

Industry Group Code: 541330 Ranks within this company's industry group: Sales: Profits:

Properties:	Financial Services:	Construction/Development:		Investments:	Specialty Services:		Brokerage:
Apartments:	Mortgages:	Commercial Construction:		REIT:	Property Management:	Y	Commercial Sales:
Malls/Shopping:	Title Insurance:	Residential Construction:			Online Services:		Residential Sales:
Offices:	Property Insurance:	Land Development:			Software/IT:		Specialty:
Hotels/Motels:		Support Services:	Y		Consulting:	Y	
Industrial/Warehouses:		Design/Engineering:	Y				
Other:							

TYPES OF BUSINESS:

Engineering Services
Facilities Management
Design Services
Consulting Services
Asset Management
Infrastructure Services
Highway Design Services
IT Services

BRANDS/DIVISIONS/AFFILIATES:

Grupo Ferrovial SA
Transportation Planning (International) Ltd.

CONTACTS: *Note: Officers with more than one job title may be intentionally listed here more than once.*

Mel Ewell, CEO
Chris Webster, COO
Andrew Nelson, Group Dir.-Finance
Chris Fenton, Dir.-Mktg.
Valerie Hughes-D'Aeth, Dir.-Human Resources
Wayne Robertson, Head-Legal
Chris Fenton, Dir.-Strategy
Steve Withers, Managing Dir.-Inter-Urban
Gillian Duggan, Managing Dir.-Built Environment
Andy Milner, Managing Dir.-Consulting
Nick Gregg, Managing Dir.-Local Gov't
Richard Mottram, Chmn.

Phone: 44-18-6571-3100	Fax: 44-18-6571-3357
Toll-Free:	
Address: The Sherard Bldg., Edmund Halley Rd., Oxford, OX4 4DQ UK	

GROWTH PLANS/SPECIAL FEATURES:

Amey plc, a subsidiary of the Spanish Grupo Ferrovial, provides business and infrastructure support services through more than 200 locations across the U.K. and Ireland. It operates in three divisions: the Market-Facing division, the Specialist division and Ventures. The Market-Facing division consists of three sub-segments: Local Government, Built Environment and Inter-Urban. The Local Government segment serves local authorities in the U.K., providing advisory, design, management and maintenance services related to highways, street lighting, waste and transportation planning, as well as facilities management. The Built Environment segment, serving the central government and aviation sectors, provides long-term facilities management, business process outsourcing and asset management services. The Inter-Urban segment offers asset management services to the U.K.'s strategic highway and rail line sectors. The Specialist division is comprised of the firm's consulting and logistics businesses. The consulting group offers design and advisory services, including engineering design, architecture, feasibility studies, planning, asset management and technology and software solutions, to clients across its three Market-Facing segments. The logistics business works with Amey's clients to provide fleet management, transportation planning and other logistics support services. The Ventures division is responsible for managing Amey's investment portfolio. In June 2010, the firm sold its equity interests in Tube Lines (Holdings) Ltd., its former Tube Services division, to Transport for London. Tube Lines Tube Lines holds a 30-year contract to upgrade and maintain London's Jubilee, Northern and Piccadilly tubes. In July 2010, Amey acquired the national rail consultancy operations of WYG Engineering Limited. In January 2011, it acquired Transportation Planning (International) Ltd.

The firm offers its employees life, dental, travel and personal accident insurance; parental leave; paid time off; and a pension plan.

FINANCIALS: Sales and profits are in thousands of dollars—add 000 to get the full amount. 2010 Note: Financial information for 2010 was not available for all companies at press time.

2010 Sales: $	2010 Profits: $	U.S. Stock Ticker: Subsidiary
2009 Sales: $2,527,580	2009 Profits: $156,160	Int'l Ticker: Int'l Exchange:
2008 Sales: $2,448,600	2008 Profits: $123,670	Employees: 9,633
2007 Sales: $	2007 Profits: $	Fiscal Year Ends: 12/31
2006 Sales: $2,613,130	2006 Profits: $127,413	Parent Company: GRUPO FERROVIAL SA

SALARIES/BENEFITS:

Pension Plan: Y	ESOP Stock Plan:	Profit Sharing:	Top Exec. Salary: $	Bonus: $
Savings Plan:	Stock Purch. Plan:		Second Exec. Salary: $	Bonus: $

OTHER THOUGHTS:

Apparent Women Officers or Directors: 2
Hot Spot for Advancement for Women/Minorities:

LOCATIONS: ("Y" = Yes)

West:	Southwest:	Midwest:	Southeast:	Northeast:	International:
					Y

AMLI RESIDENTIAL PROPERTIES TRUST

www.amli.com

Industry Group Code: 531120 Ranks within this company's industry group: Sales: Profits:

Properties:		Financial Services:	Construction/Development:		Investments:		Specialty Services:		Brokerage:
Apartments:	Y	Mortgages:	Commercial Construction:		REIT:	Y	Property Management:	Y	Commercial Sales:
Malls/Shopping:		Title Insurance:	Residential Construction:	Y			Online Services:		Residential Sales:
Offices:		Property Insurance:	Land Development:				Software/IT:		Specialty:
Hotels/Motels:			Support Services:				Consulting:		
Industrial/Warehouses:			Design/Engineering:						
Other:									

TYPES OF BUSINESS:

Real Estate Investment Trust
Apartment Communities
Construction & Landscape Services
Management & Leasing Services
Investment Services

BRANDS/DIVISIONS/AFFILIATES:

AMLI Management Company
AMLI Institutional Advisors
AMLI Residential Construction
AMLI Residential Properties, LP
Morgan Stanley Real Estate
FAMLI
AMLI Nest Egg

CONTACTS: *Note: Officers with more than one job title may be intentionally listed here more than once.*

Gregory T. Mutz, CEO
Allan J. Sweet, Pres.
Stephen C. Ross, Exec. VP-Dev.
Philip N. Tague, Exec. VP
Steve F. Hallsey, Pres./CEO-AMLI Mgmt. Co.
Mark T. Evans, Pres., AMLI Residential Construction
Taylor Bowen, Exec. VP-Dev., Texas
Gregory T. Mutz, Chmn.

Phone: 312-283-4700	Fax: 312-283-4720
Toll-Free:	
Address: 200 W. Monroe St., Ste. 2200, Chicago, IL 60606 US	

GROWTH PLANS/SPECIAL FEATURES:

AMLI Residential Properties Trust, a subsidiary of Morgan Stanley Real Estate, is a self-administered and self-managed real estate investment trust engaged in the development, acquisition and management of luxury apartment communities. The company manages 66 apartment communities in Atlanta, Georgia; Austin, Texas; Chicago, Illinois; Dallas, Texas; Denver, Colorado; West Palm Beach, Florida; Houston, Texas; Kansas City, Kansas; Kansas City, Missouri; Seattle, Washington; Morristown, New Jersey; Sherman Oaks, California; and Rancho Cucamonga, California. Overall, AMLI manages 61 apartment communities, comprised of approximately 22,000 units and about 2,000 additional apartment complexes that are in lease-up or under development. The company also provides property management, institutional advisory and construction management services through its subsidiary companies, AMLI Management Company; AMLI Institutional Advisors, Inc.; and AMLI Residential Construction, LLC. AMLI's growth strategies employ a combination of brand and market promotions, acquisition, development and co-investments with institutional investors in new apartment communities. The company offers its tenants the AMLI Nest Egg program, an equity credit plan that allows 20% of base apartment rent to be applied as non-monetary credit towards the purchase price of a new home from KB Home, Ryland Homes or Belgravia Realty Group. AMLI also created the FAMLI volunteer program as a means of connecting AMLI residents and employees with local non-profit organizations.

AMLI offers its employees a benefits package that includes health and dependent care flexible spending accounts; a 401(k) plan; bonus programs; adoption assistance; medical, dental and vision coverage; life insurance; tuition assistance; and housing discounts.

FINANCIALS: Sales and profits are in thousands of dollars—add 000 to get the full amount. 2010 Note: Financial information for 2010 was not available for all companies at press time.

2010 Sales: $	2010 Profits: $	**U.S. Stock Ticker: Subsidiary**
2009 Sales: $	2009 Profits: $	**Int'l Ticker:** Int'l Exchange:
2008 Sales: $	2008 Profits: $	Employees:
2007 Sales: $	2007 Profits: $	Fiscal Year Ends: 12/31
2006 Sales: $	2006 Profits: $	Parent Company: MORGAN STANLEY

SALARIES/BENEFITS:

Pension Plan:	ESOP Stock Plan:	Profit Sharing:	Top Exec. Salary: $	Bonus: $
Savings Plan: Y	Stock Purch. Plan:		Second Exec. Salary: $	Bonus: $

OTHER THOUGHTS:

Apparent Women Officers or Directors:
Hot Spot for Advancement for Women/Minorities:

LOCATIONS: ("Y" = Yes)

West:	Southwest:	Midwest:	Southeast:	Northeast:	International:
Y	Y	Y	Y	Y	

ANDERSON-TULLY LUMBER COMPANY

www.andersontully.com

Industry Group Code: 531120 Ranks within this company's industry group: Sales: Profits:

Properties:	Financial Services:	Construction/Development:		Investments:		Specialty Services:	Brokerage:
Apartments:	Mortgages:	Commercial Construction:		REIT:	Y	Property Management:	Commercial Sales:
Malls/Shopping:	Title Insurance:	Residential Construction:				Online Services:	Residential Sales:
Offices:	Property Insurance:	Land Development:	Y			Software/IT:	Specialty:
Hotels/Motels:		Support Services:	Y			Consulting:	
Industrial/Warehouses:		Design/Engineering:					
Other: Y							

TYPES OF BUSINESS:

Real Estate Investment Trust
Timber Tract Operations
Hardwood Products
Hardwood Flooring

BRANDS/DIVISIONS/AFFILIATES:

Anderson-Tully Worldwide
Anderson-Tully China
Anderson-Tully de Mexico
Anderson-Tully Vietnam
Louisiana Hardwood Products
International Hardwood Resource
Patton Tully Transportation, LLC
Forestland Group LLC (The)

CONTACTS: *Note: Officers with more than one job title may be intentionally listed here more than once.*

E. J. (Buddy) Irby, Jr., VP-Sales
Mike Myrick, Mgr.-Human Resources
Roy James, VP-Mfg./Dir.-Oper., Mississippi
Butch Morgan, Dir.-Oper., Louisiana
Kimberly Opiela, Mgr.-Acct.
Richard Wilkerson, Exec. VP
Norman Davis, Exec. VP-Land Acquisition & Sales

Phone: 601-629-3283	Fax: 601-629-3284
Toll-Free:	
Address: 1725 N. Washington St., P.O. Box 38, Vicksburg, MS 39181 US	

GROWTH PLANS/SPECIAL FEATURES:

Anderson-Tully Lumber Company (ATCO) is a REIT (Real Estate Investment Trust) focusing entirely on timberland investments. It is one of the few REITs that manage timberlands, and one of the only ones to focus on hardwood timberlands. Originally a crate manufacturing company, the company moved into the timberland ownership business in 1889 to provide itself with sustainable operations, eventually shifting its focus away from crates and boxes to exclusively operating its timberlands. Today, it owns approximately 300,000 acres of hardwood timber tracts along the Mississippi River in Mississippi, Louisiana and Arkansas. The firm was one of the first major Southeastern timber companies certified by the Forest Stewardship Council, an organization devoted to the promotion of responsible forestry. ATCO operates its own sawmills, lumber inspectors, holding facilities and transport networks. Customers may choose between a variety of hardwoods, including cottonwood, hackberry, pecan, poplar, red oak, sweetgum, sycamore, white ash, white oak and willow. Its operating companies include Anderson-Tully Worldwide, the firm's sales and marketing arm; Anderson-Tully China, with offices in Shanghai and Guangzhou; Anderson-Tully de Mexico, based in Mexico City; Anderson-Tully Vietnam, based in Ho Chi Minh City; and Louisiana Hardwood Products. Patton Tully Transportation, a sister company, provides shipping for the firm's products along the Mississippi, Ohio, Tombigbee, Black, Tennessee, Cumberland, Yazoo, Arkansas, Red, White and Missouri river systems. Additionally, ATCO created a network of producers called the International Hardwood Resource, designed to insure the smooth flow of hardwood to its customers. The Resource currently has six members besides ATCO subsidiaries, including five U.S. firms and one based in Italy. The firm is owned by the Heartwood Forestland Fund V, an affiliate of The Forestland Group LLC.

FINANCIALS: Sales and profits are in thousands of dollars—add 000 to get the full amount. 2010 Note: Financial information for 2010 was not available for all companies at press time.

2010 Sales: $	2010 Profits: $	U.S. Stock Ticker: Subsidiary
2009 Sales: $	2009 Profits: $	Int'l Ticker: Int'l Exchange:
2008 Sales: $	2008 Profits: $	Employees:
2007 Sales: $	2007 Profits: $	Fiscal Year Ends: 12/31
2006 Sales: $	2006 Profits: $	Parent Company: FORESTLAND GROUP LLC (THE)

SALARIES/BENEFITS:

Pension Plan:	ESOP Stock Plan:	Profit Sharing:	Top Exec. Salary: $	Bonus: $
Savings Plan:	Stock Purch. Plan:		Second Exec. Salary: $	Bonus: $

OTHER THOUGHTS:

Apparent Women Officers or Directors:
Hot Spot for Advancement for Women/Minorities:

LOCATIONS: ("Y" = Yes)

West:	Southwest:	Midwest:	Southeast:	Northeast:	International:
			Y		Y

ANNALY CAPITAL MANAGEMENT INC

www.annaly.com

Industry Group Code: 531120 Ranks within this company's industry group: Sales: 6   Profits: 3

Properties:	Financial Services:		Construction/Development:	Investments:		Specialty Services:	Brokerage:
Apartments:	Mortgages:	Y	Commercial Construction:	REIT:	Y	Property Management:	Commercial Sales:
Malls/Shopping:	Title Insurance:		Residential Construction:			Online Services:	Residential Sales:
Offices:	Property Insurance:		Land Development:			Software/IT:	Specialty:
Hotels/Motels:			Support Services:			Consulting:	
Industrial/Warehouses:			Design/Engineering:				
Other:							

TYPES OF BUSINESS:

Real Estate Investment Trust
Mortgage-Backed Securities

BRANDS/DIVISIONS/AFFILIATES:

Merganser Capital Management Inc.
Fixed Income Discount Advisory Company
RCap Securities, Inc.

CONTACTS: *Note: Officers with more than one job title may be intentionally listed here more than once.*

Michael A. J. Farrell, CEO
Wellington J. Denahan-Norris, COO
Michael A. J. Farrell, Pres.
Kathryn F. Fagan, CFO
R. Nicholas Singh, General Counsel/Sec./Exec. VP
Kathryn F. Fagen, Treas.
Wellington J. Denahan-Norris, Chief Investment Officer/Vice Chmn.
R. Nicholas Singh, Chief Compliance Officer
James P. Fortescue, Head-Liabilities/Managing Dir.
Eric Szabo, Chief Risk Officer/Managing Dir.
Michael A. J. Farrell, Chmn.

Phone: 212-696-0100	**Fax:** 212-696-9809
Toll-Free: 888-826-6259	
Address: 1211 Ave. of the Americas, Ste. 2902, New York, NY 10036 US	

GROWTH PLANS/SPECIAL FEATURES:

Annaly Capital Management, Inc. is a self-managed, self-administered real estate investment trust (REIT) that focuses entirely on owning and managing a portfolio of mortgage-backed securities. The company has three wholly-owned subsidiaries: Fixed Income Discount Advisory Company (FIDAC); Merganser Capital Management, Inc.; and RCap Securities, Inc (RCap). FIDAC and Merganser manage multiple investment vehicles and separate accounts. RCap operates as a broker dealer. The firm owns and manages a portfolio of investment securities including collateralized mortgage obligations (CMOs), mortgage pass-through certificates and agency callable debentures. All of Annaly's assets are securities issued by Fannie Mae, Ginnie Mae or Freddie Mac, carrying an AAA rating or better from Standard & Poor's, with a mix of adjustable, floating and fixed rates. Approximately 86% of the company's investment securities are fixed-rate CMOs, 13% are adjustable-rate, while 1% are CMO floaters. All of Annaly's assets are easily priced and traded in the mortgage-backed securities market. Since Annaly has elected to be taxed as a REIT, it must pay out at least 90% of its earnings to its shareholders in order to avoid taxation at the corporate level.

FINANCIALS: **Sales and profits are in thousands of dollars—add 000 to get the full amount. 2010 Note: Financial information for 2010 was not available for all companies at press time.**

2010 Sales: $2,683,134	2010 Profits: $1,267,280	**U.S. Stock Ticker: NLY**
2009 Sales: $2,922,602	2009 Profits: $1,961,471	**Int'l Ticker:** Int'l Exchange:
2008 Sales: $3,115,428	2008 Profits: $346,238	Employees: 114
2007 Sales: $2,355,447	2007 Profits: $414,384	Fiscal Year Ends: 12/31
2006 Sales: $1,221,882	2006 Profits: $93,816	Parent Company:

SALARIES/BENEFITS:

Pension Plan:	ESOP Stock Plan:	Profit Sharing:	Top Exec. Salary: $2,430,000	Bonus: $17,722,781
Savings Plan:	Stock Purch. Plan:		Second Exec. Salary: $972,000	Bonus: $7,089,113

OTHER THOUGHTS:

Apparent Women Officers or Directors: 2
Hot Spot for Advancement for Women/Minorities:

LOCATIONS: ("Y" = Yes)

West:	Southwest:	Midwest:	Southeast:	Northeast:	International:
				Y	

ANTHONY & SYLVAN POOLS

www.anthonysylvan.com

Industry Group Code: 2389 Ranks within this company's industry group: Sales: Profits:

Properties:	Financial Services:	Construction/Development:		Investments:		Specialty Services:		Brokerage:
Apartments:	Mortgages:	Commercial Construction:		REIT:		Property Management:		Commercial Sales:
Malls/Shopping:	Title Insurance:	Residential Construction:	Y			Online Services:		Residential Sales:
Offices:	Property Insurance:	Land Development:				Software/IT:		Specialty:
Hotels/Motels:		Support Services:				Consulting:		
Industrial/Warehouses:		Design/Engineering:	Y					
Other:								

TYPES OF BUSINESS:

Special Trade Contractors-Pools
Residential Swimming Pools & Spas
Pool-Related Products & Services

BRANDS/DIVISIONS/AFFILIATES:

CONTACTS:
Note: Officers with more than one job title may be intentionally listed here more than once.

Stuart D. Neidus, CEO
Howard P. Wertman, Pres.
Martin Iles, CFO
Tom Casey, VP-Sales
Ken F. Sloan, VP-Human Resources
Stuart D. Neidus, Chmn.

Phone: 732-536-1010	Fax:

Toll-Free: 877-729-7946

Address: 4215 Black Horse Pike, Ste. 110, Mays landing, NJ 08330 US

GROWTH PLANS/SPECIAL FEATURES:

Anthony & Sylvan Pools (ASP) is among the largest U.S. installers of custom-designed, in-ground concrete and fiberglass residential swimming pools and spas. Its operations span a network of sales offices serving markets in Connecticut, Delaware, New Jersey, New York, Maryland, Pennsylvania, North Carolina, Virginia, Texas and Nevada. In addition to designing and offering residential swimming pools, the company provides pool renovation services in select markets; operates retail stores that sell spa- and pool-related products such as chemicals, replacement parts, toys, accessories and equipment; and operates service centers that offer post-installation services such as weekly maintenance, as well as parts, equipment and accessories. ASP also offers eco-friendly swimming pools with filtration systems that are more energy efficient and do not require chlorine. Historically, its sales have been seasonally strongest in the second and third quarters, the peak period for pool installation and use, and weakest in the first and fourth quarters, corresponding with the colder seasons of the year. ASP sells its products primarily to residential homeowners and homebuilders. The company offers its customers financing options and warranty packages.

The firm offers employee benefits that include health care insurance; dental coverage; company-paid life insurance; discounted prescription drugs; short- and long-term disability insurance; 401(k) with company match; and career development training.

FINANCIALS:
Sales and profits are in thousands of dollars—add 000 to get the full amount. 2010 Note: Financial information for 2010 was not available for all companies at press time.

		U.S. Stock Ticker: Private
2010 Sales: $	2010 Profits: $	Int'l Ticker: Int'l Exchange:
2009 Sales: $	2009 Profits: $	Employees:
2008 Sales: $	2008 Profits: $	Fiscal Year Ends: 12/31
2007 Sales: $	2007 Profits: $	Parent Company:
2006 Sales: $	2006 Profits: $	

SALARIES/BENEFITS:

Pension Plan:	ESOP Stock Plan:	Profit Sharing:	Top Exec. Salary: $	Bonus: $
Savings Plan: Y	Stock Purch. Plan:		Second Exec. Salary: $	Bonus: $

OTHER THOUGHTS:

Apparent Women Officers or Directors:
Hot Spot for Advancement for Women/Minorities:

LOCATIONS: ("Y" = Yes)

West:	Southwest:	Midwest:	Southeast:	Northeast:	International:
Y	Y			Y	

APARTMENT INVESTMENT AND MANAGEMENT CO

www.aimco.com

Industry Group Code: 531120 Ranks within this company's industry group: Sales: 12   Profits: 58

Properties:		Financial Services:	Construction/Development:	Investments:		Specialty Services:		Brokerage:
Apartments:	Y	Mortgages:	Commercial Construction:	REIT:	Y	Property Management:	Y	Commercial Sales:
Malls/Shopping:		Title Insurance:	Residential Construction:			Online Services:		Residential Sales:
Offices:		Property Insurance:	Land Development:			Software/IT:		Specialty:
Hotels/Motels:			Support Services:			Consulting:		
Industrial/Warehouses:			Design/Engineering:					
Other:								

TYPES OF BUSINESS:

Real Estate Investment Trust
Apartment Communities
Property Management Services

BRANDS/DIVISIONS/AFFILIATES:

AIMCO
AIMCO-GP, Inc.
AIMCO-LP, Inc.
AIMCO Properties, LP

CONTACTS: *Note: Officers with more than one job title may be intentionally listed here more than once.*

Terry Considine, CEO
Ernest M. Freedman, CFO/Exec. VP
Miles Cortez, Chief Admin. Officer/Exec. VP
Lisa R. Cohn, General Counsel/Exec. VP/Sec.
Keith M. Kimmel, Exec. VP-Property Oper.
Cindy Duffy, Dir.-Corp. Comm.
Elizabeth Coalson, VP-Investor Rel.
Patti K. Fielding, Treas./Exec. VP-Securities & Debt
Dan S. Matula, Exec. VP-Redevelopment & Construction Svcs.
John E. Bezzant, Exec. VP-Transactions
Terry Considine, Chmn.

Phone: 303-757-8101	Fax: 303-759-3226
Toll-Free: 888-789-8600	
Address: 4582 S. Ulster St. Pkwy., Ste. 1100, Denver, CO 80237 US	

GROWTH PLANS/SPECIAL FEATURES:

Apartment Investment and Management Co. (AIMCO) is a self-administered and self-managed real estate investment trust (REIT) engaged in the acquisition, ownership, management and redevelopment of apartment properties. The company operates in two segments: real estate, which focuses on the owning and operating of apartments; and portfolio management, which oversees investment strategies and manages assets. AIMCO owns and operates 447 properties that include approximately 95,512 units. Additionally, it provides property management for 20 properties (representing 2,373 units) and asset management for another 301 properties (representing 24,809 units). In total, AIMCO owns and/or manages 768 properties with 122,694 units in 43 states, Washington, D.C. and Puerto Rico. The firm's portfolio is divided into two classes of properties: conventional and affordable. Conventional operations consist of market-rate apartments in which rent is paid by the resident. Affordable operations consist of mostly apartments in which rent is subsidized or paid by a government agency. Its operations are almost completely conducted through the AIMCO Properties, L.P., which is majority-held through its wholly-owned subsidiaries AIMCO-GP, Inc. and AIMCO-LP, Inc.

Employees are offered medical, dental and vision insurance; life insurance; disability coverage; a 401(k) plan; an employee assistance program; flexible spending accounts; fitness club discounts; professional certification reimbursement; a tuition aid program; an apartment discount; and discounted legal services.

FINANCIALS: Sales and profits are in thousands of dollars—add 000 to get the full amount. 2010 Note: Financial information for 2010 was not available for all companies at press time.

2010 Sales: $1,144,934	2010 Profits: $-89,624	U.S. Stock Ticker: AIV
2009 Sales: $1,131,103	2009 Profits: $-44,800	Int'l Ticker: Int'l Exchange:
2008 Sales: $1,178,878	2008 Profits: $627,002	Employees: 3,100
2007 Sales: $1,174,457	2007 Profits: $125,506	Fiscal Year Ends: 12/31
2006 Sales: $1,274,163	2006 Profits: $176,787	Parent Company:

SALARIES/BENEFITS:

Pension Plan:	ESOP Stock Plan:	Profit Sharing:	Top Exec. Salary: $600,000	Bonus: $1,349,460
Savings Plan: Y	Stock Purch. Plan:		Second Exec. Salary: $500,000	Bonus: $789,035

OTHER THOUGHTS:

Apparent Women Officers or Directors: 4
Hot Spot for Advancement for Women/Minorities: Y

LOCATIONS: ("Y" = Yes)

West:	Southwest:	Midwest:	Southeast:	Northeast:	International:
Y	Y	Y	Y	Y	Y

ARC GROUP OF COMPANIES (THE)

www.arcproperties.com

Industry Group Code: 531120 Ranks within this company's industry group: Sales: Profits:

Properties:		Financial Services:	Construction/Development:	Investments:		Specialty Services:		Brokerage:
Apartments:	Y	Mortgages:	Commercial Construction:	REIT:	Y	Property Management:	Y	Commercial Sales:
Malls/Shopping:	Y	Title Insurance:	Residential Construction:			Online Services:		Residential Sales:
Offices:	Y	Property Insurance:	Land Development:			Software/IT:		Specialty:
Hotels/Motels:			Support Services:			Consulting:		
Industrial/Warehouses:			Design/Engineering:					
Other:								

TYPES OF BUSINESS:

Real Estate Investment Trust
Credit Lease Properties

BRANDS/DIVISIONS/AFFILIATES:

ARC International Fund
ARC Corporate Realty Trust
ARC Properties, Inc.

CONTACTS: *Note: Officers with more than one job title may be intentionally listed here more than once.*

Robert J. Ambrosi, CEO
Marc Perel, COO
Marc Perel, Pres.
Bruce Nelson, CFO
Michael R. Ambrosi, Mktg. & Leasing
Gary S. Baumann, General Counsel
Gil Revera, VP-Bus. Dev.
Stephen J. O'Brien, VP-Finance
Steven L. Maloy, Sr. VP-Investments
Joseph Morena, Exec. VP
Claudia L. Gibson, VP-Capital Markets
John Pantone, Dir.-Regional
Robert J. Ambrosi, Chmn.

Phone: 973-249-1000	Fax: 973-249-1001
Toll-Free:	
Address: 1401 Broad St., Clifton, NJ 07013 US	

GROWTH PLANS/SPECIAL FEATURES:

The ARC Group of Companies consists of three operating companies: ARC International Fund; ARC Property Trust (the firm's publicly listed REIT); and ARC Properties, Inc., a development and management wing. Together the companies specialize in the acquisition and development of credit lease properties throughout the U.S., with special emphasis on metropolitan areas east of the Mississippi. Credit lease properties are general retail, office or industrial buildings leased long-term to credit-worthy clients, who in turn pay the majority or entirety of operating expenses and insurance. Major retail tenants include Home Depot, Lowe's, Staples, Walgreen's and Bed, Bath & Beyond. The company seeks undeveloped land from 1-100 acres in size, generally along the Eastern seaboard from New York City to Washington, D.C. and in Miami. Its preferences are less narrow concerning the location of its developed properties, but it tends to focus on the metropolitan areas of Miami, Florida; Boston, Massachusetts; Washington, D.C.; Philadelphia, Pennsylvania; Chicago, Illinois; and Charlotte, North Carolina. These tend to range anywhere from $1 million to $50 million. Additionally, ARC has leased residential properties near greater New York, Philadelphia and Baltimore. In early 2010, following the liquidation of the group's former REIT, Arc Corporate Realty Trust, Arc Properties, Inc. established ARC Property Trust.

FINANCIALS: Sales and profits are in thousands of dollars—add 000 to get the full amount. 2010 Note: Financial information for 2010 was not available for all companies at press time.

2010 Sales: $	2010 Profits: $	U.S. Stock Ticker: Private
2009 Sales: $	2009 Profits: $	Int'l Ticker: Int'l Exchange:
2008 Sales: $	2008 Profits: $	Employees:
2007 Sales: $	2007 Profits: $	Fiscal Year Ends: 12/31
2006 Sales: $	2006 Profits: $	Parent Company:

SALARIES/BENEFITS:

Pension Plan:	ESOP Stock Plan:	Profit Sharing:	Top Exec. Salary: $	Bonus: $
Savings Plan:	Stock Purch. Plan:		Second Exec. Salary: $	Bonus: $

OTHER THOUGHTS:

Apparent Women Officers or Directors: 1
Hot Spot for Advancement for Women/Minorities:

LOCATIONS: ("Y" = Yes)

West:	Southwest:	Midwest:	Southeast:	Northeast:	International:
	Y	Y	Y	Y	

ARCADIS NV

www.arcadis-global.com

Industry Group Code: 541330 Ranks within this company's industry group: Sales: 4   Profits: 4

Properties:	Financial Services:	Construction/Development:		Investments:	Specialty Services:		Brokerage:
Apartments:	Mortgages:	Commercial Construction:	Y	REIT:	Property Management:	Y	Commercial Sales:
Malls/Shopping:	Title Insurance:	Residential Construction:	Y		Online Services:		Residential Sales:
Offices:	Property Insurance:	Land Development:	Y		Software/IT:		Specialty:
Hotels/Motels:		Support Services:	Y		Consulting:		
Industrial/Warehouses:		Design/Engineering:	Y				
Other:							

TYPES OF BUSINESS:

Engineering Services
Consulting Services
Project Management
Environmental Services
Infrastructure Construction Management
Power Generation Facilities
Industrial & Residential Development

BRANDS/DIVISIONS/AFFILIATES:

Malcolm Pirnie, Inc.
Rise International LLC

CONTACTS: *Note: Officers with more than one job title may be intentionally listed here more than once.*

Harrie L. J. Noy, Exec. Chmn.
Renier Vree, CFO
Tom W. Haak, Dir.-Human Resources
Bartheke Weerstra, General Counsel/Corp. Sec.
Gary Coates, COO-Arcadis U.S./Pres., Environment Div.
Chuck H. Leichner, Global Dir.-Corp. Dev.
Mark Zellenrath, Dir.-Corp. Comm.
Joost Slooten, Dir.-Investor Rel.
Robert K. Goldman, Global Dir.-Environment
Yann Leblais, Global Dir.-Infrastructure
Bill Dee, Global Dir.-Water
Rijnhard W. F. van Tets, Chmn.
Steven B. Blake, CEO-Arcadis U.S.

Phone: 31-20-201-1011	Fax: 31-20-201-1002
Toll-Free:	
Address: Gustav Mahlerplein 97-103, Amsterdam, 1008 AB The Netherlands	

GROWTH PLANS/SPECIAL FEATURES:

Arcadis N.V., based in the Netherlands, is an international provider of consulting, engineering and project management services for infrastructure, environment and facilities. The company develops, designs, implements, maintains and operates projects for private and public sector clients through four divisions: Infrastructure, which accounts for 26% of Arcadis' business; Water, 19%; Environment, 36%; and Buildings, 19%. The infrastructure division consults, designs and manages the construction of infrastructure projects, including railroads, highways, airports, harbors, waterways, dikes and retention ponds. The company also develops utilities for rail signaling, safety, communications and energy supply; constructs bridges and tunnels; and develops small power plants, wind farms and hydroelectric facilities. In addition, the infrastructure division designs new industrial parks and residential areas and oversees the redevelopment of old sites. The water division oversees projects through the entire water cycle, from the supply of clean drinking water to wastewater treatment and water management services. It operates primarily through Malcolm Pirnie, Inc. The environment division provides consulting on environmental policy for companies and governments; conducts environmental impact assessments; and supports environmental management and environmentally conscious engineering practices. The division provides soil and groundwater contamination testing and develops cost-effective solutions for the remediation of contaminated soil and water. Lastly, the buildings division develops and maintains buildings, including offices, stores, commercial properties, schools, museums, prisons, stadiums and railway stations. To carry out the activities of these divisions, Arcadis works from offices in Europe, the U.S. and South America, with approximately 200 locations in 100 countries. The firm is also seeking to expand into new markets, with select offices in the Middle East, Japan and China. In December 2010, it acquired Rise International LLC.

Arcadis offers its U.S. employees benefits including medical, dental and vision coverage; flexible spending accounts; an employee assistance program; a 401(k) plan; a discount stock purchase plan; and life and AD&D insurance.

FINANCIALS: Sales and profits are in thousands of dollars—add 000 to get the full amount. 2010 Note: Financial information for 2010 was not available for all companies at press time.

2010 Sales: $2,919,410	2010 Profits: $114,270	**U.S. Stock Ticker: ARCAY**
2009 Sales: $2,426,260	2009 Profits: $98,910	**Int'l Ticker: ARCAD** Int'l Exchange: Amsterdam
2008 Sales: $2,277,630	2008 Profits: $83,350	Employees: 15,905
2007 Sales: $2,235,000	2007 Profits: $81,260	Fiscal Year Ends: 12/31
2006 Sales: $1,825,000	2006 Profits: $66,460	Parent Company:

SALARIES/BENEFITS:

Pension Plan:	ESOP Stock Plan:	Profit Sharing:	Top Exec. Salary: $	Bonus: $
Savings Plan: Y	Stock Purch. Plan: Y		Second Exec. Salary: $	Bonus: $

OTHER THOUGHTS:

Apparent Women Officers or Directors: 1
Hot Spot for Advancement for Women/Minorities:

LOCATIONS: ("Y" = Yes)

West:	Southwest:	Midwest:	Southeast:	Northeast:	International:
Y	Y	Y	Y	Y	Y

ARCHSTONE TRUST

www.archstoneapartments.com

Industry Group Code: 531110 Ranks within this company's industry group: Sales: Profits:

Properties:		Financial Services:	Construction/Development:		Investments:		Specialty Services:		Brokerage:
Apartments:	Y	Mortgages:	Commercial Construction:		REIT:	Y	Property Management:	Y	Commercial Sales:
Malls/Shopping:		Title Insurance:	Residential Construction:				Online Services:		Residential Sales:
Offices:		Property Insurance:	Land Development:	Y			Software/IT:		Specialty:
Hotels/Motels:			Support Services:				Consulting:	Y	
Industrial/Warehouses:			Design/Engineering:						
Other:									

TYPES OF BUSINESS:

Real Estate Investment Trust
Apartments
Land Development
Garden Communities

BRANDS/DIVISIONS/AFFILIATES:

Archstone Communities
Archstone B.V.
Archstone Real Estate Advisory Services
Archstone NoMa
Archstone Tech Ridge

CONTACTS: *Note: Officers with more than one job title may be intentionally listed here more than once.*

R. Scot Sellers, CEO
Charles E. Mueller, COO
Daniel E. Amedro, Chief Mktg. Officer
Daniel E. Amedro, CIO
Neil Brown, Chief Dev. Officer
Dana K. Hamilton, Pres., European Oper.
R. Scot Sellers, Chmn.
Dana K. Hamilton, Managing Dir.-Archstone B.V.

Phone: 303-708-5959	Fax: 303-708-5999
Toll-Free:	
Address: 9200 E. Panorama Cir., Ste. 400, Englewood, CO 80112 US	

GROWTH PLANS/SPECIAL FEATURES:

Archstone Trust (formerly Archstone-Smith Trust) is a real estate investment trust (REIT) focused on acquiring, developing and managing apartment properties. The company administers a portfolio concentrated on desirable neighborhoods in the Washington, D.C. metro area, Southern California, the San Francisco Bay area, the New York City metropolitan area, Boston, the Orlando metropolitan area, Chicago, Atlanta, Houston, Seattle and other major cities. The firm manages garden-style apartment complexes and high-rise apartments. All of the market areas in which the company owns property are characterized by three traits: high income levels; limited land available for new housing development; and a strong, diversified economic base. The firm also offers advisory services to lenders and investors through Archstone Real Estate Advisory Services, including asset strategy services such as market analysis, valuation, underwriting and risk modeling; development services, consisting of entitlement and pre-construction services such as permits, estimates, design management, value engineering, community outreach and public hearing facilitation; construction management services, including bidding, contracting, cost and schedule control, reporting, risk management and construction completion; and asset management services, consisting of marketing and leasing, property maintenance, asset repositioning, disposition analysis and execution and performance monitoring. Archstone's foreign subsidiary, Archstone B.V., develops and manages apartment properties in Europe. In July 2010, the company began construction of Archstone NoMa, a 469-apartment community in Washington, D.C. In September 2010, the firm opened Archstone Tech Ridge, a luxury apartment community in Austin, Texas, developed with Bluerock Real Estate LLC. In December 2010, Archstone began construction of a 389-unit apartment community in Maryland.

The firm offers its employees health, dental, vision, prescription drug, disability, life, and AD&D insurance; flexible spending accounts; wellness programs; tuition reimbursement; a 401(k) plan; relocation assistance; an employee assistance program; employee discounts; and credit union membership.

FINANCIALS: Sales and profits are in thousands of dollars—add 000 to get the full amount. 2010 Note: Financial information for 2010 was not available for all companies at press time.

2010 Sales: $	2010 Profits: $	U.S. Stock Ticker: Private
2009 Sales: $	2009 Profits: $	Int'l Ticker: Int'l Exchange:
2008 Sales: $	2008 Profits: $	Employees:
2007 Sales: $	2007 Profits: $	Fiscal Year Ends: 12/31
2006 Sales: $1,133,586	2006 Profits: $727,434	Parent Company:

SALARIES/BENEFITS:

Pension Plan:	ESOP Stock Plan:	Profit Sharing:	Top Exec. Salary: $	Bonus: $
Savings Plan: Y	Stock Purch. Plan:		Second Exec. Salary: $	Bonus: $

OTHER THOUGHTS:

Apparent Women Officers or Directors: 1
Hot Spot for Advancement for Women/Minorities:

LOCATIONS: ("Y" = Yes)

West:	Southwest:	Midwest:	Southeast:	Northeast:	International:
Y	Y		Y	Y	Y

ARDEN REALTY INC

www.ardenrealty.com

Industry Group Code: 531120 Ranks within this company's industry group: Sales: Profits:

Properties:		Financial Services:	Construction/Development:		Investments:		Specialty Services:		Brokerage:
Apartments:		Mortgages:	Commercial Construction:	Y	REIT:	Y	Property Management:	Y	Commercial Sales:
Malls/Shopping:		Title Insurance:	Residential Construction:				Online Services:	Y	Residential Sales:
Offices:	Y	Property Insurance:	Land Development:	Y			Software/IT:		Specialty:
Hotels/Motels:			Support Services:	Y			Consulting:		
Industrial/Warehouses:			Design/Engineering:	Y					
Other:									

TYPES OF BUSINESS:

Real Estate Investment Trust
Office Properties
Property & Asset Management
Property Development
Construction
Consulting-Energy Efficiency

BRANDS/DIVISIONS/AFFILIATES:

GE Real Estate
Arden At Your Service
Concierge At Large, Inc.

GROWTH PLANS/SPECIAL FEATURES:

Arden Realty, Inc., a subsidiary of GE Real Estate, is a fully-integrated real estate investment trust (REIT) that leases, manages, constructs, develops and acquires commercial properties throughout the West Coast. The company owns and manages approximately 230 buildings (101 Office buildings and 126 industrial properties) covering 27 million square feet in Southern California, Northern California, Seattle, Portland, Phoenix, Chicago and Utah. The firm's Arden at Your Service program is a free online concierge service for its tenants offered in partnership with Concierge At Large, Inc., a provider of luxury and corporate concierge services. Arden additionally surveys its tenants twice a year and provides special discounts, events and energy solutions. The company's portfolio includes a number of EPA Energy Star labeled buildings as a result of its portfolio-wide energy conservation program.

CONTACTS: *Note: Officers with more than one job title may be intentionally listed here more than once.*

Joaquin de Monet, CEO
Scott Lyle, COO
Joaquin de Monet, Pres.
David Stippich, CFO
Brooke Lauter, First VP-Mktg.
Danielle Saccone, VP-Human Resources
Noel Clark, CIO/First VP
Danielle Saccone, VP-Admin.
Scott Lyle, Sr. VP-Oper.
Brooke Lauter, First VP-Corp. Comm.
Iris Almaraz, First VP-Acct.
Lee Halford, Managing Dir.-Industrial
Gary Hansel, VP-Portfolio Oper.
Eric Hasserjian, First VP-Northern Region
Paul King, First VP-Southern Region

Phone: 310-966-2600	Fax: 310-966-2699
Toll-Free:	
Address: 11601 Wilshire Blvd., Ste. 400, Los Angeles, CA 90025 US	

FINANCIALS: Sales and profits are in thousands of dollars—add 000 to get the full amount. 2010 Note: Financial information for 2010 was not available for all companies at press time.

2010 Sales: $	2010 Profits: $	U.S. Stock Ticker: Subsidiary
2009 Sales: $	2009 Profits: $	Int'l Ticker: Int'l Exchange:
2008 Sales: $	2008 Profits: $	Employees:
2007 Sales: $	2007 Profits: $	Fiscal Year Ends: 12/31
2006 Sales: $	2006 Profits: $	Parent Company: GE REAL ESTATE

SALARIES/BENEFITS:

Pension Plan:	ESOP Stock Plan:	Profit Sharing:	Top Exec. Salary: $	Bonus: $
Savings Plan:	Stock Purch. Plan:		Second Exec. Salary: $	Bonus: $

OTHER THOUGHTS:

Apparent Women Officers or Directors: 3
Hot Spot for Advancement for Women/Minorities: Y

LOCATIONS: ("Y" = Yes)

West:	Southwest:	Midwest:	Southeast:	Northeast:	International:
Y	Y	Y			

ASSOCIATED ESTATES REALTY CORPORATION

www.associatedestates.com

Industry Group Code: 531110   Ranks within this company's industry group: Sales: 17   Profits: 13

Properties:		Financial Services:	Construction/Development:		Investments:		Specialty Services:		Brokerage:
Apartments:	Y	Mortgages:	Commercial Construction:	Y	REIT:	Y	Property Management:	Y	Commercial Sales:
Malls/Shopping:		Title Insurance:	Residential Construction:	Y			Online Services:		Residential Sales:
Offices:		Property Insurance:	Land Development:				Software/IT:		Specialty:
Hotels/Motels:			Support Services:				Consulting:		
Industrial/Warehouses:			Design/Engineering:						
Other:									

TYPES OF BUSINESS:

Real Estate Investment Trust
Apartment Communities
Multifamily
Construction Services

BRANDS/DIVISIONS/AFFILIATES:

Merit Enterprises, Inc.

CONTACTS: *Note: Officers with more than one job title may be intentionally listed here more than once.*

Jeffrey I. Friedman, CEO
Jeffrey I. Friedman, Pres.
Lou Fatica, CFO/VP/Treas.
Patrick Duffy, VP-Strategic Mktg.
Daniel E. Gold, VP-Human Resources
Bradley A. Van Auken, General Counsel/VP/Corp. Sec.
John T. Shannon, Sr. VP-Oper.
John P. Hinkle, VP-Acquisitions
John Lytell, Dir.-Corp. Comm.
Jeremy S. Goldberg, VP-Investor Rel.
Jeremy S. Goldberg, VP-Corp. Finance
Beth L. Stoll, VP-Oper.
Miria C. Rabideau, VP-Oper.
Michelle B. Creger, VP/Associate General Counsel
Jason A. Friedman, VP-Construction & Dev.
Jeffrey I. Friedman, Chmn.

Phone: 216-261-5000	Fax: 216-289-9600
Toll-Free: 800-440-2372	
Address: 1 AEC Pkwy., Richmond Heights, OH 44143-1467 US	

GROWTH PLANS/SPECIAL FEATURES:

Associated Estates Realty Corporation (AEC) is an equity real estate investment trust (REIT) engaged in property acquisition, advisory, development, construction, management, disposition, operation and ownership activities. The firm focuses on high barrier-to-entry markets in the Midwest, Mid-Atlantic and Southeastern U.S. AEC's property portfolio includes 52 owned apartment communities containing 13,662 units in eight states. In 2010, multifamily properties accounted for 88% of its total revenue. In addition to property ownership, through subsidiary Merit Enterprises, Inc., the company offers a number of construction and development services for commercial construction, including design and rehabilitation services for offices, warehouses, public and government-assisted projects; residential construction services for single family property design, development and rehabilitation; commercial and residential construction site development services; and tax credit preparation services. The firm also owns two taxable REIT subsidiaries that provide management and other services to AEC and third party owners. In 2010, the firm acquired three apartment communities in the state of Virginia and one in Dallas, Texas.

AEC offers its employees health, dental, life and vision insurance, long-term disability coverage, tuition and educational reimbursement, medical and dependent care flexible spending accounts, a 401(k) plan, employee discounts and rent discounts for employees residing in AEC-owned apartment communities.

FINANCIALS: Sales and profits are in thousands of dollars—add 000 to get the full amount. 2010 Note: Financial information for 2010 was not available for all companies at press time.

2010 Sales: $153,715	2010 Profits: $-8,585	U.S. Stock Ticker: AEC
2009 Sales: $130,419	2009 Profits: $6,263	Int'l Ticker: Int'l Exchange:
2008 Sales: $130,642	2008 Profits: $34,627	Employees: 390
2007 Sales: $126,980	2007 Profits: $10,165	Fiscal Year Ends: 12/31
2006 Sales: $119,364	2006 Profits: $27,021	Parent Company:

SALARIES/BENEFITS:

Pension Plan:	ESOP Stock Plan:	Profit Sharing:	Top Exec. Salary: $487,479	Bonus: $690,758
Savings Plan: Y	Stock Purch. Plan:		Second Exec. Salary: $290,000	Bonus: $203,580

OTHER THOUGHTS:

Apparent Women Officers or Directors: 3
Hot Spot for Advancement for Women/Minorities: Y

LOCATIONS: ("Y" = Yes)

West:	Southwest:	Midwest:	Southeast:	Northeast:	International:
Y	Y	Y	Y	Y	

ATRIA SENIOR LIVING GROUP

www.atriaseniorliving.com

Industry Group Code: 623110 Ranks within this company's industry group: Sales: Profits:

Properties:	Financial Services:	Construction/Development:	Investments:	Specialty Services:		Brokerage:
Apartments:	Mortgages:	Commercial Construction:	REIT:	Property Management:	Y	Commercial Sales:
Malls/Shopping:	Title Insurance:	Residential Construction:		Online Services:		Residential Sales:
Offices:	Property Insurance:	Land Development:		Software/IT:		Specialty:
Hotels/Motels:		Support Services:		Consulting:		
Industrial/Warehouses:		Design/Engineering:				
Other: Y						

TYPES OF BUSINESS:

Long-Term Health Care
Assisted Living Centers
Alzheimer Care
Short-Term Health Care

BRANDS/DIVISIONS/AFFILIATES:

Engage Life Program
Life Guidance Program
Independent Living Program
Assisted Living Program

CONTACTS: *Note: Officers with more than one job title may be intentionally listed here more than once.*

John A. Moore, CEO
Julie Harding, COO
Mark Jesse, CFO

Phone: 502-779-4700	**Fax:** 502-779-4701
Toll-Free: 888-287-4201	
Address: 401 S. 4th Ave., Ste. 1900, Louisville, KY 40202 US	

GROWTH PLANS/SPECIAL FEATURES:

Atria Senior Living Group is one of the nation's largest operators of facilities providing assisted living services for the country's burgeoning senior population. The company currently operates more than 120 communities across 26 states, which provide housing and support services for over 13,000 seniors. Each program that Atria offers is tailored to the individual, with residents free to bring their own furnishings and pets. Atria provides seniors with the following programs: The Independent Living program, which is a retirement lifestyle that frees seniors from the worries of home maintenance, encourages them to engage in activities and hobbies and allows them to choose their own degree of privacy or sociability; the Assisted Living program, which is available to help seniors with daily activities such as bathing, eating, dressing and medication management; the Life Guidance program, which is available at some communities to provide a separate and secure environment for seniors with Alzheimer's disease and other forms of memory impairment; and respite stay programs, which are tailored for seniors on a temporary basis for seasonal stays, hospital recovery or trial-period stays. Also, Atria's Engage Life program works to provide residents with other interesting and meaningful activities, such as book clubs, exercise classes, gardening, arts and crafts, bingo and card games which are coordinated by Engage Life Directors that spend individual time with each resident to help them plan activities according to their interests.

FINANCIALS: Sales and profits are in thousands of dollars—add 000 to get the full amount. 2010 Note: Financial information for 2010 was not available for all companies at press time.

2010 Sales: $	2010 Profits: $	**U.S. Stock Ticker: Private**
2009 Sales: $	2009 Profits: $	**Int'l Ticker:** Int'l Exchange:
2008 Sales: $	2008 Profits: $	Employees:
2007 Sales: $	2007 Profits: $	Fiscal Year Ends: 12/31
2006 Sales: $	2006 Profits: $	Parent Company:

SALARIES/BENEFITS:

Pension Plan:	ESOP Stock Plan:	Profit Sharing:	Top Exec. Salary: $	Bonus: $
Savings Plan:	Stock Purch. Plan:		Second Exec. Salary: $	Bonus: $

OTHER THOUGHTS:

Apparent Women Officers or Directors:
Hot Spot for Advancement for Women/Minorities:

LOCATIONS: ("Y" = Yes)

West:	Southwest:	Midwest:	Southeast:	Northeast:	International:
Y	Y	Y	Y	Y	

AVALONBAY COMMUNITIES INC

www.avalonbay.com

Industry Group Code: 531110 Ranks within this company's industry group: Sales: 2 Profits: 2

Properties:		Financial Services:		Construction/Development:		Investments:		Specialty Services:		Brokerage:	
Apartments:	Y	Mortgages:		Commercial Construction:		REIT:	Y	Property Management:	Y	Commercial Sales:	
Malls/Shopping:		Title Insurance:		Residential Construction:	Y			Online Services:		Residential Sales:	
Offices:		Property Insurance:		Land Development:				Software/IT:		Specialty:	
Hotels/Motels:				Support Services:				Consulting:			
Industrial/Warehouses:				Design/Engineering:							
Other:	Y										

TYPES OF BUSINESS:

Real Estate Investment Trust
Apartment Complexes
Residential Construction

BRANDS/DIVISIONS/AFFILIATES:

CONTACTS:
Note: Officers with more than one job title may be intentionally listed here more than once.

Bryce Blair, CEO
Timothy J. Naughton, Pres.
Thomas J. Sargeant, CFO
Kevin Thompson, VP-Mktg.
Suzanne Jakstavich, VP-Human Resources
Karen A. Hollinger, VP-Info. Svcs.
Mike Nootens, VP-Eng. & Maintenance
Edward M. Schulman, General Counsel/Sr. VP/Corp. Sec.
Leo S. Horey, Exec. VP-Oper.
Jonathan B. Cox, Sr. VP-Dev.
Kevin P. O'Shea, Sr. VP-Finance & Investment Mgmt.
David W. Bellman, Sr. VP-Construction
Sean J. Breslin, Exec. VP-Investments & Asset Mgmt.
Lyn C. Lansdale, Sr. VP-Strategic Bus. Svcs.
Keri A. Shea, VP-Finance/Treas.
Bryce Blair, Chmn.

Phone: 703-329-6300	Fax: 703-329-1459
Toll-Free:	
Address: 2900 Eisenhower Ave., Ste. 300, Alexandria, VA 22314 US	

GROWTH PLANS/SPECIAL FEATURES:

AvalonBay Communities, Inc. is a real estate investment trust (REIT) engaged in the development, redevelopment, acquisition, ownership and operation of multifamily communities in high barrier-to-entry markets in the U.S. The company owns or operates 173 apartment communities containing over 51,693 apartment units in 10 states and Washington, D.C. AvalonBay also has 14 communities currently under construction and holds development rights for 26 additional communities. Current properties are primarily garden-style apartment communities consisting of two- and three-story buildings in landscaped settings, as well as high-rise and mid-rise apartment communities. The firm's investments are divided into three classes: Established Communities; Other Stabilized Communities; and Development/Redevelopment Communities. Established Communities are generally operating communities that were owned and had stabilized occupancy and operating expenses as of the beginning of the prior year. Other Stabilized Communities are generally all other operating communities that have stabilized occupancy and operating expenses during the current year, but that had not achieved stabilization as of the beginning of the prior year. Development/ Redevelopment Communities consist of communities that are under construction, communities where substantial redevelopment is in progress or is planned to begin during the current year and communities under lease-up. AvalonBay's primary markets are Boston, Massachusetts; Chicago, Illinois; San Jose and Los Angeles, California; Shelton, Connecticut; Virginia Beach, Virginia; Seattle, Washington; New York City; and Washington, D.C. In January 2011, the firm acquired three apartment communities: two in California and one in New Jersey.

Employees are offered medical, dental, and vision insurance; disability benefits; accidental death and dismemberment (AD&D) insurance; flexible spending accounts; a health care account; a dependent care account; an employee assistance program; an employee stock purchase plan; relocation assistance; a 401(k) plan; professional development opportunities through AvalonBay University and tuition reimbursement; and a housing discount for employees who live at an AvalonBay community.

FINANCIALS:
Sales and profits are in thousands of dollars—add 000 to get the full amount. 2010 Note: Financial information for 2010 was not available for all companies at press time.

2010 Sales: $895,266	2010 Profits: $175,331	**U.S. Stock Ticker: AVB**
2009 Sales: $851,107	2009 Profits: $155,647	**Int'l Ticker:** Int'l Exchange:
2008 Sales: $813,764	2008 Profits: $411,487	Employees: 1,993
2007 Sales: $727,786	2007 Profits: $358,160	Fiscal Year Ends: 12/31
2006 Sales: $677,641	2006 Profits: $266,546	Parent Company:

SALARIES/BENEFITS:

Pension Plan:	ESOP Stock Plan:	Profit Sharing:	Top Exec. Salary: $855,036	Bonus: $965,389
Savings Plan: Y	Stock Purch. Plan: Y		Second Exec. Salary: $778,847	Bonus: $693,758

OTHER THOUGHTS:

Apparent Women Officers or Directors: 12
Hot Spot for Advancement for Women/Minorities: Y

LOCATIONS: ("Y" = Yes)

West:	Southwest:	Midwest:	Southeast:	Northeast:	International:
Y		Y		Y	

AVATAR HOLDINGS INC

www.avatarhomes.com

Industry Group Code: 2361 Ranks within this company's industry group: Sales: 17 Profits: 12

Properties:		Financial Services:		Construction/Development:		Investments:	Specialty Services:		Brokerage:
Apartments:	Y	Mortgages:		Commercial Construction:	Y	REIT:	Property Management:	Y	Commercial Sales:
Malls/Shopping:	Y	Title Insurance:	Y	Residential Construction:	Y		Online Services:		Residential Sales:
Offices:	Y	Property Insurance:		Land Development:	Y		Software/IT:		Specialty:
Hotels/Motels:				Support Services:	Y		Consulting:		
Industrial/Warehouses:				Design/Engineering:					
Other:	Y								

TYPES OF BUSINESS:

Property Development
Retirement Communities
Residential Properties
Commercial Properties
Home Building
Property Management
Utility Operations
Title Insurance Agency

BRANDS/DIVISIONS/AFFILIATES:

Avatar Properties, Inc.
Solivita
Poinciana
CantaMia
Seasons at Traditions
Prominent Title Insurance Agency Inc

CONTACTS:
Note: Officers with more than one job title may be intentionally listed here more than once.
Jon M. Donnell, CEO
Jon M. Donnell, Pres.
Patricia Kimball Fletcher, General Counsel/Exec. VP
Michael P. Rama, Controller
Joseph Carl Mulac III, Exec. VP/Pres., Avatar Properties, Inc.
Juanita I. Kerrigan, VP/Corp. Sec.
Joshua Lionel Nash, Chmn.

Phone: 305-442-7000	Fax: 305-443-3844
Toll-Free:	
Address: 201 Alhambra Cir., Coral Gables, FL 33134 US	

GROWTH PLANS/SPECIAL FEATURES:

Avatar Holdings, Inc. is a diversified real estate company engaged primarily in the development of lifestyle communities, including active adult and primary residential communities in Florida and Arizona. It handles development through subsidiary Avatar Properties, Inc. Avatar's chief retirement community, Solivita, is located within its master-planned community of Poinciana in central Florida and encompasses approximately 126,000 square feet of recreation and service facilities, including a fitness center, a golf clubhouse, restaurants, arts and crafts rooms, a newsstand and meeting and theater facilities. The property also features two 18-hole golf courses and other sporting and games facilities, including a softball field and five tennis courts. The community was designed to accommodate in excess of 4,000 homes. Additionally, it is currently developing the CantaMia active adult community in Goodyear, Arizona and the Seasons at Tradition community in St. Lucie County, Florida. Overall, Avatar owns over 17,000 acres of developed, partially developed or developable residential, commercial and industrial property. Within Florida and Arizona, Avatar also owns more than 15,000 acres of preserves, wetlands, open space and other areas that are not developable, but which the company considers potentially valuable for preservation or conservation purposes. Avatar's other activities include the management and operation of a small shopping center in Rio Rico, Arizona and Prominent Title Insurance Agency, Inc., a title insurance agency. In October 2010, it acquired a portfolio of real estate assets, including the CantaMia community, from JEN Partners LLC.

FINANCIALS:
Sales and profits are in thousands of dollars—add 000 to get the full amount. 2010 Note: Financial information for 2010 was not available for all companies at press time.

2010 Sales: $59,138	2010 Profits: $-35,682	**U.S. Stock Ticker:** AVTR
2009 Sales: $73,501	2009 Profits: $-28,983	**Int'l Ticker:** Int'l Exchange:
2008 Sales: $110,366	2008 Profits: $-109,876	Employees: 243
2007 Sales: $291,832	2007 Profits: $20,997	Fiscal Year Ends: 12/31
2006 Sales: $835,079	2006 Profits: $174,726	Parent Company:

SALARIES/BENEFITS:

Pension Plan:	ESOP Stock Plan:	Profit Sharing:	Top Exec. Salary: $500,000	Bonus: $500,000
Savings Plan: Y	Stock Purch. Plan:		Second Exec. Salary: $500,000	Bonus: $400,000

OTHER THOUGHTS:

Apparent Women Officers or Directors: 3
Hot Spot for Advancement for Women/Minorities: Y

LOCATIONS: ("Y" = Yes)

West:	Southwest:	Midwest:	Southeast:	Northeast:	International:
	Y		Y		

BALFOUR BEATTY PLC

www.balfourbeatty.com

Industry Group Code: 237 Ranks within this company's industry group: Sales: 10   Profits: 7

Properties:	Financial Services:	Construction/Development:		Investments:	Specialty Services:	Brokerage:
Apartments:	Mortgages:	Commercial Construction:	Y	REIT:	Property Management:	Commercial Sales:
Malls/Shopping:	Title Insurance:	Residential Construction:			Online Services:	Residential Sales:
Offices:	Property Insurance:	Land Development:			Software/IT:	Specialty:
Hotels/Motels:		Support Services:	Y		Consulting:	
Industrial/Warehouses:		Design/Engineering:				
Other:						

TYPES OF BUSINESS:

Heavy Construction
Engineering Services
Railway Services
Property Management
Utility & Roadway Infrastructure Management

BRANDS/DIVISIONS/AFFILIATES:

Heery International, Inc.
Parsons Brinckerhoff Inc
Balfour Beatty Rail, Inc.
Halsall Group

CONTACTS: *Note: Officers with more than one job title may be intentionally listed here more than once.*

Ian Tyler, CEO
Andrew McNaughton, COO
Paul Raby, Dir.-Human Resources
Andy Rose, Managing Dir.-Eng. & Safety
Chris Vaughan, General Counsel/Corp. Sec.
Peter Zinkin, Dir.-Planning & Dev.
Duncan Magrath, Dir.-Finance
Anthony Rabin, Deputy CEO
Manfred Leger, CEO-Rail
Robert Van Cleave, CEO-Construction Svcs., U.S.
Mike Peasland, CEO-Construction Svcs., U.K.
Steve Marshall, Chmn.
Brian Osborne, Dir.-Int'l Bus.

Phone: 44-20-7216-6800	Fax: 44-20-7216-6950
Toll-Free:	
Address: 130 Wilton Rd., London, SW1V 1LQ UK	

GROWTH PLANS/SPECIAL FEATURES:

Balfour Beatty plc provides engineering, construction and financial services for rail, road, power and building projects worldwide. It is one of the largest fixed rail infrastructure contracting companies in the world. Balfour Beatty divides its business into four categories: professional services, construction services, support services and infrastructure investments. The professional services division provides program and project management, architectural services, project design, technical services, planning and consultancy. This division operates in the U.S. through subsidiaries Heery International, Inc. and Parsons Brinckerhoff, Inc. Construction services include building design; construction management; refurbishment and fit-out; and mechanical and electrical services. The firm has an established presence in the U.K. and U.S., through its subsidiaries, and is expanding its business in South East Asia and the Middle East. Balfour Beatty provides ongoing operation and maintenance of assets after construction and offers business services outsourcing through its support services division. The division encompasses the company's utilities, facilities management, rail renewals and highway management activities. It conducts business mainly through long-term contracts, ranging from 5-30 years. The infrastructure investments segment is a leader in the public private partnership (PPP) contracts. It maintains 31 concessions in the U.K., primarily in the education, health and roads/street lighting sectors. The division also maintains 18 concessions in the U.S., where it is involved in the military housing market, and one concession in Singapore. Some of the company's subsidiaries include Heery International, Inc. In October 2010, the firm acquired Canadian professional services company, Halsall Group.

FINANCIALS: Sales and profits are in thousands of dollars—add 000 to get the full amount. 2010 Note: Financial information for 2010 was not available for all companies at press time.

2010 Sales: $17,143,400	2010 Profits: $549,710	U.S. Stock Ticker:
2009 Sales: $13,771,300	2009 Profits: $327,600	Int'l Ticker: BBY Int'l Exchange: London-LSE
2008 Sales: $12,658,800	2008 Profits: $396,460	Employees: 41,000
2007 Sales: $9,494,480	2007 Profits: $230,530	Fiscal Year Ends: 12/31
2006 Sales: $8,936,980	2006 Profits: $497,270	Parent Company:

SALARIES/BENEFITS:

Pension Plan:	ESOP Stock Plan:	Profit Sharing:	Top Exec. Salary: $	Bonus: $
Savings Plan:	Stock Purch. Plan:		Second Exec. Salary: $	Bonus: $

OTHER THOUGHTS:

Apparent Women Officers or Directors:
Hot Spot for Advancement for Women/Minorities:

LOCATIONS: ("Y" = Yes)

West:	Southwest:	Midwest:	Southeast:	Northeast:	International:
	Y		Y		Y

BANK OF AMERICA HOME LOANS   www8.bankofamerica.com/home-loans/overview.go

Industry Group Code: 522310 Ranks within this company's industry group: Sales: Profits:

Properties:	Financial Services:		Construction/Development:	Investments:	Specialty Services:		Brokerage:
Apartments:	Mortgages:	Y	Commercial Construction:	REIT:	Property Management:		Commercial Sales:
Malls/Shopping:	Title Insurance:		Residential Construction:		Online Services:	Y	Residential Sales:
Offices:	Property Insurance:		Land Development:		Software/IT:		Specialty:
Hotels/Motels:			Support Services:		Consulting:		
Industrial/Warehouses:			Design/Engineering:				
Other:							

TYPES OF BUSINESS:

Mortgage Banking
Banking
Insurance

BRANDS/DIVISIONS/AFFILIATES:

Bank of America Corp
Countrywide Financial Corp
Taylor, Bean & Whitaker

CONTACTS: *Note: Officers with more than one job title may be intentionally listed here more than once.*

Barbara Desoer, Pres., Bank of America Mortgage, Home Equity & Insurance Svcs.
Anne D. McCallion, CFO
Bridget O'Connor, CTO
Brian Moynihan, CEO-Bank of America
Matt Vernon, Exec.-Short Sale & Real Estate Owned BoA Home Loan
Rebecca Mairone, Exec.-National Servicing, BoA Home Loans

Phone: 818-225-3000	Fax:
Toll-Free: 800-283-8875	
Address: 4500 Park Granada, Calabasas, CA 91302 US	

GROWTH PLANS/SPECIAL FEATURES:

Bank of America Home Loans (BOAHL), formerly Countrywide Financial Corp, a wholly-owned subsidiary of Bank of America, is engaged in mortgage lending and other real estate finance-related businesses, including mortgage banking; banking and mortgage warehouse lending; securities; and insurance underwriting. The company operates in three segments: home loans, banking and insurance. Home loan products include home loans, refinancing, home equity lines of credit, construction loans and reverse mortgages. Through the banking division, BOAHL takes deposits and invests in mortgage loans and home equity lines of credit, sourced primarily through its mortgage banking operation as well as through purchases from non-affiliates. The segment also offers short-term secured financing to mortgage lenders. Banking products include certificates of deposit, money market accounts, savings accounts and credit cards. The insurance division offers property, casualty, life and disability insurance as an underwriter and as an insurance agency. Insurance products include homeowners/condo, auto, home warranty, renters, life, commercial and other products. In August 2010, the number of homeowners assisted in avoiding foreclosure through BOAHL's mortgage modification programs, including the U.S. government's Home Affordable Modification Program (HAMP) exceeded 680,000 over the last two years.

FINANCIALS: Sales and profits are in thousands of dollars—add 000 to get the full amount. 2010 Note: Financial information for 2010 was not available for all companies at press time.

2010 Sales: $	2010 Profits: $	**U.S. Stock Ticker: Subsidiary**
2009 Sales: $	2009 Profits: $	**Int'l Ticker:** Int'l Exchange:
2008 Sales: $	2008 Profits: $	Employees:
2007 Sales: $6,061,437	2007 Profits: $-703,538	Fiscal Year Ends: 12/31
2006 Sales: $11,417,128	2006 Profits: $2,674,846	Parent Company: BANK OF AMERICA CORP

SALARIES/BENEFITS:

Pension Plan:	ESOP Stock Plan:	Profit Sharing:	Top Exec. Salary: $	Bonus: $
Savings Plan: Y	Stock Purch. Plan:		Second Exec. Salary: $	Bonus: $

OTHER THOUGHTS:

Apparent Women Officers or Directors: 3
Hot Spot for Advancement for Women/Minorities: Y

LOCATIONS: ("Y" = Yes)

West:	Southwest:	Midwest:	Southeast:	Northeast:	International:
Y	Y	Y	Y	Y	Y

BANYAN TREE HOLDINGS LIMITED

www.banyantree.com

Industry Group Code: 721110 Ranks within this company's industry group: Sales: 25   Profits: 18

Properties:		Financial Services:		Construction/Development:		Investments:		Specialty Services:		Brokerage:	
Apartments:		Mortgages:		Commercial Construction:		REIT:		Property Management:	Y	Commercial Sales:	Y
Malls/Shopping:	Y	Title Insurance:		Residential Construction:				Online Services:		Residential Sales:	
Offices:		Property Insurance:		Land Development:				Software/IT:		Specialty:	
Hotels/Motels:	Y			Support Services:				Consulting:			
Industrial/Warehouses:				Design/Engineering:	Y						
Other:	Y										

TYPES OF BUSINESS:

Hotels & Resorts
Spas
Fine Art Galleries
Design Services

BRANDS/DIVISIONS/AFFILIATES:

Laguna Resorts & Hotels Public Company Limited
Architrave Design & Project Services Pte Ltd
Banyan Tree Hotels
Angsana Hotels

CONTACTS: *Note: Officers with more than one job title may be intentionally listed here more than once.*

Ariel P. Vera, Group Managing Dir.
Angelina Hue, Asst. Dir.-Mktg. Comm.
Jane Teah Seow Lian, Sec.
Ho KwonCjan, Managing Dir.-Design Oper.
Paul Chong, VP-Bus. Dev.
Claire Chiang, Managing Dir.-Retail Oper.
Ho KwonPing, Exec. Chmn.

Phone: 65-6849-5888	Fax: 65-6462-2463
Toll-Free: 800-591-0439	
Address: 211 Upper Bukit Timah Rd., Singapore, 588182 Singapore	

GROWTH PLANS/SPECIAL FEATURES:

Banyan Tree Holdings Limited, operating as Banyan Tree Hotels & Resorts, is a Singapore-based hospitality company that develops, manages, operates and invests in resorts, hotels, spas and other property. The company's portfolio includes more than 29 hotels and resorts, 65 spas, 75 retail galleries and three golf clubs across 23 countries, and the Banyan Tree and Angsana brand names. Banyan Tree's operations are split into three segments: Hotel Investments, which generated 62% of the firm's 2010 revenue; Property Sales, 9%; and Fee-based Activities, 29%. The Hotel Investments segment invests in luxury hotels that are managed by third-party operators. The Property Sales segment consists of the sales of hotel residencies, such as villas, townhomes and apartments, in Asia and Mexico under the Banyan Tree Residences and Laguna Property brands. The Fee-based Activities segment is comprised of the firm's hotel management; spa and gallery operations; and design services businesses. Banyan Tree's hotel management segment manages properties owned by other companies. The spa operations segment manages spas located within Banyan Tree's properties and other hotels, while the gallery branch offers fine art and other retail sales. Banyan Tree's in-house design division, Architrave, conducts designing services as well as operates the firm's golf properties. Other businesses include the firm's real estate hospitality funds segment, operating as Banyan Tree Capital, which seeks private equity investments for the development of the firm's business. The majority of Banyan Tree's properties and operations are located in the Asia Pacific region and Mexico, with destinations in Bahrain, China, Indonesia, Korea, Maldives, Seychelles, Thailand and the United Arab Emirates. The firm has over 30 projects currently in various stages of development across Asia and the Middle East that it plans to open through 2013.

FINANCIALS: Sales and profits are in thousands of dollars—add 000 to get the full amount. 2010 Note: Financial information for 2010 was not available for all companies at press time.

2010 Sales: $248,240	2010 Profits: $24,400	U.S. Stock Ticker: Private	
2009 Sales: $253,680	2009 Profits: $2,780	Int'l Ticker:	Int'l Exchange:
2008 Sales: $	2008 Profits: $	Employees:	
2007 Sales: $	2007 Profits: $	Fiscal Year Ends: 12/31	
2006 Sales: $	2006 Profits: $	Parent Company:	

SALARIES/BENEFITS:

Pension Plan:	ESOP Stock Plan:	Profit Sharing:	Top Exec. Salary: $	Bonus: $
Savings Plan:	Stock Purch. Plan:		Second Exec. Salary: $	Bonus: $

OTHER THOUGHTS:

Apparent Women Officers or Directors: 3
Hot Spot for Advancement for Women/Minorities: Y

LOCATIONS: ("Y" = Yes)

West:	Southwest:	Midwest:	Southeast:	Northeast:	International:
					Y

BARCELO CRESTLINE CORPORATION

www.barcelocrestline.com

Industry Group Code: 721110 Ranks within this company's industry group: Sales: Profits:

Properties:	Financial Services:	Construction/Development:	Investments:	Specialty Services:	Brokerage:
Apartments:	Mortgages:	Commercial Construction:	REIT:	Property Management: Y	Commercial Sales:
Malls/Shopping:	Title Insurance:	Residential Construction:		Online Services:	Residential Sales:
Offices:	Property Insurance:	Land Development:		Software/IT:	Specialty:
Hotels/Motels: Y		Support Services:		Consulting:	
Industrial/Warehouses:		Design/Engineering:			
Other:					

TYPES OF BUSINESS:

Hotels

BRANDS/DIVISIONS/AFFILIATES:

Barcelo Corporacion Empresarial SA
Crestline Hotels & Resorts, Inc.

CONTACTS: *Note: Officers with more than one job title may be intentionally listed here more than once.*

James Carroll, CEO
James Carroll, Pres.
Pierre Donahue, General Counsel/Sr. VP
Bruce Wardinski, Chmn.

Phone: 571-529-6000	Fax: 571-529-6050
Toll-Free:	
Address: 3950 University Dr., Ste. 301, Fairfax, VA 22030 US	

GROWTH PLANS/SPECIAL FEATURES:

Barcelo Crestline Corporation is a leading independent hospitality management company. It is a privately-owned subsidiary of Barcelo Corporacion Empresarial S.A. (based in Palma de Mallorca, Spain).   Through its operating company, wholly-owned subsidiary Crestline Hotels & Resorts, Inc. (Crestline), the company manages properties including 47 hotels, resorts and conference and convention centers with nearly 8,600 rooms in 11 states and Washington, D.C. Crestline operates 10 independent hotels, with the remainder falling under brands such as Hilton, Hilton Garden Inn, Homewood Suites by Hilton, Sheraton, Westin, TownePlace Suites, Fairfield Inn. Staybridge Suites, SpringHill Suites, Crowne Plaza, Residence Inn, Marriott and Courtyard by Marriott. Crestline typically seeks to acquire 70 to 350-room hotels in the U.S. It generally acquires boutique or premium branded limited-service hotels; or first class, full-service hotels located in either suburban or urban markets. Recently, the firm opened the 410- room Renaissance Palm Springs Hotel, formerly the Wyndham Palm Springs, in Palm Springs, California.   In March 2010, Hotel & Motel Management magazine ranked Crestline fifth on its list of Top Third Party Management Companies. In another 2010 survey, this one by HotelBusiness magazine, Crestline was again named fifth among the Top 100 Management Companies.

The firm offers its employees medical, vision and dental insurance; life and disability insurance; a 401(k) plan; and hotel discounts.

FINANCIALS: Sales and profits are in thousands of dollars—add 000 to get the full amount. 2010 Note: Financial information for 2010 was not available for all companies at press time.

2010 Sales: $	2010 Profits: $	U.S. Stock Ticker: Subsidiary
2009 Sales: $	2009 Profits: $	Int'l Ticker: Int'l Exchange:
2008 Sales: $	2008 Profits: $	Employees:
2007 Sales: $	2007 Profits: $	Fiscal Year Ends: 12/31
2006 Sales: $	2006 Profits: $	Parent Company: BARCELO CORPORATION EMPRESARIAL SA

SALARIES/BENEFITS:

Pension Plan:	ESOP Stock Plan:	Profit Sharing:	Top Exec. Salary: $	Bonus: $
Savings Plan: Y	Stock Purch. Plan:		Second Exec. Salary: $	Bonus: $

OTHER THOUGHTS:

Apparent Women Officers or Directors:
Hot Spot for Advancement for Women/Minorities:

LOCATIONS: ("Y" = Yes)

West:	Southwest:	Midwest:	Southeast:	Northeast:	International:
Y	Y	Y	Y	Y	

BEAZER HOMES USA INC

www.beazer.com

Industry Group Code: 2361 Ranks within this company's industry group: Sales: 11   Profits: 11

Properties:	Financial Services:		Construction/Development:		Investments:	Specialty Services:	Brokerage:	
Apartments:	Mortgages:	Y	Commercial Construction:		REIT:	Property Management:	Commercial Sales:	
Malls/Shopping:	Title Insurance:		Residential Construction:	Y		Online Services:	Residential Sales:	Y
Offices:	Property Insurance:		Land Development:			Software/IT:	Specialty:	
Hotels/Motels:			Support Services:			Consulting:		
Industrial/Warehouses:			Design/Engineering:	Y				
Other:								

TYPES OF BUSINESS:
Homebuilding
Home Design

BRANDS/DIVISIONS/AFFILIATES:
Beazer Mortgage Corporation

CONTACTS: *Note: Officers with more than one job title may be intentionally listed here more than once.*
Ian J. McCarthy, CEO
Michael H. Furlow, COO/Exec. VP
Ian J. McCarthy, Pres.
Allan P. Merrill, CFO/Exec. VP
Kathi James, Chief Mktg. Officer/Sr. VP
Fred Fratto, Sr. VP-Human Resources
Cindy B. Tierney, CIO/Sr. VP
Kenneth Khoury, General Counsel/Exec. VP
Carey Phelps, Dir.-Corp. Comm.
Carey Phelps, Dir.-Investor Rel.
Robert Salomon, Chief Acct. Officer/Sr. VP/Controller
Peggy J. Caldwell, Deputy General Counsel/Sr. VP
J. Marty Shaffer, Sr. VP-Process Improvement
Brian C. Beazer, Chmn.
Tony L. Callahan, Chief Procurement Officer/Sr. VP

Phone: 770-829-3700	Fax: 770-481-2808
Toll-Free:	
Address: 1000 Abernathy Rd., Ste. 1200, Atlanta, GA 30328 US	

GROWTH PLANS/SPECIAL FEATURES:
Beazer Homes USA, Inc., a top national homebuilder, designs, sells and builds single-family and multi-family homes in 15 states. Its operations are divided into three geographic regions: West, which covers markets in Arizona, California, Nevada and Texas; East, covering markets in Maryland/Delaware, New Jersey/Pennsylvania, Virginia, Indiana and Tennessee; and Southeast, which consists of Florida, Georgia, North Carolina and South Carolina. Beazer's homes are designed primarily for first-time buyers and are designed at various price points to appeal to a wide demographic. They are also generally offered for sale in advance of their construction. Most homes are built from standardized plans, which help facilitate a greater profit margin through faster construction times and standard materials. The company does offer some measure of customization in the form of flooring, cabinetry, countertop and wall covering options. Beazer's business strategy involves geographically diverse project development to minimize losses caused by local economic downturns and a localized management scheme based on local market knowledge and expertise. Part of this business strategy is the company's eSmart initiative, which engineers homes to be energy-efficient and less expensive. The company also seeks to make energy saving, water conservation and improved air quality standard components in all homes. The company's home warranties are issued, administered and insured by independent third parties. The company is a national sponsor of HomeAid America, a nonprofit national program that provides housing for the temporarily homeless. The average sales price of a Beazer home was about $221,700 in 2010, down $9,200 from the previous year. In 2010, the firm sold 1,777 homes in its West region, with an average closing price of $203,000 per home; 1,729 in its East region, averaging $258,500; and 1,007 in the Southeast, averaging $191,600.

FINANCIALS: Sales and profits are in thousands of dollars—add 000 to get the full amount. 2010 Note: Financial information for 2010 was not available for all companies at press time.

2010 Sales: $1,009,841	2010 Profits: $-34,049	U.S. Stock Ticker: BZH
2009 Sales: $971,703	2009 Profits: $-189,383	Int'l Ticker: Int'l Exchange:
2008 Sales: $1,736,727	2008 Profits: $-951,912	Employees: 883
2007 Sales: $3,036,988	2007 Profits: $-411,000	Fiscal Year Ends: 9/30
2006 Sales: $5,321,702	2006 Profits: $388,761	Parent Company:

SALARIES/BENEFITS:

Pension Plan:	ESOP Stock Plan:	Profit Sharing:	Top Exec. Salary: $1,200,000	Bonus: $1,048,105
Savings Plan:	Stock Purch. Plan:		Second Exec. Salary: $600,000	Bonus: $524,052

OTHER THOUGHTS:
Apparent Women Officers or Directors: 4
Hot Spot for Advancement for Women/Minorities: Y

LOCATIONS: ("Y" = Yes)

West:	Southwest:	Midwest:	Southeast:	Northeast:	International:
Y	Y	Y	Y	Y	

BECHTEL GROUP INC

www.bechtel.com

Industry Group Code: 237 Ranks within this company's industry group: Sales: 3 Profits:

Properties:	Financial Services:	Construction/Development:		Investments:	Specialty Services:	Brokerage:
Apartments:	Mortgages:	Commercial Construction:	Y	REIT:	Property Management:	Commercial Sales:
Malls/Shopping:	Title Insurance:	Residential Construction:			Online Services:	Residential Sales:
Offices:	Property Insurance:	Land Development:	Y		Software/IT:	Specialty:
Hotels/Motels:		Support Services:	Y		Consulting:	
Industrial/Warehouses:		Design/Engineering:	Y			
Other:						

TYPES OF BUSINESS:

Engineering, Construction & Project Management Services
Civic Engineering
Outsourcing
Financial Services
Atomic Propulsion Systems Engineering
Airport Construction
Electric Power Plant Construction
Nuclear Power Plant Construction

BRANDS/DIVISIONS/AFFILIATES:

CONTACTS: *Note: Officers with more than one job title may be intentionally listed here more than once.*

Riley P. Bechtel, CEO
Bill Dudley, COO
Bill Dudley, Pres.
Peter Dawson, CFO
John MacDonald, Head-Human Resources
Geir Ramleth, Head-Info. Systems
Geir Ramleth, Head-Tech.
Michael Bailey, General Counsel
Anette Sparks, Controller
Steve Katzman, Pres., Asia
Jim Haynes, Pres., Latin America
Susan Kubanis, Head-Sustainability Svcs.
Lorne Parker, Head-Risk Mgmt.
Riley P. Bechtel, Chmn.
David Welch, Pres., EMEA

Phone: 415-768-1234	Fax: 415-768-9038
Toll-Free:	
Address: 50 Beale St., San Francisco, CA 94105-1895 US	

GROWTH PLANS/SPECIAL FEATURES:

Bechtel Group, Inc., founded in 1906 by Warren A. Bechtel, is one of the world's largest engineering companies. The privately-owned firm offers engineering, construction and project management services, with a broad project portfolio including road and rail systems, airports and seaports, nuclear power plants, petrochemical facilities, mines, defense and aerospace facilities, environmental cleanup projects, telecommunication networks, pipelines and oil fields development. The firm has participated in such notable endeavors as the construction of the Hoover Dam, the creation of the Bay Area Rapid Transit system in San Francisco, the massive James Bay Hydroelectric Project in Quebec and the quelling of oil field fires in Kuwait following the Persian Gulf War. Bechtel also constructed the Trans-Alaska Oil Pipeline, covering 800 miles between the Prudhoe Bay oil field and Valdez. Bechtel has also been contracted to develop the New Doha International Airport in Qatar, Iraq. An 11-year, multi-billion-dollar project, the new airport will be designed to accommodate six Airbus A380-800's, the largest passenger aircraft in the world.

The firm offers employees benefits including medical, dental and vision coverage; short- and long-term disability; flexible spending accounts; an employee assistance program; life insurance; and a 401(k) plan.

FINANCIALS: Sales and profits are in thousands of dollars—add 000 to get the full amount. 2010 Note: Financial information for 2010 was not available for all companies at press time.

2010 Sales: $32,500,000	2010 Profits: $	**U.S. Stock Ticker: Private**
2009 Sales: $30,800,000	2009 Profits: $	**Int'l Ticker:** Int'l Exchange:
2008 Sales: $31,400,000	2008 Profits: $	Employees: 44,000
2007 Sales: $27,000,000	2007 Profits: $	Fiscal Year Ends: 12/31
2006 Sales: $20,500,000	2006 Profits: $	Parent Company:

SALARIES/BENEFITS:

Pension Plan: Y	ESOP Stock Plan:	Profit Sharing:	Top Exec. Salary: $	Bonus: $
Savings Plan: Y	Stock Purch. Plan:		Second Exec. Salary: $	Bonus: $

OTHER THOUGHTS:

Apparent Women Officers or Directors: 4
Hot Spot for Advancement for Women/Minorities: Y

LOCATIONS: ("Y" = Yes)

West:	Southwest:	Midwest:	Southeast:	Northeast:	International:
Y	Y	Y	Y	Y	Y

BEST WESTERN INTERNATIONAL INC

www.bestwestern.com

Industry Group Code: 721110 Ranks within this company's industry group: Sales: Profits:

Properties:	Financial Services:	Construction/Development:	Investments:	Specialty Services:	Brokerage:
Apartments:	Mortgages:	Commercial Construction:	REIT:	Property Management:	Commercial Sales:
Malls/Shopping:	Title Insurance:	Residential Construction:		Online Services:	Residential Sales:
Offices:	Property Insurance:	Land Development:		Software/IT:	Specialty:
Hotels/Motels: Y		Support Services:		Consulting:	
Industrial/Warehouses:		Design/Engineering:			
Other:					

TYPES OF BUSINESS:

Hotels

BRANDS/DIVISIONS/AFFILIATES:

Best Western Rewards
Travel Card
Speed Rewards
Best Western Premier

CONTACTS: *Note: Officers with more than one job title may be intentionally listed here more than once.*

David T. Kong, CEO
David T. Kong, Pres.
Mark Straszynski, CFO
Dorothy Dowling, Sr. VP-Mktg. & Sales
Barbara Bras, VP-Human Resources
Scott Gibson, CIO/Sr. VP-Dist. & Strategic Svcs.
Larry Cuculic, General Counsel/Sr. VP
David Velasquez, VP-Info. Systems Oper.
Mark Williams, VP-North American Dev.
Devang (Dave) Amin, Treas./Sec.
Glenn De Souza, VP-Int'l Oper. Asia
Ron Pohl, Sr. VP-Brand Mgmt. & Member Svcs.
P.G West, Chmn.
Suzi MacDonald Yoder, VP-Int'l Oper.
Rich Bennett, VP-Supply & Design

Phone: 602-957-4200	Fax: 602-957-5641
Toll-Free:	
Address: 6201 N. 24th Pkwy., Phoenix, AZ 85016 US	

GROWTH PLANS/SPECIAL FEATURES:

Best Western International, Inc. is one of the largest lodging companies in the world, providing over 308,000 rooms in 90 countries and territories worldwide through more than 4,000 independently owned and operated hotels. Its unique organizational structure allows individual hotels to maintain local control and autonomy while reaping the benefits of a large international lodging firm, such as a global reservations system. The company, which is organized as a nonprofit association of member hotels, continues to grow as it establishes new hotels in the U.S. and across the world. Its international expansion includes hotels in Europe, South America, Africa and other regions of the world. In addition, Best Western has a partnership with MasterCard that provides cardholders with special offers and benefits, as well as its own benefits program, Best Western Rewards. Some other customer benefit programs such as Speed Rewards, for race fans, and Ride Rewards for Harley-Davidson owners, offer discounted room rates, free room upgrades, meal certificates and other promotional offerings. Best Western also offers a prepaid Travel Card that can be filled with U.S. or Canadian dollars, euros, British pounds or several other international currencies and used for hotel accommodations and other services provided by Best Western hotels. Regular amenities include breakfast services, data port connections, free local calls and a variety of other services that are already offered in many locations and are currently being extended to other facilities. The company offers free high-speed Internet access to guests at all of its U.S., Canadian and Caribbean properties. Additionally, The Best Western Premier brand is applied to a select number of properties that offer greater amenities and services than the regular Best Western locations. In 2010, the firm opened its first locations in Ghana, Nigeria and Tanzania.

FINANCIALS: Sales and profits are in thousands of dollars—add 000 to get the full amount. 2010 Note: Financial information for 2010 was not available for all companies at press time.

2010 Sales: $	2010 Profits: $	**U.S. Stock Ticker: Nonprofit**
2009 Sales: $	2009 Profits: $	**Int'l Ticker:** Int'l Exchange:
2008 Sales: $231,638	2008 Profits: $-1,657	Employees:
2007 Sales: $220,911	2007 Profits: $-2,983	Fiscal Year Ends: 11/30
2006 Sales: $205,539	2006 Profits: $4,052	Parent Company:

SALARIES/BENEFITS:

Pension Plan:	ESOP Stock Plan:	Profit Sharing:	Top Exec. Salary: $	Bonus: $
Savings Plan: Y	Stock Purch. Plan:		Second Exec. Salary: $	Bonus: $

OTHER THOUGHTS:

Apparent Women Officers or Directors: 6
Hot Spot for Advancement for Women/Minorities: Y

LOCATIONS: ("Y" = Yes)

West:	Southwest:	Midwest:	Southeast:	Northeast:	International:
Y	Y	Y	Y	Y	Y

BLACK & VEATCH HOLDING COMPANY

www.bv.com

Industry Group Code: 237 Ranks within this company's industry group: Sales: Profits:

Properties:	Financial Services:	Construction/Development:		Investments:	Specialty Services:	Brokerage:
Apartments:	Mortgages:	Commercial Construction:	Y	REIT:	Property Management:	Commercial Sales:
Malls/Shopping:	Title Insurance:	Residential Construction:			Online Services:	Residential Sales:
Offices:	Property Insurance:	Land Development:			Software/IT:	Specialty:
Hotels/Motels:		Support Services:			Consulting:	
Industrial/Warehouses:		Design/Engineering:	Y			
Other:						

TYPES OF BUSINESS:

Construction, Heavy & Civil Engineering
Infrastructure & Energy Services
Environmental & Hydrologic Engineering
Consulting Services
IT Services
Power Plant Engineering and Construction
LNG and Gas Processing Plant Engineering
Climate Change Services

BRANDS/DIVISIONS/AFFILIATES:

Enspiria Solutions

CONTACTS: *Note: Officers with more than one job title may be intentionally listed here more than once.*

Leonard C. Rodman, CEO
Leonard C. Rodman, Pres.
Karen L. Daniel, CFO
Carl Petz, Dir.-Strategic Mktg. & Comm./Associate VP
Jim Lewis, Chief Admin. Officer
George Minter, Dir.-Corp. Comm. & Media Rel.
Ken Williams, Treas./Sr. VP
Daniel W. McCarthy, Pres./CEO-B&V Water
O.H. Oskvig, Pres./CEO-B&V Energy
Sheri Blauwiekel, Exec. VP/Dir.-Project Support, Global Energy Bus.
Mark Turner, Dir.-Public Safety Telecommunications Bus.
Leonard C. Rodman, Chmn.

Phone: 913-458-2000	**Fax:** 913-458-2934
Toll-Free:	
Address: 11401 Lamar Ave., Overland Park, KS 66211 US	

GROWTH PLANS/SPECIAL FEATURES:

Black & Veatch Holding Company (B&V) is an engineering, consulting and construction company specializing in infrastructure development for the energy, water, telecommunications, federal, management consulting and environmental markets. The company is employee-owned and operates over 100 offices worldwide. B&V divides its service offerings into 15 categories. The firm's asset management services include power and water asset optimization solutions. Its climate change solutions include encompass energy optimization, water planning, greenhouse gas services, climate economics and government services. The company provides construction services for energy facilities, water and wastewater treatment facilities, water distribution systems, desalination facilities, wireless sites and aerospace and defense sites. Design-build services cover engineering, procurement and construction. Its also offers engineering consulting services. Engineering and design services include power delivery, siting, new generation engineering, power plant upgrade and bulk materials handling services. The firm's information management solutions include technical consulting, data management and systems integration. The infrastructure planning segment serves the energy, water and telecommunications sectors. Management consulting services comprise enterprise management and utility efficiency solutions. Procurement services include project procurement strategy, transportation logistics and inspection services. The program management segment manages energy, water, telecom and federal programs. SAP services include supply chain support and customer relationship management. Smart utility services include utilities planning, system modeling, distribution automation and field construction. Utility cost containment solutions include call center and asset management efficiency improvement services. Finally, the firm's water spares division supplies filter floor replacements and desludging systems to the wastewater industry. In March 2010, the company acquired Enspiria Solutions, which provides smart grid solutions.

The company offers employees medical, dental, vision and prescription drug coverage; flexible spending accounts; employee assistance programs; tuition reimbursement; adoption assistance; and credit union membership.

FINANCIALS: Sales and profits are in thousands of dollars—add 000 to get the full amount. 2010 Note: Financial information for 2010 was not available for all companies at press time.

2010 Sales: $	2010 Profits: $	**U.S. Stock Ticker: Private**
2009 Sales: $2,700,000	2009 Profits: $	**Int'l Ticker:** Int'l Exchange:
2008 Sales: $3,200,000	2008 Profits: $	Employees: 8,600
2007 Sales: $3,200,000	2007 Profits: $	Fiscal Year Ends: 12/31
2006 Sales: $1,800,000	2006 Profits: $	Parent Company:

SALARIES/BENEFITS:

Pension Plan: Y	ESOP Stock Plan:	Profit Sharing: Y	Top Exec. Salary: $	Bonus: $
Savings Plan:	Stock Purch. Plan:		Second Exec. Salary: $	Bonus: $

OTHER THOUGHTS:

Apparent Women Officers or Directors: 3
Hot Spot for Advancement for Women/Minorities: Y

LOCATIONS: ("Y" = Yes)

West:	Southwest:	Midwest:	Southeast:	Northeast:	International:
Y	Y	Y	Y	Y	Y

BLUEGREEN CORPORATION   www.bluegreencorp.com

Industry Group Code: 561599 Ranks within this company's industry group: Sales: 1   Profits: 1

Properties:		Financial Services:	Construction/Development:		Investments:		Specialty Services:		Brokerage:	
Apartments:		Mortgages:	Commercial Construction:		REIT:		Property Management:	Y	Commercial Sales:	
Malls/Shopping:		Title Insurance:	Residential Construction:				Online Services:		Residential Sales:	Y
Offices:		Property Insurance:	Land Development:	Y			Software/IT:		Specialty:	
Hotels/Motels:	Y		Support Services:				Consulting:			
Industrial/Warehouses:			Design/Engineering:							
Other:	Y									

TYPES OF BUSINESS:

Timeshare Resorts
Time shares
Residential Properties
Property Development & Subdivisions
Resort Management Services

BRANDS/DIVISIONS/AFFILIATES:

Bluegreen Resorts
Bluegreen Vacation Club
Bluegreen Communities

CONTACTS: *Note: Officers with more than one job title may be intentionally listed here more than once.*

John M. Maloney, Jr., CEO
John M. Maloney, Jr., Pres.
Anthony M. Puleo, CFO/Sr. VP/Treas.
David A. Bidgood, Pres., Field Sales & Mktg.-Bluegreen Resorts
Susan J. Saturday, Chief Human Resources Officer/Sr. VP
Allan J. Herz, Sr. VP-Mortgage Oper./Assistant Treas.
David L. Pontius, Chief Strategy Officer/Sr. VP
Raymond S. Lopez, Chief Acct. Officer/VP
Daniel C. Koscher, Sr. VP/CEO/Pres., Bluegreen Communities
David L. Pontius, Pres., Bluegreen Management Svcs.
Paul Humphrey, VP-Finance & Capital Markets
Alan B. Levan, Chmn.

Phone: 561-912-8000	Fax: 561-912-8100
Toll-Free:	
Address: 4960 Conference Way N., Ste. 100, Boca Raton, FL 33431 US	

GROWTH PLANS/SPECIAL FEATURES:

Bluegreen Corporation markets and develops both residential and vacation homes. It operates in two segments: Bluegreen Resorts and Bluegreen Communities. Bluegreen Resorts markets, sells and manages real estate-based vacation ownership interests in resorts generally located in popular high-volume vacation destinations. This division also provides sales, marketing, mortgage servicing, construction management, title and resort management services to third-party resort developers and owners. Bluegreen currently markets timeshare interests for over 55 owned or managed resorts. Customers are eligible to enter the Bluegreen Vacation Club, a customer rewards system similar to a frequent flyer program. U.S. resort locations include Myrtle Beach, South Carolina; numerous locations in Florida, including Orlando, Panama City Beach and Surfside; Las Vegas, Nevada; New Orleans, Louisiana; and locations in Aruba, the Bahamas and Hawaii. Bluegreen Communities, Bluegreen's residential land and golf business, acquires, develops and subdivides property and markets residential land homesites. These homesites are generally sold directly to retail customers seeking to build a home, in some cases on properties featuring a golf course. This division's strategy is to locate its properties in popular retirement areas near major metropolitan centers but outside the perimeter of intense subdivision development. The division has sold homesites in planned residential and golf communities in 32 states, with projects located in Texas, North Carolina, Virginia, Tennessee and Georgia.

FINANCIALS: Sales and profits are in thousands of dollars—add 000 to get the full amount. 2010 Note: Financial information for 2010 was not available for all companies at press time.

2010 Sales: $365,677	2010 Profits: $-43,966	U.S. Stock Ticker: BXG
2009 Sales: $367,366	2009 Profits: $-3,572	Int'l Ticker: Int'l Exchange:
2008 Sales: $595,031	2008 Profits: $- 516	Employees: 3,825
2007 Sales: $683,917	2007 Profits: $31,926	Fiscal Year Ends: 12/31
2006 Sales: $673,373	2006 Profits: $29,817	Parent Company:

SALARIES/BENEFITS:

Pension Plan:	ESOP Stock Plan:	Profit Sharing:	Top Exec. Salary: $600,000	Bonus: $1,375,000
Savings Plan:	Stock Purch. Plan:		Second Exec. Salary: $450,000	Bonus: $150,000

OTHER THOUGHTS:

Apparent Women Officers or Directors: 1
Hot Spot for Advancement for Women/Minorities:

LOCATIONS: ("Y" = Yes)

West:	Southwest:	Midwest:	Southeast:	Northeast:	International:
Y	Y	Y	Y	Y	

BOARDWALK REAL ESTATE INVESTMENT TRUST

www.boardwalkreit.com
Industry Group Code: 531110 Ranks within this company's industry group: Sales: 7   Profits: 4

Properties:		Financial Services:		Construction/Development:	Investments:		Specialty Services:		Brokerage:	
Apartments:	Y	Mortgages:		Commercial Construction:	REIT:	Y	Property Management:	Y	Commercial Sales:	
Malls/Shopping:		Title Insurance:		Residential Construction:			Online Services:		Residential Sales:	
Offices:		Property Insurance:		Land Development:			Software/IT:		Specialty:	
Hotels/Motels:				Support Services:			Consulting:			
Industrial/Warehouses:				Design/Engineering:						
Other:										

TYPES OF BUSINESS:

Real Estate Investment Trust
Apartment Development & Management

BRANDS/DIVISIONS/AFFILIATES:

Boardwalk Equities Inc

CONTACTS: *Note: Officers with more than one job title may be intentionally listed here more than once.*

Sam Kolias, CEO
Roberto Geremia, Pres.
William Wong, CFO
Helen Mix, VP-Human Resources
Michael Guyette, CIO
Dean Burns, General Counsel/Corp. Sec.
Michael Guyette, VP-Oper., Southern Alberta & British Columbia
William Chidley, Sr. VP-Corp. Dev.
David McIlveen, Contact-Media Rel.
James Ha, Contact-Investor Rel.
Van Kolias, Sr. VP-Quality Control
Jonathan Brimmell, VP-Oper., Ontario & Quebec
Kelly Mahajan, VP-Customer Service & Process Design
Jean Denis, VP-Quebec Acquisitions
Sam Kolias, Chmn.
Ian Dingle, VP-Purchasing & Contracts

Phone: 403-531-9255	Fax: 403-531-9565
Toll-Free:	
Address: 1501 1st St. SW, Ste. 200, Calgary, AB T2R 0W1 Canada	

GROWTH PLANS/SPECIAL FEATURES:

Boardwalk Real Estate Investment Trust, formerly Boardwalk Equities, Inc., is one of Canada's largest owners and operators of multi-family rental communities. The company currently owns and operates over 225 properties with more than 35,277 units, totaling approximately 30 million rentable square feet. Boardwalk's portfolio includes properties in the provinces of Alberta, British Columbia, Saskatchewan, Ontario and Quebec, with approximately 56% of its rentable portfolio and nearly 61% of its net operating income concentrated in Alberta. The firm is not involved in construction, instead focusing on the purchase of existing structures within its acquisition program, especially mid-sized suburban and downtown apartment buildings and mid-sized community and neighborhood residential centers located in urban markets, to ensure a diversified portfolio. The company targets well-located properties that it believes have been poorly managed, creating a higher-than-average vacancy rate, and which are located in areas characterized by limited new housing supply. Boardwalk's strength is in its operating, leasing and financing capabilities and its ability to enhance the long-term value of a property. The firm attempts to acquire properties at a substantial discount to replacement cost. It then restores the apartment buildings and focuses on adding high-tech amenities, such as fiber-optic cable. Boardwalk sometimes sells its properties after renovation, either entirely to other companies or as individual condos to residents. In recent years, the firm disposed of four properties, one each in Calgary, Quebec, Levis and Surrey. In 2010, the company disposed of real estate assets in Quebec, Alberta, Saskatchewan and British Columbia comprising 1,142 apartment units.

FINANCIALS: Sales and profits are in thousands of dollars—add 000 to get the full amount. 2010 Note: Financial information for 2010 was not available for all companies at press time.

2010 Sales: $436,580	2010 Profits: $75,260	**U.S. Stock Ticker:**
2009 Sales: $437,320	2009 Profits: $65,120	**Int'l Ticker: BEI** Int'l Exchange: Toronto-TSX
2008 Sales: $440,450	2008 Profits: $47,930	Employees:
2007 Sales: $309,000	2007 Profits: $-48,880	Fiscal Year Ends: 12/31
2006 Sales: $316,200	2006 Profits: $25,100	Parent Company:

SALARIES/BENEFITS:

Pension Plan:	ESOP Stock Plan:	Profit Sharing:	Top Exec. Salary: $	Bonus: $
Savings Plan:	Stock Purch. Plan:		Second Exec. Salary: $	Bonus: $

OTHER THOUGHTS:

Apparent Women Officers or Directors: 3
Hot Spot for Advancement for Women/Minorities: Y

LOCATIONS: ("Y" = Yes)

West:	Southwest:	Midwest:	Southeast:	Northeast:	International:
					Y

BOISE CASCADE CORP

www.bc.com

Industry Group Code: 322 Ranks within this company's industry group: Sales: 1   Profits: 1

Properties:	Financial Services:	Construction/Development:		Investments:	Specialty Services:	Brokerage:
Apartments:	Mortgages:	Commercial Construction:		REIT:	Property Management:	Commercial Sales:
Malls/Shopping:	Title Insurance:	Residential Construction:			Online Services:	Residential Sales:
Offices:	Property Insurance:	Land Development:			Software/IT:	Specialty:
Hotels/Motels:		Support Services:	Y		Consulting:	
Industrial/Warehouses:		Design/Engineering:				
Other:						

TYPES OF BUSINESS:

Lumber Products, Manufacturing
Engineered Wood Products
Wholesale Building Materials Distribution
Packaging & Newsprint
Cottonwood Fiber Farming

BRANDS/DIVISIONS/AFFILIATES:

Kettle Falls Lumber
Elgin Studs
Florien Plywood
St. Jacques, NB

CONTACTS: *Note: Officers with more than one job title may be intentionally listed here more than once.*

Thomas Carlile, CEO
Wayne Rancourt, CFO/Sr. VP/Treas.
John Sahlberg, VP-Human Resources
John Sahlberg, Corp. Counsel/Sec.
Kelly Hibbs, Controller
Stanley Bell, Pres., Building Materials Dist.
Thomas Lovlien, Pres., Wood Prod.
Thomas Corrick, VP-Boise Wood Prod.
Dave Gadda, VP-Legal
Duane McDougall, Chmn.

Phone: 208-384-6161	Fax: 208-384-7189
Toll-Free:	
Address: 1111 W. Jefferson St., Ste. 300, Boise, ID 83702-5389 US	

GROWTH PLANS/SPECIAL FEATURES:

Boise Cascade Corp. is a major wholesale distributor of wood products and building materials. The firm controls significant amounts of timberland in the United States. Boise Cascade produces structural panels, lumber and particleboard, as well as engineered wood products consisting of laminated veneer lumber, wood I-joists and laminated beams. These products are used primarily in housing, industrial construction and a variety of manufactured products. The firm also offers special-order sourcing and merchandising support for its offerings. The company operates its wood products division in Louisiana, Oregon, Washington, Idaho and Canada. Operating names include Kettle Falls Lumber; Elgin Studs; Kinzua Lumber; Florien Plywood; and St. Jacques, NB. Boise Cascade's materials distribution division maintains distribution centers throughout the U.S. The firm holds many environmental sustainability certificates, including compliance with Forest Stewardship Council, Programme for Endorsement of Forest Certification and Sustainable Forestry Initiative. The company is controlled by private equity investors Madison Dearborn Partners.

The firm offers its employees health, medical, prescription drug, dental and vision coverage; flexible spending accounts; 16-31 days paid-time off; life, AD&D and long-term disability insurance; a 401(k) plan with a 4% employer match; a wellness program; and an employee assistance program.

FINANCIALS: Sales and profits are in thousands of dollars—add 000 to get the full amount. 2010 Note: Financial information for 2010 was not available for all companies at press time.

2010 Sales: $2,240,591	2010 Profits: $-6,101	**U.S. Stock Ticker:** Private
2009 Sales: $1,973,250	2009 Profits: $-19,057	**Int'l Ticker:** Int'l Exchange:
2008 Sales: $2,977,498	2008 Profits: $-287,978	Employees: 4,600
2007 Sales: $5,413,456	2007 Profits: $127,697	Fiscal Year Ends: 12/31
2006 Sales: $5,779,865	2006 Profits: $71,571	Parent Company:

SALARIES/BENEFITS:

Pension Plan:	ESOP Stock Plan:	Profit Sharing:	Top Exec. Salary: $	Bonus: $
Savings Plan: Y	Stock Purch. Plan:		Second Exec. Salary: $	Bonus: $

OTHER THOUGHTS:

Apparent Women Officers or Directors: 1
Hot Spot for Advancement for Women/Minorities:

LOCATIONS: ("Y" = Yes)

West:	Southwest:	Midwest:	Southeast:	Northeast:	International:
Y	Y	Y	Y	Y	Y

BOSTON PROPERTIES INC

www.bostonproperties.com

Industry Group Code: 531120 Ranks within this company's industry group: Sales: 8   Profits: 12

Properties:		Financial Services:	Construction/Development:	Investments:		Specialty Services:	Brokerage:
Apartments:		Mortgages:	Commercial Construction:	REIT:	Y	Property Management:	Commercial Sales:
Malls/Shopping:		Title Insurance:	Residential Construction:			Online Services:	Residential Sales:
Offices:	Y	Property Insurance:	Land Development:			Software/IT:	Specialty:
Hotels/Motels:	Y		Support Services:			Consulting:	
Industrial/Warehouses:	Y		Design/Engineering:				
Other:							

TYPES OF BUSINESS:

Real Estate Investment Trust
Offices
Hotel
Industrial Space

BRANDS/DIVISIONS/AFFILIATES:

Boston Properties Office Value-Added Fund LP
Times Square Tower
Embarcadero Center
Prudential Center
Prudential Tower
Metropolitan Square
General Motors Building
Bay Colony Corporate Center

CONTACTS: *Note: Officers with more than one job title may be intentionally listed here more than once.*

Mortimer B. Zuckerman, CEO
E. Mitchell Norville, COO/Exec. VP
Douglas T. Linde, Pres.
Michael E. LaBelle, CFO/Sr. VP
Raymond A. Ritchey, Exec. VP/Dir.-Dev. & Acquisitions
Arista Joyner, Mgr.-Investor Rel.
Michael E. LaBelle, Treas.
Bryan J. Koop, Sr. VP/Mgr.-Boston Office
Robert E. Selsam, Sr. VP/Mgr.-New York Office
Robert E. Pester, Sr. VP/Mgr.-San Francisco Office
Mitchell S. Landis, Sr. VP/Mgr.-Princeton Office
Mortimer B. Zuckerman, Chmn.

Phone: 617-236-3300	Fax: 617-536-5087
Toll-Free:	
Address: 800 Boylston St., The Prudential Ctr., Ste. 1900, Boston, MA 02199-8103 US	

GROWTH PLANS/SPECIAL FEATURES:

Boston Properties, Inc. is a fully integrated, self-administered and self-managed real estate investment trust (REIT) and one of the largest owners and developers of office properties in the U.S. The trust develops, redevelops, acquires, manages, operates and owns a diverse portfolio of Class A offices. It holds properties in the U.S., with holdings concentrated in five core markets: Boston, Massachusetts; Washington, D.C.; midtown Manhattan; San Francisco, California; and Princeton, New Jersey. The company's subsidiary, Boston Properties Limited Partnership, conducts the vast majority of its business. Boston Properties owns or has interests in 146 properties, including 140 office properties, one hotel, three retail properties and two residential properties (under construction). The sum of this property is 39.9 million net rentable square feet and 13.7 million square feet of structured parking. In addition, the trust owns or controls approximately 513.3 acres of undeveloped land. The company has a minority interest in the Boston Properties Office Value-Added Fund, L.P., which acquires deficient properties and remodels/refurbishes them for resale. Examples of the company's properties are Prudential Tower and Prudential Center in Boston; Times Square Tower and General Motors Building (60% owned) in New York; Metropolitan Square (51% owned) in Washington, D.C.; One, Two, Three and Four Embarcadero Center in San Francisco; and 17 office buildings in Carnegie Center in Princeton. In December 2010, Boston Properties acquired the John Hancock Tower and Garage in Boston, Massachusetts, for roughly $930 million. In February 2011, the firm acquired Bay Colony Corporate Center in Waltham, Massachusetts, for approximately $185 million.

The company offers employees health, dental, life, business travel accident and disability insurance; an employee assistance program; a 401(k); a stock purchase plan; paid time off; legal referral services; tuition reimbursement; commuter benefits; and a scholarship program.

FINANCIALS: Sales and profits are in thousands of dollars—add 000 to get the full amount. 2010 Note: Financial information for 2010 was not available for all companies at press time.

2010 Sales: $1,550,804	2010 Profits: $190,327	U.S. Stock Ticker: BXP
2009 Sales: $1,518,190	2009 Profits: $274,499	Int'l Ticker: Int'l Exchange:
2008 Sales: $1,469,442	2008 Profits: $125,232	Employees: 700
2007 Sales: $1,482,289	2007 Profits: $1,324,690	Fiscal Year Ends: 12/31
2006 Sales: $1,417,627	2006 Profits: $873,635	Parent Company:

SALARIES/BENEFITS:

Pension Plan:	ESOP Stock Plan:	Profit Sharing:	Top Exec. Salary: $986,538	Bonus: $2,000,000
Savings Plan: Y	Stock Purch. Plan: Y		Second Exec. Salary: $986,538	Bonus: $1,800,000

OTHER THOUGHTS:

Apparent Women Officers or Directors: 3
Hot Spot for Advancement for Women/Minorities: Y

LOCATIONS: ("Y" = Yes)

West:	Southwest:	Midwest:	Southeast:	Northeast:	International:
Y				Y	

BOUYGUES SA

www.bouygues.fr

Industry Group Code: 237 Ranks within this company's industry group: Sales: 2   Profits: 5

Properties:	Financial Services:	Construction/Development:		Investments:	Specialty Services:		Brokerage:
Apartments:	Mortgages:	Commercial Construction:	Y	REIT:	Property Management:		Commercial Sales:
Malls/Shopping:	Title Insurance:	Residential Construction:			Online Services:		Residential Sales:
Offices:	Property Insurance:	Land Development:			Software/IT:	Y	Specialty:
Hotels/Motels:		Support Services:	Y		Consulting:		
Industrial/Warehouses: Y		Design/Engineering:	Y				
Other:							

TYPES OF BUSINESS:

Construction & Telecommunications
Construction
Road Building
Property Development
Precasting
Cellular Phone Service
Media Operation
Research & Development

BRANDS/DIVISIONS/AFFILIATES:

Bouygues Construction
Bouygues Immobilier
Bouygues Telecom
Bouygues e-Lab
Colas
TF1

CONTACTS: *Note: Officers with more than one job title may be intentionally listed here more than once.*

Martin Bouygues, CEO
Philippe Marien, CFO
Jean-Claude Tostivin, Sr. VP-Human Resources
Alain Pouyat, Exec. VP-Info. Systems
Alain Pouyat, Exec. VP-New Tech.
Jean-Claude Tostivin, Sr. VP-Admin.
Jean-Francois Guillemin, Corp. Sec.
Pierre Auberger, Dir.-Corp. Comm.
Valarie Agathon, Dir.-Investor Rel.
Olivier Bouygues, Deputy CEO
Yves Gabriel, CEO-Bouygues Construction
Nonce Paolini, CEO-TF1
Francois Bertiere, CEO-Bouygues Immobilier
Martin Bouygues, Chmn.

Phone: 33-1-44-20-10-00	Fax: 33-1-30-60-4861
Toll-Free:	
Address: 32 Ave. Hoche, Paris, 75008 France	

GROWTH PLANS/SPECIAL FEATURES:

Buoygues S.A., based in Paris, France, was founded in 1952 as a construction and industrial works company. Operating through its subsidiaries, the firm now primarily serves two distinct areas: construction and telecoms/media. Company subsidiaries working within the construction sector include Bouygues Construction, dedicated to electrical contracting and civil works; Bouygues Immobilier, committed to property development; and Colas, dedicated to building roads. Subsidiaries serving the telecoms/media branch include TF1 and Buoygues Telecom. The firm also maintains the Bouygues e-Lab, a research and development center which supports all areas of the company with innovations in their particular fields and in the digital technologies sector. Recent research projects include acoustics, vibration and energy performance for the Construction sector; strategic marketing and the development of new products for the Immobilier sector; various asphalts and mixing processes for the Colas sector; television capabilities on mobile phones as well as high-definition TV for the TF1 sector; and mobile videos, broadband innovations and contactless applications for the Telecom sector. The firm maintains operations in Europe, Central and South America, North America, Asia, the Middle East and Africa.

FINANCIALS: Sales and profits are in thousands of dollars—add 000 to get the full amount. 2010 Note: Financial information for 2010 was not available for all companies at press time.

2010 Sales: $45,123,600	2010 Profits: $1,547,710	**U.S. Stock Ticker:**
2009 Sales: $41,783,500	2009 Profits: $1,757,800	**Int'l Ticker: EN** Int'l Exchange: Paris-Euronext
2008 Sales: $43,264,900	2008 Profits: $1,985,160	Employees:
2007 Sales: $39,131,900	2007 Profits: $1,819,840	Fiscal Year Ends: 12/31
2006 Sales: $36,022,600	2006 Profits: $2,157,970	Parent Company:

SALARIES/BENEFITS:

Pension Plan:	ESOP Stock Plan:	Profit Sharing:	Top Exec. Salary: $	Bonus: $
Savings Plan:	Stock Purch. Plan:		Second Exec. Salary: $	Bonus: $

OTHER THOUGHTS:

Apparent Women Officers or Directors: 6
Hot Spot for Advancement for Women/Minorities: Y

LOCATIONS: ("Y" = Yes)

West:	Southwest:	Midwest:	Southeast:	Northeast:	International:
Y		Y	Y	Y	Y

BOYD GAMING CORP

www.boydgaming.com

Industry Group Code: 721120 **Ranks within this company's industry group:** Sales: 5 Profits: 2

Properties:		Financial Services:	Construction/Development:	Investments:		Specialty Services:		Brokerage:	
Apartments:		Mortgages:	Commercial Construction:	REIT:		Property Management:	Y	Commercial Sales:	
Malls/Shopping:		Title Insurance:	Residential Construction:			Online Services:		Residential Sales:	
Offices:		Property Insurance:	Land Development:			Software/IT:		Specialty:	
Hotels/Motels:	Y		Support Services:			Consulting:			
Industrial/Warehouses:			Design/Engineering:						
Other:	Y								

TYPES OF BUSINESS:

Casinos & Hotels
Casino Management

BRANDS/DIVISIONS/AFFILIATES:

California Hotel & Casino
Borgata Hotel, Casino, & Spa
Blue Chip Hotel and Casino
Delta Downs Racetrack & Casino
Gold Coast Hotel and Casino
Fremont Hotel & Casino
Club Coast
B Connected

CONTACTS: *Note: Officers with more than one job title may be intentionally listed here more than once.*

Keith E. Smith, CEO
Paul J. Chakmak, COO/Exec. VP
Keith E. Smith, Pres.
John Hirsberg, CFO/Sr. VP/Treas.
Brian A. Larson, General Counsel/Exec. VP/Sec.
Robert L. Boughner, Chief Bus. Dev. Officer/Exec. VP
Rob Meyne, VP-Corp. Comm.
Ellie J. Bowdish, Chief Acct. Officer/VP
Marianne Boyd Johnson, Chief Diversity Officer/Exec. VP
William R. Boyd, VP
William S. Boyd, Exec. Chmn.

Phone: 702-792-7200	Fax: 702-792-7313
Toll-Free:	
Address: 3883 Howard Hughes Pkwy., 9th Fl., Las Vegas, NV 89169 US	

GROWTH PLANS/SPECIAL FEATURES:

Boyd Gaming Corp. is a multi-jurisdictional gaming company and one of the country's leading casino operators. It currently owns and operates 16 casinos totaling 972,787 square feet, and housing 24,536 slot machines, 685 table games and 10,318 hotel rooms. The firm divides its properties into four segments: Las Vegas Locals; Downtown Las Vegas; Midwest and South; and Atlantic City. The Las Vegas Locals properties include The Orleans Hotel and Casino; Sam's Town Hotel & Gambling Hall; Gold Coast Hotel and Casino; Eldorado Casino; Jokers Wild Casino; and Suncoast Hotel and Casino. Downtown Las Vegas facilities consist of the Fremont Hotel & Casino; California Hotel and Casino; and Main Street Casino, Brewery and Hotel. The Midwest and South properties include Sam's Town Hotel and Gambling Hall, in Tunica, Mississippi; the Delta Downs Racetrack and Casino, the Sam's Town Hotel and Casino Shreveport (formerly Shreveport Hotel and Casino) and the Treasure Chest Casino, in Louisiana; the Par-a-Dice Hotel and Casino in East Peoria, Illinois; and the Blue Chip Hotel and Casino in Michigan City, Indiana. The Atlantic City property, Borgata Hotel, Casino and Spa, is jointly owned with Marina District Development Holding Co., LLC. In addition to these properties, the firm owns and operates a jai-alai facility in Dania Beach, Florida; a travel agency; an insurance agency specializing in travel-related insurance; and 85 contiguous acres of land on the Las Vegas Strip. The company maintains a loyalty program which allows customers to use Club Coast or B Connected cards to earn and redeem points at any Boyd gaming property in Nevada, Illinois, Indiana, Louisiana and Mississippi. Boyd has suspended development at its multi-billion dollar Echelon property on the Las Vegas Strip.

Employees are offered medical, dental and vision coverage; a 401(k) plan; short-term disability coverage; and life insurance.

FINANCIALS: Sales and profits are in thousands of dollars—add 000 to get the full amount. 2010 Note: Financial information for 2010 was not available for all companies at press time.

2010 Sales: $2,494,724	2010 Profits: $183,938	U.S. Stock Ticker: BYD	
2009 Sales: $1,824,166	2009 Profits: $156,193	Int'l Ticker:	Int'l Exchange:
2008 Sales: $1,987,555	2008 Profits: $-153,429	Employees: 21,300	
2007 Sales: $1,997,119	2007 Profits: $303,035	Fiscal Year Ends: 12/31	
2006 Sales: $2,192,634	2006 Profits: $116,778	Parent Company:	

SALARIES/BENEFITS:

Pension Plan:	ESOP Stock Plan:	Profit Sharing:	Top Exec. Salary: $1,100,000	Bonus: $770,000
Savings Plan: Y	Stock Purch. Plan:		Second Exec. Salary: $1,100,000	Bonus: $577,500

OTHER THOUGHTS:

Apparent Women Officers or Directors: 2
Hot Spot for Advancement for Women/Minorities:

LOCATIONS: ("Y" = Yes)

West:	Southwest:	Midwest:	Southeast:	Northeast:	International:
Y		Y	Y	Y	

BRANDYWINE REALTY TRUST

www.brandywinerealty.com

Industry Group Code: 531120 Ranks within this company's industry group: Sales: 31   Profits: 53

Properties:		Financial Services:		Construction/Development:		Investments:		Specialty Services:		Brokerage:	
Apartments:		Mortgages:		Commercial Construction:		REIT:	Y	Property Management:	Y	Commercial Sales:	
Malls/Shopping:		Title Insurance:		Residential Construction:				Online Services:	Y	Residential Sales:	
Offices:	Y	Property Insurance:		Land Development:	Y			Software/IT:		Specialty:	
Hotels/Motels:				Support Services:				Consulting:	Y		
Industrial/Warehouses:	Y			Design/Engineering:							
Other:											

TYPES OF BUSINESS:

Real Estate Investment Trust
Office & Industrial Properties
Property Management Services
Development Support Services
Consulting

BRANDS/DIVISIONS/AFFILIATES:

Brandywine Operating Partnership, LP
e-tenants.com

CONTACTS: Note: Officers with more than one job title may be intentionally listed here more than once.

Gerard H. Sweeney, CEO
Gerard H. Sweeney, Pres.
Howard M. Sipzner, CFO/Exec. VP
Beth R. Glassman, VP-Human Resources
Robert J. Juliano, CIO/VP
Brad A. Molotsky, General Counsel/Sr. VP/Corp. Sec.
George D. Johnstone, Sr. VP-Oper. & Asset Management
Gabe Mainardi, Chief Acct. Officer/VP
H. Jeffrey DeVuono, Exec. VP/Sr. Managing Dir.-Pennsylvania Region
George D. Sowa, Exec. VP/Sr. Managing Dir.-NJ & DE Region
William D. Redd, Sr. VP/Managing Dir.-Richmond & Austin Region
Robert K. Wiberg, Exec. VP/Sr. Managing Dir.-Metro DC & CA Region
Walter D'Alessio, Chmn.

Phone: 610-325-5600	Fax: 610-325-5622
Toll-Free:	
Address: 555 East Lancaster Ave., Ste. 100, Radnor, PA 19087 US	

GROWTH PLANS/SPECIAL FEATURES:

Brandywine Realty Trust is a real estate investment trust (REIT) that acquires, develops, redevelops, manages and leases office and industrial properties across the U.S. The firm owns 233 properties, which consist of 20 industrial properties, 208 office properties and four mixed-use properties, containing approximately 25.6 million net rentable square feet. It also owns interests in 17 unconsolidated real estate ventures that contain approximately 6.5 million net rentable square feet and 509 acres of undeveloped land. Its portfolio is divided into seven geographic segments: Pennsylvania Suburbs; Philadelphia Central Business District; Metropolitan Washington D.C; New Jersey/Delaware; Richmond, Virginia; Austin, Texas; and California. The company's services are categorized into five segments: Asset and Property Management; Development/Construction; Marketing and Leasing Services; Property Management; and Tenant Services. Asset and property management activities include acquisition and disposition; capital allocation and deployment; and project management. Development/construction capabilities include development, site selection, land purchase, renovation and construction management. The marketing and leasing services division works with tenants to provide office space and other alternatives. As part of the company's Tenant Services offering, Brandywine launched e-tenants.com, intended to streamline delivery of service and amenities to its tenants online.

Employees are offered medical, dental, prescription drug and vision insurance; short- and long-term disability coverage; a 401(k) plan with company match; reimbursement accounts for health, dependent care and public transportation; an employee stock purchase plan; military leave with pay for training or reserve duty; tuition reimbursement; scholarships for employees' children; and business casual environment in the corporate and property management offices.

FINANCIALS: Sales and profits are in thousands of dollars—add 000 to get the full amount. 2010 Note: Financial information for 2010 was not available for all companies at press time.

2010 Sales: $566,897	2010 Profits: $-17,606	**U.S. Stock Ticker:** BDN
2009 Sales: $575,058	2009 Profits: $8,089	**Int'l Ticker:** Int'l Exchange:
2008 Sales: $580,932	2008 Profits: $38,525	Employees: 439
2007 Sales: $604,811	2007 Profits: $55,335	Fiscal Year Ends: 12/31
2006 Sales: $568,883	2006 Profits: $9,814	Parent Company:

SALARIES/BENEFITS:

Pension Plan:	ESOP Stock Plan:	Profit Sharing:	Top Exec. Salary: $600,000	Bonus: $1,050,000
Savings Plan: Y	Stock Purch. Plan:		Second Exec. Salary: $402,069	Bonus: $392,700

OTHER THOUGHTS:

Apparent Women Officers or Directors: 6
Hot Spot for Advancement for Women/Minorities: Y

LOCATIONS: ("Y" = Yes)

West:	Southwest:	Midwest:	Southeast:	Northeast:	International:
Y	Y			Y	

BRE PROPERTIES INC

www.breproperties.com

Industry Group Code: 531110 Ranks within this company's industry group: Sales: 11   Profits: 5

Properties:		Financial Services:	Construction/Development:	Investments:		Specialty Services:	Brokerage:
Apartments:	Y	Mortgages:	Commercial Construction:	REIT:	Y	Property Management:	Commercial Sales:
Malls/Shopping:		Title Insurance:	Residential Construction:			Online Services:	Residential Sales:
Offices:		Property Insurance:	Land Development:			Software/IT:	Specialty:
Hotels/Motels:			Support Services:			Consulting:	
Industrial/Warehouses:			Design/Engineering:				
Other:							

TYPES OF BUSINESS:

Real Estate Investment Trust
Apartment Communities

BRANDS/DIVISIONS/AFFILIATES:

CONTACTS: *Note: Officers with more than one job title may be intentionally listed here more than once.*

Constance B. Moore, CEO
Constance B. Moore, Pres.
John A. Schissel, CFO/Exec. VP
Deborah J. Jones, Exec. VP-Associate Rel. & Dev.
Kerry Fanwick, General Counsel/Exec. VP
Scott A. Reinert, Exec. VP-Oper.
Stephanie Andre, Treas./VP
Stephen C. Dominiak, Chief Investment Officer/Exec. VP
Irving F. Lyons III, Chmn.

Phone: 415-445-6530	Fax: 415-445-6505
Toll-Free:	
Address: 525 Market St., 4th Fl., San Francisco, CA 94105 US	

GROWTH PLANS/SPECIAL FEATURES:

BRE Properties, Inc. is a real estate investment trust (REIT) that develops, acquires and manages multifamily apartment communities. BRE operates communities in six targeted metropolitan markets of the western U.S., including 75 wholly- or majority-owned stabilized multifamily communities, including 21,318 apartment units, in California, Washington and Arizona; 13 stabilized multifamily communities owned through joint venture agreements comprised of 4,080 apartment units; and six apartment communities (1,742 units) in various stages of construction. The company's strategy for acquiring new property involves targeting high-quality communities in high-demand, supply-constrained, attractive locations, especially coastal California. Furthermore, its communities are generally built after 1980, include 100 or more units and are located near business, transportation, employment and recreation centers. The company recently acquired Fountains at River Oaks, a 226-unit community in San Jose, California, for $50.3 million; Aqua Marina del Rey, a property containing 500 units in Marina del Rey, California for $166 million; The Vistas of West Hills, a property with 220 units in Valencia, California for $56.5 million; and 2.4 acres of land in Sunnyvale California for $19 million. In 2010, the firm sold the 264-unit Bolder Creek property in Riverside, California for $24.6 million.

The company offers employees medical and dental insurance; flexible spending accounts; life and AD&D insurance; disability coverage; a 401(k) plan; scholarship programs for employees' children and grandchildren; a 529 college plan; tuition reimbursement; and an employee assistance program.

FINANCIALS: Sales and profits are in thousands of dollars—add 000 to get the full amount. 2010 Note: Financial information for 2010 was not available for all companies at press time.

2010 Sales: $341,973	2010 Profits: $54,835	**U.S. Stock Ticker:** BRE
2009 Sales: $326,180	2009 Profits: $64,340	**Int'l Ticker:** Int'l Exchange:
2008 Sales: $325,898	2008 Profits: $136,864	Employees: 628
2007 Sales: $362,561	2007 Profits: $128,081	Fiscal Year Ends: 12/31
2006 Sales: $364,586	2006 Profits: $102,195	Parent Company:

SALARIES/BENEFITS:

Pension Plan:	ESOP Stock Plan:	Profit Sharing:	Top Exec. Salary: $475,000	Bonus: $567,373
Savings Plan: Y	Stock Purch. Plan:		Second Exec. Salary: $416,000	Bonus: $409,731

OTHER THOUGHTS:

Apparent Women Officers or Directors: 5
Hot Spot for Advancement for Women/Minorities: Y

LOCATIONS: ("Y" = Yes)

West:	Southwest:	Midwest:	Southeast:	Northeast:	International:
Y					

BROOKDALE SENIOR LIVING INC

www.brookdaleliving.com

Industry Group Code: 623110 Ranks within this company's industry group: Sales: 1 Profits: 5

Properties:	Financial Services:	Construction/Development:	Investments:	Specialty Services:		Brokerage:
Apartments:	Mortgages:	Commercial Construction:	REIT:	Property Management:	Y	Commercial Sales:
Malls/Shopping:	Title Insurance:	Residential Construction:		Online Services:		Residential Sales:
Offices:	Property Insurance:	Land Development:		Software/IT:		Specialty:
Hotels/Motels:		Support Services:		Consulting:		
Industrial/Warehouses:		Design/Engineering:				
Other: Y						

TYPES OF BUSINESS:

Long-Term Health Care & Assisted Living
Retirement Communities
Assisted Living Communities
Continued Care Retirement Communities (CCRCs)
Managed Facilities

BRANDS/DIVISIONS/AFFILIATES:

Innovative Senior Care
Optimum Life
Clare Bridge

CONTACTS: *Note: Officers with more than one job title may be intentionally listed here more than once.*

Bill E. Sheriff, CEO
John P. Rijos, COO
John P. Rijos, Co-Pres.
Mark W. Ohlendorf, CFO/Co-Pres.
Bryan D. Richardson, Chief Admin. Officer/Exec. VP
T. Andrew Smith, General Counsel/Sec./Exec. VP
Gregory B. Richard, Exec. VP-Field Oper.
H. Todd Kaestner, Exec. VP-Dev.
Holly Botsford, Mgr.-Public Rel.
George T. Hicks, Exec. VP-Finance
Kristin A. Ferge, Exec. VP/Treas.
Wesley R. Edens, Chmn.

Phone: 615-221-2250	Fax: 615-221-2289
Toll-Free: 866-785-9025	
Address: 111 Westwood Place, Ste. 200, Brentwood, TN 37027 US	

GROWTH PLANS/SPECIAL FEATURES:

Brookdale Senior Living, Inc. (BSL) is one of the largest senior living facility operators in the U.S. It operates 559 owned, leased or managed senior living facilities in 34 states that can serve approximately 51,300 residents. BSL operates four segments, representing different types of facilities. It has 78 retirement centers with 14,620 beds, 427 assisted living communities with 20,988 beds, 35 continuing care retirement communities (CCRCs) with 11,919 beds and it provides management services for 19 third-party facilities with 3,786 beds. At the end of 2010, these facilities were 87.1% occupied. The facilities strive to offer residents a home-like setting and typically feature assistance with daily living, multiple forms of therapy and various home health services. For example, many locations offer the Innovative Senior Care program, which focuses on rehabilitation, fitness and educational offerings in addition to home health services. Additionally, its Optimum Life program is a nationwide wellness initiative that offers a holistic approach to health, life and aging. BSL offers a full spectrum of care options, including independent living, personalized assisted living, rehabilitation and skilled nursing. Additionally, through its Clare Bridge facilities, the firm specializes in the care of Alzheimer's and dementia patients. The company maintains its own culinary arts institute, which offers a training ground for chefs and dining staff. Leased communities generated the largest share (56.1%) of 2010 revenues, followed by owned communities (43.6%) and managed communities (0.3%). BSL generated 81% of its 2010 revenue from private pay customers, with the remainder generated by Medicare, Medicaid and other various third-party payor programs.

Employees are offered medical, dental and vision insurance; flexible spending accounts; disability coverage; an employee assistance plan; a discount stock purchase plan; access to onsite clinics that offer free healthcare services; adoption benefits; legal insurance; and tuition reimbursement.

FINANCIALS: Sales and profits are in thousands of dollars—add 000 to get the full amount. 2010 Note: Financial information for 2010 was not available for all companies at press time.

2010 Sales: $2,213,264	2010 Profits: $-48,901	**U.S. Stock Ticker:** BKD
2009 Sales: $2,023,068	2009 Profits: $-66,255	**Int'l Ticker:** **Int'l Exchange:**
2008 Sales: $1,928,054	2008 Profits: $-373,241	**Employees:** 38,600
2007 Sales: $1,839,296	2007 Profits: $-161,979	**Fiscal Year Ends:** 12/31
2006 Sales: $1,309,913	2006 Profits: $-108,087	**Parent Company:**

SALARIES/BENEFITS:

Pension Plan:	ESOP Stock Plan:	Profit Sharing:	Top Exec. Salary: $587,692	Bonus: $1,012,500
Savings Plan: Y	Stock Purch. Plan: Y		Second Exec. Salary: $486,962	Bonus: $697,333

OTHER THOUGHTS:

Apparent Women Officers or Directors: 2
Hot Spot for Advancement for Women/Minorities:

LOCATIONS: ("Y" = Yes)

West:	Southwest:	Midwest:	Southeast:	Northeast:	International:
Y	Y	Y	Y	Y	

BROOKFIELD ASSET MANAGEMENT INC

www.brookfield.com

Industry Group Code: 5311 Ranks within this company's industry group: Sales: 1 Profits: 9

Properties:		Financial Services:		Construction/Development:		Investments:		Specialty Services:		Brokerage:	
Apartments:		Mortgages:		Commercial Construction:		REIT:		Property Management:		Commercial Sales:	Y
Malls/Shopping:	Y	Title Insurance:		Residential Construction:				Online Services:		Residential Sales:	Y
Offices:	Y	Property Insurance:		Land Development:				Software/IT:		Specialty:	
Hotels/Motels:	Y			Support Services:	Y			Consulting:			
Industrial/Warehouses:				Design/Engineering:							
Other:	Y										

TYPES OF BUSINESS:

Real Estate and Industrial Investments
Asset Management
Hydroelectric Generation & Transmission
Paper Production
Agriculture
Financial Services
Timber Development
Wind Power Development

BRANDS/DIVISIONS/AFFILIATES:

Brookfield Special Situations Group
Norbord Inc
Brookfield Renewable Power Fund
Brookfield Incorporacoes SA
Brookfield Homes Corporation
Brookfield Renewable Power Inc
Brookfield Properties Corporation

CONTACTS: *Note: Officers with more than one job title may be intentionally listed here more than once.*

J. Bruce Flatt, CEO
Brian D. Lawson, CFO
Lori Pearson, Sr. VP-Human Resources
Joseph S. Freedman, General Counsel
Richard Clark, Sr. Managing Partner-Property Oper.
Jeff Blidner, Sr. Managing Partner-Strategic Planning
Katherine Vyse, Sr. VP-Comm.
Katherine Vyse, Sr. VP-Investor Rel.
Richard Legault, CEO/Pres., Brookfield Power
Marcel R. Coutu, Chmn.

Phone: 416-363-9491	**Fax:** 416-365-9642
Toll-Free:	
Address: 181 Bay St., Brookfield Pl., Ste. 300, Toronto, ON M5J 2T3 Canada	

GROWTH PLANS/SPECIAL FEATURES:

Brookfield Asset Management, Inc. is a Canadian holding company that owns and manages assets in the areas of real estate and power generation. The company maintains more than $100 billion in assets under management. Brookfield's subsidiaries include Norbord, a paper production firm; Brookfield Renewable Power, Inc., which operates 166 hydroelectric plants, two wind farms and two thermal plants hydroelectric power facilities with a combined production capacity of roughly 4,292 megawatts; Brookfield Homes Corporation, which deals in residential real estate; The Brookfield Special Situations Group, which offers long-term capital and strategic assistance to mid- market North American firms; Brookfield Properties Corporation, a commercial real estate management agency; Brookfield Renewable Power Fund, which owns assets that produce electricity exclusively from environmentally friendly hydroelectric resources; and Brookfield Incorporacoes SA, a high-end and luxury residential real estate company based in Brazil. Brookfield manages office properties and development sites located in 10 core markets: New York, Los Angeles, Houston, Denver, Minneapolis, Boston, Washington, D.C., Toronto, Ottawa and Calgary. The firm also owns retail and hotel properties in the U.K. and Brazil. The firm also sponsors The Brookfield Real Estate Opportunity Fund, which invests and manages two funds with over $1.8 billion of assets, comprised of roughly 16.87 million square feet of industrial, commercial office and multi-family residential properties. In May 2010, The Brookfield Special Situations Group acquired roughly 24.5% additional interest in Ainsworth Lumber Co., Ltd.; it now owns approximately 53.5% Ainsworth Lumber.

FINANCIALS: Sales and profits are in thousands of dollars—add 000 to get the full amount. 2010 Note: Financial information for 2010 was not available for all companies at press time.

2010 Sales: $13,623,000	2010 Profits: $1,454,000	**U.S. Stock Ticker: BAM**
2009 Sales: $12,082,000	2009 Profits: $454,000	**Int'l Ticker: BAM** Int'l Exchange: Toronto-TSX
2008 Sales: $12,909,000	2008 Profits: $649,000	Employees: 18,000
2007 Sales: $9,343,000	2007 Profits: $787,000	Fiscal Year Ends: 12/31
2006 Sales: $6,897,000	2006 Profits: $1,170,000	Parent Company:

SALARIES/BENEFITS:

Pension Plan:	ESOP Stock Plan:	Profit Sharing:	Top Exec. Salary: $374,445	Bonus: $
Savings Plan:	Stock Purch. Plan:		Second Exec. Salary: $374,445	Bonus: $

OTHER THOUGHTS:

Apparent Women Officers or Directors: 2
Hot Spot for Advancement for Women/Minorities:

LOCATIONS: ("Y" = Yes)

West:	Southwest:	Midwest:	Southeast:	Northeast:	International:
Y	Y	Y	Y	Y	Y

BROOKFIELD HOMES CORP   www.brookfieldhomes.com

Industry Group Code: 2361 Ranks within this company's industry group: Sales: 16   Profits: 6

Properties:	Financial Services:	Construction/Development:		Investments:	Specialty Services:	Brokerage:
Apartments:	Mortgages:	Commercial Construction:		REIT:	Property Management:	Commercial Sales:
Malls/Shopping:	Title Insurance:	Residential Construction:	Y		Online Services:	Residential Sales:
Offices:	Property Insurance:	Land Development:	Y		Software/IT:	Specialty:
Hotels/Motels:		Support Services:			Consulting:	
Industrial/Warehouses:		Design/Engineering:				
Other:						

TYPES OF BUSINESS:

Construction, Residential
Land Development

BRANDS/DIVISIONS/AFFILIATES:

Brookfield Bay Area Holdings LLC
Brookfield Southland Holdings LLC
Brookfield San Diego Holdings LLC
Brookfield Washington LLC
Brookfield California Land Holdings LLC
Brookfield Properties Corporation
Brookfield Residential Properties, Inc.

CONTACTS: *Note: Officers with more than one job title may be intentionally listed here more than once.*

Ian G. Cockwell, CEO
Ian G. Cockwell, Pres.
Craig J. Laurie, CFO/Exec. VP
Shane D. Pearson, General Counsel/VP
Linda T. Northwood, Dir.-Investor Rel.
Jessica Caldwell, Corp. Controller/VP
William B. Seith, Exec. VP-Risk Management
Stephen P. Doyle, Pres., Brookfield San Diego Holdings LLC
John J. Ryan, Pres., Brookfield Bay Area Holdings LLC
Robert Hubbell, Pres., Brookfield Washington LLC
Robert L. Stelzl, Chmn.

Phone: 703-270-1700	Fax: 703-270-1401
Toll-Free:	
Address: 8500 Executive Park Ave., Ste. 300, Fairfax, VA 22031 US	

GROWTH PLANS/SPECIAL FEATURES:

Brookfield Homes Corp. is a residential homebuilder and land developer. The company builds homes and develops land in master-planned communities and infill locations in four markets: Northern California, including the San Francisco Bay Area and Sacramento, which generated $71 million in sales on 66 units in 2010; Southland/Los Angeles, $83 million on 189 units; San Diego/Riverside, $54 million on 100 units; and the Washington D.C. area, $80 million on 210 units. It develops land for its own communities and sells lots to other homebuilders. In its communities, the company designs, constructs and markets single-family and multi-family homes primarily to move-up and luxury homebuyers. In each of its markets, the firm operates through a local business unit that is involved in all phases of the planning and building of master-planned communities and infill developments. These phases include sourcing and evaluating land acquisitions; site planning; obtaining entitlements; developing the land; product design; constructing, marketing and selling homes; and homebuyer customer services. The firm owns over 17,600 lots and controls another 9,000 through land options. The company's work begins with the purchase of raw or semi-developed land. It then involves itself with gaining governmental permission in regards to infrastructure development, such as new roads, water and power lines. Upon approval, single-family homes or planned communities of homes with recreational amenities are constructed. In October 2010, the firm agreed to merge its operations with and into the North American residential land and housing division of Brookfield Properties Corporation. Upon completion of the transaction, the combined company will operate as Brookfield Residential Properties, Inc.

FINANCIALS: Sales and profits are in thousands of dollars—add 000 to get the full amount. 2010 Note: Financial information for 2010 was not available for all companies at press time.

2010 Sales: $339,000	2010 Profits: $3,000	**U.S. Stock Ticker: BHS**
2009 Sales: $376,000	2009 Profits: $-33,000	**Int'l Ticker:** Int'l Exchange:
2008 Sales: $449,000	2008 Profits: $-116,000	Employees: 271
2007 Sales: $583,000	2007 Profits: $16,000	Fiscal Year Ends: 12/31
2006 Sales: $872,000	2006 Profits: $148,000	Parent Company:

SALARIES/BENEFITS:

Pension Plan:	ESOP Stock Plan:	Profit Sharing:	Top Exec. Salary: $400,000	Bonus: $630,000
Savings Plan:	Stock Purch. Plan:		Second Exec. Salary: $320,000	Bonus: $360,000

OTHER THOUGHTS:

Apparent Women Officers or Directors: 2
Hot Spot for Advancement for Women/Minorities:

LOCATIONS: ("Y" = Yes)

West:	Southwest:	Midwest:	Southeast:	Northeast:	International:
Y				Y	

BUILDING MATERIALS HOLDING CORP

www.bmcselect.com

Industry Group Code: 444130 Ranks within this company's industry group: Sales: Profits:

Properties:	Financial Services:	Construction/Development:		Investments:	Specialty Services:	Brokerage:
Apartments:	Mortgages:	Commercial Construction:		REIT:	Property Management:	Commercial Sales:
Malls/Shopping:	Title Insurance:	Residential Construction:			Online Services:	Residential Sales:
Offices:	Property Insurance:	Land Development:			Software/IT:	Specialty:
Hotels/Motels:		Support Services:	Y		Consulting:	
Industrial/Warehouses:		Design/Engineering:	Y			
Other:						

TYPES OF BUSINESS:

Building Materials & Hardware Stores, Retail
Building & Construction Services

BRANDS/DIVISIONS/AFFILIATES:

BMC West Corporation
SelectBuild Construction
BBP Companies
Campbell Companies
Leaman Building Materials
Riggs Plumbing LLC

CONTACTS: Note: Officers with more than one job title may be intentionally listed here more than once.

Peter C. Alexander, CEO
Stanley M. Wilson, COO
Stanley M. Wilson, Pres.
Daniel McQuary, CFO
Steven H. Pearson, Sr. VP-Human Resources
Paul S. Street, Chief Admin. Officer
Paul S. Street, General Counsel/Corp. Sec./Sr. VP
Jay B. Hunt, Chmn.

Phone: 208-331-4300	Fax: 208-331-4366
Toll-Free:	
Address: 720 Park Blvd., Ste. 200, Boise, ID 83712 US	

GROWTH PLANS/SPECIAL FEATURES:

Building Materials Holding Corp. (BMHC) through wholly-owned subsidiaries BMC West Corporation and SelectBuild Construction, is a leading provider of building materials and services to residential, commercial and industrial contractors as well as professional repair and remodeling contractors and builders. BMC West operates building materials centers primarily in the western U.S. The division's principal products include lumber, panel products, engineered wood products, roofing materials, pre-hung doors and millwork, roof and floor trusses, pre-assembled windows, cabinets, hardware, paint and tools. In addition, BMC West provides services such as pre-cutting lumber and pre-assembling windows to meet customer specifications. The company targets primarily professional contractors and builders engaged in residential construction and, to a lesser extent, light commercial and industrial construction. The firm's other subsidiary, SelectBuild Construction, provides construction services to high-volume production homebuilders. Services include framing, concrete, plumbing, other construction trades, managing labor and construction schedules as well as sourcing materials. BMHC's primary growth plans consist of expansion through acquisitions, focusing on those that complement existing operations in growing building markets, and those that provide entry into fast-growing, attractive new markets. In January 2010, the company emerged from Chapter 11 protection after closing all of its facilities in Nevada; consolidating its Portland operations with its Vancouver, Washington facility; consolidating its California facilities. Additional consolidations took place in Texas, Arizona and Colorado.

The company offers its employees medical, dental and health insurance.

FINANCIALS: Sales and profits are in thousands of dollars—add 000 to get the full amount. 2010 Note: Financial information for 2010 was not available for all companies at press time.

2010 Sales: $	2010 Profits: $	U.S. Stock Ticker: Private
2009 Sales: $	2009 Profits: $	Int'l Ticker: Int'l Exchange:
2008 Sales: $1,324,679	2008 Profits: $-214,809	Employees: 8,200
2007 Sales: $2,179,073	2007 Profits: $-312,713	Fiscal Year Ends: 12/31
2006 Sales: $2,951,162	2006 Profits: $102,074	Parent Company:

SALARIES/BENEFITS:

Pension Plan:	ESOP Stock Plan: Y	Profit Sharing: Y	Top Exec. Salary: $	Bonus: $833,690
Savings Plan: Y	Stock Purch. Plan:		Second Exec. Salary: $	Bonus: $

OTHER THOUGHTS:

Apparent Women Officers or Directors: 1
Hot Spot for Advancement for Women/Minorities:

LOCATIONS: ("Y" = Yes)

West:	Southwest:	Midwest:	Southeast:	Northeast:	International:
Y	Y	Y	Y	Y	

BURNS & MCDONNELL

www.burnsmcd.com

Industry Group Code: 237 Ranks within this company's industry group: Sales: Profits:

Properties:	Financial Services:	Construction/Development:		Investments:	Specialty Services:	Brokerage:
Apartments:	Mortgages:	Commercial Construction:	Y	REIT:	Property Management:	Commercial Sales:
Malls/Shopping:	Title Insurance:	Residential Construction:			Online Services:	Residential Sales:
Offices:	Property Insurance:	Land Development:			Software/IT:	Specialty:
Hotels/Motels:		Support Services:			Consulting:	
Industrial/Warehouses:		Design/Engineering:	Y			
Other:						

TYPES OF BUSINESS:

Engineering
Construction
Consulting
Environmental Consulting
Architecture & Design
Energy Transmission

BRANDS/DIVISIONS/AFFILIATES:

CONTACTS: *Note: Officers with more than one job title may be intentionally listed here more than once.*

Greg Graves, CEO
Greg Graves, Pres.
Mark Taylor, CFO
Greg Gould, CTO/VP
Mark Taylor, VP/Treas.
Greg Graves, Chmn.

Phone: 816-333-9400	Fax: 816-822-3412
Toll-Free:	
Address: 9400 Ward Pkwy., Kansas City, MO 64114 US	

GROWTH PLANS/SPECIAL FEATURES:

Burns & McDonnell provides engineering, architectural, construction, environmental and consulting services across the U.S. and worldwide. The company divides its businesses into several global practice units and an operations division. The Government and Defense unit designs and constructs airport terminals; military facilities; aerospace manufacturing facilities; runways and airfield infrastructure; and aviation support facilities. The Buildings unit provides post-construction services to companies in the power, process, aviation, infrastructure and commercial industries. The Energy unit is focused on sustainability in construction and renovation, with projects ranging from the construction of baseload coal-fired power generation plants and high-voltage transmission networks to comprehensive energy system overhauls. The Environmental unit's services include hazardous waste remediation, solid waste management and emergency response. The Environmental and Remediation unit offers permitting, ecology, studies and land management services. The Healthcare and Research Facilities unit constructs hospitals, laboratories and research facilities, and offers additional planning, management and landscape architecture services. The Water/Wastewater unit is focused on water and transportation projects, providing collection system construction, wastewater services and watershed management. The Process and Industrial unit designs manufacturing plants, refineries, warehouses and assembly facilities. The Transmission and Distribution unit includes the construction of transportation infrastructure and electrical energy transmission services. Other units include Security, Telecommunications, Transportation, Food/Consumer Products, Local Government and Sustainable Solutions. Burns & McDonnell's customers include companies in a wide variety of industries, including the energy, environmental, government and defense, healthcare, manufacturing, telecommunications and water and wastewater markets.

Employees of the firm are offered health and life insurance; short- and long-term disability; flexible spending accounts; personal time off; eight paid holidays; educational seminars; fitness center; tuition assistance; certification and membership reimbursement. The company is 100% employee-owned through its employee stock ownership plan.

FINANCIALS: Sales and profits are in thousands of dollars—add 000 to get the full amount. 2010 Note: Financial information for 2010 was not available for all companies at press time.

2010 Sales: $	2010 Profits: $	U.S. Stock Ticker: Private
2009 Sales: $	2009 Profits: $	Int'l Ticker: Int'l Exchange:
2008 Sales: $	2008 Profits: $	Employees: 2,850
2007 Sales: $	2007 Profits: $	Fiscal Year Ends: 12/31
2006 Sales: $	2006 Profits: $	Parent Company:

SALARIES/BENEFITS:

Pension Plan:	ESOP Stock Plan: Y	Profit Sharing:	Top Exec. Salary: $	Bonus: $
Savings Plan: Y	Stock Purch. Plan:		Second Exec. Salary: $	Bonus: $

OTHER THOUGHTS:

Apparent Women Officers or Directors:
Hot Spot for Advancement for Women/Minorities:

LOCATIONS: ("Y" = Yes)

West:	Southwest:	Midwest:	Southeast:	Northeast:	International:
Y	Y	Y	Y	Y	

BUTLER MANUFACTURING CO

www.butlermfg.com

Industry Group Code: 332311 Ranks within this company's industry group: Sales: Profits:

Properties:	Financial Services:	Construction/Development:		Investments:	Specialty Services:	Brokerage:
Apartments:	Mortgages:	Commercial Construction:	Y	REIT:	Property Management:	Commercial Sales:
Malls/Shopping:	Title Insurance:	Residential Construction:			Online Services:	Residential Sales:
Offices:	Property Insurance:	Land Development:			Software/IT:	Specialty:
Hotels/Motels:		Support Services:	Y		Consulting:	
Industrial/Warehouses:		Design/Engineering:	Y			
Other:						

TYPES OF BUSINESS:

Construction Materials
Prefabricated Metal Building & Component Manufacturing
Pre-Engineered Building Systems & Components
Architectural Aluminum Systems & Components
Construction & Real Estate Services

BRANDS/DIVISIONS/AFFILIATES:

BlueScope Steel, Ltd.
Butler Buildings North America
Butler Heavy Structures
BlueScope Construction

CONTACTS: *Note: Officers with more than one job title may be intentionally listed here more than once.*

Ted Wolfe, Pres.
Tom Gilligan, VP-Mktg. & Sales
Ron Miller, VP-Mktg.

Phone: 816-968-3000	Fax: 816-968-3279
Toll-Free:	
Address: 1540 Genessee St., Kansas City, MO 64102 US	

GROWTH PLANS/SPECIAL FEATURES:

Butler Manufacturing Co., a subsidiary of BlueScope Steel Limited, markets, designs and manufactures steel building systems for nonresidential buildings. It also executes construction and real estate operations. The firm manufactures five main types of product: structural systems, consisting of support systems (trusses, joists and anything else that keeps a building standing up); wall systems, which come in a variety of textures but are generally utilitarian in design; roofs; small buildings, such as climate-controlled storage units and maintenance structures; and environmental designs, mainly with a focus on reduced energy consumption. Butler's largest division designs, manufactures, markets and sells steel building systems. This division's products are mostly custom-designed and engineered one- to eight-story steel buildings for use as offices, manufacturing facilities, warehouses, schools, shopping centers, agricultural buildings and other applications. Butler's specialized construction services segment consists of BlueScope Construction, a construction company specializing in large, multiple-site projects and Butler Heavy Structures, a supplier of pre-engineered building shell materials, offering design, delivery, installation and complete turnkey construction services. The company offers specialized government construction services through Butler GSA, which has experience in military base construction, Air Force hangars, Coast Guard marine storage and maintenance facilities and more. Additionally the Butler Research Center simulates worst case scenario weather conditions designed to test Butler products and ensure their durability. The company has subsidiaries and joint-ventures located throughout the U.S., China, Europe, Japan, Saudi Arabia and Latin America.

FINANCIALS: Sales and profits are in thousands of dollars—add 000 to get the full amount. 2010 Note: Financial information for 2010 was not available for all companies at press time.

2010 Sales: $	2010 Profits: $	U.S. Stock Ticker: Subsidiary
2009 Sales: $	2009 Profits: $	Int'l Ticker: Int'l Exchange:
2008 Sales: $	2008 Profits: $	Employees:
2007 Sales: $	2007 Profits: $	Fiscal Year Ends: 6/30
2006 Sales: $	2006 Profits: $	Parent Company: BLUESCOPE STEEL LIMITED

SALARIES/BENEFITS:

Pension Plan:	ESOP Stock Plan:	Profit Sharing:	Top Exec. Salary: $	Bonus: $
Savings Plan:	Stock Purch. Plan:		Second Exec. Salary: $	Bonus: $

OTHER THOUGHTS:

Apparent Women Officers or Directors: 1
Hot Spot for Advancement for Women/Minorities:

LOCATIONS: ("Y" = Yes)

West:	Southwest:	Midwest:	Southeast:	Northeast:	International:
Y	Y	Y	Y	Y	Y

CAESARS ENTERTAINMENT CORPORATION   www.caesars.com

Industry Group Code: 721120 Ranks within this company's industry group: Sales: 1   Profits: 7

Properties:		Financial Services:	Construction/Development:	Investments:	Specialty Services:		Brokerage:
Apartments:		Mortgages:	Commercial Construction:	REIT:	Property Management:	Y	Commercial Sales:
Malls/Shopping:		Title Insurance:	Residential Construction:		Online Services:		Residential Sales:
Offices:		Property Insurance:	Land Development:		Software/IT:		Specialty:
Hotels/Motels:	Y		Support Services:		Consulting:		
Industrial/Warehouses:			Design/Engineering:				
Other:	Y						

TYPES OF BUSINESS:

Casino Hotels
Dockside & Riverboat Casinos
Racing Venues
Casino Management

BRANDS/DIVISIONS/AFFILIATES:

Harrah's Entertainment, Inc.
Caesers
Flamingo
Horseshoe
Total Rewards
World Series of Poker
Rock Ohio Caesars LLC
Hamlet Holdings LLC

CONTACTS: Note: Officers with more than one job title may be intentionally listed here more than once.

Gary W. Loveman, CEO
Gary W. Loveman, Pres.
Jonathan S. Halkyard, CFO/Sr. VP/Treas.
David Norton, Chief Mktg. Officer/Sr. VP
Mary Thomas, Sr. VP-Human Resources
Katrina Lane, CTO/Sr. VP
Tim Donovan, General Counsel/Sr. VP
Jan Jones, Sr. VP-Comm. & Gov't Rel.
Tom M. Jenkin, Pres., Western Div.
John Payne, Pres., Central Div.
Don Marrandino, Pres., Eastern Div.
John Baker, Sr. VP-Enterprise Effectiveness
Gary W. Loveman, Chmn.

Phone: 702-407-6000	Fax: 702-407-6037
Toll-Free: 800-318-0047	
Address: 1 Caesars Palace Dr., Las Vegas, NV 89109 US	

GROWTH PLANS/SPECIAL FEATURES:

Caesars Entertainment Corporation, formerly Harrah's Entertainment, Inc., is one of the largest gaming companies in the world. The firm owns or manages approximately 52 casinos throughout the world. It operates casino entertainment facilities primarily under the Harrah's, Caesars and Horseshoe brands in the U.S., including land-based casinos; riverboat or dockside casinos; casino clubs; and three racing venues. Caesars also earns fees from managing three casinos for Indian tribes: Harrah's Phoenix Ak-Chin, located near Phoenix, Arizona; Harrah's Rincon Casino and Resort, near San Diego, California; and Harrah's Cherokee Casino and Hotel, in Cherokee, North Carolina. Its international facilities are located in Canada, Uruguay, England, Scotland, Egypt and South Africa. Additional brands operated and/or owned by Caesars include Bally's; Flamingo; Grand Biloxi; Harveys; Imperial Palace; Paris; Rio; and Showboat. The company also owns and operates the World Series of Poker tournament and brand. Besides casinos, the firm's properties generally include hotel and convention space; restaurants; and non-gaming entertainment facilities. Its facilities contain an aggregate 3 million square feet of gaming space and over 42,000 hotel rooms. For returning customers in the U.S., the firm offers the Total Rewards card plan, allowing holders to earn reward credits for prizes such as vacations, event tickets and cars; Total Rewards currently has over 40 million members. In February 2010, Caesars acquired the Planet Hollywood Resort and Casino in Las Vegas, Nevada. In July 2010, the firm purchased the Thistledown Racetrack, a thoroughbred racing facility located in Cleveland, Ohio. In December 2010, it formed a joint venture with Rock Gaming LLC, Rock Ohio Caesars LLC, in order to develop casinos in Cincinnati and Cleveland.

Employees of Caesars receive medical, dental and vision plans; educational assistance; a health and wellness programs.

FINANCIALS: Sales and profits are in thousands of dollars—add 000 to get the full amount. 2010 Note: Financial information for 2010 was not available for all companies at press time.

2010 Sales: $8,818,600	2010 Profits: $-823,300	**U.S. Stock Ticker: Private**
2009 Sales: $8,907,400	2009 Profits: $846,400	**Int'l Ticker:** Int'l Exchange:
2008 Sales: $9,370,000	2008 Profits: $-5,197,200	Employees: 85,000
2007 Sales: $10,825,200	2007 Profits: $619,400	Fiscal Year Ends: 12/31
2006 Sales: $9,673,900	2006 Profits: $535,800	Parent Company: HAMLET HOLDINGS LLC

SALARIES/BENEFITS:

Pension Plan:	ESOP Stock Plan:	Profit Sharing:	Top Exec. Salary: $	Bonus: $
Savings Plan: Y	Stock Purch. Plan:		Second Exec. Salary: $	Bonus: $

OTHER THOUGHTS:

Apparent Women Officers or Directors: 3
Hot Spot for Advancement for Women/Minorities: Y

LOCATIONS: ("Y" = Yes)

West:	Southwest:	Midwest:	Southeast:	Northeast:	International:
Y	Y	Y	Y	Y	Y

CAMDEN PROPERTY TRUST   www.camdenliving.com

Industry Group Code: 531120 Ranks within this company's industry group: Sales: 28   Profits: 39

Properties:		Financial Services:	Construction/Development:	Investments:		Specialty Services:		Brokerage:
Apartments:	Y	Mortgages:	Commercial Construction:	REIT:	Y	Property Management:		Commercial Sales:
Malls/Shopping:		Title Insurance:	Residential Construction: Y			Online Services:		Residential Sales:
Offices:		Property Insurance:	Land Development:			Software/IT:		Specialty:
Hotels/Motels:			Support Services: Y			Consulting:	Y	
Industrial/Warehouses:			Design/Engineering:					
Other:								

TYPES OF BUSINESS:

Real Estate Investment Trust
Apartment Communities
Construction Services
Consulting Services

BRANDS/DIVISIONS/AFFILIATES:

Onex Real Estate Partners
Camden Plaza
Camden Main & Jamboree
Camden College Park

CONTACTS: Note: Officers with more than one job title may be intentionally listed here more than once.

Richard J. Campo, CEO
H. Malcolm Stewart, COO
D. Keith Oden, Pres.
Dennis M. Steen, CFO/Sr. VP-Finance
John Selindh, VP-Mktg.
Cynthia B. Scharringhausen, Sr. VP-Human Resources
Jimmy Whorton, VP-IT
Stephen R. Hefner, Sr. VP-Construction
Bob Fisher, General Counsel/VP/Sec.
Kim Callahan, Contact-Investor Rel.
Michael P. Gallagher, Chief Acct. Officer/VP
Ross Wehman, VP-Tax
Sarah Barletta, VP-Employee Benefits
Kip Zacharias, VP-Bus. Svcs.
Richard J. Campo, Chmn.

Phone: 713-354-2500	Fax: 713-354-2700
Toll-Free: 800-922-6336	
Address: 3 Greenway Plz., Ste. 1300, Houston, TX 77046 US	

GROWTH PLANS/SPECIAL FEATURES:

Camden Property Trust is one of the largest real estate investment trusts (REIT) in the U.S, specializing in several disciplines within the residential real estate industry. The company acquires, develops, manages, disposes and redevelops apartment home communities and offers consulting, building and construction services for third-party clients. Camden currently owns interests in and operates 185 communities consisting of approximately 63,209 apartment homes in the U.S. The company has pursued an aggressive growth strategy over the past decade, with more than a $1 billion in construction since 1996. Camden maintains a diversified portfolio of residential properties ranging from upscale urban residences to middle-class housing in established suburban neighborhoods. Camden maintains a joint venture establishment with Onex Real Estate Partners. The joint venture currently operates three projects: Camden College Park, a 508-unit property in College Park, Maryland; Camden Main & Jamboree in Irvine California, which features 290 luxury apartments; and Camden Plaza, which is a 271-unit facility in Houston, Texas. The company currently has two properties under development, and after completion, the firm's portfolio is expected to increase to 63,816 homes in 187 properties.

The firm offers employees medical, vision and dental insurance; flexible spending accounts; life & AD&D insurance; adoption assistance; a 401(k) plan; an employee stock purchase plan; an apartment discount; education assistance; scholarship funds; and an employee assistance program.

FINANCIALS: Sales and profits are in thousands of dollars—add 000 to get the full amount. 2010 Note: Financial information for 2010 was not available for all companies at press time.

2010 Sales: $610,404	2010 Profits: $23,216	**U.S. Stock Ticker:** CPT
2009 Sales: $612,010	2009 Profits: $-50,800	**Int'l Ticker:** Int'l Exchange:
2008 Sales: $612,408	2008 Profits: $70,973	Employees: 1,750
2007 Sales: $588,319	2007 Profits: $148,457	Fiscal Year Ends: 12/31
2006 Sales: $561,029	2006 Profits: $232,846	Parent Company:

SALARIES/BENEFITS:

Pension Plan:	ESOP Stock Plan:	Profit Sharing:	Top Exec. Salary: $447,700	Bonus: $408,000
Savings Plan: Y	Stock Purch. Plan: Y		Second Exec. Salary: $447,000	Bonus: $408,000

OTHER THOUGHTS:

Apparent Women Officers or Directors: 12
Hot Spot for Advancement for Women/Minorities: Y

LOCATIONS: ("Y" = Yes)

West:	Southwest:	Midwest:	Southeast:	Northeast:	International:
Y	Y	Y	Y	Y	

CAMP DRESSER & MCKEE INC

www.cdm.com

Industry Group Code: 237 Ranks within this company's industry group: Sales: Profits:

Properties:	Financial Services:	Construction/Development:		Investments:	Specialty Services:	Brokerage:
Apartments:	Mortgages:	Commercial Construction:	Y	REIT:	Property Management:	Commercial Sales:
Malls/Shopping:	Title Insurance:	Residential Construction:			Online Services:	Residential Sales:
Offices:	Property Insurance:	Land Development:			Software/IT:	Specialty:
Hotels/Motels:		Support Services:			Consulting:	
Industrial/Warehouses:		Design/Engineering:	Y			
Other:						

TYPES OF BUSINESS:

Engineering & Construction
Water Management
Environmental Services
Design Services
Information Management & Technology
Consulting
Facilities Design
Geotechnical Services

BRANDS/DIVISIONS/AFFILIATES:

CDM
CDM International Inc
CDM Constructors Inc
CDM Federal Programs Corporation
CDM Consult GmbH
Wilbur Smith Associates

CONTACTS: *Note: Officers with more than one job title may be intentionally listed here more than once.*

Richard D. Fox, CEO
John D. Manning, COO
John D. Manning, Pres.
Paul R. Brown, Chief Mktg. Officer/Exec. VP
Paul G. Camell, Chief Admin. Officer/Exec. VP
Paul R. Brown, Exec. VP-Global Market Dev.
Steve Smith, Exec. VP
Richard D. Fox, Chmn.

Phone: 617-452-6000	Fax: 617-452-8000
Toll-Free:	
Address: 50 Hampshire St., 1 Cambridge Pl., Cambridge, MA 02139 US	

GROWTH PLANS/SPECIAL FEATURES:

Camp Dresser & McKee, Inc. (CDM) provides services in engineering, consulting, construction and operations. The company has five operating units: client services - Europe, Middle East and Africa; federal services; industrial services; public services - North America east & Latin America; and public services - North America west/central & Asia. Supporting these units are the consulting services; engineering services; construction services; and the operations services units. In addition to consulting services, CDM offers engineering services such as 3D design; automation and instrumentation; and civil, electrical, geotechnical, mechanical, process and structural engineering. Construction services include constructability and value engineering reviews; cost estimating; design-build and alternative delivery methods; engineering services during construction; general contracting; procurement; and project controls. Operations services include contract management; contract operations; operations and maintenance; and operations optimization. CDM's work involves solid waste and wastewater purification facilities; municipal data management systems; airports, dams, harbors and bridges; a wildlife refuge; major universities; municipal railways; and sports facilities. The firm has a number of subsidiaries including CDM International, Inc., offering CDM's full range of services in Europe, Latin America, the Middle East and Asia; CDM Constructors, Inc., providing design, construction, remediation, general contracting and equipment fabrication services worldwide; and CDM Federal Programs Corporation, offering environmental management services for the EPA, Department of Energy, Department of Defense and other U.S. government agencies. Additionally, CDM owns a majority interest in geotechnical and environmental consulting and design firm CDM Consult GmbH, in Germany. In February 2011, the company acquired Wilbur Smith Associates, which specializes in transportation technology.

CDM offers its employees medical, dental and vision coverage; short- and long-term disability; life and AD&D insurance; commuter benefits; flexible spending accounts; a 401(k) program; profit sharing; an employee assistance program; tuition assistance; and business travel insurance.

FINANCIALS: Sales and profits are in thousands of dollars—add 000 to get the full amount. 2010 Note: Financial information for 2010 was not available for all companies at press time.

2010 Sales: $	2010 Profits: $	U.S. Stock Ticker: Private
2009 Sales: $	2009 Profits: $	Int'l Ticker: Int'l Exchange:
2008 Sales: $	2008 Profits: $	Employees: 4,500
2007 Sales: $	2007 Profits: $	Fiscal Year Ends: 12/31
2006 Sales: $	2006 Profits: $	Parent Company:

SALARIES/BENEFITS:

Pension Plan:	ESOP Stock Plan:	Profit Sharing: Y	Top Exec. Salary: $	Bonus: $
Savings Plan: Y	Stock Purch. Plan:		Second Exec. Salary: $	Bonus: $

OTHER THOUGHTS:

Apparent Women Officers or Directors:
Hot Spot for Advancement for Women/Minorities:

LOCATIONS: ("Y" = Yes)

West:	Southwest:	Midwest:	Southeast:	Northeast:	International:
Y	Y	Y	Y	Y	Y

CAPITAL AUTOMOTIVE REIT   www.capitalautomotive.com

Industry Group Code: 531120 Ranks within this company's industry group: Sales: Profits:

Properties:	Financial Services:	Construction/Development:	Investments:	Specialty Services:	Brokerage:
Apartments:	Mortgages:	Commercial Construction:	REIT: Y	Property Management:	Commercial Sales:
Malls/Shopping:	Title Insurance:	Residential Construction:		Online Services:	Residential Sales:
Offices:	Property Insurance:	Land Development:		Software/IT:	Specialty:
Hotels/Motels:		Support Services:		Consulting:	
Industrial/Warehouses:		Design/Engineering:			
Other: Y					

TYPES OF BUSINESS:

Real Estate Investment Trust
Automotive Retail Real Estate

BRANDS/DIVISIONS/AFFILIATES:

DRA Advisors LLC

CONTACTS: *Note: Officers with more than one job title may be intentionally listed here more than once.*

Thomas D. Eckert, CEO
Jay M. Ferriero, COO/Exec. VP
Thomas D. Eckert, Pres.
David S. Kay, CFO/Exec. VP
John M. Weaver, General Counsel/Exec. VP/Corp. Sec.
David S. Kay, Treas.
Joseph P. Connolly, VP-Western Region Acquisitions
Daniel E. Garces, VP/Sr. Portfolio Mgr.-Midwest Acquisitions
Willie Beck, VP-Eastern U.S. Acquisitions

Phone: 703-288-3075	Fax: 703-288-3375
Toll-Free: 877-422-7288	
Address: 8270 Greensboro Dr., Ste. 950, McLean, VA 22102 US	

GROWTH PLANS/SPECIAL FEATURES:

Capital Automotive REIT (CARS), a private real estate investment trust owned by DRA Advisors LLC, is a finance company focused on automotive retail real estate, with almost $3.8 billion invested in more than 550 automotive properties, such as automobile retailing sites, automotive storage lots and body shops. The company's properties are located in 37 states and Canada, and make up more than 17.5 million square feet of retail building space on over 3,000 acres of land. Capital's strategy is to acquire real estate throughout the U.S. and then make improvements so that operators of multi-site, multi-franchised automotive dealerships and related businesses can use the piece of property. The company engages in a sale-leaseback transaction with automotive dealers, in which the dealers sell their real estate to the firm and then lease it back. This allows the dealers to tap into 100% of their real estate equity while maintaining long-term control of their property. The initial lease term is generally 15-20 years with options for renewal. Capital seeks to invest in properties used by high-quality, well-managed dealer groups that have demonstrated a consistent growth and strong operating results in top metropolitan markets. A typical investment begins at $10 million but the firm will consider an investment as small as $5 million. The firm also purchases properties with operating partnership units, which are exchangeable for common stock. This allows dealers to defer large portions of their tax liability from selling their properties for cash.

Parent company DRA Advisors offers employees medical, dental and life insurance; a prescription drug plan; 401(k) savings and matching plans; flexible spending accounts; commuter subsidies; an employee assistance program; short- and long-term disability; a discount program; and gym memberships.

FINANCIALS: Sales and profits are in thousands of dollars—add 000 to get the full amount. 2010 Note: Financial information for 2010 was not available for all companies at press time.

2010 Sales: $	2010 Profits: $	U.S. Stock Ticker: Private
2009 Sales: $	2009 Profits: $	Int'l Ticker: Int'l Exchange:
2008 Sales: $	2008 Profits: $	Employees:
2007 Sales: $	2007 Profits: $	Fiscal Year Ends: 12/31
2006 Sales: $	2006 Profits: $	Parent Company: DRA ADVISORS LLC

SALARIES/BENEFITS:

Pension Plan:	ESOP Stock Plan:	Profit Sharing:	Top Exec. Salary: $	Bonus: $
Savings Plan: Y	Stock Purch. Plan:		Second Exec. Salary: $	Bonus: $

OTHER THOUGHTS:

Apparent Women Officers or Directors:
Hot Spot for Advancement for Women/Minorities:

LOCATIONS: ("Y" = Yes)

West:	Southwest:	Midwest:	Southeast:	Northeast:	International:
Y	Y	Y	Y	Y	

CAPITAL PACIFIC HOLDINGS INC   www.capitalpacifichomes.com

Industry Group Code: 2361 Ranks within this company's industry group: Sales: Profits:

Properties:	Financial Services:		Construction/Development:		Investments:	Specialty Services:		Brokerage:
Apartments:	Mortgages:	Y	Commercial Construction:		REIT:	Property Management:	Y	Commercial Sales:
Malls/Shopping:	Title Insurance:		Residential Construction:	Y		Online Services:		Residential Sales:
Offices:	Property Insurance:		Land Development:	Y		Software/IT:		Specialty:
Hotels/Motels:			Support Services:			Consulting:		
Industrial/Warehouses:			Design/Engineering:					
Other:								

TYPES OF BUSINESS:

Homebuilding
Land Development
Mortgage Brokerage
Commercial Properties Management

BRANDS/DIVISIONS/AFFILIATES:

Capital Pacific Homes
Capital Pacific Holdings,LLC
Makar Properties

CONTACTS: *Note: Officers with more than one job title may be intentionally listed here more than once.*

Hadi Makarechian, CEO
Hadi Makarechian, Pres.
Matthew C. Kern, CFO
Hadi Makarechian, Chmn.

Phone: 949-622-8400	Fax: 949-622-8404
Toll-Free:	
Address: 4100 MacArthur Blvd., Ste. 120, Newport Beach, CA 92660 US	

GROWTH PLANS/SPECIAL FEATURES:

Capital Pacific Holdings, Inc. (CPH) is a diversified real estate development company. The Newport Beach, California-based firm's principal activities include single-family home, residential community and mixed-use project development. CPH develops communities of new homes for buyers (under Capital Pacific Homes) with varying lifestyles and budgets throughout Arizona, California, Colorado and Texas. The company builds entry-level, move-up, and semi-custom homes, as well as commercial properties. With regards to residential construction, CPH has constructed homes for more than 27,000 customers and closes as many as 1,470 homes and lots annually. Through subsidiary Makar Properties, The firm also provides land entitlement, commercial real estate development, mixed-use development, hospitality and real estate investment management services. This subsidiary has real estate and management assets in Palm Springs and Dana Point, California, among other locations. CPH also develops new home communities for third party owners; and provides mortgage brokerage operations and residential design services.

FINANCIALS: Sales and profits are in thousands of dollars—add 000 to get the full amount. 2010 Note: Financial information for 2010 was not available for all companies at press time.

2010 Sales: $	2010 Profits: $	**U.S. Stock Ticker: Private**
2009 Sales: $	2009 Profits: $	**Int'l Ticker:** Int'l Exchange:
2008 Sales: $	2008 Profits: $	Employees:
2007 Sales: $	2007 Profits: $	Fiscal Year Ends: 2/28
2006 Sales: $	2006 Profits: $	Parent Company:

SALARIES/BENEFITS:

Pension Plan:	ESOP Stock Plan:	Profit Sharing:	Top Exec. Salary: $	Bonus: $
Savings Plan:	Stock Purch. Plan:		Second Exec. Salary: $	Bonus: $

OTHER THOUGHTS:

Apparent Women Officers or Directors:
Hot Spot for Advancement for Women/Minorities:

LOCATIONS: ("Y" = Yes)

West:	Southwest:	Midwest:	Southeast:	Northeast:	International:
Y	Y				

CAPITAL SENIOR LIVING CORP

www.capitalsenior.com

Industry Group Code: 623110 Ranks within this company's industry group: Sales: 6   Profits: 3

Properties:	Financial Services:	Construction/Development:	Investments:	Specialty Services:	Brokerage:
Apartments:	Mortgages:	Commercial Construction:	REIT:	Property Management:	Commercial Sales:
Malls/Shopping:	Title Insurance:	Residential Construction:		Online Services:	Residential Sales:
Offices:	Property Insurance:	Land Development:		Software/IT:	Specialty:
Hotels/Motels:		Support Services:		Consulting:	
Industrial/Warehouses:		Design/Engineering:			
Other: Y					

TYPES OF BUSINESS:

Long-Term Health Care
Nursing Homes
Assisted Living Services
Home Care Services

BRANDS/DIVISIONS/AFFILIATES:

Quality Home Care, Inc.

CONTACTS: Note: Officers with more than one job title may be intentionally listed here more than once.

Lawrence A. Cohen, CEO
Keith N. Johannessen, COO
Keith N. Johannessen, Pres.
Ralph A. Beattie, CFO/Exec. VP
Rob Goodpaster, VP-Nat'l Mktg.
David R. Brickman, General Counsel/VP/Sec.
David Beathard, Sr., VP-Oper.
Joseph G. Solari, VP-Corp. Dev.
Gloria Holland, VP-Finance
Robert Hollister, Property Controller
Glen H. Campbell, VP-Dev.
James A. Moore, Chmn.

Phone: 972-770-5600	Fax: 972-770-5666
Toll-Free:	
Address: 14160 Dallas Pkwy., Ste. 300, Dallas, TX 75254 US	

GROWTH PLANS/SPECIAL FEATURES:

Capital Senior Living Corp. (CSL) is one of the nation's largest operators and developers of residential communities for seniors. The firm operates 77 communities in 23 states, including 32 senior living communities that it either owned or had an ownership interest in and 45 senior living communities that are leased facilities. Its combined facilities can support approximately 11,000 residents. Approximately 95% of the company's annual revenue is generated through private pay parties at these communities. The firm provides senior living services to the elderly in four categories of assistance: independent living, assisted living, continuing care retirement communities and home care services. Its independent living communities provide residents with daily meals, transportation, social and recreational activities, laundry, housekeeping and 24-hour staffing. The firm's assisted living communities, with residents that acquire additional assistance over independent residents, provide personal care services, such as walking, eating, personal hygiene and medication assistance; and special care services for residents with certain forms of dementia. The continuing care retirement communities provide traditional long-term care through 24-hour-per-day skilled nursing care by registered nurses. The company provides home care services to residents at one senior living community through its home care agency, Quality Home Care, Inc., and through third-party providers at a majority of its senior living communities. Many of CSL's communities offer a continuum of care to meet its residents' needs as they change over time. This continuum of care, which integrates independent living, assisted living and home care through independent home care agencies or the company's home care agency, sustains residents' autonomy and independence based on their physical and mental abilities.

Employees are offered medical and dental insurance; life insurance; and a 401(k) plan.

FINANCIALS: Sales and profits are in thousands of dollars—add 000 to get the full amount. 2010 Note: Financial information for 2010 was not available for all companies at press time.

2010 Sales: $211,929	2010 Profits: $4,254	**U.S. Stock Ticker: CSU**
2009 Sales: $191,991	2009 Profits: $2,759	**Int'l Ticker:** Int'l Exchange:
2008 Sales: $193,274	2008 Profits: $3,724	Employees: 4,188
2007 Sales: $189,052	2007 Profits: $4,360	Fiscal Year Ends: 12/31
2006 Sales: $159,070	2006 Profits: $-2,600	Parent Company:

SALARIES/BENEFITS:

Pension Plan:	ESOP Stock Plan:	Profit Sharing:	Top Exec. Salary: $436,558	Bonus: $406,173
Savings Plan: Y	Stock Purch. Plan:		Second Exec. Salary: $278,538	Bonus: $209,023

OTHER THOUGHTS:

Apparent Women Officers or Directors: 2
Hot Spot for Advancement for Women/Minorities:

LOCATIONS: ("Y" = Yes)

West:	Southwest:	Midwest:	Southeast:	Northeast:	International:
Y	Y	Y	Y	Y	

CAPMARK FINANCIAL GROUP INC

www.capmark.com

Industry Group Code: 522310 Ranks within this company's industry group: Sales: Profits:

Properties:	Financial Services:		Construction/Development:	Investments:	Specialty Services:		Brokerage:
Apartments:	Mortgages:	Y	Commercial Construction:	REIT:	Property Management:		Commercial Sales:
Malls/Shopping:	Title Insurance:		Residential Construction:		Online Services:		Residential Sales:
Offices:	Property Insurance:		Land Development:		Software/IT:		Specialty:
Hotels/Motels:			Support Services:		Consulting:	Y	
Industrial/Warehouses:			Design/Engineering:				
Other:							

TYPES OF BUSINESS:

Commercial Real Estate & Construction Lending
Loan Services
Investments
Investment Research

BRANDS/DIVISIONS/AFFILIATES:

Capmark Investments LP
Capmark Bank

GROWTH PLANS/SPECIAL FEATURES:

Capmark Financial Group, Inc. is a real estate finance company. The firm has three core businesses: Capmark Bank; investments and funds management; and services. Capmark Bank has approximately $9.533 billion in assets and outstanding deposits of roughly $6.63 billion. Capmark Bank funds loans secured by commercial and multi-family real estate properties throughout the U.S. and provides trust services to servicers of commercial real estate mortgages. The investments unit, comprising subsidiary Capmark Investments LP, offers investors private funds and separate accounts in equity real estate and higher-yield mortgage plans. The firm has operations in the U.S., Japan, India and China. Capmark is currently operating under Chapter 11 bankruptcly protection. In January 2010, Capmark Investments also filed for Chapter 11 bankruptcy protection.

CONTACTS: *Note: Officers with more than one job title may be intentionally listed here more than once.*

Jay N. Levine, CEO
Jay N. Levine, Pres.
Frederick Arnold, CFO/Exec. VP
Thomas L. Fairfield, General Counsel/Exec. VP
William Gallagher, Exec. VP/Chief Risk Officer
Dennis D. Dammerman, Chmn.

Phone: 215-328-1630	Fax:
Toll-Free: 888-848-2276	
Address: 116 Welsh Rd., Horsham, PA 19044 US	

FINANCIALS: Sales and profits are in thousands of dollars—add 000 to get the full amount. 2010 Note: Financial information for 2010 was not available for all companies at press time.

2010 Sales: $	2010 Profits: $	U.S. Stock Ticker: Private
2009 Sales: $	2009 Profits: $	Int'l Ticker: Int'l Exchange:
2008 Sales: $	2008 Profits: $	Employees:
2007 Sales: $	2007 Profits: $	Fiscal Year Ends: 12/31
2006 Sales: $	2006 Profits: $	Parent Company:

SALARIES/BENEFITS:

Pension Plan:	ESOP Stock Plan:	Profit Sharing:	Top Exec. Salary: $1,549,039	Bonus: $
Savings Plan: Y	Stock Purch. Plan:		Second Exec. Salary: $500,000	Bonus: $

OTHER THOUGHTS:

Apparent Women Officers or Directors: 1
Hot Spot for Advancement for Women/Minorities:

LOCATIONS: ("Y" = Yes)

West:	Southwest:	Midwest:	Southeast:	Northeast:	International:
Y		Y	Y	Y	Y

CAPREIT INC

www.capreit.com

Industry Group Code: 531110 Ranks within this company's industry group: Sales: Profits:

Properties:		Financial Services:	Construction/Development:		Investments:		Specialty Services:		Brokerage:
Apartments:	Y	Mortgages:	Commercial Construction:		REIT:	Y	Property Management:	Y	Commercial Sales:
Malls/Shopping:		Title Insurance:	Residential Construction:				Online Services:		Residential Sales:
Offices:		Property Insurance:	Land Development:				Software/IT:		Specialty:
Hotels/Motels:			Support Services:				Consulting:		
Industrial/Warehouses:			Design/Engineering:						
Other:									

TYPES OF BUSINESS:

Real Estate Investment Trust
Apartments
Property Management

BRANDS/DIVISIONS/AFFILIATES:

CONTACTS: *Note: Officers with more than one job title may be intentionally listed here more than once.*

Dick Kadish, Pres.
Sandra Becker, Sr. VP

Phone: 301-231-8700	Fax: 301-468-8391
Toll-Free:	
Address: 11200 Rockville Pk., Ste. 100, Rockville, MD 20852 US	

GROWTH PLANS/SPECIAL FEATURES:

CAPREIT, Inc. is a real estate investment trust (REIT) and property manager. Its focus is on the acquisition of multi-family residential properties. Since its founding in 1993, CAPREIT has owned or operated over 200 rental and condominium apartment homes consisting of over 30,000 units and housing over 100,000 families. The company's current holdings include apartment units spread over a broad market area of 19 states. CAPREIT also manages a portfolio of properties for third parties. Most of its properties are spread over the Northeast and Southeast, with additional properties in the Midwest and in California. In acquiring properties, the firm stresses both a viable knowledge of the local market and establishing consistent relationships with its brokers, many of whom have made the company a preferred customer. It targets markets that have both high economic growth characteristics and identifiable barriers to entry. CAPREIT specializes in financing its acquisitions with tax-exempt multifamily housing revenue bonds and, to date, has acquired over $1.5 billion. Its acquisitions team works directly with municipal and state issuing authorities, bond trustees and monitoring agents in closing these financing transactions. CAPREIT has a team of over 400 real estate professionals that handles day-to-day on-site management of its multifamily communities.

FINANCIALS: Sales and profits are in thousands of dollars—add 000 to get the full amount. 2010 Note: Financial information for 2010 was not available for all companies at press time.

2010 Sales: $	2010 Profits: $	**U.S. Stock Ticker: Private**
2009 Sales: $	2009 Profits: $	**Int'l Ticker:** Int'l Exchange:
2008 Sales: $	2008 Profits: $	Employees:
2007 Sales: $	2007 Profits: $	Fiscal Year Ends: 12/31
2006 Sales: $	2006 Profits: $	Parent Company:

SALARIES/BENEFITS:

Pension Plan:	ESOP Stock Plan:	Profit Sharing:	Top Exec. Salary: $	Bonus: $
Savings Plan:	Stock Purch. Plan:		Second Exec. Salary: $	Bonus: $

OTHER THOUGHTS:

Apparent Women Officers or Directors: 1
Hot Spot for Advancement for Women/Minorities:

LOCATIONS: ("Y" = Yes)

West:	Southwest:	Midwest:	Southeast:	Northeast:	International:
Y	Y	Y	Y	Y	

CAPSTEAD MORTGAGE CORPORATION

www.capstead.com

Industry Group Code: 531110 Ranks within this company's industry group: Sales: 16   Profits: 3

Properties:	Financial Services:		Construction/Development:	Investments:		Specialty Services:	Brokerage:
Apartments:	Mortgages:	Y	Commercial Construction:	REIT:	Y	Property Management:	Commercial Sales:
Malls/Shopping:	Title Insurance:		Residential Construction:			Online Services:	Residential Sales:
Offices:	Property Insurance:		Land Development:			Software/IT:	Specialty:
Hotels/Motels:			Support Services:			Consulting:	
Industrial/Warehouses:			Design/Engineering:				
Other:							

TYPES OF BUSINESS:

Real Estate Investment Trust
Mortgage-Backed Securities
Commercial Real Estate

BRANDS/DIVISIONS/AFFILIATES:

CONTACTS: Note: Officers with more than one job title may be intentionally listed here more than once.

Andrew F. Jacobs, CEO
Andrew F. Jacobs, Pres.
Phillip A. Reinsch, CFO/Exec. VP
Kelly L. Sargent, Contact-Investor Rel.
Robert R. Spears, Jr., Exec. VP/Dir.-Residential Mortgage Investments
Michael W. Brown, Sr. VP-Asset & Liability Mgmt.
Jack E. Biegler, Chmn.

Phone: 214-874-2323	**Fax:** 214-874-2398
Toll-Free: 800-358-2323	
Address: 8401 N. Central Expressway, Ste. 800, Dallas, TX 75225 US	

GROWTH PLANS/SPECIAL FEATURES:

Capstead Mortgage Corporation, headquartered in Dallas, Texas, operates as a real estate investment trust earning income from investing in real estate-related assets on a leveraged basis and from other investment strategies. For the most part, these investments are limited to single-family residential adjustable-rate mortgage securities issued by such government agencies and government-sponsored entities as Fannie Mae, Freddie Mac and Ginnie Mae. The firm also invests in credit-sensitive commercial mortgage assets. Capstead tends to focus on ARM securities that reset annually or semi-annually and are particularly liquid. Up until 1998, Capstead provided mortgage servicing, but this portfolio was dispensed to GMAC Mortgage Corporation. In recent years, the company acquired an additional 25% of its commercial real estate loan joint venture with Redtail Capital Partners L.P. Capstead previously held a 75% interest; the takeover price was $4 million.

The firm offers its employees benefits such as basic life and AD&D insurance, as well as a 401(k) plan.

FINANCIALS: Sales and profits are in thousands of dollars—add 000 to get the full amount. 2010 Note: Financial information for 2010 was not available for all companies at press time.

2010 Sales: $199,778	2010 Profits: $126,896	**U.S. Stock Ticker: CMO**
2009 Sales: $314,595	2009 Profits: $129,263	**Int'l Ticker:** Int'l Exchange:
2008 Sales: $400,489	2008 Profits: $125,923	Employees: 13
2007 Sales: $311,643	2007 Profits: $24,713	Fiscal Year Ends: 12/31
2006 Sales: $243,272	2006 Profits: $3,843	Parent Company:

SALARIES/BENEFITS:

Pension Plan:	ESOP Stock Plan:	Profit Sharing:	Top Exec. Salary: $908,000	Bonus: $1,450,000
Savings Plan: Y	Stock Purch. Plan:		Second Exec. Salary: $695,500	Bonus: $1,150,000

OTHER THOUGHTS:

Apparent Women Officers or Directors: 1
Hot Spot for Advancement for Women/Minorities:

LOCATIONS: ("Y" = Yes)

West:	Southwest:	Midwest:	Southeast:	Northeast:	International:
	Y				

CARLSON HOTELS WORLDWIDE
www.carlsonhotels.com

Industry Group Code: 721110 Ranks within this company's industry group: Sales: Profits:

Properties:	Financial Services:	Construction/Development:	Investments:	Specialty Services:		Brokerage:
Apartments:	Mortgages:	Commercial Construction:	REIT:	Property Management:	Y	Commercial Sales:
Malls/Shopping:	Title Insurance:	Residential Construction:		Online Services:		Residential Sales:
Offices:	Property Insurance:	Land Development:		Software/IT:		Specialty:
Hotels/Motels: Y		Support Services:		Consulting:		
Industrial/Warehouses:		Design/Engineering:				
Other:						

TYPES OF BUSINESS:
Hotels & Resorts

BRANDS/DIVISIONS/AFFILIATES:
Carlson Companies Inc
Radisson Hotels & Resorts
Park Plaza Hotels & Resorts
Country Inns & Suites By Carlson
Park Inn Hotels
Rezidor Hotel Group

CONTACTS: *Note: Officers with more than one job title may be intentionally listed here more than once.*
Thorsten Kirschke, COO/Pres., Carlson Hotels, Americas
Beathe-Jeannette Lunde, Exec. VP-People Dev., Safety & Security
Christian Urbat, Sr. VP-Tech. Svcs., Carlson Hotels Americas
Suzanne Riesterer, Exec. VP-Admin., Carlson Hotels Americas
Javier Rosenberg, VP-Owned & Managed Oper.
Robert Kleinschmidt, Chief Dev. Officer, Carlson Hotels, The Americas
Suzanne Riesterer, Exec. VP-Finance, Carlson Hotels Americas
Hubert Joly, Pres./CEO-Carlson Companies Inc
Steve Mogck, Exec. VP/COO-Country Inns & Suites
Fredrik Korallus, Exec. VP-Global Revenue Generation
Kurt Ritter, Pres./CEO-Rezidor Hotel Group
Simon Barlow, Pres., Carlson Hotels, Asia Pacific

Phone: 763-212-4000	**Fax:**
Toll-Free:	
Address: 701 Carlson Pkwy., Minnetonka, MN 55305 US	

GROWTH PLANS/SPECIAL FEATURES:
Carlson Hotels Worldwide, a subsidiary of Carlson Companies, Inc., is one of the world's leading hotel franchisors. The firm includes more than 1,070 locations in 77 countries. Specific brands include Radisson Hotels & Resorts; Park Plaza Hotels & Resorts; Park Inn; Country Inns & Suites by Carlson; and Park Inn Hotels. The company's Radisson chain owns full-service hotels at 425 locations throughout North America, Latin America, Asia Pacific, Europe, the Middle East and Africa. Radisson Hotels offer pre-arrival online check-in; Sleep Number beds by Select Comfort; a fitness center; and free high-speed Internet access. The Park Inn is the company's economy brand with approximately 114 hotels in operation worldwide. The firm's 39 Park Plaza Hotels are generally 150 rooms or larger and include restaurants, meeting rooms, catering, suites and recreational facilities. Country Inns & Suites By Carlson is a mid-tier lodging chain with more than 488 locations in the Americas, Europe and India and 80 more under development. Specialty services include an in-hotel Read It and Return Lending Library in which guests can borrow a book and return it on their next stay. Additionally, Carlson Companies owns a 50% interest in the Rezidor Hotel Group, a developer and franchisor of hotels worldwide. Besides hotels, Carlson Companies, Inc. owns subsidiaries in the travel, restaurant and marketing industries. In April 2010, Carlson sold the Regent Hotels & Resort business, including the Regent brand, hotel management rights and the Regent Seven Seas cruise license, to Formosa International Hotels Corp. based in Taiwan. In February 2011, the firm opened its first Park Inn hotel in Mexico.

FINANCIALS: Sales and profits are in thousands of dollars—add 000 to get the full amount. 2010 Note: Financial information for 2010 was not available for all companies at press time.

2010 Sales: $	2010 Profits: $	**U.S. Stock Ticker: Subsidiary**
2009 Sales: $	2009 Profits: $	**Int'l Ticker:** Int'l Exchange:
2008 Sales: $	2008 Profits: $	Employees:
2007 Sales: $	2007 Profits: $	Fiscal Year Ends: 12/31
2006 Sales: $	2006 Profits: $	Parent Company: CARLSON COMPANIES INC

SALARIES/BENEFITS:

Pension Plan:	ESOP Stock Plan:	Profit Sharing:	Top Exec. Salary: $	Bonus: $
Savings Plan:	Stock Purch. Plan:		Second Exec. Salary: $	Bonus: $

OTHER THOUGHTS:
Apparent Women Officers or Directors: 5
Hot Spot for Advancement for Women/Minorities: Y

LOCATIONS: ("Y" = Yes)

West:	Southwest:	Midwest:	Southeast:	Northeast:	International:
Y	Y	Y	Y	Y	Y

CB RICHARD ELLIS GROUP INC (CBRE)   www.cbre.com

Industry Group Code: 531210 Ranks within this company's industry group: Sales: 1   Profits: 1

Properties:		Financial Services:		Construction/Development:	Investments:	Specialty Services:		Brokerage:	
Apartments:		Mortgages:	Y	Commercial Construction:	REIT:	Property Management:	Y	Commercial Sales:	Y
Malls/Shopping:		Title Insurance:		Residential Construction:		Online Services:		Residential Sales:	
Offices:		Property Insurance:		Land Development:		Software/IT:		Specialty:	
Hotels/Motels:				Support Services:		Consulting:	Y		
Industrial/Warehouses:				Design/Engineering:					
Other:									

TYPES OF BUSINESS:

Real Estate Brokerage
Real Estate Management Services
Mortgage Banking
Investment Management
Consulting Services
Real Estate Investment Trust

BRANDS/DIVISIONS/AFFILIATES:

CB Richard Ellis, Inc.
CBRE Capital Markets
CB Richard Ellis Ltd.
CB Richard Ellis Investors, LLC
Trammel Crow Company
CBRE Solar
PropertyOne

CONTACTS: *Note: Officers with more than one job title may be intentionally listed here more than once.*

Brett White, CEO
Bob Sulentic, Pres.
Gil Borok, CFO
Chris Kirk, Dir.-Human Resources
Laurence Midler, General Counsel/Exec. VP
Jim Groch, Global Strategy Officer/Chief Investment Officer
Arlin E. Gaffner, Chief Acct. Officer
Ray Torto, Global Chief Economist
Robert Blain, Chmn./Pres./CEO-Asia Pacific
Calvin W. Frese, Jr., Pres., Global Svcs.
Brian F. Stoffers, Pres., Capital Markets
Richard C. Blum, Chmn.
Michael J. Strong, CEO/Pres., EMEA

Phone: 310-405-8900	Fax:
Toll-Free:	
Address: 11150 Santa Monica Blvd., Ste. 1600, Los Angeles, CA 90025 US	

GROWTH PLANS/SPECIAL FEATURES:

CB Richard Ellis Group, Inc. (CBRE) is one of the world's largest commercial real estate services companies, with over 300 offices in more than 50 countries. It offers a full range of services to occupiers, owners, lenders and investors in office, retail, industrial, multi-family and other commercial real estate assets. The firm's core services include commercial property and corporate facilities management; tenant representation; property/agency leasing; property sales; valuation; real estate investment management; commercial mortgage origination and servicing; capital markets (equity and debt); development services; and proprietary research. CBRE operates in five segments: the Americas, which accounted for 62.9% of its 2010 revenue; Europe, Middle East and Africa (EMEA), 18.3%; Asia Pacific, 13.1%; Global Investment Management, 4.2%; and Development Services, 1.5%. The Americas segment operates primarily through CB Richard Ellis, Inc.; CBRE Capital Markets; and CB Richard Ellis Ltd. The EMEA segment has offices in 42 countries, with its largest operations located in the U.K., France, Spain, the Netherlands and Germany. The Asia Pacific segment operates in 12 countries, including China, India, Japan, Korea and Taiwan. In addition, the company has agreements with affiliated offices in the Philippines, Thailand, Indonesia and Vietnam that generate royalty fees and support cross-referral arrangements. Its Global Investment Management business is handled by subsidiary CB Richard Ellis Investors, LLC. Through the Trammel Crow Company, the firm provides development services primarily in the U.S. to users of and investors in commercial real estate. In March 2010, the company launched a solar energy services company, CBRE Solar. In November 2010, it acquired PropertyOne in Hong Kong. In February 2011, the firm agreed to acquire the majority of the real estate investment management business of ING Group NV.

The company offers its employees medical, dental and vision insurance; 401(k); flexible spending accounts; an employee assistance program; and paid vacation and holidays.

FINANCIALS: Sales and profits are in thousands of dollars—add 000 to get the full amount. 2010 Note: Financial information for 2010 was not available for all companies at press time.

2010 Sales: $5,115,316	2010 Profits: $156,009	**U.S. Stock Ticker: CBG**
2009 Sales: $4,165,820	2009 Profits: $33,341	**Int'l Ticker:** Int'l Exchange:
2008 Sales: $5,128,817	2008 Profits: $-1,012,066	Employees: 31,000
2007 Sales: $6,034,249	2007 Profits: $390,505	Fiscal Year Ends: 12/31
2006 Sales: $4,032,027	2006 Profits: $318,571	Parent Company:

SALARIES/BENEFITS:

Pension Plan:	ESOP Stock Plan:	Profit Sharing:	Top Exec. Salary: $781,346	Bonus: $843,200
Savings Plan: Y	Stock Purch. Plan:		Second Exec. Salary: $562,038	Bonus: $447,300

OTHER THOUGHTS:

Apparent Women Officers or Directors: 2
Hot Spot for Advancement for Women/Minorities:

LOCATIONS: ("Y" = Yes)

West:	Southwest:	Midwest:	Southeast:	Northeast:	International:
Y	Y	Y	Y	Y	Y

CBL & ASSOCIATES PROPERTIES INC

www.cblproperties.com

Industry Group Code: 531120 Ranks within this company's industry group: Sales: 15 Profits: 24

Properties:		Financial Services:	Construction/Development:	Investments:	Specialty Services:		Brokerage:
Apartments:		Mortgages:	Commercial Construction:	REIT: Y	Property Management: Y		Commercial Sales:
Malls/Shopping:	Y	Title Insurance:	Residential Construction:		Online Services:		Residential Sales:
Offices:		Property Insurance:	Land Development:		Software/IT:		Specialty:
Hotels/Motels:			Support Services:		Consulting:		
Industrial/Warehouses:			Design/Engineering:				
Other:	.						

TYPES OF BUSINESS:

Malls & Shopping Centers
Retail Property Management
Retail Property Development
Real Estate Investment Trust

BRANDS/DIVISIONS/AFFILIATES:

CBL Holdings I, Inc.
CBL Holdings II, Inc.
CBL & Associates Management, Inc.
Parkway Place
Colonial Properties Trust

CONTACTS:
Note: Officers with more than one job title may be intentionally listed here more than once.
Stephen D. Lebovitz, CEO
Augustus N. Stephas, COO/Exec. VP
Stephen D. Lebovitz, Pres.
John N. Foy, CFO/Treas./Sec.
Barbara J. Faucette, VP-Mall Mktg.
Maggie Carrington, VP-Human Resources
Steve T. Newton, VP-IT
Michael I. Lebovitz, Exec. VP-Admin.
Victoria S. Berghel, General Counsel/Sr. VP
Michael I. Lebovitz, Exec. VP-Dev.
Katie Reinsmidt, VP-Corp. Rel.
Katie Reinsmidt, VP-Investor Rel.
Farzana K. Mitchell, Exec. VP-Finance
John N. Foy, Vice Chmn.
Ben S. Landress, Exec. VP-Mgmt.
Howard B. Grody, Sr. VP-Leasing
Andrew F. Cobb, VP/Dir.-Acct.
Charles B. Lebovitz, Chmn.

Phone: 423-855-0001	Fax: 423-490-8390
Toll-Free: 800-333-7310	

Address: 2030 Hamilton Place Blvd., Ste. 500, Chattanooga, TN 37421-6000 US

GROWTH PLANS/SPECIAL FEATURES:

CBL & Associates Properties, Inc. is a self-managed, self-administered real estate investment trust (REIT) engaged in the ownership, development, acquisition, leasing, management and operation of regional shopping malls, open-air centers, community centers and office properties. The firm's properties are located principally in the Southeastern and Midwestern U.S., with its top markets in St. Louis, Missouri; Nashville, Tennessee; Kansas City, Kansas; Madison, Wisconsin; and Chattanooga, Tennessee. CBL owns, holds interests in or manages 158 properties, including 85 regional malls/open-air centers. The properties are located in 27 states. The firm also has mortgages on eight properties. The company conducts substantially all of its business through two REIT subsidiaries, CBL Holdings I, Inc. and CBL Holdings II, Inc. Additionally, the company conducts its property management operations through subsidiary CBL & Associates Management, Inc. This subsidiary operates property management at all but three of CBL's properties, Governor's Square and Governor's Plaza in Clarksville, Tennessee, and Kentucky Oaks Mall, in Paducah, Kentucky, which are owned as joint ventures and operated by third parties. CBL's key tenants include The Limited, Footlocker, Gap, Luxottica, Abercrombie & Fitch, Signet, American Eagle Outfitters, J.C. Penny, Zales and The Finish Line. The firm's on-site property management functions include leasing, management, data processing, rent collection, budgeting and promotions. In October 2010, the company acquired the remaining 50% stake in Parkway Place in Huntsville, Alabama from Colonial Properties Trust, its joint venture partner.

FINANCIALS:
Sales and profits are in thousands of dollars—add 000 to get the full amount. 2010 Note: Financial information for 2010 was not available for all companies at press time.

2010 Sales: $1,071,804	2010 Profits: $98,170	**U.S. Stock Ticker: CBL**
2009 Sales: $1,082,279	2009 Profits: $-7,065	**Int'l Ticker:** Int'l Exchange:
2008 Sales: $1,132,174	2008 Profits: $57,434	Employees: 905
2007 Sales: $1,039,944	2007 Profits: $147,608	Fiscal Year Ends: 12/31
2006 Sales: $995,502	2006 Profits: $17,501	Parent Company:

SALARIES/BENEFITS:

Pension Plan:	ESOP Stock Plan:	Profit Sharing:	Top Exec. Salary: $596,836	Bonus: $337,500
Savings Plan: Y	Stock Purch. Plan:		Second Exec. Salary: $532,906	Bonus: $337,500

OTHER THOUGHTS:

Apparent Women Officers or Directors: 8
Hot Spot for Advancement for Women/Minorities: Y

LOCATIONS: ("Y" = Yes)

West:	Southwest:	Midwest:	Southeast:	Northeast:	International:
Y	Y	Y	Y	Y	

CEMEX INC
www.cemexusa.com

Industry Group Code: 4233 Ranks within this company's industry group: Sales: Profits:

Properties:	Financial Services:	Construction/Development:		Investments:	Specialty Services:	Brokerage:
Apartments:	Mortgages:	Commercial Construction:		REIT:	Property Management:	Commercial Sales:
Malls/Shopping:	Title Insurance:	Residential Construction:			Online Services:	Residential Sales:
Offices:	Property Insurance:	Land Development:			Software/IT:	Specialty:
Hotels/Motels:		Support Services:	Y		Consulting:	
Industrial/Warehouses: Y		Design/Engineering:				
Other: Y						

TYPES OF BUSINESS:
Cement Materials & Production
Cement Materials & Production
Ready-Mix Cement

BRANDS/DIVISIONS/AFFILIATES:
CEMEX SAB de CV

CONTACTS: *Note: Officers with more than one job title may be intentionally listed here more than once.*
Gilberto Perez, Pres.
Andy Miller, Exec. VP-Human Resources
Leslie White, General Counsel/Exec. VP
Luis Oropeza, Exec. VP-Cement Oper.
Frank Angelle, Exec. VP-Planning
Sarah Engdahl, Dir.-External Comm.
Frank Craddock, Exec. VP-Commercial
Ira Fialkow, Exec. VP-Shared Service Organization
Karl Watson, Jr., Pres., Eastern Region
Steven Wise, Pres., Western Region
Juan Carlos Herrera, Exec. VP-Logistics

Phone: 713-650-6200	Fax: 713-653-6815
Toll-Free: 800-999-8529	
Address: 920 Memorial City Way, Ste. 100, Houston, TX 77024 US	

GROWTH PLANS/SPECIAL FEATURES:
CEMEX Inc., a subsidiary of Mexico-based CEMEX, S.A.B. de C.V., is among the largest cement and ready-mix companies in the U.S. Headquartered in Houston, Texas, the firm also has operations in 29 other states across the U.S. The firm's network includes 13 cement plants, 47 distribution channels, 80 aggregate quarries and 320 ready-mix concrete plants. CEMEX divides its operations into the following four categories: cement, aggregates, ready mix and related products. Cement products, which vary by region in terms of availability, include portland cement, masonry cement, low-alkali cement, plastic cement and cement lime-mix. The firm has cement plants in nine states. Aggregate products include sand, gravel and crushed stone, all of which are used in concrete products as well as in landscaping settings. The firm's ready-mix concrete, which consists of cement, water and aggregates, is a cost-effective and versatile building material used in almost all types of construction. Special ready-mix products include abrasion resistant, accelerated set, corrosion inhibited, fiber-reinforced, micro-silica, self-consolidating, shrinkage reduced and underwater concretes. The related products unit manufactures concrete block, architectural products (such as concrete pavers, concrete brick and segmental retaining wall block), asphalt, building materials (such as mortar mix, curing compounds, water proofing material, rigid insulation, floor hardeners and epoxies), gypsum, pipe, landscaping materials (primarily specialty rock products) and fly ash. Products are marketed principally to industrial, commercial, residential and municipal construction customers.

FINANCIALS: Sales and profits are in thousands of dollars—add 000 to get the full amount. 2010 Note: Financial information for 2010 was not available for all companies at press time.

2010 Sales: $	2010 Profits: $	U.S. Stock Ticker: Subsidiary
2009 Sales: $	2009 Profits: $	Int'l Ticker: Int'l Exchange:
2008 Sales: $	2008 Profits: $	Employees:
2007 Sales: $	2007 Profits: $	Fiscal Year Ends: 12/31
2006 Sales: $	2006 Profits: $	Parent Company: CEMEX SAB DE CV

SALARIES/BENEFITS:

Pension Plan:	ESOP Stock Plan:	Profit Sharing:	Top Exec. Salary: $	Bonus: $
Savings Plan:	Stock Purch. Plan:		Second Exec. Salary: $	Bonus: $

OTHER THOUGHTS:
Apparent Women Officers or Directors: 2
Hot Spot for Advancement for Women/Minorities:

LOCATIONS: ("Y" = Yes)

West:	Southwest:	Midwest:	Southeast:	Northeast:	International:
Y	Y	Y	Y	Y	

CEMEX SAB DE CV

www.cemex.com

Industry Group Code: 4233 Ranks within this company's industry group: Sales: 2   Profits: 1

Properties:	Financial Services:	Construction/Development:		Investments:	Specialty Services:	Brokerage:
Apartments:	Mortgages:	Commercial Construction:		REIT:	Property Management:	Commercial Sales:
Malls/Shopping:	Title Insurance:	Residential Construction:			Online Services:	Residential Sales:
Offices:	Property Insurance:	Land Development:			Software/IT:	Specialty:
Hotels/Motels:		Support Services:	Y		Consulting:	
Industrial/Warehouses:		Design/Engineering:				
Other:						

TYPES OF BUSINESS:

Cement & Concrete Production
Construction Materials Production

BRANDS/DIVISIONS/AFFILIATES:

CEMEX Deutschland AG
CEMEX Mexico
CEMEX Corp.
CEMEX Inc
CEMEX France Gestion SAS
CEMEX Southeast, LLC
Empresas Tolteca de Mexico
CEMEX UK

CONTACTS: *Note: Officers with more than one job title may be intentionally listed here more than once.*

Lorenzo H. Zambrano, CEO
Rodrigo Trevino, CFO
Victor M. Romo, Exec. VP-Admin.
Ramiro G. Villarreal, General Counsel
Fernando A. Gonzalez, Exec. VP-Planning & Finance
Rafael Garza, Chief Acct. Officer
Francisco Garza, Pres., Americas
Lorenzo H. Zambrano, Chmn.
Juan Romero, Pres., EMEA & Asia Region

Phone: 52-81-8888-8888	Fax: 52-81-8888-4417
Toll-Free:	
Address: Av. Ricardo Margain Zozaya 325, San Pedro Garza Garcia, 66265 Mexico	

GROWTH PLANS/SPECIAL FEATURES:

Cemex S.A.B. de C.V. founded in Mexico in 1906, is a holding company that produces, distributes, markets and sells cement, ready-mix concrete, aggregates, clinker and other construction materials through its operating subsidiaries. The company has operations in over 50 countries across five continents, with annual production levels of around 96 million tons of cement. Cemex wholly owns 63 cement plants; over 2,000 ready-mix concrete facilities; and has a minority participation in 12 cement plants. The firm also operates 391 aggregates quarries, 223 land-distribution centers and 72 marine terminals. The firm's operations in Mexico are run by subsidiaries CEMEX Mexico and Empresas Tolteca de Mexico. In the U.S., the company owns holding company CEMEX Corp., which manages companies such as CEMEX Southeast, LLC through CEMEX, Inc. The company operates through a number of subsidiaries throughout Europe: CEMEX France Gestion SAS; CEMEX UK; CEMEX Espana S.A.; CEMEX Deutchland AG in Germany; with additional operations in Poland, Croatia, the Czech Republic, Denmark, Ireland, Italy, Finland, Norway and Sweden.   In South and Central America, the company operates facilities in Venezuela, Colombia, Argentina, Costa Rica, the Dominican Republic, Panama, Nicaragua, Puerto Rico and Jamaica. CEMEX also has operations in Egypt, the U.A.E., Israel, the Philippines, Singapore, Thailand, Malaysia and Taiwan. In 2010, sales of cement represented 48% of its total sales, ready-mix concrete 34%, aggregates 14% and other products 4%. In August 2010, the company sold seven aggregates quarries, three resale aggregate distribution centers and one concrete block manufacturing facility in Kentucky to Bluegrass Materials Company, LLC. In October 2010, it agreed to acquire the outstanding interests in two joint ventures with Ready Mix USA.

FINANCIALS: Sales and profits are in thousands of dollars—add 000 to get the full amount. 2010 Note: Financial information for 2010 was not available for all companies at press time.

2010 Sales: $14,069,000	2010 Profits: $856,000	U.S. Stock Ticker: CX
2009 Sales: $14,544,000	2009 Profits: $1,165,000	Int'l Ticker: Int'l Exchange:
2008 Sales: $20,131,000	2008 Profits: $2,327,000	Employees: 47,624
2007 Sales: $21,673,000	2007 Profits: $2,971,000	Fiscal Year Ends: 12/31
2006 Sales: $21,376,700	2006 Profits: $2,785,500	Parent Company:

SALARIES/BENEFITS:

Pension Plan:	ESOP Stock Plan:	Profit Sharing:	Top Exec. Salary: $	Bonus: $
Savings Plan:	Stock Purch. Plan:		Second Exec. Salary: $	Bonus: $

OTHER THOUGHTS:

Apparent Women Officers or Directors:
Hot Spot for Advancement for Women/Minorities:

LOCATIONS: ("Y" = Yes)

West:	Southwest:	Midwest:	Southeast:	Northeast:	International:
Y	Y	Y	Y	Y	Y

CENTEX CORP

www.centex.com

Industry Group Code: 2361 Ranks within this company's industry group: Sales: Profits:

Properties:	Financial Services:		Construction/Development:		Investments:	Specialty Services:	Brokerage:	
Apartments:	Mortgages:	Y	Commercial Construction:		REIT:	Property Management:	Commercial Sales:	
Malls/Shopping:	Title Insurance:	Y	Residential Construction:	Y		Online Services:	Residential Sales:	Y
Offices:	Property Insurance:	Y	Land Development:	Y		Software/IT:	Specialty:	
Hotels/Motels:			Support Services:	Y		Consulting:		
Industrial/Warehouses:			Design/Engineering:	Y				
Other:								

TYPES OF BUSINESS:

Residential Construction
Mortgages
Real Estate Development
Commercial Construction
Construction Supply Services

BRANDS/DIVISIONS/AFFILIATES:

Centex Homes
Pulte Homes Inc
PulteGroup Inc

CONTACTS: *Note: Officers with more than one job title may be intentionally listed here more than once.*

Timothy R. Eller, CEO
Cathy R. Smith, CFO/Exec. VP
Joe Bosch, Sr. VP-Human Resources
Mark D. Kemp, Controller
Timothy R. Eller, Chmn.

Phone: 214-981-5000	Fax: 214-981-6859
Toll-Free:	
Address: 2728 N. Harwood, Dallas, TX 75201 US	

GROWTH PLANS/SPECIAL FEATURES:

Centex Corp., a subsidiary of PulteGroup, Inc. (formerly Pulte Homes, Inc.) focuses principally on residential construction and related activities, including mortgage financing. The firm's home building operations involve the purchase and development of land or lots and the construction and sale of detached and attached single-family homes, including resort and second home properties and lots, and land or lots. Centex's financial services include mortgage lending, conducted through Pulte Motrgage LLC; title insurance, handled by Commerce Title and Closing Services, LLC; and insurance with Westwood Insurance Agency, offering homeowners, auto, life and commercial insurance. In partnership with HomeTeam Pest Defense, Centex installs pest control systems in its homes as they are being built including Taexx, built-in pest control systems and Tubes Under the Slab termite control systems. All new Centex homes include energy saving features such as radiant-barrier roof decking, enhanced insulation, low-emissivity windows and Energy Star appliances. In recent years, Centex was acquired by competitor, PulteGroup, Inc. for approximately $1.4 billion.

The company offers its employees medical, dental and vision insurance; life and AD&D insurance; short- and long-term disability insurance; a 401(k) plan; a college savings plan; tuition reimbursement; and an employee assistance program.

FINANCIALS: Sales and profits are in thousands of dollars—add 000 to get the full amount. 2010 Note: Financial information for 2010 was not available for all companies at press time.

2010 Sales: $	2010 Profits: $	U.S. Stock Ticker: Subsidiary
2009 Sales: $	2009 Profits: $	Int'l Ticker: Int'l Exchange:
2008 Sales: $8,275,562	2008 Profits: $-2,657,482	Employees: 6,530
2007 Sales: $11,887,601	2007 Profits: $268,366	Fiscal Year Ends: 3/31
2006 Sales: $12,742,666	2006 Profits: $1,289,313	Parent Company: PULTEGROUP INC

SALARIES/BENEFITS:

Pension Plan:	ESOP Stock Plan:	Profit Sharing:	Top Exec. Salary: $920,000	Bonus: $216,459
Savings Plan: Y	Stock Purch. Plan:		Second Exec. Salary: $542,375	Bonus: $492,188

OTHER THOUGHTS:

Apparent Women Officers or Directors: 1
Hot Spot for Advancement for Women/Minorities:

LOCATIONS: ("Y" = Yes)

West:	Southwest:	Midwest:	Southeast:	Northeast:	International:
Y	Y	Y	Y	Y	Y

CENTRO NP LLC

www.centroprop.com

Industry Group Code: 531120 Ranks within this company's industry group: Sales: Profits:

Properties:	Financial Services:	Construction/Development:		Investments:		Specialty Services:		Brokerage:
Apartments:	Mortgages:	Commercial Construction:	Y	REIT:	Y	Property Management:	Y	Commercial Sales:
Malls/Shopping: Y	Title Insurance:	Residential Construction:				Online Services:		Residential Sales:
Offices:	Property Insurance:	Land Development:	Y			Software/IT:		Specialty:
Hotels/Motels:		Support Services:	Y			Consulting:		
Industrial/Warehouses:		Design/Engineering:						
Other:								

TYPES OF BUSINESS:

Real Estate Investment Trust
Community Shopping Centers

BRANDS/DIVISIONS/AFFILIATES:

Centro Properties Group
New Plan Excel Realty Trust, Inc.

CONTACTS: *Note: Officers with more than one job title may be intentionally listed here more than once.*

Michael Carroll, CEO
Tiffanie Fisher, CFO
Dean Bernstein, Exec. VP-Acquisitions & Depositions
Stacy Slater, Contact-Corp. Comm.

Phone: 212-869-3000	**Fax:**
Toll-Free:	
Address: 420 Lexington Ave., New York, NY 10170 US	

GROWTH PLANS/SPECIAL FEATURES:

Centro NP LLC, formerly New Plan Excel Realty Trust, Inc. (NP), is a U.S. shopping center Real Estate Investment Trust (REIT). The firm is a subsidiary of Centro Properties Group, based in Australia. The company engages in the ownership, management and development of community and neighborhood shopping centers, malls and lifestyle centers, with approximately 430 properties in 39 states comprising 69 million square feet of gross leasable area. The company's portfolio includes 151 wholly-owned properties; one property owned by a consolidated joint venture; and 278 properties held through unconsolidated joint ventures. The firm has a mix of convenience shopping and general merchandise properties, with both grocery and non-grocery anchors. In regards to new development, the firm has a policy of having a lease executed with an anchor tenant prior to making an investment. The firm's model for growth is both internal and external, focusing on aggressive management to maintain high occupancy rates and recognized anchor tenants, as well as on selective acquisitions of income-producing shopping centers or of centers that the firm can add value to through redevelopment or management. The gross leasable area of the firm's portfolio is over 86% leased. Major tenants such as Bed, Bath & Beyond, Kohl's, Kroger, Marshalls, Publix, Stop & Shop, Target, TJ Maxx, Wal-Mart, Cub Foods and Giant-Eagle serve as its anchor stores.

FINANCIALS: Sales and profits are in thousands of dollars—add 000 to get the full amount. 2010 Note: Financial information for 2010 was not available for all companies at press time.

2010 Sales: $	2010 Profits: $	**U.S. Stock Ticker: Subsidiary**
2009 Sales: $306,176	2009 Profits: $-233,052	**Int'l Ticker:** Int'l Exchange:
2008 Sales: $412,425	2008 Profits: $-546,300	Employees:
2007 Sales: $	2007 Profits: $	Fiscal Year Ends: 12/31
2006 Sales: $456,975	2006 Profits: $135,217	Parent Company: CENTRO PROPERTIES GROUP

SALARIES/BENEFITS:

Pension Plan:	ESOP Stock Plan:	Profit Sharing:	Top Exec. Salary: $1,166,769	Bonus: $1,866,438
Savings Plan:	Stock Purch. Plan:		Second Exec. Salary: $404,423	Bonus: $605,001

OTHER THOUGHTS:

Apparent Women Officers or Directors: 2
Hot Spot for Advancement for Women/Minorities:

LOCATIONS: ("Y" = Yes)

West:	Southwest:	Midwest:	Southeast:	Northeast:	International:
Y	Y	Y	Y	Y	Y

CENTRO PROPERTIES GROUP

www.centro.com.au

Industry Group Code: 5311 Ranks within this company's industry group: Sales: Profits:

Properties:		Financial Services:	Construction/Development:		Investments:		Specialty Services:		Brokerage:
Apartments:		Mortgages:	Commercial Construction:		REIT:	Y	Property Management:	Y	Commercial Sales:
Malls/Shopping:	Y	Title Insurance:	Residential Construction:				Online Services:		Residential Sales:
Offices:	Y	Property Insurance:	Land Development:	Y			Software/IT:		Specialty:
Hotels/Motels:			Support Services:				Consulting:		
Industrial/Warehouses:			Design/Engineering:	Y					
Other:									

TYPES OF BUSINESS:

Real Estate Development-Shopping Centers
Property Ownership
Leasing
Funds Management

BRANDS/DIVISIONS/AFFILIATES:

Centro US
Centro Retail Trust
Centro MCS Manager Limited

CONTACTS: *Note: Officers with more than one job title may be intentionally listed here more than once.*

Robert Tsenin, CEO/Managing Dir.
Chris Nunn, CFO
Lisa Charter, National Mgr.-Mktg.
Sue Smith, Gen. Mgr.-Human Resources
Dimitri Kiriacoulacos, General Counsel
Mark Wilson, Gen. Mgr.-Property Oper., Australia
Marjan Doroodkar, Mgr.-Mktg. & Investor Comm.
Paul Belcher, Gen. Mgr.-Finance
Michael Benett, Chief Restructuring Officer
Gerard Condon, Gen. Mgr.-Syndicate Funds Mgmt.
Krista-Lee Fogarty, National Mgr.-Health, Safety & Environment
Paul Cooper, Chmn.

Phone: 61-3-8847-0000	Fax: 61-3-8847-1868
Toll-Free:	
Address: 235 Springvale Rd., 3rd Fl., Glen Waverly, VIC 3150 Australia	

GROWTH PLANS/SPECIAL FEATURES:

Centro Properties Group (Centro) is an Australian Real Estate Investment Trust (A-REIT) concerned with property investment, property management, property development and funds management. The firm has offices in Australia, New Zealand and the U.S. In Australia and New Zealand, Centro maintains regional and neighborhood shopping centers in metropolitan and non-metropolitan markets. The network in Australia includes 123 shopping centers hosting over 7,000 stores. In the U.S., the firm manages neighborhood as well as mall and large retail shopping centers primarily based in suburban areas. Centro's shopping centers are primarily concerned with non-discretionary retail spending, focusing on fresh food, supermarkets and other everyday needs. The company also derives revenue from providing property, management, leasing and funds management services to shopping centers owned by the investment funds it manages. Centro Retail Trust is a CER, or an Australian Real Estate Investment Trust (REIT), managed by Centro subsidiary Centro MCS Manager Limited, which connects investors to over 400 Australian and U.S. shopping center investments. Subsidiary Centro US is responsible for carrying out asset management; property management and development; and leasing activities with U.S. properties. Centro Properties Group has approximately $18.6 billion in funds under management. The group is a major provider of retail space to Wesfarmers and Woolworths in Australia and TJX and Kroger in the U.S. In March 2011, Blackstone Group LP, purchased all of Centro's U.S. assets, including investments in nearly 600 shopping malls, for $9.4 billion.

FINANCIALS: Sales and profits are in thousands of dollars—add 000 to get the full amount. 2010 Note: Financial information for 2010 was not available for all companies at press time.

2010 Sales: $	2010 Profits: $	U.S. Stock Ticker:
2009 Sales: $1,850,360	2009 Profits: $-3,284,920	Int'l Ticker: CNP Int'l Exchange: Sydney-ASX
2008 Sales: $491,360	2008 Profits: $-1,467,390	Employees:
2007 Sales: $261,490	2007 Profits: $336,150	Fiscal Year Ends: 6/30
2006 Sales: $677,800	2006 Profits: $611,100	Parent Company:

SALARIES/BENEFITS:

Pension Plan:	ESOP Stock Plan:	Profit Sharing:	Top Exec. Salary: $	Bonus: $
Savings Plan:	Stock Purch. Plan:		Second Exec. Salary: $	Bonus: $

OTHER THOUGHTS:

Apparent Women Officers or Directors: 3
Hot Spot for Advancement for Women/Minorities: Y

LOCATIONS: ("Y" = Yes)

West:	Southwest:	Midwest:	Southeast:	Northeast:	International:
Y	Y	Y	Y	Y	Y

CENTURY 21 REAL ESTATE LLC

www.century21.com

Industry Group Code: 531210 Ranks within this company's industry group: Sales: Profits:

Properties:	Financial Services:		Construction/Development:		Investments:	Specialty Services:		Brokerage:	
Apartments:	Mortgages:	Y	Commercial Construction:		REIT:	Property Management:		Commercial Sales:	Y
Malls/Shopping:	Title Insurance:		Residential Construction:			Online Services:	Y	Residential Sales:	Y
Offices:	Property Insurance:		Land Development:			Software/IT:		Specialty:	Y
Hotels/Motels:			Support Services:	Y		Consulting:			
Industrial/Warehouses:			Design/Engineering:						
Other:									

TYPES OF BUSINESS:

Real Estate Brokerage
Commercial Brokerage
Residential & Specialty Brokerage
Mortgage Services

BRANDS/DIVISIONS/AFFILIATES:

Realogy Corporation
Century 21 Mortgage
Century 21 Commercial
Century 21 Fine Homes and Estates
Century 21 International
At Home with Century 21
Golden Ruler (The)

CONTACTS: *Note: Officers with more than one job title may be intentionally listed here more than once.*

Richard W. Davidson, CEO
Richard W. Davidson, Pres.
Beverly Thorne, Chief Mktg. Officer
Mark Foreman, Sr. VP-Oper.
Matt Gentile, Contact-Public Rel.
Jim Lonegran, Sr. VP-Franchise Growth
Greg Sexton, Sr. VP-Brokerage Svcs.

Phone: 877-221-2765	Fax:
Toll-Free: 866-732-6139	
Address: 1 Campus Dr., Parsippany, NJ 07054 US	

GROWTH PLANS/SPECIAL FEATURES:

Century 21 Real Estate LLC, a subsidiary of Realogy Corp., is the franchiser of one of the world's largest residential real estate sales organizations. It has more than 8,000 independently owned and operated franchised broker offices in 72 countries. The firm helps clients find, buy, sell and finance their residential property or new home, as well as find, buy, sell and sometimes lease commercial property and vacation properties. Century 21's web site gives the public access to its vast database of listed homes, as well as allowing clients to list their homes on said database. The company has offices in every state, providing customers with brokers familiar with their area and current market conditions. Century 21 Mortgage offers mortgage services to its clients in person, over the phone or online, and advertises same-day loan decisions for clients. Other subsidiaries include Century 21 Commercial, helping clients sell, buy or lease commercial real estate; Century 21 International, active in Africa, the Americas, Australia and New Zealand, the Caribbean, Europe, Asia and the Middle East; and Century 21 Fine Homes and Estates, for those looking for higher-priced luxury homes. Its bi-monthly magazine, At Home with Century 21, provides information on home improvement, decor, remodeling, organization and storage, gardening and cooking. In recent years, the firm has expanded into Albania, Slovakia, India, the Czech Republic, Thailand and Bermuda. In December 2010, the company launched an online tool called The Golden Ruler, which allows customers to view web traffic statistics for their homes listed online.

FINANCIALS: Sales and profits are in thousands of dollars—add 000 to get the full amount. 2010 Note: Financial information for 2010 was not available for all companies at press time.

2010 Sales: $	2010 Profits: $	U.S. Stock Ticker: Subsidiary
2009 Sales: $	2009 Profits: $	Int'l Ticker: Int'l Exchange:
2008 Sales: $	2008 Profits: $	Employees:
2007 Sales: $41,300	2007 Profits: $	Fiscal Year Ends: 12/31
2006 Sales: $	2006 Profits: $	Parent Company: REALOGY CORPORATION

SALARIES/BENEFITS:

Pension Plan:	ESOP Stock Plan:	Profit Sharing:	Top Exec. Salary: $	Bonus: $
Savings Plan:	Stock Purch. Plan:		Second Exec. Salary: $	Bonus: $

OTHER THOUGHTS:

Apparent Women Officers or Directors: 1
Hot Spot for Advancement for Women/Minorities:

LOCATIONS: ("Y" = Yes)

West:	Southwest:	Midwest:	Southeast:	Northeast:	International:
Y	Y	Y	Y	Y	Y

CH2M HILL COMPANIES LTD

www.ch2m.com

Industry Group Code: 541330 Ranks within this company's industry group: Sales: 2   Profits: 5

Properties:	Financial Services:	Construction/Development:		Investments:	Specialty Services:		Brokerage:
Apartments:	Mortgages:	Commercial Construction:	Y	REIT:	Property Management:	Y	Commercial Sales:
Malls/Shopping:	Title Insurance:	Residential Construction:			Online Services:		Residential Sales:
Offices:	Property Insurance:	Land Development:			Software/IT:		Specialty:
Hotels/Motels:		Support Services:	Y		Consulting:	Y	
Industrial/Warehouses:		Design/Engineering:	Y				
Other:							

TYPES OF BUSINESS:

Engineering Services-Consultation
Environmental Engineering & Consulting
Nuclear Management Services
Water & Electrical Utility Services
Decommissioning & Decontamination
Facilities Design & Construction
Project Financing & Procurement
Nanotechnology Research

BRANDS/DIVISIONS/AFFILIATES:

Operations Management International
CH2M HILL Canada, Ltd.
Lockwood Greene
Industrial Design and Construction
CH2M-IDC China
Wade & Assoicates, Inc.
Goldston Engineering, Inc.
VECO

CONTACTS: *Note: Officers with more than one job title may be intentionally listed here more than once.*

Lee A. McIntire, CEO
Mike Lucki, CFO/Sr VP
John Madia, VP-Human Resources
Margaret McLean, Corp. Sec./Chief Legal Officer/Sr. VP
JoAnn Shea, Chief Acct. Officer/Controller/VP
Jacqueline C. Rast, Sr. VP/Pres-Facilities & Infrastructure Div.
Michael E McKelvy, Pres., Gov't, Environment & Nuclear Div.
William T. Dehn, VP
Robert G Card, Sr. VP/Pres., Energy & Water Div.
Lee A. McIntire, Chmn.
Fred Brune, Pres., CH2M HILL Int'l

Phone: 303-771-0900	Fax: 720-286-9250
Toll-Free: 888-242-6445	
Address: 9191 S. Jamaica St., Englewood, CO 80112 US	

GROWTH PLANS/SPECIAL FEATURES:

CH2M HILL Companies, Ltd. is an employee-owned firm that offers engineering, consulting, design, construction, procurement, operations, maintenance and program and project management services to clients in the public and private sectors. CH2M HILL conducts business in several countries worldwide. The company's environmental services division offers its clients ecological and natural resource damage assessments, environmental consulting for remediation projects and treatment systems for properties that have been contaminated by toxic or radioactive waste. The nuclear services segment manages the decontamination and demolition of weapons production facilities and designs nuclear waste treatment and handling facilities. CH2M HILL's Operations Management International subsidiary provides water, wastewater and electrical utility services to private and public clients. CH2M HILL Canada, Ltd. is the Canadian division of the company. CH2M HILL Lockwood Greene is a major engineering and construction firm focused on national and multinational industrial and power clients worldwide. CH2M HILL Industrial Design and Construction, Inc. (IDC) is a high-technology facilities design, construction, maintenance and operations company serving process-intensive technology clients. IDC also has interests in nanotechnology research and manufacturing. CH2M-IDC China provides full-service solution to manufacturing companies that are building or have plants in China.

FINANCIALS: Sales and profits are in thousands of dollars—add 000 to get the full amount. 2010 Note: Financial information for 2010 was not available for all companies at press time.

2010 Sales: $5,422,801	2010 Profits: $93,695	**U.S. Stock Ticker: Private**
2009 Sales: $5,499,318	2009 Profits: $103,742	**Int'l Ticker:** Int'l Exchange:
2008 Sales: $5,589,900	2008 Profits: $32,056	Employees: 23,000
2007 Sales: $4,376,200	2007 Profits: $65,999	Fiscal Year Ends: 12/31
2006 Sales: $4,000,000	2006 Profits: $	Parent Company:

SALARIES/BENEFITS:

Pension Plan:	ESOP Stock Plan:	Profit Sharing:	Top Exec. Salary: $	Bonus: $
Savings Plan:	Stock Purch. Plan:		Second Exec. Salary: $	Bonus: $

OTHER THOUGHTS:

Apparent Women Officers or Directors: 3
Hot Spot for Advancement for Women/Minorities: Y

LOCATIONS: ("Y" = Yes)

West:	Southwest:	Midwest:	Southeast:	Northeast:	International:
Y	Y	Y	Y	Y	Y

CHAMPION ENTERPRISES INC

www.championhomes.com

Industry Group Code: 321991 Ranks within this company's industry group: Sales: Profits:

Properties:	Financial Services:	Construction/Development:		Investments:	Specialty Services:	Brokerage:
Apartments:	Mortgages:	Commercial Construction:		REIT:	Property Management:	Commercial Sales:
Malls/Shopping:	Title Insurance:	Residential Construction:	Y		Online Services:	Residential Sales:
Offices:	Property Insurance:	Land Development:			Software/IT:	Specialty:
Hotels/Motels:		Support Services:			Consulting:	
Industrial/Warehouses:		Design/Engineering:				
Other:						

TYPES OF BUSINESS:

Manufactured Housing
Housing Retailing
Steel-Frame Building

BRANDS/DIVISIONS/AFFILIATES:

Champion Enterprises Inc
Champion Home Centers
GO House
Genesis Homes
Building Systems Limited
Moduline Industries
SRI Homes

CONTACTS: *Note: Officers with more than one job title may be intentionally listed here more than once.*

John Lawless, CEO
John Lawless, Pres.
Kevin Flaherty, VP-Mktg.
Roger K. Scholten, General Counsel/Sr. VP/Sec.
Timothy J. Bernlohr, Chmn.

Phone: 248-614-8200	Fax: 248-273-4279
Toll-Free:	
Address: 755 W. Big Beaver, Ste. 1000, Troy, MI 48084 US	

GROWTH PLANS/SPECIAL FEATURES:

Champion Enterprises, Inc. is the holding company for a family of companies that manufacture and retail manufactured and modular housing. Founded in 1953, the company has sold over 1.7 million factory-built homes since its inception. The Champion family of companies is one of the largest housing manufacturers and retailers in the U.S., manufacturing approximately 11,000 homes annually through 27 manufacturing facilities in North America and the U.K. The company sells homes largely through its 15 company-owned retail home centers in California. The Champion family of homebuilders includes Carolina Building Solutions, Commander, Dutch, Fortune, Highland, Homes of Merit, New Era, New Image, North American, Redman, Silvercrest, Summit Crest and Titan. Most of the homes built are multi-section, ranch-style units, but one and two-story homes, colonial-style homes, Cape Cod style homes and multi-family units are also offered. Homes generally range in size from 600 to 3,000 square feet and typically include 2-4 bedrooms, a living room or family room, dining room, kitchen and two full bathrooms. Additional floor plan options include vaulted ceilings, entertainment centers, spa-style bathrooms, fireplaces, custom cabinetry and various floor covering options. In Canada, Champion produces and sells factory-built homes through two divisions: Moduline Industries, operating in western Canada; and SRI Homes, operating in western and central Canada. Additionally, Champion produces pre-engineered and steel-framed modular buildings in the U.K through Caledonian Building Systems Limited. In early 2010, the firm launched the GO House, an environmentally conscious modular home marketed under the Genesis Homes brand. In March 2010, the company's domestic and international operations were acquired by Champion Enterprises Holdings LLC.

FINANCIALS: Sales and profits are in thousands of dollars—add 000 to get the full amount. 2010 Note: Financial information for 2010 was not available for all companies at press time.

2010 Sales: $	2010 Profits: $	U.S. Stock Ticker: CJHBQ.PK
2009 Sales: $	2009 Profits: $	Int'l Ticker: Int'l Exchange:
2008 Sales: $1,033,193	2008 Profits: $-199,460	Employees: 4,100
2007 Sales: $1,273,465	2007 Profits: $7,192	Fiscal Year Ends: 12/31
2006 Sales: $1,364,648	2006 Profits: $138,308	Parent Company:

SALARIES/BENEFITS:

Pension Plan:	ESOP Stock Plan:	Profit Sharing:	Top Exec. Salary: $	Bonus: $
Savings Plan:	Stock Purch. Plan:		Second Exec. Salary: $	Bonus: $

OTHER THOUGHTS:

Apparent Women Officers or Directors:
Hot Spot for Advancement for Women/Minorities:

LOCATIONS: ("Y" = Yes)

West:	Southwest:	Midwest:	Southeast:	Northeast:	International:
Y	Y	Y	Y	Y	Y

CHICAGO BRIDGE & IRON COMPANY NV

www.cbi.com

Industry Group Code: 237 Ranks within this company's industry group: Sales: 22   Profits: 18

Properties:	Financial Services:	Construction/Development:		Investments:	Specialty Services:	Brokerage:
Apartments:	Mortgages:	Commercial Construction:		REIT:	Property Management:	Commercial Sales:
Malls/Shopping:	Title Insurance:	Residential Construction:			Online Services:	Residential Sales:
Offices:	Property Insurance:	Land Development:			Software/IT:	Specialty:
Hotels/Motels:		Support Services:	Y		Consulting:	
Industrial/Warehouses:		Design/Engineering:	Y			
Other:						

TYPES OF BUSINESS:

Heavy Construction & Civil Engineering
Specialty Engineering & Procurement Services
Liquid & Gas Storage Facilities
Maintenance & Support Services

BRANDS/DIVISIONS/AFFILIATES:

CB&I Steel Plate Structures
CB&I Lummus
Lummus Technology

CONTACTS: *Note: Officers with more than one job title may be intentionally listed here more than once.*

Phillip K. Asheman, CEO
Lasse Petterson, COO
Phillip K. Asheman, Pres.
Ronald A. Ballschmiede, CFO/Exec. VP
Jan Sieving, VP-Mktg.
Beth A. Bailey, Chief Admin. Officer/Exec. VP
David A. Delman, Chief Legal Officer/Sec./Exec. VP
E. Chip Ray, Exec. VP-Corp. Planning
Jan Sieving, VP-Corp. Comm.
Luciano Reyes, Treas./VP
Ronald E. Blum, Pres., Steel Plate Structures
Daniel M. McCarthy, Pres., Lummus Technology
Mark Coscio, VP-Corp. Planning
L. Richard Flury, Chmn.
Ronald E. Blum, Exec. VP-Global Bus. Dev.

Phone: 31-70-373-2722	Fax:
Toll-Free:	
Address: Oostduinlaan 75, Hoofddorp, The Hague, 2596JJ The Netherlands	

GROWTH PLANS/SPECIAL FEATURES:

Chicago Bridge & Iron Company N.V. (CB&I), a global engineering, procurement and construction (EPC) company, provides specialty construction for liquid and gas storage facilities.   Company operations include over 80 offices, warehouses and other facilities on six continents.   CB&I maintains three business units, operating both independently and on an integrated basis.   CB&I Steel Plate Structures provides engineering, procurement, fabrication and construction services for the petroleum, water and nuclear industries.   CB&I Lummus provides infrastructure engineering, fabrication and construction services to the upstream and downstream energy industry.   Lummus Technology provides proprietary technologies used to process natural gas, manufacture petrochemicals and convert crude oil into consumer products. Some of the many projects CB&I works on include hydrocarbon processing plants, liquid natural gas (LNG) terminals and peak shaving plants, offshore structures, pipelines, bulk liquid terminals and water storage and treatment facilities.   The company provides complete services, from the initial design and engineering through procurement and construction and maintenance.   Additionally,   it   offers   numerous complementary products and services including low temperature or cryogenic tanks and systems, primarily used by petroleum, chemical, petrochemical and other companies to store, transport and handle liquefied gases and specialty structures including iron and aluminum processing facilities and hydroelectric structures.   In May 2010, the firm was awarded a contract to design and construct a new gas processing plant at the Elk Hills oil and gas field in Central California. In October 2010, Lummus Technology signed an agreement with BP for the exclusive right to license and market BP's paraxylene recovery and isomerization technology and catalyst.

The firm offers its U.S. employees medical, dental and vision plans; employee and dependent life insurance options; a 401(k) plan; profit sharing; a stock purchase program; and an education assistance plan.

FINANCIALS: Sales and profits are in thousands of dollars—add 000 to get the full amount. 2010 Note: Financial information for 2010 was not available for all companies at press time.

2010 Sales: $3,642,318	2010 Profits: $204,559	**U.S. Stock Ticker: CBI**
2009 Sales: $4,556,503	2009 Profits: $174,289	**Int'l Ticker: BDZ** Int'l Exchange: Frankfurt-Euronext
2008 Sales: $5,944,981	2008 Profits: $-21,146	Employees: 13,000
2007 Sales: $4,363,492	2007 Profits: $165,640	Fiscal Year Ends: 12/31
2006 Sales: $3,125,307	2006 Profits: $116,968	Parent Company:

SALARIES/BENEFITS:

Pension Plan:	ESOP Stock Plan:	Profit Sharing: Y	Top Exec. Salary: $955,000	Bonus: $1,806,860
Savings Plan: Y	Stock Purch. Plan: Y		Second Exec. Salary: $546,000	Bonus: $567,840

OTHER THOUGHTS:

Apparent Women Officers or Directors: 3
Hot Spot for Advancement for Women/Minorities: Y

LOCATIONS: ("Y" = Yes)

West:	Southwest:	Midwest:	Southeast:	Northeast:	International:
Y	Y	Y	Y	Y	Y

CHINA COMMUNICATIONS CONSTRUCTION COMPANY LTD

www.ccccltd.com.cn
Industry Group Code: 23 Ranks within this company's industry group: Sales: 1   Profits: 1

Properties:	Financial Services:	Construction/Development:		Investments:	Specialty Services:	Brokerage:
Apartments:	Mortgages:	Commercial Construction:	Y	REIT:	Property Management:	Commercial Sales:
Malls/Shopping:	Title Insurance:	Residential Construction:			Online Services:	Residential Sales:
Offices:	Property Insurance:	Land Development:			Software/IT:	Specialty:
Hotels/Motels:		Support Services:	Y		Consulting:	
Industrial/Warehouses:		Design/Engineering:	Y			
Other: Y						

TYPES OF BUSINESS:

Transport Infrastructure, Construction & Design
Port Construction
Dredging
Container Cranes
Heavy Machinery Manufacturing

BRANDS/DIVISIONS/AFFILIATES:

China Harbor Engineering Co Ltd
China Road and Bridge Corporation
CCCC Tunnel Engineering Co Ltd
CCCC Tianjin Dredging Co Ltd
CCCC Highway Consultants Co Ltd
CCCC Water Transportation Consultants Co Ltd
CCCC Investment Co Ltd
China Highway Vehicle & Machinery Co Ltd

CONTACTS: Note: Officers with more than one job title may be intentionally listed here more than once.

Jichang Zhou, Exec. Dir.
Quitao Liu, Pres.
Junyuan Fu, CFO
Ming Lin, Chief Engineer
Wensheng Liu, Sec./Chief Economist
Yun Chen, VP
Yusheng Chen, VP
Jinlong Hou, VP
Liqiang Yang, VP/Head-Trade Union
Jichang Zhou, Chmn.

Phone: 86-10-8201-6655	**Fax:** 86-10-8201-6500
Toll-Free:	
Address: 85 Deshengmenwai St., Xicheng District, Beijing, 100088 China	

GROWTH PLANS/SPECIAL FEATURES:

China Communications Construction Company Ltd. (CCCC) is one of China's largest port construction and design companies, as well as one of the world's largest container crane manufacturers. The firm's principal activities include the design and construction of transportation infrastructure, dredging and heavy machinery manufacturing. CCCC's operations are separated into seven business units: infrastructure construction, infrastructure design, dredging, heavy machinery manufacturing, overseas business, investments and others. The infrastructure construction business, operating through 10 direct subsidiaries, offers construction and transportation services for ports, roads, bridges, railways and tunnel works. It currently has the only three top-tier qualification certificates granted by the Ministry of Construction for port construction work in China. The infrastructure design business, comprised of 10 subsidiaries, offers a range of design services including consulting and planning; feasibility studies; design services; engineering consulting; engineering surveys and technical studies; project management and supervision; construction; and more. The dredging business, one of the largest in the world, made up of three subsidiaries, is involved in major dredging and reclamation operations along the China coast and internationally. The heavy machinery manufacturing business, operating through two major subsidiaries, mainly supplies container cranes, and bulk material handling machinery. The overseas segment operates through subsidiaries China Harbor Engineering Co. and China Road and Bridge Corporation. The firm's investment activities are conducted through CCCC Investment Co. The other businesses, comprised of five subsidiaries, have completed projects in a variety of fields, including railway, road, bridge, machinery manufacturing, logistics services and the trading of construction materials and equipment.

FINANCIALS: Sales and profits are in thousands of dollars—add 000 to get the full amount. 2010 Note: Financial information for 2010 was not available for all companies at press time.

2010 Sales: $41,830,500	2010 Profits: $1,512,730	**U.S. Stock Ticker:** HSI
2009 Sales: $33,195,800	2009 Profits: $1,053,280	**Int'l Ticker:** Int'l Exchange:
2008 Sales: $22,008,100	2008 Profits: $881,490	Employees: 101,030
2007 Sales: $16,788,200	2007 Profits: $467,490	Fiscal Year Ends: 12/31
2006 Sales: $16,386,300	2006 Profits: $456,300	Parent Company:

SALARIES/BENEFITS:

Pension Plan:	ESOP Stock Plan:	Profit Sharing:	Top Exec. Salary: $	Bonus: $
Savings Plan:	Stock Purch. Plan:		Second Exec. Salary: $	Bonus: $

OTHER THOUGHTS:

Apparent Women Officers or Directors:
Hot Spot for Advancement for Women/Minorities:

LOCATIONS: ("Y" = Yes)

West:	Southwest:	Midwest:	Southeast:	Northeast:	International:
					Y

CHINA LODGING GROUP LTD

www.htinns.com

Industry Group Code: 721110 Ranks within this company's industry group: Sales: 24   Profits: 17

Properties:		Financial Services:	Construction/Development:	Investments:	Specialty Services:		Brokerage:
Apartments:		Mortgages:	Commercial Construction:	REIT:	Property Management:	Y	Commercial Sales:
Malls/Shopping:		Title Insurance:	Residential Construction:		Online Services:		Residential Sales:
Offices:		Property Insurance:	Land Development:		Software/IT:		Specialty:
Hotels/Motels:	Y		Support Services:		Consulting:		
Industrial/Warehouses:			Design/Engineering:				
Other:							

TYPES OF BUSINESS:

Hotels & Resorts

BRANDS/DIVISIONS/AFFILIATES:

HanTing Express Hotels
HanTing Seasons Hotels
HanTing Hi Inn
HanTing Club

CONTACTS: *Note: Officers with more than one job title may be intentionally listed here more than once.*

Tuo (Matthew) Zhang, CEO
Chang Su, COO
Min (Jenny) Zhang, CFO
Haijun Wang, Exec. VP-Oper., Northern China
Ida Yu, Mgr.-Investor Rel.
Qi Ji, Exec. Chmn.

Phone: 86-21-51539477	Fax:
Toll-Free:	
Address: 5th Fl., Bl. 57, #461 Hongcao Rd., Xuhui District, Shanghai, 200233 China	

GROWTH PLANS/SPECIAL FEATURES:

China Lodging Group Ltd. is a China-based holding group active in China's hospitality sector. The firm conducts operations through HanTing Inn & Hotels, a leading chain of economy hotels. Its properties include 438 hotels (202 of which were newly opened in 2010) with 50,438 rooms across 65 cities, primarily in western China. China Lodging employs both a lease-and-operate model, which is used to directly operate hotels in prime locations, and a franchise-and-manage model, which is used to expand network coverage. Of its 438 locations, 243 are directly operated by the company and 195 are franchised. The firm has three primary brands: HanTing Express Hotels; HanTing Seasons Hotels; and HanTing Hi Inn. The flagship HanTing Express Hotels is targeted towards value-conscious travelers and workers. The premium HanTing Seasons Hotel is geared primarily towards corporate managers and owners of small-to mid-level businesses. The HanTing Hi Inn are designed to appeal to the younger, budget conscious traveler. The firm's HanTing Club rewards program has over 2.6 million members, who represent 61% of its room nights sold. The company hopes to harness rapidly growing levels of middle-class leisure travelers with increasing amounts of disposable income in China to help fuel its growth. In 2010, the occupancy rate at its hotels was approximately 93%. In March 2010, the company became listed on the NASDAQ stock index. In 2011, it plans to open an additional 200 locations within China.

FINANCIALS: Sales and profits are in thousands of dollars—add 000 to get the full amount. 2010 Note: Financial information for 2010 was not available for all companies at press time.

2010 Sales: $263,408	2010 Profits: $33,606	U.S. Stock Ticker: HTHT
2009 Sales: $192,660	2009 Profits: $7,870	Int'l Ticker: Int'l Exchange:
2008 Sales: $116,840	2008 Profits: $-20,270	Employees: 7,801
2007 Sales: $	2007 Profits: $	Fiscal Year Ends: 12/31
2006 Sales: $	2006 Profits: $	Parent Company:

SALARIES/BENEFITS:

Pension Plan:	ESOP Stock Plan:	Profit Sharing:	Top Exec. Salary: $	Bonus: $
Savings Plan:	Stock Purch. Plan:		Second Exec. Salary: $	Bonus: $

OTHER THOUGHTS:

Apparent Women Officers or Directors: 1
Hot Spot for Advancement for Women/Minorities:

LOCATIONS: ("Y" = Yes)

West:	Southwest:	Midwest:	Southeast:	Northeast:	International:
					Y

CHINA OVERSEAS LAND & INVESTMENT LIMITED www.coli.com.hk

Industry Group Code: 5311 Ranks within this company's industry group: Sales: 4   Profits: 8

Properties:		Financial Services:	Construction/Development:		Investments:	Specialty Services:		Brokerage:
Apartments:	Y	Mortgages:	Commercial Construction:	Y	REIT:	Property Management:	Y	Commercial Sales:
Malls/Shopping:		Title Insurance:	Residential Construction:	Y		Online Services:		Residential Sales:
Offices:		Property Insurance:	Land Development:	Y		Software/IT:		Specialty:
Hotels/Motels:	Y		Support Services:	Y		Consulting:		
Industrial/Warehouses:			Design/Engineering:	Y				
Other:	Y							

TYPES OF BUSINESS:

Real Estate Holdings & Development
Property Management Services
Construction Design Services

BRANDS/DIVISIONS/AFFILIATES:

China State Construction Engineering Corporation
China Overseas Property Management
Hua Yi Designing Consultants Ltd.

CONTACTS: *Note: Officers with more than one job title may be intentionally listed here more than once.*

Jian Min Hao, CEO/Vice Chmn.
Yun Wing Nip, CFO
Liang Luo, VP/Chief Architect
Yi Zhang, VP
Yonghai Qu, VP
Dapeng Qi, VP
Qing Ping Kong, Chmn.

Phone: 852-2823-7888	**Fax:** 852-2865-5939
Toll-Free:	
Address: 3 Pacific Place, 1 Queen's Rd. East, 10th Fl., Hong Kong, China	

GROWTH PLANS/SPECIAL FEATURES:

China Overseas Land & Investment Limited (COLI) is a Hong Kong-based real estate investment holding firm and a publicly listed subsidiary of government-owned China State Construction Engineering Corporation. The firm operates in three segments: property development, property investment and other related businesses. The property development business, the company's largest business segment, engages in the development and sale of property. The property investment business holds approximately 2.5 million square feet of investment properties and about 21.5 million square feet of property under development. The firm's portfolio includes properties in 22 Chinese cities and regions, including Beijing, Shanghai, Guangzhou, Shenzhen, Chengdu, Changchun, Nanjing, Xian, Zhongshan, Foshan, Zhuhai, Suzhou, Ningbo, Chongqing, Hangzhou, Qingdao, Dalian, Shenyang, Tianjin, Jinan, Hong Kong and Macau. Some of the major properties held by the company include luxury apartment communities such as Mt. Riviera, a 1,071 unit housing and high-rise apartment complex in Hangzhou; Blossom Riverine, a 766,670 square-foot residential development in Foshan; Olympic City Phase One, a 1.2 million square-foot multi-storey apartment complex in Shenzhen; The Arch, a 293,800 square-foot luxury high-rise apartment and hotel property in Nanjing; International Community, a 4.8 million square-foot residential development in Xi'an; the Orchid Garden, a 1 million square-foot residential garden-style community in Chengdu; and One South Lake, a 293,400 square-foot upscale apartment complex in Changchun. The firm is also engaged in several related business areas, including property management, provided by subsidiary China Overseas Property Management; construction design services, offered through subsidiary Hua Yi; and several long-term investments in infrastructure and provincial facilities projects.

FINANCIALS: Sales and profits are in thousands of dollars—add 000 to get the full amount. 2010 Note: Financial information for 2010 was not available for all companies at press time.

2010 Sales: $5,703,100	2010 Profits: $1,592,430	**U.S. Stock Ticker: Subsidiary**
2009 Sales: $4,807,250	2009 Profits: $962,040	**Int'l Ticker: 0688** Int'l Exchange: Hong Kong-HKE
2008 Sales: $2,437,530	2008 Profits: $654,440	Employees: 13,991
2007 Sales: $2,145,970	2007 Profits: $544,110	Fiscal Year Ends: 12/31
2006 Sales: $	2006 Profits: $	Parent Company: CHINA STATE CONSTRUCTION ENGINEERING CORP

SALARIES/BENEFITS:

Pension Plan:	ESOP Stock Plan:	Profit Sharing:	Top Exec. Salary: $	Bonus: $
Savings Plan:	Stock Purch. Plan:		Second Exec. Salary: $	Bonus: $

OTHER THOUGHTS:

Apparent Women Officers or Directors:
Hot Spot for Advancement for Women/Minorities:

LOCATIONS: ("Y" = Yes)

West:	Southwest:	Midwest:	Southeast:	Northeast:	International:
					Y

CHINA STATE CONSTRUCTION ENGINEERING CORP

www.cscec.com.cn

Industry Group Code: 5311 Ranks within this company's industry group: Sales: Profits:

Properties:	Financial Services:	Construction/Development:		Investments:	Specialty Services:	Brokerage:
Apartments:	Mortgages:	Commercial Construction:	Y	REIT:	Property Management:	Commercial Sales:
Malls/Shopping:	Title Insurance:	Residential Construction:			Online Services:	Residential Sales:
Offices:	Property Insurance:	Land Development:	Y		Software/IT:	Specialty:
Hotels/Motels:		Support Services:			Consulting:	
Industrial/Warehouses:		Design/Engineering:				
Other:						

TYPES OF BUSINESS:

Construction & Real Estate Development
Contract Engineering
Property Development

BRANDS/DIVISIONS/AFFILIATES:

China State Construction International Co
China Construction Development Co. Ltd.
China Construction Decoration Engineering Co.
CSCEC Property Management Co.
CSC& EC (PTY) Ltd.
China Construction Namibia Co. Ltd.
China Construction American Co.

CONTACTS: *Note: Officers with more than one job title may be intentionally listed here more than once.*

Yi Jun, Pres.
Zeng Zhaohe, CFO
Zeng Zhaohe, General Counsel
Liu Jinzhang, Chief Economic Analyst/VP
Kong Qingping, VP
Wang Xiangming, VP
Li Baian, VP

Phone: 86-10-880-82888	**Fax:**
Toll-Free:	
Address: 15 Sanlihe Rd., Haidan Dist., Beijing, 100037 China	

GROWTH PLANS/SPECIAL FEATURES:

China State Construction Engineering Corp. (CSCEC), founded in 1982, is primarily engaged in real estate, construction and contract engineering. The company also conducts design and planning; property development; machinery leasing; project supervision; property management; and trading activities. The firm has worked on office buildings, public facilities, airports, hotels, educational institutions, sports facilities, residential complexes, hospitals and military buildings. Its technologies are used for many applications such as constructing high-rises; installing large industrial works; complex deep pit support and dewatering activities; concrete manufacturing; project management; and general contracting of international projects. Specific projects include the Hada Express Way, Wuhan Railway Station, Shaanxi LanShang Expressway, the Tianjin Cihan Ferris Wheel, the Beijing Subway Line 4, Hongheyan Nuclear Station and China World Trade Center. The company has various domestic affiliated companies such as China State Construction International Co; China Construction Development Co. Ltd.; China Construction Decoration Engineering Co.; and CSCEC Property Management Co. The firm also has various international affiliated companies such as China Construction (South Pacific) Development Co. Pte. Ltd. in Singapore; CSC& EC (PTY) Ltd. in Botswana; China Construction Namibia Co. Ltd. in Namibia; and China Construction American Co. in Jersey City, New Jersey, with additional branches in Algeria, Barbados, Seychelles, Thailand, the Philippines, United Arab Emirates (U.A.E.), Japan, Korea, Ireland, Russia and the Middle East.

FINANCIALS: Sales and profits are in thousands of dollars—add 000 to get the full amount. 2010 Note: Financial information for 2010 was not available for all companies at press time.

2010 Sales: $	2010 Profits: $	**U.S. Stock Ticker:**
2009 Sales: $38,078,900	2009 Profits: $837,950	**Int'l Ticker: 601668** Int'l Exchange:
2008 Sales: $29,564,000	2008 Profits: $401,630	Employees:
2007 Sales: $24,620,900	2007 Profits: $719,290	Fiscal Year Ends: 12/31
2006 Sales: $	2006 Profits: $	Parent Company:

SALARIES/BENEFITS:

Pension Plan:	ESOP Stock Plan:	Profit Sharing:	Top Exec. Salary: $	Bonus: $
Savings Plan:	Stock Purch. Plan:		Second Exec. Salary: $	Bonus: $

OTHER THOUGHTS:

Apparent Women Officers or Directors:
Hot Spot for Advancement for Women/Minorities:

LOCATIONS: ("Y" = Yes)

West:	Southwest:	Midwest:	Southeast:	Northeast:	International:
				Y	Y

CHINESE ESTATES HOLDINGS LTD

www.chineseestates.com

Industry Group Code: 5311 Ranks within this company's industry group: Sales: 26   Profits: 32

Properties:		Financial Services:		Construction/Development:		Investments:	Specialty Services:	Brokerage:
Apartments:	Y	Mortgages:		Commercial Construction:	Y	REIT:	Property Management:	Commercial Sales:
Malls/Shopping:	Y	Title Insurance:		Residential Construction:	Y		Online Services:	Residential Sales:
Offices:	Y	Property Insurance:		Land Development:	Y		Software/IT:	Specialty:
Hotels/Motels:	Y			Support Services:			Consulting:	
Industrial/Warehouses:	Y			Design/Engineering:				
Other:	Y							

TYPES OF BUSINESS:

Real Estate Holdings & Development
Commercial Property Development
Residential Property Development

BRANDS/DIVISIONS/AFFILIATES:

Chi Cheung Investment Company, Ltd.
Power Jade Limited
G-Prop (Holdings) Limited

CONTACTS: Note: Officers with more than one job title may be intentionally listed here more than once.

Luen-hung (Joseph) Lau, CEO
Sze-wan (Sue) Chan, Mgr.-Sales & Leasing Dept.
Mun-yi (Connie) Cheung, Head-Legal Dept.
Veng-va (Matthew) Cheong, Gen. Mgr.-Oper.
Alison Yeung, Dir.-Corp. Comm.
Kwong-wai Lam, Controller/Company Sec.
Chi-ming (Alec) Kong, Head-China Bus.
Ming-yan (Hazel) Lai, Sr. Mgr.-Contracts, Project Dev.
Mun-chie (Teresa) Poon, Sr. Mgr.-Project Dev. Dept.
Yik-hei (Kenneth) Ng, Sr. Mgr.-Project Dev. Dept.
Luen-hung (Joseph) Lau, Chmn.

Phone: 852-2866-6999	Fax: 852-2866-2822
Toll-Free:	
Address: 38 Gloucester Rd., 26th Fl., Wanchai, Hong Kong, China	

GROWTH PLANS/SPECIAL FEATURES:

Chinese Estates Holdings Ltd. is a Hong Kong-based property development firm. Its core business is focused on investments in properties for rent and the development of properties for sale. Over the course of its 20-year history, the company's primary work has been in Hong Kong, though in recent years it has been expanding its activities in Mainland China and Macau. The firm's property portfolio is comprised of approximately 1 million square feet of retail property and approximately 1.2 million square feet of office property, mostly situated in commercial areas of Hong Kong such as Causeway Bay, Tsim Sha Tsui and Wanchai. The company's Hong Kong rental properties include 10 shopping centers, four industrial sites and three commercial properties, including the MassMutual Tower, where the firm has its headquarters. Hong Kong properties currently for sale include 13 residential complexes, primarily consisting of high-rise apartments and condominiums. On the Chinese mainland, Chinese Estates owns a mixed-use office/shopping complex property in Shanghai; commercial buildings and a five-star hotel in Beijing; and part of a shopping arcade in Shenzhen. Mainland China properties for sale comprise two residential properties in Chengdu. The firm specializes in developing mid to high-end residential and commercial properties. It currently has a land bank totaling approximately 30 million square feet in various parts of Hong Kong, Macau and Mainland China. Chinese Estates has several partially-owned subsidiaries also engaged in property investment and development: Chi Cheung Investment Company, Ltd., in which the firm holds a 61.96% stake; Power Jade Limited, of which the company owns 50%; and G-Prop (Holdings) Limited, in which Chinese Estates hold a 41.93% stake. In addition to its Hong Kong headquarters, the company maintains offices in Beijing, Chengdu, Shanghai and Shenzhen.

FINANCIALS: Sales and profits are in thousands of dollars—add 000 to get the full amount. 2010 Note: Financial information for 2010 was not available for all companies at press time.

2010 Sales: $351,040	2010 Profits: $-1,140,050	U.S. Stock Ticker:
2009 Sales: $292,890	2009 Profits: $1,114,000	Int'l Ticker: 0127 Int'l Exchange: Hong Kong-HKE
2008 Sales: $163,200	2008 Profits: $-187,880	Employees: 665
2007 Sales: $577,770	2007 Profits: $1,075,120	Fiscal Year Ends: 12/31
2006 Sales: $	2006 Profits: $	Parent Company:

SALARIES/BENEFITS:

Pension Plan:	ESOP Stock Plan:	Profit Sharing:	Top Exec. Salary: $	Bonus: $
Savings Plan:	Stock Purch. Plan:		Second Exec. Salary: $	Bonus: $

OTHER THOUGHTS:

Apparent Women Officers or Directors: 6
Hot Spot for Advancement for Women/Minorities: Y

LOCATIONS: ("Y" = Yes)

West:	Southwest:	Midwest:	Southeast:	Northeast:	International:
					Y

CHIYODA CORPORATION

www.chiyoda-corp.com

Industry Group Code: 541330 Ranks within this company's industry group: Sales: 3 Profits: 7

Properties:	Financial Services:	Construction/Development:	Investments:	Specialty Services:		Brokerage:
Apartments:	Mortgages:	Commercial Construction:	REIT:	Property Management:		Commercial Sales:
Malls/Shopping:	Title Insurance:	Residential Construction:		Online Services:	Y	Residential Sales:
Offices:	Property Insurance:	Land Development:		Software/IT:		Specialty:
Hotels/Motels:		Support Services:		Consulting:	Y	
Industrial/Warehouses:		Design/Engineering: Y				
Other:						

TYPES OF BUSINESS:

Engineering & Construction Services
Plant Lifecycle Engineering
Computer-Aided Engineering
Risk Management
Pollution Prevention Systems
Industrial Equipment-Online Procurement

BRANDS/DIVISIONS/AFFILIATES:

Chiyoda Advanced Solutions Corporation
EUREKA
IT Engineering Limited
Chiyoda TechnoAce Co., Ltd.
Chiyoda Kosho Co., Ltd.
Chiyoda International Corporation
Chiyoda U-Tech Co., Ltd.
Toyo-Thai pcl

CONTACTS: *Note: Officers with more than one job title may be intentionally listed here more than once.*

Takashi Kubota, CEO
Takashi Kubota, Pres.
Hiroshi Shibata, CFO/Exec. VP
Hiromi Koshizuka, Managing Exec. Officer-Tech. Dev.
Shougo Shibuya, Managing Exec. Officer-Eng. & Tech.
Kenjiroh Miura, Managing Dir.-Admin. & Project Planning
Hiroshi Ogawa, Sr. Managing Exec. Officer-Project Oper.
Yoichi Kanno, Exec. VP-Corp. Planning & Mgmt.
Yoichi Kanno, Exec. VP-Finance
Sumio Nakashima, Managing Exec. Officer-Project Oper.
Satoru Yokoi, Managing Exec. Officer-Bus. Dev. Oper.
Kazuo Obokata, Managing Exec. Officer-Customer Rel. Mgmt.
Katsutoshi Kimura, Managing Dir.-Corp. Planning/Gen. Mgr.-Finance
Manabu Mitani, Managing Dir.-Projects Logistics & Construction

Phone: 81-45-521-1231	Fax: 81-45-503-0200
Toll-Free:	
Address: 12-1, Tsurumichuo, 2-Chome, Tsurumi-ku, Yokohama, 230-8601 Japan	

GROWTH PLANS/SPECIAL FEATURES:

Chiyoda Corporation is a Japanese engineering firm that operates in the hydrocarbon and chemical industries, with a focus on the refining, petrochemical, gas processing, pharmaceutical and fine chemicals sectors. Many of the firm's activities involve engineering, procurement and construction (EPC) solutions for facilities that prevent disasters, improve the environment and control pollution. Chiyoda provides comprehensive engineering services in three phases: the planning phase, which involves master planning, feasibility studies, licensing and process development support services; the EPC phase, during which the firm provides FEED (Front End Engineering Design), equipment and systems design, purchasing and transport planning, site survey and commissioning services; and the operation and maintenance phase, in which Chiyoda offers upgrade and troubleshooting services, such as process and utility system improvement, equipment reliability improvement, environmental technology consulting and maintenance consulting. The firm's EUREKA process provides a means of producing clean fuel from heavy residual materials. The first Eureka unit was installed in Japan over 30 years ago. Chiyoda has also developed many environmental preservation and pollution prevention systems, such as Biofiner, the iWater System and the CT-121 Flue Gas Desulfurization Process. Major domestic subsidiaries include Chiyoda Advanced Solutions, which provides technological support for engineering projects; Chiyoda Kosho Co., Ltd., a design and construction company; Chiyoda Keiso Co., Ltd., which constructs electrical and instrumentation facilities; Chiyoda TechnoAce Co., Ltd., which constructs pharmaceutical facilities; Chiyoda U-Tech Co., Ltd., a human resources placement company; and IT Engineering Limited, an IT consulting firm. The firm's U.S. activities are overseen by Chiyoda International Corporation, headquartered in Houston, Texas. Chiyoda has offices in countries throughout the world, including the United Arab Emirates, China, Indonesia, Korea, Qatar, Italy, Singapore and the Netherlands. The company has 19 consolidated subsidiaries and three associated companies. In December 2010, the firm acquired a 7% stake in Toyo-Thai pcl.

FINANCIALS: Sales and profits are in thousands of dollars—add 000 to get the full amount. 2010 Note: Financial information for 2010 was not available for all companies at press time.

2010 Sales: $3,693,520	2010 Profits: $34,850	**U.S. Stock Ticker:**
2009 Sales: $4,963,910	2009 Profits: $72,250	**Int'l Ticker: 6366** Int'l Exchange: Tokyo-TSE
2008 Sales: $6,035,600	2008 Profits: $96,410	Employees:
2007 Sales: $4,800,500	2007 Profits: $233,000	Fiscal Year Ends: 3/31
2006 Sales: $3,869,700	2006 Profits: $192,100	Parent Company:

SALARIES/BENEFITS:

Pension Plan:	ESOP Stock Plan:	Profit Sharing:	Top Exec. Salary: $	Bonus: $
Savings Plan:	Stock Purch. Plan:		Second Exec. Salary: $	Bonus: $

OTHER THOUGHTS:

Apparent Women Officers or Directors:
Hot Spot for Advancement for Women/Minorities:

LOCATIONS: ("Y" = Yes)

West:	Southwest:	Midwest:	Southeast:	Northeast:	International:
					Y

Note: Financial information, benefits and other data can change quickly and may vary from those stated here.

CHOICE HOTELS INTERNATIONAL INC   www.choicehotels.com

Industry Group Code: 721110 Ranks within this company's industry group: Sales: 17   Profits: 11

Properties:		Financial Services:	Construction/Development:	Investments:	Specialty Services:	Brokerage:
Apartments:		Mortgages:	Commercial Construction:	REIT:	Property Management:	Commercial Sales:
Malls/Shopping:		Title Insurance:	Residential Construction:		Online Services:	Residential Sales:
Offices:		Property Insurance:	Land Development:		Software/IT:	Specialty:
Hotels/Motels:	Y		Support Services:		Consulting:	
Industrial/Warehouses:			Design/Engineering:			
Other:						

TYPES OF BUSINESS:

Hotels
Motels
Suites
Franchising

BRANDS/DIVISIONS/AFFILIATES:

Econo Lodge
MainStay Suites
Rodeway Inn
Quality Inn
Clarion Hotels
Comfort Inn
Sleep Inn
Comfort Suites

CONTACTS: *Note: Officers with more than one job title may be intentionally listed here more than once.*

Stephen P. Joyce, CEO
Stephen P. Joyce, Pres.
David White, CFO
Bruce N. Haase, Exec. VP-Mktg. & Global Brands
Patrick Cimerola, Sr. VP-Human Resources
Patrick Pacious, Exec. VP-Tech.
Patrick Cimerola, Sr. VP-Admin.
Ronald D. Parisotto, General Counsel/Sr. VP/Sec.
Bruce Haase, Exec. VP-Oper.
Patrick Pacious, Exec. VP-Global Strategy
Anne Madison, Sr. VP-Corp. Comm.
Scott Oaksmith, Controller
William Carlson, Sr. VP-Performance Analytics
David Pepper, Sr. VP-Global Dev.
Ron Parisotto, Chief Compliance Officer
Alexandra Jaritz, Sr. VP-Brand Planning & Management
Stewart W. Bainum, Jr., Chmn.
Oliver Dupont, VP-European Dev.
Patrick Pacious, Exec. VP-Dist.

Phone: 301-592-5000	Fax: 301-592-6157
Toll-Free:	
Address: 10750 Columbia Pike, Silver Spring, MD 20901 US	

GROWTH PLANS/SPECIAL FEATURES:

Choice Hotels International, Inc. is one of the world's largest franchisers of hotel properties. It has 6,142 hotels open and 621 hotels under development in 49 states, Washington D.C. and over 35 foreign countries and territories around the globe, with over 500,000 rooms worldwide. The firm's 11 proprietary brand names include Comfort Inn, Comfort Suites, Quality, Clarion, Sleep Inn, Econo Lodge, Rodeway Inn, MainStay Suites, Suburban Extended Stay Hotel, Cambria Suites and the Ascend Collection. Choice Hotel's business is based on franchise revenues that consist of initial fees and ongoing royalty fees. The company also collects marketing and reservation fees to support centralized activities. The Econo Lodge and Rodeway Inn brands compete in the limited-service economy market; the Comfort Inn, Comfort Suites and Sleep Inn brands compete in the limited-service midscale without food and beverage market; the MainStay brand and the Extended Stay Hotel brand compete in the extended stay market; and the Clarion and Quality brands compete primarily in the full-service midscale with food and beverage market. The firm's largest brand is Comfort, which provides mid-scale rooms without food and beverage service, targeted primarily to business and leisure travelers. To support its hotel operations, Choice Hotels maintains call centers, proprietary web sites and global distribution systems to help deliver customers to franchisees through multiple channels. Through these channels, customers can check hotel rates and locations as well as make reservations and apply for the company loyalty program.

Employees are offered a 401(k) plan; an employee stock purchase plan; medical, dental, vision and prescription coverage; life insurance; accidental death and dismemberment coverage; flexible spending accounts; disability coverage; long-term care coverage; an employee assistance program; paid leave; tuition reimbursement; adoption assistance; legal services; hotel discounts; employee banking; pet insurance; and vendor/retail discounts.

FINANCIALS: Sales and profits are in thousands of dollars—add 000 to get the full amount. 2010 Note: Financial information for 2010 was not available for all companies at press time.

2010 Sales: $596,076	2010 Profits: $107,441	U.S. Stock Ticker: CHH
2009 Sales: $564,178	2009 Profits: $98,250	Int'l Ticker: Int'l Exchange:
2008 Sales: $641,680	2008 Profits: $100,211	Employees: 1,524
2007 Sales: $615,494	2007 Profits: $111,301	Fiscal Year Ends: 12/31
2006 Sales: $539,903	2006 Profits: $112,787	Parent Company:

SALARIES/BENEFITS:

Pension Plan:	ESOP Stock Plan:	Profit Sharing:	Top Exec. Salary: $775,000	Bonus: $775,000
Savings Plan: Y	Stock Purch. Plan: Y		Second Exec. Salary: $360,000	Bonus: $199,980

OTHER THOUGHTS:

Apparent Women Officers or Directors: 4
Hot Spot for Advancement for Women/Minorities: Y

LOCATIONS: ("Y" = Yes)

West:	Southwest:	Midwest:	Southeast:	Northeast:	International:
Y	Y	Y	Y	Y	Y

CHRISTIES INTERNATIONAL REAL ESTATE

www.christiesrealestate.com

Industry Group Code: 531210 Ranks within this company's industry group: Sales: Profits:

Properties:		Financial Services:	Construction/Development:	Investments:		Specialty Services:		Brokerage:	
Apartments:	Y	Mortgages:	Commercial Construction:	REIT:		Property Management:		Commercial Sales:	
Malls/Shopping:		Title Insurance:	Residential Construction:			Online Services:		Residential Sales:	Y
Offices:		Property Insurance:	Land Development:			Software/IT:		Specialty:	Y
Hotels/Motels:			Support Services:			Consulting:			
Industrial/Warehouses:			Design/Engineering:						
Other:									

TYPES OF BUSINESS:

Real Estate Brokerage
Luxury Home Sales

BRANDS/DIVISIONS/AFFILIATES:

Christie's International plc
Christie's Great Estates
Christie's International Real Estate Magazine

CONTACTS: *Note: Officers with more than one job title may be intentionally listed here more than once.*

Neil Palmer, CEO
Jarvis Slade, Managing Dir.-Americas
Giles Hannah, Dir.-London & Europe
Rick Moeser, VP/Regional Mgr.-SE, Caribbean & Latin America
Gregg Antonsen, Sr. VP/Regional Mgr.-Central Region
Lisa King, Chmn.
Mitchell Lewis, Managing Dir.-Asia Pacific

Phone: 212-468-7182	**Fax:** 212-468-7141
Toll-Free:	
Address: 20 Rockefeller Plaza, New York, NY 10020 US	

GROWTH PLANS/SPECIAL FEATURES:

Christie's International Real Estate (formerly Christie's Great Estates), a wholly-owned subsidiary of Christie's International plc, was formed when Christie's Auction House acquired Great Estates, Inc. It is the largest international network of real estate companies that are dedicated to the marketing and selling of high-end properties in the prime and super-prime market categories. The network includes over 800 real estate offices in over 45 countries. The company brings buyers and sellers of luxury real estate together throughout the world. Through an exclusive system of advertising, marketing and listing tools, the company provides access to a worldwide audience. Properties are showcased in Christie's International Real Estate magazine, which is published four times a year; in custom-designed property brochures distributed worldwide; on its web site; and in Christie's Magazine and other highly regarded international publications. The company's magazine is also available worldwide in all of the firm's offices; at newsstands and bookstores in affluent communities; and many luxury hotels and inns. Christie's real estate clients include some of the highest-salaried executives and heads of major international corporations, celebrities, sports figures and other high-net-worth individuals. In 2010, new affiliates were added in Mallorca, Spain; Milan, Italy; Stockholm, Sweden; Bordeaux, France; Luxembourg; Cancun; Cayman Islands; San Juan, Puerto Rico; and Toronto, Canada.

FINANCIALS: Sales and profits are in thousands of dollars—add 000 to get the full amount. 2010 Note: Financial information for 2010 was not available for all companies at press time.

2010 Sales: $	2010 Profits: $	**U.S. Stock Ticker:** Subsidiary
2009 Sales: $	2009 Profits: $	**Int'l Ticker:** Int'l Exchange:
2008 Sales: $	2008 Profits: $	Employees:
2007 Sales: $	2007 Profits: $	Fiscal Year Ends: 12/31
2006 Sales: $	2006 Profits: $	Parent Company: CHRISTIES INTERNATIONAL PLC

SALARIES/BENEFITS:

Pension Plan:	ESOP Stock Plan:	Profit Sharing:	Top Exec. Salary: $	Bonus: $
Savings Plan:	Stock Purch. Plan:		Second Exec. Salary: $	Bonus: $

OTHER THOUGHTS:

Apparent Women Officers or Directors: 2
Hot Spot for Advancement for Women/Minorities:

LOCATIONS: ("Y" = Yes)

West:	Southwest:	Midwest:	Southeast:	Northeast:	International:
Y	Y	Y	Y	Y	Y

CITIMORTGAGE INC

www.citimortgage.com

Industry Group Code: 522310 Ranks within this company's industry group: Sales: Profits:

Properties:	Financial Services:		Construction/Development:	Investments:	Specialty Services:	Brokerage:
Apartments:	Mortgages:	Y	Commercial Construction:	REIT:	Property Management:	Commercial Sales:
Malls/Shopping:	Title Insurance:		Residential Construction:		Online Services:	Residential Sales:
Offices:	Property Insurance:		Land Development:		Software/IT:	Specialty:
Hotels/Motels:			Support Services:		Consulting:	
Industrial/Warehouses:			Design/Engineering:			
Other:						

TYPES OF BUSINESS:

Mortgages
Refinancing
Home Equity Loans

BRANDS/DIVISIONS/AFFILIATES:

Citigroup Inc
Citi Unemployment Assist Program
Citi Foreclosure Alternatives Program
Smith Barney

CONTACTS: Note: Officers with more than one job title may be intentionally listed here more than once.

Sanjiv Das, CEO
Sanjiv Das, Pres.
Paul Ince, CFO

Phone: 636-261-2484	Fax: 636-261-2387
Toll-Free: 800-667-8424	
Address: 1000 Technology Dr., O'Fallon, MO 63368-2240 US	

GROWTH PLANS/SPECIAL FEATURES:

CitiMortgage, Inc., the mortgage lending unit of Citigroup, Inc., is one of the nation's leading residential mortgage originators, with over 100 retail branch locations throughout the country. The company offers products to help first-time homebuyers, as well as those interested in building a new home, refinancing or salvaging the equity built up in an existing home through its retail, telesales and corporate loan origination channels. CitiMortgage allows customers to apply online, by phone or in person at various locations throughout the country. Its web site provides several tools that help customers choose the right mortgage product, determine how much they can realistically expect to receive, what their rate will be and compare home equity versus refinancing and renting versus buying. The firm receives customer referrals from Citigroup and its subsidiaries, which have over 200 million customers. CitiMortgage allows the customers of its sister subsidiary, Morgan Stanley Smith Barney, a global private wealth management and equity research unit, to use its accounts as collateral for down payments. Between October 2008 and March 2009, Citigroup received $45 billion in government bailout funds. Since the mortgage crisis, Citigroup has implemented several assistance programs to aid struggling homeowners, including Citi Unemployment Assist Program, which lowers monthly mortgage payments to an average of $500 for three months; and Citi Foreclosure Alternatives Program, which began in February 2010 and allows borrowers to remain in their residence for six months while the company provides relocation counseling and financial assistance in exchange for the deed to the property at the end of six month period.

CitiMortgage offers its employees benefits including tuition reimbursement, mortgage assistance, discount banking services, stock ownership programs, LifeWorks family support, 2-4 weeks of paid vacation and 10 paid holidays per year.

FINANCIALS: Sales and profits are in thousands of dollars—add 000 to get the full amount. 2010 Note: Financial information for 2010 was not available for all companies at press time.

2010 Sales: $	2010 Profits: $	U.S. Stock Ticker: Subsidiary
2009 Sales: $	2009 Profits: $	Int'l Ticker: Int'l Exchange:
2008 Sales: $	2008 Profits: $	Employees:
2007 Sales: $	2007 Profits: $	Fiscal Year Ends: 12/31
2006 Sales: $	2006 Profits: $	Parent Company: CITIGROUP INC

SALARIES/BENEFITS:

Pension Plan:	ESOP Stock Plan:	Profit Sharing:	Top Exec. Salary: $	Bonus: $
Savings Plan: Y	Stock Purch. Plan: Y		Second Exec. Salary: $	Bonus: $

OTHER THOUGHTS:

Apparent Women Officers or Directors:
Hot Spot for Advancement for Women/Minorities:

LOCATIONS: ("Y" = Yes)

West:	Southwest:	Midwest:	Southeast:	Northeast:	International:
		Y			

CLAYTON HOMES INC

www.claytonhomes.com

Industry Group Code: 321991 Ranks within this company's industry group: Sales: Profits:

Properties:	Financial Services:		Construction/Development:		Investments:	Specialty Services:	Brokerage:	
Apartments:	Mortgages:	Y	Commercial Construction:		REIT:	Property Management:	Commercial Sales:	
Malls/Shopping:	Title Insurance:		Residential Construction:	Y		Online Services:	Residential Sales:	Y
Offices:	Property Insurance:	Y	Land Development:			Software/IT:	Specialty:	
Hotels/Motels:			Support Services:			Consulting:		
Industrial/Warehouses:			Design/Engineering:					
Other:								

TYPES OF BUSINESS:

Construction Services
Manufactured Housing
Insurance & Financing

BRANDS/DIVISIONS/AFFILIATES:

Vanderbilt Mortgage & Finance, Inc.
Berkshire Hathaway Inc
Schult
Clayton
Crest Homes
Marlette
SE Homes

CONTACTS: *Note: Officers with more than one job title may be intentionally listed here more than once.*

Kevin T. Clayton, CEO
Kevin T. Clayton, Pres.
John J. Kalec, CFO/Exec. VP
Ralph Warchol, CIO/VP

Phone: 865-380-3000	Fax: 865-380-3742
Toll-Free: 800-822-0633	
Address: 500 Clayton Rd., Maryville, TN 37804 US	

GROWTH PLANS/SPECIAL FEATURES:

Clayton Homes, Inc., a subsidiary of Berkshire Hathaway, Inc., produces, sells, finances and insures modular and manufactured homes, in addition to commercial and educational relocatable buildings. The company's 36 manufacturing plants in 12 states produce homes that are marketed in 48 states through 1,500 independent retailers and approximately 385 company-owned sales centers. Its homes are designed and built through 35 facilities. Clayton's factory-built manufactured homes are completely finished dwellings that are constructed under federal code in factories and then transported by trucks to its targeted location. The homes are designed to be permanent, owner-occupied residential sites with attached utilities. Clayton manufactures a variety of single- and multi-sectional homes from 500 to 2,000 square feet and larger under brand names such as Clayton, Schult, Crest Homes, Marlette, Karsten, Norris, Golden West, Giles and SEhomes. Standard features offered in Clayton Homes include central heating, flooring systems and wall and floor treatments. Customers can choose predesigned homes or custom-design a home by size, number of bedrooms and other features. Through Clayton's financial subsidiary, Vanderbilt Mortgage and Finance, Inc. (VMF), the firm offers financing to manufactured home customers, as well as customers purchasing homes from certain third parties. VMF's financing products include manufactured home loans, Federal Housing Authority (FHA) loans, Land Home financing and more. Clayton and its subsidiaries provide financing to 325,000 customers and insurance to 160,000 customers. Additionally, Clayton acts as a reinsurance agent for physical damage, family protection and homebuyer protection insurance and other policies issued by insurance companies in connection with the firm's homes.

Clayton offers its employees a 401(k) plan; medical, dental vision and life insurance; training programs; and tuition and fitness reimbursement.

FINANCIALS: Sales and profits are in thousands of dollars—add 000 to get the full amount. 2010 Note: Financial information for 2010 was not available for all companies at press time.

2010 Sales: $	2010 Profits: $	**U.S. Stock Ticker: Subsidiary**
2009 Sales: $	2009 Profits: $	**Int'l Ticker:** Int'l Exchange:
2008 Sales: $	2008 Profits: $	Employees:
2007 Sales: $	2007 Profits: $	Fiscal Year Ends: 6/30
2006 Sales: $	2006 Profits: $	Parent Company: BERKSHIRE HATHAWAY INC

SALARIES/BENEFITS:

Pension Plan:	ESOP Stock Plan:	Profit Sharing:	Top Exec. Salary: $	Bonus: $
Savings Plan: Y	Stock Purch. Plan:		Second Exec. Salary: $	Bonus: $

OTHER THOUGHTS:

Apparent Women Officers or Directors:
Hot Spot for Advancement for Women/Minorities:

LOCATIONS: ("Y" = Yes)

West:	Southwest:	Midwest:	Southeast:	Northeast:	International:
Y	Y	Y	Y	Y	

CLUB MEDITERRANEE SA

www.clubmed.com

Industry Group Code: 721110 Ranks within this company's industry group: Sales: 6   Profits: 23

Properties:		Financial Services:	Construction/Development:	Investments:	Specialty Services:	Brokerage:
Apartments:		Mortgages:	Commercial Construction:	REIT:	Property Management:	Commercial Sales:
Malls/Shopping:		Title Insurance:	Residential Construction:		Online Services:	Residential Sales:
Offices:		Property Insurance:	Land Development:		Software/IT:	Specialty:
Hotels/Motels:	Y		Support Services:		Consulting:	
Industrial/Warehouses:			Design/Engineering:			
Other:	Y					

TYPES OF BUSINESS:

Resort Hotels
Tour Marketing/Packaging
Cruises
Seminars, Conventions & Event Planning
Licensed Apparel Products

BRANDS/DIVISIONS/AFFILIATES:

Club Med
Club Med Decouverte
Club Med 2
Club Med Villas & Chalets

CONTACTS: *Note: Officers with more than one job title may be intentionally listed here more than once.*

Henri G. d'Estaing, CEO
Michel Wolfovski, CFO/Exec. VP
Caroline Puechoultres, VP-Strategic Mktg. & Quality
Olivier Sastre, Sr. VP-Human Resources
Thierry Orsoni, VP-Comm.
Anne Yannic, VP-Sales & Mktg., France, Belgium & Switzerland
Patrick Calvet, VP-Villages, Europe & Africa
Caroline Puechoultres, VP-Dev., Asia-Pacific
Sylvain Rabuel, VP-Sales & Mktg. New Markets, Europe & Africa
Henri G. d'Estaing, Chmn.
Janyck Daudet, CEO/Pres., Latin America

Phone: 33-1-53-35-35-53	Fax: 33-1-53-35-36-16
Toll-Free:	
Address: 11 Rue de Cambrai, Paris, 75019 France	

GROWTH PLANS/SPECIAL FEATURES:

Club Mediterranee S.A. (Club Med) is an international operator of resort hotels and tours, with properties in over 40 countries worldwide.   Club Med is known for being the originator of all-inclusive vacations packages, which group fees for every meal, drink, activity and amenity into one price. The core business of the company is the operation of vacation villages and resorts organized like small towns. These villages and villas include streets with shops and houses and feature a large number of luxury accommodations in hand-picked locations. The company operates approximately 75 properties, concentrated in equatorial locations, including the Caribbean, Southeast Asia and the Mediterranean, as well as several ski resorts. In addition, the firm offers Club Med Decouverte, a tour guide service that takes small groups to places such as Phuket, Cancun Yucatan as well as weekend getaways to Venice, Istanbul and other well-known cities. It also operates Club Med 2, a luxury sailing ship in the Mediterranean. Club Med organizes corporate events, weddings and other events at its villages and other venues. Besides vacation packages, the company sells licensed products such as sportswear and children's clothing. Through Club Med Villas & Chalets, it offers freehold real estate at its villas on the island of Mauritius and its chalet apartments in the French Alps. In February 2010, the company signed an agreement with Melco China Resorts Holding Limited to open its first Chinese resort village, the Sun Mountain Yabuli Resort. In June 2010, it announced a strategic partnership with one of China's largest conglomerates, Fosun, to develop four additional resorts in China by 2015. In September 2010, the firm sold its Sestriere resort to Italian hotel and tour operator Aurum.

FINANCIALS: Sales and profits are in thousands of dollars—add 000 to get the full amount. 2010 Note: Financial information for 2010 was not available for all companies at press time.

2010 Sales: $1,947,030	2010 Profits: $-23,320	**U.S. Stock Ticker: CU**
2009 Sales: $1,801,630	2009 Profits: $-77,750	**Int'l Ticker: CU** Int'l Exchange: Paris-Euronext
2008 Sales: $1,938,630	2008 Profits: $2,600	Employees:
2007 Sales: $1,829,630	2007 Profits: $-10,380	Fiscal Year Ends: 10/31
2006 Sales: $2,468,100	2006 Profits: $7,400	Parent Company:

SALARIES/BENEFITS:

Pension Plan:	ESOP Stock Plan:	Profit Sharing:	Top Exec. Salary: $	Bonus: $
Savings Plan:	Stock Purch. Plan:		Second Exec. Salary: $	Bonus: $

OTHER THOUGHTS:

Apparent Women Officers or Directors: 2
Hot Spot for Advancement for Women/Minorities:

LOCATIONS: ("Y" = Yes)

West:	Southwest:	Midwest:	Southeast:	Northeast:	International:
Y			Y		Y

CNL FINANCIAL GROUP INC

www.cnl.com

Industry Group Code: 531120 Ranks within this company's industry group: Sales: Profits:

Properties:		Financial Services:		Construction/Development:		Investments:		Specialty Services:		Brokerage:	
Apartments:		Mortgages:		Commercial Construction:	Y	REIT:	Y	Property Management:	Y	Commercial Sales:	
Malls/Shopping:	Y	Title Insurance:		Residential Construction:				Online Services:		Residential Sales:	
Offices:	Y	Property Insurance:		Land Development:	Y			Software/IT:		Specialty:	
Hotels/Motels:				Support Services:				Consulting:	Y		
Industrial/Warehouses:	Y			Design/Engineering:							
Other:	Y										

TYPES OF BUSINESS:

Real Estate Investment Trust
Retail, Hotel & Entertainment Properties
Commercial Financing
Investment Advisory Services
Real Estate Development & Management
Health Care & Assisted Living Properties
Industrial Properties

BRANDS/DIVISIONS/AFFILIATES:

CNL Fund Management Company
CNL Lifestyle Company LLC
CNL Lifestyle Properties
CNL Commercial Real Estate
CNL Private Equity Corp.
CNL Real Estate Advisors Company
CNL Real Estate & Development Corp.
CNL Fund Advisors Company

CONTACTS:
Note: Officers with more than one job title may be intentionally listed here more than once.
Thomas K. Sittema, CEO
Tracy G. Schmidt, CFO
Lisa A. Schultz, Chief Human Capital Officer
Joel Schwalbe, CIO
Timothy J. Manor, General Counsel
Lisa A. Schultz, Chief Comm. Officer
Kaki Rawls, Sr. VP-Tax
Robert A. Bourne, Vice Chmn.
Timothy J. Seneff, Pres., CNL Capital Markets Corp.
Tammy Tipton, Chief Acct. Officer
Paul Ellis, Pres., CNL Commercial Real Estate
James M. Seneff, Jr., Chmn.
Jeffrey R. Shafer, Head-Dist., CNL Securities Corp.

Phone: 407-650-1000	Fax: 407-650-1011

Toll-Free: 800-522-3863

Address: 450 S. Orange Ave., CNL Center at City Commons, Orlando, FL 32801-3336 US

GROWTH PLANS/SPECIAL FEATURES:

CNL Financial Group, Inc. is the flagship company for a group of real estate investment trusts (REITs) and financial services and advisory companies. CNL Fund Management Company creates and manages real estate investment products. CNL Lifestyle Company LLC is an advisor to CNL Lifestyle Properties, an REIT primarily investing in lifestyle properties in the U.S. and Canada. CNL Private Equity Corp. invests in business and real estate opportunities and manages CNL's portfolio of private offerings and investments. CNL Real Estate Advisors Company creates, administers and manages real property investments across a wide variety of sectors. CNL Real Estate & Development Corp. is a comprehensive development group specializing in master-planned communities, corporate offices, urban infill and other mixed-use projects throughout the Southeast U.S. CNL Commercial Real Estate invests in and develops commercial real estate and provides real estate services including brokerage; building management and leasing; and religious and education consultant services. CNL Securities Corp. sources capital for CNL and its joint venture partners. CNL Fund Advisors Company is an advisory company that partners with alternative asset managers. Other CNL related companies are Macquire CNL Global Income Trust, Inc., a private REIT that manages income-oriented real estate properties; and CNL Macquire Global Growth Trust, Inc., a private REIT focused on commercial real estate. In March 2010, CNL Lifestyle Properties, Inc. acquired four California marinas for $55 million from Almar Management, Inc. In May 2010, CNL Commercial Real Estate acquired Drexel Realty Partners; and acquired two marinas in Maryland. In January 2011, the firm acquired 29 senior living communities in 12 states; and CNL Lifestyle Properties acquired the Pacific Park amusement park in California.

Employees of the firm receive a 401(k) plan, educational assistance, adoption assistance, flexible spending accounts and medical, prescription, hospitalization, dental, vision, disability and life insurance.

FINANCIALS:
Sales and profits are in thousands of dollars—add 000 to get the full amount. 2010 Note: Financial information for 2010 was not available for all companies at press time.

2010 Sales: $	2010 Profits: $	**U.S. Stock Ticker: Private**
2009 Sales: $	2009 Profits: $	**Int'l Ticker:** Int'l Exchange:
2008 Sales: $	2008 Profits: $	Employees:
2007 Sales: $77,400	2007 Profits: $	Fiscal Year Ends: 12/31
2006 Sales: $	2006 Profits: $	Parent Company:

SALARIES/BENEFITS:

Pension Plan:	ESOP Stock Plan:	Profit Sharing:	Top Exec. Salary: $	Bonus: $
Savings Plan: Y	Stock Purch. Plan:		Second Exec. Salary: $	Bonus: $

OTHER THOUGHTS:

Apparent Women Officers or Directors: 3
Hot Spot for Advancement for Women/Minorities: Y

LOCATIONS: ("Y" = Yes)

West:	Southwest:	Midwest:	Southeast:	Northeast:	International:
Y	Y	Y	Y	Y	

COLDWELL BANKER REAL ESTATE LLC   www.coldwellbanker.com

Industry Group Code: 531210 Ranks within this company's industry group: Sales: Profits:

Properties:	Financial Services:		Construction/Development:	Investments:	Specialty Services:		Brokerage:	
Apartments:	Mortgages:	Y	Commercial Construction:	REIT:	Property Management:		Commercial Sales:	Y
Malls/Shopping:	Title Insurance:		Residential Construction:		Online Services:	Y	Residential Sales:	Y
Offices:	Property Insurance:		Land Development:		Software/IT:		Specialty:	Y
Hotels/Motels:			Support Services:		Consulting:			
Industrial/Warehouses:			Design/Engineering:					
Other:								

TYPES OF BUSINESS:

Real Estate Brokerage
Residential & Resort Brokerage
Commercial Brokerage
Mortgage Services
Online Information & Lending

BRANDS/DIVISIONS/AFFILIATES:

Realogy Corporation
Coldwell Banker Previews International
Coldwell Banker Concierge
Coldwell Banker Mortgage
Coldwell Banker Commercial
CBU.com
CBNet

CONTACTS: *Note: Officers with more than one job title may be intentionally listed here more than once.*

Jim Gillespie, CEO
Budge Huskey, COO
Budge Huskey, Pres.
Michael Fischer, Chief Mktg. Officer
Heather Roberts, Dir.-Public Rel.
Steve Bright, Sr. VP/Regional Dir.-Western Region
Nelson Bennett, Sr. VP/Regional Dir.-Northern Region
Frank Lindsey, Sr. VP/Regional Dir.-Southern Region
John Geha, Pres., Coldwell Banker Canada

Phone: 973-407-2000	Fax: 973-496-7217
Toll-Free:	
Address: 1 Campus Dr., Parsippany, NJ 07054 US	

GROWTH PLANS/SPECIAL FEATURES:

Coldwell Banker Real Estate LLC, a subsidiary of Realogy Corporation, offers a full array of commercial and residential real estate services including buying, selling, leasing, lending, refinancing and a variety of support services. The Coldwell Banker website provides resources for buyers and sellers of homes such as local real estate office information, agent locators, general information for first time buyers/sellers and a property locator. The website's Personal Retriever feature allows customers to keep track of properties they are interested in by creating a personal online account to which they can save home and real estate agent information as well as receive alerts when new properties are listed that meet their search criteria. The firm's Concierge Service Program provides customers with information on local service providers specializing in everything from car and truck rental to home maintenance. Coldwell's sales associates act as local market experts and can help clients with everything from selling, buying and financing to moving into a new home. The company carries out its operations through its licensed trademark brand, Coldwell Banker Commercial. Coldwell Banker Mortgage is a leading telephone- and web-based lender in the U.S. Coldwell Banker Previews International markets and sells luxury homes in the Americas, Europe, Africa, the Middle East, Asia and Australia. The firm has over 3,300 franchised residential and commercial real estate offices in 50 countries. Each office is independently owned and operated, except for offices owned and operated by NRT, Inc. Coldwell provides its brokers and sales associates with exclusive access to its Internet portal, CBNet, which has the most up-to-date information on all of the company's products and services, its listings, selling and prospecting and networking tools. Coldwell also provides CBU.com, an education site with a wide variety of classes and continuing education programs that can be taken in person, by phone or via the Internet.

FINANCIALS: Sales and profits are in thousands of dollars—add 000 to get the full amount. 2010 Note: Financial information for 2010 was not available for all companies at press time.

2010 Sales: $	2010 Profits: $	U.S. Stock Ticker: Subsidiary
2009 Sales: $	2009 Profits: $	Int'l Ticker: Int'l Exchange:
2008 Sales: $	2008 Profits: $	Employees:
2007 Sales: $	2007 Profits: $	Fiscal Year Ends: 12/31
2006 Sales: $	2006 Profits: $	Parent Company: REALOGY CORPORATION

SALARIES/BENEFITS:

Pension Plan:	ESOP Stock Plan:	Profit Sharing:	Top Exec. Salary: $	Bonus: $
Savings Plan:	Stock Purch. Plan:		Second Exec. Salary: $	Bonus: $

OTHER THOUGHTS:

Apparent Women Officers or Directors: 1
Hot Spot for Advancement for Women/Minorities:

LOCATIONS: ("Y" = Yes)

West:	Southwest:	Midwest:	Southeast:	Northeast:	International:
Y	Y	Y	Y	Y	Y

COLLIERS INTERNATIONAL PROPERTY CONSULTANTS INC

www.colliers.com

Industry Group Code: 531210 Ranks within this company's industry group: Sales: Profits:

Properties:		Financial Services:		Construction/Development:		Investments:		Specialty Services:		Brokerage:	
Apartments:		Mortgages:		Commercial Construction:		REIT:		Property Management:	Y	Commercial Sales:	Y
Malls/Shopping:		Title Insurance:		Residential Construction:				Online Services:		Residential Sales:	Y
Offices:		Property Insurance:		Land Development:	Y			Software/IT:		Specialty:	Y
Hotels/Motels:				Support Services:				Consulting:	Y		
Industrial/Warehouses:				Design/Engineering:							
Other:	Y										

TYPES OF BUSINESS:

Property Representation & Agency
Facilities Management
Commercial Sales
Consulting Services
Valuation & Advisory Services
Portfolio Management
Development & Project Management
Debt, Mezzanine & Equity Capital Financing

BRANDS/DIVISIONS/AFFILIATES:

Colliers Law Firm Services Group
Colliers Investment Services Group
Colliers MultiModal Services Group
Colliers Facility Management Group
Colliers Healthcare Services Group
Colliers Life Sciences Group
Colliers Automotive Real Estate Services Group
Colliers Land Advisory Group

CONTACTS:
Note: Officers with more than one job title may be intentionally listed here more than once.

Doug Frye, CEO
Peter Humphries, COO
Doug Frye, Global Pres.
Peter Humphries, CFO
Veresh Sita, CIO
Carolyn Sidor, Exec. VP-Oper.
Curtis Akey, Dir.-Finance
Dylan Taylor, CEO-Colliers USA
Doug Frye, Chmn.

Phone: 206-223-0866	Fax:
Toll-Free:	
Address: 601 Union St., Ste. 4800, Seattle, WA 98101 US	

GROWTH PLANS/SPECIAL FEATURES:

Colliers International Property Consultants, Inc. (CIPC), a subsidiary of FirstService, is one of the world's largest commercial real estate organizations, with over 480 offices worldwide. The company's services include property representation and agency; tenant representation; portfolio management; mergers and acquisitions; facilities management; multi-family property advisement; development and project management; valuation and advisory services; and consulting. CIPC provides its services to a wide range of clients and industries through 11 practice groups which include The Healthcare Services Group, which assists healthcare organizations in the development of real estate solutions; the Law Firm Services Group, which provides specialized services to law firms; the Colliers Investment Services Group, which serves institutional and private investors; the Life Sciences Group, which caters to research centers and pharmaceutical and biotechnology companies; the Colliers MultiModal Services Group, which provides services to the global shipping and transportation industry; the Colliers Automotive Real Estate Services Group (Cars), which offers commercial real estate to the automotive industry; the Colliers Investment Service Group, which provides market research, data on emerging capital sources and sales transaction information; and the Colliers Land Advisory Group represents both buyer and sellers in land acquisitions and dispositions. In early 2010, property management firm FirstService acquired Colliers International. In April 2010, the company acquired a majority ownership in commercial real estate firm Colliers Bennett & Kahnweiler.

FINANCIALS:
Sales and profits are in thousands of dollars—add 000 to get the full amount. 2010 Note: Financial information for 2010 was not available for all companies at press time.

2010 Sales: $	2010 Profits: $	**U.S. Stock Ticker: Subsidiary**
2009 Sales: $	2009 Profits: $	**Int'l Ticker:** Int'l Exchange:
2008 Sales: $2,000,000	2008 Profits: $	Employees: 11,000
2007 Sales: $	2007 Profits: $	Fiscal Year Ends: 12/31
2006 Sales: $	2006 Profits: $	Parent Company: FIRSTSERVICE CORPORATION

SALARIES/BENEFITS:

Pension Plan:	ESOP Stock Plan:	Profit Sharing:	Top Exec. Salary: $	Bonus: $
Savings Plan:	Stock Purch. Plan:		Second Exec. Salary: $	Bonus: $

OTHER THOUGHTS:

Apparent Women Officers or Directors: 1
Hot Spot for Advancement for Women/Minorities:

LOCATIONS: ("Y" = Yes)

West:	Southwest:	Midwest:	Southeast:	Northeast:	International:
Y	Y	Y	Y	Y	Y

COLONIAL PROPERTIES TRUST

www.colonialprop.com

Industry Group Code: 531110 **Ranks within this company's industry group:** Sales: 10   Profits: 15

Properties:		Financial Services:	Construction/Development:	Investments:		Specialty Services:		Brokerage:
Apartments:	Y	Mortgages:	Commercial Construction:	REIT:	Y	Property Management:	Y	Commercial Sales:
Malls/Shopping:	Y	Title Insurance:	Residential Construction:			Online Services:		Residential Sales:
Offices:	Y	Property Insurance:	Land Development:			Software/IT:		Specialty:
Hotels/Motels:			Support Services:			Consulting:		
Industrial/Warehouses:			Design/Engineering:					
Other:								

TYPES OF BUSINESS:

Real Estate Investment Trust
Multi-Family Apartments
Office Properties
Retail Properties
Property Management

BRANDS/DIVISIONS/AFFILIATES:

Colonial Realty, LP
Colonial Properties Services, Inc.

CONTACTS: *Note: Officers with more than one job title may be intentionally listed here more than once.*

Thomas Lowder, CEO
Paul F. Earle, COO
C. Reynolds Thompson, III, Pres.
C. Reynolds Thompson, III, CFO
John P. Rigrish, Chief Admin. Officer
John P. Rigrish, Corp. Sec.
Edward T. Wright, Exec. VP-Multifamily Dev.
Jerry A. Brewer, Exec. VP-Finance
Bradley P. Sandidge, Exec. VP-Acct.
Ed Wright, Exec. VP-Dev. & Construction
Robert A. Jackson, Exec. VP-Commercial Properties
Mary Ann Klingler, Exec. VP-Multifamily Properties
Thomas Lowder, Chmn.

Phone: 205-250-8700	**Fax:** 205-250-8890
Toll-Free: 800-645-3917	
Address: 2101 6th Ave. N., Ste. 750, Birmingham, AL 35203 US	

GROWTH PLANS/SPECIAL FEATURES:

Colonial Properties Trust is a self-administered equity real estate investment trust (REIT) that owns, develops and operates multi-family, office, retail and mixed-use properties in Alabama, Arizona, Florida, Georgia, Nevada, North Carolina, South Carolina, Tennessee, Texas and Virginia. Colonial owns and operates a diversified portfolio of 156 wholly- and partially-owned properties, including 111 multifamily apartment communities containing a total of 33,520 apartment units and 45 commercial properties containing 10.6 million square feet. The company holds an 89.1% interest in Colonial Realty, LP. Through this partnership, Colonial conducts management services for its properties as well as other business. Additionally, through Colonial Properties Services, Inc., the company provides management services for properties owned by third parties. Colonial also creates added value by managing commercial assets, primarily through joint venture investments, and pursuing development opportunities. In October 2010, it sold its 50% interest in the Parkway Place Mall in Huntsville, Alabama to joint venture partner CBL & Associates Properties, Inc. In March 2011, the firm acquired three Class A apartment communities: one each in Austin, Texas; Charlotte, North Carolina; and Las Vegas, Nevada.

Employees are offered medical, dental and vision insurance; a 401(k) plan; a stock purchase plan; flexible spending accounts; life and AD&D insurance; short- and long-term disability coverage; an employee assistance program; education assistance; adoption assistance; and access to onsite fitness facilities.

FINANCIALS: Sales and profits are in thousands of dollars—add 000 to get the full amount. 2010 Note: Financial information for 2010 was not available for all companies at press time.

2010 Sales: $367,009	2010 Profits: $-38,543	**U.S. Stock Ticker:** CLP
2009 Sales: $340,754	2009 Profits: $15,178	**Int'l Ticker:** Int'l Exchange:
2008 Sales: $344,405	2008 Profits: $-50,521	Employees: 988
2007 Sales: $421,571	2007 Profits: $342,102	Fiscal Year Ends: 12/31
2006 Sales: $466,037	2006 Profits: $203,480	Parent Company:

SALARIES/BENEFITS:

Pension Plan:	ESOP Stock Plan:	Profit Sharing:	Top Exec. Salary: $500,000	Bonus: $
Savings Plan: Y	Stock Purch. Plan: Y		Second Exec. Salary: $400,000	Bonus: $

OTHER THOUGHTS:

Apparent Women Officers or Directors: 1
Hot Spot for Advancement for Women/Minorities:

LOCATIONS: ("Y" = Yes)

West:	Southwest:	Midwest:	Southeast:	Northeast:	International:
Y	Y		Y	Y	

COLONY CAPITAL LLC

www.colonyinc.com

Industry Group Code: 5311 Ranks within this company's industry group: Sales: Profits:

Properties:	Financial Services:	Construction/Development:	Investments:	Specialty Services:	Brokerage:
Apartments:	Mortgages:	Commercial Construction:	REIT: Y	Property Management:	Commercial Sales:
Malls/Shopping:	Title Insurance:	Residential Construction:		Online Services:	Residential Sales:
Offices:	Property Insurance:	Land Development:		Software/IT:	Specialty:
Hotels/Motels: Y		Support Services:		Consulting:	
Industrial/Warehouses: Y		Design/Engineering:			
Other: Y					

TYPES OF BUSINESS:

Real Estate Investments
Private Equity

BRANDS/DIVISIONS/AFFILIATES:

Colony Reality Partners LP
Colony Investment Management LLC
La Tour
Brownfields
Carrefour SA
Challenger Financial Services
Station Casinos Inc
Meadowlands Xanadu

CONTACTS: *Note: Officers with more than one job title may be intentionally listed here more than once.*

Thomas J. Barrack Jr., CEO
Richard B. Saltzman, Pres.
Mark M. Hedstrom, CFO
Jonathan Grunzweig, CIO
Ronald M. Sanders, General Counsel/Principal
Duyen Tran, VP-Oper. & Finance
Richard S. Welch, Sr. VP-Finance
Ed C. Daily, VP-Risk Mgmt. & Asset Mgmt.
Jean-Romain Lhomme, Principal-Colony Capital Europe
Henry G. Brauer, Sr. Managing Dir.-Colony Realty Partners LLC
Justin Chang, Principal
Thomas J. Barrack Jr., Chmn.
Sebastien Bazin, CEO-Colony Capital SAS/Managing Dir.-Europe

Phone: 310-282-8820	Fax: 310-282-8808
Toll-Free:	
Address: 2450 Broadway, 6th Fl., Santa Monica, CA 90404 US	

GROWTH PLANS/SPECIAL FEATURES:

Colony Capital, LLC is a private international investment firm focusing primarily on real estate related assets and operating companies with a strategic dependence on such assets. The firm has invested over $45 billion in more than 13,000 assets since 1991. The company's current fund, its eighth, has stakes in Station Casinos, a Las Vegas locals gaming business and Native American gaming management company; Meadowlands Xanadu, a retail development of a 2.2 million-square-foot sports, leisure, shopping and entertainment location in New Jersey; Ambassy Court, a 484,000-square-foot apartment building in Beijing; Brownfields, a platform specializing in the purchase, de-pollution and resale of contaminated industrial sites in Europe; La Tour, consisting of two private hospitals in Geneva, Switzerland; Challenger Financial Services Group, an Australian financial services company with $79 billion assets in management, administration and advice; Accor SA, a French Hotel Group with 4,000 hotels and 500,000 rooms; and 9.1% public shares of Carrefour SA, a food retailer with 12,000 locations in 29 countries. The company has two subsidiaries: Colony Reality Partners L.P., a real estate investment company that acquires and manages commercial real estate properties; and Colony Investment Management LLC, which manages investments for its clients. The firm operates through offices in Santa Monica, New York, Boston, Paris, Rome, London, Madrid, Hong Kong, Beijing, Tokyo, Seoul and Taipei. In April 2010, as a co-owner with the Station executives Frank and Lorenzo Fertitta, the company formed a new entity called PropCo, which manages and has an ownership stake in five of Station's properties: Red Rock Resort, Sunset Station, Boulder Station, Palace Station and the Wild Wild West in Nevada. In January 2011, Colony Capital acquired two portfolios comprised of 1,505 residential and commercial mortgages from Federal Deposit Insurance Corporation for approximately $96 million.

FINANCIALS: Sales and profits are in thousands of dollars—add 000 to get the full amount. 2010 Note: Financial information for 2010 was not available for all companies at press time.

2010 Sales: $	2010 Profits: $	**U.S. Stock Ticker: Private**
2009 Sales: $	2009 Profits: $	**Int'l Ticker:** Int'l Exchange:
2008 Sales: $	2008 Profits: $	Employees:
2007 Sales: $475,100	2007 Profits: $	Fiscal Year Ends:
2006 Sales: $	2006 Profits: $	Parent Company:

SALARIES/BENEFITS:

Pension Plan:	ESOP Stock Plan:	Profit Sharing:	Top Exec. Salary: $	Bonus: $
Savings Plan:	Stock Purch. Plan:		Second Exec. Salary: $	Bonus: $

OTHER THOUGHTS:

Apparent Women Officers or Directors: 3
Hot Spot for Advancement for Women/Minorities: Y

LOCATIONS: ("Y" = Yes)

West:	Southwest:	Midwest:	Southeast:	Northeast:	International:
Y				Y	Y

COMFORT SYSTEMS USA INC
www.comfortsystemsusa.com

Industry Group Code: 238220 Ranks within this company's industry group: Sales: 1   Profits: 1

Properties:	Financial Services:	Construction/Development:		Investments:	Specialty Services:	Brokerage:
Apartments:	Mortgages:	Commercial Construction:		REIT:	Property Management:	Commercial Sales:
Malls/Shopping:	Title Insurance:	Residential Construction:			Online Services:	Residential Sales:
Offices:	Property Insurance:	Land Development:			Software/IT:	Specialty:
Hotels/Motels:		Support Services:	Y		Consulting:	
Industrial/Warehouses:		Design/Engineering:	Y			
Other:						

TYPES OF BUSINESS:
Plumbing, Heating & Air Conditioning Contractors
Industrial & Commercial HVAC Systems & Services
Facility Automation Services

BRANDS/DIVISIONS/AFFILIATES:
ColonialWebb Contractors Company

CONTACTS: *Note: Officers with more than one job title may be intentionally listed here more than once.*
William F. Murdy, CEO
Brian Lane, COO
Brian Lane, Pres.
William George, CFO
Trent McKenna, General Counsel/VP
Julie Shaeff, Chief Acct. Officer
Melissa Frazier, VP-Audit & Controls
W. Brewster Earle, Sr. VP-Energy Svcs.
Thomas N. Tanner, Sr. VP-Region 1
Dean Tillison, Sr. VP-Region 2
William F. Murdy, Chmn.

Phone: 713-803-9600	**Fax:** 713-830-9696
Toll-Free: 800-723-8431	
Address: 675 Bering, Ste. 400, Houston, TX 77057 US	

GROWTH PLANS/SPECIAL FEATURES:

Comfort Systems USA, Inc. is a national heating, ventilation and air conditioning (HVAC) and building automation services company with 84 locations in 70 cities nationwide. It provides installation, maintenance, repair and replacement services for a large and growing base of national, multi-location clients in both commercial and industrial markets. The company's technical experts design, install and fine-tune HVAC systems for downtown high-rises, hospitals, universities, national hotels, factories and industrial plants. Comfort offers two types of service: Installation services, accounting for 47% of revenues; and maintenance, repair and replacement services, accounting for 53% of revenues. Installation services involve the design, engineering, integration, installation and start-up of HVAC, building automation controls and related systems. The company provides design-and-build services, in which Comfort determines the needed capacity and energy efficiency of the HVAC system that best suits the proposed facility and then estimates the amount of time, labor, materials and equipment needed to build the specified system. It also provides plan-and-spec services, in which it participates in a bid process to provide labor, equipment, materials and installation based on plans and engineering specifications provided by a customer, general contractor or consulting engineer, for office buildings, retail centers, apartment complexes, manufacturing plants, health care, education and government facilities and other commercial, industrial, and institutional facilities. Additionally, the firm installs process cooling systems and building automation controls and monitoring systems. The maintenance, repair and replacement services include the maintenance, repair, replacement, reconfiguration and monitoring of HVAC systems and industrial process piping. Maintenance and repair services are provided either in response to service calls or under a service agreement. In July 2010, the firm acquired ColonialWebb Contractors Company.

FINANCIALS: Sales and profits are in thousands of dollars—add 000 to get the full amount. 2010 Note: Financial information for 2010 was not available for all companies at press time.

2010 Sales: $1,108,282	2010 Profits: $14,740	**U.S. Stock Ticker: FIX**
2009 Sales: $1,128,907	2009 Profits: $34,182	**Int'l Ticker:** Int'l Exchange:
2008 Sales: $1,321,770	2008 Profits: $49,690	Employees: 6,569
2007 Sales: $1,101,579	2007 Profits: $32,466	Fiscal Year Ends: 12/31
2006 Sales: $1,056,525	2006 Profits: $28,724	Parent Company:

SALARIES/BENEFITS:

Pension Plan:	ESOP Stock Plan:	Profit Sharing:	Top Exec. Salary: $579,000	Bonus: $632,294
Savings Plan:	Stock Purch. Plan:		Second Exec. Salary: $305,000	Bonus: $333,074

OTHER THOUGHTS:
Apparent Women Officers or Directors: 3
Hot Spot for Advancement for Women/Minorities: Y

LOCATIONS: ("Y" = Yes)

West:	Southwest:	Midwest:	Southeast:	Northeast:	International:
Y	Y	Y	Y	Y	

COMMONWEALTH REIT

www.cwhreit.com

Industry Group Code: 531120 Ranks within this company's industry group: Sales: 20   Profits: 16

Properties:	Financial Services:	Construction/Development:	Investments:	Specialty Services:	Brokerage:
Apartments:	Mortgages:	Commercial Construction:	REIT: Y	Property Management:	Commercial Sales:
Malls/Shopping:	Title Insurance:	Residential Construction:		Online Services:	Residential Sales:
Offices: Y	Property Insurance:	Land Development:		Software/IT:	Specialty:
Hotels/Motels:		Support Services:		Consulting:	
Industrial/Warehouses: Y		Design/Engineering:			
Other:					

TYPES OF BUSINESS:

Real Estate Investment Trust
Office Buildings

BRANDS/DIVISIONS/AFFILIATES:

REIT Management & Research LLC
HRPT Properties Trust
Government Properties Income Trust

CONTACTS: *Note: Officers with more than one job title may be intentionally listed here more than once.*

David M. Lepore, COO/Sr. VP
Adam D. Portnoy, Pres./Managing Trustee
John C. Popeo, CFO
Jennifer B. Clark, Sec.
Tim Bonang, VP-Investor Rel.
John C. Popeo, Treas.
William J. Sheehan, Dir.-Internal Audit & Compliance

Phone: 617-332-3990	**Fax:** 617-332-2261
Toll-Free:	
Address: 255 Washington St., 2 Newton Place, Ste. 300, Newton, MA 02458 US	

GROWTH PLANS/SPECIAL FEATURES:

CommonWealth REIT, formerly HRPT Properties Trust, is a real estate investment trust that owns and operates office and industrial buildings and leases industrial land. The company owns 481 properties, which consist of 303 office properties with a total of 33.6 million square feet and 178 industrial properties with 30.4 million square feet of space. Its properties are predominately located in central business districts and suburban areas in five major market regions: Metro Denver; Metro Philadelphia; Metro Washington, D.C.; Metro Boston; and Oahu, Hawaii. CommonWealth operates in a total of 34 states, with 17.9 million square feet of the land area of the firm's industrial properties concentrated in Oahu, Hawaii. Additionally, 11 of its properties, totaling 1.8 million square feet, are located in Australia. The firm also maintains a 24.6% interest in Government Properties Income Trust, a former subsidiary that leases properties to government tenants. In evaluating potential investments and asset sales, CommonWealth considers historic and projected rents received and operating expenses; the growth, tax and regulatory environment of the market; the quality, experience and credit worthiness of the property's tenants; the occupancy, demand for and pricing of similar properties in nearby markets; the construction quality, physical condition and design of the property; and the geographic area and type of property. Its leading tenants, as measured by percentage of square feet, include Flextronics International Ltd.; PNC Financial Services Group; GlaxoSmithKline plc; the U.S. government; and Wells Fargo Bank. CommonWealth is managed by REIT Management & Research LLC.

FINANCIALS: Sales and profits are in thousands of dollars—add 000 to get the full amount. 2010 Note: Financial information for 2010 was not available for all companies at press time.

2010 Sales: $793,370	2010 Profits: $135,409	**U.S. Stock Ticker:** CWH
2009 Sales: $770,941	2009 Profits: $164,674	**Int'l Ticker:** Int'l Exchange:
2008 Sales: $752,110	2008 Profits: $244,645	Employees: 650
2007 Sales: $783,266	2007 Profits: $124,255	Fiscal Year Ends: 12/31
2006 Sales: $744,008	2006 Profits: $250,580	Parent Company:

SALARIES/BENEFITS:

Pension Plan:	ESOP Stock Plan:	Profit Sharing:	Top Exec. Salary: $102,375	Bonus: $
Savings Plan:	Stock Purch. Plan:		Second Exec. Salary: $102,375	Bonus: $

OTHER THOUGHTS:

Apparent Women Officers or Directors: 1
Hot Spot for Advancement for Women/Minorities:

LOCATIONS: ("Y" = Yes)

West:	Southwest:	Midwest:	Southeast:	Northeast:	International:
Y	Y	Y	Y	Y	

COMMUNITY DEVELOPMENT TRUST

www.cdt.biz

Industry Group Code: 531110 Ranks within this company's industry group: Sales: Profits:

Properties:		Financial Services:		Construction/Development:	Investments:		Specialty Services:	Brokerage:
Apartments:	Y	Mortgages:	Y	Commercial Construction:	REIT:	Y	Property Management:	Commercial Sales:
Malls/Shopping:	Y	Title Insurance:		Residential Construction:			Online Services:	Residential Sales:
Offices:	Y	Property Insurance:		Land Development:			Software/IT:	Specialty:
Hotels/Motels:				Support Services:			Consulting:	
Industrial/Warehouses:				Design/Engineering:				
Other:								

TYPES OF BUSINESS:

Real Estate Investment Trust
Equity & Mortgage Investments
Apartments
Offices
Retail Properties

BRANDS/DIVISIONS/AFFILIATES:

CONTACTS:
Note: Officers with more than one job title may be intentionally listed here more than once.

Joseph F. Reilly, CEO
Joseph F. Reilly, Pres.
John J. Divers, CFO/Treas.
Patricia Tagarello, VP-Oper.
Mark W. Bolinsky, Controller
Brian Gallagher, Sr. VP-Debt
Christopher Blair, VP-Finance
Shelly Cleary, Sr. VP-Underwriting
Joan Berkowitz, Sr. VP-Asset Mgmt.
Peter J. Weidhorn, Chmn.

Phone: 212-271-5080	Fax: 212-271-5079
Toll-Free:	
Address: 1350 Broadway, Ste. 700, New York, NY 10018 US	

GROWTH PLANS/SPECIAL FEATURES:

Community Development Trust (CDT) is a real estate investment trust (REIT) entirely devoted to investment in the community development market through both an equity program and a debt program. In the past ten years, the company has committed $745 million in debt and equity capital to affordable housing properties across the country. Through CDT's debt and equity programs, the firm invests long-term debt capital by purchasing smaller, fixed-rate multifamily mortgages from community lenders and equity capital in cash or by providing a tax advantaged transition for existing properties to a new set of owners committed to long-term affordability. All of CDT's investments must satisfy Community Reinvestment Act requirements. The company currently has investments in 28,000 housing units in 40 states across the country representing a broad mix of types ranging from scattered-site developments to in-fill urban family apartments and redeveloped high rises. The firm's average investment per transaction is approximately $5 million. Major investors in CDT include Allstate Insurance; Bank of America; California Bank and Trust; Citibank Community Development; Deutsche Bank; Fannie Mae; HSBC Bank USA; JPMorgan Chase Community Development Group; Key Community Development; Local Initiatives Support Corporation; MetLife; Merrill Lynch Community Development Company LLC; NCB Capital Impact; Prudential Financial; The Reinvestment Fund; and Wells Fargo Bank.

FINANCIALS:
Sales and profits are in thousands of dollars—add 000 to get the full amount. 2010 Note: Financial information for 2010 was not available for all companies at press time.

2010 Sales: $	2010 Profits: $	**U.S. Stock Ticker: Private**
2009 Sales: $	2009 Profits: $	**Int'l Ticker:** Int'l Exchange:
2008 Sales: $	2008 Profits: $	Employees:
2007 Sales: $	2007 Profits: $	Fiscal Year Ends: 12/31
2006 Sales: $	2006 Profits: $	Parent Company:

SALARIES/BENEFITS:

Pension Plan:	ESOP Stock Plan:	Profit Sharing:	Top Exec. Salary: $	Bonus: $
Savings Plan:	Stock Purch. Plan:		Second Exec. Salary: $	Bonus: $

OTHER THOUGHTS:

Apparent Women Officers or Directors: 4
Hot Spot for Advancement for Women/Minorities: Y

LOCATIONS: ("Y" = Yes)

West:	Southwest:	Midwest:	Southeast:	Northeast:	International:
Y			Y	Y	

CORE NETWORK (THE)

www.corenetwork.org

Industry Group Code: 531210 Ranks within this company's industry group: Sales: Profits:

Properties:		Financial Services:	Construction/Development:	Investments:	Specialty Services:		Brokerage:	
Apartments:		Mortgages:	Commercial Construction:	REIT:	Property Management:	Y	Commercial Sales:	Y
Malls/Shopping:		Title Insurance:	Residential Construction:		Online Services:	Y	Residential Sales:	
Offices:		Property Insurance:	Land Development:		Software/IT:		Specialty:	Y
Hotels/Motels:			Support Services:		Consulting:	Y		
Industrial/Warehouses:			Design/Engineering:					
Other:								

TYPES OF BUSINESS:

Office & Industrial Consulting
Retail Planning
Real Estate Development
Financial Services & Mortgages
Property Management
Real Estate Brokerage

BRANDS/DIVISIONS/AFFILIATES:

Project Tracking System

CONTACTS: *Note: Officers with more than one job title may be intentionally listed here more than once.*

Perry Morita, Exec. Dir.
Michael B. Divaris, Chmn.

Phone: 972-980-3994	Fax: 972-980-3993
Toll-Free:	
Address: 15150 Preston Rd., Ste. 300, Dallas, TX 75248 US	

GROWTH PLANS/SPECIAL FEATURES:

The CORE Network is a consortium of approximately 30 mid-sized commercial real estate companies providing services to office and retail businesses. Through its member firms Core offers clients a variety of services including tenant representation, in which a specialist assists clients in negotiating leases, moving into a new facility and defining goals for surplus property and space requirements. The leasing and management service offers clients basic property management, as well as providing an evaluation of occupancy alternatives. The investment advisory services offer investors consultation in advantageous portfolio acquisitions through the firm's knowledge of local real estate opportunities. In addition, it offers finance and investment banking services to large corporate and institutional clients that consists of financing, transaction assistance, providing capital and negotiation tactics. The facility management services helps reduce cost and facilitate tenant services; construction management provides budgeting, general contracting, project and scheduling management; and development management services provides assistance to those clients wanting to occupy a property or for corporate clients entering into a joint venture. CORE's portfolio management offers tracking and administrative services to clients with numerous real estate acquisitions. The network's strategic planning and general advisory services incorporate long term consulting and analytical methods for financial growth. Additionally, CORE offers fundamental research, analysis and planning through specialized department within each member firm. The company employs the expertise of industry-specific account teams and specialists from various member firms in the network, allowing companies to provide better service collectively. Most clients of network members are major property holders with at least 100 leased or owned properties. CORE supports client projects through the Project Tracking System, which allows network members to access an index of project progress online.

FINANCIALS: Sales and profits are in thousands of dollars—add 000 to get the full amount. 2010 Note: Financial information for 2010 was not available for all companies at press time.

2010 Sales: $	2010 Profits: $	U.S. Stock Ticker: Private
2009 Sales: $	2009 Profits: $	Int'l Ticker: Int'l Exchange:
2008 Sales: $	2008 Profits: $	Employees:
2007 Sales: $	2007 Profits: $	Fiscal Year Ends:
2006 Sales: $	2006 Profits: $	Parent Company:

SALARIES/BENEFITS:

Pension Plan:	ESOP Stock Plan:	Profit Sharing:	Top Exec. Salary: $	Bonus: $
Savings Plan:	Stock Purch. Plan:		Second Exec. Salary: $	Bonus: $

OTHER THOUGHTS:

Apparent Women Officers or Directors: 1
Hot Spot for Advancement for Women/Minorities:

LOCATIONS: ("Y" = Yes)

West:	Southwest:	Midwest:	Southeast:	Northeast:	International:
Y	Y	Y	Y	Y	

CORPORATE OFFICE PROPERTIES TRUST   www.copt.com

Industry Group Code: 531120 Ranks within this company's industry group: Sales: 32   Profits: 34

Properties:		Financial Services:	Construction/Development:		Investments:		Specialty Services:		Brokerage:
Apartments:		Mortgages:	Commercial Construction:	Y	REIT:	Y	Property Management:	Y	Commercial Sales:
Malls/Shopping:		Title Insurance:	Residential Construction:				Online Services:		Residential Sales:
Offices:	Y	Property Insurance:	Land Development:	Y			Software/IT:		Specialty:
Hotels/Motels:			Support Services:	Y			Consulting:		
Industrial/Warehouses:			Design/Engineering:	Y					
Other:	Y								

TYPES OF BUSINESS:

Real Estate Investment Trust
Commercial Development & Construction Services
Office Properties
Property Management
HVAC Services
Lease, Audit & Consulting Services

BRANDS/DIVISIONS/AFFILIATES:

COPT Development & Construction Services, LLC
COPT Property Management Services, LLC
COPT Environmental Systems, LLC
LW Redstone Company, LLC

CONTACTS: Note: Officers with more than one job title may be intentionally listed here more than once.

Randall M. Griffin, CEO
Roger A. Waesche, Jr., COO
Roger A. Waesche, Jr., Pres.
Stephen E. Riffee, CFO/Exec. VP
Holly G. Edington, Sr. VP-Human Resources
Stephen B. Kutzer, CIO
Karen M. Singer, General Counsel/Sr. VP/Corp. Sec.
Frank W. Ziegler, Sr. VP-New Bus. & Dev., Gov't Svcs.
Michelle Layne, Contact-Media
Michelle Layne, Contact-Investor Rel.
Anthony Mifsud, Treas./Sr. VP-Finance
Wayne Lingafelter, Pres., COPT Dev. & Construction Svcs. LLC
Carl M. Nelson, Sr. VP-Dev. & Construction
Charles J. Fiala, Jr., Sr. VP-Gov't Svcs.
George J. Marcin, Sr. VP-Interiors
Jay H. Shidler, Chmn.

Phone: 443-285-5400	Fax: 443-285-7650
Toll-Free:	
Address: 6711 Columbia Gateway Dr., Ste. 300, Columbia, MD 21046 US	

GROWTH PLANS/SPECIAL FEATURES:

Corporate Office Properties Trust (COPT) is a real estate investment trust (REIT) focused on strategic customer relationships and specialized tenant requirements in the U.S. government and defense information technology sectors, with property investments in Washington D.C., Maryland, Virginia, Pennsylvania, Alabama, Texas and Colorado. The company wholly owns 252 office properties containing 20 million rentable square feet that were 88.2% occupied at the beginning of 2011. COPT also wholly owns 21 office properties under construction, development or redevelopment and land parcels totaling 1,497 acres. In addition, the company has partial ownership interests, primarily through joint ventures, in 20 operational properties, totaling approximately 1.1 million square feet; two properties under development; and land parcels totaling 755 acres. Subsidiary COPT Development & Construction Services, LLC (CDCS) provides development and construction services to government and private sector clients. CDCS specializes in suburban office buildings and handles all aspects of real estate development including project planning, design and construction. Subsidiary COPT Property Management Services, LLC manages most of firm's properties and provide corporate facilities management for third parties. Subsidiary COPT Environmental Systems, LLC provides heating and air conditioning installation, maintenance, repair and other services. Joint venture subsidiary LW Redstone Company, LLC oversees a 468-acre property adjacent to a U.S. Army facility in Huntsville, Alabama. COPT's largest tenant is the U.S. Government, representing approximately 16% of 2010 rental revenues. Over the course of 2010, the company made several acquisitions, including three office properties totaling 514,000 square feet and a shell-complete office property totaling 183,000 square feet acquired for a total of $205.1 million.

The company offers its employees a benefits package that includes a 401(k) plan with company match; a college savings plan; an adoption assistance program; life and disability insurance; flexible spending accounts for health and dependent care; and medical, dental and vision coverage.

FINANCIALS: Sales and profits are in thousands of dollars—add 000 to get the full amount. 2010 Note: Financial information for 2010 was not available for all companies at press time.

2010 Sales: $564,475	2010 Profits: $45,504	**U.S. Stock Ticker:** OFC
2009 Sales: $767,519	2009 Profits: $61,299	**Int'l Ticker:** Int'l Exchange:
2008 Sales: $585,605	2008 Profits: $61,316	**Employees:** 411
2007 Sales: $404,466	2007 Profits: $35,942	**Fiscal Year Ends:** 12/31
2006 Sales: $351,528	2006 Profits: $49,227	**Parent Company:**

SALARIES/BENEFITS:

Pension Plan:	ESOP Stock Plan:	Profit Sharing:	Top Exec. Salary: $625,000	Bonus: $1,558,500
Savings Plan: Y	Stock Purch. Plan:		Second Exec. Salary: $475,000	Bonus: $720,000

OTHER THOUGHTS:

Apparent Women Officers or Directors: 8
Hot Spot for Advancement for Women/Minorities: Y

LOCATIONS: ("Y" = Yes)

West:	Southwest:	Midwest:	Southeast:	Northeast:	International:
Y	Y		Y	Y	

COSTAR GROUP INC

www.costar.com

Industry Group Code: 519130 Ranks within this company's industry group: Sales: 1   Profits: 1

Properties:	Financial Services:	Construction/Development:	Investments:	Specialty Services:		Brokerage:	
Apartments:	Mortgages:	Commercial Construction:	REIT:	Property Management:		Commercial Sales:	Y
Malls/Shopping:	Title Insurance:	Residential Construction:		Online Services:	Y	Residential Sales:	
Offices:	Property Insurance:	Land Development:		Software/IT:		Specialty:	
Hotels/Motels:		Support Services:		Consulting:			
Industrial/Warehouses:		Design/Engineering:					
Other:							

TYPES OF BUSINESS:

Online Commercial Real Estate Information
Data Hosting Services
Advertising Services

BRANDS/DIVISIONS/AFFILIATES:

CoStar Property Professional
CoStar Tenant
CoStar COMPS Professional
FOCUS
CoStar UK Ltd.
Resolve Technology, Inc.
Property Portfolio Research, Inc.
Grecam S.A.S.

CONTACTS: *Note: Officers with more than one job title may be intentionally listed here more than once.*

Andrew C. Florance, CEO
Andrew C. Florance, Pres.
Brian Radecki, CFO
John Stanfill, Sr. VP-Sales & Customer Service
Jennifer Kitchen, Sr. VP-Research
Frank Simuro, CIO
Jonathan Coleman, General Counsel/Corp. Sec.
Michael R. Klein, Chmn.
Paul Marples, Managing Dir.-CoStar UK Ltd.

Phone: 202-346-6500	**Fax:** 202-346-6370
Toll-Free: 800-204-5960	
Address: 1331 L St., NW, Washington, DC 20005 US	

GROWTH PLANS/SPECIAL FEATURES:

CoStar Group, Inc. is a leading national provider of commercial real estate sales information. The company offers customers online access to a comprehensive, verified database of commercial real estate information in U.S. markets, as well as in London, other U.K. markets and France. CoStar has a highly developed data collection system that includes sales prices, income and expenses, capitalization rates, loan data, property photographs, buyers, sellers, brokers and other key details. The firm provides commercial real estate professionals with critical knowledge that enables them to complete transactions by offering the most up-to-date, consolidated and standardized information on U.S. commercial real estate. CoStar's subscription-based information services consist primarily of CoStar Property Professional, the firm's flagship service, which provides a comprehensive inventory of office, industrial, retail, multifamily properties and land in markets throughout the U.S., including for-lease and for-sales listings, historical data, building photographs, maps and floor plans; CoStar Tenant, an online business-to-business prospecting and analytical tool providing commercial real estate professionals with commercial U.S. tenant information; CoStar COMPS Professional, a provider of comprehensive coverage of comparable sales information in the U.S. commercial real estate industry; and FOCUS (offered by CoStar U.K Limited, the firm's U.K. subsidiary), a digital online service offering information on the U.K. real estate market. These services generate over 95% of the company's total revenues. A diverse portfolio of customers consists of asset managers, mortgage lenders, investors, security analysts and property managers. Other subsidiaries of the company include Resolve Technology, Inc, a real estate investment management software provider; Property and Portfolio Research, Inc., a commercial real estate market forecaster; and Grecam S.A.S., a France-based commercial property information provider. In October 2010, the firm opened its new headquarters in Washington, D.C.

The firm offers employees medical, dental and vision insurance; an employee assistance program; tuition reimbursement; life insurance; and disability coverage.

FINANCIALS: Sales and profits are in thousands of dollars—add 000 to get the full amount. 2010 Note: Financial information for 2010 was not available for all companies at press time.

2010 Sales: $226,260	2010 Profits: $13,289	**U.S. Stock Ticker: CSGP**
2009 Sales: $209,659	2009 Profits: $18,693	**Int'l Ticker:** Int'l Exchange:
2008 Sales: $212,428	2008 Profits: $24,623	Employees: 1,389
2007 Sales: $192,805	2007 Profits: $15,951	Fiscal Year Ends: 12/31
2006 Sales: $158,889	2006 Profits: $12,410	Parent Company:

SALARIES/BENEFITS:

Pension Plan:	ESOP Stock Plan:	Profit Sharing:	Top Exec. Salary: $456,560	Bonus: $385,379
Savings Plan: Y	Stock Purch. Plan:		Second Exec. Salary: $250,000	Bonus: $25,000

OTHER THOUGHTS:

Apparent Women Officers or Directors: 1
Hot Spot for Advancement for Women/Minorities:

LOCATIONS: ("Y" = Yes)

West:	Southwest:	Midwest:	Southeast:	Northeast:	International:
Y	Y	Y	Y	Y	Y

COUSINS PROPERTIES INC

www.cousinsproperties.com

Industry Group Code: 531110 Ranks within this company's industry group: Sales: 15   Profits: 14

Properties:		Financial Services:		Construction/Development:		Investments:		Specialty Services:		Brokerage:	
Apartments:		Mortgages:		Commercial Construction:		REIT:	Y	Property Management:	Y	Commercial Sales:	
Malls/Shopping:	Y	Title Insurance:		Residential Construction:	Y			Online Services:		Residential Sales:	Y
Offices:	Y	Property Insurance:		Land Development:	Y			Software/IT:		Specialty:	
Hotels/Motels:				Support Services:				Consulting:			
Industrial/Warehouses:				Design/Engineering:							
Other:	Y										

TYPES OF BUSINESS:

Real Estate Investment Trust
Residential Communities
Office Properties
Retail Properties
Property Management
Land Development
Open Air Malls
Industrial

BRANDS/DIVISIONS/AFFILIATES:

CONTACTS: *Note: Officers with more than one job title may be intentionally listed here more than once.*

Larry L. Gellerstedt, III, CEO
Larry L. Gellerstedt, III, Pres.
Greg Adzema, CFO/Exec. VP
Robert M. Jackson, General Counsel/Sr. VP/Corp. Sec.
John D. Harris, Jr, Chief Acct. Officer/Sr. VP
Craig B. Jones, Chief Investment Officer/Exec. VP
John S. McColl, Exec. VP-Dev., Office Leasing & Asset Mgmt.
J. Thad Ellis II, Sr. VP-Client Svcs.
Michael I. Cohn, Exec. VP-Retail Investments, Leasing & Asset Mgmt.
S. Taylor Glover, Chmn.

Phone: 404-407-1000	Fax: 770-857-2360
Toll-Free:	
Address: 191 Peachtree St., NE, Ste. 500, Atlanta, GA 30303 US	

GROWTH PLANS/SPECIAL FEATURES:

Cousins Properties, Inc., a real estate investment trust (REIT) located in Atlanta, Georgia, owns, develops and manages its own real estate portfolio. This company controls 22 operating office properties equaling 7.4 million square feet, 17 operating retail centers equaling 4.7 million square feet and three operating industrial properties equaling 2 million square feet. It also has 24 residential development projects, seven completed units in a for-sale multifamily project and 9,100 acres of undeveloped land. The firm's operations can be divided into three groups: The Development Group is responsible for identifying new development projects among all product types and managing all phases of the development and construction process through project stabilization or sale. This process includes not only construction management, but also leasing and tenant coordination for first generation office and retail space. It also includes marketing, selling and move-in coordination for multi-family projects. In addition, this group is responsible for all residential lot and tract development from project identification to lot and tract sales to end users. The Leasing and Property Management Group is responsible for the activities of all operating properties. These activities include property management, leasing and asset management of each property. The Client Services group provides advisory services, as well as office and retail leasing and property management, focusing primarily on acquisition, disposition, development and financing.

FINANCIALS: Sales and profits are in thousands of dollars—add 000 to get the full amount. 2010 Note: Financial information for 2010 was not available for all companies at press time.

2010 Sales: $228,506	2010 Profits: $-12,033	U.S. Stock Ticker: CUZ
2009 Sales: $214,544	2009 Profits: $29,547	Int'l Ticker: Int'l Exchange:
2008 Sales: $204,140	2008 Profits: $24,925	Employees: 320
2007 Sales: $165,357	2007 Profits: $34,578	Fiscal Year Ends: 12/31
2006 Sales: $162,288	2006 Profits: $217,441	Parent Company:

SALARIES/BENEFITS:

Pension Plan:	ESOP Stock Plan:	Profit Sharing:	Top Exec. Salary: $432,565	Bonus: $
Savings Plan: Y	Stock Purch. Plan:		Second Exec. Salary: $350,000	Bonus: $

OTHER THOUGHTS:

Apparent Women Officers or Directors: 1
Hot Spot for Advancement for Women/Minorities:

LOCATIONS: ("Y" = Yes)

West:	Southwest:	Midwest:	Southeast:	Northeast:	International:
Y	Y		Y	Y	

CRESCENT REAL ESTATE EQUITIES LP

www.crescent.com

Industry Group Code: 531120 Ranks within this company's industry group: Sales: Profits:

Properties:		Financial Services:		Construction/Development:		Investments:		Specialty Services:		Brokerage:	
Apartments:	Y	Mortgages:	Y	Commercial Construction:		REIT:	Y	Property Management:	Y	Commercial Sales:	
Malls/Shopping:		Title Insurance:		Residential Construction:	Y			Online Services:		Residential Sales:	
Offices:	Y	Property Insurance:		Land Development:	Y			Software/IT:		Specialty:	
Hotels/Motels:	Y			Support Services:				Consulting:			
Industrial/Warehouses:	Y			Design/Engineering:							
Other:											

TYPES OF BUSINESS:

Real Estate Investment Trust
Property Management
Land Development
Leasing
Offices
Hotels & Resorts
Residential Properties
Temperature-Controlled Logistics Facilities

BRANDS/DIVISIONS/AFFILIATES:

Barclays Capital
Goff Capital, Inc
Crescent Resort Development
Desert Mountain Development
Canyon Ranch
Fairmont Sonoma Mission Inn & Spa
Kelsey-Seybold Clinic
Westin Riverfront Resort & Spa (The)

CONTACTS: Note: Officers with more than one job title may be intentionally listed here more than once.

Jason Anderson, COO
Suzanne M. Stevens, CFO
Jean Suitt, Mgr.-Corp. Mktg.
Peggy Haynes, VP-Human Resources
C. Robert Baird, General Counsel/Sr. VP
Joseph Pitchford, Sr. VP-Dev.
Jean Suitt, Mgr.-Corp. Comm.
Jason Phinney, Controller/Sr. VP
Frank G. Staats, VP-Property Mgmt.
Eric Siegrist, VP-Leasing
Randall C. Kostroske, VP-Risk Mgmt.
Helen Rivero, VP-Joint Venture Mgmt.

Phone: 817-321-2100	Fax: 817-321-2000
Toll-Free:	
Address: 777 Main St., Ste. 2000, Fort Worth, TX 76102 US	

GROWTH PLANS/SPECIAL FEATURES:

Crescent Real Estate Equities LP, registered as a real estate investment trust (REIT), conducts property management, leasing and development activities. The company owns and operates 35 premier office buildings with over 17 million square feet of rentable space. The company's properties are concentrated in Dallas, Texas; Houston, Texas; Denver, Colorado; and Las Vegas, Nevada. The firm also holds five resort/spa properties in its portfolio including the Canyon Ranch in Tucson, Arizona; the Canyon Ranch in Lenox, Massachusetts; the Fairmont Sonoma Mission Inn & Spa in Sonoma, California; The Ritz-Carlton Hotel in Dallas; and The Westin Riverfront Resort & Spa at Beaver Creek Mountain in Avon, Colorado. Crescent also maintains interests in two high-end residential development corporations that include the Desert Mountain Development in Arizona and the Crescent Resort Development in both Colorado and California. The company is jointly owned by Barclays Capital & Goff Capital, Inc. In April 2010, the company opened a Kelsey-Seybold Clinic in Houston, Texas, marking the company's first venture into medical services development.

The company offers employees medical, dental and vision insurance; life and AD&D insurance; an employee assistance plan; short- and long-term disability coverage; adoption assistance; a 401(k) plan; health care and dependent care reimbursement; and scholarships for children of employees.

FINANCIALS: Sales and profits are in thousands of dollars—add 000 to get the full amount. 2010 Note: Financial information for 2010 was not available for all companies at press time.

2010 Sales: $	2010 Profits: $	U.S. Stock Ticker: Subsidiary
2009 Sales: $	2009 Profits: $	Int'l Ticker: Int'l Exchange:
2008 Sales: $	2008 Profits: $	Employees:
2007 Sales: $	2007 Profits: $	Fiscal Year Ends: 12/31
2006 Sales: $928,696	2006 Profits: $33,433	Parent Company: BARCLAYS CAPITAL

SALARIES/BENEFITS:

Pension Plan:	ESOP Stock Plan:	Profit Sharing:	Top Exec. Salary: $	Bonus: $
Savings Plan: Y	Stock Purch. Plan:		Second Exec. Salary: $	Bonus: $

OTHER THOUGHTS:

Apparent Women Officers or Directors: 6
Hot Spot for Advancement for Women/Minorities: Y

LOCATIONS: ("Y" = Yes)

West:	Southwest:	Midwest:	Southeast:	Northeast:	International:
Y	Y				

CREST NICHOLSON PLC

www.crestnicholson.com

Industry Group Code: 5311 Ranks within this company's industry group: Sales: Profits:

Properties:	Financial Services:	Construction/Development:		Investments:	Specialty Services:	Brokerage:
Apartments:	Mortgages:	Commercial Construction:		REIT:	Property Management:	Commercial Sales:
Malls/Shopping:	Title Insurance:	Residential Construction:	Y		Online Services:	Residential Sales:
Offices:	Property Insurance:	Land Development:	Y		Software/IT:	Specialty:
Hotels/Motels:		Support Services:			Consulting:	
Industrial/Warehouses:		Design/Engineering:				
Other:						

TYPES OF BUSINESS:

Real Estate Development
Environmental Communities
Mixed-Use Developments

BRANDS/DIVISIONS/AFFILIATES:

Castle Bidco Ltd
HBOS plc
West Coast Capital
Building Research Establishment
EcoHomes
Crest Nicholson Holdings Ltd

CONTACTS: *Note: Officers with more than one job title may be intentionally listed here more than once.*

Stephen Stone, CEO
D. Peter Darby, Dir.-Finance
Steve Evans, Dir.-Prod.
Kevin Maguire, Corp. Sec.
Alen Goldman, Chmn.

Phone: 44-193-258-0555	**Fax:** 44-870-336-3990
Toll-Free:	
Address: Crest House, Pyrcroft Rd., Chertsey, Surrey KT16 9GN UK	

GROWTH PLANS/SPECIAL FEATURES:

Crest Nicholson plc is a British real estate developer focusing on the construction of environmentally sound master-planned communities and mixed-use developments. The company's master planned communities feature distinctive residential areas and a good deal of open space, as well as amenities such as schools, shops and sports facilities. The company also focuses on building communities that do not rely on the use of a car, featuring designated cycling routes and integrated bus service that link outlying residential areas to the town center. Crest Nicholson actively supports the Building Research Establishment's EcoHomes rating scheme, which accesses the environmental performance of buildings in the areas of energy, transport, pollution, materials, water, land use, ecology, health and well being. In recent years, the firm became a subsidiary of Castle Bidco Ltd., a joint venture between HBOS plc and West Coast Capital. Shortly after, as part of a restructuring, Castle Bidco Ltd. was acquired by new holding company Crest Nicholson Holdings, Ltd., which is now the ultimate parent firm of Crest Nicholson plc. In March 2011, the firm received approval to build a new 132-unit housing division in West Sussex, U.K.

FINANCIALS: Sales and profits are in thousands of dollars—add 000 to get the full amount. 2010 Note: Financial information for 2010 was not available for all companies at press time.

2010 Sales: $	2010 Profits: $	**U.S. Stock Ticker:** Private
2009 Sales: $	2009 Profits: $	**Int'l Ticker:** Int'l Exchange:
2008 Sales: $	2008 Profits: $	Employees:
2007 Sales: $	2007 Profits: $	Fiscal Year Ends: 10/31
2006 Sales: $1,365,090	2006 Profits: $196,060	Parent Company: CREST NICHOLSON HOLDINGS LTD

SALARIES/BENEFITS:

Pension Plan:	ESOP Stock Plan:	Profit Sharing:	Top Exec. Salary: $	Bonus: $
Savings Plan:	Stock Purch. Plan:		Second Exec. Salary: $	Bonus: $

OTHER THOUGHTS:

Apparent Women Officers or Directors:
Hot Spot for Advancement for Women/Minorities:

LOCATIONS: ("Y" = Yes)

West:	Southwest:	Midwest:	Southeast:	Northeast:	International:
					Y

CRH PLC

www.crh.com

Industry Group Code: 327 Ranks within this company's industry group: Sales: 1   Profits: 1

Properties:	Financial Services:	Construction/Development:		Investments:	Specialty Services:	Brokerage:
Apartments:	Mortgages:	Commercial Construction:		REIT:	Property Management:	Commercial Sales:
Malls/Shopping:	Title Insurance:	Residential Construction:			Online Services:	Residential Sales:
Offices:	Property Insurance:	Land Development:			Software/IT:	Specialty:
Hotels/Motels:		Support Services:	Y		Consulting:	
Industrial/Warehouses:		Design/Engineering:				
Other:						

TYPES OF BUSINESS:

Building Materials
Aggregates
Asphalt
Cement & Concrete Products
Distribution
Glass Fabrications
Security Gates & Fencing
Insulation Products

BRANDS/DIVISIONS/AFFILIATES:

Oldcastle, Inc.
Ancon Building Products
My Home Industries Limited
Bauking

CONTACTS: *Note: Officers with more than one job title may be intentionally listed here more than once.*

Myles Lee, CEO
Albert Manifold, COO
Maeve Carlton, Dir.-Finance
Jack Golden, Dir.-Human Resources
Neil Colgan, Corp. Sec.
Philip Wheatley, Mgr.-Dev.
Elmear O'Flynn, Head-Investor Rel.
Rossa McCann, Group Treas.
Mark Towe, CEO-Old Castle, Inc.
Kieran McGowan, Chmn.

Phone: 353-1-404-1000	Fax: 353-1-404-1007
Toll-Free:	
Address: Belgard Castle, Clondalkin, Dublin, Ireland L2 22 UK	

GROWTH PLANS/SPECIAL FEATURES:

CRH plc is a building materials company focusing on three core businesses: primary materials, value-added building products and building materials distribution. With operations in 35 countries, CRH is divided into four regionally focused business segments: Europe materials; Europe products and distribution; Americas materials; and Americas products and distribution.   The European materials division, which operates in 20 countries, produces primary materials and value-added manufactured products, including cement, aggregates, ready-mixed concrete and pre-cast concrete products. The Europe products and distribution segment is comprised of four groups: concrete products, which manufactures products for architectural and structural use; clay products, which manufactures bricks and blocks; building products, which manufactures construction accessories, insulation, fences, security products, awnings and roller shutters; and distribution, comprised of 479 professional builders merchants locations in Austria, France, Germany, the Netherlands and Switzerland, and 241 DIY (do-it-yourself) stores in the Benelux, Germany, Spain and Portugal. The Americas materials segment, operating in 44 states in the U.S., produces aggregates, asphalt and ready-mixed concrete throughout the U.S. The Americas products and distribution segment, which is run by Oldcastle, Inc., has operations throughout the U.S. and Canada, with five divisions: architectural products, precast, glass, MMI (management and maintenance inspection) and distribution. The segment additionally produces clay tile products in Argentina and operates glass fabrication businesses in Argentina and Chile. The company owns stakes in several companies including My Home Industries Ltd; Jilin Yatai Group's cement operations; and Ancon Building Products. In November 2010, the company sold its Ivy Steel and Wire business in the U.S. to Insteel Industries, Inc. for $51 million. Also in November 2010, the firm acquired an additional 50% in its German distribution joint venture, Bauking, bringing its total ownership to 98%.

FINANCIALS: Sales and profits are in thousands of dollars—add 000 to get the full amount. 2010 Note: Financial information for 2010 was not available for all companies at press time.

2010 Sales: $24,505,400	2010 Profits: $626,440	**U.S. Stock Ticker: CRH**
2009 Sales: $23,288,500	2009 Profits: $801,620	**Int'l Ticker:** Int'l Exchange:
2008 Sales: $27,220,600	2008 Profits: $1,644,680	Employees: 7,000
2007 Sales: $27,357,400	2007 Profits: $1,874,040	Fiscal Year Ends: 12/31
2006 Sales: $25,450,820	2006 Profits: $2,176,520	Parent Company:

SALARIES/BENEFITS:

Pension Plan:	ESOP Stock Plan:	Profit Sharing:	Top Exec. Salary: $	Bonus: $
Savings Plan:	Stock Purch. Plan:		Second Exec. Salary: $	Bonus: $

OTHER THOUGHTS:

Apparent Women Officers or Directors: 3
Hot Spot for Advancement for Women/Minorities: Y

LOCATIONS: ("Y" = Yes)

West:	Southwest:	Midwest:	Southeast:	Northeast:	International:
Y	Y	Y	Y	Y	Y

CUSHMAN & WAKEFIELD INC
www.cushmanwakefield.com

Industry Group Code: 531210 Ranks within this company's industry group: Sales: Profits:

Properties:	Financial Services:	Construction/Development:	Investments:	Specialty Services:		Brokerage:	
Apartments:	Mortgages:	Commercial Construction:	REIT:	Property Management:	Y	Commercial Sales:	Y
Malls/Shopping:	Title Insurance:	Residential Construction:		Online Services:	Y	Residential Sales:	
Offices:	Property Insurance:	Land Development:		Software/IT:		Specialty:	
Hotels/Motels:		Support Services:		Consulting:			
Industrial/Warehouses:		Design/Engineering:					
Other:							

TYPES OF BUSINESS:
Real Estate Brokerage
Property Management
Real Estate Documentation Web Site
Advisory Services
Research Services
Property Valuation

BRANDS/DIVISIONS/AFFILIATES:
Cushman & Wakefield Sonnenblick Goldman
Cowen Commercial LLC
Ecological LLC
Laing+Simmons Commercial, Inc.
Cushman & Wakefield Residential
Cushman & Wakefield Hotels

CONTACTS: *Note: Officers with more than one job title may be intentionally listed here more than once.*
Glenn Rufrano, CEO
Glenn Rufrano, Pres.
Robert P. Rozek, CFO/Exec. VP
James M. Underhill, CEO-Americas
Sanjay Verma, CEO-Asia
John C. Santora, Pres./CEO-Client Solutions
Maxime Xantippe, Head-Capital Markets, Belgium
Carlo Sant'Albano, Chmn.
Paul Bacon, CEO-Europe

Phone: 212-841-7500	Fax: 212-841-5002
Toll-Free:	
Address: 1290 Avenue of the Americas, New York, NY 10104-6178 US	

GROWTH PLANS/SPECIAL FEATURES:
Cushman & Wakefield, Inc. (C&W), founded in 1917, is a global commercial real estate brokerage and services company with 231 offices in 58 countries. The company provides advisory services related to asset buying, selling, financing and leasing; and also provides strategic planning, portfolio analysis and space location services. The firm divides its service offerings into eight categories. Agency and brokerage services assist clients with marketing and positioning properties through landlord representation, lease advisory, offices, retail services, supply chain, tenant representation and industrial solutions. The Capital Markets Group offers real estate buying, financing and investment clients various advisory services, including agency execution, investment management and corporate disposition practice. Global consulting services comprise market access, office platform, retail consulting and supply chain solutions for business customers; and transaction and portfolio consulting for real estate customers. The Practice Groups division serves clients in selected industries, including energy and resources, healthcare, hospitality, law firms, life sciences, mission critical facilities and Japanese multinational corporations. The research division offers property research, market analysis and forecasting solutions. The firm's valuation and advisory services include appraisal, portfolio valuation, development strategy, occupancy strategy and property tax services for real estate. Cushman & Wakefield Sonnenblick Goldman, a subsidiary, provides real estate financial services, specializing in debt structuring and debt and equity placement. Finally, C&W's corporate occupier and investor services manage real estate portfolios through account, transaction and project management, lease administration and facilities management. Recent acquisitions of the company include Laing+Simmons Commercial, Inc.; Cushman & Wakefield Residential; and Cushman & Wakefield Hotels. In April 2010, the company announced the formation of two partnerships, including Ecological LLC and a partnership with Saffronart, a leading Indian auction house. In August 2010, the firm acquired Cowen Commercial LLC. In October 2010, C&W acquired the outstanding 35% of Cushman & Wakefield Sonnenblick Goldman.

FINANCIALS: Sales and profits are in thousands of dollars—add 000 to get the full amount. 2010 Note: Financial information for 2010 was not available for all companies at press time.

2010 Sales: $	2010 Profits: $	U.S. Stock Ticker: Subsidiary
2009 Sales: $	2009 Profits: $	Int'l Ticker: Int'l Exchange:
2008 Sales: $	2008 Profits: $	Employees:
2007 Sales: $	2007 Profits: $	Fiscal Year Ends: 12/31
2006 Sales: $	2006 Profits: $	Parent Company: IFIL GROUP

SALARIES/BENEFITS:

Pension Plan:	ESOP Stock Plan:	Profit Sharing:	Top Exec. Salary: $	Bonus: $
Savings Plan:	Stock Purch. Plan:		Second Exec. Salary: $	Bonus: $

OTHER THOUGHTS:
Apparent Women Officers or Directors:
Hot Spot for Advancement for Women/Minorities:

LOCATIONS: ("Y" = Yes)

West:	Southwest:	Midwest:	Southeast:	Northeast:	International:
Y	Y	Y	Y	Y	Y

CYRELA BRAZIL REALTY SA EMPREENDIMENTOS E PARTICIPACOES

www.brazilrealty.com.br

Industry Group Code: 2361 Ranks within this company's industry group: Sales: 4   Profits: 1

Properties:	Financial Services:	Construction/Development:		Investments:	Specialty Services:	Brokerage:
Apartments:	Mortgages:	Commercial Construction:		REIT:	Property Management:	Commercial Sales:
Malls/Shopping:	Title Insurance:	Residential Construction:	Y		Online Services:	Residential Sales:
Offices:	Property Insurance:	Land Development:			Software/IT:	Specialty:
Hotels/Motels:		Support Services:			Consulting:	
Industrial/Warehouses:		Design/Engineering:				
Other:						

TYPES OF BUSINESS:

Residential Construction

BRANDS/DIVISIONS/AFFILIATES:

SKR
LIDER
Irsa Cyrela
Cury Construtora e Incorporadora
Plano & Plano Construcoes e Participacoes
MAC Construtora e Incorporadora
Lucio Engenharia

CONTACTS: *Note: Officers with more than one job title may be intentionally listed here more than once.*

Elie Horn, CEO
Luis Largman, CFO
Gilson Fernando Hochman, Dir.-Sales
Claudio Carvalho de Lima, Corp. Legal Dept. Officer
Luis Largman, Investor Rel. Officer
Rogerio J. Zylbersztajn, VP
Ubirajara Spessotto de Camargo de Freitas, Gen. Exec. Officer-Cyrela Sao Paulo
Cassio Mantelmacher, Real Estate Dev. Officer
Elie Horn, Chmn.

Phone: 55-11-4502-3000	Fax: 55-11-4502-3140
Toll-Free:	
Address: 1455 Presidente Juscelino Kubitscheck Ave., 3rd Fl, Sao Paulo, SP 04543-011 Brazil	

GROWTH PLANS/SPECIAL FEATURES:

Cyrela Brazil Realty S.A. Empreendimentos e Participacoes is one of Brazil's largest developers of residential properties. In its 50 years of operation, the firm has built more than 30,000 units for 50,000 customers. The company operates in 16 states and 66 cities in Brazil; Cyrela Brazil also operates in Argentina and Uruguay. Middle class housing accounts for approximately 17% of the firm's sales; economic housing, 18%; high-end real estate, 22%; mid-high housing, 27%; and super economic housing, 16%. Cyrela Brazil also offers residential construction through seven primary joint ventures: MAC Construtora e Incorporadora and Lucio Engenharia, which both build middle and mid-high housing; Irsa Cyrela, which builds all economic levels of housing in Buenos Aires; SKR, a mid-high and luxury home builder in Sao Paulo; Cury Construtora e Incorporadora and Plano & Plano Construcoes e Participacoes, both of which build economic and super-economic housing; and LIDER, which builds all economic levels of housing in Minas Gerais and Distrito Federal, Brazil. The company owns 50% of each of these joint ventures with the exception of Plano & Plano (79% owned). The majority of Cyrela Brazil's sales are derived from Sao Paulo (47%) and Rio de Janeiro (13%).

FINANCIALS: Sales and profits are in thousands of dollars—add 000 to get the full amount. 2010 Note: Financial information for 2010 was not available for all companies at press time.

2010 Sales: $3,117,490	2010 Profits: $382,630	**U.S. Stock Ticker:**
2009 Sales: $2,606,020	2009 Profits: $464,940	**Int'l Ticker: CYRE3** Int'l Exchange: Sao Paulo-SAO
2008 Sales: $1,815,250	2008 Profits: $177,040	Employees:
2007 Sales: $	2007 Profits: $	Fiscal Year Ends: 12/31
2006 Sales: $	2006 Profits: $	Parent Company:

SALARIES/BENEFITS:

Pension Plan:	ESOP Stock Plan:	Profit Sharing:	Top Exec. Salary: $	Bonus: $
Savings Plan:	Stock Purch. Plan:		Second Exec. Salary: $	Bonus: $

OTHER THOUGHTS:

Apparent Women Officers or Directors:
Hot Spot for Advancement for Women/Minorities:

LOCATIONS: ("Y" = Yes)

West:	Southwest:	Midwest:	Southeast:	Northeast:	International:
					Y

DAELIM INDUSTRIAL CO LTD

www.daelim.co.kr

Industry Group Code: 237 Ranks within this company's industry group: Sales: 16   Profits: 14

Properties:	Financial Services:	Construction/Development:		Investments:	Specialty Services:	Brokerage:
Apartments:	Mortgages:	Commercial Construction:	Y	REIT:	Property Management:	Commercial Sales:
Malls/Shopping:	Title Insurance:	Residential Construction:	Y		Online Services:	Residential Sales:
Offices:	Property Insurance:	Land Development:	Y		Software/IT:	Specialty:
Hotels/Motels:		Support Services:			Consulting:	
Industrial/Warehouses:		Design/Engineering:	Y			
Other:						

TYPES OF BUSINESS:

Construction
Petrochemicals Distribution

BRANDS/DIVISIONS/AFFILIATES:

CONTACTS: *Note: Officers with more than one job title may be intentionally listed here more than once.*

Yong Koo Lee, CEO
Jong In Kim, Pres./CEO-Eng. & Construction Div.
Joo Hee Han, Pres./CEO-Petrochemical Div.
Yong Koo Lee, Chmn.

Phone: 82-2-2011-7114	Fax: 82-2-2011-8000
Toll-Free:	
Address: 146-12 Susong-Dong, Jongno-Gu, Seoul, 110-732 Korea	

GROWTH PLANS/SPECIAL FEATURES:

Daelim Industrial Co., Ltd. is a construction and engineering firm operating in two sectors: Engineering & Construction (E&C) and Petrochemicals. The E&C division consists of three operating segments: building & housing, civil works and plants. The building & housing division is engaged in the construction, redevelopment and remodeling of offices and apartments; cultural and assembly facilities; commercial buildings, such as markets and department stores; educational facilities, such as university buildings; medical and sports facilities, such as the King Abdul Aziz University Hospital; and others, such as the Seoul Court House Complex and the U.S. Embassy in Bangladesh. Some of the division's projects include constructing the main stadium for the 1988 Seoul Olympics, the Sejong Performing Arts Center and the main campus of the Arabian Gulf University in Bahrain, as well as work on the Meyongdong Cathedral, the Daelim Contemporary Art Museum and the main building of the Bank of Korea. The civil works division has three broad categories of projects. The first combines expressways, airports, airfields and bridges. The second encompasses railroads, subways and tunnels. The third is engaged in the construction of dams; irrigation infrastructure; and harbors and marine facilities. Some of the division's projects include constructing the King Fahad International Airport in Saudi Arabia, the Ayer Rajah Expressway in Singapore, the Hwacheon Dam and the Dintulu Deepwater Port in Malaysia. The plants segment constructs chemical plants, such as oil refineries and petrochemical processing facilities, including plants in India, the Middle East, Africa, the U.S., Southeast Asia and Korea; and nuclear and power plants, which Daelim has constructed both in Korea and abroad. The firm's Petrochemicals division engages in the production of refined oil products such as ethylene, propylene, polyethylene and polybutene, as well offering contract plant management services.

FINANCIALS: Sales and profits are in thousands of dollars—add 000 to get the full amount. 2010 Note: Financial information for 2010 was not available for all companies at press time.

		U.S. Stock Ticker:
2010 Sales: $7,086,410	2010 Profits: $325,610	Int'l Ticker: 000210 Int'l Exchange: Seoul-KRX
2009 Sales: $6,873,200	2009 Profits: $309,460	Employees:
2008 Sales: $6,942,560	2008 Profits: $95,850	Fiscal Year Ends: 12/31
2007 Sales: $3,641,270	2007 Profits: $339,070	Parent Company:
2006 Sales: $3,412,040	2006 Profits: $188,700	

SALARIES/BENEFITS:

Pension Plan:	ESOP Stock Plan:	Profit Sharing:	Top Exec. Salary: $	Bonus: $
Savings Plan:	Stock Purch. Plan:		Second Exec. Salary: $	Bonus: $

OTHER THOUGHTS:

Apparent Women Officers or Directors:
Hot Spot for Advancement for Women/Minorities:

LOCATIONS: ("Y" = Yes)

West:	Southwest:	Midwest:	Southeast:	Northeast:	International:
	Y				Y

DAYS INN WORLDWIDE INC

www.daysinn.com

Industry Group Code: 721110 Ranks within this company's industry group: Sales: Profits:

Properties:		Financial Services:	Construction/Development:	Investments:	Specialty Services:		Brokerage:
Apartments:		Mortgages:	Commercial Construction:	REIT:	Property Management:		Commercial Sales:
Malls/Shopping:		Title Insurance:	Residential Construction:		Online Services:	Y	Residential Sales:
Offices:		Property Insurance:	Land Development:		Software/IT:		Specialty:
Hotels/Motels:	Y		Support Services:		Consulting:		
Industrial/Warehouses:			Design/Engineering:				
Other:							

TYPES OF BUSINESS:
Motels

BRANDS/DIVISIONS/AFFILIATES:
Wyndham Worldwide
Days Hotel
Days Inn & Suites
Days Inn Business Place
TripRewards Card

CONTACTS: *Note: Officers with more than one job title may be intentionally listed here more than once.*
Clyde Guinn, Pres.
Eric A. Danziger, Pres./CEO-Wyndham Hotel Group
Stephen P. Holmes, Chmn./CEO-Wyndham Worldwide

Phone: 973-428-9700	Fax: 973-496-7658
Toll-Free: 800-329-7466	
Address: 1 Sylvan Way, Parsippany, NJ 07054 US	

GROWTH PLANS/SPECIAL FEATURES:

Days Inn Worldwide, Inc., a subsidiary of Wyndham Worldwide, operates one of the world's largest franchised hotel networks. Its operations span over 1,875 low-cost hotels with a total of 149,980 rooms that are located throughout the U.S. and around the world. Its worldwide locations include Argentina, Canada, China, Egypt, Hungary, India, Japan, Jordan, Korea, Mexico, Morocco, the Philippines, South Africa, the U.K. and Uruguay. The franchised hotels come in four varieties: Days Inn, a standard roadside motel; Days Hotel, a slightly larger property, usually in an urban center or near an airport, that features restaurants, lounges and meeting and banquet rooms in addition to guest rooms; Days Inn & Suites, similar to Days Inn but providing larger rooms, often for guests who plan to stay for a longer duration; and Days Inn Business Place, inns offering specialized services catering to the needs of business travelers. Some universal amenities that the chain offers its guests include free high-speed internet, complimentary breakfast, hairdryers, alarm clocks and complimentary copies of USA Today. The firm inspects and rates its properties three times per year to ensure its quality standards are met. At the company's web site customers can make reservations online and access special promotions and other information. Additionally, Wyndham's hotel group offers a best-available-rate guarantee, providing its online customers with the lowest rates available for all its hotel brands, including Days Inn. It also offers the Wyndham Rewards Card, which allows customers to earn points at any of Wyndham's hotel chains, a total of more than 7,000 hotels. The Mobile Days application allows guests to connect to the nearest Days Inn location using a mobile phone browser.

FINANCIALS: Sales and profits are in thousands of dollars—add 000 to get the full amount. 2010 Note: Financial information for 2010 was not available for all companies at press time.

2010 Sales: $	2010 Profits: $	**U.S. Stock Ticker: Subsidiary**
2009 Sales: $	2009 Profits: $	**Int'l Ticker:** Int'l Exchange:
2008 Sales: $	2008 Profits: $	Employees:
2007 Sales: $	2007 Profits: $	Fiscal Year Ends: 12/31
2006 Sales: $	2006 Profits: $	Parent Company: WYNDHAM WORLDWIDE

SALARIES/BENEFITS:

Pension Plan:	ESOP Stock Plan:	Profit Sharing:	Top Exec. Salary: $	Bonus: $
Savings Plan:	Stock Purch. Plan:		Second Exec. Salary: $	Bonus: $

OTHER THOUGHTS:
Apparent Women Officers or Directors:
Hot Spot for Advancement for Women/Minorities:

LOCATIONS: ("Y" = Yes)

West:	Southwest:	Midwest:	Southeast:	Northeast:	International:
Y	Y	Y	Y	Y	Y

DCT INDUSTRIAL TRUST INC

www.dctindustrial.com

Industry Group Code: 531120 Ranks within this company's industry group: Sales: 55   Profits: 55

Properties:	Financial Services:	Construction/Development:	Investments:	Specialty Services:	Brokerage:
Apartments:	Mortgages:	Commercial Construction:	REIT: Y	Property Management: Y	Commercial Sales:
Malls/Shopping:	Title Insurance:	Residential Construction:		Online Services:	Residential Sales:
Offices:	Property Insurance:	Land Development:		Software/IT:	Specialty:
Hotels/Motels:		Support Services:		Consulting:	
Industrial/Warehouses: Y		Design/Engineering:			
Other:					

TYPES OF BUSINESS:

Industrial Property Leasing
REIT
Property Management Services

BRANDS/DIVISIONS/AFFILIATES:

CONTACTS: *Note: Officers with more than one job title may be intentionally listed here more than once.*

Philip L. Hawkins, CEO
Philip L. Hawkins, Pres.
Stuart B. Brown, CFO
Heather S. Hagemann, Sec.
Matthew T. Murphy, Sr. VP-Finance/Treas.
Michael J. Ruen, Managing Dir.-East Region
Daryl H. Mechem, Managing Dir.-West Region
Teresa L. Corral, Sr. VP-Fund Mgmt. & Dispositions
Jeffrey F. Phelan, Managing Dir.-California/Pres., National Dev.
Thomas G. Wattles, Chmn.

Phone: 303-597-2400	Fax: 303-228-2201
Toll-Free:	
Address: 518 17th St., Ste. 800, Denver, CO 80202 US	

GROWTH PLANS/SPECIAL FEATURES:

DCT Industrial Trust, Inc., formerly Dividend Capital Trust Inc., is a real estate investment trust (REIT) specializing in the ownership, acquisition, development and management of bulk distribution and light industrial properties in the U.S. and Mexico. The company owns, manages, or has under development over 76.3 million square feet leased to approximately 810 corporate customers. DCT seeks to acquire properties that have convenient access to major transportation arteries; proximity to densely populated markets; and quality design standards that allow for easy reconfiguration of space. The firm concentrates its acquisitions into 25 key markets: Atlanta, Georgia; Nashville and Memphis, Tennessee; Baltimore, Maryland/Washington, D.C.; Orlando, Florida; Central Pennsylvania; New Jersey; Miami, Florida; Cincinnati and Columbus, Ohio; Indianapolis, Indiana; Chicago, Illinois; Charlotte, North Carolina; Louisville, Kentucky; Dallas, Houston and San Antonio, Texas; Minneapolis, Minnesota; Kansas City, Missouri; Northern California; Southern California; Phoenix, Arizona; Seattle, Washington; Denver, Colorado; and Mexico. DCT also manages and owns interests in properties through its institutional capital management program. In 2010 the company acquired a land parcel of 19.3 acres in Rancho Cucamonga, California for 4.7 million; a bulk distribution property in Southern California for $4.5 million; and three properties in Seattle, Chicago and Houston totaling 332,900 square feet for $20.2 million. In 2011, the firm acquired nine properties in Southern California for $79.5 million; two properties in Ridgefield, New Jersey and Chino, California totaling 519,990 square feet for $26 million; and a 100,000 square foot distribution building in Miami for $7.5 million.

The company offers employees medical and dental insurance; life and AD&D insurance; and a 401(k) plan.

FINANCIALS: Sales and profits are in thousands of dollars—add 000 to get the full amount. 2010 Note: Financial information for 2010 was not available for all companies at press time.

2010 Sales: $239,417	2010 Profits: $-37,830	U.S. Stock Ticker: DCT
2009 Sales: $242,665	2009 Profits: $-18,585	Int'l Ticker: Int'l Exchange:
2008 Sales: $245,982	2008 Profits: $9,486	Employees: 108
2007 Sales: $245,816	2007 Profits: $40,112	Fiscal Year Ends: 12/31
2006 Sales: $209,851	2006 Profits: $-158,043	Parent Company:

SALARIES/BENEFITS:

Pension Plan:	ESOP Stock Plan:	Profit Sharing:	Top Exec. Salary: $600,000	Bonus: $510,000
Savings Plan: Y	Stock Purch. Plan:		Second Exec. Salary: $265,000	Bonus: $205,000

OTHER THOUGHTS:

Apparent Women Officers or Directors: 2
Hot Spot for Advancement for Women/Minorities:

LOCATIONS: ("Y" = Yes)

West:	Southwest:	Midwest:	Southeast:	Northeast:	International:
Y	Y	Y	Y	Y	Y

DESARROLLADORA HOMEX SAB DE CV   www.homex.com.mx

Industry Group Code: 237 Ranks within this company's industry group: Sales: 28   Profits: 20

Properties:	Financial Services:	Construction/Development:		Investments:	Specialty Services:	Brokerage:
Apartments:	Mortgages:	Commercial Construction:		REIT:	Property Management:	Commercial Sales:
Malls/Shopping:	Title Insurance:	Residential Construction:	Y		Online Services:	Residential Sales:
Offices:	Property Insurance:	Land Development:			Software/IT:	Specialty:
Hotels/Motels:		Support Services:			Consulting:	
Industrial/Warehouses:		Design/Engineering:				
Other:						

TYPES OF BUSINESS:

Home Building
Construction

BRANDS/DIVISIONS/AFFILIATES:

Homex
Homex India Private Limited
HXMTD Las Villas de Mexico

CONTACTS: *Note: Officers with more than one job title may be intentionally listed here more than once.*

Gerardo de Nicolas Gutierrez, CEO
Carlos J. Monctezuma, CFO
Daniel Leal Diaz-Conti, VP-Sales & Mktg.
Monica Lafaire Cruz, VP-Human Resources & Social Responsibility
Ramon Lafarga Batiz, Chief Admin. Officer
Carlos J. Monctezuma, Dir.-Strategic Planning
Ramon Lafarga Batiz, Chief Acct. Officer
Ruben Izabal Gonzalez, VP-Construction
Alberto Menchaca Valenzuela, VP-Mexico Div.
Fernando Ventura Pena, VP-Tourism Div.
Eustaquio Tomas De Nicolas Gutierrez, Chmn.
Alberto Urquiza Quiroz, VP-Int'l Div.

Phone: 52-667-758-5800	Fax:
Toll-Free: 800-224-6639	

Address: Boulevard Alfonso Zaragoza M. 2204 Norte, Sinaloa, 80200 Mexico

GROWTH PLANS/SPECIAL FEATURES:

Desarrolladora Homex SAB de CV (Homex) is a homebuilding and construction company based in Culiacan, Mexico. The firm focuses primarily on building entry-level and middle-income housing throughout Mexico. Homex has operations in 34 cities in 21 states, including Culiacan, Mexico City, Puebla, Guadalajara, Acapulco, Nuevo Laredo, Juarez, Tijuana, Tuxtla, Coahuila, Queretaro, Cancun, Cuernavaca, Veracruz and Puerto Vallarta. Most of the firm's largest entry-level housing developments are located in Guadalajara, Monterrey, Tijuana, Puebla, and Nuevo Laredo. Entry-level developments range in size from 500 to 20,000 homes, which typically include one to three bedrooms and one bathroom and are sold at an average price of roughly $30,000. In 2010, sales of entry-level housing accounted for approximately 83% of the company's revenues. Its mid-level developments range in size from 400 to 2,000 homes, which include two to three bedrooms and two bathrooms and average roughly $76,000. It closed 48,442 units in 2010 (95% of which were entry-level homes), a slight increase from the previous year, when it closed a total of 46,631 homes. The firm's recently established vacation homes division, HXMTD Las Villas de Mexico, builds resort-style communities, featuring pools, fitness centers and golf courses, that are targeted at foreigners in the major tourism markets of Los Cabos, Puerto Vallarta and Cancun. In addition to its Mexican operations, the firm has expanded into the Brazilian market, with a presence in three cities in Brazil. In March 2010, the company's Indian subsidiary, Homex India Private Limited established a joint venture company with Puravankara Projects Limited to develop affordable entry-level housing in and around Chennai, in South India.

FINANCIALS: Sales and profits are in thousands of dollars—add 000 to get the full amount. 2010 Note: Financial information for 2010 was not available for all companies at press time.

2010 Sales: $1,696,580	2010 Profits: $132,730	**U.S. Stock Ticker: HXM**
2009 Sales: $1,654,710	2009 Profits: $155,880	Int'l Ticker: Int'l Exchange:
2008 Sales: $1,368,576	2008 Profits: $117,543	Employees: 23,085
2007 Sales: $1,622,300	2007 Profits: $223,300	Fiscal Year Ends: 12/31
2006 Sales: $1,344,000	2006 Profits: $139,100	Parent Company:

SALARIES/BENEFITS:

Pension Plan:	ESOP Stock Plan:	Profit Sharing:	Top Exec. Salary: $	Bonus: $
Savings Plan:	Stock Purch. Plan:		Second Exec. Salary: $	Bonus: $

OTHER THOUGHTS:

Apparent Women Officers or Directors: 2
Hot Spot for Advancement for Women/Minorities:

LOCATIONS: ("Y" = Yes)

West:	Southwest:	Midwest:	Southeast:	Northeast:	International:
					Y

DEVELOPERS DIVERSIFIED REALTY CORP   www.ddrc.com

Industry Group Code: 531110 Ranks within this company's industry group: Sales: 3   Profits: 17

Properties:		Financial Services:	Construction/Development:		Investments:		Specialty Services:		Brokerage:
Apartments:		Mortgages:	Commercial Construction:	Y	REIT:	Y	Property Management:	Y	Commercial Sales:
Malls/Shopping:	Y	Title Insurance:	Residential Construction:				Online Services:		Residential Sales:
Offices:	Y	Property Insurance:	Land Development:	Y			Software/IT:		Specialty:
Hotels/Motels:			Support Services:				Consulting:		
Industrial/Warehouses:			Design/Engineering:						
Other:									

TYPES OF BUSINESS:

Real Estate Investment Trust
Shopping Centers
Business Centers
Property Management
Commercial Construction & Land Development

BRANDS/DIVISIONS/AFFILIATES:

CONTACTS: *Note: Officers with more than one job title may be intentionally listed here more than once.*

Daniel B. Hurwitz, CEO
Daniel B. Hurwitz, Pres.
David J. Oakes, CFO/Sr. Exec. VP
Nan Zieleniec, Sr. VP-Human Resources
Kevin Moss, Sr. VP-IT
John S. Kokinchak, Chief Admin. Officer/Sr. Exec. VP
David E. Weiss, General Counsel/Exec. VP
Marc Feldman, Sr. VP-New Bus. Dev.
Christa A. Vesy, Chief Acct. Officer/Sr. VP
Francine Glandt, Sr. VP-Capital Markets/Treas.
Timothy J. Lordan, Sr. VP-Funds Mgmt.
Robin R. Walker-Gibbons, Exec. VP-Leasing
Kenneth L. Stern, Sr. VP-Peripheral Dev.
Scott A. Wolstein, Chmn.
Richard E. Brown, Exec. VP-Int'l

Phone: 216-755-5500	Fax: 216-755-1500
Toll-Free: 877-225-5337	
Address: 3300 Enterprise Pkwy., Beachwood, OH 44122 US	

GROWTH PLANS/SPECIAL FEATURES:

Developers Diversified Realty Corp. (DDR) is a self-administered and self-managed real estate investment trust (REIT).   The company is in the business of acquiring, developing, owning, leasing and managing shopping centers and business centers. The firm currently owns and manages approximately 522 shopping centers and six business centers (over 91.5 million square feet) in 41 states, Puerto Rico and Brazil. The company has 233 shopping centers that are owned through joint ventures. DDR also owns over 1,800 acres of undeveloped land. The company focuses on earning rent payments in properties already owned; and the acquisition, development, redevelopment, renovation and expansion of income-producing real estate properties (primarily shopping centers). DDR's primary interest is in open-air shopping centers and lifestyle centers between 250,000 and 1 million square feet in size. The firm prefers properties with strong national tenant anchor stores such as Wal-Mart, Circuit City, PetSmart and Lowe's Home Improvement. The Otto family is DDR's biggest individual shareholder. In the last three years, DDR has sold 137 shopping centers, including 49 properties owned through joint ventures.

FINANCIALS: Sales and profits are in thousands of dollars—add 000 to get the full amount. 2010 Note: Financial information for 2010 was not available for all companies at press time.

2010 Sales: $803,069	2010 Profits: $-209,358	**U.S. Stock Ticker: DDR**	
2009 Sales: $797,399	2009 Profits: $-356,593	**Int'l Ticker:**	Int'l Exchange:
2008 Sales: $825,068	2008 Profits: $-71,930	Employees: 682	
2007 Sales: $885,025	2007 Profits: $186,237	Fiscal Year Ends: 12/31	
2006 Sales: $773,351	2006 Profits: $253,264	Parent Company:	

SALARIES/BENEFITS:

Pension Plan:	ESOP Stock Plan:	Profit Sharing:	Top Exec. Salary: $875,000	Bonus: $4,963,522
Savings Plan:	Stock Purch. Plan:		Second Exec. Salary: $616,000	Bonus: $3,146,240

OTHER THOUGHTS:

Apparent Women Officers or Directors: 2
Hot Spot for Advancement for Women/Minorities:

LOCATIONS: ("Y" = Yes)

West:	Southwest:	Midwest:	Southeast:	Northeast:	International:
Y	Y	Y	Y	Y	Y

DIAMOND RESORTS HOLDINGS LLC   www.diamondresorts.com

Industry Group Code: 561599 Ranks within this company's industry group: Sales: Profits:

Properties:		Financial Services:	Construction/Development:	Investments:	Specialty Services:		Brokerage:
Apartments:		Mortgages:	Commercial Construction:	REIT:	Property Management:		Commercial Sales:
Malls/Shopping:		Title Insurance:	Residential Construction:		Online Services:	Y	Residential Sales:
Offices:		Property Insurance:	Land Development:		Software/IT:		Specialty:
Hotels/Motels:	Y		Support Services:		Consulting:		
Industrial/Warehouses:			Design/Engineering:				
Other:							

TYPES OF BUSINESS:
Time-Share Resorts

BRANDS/DIVISIONS/AFFILIATES:
Diamond Resorts International
THE Club
Tempus Resorts International, Ltd.
Diamond Resorts Corporation

CONTACTS: *Note: Officers with more than one job title may be intentionally listed here more than once.*
Stephen J. Cloobeck, CEO
David Palmer, Pres.
David Palmer, CFO
Michael A. Flaskey, Sr. VP-Mktg. & Sales, North America
Sarah Hulme, Sr. VP-Global Club Oper.
Frank T. Goeckel, Sr. VP-Bus. Dev.
Derek Kanoa, VP-Sales & Mktg., Western Bus. Unit
Rhett Bolling, VP-Sales & Mktg., Eastern Bus. Unit
Dennis Nau, Sr. VP-Resort Oper.
Stephen J. Cloobeck, Chmn.

Phone: 702-804-8600	Fax: 702-304-7066
Toll-Free:	
Address: 10600 W. Charleston Blvd., Las Vegas, NV 89135 US	

GROWTH PLANS/SPECIAL FEATURES:
Diamond Resorts Holdings, LLC, operating through Diamond Resorts Corporation (DRC), is a vacation ownership firm, offering 69 Diamond Resorts International-branded resorts and 127 affiliated resorts in 28 countries. Affiliated resorts are resorts that the company maintains contractual arrangements with to use a certain number of vacation units in exchange for similar usage arrangements at its managed resorts. DRC operates THE Club, a points-based vacation system with over 380,000 member-owners. Points, which are renewed annually, may be spent as currency on resort vacations, cruises, airline tickets and other travel purchases. Members may search for a resort by an activity or interest they wish to pursue, browsing through categories such as History & Heritage; Outdoor; Ski & Snow; Spa; Beaches; Family Resorts; and Golf Resorts. Alternatively, resorts may be located by geographical area; the firm currently has resorts in the U.S., the Caribbean, Mexico, Canada and 10 countries in Europe: Austria, England, France, Germany, Ireland, Italy, Malta, Portugal, Scotland and Spain. Amenities vary by resort, but may include a full bath, kitchen, dishwasher, washer/dryer, satellite TV, fireplace, deck, pool, sauna, spa, beauty salon, fitness center, movie rentals, high-speed Internet, childcare, 24-hour reception and safe deposit boxes. Besides resort reservations, DRC directly offers flight, cruise and car rental reservations (provided by various third-parties such as British Airways, Hertz and Royal Caribbean) on its DiamondResorts.com site, as well as offering hotel reservations through its Travel.ian.com site. In November 2010, the firm agreed to acquire a majority of the assets of Tempus Resorts International, Ltd.

FINANCIALS: Sales and profits are in thousands of dollars—add 000 to get the full amount. 2010 Note: Financial information for 2010 was not available for all companies at press time.

2010 Sales: $	2010 Profits: $	U.S. Stock Ticker: Private	
2009 Sales: $	2009 Profits: $	Int'l Ticker: Int'l Exchange:	
2008 Sales: $	2008 Profits: $	Employees:	
2007 Sales: $	2007 Profits: $	Fiscal Year Ends: 9/30	
2006 Sales: $	2006 Profits: $	Parent Company:	

SALARIES/BENEFITS:

Pension Plan:	ESOP Stock Plan:	Profit Sharing:	Top Exec. Salary: $	Bonus: $
Savings Plan:	Stock Purch. Plan:		Second Exec. Salary: $	Bonus: $

OTHER THOUGHTS:
Apparent Women Officers or Directors:
Hot Spot for Advancement for Women/Minorities:

LOCATIONS: ("Y" = Yes)

West:	Southwest:	Midwest:	Southeast:	Northeast:	International:
Y	Y	Y	Y	Y	Y

DITECH.COM

www.ditech.com

Industry Group Code: 522310E Ranks within this company's industry group: Sales: Profits:

Properties:	Financial Services:		Construction/Development:	Investments:	Specialty Services:	Brokerage:
Apartments:	Mortgages:	Y	Commercial Construction:	REIT:	Property Management:	Commercial Sales:
Malls/Shopping:	Title Insurance:		Residential Construction:		Online Services:	Residential Sales:
Offices:	Property Insurance:		Land Development:		Software/IT:	Specialty:
Hotels/Motels:			Support Services:		Consulting:	
Industrial/Warehouses:			Design/Engineering:			
Other:						

TYPES OF BUSINESS:

Mortgage Origination
Direct Lending
Online Services

BRANDS/DIVISIONS/AFFILIATES:

GMAC Mortgage Corporation
Real Life Plan
Ditech Equity Rewards MasterCard

CONTACTS:
Note: Officers with more than one job title may be intentionally listed here more than once.
Richard D. Powers, Gen. Mgr./Sr. VP
Phil Armstrong, VP-Mktg.

Phone:	Fax:
Toll-Free: 800-348-3243	
Address: 1100 Virginia Dr., Ft. Washington, PA 19034 US	

GROWTH PLANS/SPECIAL FEATURES:

Ditech.com, a business unit of GMAC Mortgage Corporation, is a leader in the direct lending industry. As a direct lender, customers are offered mortgages without the intermediary of a broker. The company offers a variety of products, including first mortgages, fixed-rate second mortgages, variable equity lines of credit and no-closing-cost-option equity seconds. Its online capabilities allow customers to communicate with loan agents from home, work or on the road and provide 24-hour-a-day access to information, loan calculator tools and customer service. Customers are asked to take part in a five-step process which involves determining the customer's purchasing power; the customer's goals and situation; and choosing a loan appropriate to the home they wish to purchase. The firm has found that its flat-fee program, which opened in 1995, is a popular solution for customers wary of hidden fees when refinancing. Within the first 18 months of launching the program, ditech.com had signed up over 30,000 customers for the $395 flat-fee program. The firm offers Real Life Plan, a service which combines a mortgage or refinance with a home equity line of credit, and the Ditech Equity Rewards MasterCard, to help pay down the loan principal with use.

FINANCIALS:
Sales and profits are in thousands of dollars—add 000 to get the full amount. 2010 Note: Financial information for 2010 was not available for all companies at press time.

2010 Sales: $	2010 Profits: $	**U.S. Stock Ticker: Subsidiary**
2009 Sales: $	2009 Profits: $	**Int'l Ticker:** Int'l Exchange:
2008 Sales: $	2008 Profits: $	Employees:
2007 Sales: $	2007 Profits: $	Fiscal Year Ends: 12/31
2006 Sales: $	2006 Profits: $	Parent Company: GMAC INC

SALARIES/BENEFITS:

Pension Plan:	ESOP Stock Plan:	Profit Sharing:	Top Exec. Salary: $	Bonus: $
Savings Plan:	Stock Purch. Plan:		Second Exec. Salary: $	Bonus: $

OTHER THOUGHTS:

Apparent Women Officers or Directors:
Hot Spot for Advancement for Women/Minorities:

LOCATIONS: ("Y" = Yes)

West:	Southwest:	Midwest:	Southeast:	Northeast:	International:
Y	Y				

DIVIDEND CAPITAL GROUP LLC

www.dividendcapital.com

Industry Group Code: 531120 Ranks within this company's industry group: Sales: Profits:

Properties:	Financial Services:	Construction/Development:	Investments:	Specialty Services:	Brokerage:
Apartments:	Mortgages:	Commercial Construction:	REIT: Y	Property Management:	Commercial Sales:
Malls/Shopping:	Title Insurance:	Residential Construction:		Online Services:	Residential Sales:
Offices:	Property Insurance:	Land Development:		Software/IT:	Specialty:
Hotels/Motels:		Support Services:		Consulting:	
Industrial/Warehouses: Y		Design/Engineering:			
Other:					

TYPES OF BUSINESS:

Real Estate Investment
REIT Holding
Mutual Funds
Investment Advisory Services

BRANDS/DIVISIONS/AFFILIATES:

DCT Industrial Trust, Inc.
Dividend Capital Total Realty Trust
Dividend Capital Investments
DCA Total Return Fund
DCW Total Return Fund
Industrial Income Trust
Dividend Capital Securities

CONTACTS: *Note: Officers with more than one job title may be intentionally listed here more than once.*

Eric Paul, Contact-Media
Greg Moran, Chief Investment Officer
Guy Arnold, Pres., Dividend Capital Total Realty Trust
Lainie Minnick, VP-Finance, Dividend Capital Total Realty Trust
Kris Jaenicke, Sr. VP

Phone: 303-228-2200	Fax: 303-228-0128
Toll-Free: 866-324-7348	
Address: 518 17th St., Fl. 17, Denver, CO 80202 US	

GROWTH PLANS/SPECIAL FEATURES:

Dividend Capital Group LLC (DCG) is a real estate investment holding company. Its subsidiaries are DCT Industrial Trust, Inc. (DCT); Dividend Capital Total Realty Trust (TRT); Dividend Capital Investments (DCI); and Industrial Income Trust (IIT). DCT is a public REIT that owns, operates and develops primarily bulk distribution warehouses and light industrial properties in the U.S. and Mexico. DCT invests in industrial properties through active leasing and management, which allows the company to more easily control operating expenses and maintain its properties; and an ongoing strategy of recycling capital by disposing of underperforming assets. TRT is a private REIT with a diverse portfolio of 111 properties 924.3 million square feet) in 35 markets, offering a sampling of multiple real estate sectors. DCI is the registered investment advisor for DCA Total Return Fund, a closed-end management investment company that invests in the financial, healthcare, materials, energy, information technology, industrial, consumer staples, telecommunications services and real estate sectors; and DCW Total Return Fund (formerly Dividend Capital Global Realty Exposure Fund), a non- closed-end management investment company investing in similar segments, with roughly 33.99% of its net assets invested in real estate. IIT is a private REIT with investments in industrial and distribution properties, which it leases to corporate customers. IIT invests in industrial properties principally because of industrial real estate's typically lower rent volatility; the generally lower operating costs; and larger diversity of tenants, which reduces risk of cash flow instability. Securities for DCG are offered through Dividend Capital Securities LLC. Recently, DCG acquired properties in Denver, Colorado; Perris, California; Baltimore, Maryland; and Seattle, Washington.

DCG offers its employees medical, dental and vision coverage; life, AD&D and short- and long-term disability insurance; parking and transportation plans; a health savings account; and a 401(k) plan.

FINANCIALS: Sales and profits are in thousands of dollars—add 000 to get the full amount. 2010 Note: Financial information for 2010 was not available for all companies at press time.

2010 Sales: $	2010 Profits: $	**U.S. Stock Ticker: Private**
2009 Sales: $	2009 Profits: $	**Int'l Ticker:** Int'l Exchange:
2008 Sales: $	2008 Profits: $	Employees:
2007 Sales: $	2007 Profits: $	Fiscal Year Ends: 12/31
2006 Sales: $	2006 Profits: $	Parent Company:

SALARIES/BENEFITS:

Pension Plan:	ESOP Stock Plan:	Profit Sharing:	Top Exec. Salary: $	Bonus: $
Savings Plan: Y	Stock Purch. Plan:		Second Exec. Salary: $	Bonus: $

OTHER THOUGHTS:

Apparent Women Officers or Directors:
Hot Spot for Advancement for Women/Minorities:

LOCATIONS: ("Y" = Yes)

West:	Southwest:	Midwest:	Southeast:	Northeast:	International:
Y					

DLF LIMITED

www.dlf.in

Industry Group Code: 5311 Ranks within this company's industry group: Sales: 15   Profits: 17

Properties:		Financial Services:		Construction/Development:		Investments:		Specialty Services:		Brokerage:	
Apartments:		Mortgages:		Commercial Construction:	Y	REIT:		Property Management:	Y	Commercial Sales:	
Malls/Shopping:	Y	Title Insurance:		Residential Construction:	Y			Online Services:		Residential Sales:	
Offices:	Y	Property Insurance:		Land Development:				Software/IT:		Specialty:	
Hotels/Motels:	Y			Support Services:				Consulting:			
Industrial/Warehouses:				Design/Engineering:							
Other:											

TYPES OF BUSINESS:

Real Estate Development
Commercial Real Estate Management & Leasing
Hotels
Luxury Resorts

BRANDS/DIVISIONS/AFFILIATES:

Aman Resorts

CONTACTS: Note: Officers with more than one job title may be intentionally listed here more than once.

T.C. Goyal, Managing Dir.
Kameshwar Swarup, Exec. Dir.-Legal
Subhash C. Setia, Corp. Sec./Compliance Officer
Rajiv Singh, Vice Chmn.
Kushal P. Singh, Chmn.

Phone: 91-11-4210-2030	Fax:
Toll-Free:	
Address: DLF Centre Sansad Marg, New Delhi, 110001 India	

GROWTH PLANS/SPECIAL FEATURES:

DLF Limited is an India-based real estate development and construction company. The firm has over 238 million square feet (msf) of completed development, with another 399 msf of planned projects and 56 msf of projects under construction, in cities across India. DLF is primarily engaged in the development of residential, commercial and retail properties. It is divided into two business units: development and annuity. The development unit develops mid-income, luxury and super luxury residential communities. Products offered include condominiums, duplexes, row houses and apartments. The annuity business is engaged in the rental of office and retail properties. Through subsidiary Aman Resorts the firm participates in the hospitality business, developing and managing hotels internationally, and maintains an alliance with Hilton Group for Indian hotel development and management. The firm's business model allows it to earn revenues from both development activities and the leasing of completed properties. The company hopes to continue to grow its business through projects in India's special economic zones (SEZs), which are specially legislated areas designed to encourage foreign investment and exports from the country. DLF is also one of the largest owners of wind power plants in India, managing plants with a combined installed capacity of 228.7 megawatts. The firm's clients have included GE, IBM, Microsoft, Canon, Citibank, Vertex, Hewitt, Fidelity Investments, WNS, Bank of America, Cognizant, Infosys, CSC, Symantec and Sapient. In February 2010, DLF began construction on its largest township project outside of Guragon, the Panchkula Valley project, which will include over 1,200 apartments, a community center, nursery, schools, shopping centers, offices, a hospital and a rainwater collection system. In January 2010, the firm exited a joint venture with Prudential Financial, Inc.

FINANCIALS: Sales and profits are in thousands of dollars—add 000 to get the full amount. 2010 Note: Financial information for 2010 was not available for all companies at press time.

2010 Sales: $1,751,680	2010 Profits: $383,730	**U.S. Stock Ticker:**
2009 Sales: $2,241,520	2009 Profits: $960,220	**Int'l Ticker: 532868** Int'l Exchange: Bombay-BSE
2008 Sales: $3,155,320	2008 Profits: $1,678,670	Employees: 3,542
2007 Sales: $1,085,870	2007 Profits: $415,510	Fiscal Year Ends: 3/31
2006 Sales: $	2006 Profits: $	Parent Company:

SALARIES/BENEFITS:

Pension Plan:	ESOP Stock Plan:	Profit Sharing:	Top Exec. Salary: $	Bonus: $
Savings Plan:	Stock Purch. Plan:		Second Exec. Salary: $	Bonus: $

OTHER THOUGHTS:

Apparent Women Officers or Directors:
Hot Spot for Advancement for Women/Minorities:

LOCATIONS: ("Y" = Yes)

West:	Southwest:	Midwest:	Southeast:	Northeast:	International:
					Y

DOMINION HOMES INC

www.dominionhomes.com

Industry Group Code: 2361 Ranks within this company's industry group: Sales: Profits:

Properties:	Financial Services:		Construction/Development:		Investments:	Specialty Services:	Brokerage:	
Apartments:	Mortgages:	Y	Commercial Construction:		REIT:	Property Management:	Commercial Sales:	
Malls/Shopping:	Title Insurance:		Residential Construction:	Y		Online Services:	Residential Sales:	Y
Offices:	Property Insurance:		Land Development:	Y		Software/IT:	Specialty:	
Hotels/Motels:			Support Services:			Consulting:		
Industrial/Warehouses:			Design/Engineering:					
Other:								

TYPES OF BUSINESS:

Residential Construction
Financial Services
Residential Sales

BRANDS/DIVISIONS/AFFILIATES:

Founders Collection
Metropolitan Collection
Celebration Collection
Grand Reserve Collection
Tradition Collection
Angelo Gordon & Co LP
Silver Point Capital LP
BRC Properties Inc

CONTACTS: *Note: Officers with more than one job title may be intentionally listed here more than once.*

William G. Cornely, CEO
William G. Cornely, Pres.
Michael A. Archer, Sr. VP-Sales Oper.
Douglas G. Borror, Chmn.

Phone: 614-356-5000	Fax: 614-356-6010
Toll-Free:	
Address: 4900 Tuttle Crossing Blvd., Dublin, OH 43016 US	

GROWTH PLANS/SPECIAL FEATURES:

Dominion Homes, Inc. is a leading builder of high-quality homes in central Ohio, as well as in Louisville and Lexington, Kentucky. Dominion targets entry-level and move-up home buyers, offering a variety of homes differentiated by price, size, standard features and available options. These homes range in price from approximately $90,000 to over $300,000 and in size from approximately 1,000 to 3,500 square feet. The company currently offers six distinct series of homes: the Founders Collection, a neo-traditional housing concept targeting entry-level home buyers; the Haven Collection, moderately priced homes featuring single family ranch, multi-level and two-story layouts. The Metropolitan Collection, targeting the young, single home buyer; the Celebration Collection, targeting entry-level and first-time move-up home buyers; the Tradition Collection with styles ranging from contemporary to traditional designs, targeting move-up home buyers; and the Grand Reserve Collection, which targets active adults who want luxury patio homes built in private communities with convenient amenities like pools and clubhouses. Dominion Homes is owned by investors Angelo Gordon & Co., L.P.; Silver Point Capital L.P.; and BRC Properties, Inc.

Dominion offers its employees benefits including life, accidental death, medical, dental and vision insurance; flexible spending accounts; a 401(k); training/development programs; tuition assistance; and home purchase discounts.

FINANCIALS: Sales and profits are in thousands of dollars—add 000 to get the full amount. 2010 Note: Financial information for 2010 was not available for all companies at press time.

2010 Sales: $	2010 Profits: $	U.S. Stock Ticker: Private
2009 Sales: $	2009 Profits: $	Int'l Ticker: Int'l Exchange:
2008 Sales: $	2008 Profits: $	Employees:
2007 Sales: $147,991	2007 Profits: $-82,159	Fiscal Year Ends: 12/31
2006 Sales: $256,760	2006 Profits: $-34,009	Parent Company:

SALARIES/BENEFITS:

Pension Plan:	ESOP Stock Plan:	Profit Sharing:	Top Exec. Salary: $	Bonus: $
Savings Plan: Y	Stock Purch. Plan:		Second Exec. Salary: $	Bonus: $

OTHER THOUGHTS:

Apparent Women Officers or Directors: 2
Hot Spot for Advancement for Women/Minorities:

LOCATIONS: ("Y" = Yes)

West:	Southwest:	Midwest:	Southeast:	Northeast:	International:
		Y			

DOOSAN HEAVY INDUSTRY & CONSTRUCTION CO

www.doosanheavy.com
Industry Group Code: 237 Ranks within this company's industry group: Sales: 8 Profits: 29

Properties:	Financial Services:	Construction/Development:		Investments:	Specialty Services:	Brokerage:
Apartments:	Mortgages:	Commercial Construction:	Y	REIT:	Property Management:	Commercial Sales:
Malls/Shopping:	Title Insurance:	Residential Construction:	Y		Online Services:	Residential Sales:
Offices:	Property Insurance:	Land Development:	Y		Software/IT:	Specialty:
Hotels/Motels:		Support Services:	Y		Consulting:	
Industrial/Warehouses:		Design/Engineering:	Y			
Other:						

TYPES OF BUSINESS:

Construction
Power Plant Construction
Desalination Plant Construction
Civil Works Projects
Architecture Works Projects
Casting & Forging
Material Handling Systems

BRANDS/DIVISIONS/AFFILIATES:

Doosan Power Systems
Skoda Power
Doosan Babcock Energy
DPS Europe
DPS Americas
Doosan Infracore Co., Ltd.

CONTACTS: *Note: Officers with more than one job title may be intentionally listed here more than once.*

Geewon Park, CEO
Key-sun Han, COO
Geewon Park, Pres.
Hyoung-hee Choi, CFO/Exec. VP
Ji Taik Chung, Vice Chmn.
Yong-Sung Park, Chmn.

Phone: 82-55-278-6114	**Fax:** 82-55-264-5551
Toll-Free:	
Address: 555 Gwigok-dong, Gyeongsangnam-do, Changwon, 641-792 Korea	

GROWTH PLANS/SPECIAL FEATURES:

Doosan Heavy Industry & Construction Co., established in 1962, has built over 300 thermal, coal-fired, nuclear and combined cycle power plants. It is also developing water treatment plants, wind power systems, fuel cells and other environmentally friendly energy sources. Doosan built the Shuaibah Desalination Plant Phase 3 in Saudi Arabia, one of the world's largest desalination facilities, with a daily capacity of 880,000 tons. The company also built one of the world's first hybrid desalination plants, located in Fujairah, in the United Arab Emirates. The plant combines two desalination technologies: Multi-Stage Flash (MSF), which desalinates through a repeated cycle of evaporation and condensation; and Reverse Osmosis (RO), which forces the water across a filtering membrane. The firm is one of the few with proprietary technologies in all three areas of desalination: MSF, RO and MED (Multi-Effect Distillation, where the heat from boiling one chamber is used to heat another). In addition to constructing plants, Doosan produces material handling equipment; supplies forging and casting products; and constructs highways, ports, high-speed railroads, tunnels, subways, apartments and power transmission lines. Its casting and forging products include rotor shafts and turbine casings for nuclear and thermal power plants; shells for reactors in nuclear power plants; crank shafts, marine shafts and stern frame casting for ships; components for steel mills, such as mill housing and rolls; die steel, used in the manufacture of plastic products; tool steel, used to manufacture machine tools; and shells for petrochemical applications. Material handling equipment includes container handling cranes and bulk material handling systems. In February 2010, the firm established Doosan Power Systems, a holding company, to manage its U.S. and European companies, including Doosan Babcock (U.K.); Skoda Power (Czech Republic); DPS Europe; and DPS Americas. In December 2010, the company acquired 44.83% of Doosan Infracore Co., Ltd.

FINANCIALS: Sales and profits are in thousands of dollars—add 000 to get the full amount. 2010 Note: Financial information for 2010 was not available for all companies at press time.

2010 Sales: $18,912,600	2010 Profits: $-18,450	**U.S. Stock Ticker:**
2009 Sales: $16,721,000	2009 Profits: $79,640	**Int'l Ticker: 034020** Int'l Exchange: Seoul-KRX
2008 Sales: $17,217,200	2008 Profits: $2,230	Employees:
2007 Sales: $7,651,000	2007 Profits: $48,300	Fiscal Year Ends: 12/31
2006 Sales: $5,907,300	2006 Profits: $112,000	Parent Company:

SALARIES/BENEFITS:

Pension Plan:	ESOP Stock Plan:	Profit Sharing:	Top Exec. Salary: $	Bonus: $
Savings Plan:	Stock Purch. Plan:		Second Exec. Salary: $	Bonus: $

OTHER THOUGHTS:

Apparent Women Officers or Directors:
Hot Spot for Advancement for Women/Minorities:

LOCATIONS: ("Y" = Yes)

West:	Southwest:	Midwest:	Southeast:	Northeast:	International:
	Y		Y	Y	Y

DOYLE COLLECTION (THE)

www.doylecollection.com

Industry Group Code: 721110 Ranks within this company's industry group: Sales:　Profits:

Properties:	Financial Services:	Construction/Development:	Investments:	Specialty Services:		Brokerage:
Apartments:	Mortgages:	Commercial Construction:	REIT:	Property Management:	Y	Commercial Sales:
Malls/Shopping:	Title Insurance:	Residential Construction:		Online Services:		Residential Sales:
Offices:	Property Insurance:	Land Development:		Software/IT:		Specialty:
Hotels/Motels: Y		Support Services:		Consulting:		
Industrial/Warehouses:		Design/Engineering:				
Other:						

TYPES OF BUSINESS:

Hotels
Hotel Management

BRANDS/DIVISIONS/AFFILIATES:

Jurys Doyle Hotel Group
Westbury Hotel (The)
Croke Park Hotel (The)
River Lee Hotel (The)
Normandy Hotel (The)
Courtyard by Marriott Northwest
Back Bay Hotel (The)
Marylebone Hotel (The)

CONTACTS: Note: Officers with more than one job title may be intentionally listed here more than once.

Bill Walshe, CEO
Patrick King, CFO
Seamus Daly, Corp. Sec.
Bernadette C. Gallagher, Chmn.

Phone: 353-1-607-0070	Fax: 353-1-667-2370
Toll-Free:	
Address: 146 Pembroke Rd., Ballsbridge, Dublin, Ireland 4 UK	

GROWTH PLANS/SPECIAL FEATURES:

The Doyle Collection (TDC), formerly known as Jurys Doyle Hotel Group plc, is an international hotel operator headquartered in Dublin, Ireland. It has properties in Ireland, the U.K. and the U.S.   Currently, the company offers business and leisure travelers a portfolio of 11 luxury hotels in six cities with a combined total of about 2,300 rooms. The firm's Irish properties are located in Dublin and Cork; its U.K. properties are located in London and Bristol; and its U.S. properties are located in Boston, Massachusetts and Washington, D.C. Hotels are generally located centrally in their respective cities, giving corporate clients easy access to local business and financial districts. Additionally, the firm's hotels offer corporate hospitality, conference, event and meeting suites to accommodate meetings and events of various sizes.   Several of the group's hotels have professional wedding planners on staff to help coordinate wedding and reception activities. The company's individual properties include the Westbury Hotel and the Croke Park Hotel in Dublin; The River Lee Hotel in Cork; the Marylebone Hotel, the Bloomsbury Hotel and the Kensington Hotel in London; the Bristol Hotel, in Bristol; the Normandy Hotel, the Dupont Hotel and the Courtyard by Marriott Northwest in Washington, D.C.; and the Back Bay Hotel in Boston.

The Doyle Collection offers its employees a benefits package that includes a pension plan; medical coverage; discounts on accommodation and food; death-in-service benefits; and educational assistance.

FINANCIALS: Sales and profits are in thousands of dollars—add 000 to get the full amount. 2010 Note: Financial information for 2010 was not available for all companies at press time.

2010 Sales: $	2010 Profits: $	U.S. Stock Ticker: Private
2009 Sales: $	2009 Profits: $	Int'l Ticker:　Int'l Exchange:
2008 Sales: $	2008 Profits: $	Employees:
2007 Sales: $	2007 Profits: $	Fiscal Year Ends: 12/31
2006 Sales: $	2006 Profits: $	Parent Company:

SALARIES/BENEFITS:

Pension Plan: Y	ESOP Stock Plan:	Profit Sharing:	Top Exec. Salary: $	Bonus: $
Savings Plan:	Stock Purch. Plan:		Second Exec. Salary: $	Bonus: $

OTHER THOUGHTS:

Apparent Women Officers or Directors: 1
Hot Spot for Advancement for Women/Minorities:

LOCATIONS: ("Y" = Yes)

West:	Southwest:	Midwest:	Southeast:	Northeast:	International:
				Y	Y

DR HORTON INC

www.drhorton.com

Industry Group Code: 2361 Ranks within this company's industry group: Sales: 3 Profits: 2

Properties:	Financial Services:		Construction/Development:		Investments:	Specialty Services:	Brokerage:
Apartments:	Mortgages:	Y	Commercial Construction:		REIT:	Property Management:	Commercial Sales:
Malls/Shopping:	Title Insurance:	Y	Residential Construction:	Y		Online Services:	Residential Sales:
Offices:	Property Insurance:		Land Development:			Software/IT:	Specialty:
Hotels/Motels:			Support Services:			Consulting:	
Industrial/Warehouses:			Design/Engineering:				
Other:							

TYPES OF BUSINESS:

Construction, Residential
Mortgages
Title Insurance

BRANDS/DIVISIONS/AFFILIATES:

DHI Mortgage

CONTACTS: *Note: Officers with more than one job title may be intentionally listed here more than once.*

Donald J. Tomnitz, CEO
Donald J. Tomnitz, Pres./Vice Chmn.
Bill W. Wheat, CFO/Exec. VP
Ted I. Harbour, Chief Legal Officer
Jessica Hansen, Dir.-Investor Rel.
Stacey H. Dwyer, Treas./Exec. VP
Randy Present, Pres., Financial Svcs.
Chris Chambers, Pres., West Region
Rick Horton, Pres., South Region
George Seagraves, Pres., North Region
Donald R. Horton, Chmn.

Phone: 817-390-8200	Fax: 817-390-1715
Toll-Free:	
Address: 301 Commerce St., Ste. 500, Fort Worth, TX 76102 US	

GROWTH PLANS/SPECIAL FEATURES:

D. R. Horton, Inc. is a leading national builder of single-family homes with a diversified set of holdings, and operating divisions in 26 states and 72 metropolitan markets. The firm generally builds homes between 1,000 to 4,000 square feet, ranging in price from $90,000 to $700,000, with construction often completed in three to six months. In 2010, the company closed approximately 20,875 homes, with an average closing sales price approximating $206,100. The company is divided into six regional homebuilding segments and one financial services segment. The homebuilding segments are East, operating in eight states; Midwest, four states; Southeast, three states; South Central, four states; Southwest, two states; and West, seven states. The building services section constructs residences, tailored to the particular community where they are being built, including single-family residential homes, townhouses, condominiums, duplexes and triplexes. Subcontractors under the supervision of D. R. Horton do substantially all of the actual building. The financial services segment of the company provides mortgage financing and title insurance through its wholly-owned subsidiary, DHI Mortgage. The home builder's current business strategy is to enter into new lot option contracts to purchase finished lots in selected communities to potentially increase sales volumes and profitability. The firm plans to renegotiate existing lot option contracts as necessary to reduce lot costs and better match the scheduled lot purchases with new home demand in each community. The company also manages inventory of homes under construction by selectively starting construction on unsold homes to capture new home demand, while monitoring the number and aging of unsold homes and aggressively marketing its unsold, completed homes in inventory.

FINANCIALS: Sales and profits are in thousands of dollars—add 000 to get the full amount. 2010 Note: Financial information for 2010 was not available for all companies at press time.

2010 Sales: $4,309,700	2010 Profits: $245,100	U.S. Stock Ticker: DHI
2009 Sales: $3,603,900	2009 Profits: $-549,800	Int'l Ticker: Int'l Exchange:
2008 Sales: $6,518,600	2008 Profits: $-2,633,600	Employees: 3,214
2007 Sales: $11,088,800	2007 Profits: $-712,500	Fiscal Year Ends: 9/30
2006 Sales: $14,760,500	2006 Profits: $1,233,300	Parent Company:

SALARIES/BENEFITS:

Pension Plan:	ESOP Stock Plan:	Profit Sharing:	Top Exec. Salary: $1,000,000	Bonus: $1,989,755
Savings Plan: Y	Stock Purch. Plan:		Second Exec. Salary: $900,000	Bonus: $1,989,755

OTHER THOUGHTS:

Apparent Women Officers or Directors: 2
Hot Spot for Advancement for Women/Minorities:

LOCATIONS: ("Y" = Yes)

West:	Southwest:	Midwest:	Southeast:	Northeast:	International:
Y	Y	Y	Y	Y	

DREW INDUSTRIES INC

www.drewindustries.com

Industry Group Code: 321991 Ranks within this company's industry group: Sales: 1 Profits: 1

Properties:	Financial Services:	Construction/Development:		Investments:		Specialty Services:	Brokerage:
Apartments:	Mortgages:	Commercial Construction:		REIT:		Property Management:	Commercial Sales:
Malls/Shopping:	Title Insurance:	Residential Construction:	Y			Online Services:	Residential Sales:
Offices:	Property Insurance:	Land Development:				Software/IT:	Specialty:
Hotels/Motels:		Support Services:	Y			Consulting:	
Industrial/Warehouses:		Design/Engineering:					
Other:							

TYPES OF BUSINESS:

Recreational Vehicle Components
Manufactured Housing Components
Modular Housing & Office Unit Products
Chassis & Chassis Parts

BRANDS/DIVISIONS/AFFILIATES:

Kinro Inc
Lippert Components Inc
Happijac
Michiana Mattress
Extreme Custom Trailers
Zieman Manufacturing
Seating Technology Inc
Sellers Mfg., Inc.

CONTACTS: Note: Officers with more than one job title may be intentionally listed here more than once.

Fredric M. Zinn, CEO
Fredric M. Zinn, Pres.
Joseph S. Giordano, III, CFO/Treas.
Harvey F. Milman, Chief Legal Officer/VP/Corp. Sec.
Christopher L. Smith, Controller
Jason Lippert, Chmn./CEO-Kinro Inc & Lippert Components, Inc.
Scott Mereness, Pres., Kinro Inc & Lippert Components, Inc.
Joel DeVries, Dir.-Oper., Seating Tech. & Michiana Mattress
Mark Taylor, Gen. Mgr.-Seating Tech.
Leigh J. Abrams, Chmn.

Phone: 914-428-9098	**Fax:** 914-428-4581
Toll-Free:	
Address: 200 Mamaroneck Ave., White Plains, NY 10601 US	

GROWTH PLANS/SPECIAL FEATURES:

Drew Industries, Inc., operating through its wholly-owned subsidiaries Kinro, Inc. and Lippert Components, Inc., supplies a broad array of components for recreational vehicles (RVs) and manufactured homes. The company operates in two divisions: RV products, which accounted for 83% of its 2010 sales; and manufactured home products, which accounted for the remaining 17%. Each of the firm's subsidiaries produces components and products in both segments. Kinro manufactures and markets components such as windows, doors, screens and thermoformed bath and kitchen products. Lippert Components manufactures and markets steel chassis; steel chassis parts; slide-out mechanisms and related power units; electric stabilizer jacks; leveling devices; bed lifts; suspension systems; axles; and steps. It also manufactures specialty trailers for hauling equipment, boats, personal watercraft and snowmobiles, as well as axles for specialty trailers. With 25 manufacturing facilities located in 11 states, Drew is an important supplier to nearly all of the leading producers of RVs and manufactured homes. The firm's brands include Happijac, Michiana Mattress, Extreme Custom Trailers and Zieman Manufacturing. Certain products manufactured by the subsidiaries are also used in modular homes and office units. In March 2010, Lippert Components acquired certain intellectual property and other assets from Schwintek, Inc. In April 2010, the firm announced plans to construct a manufacturing plant for Kinro, Inc. in Chester, South Carolina. In August 2010, it acquired Sellers Mfg., Inc., which manufactures the patented E-Z Cruise suspension enhancement system. In January 2011, the company acquired Home-Style Industries, Inc. and its affiliated companies, which manufacture upholstered furniture and mattresses for RVs.

FINANCIALS: Sales and profits are in thousands of dollars—add 000 to get the full amount. 2010 Note: Financial information for 2010 was not available for all companies at press time.

2010 Sales: $572,755	2010 Profits: $28,034	**U.S. Stock Ticker: DW**
2009 Sales: $397,839	2009 Profits: $-24,053	**Int'l Ticker:** Int'l Exchange:
2008 Sales: $510,506	2008 Profits: $11,678	Employees: 3,016
2007 Sales: $668,625	2007 Profits: $39,767	Fiscal Year Ends: 12/31
2006 Sales: $729,232	2006 Profits: $31,023	Parent Company:

SALARIES/BENEFITS:

Pension Plan:	ESOP Stock Plan:	Profit Sharing:	Top Exec. Salary: $700,000	Bonus: $244,569
Savings Plan: Y	Stock Purch. Plan:		Second Exec. Salary: $450,000	Bonus: $34,680

OTHER THOUGHTS:

Apparent Women Officers or Directors:
Hot Spot for Advancement for Women/Minorities:

LOCATIONS: ("Y" = Yes)

West:	Southwest:	Midwest:	Southeast:	Northeast:	International:
Y	Y	Y	Y	Y	Y

DUKE REALTY CORP
www.dukerealty.com

Industry Group Code: 531120 Ranks within this company's industry group: Sales: 10   Profits: 30

Properties:		Financial Services:		Construction/Development:		Investments:		Specialty Services:		Brokerage:	
Apartments:		Mortgages:		Commercial Construction:	Y	REIT:	Y	Property Management:		Commercial Sales:	
Malls/Shopping:	Y	Title Insurance:		Residential Construction:				Online Services:		Residential Sales:	
Offices:	Y	Property Insurance:		Land Development:	Y			Software/IT:		Specialty:	
Hotels/Motels:				Support Services:				Consulting:			
Industrial/Warehouses:	Y			Design/Engineering:	Y						
Other:											

TYPES OF BUSINESS:
Real Estate Investment Trust
Real Estate Development
Commercial Real Estate
Construction & Design Services
Commercial Construction
Warehouses

BRANDS/DIVISIONS/AFFILIATES:
Duke Realty LP
Duke Realty Services LP
Duke Construction LP

CONTACTS: *Note: Officers with more than one job title may be intentionally listed here more than once.*
Dennis D. Oklak, CEO
Christie Kelly, CFO/Exec. VP
Howard L. Feinsand, General Counsel/Exec. VP/Corp. Sec.
Steve R. Kennedy, Exec. VP-Construction
James B. Connor, Exec. VP-Midwest
Jeffrey D. Turner, Exec. VP-South & West Regions
Sam O'Briant, Exec. VP-Southeast & East Regions
Dennis D. Oklak, Chmn.

Phone: 317-808-6000	**Fax:** 317-808-6770
Toll-Free: 800-875-3366	
Address: 600 E. 96th St., Ste. 100, Indianapolis, IN 46240 US	

GROWTH PLANS/SPECIAL FEATURES:

Duke Realty Corp. is a self-administered and self-managed real estate investment trust (REIT) that operates in 18 major U.S. cities. The firm provides in-house leasing, management, development and construction services. The company's diversified portfolio of 747 office, industrial, healthcare and retail rental properties totaling 136.5 million square feet, including 108 jointly controlled in-service properties totaling roughly 22.1 million square feet. The firm's 77.5 million square feet of industrial properties consists of bulk warehouses and service center properties also known as flex buildings or light industrial properties. Office properties owned by the firm total 30.73 million square feet and are located primarily in suburban locations. Duke also owns interests in approximately 2.7 million square feet of healthcare and retail buildings. The firm's properties are roughly 89.5% occupied. The company conducts rental operations through subsidiary Duke Realty, LP. It conducts service operations through Duke Realty Services, LP, in which the company is the sole general partner. Duke Realty Corp. also operates Duke Construction, LP, which offers office, industrial, medical and retail building and design services in the Midwestern, Southeastern and Southwestern U.S. In December 2010, Duke Realty Corp. agreed to sell 20 office buildings (3.1 million square feet) to its joint venture with CB Richard Ellis Realty Trust, in which it owns 20% interest. Also in December 2010, the firm agreed to acquire 51 industrial and five office buildings (over 4.9 million square feet) and four ground leases, all located in southern Florida, from Premier Commercial Realty for $450 million.

Employees are offered life, AD&D, disability, medical, dental and vision insurance; health savings and flexible spending accounts; an employee assistance program; a 401(k) plan; a stock purchase plan; adoption assistance; a scholarship program; an employer assisted housing program; and an associate referral bonus program.

FINANCIALS: Sales and profits are in thousands of dollars—add 000 to get the full amount. 2010 Note: Financial information for 2010 was not available for all companies at press time.

2010 Sales: $1,393,603	2010 Profits: $65,262	**U.S. Stock Ticker:** DRE
2009 Sales: $1,291,741	2009 Profits: $-271,490	**Int'l Ticker:** Int'l Exchange:
2008 Sales: $1,292,183	2008 Profits: $110,408	Employees: 1,000
2007 Sales: $1,122,095	2007 Profits: $291,059	Fiscal Year Ends: 12/31
2006 Sales: $805,296	2006 Profits: $204,147	Parent Company:

SALARIES/BENEFITS:

Pension Plan:	ESOP Stock Plan:	Profit Sharing:	Top Exec. Salary: $635,385	Bonus: $400,000
Savings Plan: Y	Stock Purch. Plan: Y		Second Exec. Salary: $425,000	Bonus: $454,330

OTHER THOUGHTS:
Apparent Women Officers or Directors: 3
Hot Spot for Advancement for Women/Minorities: Y

LOCATIONS: ("Y" = Yes)

West:	Southwest:	Midwest:	Southeast:	Northeast:	International:
	Y	Y	Y	Y	

DYNEX CAPITAL INC

www.dynexcapital.com

Industry Group Code: 525990 Ranks within this company's industry group: Sales: 3   Profits: 2

Properties:	Financial Services:		Construction/Development:	Investments:	Specialty Services:	Brokerage:
Apartments:	Mortgages:	Y	Commercial Construction:	REIT:	Property Management:	Commercial Sales:
Malls/Shopping:	Title Insurance:		Residential Construction:		Online Services:	Residential Sales:
Offices:	Property Insurance:		Land Development:		Software/IT:	Specialty:
Hotels/Motels:			Support Services:		Consulting:	
Industrial/Warehouses:			Design/Engineering:			
Other:						

TYPES OF BUSINESS:

Mortgage REIT
Real Estate Investment Trust
Mortgage-Backed Securities
Commercial Mortgage Loans

BRANDS/DIVISIONS/AFFILIATES:

Issued Holdings Capital Corporation

CONTACTS: *Note: Officers with more than one job title may be intentionally listed here more than once.*

Thomas B. Akin, CEO
Stephen J. Benedetti, COO/Exec. VP
Stephen J. Benedetti, CFO/Exec. VP
John L. Goodhue, VP-Info. Systems
John L. Goodhue, VP-Tech.
Stephen J. Benedetti, Corp. Sec.
Alison G. Griffin, VP-Investor Rel.
Jeffrey L. Childress, Controller/Chief Acct. Officer/VP
Robert M. Nilson, Jr., VP-Risk Mgmt.
Wayne E. Brockwell, VP-Portfolio
Byron L Boston, Chief Investment Officer/Exec. VP
Thomas B. Akin, Chmn.

Phone: 804-217-5800	Fax: 804-217-5860
Toll-Free:	
Address: 4991 Lake Brook Dr., Ste. 100, Glen Allen, VA 23060 US	

GROWTH PLANS/SPECIAL FEATURES:

Dynex Capital, Inc., organized as a real estate investment trust (REIT), is a financial services company that invests in loans and mortgage-backed securities (MBS) issued or guaranteed by a federally chartered corporation or an agency of the U.S. government. These securities are referred to as Agency MBS. The company also invests in commercial mortgage-backed securities (CMBS) and non-Agency residential mortgage-backed securities, as well as securitized residential and commercial mortgage loans. Dynex's investments are typically financed through a combination of repurchase agreements, securitization financing and equity capital. Its investment policy allocates the firm's capital amongst short-duration, high-grade Agency MBS with less exposure to credit risk, interest rate risk and liquidity risk and CMBS rated AAA by one of the nationally recognized rating services. Dynex's primary source of income is net interest income, which is the excess of the interest income earned on its investments over the cost of financing these investments. The firm's investments consist of approximately $594.1 million in Agency MBS, $109.1 million in non-Agency securities, $150.4 million in securitized commercial mortgage loans, $62.1 million in securitized single-family residential mortgage loans and $2.1 million in unsecuritized mortgage loans.

FINANCIALS: Sales and profits are in thousands of dollars—add 000 to get the full amount. 2010 Note: Financial information for 2010 was not available for all companies at press time.

2010 Sales: $54,024	2010 Profits: $29,472	U.S. Stock Ticker: DX
2009 Sales: $39,750	2009 Profits: $17,581	Int'l Ticker: Int'l Exchange:
2008 Sales: $29,653	2008 Profits: $15,121	Employees: 15
2007 Sales: $30,778	2007 Profits: $8,899	Fiscal Year Ends: 6/30
2006 Sales: $50,449	2006 Profits: $4,909	Parent Company:

SALARIES/BENEFITS:

Pension Plan:	ESOP Stock Plan:	Profit Sharing:	Top Exec. Salary: $300,000	Bonus: $309,531
Savings Plan: Y	Stock Purch. Plan:		Second Exec. Salary: $275,000	Bonus: $325,000

OTHER THOUGHTS:

Apparent Women Officers or Directors: 1
Hot Spot for Advancement for Women/Minorities:

LOCATIONS: ("Y" = Yes)

West:	Southwest:	Midwest:	Southeast:	Northeast:	International:
				Y	

EASTGROUP PROPERTIES INC

www.eastgroup.net

Industry Group Code: 531120 Ranks within this company's industry group: Sales: 57   Profits: 42

Properties:	Financial Services:	Construction/Development:	Investments:	Specialty Services:	Brokerage:
Apartments:	Mortgages:	Commercial Construction:	REIT: Y	Property Management: Y	Commercial Sales:
Malls/Shopping:	Title Insurance:	Residential Construction:		Online Services:	Residential Sales:
Offices:	Property Insurance:	Land Development:		Software/IT:	Specialty:
Hotels/Motels:		Support Services:		Consulting:	
Industrial/Warehouses: Y		Design/Engineering:			
Other:					

TYPES OF BUSINESS:

Real Estate Investment Trust
Industrial Properties
Property Management

BRANDS/DIVISIONS/AFFILIATES:

CONTACTS:
Note: Officers with more than one job title may be intentionally listed here more than once.
David H. Hoster, II, CEO
David H. Hoster, II, Pres.
N. Keith McKey, CFO/Exec. VP/Treas.
Brian Laird, VP-IT
N. Keith McKey, Corp. Sec.
Bruce Corkern, Chief Acct. Officer/Controller/Sr. VP
William D. Petsas, Sr. VP/Head-Arizona Western Regional Office
John F. Coleman, Sr. VP-Florida Regional Office
Brent W. Wood, Sr. VP/Head-Texas Regional Office
Jann W. Puckett, VP/Asset Mgr.
Leland R. Speed, Chmn.

Phone: 601-354-3555	Fax: 601-352-1441
Toll-Free:	
Address: 190 E. Capital St., Ste. 400, Jackson, MS 39201-2195 US	

GROWTH PLANS/SPECIAL FEATURES:

EastGroup Properties, Inc. is an equity real estate investment trust (REIT) focused on the acquisition, operation and development of industrial properties in major Sunbelt markets throughout the U.S., with a concentration in the states of Florida, Texas, Arizona and California. The company acquires distribution facilities in the 5,000 to 50,000 square foot range, generally clustered near major transportation routes in supply constrained markets. The company's portfolio is comprised of 28.1 million square feet of leasable space at 247 industrial properties and one office building, with nearly 91% of its portfolio leased. EastGroup's focus is the ownership of business distribution space (76% of its portfolio), with the remainder in bulk distribution space (19%) and business service space (5%). Business distribution space properties are typically multi-tenant buildings with a building depth of 200 feet or less, clear height of 20-24 feet, office finish of 10% to 25% and truck courts with a depth of 100-120 feet. In addition to direct property acquisitions and developments, the company seeks to expand its portfolio through the acquisition of other public and private real estate companies and REITs. In 2010, the company acquired two business distribution buildings for approximately $5.3 million; and a three building complex in San Diego called the Ocean View Corporate Center for $17 million.

FINANCIALS:
Sales and profits are in thousands of dollars—add 000 to get the full amount. 2010 Note: Financial information for 2010 was not available for all companies at press time.

2010 Sales: $173,126	2010 Profits: $18,755	**U.S. Stock Ticker:** EGP
2009 Sales: $172,354	2009 Profits: $26,659	**Int'l Ticker:** Int'l Exchange:
2008 Sales: $168,503	2008 Profits: $34,142	Employees: 68
2007 Sales: $150,730	2007 Profits: $29,734	Fiscal Year Ends: 12/31
2006 Sales: $133,145	2006 Profits: $29,234	Parent Company:

SALARIES/BENEFITS:

Pension Plan:	ESOP Stock Plan:	Profit Sharing:	Top Exec. Salary: $525,000	Bonus: $420,000
Savings Plan: Y	Stock Purch. Plan:		Second Exec. Salary: $317,200	Bonus: $237,900

OTHER THOUGHTS:

Apparent Women Officers or Directors: 3
Hot Spot for Advancement for Women/Minorities: Y

LOCATIONS: ("Y" = Yes)

West:	Southwest:	Midwest:	Southeast:	Northeast:	International:
Y	Y		Y	Y	

E-LOAN INC

www.eloan.com

Industry Group Code: 522310E Ranks within this company's industry group: Sales: Profits:

Properties:	Financial Services:		Construction/Development:	Investments:	Specialty Services:		Brokerage:
Apartments:	Mortgages:	Y	Commercial Construction:	REIT:	Property Management:		Commercial Sales:
Malls/Shopping:	Title Insurance:		Residential Construction:		Online Services:	Y	Residential Sales:
Offices:	Property Insurance:		Land Development:		Software/IT:		Specialty:
Hotels/Motels:			Support Services:		Consulting:		
Industrial/Warehouses:			Design/Engineering:				
Other:							

TYPES OF BUSINESS:

Online Mortgage Broker
Debt Consolidation
Small Business Loans
Credit Cards
Education Loans

BRANDS/DIVISIONS/AFFILIATES:

Popular Inc
Banco Popular North America

CONTACTS: *Note: Officers with more than one job title may be intentionally listed here more than once.*

Mark E. Lefanowicz, Pres.
Alberto J. Paracchini, CFO/Exec. VP
Scott McKinlay, Sr. VP-Corp. Dev.
Harold (Pete) Bonnikson, Sr. VP-First Mortgage
Rick Folgmann, Sr. VP-Home Equity
Tess Koleczek, Chief Privacy Officer
Christian A. Larsen, Chmn.

Phone: 925-847-6200	Fax: 925-847-0831
Toll-Free: 888-533-5333	
Address: 6230 Stoneridge Mall Rd., Pleasanton, CA 94588 US	

GROWTH PLANS/SPECIAL FEATURES:

E-LOAN, Inc., a wholly-owned subsidiary of Banco Popular North America (a subsidiary of Popular Inc.), is an online provider and direct-to-consumer lender of a full range of mortgages; credit cards; and home equity, auto, education and personal loans. The E-LOAN web site offers a variety of services for borrowers, including comparisons of loans from the nation's leading lenders; tools for managing debt; credit reports and scores; exclusive 24-hour loan status access; automatic notification regarding new products that meet specific customer needs; and a variety of other services. E-LOAN originates loans through its web site and by telephone; funds the loans using warehouse and other lines of credit; and then sells closed loans. The gain on the sale of these loans is the company's primary source of income. The firm showcases a low-cost guarantee, assuring customers that its combination of low rate, points and lender or broker fees is the lowest-cost loan available. Products offered by E-LOAN include fixed-rate mortgage products, including 30 year and 15 year terms; adjustable rate mortgage products, including 10, seven, five and three year terms; stated income mortgage products, for individuals who are self-employed or write off a large portion of their income; and home equity lines of credit, home equity loans and installment vehicle loans. Lending partners for the company include First Street, Option One Mortgage Corporation (a subsidiary of H&R Block), Irwin Home Equity and HSBC Auto Finance. In addition, E-LOAN offers federally insured Federal Housing Administration (FHA) loans to assist consumers facing a tight credit market.

FINANCIALS: Sales and profits are in thousands of dollars—add 000 to get the full amount. 2010 Note: Financial information for 2010 was not available for all companies at press time.

2010 Sales: $	2010 Profits: $	**U.S. Stock Ticker: Subsidiary**
2009 Sales: $	2009 Profits: $	**Int'l Ticker:** Int'l Exchange:
2008 Sales: $	2008 Profits: $	Employees:
2007 Sales: $	2007 Profits: $	Fiscal Year Ends: 12/31
2006 Sales: $	2006 Profits: $	Parent Company: POPULAR INC

SALARIES/BENEFITS:

Pension Plan:	ESOP Stock Plan:	Profit Sharing:	Top Exec. Salary: $	Bonus: $
Savings Plan:	Stock Purch. Plan:		Second Exec. Salary: $	Bonus: $

OTHER THOUGHTS:

Apparent Women Officers or Directors: 1
Hot Spot for Advancement for Women/Minorities:

LOCATIONS: ("Y" = Yes)

West:	Southwest:	Midwest:	Southeast:	Northeast:	International:
Y					

EMAAR PROPERTIES PJSC

www.emaar.com

Industry Group Code: 5311 Ranks within this company's industry group: Sales: 11   Profits: 14

Properties:		Financial Services:		Construction/Development:		Investments:	Specialty Services:		Brokerage:
Apartments:	Y	Mortgages:	Y	Commercial Construction:	Y	REIT:	Property Management:	Y	Commercial Sales:
Malls/Shopping:	Y	Title Insurance:		Residential Construction:	Y		Online Services:		Residential Sales:
Offices:	Y	Property Insurance:		Land Development:	Y		Software/IT:		Specialty:
Hotels/Motels:	Y			Support Services:			Consulting:		
Industrial/Warehouses:				Design/Engineering:					
Other:	Y								

TYPES OF BUSINESS:

Real Estate Development
Retail Construction
Residential Construction
Education & Health Care Construction
Investments

BRANDS/DIVISIONS/AFFILIATES:

Burj Dubai
Emaar Malls Group LLC
Emaar Hotels and Resorts LLC
Emaar Hospitality Group LLC
Emaar Healthcare Group
Emaar Investment Holding LLC
Amlak Finance PJSC
Dubai Bank PJSC

CONTACTS: *Note: Officers with more than one job title may be intentionally listed here more than once.*

Ahmed Thani Al Matrooshi, Managing Dir.
Amit Jain, CFO
Kenneth Foong, CIO
Ayman Hamdy, Exec. Dir.-Legal/Company Sec.
Low Ping, Exec. Dir.-Finance & Risk
Nasser Rafi, CEO-Emaar Malls Group LLC
Marc-Francois Dardenne, CEO-Emaar Hospitality Group LLC
Arif Amiri, CEO-Amaar Retail LLC
Robert Booth, CEO-North America
H.E. Mohamed Bin Ali Alabbar, Chmn.
Sergio Casari, CEO-Emaar Int'l

GROWTH PLANS/SPECIAL FEATURES:

Emaar Properties PJSC is a Dubai-based real estate developer whose projects are primarily located in Dubai, though the group encompasses more than 60 active companies with operations spanning the Middle East, North Africa, Pan-Asia, Europe and North America. Emaar Properties PJSC's operating divisions include Emaar United Arab Emirates, principally active in Dubai; Emaar International, with focus on partnerships in the Middle East, North Africa and India; Emaar Malls Group LLC; Emaar Education, which manages over 100 educational institutions through a subsidiary; Emaar Healthcare Group, which plans to develop and manage hospitals and health clinics in the Middle East, North Africa and southeastern Asia; Emaar Hotels and Resorts LLC, a joint venture with Giorgio Armani SPA; Emaar Investment Holding LLC, which focuses on strategic acquisitions; Dubai Bank PJSC, Amlak Finance PJSC and EMAAR Financial Services LLC, which specializes in financing and investment; and Emaar Hospitality Group LLC, which manages the company's hospitality and leisure projects. The company's most ambitious project to-date is the Downtown Burj Dubai or Burj Khalifa in Dubai, the world's tallest tower. Other projects include the Dubai Mall, which will be one of the world's largest shopping malls; and the Old Town, a residence community designed to reflect traditional Arabian architecture including the Old Town Island, Emaar Square, the Residences and Burj Dubai Boulevard and featuring a manmade lake and fountain, as well as parks and gardens.

Phone: 971-4-367-3333	**Fax:** 971-4-367-3000
Toll-Free:	
Address: Emaar Business Park, Bldg. 3, PO Box 9440, Dubai, UAE	

FINANCIALS: Sales and profits are in thousands of dollars—add 000 to get the full amount. 2010 Note: Financial information for 2010 was not available for all companies at press time.

2010 Sales: $3,307,550	2010 Profits: $666,450	**U.S. Stock Ticker:**
2009 Sales: $2,290,040	2009 Profits: $89,090	**Int'l Ticker: EMAAR** Int'l Exchange: Abu Dhabi-ADSM
2008 Sales: $4,360,000	2008 Profits: $1,519,000	Employees:
2007 Sales: $4,865,000	2007 Profits: $1,790,000	Fiscal Year Ends: 12/31
2006 Sales: $3,813,000	2006 Profits: $1,730,000	Parent Company:

SALARIES/BENEFITS:

Pension Plan:	ESOP Stock Plan:	Profit Sharing:	Top Exec. Salary: $	Bonus: $
Savings Plan:	Stock Purch. Plan:		Second Exec. Salary: $	Bonus: $

OTHER THOUGHTS:

Apparent Women Officers or Directors: 1
Hot Spot for Advancement for Women/Minorities:

LOCATIONS: ("Y" = Yes)

West:	Southwest:	Midwest:	Southeast:	Northeast:	International:
Y					Y

EMCOR GROUP INC

www.emcorgroup.com

Industry Group Code: 238210 Ranks within this company's industry group: Sales: 1   Profits: 2

Properties:	Financial Services:	Construction/Development:		Investments:	Specialty Services:		Brokerage:
Apartments:	Mortgages:	Commercial Construction:		REIT:	Property Management:	Y	Commercial Sales:
Malls/Shopping:	Title Insurance:	Residential Construction:			Online Services:		Residential Sales:
Offices:	Property Insurance:	Land Development:			Software/IT:		Specialty:
Hotels/Motels:		Support Services:	Y		Consulting:	Y	
Industrial/Warehouses:		Design/Engineering:	Y				
Other:							

TYPES OF BUSINESS:

Electric Contractors
Mechanical Construction
Technical Consulting Services
Facilities Management

BRANDS/DIVISIONS/AFFILIATES:

EMCOR Construction Services, Inc.
EMCOR International, Inc.
EMCOR (UK) Limited
EMCOR Facilities Services, Inc.
EMCOR Mechanical/Electrical Services (East), Inc.
Scalise Industries
Harry Pepper & Associates, Inc.

CONTACTS:
Note: Officers with more than one job title may be intentionally listed here more than once.

Anthony J. Guzzi, CEO
Anthony J. Guzzi, Pres.
Mark A. Pompa, CFO/Exec. VP
Mava K. Heffler, VP-Mktg.
Joseph A. Puglisi, CIO/VP
Sheldon I. Cammaker, General Counsel/Exec. VP/Corp. Sec.
Mava K. Heffler, VP-Comm.
William E. Feher, VP-Finance & Compliance
Michael J. Parry, Pres./CEO-EMCOR Construction Svcs.
Michael P. Bordes, Pres., EMCOR Mechanical Svcs.
Arthur L. Strenkert, Pres., EMCOR Energy Svcs.
Michael W. Shelton, Chmn., EMCOR Gov't Svcs.
Frank T. MacInnis, Chmn.
Geoff Birkbeck, CEO-Comstock Canada

Phone: 203-849-7800	Fax: 203-849-7900
Toll-Free: 866-890-7794	
Address: 301 Merritt Seven, Norwalk, CT 06851 US	

GROWTH PLANS/SPECIAL FEATURES:

EMCOR Group, Inc. is a global leader in mechanical and electrical construction, energy infrastructure and facilities services. The company offers its services through more than 70 subsidiaries and joint ventures and 170 offices located throughout the U.S., as well as in Canada, the U.K. and the Middle East. Services provided to its customers include the design, integration, installation, start-up, operation and maintenance of systems for generation and distribution of electrical power; lighting systems; low-voltage systems, such as fire alarm, security, communications and process control systems; voice and data communication systems; heating, ventilation, air conditioning, refrigeration and clean-room process ventilation systems; plumbing, process and high-purity piping systems; water and wastewater treatment systems; and central plant heating and cooling systems. In addition to its construction services, EMCOR offers facilities services, such as site-based operations and maintenance, mobile maintenance and service, facilities management, installation and support for building systems, technical consulting and diagnostic services, small modification and retrofit projects and program development and management for energy systems. Most of the firm's business is done with corporations, municipalities and other government agencies, owner/developers and tenants of buildings. Additional services are provided to a range of general and specialty contractors, with EMCOR operating as a subcontractor. In 2010, approximately 86% of its revenue was generated in the U.S., with the remaining 14% coming from international business. In February 2010, the company acquired Scalise Industries. In October 2010, it acquired Harry Pepper & Associates, Inc.

Employees are offered medical, dental and vision coverage; flexible spending accounts; life insurance; disability coverage; a 401(k) plan; and an employee assistance program.

FINANCIALS:
Sales and profits are in thousands of dollars—add 000 to get the full amount. 2010 Note: Financial information for 2010 was not available for all companies at press time.

2010 Sales: $5,121,285	2010 Profits: $-86,691	U.S. Stock Ticker: EME
2009 Sales: $5,547,942	2009 Profits: $160,756	Int'l Ticker: Int'l Exchange:
2008 Sales: $6,785,242	2008 Profits: $182,204	Employees: 24,000
2007 Sales: $5,927,152	2007 Profits: $126,808	Fiscal Year Ends: 12/31
2006 Sales: $4,901,783	2006 Profits: $86,634	Parent Company:

SALARIES/BENEFITS:

Pension Plan:	ESOP Stock Plan:	Profit Sharing:	Top Exec. Salary: $950,000	Bonus: $4,077,000
Savings Plan: Y	Stock Purch. Plan:		Second Exec. Salary: $650,000	Bonus: $2,307,120

OTHER THOUGHTS:

Apparent Women Officers or Directors: 1
Hot Spot for Advancement for Women/Minorities:

LOCATIONS: ("Y" = Yes)

West:	Southwest:	Midwest:	Southeast:	Northeast:	International:
Y	Y	Y	Y	Y	Y

EMERITUS CORP

www.emeritus.com

Industry Group Code: 623110 Ranks within this company's industry group: Sales: 4   Profits: 6

Properties:	Financial Services:	Construction/Development:	Investments:	Specialty Services:		Brokerage:
Apartments:	Mortgages:	Commercial Construction:	REIT:	Property Management:	Y	Commercial Sales:
Malls/Shopping:	Title Insurance:	Residential Construction:		Online Services:		Residential Sales:
Offices:	Property Insurance:	Land Development:		Software/IT:		Specialty:
Hotels/Motels:		Support Services:		Consulting:		
Industrial/Warehouses:		Design/Engineering:				
Other: Y						

TYPES OF BUSINESS:

Long-Term Health Care
Assisted Living Communities

BRANDS/DIVISIONS/AFFILIATES:

Weston Group, Inc.

CONTACTS: *Note: Officers with more than one job title may be intentionally listed here more than once.*

Granger Cobb, CEO
Chris Hyatt, COO/Exec. VP
Granger Cobb, Pres.
Robert C. Bateman, CFO/Exec. VP-Finance
Jayne Sallerson, Exec. VP-Mktg. & Sales
Melanie Werdel, Exec. VP-Admin.
Raymond R. Brandstrom, Corp. Sec.
Chris Belford, Sr. VP-Oper.
Eric Mendelsohn, Sr. VP-Corp. Dev.
Jayne Sallerson, Exec. VP-Comm.
Jim L. Hanson, Sr. VP-Financial Svcs./Controller
Budgie Amparo, Exec. VP-Quality Svcs. & Risk Management
Martin D. Roffe, Sr. VP-Financial Planning
John Cincotta, Sr. VP-Sales
Leo Watterson, Sr. VP-Corp. Acct.
Daniel R. Baty, Chmn.

Phone: 206-298-2909	Fax: 206-301-4500
Toll-Free: 800-429-4828	
Address: 3131 Elliott Ave., Ste. 500, Seattle, WA 98121 US	

GROWTH PLANS/SPECIAL FEATURES:

Emeritus Corp. operates assisted living residential communities in the U.S. These communities cater to senior citizens who need help with daily living, but do not require the intensive care provided in skilled nursing facilities. It operates or has an interest in 306 communities, consisting of 28,277 residential rooms or suites with a capacity for 33,265 residents. The firm's communities are located in 42 states and include 165 owned communities and 141 leased communities. Additionally, the company manages 10 facilities for third-parties and 163 facilities through joint ventures. In total, its operating portfolio includes 479 communities, with 42,172 units and a capacity of 49,667 residents. Assisted living generally provides housing and 24-hour personal support services. Seniors reside in a private or semi-private residential unit for a monthly fee based on each resident's individual service needs. The company's specialty is Alzheimer's disease and dementia-related care, for which the company has developed a program that links memory training, familiar environments and personalized care services. In its other assisted living programs, Emeritus business strategy calls for customer service that addresses both physical and social health. The firm's target customers are middle to upper-middle income seniors, 75 and older, living in smaller cities (50,000 to 150,000 persons). In August 2010, Emeritus, through a joint venture with Columbia Pacific Advisors and Blackstone Real Estate Advisors, acquired 144 senior living communities from Sunwest Management. In October 2010, it agreed to acquire Weston Group, Inc., a provider of rehabilitation services and medical equipment. In December 2010, the firm acquired eight additional communities. In January 2011, Emeritus entered into a memorandum of understanding with Columbia Pacific Advisors to begin exploring the potential to develop senior housing in China.

Employees are offered health care benefits; a 401(k) plan; a stock purchase plan; tuition assistance; and sick, vacation and holiday pay.

FINANCIALS: Sales and profits are in thousands of dollars—add 000 to get the full amount. 2010 Note: Financial information for 2010 was not available for all companies at press time.

2010 Sales: $1,007,065	2010 Profits: $-57,842	**U.S. Stock Ticker: ESC**
2009 Sales: $898,732	2009 Profits: $-53,875	**Int'l Ticker:** Int'l Exchange:
2008 Sales: $772,443	2008 Profits: $-104,751	Employees: 29,300
2007 Sales: $538,874	2007 Profits: $-48,741	Fiscal Year Ends: 12/31
2006 Sales: $411,375	2006 Profits: $-14,618	Parent Company:

SALARIES/BENEFITS:

Pension Plan:	ESOP Stock Plan:	Profit Sharing:	Top Exec. Salary: $641,533	Bonus: $242,850
Savings Plan: Y	Stock Purch. Plan: Y		Second Exec. Salary: $636,952	Bonus: $243,500

OTHER THOUGHTS:

Apparent Women Officers or Directors: 3
Hot Spot for Advancement for Women/Minorities: Y

LOCATIONS: ("Y" = Yes)

West:	Southwest:	Midwest:	Southeast:	Northeast:	International:
Y	Y	Y	Y	Y	

EMPRESAS ICA SA DE CV

www.ica.com.mx

Industry Group Code: 237 Ranks within this company's industry group: Sales: 26   Profits: 24

Properties:	Financial Services:	Construction/Development:		Investments:	Specialty Services:	Brokerage:
Apartments:	Mortgages:	Commercial Construction:	Y	REIT:	Property Management:	Commercial Sales:
Malls/Shopping:	Title Insurance:	Residential Construction:	Y		Online Services:	Residential Sales:
Offices:	Property Insurance:	Land Development:	Y		Software/IT:	Specialty:
Hotels/Motels:		Support Services:			Consulting:	
Industrial/Warehouses:		Design/Engineering:	Y			
Other:						

TYPES OF BUSINESS:

Heavy Construction
Civic Construction
Industrial Construction
Transportation Infrastructure Management
Residential Construction
Design & Engineering Services
Airport Operations

BRANDS/DIVISIONS/AFFILIATES:

ICA Fluor
Rodio Kronsa
Grupo Aeroportuario del Centro Norte
ViveICA Casas
Los Portales

CONTACTS: *Note: Officers with more than one job title may be intentionally listed here more than once.*

Jose Luis Guerrero, CEO
Alonso Quintana Kawage, CFO/VP
Juan Carlos Santos, Dir.-Industrial Construction
Rodrigo Quintana Kawage, General Counsel
Sergio F. Montano Leon, Exec. VP
Luis Z. Rocha, Exec. VP-Civil Construction
Luis Urrutia Sodi, Dir.-Housing Dev.
Bernardo Quintana Isaac, Chmn.

Phone: 52-55-5272-9991	Fax: 52-55-52771428
Toll-Free:	
Address: Mineria No. 145, Edificio Central, Mexico City, 11800 Mexico	

GROWTH PLANS/SPECIAL FEATURES:

Empresas ICA S.A. de C.V. (ICA) is one of Mexico's largest engineering, procurement and construction companies. It operates three primary divisions: construction (divided into the civil construction, industrial construction and Rodio Kronsa segments), infrastructure (airports and other concessions) and housing development. The company's civil construction segment builds highways, dams, airports, bridges, tunnels, subways and port facilities primarily in Mexico, with occasional projects in Latin America, the Caribbean, Asia and the U.S. The industrial construction division, through majority owned subsidiary ICA Fluor, builds industrial factories such as refineries, petrochemical plants, cement factories, automotive factories and electrical generation plants. Its Rodio Kronsa segment is responsible for sub-soil construction projects internationally, primarily in Spain. ICA's construction divisions account for over 80% of its annual revenues. The infrastructure segment operates 13 airports, primarily in the central-north region of Mexico, through subsidiary Grupo Aeroportuario del Centro Norte (GACN), as well as highway, bridge and tunnel concessions and water distribution and water treatment concessions. The housing development segment has built over 40,000 homes across Mexico. Through its subsidiary ViveICA Casas, it actively markets housing in Mexico and offers buyer's assistance and after-sales service. The firm has entered partnerships with leading companies around the world to develop and carry out new projects. Some of its current permanent partnerships include ICA Fluor (with Fluor Corporation), a construction partnership in the U.S.; and Los Portales (with Grupo Raffo), developing real estate in Peru. In April 2010, the firm agreed to sell its concession for the management and operation of the Corredor Sur toll road in Panama to the Panamanian government for $420 million.

FINANCIALS: Sales and profits are in thousands of dollars—add 000 to get the full amount. 2010 Note: Financial information for 2010 was not available for all companies at press time.

2010 Sales: $2,364,000	2010 Profits: $68,000	**U.S. Stock Ticker: ICA**
2009 Sales: $2,441,780	2009 Profits: $-3,240	**Int'l Ticker: ICA** Int'l Exchange: Mexico City-BMV
2008 Sales: $2,020,700	2008 Profits: $58,300	Employees:
2007 Sales: $2,060,000	2007 Profits: $-72,000	Fiscal Year Ends: 12/31
2006 Sales: $1,982,000	2006 Profits: $92,000	Parent Company:

SALARIES/BENEFITS:

Pension Plan:	ESOP Stock Plan:	Profit Sharing:	Top Exec. Salary: $	Bonus: $
Savings Plan:	Stock Purch. Plan:		Second Exec. Salary: $	Bonus: $

OTHER THOUGHTS:

Apparent Women Officers or Directors:
Hot Spot for Advancement for Women/Minorities:

LOCATIONS: ("Y" = Yes)

West:	Southwest:	Midwest:	Southeast:	Northeast:	International:
					Y

ENGLOBAL CORP

www.englobal.com

Industry Group Code: 541330 Ranks within this company's industry group: Sales: 8   Profits: 8

Properties:	Financial Services:	Construction/Development:		Investments:	Specialty Services:		Brokerage:
Apartments:	Mortgages:	Commercial Construction:		REIT:	Property Management:		Commercial Sales:
Malls/Shopping:	Title Insurance:	Residential Construction:			Online Services:		Residential Sales:
Offices:	Property Insurance:	Land Development:			Software/IT:	Y	Specialty:
Hotels/Motels:		Support Services:			Consulting:	Y	
Industrial/Warehouses:		Design/Engineering:	Y				
Other:							

TYPES OF BUSINESS:

Engineering Services
Petrochemicals Industry Support Services
Control & Instrumentation Systems
Consulting & Inspection Services
Project Management

BRANDS/DIVISIONS/AFFILIATES:

CONTACTS:
Note: Officers with more than one job title may be intentionally listed here more than once.

Edward L. Pagano, CEO
Edward L. Pagano, Pres.
Robert W. Raiford, CFO
Fred Bridgewater, VP-Human Resources
Alex Schroeder, Mgr.-Corp. IT
David W. Smith, Pres., ENGlobal Engineering, Inc.
Natalie S. Hairston, Corp. Sec./Chief Governance Officer
Rochelle D. Leedy, Sr. VP-Bus. Dev.
Natalie S. Hairston, VP-Investor Rel.
Robert W. Raiford, Treas.
R. David Kelley, VP-Governmental Svcs.
William Wells, VP-Health, Safety & Environmental
Katrina Hamrick, VP-Legal Affairs
William A. Coskey, Chmn.

Phone: 281-878-1000	**Fax:** 281-878-1010
Toll-Free: 800-411-6040	
Address: 654 N. Sam Houston Pkwy E., Ste. 400, Houston, TX 77060-5914 US	

GROWTH PLANS/SPECIAL FEATURES:

ENGlobal Corp. is an international provider of engineering services and systems to the petroleum refining, petrochemical, pipeline, production and processing industries. The firm operates in five primary segments: Engineering; Construction; Automation; Land; and Government and Infrastructure. The engineering segment provides consulting services including feasibility studies, engineering, design, procurement and construction management. The segment provides these services to the upstream, midstream and downstream energy industries and branches of the U.S. military, and in some instances it delivers its services via in-plant personnel assigned throughout the U.S. and internationally. ENGlobal's construction segment provides construction management personnel and services in the areas of inspection, mechanical integrity, vendor and turnaround surveillance, field support, construction, quality assurance and plant asset management. Its customers include pipeline, refining, utility, chemical, petroleum, petrochemical, oil and gas, and power industries throughout the U.S. The automation segment provides services related to the design, fabrication, and implementation of process distributed control and analyzer systems, advanced automation and information technology projects. This segment's customers include members of the domestic and foreign energy related industries. Automation segment personnel assist in on-site commissioning, start-up and training for the company's specialized systems. The land segment provides land management, right-of-way, environmental compliance and governmental regulatory compliance services primarily to the pipeline, utility and telecom companies and other owner/operators of infrastructure facilities throughout the U.S. and Canada. ENGlobal's Government and Infrastructure unit was created to discover potential new operating markets for the firm and offer the company's technical services. In April 2010, the firm acquired certain assets of industrial automation control system provider CDI.

Employees are offered life, disability, medical, dental and vision insurance; flexible spending accounts; educational reimbursement; direct deposit services; and employee referral bonuses.

FINANCIALS:
Sales and profits are in thousands of dollars—add 000 to get the full amount. 2010 Note: Financial information for 2010 was not available for all companies at press time.

2010 Sales: $320,615	2010 Profits: $-11,752	**U.S. Stock Ticker: ENG**
2009 Sales: $343,462	2009 Profits: $1,233	**Int'l Ticker:** Int'l Exchange:
2008 Sales: $493,332	2008 Profits: $18,258	Employees: 2,030
2007 Sales: $363,227	2007 Profits: $12,464	Fiscal Year Ends: 12/31
2006 Sales: $303,090	2006 Profits: $-3,486	Parent Company:

SALARIES/BENEFITS:

Pension Plan:	ESOP Stock Plan:	Profit Sharing:	Top Exec. Salary: $260,000	Bonus: $
Savings Plan: Y	Stock Purch. Plan:		Second Exec. Salary: $245,000	Bonus: $

OTHER THOUGHTS:

Apparent Women Officers or Directors: 2
Hot Spot for Advancement for Women/Minorities:

LOCATIONS: ("Y" = Yes)

West:	Southwest:	Midwest:	Southeast:	Northeast:	International:
Y	Y	Y	Y	Y	Y

ENTERTAINMENT PROPERTIES TRUST

www.eprkc.com

Industry Group Code: 531120 Ranks within this company's industry group: Sales: 44   Profits: 25

Properties:		Financial Services:	Construction/Development:	Investments:		Specialty Services:	Brokerage:
Apartments:		Mortgages:	Commercial Construction:	REIT:	Y	Property Management:	Commercial Sales:
Malls/Shopping:	Y	Title Insurance:	Residential Construction:			Online Services:	Residential Sales:
Offices:		Property Insurance:	Land Development:			Software/IT:	Specialty:
Hotels/Motels:			Support Services:			Consulting:	
Industrial/Warehouses:			Design/Engineering:				
Other:	Y						

TYPES OF BUSINESS:

REIT-Entertainment Properties
Megaplex Movie Theaters
Entertainment Retail Centers
Ski Resorts
Vineyards & Wineries
Public Charter Schools

BRANDS/DIVISIONS/AFFILIATES:

CONTACTS: *Note: Officers with more than one job title may be intentionally listed here more than once.*

David M. Brain, CEO
Gregory K. Silvers, COO/VP
David M. Brain, Pres.
Mark A. Peterson, CFO/VP
Gregory K. Silvers, General Counsel/VP
Jonathan Weis, Dir.-Corp. Comm.
Michael Hirons, VP-Finance
Morgan G. (Jerry) Earnest, II, Chief Investment Officer/VP
Robert J. Druten, Chmn.

Phone: 816-472-1700	**Fax:** 816-472-5794
Toll-Free: 888-377-7348	
Address: 909 Walnut St., Ste. 200, Kansas City, MO 64106 US	

GROWTH PLANS/SPECIAL FEATURES:

Entertainment Properties Trust (EPR) is a self-administered REIT (Real Estate Investment Trust) with approximately 107 multiplex movie theaters, nine entertainment retail centers (ERCs) and other specialty properties. EPR's collection of properties totals approximately 13.2 million square feet, including 8.7 million square feet of multiplex theatre properties and 4.5 million square feet of retail centers, restaurant and other miscellaneous properties. Its multiplex theatres usually have at least 10 screens with elevated, stadium-style seating and amenities such as digital projection, which allow greater enhancement to audio and visual experiences for theatre patrons.   EPR's portfolio includes multiplexes in 33 U.S. states and Ontario, Canada, with theatres leased to operators such as American Multi-Cinema, Inc. (AMC), whose rental payments represented roughly 36% of the firm's 2010 revenues; Muvico Entertainment, LLC; Regal Entertainment Group; Rave Cinemas, LLC; AmStar Cinemas, LLC; Southern Theatres; and Cinemark.   The firm's ERCs are located in Colorado, New York, California, Virginia and Ontario, Canada. Land parcels are often leased to restaurant and retail operators adjacent to EPR's theater properties. Tenants of EPR's restaurant properties include Texas Roadhouse, Cherrydale Shops, Stir Crazy, Mad River Mountain, Johnny Carino's, On The Border and Wing Factory, among others. Some of its specialty properties include 10 wineries and six vineyards located in California and Washington; a metropolitan ski area in Bellefontaine, Ohio; and 27 public charter schools in eight states and Washington, D.C. In June 2010, EPR acquired 12 theatre properties located in Colorado, California, Indiana and Texas for approximately $124 million; the acquisition added 192 screens to the company's portfolio, with all of the newly acquired screens leased to Cinemark U.S.A. at the time of the transaction.   In February 2011, the firm announced plans to sell a 330,000-square-foot entertainment retail property in downtown Toronto, Ontario, for approximately $224 million.

FINANCIALS: Sales and profits are in thousands of dollars—add 000 to get the full amount. 2010 Note: Financial information for 2010 was not available for all companies at press time.

2010 Sales: $313,064	2010 Profits: $84,668	**U.S. Stock Ticker:** EPR
2009 Sales: $259,111	2009 Profits: $-22,199	**Int'l Ticker:** Int'l Exchange:
2008 Sales: $269,412	2008 Profits: $101,710	Employees: 25
2007 Sales: $235,615	2007 Profits: $81,251	Fiscal Year Ends: 12/31
2006 Sales: $195,860	2006 Profits: $70,432	Parent Company:

SALARIES/BENEFITS:

Pension Plan:	ESOP Stock Plan:	Profit Sharing:	Top Exec. Salary: $530,250	Bonus: $400,000
Savings Plan: Y	Stock Purch. Plan:		Second Exec. Salary: $383,250	Bonus: $287,500

OTHER THOUGHTS:

Apparent Women Officers or Directors:
Hot Spot for Advancement for Women/Minorities:

LOCATIONS: ("Y" = Yes)

West:	Southwest:	Midwest:	Southeast:	Northeast:	International:
Y	Y	Y	Y	Y	Y

EQUITY LIFESTYLE PROPERTIES INC
www.equitylifestyle.com

Industry Group Code: 531110 Ranks within this company's industry group: Sales: 6   Profits: 7

Properties:		Financial Services:	Construction/Development:	Investments:		Specialty Services:	Brokerage:
Apartments:		Mortgages:	Commercial Construction:	REIT:	Y	Property Management:	Commercial Sales:
Malls/Shopping:		Title Insurance:	Residential Construction:			Online Services:	Residential Sales:
Offices:		Property Insurance:	Land Development:			Software/IT:	Specialty:
Hotels/Motels:			Support Services:			Consulting:	
Industrial/Warehouses:			Design/Engineering:				
Other:	Y						

TYPES OF BUSINESS:

Real Estate Investment Trust
Manufactured Home & RV Communities

BRANDS/DIVISIONS/AFFILIATES:

MHC Operating Limited Partnership

CONTACTS: *Note: Officers with more than one job title may be intentionally listed here more than once.*

Thomas P. Heneghan, CEO
Thomas P. Heneghan, Pres.
Michael B. Berman, CFO/Exec. VP
Seth Rosenberg, Sr. VP-Sales & Mktg.
Barb Itter, VP-Human Resources
Ellen Kelleher, Corp. Sec./Exec. VP
Roger A. Maynard, Exec. VP-Asset Management
Ellen Kelleher, Exec. VP-Property Management
Samuel Zell, Chmn.

Phone: 312-279-1400	Fax: 312-279-1710
Toll-Free:	
Address: 2 N. Riverside Plz., Ste. 800, Chicago, IL 60606 US	

GROWTH PLANS/SPECIAL FEATURES:

Equity Lifestyle Properties, Inc. (ELS) is an integrated real estate investment trust (REIT) that owns and operates communities of developed residential sites as well as recreational vehicle (RV) resorts. The company primarily operates through MHC Operating Limited Partnership. The firm owns or has an interest in 307 properties in 27 U.S. states and the Canadian province of British Columbia, consisting of about 111,000 residential sites. The heaviest concentrations of these properties are located in Florida, California and Arizona, with 86 properties, 48 properties and 37 properties, respectively. Additional U.S. sites are located in Texas, Pennsylvania, Washington, Colorado, Oregon, North Carolina, Delaware, New York, Nevada, Virginia, Wisconsin, Indiana, Maine, Illinois, Massachusetts, New Jersey, Michigan, South Carolina, New Hampshire, Ohio, Tennessee, Utah, Alabama and Kentucky. These communities are designed and improved for the placement of detached, single-family manufactured homes that are produced off-site, then installed and set on residential sites within the community. The owner of each home leases the site on which it is located, while the firm handles property infrastructure issues, such as water, sewage and power. Sites typically contain centralized entrances, paved streets, curbs, gutters, parkways, clubhouses for social activities and recreation, swimming pools, shuffleboard courts, tennis courts, laundry facilities and cable television service, among other amenities. Each community is designed to attract, and is marketed to, retirees, empty-nesters, families or first-time homeowners. The company focuses on owning properties in or near large metropolitan markets, as well as popular retirement and vacation destinations.

ELS offers its employees medical coverage, life and disability insurance, a 401(k) plan and a bonus program, among other benefits.

FINANCIALS: Sales and profits are in thousands of dollars—add 000 to get the full amount. 2010 Note: Financial information for 2010 was not available for all companies at press time.

2010 Sales: $511,361	2010 Profits: $38,354	U.S. Stock Ticker: ELS
2009 Sales: $503,221	2009 Profits: $34,005	Int'l Ticker: Int'l Exchange:
2008 Sales: $463,586	2008 Profits: $18,303	Employees: 3,600
2007 Sales: $376,154	2007 Profits: $32,102	Fiscal Year Ends: 12/31
2006 Sales: $346,383	2006 Profits: $16,632	Parent Company:

SALARIES/BENEFITS:

Pension Plan:	ESOP Stock Plan:	Profit Sharing:	Top Exec. Salary: $382,454	Bonus: $573,681
Savings Plan: Y	Stock Purch. Plan:		Second Exec. Salary: $311,428	Bonus: $370,210

OTHER THOUGHTS:

Apparent Women Officers or Directors: 3
Hot Spot for Advancement for Women/Minorities: Y

LOCATIONS: ("Y" = Yes)

West:	Southwest:	Midwest:	Southeast:	Northeast:	International:
Y	Y	Y	Y	Y	Y

EQUITY OFFICE PROPERTIES TRUST

www.equityoffice.com

Industry Group Code: 531120 Ranks within this company's industry group: Sales: Profits:

Properties:		Financial Services:		Construction/Development:	Investments:		Specialty Services:		Brokerage:
Apartments:		Mortgages:		Commercial Construction:	REIT:	Y	Property Management:	Y	Commercial Sales:
Malls/Shopping:		Title Insurance:		Residential Construction:			Online Services:		Residential Sales:
Offices:	Y	Property Insurance:		Land Development:			Software/IT:		Specialty:
Hotels/Motels:				Support Services:			Consulting:		
Industrial/Warehouses:				Design/Engineering:					
Other:									

TYPES OF BUSINESS:

Real Estate Investment Trust
Office Properties
Property Management

BRANDS/DIVISIONS/AFFILIATES:

Beacon Properties, Inc.
Cornerstone Properties, Inc.
Spieker Properties, Inc.
Blackstone Group (The)
CarrAmerica Properties
Trizec Properties, Inc.
EOP Operating Limited Partnership

CONTACTS: *Note: Officers with more than one job title may be intentionally listed here more than once.*

Tom August, CEO
Tom August, Pres.
Kurt Heister, CFO
Matt Koritz, VP-General Counsel
Tom Bakke, Market Managing Dir.-Boston
Adam Goldenberg, Market Managing Dir.-New York
Joe Moe, Market Managing Dir.-Northern California
Frank Campbell, Market Managing Dir.-Southern California

Phone: 312-466-3300	Fax:
Toll-Free:	
Address: 2 N. Riverside Plz., Chicago, IL 60606 US	

GROWTH PLANS/SPECIAL FEATURES:

Equity Office Properties Trust (EOP), operating through its various affiliates and subsidiaries, is one of the largest real estate investment trusts (REITs) in the U.S. At last count, the company owned over 400 properties, most of which are Class A office buildings, in Denver, Colorado; Los Angeles, San Diego and Northern California; Seattle, Washington; Austin and Dallas Texas; Minneapolis, Minnesota; New Orleans, Louisiana; Atlanta, Georgia; Boston, Massachusetts; Columbus, Ohio; Miami, Florida; and New York City. EOP provides a wide range of office options for local, regional and national customers. The firm has a history of strategic acquisitions that have enabled it to quadruple in size since its 1997 initial public offering. These acquisitions, totaling more than $17 billion in value, include mergers with Beacon Properties, Inc.; Cornerstone Properties, Inc.; and Spieker Properties, Inc. The Blackstone Group owns the firm. Subsidiary, Equity Office Properties was merged with EOP Operating Limited Partnership and affiliates of Blackstone Real Estate Partners, including CarrAmerica Properties and Trizec Properties.

Employees of the firm are offered a benefits package that includes a 401(k) savings program with company match, health and dependent care flexible spending accounts, insurance benefits for domestic partners, adoption assistance, flexible work arrangements, educational assistance, an employee assistance program and a commuter program.

FINANCIALS: Sales and profits are in thousands of dollars—add 000 to get the full amount. 2010 Note: Financial information for 2010 was not available for all companies at press time.

2010 Sales: $	2010 Profits: $	**U.S. Stock Ticker: Private**
2009 Sales: $	2009 Profits: $	**Int'l Ticker:** Int'l Exchange:
2008 Sales: $	2008 Profits: $	Employees:
2007 Sales: $	2007 Profits: $	Fiscal Year Ends: 12/31
2006 Sales: $	2006 Profits: $	Parent Company: BLACKSTONE GROUP LP (THE)

SALARIES/BENEFITS:

Pension Plan:	ESOP Stock Plan:	Profit Sharing:	Top Exec. Salary: $	Bonus: $
Savings Plan: Y	Stock Purch. Plan:		Second Exec. Salary: $	Bonus: $

OTHER THOUGHTS:

Apparent Women Officers or Directors:
Hot Spot for Advancement for Women/Minorities:

LOCATIONS: ("Y" = Yes)

West:	Southwest:	Midwest:	Southeast:	Northeast:	International:
Y	Y	Y	Y	Y	

EQUITY ONE INC

www.equityone.net

Industry Group Code: 531120 Ranks within this company's industry group: Sales: 50   Profits: 26

Properties:		Financial Services:	Construction/Development:		Investments:		Specialty Services:		Brokerage:
Apartments:		Mortgages:	Commercial Construction:		REIT:	Y	Property Management:	Y	Commercial Sales:
Malls/Shopping:	Y	Title Insurance:	Residential Construction:				Online Services:		Residential Sales:
Offices:		Property Insurance:	Land Development:	Y			Software/IT:		Specialty:
Hotels/Motels:			Support Services:				Consulting:		
Industrial/Warehouses:			Design/Engineering:						
Other:	Y								

TYPES OF BUSINESS:

Real Estate Investment Trust
Property Management
Shopping Centers

BRANDS/DIVISIONS/AFFILIATES:

GRI-EQY I LLC
DIM Vastgoed NV
G&I VI Investment South Florida Portfolio, LLC
Capital and Counties USA, Inc.

CONTACTS: *Note: Officers with more than one job title may be intentionally listed here more than once.*

Jeffrey S. Olson, CEO
Thomas Caputo, Pres.
Mark Langer, CFO/Exec. VP/Treas.
Mark Langer, Chief Admin. Officer
Arthur L. Gallagher, General Counsel/Exec. VP/Sec.
Robert Malagon, Exec. VP-Dev.
Jason Engelman, Mgr.-Investor Rel.
Angie Valdes, Chief Acct. Officer
Lauren Holden, VP-Portfolio Mgmt./Regional Pres., Northeast
Arthur L. Gallagher, Regional Pres., South Florida
Ken Choquette, VP-Construction
Joseph Lopez, VP-Property Management/Dir.-Environmental Impact
Chaim Katzman, Chmn.

Phone: 305-947-1664	**Fax:** 305-947-1734
Toll-Free:	
Address: 1600 NE Miami Gardens Dr., North Miami Beach, FL 33179 US	

GROWTH PLANS/SPECIAL FEATURES:

Equity One, Inc. is a Florida-based real estate investment trust (REIT) that acquires, renovates, develops and manages neighborhood shopping centers anchored by national and regional supermarket chains and other necessity-oriented retailers. Its portfolio consists of 19.9 million square feet of leasable space at 182 properties located in Alabama, Connecticut, Florida, Georgia, Louisiana, Maryland, Massachusetts, Mississippi, New York, North Carolina, South Carolina, Tennessee and Virginia. These properties include 174 shopping centers, four development/redevelopment properties, six non-retail properties and five parcels of land. 21 of its shopping centers are owned through Dutch subsidiary DIM Vastgoed N.V. Additionally, it owns a 10% interest in GRI-EQY I LLC, a joint venture with Global Retail Investors LLC, which owns ten neighborhood shopping centers. It also owns a 20% interest in G&I VI Investment South Florida Portfolio, LLC, an affiliate of DRA Advisors LLC, which owns one office building and two neighborhood shopping centers. The company has leased to supermarkets, such as Albertsons, H.E.B., Kash N' Karry and Publix Super Markets (the leading Equity One tenant with 67 leases), as well as national retailers such as Office Depot, Best Buy, Blockbuster, CVS Pharmacy, Home Depot, Kmart, Lowe's, Walgreens and Wal-Mart. In April 2010, the firm acquired two shopping centers: Veranda Shoppes in Plantation, Florida, and Copps Hill Plaza in Ridgefield, Connecticut. In January 2011, through a joint venture with Capital Shopping Centres Group PLC, Equity One acquired Capital and Counties USA, Inc., which owns a portfolio of 13 properties in California. Also in January 2011, it formed joint ventures with Vestar Development Company and Rockwood Capital to acquire three shopping centers in California.

The company offers its employees benefits that include medical and dental insurance; flexible spending accounts; short- and long-term disability insurance; a 401(k) plan; an employee stock purchase plan; and a tuition assistance program.

FINANCIALS: Sales and profits are in thousands of dollars—add 000 to get the full amount. 2010 Note: Financial information for 2010 was not available for all companies at press time.

2010 Sales: $271,172	2010 Profits: $81,375	**U.S. Stock Ticker:** EQY
2009 Sales: $237,241	2009 Profits: $35,008	**Int'l Ticker:** Int'l Exchange:
2008 Sales: $239,029	2008 Profits: $35,008	Employees: 168
2007 Sales: $246,109	2007 Profits: $69,385	Fiscal Year Ends: 12/31
2006 Sales: $224,937	2006 Profits: $176,955	Parent Company:

SALARIES/BENEFITS:

Pension Plan:	ESOP Stock Plan:	Profit Sharing:	Top Exec. Salary: $672,750	Bonus: $1,164,000
Savings Plan: Y	Stock Purch. Plan:		Second Exec. Salary: $600,000	Bonus: $300,000

OTHER THOUGHTS:

Apparent Women Officers or Directors: 3
Hot Spot for Advancement for Women/Minorities: Y

LOCATIONS: ("Y" = Yes)

West:	Southwest:	Midwest:	Southeast:	Northeast:	International:
Y			Y	Y	

Note: Financial information, benefits and other data can change quickly and may vary from those stated here.

EQUITY RESIDENTIAL

www.equityapartments.com

Industry Group Code: 531110 Ranks within this company's industry group: Sales: 1   Profits: 1

Properties:		Financial Services:	Construction/Development:	Investments:		Specialty Services:		Brokerage:
Apartments:	Y	Mortgages:	Commercial Construction:	REIT:	Y	Property Management:	Y	Commercial Sales:
Malls/Shopping:		Title Insurance:	Residential Construction:			Online Services:		Residential Sales:
Offices:		Property Insurance:	Land Development:			Software/IT:		Specialty:
Hotels/Motels:			Support Services:			Consulting:		
Industrial/Warehouses:			Design/Engineering:					
Other:								

TYPES OF BUSINESS:

Real Estate Investment Trust
Apartment Communities
Property Management

BRANDS/DIVISIONS/AFFILIATES:

CONTACTS: *Note: Officers with more than one job title may be intentionally listed here more than once.*

David J. Neithercut, CEO
David J. Neithercut, Pres.
Mark J. Parrell, CFO/Exec. VP
John Powers, Exec. VP-Human Resources
Bruce C. Strohm, General Counsel/Exec. VP
David S. Santee, Exec. VP-Oper.
Mark N. Tennison, Exec. VP-Dev.
Alan W. George, Chief Investment Officer/Exec. VP
Frederick C. Tuomi, Pres., Property Management
Samuel Zell, Chmn.

Phone: 312-474-1300	Fax:
Toll-Free:	
Address: 2 N. Riverside Plz., Chicago, IL 60606 US	

GROWTH PLANS/SPECIAL FEATURES:

Equity Residential is a real estate investment trust (REIT) engaged in the acquisition, development and management of apartment properties across the U.S. The firm conducts all operations through operating partnership ERP Operating Limited Partnership, of which it owns 95.5%. One of the leading publicly traded owners and operators of multiple-family properties in the U.S., the firm owns all or a portion of 451 properties throughout 17 states and Washington, D.C., totaling around 129,604 units. The firm's most important markets include Seattle/Tacoma (with 43 apartment properties), Los Angeles (39), South Florida (38), Phoenix (36) and the San Francisco Bay Area (35). Its properties are highly diversified with respect to design and geography, ranging from high-rise to garden styles. It also owns housing units specially designed for corporate and military use. Corporate housing benefits include fully furnished units, free local calling, basic cable, short-term leases and direct billing options. Military housing provides similar benefits in addition to government credit card acceptance and military discounts. The firm's corporate housing and condominium conversion businesses are handled through subsidiaries. In 2010, the company acquired luxury apartment, 425 Mass, in Washington, D.C. for $167 million; as well as three high-rise apartment towers in Manhattan for a combined total of $475 million.

Employees are offered medical, dental and vision coverage; life and AD&D insurance; travel accident insurance; disability insurance; flexible spending accounts; a 401(k) plan; an employee stock purchase plan; profit sharing; discounts on apartment rent; home and auto insurance discounts; and credit card union membership.

FINANCIALS: Sales and profits are in thousands of dollars—add 000 to get the full amount. 2010 Note: Financial information for 2010 was not available for all companies at press time.

2010 Sales: $1,995,519	2010 Profits: $295,983	**U.S. Stock Ticker: EQR**
2009 Sales: $1,856,503	2009 Profits: $382,029	**Int'l Ticker:** Int'l Exchange:
2008 Sales: $1,886,988	2008 Profits: $436,413	Employees: 4,100
2007 Sales: $1,824,046	2007 Profits: $1,047,356	Fiscal Year Ends: 12/31
2006 Sales: $1,702,541	2006 Profits: $1,072,844	Parent Company:

SALARIES/BENEFITS:

Pension Plan:	ESOP Stock Plan:	Profit Sharing: Y	Top Exec. Salary: $625,000	Bonus: $719,063
Savings Plan: Y	Stock Purch. Plan: Y		Second Exec. Salary: $425,000	Bonus: $346,587

OTHER THOUGHTS:

Apparent Women Officers or Directors:
Hot Spot for Advancement for Women/Minorities:

LOCATIONS: ("Y" = Yes)

West:	Southwest:	Midwest:	Southeast:	Northeast:	International:
Y	Y	Y	Y	Y	

ERICKSON RETIREMENT COMMUNITIES

www.ericksonliving.com

Industry Group Code: 623110 Ranks within this company's industry group: Sales: Profits:

Properties:		Financial Services:	Construction/Development:	Investments:	Specialty Services:	Brokerage:
Apartments:	Y	Mortgages:	Commercial Construction:	REIT:	Property Management:	Commercial Sales:
Malls/Shopping:		Title Insurance:	Residential Construction:		Online Services:	Residential Sales:
Offices:		Property Insurance:	Land Development:		Software/IT:	Specialty:
Hotels/Motels:			Support Services:		Consulting:	
Industrial/Warehouses:			Design/Engineering:			
Other:	Y					

TYPES OF BUSINESS:

Retirement Communities
Supplemental Health Insurance

BRANDS/DIVISIONS/AFFILIATES:

Erickson Advantage

CONTACTS:
Note: Officers with more than one job title may be intentionally listed here more than once.
Rick Grindrod, CEO
Alan Butler, COO
Bill Butz, CFO
Tom Neubauer, Exec. VP-Sales & Mktg.
Julie Judge, Sr. VP-Human Resources
John F. Triscoli, CIO/Sr. VP
Jerry Doherty, General Counsel/Exec. VP
Kerry Jones, Sr. VP-Oper.
Adam Kane, Sr. VP-Corp. Affairs
Matthew Narrett, Exec. VP/Chief Medical Officer
Deb B. Doyle, Exec. VP-Health & Oper.
Jim Davis, Chmn.

Phone: 410-242-2880	Fax: 410-737-8854
Toll-Free:	
Address: 701 Maiden Choice Lane, Catonsville, MD 21228 US	

GROWTH PLANS/SPECIAL FEATURES:

Erickson Retirement Communities is a real estate firm focused on the development and operation of retirement communities for men and women ages 62 and up. The firm's portfolio consists of 16 properties spread throughout Colorado, Kansas, Maryland, Massachusetts, Michigan, New Jersey, Pennsylvania, Texas, and Virginia, which altogether house more than 22,000 senior citizens. The firm's communities feature apartment homes with a variety of floor plans, primarily in one- or two-bedroom options. Each apartment home is designed to promote an independent lifestyle and all Erickson communities provide residents with services including transportation, grounds maintenance, and housekeeping. Erickson's retirement communities feature amenities including restaurants, stores and a Fitness Center with full-time trainers. Additionally, each community features a medical center staffed by geriatricians who practice exclusively in Erickson communities. Residents pay an all-inclusive monthly service fee, which covers all rent and maintenance service costs. In addition to its retirement communities, Erickson provides the Erickson Advantage supplemental health insurance plan and the Erickson Health health and wellness maintenance system, which focuses on fitness and preventative wellness programs.

FINANCIALS: Sales and profits are in thousands of dollars—add 000 to get the full amount. 2010 Note: Financial information for 2010 was not available for all companies at press time.

2010 Sales: $	2010 Profits: $	U.S. Stock Ticker: Private
2009 Sales: $	2009 Profits: $	Int'l Ticker: Int'l Exchange:
2008 Sales: $	2008 Profits: $	Employees:
2007 Sales: $	2007 Profits: $	Fiscal Year Ends:
2006 Sales: $	2006 Profits: $	Parent Company:

SALARIES/BENEFITS:

Pension Plan:	ESOP Stock Plan:	Profit Sharing:	Top Exec. Salary: $	Bonus: $
Savings Plan:	Stock Purch. Plan:		Second Exec. Salary: $	Bonus: $

OTHER THOUGHTS:

Apparent Women Officers or Directors: 2
Hot Spot for Advancement for Women/Minorities:

LOCATIONS: ("Y" = Yes)

West:	Southwest:	Midwest:	Southeast:	Northeast:	International:
Y	Y	Y	Y	Y	

ESSAR GROUP LTD

www.essar.com

Industry Group Code: 523910 Ranks within this company's industry group: Sales: Profits:

Properties:	Financial Services:	Construction/Development:		Investments:	Specialty Services:	Brokerage:
Apartments:	Mortgages:	Commercial Construction:	Y	REIT:	Property Management:	Commercial Sales:
Malls/Shopping:	Title Insurance:	Residential Construction:			Online Services:	Residential Sales:
Offices:	Property Insurance:	Land Development:			Software/IT:	Specialty:
Hotels/Motels:		Support Services:			Consulting:	
Industrial/Warehouses:		Design/Engineering:				
Other:						

TYPES OF BUSINESS:

Private Equity Investments
Oil & Gas
Electric Generation
Logistics & Shipping
Steel
Construction
Communications Investments
Trucking

BRANDS/DIVISIONS/AFFILIATES:

Essar Steel
Hypermart
Essar Oil
Essar Energy
Essar Power
Essar Communications Holdings Ltd.
Vodaphone
MobileStore Ltd. (The)

CONTACTS: *Note: Officers with more than one job title may be intentionally listed here more than once.*

Prashant Ruia, CEO
V. Ashok, CFO
Adil Malia, Pres., Human Resources
Shishir Agarwal, CEO-Exploration & Prod. Bus. Group
Vikash Saraf, Dir.-Strategy, Planning, Mergers & Acquisitions
Ganesh Pai, Gen. Mgr.-Corp. Comm.
Malay Mukherjee, CEO-Steel Bus. Group
Pradeep Mittal, CEO-Minerals & Mining Bus. Group
Naresh Nayyar, CEO-Energy Bus. Group
Shashi Ruia, Chmn.

Phone: 91-22-5001-1100	Fax: 91-22-6660-1809
Toll-Free:	
Address: Essar House, 11 Kesharao Khadye Marg, Mumbai, 400 034 India	

GROWTH PLANS/SPECIAL FEATURES:

Essar Group, Ltd., based in Mumbai, is a multinational conglomerate active in the steel, energy, oil & gas, communications, construction and shipping industries, as well as other various activities. Essar Steel is an integrated flat carbon steel manufacturer with a production capacity of nearly 9.5 million tons per year. The division is involved in all aspects of production and distribution; from mining iron ore to 474 end user distribution outlets known as Essar Hypermarts. The Essar Energy Group comprises Essar Oil & Gas and Essar Power. Essar Oil operations include exploration and production of oil and gas, as well as refining and retail distribution through more than 1,300 Essar-branded service stations across India. Essar Power operates four power plants with a combined capacity of 1,220 megawatts (MW). It is currently constructing additional plants to add another 5,370 MW to its portfolio. The communications division, under Essar Communications Holdings Ltd, is partner to a joint venture with U.K. firm Vodaphone that offers GSM-based mobile telephony; has a 14% stake in Indus Towers; operates a chain of 1,300 telecom retail outlets, The MobileStore Ltd.; and through Aegis Ltd., offers integrated IT services and business process outsourcing. Essar Projects Limited is a global engineering, procurement and construction company headquartered in Dubai. Essar Shipping ports & logistics operates ports and terminals for crude oil, petroleum and coal; owns 27 sea transportation vessels; and manages an oilfield drilling business that offers on- and offshore contract drilling, with a fleet of 12 onshore rigs and one semi-submersible offshore rig. Other business areas the group is involved in include realty, minerals & mining, financial services (Essar Capital), publishing (Paprika Media) and agribusiness. In 2010, the group made several acquisitions: in May, Sallie Mae's customer service center in Texas; in June, Servosteel, a leading steel processor in the U.K.; in September, a controlling stake in AGC Networks Ltd.; and in October, the outsourcing firm Actionline based in Argentina.

FINANCIALS: Sales and profits are in thousands of dollars—add 000 to get the full amount. 2010 Note: Financial information for 2010 was not available for all companies at press time.

2010 Sales: $	2010 Profits: $	U.S. Stock Ticker: Private
2009 Sales: $	2009 Profits: $	Int'l Ticker: Int'l Exchange:
2008 Sales: $	2008 Profits: $	Employees:
2007 Sales: $	2007 Profits: $	Fiscal Year Ends:
2006 Sales: $	2006 Profits: $	Parent Company:

SALARIES/BENEFITS:

Pension Plan:	ESOP Stock Plan:	Profit Sharing:	Top Exec. Salary: $	Bonus: $
Savings Plan:	Stock Purch. Plan:		Second Exec. Salary: $	Bonus: $

OTHER THOUGHTS:

Apparent Women Officers or Directors: 1
Hot Spot for Advancement for Women/Minorities:

LOCATIONS: ("Y" = Yes)

West:	Southwest:	Midwest:	Southeast:	Northeast:	International:
	Y			Y	Y

ESSEX PROPERTY TRUST INC

www.essexpropertytrust.com

Industry Group Code: 531110 Ranks within this company's industry group: Sales: 8   Profits: 6

Properties:		Financial Services:	Construction/Development:	Investments:	Specialty Services:		Brokerage:
Apartments:	Y	Mortgages:	Commercial Construction:	REIT: Y	Property Management:	Y	Commercial Sales:
Malls/Shopping:		Title Insurance:	Residential Construction:		Online Services:		Residential Sales:
Offices:	Y	Property Insurance:	Land Development:		Software/IT:		Specialty:
Hotels/Motels:			Support Services:		Consulting:		
Industrial/Warehouses:			Design/Engineering:				
Other:							

TYPES OF BUSINESS:

Real Estate Investment Trust
Apartments
Residential Brokerage
Property Management

BRANDS/DIVISIONS/AFFILIATES:

Essex Portfolio, L.P.

CONTACTS: *Note: Officers with more than one job title may be intentionally listed here more than once.*

Michael J. Schall, CEO
Michael J. Schall, Pres.
Michael T. Dance, CFO/Exec. VP
Darcey Forbes, Dir.-Mktg.
Suzanne M. Golden, VP-Human Resources
Jamie Williams, VP-Info. Systems
Jordan E. Ritter, General Counsel/Sr. VP
John D. Eudy, Exec. VP-Dev.
Bryan G. Hunt, Chief Acct. Officer/VP
Craig K. Zimmerman, Exec. VP-Acquisitions
John F. Burkart, Exec. VP-Asset Mgmt.
Mark J. Mikl, Sr. VP-Capital Markets & Strategic Planning
Jeff Lambert, VP-Construction
George M. Marcus, Chmn.

Phone: 650-494-3700	Fax: 650-494-8743
Toll-Free:	
Address: 925 E. Meadow Dr., Palo Alto, CA 94303 US	

GROWTH PLANS/SPECIAL FEATURES:

Essex Property Trust, Inc. (EPT) is a self-administered and self-managed real estate investment trust (REIT) that acquires, develops, redevelops and manages multifamily residential properties in West Coast communities. The firm owns all of its interest in properties either directly or through Essex Portfolio, L.P., in which EPT owns about 93% general partnership interest and is the sole general partner. The company's holdings encompass 147 apartment communities, aggregating approximately 30,072 units; five office buildings, totaling roughly 215,840 square feet; and two active development projects, with 436 units in various stages of completion. Most of the firm's holdings are concentrated in coastal markets in Southern California, the San Francisco Bay area and the Seattle, Washington, metropolitan area. EPT's apartment communities are primarily suburban garden-style apartment communities and town homes comprising multiple clusters of two and three-story buildings situated on three to fifteen acres of land. The property portfolio currently includes 110 garden-style, 33 mid-rise and four high-rise apartment communities averaging approximately 205 units each. These communities contain a mixture of studio, one, two and some three-bedroom units. EPT's investment strategy has various components, including monitoring of current markets as well as the evaluation of new metropolitan markets in search of areas with relatively high rental growth potential. The company typically targets properties with over 100 units with a total value greater than $10 million. Over the course of 2010, EPT acquired 12 apartment complexes in California and Washington for a total of $584 million; the acquisitions collectively added roughly 2,100 additional units to the firm's property portfolio.

EPT offers its employees medical, dental and vision coverage; flexible spending accounts; life and disability insurance, including dependent insurance coverage; a 401(k) plan with company match; educational assistance; and a company-paid employee assistance plan, among other benefits.

FINANCIALS: Sales and profits are in thousands of dollars—add 000 to get the full amount. 2010 Note: Financial information for 2010 was not available for all companies at press time.

2010 Sales: $415,732	2010 Profits: $50,782	**U.S. Stock Ticker: ESS**
2009 Sales: $411,389	2009 Profits: $53,739	**Int'l Ticker:** Int'l Exchange:
2008 Sales: $408,434	2008 Profits: $84,395	Employees: 1,039
2007 Sales: $374,749	2007 Profits: $203,061	Fiscal Year Ends: 12/31
2006 Sales: $334,102	2006 Profits: $62,748	Parent Company:

SALARIES/BENEFITS:

Pension Plan:	ESOP Stock Plan:	Profit Sharing:	Top Exec. Salary: $350,000	Bonus: $400,000
Savings Plan: Y	Stock Purch. Plan:		Second Exec. Salary: $300,000	Bonus: $300,000

OTHER THOUGHTS:

Apparent Women Officers or Directors: 7
Hot Spot for Advancement for Women/Minorities: Y

LOCATIONS: ("Y" = Yes)

West:	Southwest:	Midwest:	Southeast:	Northeast:	International:
Y					

EVERGRANDE REAL ESTATE GROUP   www.evergrande.com

Industry Group Code: 5311 Ranks within this company's industry group: Sales: 3   Profits: 10

Properties:		Financial Services:		Construction/Development:		Investments:	Specialty Services:		Brokerage:	
Apartments:	Y	Mortgages:		Commercial Construction:	Y	REIT:	Property Management:	Y	Commercial Sales:	
Malls/Shopping:		Title Insurance:		Residential Construction:	Y		Online Services:		Residential Sales:	
Offices:	Y	Property Insurance:		Land Development:	Y		Software/IT:		Specialty:	
Hotels/Motels:	Y			Support Services:	Y		Consulting:			
Industrial/Warehouses:				Design/Engineering:	Y					
Other:										

TYPES OF BUSINESS:

Real Estate Development
Architectural Engineering Services
Architectural Design Services
Property Management Services

BRANDS/DIVISIONS/AFFILIATES:

Evergrande Real Estate Development Co., Ltd.
Evergrande Architectural Engineering Company
Evergrande Architectural Design Institute
Evergrande Property Management Company
Jinan Evergrande Oasis
Changchun Evergrande Oasis
Chongqing Evergrande Hotel

CONTACTS: *Note: Officers with more than one job title may be intentionally listed here more than once.*

Xia Haijun, CEO/Vice Chmn.
Tse Wai Wah, CFO
He Miaoling, VP-Mktg.
Jimmy Fong, Corp. Sec./VP
Li Gang, Exec. VP/Vice Chmn.
Xu Xiangwu, VP/Gen. Mgr.-Mgmt. Center
Xu Wen, VP/Chmn.-Evergrande Materials & Equipment Co.
He Maoling, VP
Hui Ka Yan, Chmn.

Phone: 86-20-3830-2222	**Fax:** 86-20-3830-2233
Toll-Free:	
Address: Tianlun Building, 45 Tianhe Rd., 23rd Fl., Guangzhou City, 510060 China	

GROWTH PLANS/SPECIAL FEATURES:

Evergrande Real Estate Group is one of the largest real estate developers in China, primarily engaged in the planning, design, construction, development and management of real estate properties. Evergrande's portfolio of real estate comprises 73 properties throughout China. Major projects, comprising high-end residential, hotel and commercial properties, include the Evergrande Palace, Evergrande Metropolis, Evergrande City, Evergrande Oasis and Evergrande Splendor. The firm has launched more than 150 major projects throughout 80 cities across China, including Guangzhou, Shanghai, Shenzhen, Tianjin, Chongqing, Shenyang, Wuhan, Chengdu, Nanjing, Xi'an, Changsha, Taiyuan, Kunming, Hefei, Guiyang, Nanchang, Changchun, Haikou, Harbin and Urumqi. Evergrande's subsidiaries include Evergrande Real Estate Development Co., Ltd., a real estate development company that has developed projects such as the Evergrande Jinbi Garden, Evergrande Royal Scenic Peninsula and Evergrande Palace; Evergrande Architectural Engineering Company, an architectural engineering company that performs industrial and civil construction, high-rise construction, equipment installation and municipal works; Evergrande Architectural Design Institute, which offers architectural design services for residential buildings ranging from planning and interior design to garden landscaping; and Evergrande Property Management Company, which manages a variety of properties throughout China, including multi-story residential buildings, high-rise residential buildings, villas and commercial properties. During 2010, the firm opened three new properties: the Jinan Evergrande Oasis; the Changchun Evergrande Oasis; and the Chongqing Evergrande Hotel.

FINANCIALS: Sales and profits are in thousands of dollars—add 000 to get the full amount. 2010 Note: Financial information for 2010 was not available for all companies at press time.

2010 Sales: $7,024,780	2010 Profits: $1,163,930	**U.S. Stock Ticker:**
2009 Sales: $877,720	2009 Profits: $160,490	**Int'l Ticker: 3333** Int'l Exchange: Hong Kong-HKEX
2008 Sales: $553,190	2008 Profits: $80,490	Employees: 19,351
2007 Sales: $	2007 Profits: $	Fiscal Year Ends: 12/31
2006 Sales: $	2006 Profits: $	Parent Company:

SALARIES/BENEFITS:

Pension Plan:	ESOP Stock Plan:	Profit Sharing:	Top Exec. Salary: $	Bonus: $
Savings Plan:	Stock Purch. Plan:		Second Exec. Salary: $	Bonus: $

OTHER THOUGHTS:

Apparent Women Officers or Directors: 3
Hot Spot for Advancement for Women/Minorities: Y

LOCATIONS: ("Y" = Yes)

West:	Southwest:	Midwest:	Southeast:	Northeast:	International:
					Y

EXTENDICARE REAL ESTATE INVESTMENT TRUST

www.extendicare.com

Industry Group Code: 623110 Ranks within this company's industry group: Sales: 2 Profits: 2

Properties:	Financial Services:	Construction/Development:	Investments:	Specialty Services:	Brokerage:
Apartments:	Mortgages:	Commercial Construction:	REIT:	Property Management:	Commercial Sales:
Malls/Shopping:	Title Insurance:	Residential Construction:		Online Services:	Residential Sales:
Offices:	Property Insurance:	Land Development:		Software/IT:	Specialty:
Hotels/Motels:		Support Services:		Consulting:	
Industrial/Warehouses:		Design/Engineering:			
Other: Y					

TYPES OF BUSINESS:

Long-Term Care
Assisted Living Facilities
Sub-Acute Care
Rehabilitative Services

BRANDS/DIVISIONS/AFFILIATES:

Extendicare Health Services Inc
Extendicare REIT
Extendicare (Canada) Inc
ProStep
ParaMed

CONTACTS: Note: Officers with more than one job title may be intentionally listed here more than once.

Timothy L. Lukenda, CEO
Timothy L. Lukenda, Pres.
Douglas J. Harris, CFO/Sr. VP
Deborah Bakti, VP-Human Resources, Extendicare (Canada), Inc.
Jillian E. Fountain, Corp. Sec.
Paul Tuttle, Pres., Canadian Oper.-Extendicare, Inc.
Elaine E. Everson, Controller/VP-Extendicare, Inc.
Elaine E. Everson, Controller/VP-Extendicare (Canada), Inc.
Katharine A. O'Reilly, VP-Quality, Extendicare (Canada), Inc.
Christina L. McKey, VP-Eastern Oper., Extendicare (Canada), Inc.
Wayne McKendrick, VP-Western Oper., Extendicare (Canada), Inc.
Mel Rhinelander, Chmn.
Roch Carter, VP/General Counsel-Extendicare Health Svcs., Inc.

Phone: 905-470-4000	Fax: 905-470-4003
Toll-Free:	
Address: 3000 Steeles Ave. E., Ste. 700, Markham, ON L3R 9W2 Canada	

GROWTH PLANS/SPECIAL FEATURES:

Extendicare Real Estate Investment Trust is a Canadian real estate investment trust (REIT) operating long-term care facilities and related services. Through its subsidiaries it operates roughly 258 (176 in the U.S.) long-term care and assisted living facilities across North America, with a total capacity of 28,800 residents (17,300 in the U.S.). Through its operations in the U.S., Extendicare offers nursing care, assisted living and related medical specialty services, while home health care services are provided in Canada. All of these facilities are operated through two operating subsidiaries: Extendicare Health Services, Inc. (EHSI), based in the U.S.; and Extendicare (Canada), Inc., based in Canada. EHSI offers, in addition to standard nursing and assistance, specialty care services such as sub-acute care and rehabilitative therapy services through ProStep, the company's progressive step rehabilitation service. Virtual Care Provider, Inc., also operating in the U.S., provides information technology services to small long-term care providers. In Canada, Extendicare offers ParaMed, which provides home health care services to subscribers. In addition to these subsidiaries and products, the firm offers management and consulting services and group supply purchasing services for third-party customers.

Extendicare offers its employees and their children educational assistance programs, as well as scholarship programs for those pursuing health care professions.

FINANCIALS: Sales and profits are in thousands of dollars—add 000 to get the full amount. 2010 Note: Financial information for 2010 was not available for all companies at press time.

2010 Sales: $2,177,380	2010 Profits: $54,410	**U.S. Stock Ticker:**
2009 Sales: $2,166,230	2009 Profits: $77,720	**Int'l Ticker: EXE** Int'l Exchange: Toronto-TSX
2008 Sales: $1,686,690	2008 Profits: $11,350	Employees: 37,700
2007 Sales: $1,441,150	2007 Profits: $57,500	Fiscal Year Ends: 12/31
2006 Sales: $1,664,300	2006 Profits: $-34,300	Parent Company:

SALARIES/BENEFITS:

Pension Plan:	ESOP Stock Plan:	Profit Sharing:	Top Exec. Salary: $821,700	Bonus: $402,794
Savings Plan:	Stock Purch. Plan: Y		Second Exec. Salary: $383,489	Bonus: $152,598

OTHER THOUGHTS:

Apparent Women Officers or Directors: 6
Hot Spot for Advancement for Women/Minorities: Y

LOCATIONS: ("Y" = Yes)

West:	Southwest:	Midwest:	Southeast:	Northeast:	International:
Y		Y		Y	Y

FAIRMONT HOMES INC   www.fairmonthomes.com

Industry Group Code: 321991 Ranks within this company's industry group: Sales: Profits:

Properties:	Financial Services:	Construction/Development:		Investments:	Specialty Services:	Brokerage:
Apartments:	Mortgages:	Commercial Construction:		REIT:	Property Management:	Commercial Sales:
Malls/Shopping:	Title Insurance:	Residential Construction:	Y		Online Services:	Residential Sales:
Offices:	Property Insurance:	Land Development:			Software/IT:	Specialty:
Hotels/Motels:		Support Services:			Consulting:	
Industrial/Warehouses:		Design/Engineering:				
Other:						

TYPES OF BUSINESS:

Manufactured Housing
Recreational Vehicles

BRANDS/DIVISIONS/AFFILIATES:

Owens Corning
Moen
Georgia-Pacific Corp
Whirpool Appliances
Gulf Stream Coach Inc
Supernova
Touring Cruiser
Canyon Trail

CONTACTS: *Note: Officers with more than one job title may be intentionally listed here more than once.*

James F. Shea, CEO
Edward Ludwick, Pres.
Rick Jones, Dir.-Human Resources
Judy Stapleton, Mgr.-Safety
James F. Shea, Chmn.
Bob Hasse, Dir.-Purchasing

Phone: 574-773-7941	Fax: 574-773-2185
Toll-Free:	
Address: 502 S. Oakland Ave., Nappanee, IN 46550 US	

GROWTH PLANS/SPECIAL FEATURES:

Fairmont Homes, Inc., a family owned and operated business, makes manufactured housing, including single- and multi-section homes with up to 2,330 square feet. It offers several floor plans that feature 2-5 bedrooms, 1-3 bathrooms and extra features such as a study, retreat room, library, utility room, family room, great room, porch, basement, den, breakfast nook, dining room, living room, sunroom, morning room, sitting room and park trailer. The company also offers luxury features such as Amish-crafted cabinetry and custom designed kitchens. Fairmont has retailers located in 21 states throughout the Midwestern and Northeastern U.S. The firm's suppliers include Owens Corning, Moen, Georgia-Pacific, Whirlpool Appliances, Trane Furnaces, Style Crest Siding, Honeywell Thermostats, Congoleum Flooring and Shaw Carpets. In addition to manufactured housing, Fairmont's Gulf Stream Coach subsidiary manufactures a full line of recreational vehicles, offering 26 brands and more than 100 models. Gulf Stream brands include the luxury brands, Scenic Cruiser, Independence, Sun Voyager, Constellation, Canyon Trail, Caribbean, Conquest, Yellowstone, Sedona, Supernova, Touring Cruiser and Montaj.

Employees of the company receive medical and dental coverage; an on-site country club with a swimming pool and golf course; a 401(k) plan; life insurance; cancer insurance; wellness benefits; and prescription plan.

FINANCIALS: Sales and profits are in thousands of dollars—add 000 to get the full amount. 2010 Note: Financial information for 2010 was not available for all companies at press time.

2010 Sales: $	2010 Profits: $	**U.S. Stock Ticker: Private**
2009 Sales: $	2009 Profits: $	**Int'l Ticker:** Int'l Exchange:
2008 Sales: $	2008 Profits: $	Employees:
2007 Sales: $	2007 Profits: $	Fiscal Year Ends: 12/31
2006 Sales: $	2006 Profits: $	Parent Company:

SALARIES/BENEFITS:

Pension Plan:	ESOP Stock Plan:	Profit Sharing:	Top Exec. Salary: $	Bonus: $
Savings Plan: Y	Stock Purch. Plan:		Second Exec. Salary: $	Bonus: $

OTHER THOUGHTS:

Apparent Women Officers or Directors: 1
Hot Spot for Advancement for Women/Minorities:

LOCATIONS: ("Y" = Yes)

West:	Southwest:	Midwest:	Southeast:	Northeast:	International:
		Y			

FAIRMONT RAFFLES HOTELS INTERNATIONAL INC

www.fairmont.com
Industry Group Code: 721110 Ranks within this company's industry group: Sales: Profits:

Properties:		Financial Services:	Construction/Development:	Investments:	Specialty Services:		Brokerage:
Apartments:		Mortgages:	Commercial Construction:	REIT:	Property Management:	Y	Commercial Sales:
Malls/Shopping:		Title Insurance:	Residential Construction:		Online Services:	Y	Residential Sales:
Offices:		Property Insurance:	Land Development:		Software/IT:		Specialty:
Hotels/Motels:	Y		Support Services:		Consulting:		
Industrial/Warehouses:			Design/Engineering:				
Other:	Y						

TYPES OF BUSINESS:
Hotels, Luxury
Spa Services
Real Estate Holdings

BRANDS/DIVISIONS/AFFILIATES:
Fairmont Hotels & Resorts
Farimont Gold
Raffles Hotels & Resorts
Fairmont Golf
Fairmont Residences
Fairmont Ski
Fairmont Chateau Whistler
Fairmont Vail

CONTACTS: *Note: Officers with more than one job title may be intentionally listed here more than once.*
William R. Fatt, CEO
Chris J. Cahill, COO
John A. Carnella, CFO/Exec. VP

Phone: 416-874-2600	Fax: 416-874-2601
Toll-Free: 800-257-7544	
Address: 155 Wellington St. W., Ste. 3300, Toronto, ON M5K 0C3 Canada	

GROWTH PLANS/SPECIAL FEATURES:
Fairmont Raffles Hotels International, Inc., created in 2006 by the combination of Fairmont Hotels and Raffles Hotels, is one of the world's largest luxury hotel firms. It operates approximately 100 hotels worldwide under the Raffles, Fairmont and Swissotel brand names. Owners of the firm include Kingdom Holding Company and Colony Capital. The firm offers many services to its business travel clients such as high-speed Internet access; a 24 hour technology help desk; work centers with photocopying services, secretarial services, a private lounge and boardroom; printers for in-room use; a 24 hour fax service; and express checkout. The Fairmont offers various types of resort accommodations including spa resorts, golf resorts, ski resorts, Fairmont Gold and Fairmont Residences. Fairmont Spas feature Willow Stream spa facilities in many of its hotels. Fairmont Golf properties are located in cities around the world such as Acapulco, Mexico; St. Andrews, Scotland; Zimbali, South Africa; and Southhampton, Bermuda. Fairmont Ski designations include the Fairmont Chateau Whistler, Fairmont Vail, Fairmont Tremblant and many others. Fairmont Gold is an exclusive, private floor of the hotel with its own private check-in and check-out desk. Fairmont Gold offers a private lounge; a healthy continental breakfast; afternoon canapes and honor bar; complimentary newspapers; computer access in lounge; in-room high-speed Internet access; and a selection of DVD's , CD's, books and games. Fairmont Residences are located worldwide in locations such as Dubai, U.A.E.; Zimbali, South Africa; and Vancouver, Canada. These properties are designed to be utilized as primary dwelling or as getaway retreats.

FINANCIALS: Sales and profits are in thousands of dollars—add 000 to get the full amount. 2010 Note: Financial information for 2010 was not available for all companies at press time.

2010 Sales: $	2010 Profits: $	U.S. Stock Ticker: Private
2009 Sales: $	2009 Profits: $	Int'l Ticker: Int'l Exchange:
2008 Sales: $	2008 Profits: $	Employees:
2007 Sales: $	2007 Profits: $	Fiscal Year Ends: 12/31
2006 Sales: $	2006 Profits: $	Parent Company:

SALARIES/BENEFITS:

Pension Plan:	ESOP Stock Plan:	Profit Sharing:	Top Exec. Salary: $	Bonus: $
Savings Plan:	Stock Purch. Plan:		Second Exec. Salary: $	Bonus: $

OTHER THOUGHTS:
Apparent Women Officers or Directors:
Hot Spot for Advancement for Women/Minorities:

LOCATIONS: ("Y" = Yes)

West:	Southwest:	Midwest:	Southeast:	Northeast:	International:
Y	Y	Y	Y	Y	Y

FANNIE MAE

www.fanniemae.com

Industry Group Code: 522310　Ranks within this company's industry group:　Sales: 1　Profits: 5

Properties:	Financial Services:		Construction/Development:	Investments:	Specialty Services:		Brokerage:
Apartments:	Mortgages:	Y	Commercial Construction:	REIT:	Property Management:		Commercial Sales:
Malls/Shopping:	Title Insurance:		Residential Construction:		Online Services:		Residential Sales:
Offices:	Property Insurance:		Land Development:		Software/IT:	Y	Specialty:
Hotels/Motels:			Support Services:		Consulting:		
Industrial/Warehouses:			Design/Engineering:				
Other:							

TYPES OF BUSINESS:

Mortgages, Secondary Market
Mortgage-Related Securities
Financial Software

BRANDS/DIVISIONS/AFFILIATES:

Federal National Mortgage Association

CONTACTS:
Note: Officers with more than one job title may be intentionally listed here more than once.

Michael J. Williams, CEO
Michael J. Williams, Pres.
David M. Johnson, CFO/Exec. VP
Edward G. Watson, Exec. VP-Tech
Timothy J. Mayopoulos, Chief Admin. Officer
Timothy J. Mayopoulos, General Counsel/Exec. VP/Corp. Sec.
Edward G. Watson, Exec. VP-Oper.
Terry Edwards, Exec. VP-Credit Portfolio Mgmt.
David Benson, Exec. VP-Capital Markets
Michael A. Shaw, Exec. VP/Chief Credit Officer
Kenneth J. Phelan, Exec. VP/Chief Risk Officer
Phillip A. Laskawy, Chmn.

Phone: 202-752-7000	Fax:
Toll-Free: 800-732-6643	
Address: 3900 Wisconsin Ave. NW, Washington, DC 20016 US	

GROWTH PLANS/SPECIAL FEATURES:

Fannie Mae is a government-sponsored enterprise chartered by the U.S. Congress under the name Federal National Mortgage Association. Fannie Mae is currently in a conservatorship under the control of the U.S. federal government. The firm's activities include providing funds to mortgage lenders through the purchase of mortgage assets, then issuing and guarantying mortgage-related securities, which facilitates the flow of additional funds into the mortgage market. Fannie Mae does not offer mortgages directly to homebuyers, but operates exclusively in the secondary mortgage market, securitizing mortgages from primary market lenders. These include commercial banks, savings and loan associations, mortgage companies and securities dealers. The company operates in three segments: single-family credit guaranty, housing and community development and capital markets. The single-family credit guaranty segment works with lender customers to securitize single-family mortgage loans into Fannie Mae mortgage-backed securities (MBS) and to facilitate the purchase of single-family mortgage loans. The housing and community development segment works with lender customers to securitize multifamily mortgage loans into Fannie Mae MBS and to facilitate the purchase of multifamily mortgage loans. The capital markets segment manages the firm's investment activity in mortgage loans and mortgage-related securities. This segment is also responsible for managing the company's assets, liabilities and its liquidity and capital positions. In 2010, Fannie Mae opened mortgage help centers in Miami, Atlanta and Chicago to assist homeowners struggling to pay their mortgages. Services available at these centers include reviewing the borrower's loan, discussing foreclosure alternatives, collecting required documents for the federal Making Home Affordable Program and reaching a decision on any pending loan workout efforts. In June 2010, the firm was ordered to delist from the New York Stock Exchange.

The company offers its employees medical and dental insurance; life insurance; and education assistance.

FINANCIALS:
Sales and profits are in thousands of dollars—add 000 to get the full amount. 2010 Note: Financial information for 2010 was not available for all companies at press time.

2010 Sales: $17,493,000	2010 Profits: $-14,018,000	**U.S. Stock Ticker: FNMA**
2009 Sales: $22,494,000	2009 Profits: $-72,022,000	**Int'l Ticker:**　Int'l Exchange:
2008 Sales: $17,436,000	2008 Profits: $-58,707,000	Employees: 7,300
2007 Sales: $11,206,000	2007 Profits: $-2,050,000	Fiscal Year Ends: 12/31
2006 Sales: $12,012,000	2006 Profits: $4,059,000	Parent Company:

SALARIES/BENEFITS:

Pension Plan: Y	ESOP Stock Plan: Y	Profit Sharing:	Top Exec. Salary: $951,923	Bonus: $
Savings Plan: Y	Stock Purch. Plan: Y		Second Exec. Salary: $788,000	Bonus: $

OTHER THOUGHTS:

Apparent Women Officers or Directors: 3
Hot Spot for Advancement for Women/Minorities: Y

LOCATIONS: ("Y" = Yes)

West:	Southwest:	Midwest:	Southeast:	Northeast:	International:
		Y	Y	Y	

FEDERAL AGRICULTURAL MORTGAGE CORP (FARMER MAC)

www.farmermac.com

Industry Group Code: 522310 Ranks within this company's industry group: Sales: 4   Profits: 1

Properties:		Financial Services:		Construction/Development:	Investments:	Specialty Services:	Brokerage:
Apartments:		Mortgages:	Y	Commercial Construction:	REIT:	Property Management:	Commercial Sales:
Malls/Shopping:		Title Insurance:		Residential Construction:		Online Services:	Residential Sales:
Offices:		Property Insurance:		Land Development:		Software/IT:	Specialty:
Hotels/Motels:				Support Services:		Consulting:	
Industrial/Warehouses:				Design/Engineering:			
Other:							

TYPES OF BUSINESS:

Mortgages
Agricultural Real Estate Loans
Rural Housing Mortgage Loans

BRANDS/DIVISIONS/AFFILIATES:

Farmer Mac I
Farmer Mac II
Rural Utilities
AgPower LOS

CONTACTS: *Note: Officers with more than one job title may be intentionally listed here more than once.*

Michael A. Gerber, CEO
Tom D. Stenson, COO/Exec. VP
Michael A. Gerber, Pres.
Timothy L. Buzby, CFO/Sr. VP
Jerome G. Oslick, General Counsel/Corp. Sec./VP
Mary K. Waters, VP-Corp. Rel.
Lowell L. Junkins, Acting Chmn.

Phone: 202-872-7700	Fax: 202-872-7713
Toll-Free: 800-879-3276	
Address: 1133 21st St. NW, Ste. 600, Washington, DC 20036 US	

GROWTH PLANS/SPECIAL FEATURES:

Federal Agricultural Mortgage Corp., known as Farmer Mac, is a secondary market for agricultural real estate and rural housing mortgage loans. Congress created the company in 1987 to improve the availability of mortgage credit to America's farmers, ranchers and rural homeowners, businesses and communities. Farmer Mac does this through providing liquidity and lending capacity to agricultural mortgage lenders by purchasing newly originated and pre-existing mortgage loans directly from lenders; guaranteeing securities backed by eligible mortgage loans, referred to as Farmer Mac I Guaranteed Securities; exchanging newly issued Farmer Mac I Guaranteed Securities for newly originated and seasoned eligible mortgage loans that back those securities in so-called swap transactions; and issuing long-term standby purchase commitments for both newly originated and seasoned mortgage loans. The firm does this through three programs: Farmer Mac I, Farmer Mac II and rural utilities. Under Farmer Mac I, Farmer Mac purchases eligible mortgage loans, securitizes purchased loans and guarantees the timely payment of principal and interest on the securities backed by the loans. Under Farmer Mac II, the company purchases the guaranteed portions of loans guaranteed by the United States Department of Agriculture (USDA) and guarantees securities backed by those USDA-guaranteed portions purchased by Farmer Mac. Under the Rural Utilities Loans program, Farmer Mac purchases qualified rural utilities loans, or guarantees the timely payment of interest and principal of securities representing interests in or obligations backed by pools of such loans. AgPower LOS (Loan Origination System) is Farmer Mac's proprietary web based system that facilitates loan submission and communication with underwriters. Although created by Congress, Farmer Mac is a publicly traded corporation owned by its stockholders. Farmer Mac's primary sources of revenue are the fees it receives from outstanding Farmer Mac Guaranteed Securities and its purchase commitments and net interest income from Farmer Mac Guaranteed Securities.

FINANCIALS: Sales and profits are in thousands of dollars—add 000 to get the full amount. 2010 Note: Financial information for 2010 was not available for all companies at press time.

2010 Sales: $94,150	2010 Profits: $22,080	**U.S. Stock Ticker: AGM**
2009 Sales: $83,055	2009 Profits: $82,298	**Int'l Ticker:** Int'l Exchange:
2008 Sales: $74,184	2008 Profits: $-154,080	Employees:
2007 Sales: $44,668	2007 Profits: $4,421	Fiscal Year Ends: 12/31
2006 Sales: $40,686	2006 Profits: $29,773	Parent Company:

SALARIES/BENEFITS:

Pension Plan:	ESOP Stock Plan:	Profit Sharing:	Top Exec. Salary: $528,990	Bonus: $648,544
Savings Plan:	Stock Purch. Plan:		Second Exec. Salary: $366,097	Bonus: $281,192

OTHER THOUGHTS:

Apparent Women Officers or Directors: 2
Hot Spot for Advancement for Women/Minorities:

LOCATIONS: ("Y" = Yes)

West:	Southwest:	Midwest:	Southeast:	Northeast:	International:
		Y		Y	

FEDERAL REALTY INVESTMENT TRUST   www.federalrealty.com

Industry Group Code: 531120 Ranks within this company's industry group: Sales: 34   Profits: 20

Properties:		Financial Services:	Construction/Development:	Investments:		Specialty Services:	Brokerage:
Apartments:		Mortgages:	Commercial Construction:	REIT:	Y	Property Management:	Commercial Sales:
Malls/Shopping:	Y	Title Insurance:	Residential Construction:			Online Services:	Residential Sales:
Offices:	Y	Property Insurance:	Land Development:			Software/IT:	Specialty:
Hotels/Motels:			Support Services:			Consulting:	
Industrial/Warehouses:			Design/Engineering:				
Other:							

TYPES OF BUSINESS:

Real Estate Investment Trust
Retail Properties
Real Estate Development & Redevelopment

BRANDS/DIVISIONS/AFFILIATES:

CONTACTS: *Note: Officers with more than one job title may be intentionally listed here more than once.*

Donald C. Wood, CEO
Dawn Becker, COO/Exec. VP
Donald C. Wood, Pres.
Andrew Blocher, CFO/Treas./Sr. VP
Lisa Denson, VP-IT & Special Projects
Debbie Colson, Sr. VP-Legal Oper.
John Hendrickson, VP/COO-Northeast Region
Don Briggs, Sr. VP-Dev.
Janelle Stevenson, Dir.-Corp. Comm.
Gina Birdsall, Dir.-Investor Rel.
Phillip Mays, Chief Acct. Officer/VP
Wendy Seher, VP-Leasing
Chris Weilminster, Sr. VP-Leasing
Jeff Berkes, Chief Investment Officer/Exec. VP
Joseph S. Vassalluzzo, Chmn.

Phone: 301-998-8100	Fax: 301-998-3700
Toll-Free: 800-658-8980	
Address: 1626 E. Jefferson St., Rockville, MD 20852-4041 US	

GROWTH PLANS/SPECIAL FEATURES:

Federal Realty Investment Trust is an equity real estate investment trust (REIT) engaged in the ownership, management, development and redevelopment of retail and mixed-use properties. Federal Realty's portfolio encompasses approximately 85 community and neighborhood shopping centers and mixed-used properties in 13 states and Washington, D.C., comprising a total of 18.3 million square feet. The company also holds a 30% share in a joint venture that owns seven properties totaling approximately 1 million square feet. The company focuses on the acquisition of commercial properties that have expansion, redevelopment and remerchandising potential. The company particularly targets affluent and densely populated communities throughout the Northeast, Mid-Atlantic and California. Its largest markets by number of developments are Maryland (with 17 properties), followed by Virginia (15), California (12) and Pennsylvania (11). Federal Realty's portfolio is 94% leased to national, regional and local retailers. Its leasing clients include Urban Outfitters, Banana Republic, Borders Books, Safeway, Crate & Barrel, TJ Maxx, Giant Food, CVS and Barnes & Noble, among many others. In January 2011, the firm acquired the Tower Shops retail center, a 372,000 square-foot development in Davie, Florida, for $66.1 million.

Employees are offered medical and dental insurance; a vision discount program; a 401(k) plan; tuition reimbursement; disability coverage; flexible spending accounts; life insurance; AD&D insurance; an incentive bonus program; and housing discounts.

FINANCIALS: Sales and profits are in thousands of dollars—add 000 to get the full amount. 2010 Note: Financial information for 2010 was not available for all companies at press time.

2010 Sales: $544,674	2010 Profits: $122,249	**U.S. Stock Ticker:** FRT
2009 Sales: $530,518	2009 Profits: $97,763	**Int'l Ticker:** Int'l Exchange:
2008 Sales: $519,611	2008 Profits: $129,246	Employees: 361
2007 Sales: $482,788	2007 Profits: $195,095	Fiscal Year Ends: 12/31
2006 Sales: $426,816	2006 Profits: $118,712	Parent Company:

SALARIES/BENEFITS:

Pension Plan:	ESOP Stock Plan:	Profit Sharing:	Top Exec. Salary: $726,154	Bonus: $1,122,000
Savings Plan: Y	Stock Purch. Plan:		Second Exec. Salary: $400,000	Bonus: $264,000

OTHER THOUGHTS:

Apparent Women Officers or Directors: 8
Hot Spot for Advancement for Women/Minorities: Y

LOCATIONS: ("Y" = Yes)

West:	Southwest:	Midwest:	Southeast:	Northeast:	International:
Y	Y	Y	Y	Y	

FELCOR LODGING TRUST INC

www.felcor.com

Industry Group Code: 531120 Ranks within this company's industry group: Sales: 17   Profits: 60

Properties:	Financial Services:	Construction/Development:	Investments:	Specialty Services:	Brokerage:
Apartments:	Mortgages:	Commercial Construction:	REIT: Y	Property Management:	Commercial Sales:
Malls/Shopping:	Title Insurance:	Residential Construction:		Online Services:	Residential Sales:
Offices:	Property Insurance:	Land Development:		Software/IT:	Specialty:
Hotels/Motels: Y		Support Services:		Consulting:	
Industrial/Warehouses:		Design/Engineering:			
Other:					

TYPES OF BUSINESS:

Real Estate Investment Trust
Hotel Ownership

BRANDS/DIVISIONS/AFFILIATES:

FelCor Lodging LP

CONTACTS: *Note: Officers with more than one job title may be intentionally listed here more than once.*

Richard A. Smith, CEO
Troy A. Pentecost, COO/Exec. VP
Richard A. Smith, Pres.
Andrew J. Welch, CFO/Exec. VP
Jonathan H. Yellen, General Counsel/Exec. VP/Corp. Sec.
Stephen A. Schafer, VP-Investor Rel.
Michael A. DeNicola, Chief Investment Officer/Exec. VP
Robert P. Carl, Sr. VP/Dir.-Design & Construction
Thomas J. Corcoran, Jr., Chmn.

Phone: 972-444-4900	**Fax:** 972-444-4949
Toll-Free:	
Address: 545 E. John Carpenter Freeway, Ste. 1300, Irving, TX 75062 US	

GROWTH PLANS/SPECIAL FEATURES:

FelCor Lodging Trust, Inc. (FelCor) is a hotel real estate investment trust (REIT) that, through its 99% partnership interest in FelCor Lodging LP, holds ownership interests in 82 hotels in 22 states and the city of Toronto in Canada, with a total of approximately 24,000 rooms and suites. The company is among the largest U.S. owners of upper-upscale, all-suite style hotel properties. Of the 82 hotels in which FelCor holds an ownership interest, it owns a 100% interest in 64 hotels, a 90% interest in entities owning three hotels, an 82% interest in an entity owning one hotel, a 60% interest in an entity owning one hotel and a 50% interest in entities owning 13 hotels. Its hotel brands include Embassy Suites Hotels (representing approximately 54% of FelCor 2010 earnings), Holiday Inn (19%), Sheraton (10%), Doubletree (7%), Renaissance (5%), Hilton (2%), Westin (2%) and Marriot (1%). FelCor's properties are located in major business and leisure travel markets including San Francisco, southern Florida, Atlanta, Los Angeles, Orlando, Dallas, San Antonio, San Diego, Boston, Minneapolis and Philadelphia. In 2010, roughly 97% of FelCor's revenue was derived from U.S. properties, with the remaining 3% derived from the properties in Canada. The firm has alliances with the four brand owners that manage most of FelCor's hotels: Hilton Worldwide, whose brands include Embassy Suites Hotels, Hilton and Doubletree; InterContinental Hotels Group, owner of the Holiday Inn brand; Starwood Hotels & Resorts, whose brands include Sheraton and Westin; and Marriott International, Inc., which owns the Marriott and Renaissance hotel brands. During 2010, FelCor acquired the Fairmont Copley Plaza in Boston for $98.5 million. The company has initiated a program of strategic disposition that is expected to eventually lead to the sale of 35 hotel properties, with 14 initial properties being listed for sale in January 2011.

FINANCIALS: Sales and profits are in thousands of dollars—add 000 to get the full amount. 2010 Note: Financial information for 2010 was not available for all companies at press time.

2010 Sales: $928,311	2010 Profits: $-225,837	**U.S. Stock Ticker:** FCH
2009 Sales: $874,395	2009 Profits: $-109,091	**Int'l Ticker:** Int'l Exchange:
2008 Sales: $1,059,394	2008 Profits: $-120,487	Employees: 68
2007 Sales: $993,834	2007 Profits: $89,824	Fiscal Year Ends: 12/31
2006 Sales: $991,038	2006 Profits: $51,045	Parent Company:

SALARIES/BENEFITS:

Pension Plan:	ESOP Stock Plan:	Profit Sharing:	Top Exec. Salary: $600,000	Bonus: $1,776,184
Savings Plan: Y	Stock Purch. Plan:		Second Exec. Salary: $321,360	Bonus: $694,828

OTHER THOUGHTS:

Apparent Women Officers or Directors: 1
Hot Spot for Advancement for Women/Minorities:

LOCATIONS: ("Y" = Yes)

West:	Southwest:	Midwest:	Southeast:	Northeast:	International:
Y	Y	Y	Y	Y	Y

FERGUSON ENTERPRISES INC

www.ferguson.com

Industry Group Code: 444130 Ranks within this company's industry group: Sales: Profits:

Properties:	Financial Services:	Construction/Development:		Investments:	Specialty Services:	Brokerage:
Apartments:	Mortgages:	Commercial Construction:		REIT:	Property Management:	Commercial Sales:
Malls/Shopping:	Title Insurance:	Residential Construction:			Online Services:	Residential Sales:
Offices:	Property Insurance:	Land Development:			Software/IT:	Specialty:
Hotels/Motels:		Support Services:	Y		Consulting:	
Industrial/Warehouses:		Design/Engineering:				
Other:						

TYPES OF BUSINESS:

Plumbing Supplies, Retail
Wholesale Distribution
Construction Supplies, Retail
Waterworks Supplies
HVAC Equipment, Retail
PVF Supplies, Retail

BRANDS/DIVISIONS/AFFILIATES:

Wolseley plc
Ferguson Xpress

CONTACTS: *Note: Officers with more than one job title may be intentionally listed here more than once.*

Frank W. Roach, CEO
Kevin Murphy, COO
Frank W. Roach, Pres.
Dave Keltner, CFO
Shawn Washington, Mgr.-Oper.
Bill Stevens, Mgr.-Bus. Dev., Ferguson Integration Svcs.
Stacy Hackworth, Gen. Mgr.-Frostproof Dist. Center
Frank W. Roach, CEO-Wolseley North America

Phone: 757-874-7795	Fax: 757-989-2501
Toll-Free:	
Address: 12500 Jefferson Ave., Newport News, VA 23602 US	

GROWTH PLANS/SPECIAL FEATURES:

Ferguson Enterprises, Inc. is one of the largest wholesale distributors of plumbing supplies in the U.S. The company has been a subsidiary of Wolseley plc, one of largest distributors of plumbing and heating products in the world, since 1982. Ferguson has approximately 1,350 retail locations in all 50 U.S. states, Washington, D.C., Puerto Rico, the Caribbean and Mexico. Additionally, the firm operates Ferguson Xpress stores, largely self-service locations that market plumbing and light commercial products to contractors. In general, Ferguson's customers include homeowners, builders, contractors, engineers and other trade professionals. Ferguson operates in eight business groups: residential; heating and cooling equipment (HVAC); industrial; commercial and mechanical; waterworks; hospitality; government; and integrated services. The company's product offerings include plumbing supplies; pipes, valves and fittings; HVAC; waterworks; lighting; appliances; tools and safety equipment; gas fireplaces; and fire protection products. An internal delivery service moves products from distribution hubs to Ferguson branches, satellites and customers. Through other divisions, the company is involved in nuclear power provision; fire protection supply; valve assembly and testing; and geosynthetic product supply to the mining industry.

Employees of Ferguson are offered medical, dental and vision coverage; a 401(k) plan; short- and long-term disability; life insurance; flexible spending accounts; educational assistance; on-site employee training courses; and a performance awards program.

FINANCIALS: Sales and profits are in thousands of dollars—add 000 to get the full amount. 2010 Note: Financial information for 2010 was not available for all companies at press time.

2010 Sales: $	2010 Profits: $	U.S. Stock Ticker: Subsidiary
2009 Sales: $	2009 Profits: $	Int'l Ticker: Int'l Exchange:
2008 Sales: $	2008 Profits: $	Employees:
2007 Sales: $9,650,000	2007 Profits: $	Fiscal Year Ends: 7/31
2006 Sales: $9,650,000	2006 Profits: $	Parent Company: WOLSELEY PLC

SALARIES/BENEFITS:

Pension Plan:	ESOP Stock Plan:	Profit Sharing:	Top Exec. Salary: $	Bonus: $
Savings Plan: Y	Stock Purch. Plan:		Second Exec. Salary: $	Bonus: $

OTHER THOUGHTS:

Apparent Women Officers or Directors: 1
Hot Spot for Advancement for Women/Minorities:

LOCATIONS: ("Y" = Yes)

West:	Southwest:	Midwest:	Southeast:	Northeast:	International:
Y	Y	Y	Y	Y	Y

FIDELITY NATIONAL FINANCIAL INC   www.fnf.com

Industry Group Code: 524127 Ranks within this company's industry group: Sales: 1   Profits: 1

Properties:	Financial Services:		Construction/Development:	Investments:	Specialty Services:	Brokerage:
Apartments:	Mortgages:		Commercial Construction:	REIT:	Property Management:	Commercial Sales:
Malls/Shopping:	Title Insurance:	Y	Residential Construction:		Online Services:	Residential Sales:
Offices:	Property Insurance:		Land Development:		Software/IT:	Specialty:
Hotels/Motels:			Support Services:		Consulting:	
Industrial/Warehouses:			Design/Engineering:			
Other:						

TYPES OF BUSINESS:

Title Insurance
Escrow Services
Collection & Trust Activities
Electronic Data Interchange Software
Payment Processing
Equipment Lease Services
Insurance Claims Management

BRANDS/DIVISIONS/AFFILIATES:

Fidelity National Title
Chicago Title
Commonwealth Land Title
Lawyers Title
Ticor Title
Security Union Title
Alamo Title
Ceridian Corporation

CONTACTS: *Note: Officers with more than one job title may be intentionally listed here more than once.*

Alan L. Stinson, CEO
George Scanlon, COO
Anthony J. Park, CFO
Brent Bickett, Exec. VP-Finance
Raymond R. Quirk, CEO-Fidelity National Title Group
Michael L. Gravelle, Corp. Sec
Daniel Kennedy Murphy, Sr. VP/Treas.
William P. Foley, II, Chmn.

Phone: 904-854-8100	Fax: 904-357-1007
Toll-Free: 888-934-3354	
Address: 601 Riverside Ave., Jacksonville, FL 32204 US	

GROWTH PLANS/SPECIAL FEATURES:

Fidelity National Financial, Inc. (FNF) is a holding company that provides outsourced products and services to a variety of industries. It offers mortgage services, title insurance, specialty insurance and information services. The company is one of the nation's largest title insurance companies through its title insurance underwriters: Fidelity National Title, Chicago Title, Commonwealth Land Title, Lawyers Title, Ticor Title, Security Union Title and Alamo Title. FNF operates in three segments: Fidelity National Title Group, Inc. (FNT); Specialty Insurance; and Corporate and Other. Fidelity National Title Group, Inc., a majority-owned, publicly traded company, is responsible for the title operations of FNF. Through its Specialty Insurance segment, FNF is a leading provider of specialty insurance products, including flood insurance, homeowners insurance, automobile insurance and home warranty insurance. The company's Corporate and Other segment includes certain other unallocated corporate overhead expenses, other smaller operations and the firm's interests in Ceridian Corporation and Remy International, Inc. Ceridian Corporation, the firm's minority-owned subsidiary, provides information services to the transportation, human resources and retail industries. Remy International, Inc. is a manufacturer, remanufacturer and distributor of Delco Remy brand heavy-duty systems and Remy brand starters and alternators, locomotive products and hybrid power technology. In May 2010, FNF sold its 32% ownership in Sedgwick Claims Management Services, Inc. to affiliates of Stone Point Capital LLC and Hellman & Friedman LLC for $224 million.

FINANCIALS: Sales and profits are in thousands of dollars—add 000 to get the full amount. 2010 Note: Financial information for 2010 was not available for all companies at press time.

2010 Sales: $5,740,300	2010 Profits: $370,100	**U.S. Stock Ticker: FNF**
2009 Sales: $5,828,400	2009 Profits: $222,300	**Int'l Ticker:** Int'l Exchange:
2008 Sales: $4,251,200	2008 Profits: $-179,016	Employees: 18,200
2007 Sales: $5,465,600	2007 Profits: $129,769	Fiscal Year Ends: 12/31
2006 Sales: $9,434,399	2006 Profits: $437,761	Parent Company:

SALARIES/BENEFITS:

Pension Plan: Y	ESOP Stock Plan:	Profit Sharing:	Top Exec. Salary: $7,215,000	Bonus: $4,438,783
Savings Plan: Y	Stock Purch. Plan: Y		Second Exec. Salary: $642,000	Bonus: $2,562,637

OTHER THOUGHTS:

Apparent Women Officers or Directors:
Hot Spot for Advancement for Women/Minorities:

LOCATIONS: ("Y" = Yes)

West:	Southwest:	Midwest:	Southeast:	Northeast:	International:
Y	Y	Y	Y	Y	Y

FIDELITY NATIONAL INFORMATION SERVICES INC

www.fisglobal.com

Industry Group Code: 522320 Ranks within this company's industry group: Sales: 1   Profits: 1

Properties:	Financial Services:	Construction/Development:	Investments:	Specialty Services:		Brokerage:
Apartments:	Mortgages:	Commercial Construction:	REIT:	Property Management:		Commercial Sales:
Malls/Shopping:	Title Insurance:	Residential Construction:		Online Services:		Residential Sales:
Offices:	Property Insurance:	Land Development:		Software/IT:	Y	Specialty:
Hotels/Motels:		Support Services:		Consulting:		
Industrial/Warehouses:		Design/Engineering:				
Other:						

TYPES OF BUSINESS:

Payment & Transaction Processing Services
IT Consulting
Outsourcing Services
Due Diligence Services
Mortgage Loan Processing

BRANDS/DIVISIONS/AFFILIATES:

GIFTS Software, Inc.
Capco
ValueCentric Marketing Group, Inc.

CONTACTS: *Note: Officers with more than one job title may be intentionally listed here more than once.*

Frank R. Martire, CEO
Gary A. Norcross, COO/Exec. VP
Frank R. Martire, Pres.
Michael D. Hayford, CFO/Exec. VP
Marcia Danzeisen, Sr. VP-Global Mktg.
Michael P. Oates, Chief Human Resources Officer/Exec. VP
Brian Hurdis, Exec. VP-Tech. Svcs.
Michael Gravelle, Chief Legal Officer/Exec. VP/Corp. Sec.
James Susoreny, Exec. VP-Bus. Dev.
Marcia Danzeisen, Sr. VP-Global Comm.
Mary K. Waggoner, Sr. VP-Investor Rel.
Brent Bickett, Exec. VP-Corp. Finance
Ram Chary, Exec. VP-Global Commercial Svcs.
Rob Heyvaert, Exec. VP
Frank D'Angelo, Exec. VP-Payment Solutions
Anthony Jabbour, Exec. VP-Financial Solutions
William P. Foley, II, Chmn.
Mark Davey, Exec. VP-Int'l

Phone: 904-854-5000	**Fax:** 904-357-1105
Toll-Free: 888-323-0310	
Address: 601 Riverside Ave., Jacksonville, FL 32204 US	

GROWTH PLANS/SPECIAL FEATURES:

Fidelity National Information Services, Inc. (FIS) offers banking/payments technology solutions, processing services and information-based services. The firm provides core financial institution processing; card issuer and transaction processing services; and outsourcing services to financial institutions and retailers worldwide. The company has processing and technology relationships with 40 of the top 50 global banks, including nine of the top 10. Headquartered in Jacksonville, Florida, FIS maintains a global presence, serving more than 14,000 financial institutions through offices in over 100 countries worldwide. The company operates in four segments: Financial Solutions, Payment Solutions, International Solutions and Corporate/Other. The Financial Solutions Group offers core processing software applications designed to run critical banking processes; channel, decision and risk management solutions; syndicated loan applications; and global commercial services. The Payment Solutions division offers settlement and card management solutions for financial institution card issuers; check and transaction ticket data capture; healthcare payments solutions; and card issuer services, enabling financial institutions and others to issue VISA and MasterCard branded credit and debit cards, private label cards, and other electronic payment cards for use by both consumer and business accounts. FIS' International Solutions segment provides the firm's services in over 100 countries. The Corporate/Other division includes corporate overhead costs that are not allocated to operating segments. In June 2010, FIS agreed to acquire Compliance Coach, Inc. In October 2010, the firm acquired ValueCentric Marketing Group, Inc. In December 2010, the company acquired Capco. In February 2011, FIS acquired GIFTS Software, Inc.

FINANCIALS: Sales and profits are in thousands of dollars—add 000 to get the full amount. 2010 Note: Financial information for 2010 was not available for all companies at press time.

2010 Sales: $5,269,500	2010 Profits: $404,500	**U.S. Stock Ticker:** FIS
2009 Sales: $3,711,100	2009 Profits: $105,900	**Int'l Ticker:** Int'l Exchange:
2008 Sales: $3,446,000	2008 Profits: $214,800	Employees: 33,000
2007 Sales: $2,892,900	2007 Profits: $561,222	Fiscal Year Ends: 12/31
2006 Sales: $2,416,500	2006 Profits: $259,087	Parent Company:

SALARIES/BENEFITS:

Pension Plan:	ESOP Stock Plan:	Profit Sharing:	Top Exec. Salary: $886,250	Bonus: $2,481,500
Savings Plan: Y	Stock Purch. Plan:		Second Exec. Salary: $627,500	Bonus: $3,067,500

OTHER THOUGHTS:

Apparent Women Officers or Directors: 2
Hot Spot for Advancement for Women/Minorities:

LOCATIONS: ("Y" = Yes)

West:	Southwest:	Midwest:	Southeast:	Northeast:	International:
Y	Y	Y	Y	Y	Y

FIRST AMERICAN FINANCIAL CORPORATION www.firstam.com

Industry Group Code: 524127 Ranks within this company's industry group: Sales: 2 Profits: 2

Properties:	Financial Services:		Construction/Development:	Investments:	Specialty Services:	Brokerage:
Apartments:	Mortgages:		Commercial Construction:	REIT:	Property Management:	Commercial Sales:
Malls/Shopping:	Title Insurance:	Y	Residential Construction:		Online Services:	Residential Sales:
Offices:	Property Insurance:		Land Development:		Software/IT:	Specialty:
Hotels/Motels:			Support Services:		Consulting:	
Industrial/Warehouses:			Design/Engineering:			
Other:						

TYPES OF BUSINESS:

Title Insurance
Real Estate Services
Escrow Services
Screening Services
Credit Reporting
Property & Casualty Insurance
Trust Services
Internet Services

BRANDS/DIVISIONS/AFFILIATES:

First American Corp.
First Title plc
First American CoreLogic
BasePoint Analytics LLC
First Advantage Corporation
CoreLogic, Inc.

CONTACTS: *Note: Officers with more than one job title may be intentionally listed here more than once.*

Dennis J. Gilmore, CEO
Max O. Valdes, CFO/Exec. VP
Mark E. Rutherford, Sr. VP-Human Resources
Kenneth D. DeGiorgio, Exec. VP/Sec.
Craig Barberio, Contact-Investor Rel.
Mark E. Seaton, Sr. VP-Finance
Parker S. Kennedy, Chmn.
Tom Grifferty, Pres., Int'l Svcs.

Phone: 714-250-3000	Fax:
Toll-Free: 800-854-3643	
Address: 1 First American Way, Santa Ana, CA 92707 US	

GROWTH PLANS/SPECIAL FEATURES:

First American Financial Corporation, formerly First American Corp., provides title insurance, as well as specialty insurance coverage for the real estate and mortgage industries. The company conducts its operations through two major units: the financial services group and the information solutions group. The financial services group includes the title insurance and services segment, which issues residential and commercial title insurance policies and provides escrow services, investment advisory services and trust services; and the specialty insurance segment, which issues property and casualty insurance policies and provides home warranties. Through FAF International, the firm offers global insurance services in certain Central and South American countries, Canada, Europe, Australia and Asia. The firm's information solutions group encompasses the information and outsourcing solutions segment, which provides tax monitoring, flood zone certification, default management services and asset management services; the data and analytic solutions segment, offering database management and appraisal services; and the risk mitigation and business solutions segment, comprised of First Advantage Corporation (FAC). FAC operates in six business groups: lender services, data services, dealer services, employer services, multifamily services and investigation and litigation support services. The lender services group provides consumer credit reporting solutions for mortgage and home equity companies. The data services group offers motor vehicle records, transportation industry credit reporting, criminal records reselling and lead generation services. In June 2010, the company spun off its two major divisions, establishing two separate legal entities; First American Financial Corp. now handles the operations of the title and financial services group, and CoreLogic, Inc. now comprises the information solutions operating segment.

Employee benefits include medical, dental, prescription drug and vision coverage; an employee assistance program; a 401(k); an employee stock purchase plan; life and AD&D insurance; group legal and auto plans; long-term care insurance; and fitness discounts.

FINANCIALS: Sales and profits are in thousands of dollars—add 000 to get the full amount. 2010 Note: Financial information for 2010 was not available for all companies at press time.

2010 Sales: $3,906,612	2010 Profits: $128,956	**U.S. Stock Ticker:** FAF
2009 Sales: $4,046,834	2009 Profits: $134,277	**Int'l Ticker:** Int'l Exchange:
2008 Sales: $4,367,725	2008 Profits: $-72,482	Employees: 16,879
2007 Sales: $8,222,383	2007 Profits: $-3,119	Fiscal Year Ends: 12/31
2006 Sales: $8,533,597	2006 Profits: $287,676	Parent Company:

SALARIES/BENEFITS:

Pension Plan:	ESOP Stock Plan:	Profit Sharing:	Top Exec. Salary: $700,000	Bonus: $490,000
Savings Plan: Y	Stock Purch. Plan: Y		Second Exec. Salary: $675,000	Bonus: $1,308,242

OTHER THOUGHTS:

Apparent Women Officers or Directors:
Hot Spot for Advancement for Women/Minorities:

LOCATIONS: ("Y" = Yes)

West:	Southwest:	Midwest:	Southeast:	Northeast:	International:
Y	Y	Y	Y	Y	Y

FIRST INDUSTRIAL REALTY TRUST INC

www.firstindustrial.com

Industry Group Code: 531120 Ranks within this company's industry group: Sales: 40 Profits: 59

Properties:	Financial Services:	Construction/Development:		Investments:		Specialty Services:		Brokerage:
Apartments:	Mortgages:	Commercial Construction:	Y	REIT:	Y	Property Management:	Y	Commercial Sales:
Malls/Shopping:	Title Insurance:	Residential Construction:				Online Services:		Residential Sales:
Offices:	Property Insurance:	Land Development:				Software/IT:		Specialty:
Hotels/Motels:		Support Services:				Consulting:		
Industrial/Warehouses: Y		Design/Engineering:						
Other:								

TYPES OF BUSINESS:

Real Estate Investment Trust-Industrial Properties
Development Services
Warehouses

BRANDS/DIVISIONS/AFFILIATES:

CONTACTS:
Note: Officers with more than one job title may be intentionally listed here more than once.

Bruce W. Duncan, CEO
Bruce W. Duncan, Pres.
Scott Musil, Interim CFO
Christopher Schneider, CIO
John Clayton, VP-Legal
Christopher Schneider, Sr. VP-Oper.
Michael Damone, Dir.-Strategic Planning
Johannson Yap, Chief Investment Officer
Donald Stoffle, Exec. Dir.-Dispositions
Robert Walter, Sr. VP-Capital Markets
David Harker, Exec. VP-Central
W. Ed Tyler, Chmn.

Phone: 312-344-4300	Fax: 312-922-6320
Toll-Free:	
Address: 311 S. Wacker Dr., Ste. 3900, Chicago, IL 60606 US	

GROWTH PLANS/SPECIAL FEATURES:

First Industrial Realty Trust, Inc. owns, manages, acquires, sells, develops and redevelops industrial real estate in the U.S. Organized as a real estate investment trust (REIT), First Industrial owns and operates approximately 783 in-service industrial properties located in 28 states and containing approximately 68.9 million square feet of gross leasable areas. These properties fall into five primary sub-groups: light industrial (of which the firm's portfolio contains approximately 369 properties), R&D flex (131 properties), bulk warehouse (174 properties), regional warehouse (89 properties) and manufacturing (20 properties). Most of its properties are located in business parks, with easy access to highways, rail lines or airports. The tenants that occupy them do business in the manufacturing, retail, wholesale trade, distribution and professional service industries. First Industrial's properties and land parcels are held through partnerships, corporations and limited liability companies controlled directly or indirectly by the firm, including a number of joint ventures.

Employees are offered medical, dental and vision insurance; retirement planning; employee stock programs; and life insurance.

FINANCIALS:
Sales and profits are in thousands of dollars—add 000 to get the full amount. 2010 Note: Financial information for 2010 was not available for all companies at press time.

2010 Sales: $351,838	2010 Profits: $-222,619	**U.S. Stock Ticker: FR**
2009 Sales: $288,541	2009 Profits: $4,186	**Int'l Ticker:** Int'l Exchange:
2008 Sales: $514,321	2008 Profits: $20,169	Employees: 229
2007 Sales: $369,874	2007 Profits: $130,368	Fiscal Year Ends: 12/31
2006 Sales: $300,183	2006 Profits: $112,082	Parent Company:

SALARIES/BENEFITS:

Pension Plan:	ESOP Stock Plan:	Profit Sharing:	Top Exec. Salary: $778,974	Bonus: $750,000
Savings Plan:	Stock Purch. Plan: Y		Second Exec. Salary: $365,000	Bonus: $400,000

OTHER THOUGHTS:

Apparent Women Officers or Directors:
Hot Spot for Advancement for Women/Minorities:

LOCATIONS: ("Y" = Yes)

West:	Southwest:	Midwest:	Southeast:	Northeast:	International:
Y	Y	Y	Y	Y	Y

FIRST MORTGAGE CORP
www.firstmortgage.com

Industry Group Code: 522310 Ranks within this company's industry group: Sales: Profits:

Properties:	Financial Services:		Construction/Development:	Investments:	Specialty Services:	Brokerage:
Apartments:	Mortgages:	Y	Commercial Construction:	REIT:	Property Management:	Commercial Sales:
Malls/Shopping:	Title Insurance:		Residential Construction:		Online Services:	Residential Sales:
Offices:	Property Insurance:		Land Development:		Software/IT:	Specialty:
Hotels/Motels:			Support Services:		Consulting:	
Industrial/Warehouses:			Design/Engineering:			
Other:						

TYPES OF BUSINESS:
Mortgages
Loan Origination
Loan Purchasing

BRANDS/DIVISIONS/AFFILIATES:

CONTACTS: *Note: Officers with more than one job title may be intentionally listed here more than once.*
Clement Ziroli, CEO
Bruce G. Norman, COO
Bruce G. Norman, Pres.
Pac W. Dong, CFO/Exec. VP
Tammy Russ, VP-Human Resources
Robyn S. Fredericks, Corp. Sec./Sr. VP
Pac W. Dong, Controller/Exec. VP
Ronald T. Vargas, Sr. VP
Scott Lehrer, Sr. VP
Clement Ziroli, Chmn.

Phone: 909-595-1996	Fax: 909-598-7351
Toll-Free: 800-395-4778	
Address: 3230 Fallow Field Dr., Diamond Bar, CA 91765 US	

GROWTH PLANS/SPECIAL FEATURES:
First Mortgage Corp. (FMC) is a mortgage banking firm. The company originates, purchases, warehouses, sells and services mortgage loans for owner-occupied residences, principally in California. The firm originates mortgage loans through three primary sources: referrals from real estate brokers and builders; direct marketing; and consumers interested in refinancing. FMC provides seven different loan programs. Its conventional loans are mortgages not insured or guaranteed by any governmental agency, and thus may be eligible for purchase on the secondary mortgage market. These loans are available with either fixed or adjustable interest rates and have individualized repayment terms. FHA loans are originated by FMC and insured by the Federal Housing Administration, have both fixed or adjustable interest rates and 30-year repayment terms. The Department of Housing and Urban Development (HUD) determines the designated maximum loan amount. Jumbo or non-conforming loans are those that exceed the maximum amount allowed for conventional loans and may be up to $1 million. These are either fixed or adjustable rate mortgages, with parameters varying depending on the down payment and actual loan amount. In addition to these, the company provides VA loans and three California-specific programs. The VA loans, guaranteed by the Veteran's Association, are for those who have served or are currently in the U.S. armed forces that meet eligibility requirements. They do not require a down payment. FMC is approved to offer California's Housing Finance Agency Homeownership Loan Program; it offers California State Teachers Retirement System loan programs; and it is an approved lender of the California Public Employees Retirement System. These California programs allow certain public officials, teachers, judges and state legislators and homebuyers to benefit from low or no down payments, reduced fees and closing cost assistance.

FINANCIALS: Sales and profits are in thousands of dollars—add 000 to get the full amount. 2010 Note: Financial information for 2010 was not available for all companies at press time.

2010 Sales: $	2010 Profits: $	U.S. Stock Ticker: Private
2009 Sales: $	2009 Profits: $	Int'l Ticker: Int'l Exchange:
2008 Sales: $	2008 Profits: $	Employees:
2007 Sales: $	2007 Profits: $	Fiscal Year Ends: 3/31
2006 Sales: $	2006 Profits: $	Parent Company:

SALARIES/BENEFITS:

Pension Plan:	ESOP Stock Plan:	Profit Sharing:	Top Exec. Salary: $	Bonus: $
Savings Plan:	Stock Purch. Plan:		Second Exec. Salary: $	Bonus: $

OTHER THOUGHTS:
Apparent Women Officers or Directors: 2
Hot Spot for Advancement for Women/Minorities:

LOCATIONS: ("Y" = Yes)

West:	Southwest:	Midwest:	Southeast:	Northeast:	International:
Y					

FIRSTCITY FINANCIAL CORP

www.fcfc.com

Industry Group Code: 522310 Ranks within this company's industry group: Sales: 5   Profits: 2

Properties:	Financial Services:		Construction/Development:	Investments:	Specialty Services:	Brokerage:
Apartments:	Mortgages:	Y	Commercial Construction:	REIT:	Property Management:	Commercial Sales:
Malls/Shopping:	Title Insurance:		Residential Construction:		Online Services:	Residential Sales:
Offices:	Property Insurance:		Land Development:		Software/IT:	Specialty:
Hotels/Motels:			Support Services:		Consulting:	
Industrial/Warehouses:			Design/Engineering:			
Other:						

TYPES OF BUSINESS:

Mortgages
Portfolio Acquisitions
Flexible Capital Structuring Arrangements

BRANDS/DIVISIONS/AFFILIATES:

VFC Partners 4 LLC

CONTACTS: *Note: Officers with more than one job title may be intentionally listed here more than once.*

James T. Sartain, CEO
Jim W. Moore, COO/Exec. VP
James T. Sartain, Pres.
J. Bryan Baker, CFO/Sr. VP
James C. Holmes, Sr. VP/Dir.-Finance
Mark B. Horrell, VP
Terry R. DeWitt, Sr. VP/Dir.-Acquisitions
Joe S. Greak, Sr. VP/Dir.-Tax
C. Ivan Wilson, Vice Chmn.
Richard E. Bean, Chmn.

Phone: 254-761-2800	Fax: 254-751-7648
Toll-Free: 800-247-4274	
Address: 6400 Imperial Dr., Waco, TX 76712 US	

GROWTH PLANS/SPECIAL FEATURES:

FirstCity Financial Corp. is a diversified financial services company. The firm has offices throughout the U.S. and Mexico, and a presence in Chile, Argentina, France, Germany and Brazil. The company operates in two segments: portfolio asset acquisition/resolution and special situations platform. FirstCity Financial purchases and resolves portfolios of performing and non-performing commercial/consumer loans, as well as other assets generally acquired at a discount. Assets are acquired either in the form of pools or single assets, and are only purchased after an extensive evaluation has been completed. This evaluation includes an examination of the local economic and market trends; and an analysis of a given asset's projected cash flow and sources of repayment. Sellers of portfolio assets have included financial institutions, insurance companies and government agencies such as the Small Business Association (SBA). FirstCity Financial's special situation platform segment provides investment capital to privately-held middle-market companies through flexible capital structuring arrangements. These capital investments are primarily senior and junior financing arrangements; other investments include common equity warrants, distressed debt transactions, direct equity investments and leveraged buyouts. FirstCity's other services include debt purchases; due diligence underwriting; loan servicing and management; and debt obligation negotiation and resolution. In May 2010, VFC Partners 4 LLC (jointly owned by FirstCity Financial and Varde Partners, Inc.) acquired underperforming commercial and residential loans on properties in Florida and New York from Intervest Mortgage Corporation and Intervest National Bank.

FINANCIALS: Sales and profits are in thousands of dollars—add 000 to get the full amount. 2010 Note: Financial information for 2010 was not available for all companies at press time.

2010 Sales: $85,564	2010 Profits: $12,503	**U.S. Stock Ticker: FCFC**
2009 Sales: $79,787	2009 Profits: $18,744	**Int'l Ticker:** Int'l Exchange:
2008 Sales: $45,196	2008 Profits: $-46,675	Employees: 264
2007 Sales: $43,656	2007 Profits: $2,185	Fiscal Year Ends: 12/31
2006 Sales: $28,387	2006 Profits: $9,802	Parent Company:

SALARIES/BENEFITS:

Pension Plan:	ESOP Stock Plan:	Profit Sharing: Y	Top Exec. Salary: $500,000	Bonus: $370,000
Savings Plan: Y	Stock Purch. Plan: Y		Second Exec. Salary: $300,000	Bonus: $325,000

OTHER THOUGHTS:

Apparent Women Officers or Directors: 1
Hot Spot for Advancement for Women/Minorities:

LOCATIONS: ("Y" = Yes)

West:	Southwest:	Midwest:	Southeast:	Northeast:	International:
Y	Y				Y

FIRSTSERVICE CORPORATION

www.firstservice.com

Industry Group Code: 5311 Ranks within this company's industry group: Sales: 14   Profits: 23

Properties:	Financial Services:	Construction/Development:		Investments:	Specialty Services:		Brokerage:	
Apartments:	Mortgages:	Commercial Construction:		REIT:	Property Management:	Y	Commercial Sales:	Y
Malls/Shopping:	Title Insurance:	Residential Construction:			Online Services:		Residential Sales:	Y
Offices:	Property Insurance:	Land Development:			Software/IT:	Y	Specialty:	
Hotels/Motels:		Support Services:	Y		Consulting:	Y		
Industrial/Warehouses:		Design/Engineering:	Y					
Other:								

TYPES OF BUSINESS:

Real Estate Services
Residential Property Management
Security Services
Maintenance Services
Outsourcing Services
IT & Logistics Support
Security Systems Design

BRANDS/DIVISIONS/AFFILIATES:

Colliers International
PGP Property Valuation
PKF Hotel & Hospitality Consulting
California Closets
Goodstein Management
Condominium First Management Services
Boer Hartog Hooft
Association Management, Inc.

CONTACTS: *Note: Officers with more than one job title may be intentionally listed here more than once.*

Jay S. Hennick, CEO
D. Scott Patterson, COO
D. Scott Patterson, Pres.
John B. Friedrichsen, CFO/Sr. VP
Douglas G. Cooke, Corp. Sec.
Roman Kocur, Sr. VP-Corp. Dev. & Strategy
Christian Mayer, VP-Finance
Elias Mulamoottil, Sr. VP-Corp. Dev. & Strategy
Neil D. Chander, VP-Tax
Douglas G. Cooke, Corp. Controller/VP
Gene Gomberg, CEO-FirtService Residential Management
Peter F. Cohen, Chmn.

Phone: 416-960-9500	**Fax:** 416-960-5333
Toll-Free:	
Address: FirstService Bldg., 1140 Bay St., Ste. 4000, Toronto, ON M5S 2B4 Canada	

GROWTH PLANS/SPECIAL FEATURES:

FirstService Corporation is a diversified provider of services to residential and commercial tenants worldwide. The company has three main operating segments: residential property management, which generated 33% of the firm's 2010 revenue; property services, 24%; and commercial real estate services, 43%. The residential property management segment oversees residential communities; provides sales and leasing brokerage; valuation and advisory services; standard property management (leasing, maintenance, etc.); and specialty management (such as pools), mostly to private residential communities. In total, the residential property management unit oversees roughly 4,600 residential communities containing over 1.2 million housing units in 18 U.S. states and two Canadian provinces. The property services segment offers property reservation services through Field Asset Services; owns and operates seven franchise systems, including Paul Davis Restoration, California Closets, CertaPro Painters, Pillar to Post and Floorcoverings International; and branchising services (the reacquisition of profitable franchises). The commercial real estate services segment, which operates primarily through its subsidiary Colliers International, offers full service commercial real estate services through over 214 offices in 38 countries. Other brands in this segment include PGP Property Valuation, PKF Hotel & Hospitality Consulting and MHPM Project Managers. In April 2010, Colliers International acquired a controlling stake in commercial real estate services company Colliers Bennett & Kahnweiler. In July 2010, the firm acquired Goodstein Management. In September 2010, FirstService acquired Condominium First Management Services, a residential property management services firm in Alberta, Canada. In November 2010, Colliers International acquired a majority interest in Dutch commercial real estate services company Boer Hartog Hooft. In December 2010, the company acquired an 80% interest in Association Management, Inc. and a majority interest in Crosby Property Management Ltd.

FINANCIALS: Sales and profits are in thousands of dollars—add 000 to get the full amount. 2010 Note: Financial information for 2010 was not available for all companies at press time.

2010 Sales: $1,986,271	2010 Profits: $47,900	**U.S. Stock Ticker: FSRV**
2009 Sales: $1,703,222	2009 Profits: $-7,279	**Int'l Ticker: FSV** Int'l Exchange: Toronto-TSX
2008 Sales: $1,549,713	2008 Profits: $34,863	Employees: 20,000
2007 Sales: $1,152,821	2007 Profits: $34,863	Fiscal Year Ends: 12/31
2006 Sales: $918,668	2006 Profits: $69,497	Parent Company:

SALARIES/BENEFITS:

Pension Plan:	ESOP Stock Plan:	Profit Sharing:	Top Exec. Salary: $1,155,300	Bonus: $3,347,300
Savings Plan:	Stock Purch. Plan:		Second Exec. Salary: $469,200	Bonus: $

OTHER THOUGHTS:

Apparent Women Officers or Directors:
Hot Spot for Advancement for Women/Minorities:

LOCATIONS: ("Y" = Yes)

West:	Southwest:	Midwest:	Southeast:	Northeast:	International:
Y	Y	Y	Y	Y	Y

FIVE STAR PRODUCTS INC

www.fivestarproducts.com

Industry Group Code: 4233 Ranks within this company's industry group: Sales: Profits:

Properties:	Financial Services:	Construction/Development:		Investments:	Specialty Services:		Brokerage:
Apartments:	Mortgages:	Commercial Construction:		REIT:	Property Management:		Commercial Sales:
Malls/Shopping:	Title Insurance:	Residential Construction:			Online Services:		Residential Sales:
Offices:	Property Insurance:	Land Development:			Software/IT:	Y	Specialty:
Hotels/Motels:		Support Services:	Y		Consulting:		
Industrial/Warehouses:		Design/Engineering:	Y				
Other:							

TYPES OF BUSINESS:

Hardware
Decorating & Finishing Products
Hardware Distribution
Painting Supplies
Technical Services

BRANDS/DIVISIONS/AFFILIATES:

National Patent Development Corporation
Merit Group Inc (The)
Five Star EZ-Cure Grout
Five Star Fluid Epoxy
Five Star High Temperature Grout
Five Star Group, Inc.
Novolac
Design-A-Spec

CONTACTS: Note: Officers with more than one job title may be intentionally listed here more than once.

David Babcock, CEO
David Babcock, Pres.
Brian Feidt, CFO
Terry Stysly, VP-Global Sales
Chris Piekos, Dir.-Technical Svcs.
Steven P. Fenelli, VP-Prod. Dev.
Bobby Carlson, Mgr.-East Region
Rick Dufresne, Mgr.-Northeast Region
Walt Cooper, Mgr.-Central Region
Simon Ross, Mgr.-Int'l Sales

Phone: 203-336-7900	Fax: 203-336-7930
Toll-Free:	
Address: 750 Commerce Dr., Fairfield, CT 06825 US	

GROWTH PLANS/SPECIAL FEATURES:

Five Star Products, Inc. (Five Star) is engaged in the wholesale distribution of home decorating, hardware and finishing products. Formerly a wholly-owned subsidiary of National Patent Development Corporation, the company was acquired by The Merit Group, Inc. in 2010. Five Star serves over 3,000 retail dealers in the Northeast and Mid Atlantic states, making it one of the largest independent distributors in the Northeastern U.S. The firm and its subsidiary, Five Star Group, Inc., operate two warehouse facilities located in Newington, Connecticut and East Hanover, New Jersey. The company has 100 patents worldwide and offers a variety of high performance cement and epoxy based construction solutions for the industrial, infrastructure and marine markets. Specific products produced by Five Star include concrete restoration, advanced vibration dampening products, waterproofing coatings, adhesives and machinery foundation systems. The firm is a major distributor of paint sundry items, interior and exterior stains, brushes, rollers, caulking compounds and hardware products. Five Star has also developed elastomeric grout, which absorbs vibration in the train and trolley industries; a line of Novolac products for coatings, structural concrete and grout; and a new computer program, Design-A-Spec, which assists engineers in selecting the proper products for applications, giving specifications for general conditions, materials, preparation, application, finishing and curing. The company offers its own line of patented products, which include Five Star Special Grout 400, Five Star Fluid Epoxy and Five Star EZ-Cure Grout. Five Star additionally offers products from manufacturers such as Valspar/Cabot Stain; William Zinsser; DAP; General Electric Corporation; Newell/Irwin; USG; Stanley Tools; Minwax; and 3M Company. It distributes its products to lumberyards, do-it-yourself centers, hardware stores and paint stores throughout the world. In January 2011, the firm began construction on a manufacturing facility in Ohio to be dedicated to the production of nuclear power products.

FINANCIALS: Sales and profits are in thousands of dollars—add 000 to get the full amount. 2010 Note: Financial information for 2010 was not available for all companies at press time.

2010 Sales: $	2010 Profits: $	U.S. Stock Ticker: Subsidiary
2009 Sales: $	2009 Profits: $	Int'l Ticker: Int'l Exchange:
2008 Sales: $	2008 Profits: $	Employees:
2007 Sales: $123,713	2007 Profits: $1,199	Fiscal Year Ends: 12/31
2006 Sales: $108,088	2006 Profits: $ 285	Parent Company: MERIT GROUP INC (THE)

SALARIES/BENEFITS:

Pension Plan:	ESOP Stock Plan:	Profit Sharing:	Top Exec. Salary: $	Bonus: $
Savings Plan:	Stock Purch. Plan:		Second Exec. Salary: $	Bonus: $

OTHER THOUGHTS:

Apparent Women Officers or Directors:
Hot Spot for Advancement for Women/Minorities:

LOCATIONS: ("Y" = Yes)

West:	Southwest:	Midwest:	Southeast:	Northeast:	International:
Y	Y	Y		Y	Y

FLUOR CORP

www.fluor.com

Industry Group Code: 237 Ranks within this company's industry group: Sales: 7   Profits: 9

Properties:	Financial Services:	Construction/Development:	Investments:	Specialty Services:		Brokerage:
Apartments:	Mortgages:	Commercial Construction:	REIT:	Property Management:	Y	Commercial Sales:
Malls/Shopping:	Title Insurance:	Residential Construction:		Online Services:		Residential Sales:
Offices:	Property Insurance:	Land Development:		Software/IT:		Specialty:
Hotels/Motels:		Support Services:		Consulting:	Y	
Industrial/Warehouses:		Design/Engineering: Y				
Other:						

TYPES OF BUSINESS:

Construction, Heavy & Civil Engineering
Power Plant Construction and Management
Facilities Management
Procurement Services
Consulting Services
Project Management
Asset Management
Staffing Services

BRANDS/DIVISIONS/AFFILIATES:

Fluor Constructors International, Inc.

CONTACTS: Note: Officers with more than one job title may be intentionally listed here more than once.

David T. Seaton, CEO
D. Michael Steuert, CFO/Sr. VP
Glenn Gilkey, Sr. VP-Human Resources
Ray F. Barnard, CIO/VP
Glenn Gilkey, Sr. VP-Admin.
Carlos M. Hernandez, Chief Legal Officer/Corp. Sec.
David E. Constable, Group Pres., Oper.
John L. Hopkins, Group Exec.-Bus. Dev.
Lee Tashjian, VP-Corp. Affairs
Kenneth H. Lockwood, VP-Investor Rel.
Kenneth H. Lockwood, VP-Corp. Finance
Wendy Hallgren, VP-Corp. Compliance
David Marventano, Sr. VP-Gov't Rel.
Joanna M. Oliva, Treas./VP
Richard P. Carter, Pres., Fluor Constructors International, Inc.
Alan L. Boeckmann, Chmn.
Kirk D. Grimes, Pres., Global Svcs.

Phone: 469-398-7000	Fax: 469-398-7255
Toll-Free:	
Address: 6700 Las Colinas Blvd., Irving, TX 75039 US	

GROWTH PLANS/SPECIAL FEATURES:

Fluor Corp. is a global provider of engineering, procurement, construction and maintenance services, with offices in over 25 countries spanning across six continents. The corporation provides logistics services in both Afghanistan and Iraq. As well as being a primary service provider to the U.S. federal government, Fluor serves a diverse set of industries including oil and gas; chemical and petrochemicals; transportation; mining and metals; power; life sciences; and manufacturing. Fluor operates in five business segments: oil and gas; industrial and infrastructure; government; global services; and power. The oil and gas segment offers design, engineering, procurement, construction and project management services to energy-related industries. The industrial and infrastructure segment provides design, engineering and construction services to the transportation, mining, life sciences, telecommunications, manufacturing, microelectronics and healthcare sectors. The government segment provides project management services, including environmental restoration, engineering, construction, site operations and maintenance, to the U.S. government, particularly to the Department of Energy, the Department of Homeland Security and the Department of Defense. The global services segment provides operations, maintenance and construction services, as well as industrial fleet outsourcing, plant turnaround services, temporary staffing, procurement services and construction-related support. The power segment provides such services as engineering, procurement, construction, program management, start-up, commissioning and maintenance to the gas fueled, solid fueled, renewable and nuclear marketplaces. Fluor Constructors International, Inc., which operates separately from the rest of the businesses, provides unionized management and construction services in the U.S. and Canada, both independently.

Employees are offered life, disability, medical, dental, vision, auto and home insurance; a retirement plan; a 401(k) savings plan; an employee assistance program; a tax savings account; education assistance; and legal services.

FINANCIALS: Sales and profits are in thousands of dollars—add 000 to get the full amount. 2010 Note: Financial information for 2010 was not available for all companies at press time.

2010 Sales: $20,849,300	2010 Profits: $441,100	**U.S. Stock Ticker:** FLR
2009 Sales: $21,990,300	2009 Profits: $732,875	**Int'l Ticker:** Int'l Exchange:
2008 Sales: $22,325,900	2008 Profits: $748,903	Employees: 36,152
2007 Sales: $16,691,000	2007 Profits: $527,961	Fiscal Year Ends: 12/31
2006 Sales: $14,078,500	2006 Profits: $263,500	Parent Company:

SALARIES/BENEFITS:

Pension Plan: Y	ESOP Stock Plan:	Profit Sharing:	Top Exec. Salary: $1,248,042	Bonus: $3,663,280
Savings Plan: Y	Stock Purch. Plan:		Second Exec. Salary: $791,835	Bonus: $1,310,540

OTHER THOUGHTS:

Apparent Women Officers or Directors: 6
Hot Spot for Advancement for Women/Minorities: Y

LOCATIONS: ("Y" = Yes)

West:	Southwest:	Midwest:	Southeast:	Northeast:	International:
Y	Y	Y	Y	Y	Y

FOMENTO DE CONSTRUCCIONES Y CONTRATAS SA (FCC)

www.fcc.es

Industry Group Code: 237 Ranks within this company's industry group: Sales: 11   Profits: 10

Properties:	Financial Services:	Construction/Development:		Investments:	Specialty Services:	Brokerage:
Apartments:	Mortgages:	Commercial Construction:	Y	REIT:	Property Management:	Commercial Sales:
Malls/Shopping:	Title Insurance:	Residential Construction:			Online Services:	Residential Sales:
Offices:	Property Insurance:	Land Development:	Y		Software/IT:	Specialty:
Hotels/Motels:		Support Services:			Consulting:	
Industrial/Warehouses:		Design/Engineering:				
Other:						

TYPES OF BUSINESS:

Heavy Construction
Airport Operations
Urban Sanitation
Alternative Energy Development
Logistics Services
Real Estate Development
Cement Manufacturing
Engineering Services

BRANDS/DIVISIONS/AFFILIATES:

Cementos Portland Valderrivas
FCC Medio Ambiente, S.A.
FCC Versia, S.A.
Aqualia, S.A.
Torre Picasso
Realia Business, S.A.

CONTACTS: *Note: Officers with more than one job title may be intentionally listed here more than once.*

Baldomero Falcones Jaquotot, CEO
Victor Pastor Fernandez, CFO
Antonio Gomez Ciria, Gen. Dir.-IT
Antonio Gomez Ciria, Gen. Dir.-Admin.
Francisco Vincent Chulia, Sec.
Dieter Kiefer, Chmn.-Cementos Portland Valderrivas SA
Jose Luis De la Torre Sanchez, Pres., FCC Servicios SA
Jose Mayor Oreja, Pres., FCC Construccion SA
Baldomero Falcones Jaquotot, Chmn.

Phone: 34-91-359-54-00	**Fax:** 34-91-359-49-23
Toll-Free:	
Address: Federico Salmon 13, Madrid, 28016 Spain	

GROWTH PLANS/SPECIAL FEATURES:

Fomento de Construcciones Y Contratas S.A. (FCC) is a Spanish construction and environmental service company. It divides its business into five categories: construction, cement, energy, real estate and environmental services. The firm's construction business consists of civil engineering, non-residential building and residential building. Construction projects have included oil and gas pipelines; highways; airports; and railways.   The firm's cement business, with operations in the U.S. as well in Argentina, Uruguay, Canada, the U.K. and Tunisia, is conducted by Cementos Portland Valderrivas, a leading Spanish cement firm with control over 15 cement factories.   The firm's environmental services are conducted by FCC itself, FCC Medio Ambiente, S.A.; FCC Versia, S.A.; and Aqualia, S.A. Services include sewer system maintenance; street cleaning; collecting, treating and eliminating solid urban waste; park and garden maintenance; full-service water management; and treating and eliminating industrial waste.   Versia's services include logistics; parking; passenger transportation; urban furniture; handling; conservation and systems; and technical vehicle inspections. Torre Picasso provides real estate services for the company, as does Realia Business, S.A., in which FCC owns a 27.2% interest.   Realia is involved in real estate development, rental and other services.   The energy business is involved in renewable energies, waste-to-power technologies and co-generation. The division maintains 14 wind farms in Spain with an installed capacity of 420.7 megawatts (MW) and 45 MW under development. It also maintains two photovoltaic farms with 20 MW in capacity, as well a waste-to-power plant. In July 2010, the firm agreed to sell its 31 car parks to insurance company, Mutua Madrilena.

FINANCIALS: Sales and profits are in thousands of dollars—add 000 to get the full amount. 2010 Note: Financial information for 2010 was not available for all companies at press time.

2010 Sales: $16,939,300	2010 Profits: $421,310	**U.S. Stock Ticker: FCC**
2009 Sales: $17,496,500	2009 Profits: $414,637	**Int'l Ticker: FCC** Int'l Exchange: Madrid-MCE
2008 Sales: $18,563,200	2008 Profits: $446,330	Employees: 33,768
2007 Sales: $17,777,800	2007 Profits: $977,430	Fiscal Year Ends: 12/31
2006 Sales: $13,747,300	2006 Profits: $776,500	Parent Company:

SALARIES/BENEFITS:

Pension Plan:	ESOP Stock Plan:	Profit Sharing:	Top Exec. Salary: $	Bonus: $
Savings Plan:	Stock Purch. Plan:		Second Exec. Salary: $	Bonus: $

OTHER THOUGHTS:

Apparent Women Officers or Directors: 3
Hot Spot for Advancement for Women/Minorities: Y

LOCATIONS: ("Y" = Yes)

West:	Southwest:	Midwest:	Southeast:	Northeast:	International:
			Y	Y	Y

FOREST CITY ENTERPRISES INC

www.forestcity.net

Industry Group Code: 5311 Ranks within this company's industry group: Sales: 22   Profits: 28

Properties:		Financial Services:	Construction/Development:		Investments:	Specialty Services:		Brokerage:
Apartments:	Y	Mortgages:	Commercial Construction:		REIT:	Property Management:	Y	Commercial Sales:
Malls/Shopping:	Y	Title Insurance:	Residential Construction:			Online Services:		Residential Sales:
Offices:	Y	Property Insurance:	Land Development:	Y		Software/IT:		Specialty:
Hotels/Motels:	Y		Support Services:			Consulting:		
Industrial/Warehouses:	Y		Design/Engineering:					
Other:								

TYPES OF BUSINESS:

Real Estate Development & Management
Office Buildings
Apartments
Retail Centers
Hotels
Land Development
Industrial Development
Military Housing

BRANDS/DIVISIONS/AFFILIATES:

New York by Gehry
New Jersey Nets

CONTACTS: *Note: Officers with more than one job title may be intentionally listed here more than once.*

Charles A. Ratner, CEO
David J. LaRue, COO/Exec. VP
Charles A. Ratner, Pres.
Robert G. O'Brien, CFO/Exec. VP
Andy Passen, Exec. VP-Human Resources
Charles L. Rau, CTO/VP
Linda M. Kane, Chief Admin. Officer/Sr. VP
Geralyn M. Presti, General Counsel/Sr. VP/Sec.
Linda M. Kane, Chief Acct. Officer
Charles D. Obert, Corp. Controller/VP
Robert F. Monchein, Pres., Land Group
Ronald A. Ratner, Exec. VP/Pres./CEO-Residential Group
Bruce C. Ratner, Exec. VP/CEO-Forest City Ratner Co.
Albert B. Ratner, Co-Chmn.
Brian S. Garrison, Managing Dir.-Forest City Int'l Limited

Phone: 216-621-6060	**Fax:** 216-263-4808
Toll-Free:	
Address: 1100 Terminal Tower, 50 Public Sq., Cleveland, OH 44113 US	

GROWTH PLANS/SPECIAL FEATURES:

Forest City Enterprises, Inc., with more than $11 billion in real estate assets, primarily owns, develops, acquires and manages premier commercial and residential real estate throughout the U.S. Its portfolio consists of hotels, office buildings, apartment communities and retail centers. It operates through three strategic business units. The Commercial Group has 98 completed projects, including 46 retail centers with 15 million square feet of leasable space; five hotels with 1,833 rooms; 47 office buildings with 13.5 million square feet; and mixed-use facilities. The Residential Group deals with rental properties, federally assisted housing, senior housing, mixed-use facilities, military housing and new condos and town homes. It has more than 34,700 units in 119 properties across 21 states and Washington, D.C.; and interests in 741 senior subsidized housing units at five properties. Its notable projects include the New York by Gehry building in New York City, which is the tallest residential structure in the Western Hemisphere. The Land Development Group acquires and sells raw land and developed lots to commercial, residential and industrial customers; and develops raw land into master-planned communities, mixed-use projects and other residential developments. It currently owns over 10,500 acres of undeveloped land. Forest City leases retail space, with its largest retail tenants consisting of Bass Pro Shops; AMC Entertainment, Inc.; Regal Entertainment Group; and The Gap. It also leases office space, with its largest tenants consisting of the City of New York; Millennium Pharmaceuticals, Inc.; and the U.S. Government. Forest City also reports its 20% ownership interest in the New Jersey Nets NBA franchise as a segment. Ownership in the Nets is the first step in a development called Atlantic Yards, which will include a new entertainment arena complex and adjacent urban developments combining housing, offices, shops and public open space.

Employees are offered medical, dental, vision and life insurance; disability coverage; tuition reimbursement and flexible spending accounts.

FINANCIALS: Sales and profits are in thousands of dollars—add 000 to get the full amount. 2010 Note: Financial information for 2010 was not available for all companies at press time.

2010 Sales: $820,645	2010 Profits: $-58,541	**U.S. Stock Ticker:** FCE.A
2009 Sales: $854,342	2009 Profits: $-113,087	**Int'l Ticker:** Int'l Exchange:
2008 Sales: $1,286,470	2008 Profits: $52,425	Employees: 2,917
2007 Sales: $1,116,639	2007 Profits: $177,251	Fiscal Year Ends: 1/31
2006 Sales: $1,085,857	2006 Profits: $83,519	Parent Company:

SALARIES/BENEFITS:

Pension Plan:	ESOP Stock Plan:	Profit Sharing:	Top Exec. Salary: $500,000	Bonus: $400,000
Savings Plan: Y	Stock Purch. Plan:		Second Exec. Salary: $475,000	Bonus: $494,000

OTHER THOUGHTS:

Apparent Women Officers or Directors: 15
Hot Spot for Advancement for Women/Minorities: Y

LOCATIONS: ("Y" = Yes)

West:	Southwest:	Midwest:	Southeast:	Northeast:	International:
Y	Y	Y		Y	

FOUR SEASONS HOTELS INC

www.fourseasons.com

Industry Group Code: 721110 Ranks within this company's industry group: Sales: Profits:

Properties:		Financial Services:		Construction/Development:		Investments:		Specialty Services:		Brokerage:	
Apartments:	Y	Mortgages:		Commercial Construction:		REIT:		Property Management:	Y	Commercial Sales:	
Malls/Shopping:		Title Insurance:		Residential Construction:				Online Services:		Residential Sales:	
Offices:		Property Insurance:		Land Development:				Software/IT:		Specialty:	
Hotels/Motels:	Y			Support Services:				Consulting:			
Industrial/Warehouses:				Design/Engineering:							
Other:	Y										

TYPES OF BUSINESS:

Hotels, Luxury
Luxury Condominiums
Conference Centers
Resort Time Shares

BRANDS/DIVISIONS/AFFILIATES:

Regent Hotels
Four Seasons Hotels
Four Seasons Private Residences

CONTACTS:
Note: Officers with more than one job title may be intentionally listed here more than once.
Kathleen Taylor, CEO
Kathleen Taylor, Pres.
John Davison, CFO
Susan Helstab, Exec. VP-Mktg.
Nick Mutton, Exec. VP-Human Resources
Nick Mutton, Exec. VP-Admin.
Jim FitzGibbon, Exec. VP/Pres., Worldwide Hotel Oper.
Scott Woroch, Exec. VP-Worldwide Dev.
Nicola Blazier, Dir.-Corp. Public Rel.
John Davison, Exec. VP-Residential
Isadore Sharp, Chmn.
Antoine Corinthios, Pres., EMEA

Phone: 416-449-1750	Fax: 416-441-4374
Toll-Free:	
Address: 1165 Leslie St., Toronto, ON M3C 2K8 Canada	

GROWTH PLANS/SPECIAL FEATURES:

Four Seasons Hotels, Inc. is a leading operator of luxury hotels and resorts. Headquartered in Toronto, the company manages 84 properties in 34 countries, mostly operated under the Four Seasons and Regent brands, owning roughly half of them. The firm offers its guests amenities such as monogrammed terry-cloth bathrobes, concierge service, in-room fax machines, overnight sandal and golf shoe repair and even in-room exercise equipment installation, if the guest should request it. The No Luggage Required program provides a variety of crucial loan-items to customers who have lost their belongings. Many hotels provide experienced meeting and conference personnel to help guests plan business events such as award galas and multimedia presentations. Moreover, the firm offers a number of branded vacation ownership properties and private residences in Jackson Hole, Wyoming; Scottsdale, Arizona; San Francisco, California; Miami, Florida; Austin, Texas; and Toronto, Canada, among others. New locations where Four Seasons Hotels have opened include the Maldives; northern Thailand; Damascus, Syria; Geneva, Switzerland; Palo Alto, California; Beirut, Lebanon and Lana'i, Hawaii. In 2010, the firm added two new hotels to its portfolio in China, with plans to open nine more by 2014.

Employees of Four Seasons receive medical and dental coverage; disability and life insurance; a retirement pension plan; complimentary stays at Four Seasons properties with discounted meals; educational assistance; and paid holidays and vacation. In 2010, for the 13th consecutive year, the Four Seasons was listed on Fortune magazine's list of the 100 Best Companies to Work For.

FINANCIALS:
Sales and profits are in thousands of dollars—add 000 to get the full amount. 2010 Note: Financial information for 2010 was not available for all companies at press time.

2010 Sales: $	2010 Profits: $	U.S. Stock Ticker: Private
2009 Sales: $	2009 Profits: $	Int'l Ticker: Int'l Exchange:
2008 Sales: $	2008 Profits: $	Employees:
2007 Sales: $	2007 Profits: $	Fiscal Year Ends: 12/31
2006 Sales: $253,425	2006 Profits: $50,287	Parent Company:

SALARIES/BENEFITS:

Pension Plan: Y	ESOP Stock Plan:	Profit Sharing:	Top Exec. Salary: $	Bonus: $
Savings Plan:	Stock Purch. Plan:		Second Exec. Salary: $	Bonus: $

OTHER THOUGHTS:

Apparent Women Officers or Directors: 3
Hot Spot for Advancement for Women/Minorities: Y

LOCATIONS: ("Y" = Yes)

West:	Southwest:	Midwest:	Southeast:	Northeast:	International:
Y	Y	Y	Y	Y	Y

FREDDIE MAC

www.freddiemac.com

Industry Group Code: 522310 Ranks within this company's industry group: Sales: Profits: 6

Properties:	Financial Services:		Construction/Development:	Investments:	Specialty Services:	Brokerage:
Apartments:	Mortgages:	Y	Commercial Construction:	REIT:	Property Management:	Commercial Sales:
Malls/Shopping:	Title Insurance:		Residential Construction:		Online Services:	Residential Sales:
Offices:	Property Insurance:		Land Development:		Software/IT:	Specialty:
Hotels/Motels:			Support Services:		Consulting:	
Industrial/Warehouses:			Design/Engineering:			
Other:						

TYPES OF BUSINESS:

Mortgage Purchasing
Credit Services

BRANDS/DIVISIONS/AFFILIATES:

Federal Home Loan Mortgage Corp.
Federal Housing Finance Agency

CONTACTS: *Note: Officers with more than one job title may be intentionally listed here more than once.*

Charles (Ed) Haldeman, Jr., CEO
Bruce M. Witherell, COO
Ross J. Kari, CFO
Keith Green, Sr. VP-Human Resources
Joseph A. Rossi, Sr. VP-Tech.
Jerry Weiss, Chief Admin. Officer/Exec. VP
Robert E. Bostrom, General Counsel/Exec. VP
Joseph A. Rossi, Sr. VP-Oper.
Edward L. Golding, Sr. VP-Economics & Strategy
Hollis McLoughlin, Sr. VP-External Rel.
Peter Federico, Treas./Sr. VP-Investments & Capital Markets
Ralph F. Boyd, Jr., Pres./CEO-Freddie Mac Foundation
Raymond G. Romano, Chief Credit Officer/Exec. VP
Subha V. Barry, Chief Diversity Officer/Sr. VP
Paige Wisdom, Chief Enterprise Risk Officer/Sr. VP
John A. Koskinen, Chmn.

Phone: 703-903-2000	Fax:
Toll-Free: 800-424-5401	
Address: 8200 Jones Branch Dr., McLean, VA 22102 US	

GROWTH PLANS/SPECIAL FEATURES:

Freddie Mac, officially known as Federal Home Loan Mortgage Corporation, is a public corporation chartered by the U.S. Congress to create a continuous flow of funds to mortgage lenders in support of home ownership and rental housing. Freddie Mac is currently in conservatorship under the control of the U.S. federal government, through the Federal Housing Finance Agency. The company purchases residential mortgages from lenders then packages them into securities, which are sold to investors worldwide. The firm purchases 30-year, 20-year, 15-year and 10-year fixed-rate single-family mortgages, adjustable-rate mortgages (ARMs) and balloon/reset mortgages. Freddie Mac's mortgage securitization business receives the mortgage payments from the original lender or loan servicer, deducts a timeliness guarantee fee and other fees, passing the remainder on to the holder or holders of the mortgage-backed securities. The company implements regular public risk-based capital stress tests, initiates public interest-rate risk sensitivity analyses, discloses credit risk sensitivity analyses and obtains annual ratings from statistical rating organizations. The Treasury has placed a cap of $900 billion on the unpaid principle balance of the firm's loan portfolio, and expects this cap to reduce by 10% per year. Following the subprime mortgage lending crisis, the U. S. Treasury initially committed to provide up to $100 billion under a senior preferred stock purchase agreement to ensure the continued operations of Freddie Mac. In February 2009 however, the Treasury increased its commitment to $200 billion.

The company provides employee benefits include health insurance, a 401(k) plan, a stock purchase and pension plan.

FINANCIALS: Sales and profits are in thousands of dollars—add 000 to get the full amount. 2010 Note: Financial information for 2010 was not available for all companies at press time.

2010 Sales: $	2010 Profits: $-14,025,000	**U.S. Stock Ticker: FMCC**
2009 Sales: $	2009 Profits: $-21,553,000	**Int'l Ticker:** Int'l Exchange:
2008 Sales: $	2008 Profits: $-50,119,000	Employees: 4,927
2007 Sales: $1,009,000	2007 Profits: $-3,094,000	Fiscal Year Ends: 12/31
2006 Sales: $42,264,000	2006 Profits: $2,327,000	Parent Company:

SALARIES/BENEFITS:

Pension Plan: Y	ESOP Stock Plan:	Profit Sharing:	Top Exec. Salary: $	Bonus: $
Savings Plan: Y	Stock Purch. Plan: Y		Second Exec. Salary: $	Bonus: $

OTHER THOUGHTS:

Apparent Women Officers or Directors: 2
Hot Spot for Advancement for Women/Minorities:

LOCATIONS: ("Y" = Yes)

West:	Southwest:	Midwest:	Southeast:	Northeast:	International:
				Y	

GABLES RESIDENTIAL TRUST

www.gables.com

Industry Group Code: 531110 Ranks within this company's industry group: Sales: Profits:

Properties:		Financial Services:		Construction/Development:	Investments:		Specialty Services:		Brokerage:
Apartments:	Y	Mortgages:	Y	Commercial Construction:	REIT:	Y	Property Management:	Y	Commercial Sales:
Malls/Shopping:		Title Insurance:		Residential Construction:			Online Services:		Residential Sales:
Offices:		Property Insurance:		Land Development:			Software/IT:		Specialty:
Hotels/Motels:				Support Services:			Consulting:	Y	
Industrial/Warehouses:				Design/Engineering:					
Other:									

TYPES OF BUSINESS:

Real Estate Investment Trust
Apartment Communities

BRANDS/DIVISIONS/AFFILIATES:

Gables Realty, LP
Gables Advantage Home Mortgage Program
Gables Corporate Accommodations
Express Luxury
ING Clarion

CONTACTS: *Note: Officers with more than one job title may be intentionally listed here more than once.*

David Fitch, CEO
Susan Ansel, COO/Exec. VP
David D. Fitch, Pres.
Dawn Severt, CFO/Exec. VP
Lynette Hegeman, VP-Mktg.
Philip Altschuler, Sr. VP-Human Resources
Robert D. Lamb, VP-IT
Cristina Sullivan, Sr. VP-Property Oper.
David Reece, Sr. VP-Finance & Capital Markets
Dennis E. Rainosek, Sr. VP-Portfolio Mgmt.
Darin Botelho, VP-Retail Oper.
Joseph Wilber, Sr. VP-Investments, East
Christopher R. Smurda, VP-Acct. Oper.
Chris D. Wheeler, Chmn.

Phone: 404-923-5500	Fax:
Toll-Free:	
Address: 3399 Peachtree Road NE, Ste. 600, Atlanta, GA 30326 US	

GROWTH PLANS/SPECIAL FEATURES:

Gables Residential Trust, owned by ING Clarion, is a real estate investment trust (REIT) engaged in the business of multi-family apartment community management, development, construction, disposition and acquisition. The company owns upscale apartment communities primarily in Atlanta, Georgia; Boston, Massachusetts; Chicago, Illinois; Houston, Austin and Dallas, Texas; Jacksonville, Orlando, Miami, Fort Lauderdale and Tampa, Florida; Memphis, Tennessee; Phoenix, Arizona; New York, New York; Newark, New Jersey; San Diego/Inland Empire, California; and Washington, D.C. Gables manages over 38,000 apartment homes in over 120 communities; owns 59 communities with over 15,000 apartment homes; and is in the process of developing an additional 5 communities. As a real estate investment trust (REIT), substantially all of the company's business is conducted through Gables Realty, LP. Management solutions offered by Gables includes NOI and performance improvement; leasing and marketing strategy; customized accounting and reporting; development; construction and renovation; and asset preservation planning. Gables offers its tenants Gables Great Awards, a program which provides carpet cleaning and home-improvements such as paint, patio/balcony detailing and vinyl replacement. Additional services provided by the firm are property management and consulting and development services. In addition to residential apartments, the company also offers Gables Corporate Accommodations, a temporary housing provider for business travel, insurance claims and entertainment industry projects. Express Luxury packages for corporate accommodations include a studio, 1-, 2- or 3-bedroom apartment with utensils, cookware, dishes, utilities, a washer and dryer and maid service.

The company offers employees medical, dental and vision coverage; flexible spending plans; a rental housing allowance; a 401(k) plan; an employee assistance plan; a bonus program; short- and long-term disability insurance; and continuing career development with Gables University.

FINANCIALS: Sales and profits are in thousands of dollars—add 000 to get the full amount. 2010 Note: Financial information for 2010 was not available for all companies at press time.

2010 Sales: $	2010 Profits: $	**U.S. Stock Ticker: Subsidiary**
2009 Sales: $	2009 Profits: $	**Int'l Ticker:** Int'l Exchange:
2008 Sales: $	2008 Profits: $	Employees:
2007 Sales: $	2007 Profits: $	Fiscal Year Ends: 12/31
2006 Sales: $	2006 Profits: $	Parent Company: ING CLARION

SALARIES/BENEFITS:

Pension Plan:	ESOP Stock Plan:	Profit Sharing:	Top Exec. Salary: $	Bonus: $
Savings Plan: Y	Stock Purch. Plan:		Second Exec. Salary: $	Bonus: $

OTHER THOUGHTS:

Apparent Women Officers or Directors: 14
Hot Spot for Advancement for Women/Minorities: Y

LOCATIONS: ("Y" = Yes)

West:	Southwest:	Midwest:	Southeast:	Northeast:	International:
Y	Y	Y	Y	Y	

GAFISA SA

www.gafisa.com.br

Industry Group Code: 5311 Ranks within this company's industry group: Sales: Profits:

Properties:		Financial Services:		Construction/Development:		Investments:		Specialty Services:		Brokerage:	
Apartments:		Mortgages:		Commercial Construction:	Y	REIT:		Property Management:	Y	Commercial Sales:	Y
Malls/Shopping:		Title Insurance:		Residential Construction:	Y			Online Services:		Residential Sales:	Y
Offices:	Y	Property Insurance:		Land Development:	Y			Software/IT:		Specialty:	
Hotels/Motels:				Support Services:				Consulting:			
Industrial/Warehouses:				Design/Engineering:							
Other:	Y										

TYPES OF BUSINESS:

Construction & Real Estate Services
Construction Services
Real Estate Services
Residential Communities
Commercial Buildings
Third Party Construction Services

BRANDS/DIVISIONS/AFFILIATES:

Gafisa Vendas
Alphaville Urbanismo S.A.
Cipesa Engenharia S.A.
Construtora Tenda S.A.

CONTACTS: *Note: Officers with more than one job title may be intentionally listed here more than once.*

Wilson Amaral de Oliveira, CEO
Mario Rocha Neto, Exec. Officer-Oper.
Alceu Duilio Calciolari, CFO
Luiz Carlos Siciliano, Exec. Officer-Mktg. & Sales
Odair Garcia Senra, Dir.-Dev.
Alceu Duilio Calciolari, Investor Rel. Officer
Sandro Gamba, Real Estate Dev. Officer
Caio Racy Mattar, Chmn.

Phone: 55-11-3025-9000	**Fax:** 55-11-3025-9348
Toll-Free:	

Address: Ave. Nacoes Unidas 8501, 19th Fl., Sao Paulo, 05425-070 Brazil

GROWTH PLANS/SPECIAL FEATURES:

Gafisa S.A., based in Sao Paulo, Brazil, provides construction and real estate services to Brazil's housing market. Since its founding, Gafisa has completed and sold more than 1,000 developments and constructed over 36 million square feet of residential space. The firm focuses primarily on residential markets, and over half of its construction revenues annually derive from middle and upper-income residential developments. Its wholly-owned subsidiary Construtora Tenda S.A. represents its activities within the low-income/entry-level housing market, while Gafisa and Alphaville are used in the middle to upper-income developments. The company's real estate services are likewise geared toward middle and upper-income customers. However, Gafisa also sells residential units, land subdivisions, commercial buildings, construction services and entry-level housing units, in large part through its brokerage subsidiary Gafisa Vendas. Gafisa provides construction services to third parties across Brazil, primarily to developers of residential and commercial projects who do not construct their own designs. The company has a presence in roughly 130 Brazilian cities, including Sao Paulo, Rio de Janeiro, Salvador, Fortaleza, Natal, Curitiba, Belo Horizonte, Manaus, Porto Alegre and Belem, across 22 states. More than half of new projects are typically located in the populous states of Sao Paulo and Rio de Janeiro. The firm owns 80% of subsidiary Alphaville Urbanismo S.A., a residential community developer focused on premium metropolitan markets; and a 70% stake in Cipesa Engenharia S.A., a homebuilding company in the state of Alagoas.

FINANCIALS: Sales and profits are in thousands of dollars—add 000 to get the full amount. 2010 Note: Financial information for 2010 was not available for all companies at press time.

2010 Sales: $	2010 Profits: $	**U.S. Stock Ticker: GFA**
2009 Sales: $1,720,150	2009 Profits: $121,510	**Int'l Ticker:** Int'l Exchange:
2008 Sales: $990,550	2008 Profits: $62,550	Employees:
2007 Sales: $682,430	2007 Profits: $52,130	Fiscal Year Ends: 12/31
2006 Sales: $411,600	2006 Profits: $28,600	Parent Company:

SALARIES/BENEFITS:

Pension Plan:	ESOP Stock Plan:	Profit Sharing:	Top Exec. Salary: $	Bonus: $
Savings Plan:	Stock Purch. Plan:		Second Exec. Salary: $	Bonus: $

OTHER THOUGHTS:

Apparent Women Officers or Directors:
Hot Spot for Advancement for Women/Minorities:

LOCATIONS: ("Y" = Yes)

West:	Southwest:	Midwest:	Southeast:	Northeast:	International:
					Y

GAYLORD ENTERTAINMENT CO
www.gaylordentertainment.com

Industry Group Code: 721110 Ranks within this company's industry group: Sales: 14 Profits: 27

Properties:		Financial Services:	Construction/Development:	Investments:	Specialty Services:	Brokerage:
Apartments:		Mortgages:	Commercial Construction:	REIT:	Property Management:	Commercial Sales:
Malls/Shopping:		Title Insurance:	Residential Construction:		Online Services:	Residential Sales:
Offices:		Property Insurance:	Land Development:		Software/IT:	Specialty:
Hotels/Motels:	Y		Support Services:		Consulting:	
Industrial/Warehouses:			Design/Engineering:			
Other:	Y					

TYPES OF BUSINESS:

Hotels & Convention Centers
Vacation Property Management
Live Entertainment Venues
Online Vacation Rental Booking
Radio Station Operation
Golf Courses
Theme Parks

BRANDS/DIVISIONS/AFFILIATES:

Gaylord Opryland Resort & Convention Center
Gaylord Palms Resort & Convention Center
Gaylord Texan Resort & Convention Center
Gaylord National Resort & Convention Center
Grand Ole Opry
General Jackson Showboat
Gaylord Springs Golf Links
Ryman Auditorium

CONTACTS:
Note: Officers with more than one job title may be intentionally listed here more than once.

Colin V. Reed, CEO
David C. Kloeppel, COO
David C. Kloeppel, Pres.
Mark Fioravanti, CFO/Sr. VP
Rich Maradik, Chief Mktg. Officer/Sr. VP
Gara Pryor, Sr. VP-Human Resources
Carter R. Todd, General Counsel/Exec. VP/Corp. Sec.
Patrick Chaffin, VP-Strategic Planning
Brian Abrahamson, VP-Corp. Comm.
Patrick Chaffin, VP-Investor Rel.
Stephen G. Buchanan, Sr. VP-Media & Entertainment
Phil Coffey, Sr. VP/Gen. Mgr.-Gaylord National Resort
Kemp Gallineau, Chief Sales Officer/Sr. VP
Bennett D. Westbrook, Sr. VP-Dev., Design & Construction
Colin V. Reed, Chmn.

Phone: 615-316-6000	Fax: 615-316-6555
Toll-Free:	
Address: 1 Gaylord Dr., Nashville, TN 37214 US	

GROWTH PLANS/SPECIAL FEATURES:

Gaylord Entertainment Co. is a hospitality company focused on the large group meetings and conventions sector of the lodging market. It operates in two divisions: hospitality operations, which generated approximately 94% of its 2010 revenues; and Opry and Attractions, which includes its Nashville attractions and assets related to the Grand Ole Opry, 6%. The firm's hospitality business includes its Gaylord branded hotels, consisting of the Gaylord Opryland Resort & Convention Center in Nashville, Tennessee; the Gaylord Palms Resort & Convention Center near Orlando, Florida; the Gaylord Texan Resort & Convention Center near Dallas, Texas; and the Gaylord National Resort & Convention Center near Washington, D.C. It also owns and operates the Radisson Hotel at Opryland in Nashville. The company's hotels incorporate lodging; meeting, convention and exhibition space; food and beverage options; and retail and spa facilities. Gaylord also owns and operates several attractions in Nashville, including the Grand Ole Opry, a live country music variety show and one of the longest-running radio shows in the U.S. The firm's Opry and Attractions group operates country radio station WSM-AM radio; the General Jackson Showboat; the Gaylord Springs Golf Links, a championship golf course; and live music venues such as the Grand Ole Opry, the Ryman Auditorium and the Wildhorse Saloon. These attractions are located on the firm's Opry Complex property in Nashville, Tennessee.

Gaylord offers its employees medical, dental, vision, prescription, life and AD&D insurance; short- and long-term disability; medical and dependent care reimbursement accounts; a 401(k) savings plan; an employee stock purchase plan; an adoption assistance program; discounts at the hotel and with local merchants; and free laundered uniforms and a meal allowance for employees who work at the hotels.

FINANCIALS:
Sales and profits are in thousands of dollars—add 000 to get the full amount. 2010 Note: Financial information for 2010 was not available for all companies at press time.

2010 Sales: $769,961	2010 Profits: $-89,128	**U.S. Stock Ticker: GET**
2009 Sales: $872,845	2009 Profits: $- 23	**Int'l Ticker:** Int'l Exchange:
2008 Sales: $930,869	2008 Profits: $4,364	Employees: 1,365
2007 Sales: $747,723	2007 Profits: $111,911	Fiscal Year Ends: 12/31
2006 Sales: $722,272	2006 Profits: $-79,435	Parent Company:

SALARIES/BENEFITS:

Pension Plan:	ESOP Stock Plan:	Profit Sharing:	Top Exec. Salary: $910,000	Bonus: $546,000
Savings Plan: Y	Stock Purch. Plan: Y		Second Exec. Salary: $662,500	Bonus: $358,915

OTHER THOUGHTS:

Apparent Women Officers or Directors: 2
Hot Spot for Advancement for Women/Minorities:

LOCATIONS: ("Y" = Yes)

West:	Southwest:	Midwest:	Southeast:	Northeast:	International:
	Y		Y	Y	

GE CAPITAL

www.gecapital.com

Industry Group Code: 522291 **Ranks within this company's industry group:** Sales: 1   Profits: 1

Properties:	Financial Services:		Construction/Development:	Investments:	Specialty Services:	Brokerage:
Apartments:	Mortgages:	Y	Commercial Construction:	REIT:	Property Management:	Commercial Sales:
Malls/Shopping:	Title Insurance:		Residential Construction:		Online Services:	Residential Sales:
Offices:	Property Insurance:		Land Development:		Software/IT:	Specialty:
Hotels/Motels:			Support Services:		Consulting:	
Industrial/Warehouses:			Design/Engineering:			
Other:						

TYPES OF BUSINESS:

Financial Products & Services
Consumer Financial Products & Services
Real Estate
Commercial Financial Products & Services

BRANDS/DIVISIONS/AFFILIATES:

General Electric
GE Money

CONTACTS: *Note: Officers with more than one job title may be intentionally listed here more than once.*

Michael A. Neal, CEO
William H. Cary, COO
Jeffrey S. Bornstein, CFO
Jack Ryan, Sr. VP-Human Resources
Martha Poulter, CIO
Keith Morgan, General Counsel/Sr. VP
Russell Wilkerson, Managing Dir.-Comm. & Public Affairs
Kathy Cassidy, Treas./Sr. VP
Michael Pilot, Chief Commercial Officer
Dmitri Stockton, Pres./CEO-Global Banking
Ronald R. Pressman, Pres./CEO-GE Capital Real Estate
Mark W. Begor, Pres./CEO-Retail Finance & Restructuring Oper.
Michael A. Neal, Chmn.
Richard A. Laxer, Pres./CEO-GE Capital, EMEA

Phone: 203-373-2211	Fax: 203-373-3131
Toll-Free:	
Address: 901 Main Ave., Norwalk, CT 06851-1168 US	

GROWTH PLANS/SPECIAL FEATURES:

GE Capital, a division of General Electric Co. (GE), manages all of the GE's lending and financial services units, as well as its real estate activities. GE Capital offers a broad range of financial products and services worldwide. Services include commercial loans, operating leases, fleet management, financial programs, home loans, credit cards, personal loans and other financial services. It divides its operations into Commercial Lending and Leasing (CLL); Consumer Finance; Energy Financial Services; Capital Aviation Services (GECAS); and Real Estate Financing. CLL offers loans, leases and other financial services to customers including manufacturers, distributors and end-users for a variety of equipment and major capital assets such as industrial-related facilities and equipment; vehicles; corporate aircraft; and equipment used in many industries, including the construction, manufacturing, transportation, telecommunications and healthcare industries. GE Consumer Finance provides financial services such as credit cards; personal loans; bank cards; auto loans and leases; mortgages; debt consolidation; home equity loans; deposit and other savings products; and small and medium enterprise lending through GE Money. GE Energy Financial Services offers structured equity, debt, leasing, partnership financing, project finance and broad-based commercial finance to the global energy and water industries. GECAS is involved in commercial aircraft leasing and finance. The unit's airport financing unit makes debt and equity investments primarily in mid-sized regional airports. Real Estate Financing offers equity capital for acquisition or development, as well as mortgages for new acquisitions or re-capitalizations of commercial real estate worldwide. During 2010, GE Capital provided roughly $90 billion of new financings in the U.S. to various companies, infrastructure projects and municipalities. The firm serves roughly 1 million commercial and over 100 million consumer customers.

FINANCIALS: Sales and profits are in thousands of dollars—add 000 to get the full amount. 2010 Note: Financial information for 2010 was not available for all companies at press time.

2010 Sales: $47,040,000	2010 Profits: $3,265,000	U.S. Stock Ticker: Subsidiary
2009 Sales: $50,622,000	2009 Profits: $2,344,000	Int'l Ticker: Int'l Exchange:
2008 Sales: $67,008,000	2008 Profits: $8,632,000	Employees: 80,500
2007 Sales: $66,301,000	2007 Profits: $12,243,000	Fiscal Year Ends: 12/31
2006 Sales: $56,378,000	2006 Profits: $10,397,000	Parent Company: GENERAL ELECTRIC CO (GE)

SALARIES/BENEFITS:

Pension Plan:	ESOP Stock Plan:	Profit Sharing:	Top Exec. Salary: $	Bonus: $
Savings Plan:	Stock Purch. Plan:		Second Exec. Salary: $	Bonus: $

OTHER THOUGHTS:

Apparent Women Officers or Directors: 2
Hot Spot for Advancement for Women/Minorities:

LOCATIONS: ("Y" = Yes)

West:	Southwest:	Midwest:	Southeast:	Northeast:	International:
Y	Y	Y	Y	Y	Y

GE CAPITAL REAL ESTATE

www.gerealestate.com

Industry Group Code: 522310 Ranks within this company's industry group: Sales: 2   Profits: 4

Properties:		Financial Services:		Construction/Development:	Investments:		Specialty Services:	Brokerage:
Apartments:	Y	Mortgages:	Y	Commercial Construction:	REIT:	Y	Property Management:	Commercial Sales:
Malls/Shopping:	Y	Title Insurance:		Residential Construction:			Online Services:	Residential Sales:
Offices:	Y	Property Insurance:		Land Development:			Software/IT:	Specialty:
Hotels/Motels:				Support Services:			Consulting:	
Industrial/Warehouses:	Y			Design/Engineering:				
Other:	Y							

TYPES OF BUSINESS:

Commercial Real Estate Operations
Commercial Real Estate Mortgages & Finance
Asset Management
Niche Equity Investments
Restructuring & Acquisition Capital

BRANDS/DIVISIONS/AFFILIATES:

General Electric Co (GE)

CONTACTS: *Note: Officers with more than one job title may be intentionally listed here more than once.*

Mark Begor, CEO
Mark Begor, Pres.
Stewart Koenigsberg, CFO
Hank Zupnick, CIO

Phone: 203-750-2900	Fax:
Toll-Free:	
Address: 901 Main Ave., Norwalk, CT 06581 US	

GROWTH PLANS/SPECIAL FEATURES:

GE Capital Real Estate, a subsidiary of General Electric Co. (GE) operating under the GE Capital division, is one of the leading global resources for commercial real estate mortgages and investment capital, with approximately $73 billion in total assets and 43 offices in 31 countries. It provides a range of financing, equity and real estate services, including direct property acquisition, joint venture partnerships and debt financing for office, multifamily, retail, industrial and hospitality properties. GE Capital Real Estate operates in five divisions: Global Investment Management; Global Asset Management; North America; Europe; and Asia Pacific. The Global Investment Management segment creates real estate investment funds for institutional investors, and controls all fundraising and investor relations activities for GE Capital Real Estate. The Global Asset Management division manages the firm's global debt and property portfolio, and manages tenant improvements and capital expenditures for property value maximization. It is responsible for creating business plans for each investment. The North America division manages property acquisition and refinancing in the U.S., Canada and Mexico. The Europe division manages direct real estate investment activities, including debt and equity, for real estate investors, developers and brokers in the U.K., France, Germany, Scandinavia, Spain and Italy, among other countries. The Asia Pacific division provides real estate investment services for clients in Australia, Japan and Korea.

FINANCIALS: Sales and profits are in thousands of dollars—add 000 to get the full amount. 2010 Note: Financial information for 2010 was not available for all companies at press time.

2010 Sales: $3,744,000	2010 Profits: $-1,741,000	**U.S. Stock Ticker: Subsidiary**
2009 Sales: $4,009,000	2009 Profits: $-1,541,000	**Int'l Ticker:** Int'l Exchange:
2008 Sales: $6,646,000	2008 Profits: $1,144,000	Employees:
2007 Sales: $7,021,000	2007 Profits: $2,285,000	Fiscal Year Ends: 12/31
2006 Sales: $	2006 Profits: $	Parent Company: GENERAL ELECTRIC CO (GE)

SALARIES/BENEFITS:

Pension Plan:	ESOP Stock Plan:	Profit Sharing:	Top Exec. Salary: $	Bonus: $
Savings Plan:	Stock Purch. Plan:		Second Exec. Salary: $	Bonus: $

OTHER THOUGHTS:

Apparent Women Officers or Directors:
Hot Spot for Advancement for Women/Minorities:

LOCATIONS: ("Y" = Yes)

West:	Southwest:	Midwest:	Southeast:	Northeast:	International:
Y	Y	Y	Y	Y	Y

GENERAL ELECTRIC CO (GE)   www.ge.com

Industry Group Code: 522220 Ranks within this company's industry group: Sales: 1   Profits: 1

Properties:	Financial Services:	Construction/Development:		Investments:	Specialty Services:	Brokerage:
Apartments:	Mortgages:	Commercial Construction:		REIT:	Property Management:	Commercial Sales:
Malls/Shopping:	Title Insurance:	Residential Construction:			Online Services:	Residential Sales:
Offices:	Property Insurance:	Land Development:			Software/IT:	Specialty:
Hotels/Motels:		Support Services:	Y		Consulting:	
Industrial/Warehouses:		Design/Engineering:				
Other:						

TYPES OF BUSINESS:

Business Leasing & Finance
Energy Systems & Consulting
Financial Services
Industrial & Electrical Equipment & Consumer Products
Television & Film Production & Distribution
Real Estate Investments & Finance
Medical Equipment
Transportation, Aircraft Engines, Rail Systems & Truck Fleet Management

BRANDS/DIVISIONS/AFFILIATES:

GE Energy Infrastructure
GE Technology Infrastructure
GE Capital
NBC Universal LLC
Orbotech Medical Solutions Ltd.
Dresser, Inc.
GE Healthcare
GE Capital Aviation Services

CONTACTS: *Note: Officers with more than one job title may be intentionally listed here more than once.*

Jeffrey R. Immelt, CEO
Keith S. Sherin, CFO
Beth Comstock, Chief Mktg. Officer/Sr. VP
John Lynch, Sr. VP-Corp. Human Resources
Mark M. Little, Sr. VP/Dir.-Global Research
Charlene Begley, CIO/Sr. VP
Brackett B. Denniston, III, General Counsel/Sr. VP
Wayne Hewett, VP-Oper.
Pamela Daley, Sr. VP-Corp. Bus. Dev.
Trevor Schauenberg, VP-Corp. Investor Comm.
Kathryn A. Cassidy, Treas./Sr. VP
John Krenicki, Jr., CEO/Pres., GE Energy Infrastructure
Michael A. Neal, Chmn./CEO-GE Capital
John G. Rice, CEO/Pres., GE Technology Infrastructure
Susan P. Peters, Chief Learning Officer/VP-Exec. Dev.
Jeffrey R. Immelt, Chmn.
Ferdinando Beccalli-Falco, CEO/Pres., GE Europe & North Asia/CEO-GE Germany

Phone: 203-373-2211	**Fax:** 203-373-3131
Toll-Free:	
Address: 3135 Easton Turnpike, Fairfield, CT 06828-0001 US	

GROWTH PLANS/SPECIAL FEATURES:

General Electric Co. (GE) is one of the largest technology, media, and financial services corporations in the world. The company's products, which range from aircraft engines, power generation, water processing, and security technology to medical imaging, business financing, media content and industrial products, are designed and manufactured by GE's five operating divisions: Energy Infrastructure, Technology Infrastructure, NBC Universal, GE Capital and Home & Business Solutions. The Energy Infrastructure division serves power generation, industrial, government and other customers worldwide with products and services related to energy production, distribution and management. The Technology Infrastructure division comprises the firm's aviation, enterprise solutions, healthcare technology and transportation technology operations. NBC Universal, 49%-owned by GE and 51% owned by Comcast, is engaged in the production and distribution of film and television programming; the operation of cable/satellite television networks around the world; the broadcast of network television; and investment and programming activities in digital media and the Internet. GE Capital manages all of the lending and financial services units of GE, including commercial lending and leasing; consumer lending; real estate activities; energy financial services; and commercial aircraft leasing and finance (through GE Capital Aviation Services). GE's Home & Business division manufactures, sells and services major home appliances, including refrigerators, freezers and residential water systems; and lighting products such as automotive, decorative and specialty bulbs. In March 2010, GE announced plans to expand its wind turbine manufacturing, engineering and service facilities in Norway, Sweden, Germany and the U.K. In January 2011, Comcast completed its acquisition of 51% of NBC Universal from GE. Though GE will retain a 49% stake in NBC, Comcast will be responsible for its operations and management. In February 2011, GE acquired Orbotech Medical Solutions Ltd. and Dresser, Inc., a global energy infrastructure technology firm.

FINANCIALS: Sales and profits are in thousands of dollars—add 000 to get the full amount. 2010 Note: Financial information for 2010 was not available for all companies at press time.

2010 Sales: $150,211,000	2010 Profits: $11,644,000	**U.S. Stock Ticker: GE**
2009 Sales: $156,783,000	2009 Profits: $11,025,000	**Int'l Ticker:** Int'l Exchange:
2008 Sales: $182,515,000	2008 Profits: $17,410,000	Employees: 304,000
2007 Sales: $172,488,000	2007 Profits: $22,208,000	Fiscal Year Ends: 12/31
2006 Sales: $151,568,000	2006 Profits: $20,742,000	Parent Company:

SALARIES/BENEFITS:

Pension Plan:	ESOP Stock Plan:	Profit Sharing:	Top Exec. Salary: $3,300,000	Bonus: $
Savings Plan: Y	Stock Purch. Plan:		Second Exec. Salary: $1,750,000	Bonus: $2,900,000

OTHER THOUGHTS:

Apparent Women Officers or Directors: 11
Hot Spot for Advancement for Women/Minorities: Y

LOCATIONS: ("Y" = Yes)

West:	Southwest:	Midwest:	Southeast:	Northeast:	International:
Y	Y	Y	Y	Y	Y

GENERAL GROWTH PROPERTIES INC

www.ggp.com

Industry Group Code: 531120 Ranks within this company's industry group: Sales: 4   Profits: 62

Properties:		Financial Services:	Construction/Development:	Investments:		Specialty Services:		Brokerage:
Apartments:		Mortgages:	Commercial Construction:	REIT:	Y	Property Management:	Y	Commercial Sales:
Malls/Shopping:	Y	Title Insurance:	Residential Construction:			Online Services:		Residential Sales:
Offices:		Property Insurance:	Land Development:			Software/IT:		Specialty:
Hotels/Motels:			Support Services:			Consulting:		
Industrial/Warehouses:			Design/Engineering:					
Other:								

TYPES OF BUSINESS:

Real Estate Investment Trust
Property Management
Shopping Malls

BRANDS/DIVISIONS/AFFILIATES:

GGP Inc
General Growth Properties Inc
Aliansce
Howard Hughes Corporation (The)

CONTACTS:
Note: Officers with more than one job title may be intentionally listed here more than once.

Sandeep Mathrani, CEO
Steve Douglas, CFO/Exec. VP
Cathie Hollowell, Sr. VP-Human Resources
Mark Brown, CIO
Mark Brown, CTO
Andrew Perel, General Counsel/Exec. VP/Sec.
Richard Pesin, Exec. VP-Dev., Anchors & Construction
David Keating, VP-Corp. Comm.
Alan Barocas, Sr. Exec. VP-Mall Leasing
Michael H. McNaughton, Exec. VP-Asset Mgmt.
Marvin Levine, Sr. VP-Real Estate Svcs.
Bruce Flatt, Chmn.

Phone: 312-960-5000	**Fax:**
Toll-Free:	
Address: 110 N. Wacker Dr., Chicago, IL 60606 US	

GROWTH PLANS/SPECIAL FEATURES:

General Growth Properties, Inc. (GGP) is a real estate investment trust (REIT) with ownership interest and management interests in 169 regional and super-regional shopping malls in 43 U.S. states. It maintains around 174 million square feet of retail space with 24,000 stores all over the U.S. The company is primarily engaged in the operation, development and management of retail and other rental property, primarily shopping centers but also including festival market places, urban mixed-use centers and strip/community centers. Of its 169 properties, 18 of them fall in the category of GGP considers to be Platinum Properties, distinguished by high-end, luxury merchants such as Tiffany, Louis Vuitton, Saks Fifth Avenue and Barney's New York and modern architectural spaces. The company's Fashion Show development on the Las Vegas Strip is exemplary of this category of development. Additionally, the company holds a 31.4% ownership interest in a joint venture in Brazil with Aliansce. Through this venture, Aliansce and its controlling interests own or manage over 20 centers throughout Brazil, with additional centers under development. In November 2010, the firm emerged from bankruptcy after a heavy burden of debt and difficulty obtaining refinancing drove it into the largest real estate bankruptcy in U.S. history in April of the previous year. Its restructuring was enacted through the contribution of approximately $6.8 billion from a consortium of five institutional investors. In the same month, it spun-off the master planned communities and strategic development properties in its real estate portfolio into a new publicly traded entity, The Howard Hughes Corporation.

Employees are offered medical, dental and vision insurance; life insurance; disability coverage; same sex domestic partner coverage; a 401(k) savings plan; flexible spending accounts; an employee assistance program; credit union membership; and various employee discounts.

FINANCIALS:
Sales and profits are in thousands of dollars—add 000 to get the full amount. 2010 Note: Financial information for 2010 was not available for all companies at press time.

2010 Sales: $2,823,486	2010 Profits: $-1,439,974	U.S. Stock Ticker: GGP
2009 Sales: $2,881,387	2009 Profits: $-1,284,689	Int'l Ticker: Int'l Exchange:
2008 Sales: $3,361,525	2008 Profits: $4,719	Employees: 3,200
2007 Sales: $3,261,801	2007 Profits: $273,642	Fiscal Year Ends: 12/31
2006 Sales: $3,256,283	2006 Profits: $59,273	Parent Company:

SALARIES/BENEFITS:

Pension Plan:	ESOP Stock Plan:	Profit Sharing:	Top Exec. Salary: $1,200,000	Bonus: $125,000
Savings Plan: Y	Stock Purch. Plan:		Second Exec. Salary: $1,059,425	Bonus: $

OTHER THOUGHTS:

Apparent Women Officers or Directors: 3
Hot Spot for Advancement for Women/Minorities: Y

LOCATIONS: ("Y" = Yes)

West:	Southwest:	Midwest:	Southeast:	Northeast:	International:
Y	Y	Y	Y	Y	Y

GEORG FISCHER LTD

www.georgfischer.com

Industry Group Code: 3363 Ranks within this company's industry group: Sales: 2   Profits: 2

Properties:	Financial Services:	Construction/Development:	Investments:	Specialty Services:	Brokerage:
Apartments:	Mortgages:	Commercial Construction:	REIT:	Property Management:	Commercial Sales:
Malls/Shopping:	Title Insurance:	Residential Construction:		Online Services:	Residential Sales:
Offices:	Property Insurance:	Land Development:		Software/IT:	Specialty:
Hotels/Motels:		Support Services:		Consulting:	
Industrial/Warehouses:		Design/Engineering: Y			
Other:					

TYPES OF BUSINESS:

Automotive Components
Iron Casting
Manufacturing Technology
Machine Tools
Piping Systems
Design
Control systems

BRANDS/DIVISIONS/AFFILIATES:

Agie Charmilles Group
Actspark
Engemaq
Mikron
Step-Tec
Central Plastics
JRG Gunzenhauser AG

CONTACTS: *Note: Officers with more than one job title may be intentionally listed here more than once.*

Yves Serra, CEO
Yves Serra, Pres.
Stephan Wittmann, Dir.-Human Resources
Roland Groebil, Sec.
Yves Serra, Corp. Dev.
Bettina Schmidt, Head-Comm.
Daniel Boesiger, Head-Investor Rel.
Roland Abt, Dir.-Finance & Controlling
Josef Edbauer, Dir.-GF Automotive
Pietro Lori, Dir.-GF Piping Systems
Jean-Pierre Wilmes, Dir.-GF AgieCharmilles
Martin Huber, Chmn.

Phone: 41-52-631-1111	Fax: 41-52-631-2837

Toll-Free:

Address: Amsler-Laffon-Strasse 9, Schaffhausen, CH-8201 Switzerland

GROWTH PLANS/SPECIAL FEATURES:

Georg Fischer Ltd. is a design and manufacturing firm with 150 subsidiaries operating through three divisions: automotive, piping systems and machine tools. The automotive division designs and manufactures cast components and systems for auto chassis, powertrains and bodies. The firm performs large-scale iron casting, sand and die-casting and pressure die casting of iron and light metals. In addition, the firm sells automotive products such as mounting plates, mounting kits and the TRILEX Wheel System. The piping systems division supplies plastic and metal piping systems for industrial applications, gas and water utilities and construction projects. Products include industrial piping systems; piping system control and regulation products; distribution systems for gas and water; drinking water installation systems; and machines and tools for jointing plastic and metal piping systems. The division has a sales presence in over 100 countries to ensure round-the-clock customer support. The machine tools segment, also known as AgieCharmilles Group, designs and manufactures precision machinery for tool and mold making. The firm's wire-cut and die sinking electric discharge machines (EDM) and high-speed milling (HSM) technologies create forms down to the micro and nano ranges. Molds are produced for the mass production of consumer goods such as phone handsets, as well as for complex, customized precision components. The segment produces products under a number of brand names, including Agie, Charmilles, Actspark, Engemaq, Mikron, Step-Tec, System 3R and Intech EDM. The firm's subsidiaries Central Plastics and JRG Gunzenhauser AG, are suppliers of piping systems to gas and water utilities.

FINANCIALS: Sales and profits are in thousands of dollars—add 000 to get the full amount. 2010 Note: Financial information for 2010 was not available for all companies at press time.

2010 Sales: $3,916,960	2010 Profits: $122,720	**U.S. Stock Ticker:**
2009 Sales: $3,302,200	2009 Profits: $-270,450	**Int'l Ticker: FI-N** Int'l Exchange: Zurich-SWX
2008 Sales: $5,073,750	2008 Profits: $78,410	Employees: 12,908
2007 Sales: $3,977,430	2007 Profits: $216,690	Fiscal Year Ends: 12/31
2006 Sales: $4,007,500	2006 Profits: $226,700	Parent Company:

SALARIES/BENEFITS:

Pension Plan:	ESOP Stock Plan:	Profit Sharing:	Top Exec. Salary: $	Bonus: $
Savings Plan:	Stock Purch. Plan:		Second Exec. Salary: $	Bonus: $

OTHER THOUGHTS:

Apparent Women Officers or Directors: 1
Hot Spot for Advancement for Women/Minorities:

LOCATIONS: ("Y" = Yes)

West:	Southwest:	Midwest:	Southeast:	Northeast:	International:
Y			Y		Y

GLENBOROUGH LLC

www.glenborough.com

Industry Group Code: 531120 Ranks within this company's industry group: Sales: Profits:

Properties:		Financial Services:		Construction/Development:		Investments:		Specialty Services:		Brokerage:	
Apartments:		Mortgages:		Commercial Construction:		REIT:		Property Management:	Y	Commercial Sales:	
Malls/Shopping:		Title Insurance:		Residential Construction:				Online Services:		Residential Sales:	
Offices:	Y	Property Insurance:		Land Development:				Software/IT:		Specialty:	
Hotels/Motels:				Support Services:	Y			Consulting:			
Industrial/Warehouses:	Y			Design/Engineering:							
Other:											

TYPES OF BUSINESS:

Real Estate Investment Trust
Office Properties
Property Management
Property Development

BRANDS/DIVISIONS/AFFILIATES:

CONTACTS: *Note: Officers with more than one job title may be intentionally listed here more than once.*

Andrew Batinovich, CEO
Michael A. Steele, COO/Exec. VP
Andrew Batinovich, Pres.
Brian S. Peay, CFO/Exec. VP
Carlos Santmaria, VP-Eng. Svcs.
G. Lee Burns, General Counsel/Sec./Sr. VP
Sandra L. Boyle, Exec. VP-Dev.
Terri Garnick, Sr. VP-Acct.
Sandra L. Boyle, Exec. VP-Project Mgmt.
Michael Williams, VP-Property Mgmt., Eastern Region
Edward Edmiston, VP-Property Mgmt., Western Region
Alan Shapiro, VP-Acquisitions

Phone: 650-343-9300	Fax: 650-343-7438
Toll-Free:	
Address: 400 S. El Camino Real, San Mateo, CA 94402-1708 US	

GROWTH PLANS/SPECIAL FEATURES:

Glenborough, LLC is a firm focused on acquiring, managing, leasing and developing high-quality office properties. The company holds a portfolio of 45 properties, primarily high-quality, multi-tenant office properties, with some industrial and multi-use buildings. Of these, two properties are under development.   The company's portfolio encompasses approximately 4 million square feet in seven core markets: Southern California; Denver, Colorado; Washington, D.C.; San Francisco, California; Tampa, Florida; Las Vegas, Nevada; and New Jersey. In addition, the firm participates in several alliances to develop property both for its portfolio and for sale to third parties. The company performs all property management, leasing, construction supervision, accounting, finance, acquisition and disposition activities for its portfolio of properties. Glenborough has projects under development constituting over 44,000 square feet of office space and 160,000 square feet of retail space. It also performs all portfolio management activities, including on-site property management, lease negotiations and construction supervision of tenant improvements, property renovations and capital expenditures. The firm is owned by Morgan Stanley Real Estate. The firm recently completed development of its Foundry Square I, Lima Ridge Professional Center, Three Parkside and Vanderbilt Plaza properties.

FINANCIALS: Sales and profits are in thousands of dollars—add 000 to get the full amount. 2010 Note: Financial information for 2010 was not available for all companies at press time.

2010 Sales: $	2010 Profits: $	U.S. Stock Ticker: Private
2009 Sales: $	2009 Profits: $	Int'l Ticker: Int'l Exchange:
2008 Sales: $	2008 Profits: $	Employees:
2007 Sales: $	2007 Profits: $	Fiscal Year Ends: 12/31
2006 Sales: $	2006 Profits: $	Parent Company:

SALARIES/BENEFITS:

Pension Plan:	ESOP Stock Plan:	Profit Sharing:	Top Exec. Salary: $	Bonus: $
Savings Plan:	Stock Purch. Plan:		Second Exec. Salary: $	Bonus: $

OTHER THOUGHTS:

Apparent Women Officers or Directors: 2
Hot Spot for Advancement for Women/Minorities:

LOCATIONS: ("Y" = Yes)

West:	Southwest:	Midwest:	Southeast:	Northeast:	International:
Y			Y	Y	

GLIMCHER REALTY TRUST

www.glimcher.com

Industry Group Code: 531120 Ranks within this company's industry group: Sales: 49   Profits: 46

Properties:	Financial Services:	Construction/Development:	Investments:	Specialty Services:	Brokerage:
Apartments:	Mortgages:	Commercial Construction:	REIT: Y	Property Management:	Commercial Sales:
Malls/Shopping: Y	Title Insurance:	Residential Construction:		Online Services:	Residential Sales:
Offices:	Property Insurance:	Land Development:		Software/IT:	Specialty:
Hotels/Motels:		Support Services:		Consulting:	
Industrial/Warehouses:		Design/Engineering:			
Other:					

TYPES OF BUSINESS:

Real Estate Investment Trust
Malls & Shopping Centers

BRANDS/DIVISIONS/AFFILIATES:

CONTACTS: *Note: Officers with more than one job title may be intentionally listed here more than once.*

Michael P. Glimcher, CEO
Marshall A. Loeb, COO
Marshall A. Loeb, Pres.
Mark E. Yale, CFO/Exec. VP/Treas.
Grace E. Schmitt, VP-Human Resources
Cheryl M. Southworth, VP-Info. Svcs.
Kim A. Rieck, General Counsel/Corp. Sec./Sr. VP
Melissa Indest, VP-Finance & Acct.
George A. Schmidt, Chief Investment Officer/Exec. VP
Thomas J. Drought, Jr., Exec. VP/Dir.-Leasing
Steve Bruch, VP-Construction & Dev.
Armand Mastropietro, Sr. VP-Property Mgmt.
Michael P. Glimcher, Chmn.

Phone: 614-621-9000	**Fax:** 614-621-9321
Toll-Free:	
Address: 180 E. Broad St., Columbus, OH 43215 US	

GROWTH PLANS/SPECIAL FEATURES:

Glimcher Realty Trust is a fully integrated, self-administered and self-managed real estate investment trust (REIT) that owns, leases, acquires, develops and operates a portfolio of retail properties consisting of enclosed regional and super-regional malls and community shopping centers (including single-tenant retail properties) located in 14 states. The company's portfolio consists of 23 malls containing an aggregate of 20.5 million square feet of gross leasable area (GLA), and four community centers containing 779,000 square feet of GLA. Glimcher's malls are anchored by multiple department stores, such as Dillard's, Herberger's, JCPenney, Kohl's, Macy's, Nordstrom, Saks and Sears. Mall stores include national retailers such as Abercrombie & Fitch, American Eagle Outfitters, Banana Republic, Barnes & Noble, Footlocker, Gap, Hallmark, The Limited, Forever 21, Pacific Sunwear, Radio Shack and Victoria's Secret. Malls also generally include at least one restaurant, a food court and movie theaters or other entertainment. The firm's community centers are designed to attract local and regional area customers and are typically anchored by a combination of discount department stores, supermarkets and/or drug stores, including retailers such as Target and supermarkets such as Kroger. Tenants typically offer day-to-day necessities and value-oriented merchandise.

FINANCIALS: Sales and profits are in thousands of dollars—add 000 to get the full amount. 2010 Note: Financial information for 2010 was not available for all companies at press time.

2010 Sales: $274,772	2010 Profits: $5,853	**U.S. Stock Ticker: GRT**
2009 Sales: $308,425	2009 Profits: $4,581	**Int'l Ticker:** Int'l Exchange:
2008 Sales: $319,725	2008 Profits: $16,769	Employees: 1,040
2007 Sales: $302,900	2007 Profits: $39,992	Fiscal Year Ends: 12/31
2006 Sales: $292,551	2006 Profits: $-77,165	Parent Company:

SALARIES/BENEFITS:

Pension Plan:	ESOP Stock Plan:	Profit Sharing:	Top Exec. Salary: $561,731	Bonus: $393,914
Savings Plan: Y	Stock Purch. Plan:		Second Exec. Salary: $415,192	Bonus: $171,267

OTHER THOUGHTS:

Apparent Women Officers or Directors: 4
Hot Spot for Advancement for Women/Minorities: Y

LOCATIONS: ("Y" = Yes)

West:	Southwest:	Midwest:	Southeast:	Northeast:	International:
Y	Y	Y	Y	Y	

GOLDEN TULIP HOSPITALITY GROUP

www.goldentulip.com

Industry Group Code: 721110 Ranks within this company's industry group: Sales: Profits:

Properties:		Financial Services:		Construction/Development:		Investments:		Specialty Services:		Brokerage:	
Apartments:		Mortgages:		Commercial Construction:		REIT:		Property Management:	Y	Commercial Sales:	
Malls/Shopping:		Title Insurance:		Residential Construction:				Online Services:		Residential Sales:	
Offices:		Property Insurance:		Land Development:				Software/IT:		Specialty:	
Hotels/Motels:	Y			Support Services:				Consulting:			
Industrial/Warehouses:				Design/Engineering:							
Other:											

TYPES OF BUSINESS:

Hotels & Resorts

BRANDS/DIVISIONS/AFFILIATES:

Golden Tulip Hotels
Tulip Inns
Royal Tulip
Branche Restaurant, Bar & Lounge
Golden Tulip Resort
Tulip Residences

CONTACTS: *Note: Officers with more than one job title may be intentionally listed here more than once.*

Pierre-Frederic Roulot, Pres.
Haike Blaauw, Sr. VP-Franchise Oper.

Phone: 33-01-4291-4600	Fax: 33-01-4291-4601
Toll-Free:	
Address: 50 Place de L'Ellipse, Village 5, Paris, CS 70050 France	

GROWTH PLANS/SPECIAL FEATURES:

Golden Tulip Hospitality Group is a Swiss hospitality company with over 230 branded and hotels featuring more than 27,000 rooms in more than 40 countries. Since the company's acquisition in recent years by Starwood Capital Group, owner of Louvre Hotels, Golden Tulip has expanded its network of hotels to include 1072 hotels with the addition of Louvre Hotels brands, Kyriad, Kyriad Prestige, Campanile and Premiere Classe. The company's original brands include Royal Tulip, reserved for five-star hotels located in prime areas near city centers and business districts; Golden Tulip Hotels, which are four-star hotels situated in key locations near city centers, airports, conference venues and business districts; and Tulip Inns, which are three-star budget hotels with fewer amenities than company's other brands. Golden Tulip also owns and operates the Branche Restaurant, Bar & Lounge chain; George & Co. casual dining restaurants; and The State Room, exclusively in Royal Tulip Hotels. These facilities are generally located in or near a Golden Tulip hotel. In addition to its facilities, the company offers several services to business customers including group rates and the Golden Tulip Central Meeting Line, a reservation and planning service for businesses or large groups. The Ambassador Club is the company's frequent stay program through which guests have access to special events and discounts. Golden Tulip franchises and manages hotels in Europe, the Middle East and Africa, the Asia-Pacific Region and the Americas. In recent years, the company has added a new brand concept, Tulip Residences, which provides travelers with extended-stay studios and one-bedroom suites. The accommodations are four-star rated and offer amenities such as high-definition televisions, free Wi-Fi connection, en suite bathrooms and a fully equipped kitchen facility. In 2010, the company opened several new hotels in countries such as Thailand, Brazil and India.

FINANCIALS: Sales and profits are in thousands of dollars—add 000 to get the full amount. 2010 Note: Financial information for 2010 was not available for all companies at press time.

2010 Sales: $	2010 Profits: $	U.S. Stock Ticker: Private
2009 Sales: $	2009 Profits: $	Int'l Ticker: Int'l Exchange:
2008 Sales: $	2008 Profits: $	Employees:
2007 Sales: $	2007 Profits: $	Fiscal Year Ends:
2006 Sales: $	2006 Profits: $	Parent Company: STARWOOD CAPITAL GROUP GLOBAL LLC

SALARIES/BENEFITS:

Pension Plan:	ESOP Stock Plan:	Profit Sharing:	Top Exec. Salary: $	Bonus: $
Savings Plan:	Stock Purch. Plan:		Second Exec. Salary: $	Bonus: $

OTHER THOUGHTS:

Apparent Women Officers or Directors:
Hot Spot for Advancement for Women/Minorities:

LOCATIONS: ("Y" = Yes)

West:	Southwest:	Midwest:	Southeast:	Northeast:	International:
				Y	Y

GRANITE CONSTRUCTION INC

www.graniteconstruction.com

Industry Group Code: 237 Ranks within this company's industry group: Sales: 27   Profits: 30

Properties:	Financial Services:	Construction/Development:		Investments:	Specialty Services:	Brokerage:
Apartments:	Mortgages:	Commercial Construction:	Y	REIT:	Property Management:	Commercial Sales:
Malls/Shopping:	Title Insurance:	Residential Construction:			Online Services:	Residential Sales:
Offices:	Property Insurance:	Land Development:			Software/IT:	Specialty:
Hotels/Motels:		Support Services:			Consulting:	
Industrial/Warehouses:		Design/Engineering:				
Other:						

TYPES OF BUSINESS:

Construction, Heavy & Civil Engineering
Infrastructure Projects
Site Preparation Services
Construction Materials Processing
Heavy Construction Equipment

BRANDS/DIVISIONS/AFFILIATES:

Granite Construction Northeast Inc
Granite Northwest Inc
Granite Land Company
Granite Construction Supply
Intermountain Slurry Seal Inc

CONTACTS:
Note: Officers with more than one job title may be intentionally listed here more than once.

James H. Roberts, CEO
James H. Roberts, Pres.
Laurel J. Krzeminski, CFO/Sr. VP
Terry K. Eller, General Counsel/VP/Sec.
Kent H. Marshall, VP/Dir.-Bus. Dev.
Jigisha Desai, Treas./VP
Michael F. Donnino, Sr. VP/Group Mgr.
Thomas S. Case, VP/Group Mgr.
Jay L. McQuillen, Jr., VP/Group Mgr.
John A. Franich, VP/Group Mgr.
William H. Powell, Chmn.

Phone: 831-724-1011	Fax: 831-722-9657
Toll-Free:	
Address: 585 W. Beach St., Watsonville, CA 95076 US	

GROWTH PLANS/SPECIAL FEATURES:

Granite Construction, Inc. is one of the largest heavy civil construction contractors in the U.S. The firm operates nationwide, serving both public and private sector clients. Within the public sector, the company primarily concentrates on infrastructure projects, including the construction of roads, highways, bridges, dams, tunnels, canals, mass transit facilities and airports. Within the private sector, it performs site preparation services for commercial/industrial buildings, residential buildings and other facilities. Granite owns and leases substantial aggregate reserves and owns many construction materials processing plants. In addition, the company has one of the largest contractor-owned heavy construction equipment fleets in the U.S., with roughly 6,664 units. Granite operates in four segments: Construction, Large Project Construction, Construction Materials and Real Estate. The Construction division operates out of 14 branch offices that serve local markets, as well as major infrastructure projects in the western region of the U.S. Each of its branch locations is aligned under one of three operating groups: Northwest, Northern California and Southwest. The Large Project Construction segment focuses on the firm's larger projects, such as mass transit facilities, highways, dams, bridges and airports. It operates out of three regional offices in Lewisville, Texas; Tampa, Florida; and Tarrytown, New York. The Construction Materials division (Granite Construction Supply) produces concrete, gravel, ready-mix asphalt, sand, and other products. Granite Construction's Real Estate segment, formerly Granite Land Company, purchases, develops, operates, sells and invests in real estate. Its current portfolio includes residential, retail and office site development projects held for rental income or for sale to home and commercial property developers. Granite's subsidiaries and affiliates include Granite Construction Northeast, Inc.; Granite Northwest, Inc.; and Intermountain Slurry Seal, Inc.

Employee benefits include life, AD&D, medical, dental and vision coverage; a 401(k); stock purchase plan; flexible spending accounts; education reimbursement; and domestic partner benefits.

FINANCIALS:
Sales and profits are in thousands of dollars—add 000 to get the full amount. 2010 Note: Financial information for 2010 was not available for all companies at press time.

2010 Sales: $1,762,965	2010 Profits: $-62,448	U.S. Stock Ticker: GVA
2009 Sales: $1,963,479	2009 Profits: $100,201	Int'l Ticker: Int'l Exchange:
2008 Sales: $2,674,244	2008 Profits: $122,404	Employees: 3,400
2007 Sales: $2,737,914	2007 Profits: $112,065	Fiscal Year Ends: 12/31
2006 Sales: $2,969,604	2006 Profits: $80,509	Parent Company:

SALARIES/BENEFITS:

Pension Plan:	ESOP Stock Plan:	Profit Sharing:	Top Exec. Salary: $500,000	Bonus: $503,606
Savings Plan: Y	Stock Purch. Plan: Y		Second Exec. Salary: $400,000	Bonus: $279,590

OTHER THOUGHTS:

Apparent Women Officers or Directors: 2
Hot Spot for Advancement for Women/Minorities:

LOCATIONS: ("Y" = Yes)

West:	Southwest:	Midwest:	Southeast:	Northeast:	International:
Y	Y	Y	Y	Y	

GROUPE DU LOUVRE

www.groupedulouvre.com

Industry Group Code: 721110 Ranks within this company's industry group: Sales: Profits:

Properties:		Financial Services:	Construction/Development:	Investments:	Specialty Services:		Brokerage:
Apartments:		Mortgages:	Commercial Construction:	REIT:	Property Management:	Y	Commercial Sales:
Malls/Shopping:		Title Insurance:	Residential Construction:		Online Services:		Residential Sales:
Offices:		Property Insurance:	Land Development:		Software/IT:		Specialty:
Hotels/Motels:	Y		Support Services:		Consulting:		
Industrial/Warehouses:			Design/Engineering:				
Other:	Y						

TYPES OF BUSINESS:

Hotels
Luxury Goods
Perfume House

BRANDS/DIVISIONS/AFFILIATES:

Starwood Capital Group
Crillon
Concorde
Kyriad Prestige
Campanile
Premiere Classe
Annick Goutal
Baccarat

CONTACTS: *Note: Officers with more than one job title may be intentionally listed here more than once.*

Steve Goldman, CEO
Pascal Malbequi, General Counsel
Jean-Yves Schapiro, VP-Finance
Brigitte Taitttinger, Pres., Annick Goutal
Bernard Granier, COO-Concorde Hotels & Resorts
Pierre Frederic Roulot, Pres., Louvre Hotels
Herve Martin, Pres., Baccarat
Barry Sternlicht, Chmn.

Phone: 33-1-42-91-4500	Fax:
Toll-Free:	
Address: Village 5, 50 Place de l'Ellipse, Paris, 92081 France	

GROWTH PLANS/SPECIAL FEATURES:

Groupe du Louvre (Louvre) is a French hotel and luxury goods company. It is owned by an affiliate of private equity firm, Starwood Capital Group. The company operates in four segments: luxury hotel, budget hotel, crystal manufacturer and perfume house. The luxury hotel division encompasses the Crillon and Concorde hotels and resorts. The segment gathers more than 30 prestigious hotels in locations such as Amsterdam, Barcelona, Cannes, London, Nice, Paris, Prague and Tokyo. The budget hotel division is comprised of more than 800 hotels with a capacity of roughly 52,000 rooms in nine European countries under four brands: Kyriad Prestige, Kyriad, Campanile and Premiere Classe. The crystal manufacturer division operates through subsidiary Societe du Louvre, which is the majority shareholder of Baccarat, one of the most prestigious crystal manufacturers in the world. Products, which include jewelry, accessories and wristwatches, are sold through a network of 47 owned stores and points of sales worldwide. The perfume house division operates through Annick Goutal, a unique luxury perfume house created in 1980 that distributes products in a selective way in more than 20 countries. Annick Goutal offers more than 25 fragrances composed mainly of natural elements, as well as a skin care line with active rose serum. The perfumery has 11 boutiques and 1,000 prestigious points of sale such as Saks Avenue, Isetan, Bergdorf Goodman, Harrods and Harvey Nichols.

FINANCIALS: Sales and profits are in thousands of dollars—add 000 to get the full amount. 2010 Note: Financial information for 2010 was not available for all companies at press time.

2010 Sales: $	2010 Profits: $	**U.S. Stock Ticker: Private**
2009 Sales: $	2009 Profits: $	**Int'l Ticker:** Int'l Exchange:
2008 Sales: $	2008 Profits: $	Employees:
2007 Sales: $	2007 Profits: $	Fiscal Year Ends: 12/31
2006 Sales: $	2006 Profits: $	Parent Company: STARWOOD CAPITAL GROUP GLOBAL LLC

SALARIES/BENEFITS:

Pension Plan:	ESOP Stock Plan:	Profit Sharing:	Top Exec. Salary: $	Bonus: $
Savings Plan:	Stock Purch. Plan:		Second Exec. Salary: $	Bonus: $

OTHER THOUGHTS:

Apparent Women Officers or Directors: 1
Hot Spot for Advancement for Women/Minorities:

LOCATIONS: ("Y" = Yes)

West:	Southwest:	Midwest:	Southeast:	Northeast:	International:
					Y

GRUBB & ELLIS CO

www.grubb-ellis.com

Industry Group Code: 531210   Ranks within this company's industry group: Sales: 2   Profits: 3

Properties:	Financial Services:	Construction/Development:	Investments:		Specialty Services:		Brokerage:	
Apartments:	Mortgages:	Commercial Construction:	REIT:	Y	Property Management:	Y	Commercial Sales:	Y
Malls/Shopping:	Title Insurance:	Residential Construction:			Online Services:		Residential Sales:	
Offices:	Property Insurance:	Land Development:			Software/IT:		Specialty:	Y
Hotels/Motels:		Support Services:			Consulting:	Y		
Industrial/Warehouses:		Design/Engineering: Y						
Other:								

TYPES OF BUSINESS:

Real Estate Brokerage & Leasing
Property Management
Engineering Services
Strategic Planning
Market Research
Retail Services
Valuation Services
Consulting Services

BRANDS/DIVISIONS/AFFILIATES:

Grubb & Ellis Realty Investors LLC
Grubb & Ellis Securities, Inc.
Energy & Infrastructure Advisors, LLC
Grubb & Ellis Healthcare REIT II, Inc.
Grubb & Ellis Apartment REIT, Inc.

CONTACTS: *Note: Officers with more than one job title may be intentionally listed here more than once.*

Thomas P. D'Arcy, CEO
Jack Van Berkel, COO/Exec. VP
Thomas P. D'Arcy, Pres.
Michael J. Rispoli, CFO/Exec. VP
Mathieu B. Streiff, General Counsel/Exec. VP/Corp. Sec.
Matthew A. Engel, Exec. VP-Finance
Jack Van Berkel, Pres., Real Estate Svcs.
Jeffrey T. Hanson, CEO/Pres., Grubb & Ellis Equity Advisors, LLC
Jay P. Leupp, Exec. VP/Pres., Grubb & Ellis Alesco Global
Thomas P. D'Arcy, Chmn.

Phone: 714-667-8252	Fax:
Toll-Free: 800-877-9066	
Address: 1551 N. Tustin Ave., Ste. 300, Santa Ana, CA 92705 US	

GROWTH PLANS/SPECIAL FEATURES:

Grubb & Ellis Co. (G&E) is a commercial real estate services and investment management company operating through 126 owned and affiliate offices worldwide. The firm provides property owners, corporate occupants and program investors with transactions, management, consulting and investment advisory services. G&E operates through three segments: Investment Management, Transaction Services and Management Services. Its Investment Management segment provides acquisition, financing and disposition services with respect to its programs; asset management services related to its programs; and dealer-manager services by its securities broker-dealer, which facilitates capital raising transactions for its tenant-in-common (TIC), REIT and other investment programs. Investment management products are distributed through G&E's subsidiary Grubb & Ellis Securities, Inc. The firm's Transaction Services segment comprises its real estate brokerage operations, which are conducted through over 1,800 brokers. G&E's Management Services segment includes property, corporate facilities and project management; client accounting; business services; and engineering services for unrelated third parties and the properties owned by the programs it sponsors. Energy & Infrastructure Advisors, LLC, a joint venture between G&E and the Meridian Companies, sponsors retail and institutional products focused on investment opportunities in the energy and infrastructure sector. In early 2010, the company's Grubb & Ellis Healthcare REIT II, Inc. fund acquired the Center for Neurosurgery and Spine in Minnesota; Lacombe Medical Office Building in Louisiana; and Parkway Medical Center in Ohio. In March 2010, another fund, Grubb & Ellis Apartment REIT, Inc., acquired Bella Ruscello Luxury Apartment Homes in Texas. In August 2010, the company announced that it would acquire nine multifamily residential properties, located in North Carolina, Tennessee and Texas, in a transaction valued at approximately $182 million. In September 2010, the firm's Grubb & Ellis Healthcare REIT II acquired a portfolio of seven nursing facilities in Virginia for roughly $45 million.

FINANCIALS: Sales and profits are in thousands of dollars—add 000 to get the full amount. 2010 Note: Financial information for 2010 was not available for all companies at press time.

2010 Sales: $575,457	2010 Profits: $-66,780	U.S. Stock Ticker: GBE
2009 Sales: $527,914	2009 Profits: $-78,838	Int'l Ticker: Int'l Exchange:
2008 Sales: $619,678	2008 Profits: $-330,870	Employees: 4,500
2007 Sales: $229,657	2007 Profits: $21,072	Fiscal Year Ends: 12/31
2006 Sales: $108,543	2006 Profits: $19,971	Parent Company:

SALARIES/BENEFITS:

Pension Plan:	ESOP Stock Plan:	Profit Sharing:	Top Exec. Salary: $560,000	Bonus: $
Savings Plan: Y	Stock Purch. Plan:		Second Exec. Salary: $412,500	Bonus: $200,000

OTHER THOUGHTS:

Apparent Women Officers or Directors:
Hot Spot for Advancement for Women/Minorities:

LOCATIONS: ("Y" = Yes)

West:	Southwest:	Midwest:	Southeast:	Northeast:	International:
Y	Y	Y	Y	Y	Y

GRUBB & ELLIS REALTY INVESTORS LLC

equityadvisors.grubb-ellis.com

Industry Group Code: 531120 Ranks within this company's industry group: Sales: Profits:

Properties:	Financial Services:	Construction/Development:	Investments:		Specialty Services:		Brokerage:	
Apartments:	Mortgages:	Commercial Construction:	REIT:	Y	Property Management:	Y	Commercial Sales:	
Malls/Shopping:	Title Insurance:	Residential Construction:			Online Services:		Residential Sales:	
Offices:	Property Insurance:	Land Development:			Software/IT:		Specialty:	Y
Hotels/Motels:		Support Services:			Consulting:	Y		
Industrial/Warehouses:		Design/Engineering:						
Other:								

TYPES OF BUSINESS:

Real Estate Investment Trust
Commercial Properties
Advising & Redevelopment Services

BRANDS/DIVISIONS/AFFILIATES:

Grubb & Ellis Co

CONTACTS: *Note: Officers with more than one job title may be intentionally listed here more than once.*

Jeffrey T. Hanson, CEO
Jeffrey T. Hanson, Pres.
Michael Rispoli, CFO/Exec. VP
Mathieu Streiff, Chief Real Estate Counsel
Mathieu Streiff, Sr. VP-Investment Oper.
Mathieu Streiff, Sr. VP-Investment Programs
Danny Prosky, Exec. VP-Health Care Real Estate
Richard Arnitz, CEO & Pres., Grubb & Ellis Securities, Inc.
Charles Huang, COO-Grubb & Ellis Securities, Inc.
Thomas P. D'Arcy, Chmn.

Phone: 714-667-8252	Fax: 714-667-6860
Toll-Free: 877-888-7348	
Address: 1551 N. Tustin Ave., Ste. 300, Santa Ana, CA 92705 US	

GROWTH PLANS/SPECIAL FEATURES:

Grubb & Ellis Realty Investors, LLC (GERI) is the asset management and real estate investment subsidiary of Grubb & Ellis Company. GERI and its affiliates manage more than $5.8 billion in assets in 31 states on behalf of about 50,000 investors. The company specializes in tenant-in-common (TIC) investment strategies for investors structuring like-kind or tax-deferred exchanges under Section 1031 of the Tax Code, which allows a property owner to sell a property, buy another and defer the sale-generated taxable income. In addition to TIC programs, the firm has experience in non-traded public real estate investment trusts (REITs); multi-member limited liability companies (LLCs); and other institutional investments. GERI offers high net worth investors specialized, comprehensive programs through Grubb & Ellis Private Client Management. In late 2010, the company acquired a number of properties, including nine family properties in several states and the property management business Mission Residential Management, LLC in August; the Joplin Long-Term Acute Care Hospital in Missouri and seven Virginia-based skilled nursing facilities in September; the Rock Ridge Apartments in Texas; the Athens Long-Term Acute Care Hospital in Georgia and the North Carolina-based Sylva Medical Office Building in November; and the Humble Surgical Hospital in Texas in December. In November 2010, the firm severed relations with Grubb & Ellis Apartment REIT. In early 2011, G&E acquired four medical buildings in Texas, Oklahoma and Missouri.

FINANCIALS: Sales and profits are in thousands of dollars—add 000 to get the full amount. 2010 Note: Financial information for 2010 was not available for all companies at press time.

2010 Sales: $	2010 Profits: $	**U.S. Stock Ticker:** Subsidiary
2009 Sales: $	2009 Profits: $	**Int'l Ticker:** Int'l Exchange:
2008 Sales: $	2008 Profits: $	Employees:
2007 Sales: $	2007 Profits: $	Fiscal Year Ends: 12/31
2006 Sales: $	2006 Profits: $	Parent Company: GRUBB & ELLIS CO

SALARIES/BENEFITS:

Pension Plan:	ESOP Stock Plan:	Profit Sharing:	Top Exec. Salary: $	Bonus: $
Savings Plan:	Stock Purch. Plan:		Second Exec. Salary: $	Bonus: $

OTHER THOUGHTS:

Apparent Women Officers or Directors: 3
Hot Spot for Advancement for Women/Minorities: Y

LOCATIONS: ("Y" = Yes)

West:	Southwest:	Midwest:	Southeast:	Northeast:	International:
Y	Y	Y	Y		

GRUPO ACS

www.grupoacs.com

Industry Group Code: 237 Ranks within this company's industry group: Sales: 6   Profits: 4

Properties:	Financial Services:	Construction/Development:		Investments:	Specialty Services:		Brokerage:
Apartments:	Mortgages:	Commercial Construction:	Y	REIT:	Property Management:		Commercial Sales:
Malls/Shopping:	Title Insurance:	Residential Construction:			Online Services:	Y	Residential Sales:
Offices:	Property Insurance:	Land Development:			Software/IT:		Specialty:
Hotels/Motels:		Support Services:	Y		Consulting:	Y	
Industrial/Warehouses:		Design/Engineering:	Y				
Other:							

TYPES OF BUSINESS:

Heavy Construction
Engineering Services
Civic Construction & Infrastructure
Industrial Services
Facility Maintenance
Passenger Transportation
Transportation Concessions

BRANDS/DIVISIONS/AFFILIATES:

Grupo Dragados, S.A.
Vias
Drace
Geocisa
Tecsa Empresa
Constructora S.A.
FPS
John Picone

CONTACTS: *Note: Officers with more than one job title may be intentionally listed here more than once.*

Florentino P. Rodriguez, CEO
Angel G. Altozano, Corp. Gen. Mgr.
Jose L. V. Perez, Sec.
Antonio G. Ferrer, Exec. Vice Chmn.
Marcelino F. Verdes, CEO-Construction
Jose Maria Aguirre Fernandez, Gen. Mgr.-Tecsa
Alejandro C. Botteghelz, CEO-Seis
Florentino P. Rodriguez, Chmn.

Phone: 34-91-343-92-00	Fax: 34-91-343-94-56
Toll-Free:	
Address: Avda. Pio XII, No. 102, Madrid, 28036 Spain	

GROWTH PLANS/SPECIAL FEATURES:

Grupo ACS is a leading Spanish construction and engineering firm that services a wide variety of sectors, including transportation infrastructure, real estate, offshore activities, energy, hydraulics, environment, industrial equipment, concessions and maintenance. The company performs operates through many subsidiaries, the most significant being Grupo Dragados, S.A., the Spanish construction giant. Other ACS companies include Vias Y Construcciones S.A., Drace Medio Ambiente, Geocisa, Tecsa Empresa Constructora S.A., FPS, Schiavone, Seis and John Picone. The firm has operations in 43 countries. ACS operates primarily in four major areas: construction; concessions; environmental & logistical services; and industrial services. The construction business, builds a variety of civil works projects, as well as commercial and residential structures. The concessions segment is managed by Iridium, which promotes concessions and private-public partnership contracts for infrastructural projects such as toll ways and public facilities services. The environmental and logistical services segment specializes in waste management and recycling and treatment. This segment also manages port activities such as the handling of bulk materials, general cargo and perishables. The industrial services division largely serves the energy and communications sectors through its applied design, installation and maintenance of the industrial infrastructure.

FINANCIALS: Sales and profits are in thousands of dollars—add 000 to get the full amount. 2010 Note: Financial information for 2010 was not available for all companies at press time.

2010 Sales: $21,514,800	2010 Profits: $1,836,730	**U.S. Stock Ticker:**
2009 Sales: $20,818,700	2009 Profits: $2,642,050	**Int'l Ticker: ACS** Int'l Exchange: Barcelona-BME
2008 Sales: $19,320,500	2008 Profits: $1,769,040	Employees: 141,002
2007 Sales: $16,713,900	2007 Profits: $3,505,000	Fiscal Year Ends: 12/31
2006 Sales: $19,016,796	2006 Profits: $1,721,450	Parent Company:

SALARIES/BENEFITS:

Pension Plan:	ESOP Stock Plan:	Profit Sharing:	Top Exec. Salary: $	Bonus: $
Savings Plan:	Stock Purch. Plan:		Second Exec. Salary: $	Bonus: $

OTHER THOUGHTS:

Apparent Women Officers or Directors: 1
Hot Spot for Advancement for Women/Minorities:

LOCATIONS: ("Y" = Yes)

West:	Southwest:	Midwest:	Southeast:	Northeast:	International:
					Y

GRUPO FERROVIAL SA   www.ferrovial.com

Industry Group Code: 237 Ranks within this company's industry group: Sales: 9   Profits: 1

Properties:	Financial Services:	Construction/Development:		Investments:	Specialty Services:		Brokerage:
Apartments:	Mortgages:	Commercial Construction:	Y	REIT:	Property Management:	Y	Commercial Sales:
Malls/Shopping:	Title Insurance:	Residential Construction:			Online Services:		Residential Sales:
Offices:	Property Insurance:	Land Development:	Y		Software/IT:		Specialty:
Hotels/Motels:		Support Services:			Consulting:		
Industrial/Warehouses:		Design/Engineering:					
Other: Y							

TYPES OF BUSINESS:

Airport Management
Construction
Infrastructure Services
Toll Roads
Civil Engineering

BRANDS/DIVISIONS/AFFILIATES:

Cintra
Webber
BAA PLC
Cespa
Cadagua
Budimex
Amey PLC

CONTACTS: *Note: Officers with more than one job title may be intentionally listed here more than once.*

Inigo Meiras, CEO
Ernesto Lopez Mozo, CFO
Jaime Aguirre de Carcer Y Moreno, Dir.-Human Resources
Federico Florez Gutierrez, CIO
Santiago Ortiz, Sec.
Rafael del Pino, Chmn.

Phone: 34-91-586-25-00	**Fax:** 34-91-586-26-77
Toll-Free:	
Address: Principe de Vergara, 135, Madrid, 28002 Spain	

GROWTH PLANS/SPECIAL FEATURES:

Grupo Ferrovial S.A. is a leading infrastructure and industrial group with operations in 49 countries worldwide. The company's investments target four business areas: airports; toll roads, services and construction. Ferrovial's airports segment is one of the leading private airport operators in the world, with seven airports owned by BBA PLC. BAA manages six airports in the U.K.: Heathrow, Stansted, Southampton, Glasgow, Edinburgh and Aberdeen. The firm's other airport is the Cerro Moreno Airport in Chile. Cintra is the firm's toll road and car parks division. It manages a total of 23 toll roads in Spain, Portugal, Greece, Chile, Canada and the U.S.   The company's services segment consists of Amey, a British infrastructure maintenance subsidiary; Ferroser, an infrastructure management company in Spain; Cespa, a municipal and waste-water treatment subsidiary; and various other infrastructure and maintenance companies, chiefly in Spain and Portugal. Construction, the firm's original business, covers all aspects of civil engineering and building, including roads, railways, hydraulic works, maritime works, hydroelectric and industrial works. This division includes several subsidiaries: Cadagua, a water and waste treatment plant engineering and construction company; Ferrovial Agroman, the group's flagship construction company, engaged in civil engineering; Budimex, one of Poland's largest construction companies; and Webber, a construction group in Texas. In 2010, BAA sold its interest in Naples International Airport. In February 2011, the company sold its airport handling services subsidiary, Swissport.

FINANCIALS: Sales and profits are in thousands of dollars—add 000 to get the full amount. 2010 Note: Financial information for 2010 was not available for all companies at press time.

2010 Sales: $17,714,200	2010 Profits: $3,148,640	**U.S. Stock Ticker: GRFRF.PK**
2009 Sales: $14,836,800	2009 Profits: $-112,860	**Int'l Ticker: FER** Int'l Exchange: Madrid-MCE
2008 Sales: $18,672,700	2008 Profits: $43,600	Employees: 100,995
2007 Sales: $21,360,000	2007 Profits: $1,070,000	Fiscal Year Ends: 12/31
2006 Sales: $17,033,300	2006 Profits: $1,965,970	Parent Company:

SALARIES/BENEFITS:

Pension Plan:	ESOP Stock Plan:	Profit Sharing:	Top Exec. Salary: $	Bonus: $
Savings Plan:	Stock Purch. Plan:		Second Exec. Salary: $	Bonus: $

OTHER THOUGHTS:

Apparent Women Officers or Directors:
Hot Spot for Advancement for Women/Minorities:

LOCATIONS: ("Y" = Yes)

West:	Southwest:	Midwest:	Southeast:	Northeast:	International:
	Y	Y			Y

GS ENGINEERING & CONSTRUCTION CORP   www.gsconst.co.kr

Industry Group Code: 237 Ranks within this company's industry group: Sales: 15   Profits: 13

Properties:	Financial Services:	Construction/Development:		Investments:	Specialty Services:	Brokerage:
Apartments:	Mortgages:	Commercial Construction:	Y	REIT:	Property Management:	Commercial Sales:
Malls/Shopping:	Title Insurance:	Residential Construction:			Online Services:	Residential Sales:
Offices:	Property Insurance:	Land Development:	Y		Software/IT:	Specialty:
Hotels/Motels:		Support Services:			Consulting:	
Industrial/Warehouses:		Design/Engineering:	Y			
Other:						

TYPES OF BUSINESS:
Construction

BRANDS/DIVISIONS/AFFILIATES:
Xi
Eclat

CONTACTS: *Note: Officers with more than one job title may be intentionally listed here more than once.*
Myung-Soo Huh, CEO
Myung-Soo Huh, Pres.
Si-Min Kim, CFO
Hwi-Sung Lee, Sr. Exec. VP-Domestic Sales/Chief Safety Officer
Jong-Gyu Kim, Sr. VP-Human Resources
Young-Nam Lee, CTO/Sr. Exec. VP
Jong-In Park, Sr. Exec. VP-Civil Eng.
Yong-Deug Ha, Chief Legal Officer
Chang-Deuk Do, Exec. VP-Strategic Planning
Yong-Deug Ha, Sr. Exec. VP-Public Rel.
Si-Min Kim, Sr. Exec. VP-Finance
In-Seoug Son, Exec. VP-Architecture
Chung-Hee Lim, Exec. VP-Housing
Jung-Jae Huh, Sr. Exec. VP-Power & Environment
Jong-Tae Jeong, Sr. VP-Plant Eng.
Chang-Soo Huh, Chmn.
Kee-Ju Jang, Exec. VP-Procurement & Project Monitoring

Phone: 82-2-2005-1114	Fax:
Toll-Free:	
Address: GS Yeokjeon Twr., 537 Namdaemun-ro 5-ga, Joong-gu, Seoul, Korea	

GROWTH PLANS/SPECIAL FEATURES:
GS Engineering & Construction Corp. (GS E&C), established in 1969, has six main construction divisions: Civil Engineering, Plant, Environment, Architecture, Housing and Power. The Civil Engineering division focuses on roads, bridges and railroads; underground spaces; and harbors and dredging. Notable projects include the 4.54 mile West Sea Grand Bridge, the Hopo Subway Yard in Busan and an LPG (Liquefied Petroleum Gas) offloading terminal in Incheon. The Plant division constructs oil refineries and gas processing plants; petrochemical plants; and power plants and other energy related facilities, such as pipelines and storage facilities. Some of its major projects include the Azerpetrochim refinery in Azerbaijan, the QP Refinery Expansion in Qatar and a VCM/PVC (Vinyl Chloride Monomer is used to make Polyvinyl Chloride) plant in Saudi Arabia. The Environment division handles water and wastewater treatment facilities, as well as waste treatment and recycling facilities. Some of its projects include the China Sanghae Songjiang sewage treatment facilities and the Incheon Namdong-gu food waste recycling center. The Architecture division constructs intelligent buildings; research, educational and medical health care facilities; and cultural and sports facilities. Major projects include the COEX Convention Center, the Buddhist Hospital for Dongkook University and the main stadium for Iman University in Saudi Arabia. GS E&C's Housing division constructs residential complexes under the Xi brand and studio apartments under the Eclat brand. One of its major accomplishments was being selected as the contractor for the Korea National Housing Corp. project. The Power segment focuses on the construction of combined cycle and thermal fired power plants; co-generation plants and district heating; and nuclear power plants. This division is currently constructing Nuclear Power Plant No.1 & 2 in the southeastern part of Korea. In March 2010, the company signed a $3.63 billion contract to expand oil refinery facilities in the United Arab Emirates.

FINANCIALS: Sales and profits are in thousands of dollars—add 000 to get the full amount. 2010 Note: Financial information for 2010 was not available for all companies at press time.

2010 Sales: $7,669,380	2010 Profits: $370,010	**U.S. Stock Ticker:**
2009 Sales: $6,822,640	2009 Profits: $339,260	**Int'l Ticker: 006360** Int'l Exchange: Seoul-KRX
2008 Sales: $4,971,500	2008 Profits: $266,300	Employees:
2007 Sales: $4,431,100	2007 Profits: $294,850	Fiscal Year Ends: 12/31
2006 Sales: $4,234,760	2006 Profits: $285,220	Parent Company:

SALARIES/BENEFITS:

Pension Plan:	ESOP Stock Plan:	Profit Sharing:	Top Exec. Salary: $	Bonus: $
Savings Plan:	Stock Purch. Plan:		Second Exec. Salary: $	Bonus: $

OTHER THOUGHTS:
Apparent Women Officers or Directors:
Hot Spot for Advancement for Women/Minorities:

LOCATIONS: ("Y" = Yes)

West:	Southwest:	Midwest:	Southeast:	Northeast:	International:
					Y

GUOMAN HOTELS LIMITED

www.guoman.com

Industry Group Code: 721110 **Ranks within this company's industry group:** Sales: Profits:

Properties:	Financial Services:	Construction/Development:	Investments:	Specialty Services:		Brokerage:
Apartments:	Mortgages:	Commercial Construction:	REIT:	Property Management:	Y	Commercial Sales:
Malls/Shopping:	Title Insurance:	Residential Construction:		Online Services:		Residential Sales:
Offices:	Property Insurance:	Land Development:		Software/IT:		Specialty:
Hotels/Motels: Y		Support Services:		Consulting:		
Industrial/Warehouses:		Design/Engineering:				
Other:						

TYPES OF BUSINESS:

Hotels
Hotel Management

BRANDS/DIVISIONS/AFFILIATES:

Thistle Hotels plc
GuocoLeisure Limited
BIL International Limited
Thistle Marble Arch
Charing Cross
Otium Health and Leisure Club
Guoman Hotel Shanghai

CONTACTS: *Note: Officers with more than one job title may be intentionally listed here more than once.*

Timothy J. Scoble, CEO
Jeff Karlson, VP-Global Sales
Heiko Figge, Managing Dir.-Hotel Oper., UK
Tan Sri Quek Leng Chan, Chmn.
Sanjay Nijhawan, COO-Int'l

Phone: 44-20-7138-0000	Fax: 44-20-7138-0001
Toll-Free:	
Address: Bath Rd., Uxbridge, UB8 9FH UK	

GROWTH PLANS/SPECIAL FEATURES:

Guoman Hotels Limited owns and operates a chain of 40 hotels located in the U.K. and Malaysia, primarily under the Guoman and Thistle brands. The company is owned by GuocoLeisure Limited, an investment company based in Shanghai. Guoman features 16 hotels in London alone. These hotels include the Thistle Marble Arch, overlooking Oxford Street; the Charing Cross Hotel, near Trafalgar Square; and the Tower Hotel, with views of the Tower of London and Tower Bridge. All of Guoman's properties are located near financial centers, tourist attractions and shopping districts. The company has locations in most business centers and resort areas of the U.K., including Birmingham, Bristol, Edinburgh, Glasgow, Liverpool, Manchester and Newcastle. Hotel amenities include computer and modem hookups, conference rooms, Roomexpress (its delivery room service), lounges and coffee shops. In addition, Guoman properties feature a portfolio of restaurant brands, including CoMotion, a fusion of a New York deli and Italian café, and Gengis, a mixture of Asian and Mediterranean food. Many sites feature Otium Health and Leisure Clubs that have swimming pools, whirlpools and fitness centers; others have Just Gym workout facilities; while some include full-service spas. In 2010, the firm opened the 448 room Guoman Hotel Shanghai, its first property in China.

FINANCIALS: Sales and profits are in thousands of dollars—add 000 to get the full amount. 2010 Note: Financial information for 2010 was not available for all companies at press time.

2010 Sales: $	2010 Profits: $	**U.S. Stock Ticker:** Subsidiary
2009 Sales: $	2009 Profits: $	**Int'l Ticker:** Int'l Exchange:
2008 Sales: $	2008 Profits: $	Employees:
2007 Sales: $	2007 Profits: $	Fiscal Year Ends: 12/31
2006 Sales: $	2006 Profits: $	Parent Company: GUOCOLEISURE LTD

SALARIES/BENEFITS:

Pension Plan:	ESOP Stock Plan:	Profit Sharing:	Top Exec. Salary: $	Bonus: $
Savings Plan:	Stock Purch. Plan:		Second Exec. Salary: $	Bonus: $

OTHER THOUGHTS:

Apparent Women Officers or Directors: 1
Hot Spot for Advancement for Women/Minorities:

LOCATIONS: ("Y" = Yes)

West:	Southwest:	Midwest:	Southeast:	Northeast:	International:
					Y

HANG LUNG GROUP LTD

www.hanglunggroup.com

Industry Group Code: 5311 Ranks within this company's industry group: Sales: 16   Profits: 7

Properties:		Financial Services:		Construction/Development:		Investments:	Specialty Services:		Brokerage:
Apartments:	Y	Mortgages:		Commercial Construction:		REIT:	Property Management:	Y	Commercial Sales:
Malls/Shopping:	Y	Title Insurance:		Residential Construction:			Online Services:		Residential Sales:
Offices:	Y	Property Insurance:		Land Development:	Y		Software/IT:		Specialty:
Hotels/Motels:	Y			Support Services:			Consulting:		
Industrial/Warehouses:				Design/Engineering:					
Other:									

TYPES OF BUSINESS:

Real Estate Holdings & Development
Carpark Management
Hotel Management
Dry Cleaning

BRANDS/DIVISIONS/AFFILIATES:

Hang Lung Properties Limited
Hang Lung-Hakuyosha Dry Cleaning
AP City Limited
AP Success Limited
AP Win Limited
Bonna Estates Company Limited

CONTACTS: *Note: Officers with more than one job title may be intentionally listed here more than once.*

Nelson Wai Leung Yuen, Managing Dir.
Christina Yiu Chee Leung, Head-Human Resources
Walter King Yee Wong, Sr. Manager-IT
Velencia Lee, Corp. Sec.
Andrew Chee Man Lee, Sr. Manager-Finance
Ronnie Chichung Chan, Chmn.

Phone: 852-2879-0111	Fax: 852-2868-6086
Toll-Free:	
Address: 4 Des Voeux Rd., 28th Fl., Hong Kong, China	

GROWTH PLANS/SPECIAL FEATURES:

Hang Lung Group LTD, through its subsidiary, Hang Lung Properties Limited, develops property in Hong Kong and China for both sale and lease. The company's Hong Kong portfolio, accounting for approximately 55% of revenue, consists of residential, office and commercial properties. Its China portfolio, accounting for nearly 45% of revenue, includes two large scale developments in Shanghai: The Grand Gateway, a commercial, office and residential structure; and Plaza 66, a commercial and office complex. The firm is currently expanding in other large cities such as Tianjin, Shenyang, Wuxi and Jinan, where it is developing a variety of mixed use commercial, office and residential buildings. The Hang Lung Group also manages shopping centers, office buildings, apartments and car parks and the Wesley Hotel in Hong Kong. The Group derives the majority of its revenue from Hang Lung Properties Limited. The company owns a 50% stake in Hang Lung-Hakuyosha Dry Cleaning, a joint-venture. The company's subsidiaries include AP City Limited, AP Properties Limited, AP Success Limited, AP Win Limited and Bonna Estates Company Limited.

FINANCIALS: Sales and profits are in thousands of dollars—add 000 to get the full amount. 2010 Note: Financial information for 2010 was not available for all companies at press time.

2010 Sales: $1,657,780	2010 Profits: $1,595,900	**U.S. Stock Ticker: HNLGF**
2009 Sales: $649,410	2009 Profits: $339,790	**Int'l Ticker: 0010** Int'l Exchange: Hong Kong-HKE
2008 Sales: $1,361,630	2008 Profits: $969,770	Employees: 2,479
2007 Sales: $616,490	2007 Profits: $617,530	Fiscal Year Ends: 6/30
2006 Sales: $552,750	2006 Profits: $365,540	Parent Company:

SALARIES/BENEFITS:

Pension Plan:	ESOP Stock Plan:	Profit Sharing:	Top Exec. Salary: $	Bonus: $
Savings Plan:	Stock Purch. Plan:		Second Exec. Salary: $	Bonus: $

OTHER THOUGHTS:

Apparent Women Officers or Directors: 8
Hot Spot for Advancement for Women/Minorities: Y

LOCATIONS: ("Y" = Yes)

West:	Southwest:	Midwest:	Southeast:	Northeast:	International:
					Y

HANG LUNG PROPERTIES LIMITED

www.hanglung.com

Industry Group Code: 5311 Ranks within this company's industry group: Sales: 18   Profits: 3

Properties:		Financial Services:		Construction/Development:		Investments:	Specialty Services:	Brokerage:
Apartments:	Y	Mortgages:		Commercial Construction:		REIT:	Property Management:	Commercial Sales:
Malls/Shopping:	Y	Title Insurance:		Residential Construction:			Online Services:	Residential Sales:
Offices:	Y	Property Insurance:		Land Development:	Y		Software/IT:	Specialty:
Hotels/Motels:	Y			Support Services:			Consulting:	
Industrial/Warehouses:	Y			Design/Engineering:				
Other:	Y							

TYPES OF BUSINESS:

Real Estate Holdings & Development
Leasing

BRANDS/DIVISIONS/AFFILIATES:

Harbourside
Summit (The)
Grand Gateway 66
Wesley (The)
Hang Lung Group Ltd
AP City Limited
AP Properties Limited
AP Success Limited

CONTACTS: *Note: Officers with more than one job title may be intentionally listed here more than once.*

Philip N.L. Chen, Managing Dir.
Eric Wing Hong Szeto, Sr. Mgr.-Mktg.
Christina Yiu Chee Leung, Head-Human Resources & Training
Walter King Yee Wong, Sr. Mgr.-IT
Velencia Lee, Corp. Sec./Asst. Dir.-Finance & Admin.
Yun Zhang, Sr. Mgr.-Legal
May Lam K., Sr. Mgr.-Corp. Comm.
Andrew Chee Man Lee, Sr. Mgr.-Finance
Mina Pou Lam Lai, Sr. Mgr.-Leasing & Mgmt.
Shiu Wo Lam, Sr. Mgr.-Project. Dev.
Thomas Wai Ho Ng, Sr. Mgr.-Project Dev.
Desmond Chun Cheong Lai, Sr. Mgr.-Internal Audit
Ronnie C. Chan, Chmn.

Phone: 852-2879-0111   **Fax:** 852-2868-6086
Toll-Free:
Address: 4 Des Voeux Rd., 28th Fl., Hong Kong,   China

GROWTH PLANS/SPECIAL FEATURES:

Hang Lung Properties Limited (HLPL) is a property investment holding company with interests in the retail, commercial, residential and industrial sectors. As a publicly listed subsidiary of Hang Lung Group Ltd., the firm operates in both Hong Kong and mainland China, with approximately 55% of its investment properties located in Hong Kong and the remainder in mainland China. In Hong Kong, HLPL has developed shopping malls, and mixed use commercial and residential complexes concentrated along the MTR Line, the city's mass transit system. The company also develops luxury residential properties such as The Summit and HarbourSide, which consists of three blocks of 80 story residences. Its mainland China developments include Plaza 66, a five story shopping mall and office building, and Grand Gateway 66, a complex consisting of retail, office and residential facilities in Shanghai. Development projects are also underway in the mainland Chinese cities of Tianjin, Shenyang, Wuxi, Jinan and Dalian. In addition, HLPL is involved in property leasing activities. Its commercial leasing portfolio in Hong Kong includes properties in strategic locations along busy shopping centers in the city, such as Causeway Bay and Mongkok. Its office properties are located along mass transit railway lines and other transportation networks. The Summit, with 60 stories is one of the company's luxury leasing residences. It also leases its Plaza 66 and Grand Gateway 66 properties in Shanghai, China and recently completed construction at its 360,000 square foot Palace 66 shopping mall in Shenyang. The firm operates car parks located in densely populated areas and manages The Wesley Hotel in Hong Kong, a 250 room property accommodating both commercial and business travelers.

FINANCIALS: Sales and profits are in thousands of dollars—add 000 to get the full amount. 2010 Note: Financial information for 2010 was not available for all companies at press time.

2010 Sales: $1,572,610	2010 Profits: $2,863,450	**U.S. Stock Ticker:** HLPPY
2009 Sales: $539,870	2009 Profits: $531,490	**Int'l Ticker: 0101** Int'l Exchange: Hong Kong-HKE
2008 Sales: $1,300,600	2008 Profits: $661,010	Employees: 2,324
2007 Sales: $566,300	2007 Profits: $264,250	Fiscal Year Ends: 6/30
2006 Sales: $	2006 Profits: $	Parent Company: HANG LUNG GROUP LTD

SALARIES/BENEFITS:

Pension Plan:	ESOP Stock Plan:	Profit Sharing:	Top Exec. Salary: $	Bonus: $
Savings Plan:	Stock Purch. Plan:		Second Exec. Salary: $	Bonus: $

OTHER THOUGHTS:

Apparent Women Officers or Directors: 7
Hot Spot for Advancement for Women/Minorities: Y

LOCATIONS: ("Y" = Yes)

West:	Southwest:	Midwest:	Southeast:	Northeast:	International:
					Y

HANJIN HEAVY INDUSTRIES CO LTD   www.hhic-holdings.com

Industry Group Code: 3366 Ranks within this company's industry group: Sales: 1   Profits: 1

Properties:	Financial Services:	Construction/Development:		Investments:	Specialty Services:	Brokerage:
Apartments:	Mortgages:	Commercial Construction:	Y	REIT:	Property Management:	Commercial Sales:
Malls/Shopping:	Title Insurance:	Residential Construction:	Y		Online Services:	Residential Sales:
Offices:	Property Insurance:	Land Development:	Y		Software/IT:	Specialty:
Hotels/Motels:		Support Services:	Y		Consulting:	
Industrial/Warehouses:		Design/Engineering:	Y			
Other:						

TYPES OF BUSINESS:

Construction & Manufacturing
Shipbuilding
Civil Engineering
Tourism Facilities
Gas & Energy Supply

BRANDS/DIVISIONS/AFFILIATES:

CONTACTS: *Note: Officers with more than one job title may be intentionally listed here more than once.*

N.H. Cho, CEO/Gen. Mgr.
Shin Hyun Jin, Contact-Investor Rel.
J.H. Kim, Gen. Mgr./CEO-Shipbuilding Div.
S.I. Hong, Pres., Shipbuilding Div.
J.W. Kim, CEO/Pres., Construction Div.
N.H. Cho, Chmn.

Phone: 82-2-2006-7114	**Fax:** 82-2-2006-7054
Toll-Free:	
Address: No. 22-1, Jungangro 4-ga, Jung-gu, Busan, 600-751 Korea	

GROWTH PLANS/SPECIAL FEATURES:

Hanjin Heavy Industries and Construction Co., Ltd. (HHIC), established in 1937, operates in five divisions: shipbuilding; construction; engineering; city gas; and leisure. Hanjin's oldest division, shipbuilding, manufactures LNG (liquefied natural gas) carriers, container carriers, bulk carriers, ore/coal carriers, cable ships, landing ships, battleships, high-speed vessels, towing vessels and fire-fighting vessels. It also repairs, converts and dismantles ships; manufactures and installs ship machinery, machine tools, industrial machines, industrial robots, automobile equipment and automation equipment. The construction division's operations encompass the development of steel mills, power generating facilities, environmental facilities, cranes, logistics terminals, farming facilities, housing, mines, sewage disposal and treatment facilities, fish farms; and infrastructure projects such as roads, harbors, subway, electric railway, tunnels, bridges, aviation, logistics complexes and parking lots. Engineering operations cover infrastructure and construction projects such as signal lights for airport runways, power lines and electrified railway tracks and planning for water resources, civil engineering, railways and electrical equipment. The city gas division manages power supply facilities, urban local heating and industrial complex energy supply businesses, in addition to operating a city gas business. Finally, the leisure division includes tourism facility construction and maintenance, golf course development, cultural works, landscaping and the operation of bathhouses. The firm's shipbuilding research and development efforts include structural analysis, such as collision analysis; hydrodynamic performance, such as hull form development and propeller performance research; vibration and noise analysis; and automated ship manufacturing systems, including laser sensing technology and multi-axis welding robotics research.

FINANCIALS: Sales and profits are in thousands of dollars—add 000 to get the full amount. 2010 Note: Financial information for 2010 was not available for all companies at press time.

2010 Sales: $3,925,870	2010 Profits: $4,460	**U.S. Stock Ticker:**
2009 Sales: $4,278,760	2009 Profits: $6,760	**Int'l Ticker: 003480** Int'l Exchange: Seoul-KRX
2008 Sales: $3,943,050	2008 Profits: $76,180	Employees:
2007 Sales: $1,071,120	2007 Profits: $21,060	Fiscal Year Ends: 12/31
2006 Sales: $1,924,560	2006 Profits: $72,490	Parent Company:

SALARIES/BENEFITS:

Pension Plan:	ESOP Stock Plan:	Profit Sharing:	Top Exec. Salary: $	Bonus: $
Savings Plan:	Stock Purch. Plan:		Second Exec. Salary: $	Bonus: $

OTHER THOUGHTS:

Apparent Women Officers or Directors:
Hot Spot for Advancement for Women/Minorities:

LOCATIONS: ("Y" = Yes)

West:	Southwest:	Midwest:	Southeast:	Northeast:	International:
					Y

HCP INC

www.hcpi.com

Industry Group Code: 531120 Ranks within this company's industry group: Sales: 11 Profits: 9

Properties:	Financial Services:	Construction/Development:	Investments:	Specialty Services:	Brokerage:
Apartments:	Mortgages:	Commercial Construction:	REIT: Y	Property Management:	Commercial Sales:
Malls/Shopping:	Title Insurance:	Residential Construction:		Online Services:	Residential Sales:
Offices:	Property Insurance:	Land Development:		Software/IT:	Specialty:
Hotels/Motels:		Support Services:		Consulting:	
Industrial/Warehouses:		Design/Engineering:			
Other: Y					

TYPES OF BUSINESS:

Real Estate Investment Trust
Health Care Properties

BRANDS/DIVISIONS/AFFILIATES:

Investment Management Program

CONTACTS: *Note: Officers with more than one job title may be intentionally listed here more than once.*

James F. (Jay) Flaherty, III, CEO
Thomas M. Herzog, CFO/Exec. VP
J. Alberto Gonzalez-Pita, General Counsel/Exec. VP/Sec.
Thomas D. Kirby, Exec. VP-Acquisitions & Valuations
Paul F. Gallagher, Chief Investment Officer/Exec. VP
Thomas M. Klaritch, Exec. VP-Medical Office Properties
Susan M. Tate, Exec VP-Asset Mgmt. & Senior Housing
Timothy M. Schoen, Exec. VP-Life Science & Investment Mgmt.
James F. (Jay) Flaherty, III, Chmn.

Phone: 562-733-5100	Fax: 562-733-5200
Toll-Free: 888-604-1990	
Address: 3760 Kilroy Airport Way, Ste. 300, Long Beach, CA 90806 US	

GROWTH PLANS/SPECIAL FEATURES:

HCP, Inc. invests primarily in real estate serving the healthcare industry in the U.S. Headquartered in Long Beach, California, the firm has additional offices in Nashville and San Francisco. HCP's portfolio of investments is comprised of 251 senior housing facilities, 102 life science facilities, 253 medical offices, 21 hospitals and 45 skilled nursing facilities in 42 states. Included in its portfolio are joint venture investments through its Investment Management Program in 25 senior housing facilities, four life science facilities, 66 medical offices and four hospitals. Senior housing facilities include independent living facilities, assisted living facilities and continuing care retirement communities. HCP's life science properties are primarily configured in business park formats and contain laboratory and office space primarily for scientific research institutions, government agencies and biotechnology and pharmaceutical companies. The firm's medical office facilities typically contain physicians' offices and examination rooms, and may also include pharmacies, hospital ancillary service space and outpatient services such as diagnostic centers, rehabilitation clinics and day-surgery operating rooms. All of the company's hospitals, which include acute care hospitals, long-term acute care hospitals, specialty hospitals and rehabilitation hospitals, are leased to single tenants under net lease structures. HCP's skilled nursing facilities offer restorative, rehabilitative and custodial nursing care for people not requiring the more extensive and sophisticated treatment available at hospitals. In December 2010, the firm agreed to acquire the real estate assets of private company, HRC ManorCare, Inc., for $6.1 billion. Included in this acquisition are 338 skilled nursing and assisted living facilities located in 30 states.

FINANCIALS: Sales and profits are in thousands of dollars—add 000 to get the full amount. 2010 Note: Financial information for 2010 was not available for all companies at press time.

2010 Sales: $1,255,134	2010 Profits: $344,395	**U.S. Stock Ticker: HCP**
2009 Sales: $1,148,902	2009 Profits: $146,151	**Int'l Ticker:** Int'l Exchange:
2008 Sales: $1,144,996	2008 Profits: $470,983	Employees: 148
2007 Sales: $953,743	2007 Profits: $614,115	Fiscal Year Ends: 12/31
2006 Sales: $464,247	2006 Profits: $396,417	Parent Company:

SALARIES/BENEFITS:

Pension Plan:	ESOP Stock Plan:	Profit Sharing:	Top Exec. Salary: $600,000	Bonus: $1,462,500
Savings Plan: Y	Stock Purch. Plan:		Second Exec. Salary: $350,000	Bonus: $650,000

OTHER THOUGHTS:

Apparent Women Officers or Directors: 3
Hot Spot for Advancement for Women/Minorities: Y

LOCATIONS: ("Y" = Yes)

West:	Southwest:	Midwest:	Southeast:	Northeast:	International:
Y			Y		

HDR INC

www.hdrinc.com

Industry Group Code: 237 Ranks within this company's industry group: Sales: Profits:

Properties:	Financial Services:	Construction/Development:	Investments:	Specialty Services:	Brokerage:
Apartments:	Mortgages:	Commercial Construction:	REIT:	Property Management:	Commercial Sales:
Malls/Shopping:	Title Insurance:	Residential Construction:		Online Services:	Residential Sales:
Offices:	Property Insurance:	Land Development:		Software/IT:	Specialty:
Hotels/Motels:		Support Services:		Consulting:	
Industrial/Warehouses:		Design/Engineering: Y			
Other:					

TYPES OF BUSINESS:

Engineering Services
Architectural Services
Consulting Services

BRANDS/DIVISIONS/AFFILIATES:

E.T. Archer Corporation
Claunch & Miller Inc.
TransDec
RailDec
GradeDec
RAP
AirLib
Doherty & Associates

CONTACTS: Note: Officers with more than one job title may be intentionally listed here more than once.

Richard R. Bell, CEO
Terrence C. Cox, CFO
Micheal Geppert, CIO
George A. Little, Vice Chmn./Pres., HDR Eng., Inc.
Merle S. Bachman, Pres., HDR Architecture
Richard R. Bell, Chmn.

Phone: 402-399-1000	Fax: 402-399-1238
Toll-Free: 800-366-4411	
Address: 8404 Indian Hills Dr., Omaha, NE 68114-4049 US	

GROWTH PLANS/SPECIAL FEATURES:

HDR, Inc. is an architectural, engineering and consulting firm that specializes in managing complex projects and solving engineering and architectural challenges for its clients. The company has more than 185 locations globally, including operations in all 50 states and within 60 countries worldwide. The employee-owned firm offers design-build services and program management for a variety of markets, including community architecture; hospitals and other health care projects; science and technology construction; transportation; power; justice; and wastewater and water resources. HDR's economic tools include StratBENCOST, an investment analysis tool for state and local transportation agencies engaged in multi-year strategic planning and budgeting for highways; TransDec, a cost-benefit analysis tool for both large and small urban areas and projects; RailDec, a decision support tool for state and local transportation agencies engaged in strategic planning and budgeting for rail and rail-related intermodal projects; GradeDec, a highway-rail grade crossing investment analysis tool; RAP, a suite of risk analysis tools; AirLib, a model for investigating the costs and benefits associated with liberalizing international air travel agreements; Interactive Value Assessment (IVA), a tool for conducting real-time business case evaluations; and Sustainability Business Case Tool (SBC), a tool for assessing the costs and benefits related to sustainable design. Repeat clients account for roughly 80% of the company's business. Subsidiaries of the firm include, E.T. Archer Corporation, Claunch & Miller, Inc., and Doherty & Associates.

Employees are offered medical, dental and vision coverage; tuition assistance; a 401(k) plan; a flexible spending accounts; life insurance; short- and long-term disability; and part-time employee benefits (for employees who work a minimum of 30 hours per week).

FINANCIALS: Sales and profits are in thousands of dollars—add 000 to get the full amount. 2010 Note: Financial information for 2010 was not available for all companies at press time.

2010 Sales: $	2010 Profits: $	U.S. Stock Ticker: Private
2009 Sales: $	2009 Profits: $	Int'l Ticker: Int'l Exchange:
2008 Sales: $	2008 Profits: $	Employees:
2007 Sales: $	2007 Profits: $	Fiscal Year Ends: 12/31
2006 Sales: $	2006 Profits: $	Parent Company:

SALARIES/BENEFITS:

Pension Plan:	ESOP Stock Plan: Y	Profit Sharing:	Top Exec. Salary: $	Bonus: $
Savings Plan: Y	Stock Purch. Plan:		Second Exec. Salary: $	Bonus: $

OTHER THOUGHTS:

Apparent Women Officers or Directors: 1
Hot Spot for Advancement for Women/Minorities:

LOCATIONS: ("Y" = Yes)

West:	Southwest:	Midwest:	Southeast:	Northeast:	International:
Y	Y	Y	Y	Y	Y

HEALTH CARE REIT INC

www.hcreit.com

Industry Group Code: 531120 Ranks within this company's industry group: Sales: 24   Profits: 19

Properties:		Financial Services:	Construction/Development:		Investments:		Specialty Services:		Brokerage:	
Apartments:		Mortgages:	Commercial Construction:		REIT:	Y	Property Management:	Y	Commercial Sales:	
Malls/Shopping:		Title Insurance:	Residential Construction:				Online Services:		Residential Sales:	
Offices:	Y	Property Insurance:	Land Development:	Y			Software/IT:		Specialty:	
Hotels/Motels:			Support Services:	Y			Consulting:			
Industrial/Warehouses:			Design/Engineering:							
Other:	Y									

TYPES OF BUSINESS:

Real Estate Investment Trust
Health Care Properties

BRANDS/DIVISIONS/AFFILIATES:

Paramount Real Estate Services Inc
HCN Development Services Group Inc
Windrose Southside Properties Ltd
Lake Mead Medical Investors LP
Med Properties Asset Group LLC
Windrose Medical Properties Management LLC
HCRI Eden Holdings Inc

CONTACTS: *Note: Officers with more than one job title may be intentionally listed here more than once.*

George L. Chapman, CEO
George L. Chapman, Pres.
Scott A. Estes, CFO/Exec. VP
Mercedes Kerr, Sr. VP-Mktg.
Erin C. Ibele, Sr. VP-Admin./Corp. Sec.
Jeffrey H. Miller, General Counsel
Jeffrey H. Miller, Exec. VP-Oper.
Michael A. Crabtree, Sr. VP/Treas.
Charles J. Herman, Jr., Chief Investment Officer/Exec. VP
John T. Thomas, Exec. VP-Medical Facilities
Daniel R. Loftus, Sr. VP
Stephanie Anderson, Chief Acquisitions Officer-Senior Housing
George L. Chapman, Chmn.

Phone: 419-247-2800	Fax: 419-247-2826
Toll-Free:	
Address: 4500 Dorr St., Toledo, OH 43615 US	

GROWTH PLANS/SPECIAL FEATURES:

Health Care REIT, Inc. (HCR) is a self-managed and self-administered real estate investment trust (REIT) that owns, acquires, manages and develops real estate properties in the health care industry. HCR's investment portfolio consists of 683 properties in 41 states. The company's portfolio is comprised of five primary facility types: 303 senior housing facilities, which represent 49% of its total investments; 180 skilled nursing facilities, 14% of its total investments; 31 hospitals, 9% of investments; 162 medical office buildings, 24%; and seven life science buildings, 4%. The firm's senior care and skilled nursing investments consist of independent living, continuing care retirement, assisted living and Alzheimer's/dementia care facilities. HCR's hospital investments include acute care hospitals, inpatient rehabilitation hospitals and long-term acute care hospitals. Its medical office buildings house ambulatory care and surgery centers; physician's clinics; specialty outpatient and inpatient facilities; and other specialty healthcare operations. Its life science investments are comprised of a joint venture with Forest City Enterprises, which owns a seven-building life science campus located in Cambridge, Massachusetts adjacent to the Massachusetts Institute of Technology. In 2010, the firm made net investments of $3 billion. In February 2011, the company agreed to acquire the real estate assets of Genesis HealthCare for $2.4 billion.

FINANCIALS:

Sales and profits are in thousands of dollars—add 000 to get the full amount. 2010 Note: Financial information for 2010 was not available for all companies at press time.

2010 Sales: $680,530	2010 Profits: $128,884	**U.S. Stock Ticker:** HCN
2009 Sales: $546,092	2009 Profits: $192,927	**Int'l Ticker:** Int'l Exchange:
2008 Sales: $504,525	2008 Profits: $283,425	Employees: 263
2007 Sales: $429,486	2007 Profits: $138,593	Fiscal Year Ends: 12/31
2006 Sales: $288,242	2006 Profits: $89,975	Parent Company:

SALARIES/BENEFITS:

Pension Plan:	ESOP Stock Plan:	Profit Sharing:	Top Exec. Salary: $837,045	Bonus: $1,352,165
Savings Plan: Y	Stock Purch. Plan:		Second Exec. Salary: $640,338	Bonus: $1,254,452

OTHER THOUGHTS:

Apparent Women Officers or Directors: 4
Hot Spot for Advancement for Women/Minorities: Y

LOCATIONS: ("Y" = Yes)

West:	Southwest:	Midwest:	Southeast:	Northeast:	International:
Y	Y	Y	Y	Y	

HEALTHCARE REALTY TRUST INC   www.healthcarerealty.com

Industry Group Code: 531120 Ranks within this company's industry group: Sales: 52   Profits: 45

Properties:		Financial Services:		Construction/Development:		Investments:		Specialty Services:		Brokerage:	
Apartments:		Mortgages:	Y	Commercial Construction:	Y	REIT:	Y	Property Management:	Y	Commercial Sales:	
Malls/Shopping:		Title Insurance:		Residential Construction:				Online Services:		Residential Sales:	
Offices:	Y	Property Insurance:		Land Development:				Software/IT:		Specialty:	
Hotels/Motels:				Support Services:				Consulting:			
Industrial/Warehouses:				Design/Engineering:							
Other:	Y										

TYPES OF BUSINESS:
Real Estate Investment Trust
Health Care Properties
Medical Facility Construction
Property Management
Mortgages

BRANDS/DIVISIONS/AFFILIATES:
Healthcare Realty Services, Inc.

CONTACTS: *Note: Officers with more than one job title may be intentionally listed here more than once.*
David R. Emery, CEO
B. Douglas Whitman, II, COO/Exec. VP
Scott W. Holmes, CFO/Exec. VP
Revell Michael, Dir-Mktg./Associate VP
Rebecca T. Oberlander, Associate VP-Human Resources
John M. Bryant, Jr., General Counsel/Exec. VP
Gabrielle Andres, Dir.-Corp. Comm.
David Travis, Chief Acct. Officer/Sr. VP
Todd Meredith, Exec. VP-Investments
Julie A. Wilson, Sr. VP/Dir.-Asset Mgmt.
Christine Acosta, Associate VP/Dir.-Real Estate, Western Region
Kris Douglas, Sr. VP-Asset Admin.
David R. Emery, Chmn.

Phone: 615-269-8175	**Fax:** 615-269-8461
Toll-Free:	
Address: 3310 West End Ave., 4th Fl., Ste. 700, Nashville, TN 37203 US	

GROWTH PLANS/SPECIAL FEATURES:
Healthcare Realty Trust, Inc. (HRT) is a self-managed and self-administered real estate investment trust (REIT) that owns, acquires, manages and develops real estate properties in the health care industry. HRT's portfolio includes approximately $2.6 billion in mortgage investments in 209 real estate properties in 28 states with approximately 13.3 million square feet. The company also provides property management services for 137 healthcare-related properties nationwide, totaling approximately 9.2 million square feet. Its portfolio consists of six major facility types, including medical offices, which represent 80% of its total investments by square feet; physician clinics; inpatient rehabilitation facilities; surgical facilities; specialty outpatient; and other specialty healthcare fields. Unlike the majority of real estate firms, HRT funds a majority of its acquisitions and developments from internal capital instead of third-party lenders or equity partners, which allows the firm to expedite investments and accept shorter operating leases. HRT has constructed over two dozen medical real estate facilities valued at more than $750 million in an effort to improve acute care facilities, technology and services for healthcare providers. Although HRT invests in properties nationwide, the majority of its investments are concentrated in the Southern and Western U.S. In 2010, the company disposed of nine real estate properties and acquired approximately $311.5 million in real estate assets. In January 2011, it sold a medical office building located in Maryland. In February 2011, it sold a physician clinic in Florida.

FINANCIALS: Sales and profits are in thousands of dollars—add 000 to get the full amount. 2010 Note: Financial information for 2010 was not available for all companies at press time.

2010 Sales: $258,394	2010 Profits: $8,247	**U.S. Stock Ticker:** HR
2009 Sales: $246,838	2009 Profits: $51,148	**Int'l Ticker:** Int'l Exchange:
2008 Sales: $206,394	2008 Profits: $41,760	Employees: 240
2007 Sales: $197,081	2007 Profits: $60,062	Fiscal Year Ends: 12/31
2006 Sales: $198,219	2006 Profits: $39,719	Parent Company:

SALARIES/BENEFITS:

Pension Plan:	ESOP Stock Plan:	Profit Sharing:	Top Exec. Salary: $959,711	Bonus: $
Savings Plan: Y	Stock Purch. Plan: Y		Second Exec. Salary: $411,521	Bonus: $

OTHER THOUGHTS:
Apparent Women Officers or Directors: 11
Hot Spot for Advancement for Women/Minorities: Y

LOCATIONS: ("Y" = Yes)

West:	Southwest:	Midwest:	Southeast:	Northeast:	International:
Y	Y	Y	Y	Y	

HENDERSON LAND DEVELOPMENT COMPANY LIMITED
www.hld.com
Industry Group Code: 5311 Ranks within this company's industry group: Sales: 21   Profits: 5

Properties:		Financial Services:	Construction/Development:		Investments:	Specialty Services:		Brokerage:
Apartments:	Y	Mortgages:	Commercial Construction:	Y	REIT:	Property Management:	Y	Commercial Sales:
Malls/Shopping:	Y	Title Insurance:	Residential Construction:	Y		Online Services:		Residential Sales:
Offices:	Y	Property Insurance:	Land Development:	Y		Software/IT:		Specialty:
Hotels/Motels:	Y		Support Services:			Consulting:		
Industrial/Warehouses:			Design/Engineering:					
Other:								

TYPES OF BUSINESS:
Real Estate Holdings & Development
Property Management
Construction
Hotel Operation

BRANDS/DIVISIONS/AFFILIATES:
Hong Kong Ferry (Holdings) Company Limited
Henderson Investment Limited
Hong Kong & China Gas Company Limited (The)
Miramar Hotel & Investment Company, Limited
Towngas China
Citistore

CONTACTS: *Note: Officers with more than one job title may be intentionally listed here more than once.*
Tat Man Lam, Gen. Mgr-Sales
Wing Hoo Wong, Gen. Mgr-Construction
Cheung Yuen Liu, Corp. Sec.
David Francis Dumigan, Gen. Mgr.-Project Mgmt. Unit
Ho Ming Wong, Gen. Mgr.-Property Dev.
Kam Leung Leung, Gen. Mgr-Property Planning
Wing Kee Wong, Gen. Mgr.-Accounts
Shau Kee Lee, Chmn.

Phone: 852-2908-8888	**Fax:** 852-2908-8838
Toll-Free:	
Address: 2 Int'l Finance Centre, 8 Finance St., Fl. 72-76, Hong Kong, China	

GROWTH PLANS/SPECIAL FEATURES:
Henderson Land Development Company Limited is an investment holding firm that focuses on property development and investment; property management; construction; and hotel operation in Hong Kong and China. The total land bank of the company and its subsidiaries in Hong Kong equals approximately 19 million square feet of total attributable floor space. It also holds 32.8 million square feet of agricultural land. The firm develops property in both urban and suburban areas in Hong Kong. Its investment portfolio in Hong Kong is around 20 million square feet. Henderson's landmark investment project in the city is the International Finance Centre, which consists of retail shopping centers and office buildings, which account for 85% of the company's investment properties. Henderson also participates in hotel development, having established the Mira Hong Kong, Four Seasons Hotel Hong Kong and Newton Hotel Hong Kong. In addition, the company holds a place in the department store market, under the trade name, Citistore, which targets young and fashion forward clientele. The firm's total land bank in China is approximately 146.2 million square feet in developable gross floor area. Henderson has participated in the development and investment of the Henderson Centre in Beijing, Office Tower II of The Grand Gateway in Shanghai, the Shanghai Skycity and the Heng Bao Garden in Guangzhou. The company's subsidiaries include Hong Kong Ferry (Holdings) Company Limited, which focuses on property development and investment; Henderson Investment Limited, which is involved in infrastructure; The Hong Kong and China Gas Company Limited, which produces and distributes gas in Hong Kong and China; Miramar Hotel and Investment Company, Limited, which is involved in hotel operation and the travel business; and Towngas China, a distributor of liquefied petroleum and natural gas in China.

FINANCIALS: Sales and profits are in thousands of dollars—add 000 to get the full amount. 2010 Note: Financial information for 2010 was not available for all companies at press time.

2010 Sales: $912,460	2010 Profits: $2,035,400	**U.S. Stock Ticker:**
2009 Sales: $1,341,060	2009 Profits: $1,693,750	**Int'l Ticker: 0012** Int'l Exchange: Hong Kong-HKE
2008 Sales: $1,754,000	2008 Profits: $2,011,400	Employees: 8,000
2007 Sales: $1,086,300	2007 Profits: $1,276,300	Fiscal Year Ends: 12/31
2006 Sales: $880,500	2006 Profits: $1,761,300	Parent Company:

SALARIES/BENEFITS:

Pension Plan:	ESOP Stock Plan:	Profit Sharing:	Top Exec. Salary: $	Bonus: $
Savings Plan:	Stock Purch. Plan:		Second Exec. Salary: $	Bonus: $

OTHER THOUGHTS:
Apparent Women Officers or Directors: 3
Hot Spot for Advancement for Women/Minorities: Y

LOCATIONS: ("Y" = Yes)

West:	Southwest:	Midwest:	Southeast:	Northeast:	International:
					Y

HIGHWOODS PROPERTIES INC

www.highwoods.com

Industry Group Code: 531120 Ranks within this company's industry group: Sales: 37   Profits: 28

Properties:		Financial Services:		Construction/Development:		Investments:		Specialty Services:		Brokerage:	
Apartments:	Y	Mortgages:		Commercial Construction:		REIT:	Y	Property Management:	Y	Commercial Sales:	
Malls/Shopping:		Title Insurance:		Residential Construction:				Online Services:		Residential Sales:	
Offices:	Y	Property Insurance:		Land Development:	Y			Software/IT:	Y	Specialty:	
Hotels/Motels:				Support Services:	Y			Consulting:			
Industrial/Warehouses:	Y			Design/Engineering:							
Other:											

TYPES OF BUSINESS:

Real Estate Investment Trust
Real Estate Development
Property Management & Leasing
Office, Retail & Industrial Properties
Apartments
Construction Services
Asset Management
Corporate Hosting

BRANDS/DIVISIONS/AFFILIATES:

Highwoods Realty Limited Partnership
ServiceLink

CONTACTS: *Note: Officers with more than one job title may be intentionally listed here more than once.*

Edward J. Fritsch, CEO
Michael E. Harris, COO/Exec. VP
Edward J. Fritsch, Pres.
Terry L. Stevens, CFO/Sr. VP
Art H. McCann, CIO
Jeffrey D. Miller, General Counsel/Corp. Sec./VP
Kevin E. Penn, VP-Strategy
Tabitha N. Zane, VP-Corp. Comm.
Tabitha N. Zane, VP-Investor Rel.
Daniel L. Clemmens, Chief Acct. Officer/VP
S. Hugh Esleek, Treas.
Carman J. Liuzzo, VP-Investments
Michael D. Starchville, VP-Asset Mgmt.
W. Brian Reames, Sr. VP-Nashville
O. Temple Sloan, Jr., Chmn.

Phone: 919-872-4924	**Fax:** 919-876-2448
Toll-Free: 866-449-6637	
Address: 3100 Smoketree Ct., Ste. 600, Raleigh, NC 27604 US	

GROWTH PLANS/SPECIAL FEATURES:

Highwoods Properties, Inc. is a self-administered real estate investment trust (REIT) engaged in the acquisition, development and operation of rental real estate properties, including office, industrial, retail and residential properties. Highwoods conducts nearly all of its activities through the Highwoods Realty Limited Partnership, in which it is the sole general partner. The firm's property holdings consist of 295 wholly-owned, in-service office, industrial and retail properties with over 27 million square feet of space; 96 rental residential units; an interest in approximately 35 in-service office and industrial properties with 5.2 million square feet of rentable space; 611 acres of wholly-owned undeveloped land; and 26 for-sale residential condominiums. The company's properties and development land are located in Florida, Georgia, Iowa, Mississippi, Missouri, North Carolina, South Carolina, Tennessee and Virginia. Its three largest tenants, by rental revenues, are the U.S. government, AT&T and PricewaterhouseCoopers. Highwoods also provides services including asset management, tenant services and corporate hosting. Highwoods' tenant services include ServiceLink, its customer service system enabling telephone or online system access, wireless service technician notification and online real-time service request tracking. In December 2010, the company acquired Independence Park, a 33-acre, multi-building development property in Tampa, Florida.

Employees are offered medical, dental and vision insurance; life insurance; flexible reimbursement accounts; disability coverage; a 401(k) savings plan; an employee stock purchase plan; educational assistance; credit union membership; an interest free computer purchase program; and discounted auto and homeowner's insurance.

FINANCIALS: Sales and profits are in thousands of dollars—add 000 to get the full amount. 2010 Note: Financial information for 2010 was not available for all companies at press time.

2010 Sales: $463,321	2010 Profits: $72,303	**U.S. Stock Ticker:** HIW
2009 Sales: $450,154	2009 Profits: $61,694	**Int'l Ticker:** Int'l Exchange:
2008 Sales: $445,268	2008 Profits: $35,610	Employees: 397
2007 Sales: $418,409	2007 Profits: $97,095	Fiscal Year Ends: 12/31
2006 Sales: $401,304	2006 Profits: $53,744	Parent Company:

SALARIES/BENEFITS:

Pension Plan:	ESOP Stock Plan:	Profit Sharing:	Top Exec. Salary: $540,750	Bonus: $1,054,461
Savings Plan: Y	Stock Purch. Plan: Y		Second Exec. Salary: $360,500	Bonus: $513,712

OTHER THOUGHTS:

Apparent Women Officers or Directors: 3
Hot Spot for Advancement for Women/Minorities: Y

LOCATIONS: ("Y" = Yes)

West:	Southwest:	Midwest:	Southeast:	Northeast:	International:
		Y	Y	Y	

  Plunkett Research, Ltd.

HILTON HOTELS CORP

www.hiltonworldwide.com

Industry Group Code: 721110 Ranks within this company's industry group: Sales: Profits:

Properties:		Financial Services:	Construction/Development:	Investments:	Specialty Services:		Brokerage:	
Apartments:		Mortgages:	Commercial Construction:	REIT:	Property Management:	Y	Commercial Sales:	
Malls/Shopping:		Title Insurance:	Residential Construction:		Online Services:	Y	Residential Sales:	
Offices:		Property Insurance:	Land Development:		Software/IT:		Specialty:	
Hotels/Motels:	Y		Support Services:		Consulting:			
Industrial/Warehouses:			Design/Engineering:					
Other:	Y							

TYPES OF BUSINESS:

Hotels & Resorts
Timeshare Properties
Conference Centers
Franchising
Management Services
Online Reservations

BRANDS/DIVISIONS/AFFILIATES:

Hilton
Hilton Garden Inn
Hampton Inn
Conrad Hotels and Resorts
Waldorf Astoria Collection
Embassy Suites
Hilton Garden Vacations Company LLC
Home2 Suites by Hilton

CONTACTS: Note: Officers with more than one job title may be intentionally listed here more than once.

Christopher Nassetta, CEO
Christopher J. Nassetta, Pres.
Tom Kennedy, CFO/Exec. VP
Matthew W. Schuyler, Chief Human Resources Officer/Exec. VP
Ian R. Carter, Pres., Global Oper. & Dev.
Kevin Jacobs, Sr. VP-Corp. Strategy
Ellen Gonda, Sr. VP-Global Corp. Comm.
Kevin Jacobs, Treas.
Paul Brown, Pres., Global Brands & Commercial Svcs.
Mark Wang, Pres., Hilton Grand Vacations Co., LLC
Matt Richardson, Head-Architecture,/Design/Construction/Real Estate

Phone: 703-883-1000	Fax:
Toll-Free: 800-445-8667	
Address: 7930 Jones Branch Dr., Ste. 1100, McLean, VA 22102 US	

GROWTH PLANS/SPECIAL FEATURES:

Hilton Hotels Corp. (HHC), founded in 1919, owns, manages and develops hotels, resorts and timeshare properties; and franchises lodging properties. HHC consists of 10 hotel brands and more than 3,600 hotels in 81 countries around the world. Its hotel brands include Hilton, Hilton Garden Inn, Doubletree, Embassy Suites, Homewood Suites, Home2 Suites, Hampton Inn, Conrad Hotels and Resorts and The Waldorf Astoria Collection. HHC owns the worldwide rights to develop and market Hilton and Conrad brands. Although the majority of the company's hotels are located within the U.S., the company also operates luxury lodgings in locations such as Thailand, Ireland, Singapore, Uruguay, Indonesia and Egypt. Hilton Worldwide Resorts offers 54 self-contained resorts in the Middle East, Asia Pacific, Europe, the Americas, the Indian Ocean and the Caribbean. Through Hilton Garden Vacations Company, LLC, the firm also owns and manages several vacation timeshare properties with three more under development. HHonors, the firm's loyalty enrollment program for returning customers, has over 25 million members and includes partner benefits with JetBlue Airlines. The firm is investing in technologies such as check-in kiosks to facilitate an easier and faster check-in process for its customers in partnership with IBM. HHC, in separate deals with three real estate groups, is developing over 55 properties in Russia, the U.K. and Central America, all planned to be completed by 2012. In July 2010, AT&T agreed to provide a fully-managed suite of Wi-Fi and Internet services to all Hilton brand hotels. In October 2010, the firm opened to national sales office in Abu Dhabi and Dubai. In February 2011, Home2 Suites by Hilton opened its first property in Fayetteville, North Carolina. In March 2011, Doubletree opened a hotel in Aqaba, Jordan.

FINANCIALS: Sales and profits are in thousands of dollars—add 000 to get the full amount. 2010 Note: Financial information for 2010 was not available for all companies at press time.

2010 Sales: $9,000,000	2010 Profits: $	**U.S. Stock Ticker: Private**
2009 Sales: $8,000,000	2009 Profits: $	**Int'l Ticker:** Int'l Exchange:
2008 Sales: $7,770,000	2008 Profits: $	Employees: 130,000
2007 Sales: $8,090,000	2007 Profits: $121,000	Fiscal Year Ends: 12/31
2006 Sales: $7,438,000	2006 Profits: $572,000	Parent Company: BLACKSTONE GROUP LP (THE)

SALARIES/BENEFITS:

Pension Plan:	ESOP Stock Plan:	Profit Sharing:	Top Exec. Salary: $	Bonus: $
Savings Plan: Y	Stock Purch. Plan:		Second Exec. Salary: $	Bonus: $

OTHER THOUGHTS:

Apparent Women Officers or Directors: 1
Hot Spot for Advancement for Women/Minorities:

LOCATIONS: ("Y" = Yes)

West:	Southwest:	Midwest:	Southeast:	Northeast:	International:
Y	Y	Y	Y	Y	Y

HINES INTERESTS LP

www.hines.com

Industry Group Code: 5311 Ranks within this company's industry group: Sales: Profits:

Properties:		Financial Services:		Construction/Development:		Investments:		Specialty Services:		Brokerage:	
Apartments:	Y	Mortgages:		Commercial Construction:	Y	REIT:	Y	Property Management:	Y	Commercial Sales:	
Malls/Shopping:		Title Insurance:		Residential Construction:	Y			Online Services:		Residential Sales:	
Offices:	Y	Property Insurance:		Land Development:	Y			Software/IT:		Specialty:	
Hotels/Motels:	Y			Support Services:	Y			Consulting:			
Industrial/Warehouses:	Y			Design/Engineering:	Y						
Other:	Y										

TYPES OF BUSINESS:

Real Estate Development
Property Management
Property Development
Engineering Services
Office Buildings
Industrial Properties
Hotels
Residential Properties

BRANDS/DIVISIONS/AFFILIATES:

CONTACTS: *Note: Officers with more than one job title may be intentionally listed here more than once.*

Jeffrey C. Hines, CEO
Jeffrey C. Hines, Pres.
C. Hastings Johnson, CFO
Stephanie Fore, Sr. VP-Human Resources
Jesse Carrillo, CIO
Clayton Ulrich, Sr. VP-Eng. Svcs.
David LeVrier, Chief Admin. Officer/Sr. VP
Ilene Allen, VP-Corp. Oper. Svcs.
George C. Lancaster, Sr. VP-Corp. Comm.
Kay P. Forbes, Sr. VP-Corp. Finance
Charles M. Baughn, Exec. VP/CEO-Capital Markets
Jerrold P. Lea, Sr. VP-Conceptual Construction
Tom Owens, Chief Risk Officer/Exec. VP
James C. Buie, Jr., Exec. VP/CEO-West Region
Gerald D. Hines, Chmn.
E. Staman Ogilvie, CEO-Eurasia

Phone: 713-621-8000	Fax: 713-966-2636
Toll-Free:	
Address: 2800 Post Oak Blvd., Williams Tower, Houston, TX 77056-6118 US	

GROWTH PLANS/SPECIAL FEATURES:

Hines Interests, LP is a private commercial real estate development firm handling many aspects of development, including site selection, acquisition, zoning, design, construction management, financing and property management. The company has offices in 68 U.S. cities and 17 other countries in Europe, South America and North America and controls assets valued at approximately $22.9 billion. Hines' portfolio of projects completed, underway, acquired and managed for third parties includes more than 760 properties representing over 247 million square feet of office, mixed-use, industrial, hotel, medical, sports facilities and residential properties, as well as large, master-planned communities and land developments. The firm specializes in integrated design projects, working with potential tenants and other clients in order to develop the most valuable and most beautiful buildings and rentable spaces possible. Hines' services include investment management; development; asset and property management; acquisition and disposition; and marketing and leasing. Throughout its history, the company has worked on such notable properties as Pennzoil Place and the J.P. Morgan Chase Tower in Houston, Texas; the EDF Tower in Paris, France; the GM Renaissance Center in Detroit, Michigan; and the Torre Del Angel and Del Bosque in Mexico City, Mexico. Hines has worked in partnership with many of the most notable architects in the world, including Frank Gehry, I.M. Pei and Philip Johnson. Recently, Hines acquired properties in London, U.K.; Austin, Texas; Minneapolis, Minnesota; Irvine, California; and Durham, North Carolina. In April 2010, the company sold three properties in Brazil. In May 2010, the firm began construction on a 43-story, 275-unit residential building located in Warsaw, Poland.

Hines offers its employees medical, dental and vision coverage; short- and long-term disability coverage; life and AD&D insurance; adoption assistance; an employee assistance program; access to a credit union; tuition reimbursement; employee referral bonuses; and wellness benefits.

FINANCIALS: Sales and profits are in thousands of dollars—add 000 to get the full amount. 2010 Note: Financial information for 2010 was not available for all companies at press time.

2010 Sales: $	2010 Profits: $	**U.S. Stock Ticker:** Private
2009 Sales: $	2009 Profits: $	**Int'l Ticker:** Int'l Exchange:
2008 Sales: $	2008 Profits: $	Employees:
2007 Sales: $	2007 Profits: $	Fiscal Year Ends: 12/31
2006 Sales: $	2006 Profits: $	Parent Company:

SALARIES/BENEFITS:

Pension Plan:	ESOP Stock Plan:	Profit Sharing:	Top Exec. Salary: $	Bonus: $
Savings Plan: Y	Stock Purch. Plan:		Second Exec. Salary: $	Bonus: $

OTHER THOUGHTS:

Apparent Women Officers or Directors: 3
Hot Spot for Advancement for Women/Minorities: Y

LOCATIONS: ("Y" = Yes)

West:	Southwest:	Midwest:	Southeast:	Northeast:	International:
Y	Y	Y	Y	Y	Y

HOCHTIEF AG

www.hochtief.de

Industry Group Code: 237 Ranks within this company's industry group: Sales: 4   Profits: 11

Properties:	Financial Services:	Construction/Development:		Investments:	Specialty Services:	Brokerage:
Apartments:	Mortgages:	Commercial Construction:	Y	REIT:	Property Management:	Commercial Sales:
Malls/Shopping:	Title Insurance:	Residential Construction:			Online Services:	Residential Sales:
Offices:	Property Insurance:	Land Development:			Software/IT:	Specialty:
Hotels/Motels:		Support Services:			Consulting:	
Industrial/Warehouses:		Design/Engineering:				
Other:						

TYPES OF BUSINESS:

Heavy Construction
Airport Management & Consulting Services
Infrastructure Development
Geothermal Plant Construction
Green Building Engineering Services

BRANDS/DIVISIONS/AFFILIATES:

Turner Construction Company
HOCHTIEF do Brasil
HOCHTIEF Construction A.G.
HOCHTIEF Facility Management GmbH
HOCHTIEF Property Management
HOCHTIEF Projektentwicklung
HOCHTIEF PPP Solutions
HOCHTIEF AirPort

CONTACTS: Note: Officers with more than one job title may be intentionally listed here more than once.

Herbert Lutkestratkotter, CEO
Burkhard Lohr, CFO
Burkhard Lohr, Dir.-Human Resources
Herbert Lutkestratkotter, Dir.-Corp. Dev.
Herbert Lutkestratkotter, Dir.-Corp. Comm.
Burkhard Lohr, Dir.-Investor Rel.
Burkhard Lohr, Dir.-Finance
Martin Rohr, Dir.-Hochtief Americas
Frank Stieler, Dir.-Europe
Frank Stieler, Dir.-Real Estate & Svcs.
Peter Noe, Dir.-Concessions
Detlev Bremkamp, Chmn.
Peter Noe, Dir.-Asia Pacific
Frank Stieler, Dir.-Global Procurement

Phone: 49-201-824-0	Fax: 49-201-824-2777
Toll-Free:	
Address: Opernplatz 2, Essen, 45128 Germany	

GROWTH PLANS/SPECIAL FEATURES:

HOCHTIEF AG is a construction services provider that designs, builds, finances and operates facilities worldwide. The company operates through six divisions: HOCHTIEF Americas; HOCHTIEF Europe; HOCHTIEF Asia Pacific; HOCHTIEF Concessions; HOCHTIEF Real Estate; and HOCHTIEF Services. The Americas division includes the activities of subsidiaries in the U.S. and Brazil, including Turner Construction Company, a U.S. general construction contractor and green building engineering firm, and HOCHTIEF do Brasil, providing construction and facilities management services. The Europe division's leading company, HOCHTIEF Construction A.G., provides civil and structural engineering, as well as building construction services. The core of the Asia-Pacific division is Leighton Holdings, Ltd., which operates the Australian subsidiaries Leighton Contractors Pty., Leighton Properties Pty., John Holland Group Pty., Thiess Pty.; and Leighton Asia (Northern), Ltd. and Leighton Asia (Southern), Ltd., in Hong Kong. The concessions division covers business areas such as airports, roads, municipal infrastructure and public-private partnership (PPP) projects, including the operations of subsidiaries HOCHTIEF AirPort and HOCHTIEF PPP Solutions. The company's concessions portfolio contains approximately six airports, seven roads, more than 100 schools, several municipal buildings, a military base and two geothermal energy projects. The real estate division develops, markets and manages a range of property types through such subsidiaries as HOCHTIEF Projektentwicklung, an inner-city property developer; HOCHTIEF Property Management, which manages real estate for various investors; and joint venture subsidiary Aurelis Real Estate GmbH & Co. KG, which redevelops urban retail sites in Germany. The services division includes subsidiaries HOCHTIEF Facility Management GmbH and HOCHTIEF Energy Management, which works with clients to improve the energy efficiency of both public and private buildings. In addition to these primary divisions, subsidiary HOCHTIEF Insurance Broking & Risk Management Solutions handles insurance services for the company's units, while HOCHTIEF ViCon offers virtual design and construction services to HOCHTIEF units and outside clients.

FINANCIALS: Sales and profits are in thousands of dollars—add 000 to get the full amount. 2010 Note: Financial information for 2010 was not available for all companies at press time.

2010 Sales: $29,120,500	2010 Profits: $416,020	**U.S. Stock Ticker: HOCFF.PK**
2009 Sales: $24,519,300	2009 Profits: $263,470	**Int'l Ticker: HOT** Int'l Exchange: Frankfurt-Euronext
2008 Sales: $25,783,870	2008 Profits: $419,100	Employees: 70,657
2007 Sales: $22,205,420	2007 Profits: $165,870	Fiscal Year Ends: 12/31
2006 Sales: $21,065,480	2006 Profits: $273,520	Parent Company:

SALARIES/BENEFITS:

Pension Plan:	ESOP Stock Plan:	Profit Sharing:	Top Exec. Salary: $	Bonus: $
Savings Plan:	Stock Purch. Plan:		Second Exec. Salary: $	Bonus: $

OTHER THOUGHTS:

Apparent Women Officers or Directors:
Hot Spot for Advancement for Women/Minorities:

LOCATIONS: ("Y" = Yes)

West:	Southwest:	Midwest:	Southeast:	Northeast:	International:
Y	Y	Y	Y	Y	Y

HOME DEPOT INC

www.homedepot.com

Industry Group Code: 444110 Ranks within this company's industry group: Sales: 1   Profits: 1

Properties:		Financial Services:	Construction/Development:		Investments:	Specialty Services:		Brokerage:
Apartments:		Mortgages:	Commercial Construction:		REIT:	Property Management:		Commercial Sales:
Malls/Shopping:	Y	Title Insurance:	Residential Construction:			Online Services:	Y	Residential Sales:
Offices:		Property Insurance:	Land Development:			Software/IT:		Specialty:
Hotels/Motels:			Support Services:	Y		Consulting:		
Industrial/Warehouses:			Design/Engineering:					
Other:								

TYPES OF BUSINESS:

Home Centers, Retail
Home Improvement Products
Building Materials
Lawn & Garden Products
Online & Catalog Sales
Tool & Truck Rental
Installation & Design Services

BRANDS/DIVISIONS/AFFILIATES:

Husky
Hampton Bay
Behr Premium Plus
RIDGID
Ryobi
Glacier
Vigoro
Martha Stewart Living

CONTACTS: *Note: Officers with more than one job title may be intentionally listed here more than once.*

Francis S. Blake, CEO
Carol B. Tome, CFO/Exec. VP-Corp. Svcs.
Frank Bifulco, Chief Mktg. Officer/Sr. VP
Timothy M. Crow, Exec. VP-Human Resources
Matt Carey, CIO/Exec. VP
Craig A. Menear, Exec. VP-Merch.
Jack A. VanWoerkom, General Counsel/Exec. VP/Corp. Sec.
Mark Powers, Sr. VP-Oper.
Hal Lawton, Pres., Online
Brad Shaw, VP-Corp Comm. & External Affairs
Ted Decker, Sr. VP-U.S. Retail Finance
Jim Kane, Pres., Northern Div.
Ricardo E. Saldivar, Pres., The Home Depot Mexico
Anne-Marie Campbell, Pres., Southern Div.
Marvin R. Ellison, Exec. VP-U.S. Stores
Francis S. Blake, Chmn.
Annette M. Verschuren, Pres., The Home Depot Canada & Asia
Mark Holifield, Sr. VP-Supply Chain

Phone: 770-433-8211	Fax: 770-384-2356
Toll-Free: 800-553-3199	
Address: 2455 Paces Ferry Rd. N.W., Atlanta, GA 30339 US	

GROWTH PLANS/SPECIAL FEATURES:

Home Depot, Inc. is one of the world's largest home improvement retailers. The company operates approximately 2,244 Home Depot stores throughout the U.S., Canada, China, Puerto Rico, the Virgin Islands and Mexico. A typical store encompasses 105,000 square feet of enclosed space with a 24,000 square foot outdoor garden center; these locations usually stock between 30,000 and 40,000 items. These stores sell an assortment of building materials, plumbing materials, electrical materials, kitchen products, hardware, seasonal items, paint, flooring and wall coverings. The firm's proprietary brands include Hampton Bay lighting; Husky hand tools; Behr Premium Plus paint; Vigoro lawn care products; RIDGID and Ryobi power tools; and Glacier Bay bath fixtures. Home Depot markets its products primarily to three types of customers: professional customers, such as remodelers, contractors, repairmen and small business owners; do-it-for-me shoppers, who are homeowners that personally purchase Home Depot products but hire third party individuals for installation and/or project completion; and do-it-yourself customers, who are homeowners that both shop for and personally install and/or utilize the firm's materials.

The company offers its employees medical, dental, vision, life, AD&D and disability insurance; a 401(k) plan; a stock purchase plan; adoption, education and relocation assistance; flexible spending accounts; a legal services plan; auto and homeowners insurance; and veterinary coverage.

FINANCIALS: Sales and profits are in thousands of dollars—add 000 to get the full amount. 2010 Note: Financial information for 2010 was not available for all companies at press time.

2010 Sales: $66,176,000	2010 Profits: $2,661,000	**U.S. Stock Ticker:** HD
2009 Sales: $71,288,000	2009 Profits: $2,260,000	**Int'l Ticker:** Int'l Exchange:
2008 Sales: $77,349,000	2008 Profits: $4,395,000	Employees: 322,000
2007 Sales: $79,022,000	2007 Profits: $5,761,000	Fiscal Year Ends: 1/31
2006 Sales: $77,019,000	2006 Profits: $5,838,000	Parent Company:

SALARIES/BENEFITS:

Pension Plan:	ESOP Stock Plan:	Profit Sharing:	Top Exec. Salary: $1,025,000	Bonus: $2,107,730
Savings Plan: Y	Stock Purch. Plan: Y		Second Exec. Salary: $910,000	Bonus: $1,169,533

OTHER THOUGHTS:

Apparent Women Officers or Directors: 6
Hot Spot for Advancement for Women/Minorities: Y

LOCATIONS: ("Y" = Yes)

West:	Southwest:	Midwest:	Southeast:	Northeast:	International:
Y	Y	Y	Y	Y	Y

HOME INNS & HOTELS MANAGEMENT INC

www.homeinns.com

Industry Group Code: 721110 Ranks within this company's industry group: Sales: 20   Profits: 15

Properties:		Financial Services:	Construction/Development:	Investments:	Specialty Services:		Brokerage:
Apartments:		Mortgages:	Commercial Construction:	REIT:	Property Management:	Y	Commercial Sales:
Malls/Shopping:		Title Insurance:	Residential Construction:		Online Services:		Residential Sales:
Offices:		Property Insurance:	Land Development:		Software/IT:		Specialty:
Hotels/Motels:	Y		Support Services:		Consulting:		
Industrial/Warehouses:			Design/Engineering:				
Other:							

TYPES OF BUSINESS:

Economy Hotels
Midscale Hotels

BRANDS/DIVISIONS/AFFILIATES:

Home Inns
Yitel

CONTACTS: *Note: Officers with more than one job title may be intentionally listed here more than once.*

David Sun, CEO
Jason Zong, COO
Huiping Yan, CFO
May Wu, Chief Strategy Officer
Ethan Ruan, Mgr.-Investor Rel.
Neil Shen, Co-Chmn.
Yunxin Mei, Co-Chmn.

Phone: 86-21-3401-9898	**Fax:** 86-21-6483-5660
Toll-Free:	
Address: Number 124, Caobao Rd., Shanghai, 200235 China	

GROWTH PLANS/SPECIAL FEATURES:

Home Inns & Hotels Management, Inc. (Home Inns) is an economy hotel chain in China, with 818 locations in 146 Chinese cities under its Home Inns brand. Home Inns leases real estate properties on which it develops; operates hotels; franchises its brand to hotel owners; and manages these hotel properties. For the leased and operated hotels, the company is responsible for hotel development and customization to conform to the standards of Home Inns, as well as repairs, maintenance and operating expenses. For the franchised and managed hotels, Home Inns is responsible for managing the hotel, while the franchisee is responsible for cost of development and customization. The company's hotel chain consists of 454 leased-and-operated hotels in operation and 364 franchised-and-managed hotels. Additionally, the firm has 90 hotels currently contracted or under construction. A typical Home Inns hotel has 80-160 guest rooms. Each hotel has a standardized design, appearance, decor, color scheme, lighting scheme and set of guest amenities in each room, including free in-room broadband Internet access, a work space, air conditioning and a supply of cold and hot drinking water. Home Inns' hotels are strategically located to provide guests with convenient access to major business districts, ground transportation hubs, major highways, shopping centers, industrial development zones, colleges and universities, and large residential neighborhoods. In 2010, it opened 208 new hotels and plans to open 260-280 new locations in 2011. The company has also announced plans to enter China's midscale hotel market with the opening of three to four hotels under the Yitel brand in 2011.

FINANCIALS: Sales and profits are in thousands of dollars—add 000 to get the full amount. 2010 Note: Financial information for 2010 was not available for all companies at press time.

2010 Sales: $450,912	2010 Profits: $55,545	**U.S. Stock Ticker:** HMIN
2009 Sales: $357,706	2009 Profits: $38,158	**Int'l Ticker:** Int'l Exchange:
2008 Sales: $257,922	2008 Profits: $14,838	Employees: 15,810
2007 Sales: $130,098	2007 Profits: $4,902	Fiscal Year Ends: 12/31
2006 Sales: $71,055	2006 Profits: $6,009	Parent Company:

SALARIES/BENEFITS:

Pension Plan:	ESOP Stock Plan: Y	Profit Sharing:	Top Exec. Salary: $	Bonus: $
Savings Plan:	Stock Purch. Plan:		Second Exec. Salary: $	Bonus: $

OTHER THOUGHTS:

Apparent Women Officers or Directors: 1
Hot Spot for Advancement for Women/Minorities:

LOCATIONS: ("Y" = Yes)

West:	Southwest:	Midwest:	Southeast:	Northeast:	International:
					Y

HOME PROPERTIES INC

www.homeproperties.com

Industry Group Code: 531110 Ranks within this company's industry group: Sales: 5   Profits: 10

Properties:		Financial Services:	Construction/Development:	Investments:		Specialty Services:		Brokerage:
Apartments:	Y	Mortgages:	Commercial Construction:	REIT:	Y	Property Management:	Y	Commercial Sales:
Malls/Shopping:		Title Insurance:	Residential Construction:			Online Services:		Residential Sales:
Offices:		Property Insurance:	Land Development:			Software/IT:		Specialty:
Hotels/Motels:			Support Services:			Consulting:		
Industrial/Warehouses:			Design/Engineering:					
Other:								

TYPES OF BUSINESS:

Real Estate Investment Trust
Apartment Communities
Property Management

BRANDS/DIVISIONS/AFFILIATES:

Home Properties LP
Home Properties Resident Services Inc

CONTACTS: *Note: Officers with more than one job title may be intentionally listed here more than once.*

Edward J. Pettinella, CEO
Edward J. Pettinella, Pres.
David P. Gardner, CFO/Exec. VP
Lisa M. Critchley, Sr. VP-Human Resources
Ann M. McCormick, General Counsel/Exec. VP/Corp. Sec.
Bernard J. Quinn, Sr. VP-Property Mgmt. Oper.
Donald R. Hague, Sr. VP-Dev.
Robert J. Luken, Chief Acct. Officer/Treas./Sr. VP
Scott A. Doyle, Sr. VP-Strategic Property Mgmt.
John E. Smith, Sr. VP/Chief Investment Officer
Norman P. Leenhouts, Co-Chmn.
Nelson B. Leenhouts, Co-Chmn.

Phone: 585-546-4900	**Fax:** 585-546-5433
Toll-Free: 866-243-6256	
Address: 850 Clinton Sq., Rochester, NY 14604 US	

GROWTH PLANS/SPECIAL FEATURES:

Home Properties, Inc. specializes in the acquisition, development, rehabilitation, ownership and operation of apartment complexes. The company is a self-administered and self-managed real estate investment trust (REIT). Home Properties operates in Washington, D.C., and the following states: Florida; Illinois; Maine; Massachusetts; Virginia; Pennsylvania; Maryland; New Jersey; and New York. The firm conducts its business through Home Properties, L.P., in which it owns about 77.1% interest; and its management subsidiary Home Properties Resident Services, Inc. Home Properties operates 116 complexes totaling approximately 38,861 apartment units. The company typically manages and owns apartment communities with 150 or more units, which are 20-40 years old and located in suburban markets with substantial barriers to new development. Other characteristics the firm uses to evaluate markets include acquisition opportunities below replacement costs, a mature housing stock, high average single-family home prices and stable or moderate job growth. The suburban areas the trust has targeted for growth are the suburbs of New York City, Baltimore, Boston, Philadelphia, and Washington, D.C. Home Properties' business strategy involves aggressively managing and improving communities to achieve increased net operating income, as well as maintaining a conservative capital structure with efficient access to the capital markets. In April 2010, the firm acquired Westminster Apartments and Middlebrooke Apartments, which consist of a combined 318 units. In June 2010, the company acquired the 282-unit Annapolis Roads Apartments for $32.5 million. In July 2010, Home Properties opened part of its new The Courts at Huntington Station complex. In October 2010, the firm acquired three communities totaling nearly 1,500 units for $204.4 million.

The company offers its employees life, medical and dental insurance; a 401(k) plan; paid time off; an employee stock purchase program; apartment rental discounts; and flexible spending accounts.

FINANCIALS: Sales and profits are in thousands of dollars—add 000 to get the full amount. 2010 Note: Financial information for 2010 was not available for all companies at press time.

2010 Sales: $516,579	2010 Profits: $26,318	**U.S. Stock Ticker:** HME
2009 Sales: $499,176	2009 Profits: $47,078	**Int'l Ticker:** Int'l Exchange:
2008 Sales: $489,767	2008 Profits: $93,205	Employees: 1,100
2007 Sales: $472,973	2007 Profits: $82,509	Fiscal Year Ends: 12/31
2006 Sales: $424,061	2006 Profits: $110,485	Parent Company:

SALARIES/BENEFITS:

Pension Plan:	ESOP Stock Plan:	Profit Sharing:	Top Exec. Salary: $550,000	Bonus: $346,071
Savings Plan: Y	Stock Purch. Plan: Y		Second Exec. Salary: $334,970	Bonus: $145,913

OTHER THOUGHTS:

Apparent Women Officers or Directors: 3
Hot Spot for Advancement for Women/Minorities: Y

LOCATIONS: ("Y" = Yes)

West:	Southwest:	Midwest:	Southeast:	Northeast:	International:
		Y	Y	Y	

HOMESERVICES OF AMERICA INC
www.homeservices.com

Industry Group Code: 531210 Ranks within this company's industry group: Sales: Profits:

Properties:	Financial Services:	Construction/Development:	Investments:	Specialty Services:	Brokerage:	
Apartments:	Mortgages:	Commercial Construction:	REIT:	Property Management:	Commercial Sales:	Y
Malls/Shopping:	Title Insurance:	Residential Construction:		Online Services:	Residential Sales:	Y
Offices:	Property Insurance:	Land Development:		Software/IT:	Specialty:	
Hotels/Motels:		Support Services:		Consulting:		
Industrial/Warehouses:		Design/Engineering:				
Other:						

TYPES OF BUSINESS:

Real Estate Brokerage
Settlement Services
Title Services
Mortgage Services

BRANDS/DIVISIONS/AFFILIATES:

Woods Bros. Realty
Rector-Hayden Realtors
HomeServices of Kentucky, Inc.
Prudential Carolinas Realty
Long Realty Companies
CBSHOME Real Estate
HomeServices of Nebraska
Huff Realty

CONTACTS: Note: Officers with more than one job title may be intentionally listed here more than once.

Ronald J. Peltier, CEO
Robert R. Moline, COO
Robert R. Moline, Pres.
Cynthia L. Sattler, CFO/Sr. VP
Clifford Faddis Jr., Sr. VP-Human Resources
Patty Czepowski, VP-IT
Dana Strandmo, General Counsel/Sr. VP-Legal
Mike Warmka, Chief Acct. Officer/Sr. VP
Mary Lee Blaylock, Pres., HomeServices of America Relocation LLC
Melissa J. Buscho, Pres., HomeServices Insurance, Inc.
Todd Johnson, Managing Dir./Pres., HomeServices Lending LLC
Greg Mason, Managing Dir.-Title Services
Ronald J. Peltier, Chmn.

Phone:	Fax: 612-336-5590
Toll-Free: 888-485-0018	
Address: 333 S. 7th St., 27th Fl., Minneapolis, MN 55402 US	

GROWTH PLANS/SPECIAL FEATURES:

HomeServices of America, Inc., a subsidiary of MidAmerican Energy Holdings Co. (which is owned by Berkshire Hathaway, Inc.), is a real estate brokerage firm and provider of brokerage-owned settlement services. The firm is comprised of 20 real-estate brands and operates through several offices and more than 17,000 sales associates in 19 states. Though HomeServices maintains operations all over the U.S. Midwest brands include Edina Realty Home Services; CBSHOME Real Estate; Home Real Estate; Prudential First Realty; Rector-Hayden Realtors; Woods Bros. Realty; Iowa Realty; Semonin Realtors; Champion Realty; and Huff Realty. Brands in the Northeast and Southeast include Prudential Carolinas Realty; Harry Norman Realtors; Prudential York Simpson Underwood Realty; Esslinger-Wooten-Maxwell Realtors; and RealtySouth. In the Western portion of the U.S., brands include Prudential California Realty and Long Realty Company. Of the aforementioned brands, Edina Realty Home Services in one of the largest. Started by a housewife in Edina, Minnesota in 1955, the firm is now one of the nation's largest real estate companies, currently overseeing the following companies: Edina Realty; Edina Realty Title; Edina Realty Mortgage; and Edina Realty Relocation. In April 2010, the firm acquired Schiller Real Estate, an Illinois-based residential real estate firm. In November 2010, the firm acquired Yost & Little Realty, a North Carolina-based residential real estate brokerage firm. In January 2011, the company acquired Arizona-based ZipRealty. In February 2011, the company acquired Hansen Realty and merged it into CBSHOME Real Estate.

FINANCIALS: Sales and profits are in thousands of dollars—add 000 to get the full amount. 2010 Note: Financial information for 2010 was not available for all companies at press time.

2010 Sales: $	2010 Profits: $	U.S. Stock Ticker: Subsidiary
2009 Sales: $	2009 Profits: $	Int'l Ticker: Int'l Exchange:
2008 Sales: $	2008 Profits: $	Employees:
2007 Sales: $	2007 Profits: $	Fiscal Year Ends: 12/31
2006 Sales: $	2006 Profits: $	Parent Company: MIDAMERICAN ENERGY HOLDINGS CO

SALARIES/BENEFITS:

Pension Plan:	ESOP Stock Plan:	Profit Sharing:	Top Exec. Salary: $	Bonus: $
Savings Plan:	Stock Purch. Plan:		Second Exec. Salary: $	Bonus: $

OTHER THOUGHTS:

Apparent Women Officers or Directors: 3
Hot Spot for Advancement for Women/Minorities: Y

LOCATIONS: ("Y" = Yes)

West:	Southwest:	Midwest:	Southeast:	Northeast:	International:
Y	Y	Y	Y	Y	

HOMETOWN AMERICA LLC

www.hometownamerica.com

Industry Group Code: 531110 Ranks within this company's industry group: Sales: Profits:

Properties:	Financial Services:	Construction/Development:	Investments:	Specialty Services:		Brokerage:	
Apartments:	Mortgages:	Commercial Construction:	REIT:	Property Management:	Y	Commercial Sales:	
Malls/Shopping:	Title Insurance:	Residential Construction:		Online Services:		Residential Sales:	Y
Offices:	Property Insurance:	Land Development:		Software/IT:		Specialty:	
Hotels/Motels:		Support Services:		Consulting:			
Industrial/Warehouses:		Design/Engineering:					
Other: Y							

TYPES OF BUSINESS:

Manufactured Home Communities
RV Parks
Property Management
Brokerage Services

BRANDS/DIVISIONS/AFFILIATES:

Hometown America Family Communities
Hometown America
Providence Age-qualified Communities
Providence
Hometown America Foundation

CONTACTS: Note: Officers with more than one job title may be intentionally listed here more than once.

Richard G. Cline, Jr., CEO
Gregory A. O'Berry, COO
Gregory O'Berry, Pres.
Thomas Curatolo, VP-Finance
Richard G. Cline, Jr., Vice Chmn.

Phone: 312-604-7500	Fax: 312-604-7501
Toll-Free: 888.735.4310	
Address: 150 N. Wacker Dr., Ste. 2800, Chicago, IL 60606-1610 US	

GROWTH PLANS/SPECIAL FEATURES:

Hometown America, LLC develops, acquires and manages manufactured housing communities and age-qualified communities. Hometown currently owns over 120 communities with over 45,000 home sites in 20 states. The company operates through two divisions: The Hometown America Family Communities division and the Providence Age-qualified Communities division. The Providence communities are targeted toward active seniors. All of the firm's communities are provided with on-site management and new home and resale brokerage services. The Hometown America Foundation provides funding to nonprofit organizations that addresses the needs of the homelessness. Many of Hometown's communities feature recreational facilities such as swimming pools, clubhouses, golf courses and basketball courts. Nearly half of Hometown's properties are located in Florida and Michigan.

Employees of the company are offered an employee assistance program; comprehensive medical, dental, vision, life and short- and long-term disability insurance; bonus opportunities; paid vacation; sick and holiday pay; and dependent care flexible spending accounts.

FINANCIALS: Sales and profits are in thousands of dollars—add 000 to get the full amount. 2010 Note: Financial information for 2010 was not available for all companies at press time.

2010 Sales: $	2010 Profits: $	U.S. Stock Ticker: Private
2009 Sales: $	2009 Profits: $	Int'l Ticker: Int'l Exchange:
2008 Sales: $	2008 Profits: $	Employees:
2007 Sales: $	2007 Profits: $	Fiscal Year Ends: 12/31
2006 Sales: $	2006 Profits: $	Parent Company:

SALARIES/BENEFITS:

Pension Plan:	ESOP Stock Plan:	Profit Sharing:	Top Exec. Salary: $	Bonus: $
Savings Plan: Y	Stock Purch. Plan:		Second Exec. Salary: $	Bonus: $

OTHER THOUGHTS:

Apparent Women Officers or Directors:
Hot Spot for Advancement for Women/Minorities:

LOCATIONS: ("Y" = Yes)

West:	Southwest:	Midwest:	Southeast:	Northeast:	International:
Y	Y	Y	Y	Y	

HONGKONG AND SHANGHAI HOTELS LTD   www.hshgroup.com

Industry Group Code: 721110 Ranks within this company's industry group: Sales: 16   Profits: 4

Properties:		Financial Services:	Construction/Development:		Investments:	Specialty Services:		Brokerage:
Apartments:	Y	Mortgages:	Commercial Construction:	Y	REIT:	Property Management:	Y	Commercial Sales:
Malls/Shopping:	Y	Title Insurance:	Residential Construction:			Online Services:		Residential Sales:
Offices:	Y	Property Insurance:	Land Development:			Software/IT:		Specialty:
Hotels/Motels:	Y		Support Services:			Consulting:		
Industrial/Warehouses:			Design/Engineering:	Y				
Other:	Y							

TYPES OF BUSINESS:

Hotels
Commercial Properties
Resorts & Luxury Clubs
Apartments
Golf Courses
Property Management
Laundry Services
Park Attractions & Tramways

BRANDS/DIVISIONS/AFFILIATES:

Peninsula Group (The)
Landmark (The)
Peninsula Merchandising, Ltd.
Peak Tramways
Peninsula Office Tower
Peninsula Hong Kong
Peninsula Clubs and Consultancy Services, Ltd.
Tai Pan Laundry & Dry Cleaning Services, Ltd.

CONTACTS: *Note: Officers with more than one job title may be intentionally listed here more than once.*

Clement K. M. Kwok, CEO
Peter C. Borer, COO
Neil J. Galloway, CFO
Jean Forrest, Gen. Mgr.-Mktg.
Sindy Tsui, Gen. Mgr.-Human Resources
Ingvar Herland, Gen. Mgr.-R&D
Shane Izaks, Gen. Mgr.-IT
Ingvar Herland, Gen. Mgr.-Tech.
Christobelle Liao, Corp. Counsel/Sec.
David Batchelor, Gen. Mgr.-Oper.
John H. Miller, Gen. Mgr.-Design & Planning
Offer Nissenbaum, Managing Dir.-Peninsula Beverly Hills
Jonathan Crook, Gen. Mgr.-Peninsula Manila
Rainy Chan, Area VP-Hong Kong & Bangkok
Nicolas Beliard, Gen. Mgr.-Peninsula Bangkok
Michael Kadoorie, Chmn.
Maria Razumich-Zec, Regional VP-USA East Coast, Chicago & New York

Phone: 852-2840-7788	Fax: 852-2810-4306
Toll-Free:	
Address: 2 Ice House St., St. George's Bldg., 8th Fl., Hong Kong, China	

GROWTH PLANS/SPECIAL FEATURES:

Hongkong and Shanghai Hotels, Ltd. (HSH) owns and operates luxury hotels, resorts and other commercial properties. The Peninsula Group is HSH's hotel management division. The firm's Peninsula hotels are located in Hong Kong, Beijing, Chicago, New York, Bangkok, Manila, Beverly Hills, Tokyo and Shanghai. HSH also owns the Repulse Bay, a self-contained residential, retail and commercial complex. The firm's Landmark property in Ho Chi Minh City features 65 fully furnished apartments on the upper floors, a restaurant, a bar, a rooftop swimming pool with a poolside bar, deck, gymnasium, sauna and squash court and office space on the lower levels. HSH owns the Peninsula Office Tower, part of the extension of the Peninsula Hong Kong. The Office Tower includes nine floors of high-end office space with office units ranging from 6,200 to 11,200 square feet. Another office property owned by HSH is the St. John's Building in Hong Kong, with 21 floors of office space. The company's subsidiary Peninsula Clubs and Consultancy Services, Ltd., manages high-end clubs such as The Hong Kong Club, The Hong Kong Bankers Club and Butterfield's. The Thai Country Club, a 72-hole golf course in Thailand is 75% owned by HSH. The firm's other operations include Peak Tramways (one of the oldest operating funicular railways in the world) operating out of Hong Kong, Peninsula Merchandising, Ltd. (a subsidiary that owns and operates boutiques selling Peninsula-brand products) and Tai Pan Laundry & Dry Cleaning Services, Ltd. (a commercial laundry service for major hotels, clubs and restaurants, as well as a valet service). The company's latest project, The Peninsula Paris is scheduled to open in 2012.

FINANCIALS: Sales and profits are in thousands of dollars—add 000 to get the full amount. 2010 Note: Financial information for 2010 was not available for all companies at press time.

2010 Sales: $605,600	2010 Profits: $387,010	**U.S. Stock Ticker:**
2009 Sales: $543,330	2009 Profits: $296,010	**Int'l Ticker: 0045** Int'l Exchange: Hong Kong-HKEX
2008 Sales: $637,140	2008 Profits: $27,870	Employees: 6,544
2007 Sales: $590,500	2007 Profits: $446,800	Fiscal Year Ends: 12/31
2006 Sales: $483,200	2006 Profits: $272,200	Parent Company:

SALARIES/BENEFITS:

Pension Plan:	ESOP Stock Plan:	Profit Sharing:	Top Exec. Salary: $	Bonus: $
Savings Plan:	Stock Purch. Plan:		Second Exec. Salary: $	Bonus: $

OTHER THOUGHTS:

Apparent Women Officers or Directors: 7
Hot Spot for Advancement for Women/Minorities: Y

LOCATIONS: ("Y" = Yes)

West:	Southwest:	Midwest:	Southeast:	Northeast:	International:
Y		Y		Y	Y

HONGKONG LAND HOLDINGS LTD

www.hkland.com

Industry Group Code: 5311 Ranks within this company's industry group: Sales: 19   Profits: 1

Properties:		Financial Services:	Construction/Development:		Investments:	Specialty Services:		Brokerage:
Apartments:	Y	Mortgages:	Commercial Construction:		REIT:	Property Management:	Y	Commercial Sales:
Malls/Shopping:	Y	Title Insurance:	Residential Construction:			Online Services:		Residential Sales:
Offices:	Y	Property Insurance:	Land Development:	Y		Software/IT:		Specialty:
Hotels/Motels:			Support Services:	Y		Consulting:		
Industrial/Warehouses:			Design/Engineering:					
Other:	Y							

TYPES OF BUSINESS:

Property Investment, Management & Development
Office Properties
Homes & Apartments
Highway Development
Water Company Development

BRANDS/DIVISIONS/AFFILIATES:

Alexandra House
Jardine House
CityLink Mall
Gaysorn
Central Park
Marina Bay Suites
MCL Land
Jardine Matheson Group

CONTACTS: *Note: Officers with more than one job title may be intentionally listed here more than once.*

Y. K. Pang, CEO
A. J. L. Nightingale, Managing Dir.
John R. Witt, CFO
Catherine Chau, Head-Human Resources
Angie Fung, Head-Administrative & Secretarial Svcs.
Cissy Leung, Head-Legal Svcs.
Angela Yeung, Head-Comm.
Simon Keswick, Chmn.

Phone: 852-2842-8428	Fax: 852-2845-9226
Toll-Free:	
Address: 8th Fl., 1 Exchange Sq. Central, Hong Kong, China	

GROWTH PLANS/SPECIAL FEATURES:

Hongkong Land Holdings Ltd., founded in 1889, is a property investment, management and development group with a portfolio encompassing approximately 5 million square feet of commercial and residential property in Hong Kong. The firm operates in two main sectors: Commercial and Residential. The Commercial sector owns several prime office and retail locations in Hong Kong's Central Business District, as well as other high-end retail properties and prime office locations in South East Asia. Its commercial Hong Kong properties include Alexandra House; Chater House; One & Two Exchange Square; Three Exchange Square; Jardine House; The Landmark; Edinburgh Tower; Gloucester Tower; York House; Prince's Building; and Tradeport Hong Kong. Its other commercial properties include One Raffles Link, CityLink Mall, One Raffles Quay and Marina Bay Financial Centre, in Singapore; Gaysorn, in Thailand; Central Building and 63 Ly Thai To, in Vietnam; One Central, in Macau; and Jakarta Land, in Indonesia. The Residential sector focuses on luxury and high-end properties in Hong Kong and Southeast Asia. Its Hong Kong residential properties consist of the Serenade residential towers and The Sail at Victoria. Its other Asian properties include Central Park and Maple Place at Beijing Riviera, in Beijing; Bamboo Grove, in Chongqing; One Central Residences, in Macau; Marina Bay Suites and Marina Bay Residences, in Singapore; and NorthPine and Roxas Triangle Tower, in the Philippines. The firm's assets in Hong Kong represent approximately 66% of its portfolio. The company also holds a 77% ownership interest in Singapore-based residential property developer MCL Land. Asian-based trading group Jardine Matheson owns a 49% stake in Hongkong Land.

FINANCIALS: Sales and profits are in thousands of dollars—add 000 to get the full amount. 2010 Note: Financial information for 2010 was not available for all companies at press time.

2010 Sales: $1,340,600	2010 Profits: $4,739,400	**U.S. Stock Ticker: HNGKY.PK**
2009 Sales: $1,322,600	2009 Profits: $1,813,000	**Int'l Ticker: H78** Int'l Exchange: Singapore-SIN
2008 Sales: $1,022,300	2008 Profits: $-109,400	Employees: 1,144
2007 Sales: $933,200	2007 Profits: $3,037,700	Fiscal Year Ends: 12/31
2006 Sales: $556,900	2006 Profits: $358,400	Parent Company:

SALARIES/BENEFITS:

Pension Plan:	ESOP Stock Plan:	Profit Sharing:	Top Exec. Salary: $	Bonus: $
Savings Plan:	Stock Purch. Plan:		Second Exec. Salary: $	Bonus: $

OTHER THOUGHTS:

Apparent Women Officers or Directors: 4
Hot Spot for Advancement for Women/Minorities: Y

LOCATIONS: ("Y" = Yes)

West:	Southwest:	Midwest:	Southeast:	Northeast:	International:
					Y

HORTON HOMES INC

www.hortonhomes.com

Industry Group Code: 321991 Ranks within this company's industry group: Sales: Profits:

Properties:	Financial Services:	Construction/Development:		Investments:	Specialty Services:	Brokerage:
Apartments:	Mortgages:	Commercial Construction:		REIT:	Property Management:	Commercial Sales:
Malls/Shopping:	Title Insurance:	Residential Construction:	Y		Online Services:	Residential Sales:
Offices:	Property Insurance:	Land Development:			Software/IT:	Specialty:
Hotels/Motels:		Support Services:			Consulting:	
Industrial/Warehouses:		Design/Engineering:				
Other:						

TYPES OF BUSINESS:

Manufactured & Modular Homes

BRANDS/DIVISIONS/AFFILIATES:

Horton Industries
Dynasty Homes
Modular Builder's Series

CONTACTS:
Note: Officers with more than one job title may be intentionally listed here more than once.

Nevils D. Horton, Jr., CEO
Nevils D. Horton, Jr., Pres.
Steve M. Sinclair, CFO/VP
Rus W. Hicks, VP-Sales
Nevils D. Horton, Jr., Chmn.

Phone: 706-485-8506	Fax: 706-485-4446
Toll-Free: 800-657-4000	
Address: 101 Industrial Blvd., Eatonton, GA 31024 US	

GROWTH PLANS/SPECIAL FEATURES:

Horton Homes, Inc., a subsidiary of Horton Industries, is a leading manufacturer of houses and modular homes for sale in the southeastern U.S. Its sister subsidiary, Dynasty Homes, also makes manufactured houses. Horton produces approximately 100 floors a week at its 100-acre facility in Georgia. Manufactured homes are homes made or manufactured in a factory and designed to be transported to a site. They can be large or small, and while they are constructed in the same manner as mobile homes, manufactured homes are permanently attached to the site using conventional on-site construction, as opposed to mobile homes, which can be moved from one location to another. The company sells its houses through more than 90 retail centers in seven states, where buyers can choose from more than 80 floor plans, including 14-feet, 16-feet, 24-feet, 27-feet, 32-feet and 41-feet wide. The firm's homes feature brand-name appliances, a 30- or 50-gallon water heater and moisture-protected deck flooring, as well as the option of various amenities, such as bay windows, vaulted ceilings, walk-in closets and skylights. The firm's modular division, the Modular Builder's Series, builds modular homes (offering five floor plans) for the commercial modular industry. These modular buildings are mainly used for construction offices, classrooms, church assembly buildings, retail offices and golf proshops, and are marketed throughout 11 Southeastern states

FINANCIALS:
Sales and profits are in thousands of dollars—add 000 to get the full amount. **2010 Note: Financial information for 2010 was not available for all companies at press time.**

2010 Sales: $	2010 Profits: $	U.S. Stock Ticker: Subsidiary	
2009 Sales: $	2009 Profits: $	Int'l Ticker: Int'l Exchange:	
2008 Sales: $	2008 Profits: $	Employees:	
2007 Sales: $	2007 Profits: $	Fiscal Year Ends: 8/31	
2006 Sales: $	2006 Profits: $	Parent Company: HORTON INDUSTRIES INC	

SALARIES/BENEFITS:

Pension Plan:	ESOP Stock Plan:	Profit Sharing:	Top Exec. Salary: $	Bonus: $
Savings Plan:	Stock Purch. Plan:		Second Exec. Salary: $	Bonus: $

OTHER THOUGHTS:

Apparent Women Officers or Directors:
Hot Spot for Advancement for Women/Minorities:

LOCATIONS: ("Y" = Yes)

West:	Southwest:	Midwest:	Southeast:	Northeast:	International:
			Y	Y	

HOSPITALITY PROPERTIES TRUST
www.hptreit.com

Industry Group Code: 531120 Ranks within this company's industry group: Sales: 14   Profits: 40

Properties:	Financial Services:	Construction/Development:	Investments:	Specialty Services:	Brokerage:
Apartments:	Mortgages:	Commercial Construction:	REIT: Y	Property Management:	Commercial Sales:
Malls/Shopping:	Title Insurance:	Residential Construction:		Online Services:	Residential Sales:
Offices:	Property Insurance:	Land Development:		Software/IT:	Specialty:
Hotels/Motels: Y		Support Services:		Consulting:	
Industrial/Warehouses:		Design/Engineering:			
Other: Y					

TYPES OF BUSINESS:
Real Estate Investment Trust
Hotels
Travel Centers

BRANDS/DIVISIONS/AFFILIATES:
REIT Management & Research LLC

CONTACTS: *Note: Officers with more than one job title may be intentionally listed here more than once.*
John G. Murray, COO
John G. Murray, Pres.
Mark L. Kleifges, CFO
Jennifer B. Clark, Sec.
Timothy A. Bonang, VP-Investor Rel.
Mark L. Kleifges, Treas.
Ethan S. Bornstein, Sr. VP-Asset Mgmt.
William J. Sheehan, Dir.-Internal Audit & Compliance

Phone: 617-964-8389	Fax: 617-969-5730
Toll-Free:	
Address: 255 Washington St., 2 Newton Place, Ste. 300, Newton, MA 02458 US	

GROWTH PLANS/SPECIAL FEATURES:
Hospitality Properties Trust (HPT) is a real estate investment trust (REIT) that owns 289 hotels with 42,880 rooms or suites, as well as 185 travel centers, located in 44 U.S. states, Puerto Rico and Canada. All of its properties are operated by unaffiliated hospitality management companies as part of 13 combination management or lease agreements. HPT's hotel properties currently include the following brands: Courtyard by Marriott, Candlewood Suites, Staybridge Suites, Residence Inn by Marriott, Crowne Plaza Hotels & Resorts, Hyatt Place, InterContinental Hotels & Resorts, Marriott Hotels and Resorts, Radisson Hotels & Resorts, TownePlace Suites by Marriott, Country Inns & Suites by Carlson, Holiday Inn Hotels & Resorts, SpringHill Suites by Marriott and Park Plaza Hotels & Resorts. The company's 185 travel centers include 145 operated under the TravelCenters of America brand and 40 operated under the Petro Stopping Centers brand name. All of HPT's management agreements or leases share eight points: first, managers are required to pay a fixed minimum rent; second, operators must pay percentage returns on gross hotel revenues exceeding a certain threshold; third, all agreements are long-term (15 years or more); fourth, each hotel is a part of a combination of hotels and is subject to cross-default obligations with respect to all other hotels in the same combination; fifth, each combination of hotels is geographically diverse; sixth, contract renewals may only be pursued for a combination of hotels, not for each hotel individually; seventh, the firm's agreements require the deposit of 5% to 6% of gross hotel revenues into escrows to fund periodic renovations; finally, each management agreement or lease includes security terms to ensure payments to HPT.

FINANCIALS: Sales and profits are in thousands of dollars—add 000 to get the full amount. 2010 Note: Financial information for 2010 was not available for all companies at press time.

2010 Sales: $1,085,488	2010 Profits: $21,351	U.S. Stock Ticker: HPT
2009 Sales: $1,037,033	2009 Profits: $193,341	Int'l Ticker: Int'l Exchange:
2008 Sales: $1,251,362	2008 Profits: $133,995	Employees: 650
2007 Sales: $1,285,479	2007 Profits: $330,968	Fiscal Year Ends: 12/31
2006 Sales: $1,022,946	2006 Profits: $169,039	Parent Company:

SALARIES/BENEFITS:

Pension Plan:	ESOP Stock Plan:	Profit Sharing:	Top Exec. Salary: $132,060	Bonus: $
Savings Plan:	Stock Purch. Plan:		Second Exec. Salary: $132,060	Bonus: $

OTHER THOUGHTS:
Apparent Women Officers or Directors: 1
Hot Spot for Advancement for Women/Minorities:

LOCATIONS: ("Y" = Yes)

West:	Southwest:	Midwest:	Southeast:	Northeast:	International:
Y	Y	Y	Y	Y	Y

HOST HOTELS & RESORTS LP

www.hosthotels.com

Industry Group Code: 531120 Ranks within this company's industry group: Sales: 1 Profits: 17

Properties:	Financial Services:	Construction/Development:	Investments:	Specialty Services:	Brokerage:
Apartments:	Mortgages:	Commercial Construction:	REIT: Y	Property Management: Y	Commercial Sales:
Malls/Shopping:	Title Insurance:	Residential Construction:		Online Services:	Residential Sales:
Offices:	Property Insurance:	Land Development:		Software/IT:	Specialty:
Hotels/Motels: Y		Support Services:		Consulting:	
Industrial/Warehouses:		Design/Engineering:			
Other:					

TYPES OF BUSINESS:

Real Estate Investment Trust
Hotels

BRANDS/DIVISIONS/AFFILIATES:

Marriott
Ritz-Carlton
Four Seasons
Hilton/Embassy Suites
Hyatt
Westin
Sheraton
Host Hotels & Resorts, Inc.

CONTACTS: Note: Officers with more than one job title may be intentionally listed here more than once.

W. Edward Walter, CEO
W. Edward Walter, Pres.
Larry K. Harvey, CFO/Exec. VP/Treas.
Joanne G. Hamilton, Exec. VP-Human Resources
Elizabeth A. Abdoo, General Counsel/Sec./Exec. VP
Brian G. Macnamara, Sr. VP/Corp. Controller
Minaz Abji, Exec. VP-Asset Mgmt.
Gregory J. Larson, Exec. VP-Corp. Strategy & Fund Mgmt.
James F. Risoleo, Chief Investment Officer/Exec. VP
Richard E. Marriott, Chmn.

Phone: 240-744-1000	Fax:
Toll-Free:	
Address: 6903 Rockledge Dr., Ste. 1500, Bethesda, MD 20817 US	

GROWTH PLANS/SPECIAL FEATURES:

Host Hotels & Resorts, L.P. (HHR) is a leading hotel real estate investment trust (REIT). HHR operates a portfolio of 120 upper upscale and luxury full-service hotels consisting of 63,000 rooms in 25 states in the U.S. and international locations in the U.K., Brazil, Mexico, Chile, Canada and New Zealand. Its brands include Marriott (with 66 locations); Westin (12); Ritz-Carlton (8); Sheraton (seven); Hyatt (six); Novotel (four); W Hotel (three); ibis (three); Four Seasons (two); Hilton/Embassy Suites (two); and one of each of the following, Le Meridien, St. Regis, The Luxury Collection, Fairmont, Swissotel and Delta. Additionally, the firm owns a 32.1% interest in a European joint venture that owns 11 luxury hotels containing 3,510 rooms located in Italy, Spain, Belgium, the U.K., Poland and the Netherlands and a 25% stake in an Indian hotel development joint venture. All hotel locations are generally confined in the business districts of major cities, airports areas, resorts and convention destinations. Its properties typically include meeting and banquet facilities; a variety of restaurants and lounges; swimming pools; exercise facilities and/or spas; gift shops; and parking facilities. The firm conducts the entirety of its business through an umbrella partnership structure with Host Hotels & Resorts, Inc. as its sole general partner. Host Hotels & Resorts, Inc. holds 98% of HHR's outstanding partnership interests. In 2010, the operations of the Marriott properties generated 58% of the firm's total revenue. In March 2011, it acquired the 1,625-room Manchester Grand Hyatt San Diego and the 775-room New York Helmsley Hotel.

HHR offers its employees medical, dental, prescription, vision and hearing coverage; free on-site fitness centers; associate assistance programs; long- and short-term disability and life insurance; a 401(k); company paid parking; hotel discounts; health and dependent care spending accounts; long-term care coverage; employee stock purchase plan; and tuition assistance.

FINANCIALS: Sales and profits are in thousands of dollars—add 000 to get the full amount. 2010 Note: Financial information for 2010 was not available for all companies at press time.

2010 Sales: $4,437,000	2010 Profits: $132,000	**U.S. Stock Ticker: HST**
2009 Sales: $4,144,000	2009 Profits: $-258,000	**Int'l Ticker:** Int'l Exchange:
2008 Sales: $5,119,000	2008 Profits: $414,000	Employees: 203
2007 Sales: $5,249,000	2007 Profits: $734,000	Fiscal Year Ends: 12/31
2006 Sales: $4,802,000	2006 Profits: $738,000	Parent Company:

SALARIES/BENEFITS:

Pension Plan:	ESOP Stock Plan:	Profit Sharing:	Top Exec. Salary: $704,589	Bonus: $673,154
Savings Plan: Y	Stock Purch. Plan: Y		Second Exec. Salary: $500,000	Bonus: $350,769

OTHER THOUGHTS:

Apparent Women Officers or Directors: 3
Hot Spot for Advancement for Women/Minorities: Y

LOCATIONS: ("Y" = Yes)

West:	Southwest:	Midwest:	Southeast:	Northeast:	International:
Y	Y	Y	Y	Y	Y

HOTEL PROPERTIES LTD

www.hotelprop.com

Industry Group Code: 721110 Ranks within this company's industry group: Sales: 23   Profits: 9

Properties:		Financial Services:	Construction/Development:	Investments:	Specialty Services:	Brokerage:
Apartments:	Y	Mortgages:	Commercial Construction:	REIT:	Property Management:	Commercial Sales:
Malls/Shopping:	Y	Title Insurance:	Residential Construction:		Online Services:	Residential Sales:
Offices:		Property Insurance:	Land Development:		Software/IT:	Specialty:
Hotels/Motels:	Y		Support Services:		Consulting:	
Industrial/Warehouses:			Design/Engineering:			
Other:	Y					

TYPES OF BUSINESS:

Hotels
Condominiums
Restaurants
Retail Properties & Operations
Food Distribution

BRANDS/DIVISIONS/AFFILIATES:

Four Seasons Resort
Hard Rock Hotel
Rihiveli Beach Resort
Concorde Hotel
Lakehouse (The)
Hard Rock Café
Planet Hollywood
Haagen-Dazs

CONTACTS: *Note: Officers with more than one job title may be intentionally listed here more than once.*

Ong Beng Seng, Managing Dir.
Chuang Sheue Ling, Corp. Sec.
Buong Lik Lau, Head-Hotel Div.
Tien Lock Lim, Exec. Dir.
Joseph Grimberg, Chmn.

Phone: 65-734-5250	**Fax:** 65-732-0347
Toll-Free:	
Address: 50 Cuscaden Rd., 08-01 HPL House, Singapore, 249724 Singapore	

GROWTH PLANS/SPECIAL FEATURES:

Hotel Properties Ltd. (HPL) is a diversified hotel holding company headquartered in Singapore that invests in premium commercial and residential properties in Asia and the Pacific, including hotels, condominiums, shopping centers, restaurants, a food distribution chain and retail operations. It owns or has interests in 21 hotels in Singapore, Malaysia, Thailand, Indonesia, Bhutan, Seychelles, Vanuatu and the Maldives. These include three Four Seasons properties and a Hard Rock Hotel in Indonesia; two Four Seasons Resorts, one Holiday Inn Resort and the Rihiveli Beach Resort in the Maldives; two Concorde Hotels, a Casa Del Mar, a Hard Rock Hotel and The Lakehouse Cameron Highlands in Malaysia; a Four Seasons Hotel, a Hilton, a Four Seasons and a Concorde Hotel in Singapore; a Hard Rock Hotel and a Metropolitan in Thailand; a Four Seasons Resort in Seychelles; and the Palms Resort and Casino in Vanuatu. The company owns three shopping centers and five residential areas in Singapore, as well as a residential property in Thailand. In its Lifestyle division, the company owns Hard Rock Cafes in China, Hong Kong, Indonesia, Malaysia, Philippines, Singapore, and Thailand. In addition, it owns a Planet Hollywood restaurant in Malaysia and Haagen-Dazs ice cream stores in Malaysia and Singapore.

FINANCIALS: Sales and profits are in thousands of dollars—add 000 to get the full amount. 2010 Note: Financial information for 2010 was not available for all companies at press time.

2010 Sales: $357,860	2010 Profits: $113,570	**U.S. Stock Ticker:**
2009 Sales: $323,320	2009 Profits: $25,680	**Int'l Ticker: H15** Int'l Exchange: Singapore-SIN
2008 Sales: $451,528	2008 Profits: $29,524	Employees:
2007 Sales: $	2007 Profits: $	Fiscal Year Ends: 12/31
2006 Sales: $	2006 Profits: $	Parent Company:

SALARIES/BENEFITS:

Pension Plan:	ESOP Stock Plan:	Profit Sharing:	Top Exec. Salary: $	Bonus: $
Savings Plan:	Stock Purch. Plan:		Second Exec. Salary: $	Bonus: $

OTHER THOUGHTS:

Apparent Women Officers or Directors:
Hot Spot for Advancement for Women/Minorities:

LOCATIONS: ("Y" = Yes)

West:	Southwest:	Midwest:	Southeast:	Northeast:	International:
					Y

HOVNANIAN ENTERPRISES INC

www.khov.com

Industry Group Code: 2361 Ranks within this company's industry group: Sales: 9   Profits: 7

Properties:	Financial Services:	Construction/Development:		Investments:	Specialty Services:	Brokerage:
Apartments:	Mortgages:	Commercial Construction:	Y	REIT:	Property Management:	Commercial Sales:
Malls/Shopping:	Title Insurance:	Residential Construction:	Y		Online Services:	Residential Sales:
Offices:	Property Insurance:	Land Development:			Software/IT:	Specialty:
Hotels/Motels:		Support Services:			Consulting:	
Industrial/Warehouses:		Design/Engineering:	Y			
Other:						

TYPES OF BUSINESS:

Home Building
Mortgages
Title Insurance
Residential Communities
Commercial Construction

BRANDS/DIVISIONS/AFFILIATES:

K. Hovnanian American Mortgage, LLC

CONTACTS: *Note: Officers with more than one job title may be intentionally listed here more than once.*

Ara K. Hovnanian, CEO
Thomas J. Pellerito, COO
Ara K. Hovnanian, Pres.
J. Larry Sorsby, CFO/Exec. VP
Robyn T. Mingle, Sr. VP-Human Resources
Nicholas Colisto, CIO/VP
Peter S. Reinhart, General Counsel/Sr. VP
Paul W. Buchanan, Sr. VP/Chief Acct. Officer
Ara K. Hovnanian, Chmn.

Phone: 732-747-7800	Fax: 732-747-7159
Toll-Free:	
Address: 110 W. Front St., Red Bank, NJ 07701 US	

GROWTH PLANS/SPECIAL FEATURES:

Hovnanian Enterprises, Inc. designs, constructs, markets and sells single-family detached homes, attached townhomes and condominiums, mid-rise and high-rise condominiums, urban infill and active adult homes in planned residential communities. The firm organizes its operations into two divisions: homebuilding and financial services. Homebuilding operations are conducted in six geographic segments: Northeast, Mid-Atlantic, Midwest, Southeast, Southwest and West. With more than 291,000 total homes sold since its inception in 1959, including 5,009 homes delivered in 2010, the firm is one of the largest homebuilders in the U.S. Its homes are available in 192 communities in 40 markets in 18 states, and are generally located in suburban areas easily accessible through public and personal transportation. Base home prices range from $74,000 to $1,104,000 in the Northeast; from $170,000 to $1,660,000 in the Mid-Atlantic; from $34,000 to $330,000 in the Midwest; from $100,000 to $492,000 in the Southeast; from $83,000 to $675,000 in the Southwest; and from $129,000 to $544,000 in the West, with an average sales price of $289,808 in 2010. Development activities include site planning and engineering; obtaining environmental and other regulatory approvals; constructing roads, sewer, water and drainage facilities; and recreational facilities and other amenities for residential developments. Hovnanian's financial services operations provide mortgage loans and title services to its homebuyers. In December 2010, the firm entered into a joint venture with GTIS Partners to acquire a portfolio of homebuilding projects at two communities in California and one community in Virginia.

Employees are offered medical, dental and vision insurance; an employee assistance program; flexible spending accounts; life insurance; short- and long-term disability; a 401(k) plan; a 529 college bound savings plan; tuition assistance; US government bonds; a home purchase discount; entertainment discounts; and discounted home, auto, boater's and renter's insurance.

FINANCIALS: Sales and profits are in thousands of dollars—add 000 to get the full amount. 2010 Note: Financial information for 2010 was not available for all companies at press time.

2010 Sales: $1,371,842	2010 Profits: $2,588	**U.S. Stock Ticker:** HOV
2009 Sales: $1,596,290	2009 Profits: $-716,712	**Int'l Ticker:** Int'l Exchange:
2008 Sales: $3,308,111	2008 Profits: $-1,124,590	Employees: 1,629
2007 Sales: $4,798,921	2007 Profits: $-627,119	Fiscal Year Ends: 10/31
2006 Sales: $6,148,235	2006 Profits: $149,533	Parent Company:

SALARIES/BENEFITS:

Pension Plan:	ESOP Stock Plan:	Profit Sharing:	Top Exec. Salary: $1,092,606	Bonus: $949,500
Savings Plan: Y	Stock Purch. Plan:		Second Exec. Salary: $572,308	Bonus: $350,000

OTHER THOUGHTS:

Apparent Women Officers or Directors: 1
Hot Spot for Advancement for Women/Minorities:

LOCATIONS: ("Y" = Yes)

West:	Southwest:	Midwest:	Southeast:	Northeast:	International:
Y	Y	Y	Y	Y	

HOWARD JOHNSON INTERNATIONAL INC

www.hojo.com

Industry Group Code: 721110 Ranks within this company's industry group: Sales: Profits:

Properties:	Financial Services:	Construction/Development:	Investments:	Specialty Services:	Brokerage:
Apartments:	Mortgages:	Commercial Construction:	REIT:	Property Management:	Commercial Sales:
Malls/Shopping:	Title Insurance:	Residential Construction:		Online Services:	Residential Sales:
Offices:	Property Insurance:	Land Development:		Software/IT:	Specialty:
Hotels/Motels: Y		Support Services:		Consulting:	
Industrial/Warehouses:		Design/Engineering:			
Other:					

TYPES OF BUSINESS:

Hotels
Restaurants
Vacation Specials
Travel Packages

BRANDS/DIVISIONS/AFFILIATES:

Wyndham Worldwide
Hotel Package Deals
TripFinder Vacation Packages
Guaranteed Best Rate
Wyndham Rewards
Rise & Dine

CONTACTS: *Note: Officers with more than one job title may be intentionally listed here more than once.*

Ken Greene, Pres.
Rui Barros, Sr. VP-Brand

Phone: 973-428-9700	**Fax:** 973-496-7658
Toll-Free: 800-544-9881	
Address: 22 Sylvan Way, Parsippany, NJ 07054 US	

GROWTH PLANS/SPECIAL FEATURES:

Howard Johnson International, Inc., a subsidiary of Wyndham Worldwide, owns and franchises mid-priced hotels. Its portfolio currently includes over 490 hotels located in the U.S., China, Mexico and other international regions. The firm's Hotel Package Deals feature several destinations for a given week, offering various packages viewable on the firm's web site. These packaged specials often include discounted hotel fees and location-specific promotions. TripFinder Vacation Packages offer a travel package program through which costumers can rent cars or purchase airlines in addition to securing hotel reservations. Howard Johnson additionally features the Guaranteed Best Rate program, which guarantees customers a 10% lower price than any competitor. Howard Johnson participates in the Wyndham Rewards, which is a free program that offers customers redeemable points or airline miles for staying at any one of Wyndham's hotel locations. Howard Johnson's hotels feature a variety of amenities. Customers can search for a hotel on the firm's web site using any or all of these amenities as search criteria. Amenities include an airport shuttle, business center, free high-speed Internet, free Rise & Dine breakfast, gym/fitness center, meeting/banquet facilities, pet friendly, pool and restaurant.

FINANCIALS: Sales and profits are in thousands of dollars—add 000 to get the full amount. 2010 Note: Financial information for 2010 was not available for all companies at press time.

2010 Sales: $	2010 Profits: $	**U.S. Stock Ticker: Subsidiary**
2009 Sales: $	2009 Profits: $	**Int'l Ticker:** Int'l Exchange:
2008 Sales: $	2008 Profits: $	Employees:
2007 Sales: $	2007 Profits: $	Fiscal Year Ends: 12/31
2006 Sales: $	2006 Profits: $	Parent Company: WYNDHAM WORLDWIDE

SALARIES/BENEFITS:

Pension Plan:	ESOP Stock Plan:	Profit Sharing:	Top Exec. Salary: $	Bonus: $
Savings Plan:	Stock Purch. Plan:		Second Exec. Salary: $	Bonus: $

OTHER THOUGHTS:

Apparent Women Officers or Directors:
Hot Spot for Advancement for Women/Minorities:

LOCATIONS: ("Y" = Yes)

West:	Southwest:	Midwest:	Southeast:	Northeast:	International:
Y	Y	Y	Y	Y	Y

HUTCHISON WHAMPOA PROPERTIES LTD   www.hwpg.com

Industry Group Code: 5311 Ranks within this company's industry group: Sales: Profits:

Properties:		Financial Services:		Construction/Development:		Investments:		Specialty Services:		Brokerage:	
Apartments:	Y	Mortgages:		Commercial Construction:		REIT:		Property Management:	Y	Commercial Sales:	
Malls/Shopping:	Y	Title Insurance:		Residential Construction:				Online Services:	Y	Residential Sales:	
Offices:	Y	Property Insurance:		Land Development:				Software/IT:		Specialty:	
Hotels/Motels:	Y			Support Services:	Y			Consulting:			
Industrial/Warehouses:	Y			Design/Engineering:	Y						
Other:	Y										

TYPES OF BUSINESS:

Real Estate Operations & Development
Hotels
Office & Industrial Properties
Residential Properties
Marine Docks & Repair Yards

BRANDS/DIVISIONS/AFFILIATES:

Hutchison Whampoa Limited
Property & Hotels Group
Hongkong & Whampoa Dock Company Limited
Hutchison Properties Limited
Cavendish International Holdings Limited
Hutchison Premium Services
Pacific Property Net
Harbour Plaza Hotels & Resorts

CONTACTS: *Note: Officers with more than one job title may be intentionally listed here more than once.*

Ka-shing Li, Chmn.

Phone: 852-2128-7500	Fax: 852-2128-7888
Toll-Free:	
Address: 3/F, 1 Harbourfront, 18 Tak Fung St., Hunghom, Hong Kong, China	

GROWTH PLANS/SPECIAL FEATURES:

Hutchison Whampoa Properties Ltd. (Hutchison) is the property development and investment subsidiary of Hutchison Whampoa Limited (HWL). Hutchison was established by HWL to hold the property interests of Hongkong & Whampoa Dock Company Limited (HWD), Hutchison Properties Limited (HPL) and Cavendish International Holdings Limited (CIHL). The company operates within HWL's Property & Hotels Group, which was established through the merger of HWD and HPL in 1980. HWL's other Property & Hotels Group subsidiary is joint-venture Harbour Plaza Hotels & Resorts. Hutchison's properties are organized by type into six categories: residential, office, industrial, commercial, hotel and golf. The company has numerous residential properties in such locations as Hong Kong, London, Singapore, the Bahamas, Beijing and Shanghai. Hutchinson has office properties in seven different locations throughout China. The firm's five industrial properties are all located in Hong Kong. Its commercial properties are located in London and 12 locations throughout China. The company's hotels are located in the Bahamas and Hong Kong, Chongqing and Kunming, China. Hutchison has one golf property located Dongguan, China. The firm's services include property management, project management, marketing and e-business. Property management services offered by Hutchison include the deployment of security guards, caretakers and maintenance workers. The company's project management team is comprised of architects, engineers and quantity surveyors who supervise and coordinate the design and construction of its developments through external consultants and contractors. Hutchison's in-house marketing team is responsible for the leasing and sale of its properties, and provides property-related services to other HWL subsidiaries, including tenancy negotiations, valuations, feasibility studies and general real estate guidance. The company's e-business operations comprise subsidiaries Hutchison Premium Services and Pacific Property Net, both of which operate real estate web sites.

FINANCIALS: Sales and profits are in thousands of dollars—add 000 to get the full amount. 2010 Note: Financial information for 2010 was not available for all companies at press time.

2010 Sales: $	2010 Profits: $	**U.S. Stock Ticker: Subsidiary**
2009 Sales: $	2009 Profits: $	**Int'l Ticker:** Int'l Exchange:
2008 Sales: $	2008 Profits: $	Employees:
2007 Sales: $	2007 Profits: $	Fiscal Year Ends: 12/31
2006 Sales: $	2006 Profits: $	Parent Company: HUTCHISON WHAMPOA LIMITED

SALARIES/BENEFITS:

Pension Plan:	ESOP Stock Plan:	Profit Sharing:	Top Exec. Salary: $	Bonus: $
Savings Plan:	Stock Purch. Plan:		Second Exec. Salary: $	Bonus: $

OTHER THOUGHTS:

Apparent Women Officers or Directors:
Hot Spot for Advancement for Women/Minorities:

LOCATIONS: ("Y" = Yes)

West:	Southwest:	Midwest:	Southeast:	Northeast:	International:
					Y

HVM LLC

www.extendedstayhotels.com

Industry Group Code: 721110 Ranks within this company's industry group: Sales: Profits:

Properties:	Financial Services:	Construction/Development:	Investments:	Specialty Services:	Brokerage:
Apartments:	Mortgages:	Commercial Construction:	REIT:	Property Management:	Commercial Sales:
Malls/Shopping:	Title Insurance:	Residential Construction:		Online Services:	Residential Sales:
Offices:	Property Insurance:	Land Development:		Software/IT:	Specialty:
Hotels/Motels: Y		Support Services:		Consulting:	
Industrial/Warehouses:		Design/Engineering:			
Other:					

TYPES OF BUSINESS:

Hotels, Extended Stay
Hotels

BRANDS/DIVISIONS/AFFILIATES:

Lightstone Group (The)
Homestead Studio Suites
Extended Stay Hotels
Extended Stay Deluxe
Studio PLUS
Crossland
Extended Stay America
Lowest Internet Price Guarantee

CONTACTS: *Note: Officers with more than one job title may be intentionally listed here more than once.*

Gary A. DeLapp, CEO
Gary A. DeLapp, Pres.
Stephen T. Woolridge, Sr. Exec. VP-Oper.
Joseph Rodgers, Exec. VP-Acct.

Phone: 864-573-1600	Fax: 864-573-1695
Toll-Free: 800-804-3724	
Address: 100 Dunbar St., Spartanburg, SC 29306 US	

GROWTH PLANS/SPECIAL FEATURES:

HVM, LLC, formerly Homestead Village Management, LLC, is the operator of the Extended Stay Hotels network, which has nearly 700 extended-stay properties in Canada and most of the major metro areas in the U.S. The firm is a subsidiary of the Lightstone Group. The company owns and manages moderately price extended-stay hotels under five brand names: Crossland (34 hotels), Extended Stay America (363 hotels), Homestead Studio Suites (131 hotels), Extended Stay Deluxe (109 hotels) and Studio PLUS (46 hotels). The typical guest travels for training, temporary business assignments or relocation. Many are employed in fields prone to extended-stay travel, including technology, telecommunications and consulting. HVM targets large corporate customers with multi-location extended-stay needs and has customized its rooms for this purpose with full kitchens, Internet connections and work/study areas. It offers daily, weekly and monthly rates with discounts for extended stays. HVM hotels all include kitchen, living and dining areas; laundry facilities; and pet accommodations; certain locations offer pools, fitness rooms and individual DVD players. The company's properties are typically located near business centers, airports and entertainment areas. The company recently launched its Lowest Internet Price Guarantee; the program offers customers who find a lower, publicly available average hotel rate than that of a HVM hotel price matching plus an additional 10% discount.

FINANCIALS: Sales and profits are in thousands of dollars—add 000 to get the full amount. 2010 Note: Financial information for 2010 was not available for all companies at press time.

2010 Sales: $	2010 Profits: $	U.S. Stock Ticker: Private
2009 Sales: $	2009 Profits: $	Int'l Ticker: Int'l Exchange:
2008 Sales: $	2008 Profits: $	Employees:
2007 Sales: $101,000	2007 Profits: $	Fiscal Year Ends: 12/31
2006 Sales: $	2006 Profits: $	Parent Company: LIGHTSTONE GROUP (THE)

SALARIES/BENEFITS:

Pension Plan:	ESOP Stock Plan:	Profit Sharing:	Top Exec. Salary: $	Bonus: $
Savings Plan: Y	Stock Purch. Plan:		Second Exec. Salary: $	Bonus: $

OTHER THOUGHTS:

Apparent Women Officers or Directors:
Hot Spot for Advancement for Women/Minorities:

LOCATIONS: ("Y" = Yes)

West:	Southwest:	Midwest:	Southeast:	Northeast:	International:
Y	Y	Y	Y	Y	Y

HYATT HOTELS CORPORATION

www.hyatt.com

Industry Group Code: 721110 Ranks within this company's industry group: Sales: 5 Profits: 14

Properties:		Financial Services:	Construction/Development:	Investments:	Specialty Services:		Brokerage:
Apartments:		Mortgages:	Commercial Construction:	REIT:	Property Management:	Y	Commercial Sales:
Malls/Shopping:		Title Insurance:	Residential Construction:		Online Services:		Residential Sales:
Offices:		Property Insurance:	Land Development:		Software/IT:		Specialty:
Hotels/Motels:	Y		Support Services:		Consulting:		
Industrial/Warehouses:			Design/Engineering:				
Other:	Y						

TYPES OF BUSINESS:

Hotel Ownership & Management
Timeshares
Golf Courses
Gaming
Retirement Communities
Motels & Inns
Hotel Franchising

BRANDS/DIVISIONS/AFFILIATES:

Hyatt Regency
Grand Hyatt
Hyatt Resorts
Hyatt Summerfield Suites
Andaz
Hyatt Vacation Club
Hyatt Gold Passport
Park Hyatt

CONTACTS: *Note: Officers with more than one job title may be intentionally listed here more than once.*

Mark S. Hoplamazian, CEO
Mark S. Hoplamazian, Pres.
Harmit J. Singh, CFO
John Wallis, Global Head-Mktg. & Brand Strategy
Robert W. K. Webb, Chief Human Resources Officer
Rena Hozore Reiss, General Counsel/Sec.
H. Charles Floyd, COO-North America Oper.
Stephen G. Haggerty, Global Head-Dev. & Real Estate
Katie Meyer, VP-Corp. Comm.
Atish Shah, Sr. VP-Investor Rel.
Steve Sokal, Sr. VP-Global Asset Mgmt.
Sal Mendoza, VP-Diversity & Inclusion
Thomas J. Pritzker, Chmn.
Rakesh Sarna, COO-Int'l Oper.

Phone: 312-750-1234	Fax: 312-750-8550
Toll-Free:	
Address: 71 S. Wacker Dr., 12th Fl., Chicago, IL 60606 US	

GROWTH PLANS/SPECIAL FEATURES:

Hyatt Hotels Corporation (Hyatt) owns, operates, manages and franchises full-service luxury hotels in 45 countries across the globe. Its portfolio of 453 Hyatt-branded properties includes 177 managed hotels for third-party owners; 132 franchised hotels; 90 owned properties; 24 properties managed by Hyatt owned by unconsolidated hospitality ventures; 15 managed vacation ownership properties; and nine residential properties. Hyatt's operations consist of eight brands. Its best known brand, Hyatt Regency, caters mainly to corporate travel clients. Grand Hyatt hotels cater to leisure and business travelers and include accommodations for banquets and conferences. Hyatt Resorts often feature professional, PGA golf courses; adventure travel opportunities, such as scuba diving, biking, hot air balloon trips or horseback riding; Hyatt Pure spas; and activities for kids and families. Hyatt Summerfield Suites, an all-suites hotel concept designed to feel more like home, offers 32-inch HDTVs, a full kitchen and complementary shopping service for its outdoor BBQ-pits. Hyatt Place hotels feature high-tech amenities such as 42-inch HDTVs in every room, free Wi-Fi Internet access and a 24-hour, touch-screen room service ordering system. Park Hyatt hotels are smaller, full-service luxury hotels featuring world class art and restaurants in a few of the world's most visited cities. The Andaz branded hotels are boutique-style hotels that feature restaurants and bars aimed at local clientele as well as single travelers. Hyatt Vacation Club offers vacation ownership and vacation rental opportunities, offering members timeshare or points-based resort vacation opportunities. Hyatt's rewards program, Hyatt Gold Passport, has over 10 million members. In October 2010, Hyatt announced management agreements for 11 new Hyatt-branded hotels in China. In March 2011, it signed management agreements for nine new hotels in India, bringing total development in the country to 38 properties.

Employees of Hyatt receive complementary hotel rooms; medical, dental, vision and prescription drug coverage; tuition assistance; and life insurance.

FINANCIALS: Sales and profits are in thousands of dollars—add 000 to get the full amount. 2010 Note: Financial information for 2010 was not available for all companies at press time.

2010 Sales: $3,527,000	2010 Profits: $66,000	U.S. Stock Ticker: H
2009 Sales: $3,330,000	2009 Profits: $-43,000	Int'l Ticker: Int'l Exchange:
2008 Sales: $3,835,000	2008 Profits: $168,000	Employees: 130,000
2007 Sales: $3,750,000	2007 Profits: $	Fiscal Year Ends: 12/31
2006 Sales: $3,500,000	2006 Profits: $	Parent Company:

SALARIES/BENEFITS:

Pension Plan:	ESOP Stock Plan:	Profit Sharing:	Top Exec. Salary: $979,167	Bonus: $983,000
Savings Plan: Y	Stock Purch. Plan:		Second Exec. Salary: $581,000	Bonus: $370,000

OTHER THOUGHTS:

Apparent Women Officers or Directors: 2
Hot Spot for Advancement for Women/Minorities:

LOCATIONS: ("Y" = Yes)

West:	Southwest:	Midwest:	Southeast:	Northeast:	International:
Y	Y	Y	Y	Y	Y

HYPO REAL ESTATE HOLDING AG (HYPO BANK)

www.hyporealestate.com
Industry Group Code: 5311 Ranks within this company's industry group: Sales: Profits:

Properties:	Financial Services:		Construction/Development:	Investments:	Specialty Services:	Brokerage:
Apartments:	Mortgages:	Y	Commercial Construction:	REIT:	Property Management:	Commercial Sales:
Malls/Shopping:	Title Insurance:		Residential Construction:		Online Services:	Residential Sales:
Offices:	Property Insurance:		Land Development:		Software/IT:	Specialty:
Hotels/Motels:			Support Services:		Consulting:	
Industrial/Warehouses:			Design/Engineering:			
Other:						

TYPES OF BUSINESS:

Commercial Real Estate Financing
Mortgages
Asset Management

BRANDS/DIVISIONS/AFFILIATES:

Deutsche Pfandbriefbank AG
DEPFA Bank plc
Flint Nominees Ltd.
Hypo Real Estate Capital Corp.
Hypo Real Estate Capital Japan Corporation
Hypo Real Estate Transactions S.A.S.
Hypo Real Estate Capital India Corp. Private Ltd.
Hypo Pfandbrief Bank International S.A.

CONTACTS: *Note: Officers with more than one job title may be intentionally listed here more than once.*

Manuela Better, Interim CEO
Frank Krings, COO
Kai Wilhelm Franzmeyer, Treas.
Bernhard Scholz, Head-Real Estate Finance
Bernd Thiemann, Chmn.

Phone: 49-89-2880-0	**Fax:** 49-89-2880-10319
Toll-Free:	
Address: Freisinger St. 5, Unterschleissheim, D-85716 Germany	

GROWTH PLANS/SPECIAL FEATURES:

Hypo Real Estate Holding AG (Hypo Bank) is a financial holding company with interests in real estate and related areas such as financing, consulting, brokering and other services. It does not have any direct banking operations. The firm's businesses include credit and financial service institutions, Deutsche Pfandbriefbank AG (Munich) and DEPFA Bank Plc (Dublin). Deutsche Pfandbriefbank AG, headquartered in Munich, Germany, was formed by the merger of Hypo Real Estate Bank and DEPFA Deutsche Pfandbriefbank AG. Subsidiaries of Deutsche Pfandbriefbank include Flint Nominees Ltd. in London; Hypo Real Estate Capital Corp. in New York; Hypo Real Estate Capital Japan Corporation, based in Tokyo; Hypo Real Estate Transactions S.A.S., with headquarters in Paris; Mumbai-based Hypo Real Estate Capital India Corp. Private Ltd.; and Hypo Real Estate Capital Singapore Corp. Private Ltd. DEPFA Bank plc, headquartered in Dublin, is the parent of Hypo Pfandbrief Bank International S.A. of Luxembourg; DEPFA ACS Bank in Dublin; and Hypo Public Finance Bank Dublin. Both Deutsche Pfandbriefbank AG and DEPFA bank plc are currently restructuring following the firm's recent takeover by the German Financial Markets Stabilization Fund, known as SoFFin. As part of the restructuring plan, the banks will become specialist institutions focused on real estate and public finance and will take on a more regional approach, concentrating its activities primarily in Germany and Europe. In October 2010, Hypo Bank transferred $244.6 billion worth of loans and securities to FMS Wertmanagement.

FINANCIALS: Sales and profits are in thousands of dollars—add 000 to get the full amount. 2010 Note: Financial information for 2010 was not available for all companies at press time.

2010 Sales: $	2010 Profits: $	**U.S. Stock Ticker:**
2009 Sales: $	2009 Profits: $	**Int'l Ticker:** HRXG.DE Int'l Exchange: Frankfurt-Euronext
2008 Sales: $309,400	2008 Profits: $594,100	Employees: 2,000
2007 Sales: $376,000	2007 Profits: $722,100	Fiscal Year Ends: 12/31
2006 Sales: $300,200	2006 Profits: $856,400	Parent Company:

SALARIES/BENEFITS:

Pension Plan:	ESOP Stock Plan:	Profit Sharing:	Top Exec. Salary: $	Bonus: $
Savings Plan:	Stock Purch. Plan:		Second Exec. Salary: $	Bonus: $

OTHER THOUGHTS:

Apparent Women Officers or Directors: 1
Hot Spot for Advancement for Women/Minorities:

LOCATIONS: ("Y" = Yes)

West:	Southwest:	Midwest:	Southeast:	Northeast:	International:
				Y	Y

HYSAN DEVELOPMENT CO LTD

www.hysan.com.hk

Industry Group Code: 5311 Ranks within this company's industry group: Sales: 29   Profits: 16

Properties:		Financial Services:	Construction/Development:		Investments:	Specialty Services:		Brokerage:
Apartments:	Y	Mortgages:	Commercial Construction:		REIT:	Property Management:	Y	Commercial Sales:
Malls/Shopping:	Y	Title Insurance:	Residential Construction:			Online Services:		Residential Sales:
Offices:	Y	Property Insurance:	Land Development:	Y		Software/IT:		Specialty:
Hotels/Motels:			Support Services:			Consulting:		
Industrial/Warehouses:			Design/Engineering:					
Other:	Y							

TYPES OF BUSINESS:

Real Estate Development, Management & Investment
Apartments
Shopping Centers
Office Buildings
Car Parks

BRANDS/DIVISIONS/AFFILIATES:

Service-Scan
Lee Gardens (The)
Leighton Centre
Sunning Plaza
Lee Theatre Plaza
Bamboo Grove
Causeway Bay
Lee Gardens Two

CONTACTS: Note: Officers with more than one job title may be intentionally listed here more than once.

Gerry Lui Fai Yim, CEO
Cissy Ching Sze Chan, Dir.-Mktg. & Retail Portfolio
Wendy Wen Yee Yung, Corp. Sec./Exec. Dir.
Mark Tung, Head-Corp. Comm.
Shu Yan Hao, Controller
Lai Kiu Chan, Dir.-Design & Project Affairs
Yiu Cho Mak, Gen. Mgr.-Property Svcs.
David Akers-Jones, Chmn.

Phone: 852-2895-5777   **Fax:** 852-2577-5153

Toll-Free:

Address: 33 Hysan Ave., 49th Fl., The Lee Gardens, Hong Kong, China

GROWTH PLANS/SPECIAL FEATURES:

Hysan Development Co., Ltd. is a Hong Kong property development and investment firm that derives revenues by leasing space to commercial and residential tenants. Its investment portfolio totals approximately 4 million square feet of space, located primarily in the Causeway Bay district of Hong Kong. In addition, Hysan owns and manages about 1,200 carparks. The firm's commercial properties encompass office and retail space. Most of the firm's commercial properties combine office and retail within a single building, these holdings include: The Lee Gardens (53 floors); Lee Gardens Two (34 floors); Leighton Centre (28 floors); One Hysan Avenue (26 floors); Sunning Plaza (30 floors); and 111 Leighton Road (24 floors). The firm also owns Lee Theatre Plaza, a shopping and dining complex. Hysan's residential holdings encompass the 345-unit residential complex Bamboo Grove, which includes a club house and sports facilities; and the 59-unit Sunning Court. The firm's development investments consist of a 24.7% interest in The Grand Gateway, a mixed-use commercial, dining, office and residential complex in Shanghai. Additionally, the company provides property management services, based on its proprietary model, Service-Scan, and through its Satisfaction Management System, aims to monitor tenant satisfaction and respond accordingly to keep occupancy rates high.

FINANCIALS: Sales and profits are in thousands of dollars—add 000 to get the full amount. 2010 Note: Financial information for 2010 was not available for all companies at press time.

2010 Sales: $226,960	2010 Profits: $494,570	**U.S. Stock Ticker: HYSNY**
2009 Sales: $216,400	2009 Profits: $349,850	**Int'l Ticker: 0014** Int'l Exchange: Hong Kong-HKEX
2008 Sales: $212,900	2008 Profits: $207,200	Employees: 495
2007 Sales: $177,800	2007 Profits: $513,400	Fiscal Year Ends: 12/31
2006 Sales: $164,900	2006 Profits: $402,800	Parent Company:

SALARIES/BENEFITS:

Pension Plan:	ESOP Stock Plan:	Profit Sharing:	Top Exec. Salary: $	Bonus: $
Savings Plan:	Stock Purch. Plan:		Second Exec. Salary: $	Bonus: $

OTHER THOUGHTS:

Apparent Women Officers or Directors: 4
Hot Spot for Advancement for Women/Minorities: Y

LOCATIONS: ("Y" = Yes)

West:	Southwest:	Midwest:	Southeast:	Northeast:	International:
					Y

HYUNDAI ELEVATOR CO LTD

www.hyundaielevator.co.kr

Industry Group Code: 333 Ranks within this company's industry group: Sales: 1   Profits: 1

Properties:	Financial Services:	Construction/Development:		Investments:	Specialty Services:	Brokerage:
Apartments:	Mortgages:	Commercial Construction:		REIT:	Property Management:	Commercial Sales:
Malls/Shopping:	Title Insurance:	Residential Construction:			Online Services:	Residential Sales:
Offices:	Property Insurance:	Land Development:			Software/IT:	Specialty:
Hotels/Motels:		Support Services:	Y		Consulting:	
Industrial/Warehouses:		Design/Engineering:	Y			
Other:						

TYPES OF BUSINESS:

Elevator Manufacture & Design
Escalator Manufacture & Design
Moving Walk Manufacture & Design
Material Handling System Manufacture & Design
Platform Screen Door Manufacture & Design
Auto Parking System Manufacture & Design

BRANDS/DIVISIONS/AFFILIATES:

Hyundai Corporation
i-XEL Elevators
PASSENGER Elevators
LUXEN Elevators
YZER Elevators
Millenium Escalators
Modular Escalators
H-Series Escalators

CONTACTS: *Note: Officers with more than one job title may be intentionally listed here more than once.*

Jeong Eun Hyun, CEO
Hong Hwan Ahn, VP
Gi Ryung Suhk, Managing Dir.
Yeong Min Gwon, Assistant Managing Dir.
Min Yeong Shin, Assistant Managing Dir.
Jeong Eun Hyun, Chmn.

Phone: 82-2-3670-0665	Fax: 82-2-3672-8763
Toll-Free:	
Address: San 136-1, Ami-ri Boobal-eup, Icheon-si, Gyeonggi-do, 467-734 Korea	

GROWTH PLANS/SPECIAL FEATURES:

Hyundai Elevator Co., Ltd., an affiliate of the Hyundai Business Group, manufactures, sells, installs and maintains elevators, escalators and moving walkways, auto parking systems, material handling systems, platform screen doors. Hyundai Elevator manufactures passenger, observation, hospital bed, automobile, freight and marine elevators, and modernizes existing outdated elevators. Passenger elevators, sold under the i-XEL, PASSENGER, LUXEN and YZER brands, comprise high-speed traction elevators for heavy traffic high-rise commercial buildings and medium-speed traction elevators for residential or mid-rise commercial buildings. Observation elevators, with a glass wall, are designed to provide an aesthetic architectural detail to hotels, shopping centers, office buildings, banks, hospitals and observation towers. Hyundai Elevator's hospital bed elevators are designed for hospitals and other clinics. The firm's automobile elevators transport automobiles from one floor to another in parking garages. Its freight elevators include designs for lightweight cargoes as well as forklifts and heavier loads; these products are used at several museums. Hyundai Elevator's marine elevators are designed for numerous ship types, including tankers, bulk carriers, containerships, Ro-Ro (roll-on roll-off, for wheeled cargo), ferries and navy vessels. Elevator renovations include the replacement of drive control systems, traction machines, controllers, as well as car/entrance design and signal fixture. The firm sells escalators under such brands as Millennium, designed for hotels, shopping malls, banks and department stores; Modular, designed for heavy-duty use; and H-Series, designed for installation in subway stations, sports complexes, conference halls and airports. Its moving walkways include horizontal, 12-degree inclined and combination designs. Material handling systems include stacker cranes, automated guided vehicles and robotic transfer vehicles. Auto parking systems cover vertical, rotating, elevator and horizontal parking solutions. Hyundai Elevator's platform screen doors, designed to separate subway and light rail transit platforms from railways, include hermetic, semi-hermetic and handrail varieties.

FINANCIALS: Sales and profits are in thousands of dollars—add 000 to get the full amount. 2010 Note: Financial information for 2010 was not available for all companies at press time.

2010 Sales: $629,660	2010 Profits: $27,500	U.S. Stock Ticker:
2009 Sales: $531,230	2009 Profits: $138,330	Int'l Ticker: 017800 Int'l Exchange: Seoul-KRX
2008 Sales: $461,710	2008 Profits: $40,770	Employees:
2007 Sales: $	2007 Profits: $	Fiscal Year Ends:
2006 Sales: $	2006 Profits: $	Parent Company:

SALARIES/BENEFITS:

Pension Plan:	ESOP Stock Plan:	Profit Sharing:	Top Exec. Salary: $	Bonus: $
Savings Plan:	Stock Purch. Plan:		Second Exec. Salary: $	Bonus: $

OTHER THOUGHTS:

Apparent Women Officers or Directors: 1
Hot Spot for Advancement for Women/Minorities:

LOCATIONS: ("Y" = Yes)

West:	Southwest:	Midwest:	Southeast:	Northeast:	International:
Y					Y

HYUNDAI ENGINEERING & CONSTRUCTION COMPANY LTD

www.hdec.co.kr

Industry Group Code: 237 Ranks within this company's industry group: Sales: 12   Profits: 8

Properties:	Financial Services:	Construction/Development:		Investments:	Specialty Services:	Brokerage:
Apartments:	Mortgages:	Commercial Construction:	Y	REIT:	Property Management:	Commercial Sales:
Malls/Shopping:	Title Insurance:	Residential Construction:	Y		Online Services:	Residential Sales:
Offices:	Property Insurance:	Land Development:	Y		Software/IT:	Specialty:
Hotels/Motels:		Support Services:			Consulting:	
Industrial/Warehouses:		Design/Engineering:				
Other:						

TYPES OF BUSINESS:

Construction, Heavy & Civil Engineering
Power Plant Construction
Highway & Bridge Construction
Residential Construction
Commercial Construction

BRANDS/DIVISIONS/AFFILIATES:

Hillstate
Hyundai Engineering Co., Ltd.
Hyperion

CONTACTS: Note: Officers with more than one job title may be intentionally listed here more than once.

Joong-Kyum Kim, CEO
Joong-Kyum Kim, Pres.
Kyung-Ho Kim, Exec. VP-Human Resources
Dong-Kyu Paik, Exec. VP/Head-Tech. Institute & Quality Dev.
Ok-Kyun Jung, Exec. VP/Head-Corp. Bus. & Mgmt.
Dong-Ho Lee, Head-Public Rel. Office
Dong-Kwon Jang, VP/Head-Planning & Budget Office
Sung-Real Lee, Sr. Exec. VP/Head-Investment & Bus. Dev. Div.
Jong-Ho Kim, Sr. Exec. VP/Head-Power & Energy Div.
Hyo-Won Sohn, Sr. Exec. VP/Head-Building Works Div.
Seung-Taek Lee, Exec. VP/Head-Plant Div.
Lee Ji-Song, Chmn.
Ho-Sang Kim, Exec. VP/Head-Overseas Div.
Jong-Ho Lee, VP-Procurement

Phone: 82-2-746-1114	Fax: 82-2-743-8963
Toll-Free:	
Address: 140-2, Kye-dong, Chongro-ku, Seoul, Korea	

GROWTH PLANS/SPECIAL FEATURES:

Hyundai Engineering & Construction Company Ltd. (HDEC) is an international construction company based in South Korea. HDEC has expertise in a variety of structures, such as civil works, highways and bridges, housing, shipyards, dams, power plants (including nuclear power), airports, stadiums, hotels and retail complexes. The company is organized into five divisions: Civil & Environment; Building Works; Plants; Power & Energy; and Investment & Business Development. The Civil & Environment division is responsible for the engineering and construction of roads, highways and other infrastructure developments across Korea and overseas. Its major projects include the Gyeongbu Expressway, the Gyeongbu High-speed Railway, the Soyang Multi purpose Dam, Busan Harbor and Incheon International Airport. The Building Works division builds skyscrapers, residential housing and other large-scale architectural projects in both the Korean and international markets. Some of its notable projects include Hamad Medical Center in Qatar, the Hwaseong Stadium in Korea, the Jangbogo Antarctic Research Station, the Four Seasons Hotel in Cairo and the National Center for Korean Traditional Performing Arts. The Plants division constructs hydrocarbon processing and industrial plants, including LNG receiving terminals, LNG supply pipelines, multi-purpose water gate facilities and integrated steel works. The Power & Energy segment specializes in the construction of fossil fuel-based and nuclear power plants, as well as water desalination plants, transmission and substation facilities and renewable energy projects. Lastly, the Investment & Business Development division handles the firm's investments in the areas of high technology, infrastructure projects and renewable energy development, among others. The firm has offices in the Pacific Rim, the Middle East, Africa, the U.K. and the U.S. Subsidiaries of the company include Hyundai Engineering Co., Ltd.; Hillstate, a construction company; and Hyperion, an upscale apartment builder.

FINANCIALS: Sales and profits are in thousands of dollars—add 000 to get the full amount. 2010 Note: Financial information for 2010 was not available for all companies at press time.

2010 Sales: $10,274,800	2010 Profits: $476,880	**U.S. Stock Ticker:**
2009 Sales: $9,309,980	2009 Profits: $408,040	**Int'l Ticker: 000720** Int'l Exchange: Seoul-KRX
2008 Sales: $5,782,184	2008 Profits: $296,997	Employees:
2007 Sales: $4,492,324	2007 Profits: $220,584	Fiscal Year Ends:
2006 Sales: $5,410,300	2006 Profits: $	Parent Company:

SALARIES/BENEFITS:

Pension Plan:	ESOP Stock Plan:	Profit Sharing:	Top Exec. Salary: $	Bonus: $
Savings Plan:	Stock Purch. Plan:		Second Exec. Salary: $	Bonus: $

OTHER THOUGHTS:

Apparent Women Officers or Directors:
Hot Spot for Advancement for Women/Minorities:

LOCATIONS: ("Y" = Yes)

West:	Southwest:	Midwest:	Southeast:	Northeast:	International:
				Y	Y

ICAHN ENTERPRISES LP

www.ielp.com

Industry Group Code: 5311 Ranks within this company's industry group: Sales: 2   Profits: 12

Properties:		Financial Services:		Construction/Development:		Investments:	Specialty Services:		Brokerage:
Apartments:	Y	Mortgages:	Y	Commercial Construction:		REIT:	Property Management:	Y	Commercial Sales:
Malls/Shopping:	Y	Title Insurance:		Residential Construction:	Y		Online Services:		Residential Sales:
Offices:	Y	Property Insurance:	Y	Land Development:	Y		Software/IT:		Specialty:
Hotels/Motels:	Y			Support Services:			Consulting:		
Industrial/Warehouses:	Y			Design/Engineering:					
Other:	Y								

TYPES OF BUSINESS:

Real Estate Operations
Property Leasing, Retail & Corporate
Casinos, Hotels & Resorts
Residential Development
Home Furnishings
Automotive Parts & Components
Debt & Equity Investments
Railcar Manufacturing & Servicing

BRANDS/DIVISIONS/AFFILIATES:

American Real Estate Partners
WestPoint International, Inc.
PSC Metals, Inc.
Federal-Mogul Corporation
Tropicana Entertainment, Inc.
American Railcar Industries, Inc.
Viskase Companies, Inc.
Dynegy Inc

CONTACTS: *Note: Officers with more than one job title may be intentionally listed here more than once.*

Daniel A. Ninivaggi, Pres.
Dominick Ragone, CFO
Carl C. Icahn, Chmn.

Phone: 212-702-4300	**Fax:** 212-750-5841
Toll-Free: 800-255-2737	
Address: 767 Fifth Ave., 47th Fl., New York, NY 10153 US	

GROWTH PLANS/SPECIAL FEATURES:

Icahn Enterprises L.P., formerly American Real Estate Partners, is a holding company with businesses in several areas, including real estate, investment management, gaming, metals, food packaging, home fashion, railcar and automotive. In real estate, the company leases retail, office and industrial properties to corporations, and it constructs and sells residential property, including single-family homes, multiple-family complexes and residential lots. It owns and operates several resort properties near some of its residential development sites, namely, the New Seabury Resort in Massachusetts and several golf courses, athletic facilities and clubhouses in Vero Beach, Florida. Icahn's investment segment focuses on real estate development companies and mezzanine loans. Gaming operations are conducted through Tropicana Entertainment, Inc., which owns 10 casino properties in the U.S. and Aruba. The firm's metal division is operated through its subsidiary, PSC Metals, Inc., and is principally engaged in collecting, processing and selling ferrous and non-ferrous metals. Its food packaging holdings consist of a 71% interest in Viskase Companies, Inc., a provider of casings for hot dogs, sausages, lunch meats and other processed meat and poultry products. Icahn conducts its home fashion operations through WestPoint International, Inc., a manufacturer and distributor of home fashion consumer products. The railcar segment consists of Icahn's 54% stake in American Railcar Industries, a freight car manufacturing and servicing company. In the automotive sector, through subsidiary Federal-Mogul, the firm is a global supplier of vehicle technologies and products related to fuel economy, alternative energies, environment and safety systems, with customers primarily including original equipment manufacturers (OEMs) in the automotive, light commercial, heavy duty, agricultural, aerospace, marine, rail and off-road vehicle markets. In November 2010, it increased its interests in Tropicana Entertainment, Inc. from 48.9% to 51.5%. In December 2010, the firm agreed to acquire energy company Dynegy, Inc. for $665 million.

FINANCIALS: Sales and profits are in thousands of dollars—add 000 to get the full amount. 2010 Note: Financial information for 2010 was not available for all companies at press time.

2010 Sales: $7,934,000	2010 Profits: $743,000	**U.S. Stock Ticker:** IEP
2009 Sales: $6,790,000	2009 Profits: $1,225,000	**Int'l Ticker:** Int'l Exchange:
2008 Sales: $8,430,000	2008 Profits: $-2,657,000	Employees:
2007 Sales: $2,491,000	2007 Profits: $564,000	Fiscal Year Ends: 12/31
2006 Sales: $3,006,000	2006 Profits: $1,107,726	Parent Company:

SALARIES/BENEFITS:

Pension Plan: Y	ESOP Stock Plan:	Profit Sharing:	Top Exec. Salary: $1,229,743	Bonus: $972,603
Savings Plan: Y	Stock Purch. Plan:		Second Exec. Salary: $400,000	Bonus: $

OTHER THOUGHTS:

Apparent Women Officers or Directors:
Hot Spot for Advancement for Women/Minorities:

LOCATIONS: ("Y" = Yes)

West:	Southwest:	Midwest:	Southeast:	Northeast:	International:
Y	Y	Y	Y	Y	Y

IMPAC MORTGAGE HOLDINGS INC   www.impaccompanies.com

Industry Group Code: 525990 Ranks within this company's industry group: Sales: 1   Profits: 3

Properties:		Financial Services:		Construction/Development:		Investments:		Specialty Services:		Brokerage:	
Apartments:		Mortgages:	Y	Commercial Construction:		REIT:	Y	Property Management:		Commercial Sales:	
Malls/Shopping:		Title Insurance:		Residential Construction:				Online Services:		Residential Sales:	
Offices:		Property Insurance:		Land Development:				Software/IT:		Specialty:	
Hotels/Motels:				Support Services:				Consulting:			
Industrial/Warehouses:				Design/Engineering:							
Other:											

TYPES OF BUSINESS:

REIT-Mortgages
Real Estate Investment Trust
Real Estate & Mortgage Services

BRANDS/DIVISIONS/AFFILIATES:

IMH Assets Corp.
Impac Funding Corporation
Impac Secured Assets Corp.
Impac Warehouse Lending Group Inc.
Impac Commercial Capital Corporation
Integrated Real Estate Service Corporation

CONTACTS: *Note: Officers with more than one job title may be intentionally listed here more than once.*

Joseph R. Tomkinson, CEO
William S. Ashmore, Pres.
Todd R. Taylor, CFO/Sr. VP
Ronald M. Morrison, General Counsel/Exec. VP/Sec.
Justin Moisio, Dir.-Investor Rel.
Nancy Pollard, Exec. VP-Asset Mgmt.
Jim Malloy, Sr. VP-Structured Finance & Capital Markets
Joseph R. Tomkinson, Chmn.

Phone: 949-475-3600	Fax:
Toll-Free: 800-597-4101	
Address: 19500 Jamboree Rd., Irvine, CA 92612 US	

GROWTH PLANS/SPECIAL FEATURES:

Impac Mortgage Holdings, Inc. (IMH) is a mortgage real estate investment trust. Following the episode of distress within the mortgage lending and securitization markets, IMH has shifted its focus away from past interests in long-term investments of non-conforming Alt-A residential mortgages. Now, through subsidiary Integrated Real Estate Service Corporation (IRES), the firm's primary goal is to create an integrated services platform to provide solutions to the mortgage and real estate markets. These fee-based services include loan modifications, loss mitigation, real estate disposition, monitoring and surveillance services, real estate brokerage, mortgage lending, and title and escrow services. IMH and subsidiary IMH Assets maintain master servicing rights on the portfolio of long-term investments that include various adjustable rate, fixed rate and hybrid ARM residential and commercial mortgages acquired and originated by its discontinued mortgage and commercial operations.

FINANCIALS: Sales and profits are in thousands of dollars—add 000 to get the full amount. 2010 Note: Financial information for 2010 was not available for all companies at press time.

2010 Sales: $1,048,614	2010 Profits: $10,294	**U.S. Stock Ticker: IMH**
2009 Sales: $1,837,065	2009 Profits: $10,837	Int'l Ticker: Int'l Exchange:
2008 Sales: $1,572,556	2008 Profits: $-44,723	Employees: 376
2007 Sales: $1,224,821	2007 Profits: $-2,047,090	Fiscal Year Ends: 12/31
2006 Sales: $1,134,002	2006 Profits: $-75,273	Parent Company:

SALARIES/BENEFITS:

Pension Plan:	ESOP Stock Plan:	Profit Sharing:	Top Exec. Salary: $600,000	Bonus: $850,471
Savings Plan:	Stock Purch. Plan:		Second Exec. Salary: $575,000	Bonus: $900,471

OTHER THOUGHTS:

Apparent Women Officers or Directors: 1
Hot Spot for Advancement for Women/Minorities:

LOCATIONS: ("Y" = Yes)

West:	Southwest:	Midwest:	Southeast:	Northeast:	International:
Y					

IMPREGILO SPA

www.impregilo.it

Industry Group Code: 237 Ranks within this company's industry group: Sales: 25   Profits: 19

Properties:	Financial Services:	Construction/Development:		Investments:	Specialty Services:	Brokerage:
Apartments:	Mortgages:	Commercial Construction:	Y	REIT:	Property Management:	Commercial Sales:
Malls/Shopping:	Title Insurance:	Residential Construction:			Online Services:	Residential Sales:
Offices:	Property Insurance:	Land Development:			Software/IT:	Specialty:
Hotels/Motels:		Support Services:			Consulting:	
Industrial/Warehouses:		Design/Engineering:	Y			
Other:						

TYPES OF BUSINESS:

Heavy Construction
Civil Engineering
Environmental Engineering
Infrastructure Management
Airport Operations

BRANDS/DIVISIONS/AFFILIATES:

Fisia Italimpianti
Fisia Babcock
IGLI SpA

CONTACTS: *Note: Officers with more than one job title may be intentionally listed here more than once.*

Alberto Rubegni, CEO
Rosario Fiumara, CFO
Massimo Ponzellini, Chmn.

Phone: 39-02-244-22111	**Fax:** 39-02-244-22293
Toll-Free:	
Address: Viale Italia 1, Sesto San Giovanni, Milan, 20099 Italy	

GROWTH PLANS/SPECIAL FEATURES:

Impregilo S.p.A., 29%-owned by IGLI S.p.A., is a leading Italian civil engineering and construction company with over a century of experience and operations in approximately 30 countries, including the U.S. The Impregilo group is divided into three primary business segments: infrastructures, engineering and plant construction and concessions. The infrastructures unit is responsible for public-sector projects such as dams, hydroelectric plants, roads, bridges, airports, underground works and high-capacity rail projects. The engineering and plant construction segment supplies technical assistance for desalinization, water treatment, solid waste power plant facilities and remediation of contaminated areas on land and sea. It operates through Fisia Italimpianti and Fisia Babcock (Germany) and furnishes a laboratory and research center that provides backup for the segment's operations. The concessions unit manages motorways, airports, water distribution and treatment and renewable energy power production facilities. Impregilo group has had construction projects in Iceland (Karahnjukar), the Dominican Republic (Guaigui), Venezuela (Tocoma) and Ecuador (Mazar). It is currently working on the Gotthard Base Tunnel, a railway tunnel in Switzerland, expected to be completed in 2015; and the expansion of the Panama Canal, a project in which the company will create a third system of locks that will accommodate larger vessels and recycle substantially more water, is expected to be completed in 2014. In October 2010, Impreglio signed a letter of intent with Shanghai Electric Group Co., Ltd., Mandarin Capital Partners S.C.A. SICAR, and China Development Bank Securities to cooperate in the desalination industry.

FINANCIALS: Sales and profits are in thousands of dollars—add 000 to get the full amount. 2010 Note: Financial information for 2010 was not available for all companies at press time.

2010 Sales: $2,790,090	2010 Profits: $185,480	**U.S. Stock Ticker: IPG**
2009 Sales: $3,503,760	2009 Profits: $104,740	**Int'l Ticker: IPG** Int'l Exchange: Milan-BI
2008 Sales: $3,991,960	2008 Profits: $226,220	Employees:
2007 Sales: $3,770,300	2007 Profits: $60,700	Fiscal Year Ends: 12/31
2006 Sales: $3,734,700	2006 Profits: $210,800	Parent Company:

SALARIES/BENEFITS:

Pension Plan:	ESOP Stock Plan:	Profit Sharing:	Top Exec. Salary: $	Bonus: $
Savings Plan:	Stock Purch. Plan:		Second Exec. Salary: $	Bonus: $

OTHER THOUGHTS:

Apparent Women Officers or Directors: 1
Hot Spot for Advancement for Women/Minorities:

LOCATIONS: ("Y" = Yes)

West:	Southwest:	Midwest:	Southeast:	Northeast:	International:
					Y

INDIAN HOTELS COMPANY LIMITED (THE)

www.tajhotels.com

Industry Group Code: 721110 Ranks within this company's industry group: Sales: Profits:

Properties:		Financial Services:	Construction/Development:	Investments:	Specialty Services:		Brokerage:
Apartments:		Mortgages:	Commercial Construction:	REIT:	Property Management:	Y	Commercial Sales:
Malls/Shopping:		Title Insurance:	Residential Construction:		Online Services:		Residential Sales:
Offices:		Property Insurance:	Land Development:		Software/IT:		Specialty:
Hotels/Motels:	Y		Support Services:		Consulting:		
Industrial/Warehouses:			Design/Engineering:				
Other:							

TYPES OF BUSINESS:

Hotels
Spas
Apartments
Private Jet Rental
Air Catering
Travel Agency

BRANDS/DIVISIONS/AFFILIATES:

Indian Hotels Company Ltd. (The)
Tata Group
Taj Luxury Residences
TajAir Ltd.
TajSATS Air Catering Ltd.
IndiTravel Private Limited
Roots Corporation Ltd
Jiva Spas

CONTACTS: Note: Officers with more than one job title may be intentionally listed here more than once.

Raymond N. Bickson, CEO/Managing Dir.
Rajiv Gujral, COO
Anil P. Goel, Exec. Dir.-Finance
Ajoy K. Misra, Sr. VP-Sales & Mktg.
H. N. Shrinivas, Sr. VP-Human Resources
Prakash V. Shukla, CIO
Prakash V. Shukla, Sr. VP-Tech.
Abhijit Mukerji, Exec. Dir.-Hotel Oper.
Rajiv Gujral, Sr. VP-Mergers, Acquisitions & Dev.
Sarita Hegde, Dir.-Public Rel.
Veer Vijay Singh, COO-Upper Upscale Hotels
Prabhat Pani, CEO-Roots Corp. Ltd.
Jyoti Narang, COO-Luxury Div.
Kanak Kothari, VP-Projects
Ratan N. Tata, Chmn.

Phone: 91-22-6665-1000	Fax: 91-22-2284-6680

Toll-Free:

Address: Oxford House, 15/17 N.F. Rd, Apollo Bunder, Mumbai, 400 001 India

GROWTH PLANS/SPECIAL FEATURES:

The Indian Hotels Company Limited (IHCL), which, together with its subsidiaries, does business as Taj Hotels, Resorts and Palaces (Taj), is one of the world's premier operators of luxury hotels. Part of Indian conglomerate Tata Group, Taj owns more than 65 hotels in 42 locations across India and 16 additional hotels in Sri Lanka, Bhutan, Malaysia, Australia, Africa, the Middle East, the U.S. and the U.K. IHCL operates hotels in the value, mid-market, premium and luxury segments. The firm's hotel brands include Taj, a chain of luxury full-service resorts, hotels and palaces include historic properties, modern business-oriented hotels, beach resorts and safari lodges; Taj Exotica, a resort and spa brand; Taj Safaris, ecotourism lodges in the Indian jungle; The Gateway Hotel, a mid to upscale full-service hotel and resort brand; Ginger, a line of economy hotels operated by wholly-owned subsidiary Roots Corporation Ltd; and Vivanta by Taj, a luxury upper upscale brand catering to international travelers. Taj offers a variety of services through Jiva Spas including yoga, meditation, Indian healing ceremonies and other treatments. Besides hotels, IHCL offers chartered private luxury jets through subsidiary TajAir Ltd., and catering services for over 26 domestic and international airlines through TajSATS Air Catering Ltd. Subsidiary Taj Luxury Residences offers apartments in three locations, staffed with personal butlers, a round-the-clock concierge and 24-hour-a-day babysitting service. Finally, IndiTravel Private Limited offers travel services from ticketing to car rentals and passport assistance. In March 2010, Taj Cape Town, a luxury hotel in Cape Town, South Africa owned through a joint venture with Euro Cape, opened for business.

FINANCIALS: Sales and profits are in thousands of dollars—add 000 to get the full amount. 2010 Note: Financial information for 2010 was not available for all companies at press time.

2010 Sales: $	2010 Profits: $	U.S. Stock Ticker: Subsidiary
2009 Sales: $	2009 Profits: $	Int'l Ticker: Int'l Exchange:
2008 Sales: $	2008 Profits: $	Employees:
2007 Sales: $	2007 Profits: $	Fiscal Year Ends: 3/31
2006 Sales: $	2006 Profits: $	Parent Company: TATA GROUP

SALARIES/BENEFITS:

Pension Plan:	ESOP Stock Plan:	Profit Sharing:	Top Exec. Salary: $	Bonus: $
Savings Plan:	Stock Purch. Plan:		Second Exec. Salary: $	Bonus: $

OTHER THOUGHTS:

Apparent Women Officers or Directors: 1
Hot Spot for Advancement for Women/Minorities:

LOCATIONS: ("Y" = Yes)

West:	Southwest:	Midwest:	Southeast:	Northeast:	International:
Y				Y	Y

INDUSTRIAL DEVELOPMENTS INTERNATIONAL INC www.idi.com

Industry Group Code: 5311 Ranks within this company's industry group: Sales: Profits:

Properties:		Financial Services:	Construction/Development:		Investments:	Specialty Services:		Brokerage:
Apartments:		Mortgages:	Commercial Construction:	Y	REIT:	Property Management:	Y	Commercial Sales:
Malls/Shopping:		Title Insurance:	Residential Construction:			Online Services:		Residential Sales:
Offices:		Property Insurance:	Land Development:	Y		Software/IT:		Specialty:
Hotels/Motels:			Support Services:			Consulting:		
Industrial/Warehouses:	Y		Design/Engineering:					
Other:								

TYPES OF BUSINESS:

Real Estate Development
Industrial Business Parks
Warehouses
Facility Management & Leasing
Construction Management Services

BRANDS/DIVISIONS/AFFILIATES:

IDI Investment Management

CONTACTS: *Note: Officers with more than one job title may be intentionally listed here more than once.*

Tim Gunter, CEO
David Birdwell, COO/Exec. VP
Tim Gunter, Pres.
Linda Booker, CFO/Sr. VP
Rita Skaggs, VP-Mktg.
Debbie Kvietkus, Dir.-Human Resources
Matt O'Sullivan, Chief Dev. Officer/Exec. VP
Rita Skaggs, VP-Comm.
Greg Ryan, Sr. VP/Managing Dir.-Acquisitions
G. Bryan Blasingame, Jr., Chief Investment Officer/Sr. VP-Investment Mgmt.
S. Michael Parks, Sr. VP-National Bus. Dev.
Paul Philips, Sr. VP-Investment Mgmt.

Phone: 404-479-4000	Fax: 404-479-4162
Toll-Free:	
Address: 1100 Peachtree St., Ste. 1100, Atlanta, GA 30309 US	

GROWTH PLANS/SPECIAL FEATURES:

Industrial Developments International, Inc. (IDI), founded in 1989, is a national, privately held, full-service industrial real estate developer that provides development, investment management, and property management and leasing services to tenants with distribution, warehouse and light manufacturing needs. Since its inception, the firm has acquired and developed over 127 million square feet of industrial space in business parks in the U.S., Canada and Mexico. The company manages a portfolio of about 70 million square feet. IDI operates through eight development offices in Georgia, Illinois, Ohio, Texas, Florida, California, Tennessee and Pennsylvania. The company divides its operations among three business groups: the development group, the investment management group and the property management group. The firm's development group includes its build-to-suit services group, which offers comprehensive development services for single properties and multiple-market rollouts. Its project management services include site selection, due diligence, LEED/sustainable design consulting, permitting/incentive coordination, construction management and project financing. The investment management group is a leading buyer, seller, operating partner and investment advisor focusing on industrial real estate assets. This group includes IDI's Acquisitions division, which actively seeks to purchase warehouse and distribution facilities in the U.S. and Canada; and its Dispositions division, which directly markets and sells buildings under IDI development, as well as jointly owned buildings. The property management group provides property management, leasing, building service engineer programs and tenant-improvement construction management services to IDI and third parties, as well as leasing services for third-party owners of IDI-managed properties.

IDI offers its employees medical, dental and vision coverage; life insurance; short- and long-term disability insurance; flexible spending accounts; and a 401(k) plan.

FINANCIALS: Sales and profits are in thousands of dollars—add 000 to get the full amount. 2010 Note: Financial information for 2010 was not available for all companies at press time.

2010 Sales: $	2010 Profits: $	U.S. Stock Ticker: Private
2009 Sales: $	2009 Profits: $	Int'l Ticker: Int'l Exchange:
2008 Sales: $	2008 Profits: $	Employees:
2007 Sales: $262,700	2007 Profits: $	Fiscal Year Ends: 12/31
2006 Sales: $	2006 Profits: $	Parent Company:

SALARIES/BENEFITS:

Pension Plan:	ESOP Stock Plan:	Profit Sharing:	Top Exec. Salary: $	Bonus: $
Savings Plan: Y	Stock Purch. Plan:		Second Exec. Salary: $	Bonus: $

OTHER THOUGHTS:

Apparent Women Officers or Directors: 3
Hot Spot for Advancement for Women/Minorities: Y

LOCATIONS: ("Y" = Yes)

West:	Southwest:	Midwest:	Southeast:	Northeast:	International:
Y	Y	Y	Y	Y	

INLAND AMERICAN REAL ESTATE TRUST INC

www.inland-american.com

Industry Group Code: 531120 Ranks within this company's industry group: Sales: Profits:

Properties:		Financial Services:	Construction/Development:	Investments:		Specialty Services:	Brokerage:
Apartments:	Y	Mortgages:	Commercial Construction:	REIT:	Y	Property Management:	Commercial Sales:
Malls/Shopping:	Y	Title Insurance:	Residential Construction:			Online Services:	Residential Sales:
Offices:	Y	Property Insurance:	Land Development:			Software/IT:	Specialty:
Hotels/Motels:	Y		Support Services:			Consulting:	
Industrial/Warehouses:	Y		Design/Engineering:				
Other:							

TYPES OF BUSINESS:

Real Estate Investment Trust

BRANDS/DIVISIONS/AFFILIATES:

Inland Real Estate Group of Companies Inc (The)
Inland American Winston Hotels, Inc
Inland American Orchard Hotels, Inc
Inland American Urban Hotels, Inc
Inland American Lodging Corporation
Inland American Retail Management LLC
Inland American Industrial Management LLC
Inland American Office Management LLC

CONTACTS:
Note: Officers with more than one job title may be intentionally listed here more than once.

Brenda G. Gujral, Pres.
Lori J. Foust, CFO/Treas.
Roberta S. Matlin, VP-Admin.
Scott W. Wilton, Corp. Sec.
Jack Potts, Principal Acct. Officer
Robert D. Parks, Chmn.

Phone: 630-218-8000	**Fax:** 630-218-4957
Toll-Free: 800-826-8228	
Address: 2901 Butterfield Rd., Oak Brook, IL 60523 US	

GROWTH PLANS/SPECIAL FEATURES:

Inland American Real Estate Trust, Inc. is a Real Estate Investment Trust (REIT) and a member of the Inland Real Estate Group of Companies. The firm operates in five segments, divided by property types. Inland American Retail Management LLC, segment consists of 980 properties totaling approximately 48.3 million square feet. The Inland American Lodging Corporation segment consists of the operations of three subsidiaries, namely Inland American Winston Hotels, Inc., Inland American Orchard Hotels, Inc., and Inland American Urban Hotels, Inc. Between them, these subsidiaries own 99 hotel properties primarily operating under the Marriot and Hilton brand names, containing an approximately 15,380 rooms. The Inland American Industrial Management LLC segment owns approximately 72 properties totaling approximately 16.0 million square feet of industrial space. The Inland American Office Management LLC segment includes approximately 47 properties totaling approximately 10.6 million square feet. The firm's Inland American Apartment Management LLC segment consists of approximately 27 multi-family residential properties containing 9,790 units. Inland American's properties are located throughout the U.S., and it generally aims to acquire multiple properties grouped around major metropolitan markets. The company typically seeks properties with existing net leases, requiring tenants to cover various operating expenses such as real estate taxes, insurance and general maintenance costs. Inland American also engages in sale-leaseback transactions, in which the firm purchases a property, and then leases it back to the seller. The company's two largest customers are SunTrust Banks, Inc. and AT&T, Inc. In 2010, the company acquired about 30 new properties, including several shopping centers and hotels.

Employees of the company are offered medical and dental insurance; a flexible savings plan for health and dependent care needs; a 401(k) plan; life and AD&D insurance; and both short- and long-term disability insurance.

FINANCIALS:
Sales and profits are in thousands of dollars—add 000 to get the full amount. 2010 Note: Financial information for 2010 was not available for all companies at press time.

2010 Sales: $	2010 Profits: $	**U.S. Stock Ticker: Subsidiary**
2009 Sales: $	2009 Profits: $	**Int'l Ticker:** Int'l Exchange:
2008 Sales: $	2008 Profits: $	Employees:
2007 Sales: $	2007 Profits: $	Fiscal Year Ends: 12/31
2006 Sales: $	2006 Profits: $	Parent Company: INLAND REAL ESTATE GROUP OF COMPANIES INC (THE)

SALARIES/BENEFITS:

Pension Plan:	ESOP Stock Plan:	Profit Sharing:	Top Exec. Salary: $	Bonus: $
Savings Plan: Y	Stock Purch. Plan:		Second Exec. Salary: $	Bonus: $

OTHER THOUGHTS:

Apparent Women Officers or Directors: 2

Hot Spot for Advancement for Women/Minorities:

LOCATIONS: ("Y" = Yes)

West:	Southwest:	Midwest:	Southeast:	Northeast:	International:
	Y	Y		Y	

INLAND REAL ESTATE CORPORATION   www.inlandrealestate.com

Industry Group Code: 531120 Ranks within this company's industry group: Sales: 58   Profits: 49

Properties:		Financial Services:	Construction/Development:	Investments:		Specialty Services:		Brokerage:
Apartments:		Mortgages:	Commercial Construction:	REIT:	Y	Property Management:	Y	Commercial Sales:
Malls/Shopping:	Y	Title Insurance:	Residential Construction:			Online Services:		Residential Sales:
Offices:		Property Insurance:	Land Development:			Software/IT:		Specialty:
Hotels/Motels:			Support Services:			Consulting:		
Industrial/Warehouses:			Design/Engineering:					
Other:								

TYPES OF BUSINESS:

Real Estate Investment Trust
Property Management
Retail Properties

BRANDS/DIVISIONS/AFFILIATES:

Inland Real Estate Group of Companies Inc (The)

CONTACTS: *Note: Officers with more than one job title may be intentionally listed here more than once.*

Mark E. Zalatoris, CEO
Mark E. Zalatoris, Pres.
Brett A. Brown, CFO/Sr. VP
Beth Sprecher Brooks, General Counsel/Sr. VP/Corp. Sec.
Dawn Benchelt, Dir.-Investor Rel.
Brett A. Brown, Treas.
William W. Anderson, VP-Transactions
D. Scott Carr, Pres., Property Management
Thomas P. D'Arcy, Chmn.

Phone: 708-218-8000	Fax:
Toll-Free: 888-331-4732	
Address: 2901 Butterfield Rd., Oak Brook, IL 60523 US	

GROWTH PLANS/SPECIAL FEATURES:

Inland Real Estate Corporation (IRC), a member of The Inland Real Estate Group of Companies, Inc., is a self-administered real estate investment trust (REIT) that acquires, owns, operates and develops open-air neighborhood, community and lifestyle shopping centers and single-tenant retail properties located primarily in the Midwestern U.S. IRC owns or has interests in approximately 142 retail properties comprised of 61 neighborhood retail centers, 29 power centers, 22 community centers, one lifestyle center and 29 single-user retail properties, with more than 14 million square feet of total rentable space and approximately $1.7 billion in assets. Most of IRC's properties are located within a 400-mile radius of its suburban Chicago headquarters and consist of grocery anchored, discount anchored, fashion anchored and convenience retail centers. The firm will also purchase freestanding properties leased by single credit tenants, located anywhere in the country. IRC acquires both single assets and entire portfolios. Its emphasis remains on well-tenanted, well-located properties, from 75,000 to 300,000 square feet. Prominent tenants of the company include Cub Foods, a subsidiary of SUPERVALU, Inc.; Dominick's Finer Foods, a subsidiary of Safeway; Bank of America; Bally's Total Fitness; Carmax; Food 4 Less; Michael's; and PetSmart.

Employees of the company are offered medical and dental insurance; a flexible savings plan for health and dependent care needs; a 401(k) plan; life and AD&D insurance; and both short- and long-term disability insurance.

FINANCIALS: Sales and profits are in thousands of dollars—add 000 to get the full amount. 2010 Note: Financial information for 2010 was not available for all companies at press time.

2010 Sales: $167,029	2010 Profits: $ 43	**U.S. Stock Ticker: IRC**
2009 Sales: $168,025	2009 Profits: $8,629	**Int'l Ticker:** Int'l Exchange:
2008 Sales: $185,885	2008 Profits: $30,425	Employees: 113
2007 Sales: $184,664	2007 Profits: $42,095	Fiscal Year Ends: 12/31
2006 Sales: $175,856	2006 Profits: $45,184	Parent Company: INLAND REAL ESTATE GROUP OF COMPANIES INC (THE)

SALARIES/BENEFITS:

Pension Plan:	ESOP Stock Plan:	Profit Sharing:	Top Exec. Salary: $450,000	Bonus: $70,000
Savings Plan: Y	Stock Purch. Plan:		Second Exec. Salary: $300,000	Bonus: $22,500

OTHER THOUGHTS:

Apparent Women Officers or Directors: 2
Hot Spot for Advancement for Women/Minorities:

LOCATIONS: ("Y" = Yes)

West:	Southwest:	Midwest:	Southeast:	Northeast:	International:
		Y	Y		

INNKEEPERS USA TRUST

www.innkeepersusa.com

Industry Group Code: 531120 Ranks within this company's industry group: Sales: Profits:

Properties:	Financial Services:	Construction/Development:	Investments:	Specialty Services:	Brokerage:
Apartments:	Mortgages:	Commercial Construction:	REIT: Y	Property Management:	Commercial Sales:
Malls/Shopping:	Title Insurance:	Residential Construction:		Online Services:	Residential Sales:
Offices:	Property Insurance:	Land Development:		Software/IT:	Specialty:
Hotels/Motels: Y		Support Services:		Consulting:	
Industrial/Warehouses:		Design/Engineering:			
Other:					

TYPES OF BUSINESS:

Real Estate Investment Trust
Hotels
Hotel Development

BRANDS/DIVISIONS/AFFILIATES:

Island Hospitality Management

CONTACTS: *Note: Officers with more than one job title may be intentionally listed here more than once.*

Tim Walker, CEO
Tim Walker, Pres.
Nathan Cook, CFO
Mark A. Murphy, General Counsel/Sec.
Richard F. Fenton, VP-Financial Planning & Analysis
Linda K. Price, VP/Controller
Bob Martin, VP-Construction & Renovation
Marc A.Beilinson, Chief Restructuring Officer
Richard F. Fenton, VP-Financial Planning & Analysis
Jeffrey H. Fisher, Chmn.

Phone: 561-835-1800	Fax: 561-835-0457
Toll-Free:	
Address: 340 Royal Poinciana Way, Ste. 306, Palm Beach, FL 33480 US	

GROWTH PLANS/SPECIAL FEATURES:

Innkeepers USA Trust, a subsidiary of Apollo Investment Corp., is a real estate investment trust (REIT) that specializes in the ownership of multi-brand, upscale, extended-stay hotels in the U.S. The firm seeks to acquire hotel properties in markets with high barriers to entry and with strong underlying demand growth. Innkeepers USA owns interests in 73 hotels with an aggregate of 10,000 rooms/suites in 19 states and Washington, D.C. 72 of these hotels are managed by Island Hospitality Management. The firm's hotels operate under the following brands: Residence Inn, TownePlace Suites and Courtyard by Marriott; Sheraton; Double Tree; Embassy Suites; Hyatt Summerfield Suites; Westin; Best Western; Bulfinch Hotel; Hampton Inn; and Hilton. In addition to its acquisitions of existing hotels in the upscale and extended-stay market, Innkeepers also acquires under-performing mid-priced and full service hotels that have the potential for strategic repositioning or re-flagging to a premium franchise brand in the upscale segment. In July 2010, burdened with a large debt load, the firm filed for bankruptcy.

FINANCIALS: Sales and profits are in thousands of dollars—add 000 to get the full amount. 2010 Note: Financial information for 2010 was not available for all companies at press time.

2010 Sales: $	2010 Profits: $	U.S. Stock Ticker: Private
2009 Sales: $	2009 Profits: $	Int'l Ticker: Int'l Exchange:
2008 Sales: $	2008 Profits: $	Employees:
2007 Sales: $	2007 Profits: $	Fiscal Year Ends: 12/31
2006 Sales: $286,713	2006 Profits: $30,487	Parent Company:

SALARIES/BENEFITS:

Pension Plan:	ESOP Stock Plan:	Profit Sharing:	Top Exec. Salary: $	Bonus: $
Savings Plan:	Stock Purch. Plan:		Second Exec. Salary: $	Bonus: $

OTHER THOUGHTS:

Apparent Women Officers or Directors: 1
Hot Spot for Advancement for Women/Minorities:

LOCATIONS: ("Y" = Yes)

West:	Southwest:	Midwest:	Southeast:	Northeast:	International:
Y	Y	Y	Y	Y	

INSITUFORM TECHNOLOGIES

www.insituform.com

Industry Group Code: 2389 Ranks within this company's industry group: Sales: 2 Profits: 2

Properties:	Financial Services:	Construction/Development:		Investments:	Specialty Services:	Brokerage:
Apartments:	Mortgages:	Commercial Construction:		REIT:	Property Management:	Commercial Sales:
Malls/Shopping:	Title Insurance:	Residential Construction:			Online Services:	Residential Sales:
Offices:	Property Insurance:	Land Development:			Software/IT:	Specialty:
Hotels/Motels:		Support Services:	Y		Consulting:	
Industrial/Warehouses:		Design/Engineering:	Y			
Other:						

TYPES OF BUSINESS:

Construction, Heavy & Civil Engineering
Sewer & Pipe Rehabilitation Services

BRANDS/DIVISIONS/AFFILIATES:

Insituform CIPP Process
Insituform Blue
United Pipeline Systems
Corrpro Companies, Inc.
Bayou Companies (The)
Insitu Envirotech (S.E. Asia) Pte Ltd.

CONTACTS: *Note: Officers with more than one job title may be intentionally listed here more than once.*

J. Joseph Burgess, CEO
J. Joseph Burgess, Pres.
David A. Martin, CFO/VP
Holly Sharp, VP-Human Resources
David F. Morris, Chief Admin. Officer/Sr. VP
David F. Morris, General Counsel/Corp. Sec.
Kenneth Young, Treas./VP
Holly Sharp, VP-Environmental, Health & Safety
Charles Voltz, Sr. VP-North American Rehabilitation
Dorwin Hawn, Sr. VP-Energy & Mining
Daniel Cowan, VP-APAC
Alfred L. Woods, Chmn.
Alex Buehler, VP-Europe

Phone: 636-530-8000	**Fax:** 636-519-8010
Toll-Free: 800-234-2992	
Address: 17988 Edison Ave., Chesterfield, MO 63005-3700 US	

GROWTH PLANS/SPECIAL FEATURES:

Insituform Technologies is provider of proprietary technologies and pipeline rehabilitation services to the sewer, water, energy and mining infrastructure markets. The firm's products are sold in over 70 countries on six continents. Most of Insituform's installation operations are project-oriented contracts for municipal entities, concerning the maintenance of municipal sewers, commercial pipes and water mains. The company and its subsidiaries operate principally in the U.S., Canada, the Netherlands, the U.K., Portugal France, Switzerland, Chile, Spain, Poland, Mexico, Belgium, Romania and India. The firm's operations comprise the five following operating segments: North American Sewer Rehabilitation; European Sewer Rehabilitation; Asia-Pacific Sewer Rehabilitation; Water Rehabilitation; and Energy and Mining. Sewer rehabilitation services include the firm's proprietary Insituform Cured-In-Place Pipe (CIPP) process, a trenchless technology allowing pipeline to be repaired without digging and major service disruptions. Insituform's CIPP process involves saturating a synthetic fiber tube with a thermosetting resin, installing the tube into a host pipe and then hardening the resin, forming a new rigid pipe-within-a-pipe. Water rehabilitation activities are focused on pipelines carrying drinking water and include the firm's Insituform Blue brand of potable water pipe restoration services. The company's subsidiaries include United Pipeline Systems, a provider of high-density polyethylene (HDPE) lining systems used for the protection of internal pipelines; Corrpro Companies, Inc., a provider of corrosion protection and pipeline maintenance services in North America; and The Bayou Companies, a provider of pipeline services to energy and infrastructure firms, primarily in the Gulf of Mexico and North America. In early 2010, the firm acquired its former Singaporean licensee, Insitu Envirotech (S.E. Asia) Pte Ltd., for $1.3 million.

Employees are offered retirement plans; a 401(k) plan; disability coverage; and life insurance.

FINANCIALS: Sales and profits are in thousands of dollars—add 000 to get the full amount. 2010 Note: Financial information for 2010 was not available for all companies at press time.

2010 Sales: $914,975	2010 Profits: $60,462	**U.S. Stock Ticker:** INSU
2009 Sales: $726,866	2009 Profits: $26,171	**Int'l Ticker:** Int'l Exchange:
2008 Sales: $536,664	2008 Profits: $21,640	Employees: 3,200
2007 Sales: $495,570	2007 Profits: $2,543	Fiscal Year Ends: 12/31
2006 Sales: $527,419	2006 Profits: $24,678	Parent Company:

SALARIES/BENEFITS:

Pension Plan: Y	ESOP Stock Plan:	Profit Sharing:	Top Exec. Salary: $565,000	Bonus: $882,768
Savings Plan: Y	Stock Purch. Plan:		Second Exec. Salary: $345,000	Bonus: $349,151

OTHER THOUGHTS:

Apparent Women Officers or Directors: 3
Hot Spot for Advancement for Women/Minorities: Y

LOCATIONS: ("Y" = Yes)

West:	Southwest:	Midwest:	Southeast:	Northeast:	International:
Y	Y	Y	Y	Y	Y

INTEGRATED ELECTRICAL SERVICES

www.ies-co.com

Industry Group Code: 238210 Ranks within this company's industry group: Sales: 2   Profits: 1

Properties:	Financial Services:	Construction/Development:		Investments:	Specialty Services:	Brokerage:
Apartments:	Mortgages:	Commercial Construction:		REIT:	Property Management:	Commercial Sales:
Malls/Shopping:	Title Insurance:	Residential Construction:			Online Services:	Residential Sales:
Offices:	Property Insurance:	Land Development:			Software/IT:	Specialty:
Hotels/Motels:		Support Services:	Y		Consulting:	
Industrial/Warehouses:		Design/Engineering:	Y			
Other:						

TYPES OF BUSINESS:

Electric Contractors
Electrical & Communications Installation & Maintenance
Residential Building & Remodeling
Commercial & Industrial Renovations

BRANDS/DIVISIONS/AFFILIATES:

Key Electric Supply
Tesla Power & Automation

CONTACTS: Note: Officers with more than one job title may be intentionally listed here more than once.

Michael J. Caliel, CEO
Michael J. Caliel, Pres.
Terryy L. Freeman, CFO/Sr. VP
Bill Fiedler, General Counsel/Sr. VP/Corp. Sec.
Harvey Hammock, VP-Safety & Productivity
Michael J. Caliel, Acting Head-IES Commercial & Industrial
Richard Nix, VP-IES Residential
James M. Lindstrom, Chmn.

Phone: 713-860-1500	Fax: 713-222-1214
Toll-Free: 877-437-6285	
Address: 1800 W. Loop S., Ste. 500, Houston, TX 77027 US	

GROWTH PLANS/SPECIAL FEATURES:

Integrated Electrical Services (IES) is a provider of electrical contracting services in the U.S., with approximately 69 locations in the continental 48 states. The firm's offerings include: design of the electrical distribution systems within a building; procurement and installation of wiring; connection to power sources, end-use equipment and fixtures; and long-term contract maintenance. IES works in the commercial/industrial, communications and residential markets and its customer base encompasses general contractors; property managers and developers; corporations; government agencies and municipalities; and homeowners. The types of projects the firm engages in include high-rise residential and office buildings; power plants; manufacturing facilities; municipal infrastructure; health care facilities; and residential developments. To complement its electrical contracting services, IES provides low voltage services, utility services and maintenance services. The company's low voltage services include design and installation of external cables for corporations, universities, data centers and switching stations for data communications companies as well as the installation of fire and security alarm systems. Its utility services consist of overhead and underground installation and maintenance of electrical and other utilities transmission and distribution networks; installation and splicing of high-voltage transmission and distribution lines; substation construction; and substation and right-of-way maintenance. Maintenance is a general service provided by IES. Commercial and industrial work generates roughly 59.6% of the firm's revenue; residential work generates 22.6%; and communications work accounts for 17.5%. In December 2010, IES agreed to sell its light manufacturing plant, Tesla Power & Automation to Siemens Energy, Inc. In February 2011, the firm sold its electrical distribution operation, Key Electric Supply. In March 2011, the company opened a new office in California.

FINANCIALS: Sales and profits are in thousands of dollars—add 000 to get the full amount. 2010 Note: Financial information for 2010 was not available for all companies at press time.

2010 Sales: $460,633	2010 Profits: $-32,147	**U.S. Stock Ticker: IESC**
2009 Sales: $665,997	2009 Profits: $-11,820	**Int'l Ticker:** Int'l Exchange:
2008 Sales: $818,287	2008 Profits: $- 187	Employees: 2,921
2007 Sales: $890,351	2007 Profits: $-4,412	Fiscal Year Ends: 9/30
2006 Sales: $933,800	2006 Profits: $- 400	Parent Company:

SALARIES/BENEFITS:

Pension Plan:	ESOP Stock Plan:	Profit Sharing:	Top Exec. Salary: $610,000	Bonus: $
Savings Plan: Y	Stock Purch. Plan:		Second Exec. Salary: $350,000	Bonus: $

OTHER THOUGHTS:

Apparent Women Officers or Directors:
Hot Spot for Advancement for Women/Minorities:

LOCATIONS: ("Y" = Yes)

West:	Southwest:	Midwest:	Southeast:	Northeast:	International:
Y	Y	Y	Y	Y	

INTERCONTINENTAL HOTELS GROUP PLC   www.ihgplc.com

Industry Group Code: 721110 Ranks within this company's industry group: Sales: 9   Profits: 7

Properties:		Financial Services:	Construction/Development:	Investments:	Specialty Services:		Brokerage:
Apartments:		Mortgages:	Commercial Construction:	REIT:	Property Management:	Y	Commercial Sales:
Malls/Shopping:		Title Insurance:	Residential Construction:		Online Services:		Residential Sales:
Offices:		Property Insurance:	Land Development:		Software/IT:		Specialty:
Hotels/Motels:	Y		Support Services:		Consulting:		
Industrial/Warehouses:			Design/Engineering:				
Other:							

TYPES OF BUSINESS:

Hotel & Motel Development & Management
Hotels

BRANDS/DIVISIONS/AFFILIATES:

InterContinental Hotels and Resorts
Crowne Plaza Hotels and Resorts
Hotel Indigo
Staybridge Suites
Holiday Inn
Holiday Inn Express
Candlewood Suites
Priority Club Rewards

CONTACTS: *Note: Officers with more than one job title may be intentionally listed here more than once.*

Andrew Cosslett, CEO
Richard Solomons, CFO/Head-Commercial Dev.
Tom Seddon, Chief Mktg. Officer/Exec. VP
Tracy Robbins, Exec. VP-Global Human Resources & Oper. Support
Tom Conophy, CIO/Exec. VP
George Turner, General Counsel/Exec. VP/Corp. Sec.
James R. Abrahamson, Pres., Americas
Keith Barr, Managing Dir.-Greater China
Jan Smits, Managing Dir.-Asia & Australiasia
William Morris, Managing Dir.-U.K. & Ireland
David Webster, Chmn.
Kirk Kinsell, Pres., EMEA

Phone: 44-1895-512-000	**Fax:** 44-1895-512-101
Toll-Free:	
Address: Broadwater Park, Denham, UB9 5HR UK	

GROWTH PLANS/SPECIAL FEATURES:

InterContinental Hotels Group plc (IHG) is an international hotel and hospitality firm operating eight hotel brands: Holiday Inn, Holiday Inn Express, Holiday Inn Club Vacations, Hotel Indigo, Crowne Plaza, InterContinental, Staybridge Suites and Candlewood Suites. IHG franchises, manages or owns/leases approximately 4,395 hotels (over 645,000 rooms) in over 100 countries and territories. Its properties accommodate over 146 million stays per year. Mid-scale, full-service Holiday Inn is most prevalent in the U.S., the U.K. and China. It currently operates 1,241 Holiday Inn-branded locations. Its 2,075 Holiday Inn Express properties are value-priced, limited-service hotels primarily operated by franchisees. Its newly introduced Holiday Inn Club Vacations properties are resorts located in six U.S. vacation destinations: Orlando and Panama City, Florida; Myrtle Beach, South Carolina; Lake Geneva, Wisconsin; Brownsville, Vermont; and Gatlinburg, Tennessee. The firm's 38 Hotel Indigo properties are boutique hotels located in urban, mid-town and suburban areas that are in close proximity to restaurants, businesses and entertainment venues throughout the U.S. The 388 Crowne Plaza and 171 InterContinental hotels cater to business and leisure travelers in nearly 60 countries. Its 188 Staybridge Suites and 288 Candlewood Suites provide extended-stay options. IHG offers Priority Club Rewards, which provides benefits like free stays and frequent flyer miles. It currently has more than 56 million active members. In 2010, revenues generated by geographic segment were as follows: Americas, 50%; EMEA, 25%; Asia Pacific, 19%; and Central, 6%. In October 2010, it signed a ten-year license agreement with Las Vegas Sands Corp. to affiliate The Venetian and The Palazzo with the InterContinental's global portfolio.

The firm typically offers employees benefits including life, disability, medical and dental insurance; paid time off; employee discounts; a 401(k); incentive programs; and educational assistance.

FINANCIALS: Sales and profits are in thousands of dollars—add 000 to get the full amount. 2010 Note: Financial information for 2010 was not available for all companies at press time.

2010 Sales: $1,628,000	2010 Profits: $280,000	**U.S. Stock Ticker: IHG**
2009 Sales: $1,538,000	2009 Profits: $214,000	**Int'l Ticker: IHG** Int'l Exchange: London-LSE
2008 Sales: $1,897,000	2008 Profits: $262,000	Employees: 7,858
2007 Sales: $1,771,000	2007 Profits: $444,000	Fiscal Year Ends: 12/31
2006 Sales: $1,548,400	2006 Profits: $797,900	Parent Company:

SALARIES/BENEFITS:

Pension Plan: Y	ESOP Stock Plan:	Profit Sharing:	Top Exec. Salary: $	Bonus: $
Savings Plan: Y	Stock Purch. Plan:		Second Exec. Salary: $	Bonus: $

OTHER THOUGHTS:

Apparent Women Officers or Directors: 3
Hot Spot for Advancement for Women/Minorities: Y

LOCATIONS: ("Y" = Yes)

West:	Southwest:	Midwest:	Southeast:	Northeast:	International:
Y	Y	Y	Y	Y	Y

INTERSTATE HOTELS & RESORTS INC

www.ihrco.com

Industry Group Code: 721110 Ranks within this company's industry group: Sales: Profits:

Properties:		Financial Services:	Construction/Development:		Investments:	Specialty Services:		Brokerage:
Apartments:		Mortgages:	Commercial Construction:	Y	REIT:	Property Management:	Y	Commercial Sales:
Malls/Shopping:		Title Insurance:	Residential Construction:			Online Services:		Residential Sales:
Offices:		Property Insurance:	Land Development:			Software/IT:		Specialty:
Hotels/Motels:	Y		Support Services:	Y		Consulting:		
Industrial/Warehouses:			Design/Engineering:	Y				
Other:								

TYPES OF BUSINESS:

Hotel Management
Corporate Hotel Management
Engineering & Design Consulting
Construction Management
Procurement Services

BRANDS/DIVISIONS/AFFILIATES:

Hotel Acquisition Company LLC
Thayer Hotel Investors
Shanghai Jin Jiang International Hotels
Continental Design & Supply Company
Crowne Plaza Milwaukee Airport
TownePlace Suites Bethlehem-Easton
Hilton Garden Inn Baton Rouge Airport
Interstate China Hotels & Resorts

CONTACTS:
Note: *Officers with more than one job title may be intentionally listed here more than once.*

Thomas F. Hewitt, CEO
George J. Brennan, Exec. VP-Mktg. & Sales
Christopher L. Bennett, General Counsel/Exec. VP
Samuel E. Knighton, Pres., Hotel Oper.
Martin Reid, Exec. VP-Dev. & Acquisitions
Joseph A. Klam, Exec. VP-Finance
Leslie Ng, Chief Investment Officer
Thomas J. Bardenett, Exec. VP-Oper., Crossroads
Thomas F. Hewitt, Chmn.
Kenneth W. McLaren, Exec. VP-Int'l Oper.

Phone: 703-387-3100	Fax: 703-543-0633
Toll-Free:	
Address: 4501 N. Fairfax Dr., Arlington, VA 22203 US	

GROWTH PLANS/SPECIAL FEATURES:

Interstate Hotels & Resorts, Inc. is one of the world's largest independent hotel management companies. The company is a subsidiary of Hotel Acquisition Company LLC, a joint venture between subsidiaries of Thayer Hotel Investors V-A LP, a private equity fund, and Shanghai Jin Jiang International Hotels. The firm divides its operations into three primary categories: hotel management services, hotel development services and design and construction services. Interstate's hotel management services consist of finance and accounting services, including accounting, internal audit and risk management; sales and marketing services; food and beverage services, including concept development and staff training; business intelligence services; and international platform management. Interstate manages luxury, full-service, select-service and extended-stay hospitality properties, consisting of 311 properties. These properties are located in 39 U.S. states, Washington, D.C., Belgium, Canada, Ireland, England, Russia, Mexico and India. The company's development services comprise hotel and resort investment, business development, financing, acquisitions, franchising, owner relations and hotel operations solutions. Finally, its design and construction services, provided through subsidiary Continental Design & Supply Company, consist of supply and equipment procurement, design management, project and construction management and engineering consulting services. The company's brand portfolio includes Best Western; Comfort Inn; Courtyard by Marriott; Crowne Plaza; Days Inn; Doubletree; Embassy Suites; Fairfield Inn by Marriott; Hampton Inn; Hilton; Holiday Inn; Homewood Suites; Hyatt Place; Marriott; Radisson; Renaissance; Residence Inn by Marriott; Sheraton; Super 8; Travelodge; and Westin. In March 2010, the company was acquired by joint venture Hotel Acquisition Company. In April 2010, the firm entered into a joint venture with Jin Jiang Hotels Company Limited to create Interstate China Hotels & Resorts, a hotel management company based in China. Also in April 2010, the company entered into a strategic alliance with International Hotel Investments Ltd. to operates and invest in European hotels.

FINANCIALS:
Sales and profits are in thousands of dollars—add 000 to get the full amount. 2010 Note: Financial information for 2010 was not available for all companies at press time.

2010 Sales: $	2010 Profits: $	**U.S. Stock Ticker: Joint Venture**
2009 Sales: $	2009 Profits: $	**Int'l Ticker:** Int'l Exchange:
2008 Sales: $779,453	2008 Profits: $-18,023	Employees: 19,000
2007 Sales: $800,131	2007 Profits: $22,828	Fiscal Year Ends: 12/31
2006 Sales: $975,165	2006 Profits: $29,779	Parent Company:

SALARIES/BENEFITS:

Pension Plan:	ESOP Stock Plan:	Profit Sharing:	Top Exec. Salary: $500,000	Bonus: $125,000
Savings Plan:	Stock Purch. Plan:		Second Exec. Salary: $374,071	Bonus: $93,518

OTHER THOUGHTS:

Apparent Women Officers or Directors:
Hot Spot for Advancement for Women/Minorities:

LOCATIONS: ("Y" = Yes)

West:	Southwest:	Midwest:	Southeast:	Northeast:	International:
Y	Y	Y	Y	Y	Y

INTOWN SUITES MANAGEMENT INC

www.intownsuites.com

Industry Group Code: 721110 Ranks within this company's industry group: Sales: Profits:

Properties:		Financial Services:	Construction/Development:		Investments:	Specialty Services:		Brokerage:
Apartments:		Mortgages:	Commercial Construction:		REIT:	Property Management:	Y	Commercial Sales:
Malls/Shopping:		Title Insurance:	Residential Construction:			Online Services:		Residential Sales:
Offices:		Property Insurance:	Land Development:			Software/IT:		Specialty:
Hotels/Motels:	Y		Support Services:			Consulting:		
Industrial/Warehouses:			Design/Engineering:					
Other:								

TYPES OF BUSINESS:

Hotels
Extended-Stay Hotels

BRANDS/DIVISIONS/AFFILIATES:

Westmont Hospitality Group

CONTACTS: *Note: Officers with more than one job title may be intentionally listed here more than once.*

Scott Griffith, CEO
Dennis Cassel, CFO
Stephen Bell, Dir.-IT

Phone: 770-799-5000	**Fax:** 770-437-8190
Toll-Free: 800-553-9338	
Address: 2727 Paces Ferry Rd., Ste. 2-1200, Atlanta, GA 30339 US	

GROWTH PLANS/SPECIAL FEATURES:

Intown Suites Management, Inc. is a private corporation that develops, owns and operates budget extended-stay properties. The company does not offer reservations for less than seven days and prefers long-term commitments or apartment leases. A seven-day stay at Intown Suites is generally cheaper than renting a nightly room at a traditional hotel for a few days. Most facilities are located in predominately retail-oriented locations near shops, restaurants and movie theaters, with proximity to major metropolitan areas, spanning 130 locations in 21 states. Intown's properties typically feature 121 studio suites with full amenities, including complete kitchens, high-speed Internet, a dining area, cable TV, a full size bath, voicemail service, laundry facilities, pool areas and weekly housekeeping. Intown Suites was one of the first hotel chains in the U.S. to offer free high-speed Internet access in all of its hotel rooms. The company also offers specialized services for corporate customers. Intown is currently focused on accelerating the growth of its operations, and it will convert all newly acquired properties to the Intown Suites brand. Certain locations are also undergoing renovation and development, which in some cases significantly increasing the number of rooms. Westmont Hospitality Group operates InTown Suites' properties.

FINANCIALS: Sales and profits are in thousands of dollars—add 000 to get the full amount. 2010 Note: Financial information for 2010 was not available for all companies at press time.

2010 Sales: $	2010 Profits: $	**U.S. Stock Ticker: Private**
2009 Sales: $	2009 Profits: $	**Int'l Ticker:** Int'l Exchange:
2008 Sales: $	2008 Profits: $	Employees:
2007 Sales: $	2007 Profits: $	Fiscal Year Ends: 12/31
2006 Sales: $	2006 Profits: $	Parent Company:

SALARIES/BENEFITS:

Pension Plan:	ESOP Stock Plan:	Profit Sharing:	Top Exec. Salary: $	Bonus: $
Savings Plan:	Stock Purch. Plan:		Second Exec. Salary: $	Bonus: $

OTHER THOUGHTS:

Apparent Women Officers or Directors:
Hot Spot for Advancement for Women/Minorities:

LOCATIONS: ("Y" = Yes)

West:	Southwest:	Midwest:	Southeast:	Northeast:	International:
Y	Y	Y	Y	Y	

INVESTORS REAL ESTATE TRUST

www.iret.com

Industry Group Code: 531110 Ranks within this company's industry group: Sales: 14   Profits: 11

Properties:		Financial Services:		Construction/Development:	Investments:		Specialty Services:	Brokerage:
Apartments:	Y	Mortgages:	Y	Commercial Construction:	REIT:	Y	Property Management:	Commercial Sales:
Malls/Shopping:	Y	Title Insurance:	Y	Residential Construction:			Online Services:	Residential Sales:
Offices:	Y	Property Insurance:	Y	Land Development:			Software/IT:	Specialty:
Hotels/Motels:				Support Services:			Consulting:	
Industrial/Warehouses:	Y			Design/Engineering:				
Other:	Y							

TYPES OF BUSINESS:

Real Estate Investment Trust
Apartment Communities
Retail, Office & Industrial Properties
Medical Properties

BRANDS/DIVISIONS/AFFILIATES:

IRET Properties, LP

CONTACTS: *Note: Officers with more than one job title may be intentionally listed here more than once.*

Timothy P. Mihalick, CEO
Thomas A. Wentz, Jr., COO/Sr. VP
Timothy P. Mihalick, Pres.
Diane K. Bryantt, CFO/Sr. VP
Thomas A. Wentz, Sr., CIO/Sr. VP
Michael Bosh, General Counsel/Sr. VP
Karin M. Wentz, Sr. VP/Corp. Sec./Associate General Counsel
Charles A. Greenberg, Sr. VP-Asset Management Group
Jeffrey L. Miller, Chmn.

Phone: 701-837-4738	**Fax:** 701-838-7785
Toll-Free: 888-478-4738	
Address: 3015 16th St. SW, Ste. 100, Minot, ND 58702-1988 US	

GROWTH PLANS/SPECIAL FEATURES:

Investors Real Estate Trust is a self-advised real estate investment trust (REIT) involved in the ownership and operation of multi-family residential, commercial office, medical, industrial and retail properties. The firm conducts its business operations through its operating partnership, IRET Properties. By category, the portfolio contains approximately 78 multi-family residential properties, with a total of 9,691 apartment units; 67 office properties containing 5 million square feet of leasable space; 54 medical properties, including senior housing properties, for a total of approximately 2.6 million square feet of leasable space; 19 industrial properties, with a total of 3 million square feet of leasable space; and 33 retail properties, containing approximately 1.4 million square feet of leasable space. These property types also represent the company's five business segments. Gauged by investment amount, approximately 33% of the company's portfolio consists of office properties; 28.5% consists of multi-family residential properties; and 25.3% is made up of medical properties, while industrial properties and retail properties make up the remaining 6.8% and 6.4% of the portfolio, respectively. Investors Real Estate Trust outsources the day-to-day management of many of its properties to other companies; however, during 2010 the firm began to transfer the management of some of its multi-family residential properties to its own employees. The trust's main geographical area of concentration is in the upper Midwest, primarily Minnesota and North Dakota, with these two states together representing approximately 67.4% of 2010 revenue. The firm also owns properties in Colorado, Kansas, Nebraska, South Dakota, Wyoming, Montana, Idaho, Missouri, Iowa, Wisconsin and Michigan. Over the course of 2010, the company acquired two multi-family residential properties, one office property, five medical properties, one industrial property and a plot of unimproved land for purchase prices totaling approximately $55.4 million.

FINANCIALS: Sales and profits are in thousands of dollars—add 000 to get the full amount. 2010 Note: Financial information for 2010 was not available for all companies at press time.

2010 Sales: $242,775	2010 Profits: $4,585	**U.S. Stock Ticker: IRETS**
2009 Sales: $240,005	2009 Profits: $8,526	**Int'l Ticker:** Int'l Exchange:
2008 Sales: $221,170	2008 Profits: $12,088	Employees: 218
2007 Sales: $197,817	2007 Profits: $14,110	Fiscal Year Ends: 4/30
2006 Sales: $170,448	2006 Profits: $11,567	Parent Company:

SALARIES/BENEFITS:

Pension Plan:	ESOP Stock Plan:	Profit Sharing:	Top Exec. Salary: $363,958	Bonus: $47,500
Savings Plan: Y	Stock Purch. Plan:		Second Exec. Salary: $307,813	Bonus: $40,625

OTHER THOUGHTS:

Apparent Women Officers or Directors: 2
Hot Spot for Advancement for Women/Minorities:

LOCATIONS: ("Y" = Yes)

West:	Southwest:	Midwest:	Southeast:	Northeast:	International:
Y		Y			

INVESTORS TITLE COMPANY

www.invtitle.com

Industry Group Code: 524127 Ranks within this company's industry group: Sales: 4   Profits: 3

Properties:		Financial Services:		Construction/Development:	Investments:	Specialty Services:	Brokerage:
Apartments:		Mortgages:		Commercial Construction:	REIT:	Property Management:	Commercial Sales:
Malls/Shopping:		Title Insurance:	Y	Residential Construction:		Online Services:	Residential Sales:
Offices:		Property Insurance:	Y	Land Development:		Software/IT:	Specialty:
Hotels/Motels:				Support Services:		Consulting:	
Industrial/Warehouses:				Design/Engineering:			
Other:							

TYPES OF BUSINESS:

Title Insurance
Tax-Deferred Exchange Services
Reinsurance

BRANDS/DIVISIONS/AFFILIATES:

Investors Title Insurance Company (ITIC)
National Investors Title Insurance (NITIC)
Investors Title Exchange Corporation (ITEC)
Investors Title Accommodation Corporation (ITAC)
Investors Capital Management Company
Investors Title Management Services
Investors Trust Company

CONTACTS: *Note: Officers with more than one job title may be intentionally listed here more than once.*

J. Allen Fine, CEO
James A. Fine, Jr., Pres.
W. Morris Fine, Exec. VP/Sec.
James A. Fine, Jr., Treas.
W. Morris Fine, Pres./COO-Investors Title Insurance Company
J. Allen Fine, Chmn.

Phone: 919-968-2200	**Fax:** 919-968-2235
Toll-Free: 800-326-4842	
Address: 121 N. Columbia St., Chapel Hill, NC 27514 US	

GROWTH PLANS/SPECIAL FEATURES:

Investors Title Company is a holding company that, through its subsidiaries, issues and underwrites title insurance policies. Through its subsidiaries, Investors Title Insurance Company (ITIC) and National Investors Title Insurance (NITIC), the company underwrites land title insurance for owners and mortgages as a primary insurer and as a reinsurer for other title insurance companies. ITIC markets title insurance through issuing agents and branch offices in 23 states. NITIC writes title insurance as a primary insurer and as a reinsurer in the state of New York and is also licensed to write title insurance in 19 additional states and Washington, D.C. Additionally, the company provides management services to title insurance agencies through Investors Title Management Services. Investors Title also provides tax-deferred real property exchange services through subsidiaries Investors Title Exchange Corporation (ITEC) and Investors Title Accommodation Corporation (ITAC). ITEC acts as an intermediary in tax-deferred exchanges of property held for productive use in a business or for investments. The subsidiary's income is primarily derived from fees for handling exchange transactions. ITAC serves as an exchange accommodation titleholder, offering services for accomplishing reverse exchanges when a taxpayer must acquire replacement property before selling the relinquished property. Through Investors Trust Company and Investors Capital Management Company, the firm offers investment management and trust services to individuals, companies, banks and trusts.

Employees are offered medical, dental and vision insurance; disability coverage; life and AD&D insurance; flexible spending accounts; an employee assistance program; and a 401(k) plan.

FINANCIALS: Sales and profits are in thousands of dollars—add 000 to get the full amount. 2010 Note: Financial information for 2010 was not available for all companies at press time.

2010 Sales: $71,309	2010 Profits: $6,373	**U.S. Stock Ticker:** ITIC
2009 Sales: $71,308	2009 Profits: $4,829	**Int'l Ticker:** Int'l Exchange:
2008 Sales: $71,123	2008 Profits: $-1,183	Employees: 196
2007 Sales: $84,942	2007 Profits: $8,402	Fiscal Year Ends: 12/31
2006 Sales: $86,662	2006 Profits: $13,185	Parent Company:

SALARIES/BENEFITS:

Pension Plan:	ESOP Stock Plan:	Profit Sharing:	Top Exec. Salary: $303,360	Bonus: $90,000
Savings Plan: Y	Stock Purch. Plan:		Second Exec. Salary: $255,560	Bonus: $130,000

OTHER THOUGHTS:

Apparent Women Officers or Directors:
Hot Spot for Advancement for Women/Minorities:

LOCATIONS: ("Y" = Yes)

West:	Southwest:	Midwest:	Southeast:	Northeast:	International:
		Y		Y	

ISTAR FINANCIAL INC

www.istarfinancial.com

Industry Group Code: 531120 Ranks within this company's industry group: Sales: 30   Profits: 27

Properties:		Financial Services:		Construction/Development:	Investments:		Specialty Services:		Brokerage:
Apartments:		Mortgages:	Y	Commercial Construction:	REIT:	Y	Property Management:		Commercial Sales:
Malls/Shopping:	Y	Title Insurance:		Residential Construction:			Online Services:		Residential Sales:
Offices:	Y	Property Insurance:		Land Development:			Software/IT:		Specialty:
Hotels/Motels:	Y			Support Services:			Consulting:		
Industrial/Warehouses:	Y			Design/Engineering:					
Other:									

TYPES OF BUSINESS:

Financial Services
Real Estate Investment Trust
Mortgages & Loans
Asset Services
Corporate Finance
Corporate Leasing

BRANDS/DIVISIONS/AFFILIATES:

South of Fifth

CONTACTS:
Note: Officers with more than one job title may be intentionally listed here more than once.

Jay Sugarman, CEO
David M. DiStaso, CFO
Andrew G. Backman, Sr. VP-Mktg.
Nina B. Matis, Chief Legal Officer
Andrew G. Backman, Sr. VP-Investor Rel.
Collin Cochrane, Chief Acct. Officer
Nina B. Matis, Chief Investment Officer
Chase S. Curtis, Jr., Exec. VP-Credit
Michelle M. MacKay, Exec. VP-Investments
Barbara Rubin, Pres., iStar Asset Svcs.
Jay Sugarman, Chmn.

Phone: 212-930-9400	**Fax:** 212-930-9494
Toll-Free:	
Address: 1114 Ave. of the Americas, 39th Fl., New York, NY 10036 US	

GROWTH PLANS/SPECIAL FEATURES:

iStar Financial, Inc. is a finance company focused on the commercial real estate industry and is taxed as a real estate investment trust (REIT). The firm provides custom-tailored financing to high-end private and corporate owners of real estate. iStar's primary lines of business are lending and corporate tenant leasing. The lending business is primarily comprised of senior and mezzanine real estate loans that typically range in size from $20 million to $150 million and have maturities generally ranging from three to 10 years. The corporate tenant leasing business operates by purchase or leasebacks and by acquiring facilities subject to existing long-term net leases such as mission-critical headquarters or distribution facilities and general-purpose real estate with residual values that represent a discount to current market values and replacement costs. The company is focused on expanding its market-leading platforms; adding key personnel; building strategic relationships; and working to deliver comprehensive capital result to the marketplace. iStar generally seeks corporate customers that are established companies with a stable core and businesses or market leadership in growing industries. Approximately 46% of iStar's assets are in first mortgages/senior debt; corporate tenant leases make up 24%; REHI makes up 9%; OREO accounts for 8%; mezzanine/subordinated debt makes up 7%; and other investments make up the final 6%. The company's properties are broken into the following categories: Apartment/Residential, 23%; Land, 16%; Retail, 12%; Office, 10%; Industrial, 9%; Entertainment/Leisure, 9%; Hotel, 7%; Mixed Use, 6%; and Other, 8%. Approximately 4% of the firm's portfolio is outside the U.S. In January 2011, iStar acquired all remaining interest in South of Fifth, a luxury condominium project in Miami Beach, Florida.

iStar provides employees benefits including health, life and disability insurance plans; a 401(k) plan; and paid time off.

FINANCIALS:
Sales and profits are in thousands of dollars—add 000 to get the full amount. **2010 Note: Financial information for 2010 was not available for all companies at press time.**

2010 Sales: $575,251	2010 Profits: $80,206	**U.S. Stock Ticker:** SFI
2009 Sales: $766,198	2009 Profits: $-769,847	**Int'l Ticker:** Int'l Exchange:
2008 Sales: $1,229,044	2008 Profits: $-181,767	Employees: 200
2007 Sales: $1,404,459	2007 Profits: $236,602	Fiscal Year Ends: 12/31
2006 Sales: $933,752	2006 Profits: $374,827	Parent Company:

SALARIES/BENEFITS:

Pension Plan:	ESOP Stock Plan:	Profit Sharing:	Top Exec. Salary: $1,000,000	Bonus: $1,999,000
Savings Plan: Y	Stock Purch. Plan:		Second Exec. Salary: $350,000	Bonus: $1,350,000

OTHER THOUGHTS:

Apparent Women Officers or Directors: 4
Hot Spot for Advancement for Women/Minorities: Y

LOCATIONS: ("Y" = Yes)

West:	Southwest:	Midwest:	Southeast:	Northeast:	International:
Y	Y	Y	Y	Y	

JACOBS ENGINEERING GROUP INC

www.jacobs.com

Industry Group Code: 237 Ranks within this company's industry group: Sales: 13   Profits: 16

Properties:	Financial Services:	Construction/Development:		Investments:	Specialty Services:		Brokerage:
Apartments:	Mortgages:	Commercial Construction:	Y	REIT:	Property Management:	Y	Commercial Sales:
Malls/Shopping:	Title Insurance:	Residential Construction:			Online Services:		Residential Sales:
Offices:	Property Insurance:	Land Development:			Software/IT:		Specialty:
Hotels/Motels:		Support Services:			Consulting:	Y	
Industrial/Warehouses:		Design/Engineering:	Y				
Other:							

TYPES OF BUSINESS:

Engineering & Design Services
Facility Management
Construction & Field Services
Technical Consulting Services
Environmental Services

BRANDS/DIVISIONS/AFFILIATES:

TechTeam Government Solutions, Inc.
LeighFisher, Inc.
Jacobs Engineering SA

CONTACTS: *Note: Officers with more than one job title may be intentionally listed here more than once.*

Craig Martin, CEO
Craig Martin, Pres.
Andrew F. Kremer, Sr. VP-Global Sales
Patricia H. Summers, Sr. VP-Human Resources
Cora L. Carmody, Sr. VP-IT
John W. Prosser, Jr., Exec. VP-Admin.
William C. Markley III, General Counsel/Sec./Sr. VP
Thomas R. Hammond, Exec. VP-Oper.
John McLachlan, Sr. VP-Strategy & Acquisitions
John W. Prosser, Jr., Exec. VP-Finance/Treas.
John Machlan, Sr. VP-Acquisitions
George A. Kunberger, Jr., Exec. VP-Oper.
Rogers F. Starr, Pres., Jacobs Technology, Inc.
Nazim Thawerbhoy, Sr. VP/Controller
Noel G. Watson, Chmn.

Phone: 626-578-3500	Fax: 626-568-7144
Toll-Free:	
Address: 1111 S. Arroyo Pkwy., Pasadena, CA 91105 US	

GROWTH PLANS/SPECIAL FEATURES:

Jacobs Engineering Group, Inc. offers technical, professional, and construction services to industrial, commercial and governmental clients throughout North America, Europe, Asia, South America, India, the U.K. and Australia. The company's global network includes more than 160 offices in over 20 countries. The company provides project services, which include engineering, design and architecture; process, scientific, and systems consulting services; operations and maintenance services; and construction services, which include direct-hire construction and management services. Services are offered to selected industry groups such as oil and gas exploration, production, and refining; programs for various federal governments; pharmaceuticals and biotechnology; chemicals and polymers; buildings, which includes projects in the fields of health care and education as well as civic, governmental, and other buildings; infrastructure; technology and manufacturing; and pulp and paper, among others. Jacobs also provides pricing studies, project feasibility reports and automation and control system analysis for U.S. government agencies involved in defense and aerospace programs. In addition, the company is one of the leading providers of environmental engineering and consulting services in the U.S. and abroad, including hazardous and nuclear waste management and site cleanup and closure, providing support in such areas as underground storage tank removal, contaminated soil and water remediation, and long-term groundwater monitoring. Jacobs also designs, builds, installs, operates and maintains various types of soil and groundwater cleanup systems. In March 2010, the company formed Jacobs Engineering SA, a joint venture with OCP SA, to provide industrial services in Morocco. In July 2010, Jacobs established management and strategy consultancy subsidiary LeighFisher, Inc. In October 2010, the firm acquired TechTeam Government Solutions, Inc. from TechTeam Global, Inc. In February 2011, the company acquired several process and construction operations of Aker Solutions.

Jacobs offers its employees medical, disability, life and AD&D insurance; an employee tock purchase plan; tuition reimbursement; retirement benefits and more.

FINANCIALS: Sales and profits are in thousands of dollars—add 000 to get the full amount. 2010 Note: Financial information for 2010 was not available for all companies at press time.

2010 Sales: $9,915,517	2010 Profits: $245,974	**U.S. Stock Ticker: JEC**
2009 Sales: $11,467,376	2009 Profits: $399,854	**Int'l Ticker:** Int'l Exchange:
2008 Sales: $11,252,159	2008 Profits: $420,742	Employees: 38,500
2007 Sales: $8,473,970	2007 Profits: $287,130	Fiscal Year Ends: 9/30
2006 Sales: $7,421,270	2006 Profits: $196,883	Parent Company:

SALARIES/BENEFITS:

Pension Plan:	ESOP Stock Plan:	Profit Sharing:	Top Exec. Salary: $1,165,385	Bonus: $674,062
Savings Plan: Y	Stock Purch. Plan: Y		Second Exec. Salary: $694,615	Bonus: $401,768

OTHER THOUGHTS:

Apparent Women Officers or Directors: 4
Hot Spot for Advancement for Women/Minorities: Y

LOCATIONS: ("Y" = Yes)

West:	Southwest:	Midwest:	Southeast:	Northeast:	International:
Y	Y	Y	Y	Y	Y

JAMESON INN INC

www.jamesoninns.com

Industry Group Code: 721110 Ranks within this company's industry group: Sales: Profits:

Properties:		Financial Services:	Construction/Development:	Investments:	Specialty Services:		Brokerage:
Apartments:		Mortgages:	Commercial Construction:	REIT:	Property Management:	Y	Commercial Sales:
Malls/Shopping:		Title Insurance:	Residential Construction:		Online Services:		Residential Sales:
Offices:		Property Insurance:	Land Development:		Software/IT:		Specialty:
Hotels/Motels:	Y		Support Services:		Consulting:		
Industrial/Warehouses:			Design/Engineering:				
Other:							

TYPES OF BUSINESS:

Hotels

BRANDS/DIVISIONS/AFFILIATES:

JER Partners
Longhouse Hospitality
Park Management Group
J.E. Robert Companies
Signature Inn

CONTACTS: *Note: Officers with more than one job title may be intentionally listed here more than once.*

Thomas W. Kitchen, CEO
Steven A. Curlee, General Counsel/Sec./VP-Legal
Thomas W. Kitchen, Chmn.

Phone: 404-350-9990	Fax: 404-601-6106
Toll-Free: 800-526-3766	
Address: 4770 S. Atlanta Rd., Smyrna, GA 30080 US	

GROWTH PLANS/SPECIAL FEATURES:

Jameson Inn, Inc., a subsidiary of the private equity firm JER Partners, operates hotels in 13 states in the southeastern and Midwestern U.S. Jameson is a part of JER Partners' Longhouse Hospitality. JER Partners is the private equity investment arm of the J.E. Robert Companies. Jameson owns more than 160 hotels under the Jameson Inn, Crestwood Suites, Sun Suites, Lodge America and Signature Inn brands. The firm's hotels are managed by Park Management Group. All hotels owned by the firm typically offer amenities such as swimming pools, fitness centers, executive workstations, free cable, free USA Today, voicemail, refrigerators, microwaves and daily breakfast. In order to attract more business travelers, Jameson Inn offers workstations equipped with data ports, meeting spaces and fax and photocopy machines. Executive meeting rooms at Jameson Inn are approximately 300 square feet, with a capacity of 12 people, while the Signature Inn meeting rooms range from 300-900 square feet, with a capacity of 12-80 people.

The company offers its employees health, dental, vision, life and short- and long-term disability insurance; a 401(k) plan; paid holidays and time off; and discounts at company hotels.

FINANCIALS: Sales and profits are in thousands of dollars—add 000 to get the full amount. 2010 Note: Financial information for 2010 was not available for all companies at press time.

2010 Sales: $	2010 Profits: $	U.S. Stock Ticker: Subsidiary
2009 Sales: $	2009 Profits: $	Int'l Ticker: Int'l Exchange:
2008 Sales: $	2008 Profits: $	Employees:
2007 Sales: $	2007 Profits: $	Fiscal Year Ends: 12/31
2006 Sales: $	2006 Profits: $	Parent Company: JER PARTNERS

SALARIES/BENEFITS:

Pension Plan:	ESOP Stock Plan:	Profit Sharing:	Top Exec. Salary: $	Bonus: $
Savings Plan: Y	Stock Purch. Plan:		Second Exec. Salary: $	Bonus: $

OTHER THOUGHTS:

Apparent Women Officers or Directors:
Hot Spot for Advancement for Women/Minorities:

LOCATIONS: ("Y" = Yes)

West:	Southwest:	Midwest:	Southeast:	Northeast:	International:
		Y	Y	Y	

JANUS HOTELS AND RESORTS INC   www.janushotels.com

Industry Group Code: 721110 Ranks within this company's industry group: Sales: Profits:

Properties:	Financial Services:	Construction/Development:	Investments:	Specialty Services:		Brokerage:
Apartments:	Mortgages:	Commercial Construction:	REIT:	Property Management:	Y	Commercial Sales:
Malls/Shopping:	Title Insurance:	Residential Construction:		Online Services:		Residential Sales:
Offices:	Property Insurance:	Land Development:		Software/IT:		Specialty:
Hotels/Motels: Y		Support Services:		Consulting:	Y	
Industrial/Warehouses:		Design/Engineering:				
Other:						

TYPES OF BUSINESS:

Hotel Management
Management, Financial & Legal Consulting
Food & Beverage Services
Staffing Services

GROWTH PLANS/SPECIAL FEATURES:

Janus Hotels and Resorts, Inc. is one of the largest independently-owned full-service hotel management companies. It owns or manages approximately 40 hotels with approximately 8,000 guest rooms, concentrated in Florida. Its locations sit under the signposts of nationally recognized brands, including Days Inn, Holiday Inn, Radisson and Best Western. Janus operates each hotel according to a business plan specifically tailored to the characteristics of the hotel and its market, employing centralized management, accounting and purchasing systems to reduce cost and increase operating margins. The firm focuses primarily on continuing sales and marketing to increase revenue. Janus also provides food and beverage services, including lounges, coffee shops and locally and nationally branded restaurants. The company offers support services in the areas of administration, legal issues, brand relationships, maintenance of property, staffing, cash controls, liquor license issues, financial review and management, property development and customer service strategies. The firm also provides receivership services that involve quickly securing the asset; providing management services designed to stabilize the property; and services aimed at restoring staff and customer confidence in addition to its general offerings.

BRANDS/DIVISIONS/AFFILIATES:

CONTACTS: *Note: Officers with more than one job title may be intentionally listed here more than once.*

Louis Beck, CEO
Michael Nanosky, Pres.
Rick Tonges, CFO
Greg Cappel, VP-Mktg. & Sales
Jim Cordoba, Head-IT
Burton M. Bongard, Dir.-Prod. Dev.
Fred Schappacher, Corp. Engineer
Eric Glazer, General Counsel
Deborah Chamberlin, Exec. VP-Oper.
Jim Cordoba, Head-Web Tech.
Magda Khalil, Head-Corp. Acct.
Scott Wielkiewicz, Corp. Controller
Barb Soete, Controller
Burton M. Bongard, Pres., Alexander Investment Group
Louis Beck, Chmn.
Rick Ziegelmeyer, VP-Purchasing & Renovations

Phone: 561-997-2325	**Fax:** 561-997-5331
Toll-Free:	
Address: 2300 Corporate Blvd. NW, Ste. 232, Boca Raton, FL 33431-8596 US	

FINANCIALS: Sales and profits are in thousands of dollars—add 000 to get the full amount. 2010 Note: Financial information for 2010 was not available for all companies at press time.

2010 Sales: $	2010 Profits: $	**U.S. Stock Ticker: Private**
2009 Sales: $	2009 Profits: $	**Int'l Ticker:** Int'l Exchange:
2008 Sales: $	2008 Profits: $	Employees:
2007 Sales: $	2007 Profits: $	Fiscal Year Ends: 12/31
2006 Sales: $	2006 Profits: $	Parent Company:

SALARIES/BENEFITS:

Pension Plan:	ESOP Stock Plan:	Profit Sharing:	Top Exec. Salary: $	Bonus: $
Savings Plan:	Stock Purch. Plan:		Second Exec. Salary: $	Bonus: $

OTHER THOUGHTS:

Apparent Women Officers or Directors: 6
Hot Spot for Advancement for Women/Minorities: Y

LOCATIONS: ("Y" = Yes)

West:	Southwest:	Midwest:	Southeast:	Northeast:	International:
	Y	Y	Y	Y	

JOHN LAING PLC

www.john-laing.com

Industry Group Code: 5311 Ranks within this company's industry group: Sales: Profits:

Properties:	Financial Services:	Construction/Development:		Investments:	Specialty Services:	Brokerage:
Apartments:	Mortgages:	Commercial Construction:	Y	REIT:	Property Management:	Commercial Sales:
Malls/Shopping:	Title Insurance:	Residential Construction:			Online Services:	Residential Sales:
Offices:	Property Insurance:	Land Development:			Software/IT:	Specialty:
Hotels/Motels:		Support Services:	Y		Consulting:	
Industrial/Warehouses:		Design/Engineering:				
Other:						

TYPES OF BUSINESS:

Investor & Developer, Infrastructure Projects
Public Infrastructure Management
Rail Operations
Facilities Management
Private Finance Initiative Investor

BRANDS/DIVISIONS/AFFILIATES:

Henderson Group plc
Henderson Private Equity

CONTACTS: Note: Officers with more than one job title may be intentionally listed here more than once.

Adrian Ewer, CEO
Chris Waples, Dir.-Oper.
Lynn Krige, Dir.-Finance
Roger Miller, Sec.
Derek Potts, Managing Dir.-Bus. Dev.
Phil Nolan, Chmn.

Phone: 44-20-7901-3200	Fax: 44-20-7901-3520
Toll-Free:	
Address: 150 Victoria St., Allington House, London, SW1E 5LB UK	

GROWTH PLANS/SPECIAL FEATURES:

John Laing plc, owned by Henderson Private Equity, the private equity branch of Henderson Group plc, operates as a long-term investor, developer and operator of privately financed, public sector infrastructure such as roads, railways, hospitals, schools and other major projects in the U.K. and overseas. The firm's clients include local and education authorities, health trusts, the U.K. Ministry of Defense (MoD) and various police departments. The company operates in 11 business segments: police and criminal justice; defense; education; further education; health care; rail infrastructure; housing and community regeneration; local authority estates and regeneration; roads and bridges; street lighting and highway maintenance; and waste, renewable energy and utilities. In the criminal justice and police segment, John Laing serves the Department for Constitutional Affairs across all of its procurement methods, including private finance initiative (PFI), public-private partnership (PPP) and private developer schemes (PDS). In its defense segment, the company has been involved in three major MoD projects, including the Joint Services Command and Staff College in Shrivenham and the MoD Main Building in Whitehall, both of which won awards. John Laing's education portfolio includes over 80 projects, which it delivers through PPP and PFI deals. In health care, the company is a leading provider for the Local Improvement Finance Trust (LIFT), a major government initiative designed to stimulate investment in local primary and social care facilities, for which it established joint-venture Primary Plus with the Bank of Scotland, providing financing and project management expertise. John Laing is involved in the development of over 30 police facilities, including stations and firearm training facilities. Its infrastructure operations include park-and-ride rail lines; roads and bridges throughout Europe; and more than 120,000 lighting columns and illuminated traffic signs. The company provides facilities management services through subsidiary John Laing Integrated Services.

FINANCIALS: Sales and profits are in thousands of dollars—add 000 to get the full amount. 2010 Note: Financial information for 2010 was not available for all companies at press time.

2010 Sales: $	2010 Profits: $	U.S. Stock Ticker: Private
2009 Sales: $	2009 Profits: $	Int'l Ticker: Int'l Exchange:
2008 Sales: $	2008 Profits: $	Employees:
2007 Sales: $	2007 Profits: $	Fiscal Year Ends: 12/31
2006 Sales: $	2006 Profits: $	Parent Company: HENDERSON GROUP PLC

SALARIES/BENEFITS:

Pension Plan:	ESOP Stock Plan:	Profit Sharing:	Top Exec. Salary: $	Bonus: $
Savings Plan:	Stock Purch. Plan:		Second Exec. Salary: $	Bonus: $

OTHER THOUGHTS:

Apparent Women Officers or Directors: 1
Hot Spot for Advancement for Women/Minorities:

LOCATIONS: ("Y" = Yes)

West:	Southwest:	Midwest:	Southeast:	Northeast:	International:
					Y

JOHN Q HAMMONS HOTELS LLC

www.jqhhotels.com

Industry Group Code: 721110 Ranks within this company's industry group: Sales: Profits:

Properties:	Financial Services:	Construction/Development:	Investments:	Specialty Services:	Brokerage:
Apartments:	Mortgages:	Commercial Construction:	REIT:	Property Management:	Commercial Sales:
Malls/Shopping:	Title Insurance:	Residential Construction:		Online Services:	Residential Sales:
Offices:	Property Insurance:	Land Development:		Software/IT:	Specialty:
Hotels/Motels: Y		Support Services:		Consulting:	
Industrial/Warehouses:		Design/Engineering:			
Other:					

TYPES OF BUSINESS:

Hotels

BRANDS/DIVISIONS/AFFILIATES:

Chateau on the Lake
World Golf Village Renaissance Resort
John Q. Hammons Hotels Management LLC
Renaissance
Marriott
Hilton
Radisson
Residence Inn by Marriott

CONTACTS: *Note: Officers with more than one job title may be intentionally listed here more than once.*

John Q. Hammons, CEO
Phill Burgess, VP-Sales & Revenue Mgmt.
Kent Foster, VP-Human Resources
Matt Bortniker, VP-IT
John Fulton, VP-Design
Christopher Smith, Sr. VP-Admin. & Control
Justin Harris, General Counsel
Joe Morrissey, Sr. VP-Oper.
L. Scott Tarwater, Exec. VP-Bus. Dev.
Steve Minton, Sr. VP-Architecture
Rod Dornbusch, VP-Capital Planning & Asset Protection
Bill Mead, Regional VP
Paul Francisco, Regional VP
John Q. Hammons, Chmn.
John Fulton, VP-Purchasing

Phone: 417-864-4300	Fax:
Toll-Free: 800-641-4026	
Address: 300 John Q. Hammons Pkwy., Ste. 900, Springfield, MO 65806 US	

GROWTH PLANS/SPECIAL FEATURES:

John Q. Hammons Hotels LLC is a leading company that owns, manages and develops low-cost upscale hotels in main traffic areas. The company owns and operates more than 80 hotels in 25 states. These properties operate primarily under the Embassy Suites, Renaissance, Marriott, Hilton, Sheraton, Radisson, Residence Inn by Marriott, Homewood Suites by Hilton, Hampton Inn & Suites, Holiday Inn and Courtyard by Marriott trade names and are marketed to a range of customers, including frequent business travelers; groups and conventions; and leisure travelers. John Q. Hammons Hotels Management LLC manages all of the firm's hotels, which are generally located near a state capitol, university, airport, corporate headquarters or other major facility. Most of the hotels contain a multi-storied atrium, extensive meeting space and large rooms or suites. In addition, the firm owns two resorts: Chateau on the Lake, located in Branson, Missouri, and the World Golf Village Renaissance Resort in St. Augustine, Florida.

FINANCIALS: Sales and profits are in thousands of dollars—add 000 to get the full amount. 2010 Note: Financial information for 2010 was not available for all companies at press time.

2010 Sales: $	2010 Profits: $	U.S. Stock Ticker: Private
2009 Sales: $	2009 Profits: $	Int'l Ticker: Int'l Exchange:
2008 Sales: $	2008 Profits: $	Employees:
2007 Sales: $	2007 Profits: $	Fiscal Year Ends: 12/31
2006 Sales: $	2006 Profits: $	Parent Company:

SALARIES/BENEFITS:

Pension Plan:	ESOP Stock Plan:	Profit Sharing:	Top Exec. Salary: $	Bonus: $
Savings Plan: Y	Stock Purch. Plan:		Second Exec. Salary: $	Bonus: $

OTHER THOUGHTS:

Apparent Women Officers or Directors:
Hot Spot for Advancement for Women/Minorities:

LOCATIONS: ("Y" = Yes)

West:	Southwest:	Midwest:	Southeast:	Northeast:	International:
Y	Y	Y	Y	Y	

Note: Financial information, benefits and other data can change quickly and may vary from those stated here.

JOHNSON CONTROLS INC

www.johnsoncontrols.com

Industry Group Code: 3363 Ranks within this company's industry group: Sales: 1   Profits: 1

Properties:	Financial Services:	Construction/Development:		Investments:	Specialty Services:		Brokerage:
Apartments:	Mortgages:	Commercial Construction:		REIT:	Property Management:	Y	Commercial Sales:
Malls/Shopping:	Title Insurance:	Residential Construction:			Online Services:		Residential Sales:
Offices:	Property Insurance:	Land Development:			Software/IT:		Specialty:
Hotels/Motels:		Support Services:	Y		Consulting:		
Industrial/Warehouses:		Design/Engineering:					
Other:							

TYPES OF BUSINESS:

Automobile Parts & Controls
Automotive Batteries
Facilities Management
Automotive Interior Components
Energy Management Services
Building Security, Lighting & HVAC Systems

BRANDS/DIVISIONS/AFFILIATES:

National Energy Services
Johnson Controls-Saft Advanced Power Solutions
C. Rob. Hammerstein Group
KEIPER
Varta
Metasys Sustainability Manager
Heliar
LTH

CONTACTS: Note: Officers with more than one job title may be intentionally listed here more than once.

Stephen A. Roell, CEO
Keith Wandell, COO
Stephen A. Roell, Pres.
R. Bruce McDonald, CFO/Exec. VP
Susan F. Davis, Exec. VP-Human Resources
Colin Boyd, CIO/VP-IT
Jerome D. Okarma, General Counsel/VP/Sec.
Jacqueline F. Strayer, VP-Corp. Comm.
Glen Ponczak, Exec. Dir.-Investor Rel.
Frank A. Voltolina, Corp. Treas./VP
C. David Meyers, VP/Pres., Building Efficiency
Jeffrey G. Augustin, VP-Finance, Building Efficiency
Alex A. Molinaroli, VP/Pres., Power Solutions
Charles A. Harvey, VP-Public Affairs & Diversity
Stephen A. Roell, Chmn.
Jeffrey S. Edwards, VP-Automotive Experience, Japan & APAC

Phone: 414-524-1200	Fax: 414-524-2070
Toll-Free: 800-524-6220	
Address: 5757 N. Green Bay Ave., Milwaukee, WI 53209 US	

GROWTH PLANS/SPECIAL FEATURES:

Johnson Controls, Inc. is a leader in automotive interiors/batteries, building efficiency and facility management. The firm's Automotive Experience segment, which accounts for roughly 49% of the company's sales, designs and manufactures concept cars; complete seat systems; seating components; electronics; instrument panels; overhead, door and cargo management systems; cockpits; and interior trim for manufacturers of cars and light trucks. The division operates approximately 175 wholly- and majority-owned manufacturing/assembly plants in 27 countries. Johnson Control's Power Solutions division (14% of sales) manufactures and replaces automotive batteries, focusing on innovations for hybrid electric vehicles. Its battery brands include Optima, Varta, Heliar (in South America), and LTH (in Mexico). The segment produces roughly 120 million lead-acid batteries annually in approximately 55 wholly- and majority-owned manufacturing/assembly facilities in 18 countries. The Building Efficiency division (37% of sales) operates in 59 countries, supplying systems designed for heating; ventilation; air conditioning; lighting; security; and fire management. The U.S. Department of Defense utilizes Johnson Controls for the Pentagon's energy management and environmental control systems. Global WorkPlace Solutions, part of Building Efficiency, provides companies with a real-estate based approach to shareholder value. The Building Efficiency division also does facility management, using its patented Metasys Building Management System. It handles school districts, hospitals, factories, airports and government facilities. Johnson Controls has a joint venture with Saft SA, a battery company, called Johnson Controls-Saft Advanced Power Solutions. In March 2010, Johnson Controls acquired lighting services firm National Energy Services. In December 2010, the firm agreed to acquire German recliner system technology group KEIPER and the automotive sport and specialty seat operations of Recaro. In February 2011, Johnson Controls acquired metal seat manufacturer C. Rob. Hammerstein Group.

The firm offers employees benefits including health care coverage, tuition reimbursement and a 401(k) plan.

FINANCIALS: Sales and profits are in thousands of dollars—add 000 to get the full amount. 2010 Note: Financial information for 2010 was not available for all companies at press time.

2010 Sales: $34,305,000	2010 Profits: $1,491,000	**U.S. Stock Ticker: JCI**
2009 Sales: $28,497,000	2009 Profits: $-338,000	**Int'l Ticker:** Int'l Exchange:
2008 Sales: $38,062,000	2008 Profits: $979,000	Employees: 137,000
2007 Sales: $34,624,000	2007 Profits: $1,252,000	Fiscal Year Ends: 9/30
2006 Sales: $32,235,000	2006 Profits: $1,028,000	Parent Company:

SALARIES/BENEFITS:

Pension Plan:	ESOP Stock Plan:	Profit Sharing:	Top Exec. Salary: $1,365,000	Bonus: $6,317,000
Savings Plan: Y	Stock Purch. Plan:		Second Exec. Salary: $835,000	Bonus: $1,826,000

OTHER THOUGHTS:

Apparent Women Officers or Directors: 4
Hot Spot for Advancement for Women/Minorities: Y

LOCATIONS: ("Y" = Yes)

West:	Southwest:	Midwest:	Southeast:	Northeast:	International:
Y	Y	Y	Y	Y	Y

JOIE DE VIVRE HOSPITALITY

www.jdvhotels.com

Industry Group Code: 721110 Ranks within this company's industry group: Sales: Profits:

Properties:		Financial Services:	Construction/Development:	Investments:	Specialty Services:		Brokerage:
Apartments:	Y	Mortgages:	Commercial Construction:	REIT:	Property Management:	Y	Commercial Sales:
Malls/Shopping:		Title Insurance:	Residential Construction:		Online Services:		Residential Sales:
Offices:		Property Insurance:	Land Development:		Software/IT:		Specialty:
Hotels/Motels:	Y		Support Services:		Consulting:	Y	
Industrial/Warehouses:			Design/Engineering:				
Other:	Y						

TYPES OF BUSINESS:

Hotels
Day Spas
Restaurants
Hospitality Consulting
Condominium Management

BRANDS/DIVISIONS/AFFILIATES:

Hotel Rex
Phoenix Hotel
Hotel Tomo
Kabuki Springs & Spa
Spa Vitale
Millennium Restaurant
Soma Grand Condos
Shorebreak Hotel

CONTACTS: *Note: Officers with more than one job title may be intentionally listed here more than once.*

Gary Beasley, CEO
Ingrid Summerfield, COO
Ingrid Summerfield, Pres.
Michael J. Wisner, CFO
Peter Gamez, Sr. VP-Sales & Bus. Dev.
Jane Howard, Chief People Officer
Michael Stano, VP-Tech.
Anne Conley, VP-Admin.
Karlene Holloman, Sr. VP-Oper.
Christian Strobel, Chief Dev. Officer
Lori Lincoln, Dir.-Public Rel.
Linda Palermo, Chief Revenue Officer
Morgan Plant, VP-Food & Beverage
Rick Patten, Regional VP-Oper.
Mark Polochak, Regional VP-Oper.
Chip Conley, Chmn.

Phone: 415-835-0300	**Fax:** 415-835-0317
Toll-Free: 800-738-7477	
Address: 530 Bush St., Ste 501, San Francisco, CA 94108 US	

GROWTH PLANS/SPECIAL FEATURES:

Joie de Vivre Hospitality (JdV) operates primarily through subsidiary Joie de Vivre Hotels, one of California's largest independent boutique hotel operators. The company has locations throughout California, including almost 30 boutique hotels featuring a combined 20 restaurants and five bars and approximately 3,800 guest rooms. JdV's boutique hotels each target a niche audience by embodying a particular lifestyle or theme, such as arts and literature, featured at the Hotel Rex; rock and roll, at the Phoenix Hotel; or Japanese pop-culture, at Hotel Tomo. It also owns and operates the Kabuki Springs & Spa in San Francisco; Spa Vitale at Hotel Vitale; Spa Elia, a day spa at the Hotel Los Gatos in Silicon Valley; and a spa located in the Ventana Inn near Big Sur. JdV's restaurants and bars are usually attached to its hotels, such as Zimzala Restaurant & Bar in the Shorebreak Hotel; however, it also has free-standing restaurants such as Millennium Restaurant in Union Square, San Francisco. The firm offers approximately 150,000 combined square feet of business meeting space, with some locations able to accommodate groups of up to 1,000 people. JdV also manages an upscale residential community, Soma Grand Condos, in downtown San Francisco. The company's web site features the Yvette the Hotel Matchmaker service, which matches guests to particular hotels based on personality. In addition to managing its hotels, spas and restaurants, JdV provides hospitality consulting services, including general concept development and creative brainstorming for new projects.

FINANCIALS: Sales and profits are in thousands of dollars—add 000 to get the full amount. 2010 Note: Financial information for 2010 was not available for all companies at press time.

2010 Sales: $	2010 Profits: $	**U.S. Stock Ticker: Private**
2009 Sales: $	2009 Profits: $	**Int'l Ticker:** Int'l Exchange:
2008 Sales: $	2008 Profits: $	Employees:
2007 Sales: $	2007 Profits: $	Fiscal Year Ends: 12/31
2006 Sales: $	2006 Profits: $	Parent Company:

SALARIES/BENEFITS:

Pension Plan:	ESOP Stock Plan:	Profit Sharing:	Top Exec. Salary: $	Bonus: $
Savings Plan:	Stock Purch. Plan:		Second Exec. Salary: $	Bonus: $

OTHER THOUGHTS:

Apparent Women Officers or Directors: 8
Hot Spot for Advancement for Women/Minorities: Y

LOCATIONS: ("Y" = Yes)

West:	Southwest:	Midwest:	Southeast:	Northeast:	International:
Y					

JONES LANG LASALLE INC

www.joneslanglasalle.com

Industry Group Code: 5311 Ranks within this company's industry group: Sales: 13   Profits: 19

Properties:	Financial Services:	Construction/Development:	Investments:	Specialty Services:		Brokerage:	
Apartments:	Mortgages:	Commercial Construction:	REIT:	Property Management:	Y	Commercial Sales:	Y
Malls/Shopping:	Title Insurance:	Residential Construction:		Online Services:		Residential Sales:	
Offices:	Property Insurance:	Land Development:		Software/IT:		Specialty:	
Hotels/Motels:		Support Services:		Consulting:	Y		
Industrial/Warehouses:		Design/Engineering:					
Other:							

TYPES OF BUSINESS:

Real Estate Rental, Leasing & Management
Investment Management
Project Management
Consulting Services
Real Estate Investment Banking
Properties Brokerage

BRANDS/DIVISIONS/AFFILIATES:

LaSalle Investment Management, Inc.

CONTACTS: *Note: Officers with more than one job title may be intentionally listed here more than once.*

Colin Dyer, CEO
Lauralee E. Martin, COO
Colin Dyer, Pres.
Lauralee E. Martin, CFO
Charles Doyle, Chief Mktg. Officer
Nazneen Razi, Chief Human Resources Officer
David Johnson, CIO
Mark Ohringer, General Counsel/Corp. Sec.
Joe Romenesko, Global Treas.
Jeff Jacobson, CEO-LaSalle Investment Mgmt.
Peter C. Roberts, CEO-Americas
Christian Ulbrich, CEO-EMEA
James Jasionowski, Global Dir.-Tax
Sheila A. Penrose, Chmn.
Alastair Hughes, CEO-APAC

Phone: 312-782-5800	Fax: 312-782-4339
Toll-Free:	
Address: 200 E. Randolph Dr., Chicago, IL 60601 US	

GROWTH PLANS/SPECIAL FEATURES:

Jones Lang LaSalle, Inc. (JLL) is a real estate money management firm that provides integrated real estate and investment management expertise on a local, regional and global level to owner, occupier and investor clients. The firm is active in the area of property and corporate facility management services, with a portfolio encompassing roughly 1.6 billion square feet worldwide. JLL offers its real estate services across three geographically-aligned business segments: the Americas; Europe, the Middle East and Africa; and Asia Pacific. The company's range of real estate service areas includes agency leasing; property management; project and development management; valuations; brokerage of properties; capital markets; real estate investment banking and merchant banking; corporate finance; hotel advisory; space acquisition and disposition; facilities management; strategic consulting; energy management and sustainability; value recovery and receivership services; and money management. These services are offered to for-profit and not-for-profit firms, as well as to governmental entities and public-private partnerships, across a wide variety of property categories including offices, hotels, industrial, retail, multi-family residential, hospitals, data centers, sporting facilities, cultural institutions and transportation centers. A fourth business segment encompasses the operations of subsidiary LaSalle Investment Management, a leading diversified real estate investment management firm with over $41 billion in assets under management globally. JLL has operations in over 1,000 locations in 60 countries worldwide, including 185 corporate offices.

JLL offers employee benefits including medical, dental and vision coverage; health savings accounts and flexible spending accounts; discounted gym memberships; life and disability insurance; a 401(k) plan; a discount stock purchase plan; an education assistance program; adoption assistance; and an employee assistance program.

FINANCIALS: Sales and profits are in thousands of dollars—add 000 to get the full amount. 2010 Note: Financial information for 2010 was not available for all companies at press time.

2010 Sales: $2,925,613	2010 Profits: $154,439	**U.S. Stock Ticker: JLL**
2009 Sales: $2,480,736	2009 Profits: $-3,595	**Int'l Ticker:** Int'l Exchange:
2008 Sales: $2,697,586	2008 Profits: $84,883	Employees: 40,300
2007 Sales: $2,652,075	2007 Profits: $257,832	Fiscal Year Ends: 12/31
2006 Sales: $2,013,578	2006 Profits: $176,401	Parent Company:

SALARIES/BENEFITS:

Pension Plan:	ESOP Stock Plan:	Profit Sharing:	Top Exec. Salary: $750,000	Bonus: $1,162,500
Savings Plan: Y	Stock Purch. Plan: Y		Second Exec. Salary: $425,000	Bonus: $880,000

OTHER THOUGHTS:

Apparent Women Officers or Directors: 5
Hot Spot for Advancement for Women/Minorities: Y

LOCATIONS: ("Y" = Yes)

West:	Southwest:	Midwest:	Southeast:	Northeast:	International:
Y	Y	Y	Y	Y	Y

KB HOME

www.kbhome.com

Industry Group Code: 2361 Ranks within this company's industry group: Sales: 7   Profits: 14

Properties:	Financial Services:		Construction/Development:		Investments:	Specialty Services:	Brokerage:
Apartments:	Mortgages:	Y	Commercial Construction:	Y	REIT:	Property Management:	Commercial Sales:
Malls/Shopping:	Title Insurance:		Residential Construction:	Y		Online Services:	Residential Sales:
Offices:	Property Insurance:		Land Development:			Software/IT:	Specialty:
Hotels/Motels:			Support Services:			Consulting:	
Industrial/Warehouses:			Design/Engineering:				
Other:							

TYPES OF BUSINESS:

Residential Construction Services
Mortgage Services
Home Construction

BRANDS/DIVISIONS/AFFILIATES:

KB Home Mortgage Company
KBnxt
KB Home Studios
My Home. My Earth

CONTACTS: *Note: Officers with more than one job title may be intentionally listed here more than once.*

Jeffrey T. Mezger, CEO
Jeffrey T. Mezger, Pres.
Jeff Kaminski, CFO/Exec. VP
Wendy Marlett, Sr. VP-Sales & Mktg.
Thomas Norton, Sr. VP-Human Resources
Brian Woram, General Counsel/Exec. VP/Sec.
Wendy Marlett, Sr. VP-Comm.
Katoiya Marshall, Mgr.-Investor Rel.
William R. Hollinger, Chief Acct. Officer/Sr. VP
Cory F. Cohen, Sr. VP-Tax
Glen Barnard, Sr. VP-KBnxt Group
Thad Johnson, Treas.
Stephen F. Bollenbach, Chmn.

Phone: 310-231-4000	Fax: 310-231-4222
Toll-Free: 888-524-6637	
Address: 10990 Wilshire Blvd., Los Angeles, CA 90024 US	

GROWTH PLANS/SPECIAL FEATURES:

KB Home is one of the largest homebuilders in the U.S., with operations in nine states. The firm's major markets are Arizona, California, Colorado, Florida, Nevada, North Carolina, Maryland, Virginia and Texas. The company delivers approximately 7,346 houses per year at an average selling price of $214,500. KB Home builds innovatively designed homes catering to first-time and first-move-up homebuyers, generally in medium-sized developments close to major metropolitan areas, as well as to luxury home buyers. Through its KBnxt business model, KB Home seeks to keep construction costs and base prices as low as possible while promoting customer choice. Potential buyers may visit one of the firm's large KB Home Studios locations to select options for their home. KB Home's houses sell for an average price of approximately $207,100. KB Home also provides mortgage-banking, title and insurance services through KB Home Mortgage, LLC, a joint venture between the company and CWB Venture Management Corporation, a subsidiary of Bank of America, N.A. The firm's environmental initiative, My Home. My Earth, embodies the firm's commitment to become a leading environmentally friendly national company. The company currently installs exclusively ENERYSTAR appliances in all of its new homes, committed to build all new communities to ENERGY STAR guidelines, meaning that they must be more efficient and use less energy than typical houses. In June 2010, KB Home agreed to acquire 664 home sites in California from the Lewis Group of Companies. In March 2011, the firm announced a new initiative by which it will install solar panels in all of its new houses being built in 10 communities in California.

FINANCIALS: Sales and profits are in thousands of dollars—add 000 to get the full amount. 2010 Note: Financial information for 2010 was not available for all companies at press time.

2010 Sales: $1,589,996	2010 Profits: $-69,368	U.S. Stock Ticker: KBH
2009 Sales: $1,824,850	2009 Profits: $-101,784	Int'l Ticker: Int'l Exchange:
2008 Sales: $3,033,936	2008 Profits: $-976,131	Employees: 1,300
2007 Sales: $6,416,526	2007 Profits: $-929,414	Fiscal Year Ends: 11/30
2006 Sales: $9,359,843	2006 Profits: $482,351	Parent Company:

SALARIES/BENEFITS:

Pension Plan:	ESOP Stock Plan:	Profit Sharing:	Top Exec. Salary: $1,000,000	Bonus: $2,750,000
Savings Plan: Y	Stock Purch. Plan:		Second Exec. Salary: $365,000	Bonus: $350,000

OTHER THOUGHTS:

Apparent Women Officers or Directors: 3
Hot Spot for Advancement for Women/Minorities: Y

LOCATIONS: ("Y" = Yes)

West:	Southwest:	Midwest:	Southeast:	Northeast:	International:
Y	Y	Y	Y	Y	

KERZNER INTERNATIONAL HOLDINGS LIMITED www.kerzner.com

Industry Group Code: 721120 Ranks within this company's industry group: Sales: Profits:

Properties:		Financial Services:	Construction/Development:	Investments:	Specialty Services:	Brokerage:
Apartments:		Mortgages:	Commercial Construction:	REIT:	Property Management:	Commercial Sales:
Malls/Shopping:		Title Insurance:	Residential Construction:		Online Services:	Residential Sales:
Offices:		Property Insurance:	Land Development:		Software/IT:	Specialty:
Hotels/Motels:	Y		Support Services:		Consulting:	
Industrial/Warehouses:			Design/Engineering:			
Other:	Y					

TYPES OF BUSINESS:

Casino Hotels
Luxury Resort Hotels
Resort Development

BRANDS/DIVISIONS/AFFILIATES:

Atlantis
Atlantis, The Palm Dubai
Cove Atlantis (The)
One&Only
Mazagan Beach Resort

CONTACTS: *Note: Officers with more than one job title may be intentionally listed here more than once.*

Solomon Kerzner, CEO
Paul O'Neil, COO
Bonnie S. Biumi, Pres.
Bruce Himelstein, Chief Mktg. Officer/Exec. VP
Megan Marchesini, Contact-Media
Solomon Kerzner, Chmn.

Phone: 242-363-6000	Fax: 954-809-2337
Toll-Free:	
Address: 1 Casino Dr., Paradise Island, C5 Bahamas	

GROWTH PLANS/SPECIAL FEATURES:

Kerzner International Holdings Limited is a resort and gaming company that develops, operates and manages premier resorts, casinos and luxury hotels. The company's flagship property is the Atlantis Paradise Island in the Bahamas. The over 2,300-room ocean themed resort features three interconnected hotel towers built around 100 acres of pools and marine environments, home to over 50,000 marine animals. Additionally, the resort features the world's largest open-air aquarium. The firm also operates Atlantis The Palm, Dubai, an approximately 1,500-room ocean themed resort located on the manmade island of Palm Jumeirah; The Cove Atlantis; and six One&Only Resorts, exclusive luxury resorts, located in the Bahamas, Mexico, Mauritius, South Africa, the Maldives and Dubai; Mazagan Beach Resort, an approximately 500-room casino resort in Morocco which features a golf course, lagoon, swimming patio and a 180 degree view of the Atlantic Ocean; and the One&Only resort, which operates resorts in the Bahamas, Dubai, Maldives, Mauritius, Mexico and South Africa.

FINANCIALS: Sales and profits are in thousands of dollars—add 000 to get the full amount. 2010 Note: Financial information for 2010 was not available for all companies at press time.

2010 Sales: $	2010 Profits: $	U.S. Stock Ticker: Private
2009 Sales: $	2009 Profits: $	Int'l Ticker: Int'l Exchange:
2008 Sales: $	2008 Profits: $	Employees:
2007 Sales: $	2007 Profits: $	Fiscal Year Ends: 12/31
2006 Sales: $	2006 Profits: $	Parent Company:

SALARIES/BENEFITS:

Pension Plan:	ESOP Stock Plan:	Profit Sharing:	Top Exec. Salary: $	Bonus: $
Savings Plan:	Stock Purch. Plan:		Second Exec. Salary: $	Bonus: $

OTHER THOUGHTS:

Apparent Women Officers or Directors: 2
Hot Spot for Advancement for Women/Minorities:

LOCATIONS: ("Y" = Yes)

West:	Southwest:	Midwest:	Southeast:	Northeast:	International:
				Y	Y

KILROY REALTY CORPORATION

www.kilroyrealty.com

Industry Group Code: 531120 Ranks within this company's industry group: Sales: 45   Profits: 41

Properties:		Financial Services:		Construction/Development:		Investments:		Specialty Services:		Brokerage:	
Apartments:		Mortgages:		Commercial Construction:		REIT:	Y	Property Management:	Y	Commercial Sales:	
Malls/Shopping:		Title Insurance:		Residential Construction:				Online Services:		Residential Sales:	
Offices:	Y	Property Insurance:		Land Development:				Software/IT:		Specialty:	
Hotels/Motels:				Support Services:	Y			Consulting:			
Industrial/Warehouses:	Y			Design/Engineering:							
Other:											

TYPES OF BUSINESS:

Real Estate Investment Trust
Office & Industrial Properties
Property Management
Financial Services
Leasing
Construction Management

BRANDS/DIVISIONS/AFFILIATES:

Kilroy Realty, L.P.
Kilroy Realty Finance Partnership
Kilroy Realty Finance, Inc.
Kilroy Services, LLC
Kilroy Realty TRS, Inc.
Kilroy RB LLC
Kilroy RB II LLC

CONTACTS: *Note: Officers with more than one job title may be intentionally listed here more than once.*

John B. Kilroy, Jr., CEO
Jeffrey C. Hawken, COO/Exec. VP
John B. Kilroy, Jr., Pres.
Tyler H. Rose, CFO/Exec. VP
Tyler H. Rose, Sec.
Chris Corpuz, Exec. VP-Acquisitions & Strategic Initiatives
Heidi Roth, Controller/Sr. VP
John T. Fucci, Sr. VP-Asset Mgmt.
Steven R. Scott, Sr. VP-San Diego
Justin W. Smart, Sr. VP-Dev.
Eli Khouri, Chief Investment Officer/Exec. VP
John B. Kilroy, Sr., Chmn.

Phone: 310-481-8400	**Fax:** 310-481-6501
Toll-Free:	
Address: 12200 W. Olympic Blvd., Ste. 200, Los Angeles, CA 90064 US	

GROWTH PLANS/SPECIAL FEATURES:

Kilroy Realty Corporation (KRC) is a REIT (Real Estate Investment Trust) that owns, operates, develops and acquires Class A office and industrial real estate in suburban markets, primarily in southern California. Its portfolio of operating properties consists of 100 office buildings and 40 industrial buildings, aggregating approximately 10.4 million and 3.6 million rentable square feet, respectively. The office properties were 87.5% leased to 365 tenants and the industrial properties were 93.9% leased to 58 tenants. The firm's tenants can be broken down into the following industry categories: Technology and media, which generated 29% of the firm's rental revenue; education and health services, 22%; manufacturing, 14%; finance, insurance and real estate, 14%; professional and business services, 12%; wholesale and retail trade, 3%; construction, 2%; government, 2%; leisure and hospitality, 1%; and transportation, warehousing and public utilities, 1%. Its largest tenants include Intuit, Inc.; Bridgeport Education, Inc.; DIRECTV, Inc.; Scripps Health; CareFusion Corporation; Hewlett-Packard Company; Wells Fargo; and BP Biofuels North America. KRC owns all of its properties through subsidiary Kilroy Realty, L.P. (KRLP), which in turn owns Kilroy Realty Finance Partnership, L.P. KRLP's wholly-owned subsidiary Kilroy Services, LLC conducts substantially all of the firm's development activities. In November 2010, the company acquired two office buildings: the 100 First Plaza building in San Francisco's financial district and the Overlake Office Center in the Greater Seattle, Washington area.

FINANCIALS: Sales and profits are in thousands of dollars—add 000 to get the full amount. 2010 Note: Financial information for 2010 was not available for all companies at press time.

2010 Sales: $301,980	2010 Profits: $19,886	**U.S. Stock Ticker:** KRC
2009 Sales: $279,434	2009 Profits: $38,015	**Int'l Ticker:** Int'l Exchange:
2008 Sales: $289,355	2008 Profits: $46,911	Employees: 141
2007 Sales: $227,811	2007 Profits: $123,317	Fiscal Year Ends: 12/31
2006 Sales: $241,541	2006 Profits: $81,864	Parent Company:

SALARIES/BENEFITS:

Pension Plan:	ESOP Stock Plan:	Profit Sharing:	Top Exec. Salary: $1,050,000	Bonus: $2,500,000
Savings Plan:	Stock Purch. Plan:		Second Exec. Salary: $525,000	Bonus: $1,441,280

OTHER THOUGHTS:

Apparent Women Officers or Directors: 1
Hot Spot for Advancement for Women/Minorities:

LOCATIONS: ("Y" = Yes)

West:	Southwest:	Midwest:	Southeast:	Northeast:	International:
Y					

KIMCO REALTY CORP

www.kimcorealty.com

Industry Group Code: 531120 Ranks within this company's industry group: Sales: 19   Profits: 47

Properties:		Financial Services:		Construction/Development:		Investments:		Specialty Services:		Brokerage:	
Apartments:		Mortgages:		Commercial Construction:	Y	REIT:	Y	Property Management:	Y	Commercial Sales:	
Malls/Shopping:	Y	Title Insurance:		Residential Construction:				Online Services:		Residential Sales:	
Offices:	Y	Property Insurance:		Land Development:	Y			Software/IT:		Specialty:	
Hotels/Motels:				Support Services:				Consulting:	Y		
Industrial/Warehouses:				Design/Engineering:							
Other:											

TYPES OF BUSINESS:

Real Estate Investment Trust
Commercial Development
Property Services
Leasing
Consulting Services
Shopping Centers
Regional Malls
Property Management

BRANDS/DIVISIONS/AFFILIATES:

CONTACTS: *Note: Officers with more than one job title may be intentionally listed here more than once.*

David B. Henry, CEO
Michael V. Pappagallo, COO
David B. Henry, Pres.
Glenn G. Cohen, CFO/Exec. VP
Leah Landro, VP-Human Resources
Thomas R. Taddeo, CIO/VP
Barbara M Pooley, Chief Admin. Officer/Exec. VP
Bruce Rubenstein, General Counsel/VP/Sec.
William L. Brown, Pres., Dev.
Glenn G. Cohen, Treas.
Chris Freeman, VP-Property Mgmt.
Scott G. Onufrey, VP/Managing Dir.-Kimco Realty Advisors
Frederick N Kurz, VP/Gen. Mgr.-Investments & Risk Management
Kelly Smith, Managing Dir.-Canadian Oper.
Milton Cooper, Chmn.
Mike Melson, Managing Dir.-Latin America Oper.

Phone: 516-869-9000	Fax: 516-869-9001

Toll-Free: 800-285-4626

Address: 3333 New Hyde Park Rd., Ste. 100, New Hyde Park, NY 11042 US

GROWTH PLANS/SPECIAL FEATURES:

Kimco Realty Corp. is a U.S. is a real estate investment trust (REIT) that owns and operates shopping centers. The firm owns interest in approximately 1,857 properties, including shopping centers, retail store leases, development projects and undeveloped land. These properties are located in 44 states, Puerto Rico, Canada, Mexico, Brazil, Peru and Chile. Kimco's shopping centers are anchored by department store, supermarket or drug store tenants offering day-to-day necessities. Its five largest tenants, based on rental revenues, are The Home Depot, TJX Companies, Wal-Mart, Sears Holdings and Best Buy. Kimco's Property Services division provides property management services relating to the management, operation, supervision and maintenance of properties. The Leasing Department assists potential renters in finding the best locations for their business ventures. The firm focuses on acquiring properties that have opportunities for redevelopment and renovation, as well as other value increasing characteristics. Generally, the company can close a transaction in 45 to 60 days. Kimco also offers retail store owners and developers preferred equity debt. In April 2010, the firm established a joint venture with the Canada Pension Plan Investment Board to acquire shopping centers in well established neighborhoods in the U.S. The company will own a 55% interest in the venture. In May 2010, it established a similar joint venture with BIG Shopping Centers.

Employees are offered medical and dental insurance; disability coverage; life insurance; healthcare and dependent care reimbursement accounts; a 401(k) savings plan; and tuition assistance.

FINANCIALS: Sales and profits are in thousands of dollars—add 000 to get the full amount. 2010 Note: Financial information for 2010 was not available for all companies at press time.

2010 Sales: $849,549	2010 Profits: $2,377	**U.S. Stock Ticker: KIM**
2009 Sales: $773,423	2009 Profits: $-3,942	**Int'l Ticker:** Int'l Exchange:
2008 Sales: $751,196	2008 Profits: $249,902	Employees:
2007 Sales: $674,534	2007 Profits: $442,830	Fiscal Year Ends: 12/31
2006 Sales: $580,551	2006 Profits: $428,259	Parent Company:

SALARIES/BENEFITS:

Pension Plan:	ESOP Stock Plan:	Profit Sharing:	Top Exec. Salary: $750,000	Bonus: $876,818
Savings Plan: Y	Stock Purch. Plan:		Second Exec. Salary: $750,000	Bonus: $876,818

OTHER THOUGHTS:

Apparent Women Officers or Directors: 3
Hot Spot for Advancement for Women/Minorities: Y

LOCATIONS: ("Y" = Yes)

West:	Southwest:	Midwest:	Southeast:	Northeast:	International:
Y	Y	Y	Y	Y	Y

Note: Financial information, benefits and other data can change quickly and may vary from those stated here.

KIMPTON HOTEL & RESTAURANT GROUP LLC

www.kimptonhotels.com

Industry Group Code: 721110 Ranks within this company's industry group: Sales: Profits:

Properties:		Financial Services:		Construction/Development:		Investments:	Specialty Services:		Brokerage:	
Apartments:		Mortgages:		Commercial Construction:	Y	REIT:	Property Management:	Y	Commercial Sales:	
Malls/Shopping:		Title Insurance:		Residential Construction:			Online Services:		Residential Sales:	
Offices:		Property Insurance:		Land Development:			Software/IT:		Specialty:	
Hotels/Motels:	Y			Support Services:			Consulting:			
Industrial/Warehouses:				Design/Engineering:						
Other:	Y									

TYPES OF BUSINESS:

Hotels
Restaurants
Hotel Management Services

BRANDS/DIVISIONS/AFFILIATES:

Hotel Vintage Plaza
Monticello Inn
Hotel Vintage Park
Hotel Burnham
Cafe Pescatore
Sazerac
Silverleaf Tavern
Surfcomber Hotel

CONTACTS: *Note: Officers with more than one job title may be intentionally listed here more than once.*

Michael Depatie, CEO
Niki Leondakis, COO
Niki Leondakis, Pres.
Ben Rowe, CFO/Exec. VP
Steve Pinetti, Sr. VP-Mktg. & Sales
Leslie Lerude, VP-People & Culture
Kris Singleton, CIO
Kris Singleton, VP-Tech.
Judy Miles, General Counsel/Exec. VP
Mike DeFrino, Sr. VP-Hotel Oper.
Joe Long, Exec. VP-Dev./Chief Investment Officer
Ken Reynolds, Sr. VP-Construction
Greg LaMothe, VP-Concepts & Hospitality
David Sussman, Sr. VP-Hotel Dev. & Design
John Inserra, Sr. VP-Restaurant Oper.

Phone: 415-397-5572	Fax: 415-296-8031
Toll-Free: 800-546-7866	
Address: 222 Kearny St., Ste. 200, San Francisco, CA 94108 US	

GROWTH PLANS/SPECIAL FEATURES:

Kimpton Hotel & Restaurant Group, LLC, based in San Francisco, owns over 50 lifestyle boutique hotels in 15 states and Washington D.C. Its holdings consist of 9,711 rooms, in addition to 50 restaurants and bars next to or within its hotels. The firm specializes in renovating old, disused buildings to transform them into unique hotels and small, European-style restaurants. Its themed hotels include Hotel Vintage Plaza in Portland, Oregon, which has an Italian romance theme; Monticello Inn in San Francisco, reminiscent of Thomas Jefferson's estate; Hotel Vintage Park in Seattle, highlighting local Washington wines; and Hotel Burnham in Chicago, which focuses on its significance in Chicago's history. Some notable restaurants run by Kimpton include San Francisco bistros Cafe Pescatore, Scala's Bistro and Puccini & Pinetti; as well as Sazerac in Seattle; Atwood Cafe in Chicago; Area 31 in Miami; Firefly in Washington, D.C.; Ruby Room in Boston; and Silverleaf Tavern in New York City. Special services offered by its hotels include the Mind, Body, Spa Program, which offers in-room massage, yoga, Pilates and meditation; pet packages, which include pet-friendly amenities and services; and Hosted Evening Wine Hour. In addition to owning and running its own hotels, the company is engaged in comprehensive management services for other companies, offering everything from financial management to facilities renovation. It currently has three properties under development: the Surfcomber Hotel in South Beach, Florida scheduled to open in mid-2011; the Hotel Monaco in Philadelphia's historic Lafayette Building scheduled to open in 2012; and the Hotel Palomar in Phoenix, Arizona, which is also scheduled to open in 2012.

Employees of the firm are offered medical, dental, vision and basic life insurance; long- and short-term disability; pet care programs; paid vacation time; tuition reimbursement; and employee discounts.

FINANCIALS: Sales and profits are in thousands of dollars—add 000 to get the full amount. 2010 Note: Financial information for 2010 was not available for all companies at press time.

2010 Sales: $	2010 Profits: $	U.S. Stock Ticker: Private
2009 Sales: $	2009 Profits: $	Int'l Ticker: Int'l Exchange:
2008 Sales: $	2008 Profits: $	Employees:
2007 Sales: $	2007 Profits: $	Fiscal Year Ends: 12/31
2006 Sales: $	2006 Profits: $	Parent Company:

SALARIES/BENEFITS:

Pension Plan:	ESOP Stock Plan:	Profit Sharing:	Top Exec. Salary: $	Bonus: $
Savings Plan:	Stock Purch. Plan:		Second Exec. Salary: $	Bonus: $

OTHER THOUGHTS:

Apparent Women Officers or Directors: 8
Hot Spot for Advancement for Women/Minorities: Y

LOCATIONS: ("Y" = Yes)

West:	Southwest:	Midwest:	Southeast:	Northeast:	International:
Y	Y	Y	Y	Y	

Note: Financial information, benefits and other data can change quickly and may vary from those stated here.

KUMHO INDUSTRIAL CO LTD

www.kumhoenc.com

Industry Group Code: 237 Ranks within this company's industry group: Sales: 17   Profits: 22

Properties:	Financial Services:	Construction/Development:		Investments:	Specialty Services:	Brokerage:
Apartments:	Mortgages:	Commercial Construction:	Y	REIT:	Property Management:	Commercial Sales:
Malls/Shopping:	Title Insurance:	Residential Construction:	Y		Online Services:	Residential Sales:
Offices:	Property Insurance:	Land Development:	Y		Software/IT:	Specialty:
Hotels/Motels:		Support Services:			Consulting:	
Industrial/Warehouses:		Design/Engineering:	Y			
Other:						

TYPES OF BUSINESS:

Engineering & Construction
Research & Development
Sewage Treatment

BRANDS/DIVISIONS/AFFILIATES:

Kumho E&C
Kumho Asiana Group
KIDEA
ECOS

CONTACTS: *Note: Officers with more than one job title may be intentionally listed here more than once.*

Ock Kee, CEO
Bok Sang Jang, Head-Oper.
Seong San Kim, Pres.
Jong Geun Kim, VP
Jin Ryeol Seo, VP

Phone: 82-2-6303-0114	**Fax:** 82-2-6303-0736
Toll-Free:	
Address: 115 Sinmunno 1-Ga, Jongno-gu, Seoul, 100-061 Korea	

GROWTH PLANS/SPECIAL FEATURES:

Kumho Industrial Co. Ltd., doing business as Kumho Engineering & Construction (Kumho E&C), offers a wide range of building services. It has worked on general architectural construction projects, building commercial centers, warehouses, leisure facilities and even whole cities. Kumho E&C's civil engineering projects have run the gamut from airports, railroads and highways to tunnels and bridges. The firm has built over 60,000 new homes, including state-of-the-art apartment complexes and high-rise residential buildings. Kumho E&C's plant engineering projects have included constructing petrochemical plants; installing factory automation equipment; building environmental facilities such as incinerators and water and sewage treatment plants; and energy-related facilities, including gasoline tanks, LNG (liquefied natural gas) pipelines and power plants. The firm operates a research and development institute near its office dedicated to finding environmentally friendly building materials; stronger and faster building techniques; and new architectural designs maximizing heating and cooling systems, water-proofing and structural integrity. The firm's Electrode Contract Oxydation System (ECOS) is a process that facilitates the decomposition of sewage and is used in the removal of pollutants. Another sewage treatment is the KIDEA process, which was developed jointly by the company and the Korea Institute of Science & Technology, and removes 70% to 80% of nutrient salt from sewage. Kumho E&C is part of the Kumho Asiana Group.

FINANCIALS: Sales and profits are in thousands of dollars—add 000 to get the full amount. 2010 Note: Financial information for 2010 was not available for all companies at press time.

2010 Sales: $7,004,810	2010 Profits: $93,310	**U.S. Stock Ticker:**
2009 Sales: $2,096,050	2009 Profits: $-2,137,490	**Int'l Ticker: 002990** Int'l Exchange: Seoul-KRX
2008 Sales: $6,072,700	2008 Profits: $27,600	Employees:
2007 Sales: $5,339,000	2007 Profits: $135,000	Fiscal Year Ends:
2006 Sales: $6,207,400	2006 Profits: $56,900	Parent Company:

SALARIES/BENEFITS:

Pension Plan:	ESOP Stock Plan:	Profit Sharing:	Top Exec. Salary: $	Bonus: $
Savings Plan:	Stock Purch. Plan:		Second Exec. Salary: $	Bonus: $

OTHER THOUGHTS:

Apparent Women Officers or Directors:
Hot Spot for Advancement for Women/Minorities:

LOCATIONS: ("Y" = Yes)

West:	Southwest:	Midwest:	Southeast:	Northeast:	International:
					Y

LAS VEGAS SANDS CORP (THE VENETIAN) www.lasvegassands.com

Industry Group Code: 721120 Ranks within this company's industry group: Sales: 2 Profits: 1

Properties:		Financial Services:		Construction/Development:	Investments:		Specialty Services:		Brokerage:	
Apartments:		Mortgages:		Commercial Construction:	REIT:		Property Management:		Commercial Sales:	
Malls/Shopping:	Y	Title Insurance:		Residential Construction:			Online Services:		Residential Sales:	
Offices:		Property Insurance:		Land Development:			Software/IT:		Specialty:	
Hotels/Motels:	Y			Support Services:			Consulting:			
Industrial/Warehouses:				Design/Engineering:						
Other:	Y									

TYPES OF BUSINESS:

Hotel Casinos
Convention & Conference Centers
Shopping Center Development
Casino Property Development

BRANDS/DIVISIONS/AFFILIATES:

Venetian Resort Hotel Casino (The)
Sands Expo and Convention Center (The)
Congress Center (The)
Sands Macao Casino (The)
Palazzo Resort Hotel Casino (The)
Venetian Macao Resort Hotel (The)
Marina Bay Sands
Cotai Strip

CONTACTS: *Note: Officers with more than one job title may be intentionally listed here more than once.*

Sheldon G. Adelson, CEO
Michael A. Leven, COO
Michael A. Leven, Pres.
Kenneth J. Kay, CFO/Sr. VP
Gayle M. Hyman, General Counsel/Sr. VP
Robert G. Goldstein, Pres., Gaming Oper.
Leonard DeAngelo, Sr. VP-Asia Oper., Marina Bay Sands
Nigel Roberts, Pres., Marina Bay Sands
Sheldon G. Adelson, Chmn.
Steven C. Jacobs, CEO-Sands China Ltd.

Phone: 702-414-1000	**Fax:** 702-414-4884
Toll-Free:	
Address: 3355 Las Vegas Blvd. S., Las Vegas, NV 89109 US	

GROWTH PLANS/SPECIAL FEATURES:

Las Vegas Sands Corp. (The Venetian) (LVSC) is an international hotel, resort and casino firm. Its flagship property is The Venetian Resort Hotel Casino, which is connected to the firm's The Palazzo Resort Hotel Casino. Together, The Venetian and The Palazzo offer 225,000 square feet (sq. ft.) of gaming space with 230 table games and 2,640 slot machines; 7,100 hotel suites; and 840,000 sq. ft. of dining, retail and entertainment space, including The Shoppes at The Palazzo. LVSC also runs the 1.2 million sq. ft. convention and trade show facility, The Sands Expo and Convention Center, and a supplemental event and conference center, The Congress Center, that connects to The Venetian. These properties feature 1.2 million sq. ft. of meeting, exhibition and convention space; 1 million sq. ft. of retail and dining space; and the 15,000 seat Venetian Arena. The company's largest development project, the multi-billion dollar Cotai Strip, is a collection of hotel properties, casinos and entertainment venues in Macao, China, the resort and gaming hub for China's population. The firm runs The Sands Macao and The Venetian Macao Resort Hotel, the anchor property on the Cotai Strip. Other properties on the Cotai Strip include the Four Seasons Hotel Macao and the Plaza Casino. One of the company's newest properties is the Sands Casino Resort Bethlehem, Philadelphia, featuring 3,000 slot machines and various entertainment options. Construction on the tower of the Sands Casino Resort Bethlehem is to be completed by mid-2011. The firm's newest international hotel and casino, Marina Bay Sands, opened in April 2010, in Singapore, Malaysia. In October 2010, it signed a ten-year license agreement with InterContinental Hotels Group plc to affiliate The Venetian and The Palazzo with the InterContinental's global portfolio.

FINANCIALS: Sales and profits are in thousands of dollars—add 000 to get the full amount. 2010 Note: Financial information for 2010 was not available for all companies at press time.

2010 Sales: $7,317,937	2010 Profits: $781,603	**U.S. Stock Ticker: LVS**
2009 Sales: $4,929,444	2009 Profits: $-368,743	**Int'l Ticker:** Int'l Exchange:
2008 Sales: $4,735,126	2008 Profits: $-168,325	Employees: 34,000
2007 Sales: $3,104,422	2007 Profits: $116,688	Fiscal Year Ends: 12/31
2006 Sales: $2,340,178	2006 Profits: $442,003	Parent Company:

SALARIES/BENEFITS:

Pension Plan:	ESOP Stock Plan:	Profit Sharing:	Top Exec. Salary: $1,561,539	Bonus: $
Savings Plan: Y	Stock Purch. Plan:		Second Exec. Salary: $1,000,000	Bonus: $

OTHER THOUGHTS:

Apparent Women Officers or Directors: 1
Hot Spot for Advancement for Women/Minorities:

LOCATIONS: ("Y" = Yes)

West:	Southwest:	Midwest:	Southeast:	Northeast:	International:
Y				Y	Y

LASALLE HOTEL PROPERTIES

www.lasallehotels.com

Industry Group Code: 531120 Ranks within this company's industry group: Sales: 29 Profits: 48

Properties:	Financial Services:	Construction/Development:	Investments:	Specialty Services:	Brokerage:
Apartments:	Mortgages:	Commercial Construction:	REIT: Y	Property Management:	Commercial Sales:
Malls/Shopping:	Title Insurance:	Residential Construction:		Online Services:	Residential Sales:
Offices:	Property Insurance:	Land Development:		Software/IT:	Specialty:
Hotels/Motels: Y		Support Services:		Consulting:	
Industrial/Warehouses:		Design/Engineering:			
Other:					

TYPES OF BUSINESS:

Real Estate Investment Trust
Luxury Hotels
Property Investment

BRANDS/DIVISIONS/AFFILIATES:

Le Montrose Suite Hotel
Indianapolis Marriott Downtown
Westin Copley Place
Hilton San Diego Gaslamp Quarter
Westin Copley Place
Westin Michigan Avenue
Hotel Solamar

CONTACTS: *Note: Officers with more than one job title may be intentionally listed here more than once.*

Michael D. Barnello, CEO
Alfred L. Young, COO
Michael D. Barnello, Pres.
Hans S. Weger, CFO
Hans S. Weger, Corp. Sec.
Hans S. Weger, Treas./Exec. VP
Stuart L. Scott, Chmn.

Phone: 301-941-1500	Fax: 301-941-1553
Toll-Free:	
Address: 3 Bethesda Metro Ctr., Ste. 1200, Bethesda, MD 20814 US	

GROWTH PLANS/SPECIAL FEATURES:

LaSalle Hotel Properties is a self-managed and self-administered real estate investment trust (REIT) that owns and invests in luxury hotels. The firm primarily works with hotels located in convention, resort or major urban business markets. The company currently owns interests in 35 upscale and luxury full-service hotels with approximately 9,100 rooms/suites located in 10 states and Washington, D.C. The firm is comprised of hotel investors, asset managers and financial experts, rather than hotel operators. LaSalle's hotels are operated and managed by unrelated hotel operating companies. LaSalle maintains strategic relationships with internationally recognized hotel operating companies such as Westin Hotels and Resorts; Noble House Hotels & Resorts; Hilton Hotels Corporation; Hyatt Hotels Corporation; Sandcastle Hotels and Resorts; and others. The firm seeks to improve revenue growth through renovations, redevelopment and/or expansions; brand or franchise conversion; acquisitions of appropriate full-service hotels in the U.S. and abroad; and selective development of hotel properties in favorable upscale markets. Properties include the Le Montrose Suite Hotel, Indianapolis Marriott Downtown; Hilton San Diego Gaslamp Quarter; Westin Copley Place; Westin Michigan Avenue; and Hotel Solamar. Throughout late 2010 and early 2011, LaSalle purchased six and sold two hotels.

FINANCIALS: Sales and profits are in thousands of dollars—add 000 to get the full amount. 2010 Note: Financial information for 2010 was not available for all companies at press time.

2010 Sales: $600,357	2010 Profits: $1,770	**U.S. Stock Ticker:** LHO
2009 Sales: $542,646	2009 Profits: $7,970	**Int'l Ticker:** Int'l Exchange:
2008 Sales: $607,752	2008 Profits: $38,366	Employees: 29
2007 Sales: $661,710	2007 Profits: $89,755	Fiscal Year Ends: 12/31
2006 Sales: $593,831	2006 Profits: $99,060	Parent Company:

SALARIES/BENEFITS:

Pension Plan:	ESOP Stock Plan:	Profit Sharing:	Top Exec. Salary: $600,000	Bonus: $900,000
Savings Plan:	Stock Purch. Plan:		Second Exec. Salary: $425,034	Bonus: $398,438

OTHER THOUGHTS:

Apparent Women Officers or Directors: 1
Hot Spot for Advancement for Women/Minorities:

LOCATIONS: ("Y" = Yes)

West:	Southwest:	Midwest:	Southeast:	Northeast:	International:
Y	Y	Y		Y	

LAYNE CHRISTENSEN COMPANY

www.laynechristensen.com

Industry Group Code: 237 Ranks within this company's industry group: Sales: 29 Profits: 28

Properties:	Financial Services:	Construction/Development:		Investments:	Specialty Services:		Brokerage:
Apartments:	Mortgages:	Commercial Construction:		REIT:	Property Management:		Commercial Sales:
Malls/Shopping:	Title Insurance:	Residential Construction:			Online Services:		Residential Sales:
Offices:	Property Insurance:	Land Development:			Software/IT:		Specialty:
Hotels/Motels:		Support Services:	Y		Consulting:	Y	
Industrial/Warehouses:		Design/Engineering:	Y				
Other:							

TYPES OF BUSINESS:

Construction & Civil Engineering Services
Water Treatment Plant Development
Drilling Services
Oil & Gas Field Services
Unconventional Natural Gas Production

BRANDS/DIVISIONS/AFFILIATES:

W.L. Hailey & Company, Inc.
Intevras Technologies, LLC
Industrial Water Treatment Processes
Diberil Sociedad Anonima
Costa Fortuna

CONTACTS: Note: Officers with more than one job title may be intentionally listed here more than once.

Andrew B. Schmitt, CEO
Andrew B. Schmitt, Pres.
Steven F. Crooke, General Counsel/VP/Sec.
Jerry W. Fanska, VP-Finance/Treas.
Gregory F. Aluce, Sr. VP/Pres., Water Resources Div.
Eric Despain, Sr. VP/Pres., Mineral Exploration
Phil Winner, Pres., Layne Energy
Jeffrey J. Reynolds, Exec. VP/Pres., Water Infrastructure Div.
David A. B. Brown, Chmn.

Phone: 913-677-6800	Fax: 913-362-0133
Toll-Free:	
Address: 1900 Shawnee Mission Pkwy., Mission Woods, KS 66205 US	

GROWTH PLANS/SPECIAL FEATURES:

Layne Christensen Company provides drilling and construction services and related products in two principal markets: water infrastructure and mineral exploration. In addition, the company is a producer of unconventional natural gas for the energy market. The firm operates in four segments: Water Infrastructure, Mineral Exploration, Energy Services and Other. Through the Water Infrastructure division, Layne Christensen provides water systems services, such as test hole drilling, well construction, well development and testing, pump selection, equipment installation and pipeline construction; well and pump rehabilitation services; water and wastewater treatment and plant construction services; sewer rehabilitation; and environmental assessment drilling. The Mineral Exploration division conducts aboveground and underground drilling activities for the global mineral exploration industry. The Energy Services segment provides the exploration for, and acquisition, development, and production of, unconventional natural gas. The other segment includes two small specialty energy service companies and any other specialty operations not included in the other divisions. The firm operates throughout North America, as well as Africa, Australia, Europe, Brazil and, through its affiliates, in South America. Layne Christensen's customers include municipalities, investor-owned water utilities, industrial companies, global mining companies, consulting engineering firms, heavy civil construction contractors, oil and gas companies and agribusiness. In July 2010, the firm purchased Intevras Technologies, LLC, the holding company of Austin-based Industrial Water Treatment Processes, for $5.5 million. In August of the same year, the company acquired a 50% stake in Uruguayan firm, Diberil Sociedad Anonima, the parent of geotechnical firm, Costa Fortuna.

FINANCIALS: Sales and profits are in thousands of dollars—add 000 to get the full amount. 2010 Note: Financial information for 2010 was not available for all companies at press time.

2010 Sales: $866,417	2010 Profits: $1,365	**U.S. Stock Ticker:** LAYN
2009 Sales: $1,008,063	2009 Profits: $26,534	**Int'l Ticker:** Int'l Exchange:
2008 Sales: $868,274	2008 Profits: $37,256	Employees: 3,900
2007 Sales: $722,768	2007 Profits: $26,252	Fiscal Year Ends: 1/31
2006 Sales: $463,015	2006 Profits: $14,681	Parent Company:

SALARIES/BENEFITS:

Pension Plan:	ESOP Stock Plan:	Profit Sharing:	Top Exec. Salary: $618,462	Bonus: $562,437
Savings Plan:	Stock Purch. Plan:		Second Exec. Salary: $363,231	Bonus: $248,334

OTHER THOUGHTS:

Apparent Women Officers or Directors:
Hot Spot for Advancement for Women/Minorities:

LOCATIONS: ("Y" = Yes)

West:	Southwest:	Midwest:	Southeast:	Northeast:	International:
Y	Y	Y	Y	Y	Y

LB FOSTER COMPANY

www.lbfoster.com

Industry Group Code: 4233 Ranks within this company's industry group: Sales: 3 Profits: 2

Properties:	Financial Services:	Construction/Development:		Investments:	Specialty Services:	Brokerage:
Apartments:	Mortgages:	Commercial Construction:	Y	REIT:	Property Management:	Commercial Sales:
Malls/Shopping:	Title Insurance:	Residential Construction:			Online Services:	Residential Sales:
Offices:	Property Insurance:	Land Development:			Software/IT:	Specialty:
Hotels/Motels:		Support Services:	Y		Consulting:	
Industrial/Warehouses:		Design/Engineering:	Y			
Other:						

TYPES OF BUSINESS:

Engineered Building Materials
Railroad Materials

BRANDS/DIVISIONS/AFFILIATES:

LB Pipe & Coupling Products LLC
Portec Rail Products, Inc.
Foster Thomas Company

CONTACTS: *Note: Officers with more than one job title may be intentionally listed here more than once.*

Stan L. Hasselbusch, CEO
Stan L. Hasselbusch, Pres.
David J. Russo, CFO/Sr. VP/Treas.
Gregory W. Lippard, VP-Sales, Rail Prod.
Brian H. Kelly, VP-Human Resources
John F. Kasel, Sr. VP-Mfg.
David L. Voltz, General Counsel/VP/Corp. Sec.
John F. Kasel, Sr. VP-Oper.
David R. Sauder, VP-Global Bus. Dev.
Linda K. Patterson, Controller
Samuel K. Fisher, Sr. VP-Rail Prod.
Donald L. Foster, Sr. VP-Construction Prod.
Kevin R. Haugh, Pres., CXT, Inc.
Merry L. Brumbaugh, VP-Tubular Prod.
Lee B. Foster, II, Chmn.

Phone: 412-928-3417	Fax: 412-928-7891
Toll-Free:	
Address: 415 Holiday Dr., Pittsburgh, PA 15220 US	

GROWTH PLANS/SPECIAL FEATURES:

L.B. Foster Company, founded in 1902, manufactures, fabricates and distributes products and services for the rail, construction, energy and utility industries. The company operates in three business segments: rail products, construction products and tubular products. The rail products segment, serving the railroad industry, provides a full line of new and used rail, trackwork, and related accessories to the railroad, mining and industrial markets. L.B. Foster also designs and produces insulated rail joints, power rail, concrete railroad ties, track fasteners, coverboards and special accessories for mass transit and other rail systems worldwide. The construction products division manufactures and sells steel sheet piling, H-bearing piling and pipe piling, as well as providing rental sheet piling for foundation requirements. In addition, L.B. Foster supplies fabricated structural steel, bridge decking, bridge railing, expansion joints and other products for highway construction and repair. L.B. Foster's tubular products segment supplies pipe coatings for natural gas pipelines and utilities. The firm also produces threaded pipe products for industrial water well and irrigation markets and sells micropiles for construction foundation repair and slope stabilization. The company maintains 15 sales offices, as well as 22 warehouses and plants located throughout the U.S. Rail products account for approximately 49% of the L.B. Foster's revenues; construction products account for 48%; and tubular products account for 6%. Joint venture, L.B. Pipe & Coupling Products, LLC (with Jim Legg and Lally Pipe & Tube) manufactures couplings. In December 2010, L.B. Foster acquired Portec Rail Products, Inc.; sold Portec's rail joint operations to Koppers, Inc.; and merged subsidiary Foster Thomas Company into Portec.

L.B. Foster offers its employees benefits which include life, AD&D, disability, medical, dental and vision insurance; flexible spending accounts; profit sharing; and an employee assistance plan.

FINANCIALS: **Sales and profits are in thousands of dollars—add 000 to get the full amount. 2010 Note: Financial information for 2010 was not available for all companies at press time.**

2010 Sales: $475,050	2010 Profits: $20,492	**U.S. Stock Ticker: FSTR**
2009 Sales: $404,020	2009 Profits: $15,727	**Int'l Ticker:** Int'l Exchange:
2008 Sales: $539,236	2008 Profits: $27,746	Employees: 866
2007 Sales: $508,981	2007 Profits: $110,724	Fiscal Year Ends: 12/31
2006 Sales: $389,788	2006 Profits: $10,715	Parent Company:

SALARIES/BENEFITS:

Pension Plan:	ESOP Stock Plan:	Profit Sharing: Y	Top Exec. Salary: $438,000	Bonus: $218,194
Savings Plan: Y	Stock Purch. Plan:		Second Exec. Salary: $248,333	Bonus: $96,820

OTHER THOUGHTS:

Apparent Women Officers or Directors: 4
Hot Spot for Advancement for Women/Minorities: Y

LOCATIONS: ("Y" = Yes)

West:	Southwest:	Midwest:	Southeast:	Northeast:	International:
Y	Y	Y	Y	Y	

LBA REALTY LLC

www.lbarealty.com

Industry Group Code: 5311 Ranks within this company's industry group: Sales: Profits:

Properties:	Financial Services:	Construction/Development:		Investments:	Specialty Services:		Brokerage:
Apartments:	Mortgages:	Commercial Construction:	Y	REIT:	Property Management:	Y	Commercial Sales:
Malls/Shopping:	Title Insurance:	Residential Construction:			Online Services:		Residential Sales:
Offices: Y	Property Insurance:	Land Development:			Software/IT:		Specialty:
Hotels/Motels:		Support Services:			Consulting:		
Industrial/Warehouses: Y		Design/Engineering:					
Other: Y							

TYPES OF BUSINESS:

Real Estate Operations & Development
Real Estate Management

BRANDS/DIVISIONS/AFFILIATES:

CONTACTS: *Note: Officers with more than one job title may be intentionally listed here more than once.*

Mike Memoly, CFO
Claudine Gamboa, Dir.-Human Resources & Employment
Paul Thometz, Dir.-Design & Construction
Perry Schonfeld, Principal-Oper.
Phil Belling, Principal-Strategy & Acquisitions
Tom Rutherford, Sr. VP-Finance
Alice Wilson, VP-Corp. Svcs.
Melanie Colbert, Sr. VP-Property Mgmt. Svcs.
Bill Kearns, Principal-Acquisitions & Leasing
Steve Layton, Principal-Corp. Svcs.

Phone: 949-833-0400	Fax:
Toll-Free:	
Address: 17901 Von Karman Ave, Ste. 950, Irvine, CA 92614 US	

GROWTH PLANS/SPECIAL FEATURES:

LBA Realty LLC is a leading real estate investment and management company based in California, with operations primary in the western half of the U.S. The firm has multiple properties throughout Arizona, Nevada, California, Colorado, Oregon, Texas, Utah and Washington. The company's portfolio consists of large, mixed-use properties, single and multi-tenant office buildings and industrial properties such as warehouse, distribution, light manufacturing & business park facilities. The firm has three primary acquisition targets: office and industrial properties including warehouses, multi-tenant business parks, and R&D facilities; corporate-owned facilities including industrial, office and R&D; and development opportunities such as office in select markets, industrial and R&D. LBA has acquired approximately $4 billion in real estate assets since 1995. The company's major tenants include AT&T; Colorado State Bank; Comcast; DeVry; Isuzu Motors; Liberty Mutual; Microsoft; United Healthcare; QWEST; Sun Microsystems; State Farm; Sony; Starbucks; State of California; Time Warner; Jackson National Life; University of Phoenix; Verizon; and Noble Energy.

Employees of the firm are offered medical, dental and vision coverage; a 401(k) plan; life insurance; gym membership discounts; college 529 plan; a long-term care program; and a flexible spending account program.

FINANCIALS: Sales and profits are in thousands of dollars—add 000 to get the full amount. 2010 Note: Financial information for 2010 was not available for all companies at press time.

2010 Sales: $	2010 Profits: $	**U.S. Stock Ticker: Private**
2009 Sales: $	2009 Profits: $	Int'l Ticker: Int'l Exchange:
2008 Sales: $	2008 Profits: $	Employees:
2007 Sales: $	2007 Profits: $	Fiscal Year Ends: 12/31
2006 Sales: $	2006 Profits: $	Parent Company:

SALARIES/BENEFITS:

Pension Plan:	ESOP Stock Plan:	Profit Sharing:	Top Exec. Salary: $	Bonus: $
Savings Plan: Y	Stock Purch. Plan:		Second Exec. Salary: $	Bonus: $

OTHER THOUGHTS:

Apparent Women Officers or Directors: 3
Hot Spot for Advancement for Women/Minorities: Y

LOCATIONS: ("Y" = Yes)

West:	Southwest:	Midwest:	Southeast:	Northeast:	International:
Y	Y				

LENDER PROCESSING SERVICES INC

www.lpsvcs.com

Industry Group Code: 511210 Ranks within this company's industry group: Sales: 1 Profits: 1

Properties:	Financial Services:		Construction/Development:	Investments:	Specialty Services:	Brokerage:
Apartments:	Mortgages:	Y	Commercial Construction:	REIT:	Property Management:	Commercial Sales:
Malls/Shopping:	Title Insurance:		Residential Construction:		Online Services:	Residential Sales:
Offices:	Property Insurance:		Land Development:		Software/IT:	Specialty:
Hotels/Motels:			Support Services:		Consulting:	
Industrial/Warehouses:			Design/Engineering:			
Other:						

TYPES OF BUSINESS:

Mortgage Processing & Management Systems
Settlement Services
Data & Technology Solutions
Loan Facilitation Services

BRANDS/DIVISIONS/AFFILIATES:

Rising Tide Auctions

CONTACTS:
Note: Officers with more than one job title may be intentionally listed here more than once.

Jeffrey S. Carbiener, CEO
Daniel T. Scheuble, Co-COO/Exec. VP
Jeffrey S. Carbiener, Pres.
Francis K. Chan, CFO/Exec. VP
Michelle Kersch, Sr. VP-Mktg.
Greg Williamson, Sr. VP-Human Resources
Joseph M. Nackashi, CIO/Exec. VP
Todd C. Johnson, General Counsel/Exec. VP/Sec.
Parag Bhansali, Exec. VP-Corp. Dev.
Michelle Kersch, Sr. VP-Corp. Comm.
Christopher P. Breakiron, Chief Acct. Officer/Sr. VP
Eric D. Swenson, Co-COO/Exec. VP
Pete Maselli, Sr. VP-Strategy & Bus. Dev.
Grace Brasington, Chief Risk Officer/Exec. VP
Lee A. Kennedy, Chmn.

Phone: 904-854-5100	Fax: 904-854-4124
Toll-Free: 800-991-1274	
Address: 601 Riverside Ave., Jacksonville, FL 32204 US	

GROWTH PLANS/SPECIAL FEATURES:

Lender Processing Services, Inc. is a provider of integrated technology and outsourced services to the mortgage lending industry. The company provides mortgage processing services, settlement services, default services and integrated data and technology services through two operating segments: Technology, Data and Analytics; and Loan Transaction Services. The Technology, Data and Analytics segment provides mortgage processing and workflow management services to mortgage lenders and other lending institutions, along with related support and services. This segment constitutes approximately 30% of Lender Processing Services' consolidated revenue. The Loan Transaction Services segment consists primarily of the firm's loan facilitation services, including settlement services, property appraisals and other real estate-related services; and its default management services provided to national lenders and loan servicers. This segment accounts for approximately 70% of revenue. The firm serves more than 1,000 financial institutions, including many of the top 50 U.S. banks, as well as other financial groups, mortgage lenders, mortgage loan service providers and real estate service providers.

FINANCIALS:
Sales and profits are in thousands of dollars—add 000 to get the full amount. 2010 Note: Financial information for 2010 was not available for all companies at press time.

2010 Sales: $2,456,335	2010 Profits: $302,344	**U.S. Stock Ticker:** LPS
2009 Sales: $2,370,548	2009 Profits: $275,729	**Int'l Ticker:** Int'l Exchange:
2008 Sales: $1,837,590	2008 Profits: $230,888	Employees: 8,700
2007 Sales: $1,638,622	2007 Profits: $256,805	Fiscal Year Ends: 12/31
2006 Sales: $	2006 Profits: $	Parent Company:

SALARIES/BENEFITS:

Pension Plan:	ESOP Stock Plan:	Profit Sharing:	Top Exec. Salary: $850,000	Bonus: $2,550,000
Savings Plan: Y	Stock Purch. Plan: Y		Second Exec. Salary: $544,500	Bonus: $1,365,000

OTHER THOUGHTS:

Apparent Women Officers or Directors: 2
Hot Spot for Advancement for Women/Minorities:

LOCATIONS: ("Y" = Yes)

West:	Southwest:	Midwest:	Southeast:	Northeast:	International:
Y	Y	Y	Y	Y	

LENDINGTREE LLC

www.lendingtree.com

Industry Group Code: 522310E Ranks within this company's industry group: Sales: Profits:

Properties:	Financial Services:	Construction/Development:	Investments:	Specialty Services:		Brokerage:
Apartments:	Mortgages:	Commercial Construction:	REIT:	Property Management:		Commercial Sales:
Malls/Shopping:	Title Insurance:	Residential Construction:		Online Services:	Y	Residential Sales:
Offices:	Property Insurance:	Land Development:		Software/IT:		Specialty:
Hotels/Motels:		Support Services:		Consulting:		
Industrial/Warehouses:		Design/Engineering:				
Other:						

TYPES OF BUSINESS:

Consumer Loans & Mortgages Internet Portal
Online Financial Information & Tools
Online Realty Services
Settlement Services
Online Homeowner Resources

BRANDS/DIVISIONS/AFFILIATES:

Tree.com, Inc
Home Loan Center, Inc. (The)
LendingTree Loans
RealEstate.com
LendingTree.com
GetSmart.com
ARM Central

CONTACTS: *Note: Officers with more than one job title may be intentionally listed here more than once.*

Douglas Lebda, CEO
Matthew Packey, CFO/Sr. VP
Mona Marimow, Sr. VP-Mktg
Claudette Hampton, Sr. VP-Human Resources
Kamelia Dianati, Sr. VP-Tech.
Mark W. Fowler, Sr. VP-Oper. & Sales
Greg Hanson, Sr. VP/Gen. Mgr.-Tree.com & RealEstate.com
Tamara Kotronis, Sr. VP-Investor Rel.
Chris Hayek, Chief Acct. Officer/Sr. VP
David Norris, Pres., Lending Tree Loans
Tamara Kotronis, Sr. VP-Financial Planning & Analysis
Douglas Lebda, Chmn.

Phone: 704-541-5351	Fax: 704-541-1824
Toll-Free: 800-555-8733	
Address: 11115 Rushmore Dr., Charlotte, NC 28277 US	

GROWTH PLANS/SPECIAL FEATURES:

LendingTree, LLC., a subsidiary of Tree.com, Inc., is an online lending and realty services exchange. The company operates LendingTree.com a leading online loan facilitator that brings consumers together with a network of lenders competing for their business. LendingTree.com provides consumers with resources to purchase and refinance home loans, home equity loans, lines of credit, auto loans, personal loans and credit cards. It also offers these services over the phone at 800-555-TREE. Customers begin by completing the firm's online loan request, which requires information concerning desired loan(s) and personal financial information. The customer's data and credit scores are then automatically compared to the underwriting criteria of participating lenders. Subsidiary, The Home Loan Center, Inc., operating under the name LendingTree Loans, is a licensed mortgage lender in every state and originates, processes and funds consumer mortgage loans. Instead of using the LendingTree network of lenders, qualifying consumers may be matched with a single loan officer who will provide up to four loan offers based on rates and terms given to LendingTree Loans from its wholesale mortgage banks and investors. Its loans and loan servicing rights are then sold to investors on the secondary market. RealEstate.com and 1-800-REALESTATE, LendingTree's real estate brokerage businesses, operate in 20 U.S. markets. Other LendingTree websites and resources include getsmart.com, a web site that offers access to a range of loan services, including loan refinancing, mortgage loans, home equity loans, debt consolidation and credit reports; JustThrive.com, a personal finance management website; and ARM Central, a resource for homeowners facing an adjustable rate mortgage reset. In November 2010, LendingTree Loans agreed to acquire SurePoint Lending, a loan originator.

Employees of Tree.com receive medical, dental and vision insurance; flexible spending accounts; life and AD&D insurance; a 401(k); adoption assistance; and education assistance.

FINANCIALS: Sales and profits are in thousands of dollars—add 000 to get the full amount. 2010 Note: Financial information for 2010 was not available for all companies at press time.

2010 Sales: $	2010 Profits: $	**U.S. Stock Ticker:** Subsidiary
2009 Sales: $	2009 Profits: $	**Int'l Ticker:** Int'l Exchange:
2008 Sales: $	2008 Profits: $	Employees:
2007 Sales: $356,200	2007 Profits: $-42,700	Fiscal Year Ends: 12/31
2006 Sales: $485,700	2006 Profits: $42,300	Parent Company: TREE.COM INC

SALARIES/BENEFITS:

Pension Plan:	ESOP Stock Plan:	Profit Sharing:	Top Exec. Salary: $	Bonus: $178,900
Savings Plan: Y	Stock Purch. Plan:		Second Exec. Salary: $	Bonus: $

OTHER THOUGHTS:

Apparent Women Officers or Directors: 4
Hot Spot for Advancement for Women/Minorities: Y

LOCATIONS: ("Y" = Yes)

West:	Southwest:	Midwest:	Southeast:	Northeast:	International:
Y				Y	

LENNAR CORPORATION

www.lennar.com

Industry Group Code: 2361 Ranks within this company's industry group: Sales: 5   Profits: 4

Properties:	Financial Services:		Construction/Development:		Investments:	Specialty Services:	Brokerage:
Apartments:	Mortgages:	Y	Commercial Construction:	Y	REIT:	Property Management:	Commercial Sales:
Malls/Shopping:	Title Insurance:	Y	Residential Construction:	Y		Online Services:	Residential Sales:
Offices:	Property Insurance:		Land Development:	Y		Software/IT:	Specialty:
Hotels/Motels:			Support Services:			Consulting:	
Industrial/Warehouses:			Design/Engineering:	Y			
Other:							

TYPES OF BUSINESS:

Home Building
Mortgages
Title Insurance & Services

BRANDS/DIVISIONS/AFFILIATES:

Universal American Mortgage LLC
Eagle Home Mortgage LLC
Railto Investments
North American Title Insurance Company

CONTACTS: *Note: Officers with more than one job title may be intentionally listed here more than once.*

Stuart A. Miller, CEO
Jonathan M. Jaffe, COO/VP
Rick Beckwitt, Pres.
Bruce E. Gross, CFO/VP
John R. Nygard, III, CIO
Mark Sustana, General Counsel/Corp. Sec.
Kay L. Howard, Dir.-Comm.
Diane J. Bessette, Treas./VP
Michael Petrolino, VP-Taxation
Linda Reed, Exec. VP-Lennar Financial Svcs. LLC
David Collins, Controller
David J. Kaiserman, Pres., Lennar Ventures
Stuart A. Miller, Chmn.

Phone: 305-559-4000	Fax: 305-228-8383
Toll-Free: 800-741-4663	
Address: 700 NW 107th Ave., Ste. 400, Miami, FL 33172 US	

GROWTH PLANS/SPECIAL FEATURES:

Lennar Corporation is a U.S. homebuilder and provider of financial services operating in 14 states. The firm sells single-family attached and detached homes and, to a lesser extent, multi-level residential buildings primarily under the Lennar brand name, in communities targeted to first-time, move-up and active adult homebuyers. The company also purchases, develops and sells residential land. Lennar divides its homebuilding operations into five segments: East (which includes Florida, Maryland, New Jersey and Virginia), Central (including Arizona, Colorado and Texas, excluding Houston), West (California and Nevada), Houston and Other (which includes Georgia, Illinois, Minnesota, North Carolina and South Carolina). Lennar's homes have an average sale price of about $243,000. In 2010, it delivered 10,995 homes to buyers. Lennar generally supervises and controls the development of land and the design and building of its residential communities with a relatively small labor force, hiring subcontractors for site improvements and virtually all of the work involved in the construction of homes. Through its financial services subsidiaries, Universal American Mortgage Company; Eagle Home Mortgage; and North American Title Insurance Company, the firm provides mortgage financing, title insurance and closing services for both buyers of its homes and third parties. Lennar's subsidiaries provide loans to roughly 85% of its homebuyers who obtain mortgage financing in areas where it offers services. The Railto Investments segment provides advisory services, ongoing asset management services and acquisition and monetization services related to distressed loans and securities portfolios.

Employees are offered medical, dental and vision insurance; home and auto insurance; mortgage and title benefits; short- and long-term disability coverage; life insurance; and health and dependent care spending accounts.

FINANCIALS: Sales and profits are in thousands of dollars—add 000 to get the full amount. 2010 Note: Financial information for 2010 was not available for all companies at press time.

2010 Sales: $3,074,022	2010 Profits: $95,261	**U.S. Stock Ticker:** LEN
2009 Sales: $3,119,387	2009 Profits: $-417,147	**Int'l Ticker:** Int'l Exchange:
2008 Sales: $4,575,417	2008 Profits: $-1,109,085	Employees: 4,704
2007 Sales: $10,186,781	2007 Profits: $-1,941,081	Fiscal Year Ends: 11/30
2006 Sales: $16,266,662	2006 Profits: $593,869	Parent Company:

SALARIES/BENEFITS:

Pension Plan:	ESOP Stock Plan:	Profit Sharing:	Top Exec. Salary: $1,000,000	Bonus: $1,000,000
Savings Plan: Y	Stock Purch. Plan:		Second Exec. Salary: $800,000	Bonus: $1,000,000

OTHER THOUGHTS:

Apparent Women Officers or Directors: 3
Hot Spot for Advancement for Women/Minorities: Y

LOCATIONS: ("Y" = Yes)

West:	Southwest:	Midwest:	Southeast:	Northeast:	International:
Y	Y	Y	Y	Y	

LEXINGTON REALTY TRUST

www.lxp.com

Industry Group Code: 531120 Ranks within this company's industry group: Sales: 42   Profits: 54

Properties:		Financial Services:	Construction/Development:	Investments:		Specialty Services:	Brokerage:
Apartments:		Mortgages:	Commercial Construction:	REIT:	Y	Property Management:	Commercial Sales:
Malls/Shopping:	Y	Title Insurance:	Residential Construction:			Online Services:	Residential Sales:
Offices:	Y	Property Insurance:	Land Development:			Software/IT:	Specialty:
Hotels/Motels:			Support Services:			Consulting:	
Industrial/Warehouses:	Y		Design/Engineering:				
Other:							

TYPES OF BUSINESS:

Real Estate Investment Trust
Investment & Asset Management
Property Management & Leasing
Office & Industrial Properties
Retail Properties
Construction Financing

BRANDS/DIVISIONS/AFFILIATES:

Lex-Win Concord LLC
Lepercq Corporate Income Fund L.P.
Lepercq Corporate Income Fund II L.P.

CONTACTS: *Note: Officers with more than one job title may be intentionally listed here more than once.*

T. Wilson Eglin, CEO
T. Wilson Eglin, COO
T. Wilson Eglin, Pres.
Patrick Carroll, CFO/Exec. VP/Treas.
Joseph Bonventre, General Counsel/Exec. VP
Natasha Roberts, Exec. VP/Dir.-Acquisitions
Mona Manucom, Contact-Investor Rel.
Paul R. Wood, Chief Acct. Officer/VP/Corp. Sec.
Richard J. Rouse, Chief Investment Officer/Vice Chmn.
Brendan P. Mullinix, Exec. VP-Capital Markets
Lara Sweeney Johnson, Exec. VP-Strategic Transactions
E. Robert Roskind, Chmn.

Phone: 212-692-7200	**Fax:** 212-594-6600
Toll-Free:	
Address: 1 Penn Plz., Ste. 4015, New York, NY 10119-4015 US	

GROWTH PLANS/SPECIAL FEATURES:

Lexington Realty Trust (formerly Lexington Corporate Properties Trust) is a self-managed and self-administered real estate investment trust (REIT) that primarily acquires, owns and manages a portfolio of net leased office, industrial and retail properties. Lexington also acquires and holds investments in loan assets and debt securities related to real estate, primarily acquired through a 50% interest in Lex-Win Concord LLC. The majority of the company's properties are subject to triple-net or similar leases, in which the tenant bears all or substantially all of the costs and cost increases for real estate taxes, utilities, insurance and ordinary repairs. Lexington has ownership interests in roughly 195 properties in 40 states and the Netherlands, for a total of approximately 36.9 million square feet. The company has diversified its portfolio by geographical location, tenant industry segment, lease term expiration and property type in an effort to insulate itself from regional recession, industry specific downturns and price fluctuations by property type. Lexington is structured as an umbrella partnership REIT, with a portion of its business conducted through its two operating subsidiaries: Lepercq Corporate Income Fund L.P. and Lepercq Corporate Income Fund II L.P. During 2010, the firm sold 13 properties to third parties for a combined total of $158.1 million. Also during 2010, the company acquired several properties, including 105,000-square-foot office property in Columbus, Ohio, purchased for $16.7 million; a parking lot in Las Vegas, Nevada, purchased in for $3.3 million; and a plot of land adjacent to an existing property in Beaumont, Texas, purchased for approximately $500,000.

Lexington Realty Trust offers its employees a tuition assistance program; a 529 college savings plan; a 401(k) plan with company match; a stock purchase plan; flexible spending accounts; a tuition assistance program; and medical, dental, life and disability insurance.

FINANCIALS: Sales and profits are in thousands of dollars—add 000 to get the full amount. 2010 Note: Financial information for 2010 was not available for all companies at press time.

2010 Sales: $342,855	2010 Profits: $-37,410	**U.S. Stock Ticker:** LXP
2009 Sales: $356,316	2009 Profits: $-211,272	**Int'l Ticker:** Int'l Exchange:
2008 Sales: $375,618	2008 Profits: $-3,468	Employees: 53
2007 Sales: $401,176	2007 Profits: $91,929	Fiscal Year Ends: 12/31
2006 Sales: $185,963	2006 Profits: $7,753	Parent Company:

SALARIES/BENEFITS:

Pension Plan:	ESOP Stock Plan:	Profit Sharing:	Top Exec. Salary: $550,000	Bonus: $275,000
Savings Plan: Y	Stock Purch. Plan: Y		Second Exec. Salary: $475,000	Bonus: $195,000

OTHER THOUGHTS:

Apparent Women Officers or Directors: 3
Hot Spot for Advancement for Women/Minorities: Y

LOCATIONS: ("Y" = Yes)

West:	Southwest:	Midwest:	Southeast:	Northeast:	International:
Y	Y	Y	Y	Y	Y

# LIBERTY PROPERTY TRUST								www.libertyproperty.com

Industry Group Code: 531120 Ranks within this company's industry group: Sales: 23   Profits: 13

Properties:		Financial Services:		Construction/Development:		Investments:		Specialty Services:		Brokerage:	
Apartments:		Mortgages:		Commercial Construction:		REIT:	Y	Property Management:	Y	Commercial Sales:	
Malls/Shopping:		Title Insurance:		Residential Construction:				Online Services:		Residential Sales:	
Offices:	Y	Property Insurance:		Land Development:				Software/IT:		Specialty:	
Hotels/Motels:				Support Services:				Consulting:			
Industrial/Warehouses:	Y			Design/Engineering:							
Other:											

TYPES OF BUSINESS:

Real Estate Investment Trust
Industrial & Office Properties
Property Management
Property Development

BRANDS/DIVISIONS/AFFILIATES:

Liberty Property, LP

CONTACTS: *Note: Officers with more than one job title may be intentionally listed here more than once.*

William P. Hankowsky, CEO
Robert E. Fenza, COO/Exec. VP
William P. Hankowsky, Pres.
George J. Alburger, Jr., CFO/Exec. VP
Caren Hosansky, Sr. VP-Human Resources
Steven E. Messaros, CIO
James J. Bowes, General Counsel/Sec.
Jim Lutz, Sr. VP-Dev.
Jeanne A. Leonard, VP-Corp. Comm.
Mary Beth Morrissey, Sr. VP-Finance & Acct.
Donna Wagner, Sr. VP-Acquisitions
Michael T. Hagan, Chief Investment Officer/Sr. VP
Shelby Christensen, Sr. VP/National Dir.-Property Management
James V. Maneri, Sr. VP-National Leasing & Bus. Dev.
William P. Hankowsky, Chmn.
Andrew Blevins, Managing Dir.-UK Portfolio

Phone: 610-648-1700	**Fax:** 610-644-4129
Toll-Free:	
Address: 500 Chesterfield Pkwy., Malvern, PA 19355 US	

GROWTH PLANS/SPECIAL FEATURES:

Liberty Property Trust, headquartered in Pennsylvania, is a self-administered and self-managed real estate investment trust (REIT). Nearly all of the firm's assets and operations are owned and conducted through its subsidiary, Liberty Property, LP, a Pennsylvania limited partnership. Liberty's portfolio consists of 345 industrial and 292 office properties, totaling 65.2 million square feet, in 12 states and the U.K. Through joint ventures, the firm owns interest in an additional 98 properties (48 industrial and 50 office), totaling 14.4 million square feet. Liberty groups its properties according to six geographic segments: Northeast, representing 42% of its total wholly-owned square footage; Midwest, 9%; Mid-Atlantic, 22%; South, 24%; Philadelphia/Washington D.C., 2%; and the U.K., less than 1%. Industrial properties include warehouse, distribution, service, assembly, light manufacturing and research and development facilities. Office properties include single- and multi-story office buildings located principally in suburban mixed-use developments or office parks. The company provides leasing, property management, development, acquisition and other tenant-related services for its properties. It provides property management services to over 2,000 companies; leasing representatives with knowledge of the particular local market; and architects and space planners that aid in the design and use of tenants' leased space. Liberty also owns three properties under development and 1,347 acres of developable land, substantially all of which is zoned for commercial use.

Liberty offers its employees medical, dental and vision insurance; short- and long-term disability; paid time off; a 401(k); a health care spending account; a dependent care spending account; a work-life balance support program; wellness programs; an employee stock purchase plan; an employee referral program; educational assistance that includes both tuition reimbursement and professional certification support; employee discounts; commuter assistance; life insurance; and dependent, supplemental and AD&D insurance.

FINANCIALS: Sales and profits are in thousands of dollars—add 000 to get the full amount. 2010 Note: Financial information for 2010 was not available for all companies at press time.

2010 Sales: $746,830	2010 Profits: $153,375	**U.S. Stock Ticker:** LRY
2009 Sales: $739,379	2009 Profits: $78,992	**Int'l Ticker:** Int'l Exchange:
2008 Sales: $725,451	2008 Profits: $180,106	Employees: 461
2007 Sales: $669,144	2007 Profits: $190,310	Fiscal Year Ends: 12/31
2006 Sales: $607,562	2006 Profits: $266,574	Parent Company:

SALARIES/BENEFITS:

Pension Plan:	ESOP Stock Plan:	Profit Sharing:	Top Exec. Salary: $525,000	Bonus: $239,715
Savings Plan: Y	Stock Purch. Plan: Y		Second Exec. Salary: $400,000	Bonus: $ 500

OTHER THOUGHTS:

Apparent Women Officers or Directors: 5
Hot Spot for Advancement for Women/Minorities: Y

LOCATIONS: ("Y" = Yes)

West:	Southwest:	Midwest:	Southeast:	Northeast:	International:
	Y	Y	Y	Y	Y

LIGHTSTONE GROUP LLC (THE)

www.lightstonegroup.com

Industry Group Code: 531110 Ranks within this company's industry group: Sales: Profits:

Properties:		Financial Services:	Construction/Development:	Investments:		Specialty Services:		Brokerage:
Apartments:		Mortgages:	Commercial Construction:	REIT:	Y	Property Management:	Y	Commercial Sales:
Malls/Shopping:	Y	Title Insurance:	Residential Construction:			Online Services:		Residential Sales:
Offices:	Y	Property Insurance:	Land Development:			Software/IT:		Specialty:
Hotels/Motels:	Y		Support Services:			Consulting:		
Industrial/Warehouses:			Design/Engineering:					
Other:								

TYPES OF BUSINESS:

Real Estate Company
Outlet Retail Properties
Office Building Properties
Lodging Facilities Properties
Real Estate Investment Trust

BRANDS/DIVISIONS/AFFILIATES:

Beacon Management

CONTACTS: Note: Officers with more than one job title may be intentionally listed here more than once.

Peyton (Chip) Owen, Jr., COO
Peyton (Chip) Owen, Jr., Pres.
Michael M. Schurer, CFO
Pamela Meadows, Exec. VP-Human Resources
Joseph E. Teichman, General Counsel/Exec. VP
Akiva Elazary, VP-Acquisitions
Robert Brvenik, Pres., Prime Retail
Bruno de Vinck, Sr. VP-Special Projects
Jeffrey Dash, VP-Retail Leasing
David Lichtenstein, Chmn.

Phone: 212-616-9969	Fax:
Toll-Free:	
Address: 460 Park Ave., 13th Fl., New York, NY 10022 US	

GROWTH PLANS/SPECIAL FEATURES:

The Lightstone Group LLC is one of the largest privately-owned real estate companies in the U.S. It currently boasts a portfolio of diversified properties in 22 U.S. states, Washington, D.C. and Puerto Rico with holdings in excess of 11,000 residential units. The company's assets include more than 20.5 million square feet of commercial space. The firm's commercial interests generally include retail and industrial properties such as enclosed malls, outlet centers, open air centers and warehouses in excess of 150,000 square feet. Subsidiary Beacon Management is one of the foremost players in the multi-family residential housing sector, with corporate offices in the Northeast, Southeast and Midwest regions of the U.S. In February 2011, Lightstone ended its administrative role in the Prime Office Company, LLC. In the same month, the company acquired the Everson Pointe Shopping Center in Snellville, Georgia, and the Festival Bay Mall in Orlando, Florida. In March 2011, the firm acquired the Crowne Plaza Hotel in Danvers, Massachusetts.

FINANCIALS: Sales and profits are in thousands of dollars—add 000 to get the full amount. 2010 Note: Financial information for 2010 was not available for all companies at press time.

2010 Sales: $	2010 Profits: $	U.S. Stock Ticker: Private
2009 Sales: $	2009 Profits: $	Int'l Ticker: Int'l Exchange:
2008 Sales: $	2008 Profits: $	Employees:
2007 Sales: $	2007 Profits: $	Fiscal Year Ends: 12/31
2006 Sales: $	2006 Profits: $	Parent Company:

SALARIES/BENEFITS:

Pension Plan:	ESOP Stock Plan:	Profit Sharing:	Top Exec. Salary: $	Bonus: $
Savings Plan:	Stock Purch. Plan:		Second Exec. Salary: $	Bonus: $

OTHER THOUGHTS:

Apparent Women Officers or Directors: 2
Hot Spot for Advancement for Women/Minorities:

LOCATIONS: ("Y" = Yes)

West:	Southwest:	Midwest:	Southeast:	Northeast:	International:
	Y	Y	Y	Y	

LILLIBRIDGE HEALTHCARE REAL ESTATE TRUST

www.lillibridge.com

Industry Group Code: 531120 Ranks within this company's industry group: Sales: Profits:

Properties:	Financial Services:	Construction/Development:	Investments:	Specialty Services:	Brokerage:
Apartments:	Mortgages:	Commercial Construction:	REIT: Y	Property Management: Y	Commercial Sales:
Malls/Shopping:	Title Insurance:	Residential Construction:		Online Services:	Residential Sales:
Offices:	Property Insurance:	Land Development:		Software/IT:	Specialty:
Hotels/Motels:		Support Services:		Consulting: Y	
Industrial/Warehouses:		Design/Engineering:			
Other: Y					

TYPES OF BUSINESS:

Real Estate Investment Trust
Property Management
Health Care Properties
Consulting Services

BRANDS/DIVISIONS/AFFILIATES:

Ventas Inc

CONTACTS: *Note: Officers with more than one job title may be intentionally listed here more than once.*

Todd Lillibridge, CEO
Joe Kurzydym, CFO
Carla M. Lyons, VP-Mktg.
Mary Fitzpatrick, Dir.-Human Resources
David Lichterman, Sr. VP-Oper.
Michael Lincoln, Exec. VP-Bus. Dev.
Carla M. Lyons, Contact-Media
Vince Cozzi, Exec. VP/Chief Investment Officer
John Montgomery, Exec. VP-Facility Dev.
Chuck Fendrich, Exec. VP-Property Mgmt.
Kevin Geraghty, Exec. VP-Asset & Portfolio Mgmt.
Todd Lillibridge, Chmn.

Phone: 312-408-1370	Fax: 312-408-1415
Toll-Free: 877-545-5430	
Address: 200 W. Madison St., 32 Fl., Chicago, IL 60606 US	

GROWTH PLANS/SPECIAL FEATURES:

Lillibridge Healthcare Real Estate Trust, a wholly-owned subsidiary of Ventas Inc., is a leading national health care real estate investment trust (REIT) that focuses on nonprofit hospitals and other healthcare facilities. The company acquires, develops and manages its properties. The firm's operations, including owned and managed property, encompasses 64 medical office facilities, totaling 8.8 million square feet across 67 local healthcare markets and across 20 states. The business serves over 6,000 physicians and hospital tenants nationwide. Lillibridge's acquisition branch purchases a client's medical office buildings. After a purchase, the development branch of the company plans the campus, physician recruitment and other operations associated with the new facility or its renovation. Lillibridge also manages the property for clients and handles compliance issues that consistently come up in the health care field when new federal and state laws are passed. The firm has developed a compliance risk-assessment checklist and paperwork that aids clients in evaluating and learning about compliance issues. Lillibridge consulting services help clients inventory strategic and non-strategic real estate assets, improve performance through operations assessment, determine the impact of a monetization on the financial position of the hospital and create an ambulatory network or leasing strategy. In June 2010, the firm was acquired by Ventas, Inc.

FINANCIALS: Sales and profits are in thousands of dollars—add 000 to get the full amount. 2010 Note: Financial information for 2010 was not available for all companies at press time.

2010 Sales: $	2010 Profits: $	U.S. Stock Ticker: Subsidiary
2009 Sales: $	2009 Profits: $	Int'l Ticker: Int'l Exchange:
2008 Sales: $	2008 Profits: $	Employees:
2007 Sales: $	2007 Profits: $	Fiscal Year Ends: 12/31
2006 Sales: $	2006 Profits: $	Parent Company: VENTAS INC

SALARIES/BENEFITS:

Pension Plan:	ESOP Stock Plan:	Profit Sharing:	Top Exec. Salary: $	Bonus: $
Savings Plan: Y	Stock Purch. Plan:		Second Exec. Salary: $	Bonus: $

OTHER THOUGHTS:

Apparent Women Officers or Directors: 2
Hot Spot for Advancement for Women/Minorities:

LOCATIONS: ("Y" = Yes)

West:	Southwest:	Midwest:	Southeast:	Northeast:	International:
	Y	Y			

LINK REAL ESTATE INVESTMENT TRUST (THE) www.thelinkreit.com

Industry Group Code: 531120 Ranks within this company's industry group: Sales: 27   Profits: 2

Properties:		Financial Services:	Construction/Development:	Investments:		Specialty Services:	Brokerage:
Apartments:		Mortgages:	Commercial Construction:	REIT:	Y	Property Management:	Commercial Sales:
Malls/Shopping:	Y	Title Insurance:	Residential Construction:			Online Services:	Residential Sales:
Offices:		Property Insurance:	Land Development:			Software/IT:	Specialty:
Hotels/Motels:			Support Services:			Consulting:	
Industrial/Warehouses:	Y		Design/Engineering:				
Other:	Y						

TYPES OF BUSINESS:

Real Estate Investment Trust
Asset Enhancement

BRANDS/DIVISIONS/AFFILIATES:

CONTACTS: *Note: Officers with more than one job title may be intentionally listed here more than once.*

Georg Kwok Lung Hongchoy, CEO
Andy Cheung Lee Ming, CFO
Tony Lam Kwok Tai, Dir.-Human Resources
Ricky Chan Ming Tak, Dir.-Legal
Edward Tse Siu Cheung, Dir.-Dev. & Projects
KT Poon, Dir.-Corp. Comm.
Nicholas Robert Sallnow-Smith, Chmn.

Phone: 852-2175-1800	**Fax:** 852-2175-1900
Toll-Free:	
Address: 100 How Ming St., One Landmark East, Hong Kong, China	

GROWTH PLANS/SPECIAL FEATURES:

The Link Real Estate Investment Trust is one of Hong Kong's largest real estate investment trusts (REIT). The company's portfolio consists of 180 retail and car park facilities, with 11 million square feet of retail space and 80,000 individual car spaces. The firm's facilities encompass a variety of tenants, including well known retail and restaurant brands. The Link's strategy is to invest in properties in Hong Kong that are primarily for car park and retail usage and to increase their value by enhancing physical structure, customer service, and developing promotional activities. Current asset enhancement projects include introducing more popular restaurants at Hau Tak Shopping Centre; remodeling vacant floors into shopping areas for the Tsz Wan Shan Shopping Centre; aligning the walkway with retail outlets and adding a coffee shop at Lung Cheung Mall; and converting a market to a retail area and therefore adding more shopping space to the Ming Tak Shopping Centre.

Employees are offered retirement savings; health coverage; and life insurance.

FINANCIALS: Sales and profits are in thousands of dollars—add 000 to get the full amount. 2010 Note: Financial information for 2010 was not available for all companies at press time.

2010 Sales: $642,010	2010 Profits: $1,333,300	**U.S. Stock Ticker:**
2009 Sales: $580,040	2009 Profits: $80,120	**Int'l Ticker: 0823** Int'l Exchange: Hong Kong-HKE
2008 Sales: $545,900	2008 Profits: $668,100	Employees: 729
2007 Sales: $514,000	2007 Profits: $566,000	Fiscal Year Ends: 3/31
2006 Sales: $528,100	2006 Profits: $811,600	Parent Company:

SALARIES/BENEFITS:

Pension Plan:	ESOP Stock Plan:	Profit Sharing:	Top Exec. Salary: $	Bonus: $
Savings Plan: Y	Stock Purch. Plan:		Second Exec. Salary: $	Bonus: $

OTHER THOUGHTS:

Apparent Women Officers or Directors:
Hot Spot for Advancement for Women/Minorities:

LOCATIONS: ("Y" = Yes)

West:	Southwest:	Midwest:	Southeast:	Northeast:	International:
					Y

LODGIAN INC

www.lodgian.com

Industry Group Code: 721110 **Ranks within this company's industry group:** Sales: Profits:

Properties:		Financial Services:	Construction/Development:	Investments:	Specialty Services:		Brokerage:
Apartments:		Mortgages:	Commercial Construction:	REIT:	Property Management:	Y	Commercial Sales:
Malls/Shopping:		Title Insurance:	Residential Construction:		Online Services:		Residential Sales:
Offices:		Property Insurance:	Land Development:		Software/IT:		Specialty:
Hotels/Motels:	Y		Support Services:		Consulting:		
Industrial/Warehouses:			Design/Engineering:				
Other:							

TYPES OF BUSINESS:
Hotels

BRANDS/DIVISIONS/AFFILIATES:
Lone Star Funds

CONTACTS: *Note: Officers with more than one job title may be intentionally listed here more than once.*
Dana M. Ciraldo, CEO
Dana M. Ciraldo, Pres.
Daniel E. Ellis, General Counsel/Exec. VP/Corp. Sec.
Thomas Rosati, Sr. VP-Oper.
Amy Quinn, Sr. VP-Finance & Acct.

Phone: 404-364-9400	Fax: 404-364-0088
Toll-Free:	
Address: 3445 Peachtree Rd. NE, Ste. 700, Atlanta, GA 30326 US	

GROWTH PLANS/SPECIAL FEATURES:

Lodgian, Inc. is an independent owner and operator of 21 hotels located in 14 states. Of the firm's 21 hotels, 11 are InterContinental Hotels Group brands (Crowne Plaza and Holiday Inn), five are Marriott brands (Marriott, Courtyard by Marriott, SpringHill Suites by Marriott and Residence Inn by Marriott), one Hilton and four are associated with other franchisors such as Starwood, Wyndham and Carlson. The company's hotels are primarily full-service properties that offer food and beverage services; meeting and banquet facilities; and compete in the midscale and upscale market segments of the lodging industry. Lodgian operates hotel brands in the Upper Upscale; Upscale; Midscale with Food & Beverage; and Midscale without Food & Beverage segments. In April 2010, the company was acquired by an affiliate of global investment company Lone Star Funds.

Employees are offered medical, dental and vision insurance; disability coverage; life insurance; a 401(k) plan; educational assistance; and discounts on hotel stays.

FINANCIALS: Sales and profits are in thousands of dollars—add 000 to get the full amount. 2010 Note: Financial information for 2010 was not available for all companies at press time.

2010 Sales: $	2010 Profits: $	U.S. Stock Ticker: Private
2009 Sales: $188,544	2009 Profits: $-53,902	Int'l Ticker: Int'l Exchange:
2008 Sales: $228,194	2008 Profits: $-11,984	Employees: 2,362
2007 Sales: $229,875	2007 Profits: $-8,446	Fiscal Year Ends: 12/31
2006 Sales: $227,635	2006 Profits: $-15,176	Parent Company: LONE STAR FUNDS

SALARIES/BENEFITS:

Pension Plan:	ESOP Stock Plan:	Profit Sharing:	Top Exec. Salary: $413,732	Bonus: $
Savings Plan: Y	Stock Purch. Plan:		Second Exec. Salary: $357,815	Bonus: $35,000

OTHER THOUGHTS:
Apparent Women Officers or Directors: 5
Hot Spot for Advancement for Women/Minorities: Y

LOCATIONS: ("Y" = Yes)

West:	Southwest:	Midwest:	Southeast:	Northeast:	International:
Y	Y	Y	Y	Y	

LOEWS HOTELS HOLDING CORPORATION

www.loewshotels.com

Industry Group Code: 721110 Ranks within this company's industry group: Sales: Profits:

Properties:		Financial Services:	Construction/Development:	Investments:	Specialty Services:		Brokerage:
Apartments:		Mortgages:	Commercial Construction:	REIT:	Property Management:	Y	Commercial Sales:
Malls/Shopping:		Title Insurance:	Residential Construction:		Online Services:		Residential Sales:
Offices:		Property Insurance:	Land Development:		Software/IT:		Specialty:
Hotels/Motels:	Y		Support Services:		Consulting:		
Industrial/Warehouses:			Design/Engineering:				
Other:							

TYPES OF BUSINESS:

Hotels, Luxury
Hotel Management Services

BRANDS/DIVISIONS/AFFILIATES:

Loews Corporation
Loews Miami Beach Hotel
Loews Philadelphia Hotel
Loews Royal Pacific Resort at Universal Orlando
Loews Portofino Bay Hotel at Universal Orlando
Loews Lake Las Vegas Resort
Don CeSar Beach Resort & Spa
Loews Le Concorde

CONTACTS: *Note: Officers with more than one job title may be intentionally listed here more than once.*

Jonathan M. Tisch, CEO
Jack Adler, COO
Jack Adler, Pres.
Jonathan M. Tisch, Chmn.

Phone: 212-521-2000	Fax: 212-521-2525
Toll-Free:	
Address: 667 Madison Ave., New York, NY 10021 US	

GROWTH PLANS/SPECIAL FEATURES:

Loews Hotels Holding Corporation, a subsidiary of the Loews Corporation, currently has a portfolio of 20 owned and/or operated luxury hotels and resorts, with a combined 8,073 rooms. In all, the company owns six hotels; has a land lease on three hotels; and operates the remaining nine hotels under management contracts. Located in 16 cities throughout the U.S. and Canada, the firm's properties include the 790-room Loews Miami Beach Hotel in Florida; the 585-room Loews Philadelphia Hotel; the 493-room Loews Lake Las Vegas Resort; the 405-room Loews Le Concorde in Quebec City; and the 140-room Loews Hotel Vogue in Montreal. Loews Hotels operates three joint venture hotels with Universal Studios in Orlando, Florida: Loews Royal Pacific Resort at Universal Orlando, its largest hotel with 1,000 rooms; the 750-room Loews Portofino Bay Hotel at Universal Orlando; and the 650-room Hard Rock Hotel at Universal Orlando. Additionally, a subsidiary of the firm owns 20% of the Don CeSar Beach Resort in St. Pete Beach, Florida, which the firm manages. Loews Hotels' business amenities include high-speed Internet access; a power breakfast with notable business leaders; notarization services; private dining rooms; boardrooms; and concierge services. The YouFirst Loyalty Program rewards guests based on number of stays and offers free Internet access, late checkout, guaranteed rooms and upgrades for guests who visit at least twice a year. Loews Hotels offers facilities for weddings, meetings and special events; and special programs and services designed for people traveling with pets, children and teenagers.

FINANCIALS: Sales and profits are in thousands of dollars—add 000 to get the full amount. 2010 Note: Financial information for 2010 was not available for all companies at press time.

2010 Sales: $	2010 Profits: $	**U.S. Stock Ticker: Subsidiary**	
2009 Sales: $	2009 Profits: $	**Int'l Ticker:** Int'l Exchange:	
2008 Sales: $	2008 Profits: $	Employees:	
2007 Sales: $	2007 Profits: $	Fiscal Year Ends: 12/31	
2006 Sales: $	2006 Profits: $	Parent Company: LOEWS CORPORATION	

SALARIES/BENEFITS:

Pension Plan: Y	ESOP Stock Plan:	Profit Sharing:	Top Exec. Salary: $	Bonus: $
Savings Plan: Y	Stock Purch. Plan:		Second Exec. Salary: $	Bonus: $

OTHER THOUGHTS:

Apparent Women Officers or Directors:
Hot Spot for Advancement for Women/Minorities:

LOCATIONS: ("Y" = Yes)

West:	Southwest:	Midwest:	Southeast:	Northeast:	International:
Y	Y		Y	Y	Y

LOUIS BERGER GROUP INC (THE)

www.louisberger.com

Industry Group Code: 237 Ranks within this company's industry group: Sales: Profits:

Properties:	Financial Services:	Construction/Development:		Investments:	Specialty Services:	Brokerage:
Apartments:	Mortgages:	Commercial Construction:		REIT:	Property Management:	Commercial Sales:
Malls/Shopping:	Title Insurance:	Residential Construction:			Online Services:	Residential Sales:
Offices:	Property Insurance:	Land Development:			Software/IT:	Specialty:
Hotels/Motels:		Support Services:			Consulting:	
Industrial/Warehouses:		Design/Engineering:	Y			
Other:						

TYPES OF BUSINESS:

Architectural & Engineering Services
Civil Engineering
Environmental Engineering
Transportation Infrastructure
Project Management
Consulting Services
Hydrologic Engineering
Seismic & Geotechnical Services

BRANDS/DIVISIONS/AFFILIATES:

Louis Berger SAS
Ammann & Whitney Consulting Engineers Inc
Berger/ABAM Engineers Inc
Berger Devine Yaeger Inc
Klohn Crippen Berger Ltd
Berger, Lehman Associates PC
CHELBI Engineering Consultants Inc
RBA Group Inc (The)

CONTACTS: Note: Officers with more than one job title may be intentionally listed here more than once.

James G. Bach, COO
Larry D. Walker, Pres.
Luke McKinnon, CFO
Susan Knauf, VP/Chief Learning Officer
Charles Bell, Group VP
Carlos Marcenaro, Group VP
D. James Stamatis, Group VP
Fredric S. Berger, Chmn.

Phone: 973-407-1000	Fax: 973-267-6468
Toll-Free:	
Address: 412 Mt. Kemble Ave., Morristown, NJ 07960-6654 US	

GROWTH PLANS/SPECIAL FEATURES:

The Louis Berger Group, Inc. (Berger) is an infrastructure engineering, environmental science and economic development company with more than 140 offices throughout the U.S. and in more than 90 countries worldwide. Berger offers services in such areas as civil, structural, mechanical, electrical and environmental engineering; program management; planning; environmental sciences; cultural resources; information science; finance; economics; and construction management. The group operates through a number of subsidiary companies. Louis Berger SAS, based in Paris, France, provides design and supervision services for transportation and privately financed infrastructure projects, water supply and urban sanitation systems. It also offers management and human resource development services. Berger Avart, Inc. offers architectural and engineering services within Florida. Ammann & Whitney Consulting Engineers, Inc. provides structural, civil, architectural, mechanical, electrical engineering and construction inspection services for such projects as bridges, highways, airports, transit stations, schools and government and military installations. Berger/ABAM Engineers, Inc. offers planning, environmental science, civil and structural engineering, project management and construction support consulting services. Berger Devine Yaeger, Inc. provides architectural, engineering, planning and surveying solutions. Klohn Crippen Berger Ltd. designs hydroelectric power plants, dams, tunnels and pumped storage schemes; serves mining clients internationally; and provides seismic and geotechnical services throughout Canada. Berger, Lehman Associates, P.C. is one of the largest engineering, economic and environmental planning organizations in the U.S., serving state, municipal and local agencies as well as corporate and industrial clients. CHELBI Engineering Consultants, Inc. provides project support services in China. The RBA Group, Inc. offers its clients engineering, planning and architectural services.

Employees are offered medical and dental coverage; life and travel insurance; a new employee hiring referral award; tuition reimbursement; flexible spending accounts; a cafeteria plan; and registration fee payment for professional licenses.

FINANCIALS: Sales and profits are in thousands of dollars—add 000 to get the full amount. 2010 Note: Financial information for 2010 was not available for all companies at press time.

2010 Sales: $	2010 Profits: $	U.S. Stock Ticker: Private
2009 Sales: $	2009 Profits: $	Int'l Ticker: Int'l Exchange:
2008 Sales: $	2008 Profits: $	Employees:
2007 Sales: $	2007 Profits: $	Fiscal Year Ends: 6/30
2006 Sales: $	2006 Profits: $	Parent Company:

SALARIES/BENEFITS:

Pension Plan:	ESOP Stock Plan:	Profit Sharing:	Top Exec. Salary: $	Bonus: $
Savings Plan: Y	Stock Purch. Plan:		Second Exec. Salary: $	Bonus: $

OTHER THOUGHTS:

Apparent Women Officers or Directors: 1
Hot Spot for Advancement for Women/Minorities:

LOCATIONS: ("Y" = Yes)

West:	Southwest:	Midwest:	Southeast:	Northeast:	International:
Y	Y	Y	Y	Y	Y

LOWE'S COMPANIES INC

www.lowes.com

Industry Group Code: 444110 Ranks within this company's industry group: Sales: 2   Profits: 2

Properties:		Financial Services:	Construction/Development:		Investments:	Specialty Services:	Brokerage:
Apartments:		Mortgages:	Commercial Construction:		REIT:	Property Management:	Commercial Sales:
Malls/Shopping:	Y	Title Insurance:	Residential Construction:			Online Services:	Residential Sales:
Offices:		Property Insurance:	Land Development:			Software/IT:	Specialty:
Hotels/Motels:			Support Services:	Y		Consulting:	
Industrial/Warehouses:			Design/Engineering:				
Other:							

TYPES OF BUSINESS:

Home Centers, Retail
Home Improvement Products
Home Installation Services
Special Order Sales

BRANDS/DIVISIONS/AFFILIATES:

Aquasource
Kobalt
Portfolio
Harbor Breeze
Reliabilt
Utilitech
Top-Choice
Garden Treasures

CONTACTS: *Note: Officers with more than one job title may be intentionally listed here more than once.*

Robert A. Niblock, CEO
Larry D. Stone, COO
Larry D. Stone, Pres.
Robert F. Hull, Jr., CFO/Exec. VP
Thomas J. Lamb, Sr. VP-Mktg. & Advertising
Maureen K. Ausura, Sr. VP-Human Resources
Steven M. Stone, CIO/Sr. VP
Charles W. Canter, Jr., Exec. VP-Merch.
Gary E. Wyatt, Sr. VP-Eng., Real Estate & Construction
Gaither M. Keener, Jr., General Counsel/Sr. VP/Corp. Sec.
Michael K. Brown, Exec. VP-Store Oper.
Gregory M. Bridgeford, Exec. VP-Bus. Dev.
N. Brian Peace, Sr. VP-Corp. Affairs
Matthew V. Hollifield, Chief Acct. Officer/Sr. VP
Theresa A. Anderson, Sr. VP-Store Oper., Southeast Div.
Patricia M. Price, Sr. VP/Gen. Merch. Mgr.-Outdoor Living
Marshall A. Croom, Sr. VP/Chief Risk Officer
Clinton T. Davis, Sr. VP/Gen. Merch. Mgr.-Kitchen & Bath
Robert A. Niblock, Chmn.
Joseph M. Mabry, Jr., Exec. VP-Logistics & Dist.

Phone: 704-758-1000	**Fax:** 336-6584766
Toll-Free: 800-445-6937	
Address: 1000 Lowe's Blvd., Mooresville, NC 28117 US	

GROWTH PLANS/SPECIAL FEATURES:

Lowe's Companies, Inc. is one of the largest home improvement retailers in the world. The company owns over 1,710 superstores in 50 states and Canada, each carrying approximately 40,000 products. Hundreds of thousands of items are also available through the firm's special order system. Lowe's stores chiefly serve do-it-yourself homeowners and commercial business customers, including contractors, landscapers, electricians, painters and plumbers. Its home improvement product categories include building materials; lighting; cabinets and countertops; seasonal living; millwork; lumber; flooring; lawn and landscaping items; hardware; fashion and rough plumbing; appliances; paint; tools; plants and plant pots; outdoor power equipment; rough electrical; home environment and organization; and windows and walls. Each Lowe's store carries a wide selection of national brand name merchandise such as KitchenAid, Samsung, Whirlpool, Pella, Werner, Kohler, DeWalt, John Deere, Troy-Bilt, Jenn-Air and Bosch; and exclusive brand names such as Garden Treasures, Kobalt, Aquasource, Portfolio, Harbor Breeze, Reliabilt, Utilitech and Top-Choice. The company's web site, Lowes.com, facilitates customers researching, comparing and buying Lowe's products and services. Lowes.com and the firm's electronic catalogs offer customers to special order products that are not carried in its physical store locations. Lowe's expected to open approximately 40 to 45 new stores throughout 2010. The company's joint venture with Woolworths Limited, an Australian firm with over 3,000 retail outlets, of which Lowe's owns 33.3%, is expected to open its first home improvement store location in 2011.

Lowe's offers its employees benefits such as life, disability, accident, auto, home, health, dental and vision insurance; merchandise discounts; employee assistance programs; employee discounts; tuition reimbursement; paid time off; a 401(k); and flexible spending accounts.

FINANCIALS: Sales and profits are in thousands of dollars—add 000 to get the full amount. 2010 Note: Financial information for 2010 was not available for all companies at press time.

2010 Sales: $47,220,000	2010 Profits: $1,783,000	**U.S. Stock Ticker: LOW**
2009 Sales: $48,230,000	2009 Profits: $2,195,000	**Int'l Ticker:** Int'l Exchange:
2008 Sales: $48,283,000	2008 Profits: $2,809,000	Employees: 234,000
2007 Sales: $46,927,000	2007 Profits: $3,105,000	Fiscal Year Ends: 1/31
2006 Sales: $43,243,000	2006 Profits: $2,765,000	Parent Company:

SALARIES/BENEFITS:

Pension Plan:	ESOP Stock Plan:	Profit Sharing:	Top Exec. Salary: $1,100,000	Bonus: $2,839,683
Savings Plan: Y	Stock Purch. Plan: Y		Second Exec. Salary: $840,000	Bonus: $1,734,012

OTHER THOUGHTS:

Apparent Women Officers or Directors: 5
Hot Spot for Advancement for Women/Minorities: Y

LOCATIONS: ("Y" = Yes)

West:	Southwest:	Midwest:	Southeast:	Northeast:	International:
Y	Y	Y	Y	Y	Y

LQ MANAGEMENT LLC

www.lq.com

Industry Group Code: 721110 Ranks within this company's industry group: Sales: Profits:

Properties:		Financial Services:	Construction/Development:	Investments:		Specialty Services:		Brokerage:	
Apartments:		Mortgages:	Commercial Construction:	REIT:	Y	Property Management:	Y	Commercial Sales:	
Malls/Shopping:		Title Insurance:	Residential Construction:			Online Services:	Y	Residential Sales:	
Offices:		Property Insurance:	Land Development:			Software/IT:		Specialty:	
Hotels/Motels:	Y		Support Services:			Consulting:			
Industrial/Warehouses:			Design/Engineering:						
Other:									

TYPES OF BUSINESS:

Hotels, Motels & Suites
Hotel Management
Franchising
REIT

BRANDS/DIVISIONS/AFFILIATES:

La Quinta Properties
La Quinta Inns
La Quinta Inns and Suites
Budgetel
Baymont Inns and Suites
Woodfield Suites
Blackstone Group LP (The)

CONTACTS:
Note: Officers with more than one job title may be intentionally listed here more than once.

Wayne B. Goldberg, CEO
Angelo J. Lombardi, COO/Exec. VP
Wayne Goldberg, Pres.
Temple H. Weiss, CFO/Exec. VP
Julie M. Cary, Chief Mktg. Officer/Exec. VP
Jeffrey M. Schagren, Exec. VP-Human Resources
Vivek Shaiva, CIO/Exec. VP
Mark M. Chloupek, General Counsel/Exec. VP
Rajiv K. Trivedi, Chief Dev. Officer
Teresa Ferguson, Dir.-Comm. & Public Rel.
Murry J. Cathlina, Exec. VP-Design & Construction
Feliz P. Jarvis, Exec. VP-Sales
Rajiv K. Trivedi, Exec. VP-Franchise

Phone: 214-492-6600	Fax: 214-492-6616
Toll-Free:	
Address: 909 Hidden Ridge, Ste. 600, Irving, TX 75038 US	

GROWTH PLANS/SPECIAL FEATURES:

LQ Management LLC, a subsidiary of the Blackstone Group, is the operator of the La Quinta motels and suites properties. La Quinta is a leading limited-service lodging brand that provides comfortable guest rooms in convenient locations at affordable prices. The firm is one of the largest owners and operators of limited-service hotels in the U.S. It boasts more than 800 hotels and 65,000 rooms in 45 states under the brands La Quinta Inns; La Quinta Inns and Suites; Baymont Inns and Suites; Woodfield Suites; and Budgetel. The firm also licenses its brand name to franchisees for royalty and other fees. The company markets its services to both leisure guests and business travelers. All of the firm's hotels are owned through La Quinta Properties, a real estate investment trust (REIT). A typical La Quinta Inn features approximately 130 guest rooms with amenities including movies-on-demand; interactive video games; free high-speed Internet; complimentary continental breakfast; a swimming pool; fax services; and 24-hour front desk message services. La Quinta Inn and Suites properties also feature deluxe two-room suites with microwaves and refrigerators, as well as fitness centers, courtyards and expanded food offerings. In July 2010, the firm opened three hotels in Idaho.

Employees of the firm are offered medical, dental and vision coverage; life insurance; long-term disability; an employee assistance program; flexible spending accounts; a 401(k) plan; tuition reimbursement; internal referral bonus program; direct deposit and room rate discounts.

FINANCIALS:
Sales and profits are in thousands of dollars—add 000 to get the full amount. 2010 Note: Financial information for 2010 was not available for all companies at press time.

2010 Sales: $	2010 Profits: $	U.S. Stock Ticker: Private
2009 Sales: $	2009 Profits: $	Int'l Ticker: Int'l Exchange:
2008 Sales: $	2008 Profits: $	Employees:
2007 Sales: $	2007 Profits: $	Fiscal Year Ends: 12/31
2006 Sales: $	2006 Profits: $	Parent Company: BLACKSTONE GROUP LP (THE)

SALARIES/BENEFITS:

Pension Plan:	ESOP Stock Plan:	Profit Sharing:	Top Exec. Salary: $	Bonus: $
Savings Plan: Y	Stock Purch. Plan:		Second Exec. Salary: $	Bonus: $

OTHER THOUGHTS:

Apparent Women Officers or Directors: 2
Hot Spot for Advancement for Women/Minorities:

LOCATIONS: ("Y" = Yes)

West:	Southwest:	Midwest:	Southeast:	Northeast:	International:
Y	Y	Y	Y	Y	Y

M/I HOMES INC

www.mihomes.com

Industry Group Code: 2361 Ranks within this company's industry group: Sales: 15   Profits: 10

Properties:	Financial Services:		Construction/Development:		Investments:	Specialty Services:	Brokerage:	
Apartments:	Mortgages:	Y	Commercial Construction:		REIT:	Property Management:	Commercial Sales:	
Malls/Shopping:	Title Insurance:	Y	Residential Construction:	Y		Online Services:	Residential Sales:	Y
Offices:	Property Insurance:		Land Development:	Y		Software/IT:	Specialty:	
Hotels/Motels:			Support Services:			Consulting:		
Industrial/Warehouses:			Design/Engineering:	Y				
Other:								

TYPES OF BUSINESS:

Construction, Residential
Real Estate Development
Mortgage Services
Title Services

BRANDS/DIVISIONS/AFFILIATES:

Showcase Homes
M/I Financial
TransOhio Residential Title Agency
M/I Title Agency
Washington/Metro Residential Title Agency
Confidence Builder Program
Personal Construction Supervisor

CONTACTS: *Note: Officers with more than one job title may be intentionally listed here more than once.*

Robert H. Schottenstein, CEO
Robert H. Schottenstein, Pres.
Phillip G. Creek, CFO/Exec. VP
J. Thomas Mason, General Counsel/Sec./Exec. VP
Ann Marier Hunker, Investor Rel.
Robert H. Schottenstein, Chmn.

Phone: 614-418-8000	Fax: 614-418-8080
Toll-Free: 888-644-4111	
Address: 3 Easton Oval, Ste. 500, Columbus, OH 43219 US	

GROWTH PLANS/SPECIAL FEATURES:

M/I Homes, Inc. is a leading builder of single-family homes sold to first-time homebuyers, move-up buyers, empty nesters and luxury buyers under the M/I Homes and Showcase Homes trade names. The company delivered 2,434 homes in 2010, with an average sales price of $247,000. M/I sells its homes in Columbus and Cincinnati, Ohio; Tampa and Orlando, Florida; Charlotte and Raleigh, North Carolina; Indianapolis, Indiana; Chicago, Illinois; Houston, Texas; and the Virginia and Maryland suburbs of Washington, D.C. M/I operates in four segments: Midwest homebuilding, Southern homebuilding, Mid-Atlantic homebuilding and financial services. The firm's homebuilding operations comprise over 98% of its revenues. The homebuilding operations include the acquisition and development of land; the sale and construction of single-family attached and detached homes; and the occasional sale of lots and land to third parties. M/I's financial services operations generate revenue from originating and selling mortgages; collecting fees for title insurance, as well as and closing services. Subsidiary M/I Financial provides financing services in its housing markets, while title services are provided through subsidiaries TransOhio Residential Title Agency, M/I Title Agency and majority-owned Washington/Metro Residential Title Agency. The company offers roughly 400 floor plans and spent $2.4 million in 2010 on research and development of its homes. The firm's Confidence Builder Program includes a pre-construction conference between the client and a Personal Construction Supervisor. The supervisors manage the development and construction process, for which M/I utilizes independent subcontractors.

Employees are offered medical, dental and vision insurance; life insurance; disability coverage; an employee assistance program; a 401(k) plan; an employee stock purchase plan; and an employee home purchase plan.

FINANCIALS: Sales and profits are in thousands of dollars—add 000 to get the full amount. 2010 Note: Financial information for 2010 was not available for all companies at press time.

2010 Sales: $616,377	2010 Profits: $-26,269	**U.S. Stock Ticker: MHO**
2009 Sales: $569,949	2009 Profits: $-62,109	**Int'l Ticker:** Int'l Exchange:
2008 Sales: $607,659	2008 Profits: $-250,323	Employees: 522
2007 Sales: $1,016,460	2007 Profits: $-135,439	Fiscal Year Ends: 12/31
2006 Sales: $1,274,145	2006 Profits: $38,875	Parent Company:

SALARIES/BENEFITS:

Pension Plan:	ESOP Stock Plan:	Profit Sharing:	Top Exec. Salary: $750,000	Bonus: $356,501
Savings Plan: Y	Stock Purch. Plan: Y		Second Exec. Salary: $500,000	Bonus: $169,763

OTHER THOUGHTS:

Apparent Women Officers or Directors: 2
Hot Spot for Advancement for Women/Minorities:

LOCATIONS: ("Y" = Yes)

West:	Southwest:	Midwest:	Southeast:	Northeast:	International:
	Y	Y	Y	Y	

MACERICH COMPANY (THE)

www.macerich.com

Industry Group Code: 531120 Ranks within this company's industry group: Sales: 22   Profits: 38

Properties:		Financial Services:		Construction/Development:		Investments:		Specialty Services:		Brokerage:
Apartments:		Mortgages:		Commercial Construction:		REIT:	Y	Property Management:	Y	Commercial Sales:
Malls/Shopping:	Y	Title Insurance:		Residential Construction:				Online Services:		Residential Sales:
Offices:		Property Insurance:		Land Development:	Y			Software/IT:		Specialty:
Hotels/Motels:				Support Services:				Consulting:		
Industrial/Warehouses:				Design/Engineering:						
Other:										

TYPES OF BUSINESS:

Real Estate Investment Trust
Regional Shopping Centers
Community Shopping Centers
Property Management
Property Redevelopment

BRANDS/DIVISIONS/AFFILIATES:

Macerich Partnership, L.P.
Macerich Property Management Company, LLC
Westcor Partners, LLC
Macerich Management Company

CONTACTS: *Note: Officers with more than one job title may be intentionally listed here more than once.*

Arthur M. Coppola, CEO
Tony Grossi, COO/Sr. VP
Edward C. Coppola, Pres.
Thomas E. O'Hern, CFO/Sr. Exec. VP/Treas.
Tracey Gotsis, Exec. VP-Mktg. & Dev.
Genene Kruger, Sr. VP-Human Resources
J.P. Jones, CIO/Sr. VP
Steve Spector, General Counsel/Sr. VP
Eric Salo, Exec. VP-Bus. Dev., Asset Management & Properties
Scott Kingsmore, Sr. VP-Finance
Richard A. Bayer, Chief Legal Officer/Sr. Exec. VP/Sec.
Don Foster, Sr. VP-Design & Construction
Randy Brant, Exec. VP-Real Estate
Michael J. Busenhart, Sr. VP-Acquisitions
Arthur M. Coppola, Chmn.

Phone: 310-394-6000	Fax: 310-395-2791
Toll-Free:	
Address: 401 Wilshire Blvd., Ste. 700, Santa Monica, CA 90401 US	

GROWTH PLANS/SPECIAL FEATURES:

The Macerich Company is a real estate investment trust (REIT) involved in the acquisition, ownership, redevelopment, management and leasing of regional and community shopping centers located throughout the U.S. The firm is the sole general partner and has an 89% ownership interest in the Macerich Partnership, L.P. (MP), which owns or maintains ownership interests in 71 regional shopping centers and 13 community shopping centers, totaling approximately 73 million square feet of leasable area. Other subsidiaries include Macerich Property Management Company; Westcor Partners; and Macerich Management Company. Macerich's largest markets include California and Arizona, both with 20 or more shopping centers. Other properties are located in Colorado, Connecticut, Iowa, Illinois, Indiana, Kentucky, Maryland, Montana, New Jersey, New York, Oregon, South Dakota, Texas, Utah, Virginia and Washington. Macerich's integrated operations include in-house accounting, finance, legal, marketing, property management and redevelopment expertise. Its regional shopping centers are generally enclosed; offer a variety of small and mid-size stores anchored by several department stores or other large retailers; and range in size from approximately 315,000 to over two million square feet, with an average of 942,000 square feet. The firm's community shopping centers, which are generally smaller open-air centers designed to attract local and neighborhood customers with anchors such as supermarkets and drug stores, average 292,000 square feet. Some key tenants in the company's properties include The Gap, Inc.; Limited Brands, Inc.; Foot Locker, Inc.; Forever 21, Inc.; AT&T Mobility, LLC; Abercrombie & Fitch Co.; Luxottica Group; and American Eagle Outfitters, Inc. Anchors in the firm's regional malls include Macy's, Sears, J.C. Penney, Dillard's, Nordstrom and Target. In January 2011, the firm agreed to acquire a 400,000 square foot community center in Queens, New York through a 50/50 joint venture.

FINANCIALS: Sales and profits are in thousands of dollars—add 000 to get the full amount. 2010 Note: Financial information for 2010 was not available for all companies at press time.

2010 Sales: $758,559	2010 Profits: $28,420	**U.S. Stock Ticker: MAC**
2009 Sales: $805,654	2009 Profits: $139,250	**Int'l Ticker:** Int'l Exchange:
2008 Sales: $880,871	2008 Profits: $195,015	Employees: 2,658
2007 Sales: $800,842	2007 Profits: $106,062	Fiscal Year Ends: 12/31
2006 Sales: $749,619	2006 Profits: $244,549	Parent Company:

SALARIES/BENEFITS:

Pension Plan:	ESOP Stock Plan:	Profit Sharing: Y	Top Exec. Salary: $950,000	Bonus: $3,800,000
Savings Plan: Y	Stock Purch. Plan: Y		Second Exec. Salary: $800,000	Bonus: $3,200,000

OTHER THOUGHTS:

Apparent Women Officers or Directors: 5
Hot Spot for Advancement for Women/Minorities: Y

LOCATIONS: ("Y" = Yes)

West:	Southwest:	Midwest:	Southeast:	Northeast:	International:
Y	Y	Y	Y	Y	

MACK-CALI REALTY CORP   www.mack-cali.com

Industry Group Code: 531120 Ranks within this company's industry group: Sales: 21   Profits: 32

Properties:		Financial Services:	Construction/Development:	Investments:		Specialty Services:		Brokerage:
Apartments:		Mortgages:	Commercial Construction:	REIT:	Y	Property Management:	Y	Commercial Sales:
Malls/Shopping:		Title Insurance:	Residential Construction:			Online Services:		Residential Sales:
Offices:	Y	Property Insurance:	Land Development:			Software/IT:		Specialty:
Hotels/Motels:			Support Services:			Consulting:		
Industrial/Warehouses:	Y		Design/Engineering:					
Other:								

TYPES OF BUSINESS:
Real Estate Investment Trust
Office & Industrial Properties
Property Management

BRANDS/DIVISIONS/AFFILIATES:
Gale Construction Company

CONTACTS: *Note: Officers with more than one job title may be intentionally listed here more than once.*
Mitchell E. Hersh, CEO
Mitchell E. Hersh, Pres.
Barry Lefkowitz, CFO/Exec. VP
Janice H. Torchinsky, VP-Human Resources
Nicholas Mitarotonda, Jr., VP-Info. Systems
Roger W. Thomas, General Counsel/Exec. VP/Corp. Sec.
John J. Crandall, Sr. VP-Dev.
Anthony Krug, Sr. VP-Finance
Giovanni M. DeBari, VP/Corp. Controller
William Fitzpatrick, VP/Treas.
John Adderly, VP-Leasing
James A. Bell, VP-Property Mgmt.
William L. Mack, Chmn.

Phone: 732-590-1000	Fax: 732-205-8237
Toll-Free:	
Address: 343 Thornall St., Edison, NJ 08837-2206 US	

GROWTH PLANS/SPECIAL FEATURES:
Mack-Cali Realty Corp. is a fully integrated, self-administered and self-managed real estate investment trust (REIT) that owns and operates a portfolio made up predominantly of Class A office and office/flex properties, located primarily in suburban markets in the Northeast U.S. The trust performs substantially all commercial real estate leasing, management, acquisition, development and construction services on an in-house basis. The company owns or has interests in 277 properties, totaling approximately 32.2 million square feet of Class A office, office/flex properties, warehouse/industrial and stand alone retail space that is leased to more than 2,000 tenants. Mack-Cali's portfolio is approximately 89.1% leased. Many of the firm's properties have adjacent company-controlled developable land. Its major tenants include AT&T Corp.; Prentice-Hall, Inc; Forest Research Institute, Inc.; Credit Suisse (USA), Inc.; KPMG, LLP; IBM Corp.; Daiichi Sankyo, Inc.; and Allstate Insurance Company. Through joint ventures, the company has interests in an additional 20 buildings, primarily office properties, totaling about 1.2 million square feet, and a 350-room hotel. Its subsidiary, Gale Construction Company, offers development management, construction advisory services, construction management services, design services and general contracting.

FINANCIALS: Sales and profits are in thousands of dollars—add 000 to get the full amount. 2010 Note: Financial information for 2010 was not available for all companies at press time.

2010 Sales: $787,480	2010 Profits: $52,900	**U.S. Stock Ticker: CLI**
2009 Sales: $758,925	2009 Profits: $52,568	**Int'l Ticker:** Int'l Exchange:
2008 Sales: $722,780	2008 Profits: $51,726	Employees: 390
2007 Sales: $808,350	2007 Profits: $108,466	Fiscal Year Ends: 12/31
2006 Sales: $732,012	2006 Profits: $142,666	Parent Company:

SALARIES/BENEFITS:

Pension Plan:	ESOP Stock Plan:	Profit Sharing:	Top Exec. Salary: $1,050,000	Bonus: $1,000,000
Savings Plan:	Stock Purch. Plan:		Second Exec. Salary: $420,000	Bonus: $505,000

OTHER THOUGHTS:
Apparent Women Officers or Directors: 3
Hot Spot for Advancement for Women/Minorities: Y

LOCATIONS: ("Y" = Yes)

West:	Southwest:	Midwest:	Southeast:	Northeast:	International:
				Y	

MANDARIN ORIENTAL INTERNATIONAL LTD

www.mandarinoriental.com
Industry Group Code: 721110 **Ranks within this company's industry group: Sales: 19   Profits: 16**

Properties:		Financial Services:		Construction/Development:		Investments:		Specialty Services:		Brokerage:	
Apartments:		Mortgages:		Commercial Construction:	Y	REIT:		Property Management:	Y	Commercial Sales:	
Malls/Shopping:		Title Insurance:		Residential Construction:				Online Services:		Residential Sales:	
Offices:		Property Insurance:		Land Development:				Software/IT:		Specialty:	
Hotels/Motels:	Y			Support Services:				Consulting:			
Industrial/Warehouses:				Design/Engineering:							
Other:	Y										

TYPES OF BUSINESS:

Hotels, Luxury
Condominiums

BRANDS/DIVISIONS/AFFILIATES:

Mandarin Oriental Holding Company Limited
Mandarin Oriental
Residences at Mandarin Oriental
Spa at Mandarin Oriental

CONTACTS: *Note: Officers with more than one job title may be intentionally listed here more than once.*

Edouard Ettedgui, CEO
Stuart Dickie, CFO
Michael Hobson, Dir.-Sales & Mktg.
Terry L. Stinson, Dir.-Dev.
Jill Kluge, Group Dir.-Brand Comm.
Christoph Mares, Dir.-Oper., EMEA
Andrew Hirst, Dir.-Oper., Asia
Richard Baker, Exec. VP-Americas Oper.
Simon L. Keswick, Chmn.
Terry L. Stinson, Pres., The Americas

Phone: 852-2895-9288	Fax: 852-2837-3500
Toll-Free:	
Address: 281 Gloucester Rd., 7th Fl., Hong Kong, China	

GROWTH PLANS/SPECIAL FEATURES:

Mandarin Oriental International, Ltd. (MOI) is an international hotel investment and management group. MOI operates in two business segments, hotel ownership and hotel management, and four geographical regions: Hong Kong and Macau; Other Asia; Europe; and the Americas. The company operates or is in the process of developing 42 luxury and first class hotels with over 10,000 rooms and a presence in 27 countries worldwide. MOI has 18 hotel properties in Asia, 12 in the Americas and 12 in Europe, the Middle East and North Africa. These include the original flagship properties of the Mandarin Oriental in Hong Kong and the Oriental in Bangkok, as well as locations such as Singapore, Jakarta, Kuala Lumpur, Macau, Manila, London, Geneva, Tokyo, Munich, Prague and Bermuda. The company has U.S. hotels in New York City, San Francisco, Boston, Miami, Las Vegas and Washington, D.C. In addition to hotel rooms, the Mandarin Oriental New York also offers the Residences at Mandarin Oriental, 65 luxury condominiums located above the hotel. Another 12 of the firm's properties also feature the Residences at Mandarin Oriental condominiums. The Spa at Mandarin Oriental can also be found in many of the firm's hotels worldwide, including in London, Miami, Boston and New York City. Each spa is unique and offers specialized treatments to clients. Properties currently under development include the Mandarin Oriental Hotels in Beijing, Guangzhou, Maldives, Shanghai, Taipei, Costa Rica, Turks and Caicos, St. Kitts, Abu Dhabi, Doha, Marbella, Marrakech, Milan, Moscow and Paris. In 2010, the company opened new hotels in Shanghai, Doha, Macau and Abu Dhabi.

FINANCIALS: Sales and profits are in thousands of dollars—add 000 to get the full amount. 2010 Note: Financial information for 2010 was not available for all companies at press time.

		U.S. Stock Ticker:
2010 Sales: $513,200	2010 Profits: $41,400	**Int'l Ticker: M04** Int'l Exchange: Singapore-SIN
2009 Sales: $438,000	2009 Profits: $83,300	Employees:
2008 Sales: $530,000	2008 Profits: $66,200	Fiscal Year Ends: 12/31
2007 Sales: $529,500	2007 Profits: $107,400	Parent Company:
2006 Sales: $404,600	2006 Profits: $80,200	

SALARIES/BENEFITS:

Pension Plan:	ESOP Stock Plan:	Profit Sharing:	Top Exec. Salary: $	Bonus: $
Savings Plan:	Stock Purch. Plan:		Second Exec. Salary: $	Bonus: $

OTHER THOUGHTS:

Apparent Women Officers or Directors: 1
Hot Spot for Advancement for Women/Minorities:

LOCATIONS: ("Y" = Yes)

West:	Southwest:	Midwest:	Southeast:	Northeast:	International:
Y			Y	Y	Y

MANOR CARE INC

www.hcr-manorcare.com

Industry Group Code: 623110 **Ranks within this company's industry group:** Sales: Profits:

Properties:	Financial Services:	Construction/Development:	Investments:	Specialty Services:	Brokerage:
Apartments:	Mortgages:	Commercial Construction:	REIT:	Property Management:	Commercial Sales:
Malls/Shopping:	Title Insurance:	Residential Construction:		Online Services:	Residential Sales:
Offices:	Property Insurance:	Land Development:		Software/IT:	Specialty:
Hotels/Motels:		Support Services:		Consulting:	
Industrial/Warehouses:		Design/Engineering:			
Other: Y					

TYPES OF BUSINESS:

Long-Term Health Care/Nursing Homes
Home Health Care
Short-Term Care Facilities
Assisted Living Facilities
Rehabilitation Clinics

BRANDS/DIVISIONS/AFFILIATES:

HCR Manor Care
Heartland
ManorCare Health Services
Arden Courts
Carlyle Group (The)

CONTACTS: *Note: Officers with more than one job title may be intentionally listed here more than once.*

Paul A. Ormond, CEO
Stephen L. Guillard, COO/Exec. VP
Paul A. Ormond, Pres.
Steven M. Cavanaugh, CFO/VP
Paul A. Ormond, Chmn.

Phone: 419-252-5500	Fax: 419-252-6404
Toll-Free:	
Address: 333 N. Summit St., Toledo, OH 43604-2617 US	

GROWTH PLANS/SPECIAL FEATURES:

Manor Care, Inc., doing business as HCR Manor Care, provides a range of health care services, including skilled nursing care, assisted living, post-acute medical care, hospice care, home health care and rehabilitation therapy. Manor Care operates over 500 properties in 32 states, with facilities operating primarily under the Heartland, ManorCare Health Services and Arden Courts names. Manor Care's long-term care services consist of skilled nursing centers, assisted living services, post-acute medical and rehabilitation care and Alzheimer's care. The skilled nursing centers use interdisciplinary teams of experienced medical professionals, including registered nurses, licensed practical nurses and certified nursing assistants, to provide services prescribed by physicians. Other services include the design of Quality of Life programs to give the highest practicable level of functional independence to patients, provide physical, speech, respiratory and occupational therapy and provide quality nutrition services, social services, activities and housekeeping and laundry services. Manor Care's assisted living services provide personal care services and assistance with general activities of daily living such as dressing, bathing, meal preparation and medication management. The firm is owned by The Carlyle Group.

Manor Care Inc. offers its employees benefits including vision, dental, life and AD&D insurance; flexible spending accounts; legal assistance; an employee assistance program; a 401(k) savings plan; adoption assistance; and education assistance.

FINANCIALS: Sales and profits are in thousands of dollars—add 000 to get the full amount. 2010 Note: Financial information for 2010 was not available for all companies at press time.

2010 Sales: $	2010 Profits: $	U.S. Stock Ticker: Private
2009 Sales: $4,000,000	2009 Profits: $	Int'l Ticker: Int'l Exchange:
2008 Sales: $3,850,000	2008 Profits: $	Employees: 60,000
2007 Sales: $3,800,000	2007 Profits: $	Fiscal Year Ends: 12/31
2006 Sales: $3,613,185	2006 Profits: $169,560	Parent Company: CARLYLE GROUP (THE)

SALARIES/BENEFITS:

Pension Plan:	ESOP Stock Plan:	Profit Sharing:	Top Exec. Salary: $	Bonus: $
Savings Plan: Y	Stock Purch. Plan:		Second Exec. Salary: $	Bonus: $

OTHER THOUGHTS:

Apparent Women Officers or Directors:
Hot Spot for Advancement for Women/Minorities:

LOCATIONS: ("Y" = Yes)

West:	Southwest:	Midwest:	Southeast:	Northeast:	International:
Y	Y	Y	Y	Y	

MARCUS CORPORATION (THE)

www.marcuscorp.com

Industry Group Code: 721110 Ranks within this company's industry group: Sales: 22   Profits: 19

Properties:		Financial Services:		Construction/Development:		Investments:		Specialty Services:		Brokerage:	
Apartments:		Mortgages:		Commercial Construction:		REIT:		Property Management:	Y	Commercial Sales:	
Malls/Shopping:		Title Insurance:		Residential Construction:				Online Services:		Residential Sales:	
Offices:		Property Insurance:		Land Development:				Software/IT:		Specialty:	
Hotels/Motels:	Y			Support Services:				Consulting:			
Industrial/Warehouses:				Design/Engineering:							
Other:	Y										

TYPES OF BUSINESS:

Hotels & Motels
Movie & IMAX Theaters
Hotels/Resorts

BRANDS/DIVISIONS/AFFILIATES:

Marcus Theatres
Funset Boulevard
Marcus Majestic of Brookfield (The)
UltraScreen
AT&T Palladium
Marcus Hotels and Resorts
Skirvin Hilton
Marcus Midtown Cinema

CONTACTS: *Note: Officers with more than one job title may be intentionally listed here more than once.*

Gregory S. Marcus, CEO
Gregory S. Marcus, Pres.
Douglas A. Neis, CFO
Karen Y. Spindler, Dir.-Corp. Human Resources
Jane Durment, CIO
Thomas F. Kissinger, General Counsel/Corp. Sec./VP
Douglas A. Neis, Treas.
Bruce J. Olson, Sr. VP/Pres., Marcus Theatres Corp.
William J. Otto, Pres., Marcus Hotels & Resorts
Stephen H. Marcus, Chmn.

Phone: 414-905-1100	Fax: 414-905-2879
Toll-Free:	
Address: 100 E. Wisconsin Ave., Ste. 1900, Milwaukee, WI 53202-4125 US	

GROWTH PLANS/SPECIAL FEATURES:

The Marcus Corporation is an owner and operator of movie theatres, hotels and resorts. The firm operates in two segments: Theatres and Hotels/Resorts. Through its Marcus Theatres subsidiary, the company owns 52 movie theatres in Wisconsin, Ohio, Illinois, Minnesota, North Dakota, Nebraska and Iowa, with 657 screens. The company also manages two movie theaters with 11 combined screens in Wisconsin owned by a third party. Marcus operates a family entertainment center, called Funset Boulevard, which is adjacent to one of its theatres in Appleton, Wisconsin. The company's 52 owned facilities include 32 megaplex theatres (12 or more screens), 19 multiplex theatres (two to 11 screens) and one single-screen theatre. The Marcus Majestic in Brookfield, Washington, features two 72-feet-wide UltraScreens and a multi-use auditorium called the AT&T Palladium with an attached kitchen, which offers a full menu. Through subsidiary Marcus Hotels and Resorts, Marcus owns and operates eight hotels and resorts and manages 11 hotels, resorts and other properties for third parties. Marcus' owned hotels and resorts include the Pfister Hotel, the InterContinental Milwaukee and The Hilton Milwaukee City Center in Milwaukee, Wisconsin; the Hilton Madison at Monona Terrace in Madison, Wisconsin; The Grand Geneva Resort & Spa in Lake Geneva, Wisconsin; the Hotel Phillips in Kansas City, Missouri; the Four Points by Sheraton Chicago Downtown/Magnificent Mile in Chicago, Illinois; and the Skirvin Hilton in Oklahoma City, Oklahoma. Marcus Theatres and Marcus Hotels and Resorts account for about 53.2% and 46.8% of Marcus' total revenue, respectively. In September 2010, the firm announced plans to install additional digital 3D systems in three of its theaters; and agree to acquire College Avenue 16 Cinema in Wisconsin from Regal Entertainment Group. In November 2010, Marcus agreed to acquire 10 acres in Milwaukee to build a new theatre.

FINANCIALS: Sales and profits are in thousands of dollars—add 000 to get the full amount. 2010 Note: Financial information for 2010 was not available for all companies at press time.

2010 Sales: $379,069	2010 Profits: $16,115	**U.S. Stock Ticker: MCS**
2009 Sales: $383,496	2009 Profits: $17,200	**Int'l Ticker:** Int'l Exchange:
2008 Sales: $371,075	2008 Profits: $20,486	Employees: 6,200
2007 Sales: $327,631	2007 Profits: $33,297	Fiscal Year Ends: 5/31
2006 Sales: $289,244	2006 Profits: $28,271	Parent Company:

SALARIES/BENEFITS:

Pension Plan:	ESOP Stock Plan:	Profit Sharing:	Top Exec. Salary: $500,000	Bonus: $162,557
Savings Plan: Y	Stock Purch. Plan:		Second Exec. Salary: $413,962	Bonus: $93,869

OTHER THOUGHTS:

Apparent Women Officers or Directors: 3
Hot Spot for Advancement for Women/Minorities: Y

LOCATIONS: ("Y" = Yes)

West:	Southwest:	Midwest:	Southeast:	Northeast:	International:
Y	Y	Y			

MARRIOTT INTERNATIONAL INC   www.marriott.com

Industry Group Code: 721110 Ranks within this company's industry group: Sales: 1   Profits: 3

Properties:		Financial Services:		Construction/Development:		Investments:		Specialty Services:		Brokerage:	
Apartments:	Y	Mortgages:		Commercial Construction:	Y	REIT:		Property Management:	Y	Commercial Sales:	
Malls/Shopping:		Title Insurance:		Residential Construction:				Online Services:		Residential Sales:	
Offices:		Property Insurance:		Land Development:				Software/IT:		Specialty:	
Hotels/Motels:	Y			Support Services:				Consulting:			
Industrial/Warehouses:				Design/Engineering:	Y						
Other:	Y										

TYPES OF BUSINESS:

Hotels & Resorts
Suites Hotels
Corporate Apartments
Extended Stay Lodging
Luxury Hotels
Business Hotels

BRANDS/DIVISIONS/AFFILIATES:

Marriott Hotels and Resorts
Ritz-Carlton (The)
Bulgari Hotel and Resort
Renaissance Hotels, Resorts and ClubSport
Courtyard Residence Inn
Fairfield Inn
ExecuStay
TownePlace Suites

CONTACTS: *Note: Officers with more than one job title may be intentionally listed here more than once.*

J. W. Marriott, Jr., CEO
Arne M. Sorenson, COO
Arne M. Sorenson, Pres.
Carl T. Berquist, CFO/Exec. VP
David A. Rodriguez, Exec. VP-Global Human Resources
Carl Wilson, CIO/Exec. VP
Edward A. Ryan, General Counsel/Exec. VP
Anthony G. Capuano, Exec. VP-Global Dev.
Kathleen Matthews, Exec. VP-Global Comm. & Public Affairs
Laura E. Paugh, Sr. VP-Investor Rel.
David J. Grissen, Pres., Americas
Robert J. McCarthy, Pres., Americas & Global Lodging Svcs.
Simon F. Cooper, Pres., Asia Pacific
Amy C. McPherson, Pres., Europe
J. W. Marriott, Jr., Chmn.
Edwin D. Fuller, Pres./Managing Dir.-Marriott Lodging Int'l

Phone: 301-380-3000	Fax: 301-380-3967
Toll-Free: 800-721-7033	
Address: 10400 Fernwood Rd., Bethesda, MD 20817 US	

GROWTH PLANS/SPECIAL FEATURES:

Marriott International, Inc. operates 3,545 hotels and related lodging facilities in the U.S. and about 70 other countries and territories. Though primarily known for the firm's various hotel brands, Marriot also has operations in time shares. The company operates through five segments: North American Full-Service; North American Limited-Service; International; Luxury; and Timeshare. Marriott develops, operates and franchises hotels under various brand names, including Marriott Hotels and Resorts; JW Marriott Hotels and Resorts; the Ritz-Carlton, featuring luxury hotels and resorts; Bulgari Hotel and Resort; Renaissance Hotels, Resorts and ClubSport; Courtyard; Residence Inn, the firm's extended-stay brand; Fairfield Inn; SpringHill Suites; and TownePlace Suites. The firm also provides furnished corporate housing units in 41 major markets through its ExecuStay brand, as well as operating 20 upscale serviced apartments through Marriott Executive Apartments. The company also develops, markets and operates timeshare, fractional ownership and residential properties under four separate brand names in over 70 locations. The resorts are usually adjacent to the firm's hotels, bearing the brand names Marriott Vacation Club International, Horizons by Marriott Vacation Club International, Ritz-Carlton Club and Grand Residences by Marriott. Additionally, Marriott manages approximately 43 golf resorts worldwide. The company also operates 14 systemwide hotel reservation centers: eight in the U.S. and Canada, and six in other countries and territories. In late 2010, the firm announced a joint venture with AC Hotels of Spain to launch the AC Hotels by Marriott brand in Spain, Italy and Portugal. Marriott plans to spin-off its timeshare business as a free-standing company.

Employees are offered medical, dental and disability insurance; a 401(k) plan; tuition reimbursement; discounts on hotel rooms, food and beverages; and work/family programs and services. Marriot was named one of the 100 Best Companies to Work For and one of the Best Companies for Hourly Workers by Working Mother Magazine.

FINANCIALS: **Sales and profits are in thousands of dollars—add 000 to get the full amount. 2010 Note: Financial information for 2010 was not available for all companies at press time.**

2010 Sales: $11,691,000	2010 Profits: $458,000	**U.S. Stock Ticker: MAR**
2009 Sales: $10,908,000	2009 Profits: $-346,000	**Int'l Ticker:** Int'l Exchange:
2008 Sales: $12,879,000	2008 Profits: $359,000	Employees: 129,000
2007 Sales: $12,990,000	2007 Profits: $696,000	Fiscal Year Ends: 12/31
2006 Sales: $11,995,000	2006 Profits: $608,000	Parent Company:

SALARIES/BENEFITS:

Pension Plan:	ESOP Stock Plan:	Profit Sharing:	Top Exec. Salary: $1,253,063	Bonus: $2,268,419
Savings Plan: Y	Stock Purch. Plan:		Second Exec. Salary: $1,018,750	Bonus: $1,298,296

OTHER THOUGHTS:

Apparent Women Officers or Directors: 7
Hot Spot for Advancement for Women/Minorities: Y

LOCATIONS: ("Y" = Yes)

West:	Southwest:	Midwest:	Southeast:	Northeast:	International:
Y	Y	Y	Y	Y	Y

MATRIX SERVICE COMPANY

www.matrixservice.com

Industry Group Code: 237 Ranks within this company's industry group: Sales: 30   Profits: 27

Properties:	Financial Services:	Construction/Development:		Investments:	Specialty Services:	Brokerage:
Apartments:	Mortgages:	Commercial Construction:		REIT:	Property Management:	Commercial Sales:
Malls/Shopping:	Title Insurance:	Residential Construction:			Online Services:	Residential Sales:
Offices:	Property Insurance:	Land Development:			Software/IT:	Specialty:
Hotels/Motels:		Support Services:	Y		Consulting:	
Industrial/Warehouses:		Design/Engineering:				
Other:						

TYPES OF BUSINESS:

Heavy Construction & Civil Engineering
Plant Maintenance Services
Storage Tank Services
Petrochemical Industry Services

BRANDS/DIVISIONS/AFFILIATES:

Matrix Service Industrial Contractors, Inc.
Matrix Service, Inc.

CONTACTS: Note: Officers with more than one job title may be intentionally listed here more than once.

Michael J. Bradley, CEO
Joseph F. Montalbano, COO
Michael J. Bradley, Pres.
Thomas E. Long, CFO/VP
Nancy E. Austin, VP-Human Resources
Lansing G. Smith, VP-Eng. & Fabrication
Robert A. Long, VP-Gulf Coast Oper.
Kevin S. Cavanah, VP-Acct. & Financial Reporting
James P. Ryan, Pres., Matrix Service, Inc.
Matthew J. Petrizzo, Pres., Matrix Service Industrial Contractors, Inc.
Jason W. Turner, Treas./VP
Michael J. Hall, Chmn.
Lansing G. Smith, VP-Procurement

Phone:	**Fax:** 918-838-8810
Toll-Free: 866-367-6879	
Address: 5100 E. Skelly Dr., Ste. 700, Tulsa, OK 74135 US	

GROWTH PLANS/SPECIAL FEATURES:

Matrix Service Company and its subsidiaries provide construction, repair and maintenance services, primarily to the petroleum, pipeline, bulk storage terminal and industrial gas markets. The company operates in two segments: construction services and repair and maintenance services. Construction services include turnkey projects; renovations, upgrades and expansions for large and small projects, electrical and instrumentation; mechanical, piping and equipment installations; tank engineering, design, fabrication and erection; and steel, steel plate, vessel and pipe fabrication. The company's repair and maintenance services include plant maintenance, turnaround services, outages, industrial cleaning, hydroblasting and substation and above ground storage tank repair and maintenance. Matrix's major customers are Public Service Enterprise Group, British Petroleum and Chevron. Subsidiaries of the company include Matrix Service, Inc. and Matrix Service Industrial Contractors, Inc.

Employees are offered medical, dental and vision insurance; life and AD&D insurance; medical and dependant care flexible spending accounts; pre-paid legal services; and an employee assistance program.

FINANCIALS: Sales and profits are in thousands of dollars—add 000 to get the full amount. 2010 Note: Financial information for 2010 was not available for all companies at press time.

2010 Sales: $550,814	2010 Profits: $4,876	**U.S. Stock Ticker: MTRX**
2009 Sales: $689,720	2009 Profits: $30,589	**Int'l Ticker:** Int'l Exchange:
2008 Sales: $731,301	2008 Profits: $21,414	Employees: 2,477
2007 Sales: $639,846	2007 Profits: $19,171	Fiscal Year Ends: 5/31
2006 Sales: $493,927	2006 Profits: $7,653	Parent Company:

SALARIES/BENEFITS:

Pension Plan:	ESOP Stock Plan:	Profit Sharing:	Top Exec. Salary: $670,000	Bonus: $335,000
Savings Plan: Y	Stock Purch. Plan:		Second Exec. Salary: $350,000	Bonus: $175,000

OTHER THOUGHTS:

Apparent Women Officers or Directors: 1
Hot Spot for Advancement for Women/Minorities:

LOCATIONS: ("Y" = Yes)

West:	Southwest:	Midwest:	Southeast:	Northeast:	International:
Y	Y	Y		Y	Y

MAX PROPERTY GROUP PLC

www.maxpropertygroup.com

Industry Group Code: 5311 Ranks within this company's industry group: Sales: Profits:

Properties:		Financial Services:	Construction/Development:	Investments:	Specialty Services:		Brokerage:
Apartments:		Mortgages:	Commercial Construction:	REIT:	Property Management:	Y	Commercial Sales:
Malls/Shopping:	Y	Title Insurance:	Residential Construction:		Online Services:		Residential Sales:
Offices:	Y	Property Insurance:	Land Development:		Software/IT:		Specialty:
Hotels/Motels:			Support Services:		Consulting:		
Industrial/Warehouses:	Y		Design/Engineering:				
Other:	Y						

TYPES OF BUSINESS:

Real Estate Investment

BRANDS/DIVISIONS/AFFILIATES:

Solent Business Park
Overbridge Square
New Bond House
Concorde Business Park
Brooklands Business Campus
Workplace Systems Rooksley
Silbury Court
Centric MK

CONTACTS: Note: Officers with more than one job title may be intentionally listed here more than once.

Aubrey Adams, Chmn.

Phone: 534-814814	Fax: 534-814815
Toll-Free:	
Address: 26 New St., St. Helier, Jersey JE2 3RA Channel Islands	

GROWTH PLANS/SPECIAL FEATURES:

Max Property Group plc is a firm engaged in the acquisition and operation of commercial properties in the U.K. It controls more than 80 properties comprising over 7.1 million square feet (sq. ft.) of leasable space and housing approximately 800 tenants. The company's portfolio includes over 1,250 leaseable units with an average unit size of 5,700 sq. ft. Industrial properties comprise 75% of its portfolio, office properties 15% and 10% healthcare facilities. Max Property Group's commercial ventures include the Solent Business Park (71,000 sq. ft.) in Fareham, U.K.; the Overbridge Square in (66,000 sq. ft.) Newbury, U.K.; New Bond House (47,000 sq. ft.) in Bristol, U.K.; Aldrin Place (24,000 sq. ft.) in Farnborough, U.K.; Concorde Business Park (124,000 sq. ft.) and Westpoint(104,000 sq. ft.) in Manchester, U.K.; Brooklands Business Campus (116,000 sq. ft.) in Horsham, U.K.; and Workplace Systems Rooksley (27,000 sq. ft.), Centric MK (107,000 sq. ft.) and Silbury Court (77,000 sq. ft.) in Milton Keynes, U.K. In January 2010, Max Properties acquired a portfolio of office properties for approximately $59.4 million. In May 2010, it purchased a portfolio of four freehold private hospitals in Blackburn, Liverpool, Ayr and Stirling through a joint venture with Lloyds Banking Group. In October 2010, it acquired a portfolio of 14 nightclubs in various U.K. cities. In January 2011, the firm acquired a portfolio of 29 pubs in and around central London.

FINANCIALS: Sales and profits are in thousands of dollars—add 000 to get the full amount. 2010 Note: Financial information for 2010 was not available for all companies at press time.

		U.S. Stock Ticker:
2010 Sales: $	2010 Profits: $	Int'l Ticker: MAX Int'l Exchange: London-LSE
2009 Sales: $	2009 Profits: $	Employees:
2008 Sales: $	2008 Profits: $	Fiscal Year Ends: 3/31
2007 Sales: $	2007 Profits: $	Parent Company:
2006 Sales: $	2006 Profits: $	

SALARIES/BENEFITS:

Pension Plan:	ESOP Stock Plan:	Profit Sharing:	Top Exec. Salary: $	Bonus: $
Savings Plan:	Stock Purch. Plan:		Second Exec. Salary: $	Bonus: $

OTHER THOUGHTS:

Apparent Women Officers or Directors:
Hot Spot for Advancement for Women/Minorities:

LOCATIONS: ("Y" = Yes)

West:	Southwest:	Midwest:	Southeast:	Northeast:	International:
					Y

MCDERMOTT INTERNATIONAL INC

www.mcdermott.com

Industry Group Code: 541330 Ranks within this company's industry group: Sales: 5   Profits: 2

Properties:	Financial Services:	Construction/Development:		Investments:	Specialty Services:	Brokerage:
Apartments:	Mortgages:	Commercial Construction:	Y	REIT:	Property Management:	Commercial Sales:
Malls/Shopping:	Title Insurance:	Residential Construction:			Online Services:	Residential Sales:
Offices:	Property Insurance:	Land Development:			Software/IT:	Specialty:
Hotels/Motels:		Support Services:	Y		Consulting:	
Industrial/Warehouses:		Design/Engineering:	Y			
Other:						

TYPES OF BUSINESS:

Engineering Services
Power Generation Services
Nuclear Fuel Assemblies
Government Services
Marine Construction
Procurement Services
Project Management
Consulting

BRANDS/DIVISIONS/AFFILIATES:

J. Ray McDermott, S.A.
J. Ray McDermott Holdings, LLC
Babcock & Wilcox Nuclear Operations Group, Inc
Babcock & Wilcox Technical Services Group, Inc
Babcock & Wilcox Power Generation Group, Inc
Babcock & Wilcox Modular Nuclear Energy, LLC

CONTACTS: Note: Officers with more than one job title may be intentionally listed here more than once.

Stephen M. Johnson, CEO
John T. Nesser, III, COO
Stephen M. Johnson, Pres.
Perry L. Elders, CFO/Sr. VP
Gary L. Carlson, Chief Human Resources Officer/Sr. VP
William L. Soester, VP-Eng.
Liane K. Hinrichs, General Counsel/Sr. VP/Corp. Sec.
John T. McCormack, Sr. VP-Oper.
Peter A. Marler, VP-Bus. Dev.
Jeff J. Hightower, VP-Finance
David P. Roquemore, Sr. VP-Oper.
Daniel M. Houser, VP-Global Marine
Claire P. Hunter, VP-Litigation, Claims & Disputes
Thomas A. Henzler, VP/Corp. Compliance officer
Ronald C. Cambre, Chmn.
Stewart A. Mitchell, VP/Gen. Mgr.-Middle East

Phone: 281-870-5901	Fax:
Toll-Free:	
Address: 777 N. Eldridge Pkwy., Houston, TX 77079 US	

GROWTH PLANS/SPECIAL FEATURES:

McDermott International, Inc. is a multinational engineering and construction services company. The firm operates in three main business segments: offshore oil and gas construction services; government operations; and power generation systems. The offshore construction services are provided through subsidiaries J. Ray McDermott, S.A. and J. Ray McDermott Holdings, LLC, as well as their respective subsidiaries. This segment designs, engineers, fabricates and installs offshore drilling and production facilities, marine pipelines and subsea production systems. It operates in most major offshore oil and gas producing regions throughout the world, including the U.S., Mexico, Canada, the Middle East, India, the Caspian Sea and Asia Pacific Presently, this segment also operates fabrication facilities located in Indonesia on Batam Island; in Dubai, U.A.E.; Altamira, Mexico; and near Morgan City, Louisiana. These facilities construct a full range of offshore structures, from conventional jacket-type fixed platforms to intermediate water and deepwater platform configurations. The government operations segment operates through Babcock & Wilcox Nuclear Operations Group, Inc.; Babcock & Wilcox Technical Services Group, Inc.; and their respective subsidiaries. This division supplies nuclear components to the U.S. government, processes uranium, provides environmental site restoration services and manages and operates U.S. government-owned facilities, primarily within the nuclear weapons complex of the U.S. Department of Energy. Facilities served by the segment include the Y-12 National Security Complex, the Pantex Plant and Los Alamos National Laboratory. The power generation systems segment, run by Babcock & Wilcox Power Generation Group, Inc.; Babcock & Wilcox Nuclear Power Generation Group, Inc.; and Babcock & Wilcox Modular Nuclear Energy LLC, provides a variety of services, equipment and systems to generate steam and electric power at energy facilities worldwide. In March 2010, the company signed an agreement to acquire the electrostatic precipitator and emissions monitoring businesses of GE Energy.

FINANCIALS: Sales and profits are in thousands of dollars—add 000 to get the full amount. 2010 Note: Financial information for 2010 was not available for all companies at press time.

2010 Sales: $2,403,743	2010 Profits: $201,666	**U.S. Stock Ticker: MDR**
2009 Sales: $3,281,790	2009 Profits: $387,056	**Int'l Ticker:** Int'l Exchange:
2008 Sales: $3,098,104	2008 Profits: $429,302	Employees: 15,000
2007 Sales: $5,631,610	2007 Profits: $607,828	Fiscal Year Ends: 12/31
2006 Sales: $4,120,141	2006 Profits: $330,515	Parent Company:

SALARIES/BENEFITS:

Pension Plan: Y	ESOP Stock Plan:	Profit Sharing:	Top Exec. Salary: $900,000	Bonus: $1,665,000
Savings Plan: Y	Stock Purch. Plan:		Second Exec. Salary: $526,200	Bonus: $663,012

OTHER THOUGHTS:

Apparent Women Officers or Directors: 2
Hot Spot for Advancement for Women/Minorities:

LOCATIONS: ("Y" = Yes)

West:	Southwest:	Midwest:	Southeast:	Northeast:	International:
Y	Y	Y	Y	Y	Y

MDC HOLDINGS INC

www.richmondamerican.com

Industry Group Code: 2361 Ranks within this company's industry group: Sales: 12   Profits: 13

Properties:		Financial Services:		Construction/Development:		Investments:		Specialty Services:		Brokerage:	
Apartments:		Mortgages:	Y	Commercial Construction:		REIT:		Property Management:		Commercial Sales:	
Malls/Shopping:		Title Insurance:	Y	Residential Construction:	Y			Online Services:		Residential Sales:	Y
Offices:		Property Insurance:	Y	Land Development:	Y			Software/IT:		Specialty:	
Hotels/Motels:				Support Services:				Consulting:			
Industrial/Warehouses:				Design/Engineering:	Y						
Other:											

TYPES OF BUSINESS:

Residential Construction
Land Development
Mortgages
Title Services
Insurance

BRANDS/DIVISIONS/AFFILIATES:

Richmond American Homes
HomeAmerican Mortgage Corporation
American Home Insurance Agency
American Home Title and Escrow Company
Allegiant Insurance Company Inc
StarAmerican Insurance Ltd

CONTACTS: *Note: Officers with more than one job title may be intentionally listed here more than once.*

Larry A. Mizel, CEO
David D. Mandarich, COO
David D. Mandarich, Pres.
Zane DeHerrera, VP-Mktg./Chief Mktg. Officer
Karen Gard, VP-Human Resources/Chief Human Resources Officer
James McClanahan, VP-IT/CIO
Joseph H. Fretz, General Counsel/Corp. Sec.
Chad Yetka, Sr. VP-Oper.
Robert N. Martin, VP-Bus. Dev.
Zane DeHerrera, VP-Corp. Comm.
Robert N. Martin, VP-Finance
Ed Gwynn, VP-Tax
John J. Heaney, Sr. VP/Treas.
Jeff Handlin, VP-National Land Acquisition
Shelley Casagrande, VP-Internal Audit
Larry A. Mizel, Chmn.

Phone: 303-773-1100	**Fax:**
Toll-Free: 888-402-4663	
Address: 4350 S. Monaco St., Ste. 500, Denver, CO 80237 US	

GROWTH PLANS/SPECIAL FEATURES:

M.D.C. Holdings, Inc. is a holding company engaged in homebuilding and financial services. The company's homebuilding segment, which operates through subsidiary Richmond American Homes, builds and sells single-family homes through the following geographic segments: West (California, Nevada and Arizona); Mountain (Colorado and Utah); East (Maryland, Pennsylvania, Delaware, New Jersey, West Virginia and Virginia); and other homebuilding (Florida, and Illinois). The company is in the process of exiting the Illinois market. Other operations of the homebuilding segment include land acquisition and development, home construction purchasing, sales and marketing and customer service. M.D.C. also acquires entitled land for development into finished lots. The base price for its homes generally ranges from $170,000 to $450,000. M.D.C. maintains a variety of home styles in each of its markets, targeting generally first-time and first-time move-up homebuyers, and building a limited number of homes for the second-time move-up and luxury homebuyers. The firm's financial services segment consists principally of the operations of HomeAmerican Mortgage Corporation, which originates mortgage loans primarily for its homebuyers; American Home Title and Escrow Company, which provides title agency services to M.D.C. and its homebuyers in Maryland, Florida, Nevada, Colorado and Virginia; and American Home Insurance Agency, which offers third-party insurance products to its homebuyers. The segment also includes risk retention firm Allegiant Insurance Company, Inc. and reinsurer StarAmerican Insurance, Ltd.

M.D.C. offers its employees medical, dental, vision, life, AD&D and disability insurance; education reimbursement; a 401(k); home purchase discounts; paid time off; floating and paid holidays; and flexible spending accounts.

FINANCIALS: Sales and profits are in thousands of dollars—add 000 to get the full amount. 2010 Note: Financial information for 2010 was not available for all companies at press time.

2010 Sales: $958,655	2010 Profits: $-64,770	**U.S. Stock Ticker:** MDC
2009 Sales: $898,303	2009 Profits: $24,679	**Int'l Ticker:** Int'l Exchange:
2008 Sales: $1,458,108	2008 Profits: $-380,545	Employees: 1,119
2007 Sales: $2,885,659	2007 Profits: $-636,940	Fiscal Year Ends: 12/31
2006 Sales: $4,793,569	2006 Profits: $214,253	Parent Company:

SALARIES/BENEFITS:

Pension Plan:	ESOP Stock Plan:	Profit Sharing:	Top Exec. Salary: $1,000,000	Bonus: $2,500,000
Savings Plan: Y	Stock Purch. Plan:		Second Exec. Salary: $830,000	Bonus: $2,500,000

OTHER THOUGHTS:

Apparent Women Officers or Directors: 3
Hot Spot for Advancement for Women/Minorities: Y

LOCATIONS: ("Y" = Yes)

West:	Southwest:	Midwest:	Southeast:	Northeast:	International:
Y	Y		Y	Y	

MEADOW VALLEY CORPORATION

www.meadowvalley.com

Industry Group Code: 237 Ranks within this company's industry group: Sales: Profits:

Properties:	Financial Services:	Construction/Development:		Investments:	Specialty Services:	Brokerage:
Apartments:	Mortgages:	Commercial Construction:	Y	REIT:	Property Management:	Commercial Sales:
Malls/Shopping:	Title Insurance:	Residential Construction:			Online Services:	Residential Sales:
Offices:	Property Insurance:	Land Development:			Software/IT:	Specialty:
Hotels/Motels:		Support Services:	Y		Consulting:	
Industrial/Warehouses:		Design/Engineering:	Y			
Other:						

TYPES OF BUSINESS:

Heavy Construction & Civil Engineering
Construction Materials-Concrete, Sand & Gravel
Design Services
Mining
Ready-Mix Concrete
Technical Services

BRANDS/DIVISIONS/AFFILIATES:

Meadow Valley Contractors, Inc.
Insight Equity Holdings LLC

CONTACTS: Note: Officers with more than one job title may be intentionally listed here more than once.

Bradley E. Larson, CEO
David D. Doty, CFO
Lance Faber, Dir.-Info. Svcs.
Kenneth D. Nelson, Chief Admin. Officer
Grant E. Larson, VP-Bus. Dev.
Nicole R. Smith, Controller
Norm Watkins, Dir.-Safety/Compliance Officer

Phone: 602-437-5400	Fax: 602-437-1681
Toll-Free:	
Address: 4602 E. Thomas Rd., Phoenix, AZ 85018 US	

GROWTH PLANS/SPECIAL FEATURES:

Meadow Valley Corporation, operates as Meadow Valley Contractors Inc., is engaged in the construction industry. Based in Phoenix, Arizona, the firm is a provider of construction services and a supplier of construction materials. The construction services segment (CSS) specializes in structural concrete construction of highway bridges and overpasses and the paving of highways and airport runways. The construction materials segment (CMS) provides ready-mix concrete, sand and gravel products to both itself and other contractors. The company operates throughout Nevada, Arizona and Utah, with principal operations in the Las Vegas, Nevada and Phoenix, Arizona metropolitan areas. The firm operates for both public and private infrastructure projects, including the construction of bridges and overpasses, channels, roadways, highways and airport runways. The company owns 53% of Ready Mix, Inc., which manufactures and distributes ready mix concrete, crushed landscaping rock and other miscellaneous rock and sand products. Meadow Valley owns or leases most of the equipment used in its business, including cranes, backhoes, graders, loaders, trucks, trailers, pavers, rollers, construction materials processing plants, batch plants and related equipment. The raw materials necessary for most operations are obtained from multiple sources. CMS does have one full-time mining operation in Nephi, Utah. Recently, Dallas-based private equity firm Insight Equity Holdings LLC acquired the company for approximately $61 million.

FINANCIALS: Sales and profits are in thousands of dollars—add 000 to get the full amount. 2010 Note: Financial information for 2010 was not available for all companies at press time.

2010 Sales: $	2010 Profits: $	U.S. Stock Ticker: Private
2009 Sales: $	2009 Profits: $	Int'l Ticker: Int'l Exchange:
2008 Sales: $	2008 Profits: $	Employees:
2007 Sales: $205,919	2007 Profits: $4,061	Fiscal Year Ends: 12/31
2006 Sales: $195,522	2006 Profits: $4,166	Parent Company: INSIGHT EQUITY HOLDING LLC

SALARIES/BENEFITS:

Pension Plan:	ESOP Stock Plan:	Profit Sharing:	Top Exec. Salary: $	Bonus: $363,785
Savings Plan:	Stock Purch. Plan:		Second Exec. Salary: $	Bonus: $

OTHER THOUGHTS:

Apparent Women Officers or Directors: 1
Hot Spot for Advancement for Women/Minorities:

LOCATIONS: ("Y" = Yes)

West:	Southwest:	Midwest:	Southeast:	Northeast:	International:
Y	Y				

MERITAGE HOMES CORP

www.meritagehomes.com

Industry Group Code: 2361 Ranks within this company's industry group: Sales: 13   Profits: 5

Properties:	Financial Services:	Construction/Development:		Investments:	Specialty Services:	Brokerage:
Apartments:	Mortgages:	Commercial Construction:		REIT:	Property Management:	Commercial Sales:
Malls/Shopping:	Title Insurance:	Residential Construction:	Y		Online Services:	Residential Sales:
Offices:	Property Insurance:	Land Development:			Software/IT:	Specialty:
Hotels/Motels:		Support Services:			Consulting:	
Industrial/Warehouses:		Design/Engineering:	Y			
Other:						

TYPES OF BUSINESS:

Residential Construction
Home Design Services
Home Building Services

BRANDS/DIVISIONS/AFFILIATES:

Legacy Homes
Meritage Homes
Monterey Homes
Province
Simply Smart Series

CONTACTS:
Note: Officers with more than one job title may be intentionally listed here more than once.

Steven J. Hilton, CEO
Steven M. Davis, COO/Exec. VP
Larry W. Seay, CFO/Exec. VP
Jane Hays, VP-Corp. Mktg.
C. Timothy White, General Counsel/Exec. VP/Sec.
Jane Hays, VP-Corp. Comm.
Brent Anderson, VP-Investor Rel.
Hilla Sferruzza, Chief Acct. Officer/Controller/VP
Steven J. Hilton, Chmn.

Phone: 480-515-8100	**Fax:** 480-998-9162
Toll-Free: 877-275-6374	
Address: 17851 N. 85th St., Ste. 300, Scottsdale, AZ 85255 US	

GROWTH PLANS/SPECIAL FEATURES:

Meritage Home Corp. is a designer and builder of single-family attached and detached homes in the southern and western U.S. It offers a variety of homes that are designed to appeal to a wide range of homebuyers, including first-time, move-up, luxury and active adult buyers. The company has operations in three regions: west, central and east, which comprise 12 metropolitan areas in six states. These three regions are the firm's principal operating segments. The firm also holds a minority interest in three joint ventures with other development companies and real estate investors. Meritage's homebuilding and marketing activities are conducted under the name of Meritage Homes in each of its markets, except for certain communities in Arizona, where it operates under the name of Monterey Homes; and in Texas, where it operates in certain communities as Legacy Homes and Monterey Homes. The company sells homes in 151 communities, with base prices ranging from roughly $90,000 to $972,000. Doing business primarily on an individual basis with contractors and suppliers, Meritage usually completes its homes within two to four months of construction. Main strategies of the company include purchasing land subject to complete entitlement; developing smaller parcels that can be completed within a three-year period; and managing housing inventory by pre-selling and obtaining substantial customer deposits on homes prior to beginning construction. The company is also focused on offering more affordable houses in order to target first time homebuyers. In 2010, the firm introduced Simply Smart Series, homes that include a low monthly payment and are marketed toward renters and first-time buyers; and Your Home. Your Way. 99 Days Guaranteed, a program which guarantees that the firm will build a new home for a customer within 99 days of signing the sales contract.

FINANCIALS:
Sales and profits are in thousands of dollars—add 000 to get the full amount. 2010 Note: Financial information for 2010 was not available for all companies at press time.

2010 Sales: $941,656	2010 Profits: $7,150	**U.S. Stock Ticker:** MTH
2009 Sales: $970,313	2009 Profits: $-66,456	**Int'l Ticker:** Int'l Exchange:
2008 Sales: $1,523,068	2008 Profits: $-291,935	Employees: 650
2007 Sales: $2,343,594	2007 Profits: $-288,851	Fiscal Year Ends: 12/31
2006 Sales: $3,461,320	2006 Profits: $225,354	Parent Company:

SALARIES/BENEFITS:

Pension Plan:	ESOP Stock Plan:	Profit Sharing:	Top Exec. Salary: $800,000	Bonus: $
Savings Plan: Y	Stock Purch. Plan:		Second Exec. Salary: $525,000	Bonus: $250,000

OTHER THOUGHTS:

Apparent Women Officers or Directors: 2
Hot Spot for Advancement for Women/Minorities:

LOCATIONS: ("Y" = Yes)

West:	Southwest:	Midwest:	Southeast:	Northeast:	International:
Y	Y		Y		

MERITUS HOTELS & RESORTS INC

www.meritus-hotels.com

Industry Group Code: 721110 Ranks within this company's industry group: Sales: Profits:

Properties:		Financial Services:	Construction/Development:	Investments:	Specialty Services:	Brokerage:
Apartments:		Mortgages:	Commercial Construction:	REIT:	Property Management:	Commercial Sales:
Malls/Shopping:		Title Insurance:	Residential Construction:		Online Services:	Residential Sales:
Offices:		Property Insurance:	Land Development:		Software/IT:	Specialty:
Hotels/Motels:	Y		Support Services:		Consulting:	
Industrial/Warehouses:			Design/Engineering:			
Other:						

TYPES OF BUSINESS:

Hotels & Resorts

BRANDS/DIVISIONS/AFFILIATES:

Overseas Union Enterprise Ltd
Mandarin Orchard Singapore
Meritus Mandarin Haikou
Meritus Pelangi Beach Resort & Spa, Langkawi
Meritus Shantou China
Shanghai JC Mandarin
Marina Mandarin Singapore

CONTACTS:
Note: Officers with more than one job title may be intentionally listed here more than once.

Kim Seng Tan, Pres.
Joyce Yeung, Mgr.-Mktg. Comm.
Lim Ee Jin, Assistant VP-Comm.
Lim Ee Jin, Assistant VP-Investor Rel.
Elaine Heng, Mgr.-Mktg. Comm.
Dorothy Lim, Assistant Mgr.-Mktg. Comm.
Linda Su, Assistant Mgr.-Mktg. Comm.
Chitty Jiang, Mgr.-Mktg. Comm., Meritus Shantou China

Phone: 65-6235-7788	Fax: 65-6235 6688
Toll-Free:	
Address: 333 Orchard Rd., 37th Fl., Main Tower, Singapore, 238867 Singapore	

GROWTH PLANS/SPECIAL FEATURES:

Meritus Hotels & Resorts, Inc. is a hotel management firm based in Singapore. The firm is a subsidiary of Overseas Union Enterprise Limited, a Singapore-based hospitality services, property investment and investment holding firm. Meritus operates six hotels and resorts: Mandarin Orchard Singapore; Meritus Mandarin Haikou; Meritus Pelangi Beach Resort & Spa, Langkawi (Meritus Pelangi); Meritus Shantou China; Shanghai JC Mandarin; and Marina Mandarin Singapore. Mandarin Orchard Singapore is the company's flagship 1,051-room resort; it features a swimming pool, tennis court, fitness center, wireless Internet, three restaurants, one café; one bar; eight meeting suites, 34 suites, two Presidential suites and several banquet halls. Meritus Mandarin Haikou is a 318-room hotel with three restaurants, one lounge, a ballroom with a capacity of 1,000, two swimming pools and two outdoor tennis courts. Meritus Pelangi is a 31-acre spa in Malaysia that features 331 rooms, several restaurants, 12 meeting rooms, water sports, snorkeling, jungle trekking, swimming pools and spas. Meritus Shantou China is a 21-storey, 318-room hotel with five bars/restaurants, three recreational facilities and several meeting rooms. Shanghai JC Mandarin features 514 rooms, a pastry shop, five restaurants/lounges, a beauty salon, a swimming pool and a tennis court.   Marina Mandarin Singapore is a Marina Bay waterfront hotel with 575 rooms, 19 suites, one Presidential suite, a spa, a 24-hour fitness center and several restaurants/lounges.

FINANCIALS:
Sales and profits are in thousands of dollars—add 000 to get the full amount. 2010 Note: Financial information for 2010 was not available for all companies at press time.

2010 Sales: $	2010 Profits: $	**U.S. Stock Ticker: Subsidiary**
2009 Sales: $	2009 Profits: $	**Int'l Ticker:** Int'l Exchange:
2008 Sales: $	2008 Profits: $	Employees:
2007 Sales: $	2007 Profits: $	Fiscal Year Ends:
2006 Sales: $	2006 Profits: $	Parent Company: OVERSEAS UNION ENTERPRISE LTD

SALARIES/BENEFITS:

Pension Plan:	ESOP Stock Plan:	Profit Sharing:	Top Exec. Salary: $	Bonus: $
Savings Plan:	Stock Purch. Plan:		Second Exec. Salary: $	Bonus: $

OTHER THOUGHTS:

Apparent Women Officers or Directors: 5
Hot Spot for Advancement for Women/Minorities: Y

LOCATIONS: ("Y" = Yes)

West:	Southwest:	Midwest:	Southeast:	Northeast:	International:
				Y	Y

MFA FINANCIAL INC

www.mfa-reit.com

Industry Group Code: 525990 **Ranks within this company's industry group:** Sales: 2   Profits: 1

Properties:		Financial Services:		Construction/Development:	Investments:		Specialty Services:	Brokerage:
Apartments:	Y	Mortgages:	Y	Commercial Construction:	REIT:	Y	Property Management:	Commercial Sales:
Malls/Shopping:		Title Insurance:		Residential Construction:			Online Services:	Residential Sales:
Offices:		Property Insurance:		Land Development:			Software/IT:	Specialty:
Hotels/Motels:				Support Services:			Consulting:	
Industrial/Warehouses:				Design/Engineering:				
Other:								

TYPES OF BUSINESS:

Mortgage-Backed Securities
Mortgage REIT
Apartment Properties

BRANDS/DIVISIONS/AFFILIATES:

CONTACTS: *Note: Officers with more than one job title may be intentionally listed here more than once.*

Stewart Zimmerman, CEO
William S. Gorin, Pres.
Stephen D. Yarad, CFO
Timothy W. Korth II, General Counsel/Corp. Sec.
Timothy W. Korth II, Sr. VP-Bus. Dev.
Teresa D. Covello, Chief Acct. Officer/Treas./Sr. VP
Ronald A. Freydberg, Chief Investment Officer/Exec. VP
Kathleen A. Hanrahan, Sr. VP-Acct.
Craig L. Knutson, Exec. VP-RMBS Bus.
Stewart Zimmerman, Chmn.

Phone: 212-207-6400	Fax: 212-207-6420
Toll-Free: 800-892-7547	
Address: 350 Park Ave., 21st Fl., New York, NY 10022 US	

GROWTH PLANS/SPECIAL FEATURES:

MFA Financial, Inc., formerly, MFA Mortgage Investments, Inc., is a mortgage real estate investment trust (REIT), primarily engaged in the business of investing, on a leveraged basis, in residential agency and non-agency adjustable-rate mortgage-backed securities (ARM-MBS), which are secured by pools of residential mortgages. The company's operating policies require that at least 50% of its investment portfolio consist of ARM-MBS that are either issued or guaranteed by an agency of the U.S. government or a federally chartered corporation (Agency MBS), or rated in one of the two highest rating categories by at least one nationally recognized rating agency. The remaining 50% may be comprised of investments in other types of MBS and residential mortgage loans; other mortgage and real estate-related debt and equity; other yield instruments; and other types of assets approved by the board of directors. MFA has $8.687 billion in assets, of which $8.06 billion, or 93%, represent its MBS portfolio. Of these MBS assets, 74% are Agency MBS, and approximately 26% are non-agency MBS. MFA also has an indirect investment in a multi-family apartment property. Utilizing repurchase agreements, the firm finances the acquisition of these assets by pledging its MBS as collateral to secure loans with lenders. At the maturity of a repurchase agreement, MFA is required to repurchase its collateral at a higher price, corresponding to the interest expense, or renew its agreement at the then prevailing market interest rate. To reduce its lender-related risk, the company generally maintains repurchase agreements with multiple lenders with a maximum loan from any lender of no more than three times its stockholders' equity.

FINANCIALS: Sales and profits are in thousands of dollars—add 000 to get the full amount. 2010 Note: Financial information for 2010 was not available for all companies at press time.

2010 Sales: $390,953	2010 Profits: $269,762	**U.S. Stock Ticker: MFA**
2009 Sales: $504,464	2009 Profits: $268,189	Int'l Ticker: Int'l Exchange:
2008 Sales: $519,788	2008 Profits: $45,797	Employees: 29
2007 Sales: $380,328	2007 Profits: $30,210	Fiscal Year Ends: 12/31
2006 Sales: $216,871	2006 Profits: $8,758	Parent Company:

SALARIES/BENEFITS:

Pension Plan:	ESOP Stock Plan:	Profit Sharing:	Top Exec. Salary: $900,000	Bonus: $1,500,000
Savings Plan:	Stock Purch. Plan:		Second Exec. Salary: $800,000	Bonus: $1,150,000

OTHER THOUGHTS:

Apparent Women Officers or Directors: 2
Hot Spot for Advancement for Women/Minorities:

LOCATIONS: ("Y" = Yes)

West:	Southwest:	Midwest:	Southeast:	Northeast:	International:
				Y	

MGM RESORTS INTERNATIONAL

www.mgmresorts.com

Industry Group Code: 721120 Ranks within this company's industry group: Sales: 3   Profits: 8

Properties:		Financial Services:		Construction/Development:		Investments:		Specialty Services:		Brokerage:	
Apartments:		Mortgages:		Commercial Construction:		REIT:		Property Management:	Y	Commercial Sales:	
Malls/Shopping:		Title Insurance:		Residential Construction:				Online Services:		Residential Sales:	
Offices:		Property Insurance:		Land Development:				Software/IT:		Specialty:	
Hotels/Motels:	Y			Support Services:				Consulting:			
Industrial/Warehouses:				Design/Engineering:							
Other:	Y										

TYPES OF BUSINESS:

Casino Hotels & Resorts
Casino & Resort Management

BRANDS/DIVISIONS/AFFILIATES:

Bellagio
MGM Grand Las Vegas
Mandalay Bay
Mirage (The)
Luxor
Excalibur
CityCenter
MGM Mirage

CONTACTS: *Note: Officers with more than one job title may be intentionally listed here more than once.*

James J. Murren, CEO
Corey I. Sanders, COO
James J. Murren, Pres.
Daniel J. D'Arrigo, CFO/Exec. VP/Treas.
William J. Hornbuckle, Chief Mktg. Officer
Robert H. Baldwin, Chief Design & Construction Officer
Aldo Manzini, Chief Admin. Officer/Exec. VP
John McManus, General Counsel/Exec. VP/Sec.
William M. Scott IV, Exec. VP-Corp. Strategy/Special Counsel
Alan M. Feldman, Sr. VP-Public Affairs
Robert C. Selwood, Chief Acct. Officer/Exec. VP
Shawn T. Sani, Sr. VP-Taxes
Rick Arpin, Controller/Sr. VP
Robert H. Baldwin, Pres./CEO-CityCenter
Gamal Aziz, Pres./CEO-MGM Hospitality
James J. Murren, Chmn.

Phone: 702-693-7120	Fax: 702-693-8626
Toll-Free:	
Address: 3600 Las Vegas Blvd. S., Las Vegas, NV 89109 US	

GROWTH PLANS/SPECIAL FEATURES:

MGM Resorts International (MGM) and its subsidiaries operate 15 casino resorts in Nevada, Mississippi and Michigan, as well as four jointly-owned casino resorts in Nevada, Macau and Illinois. Its Las Vegas Strip casino resorts include Bellagio, CityCenter (50% owned), MGM Grand Las Vegas, Mandalay Bay, The Mirage, Luxor, New York-New York, Excalibur, Monte Carlo and Circus Circus Las Vegas. Combined, they feature 40,889 guestrooms, more than 1.2 million square feet of gaming space, 17,446 slot machines and 940 gaming tables. CityCenter, which MGM manages for a fee, consists of several casinos, resorts and hotels, including Aria, Mandarin Oriental Las Vegas and some rooms for rent at Vdara. Its other Nevada properties, including Circus Circus Reno, Silver Legacy (50% owned), Gold Strike and Railroad Pass, offer 4,211 guestrooms, 207,000 square feet of gaming space, 3,331 slot machines and 113 gaming tables. Finally, its other operations include MGM Grand Detroit, Beau Rivage and Gold Strike (both in Mississippi), all wholly-owned; and MGM Grand Macau (located in China) and Grand Victoria (in Elgin, Illinois), both 50%-owned. These facilities offer 3,866 guestrooms, 474,000 square feet of gaming space, 8,514 slot machines and 675 gaming tables. MGM's casinos often feature hotel, dining, entertainment, retail and other amenities. Subsidiary MGM Mirage Hospitality manages casino and non-casino resorts internationally. Over half of MGM's revenue is generated by non-gaming activities. In March 2010, MGM agreed to sell its 50% stake in Borgata Hotel Casino and Spa located in Atlantic City.

MGM offers its employees health plans, a college savings plan, a 401(k) plan, an employee assistance program, life and disability insurance, adoption assistance, flexible spending accounts, healthy living programs and Children's Choice Learning Centers for employees' children.

FINANCIALS: Sales and profits are in thousands of dollars—add 000 to get the full amount. 2010 Note: Financial information for 2010 was not available for all companies at press time.

2010 Sales: $6,019,233	2010 Profits: $-1,437,397	U.S. Stock Ticker: MGM
2009 Sales: $5,978,589	2009 Profits: $-1,291,682	Int'l Ticker: Int'l Exchange:
2008 Sales: $7,208,767	2008 Profits: $-855,286	Employees: 61,000
2007 Sales: $7,691,637	2007 Profits: $1,584,419	Fiscal Year Ends: 12/31
2006 Sales: $7,175,956	2006 Profits: $648,264	Parent Company:

SALARIES/BENEFITS:

Pension Plan:	ESOP Stock Plan:	Profit Sharing:	Top Exec. Salary: $2,038,462	Bonus: $3,955,368
Savings Plan: Y	Stock Purch. Plan:		Second Exec. Salary: $1,500,000	Bonus: $1,914,294

OTHER THOUGHTS:

Apparent Women Officers or Directors: 4
Hot Spot for Advancement for Women/Minorities: Y

LOCATIONS: ("Y" = Yes)

West:	Southwest:	Midwest:	Southeast:	Northeast:	International:
Y		Y	Y		Y

MID-AMERICA APARTMENT COMMUNITIES INC   www.maac.net

Industry Group Code: 531110 Ranks within this company's industry group: Sales: 9   Profits: 9

Properties:		Financial Services:	Construction/Development:		Investments:		Specialty Services:		Brokerage:
Apartments:	Y	Mortgages:	Commercial Construction:		REIT:	Y	Property Management:	Y	Commercial Sales:
Malls/Shopping:		Title Insurance:	Residential Construction:	Y			Online Services:		Residential Sales:
Offices:		Property Insurance:	Land Development:				Software/IT:		Specialty:
Hotels/Motels:			Support Services:				Consulting:		
Industrial/Warehouses:			Design/Engineering:						
Other:									

TYPES OF BUSINESS:
Real Estate Investment Trust
Apartment Communities

BRANDS/DIVISIONS/AFFILIATES:
Mid-America Apartments LP
MAC II of Delaware Inc
Mid-America Multifamily Fund I LLC
Mid-America Multifamily Fund II LLC
Alamo Ranch

CONTACTS: *Note: Officers with more than one job title may be intentionally listed here more than once.*
H. Eric Bolton, Jr., CEO
Albert M. Campbell, III, CFO/Exec. VP
Melintha Ogle, VP/Dir.-Mktg.
Melanie Carpenter, VP-Human Resources
Shelton Barron, VP/Dir.-MIS
Leslie Wolfgang, Corp. Sec./Sr. VP/Dir.-External Reporting
Thomas L. Grimes, Jr., Exec. VP/Dir.-Property Mgmt. Oper.
Ginny Doane, Sr. VP/Dir.-Dev. & Training
Rick Barton, Controller/Sr. VP
James Maclin, Sr. VP/Dir.-Corp. Support
Kevin P. Perkins, Sr. VP/Dir.-Physical Assets
James Andrew Taylor, Exec. VP/Dir.-Asset Mgmt.
Doug Clark, VP/Dir.-Risk Mgmt.
H. Eric Bolton, Jr., Chmn.

Phone: 901-682-6600	**Fax:** 901-682-6667
Toll-Free:	
Address: 6584 Poplar Ave., Memphis, TN 38138 US	

GROWTH PLANS/SPECIAL FEATURES:
Mid-America Apartment Communities, Inc. (MAAC) is a self-administered and self-managed real estate investment trust (REIT) that acquires, owns and operates apartment communities in the south-east and south-central U.S. The firm manages approximately 44,349 apartment homes in 151 communities, conducting business primarily through its subsidiary and sole general partner, Mid-America Apartments, LP. MAAC also maintains an REIT subsidiary, MAC II of Delaware, Inc. The company also has a 33.33% share in Mid-America Multifamily Fund I LLC and Mid-America Multifamily Fund II, LLC, which own six properties combined, with a total of 1,961 units. The firm's current investment focus involves acquiring relatively new properties (7-15 years old) within its present geographic area with the potential for above-average growth. MAAC also provides on-site property management, through which the firm handles matters concerning rent, occupancy limits and regulations. MAAC maintains an 18 month management training program for property managers, and a large majority of its property managers are Certified Apartment Managers, a designation established by the National Apartment Association. MAAC also maintains each property's physical condition through regular landscaping and exterior improvements. The company recently acquired nine properties, with a total of 2,138 apartments, located in Texas, North Carolina, South Carolina, Tennessee and Florida. Through its interest in Fund I and Fund II, MAAC acquired a one-third share in three properties with 1,041 units located in Texas. In January 2011, the firm acquired Alamo Ranch, a 340-unit community in San Antonio, Texas.

MAAC offers its employees life, disability, medical and dental insurance; a 401(k); a stock ownership plan; bonuses; apartment discounts; scholarships; and an employee assistance program. In addition, as employees stay with the firm over time, benefits packages are enhanced with higher bonuses, higher company contribution to retirement savings plans, decreased healthcare costs and additional vacation and leave time.

FINANCIALS: Sales and profits are in thousands of dollars—add 000 to get the full amount. 2010 Note: Financial information for 2010 was not available for all companies at press time.

2010 Sales: $401,549	2010 Profits: $29,761	**U.S. Stock Ticker:** MAA
2009 Sales: $378,251	2009 Profits: $37,211	**Int'l Ticker:** Int'l Exchange:
2008 Sales: $370,011	2008 Profits: $30,249	Employees: 1,282
2007 Sales: $347,444	2007 Profits: $39,946	Fiscal Year Ends: 12/31
2006 Sales: $318,370	2006 Profits: $20,945	Parent Company:

SALARIES/BENEFITS:

Pension Plan:	ESOP Stock Plan: Y	Profit Sharing:	Top Exec. Salary: $407,753	Bonus: $816,006
Savings Plan: Y	Stock Purch. Plan: Y		Second Exec. Salary: $265,907	Bonus: $532,314

OTHER THOUGHTS:
Apparent Women Officers or Directors: 9
Hot Spot for Advancement for Women/Minorities: Y

LOCATIONS: ("Y" = Yes)

West:	Southwest:	Midwest:	Southeast:	Northeast:	International:
	Y	Y	Y	Y	

MILLENNIUM & COPTHORNE HOTELS PLC

www.mill-cop.com

Industry Group Code: 721110 Ranks within this company's industry group: Sales: 11   Profits: 8

Properties:		Financial Services:	Construction/Development:	Investments:		Specialty Services:		Brokerage:
Apartments:	Y	Mortgages:	Commercial Construction:	REIT:	Y	Property Management:	Y	Commercial Sales:
Malls/Shopping:		Title Insurance:	Residential Construction:			Online Services:		Residential Sales:
Offices:		Property Insurance:	Land Development:			Software/IT:		Specialty:
Hotels/Motels:	Y		Support Services:			Consulting:		
Industrial/Warehouses:			Design/Engineering:					
Other:	Y							

TYPES OF BUSINESS:

Hotels, Luxury
Restaurants
Property Management
Apartments
Conference & Event Centers
Casino
Theaters
Fitness & Spa Facilities

BRANDS/DIVISIONS/AFFILIATES:

Millennium Hotels and Resorts
Copthorne Hotels
Kingsgate

CONTACTS: *Note: Officers with more than one job title may be intentionally listed here more than once.*

Richard Hartman, CEO
Adrian Bushnell, Corp. Sec.
Wong Hong Ren, Executive Dir.
Kwek Leng Beng, Chmn.
John Arnett, Head-North America

Phone: 44-0207-872-2444	**Fax:** 44-0207-872-2460
Toll-Free: 866-866-8086	
Address: Scarsdale Place, Kensington, London, W8 5SR UK	

GROWTH PLANS/SPECIAL FEATURES:

Millennium & Copthorne Hotels plc (MCH) is a global hotel company that owns, manages and/or operates over approximately 104 hotels in 17 countries worldwide, primarily located in Europe. The company's 24 European locations, branded under the Millennium Hotels and Resorts, Millennium, Copthorne labels, can be found in major business centers in the U.K. (including Birmingham, Cardiff, Glasgow, London, Manchester and Newcastle) as well as France and Germany. MCH's European locations include standard rooms, club accommodation and suites, as well as a club lounge, fully equipped business center and in-room business facilities. Meetings and events facilities operated by the firm include the Millennium Conference Centre in London; the Ballroom at Millennium Hotel London Mayfair; the Millennium Conference Centre at Effingham Park; and the Millennium Hotel and Resort Stuttgart with the SI-Entertainment-Centre, which features two full-scale musical theaters, 17 conference and banquet rooms, a six-screen movie theater, casino and 19 restaurants. Many hotel locations also offer health-club and fitness-spa facilities. In addition to MCH's European locations, the company has 22 hotels in the U.S., 29 in New Zealand (13 under the Kingsgate label), six in Singapore, six in the United Arab Emirates, six locations in China, two in Hong Kong, two in Malaysia and locations in Indonesia, the Philippines, South Korea, Taiwan, Thailand and Kuwait.

FINANCIALS: Sales and profits are in thousands of dollars—add 000 to get the full amount. 2010 Note: Financial information for 2010 was not available for all companies at press time.

2010 Sales: $1,225,410	2010 Profits: $158,510	**U.S. Stock Ticker:**
2009 Sales: $1,005,580	2009 Profits: $107,790	**Int'l Ticker: MLC** Int'l Exchange: London-LSE
2008 Sales: $1,158,530	2008 Profits: $116,860	Employees: 12,778
2007 Sales: $1,325,800	2007 Profits: $295,800	Fiscal Year Ends: 12/31
2006 Sales: $1,279,700	2006 Profits: $198,200	Parent Company:

SALARIES/BENEFITS:

Pension Plan:	ESOP Stock Plan:	Profit Sharing:	Top Exec. Salary: $	Bonus: $
Savings Plan:	Stock Purch. Plan:		Second Exec. Salary: $	Bonus: $

OTHER THOUGHTS:

Apparent Women Officers or Directors:
Hot Spot for Advancement for Women/Minorities:

LOCATIONS: ("Y" = Yes)

West:	Southwest:	Midwest:	Southeast:	Northeast:	International:
Y	Y	Y	Y	Y	Y

MISSION WEST PROPERTIES INC

www.missionwest.com

Industry Group Code: 531120 **Ranks within this company's industry group:** Sales: 60   Profits: 44

Properties:		Financial Services:		Construction/Development:		Investments:		Specialty Services:		Brokerage:	
Apartments:		Mortgages:		Commercial Construction:		REIT:	Y	Property Management:	Y	Commercial Sales:	
Malls/Shopping:		Title Insurance:		Residential Construction:				Online Services:		Residential Sales:	
Offices:	Y	Property Insurance:		Land Development:	Y			Software/IT:		Specialty:	
Hotels/Motels:				Support Services:				Consulting:			
Industrial/Warehouses:				Design/Engineering:							
Other:	Y										

TYPES OF BUSINESS:

Real Estate Investment Trust
Research & Development Properties
Real Estate Rental, Leasing & Management
Commercial Land Development

BRANDS/DIVISIONS/AFFILIATES:

Berg Group (The)

CONTACTS: *Note: Officers with more than one job title may be intentionally listed here more than once.*

Carl E. Berg, CEO
Raymond V. Marino, COO
Raymond V. Marino, Pres.
Wayne N. Pham, VP-Finance/Controller
Carl E. Berg, Chmn.

Phone: 408-725-0700	**Fax:** 408-725-1626
Toll-Free:	
Address: 10050 Bandley Dr., Cupertino, CA 95014 US	

GROWTH PLANS/SPECIAL FEATURES:

Mission West Properties, Inc. is a self-managed, self-administered real estate investment trust (REIT). The firm acquires, markets, leases and manages commercial research and development properties, primarily located in the Silicon Valley portion of the San Francisco Bay area. Much of the company's business is undertaken through four general partnerships with the Berg Group, whose properties Mission West purchased at the inception of its operations. The Berg Group maintains architectural and construction personnel and therefore is responsible for the land acquisition, development and construction activities for the research and development properties in which the firm is interested. The properties, designed both for research and development and office use, in some cases include space for light manufacturing operations and logistics installations, such as loading docks. The company currently owns and manages 111 properties, totaling approximately 8 million square feet. Mission West focuses on single-tenant properties, which it leases primarily through triple net leases, in which the lessee agrees to pay real estate taxes, building insurance and many of the maintenance costs associated with the properties. The firm has approximately 71 combined tenants leasing its properties. Some of Mission West's biggest tenants include Microsoft Corporation; Apple, Inc.; JDS Uniphase Corporation; Tyco Electronics Corporation; and Fujitsu.

FINANCIALS: Sales and profits are in thousands of dollars—add 000 to get the full amount. 2010 Note: Financial information for 2010 was not available for all companies at press time.

2010 Sales: $99,428	2010 Profits: $8,473	**U.S. Stock Ticker:** MSW
2009 Sales: $104,890	2009 Profits: $8,391	**Int'l Ticker:** Int'l Exchange:
2008 Sales: $99,440	2008 Profits: $10,134	Employees: 6
2007 Sales: $151,583	2007 Profits: $18,888	Fiscal Year Ends: 12/31
2006 Sales: $120,852	2006 Profits: $14,630	Parent Company:

SALARIES/BENEFITS:

Pension Plan:	ESOP Stock Plan:	Profit Sharing:	Top Exec. Salary: $250,000	Bonus: $
Savings Plan: Y	Stock Purch. Plan:		Second Exec. Salary: $138,000	Bonus: $

OTHER THOUGHTS:

Apparent Women Officers or Directors:
Hot Spot for Advancement for Women/Minorities:

LOCATIONS: ("Y" = Yes)

West:	Southwest:	Midwest:	Southeast:	Northeast:	International:
Y					

MODTECH HOLDINGS INC

www.modtech.com

Industry Group Code: 321991 Ranks within this company's industry group: Sales: Profits:

Properties:	Financial Services:	Construction/Development:		Investments:	Specialty Services:	Brokerage:
Apartments:	Mortgages:	Commercial Construction:	Y	REIT:	Property Management:	Commercial Sales:
Malls/Shopping:	Title Insurance:	Residential Construction:	Y		Online Services:	Residential Sales:
Offices:	Property Insurance:	Land Development:			Software/IT:	Specialty:
Hotels/Motels:		Support Services:			Consulting:	
Industrial/Warehouses:		Design/Engineering:	Y			
Other:						

TYPES OF BUSINESS:

Modular Construction
Modular Design Services
Modular Educational Facilities

BRANDS/DIVISIONS/AFFILIATES:

CONTACTS:
Note: Officers with more than one job title may be intentionally listed here more than once.
Dennis L. Shogren, CEO
Dennis L. Shogren, Pres.
Kenneth Cragun, CFO
Ronald Savona, Sr. VP-Oper.
Charles C. McGettigan, Chmn.

Phone: 951-943-4014	Fax: 951-943-3725
Toll-Free:	
Address: 1660 Chicago Ave., Ste. P-15, Perris, CA 92501 US	

GROWTH PLANS/SPECIAL FEATURES:

Modtech Holdings, Inc. designs, manufactures, markets and installs permanent and temporary modular, relocatable buildings for education, residential, commercial, healthcare, daycare and government applications. The company has three manufacturing facilities with approximately 1.2 million square feet of space on 132 acres, through which it provides design, modular construction, site work and commissioning solutions. Modtech aims to increase quality and strength of units, as well as achieve savings in construction time and overall costs through off-site building. Its service area includes California, Arizona and Florida, though most of its business is done in California. The company provides pre-manufactured student facilities for schools with overcrowded classrooms. These facilities are made up of not only standard classrooms but also libraries, gymnasiums, computer labs and bathrooms. Additionally, the company is a designer, manufacturer and wholesaler of commercial and light industrial modular buildings. Modtech designs and builds modular buildings to customer specifications for a wide array of industries, including multi-family residential, townhouse, apartment, condominium and modular home properties; office buildings, bank branches and retail locations; government and military buildings; barracks; justice centers; police departments and fire station buildings; and healthcare buildings, clinics and fitness and wellness centers. Modtech endeavors to embrace environmentally friendly manufacturing processes, including the recycling and reuse of cardboard, copper wire, wood and steel.

FINANCIALS:
Sales and profits are in thousands of dollars—add 000 to get the full amount. 2010 Note: Financial information for 2010 was not available for all companies at press time.

2010 Sales: $	2010 Profits: $	U.S. Stock Ticker: MODT
2009 Sales: $	2009 Profits: $	Int'l Ticker: Int'l Exchange:
2008 Sales: $	2008 Profits: $	Employees:
2007 Sales: $87,323	2007 Profits: $-56,908	Fiscal Year Ends: 12/31
2006 Sales: $156,033	2006 Profits: $-54,691	Parent Company:

SALARIES/BENEFITS:

Pension Plan:	ESOP Stock Plan:	Profit Sharing:	Top Exec. Salary: $	Bonus: $
Savings Plan:	Stock Purch. Plan:		Second Exec. Salary: $	Bonus: $

OTHER THOUGHTS:

Apparent Women Officers or Directors:
Hot Spot for Advancement for Women/Minorities:

LOCATIONS: ("Y" = Yes)

West:	Southwest:	Midwest:	Southeast:	Northeast:	International:
Y					

MORGANS HOTEL GROUP CO

www.morganshotelgroup.com

Industry Group Code: 721110 Ranks within this company's industry group: Sales: 26   Profits: 26

Properties:	Financial Services:	Construction/Development:	Investments:	Specialty Services:		Brokerage:
Apartments:	Mortgages:	Commercial Construction:	REIT:	Property Management:	Y	Commercial Sales:
Malls/Shopping:	Title Insurance:	Residential Construction:		Online Services:		Residential Sales:
Offices:	Property Insurance:	Land Development:		Software/IT:		Specialty:
Hotels/Motels: Y		Support Services:		Consulting:		
Industrial/Warehouses:		Design/Engineering:				
Other: Y						

TYPES OF BUSINESS:

Boutique Luxury Hotels & Resorts
Boutique Hotels
Property Management

BRANDS/DIVISIONS/AFFILIATES:

Morgans
Royalton
Hudson
Delano South Beach
Mondrian Los Angeles
Clift
Modrian SoHo
Ames

CONTACTS: *Note: Officers with more than one job title may be intentionally listed here more than once.*

Michael Gross, CEO
Marc Gordon, Pres.
Richard Szymanksi, CFO
Fernando Cerna, Dir.-Global Sales
David Smail, General Counsel/Exec. VP
David Weidlich, Exec. VP-Oper.
James Zito, VP-Interactive Mktg.
Yoav Gery, Chief Investment Officer
David T. Hamamoto, Chmn.

Phone: 212-277-4100	Fax: 212-277-4260
Toll-Free:	
Address: 475 10th Ave., New York, NY 10018 US	

GROWTH PLANS/SPECIAL FEATURES:

Morgans Hotel Group Co. (MHG) operates, owns, develops and redevelops luxury hotels. The firm, which is known for its establishment of the boutique hotel sector, primarily maintains hotels in gateway cities and select resort markets in the U.S. and Europe that feature avant-garde modern design. MHG owns/partially owns and operates 12 hotel properties in New York, Miami, Los Angeles, San Francisco, London and Boston. The firm's fully-owned and managed hotels include the Morgans, Royalton, Hudson, Delano South Beach, Mondrian SoHo, Mondrian Los Angeles and Clift. The company also manages and owns a 50% interest in two hotels (St. Martins Lane and Sanderson) in London; a 50% interest in Mondrian South Beach in Miami; a 7% interest in the Shore Club in Miami; and a 31% interest in Ames in Boston. Significant media attention has been devoted to MHG's hotels, which it attributes to the public spaces, modern design, celebrity guests and high-profile events for which its hotels are known. Designers of MHG's hotels have included Phillippe Starck, Benjamin Noriega-Ortiz, Andree Putman and David Chipperfield. The lobby of the company's Royalton in midtown Manhattan spans a full city block and includes a series of iconic spaces. Delano South Beach features a simple white Art Deco design and the Water Salon and Orchard, comprised of a landscaped orchard and 100-foot long pool. The Sanderson, located on London's Soho district, features wall-less guest rooms in which the dressing room and bathroom are encased in a glass box wrapped in layered sheer curtains. In October 2010, the firm opened a new cocktail bar, Forty Four at Royalton. In March 2011, MHG opened Mondrian SoHo in the SoHo neighborhood of New York.

FINANCIALS: Sales and profits are in thousands of dollars—add 000 to get the full amount. 2010 Note: Financial information for 2010 was not available for all companies at press time.

2010 Sales: $236,370	2010 Profits: $-83,648	U.S. Stock Ticker: MHGC
2009 Sales: $225,051	2009 Profits: $-101,605	Int'l Ticker: Int'l Exchange:
2008 Sales: $300,679	2008 Profits: $-54,569	Employees: 4,600
2007 Sales: $322,985	2007 Profits: $-14,796	Fiscal Year Ends: 12/31
2006 Sales: $281,883	2006 Profits: $-13,925	Parent Company:

SALARIES/BENEFITS:

Pension Plan:	ESOP Stock Plan:	Profit Sharing:	Top Exec. Salary: $936,000	Bonus: $374,400
Savings Plan:	Stock Purch. Plan:		Second Exec. Salary: $709,800	Bonus: $709,800

OTHER THOUGHTS:

Apparent Women Officers or Directors: 1
Hot Spot for Advancement for Women/Minorities:

LOCATIONS: ("Y" = Yes)

West:	Southwest:	Midwest:	Southeast:	Northeast:	International:
Y			Y	Y	Y

MOVE INC

www.move.com

Industry Group Code: 519130 Ranks within this company's industry group: Sales: 2   Profits: 2

Properties:	Financial Services:	Construction/Development:	Investments:	Specialty Services:		Brokerage:
Apartments:	Mortgages:	Commercial Construction:	REIT:	Property Management:		Commercial Sales:
Malls/Shopping:	Title Insurance:	Residential Construction:		Online Services:	Y	Residential Sales:
Offices:	Property Insurance:	Land Development:		Software/IT:	Y	Specialty:
Hotels/Motels:		Support Services:		Consulting:		
Industrial/Warehouses:		Design/Engineering:				
Other:						

TYPES OF BUSINESS:

Online Portal-Real Estate Data
Real Estate Software
Real Estate Publishing
Real Estate Advertising

BRANDS/DIVISIONS/AFFILIATES:

Realtor.com
Move.com
Top Producer 8i
Moving.com
Move New Homes
Move Rentals

CONTACTS: *Note: Officers with more than one job title may be intentionally listed here more than once.*

Steven Berkowitz, CEO
Rob Krolik, CFO
Matthew Moore, Exec. VP-Mktg. & Sales
Carol Brummer, VP-Human Resources
David Story, CTO
Scott Boeker, Chief Prod. Officer
Tracy Mahnken, Chief of Staff/Sr. VP
James S. Caulfield, General Counsel/Exec. VP/Sec.
Errol Samuelson, Chief Revenue Officer
Joe F. Hanauer, Chmn.

Phone: 805-557-2300	Fax:
Toll-Free:	
Address: 910 E. Hamilton Ave., 6th Fl., Campbell, CA 95008 US	

GROWTH PLANS/SPECIAL FEATURES:

Move, Inc. and its subsidiaries operate a leading network of web sites for real estate search, finance, moving and home enthusiasts and provide a resource for consumers seeking information and connections needed before, during and after a move. Its flagship consumer websites are Move.com, Realtor.com and Moving.com. The company's Realtor.com, Top Producer and Move Rentals businesses provide marketing services that allow real estate professionals connect with the consumer audience it has attracted to its web sites. Realtor.com, which is the official web site of the National Association of Realtors, offers consumers a suite of services, tools and content for all aspects of the residential real estate transaction. Move's primary Top Producer product, 8i, is a web-based customer relationship management (CRM) software. The Move new homes channel of Move.com aggregates and displays new home listings nationwide, while the rentals segment aggregates and displays rental listings. The firm also offers SeniorHousingNet.com, a searchable web site for locating housing for senior citizens. The company's consumer media business segment provides advertisers such as mortgage companies, home improvement retailers, moving service providers and other consumer product and service companies with products and services designed to help them target consumers during the move cycle. These products and services include advertising products and lead generation tools including display; text-link and rich media advertising positions; directory products; price quote tools and content sponsorships on Move.com and other related web sites as well as lead generation products for professional moving, truck rental and self-storage businesses on the Move.com web site.

FINANCIALS: Sales and profits are in thousands of dollars—add 000 to get the full amount. 2010 Note: Financial information for 2010 was not available for all companies at press time.

2010 Sales: $197,503	2010 Profits: $-15,472	**U.S. Stock Ticker: MOVE**
2009 Sales: $212,009	2009 Profits: $-6,946	**Int'l Ticker:** Int'l Exchange:
2008 Sales: $242,069	2008 Profits: $-29,190	Employees: 951
2007 Sales: $248,919	2007 Profits: $- 316	Fiscal Year Ends: 12/31
2006 Sales: $280,112	2006 Profits: $22,105	Parent Company:

SALARIES/BENEFITS:

Pension Plan:	ESOP Stock Plan:	Profit Sharing:	Top Exec. Salary: $491,093	Bonus: $300,000
Savings Plan: Y	Stock Purch. Plan:		Second Exec. Salary: $325,000	Bonus: $215,715

OTHER THOUGHTS:

Apparent Women Officers or Directors: 2
Hot Spot for Advancement for Women/Minorities:

LOCATIONS: ("Y" = Yes)

West:	Southwest:	Midwest:	Southeast:	Northeast:	International:
Y	Y			Y	Y

MPG OFFICE TRUST INC

www.maguireproperties.com

Industry Group Code: 5311 Ranks within this company's industry group: Sales: 25   Profits: 31

Properties:		Financial Services:		Construction/Development:		Investments:		Specialty Services:		Brokerage:	
Apartments:		Mortgages:		Commercial Construction:		REIT:	Y	Property Management:	Y	Commercial Sales:	Y
Malls/Shopping:		Title Insurance:		Residential Construction:				Online Services:		Residential Sales:	
Offices:	Y	Property Insurance:		Land Development:				Software/IT:		Specialty:	
Hotels/Motels:	Y			Support Services:	Y			Consulting:			
Industrial/Warehouses:				Design/Engineering:	Y						
Other:											

TYPES OF BUSINESS:

Real Estate Investment, Development & Management
Office Properties
Property Management
Asset Management

BRANDS/DIVISIONS/AFFILIATES:

Maguire Properties, Inc.
MPG Office, L.P.
MPG TRS Holdings, Inc.
MPG TRS Holdings II, Inc.
MPG Trust Services, Inc.

CONTACTS: *Note: Officers with more than one job title may be intentionally listed here more than once.*

David L. Weinsten, CEO
David L. Weinsten, Pres.
Shant Koumrigian, CFO/Exec. VP
Peggy Moretti, Chief Admin. Officer
Jonathan L. Abrams, General Counsel/Sr. VP/Corp. Sec.
Peggy Moretti, Exec. VP-Public Rel.
Peggy Moretti, Exec. VP-Investor Rel.
Peter K. Johnston, Sr. VP-Leasing
Christopher M. Norton, Sr. VP-Transactions
Paul M. Watson, Chmn.

Phone: 213-626-3300	**Fax:** 213-687-4758
Toll-Free:	
Address: 355 S. Grand Ave., Ste. 3300, Los Angeles, CA 90071 US	

GROWTH PLANS/SPECIAL FEATURES:

MPG Office Trust, Inc., formerly Maguire Properties, Inc., is a self-administered and self-managed real estate investment trust (REIT). The firm owns and operates high-quality office properties in the Los Angeles central business district. The company is primarily focused on owning, managing, leasing, acquiring and developing properties in Southern California. The firm operates through its controlling 88.4% interest in MPG Office, L.P., and subsidiaries such as MPG TRS Holdings, Inc.; MPG TRS Holdings II, Inc.; and MPG Trust Services, Inc. It currently has properties in the greater Los Angeles area, Orange County and San Diego; and has an interest in one property Denver, Colorado. The company operates through two segments: office properties and hotel. The firm's portfolio totals approximately 15 million square feet, consisting of 24 office and retail buildings; a 350-room hotel with 266,000 square feet; and off-site parking garages and on-site structured and surface parking totaling 9 million square feet with the ability to accommodate 27,000 vehicles. Office properties are typically leased to high credit tenants for terms ranging from 5-10 years. In May 2010, the company changed its name from Maguire Properties, Inc. to MPG Office Trust, Inc.

FINANCIALS: Sales and profits are in thousands of dollars—add 000 to get the full amount. 2010 Note: Financial information for 2010 was not available for all companies at press time.

2010 Sales: $406,896	2010 Profits: $-197,938	**U.S. Stock Ticker: MPG**
2009 Sales: $423,841	2009 Profits: $-869,727	**Int'l Ticker:** Int'l Exchange:
2008 Sales: $439,546	2008 Profits: $-323,338	Employees: 136
2007 Sales: $462,542	2007 Profits: $19,359	Fiscal Year Ends: 12/31
2006 Sales: $431,402	2006 Profits: $70,326	Parent Company:

SALARIES/BENEFITS:

Pension Plan:	ESOP Stock Plan:	Profit Sharing:	Top Exec. Salary: $831,250	Bonus: $
Savings Plan:	Stock Purch. Plan:		Second Exec. Salary: $375,000	Bonus: $370,000

OTHER THOUGHTS:

Apparent Women Officers or Directors: 2
Hot Spot for Advancement for Women/Minorities:

LOCATIONS: ("Y" = Yes)

West:	Southwest:	Midwest:	Southeast:	Northeast:	International:
Y					

MRV ENGENHARIA E PARTICIPACOES SA

www.mrv.com.br

Industry Group Code: 5311 Ranks within this company's industry group: Sales: Profits:

Properties:	Financial Services:	Construction/Development:		Investments:	Specialty Services:	Brokerage:
Apartments:	Mortgages:	Commercial Construction:		REIT:	Property Management:	Commercial Sales:
Malls/Shopping:	Title Insurance:	Residential Construction:	Y		Online Services:	Residential Sales:
Offices:	Property Insurance:	Land Development:	Y		Software/IT:	Specialty:
Hotels/Motels:		Support Services:			Consulting:	
Industrial/Warehouses:		Design/Engineering:				
Other:						

TYPES OF BUSINESS:

Real Estate Development

BRANDS/DIVISIONS/AFFILIATES:

Parque
Spazio
Village
Minha Casa, Minha Vida

CONTACTS:
Note: Officers with more than one job title may be intentionally listed here more than once.
Rubens M.T. de Souza, CEO
Leonardo G.Correa, CFO
Homero Aguiar Paiva, Chief Prod. Officer
Maria F.N.M.T. de Souza Maia, Chief Legal Officer
Lucas Cabaleiro Fernandez, CEO-Real Estate Dev.
Monica F.G. Simao, Chief Investor Rel. Officer
Eduardo P. Barreto, Chief Commercial Officer
Jose A.T. Simao, CEO-Real Estate Financing
Junia M. de Sousa Lima Galvao, Chief Mgmt. & Shared Service Center Officer
Rubens M.T. de Souza, Chmn.

Phone: 55-31-3348-7133   **Fax:** 55-31-3348-7155

Toll-Free:

Address: 2720 Raja Gabaglia Ave., Estoril Belo Horizonte, MG 30350-540 Brazil

GROWTH PLANS/SPECIAL FEATURES:

MRV Engenharia e Participacoes S.A. is a Brazilian developer and builder of low-income residential real estate. The firm offers three products directed to low-income customers: the Parque line, featuring units with between 430.56 and 592 square feet of usable area and a maximum sale price of approximately $55,310; the Spazio line, which offers units with between 452 and 753.47 square feet of usable area and prices ranging between $38,728 and $77,455; and the Village line, featuring units with between 753.47 and 1,291.67 square feet of usable area and prices ranging from $55,325 to $165,975. Both the Parque and Spazio units are vertically designed condominiums with a maximum of five floors; the village line of condominiums feature a horizontal layout. MRV Engenharia operates in 85 cities located in the Federal District and the following 14 states: Sao Paulo, Rio de Janeiro, Minas Gerais, Rio Grande do Norte, Goias, Espirito Santo, Parana, Santa Catarina, Rio Grande do Sul, Bahia, Ceara, Mato Grosso, Mato Grosso do Sul and Pernambuco. Approximately 84% of the firm's customers pay for their condominiums using CEF-associative credit financing; 10% utilize bank financing; 5% pay cash; and 1% use direct financing from MRV Engenharia. The company is a member of Minha Casa, Minha Vida (My Home, My Life), a program funded by the Brazilian government to promote homeownership in the country. The program, which aims to build 1 million new houses for families earning up to 10 times Brazil's minimum wage.

FINANCIALS:
Sales and profits are in thousands of dollars—add 000 to get the full amount. 2010 Note: Financial information for 2010 was not available for all companies at press time.

2010 Sales: $	2010 Profits: $	**U.S. Stock Ticker:**
2009 Sales: $940,540	2009 Profits: $198,320	**Int'l Ticker: MRVE3** Int'l Exchange: Sao Paulo-SAO
2008 Sales: $634,050	2008 Profits: $131,870	Employees:
2007 Sales: $228,110	2007 Profits: $12,730	Fiscal Year Ends: 12/31
2006 Sales: $	2006 Profits: $	Parent Company:

SALARIES/BENEFITS:

Pension Plan:	ESOP Stock Plan:	Profit Sharing:	Top Exec. Salary: $	Bonus: $
Savings Plan:	Stock Purch. Plan:		Second Exec. Salary: $	Bonus: $

OTHER THOUGHTS:

Apparent Women Officers or Directors: 3
Hot Spot for Advancement for Women/Minorities: Y

LOCATIONS: ("Y" = Yes)

West:	Southwest:	Midwest:	Southeast:	Northeast:	International:
					Y

MUNICIPAL MORTGAGE & EQUITY

www.munimae.com

Industry Group Code: 522310 Ranks within this company's industry group: Sales: 3   Profits: 3

Properties:	Financial Services:		Construction/Development:	Investments:	Specialty Services:	Brokerage:
Apartments:	Mortgages:	Y	Commercial Construction:	REIT:	Property Management:	Commercial Sales:
Malls/Shopping:	Title Insurance:		Residential Construction:		Online Services:	Residential Sales:
Offices:	Property Insurance:		Land Development:		Software/IT:	Specialty:
Hotels/Motels:			Support Services:		Consulting:	
Industrial/Warehouses:			Design/Engineering:			
Other:						

TYPES OF BUSINESS:

Mortgages
Real Estate Services

BRANDS/DIVISIONS/AFFILIATES:

MuniMae
MuniMae TE Bond Subsidiary, LLC
International Housing Solutions
MMA Renewable Ventures, LLC
MMA Equity
MMA Financial TC Corp

CONTACTS: *Note: Officers with more than one job title may be intentionally listed here more than once.*

Michael L. Falcone, CEO
Michael L. Falcone, Pres.
David Kay, CFO
Jessica C. Sanzone, Dir.-Investor Rel.
Gary A. Mentesana, Exec. VP/Chief Capital Officer
Earl W. Cole III, Exec. VP-Corp. Credit & Portfolio Mgmt.
Mark K. Joseph, Chmn.

Phone: 443-263-2900	Fax: 410-727-5387
Toll-Free:	
Address: 621 E. Pratt St., Ste. 300, Baltimore, MD 21202 US	

GROWTH PLANS/SPECIAL FEATURES:

Municipal Mortgage & Equity (MuniMae) is a real estate finance company. Following a major restructuring effort in which the company sold large portions of its non-core business segments, the company primarily invests in bonds issued by state and local governments or their agencies or authorities to finance affordable multifamily housing, student housing and assisted living properties. These bonds are secured by an assignment of the related mortgage loans and a general assignment of rents of the underlying properties. The firm's wholly-owned subsidiary, MuniMae TE Bond Subsidiary, LLC, holds the majority of its 153 tax exempt bonds, which stand at a fair value basis of $1.15 billion. Additionally, the company has an investment interest in the private equity firm International Housing Solutions. Other miscellaneous assets remaining in MuniMae's portfolio consist of commercial real estate loans and certain retained low income housing tax credit funds, as well as sundry investments received in its sales of assets and two solar funds and two solar projects. In total, outside of the bond investments, the firm has 47 loans in its portfolio, a significant portion of which are in default.

FINANCIALS: Sales and profits are in thousands of dollars—add 000 to get the full amount. 2010 Note: Financial information for 2010 was not available for all companies at press time.

2010 Sales: $107,677	2010 Profits: $-28,709	U.S. Stock Ticker: MMAB.PK
2009 Sales: $134,771	2009 Profits: $-143,840	Int'l Ticker: Int'l Exchange:
2008 Sales: $	2008 Profits: $	Employees: 40
2007 Sales: $	2007 Profits: $	Fiscal Year Ends: 12/31
2006 Sales: $	2006 Profits: $	Parent Company:

SALARIES/BENEFITS:

Pension Plan:	ESOP Stock Plan:	Profit Sharing:	Top Exec. Salary: $423,077	Bonus: $600,000
Savings Plan: Y	Stock Purch. Plan:		Second Exec. Salary: $313,573	Bonus: $525,000

OTHER THOUGHTS:

Apparent Women Officers or Directors:
Hot Spot for Advancement for Women/Minorities:

LOCATIONS: ("Y" = Yes)

West:	Southwest:	Midwest:	Southeast:	Northeast:	International:
Y	Y	Y	Y	Y	

MWH GLOBAL INC

www.mw.com

Industry Group Code: 237 Ranks within this company's industry group: Sales: Profits:

Properties:	Financial Services:	Construction/Development:	Investments:	Specialty Services:	Brokerage:
Apartments:	Mortgages:	Commercial Construction:	REIT:	Property Management:	Commercial Sales:
Malls/Shopping:	Title Insurance:	Residential Construction:		Online Services:	Residential Sales:
Offices:	Property Insurance:	Land Development:		Software/IT:	Specialty:
Hotels/Motels:		Support Services:		Consulting:	
Industrial/Warehouses:		Design/Engineering: Y			
Other:					

TYPES OF BUSINESS:

Engineering & Construction Services
Environmental Engineering
Water & Waste Treatment Analysis
Facilities Development
Infrastructure Asset Management
Consulting
Government Relations & Lobbying
Software & IT Services

BRANDS/DIVISIONS/AFFILIATES:

KnowledgeNet
MWH Laboratories
mCapitol Management
MWH Soft
H2ONET
Biwater Services Limited

CONTACTS: *Note: Officers with more than one job title may be intentionally listed here more than once.*

Robert B. Uhler, CEO
Alan J. Krause, COO
Alan J. Krause, Pres.
David Barnes, CFO
Jack Shandley, Chief Human Resources Officer
Micki Nelson, CIO
Don Ungemah, Chief Legal Officer/Chief Risk Officer
Garry Sanderson, Chief-Global Strategic Planning
Meg Vanderlaan, VP-Corp. Comm.
Dan McConville, Pres., MWH Americas, Inc.
Joseph D. Adams, Jr., Pres., MWH Constructors, Inc.
Paul F. Boulos, Pres., MWH Soft, Inc. & Middle East
Bruce K. Howard, Pres., MWH Bus. Solutions
Robert B. Uhler, Chmn.
Marshall Davert, Pres., APAC

Phone: 303-533-1900	Fax: 303-533-1901
Toll-Free:	
Address: 370 Interlocken Crescent, Ste. 200, Broomfield, CO 80021 US	

GROWTH PLANS/SPECIAL FEATURES:

MWH Global, Inc. is one of the world's leading providers of consulting, engineering, construction and management services to the water, natural resources and infrastructure industries. Through over 120 global offices, MWH specializes in proprietary software and process automation packages in the areas of environmental engineering, power generation, facilities development, laboratory services, construction, asset management, financial services, IT consulting and government relations. One of these packages, KnowledgeNet, links the firm's worldwide employee base, allowing instant collaboration on projects and the elimination of redundancies in its system. MWH conducts its operations through several independent divisions: environmental engineering, power solutions, facilities, program management, laboratory services, asset management, financial consulting, construction, information technology, applied research and government relations. Some of its affiliates include MWH Laboratories, providing water and wastewater analysis services; mCapitol Management, which offers government relations, marketing and business development services; and MWH Soft is the creator of H2ONET, an integrated water distribution analysis software package. In early 2010, the company introduced mCO2, a new reporting program that calculates carbon emissions. In January 2011, the firm acquired Biwater Services Limited, a U.K.-based company focused on the process engineering of water, waste water and environmental services.

FINANCIALS: Sales and profits are in thousands of dollars—add 000 to get the full amount. 2010 Note: Financial information for 2010 was not available for all companies at press time.

2010 Sales: $	2010 Profits: $	**U.S. Stock Ticker: Private**
2009 Sales: $	2009 Profits: $	**Int'l Ticker:** Int'l Exchange:
2008 Sales: $	2008 Profits: $	Employees:
2007 Sales: $	2007 Profits: $	Fiscal Year Ends: 9/30
2006 Sales: $	2006 Profits: $	Parent Company:

SALARIES/BENEFITS:

Pension Plan:	ESOP Stock Plan:	Profit Sharing:	Top Exec. Salary: $	Bonus: $
Savings Plan:	Stock Purch. Plan:		Second Exec. Salary: $	Bonus: $

OTHER THOUGHTS:

Apparent Women Officers or Directors: 3
Hot Spot for Advancement for Women/Minorities: Y

LOCATIONS: ("Y" = Yes)

West:	Southwest:	Midwest:	Southeast:	Northeast:	International:
Y	Y	Y	Y	Y	Y

NAI GLOBAL INC

www.naiglobal.com

Industry Group Code: 531210 Ranks within this company's industry group: Sales: Profits:

Properties:	Financial Services:	Construction/Development:	Investments:	Specialty Services:		Brokerage:	
Apartments:	Mortgages:	Commercial Construction:	REIT:	Property Management:	Y	Commercial Sales:	Y
Malls/Shopping:	Title Insurance:	Residential Construction:		Online Services:	Y	Residential Sales:	
Offices:	Property Insurance:	Land Development:		Software/IT:	Y	Specialty:	
Hotels/Motels:		Support Services:		Consulting:	Y		
Industrial/Warehouses:		Design/Engineering:					
Other:							

TYPES OF BUSINESS:

Brokerage Services
Consulting & Advisory Services
Property Management
Online Transaction Services
IT Services
Real Estate Software

BRANDS/DIVISIONS/AFFILIATES:

REALTrac Online

CONTACTS: *Note: Officers with more than one job title may be intentionally listed here more than once.*

Jeffrey Finn, CEO
Ed Finn, COO
Jeffrey Finn, Pres.
Mark Klionsky, Sr. VP-Mktg.
Shawn Stumbaugh, Exec. VP-Info. Systems
Shawn Stumbaugh, CTO
Ed Finn, General Counsel
Bobbi Jean Formosa, Exec. VP-Oper.
Marjy Smith, Sr. VP-Finance
David Blanchard, Exec. VP-Member Svcs.
Ted Parcel, Exec. VP-Corp. Svcs.
Patricia Faulkner, Sr. VP-Client Dev.
Gerald S. Monash, Exec. VP-Investment Svcs.
Gerald Finn, Chmn.
David Perry, VP-EMEA

Phone: 609-945-4000	Fax: 609-945-4001
Toll-Free:	
Address: 4 Independence Way, Ste. 400, Princeton, NJ 08540 US	

GROWTH PLANS/SPECIAL FEATURES:

NAI Global, Inc., formerly New America International, is an international commercial real estate network with more than 350 offices in 55 countries worldwide. The company manages over 200 million square feet of commercial space, with services provided local, regional, national and international businesses. The company offers leasing and brokerage agencies; disposition services; financial and investment strategies; leasing; property management; tenant representation; valuation and advice; and practice groups. Some of NAI's value-added operations include auction services, build-to-suit development services, commercial real estate due diligence, cost segregation, facilities management, lease audits, relocation studies, tax appeals, roof portfolio management and title insurance services. NAI also runs several specialty segments focusing on government; life sciences; location advisory; logistics; capital markets; investment sales; NAFTA advisory; process industries; supply chain services; and the office, industrial, retail, multifamily, hotel and land markets. The company also publishes market analysis reports and newsletters, including international and industry-specific reports, city-specific reports, country-specific reports and regional reports (the biggest being the NAI Asia Pacific Regional Overview). NAI runs REALTrac Online, an active platform for management of all company client transactions, with a leaning towards project coordination and transaction cycles. The company offers software for portfolio management, lease administration, online property marketing, financial analysis and demographics mapping. In May 2010, the firm launched a new joint venture with Chesterfield Faring Ltd. to help clients with restructuring operations. In November 2010, NAI started a new office in Colombia to better serve that country's market. In March 2011, the company expanded its operations in the U.K. and in the Caribbean.

FINANCIALS: Sales and profits are in thousands of dollars—add 000 to get the full amount. 2010 Note: Financial information for 2010 was not available for all companies at press time.

2010 Sales: $	2010 Profits: $	**U.S. Stock Ticker: Private**
2009 Sales: $	2009 Profits: $	**Int'l Ticker:** Int'l Exchange:
2008 Sales: $	2008 Profits: $	Employees:
2007 Sales: $	2007 Profits: $	Fiscal Year Ends: 6/30
2006 Sales: $	2006 Profits: $	Parent Company:

SALARIES/BENEFITS:

Pension Plan:	ESOP Stock Plan:	Profit Sharing:	Top Exec. Salary: $	Bonus: $
Savings Plan:	Stock Purch. Plan:		Second Exec. Salary: $	Bonus: $

OTHER THOUGHTS:

Apparent Women Officers or Directors: 4
Hot Spot for Advancement for Women/Minorities: Y

LOCATIONS: ("Y" = Yes)

West:	Southwest:	Midwest:	Southeast:	Northeast:	International:
Y	Y	Y	Y	Y	Y

NATIONAL HEALTH INVESTORS INC   www.nhinvestors.com

Industry Group Code: 531120 Ranks within this company's industry group: Sales: 62   Profits: 29

Properties:	Financial Services:	Construction/Development:	Investments:	Specialty Services:	Brokerage:
Apartments:	Mortgages:	Commercial Construction:	REIT: Y	Property Management:	Commercial Sales:
Malls/Shopping:	Title Insurance:	Residential Construction:		Online Services:	Residential Sales:
Offices:	Property Insurance:	Land Development:		Software/IT:	Specialty:
Hotels/Motels:		Support Services:		Consulting:	
Industrial/Warehouses:		Design/Engineering:			
Other: Y					

TYPES OF BUSINESS:

Real Estate Investment Trust
Health Care Facilities
Long-Term Care Facilities
Retirement Centers
Mortgages

BRANDS/DIVISIONS/AFFILIATES:

National HealthCare Corporation
Sun Healthcare

CONTACTS: Note: Officers with more than one job title may be intentionally listed here more than once.

J. Justin Hutchens, CEO
J. Justin Hutchens, Pres.
Roger R. Hopkins, Chief Acct. Officer
Kristin S. Gaines, Chief Credit Officer
Kevin Pascoe, VP-Asset Mgmt.
W. Andrew Adams, Chmn.

Phone: 615-890-9100	**Fax:** 615-225-3030
Toll-Free:	
Address: 222 Robert Rose Dr., Murfreesboro, TN 37129 US	

GROWTH PLANS/SPECIAL FEATURES:

National Health Investors, Inc. (NHI) is a self-managed, self-administered real estate investment trust (REIT). The firm invests in healthcare properties including long-term care facilities, acute care hospitals, medical office buildings, retirement centers and assisted living facilities. NHI's portfolio includes real estate and mortgage investments in 118 health care facilities located in 23 states. These facilities consist of approximately 78 long-term care facilities, 31 assisted living facilities, two medical office buildings, four independent living centers, one acute psychiatric hospital, one transitional rehabilitation center and one acute care hospital. Of these facilities, 41 are leased to National HealthCare Corporation (NHC). All of NHI's long-term care facilities provide some combination of skilled and intermediate nursing and rehabilitative care, including speech, physical and occupational therapy. The firm's medical office buildings are specifically configured office buildings whose tenants are primarily physicians and other medical practitioners. Each of NHI's medical office buildings is leased to one lessee, who then leases out individual office space. Its assisted living facilities are either free-standing or attached to long-term care or retirement facilities and provide basic room and board functions for the elderly. NHI's independent living centers offer specially designed residential units for the active and ambulatory elderly and provide various ancillary services for their residents including restaurants, activity rooms and social areas. Three of the centers are leased to NHC and one is leased to Sun Healthcare. The company's acute care hospital offers a wide range of inpatient and outpatient services. In early 2010, the firm acquired six skilled nursing facilities in Florida from Care Foundation of America, Inc. for roughly $67 million. In July 2010, NHI sold two long-term care facilities in Texas to Legend Healthcare for $6.2 million.

FINANCIALS: Sales and profits are in thousands of dollars—add 000 to get the full amount. 2010 Note: Financial information for 2010 was not available for all companies at press time.

2010 Sales: $78,396	2010 Profits: $69,421	**U.S. Stock Ticker: NHI**
2009 Sales: $63,157	2009 Profits: $64,229	**Int'l Ticker:** Int'l Exchange:
2008 Sales: $56,941	2008 Profits: $57,510	Employees:
2007 Sales: $57,506	2007 Profits: $96,435	Fiscal Year Ends: 12/31
2006 Sales: $60,770	2006 Profits: $69,228	Parent Company:

SALARIES/BENEFITS:

Pension Plan:	ESOP Stock Plan:	Profit Sharing:	Top Exec. Salary: $386,138	Bonus: $630,000
Savings Plan:	Stock Purch. Plan:		Second Exec. Salary: $247,000	Bonus: $409,500

OTHER THOUGHTS:

Apparent Women Officers or Directors: 1
Hot Spot for Advancement for Women/Minorities:

LOCATIONS: ("Y" = Yes)

West:	Southwest:	Midwest:	Southeast:	Northeast:	International:
Y	Y	Y	Y	Y	

NATIONWIDE HEALTH PROPERTIES INC

www.nhp-reit.com

Industry Group Code: 531120 Ranks within this company's industry group: Sales: 39 Profits: 14

Properties:		Financial Services:		Construction/Development:	Investments:		Specialty Services:		Brokerage:
Apartments:		Mortgages:	Y	Commercial Construction:	REIT:	Y	Property Management:	Y	Commercial Sales:
Malls/Shopping:		Title Insurance:		Residential Construction:			Online Services:		Residential Sales:
Offices:	Y	Property Insurance:		Land Development:			Software/IT:		Specialty:
Hotels/Motels:				Support Services:			Consulting:		
Industrial/Warehouses:				Design/Engineering:					
Other:	Y								

TYPES OF BUSINESS:

Real Estate Investment Trust
Health Care Facilities
Nursing & Assisted Living Facilities
Retirement Communities
Mortgage Loans

BRANDS/DIVISIONS/AFFILIATES:

Ventas Inc

CONTACTS: *Note: Officers with more than one job title may be intentionally listed here more than once.*

Douglas M. Pasquale, CEO
Abdo H. Khoury, CFO/Exec. VP/Chief Portfolio Officer
Derrick D. Pete, Sr. VP-Corp. Dev.
Danion Fielding, VP-Finance
Donald D. Bradley, Chief Investment Officer/Exec. VP
Craig S. Jones, Managing Dir.-Specialty Finance
David M. Boitano, Sr. Investment Officer-West/Sr. VP
William M. Wagner, Controller/VP
Douglas M. Pasquale, Chmn.

Phone: 949-718-4400	**Fax:** 919-759-6876
Toll-Free:	
Address: 610 Newport Center Dr., Ste. 1150, Newport Beach, CA 92660 US	

GROWTH PLANS/SPECIAL FEATURES:

Nationwide Health Properties, Inc. (NHP) is a real estate investment trust (REIT) that invests primarily in healthcare-related senior housing, long-term care properties and medical office buildings. NHP has investments in 663 healthcare facilities located in 42 states, comprised of 298 assisted and independent living facilities; 212 skilled nursing facilities; 12 continuing care retirement communities; seven specialty hospitals; 51 triple-net medical office buildings; and 83 multi-tenant medical office buildings. NHP's operates through two segments: triple net leases and multi-tenant leases. In the triple net leases segment, the firm invests in healthcare-related properties, which it leases to unaffiliated tenants under leases that transfer the obligation for all facility operating costs, including maintenance, repairs, taxes and insurance, to the tenant. In the multi-tenant leases segment, NHP invests in medical office buildings that have several tenants under separate leases per building, thus requiring active management. NHP's directly owned properties are operated by approximately 88 healthcare providers, including Assisted Living Concepts, Inc., operating four facilities; Brookdale Senior Living, Inc., operating 93 facilities; Emeritus Corporation, operating six facilities; HealthSouth Corporation, operating two facilities; and Sun Healthcare Group, Inc., operating four facilities. In February 2011, the company agreed to be acquired by the REIT Ventas, Inc. for $7.4 billion.

FINANCIALS: Sales and profits are in thousands of dollars—add 000 to get the full amount. 2010 Note: Financial information for 2010 was not available for all companies at press time.

2010 Sales: $439,251	2010 Profits: $142,123	**U.S. Stock Ticker: NHP**
2009 Sales: $383,853	2009 Profits: $149,058	**Int'l Ticker:** Int'l Exchange:
2008 Sales: $360,869	2008 Profits: $268,007	Employees: 41
2007 Sales: $306,269	2007 Profits: $224,458	Fiscal Year Ends: 12/31
2006 Sales: $222,910	2006 Profits: $185,577	Parent Company:

SALARIES/BENEFITS:

Pension Plan:	ESOP Stock Plan:	Profit Sharing:	Top Exec. Salary: $562,500	Bonus: $1,153,750
Savings Plan:	Stock Purch. Plan:		Second Exec. Salary: $330,000	Bonus: $500,000

OTHER THOUGHTS:

Apparent Women Officers or Directors:
Hot Spot for Advancement for Women/Minorities:

LOCATIONS: ("Y" = Yes)

West:	Southwest:	Midwest:	Southeast:	Northeast:	International:
Y	Y	Y	Y	Y	

NCI BUILDING SYSTEMS INC

www.ncilp.com

Industry Group Code: 332311 Ranks within this company's industry group: Sales: 1 Profits: 1

Properties:	Financial Services:	Construction/Development:		Investments:	Specialty Services:	Brokerage:
Apartments:	Mortgages:	Commercial Construction:		REIT:	Property Management:	Commercial Sales:
Malls/Shopping:	Title Insurance:	Residential Construction:			Online Services:	Residential Sales:
Offices:	Property Insurance:	Land Development:			Software/IT:	Specialty:
Hotels/Motels:		Support Services:	Y		Consulting:	
Industrial/Warehouses:		Design/Engineering:	Y			
Other:						

TYPES OF BUSINESS:

Prefabricated Metal Buildings
Metal Building Components
Engineered Building Systems

BRANDS/DIVISIONS/AFFILIATES:

Metallic Building Company
Heritage Building Systems
Steel Systems
All American Systems
Metal Coaters
Metal Prep
Garco Building Systems
Ceco Building Systems

CONTACTS: *Note: Officers with more than one job title may be intentionally listed here more than once.*

Norman C. Chambers, CEO
Mark W. Dobbins, COO/Exec. VP
Norman C. Chambers, Pres.
Mark E. Johnson, CFO
Eric J. Brown, CIO/Exec. VP
Todd R. Moore, General Counsel/Sec./Exec. VP
Mark T. Golladay, VP-Corp. Dev.
Mark E. Johnson, Treas./Exec. VP
C. Wayne Dickinson, Pres., Metal Components Div.
Bradley D. Robeson, Pres., NCI Buildings
John Kuzdal, Pres., Metal Coil Coating Div.
Bradley D. Robeson, Pres., Robertson-Ceco Buildings
Norman C. Chambers, Chmn.

Phone: 281-897-7788	Fax: 281-477-9674
Toll-Free: 888-624-8677	
Address: 10943 N. Sam Houston Pkwy. W., Houston, TX 77064 US	

GROWTH PLANS/SPECIAL FEATURES:

NCI Building Systems, Inc. is one of North America's largest manufacturers of metal products for the construction and building industry. Comprised of a family of companies and 32 manufacturing facilities located throughout the U.S. states and Mexico, the company is a viable national presence, offering a diversified product line. The firm operates in three business segments: metal components; engineered building systems; and metal coil coating services. The metal component segment produces metal roof and wall systems, metal partitions, metal trim, doors and other related accessories. These products are used in new construction and repair applications for industrial, commercial, institutional, agricultural and rural use. Some of this segment's brand names are Metal Building Components (MBCI); American Building Components; Insulated Panel Systems (IPS); NCI Metal Depots; and Doors and Buildings Components (DBCI). The engineered building systems segment encompasses the manufacturing of structural framing, complemented by engineering and drafting services, and includes the manufacturing of main house frames. It also offers value-added engineering and drafting services, which are typically not part of metal building component or metal coil coating products or services. This segment's brand names include A & S Building Systems; All American Systems; Ceco Building Systems; Garco Building Systems; Heritage Building Systems; Mesco Building Solutions; Metallic Building Company; and Steel Systems. The metal coil coating business, operating as Metal Coaters and Metal-Prep, is engaged in the cleaning, treating and painting of continuous steel coils before the steel is fabricated for use by construction and industrial users. In June 2010, NCI Building Systems' subsidiary NCI Group, Inc. acquired a 170,000 square foot coil coating facility in Ohio from MSC Pre Finish Metals (MT), Inc.for roughly $4.9 million.

Employees are offered medical, dental and vision benefits; a 401(k) plan; life and AD&D insurance; dependent life insurance; short- and long-term disability coverage; an employee assistance program; and credit union membership.

FINANCIALS: Sales and profits are in thousands of dollars—add 000 to get the full amount. 2010 Note: Financial information for 2010 was not available for all companies at press time.

2010 Sales: $870,526	2010 Profits: $-26,877	**U.S. Stock Ticker: NCS**
2009 Sales: $965,252	2009 Profits: $-750,796	**Int'l Ticker:** Int'l Exchange:
2008 Sales: $1,762,740	2008 Profits: $73,278	Employees: 3,606
2007 Sales: $1,625,068	2007 Profits: $63,729	Fiscal Year Ends: 10/31
2006 Sales: $1,571,183	2006 Profits: $73,796	Parent Company:

SALARIES/BENEFITS:

Pension Plan:	ESOP Stock Plan:	Profit Sharing:	Top Exec. Salary: $750,000	Bonus: $
Savings Plan: Y	Stock Purch. Plan:		Second Exec. Salary: $332,000	Bonus: $

OTHER THOUGHTS:

Apparent Women Officers or Directors: 1
Hot Spot for Advancement for Women/Minorities:

LOCATIONS: ("Y" = Yes)

West:	Southwest:	Midwest:	Southeast:	Northeast:	International:
Y	Y	Y	Y	Y	Y

NEW WORLD DEVELOPMENT COMPANY LIMITED www.nwd.com.hk

Industry Group Code: 5311 Ranks within this company's industry group: Sales: 7 Profits: 6

Properties:		Financial Services:		Construction/Development:		Investments:	Specialty Services:		Brokerage:
Apartments:	Y	Mortgages:		Commercial Construction:	Y	REIT:	Property Management:	Y	Commercial Sales:
Malls/Shopping:	Y	Title Insurance:		Residential Construction:	Y		Online Services:		Residential Sales:
Offices:	Y	Property Insurance:	Y	Land Development:	Y		Software/IT:		Specialty:
Hotels/Motels:	Y			Support Services:	Y		Consulting:		
Industrial/Warehouses:	Y			Design/Engineering:	Y				
Other:	Y								

TYPES OF BUSINESS:
Real Estate Holdings & Development

BRANDS/DIVISIONS/AFFILIATES:
New World China Land Limited
Hong Kong Property
Mainland China Property
Hotel Investment
New World Insurance
Hip Hing Construction
Taifook Securities
New World China Enterprises Projects Limited

CONTACTS: *Note: Officers with more than one job title may be intentionally listed here more than once.*
Henry Cheng Kar-Shun, Managing Dir.
Adrian Cheng Chi-Kong, Exec. Dir.
Cheng Chi-Heng, Exec. Dir.
David Liang Chong-Hou, Exec. Dir.
David Sin Wai-Kin, Exec. Dir.
Cheng Yu-Tung, Chmn.

Phone: 852-2523-1056	Fax: 852-2810-4673
Toll-Free:	
Address: 18 Queen's Rd. Central, New World Tower, 30th Fl., Hong Kong, China	

GROWTH PLANS/SPECIAL FEATURES:

New World Development Company Limited is a Hong Kong-based real estate investment holding firm operating in three primary segments: Property; Infrastructure and Service; and Department Store. The Property segment operates in three divisions: Hong Kong Property, Mainland China Property and Hotel Investment. Its Hong Kong property includes 27 projects totaling over 7.2 million square feet. Mainland China property is managed by subsidiary New World China Land Limited and encompasses properties in over 20 metropolitan areas totaling over 27 million square feet of developable floor area. The hotel division has investments in 18 operational hotels throughout Hong Kong, Mainland China and Southeast Asia. The Infrastructure and Service segment is involved in infrastructure investments and facility management. It is focused on investments in energy, roads, water and ports projects, with a portfolio encompassing 384 miles of toll roads; a number of power plants; a coal trading company; wastewater treatment facilities; and container terminals with an annual capacity of 7.1 million twenty-foot equivalent units (TEUs). Its main facility management operations include the management of the Hong Kong Convention & Exhibition Centre and the ATL Logistics Centre; contracting activities, performed mostly through subsidiaries Hip Hing Construction and NWS Engineering; and financial services, offered through subsidiaries Taifook Securities and New World Insurance. The Department Store segment includes the activities of subsidiary New World Department Store China Limited, which operates 36 department stores totaling over 3 million square feet, located in 17 cities in Mainland China. The firm, through wholly-owned subsidiary New World Strategic Investment Limited, also invests in growing private companies that are within one to three years of an initial public stock listing in a variety of industries. New World China Enterprises Projects Limited, another subsidiary, provides project management services to several of the company's businesses.

FINANCIALS: Sales and profits are in thousands of dollars—add 000 to get the full amount. 2010 Note: Financial information for 2010 was not available for all companies at press time.

		U.S. Stock Ticker:
2010 Sales: $3,888,470	2010 Profits: $1,912,150	Int'l Ticker: 0017 Int'l Exchange: Hong Kong-HKE
2009 Sales: $3,144,740	2009 Profits: $268,360	Employees:
2008 Sales: $3,788,350	2008 Profits: $1,248,270	Fiscal Year Ends: 6/30
2007 Sales: $3,004,340	2007 Profits: $556,480	Parent Company:
2006 Sales: $	2006 Profits: $	

SALARIES/BENEFITS:

Pension Plan:	ESOP Stock Plan:	Profit Sharing:	Top Exec. Salary: $	Bonus: $
Savings Plan:	Stock Purch. Plan:		Second Exec. Salary: $	Bonus: $

OTHER THOUGHTS:
Apparent Women Officers or Directors: 1
Hot Spot for Advancement for Women/Minorities:

LOCATIONS: ("Y" = Yes)

West:	Southwest:	Midwest:	Southeast:	Northeast:	International:
					Y

NEWCASTLE INVESTMENT CORP

www.newcastleinv.com

Industry Group Code: 531120 Ranks within this company's industry group: Sales: 46 Profits: 8

Properties:		Financial Services:		Construction/Development:		Investments:		Specialty Services:		Brokerage:	
Apartments:		Mortgages:	Y	Commercial Construction:		REIT:	Y	Property Management:	Y	Commercial Sales:	
Malls/Shopping:		Title Insurance:		Residential Construction:				Online Services:		Residential Sales:	
Offices:		Property Insurance:		Land Development:				Software/IT:		Specialty:	
Hotels/Motels:				Support Services:				Consulting:			
Industrial/Warehouses:				Design/Engineering:							
Other:											

TYPES OF BUSINESS:

Real Estate Investment Trust
Real Estate Securities
Real Estate Loan Investments
Loans & Mortgages
Property Management

BRANDS/DIVISIONS/AFFILIATES:

Fortress Investment Group LLC

CONTACTS: *Note: Officers with more than one job title may be intentionally listed here more than once.*

Kenneth M. Riis, CEO
Jonathan Ashley, COO
Kenneth M. Riis, Pres.
Brian C. Sigman, CFO
Randal A. Nardone, Corp. Sec.
Nadean Novogratz, Contact-Investor Rel.
Phillip J. Evanski, Chief Investment Officer
Wesley R. Edens, Chmn.

Phone: 212-798-6100	Fax: 212-798-6133
Toll-Free:	
Address: 1345 Ave. of the Americas, New York, NY 10105 US	

GROWTH PLANS/SPECIAL FEATURES:

Newcastle Investment Corp. is a REIT (Real Estate Investment Trust) and finance company that invests in real estate securities and other real estate-related assets. An affiliate of Fortress Investment Group LLC provides day-to-day management of the firm's operations. Fortress owns approximately 8.6% of Newcastle. The company has a $4.3 billion investment portfolio, consisting of $2.8 billion in commercial assets, $900 million in residential assets and $600 million in corporate assets. Its activities cover four major categories: Real Estate Securities, which represent 50.5% of Newcastle's assets; Real Estate Related Loans, 21.1%; Residential Mortgage Loans, 10.3%; and Operating Real Estate, 0.9%. Additionally, 17.2% of its assets consist of restricted and unrestricted cash and other miscellaneous net assets. The firm's Real Estate Securities activities consist of diversified, credit-sensitive real estate securities, including commercial mortgage-backed securities, asset backed securities, REIT debt and Federal National Mortgage Association (Fannie Mae) and Federal Home Loan Mortgage Corporation (Freddie Mac) securities. Its Real Estate Related Loans activities consist of acquired and company-originated loans made to well-capitalized real estate owners, including B-notes, mezzanine loans, corporate bank loans and real estate loans. Newcastle's Residential Mortgage Loans activities consist of acquiring residential loans, manufactured housing loans and subprime mortgage loans. The Operating Real Estate activities consist of acquiring and managing direct and indirect interests in the operating real estate sector.

FINANCIALS: Sales and profits are in thousands of dollars—add 000 to get the full amount. 2010 Note: Financial information for 2010 was not available for all companies at press time.

2010 Sales: $300,272	2010 Profits: $621,662	**U.S. Stock Ticker: NCT**
2009 Sales: $361,866	2009 Profits: $-209,904	**Int'l Ticker:** Int'l Exchange:
2008 Sales: $468,867	2008 Profits: $-2,985,352	Employees:
2007 Sales: $680,535	2007 Profits: $-65,457	Fiscal Year Ends: 12/31
2006 Sales: $529,818	2006 Profits: $127,923	Parent Company:

SALARIES/BENEFITS:

Pension Plan:	ESOP Stock Plan:	Profit Sharing:	Top Exec. Salary: $	Bonus: $
Savings Plan:	Stock Purch. Plan:		Second Exec. Salary: $	Bonus: $

OTHER THOUGHTS:

Apparent Women Officers or Directors: 1
Hot Spot for Advancement for Women/Minorities:

LOCATIONS: ("Y" = Yes)

West:	Southwest:	Midwest:	Southeast:	Northeast:	International:
				Y	Y

NEWHALL LAND & FARMING COMPANY

www.valencia.com

Industry Group Code: 5311 Ranks within this company's industry group: Sales: Profits:

Properties:		Financial Services:		Construction/Development:		Investments:		Specialty Services:		Brokerage:	
Apartments:	Y	Mortgages:		Commercial Construction:	Y	REIT:		Property Management:	Y	Commercial Sales:	Y
Malls/Shopping:	Y	Title Insurance:		Residential Construction:	Y			Online Services:		Residential Sales:	Y
Offices:	Y	Property Insurance:		Land Development:	Y			Software/IT:		Specialty:	Y
Hotels/Motels:				Support Services:				Consulting:			
Industrial/Warehouses:	Y			Design/Engineering:							
Other:	Y										

TYPES OF BUSINESS:

Real Estate Investment & Development
Master-Planned Communities
Commercial Property Management
Agricultural Land Management
Residential Development
Land Sales

BRANDS/DIVISIONS/AFFILIATES:

LandSource Communities Development LLC
Newhall Land Development LLC
West Hills
RiverVillage
Valencia
Newhall Ranch
West Creek

CONTACTS: Note: Officers with more than one job title may be intentionally listed here more than once.

Gregory H. McWilliams, Pres.
Donald L. Kimball, CFO/Sr. VP
Gary M. Cusumano, Chmn.

Phone: 661-255-4000	Fax: 661-255-3960
Toll-Free: 888-897-6815	
Address: 23823 Valencia Blvd., Valencia, CA 91355 US	

GROWTH PLANS/SPECIAL FEATURES:

Newhall Land & Farming Company, a subsidiary of Newhall Land Development LLC (formerly LandSource Communities Development LLC), develops new towns and master-planned, mixed-use communities. Newhall owns 15,000 acres in California from the original 48,000 acres acquired by Henry Mayo Newhall in 1882. The land, initially used for ranching, agriculture and oil production, today includes the towns of Valencia, 30 miles north of downtown Los Angeles, and Newhall Ranch, which is being planned to include 20,000 homes on 12,000 acres adjacent to Valencia. Since 1965, Newhall has been developing the town of Valencia on a portion of the company's landholdings, which now provides over 60,000 jobs. Valencia is notable for its environmentally sensitive planning, with natural amenities such as an extensive network of pedestrian walkways, 10 square miles acres of open space, long range water planning and 30 miles of the free-flowing Santa Clara River. Valencia is comprised of villages West Creek, West Hills and RiverVillage. Within its communities, Newhall sells residential lots to merchant builders, operates a portfolio of commercial properties, provides building-ready sites for sale to industrial and commercial developers and users and owns a public water utility, the Valencia Water Company.

FINANCIALS: Sales and profits are in thousands of dollars—add 000 to get the full amount. 2010 Note: Financial information for 2010 was not available for all companies at press time.

			U.S. Stock Ticker: Subsidiary
2010 Sales: $	2010 Profits: $		U.S. Stock Ticker: Subsidiary
2009 Sales: $	2009 Profits: $		Int'l Ticker: Int'l Exchange:
2008 Sales: $	2008 Profits: $		Employees:
2007 Sales: $	2007 Profits: $		Fiscal Year Ends: 12/31
2006 Sales: $	2006 Profits: $		Parent Company: NEWHALL LAND DEVELOMENT LLC

SALARIES/BENEFITS:

Pension Plan:	ESOP Stock Plan:	Profit Sharing:	Top Exec. Salary: $	Bonus: $
Savings Plan: Y	Stock Purch. Plan:		Second Exec. Salary: $	Bonus: $

OTHER THOUGHTS:

Apparent Women Officers or Directors:
Hot Spot for Advancement for Women/Minorities:

LOCATIONS: ("Y" = Yes)

West:	Southwest:	Midwest:	Southeast:	Northeast:	International:
Y					

                                                                    Plunkett Research, Ltd.

NH HOTELES SA   www.nh-hotels.com

Industry Group Code: 721110 Ranks within this company's industry group: Sales: 7   Profits: 24

Properties:	Financial Services:	Construction/Development:		Investments:	Specialty Services:		Brokerage:
Apartments:	Mortgages:	Commercial Construction:	Y	REIT:	Property Management:	Y	Commercial Sales:
Malls/Shopping:	Title Insurance:	Residential Construction:	Y		Online Services:		Residential Sales:
Offices:	Property Insurance:	Land Development:	Y		Software/IT:		Specialty:
Hotels/Motels: Y		Support Services:			Consulting:		
Industrial/Warehouses:		Design/Engineering:					
Other: Y							

TYPES OF BUSINESS:

Hotels
Golf Courses
Restaurants

BRANDS/DIVISIONS/AFFILIATES:

Sotogrande SA
Aymerich Golf Management
Grande Jolly Srl
Compagnia Italiana dei Jolly Hotels SpA

CONTACTS: *Note: Officers with more than one job title may be intentionally listed here more than once.*

Mariano Perez Claver, CEO
Francisco Zinser, COO
Mariano Perez Claver, Pres.
Roberto Chollet, CFO
Inigio Capell, Dir.-Human Resources
Francisco Souto, Dir.-IT
Luis Ortega, Dir.-Eng. & Environment
Manuel Fernandez Marcote, Dir.-Admin.
Leopoldo Gonzalez, General Counsel/Sec.
Ignacio Aranguren, Chief Strategy Officer
Ida Gutierrez, Dir.-Comm. & Institutional Rel.
Chema Garcia, Dir.-Investor Rel. & Investments
Joaquin de Entrambasaguas, Dir.-Finance
Santiago Lopez, Dir.-Projects & Construction
Tamara Wegmann, Dir.-Legal Affairs
Javier Carazo, Dir.-Quality & Procedures
Jordi Caralt, Dir.-Resorts
Mariano Perez Claver, Chmn.
Gonzalo Alcaraz, Dir.-Caribbean Hotels
Pedro Martínez, Dir.-Purchasing

Phone: 34-91-451-97-18	Fax: 34-91-451-97-64
Toll-Free: 800-232-9860	
Address: Santa Engracia 120, Edifico Central, Madrid, 28003 Spain	

GROWTH PLANS/SPECIAL FEATURES:

NH Hoteles S.A., based in Spain, is a hotel operator with nearly 400 hotels with 60,000 rooms in 24 countries across Europe, the Americas and Africa, ranging from budget hotels to four-star resorts.   In Europe, NH has hotels in Spain, Andorra, Germany, Italy, Luxembourg, Switzerland, the Netherlands, Belgium, Austria, the U.K., France, Portugal, Poland, the Czech Republic, Romania and Hungary. In the Americas, the firm has hotels in Mexico, the U.S., Argentina, Cuba, Chile, Uruguay and the Dominican Republic. In South Africa, the company has two hotels, one in Plettenberg Bay and the other in Cape Town.   Subsidiary Sotogrande S.A. operates a residential property development site in Spain and controls a 55% interest in Aymerich Golf Management, a golf course management and development company with approximately 40 active courses in Spain and Portugal. Also, through majority-owned subsidiary Grande Jolly S.r.l., the firm maintains an interest in Compagnia Italiana dei Jolly Hotels S.p.A., which operates approximately 45 hotels in Europe and one in the U.S., the Jolly Hotel Madison Towers in New York City. In 2010, the firm's revenue from its hotel operations in Spain & Portugal represented 28% of its total, Italy 15%, Benelux countries 25%, Central & Eastern Europe 5%, Germany 21% and the Americas 6%. In February 2010, the firm sold three of its Hilton-branded properties in Mexico for $57 million. In April 2010, it sold the Jolly St. Ermin's Hotel in London to investors Angelo, Gordon & Co.; Amerimar Enterprises; and Gracemark Invesments.   In March 2011, it entered a strategic alliance with AMResorts to join commercial efforts in the Dominican Republic.

FINANCIALS: Sales and profits are in thousands of dollars—add 000 to get the full amount. 2010 Note: Financial information for 2010 was not available for all companies at press time.

2010 Sales: $1,883,620	2010 Profits: $-60,650	**U.S. Stock Ticker: NHHEY.PK**
2009 Sales: $1,615,110	2009 Profits: $-129,530	**Int'l Ticker: NHH** Int'l Exchange: Madrid-MCE
2008 Sales: $1,997,070	2008 Profits: $34,930	Employees:
2007 Sales: $1,962,270	2007 Profits: $100,870	Fiscal Year Ends: 12/31
2006 Sales: $1,630,100	2006 Profits: $91,800	Parent Company:

SALARIES/BENEFITS:

Pension Plan:	ESOP Stock Plan:	Profit Sharing:	Top Exec. Salary: $	Bonus: $
Savings Plan:	Stock Purch. Plan:		Second Exec. Salary: $	Bonus: $

OTHER THOUGHTS:

Apparent Women Officers or Directors: 3
Hot Spot for Advancement for Women/Minorities: Y

LOCATIONS: ("Y" = Yes)

West:	Southwest:	Midwest:	Southeast:	Northeast:	International:
	Y		Y	Y	Y

NRT LLC

www.nrtinc.com

Industry Group Code: 531210 **Ranks within this company's industry group:** Sales: Profits:

Properties:	Financial Services:		Construction/Development:	Investments:	Specialty Services:	Brokerage:	
Apartments:	Mortgages:	Y	Commercial Construction:	REIT:	Property Management:	Commercial Sales:	Y
Malls/Shopping:	Title Insurance:		Residential Construction:		Online Services:	Residential Sales:	Y
Offices:	Property Insurance:		Land Development:		Software/IT:	Specialty:	
Hotels/Motels:			Support Services:		Consulting:		
Industrial/Warehouses:			Design/Engineering:				
Other:							

TYPES OF BUSINESS:

Real Estate Brokerage
Mortgage Lending
Real Estate Services

BRANDS/DIVISIONS/AFFILIATES:

Realogy Corporation
Coldwell Banker Real Estate Corp
ERA
Sotheby's International Realty
Corcoran Group (The)
Coldwell Banker Commercial NRT
Coldwell Banker Preferred
Coldwell Banker Residential Brokerage

CONTACTS: Note: Officers with more than one job title may be intentionally listed here more than once.

Bruce G. Zipf, CEO
Bruce G. Zipf, Pres.
Kevin Greene, CFO/Sr. VP
Dan Barnett, Sr. VP-Mktg.
Lauren De Simon Johnson, Sr. VP-Human Resources
Ken Hoffert, General Counsel/Sr. VP
Peter J. Sobeck, Sr. VP-Bus. Dev.
Kathy Borruso, Contact-Media Rel.
Jeff Culbertson, Exec. VP-Southwest Region
Kate Rossi, Exec. VP-Southeast Region
Greg Macres, Exec. VP-Western Region
Monty D. Smith, Sr. VP-Strategic Initiatives
Robert M. Becker, Chmn.

Phone: 973-407-5296	Fax: 973-407-7999
Toll-Free:	
Address: 1 Campus Dr., Parsippany, NJ 07054 US	

GROWTH PLANS/SPECIAL FEATURES:

NRT LLC, a subsidiary of Realogy Corporation, is a leading residential real estate brokerage company. The company, through subsidiaries Coldwell Banker, ERA, Sotheby's International Realty and The Corcoran Group, has operations in 35 of the largest markets in the U.S., with about 750 offices in its extended family. Coldwell Banker operates through a handful of various divisions, which offer commercial and residential real estate brokerage services and mortgage lending. Coldwell Banker Commercial NRT is the firm's commercial real estate brokerage division, with operation in 21 states. Additionally, Coldwell Banker Commercial affiliates operate throughout North America, South America, Europe, Africa, Asia and Australia. ERA is a worldwide franchised real estate brokerage that also provides mortgage lending through its subsidiary ERA Mortgage. Sotheby's International Realty, acquired from Sotheby Holding Corporation, the owners of Sotheby Auction House, specializes in luxury commercial and residential real estate worldwide. The Corcoran Group operates in New York, the Hamptons and Palm Beach. NRT's growth strategy involves an aggressive attitude towards expansion focusing on companies that have established themselves locally. Acquired companies are then affiliated with one of NRT's brands and allowed to continue a relatively independent management, simply building upon pre-established success and local identity. In April 2010, Coldwell Banker acquired Fine Homes Connecticut/USA of Westport, Connecticut. In October 2010, NRT acquired Philadelphia-based franchise Coldwell Banker Preferred. In November 2010, the firm, through Coldwell Banker Residential Brokerage, acquired brokerage group Cashin Company Realtors; and Sotheby's International Realty acquired the assets of Santa Fe Realty Partners. In February 2011, Coldwell Banker Preferred acquired residential real estate firm Baird & Bird, Inc.

FINANCIALS: Sales and profits are in thousands of dollars—add 000 to get the full amount. 2010 Note: Financial information for 2010 was not available for all companies at press time.

2010 Sales: $	2010 Profits: $	**U.S. Stock Ticker: Subsidiary**
2009 Sales: $	2009 Profits: $	**Int'l Ticker:** Int'l Exchange:
2008 Sales: $	2008 Profits: $	Employees:
2007 Sales: $	2007 Profits: $	Fiscal Year Ends: 12/31
2006 Sales: $	2006 Profits: $	Parent Company: REALOGY CORPORATION

SALARIES/BENEFITS:

Pension Plan:	ESOP Stock Plan:	Profit Sharing:	Top Exec. Salary: $	Bonus: $
Savings Plan:	Stock Purch. Plan:		Second Exec. Salary: $	Bonus: $

OTHER THOUGHTS:

Apparent Women Officers or Directors: 6
Hot Spot for Advancement for Women/Minorities: Y

LOCATIONS: ("Y" = Yes)

West:	Southwest:	Midwest:	Southeast:	Northeast:	International:
Y	Y	Y	Y	Y	Y

NVR INC

www.nvrinc.com

Industry Group Code: 2361 Ranks within this company's industry group: Sales: 6   Profits: 3

Properties:	Financial Services:		Construction/Development:		Investments:	Specialty Services:	Brokerage:	
Apartments:	Mortgages:	Y	Commercial Construction:		REIT:	Property Management:	Commercial Sales:	
Malls/Shopping:	Title Insurance:	Y	Residential Construction:	Y		Online Services:	Residential Sales:	Y
Offices:	Property Insurance:		Land Development:			Software/IT:	Specialty:	
Hotels/Motels:			Support Services:			Consulting:		
Industrial/Warehouses:			Design/Engineering:					
Other:								

TYPES OF BUSINESS:

Residential Construction
Mortgages
Townhouse Construction
Condominium Construction

BRANDS/DIVISIONS/AFFILIATES:

Ryan Homes
NVHomes
Fox Ridge Homes
NVR Mortgage Finance Inc
Rymarc Homes

CONTACTS: *Note: Officers with more than one job title may be intentionally listed here more than once.*

Paul C. Saville, CEO
Dennis M. Seremet, CFO
Robert Henley, Controller
Robert A. Goethe, Pres., NVR Mortgage Finance, Inc.
Dwight C. Schar, Chmn.

Phone: 703-956-4000	Fax: 703-956-4750
Toll-Free:	
Address: 11700 Plz. America Dr., Ste. 500, Reston, VA 20190 US	

GROWTH PLANS/SPECIAL FEATURES:

NVR, Inc. is primarily engaged in the construction and sale of single-family detached homes, townhomes and condominium buildings. Additionally, NVR offers mortgage banking services through its subsidiary NVR Mortgage Finance, Inc. (NVRM). The company operates in 14 states, with concentration in the Washington, D.C. and Baltimore, Maryland metropolitan areas, which accounted for 48% of revenues. NVR's homebuilding operations include the sale and construction of single-family detached homes, townhomes and condominium buildings under four brand names: Ryan Homes, NVHomes, Fox Ridge Homes and Rymarc Homes. The Ryan, Fox Ridge and Rymarc products are moderately priced and marketed primarily to first-time homeowners and first-time move-up buyers. Ryan Homes are currently sold in 23 metropolitan areas, including Maryland, Virginia, West Virginia, Pennsylvania, New York, Indiana, Florida, North Carolina, South Carolina, Ohio, New Jersey, Delaware and Kentucky. NVHomes are marketed primarily to move-up and upscale buyers and is sold in the Washington, D.C., Baltimore, Philadelphia and the Maryland Eastern Shore metropolitan areas. The Fox Ridge product is sold in the Nashville, Tennessee, metropolitan area and Rymarc homes are sold in Columbia, South Carolina. The firm's houses are priced between $97,000 and $1.7 million, while the average price of a unit sold is roughly $297,100. NVR also provides mortgage-related services through its mortgage banking operations, which include subsidiaries that broker title insurance and perform title searches. NVRM originates mortgage loans for NVR's homebuilding customers, making it dependent on the homebuilding operations. NVRM sells all mortgage loans it closes to investors in the secondary markets on a servicing released basis; it is an approved seller/servicer for FHLMC, VA, FNMA, GNMA and FHA mortgage loans.

Employees are offered benefits including life, AD&D, medical and dental insurance; home purchase, mortgage and settlement services discounts; paid holidays; an employee assistance program; and dependent scholarship awards.

FINANCIALS: Sales and profits are in thousands of dollars—add 000 to get the full amount. 2010 Note: Financial information for 2010 was not available for all companies at press time.

2010 Sales: $2,980,758	2010 Profits: $206,005	**U.S. Stock Ticker: NVR**
2009 Sales: $2,683,467	2009 Profits: $192,180	**Int'l Ticker:** Int'l Exchange:
2008 Sales: $3,638,702	2008 Profits: $100,892	Employees: 2,822
2007 Sales: $5,048,187	2007 Profits: $333,955	Fiscal Year Ends: 12/31
2006 Sales: $6,036,236	2006 Profits: $587,412	Parent Company:

SALARIES/BENEFITS:

Pension Plan:	ESOP Stock Plan: Y	Profit Sharing: Y	Top Exec. Salary: $800,000	Bonus: $481,299
Savings Plan: Y	Stock Purch. Plan:		Second Exec. Salary: $475,000	Bonus: $285,772

OTHER THOUGHTS:

Apparent Women Officers or Directors:
Hot Spot for Advancement for Women/Minorities:

LOCATIONS: ("Y" = Yes)

West:	Southwest:	Midwest:	Southeast:	Northeast:	International:
		Y	Y	Y	

OAKWOOD WORLDWIDE

www.oakwood.com

Industry Group Code: 721110 Ranks within this company's industry group: Sales: Profits:

Properties:	Financial Services:	Construction/Development:	Investments:	Specialty Services:	Brokerage:
Apartments:	Mortgages:	Commercial Construction:	REIT:	Property Management:	Commercial Sales:
Malls/Shopping:	Title Insurance:	Residential Construction:		Online Services:	Residential Sales:
Offices:	Property Insurance:	Land Development:		Software/IT:	Specialty:
Hotels/Motels: Y		Support Services:		Consulting:	
Industrial/Warehouses:		Design/Engineering:			
Other:					

TYPES OF BUSINESS:

Rental Housing
Temporary Housing
Corporate Apartments

BRANDS/DIVISIONS/AFFILIATES:

Oakwood Corporate Housing
Oakwood Premier
Oakwood Residence
Oakwood Apartment

CONTACTS: *Note: Officers with more than one job title may be intentionally listed here more than once.*

Howard Ruby, COO
Ric Villarreal, Pres.
Bill Foltz, CFO/Sr. VP
Jill Chapman, Sr. VP-Corp. Sales & Mktg.
Bill Maxwell, Sr. VP-Human Resources
Marina Lubinsky, CIO/Sr. VP
Matt Hagler, Sr. VP-Oper. & Service Excellence
Howard Ruby, Chmn.

Phone: 310-478-1021	Fax: 310-444-2210
Toll-Free: 877-902-0832	
Address: 2222 Corinth Ave., Los Angeles, CA 90064 US	

GROWTH PLANS/SPECIAL FEATURES:

Oakwood Worldwide offers temporary housing, corporate housing and multifamily property management. The firm provides approximately 25,000 furnished and unfurnished accommodations in roughly 4,000 locations throughout the U.S., the U.K., and the Asia Pacific region through its Oakwood Corporate Housing, Oakwood Premier, Oakwood Residence and Oakwood Apartment brands. Each apartment is equipped with fine furnishings, housewares, telephone service and cable television service. Oakwood services for temporary housing include weekly housekeeping, an on-call concierge and maintenance services. These services are available in most areas nationwide on a day-by-day pay schedule, and are often used by production crews for the footage of television shows or movies. The company also manages traditional long-term apartment residences through its 40 apartment communities in the U.S., with both furnished and unfurnished apartments. Oakwood has apartments of all styles, residing in differing natural environments, and will custom fit its models to its clients.

Oakwood offers its employees medical, dental, vision, prescription, life and AD&D insurance; short- and long-term disability; a 401(k) plan; access to a credit union; career development through Oakwood University; educational reimbursement; an employee assistance program; corporate discounts; bonus opportunities; annual company functions; flexible spending accounts; and referral bonuses.

FINANCIALS: Sales and profits are in thousands of dollars—add 000 to get the full amount. 2010 Note: Financial information for 2010 was not available for all companies at press time.

2010 Sales: $	2010 Profits: $	**U.S. Stock Ticker: Private**
2009 Sales: $	2009 Profits: $	**Int'l Ticker:** Int'l Exchange:
2008 Sales: $	2008 Profits: $	Employees:
2007 Sales: $	2007 Profits: $	Fiscal Year Ends:
2006 Sales: $	2006 Profits: $	Parent Company:

SALARIES/BENEFITS:

Pension Plan:	ESOP Stock Plan:	Profit Sharing:	Top Exec. Salary: $	Bonus: $
Savings Plan: Y	Stock Purch. Plan:		Second Exec. Salary: $	Bonus: $

OTHER THOUGHTS:

Apparent Women Officers or Directors: 1
Hot Spot for Advancement for Women/Minorities:

LOCATIONS: ("Y" = Yes)

West:	Southwest:	Midwest:	Southeast:	Northeast:	International:
Y	Y	Y	Y	Y	Y

OBEROI GROUP (EIH LTD)   www.oberoihotels.com

Industry Group Code: 721110 Ranks within this company's industry group: Sales: Profits:

Properties:	Financial Services:	Construction/Development:	Investments:	Specialty Services:		Brokerage:
Apartments:	Mortgages:	Commercial Construction:	REIT:	Property Management:	Y	Commercial Sales:
Malls/Shopping:	Title Insurance:	Residential Construction:		Online Services:		Residential Sales:
Offices:	Property Insurance:	Land Development:		Software/IT:		Specialty:
Hotels/Motels: Y		Support Services:		Consulting:		
Industrial/Warehouses:		Design/Engineering:				
Other:						

TYPES OF BUSINESS:

Luxury Hotels
Commercial Hotels
Cruise Ships
Travel Agency
Charter Aircraft
Tour Services
In-flight Catering
Car Rental

BRANDS/DIVISIONS/AFFILIATES:

EIH Limited
Trident Hotels
Oberoi Hotels and Resorts
Maidens Hotel
Clarke's Hotel

CONTACTS: *Note: Officers with more than one job title may be intentionally listed here more than once.*

P.R.S. Oberoi, CEO
Vikram Oberoi, COO
Amrita Bhalla, Exec. VP-Human Resources
Gautam Ganguli, Corp. Sec./Chief Compliance Officer
Arjun Oberoi, Chief Planning Officer
P.R.S. Oberoi, Chmn.

Phone: 91-11-2389-0505	**Fax:** 91-11-2389-0582
Toll-Free: 800-562-3764	
Address: 7 Sham Nath Marg, Delhi, 110 054 India	

GROWTH PLANS/SPECIAL FEATURES:

Oberoi Group, also known as EIH, Ltd., owns or manages about 30 Oberoi and Trident brand luxury hotels and three small cruiser ships in five countries. Additionally, the group operates airport restaurants, travel and tour services, in-flight catering, car rentals, project management and corporate air charters. The firm has Oberoi locations across the Asia-Pacific region: 12 hotels in India; two hotels in Indonesia; two hotels and two Nile river boats in Egypt; one hotel in Mauritius; and one hotel in Saudi Arabia. The company also operates two heritage hotels, the Maidens Hotel and the Clarke's Hotel, which are located in historic colonial areas. The firm offers a member program called Connections, which rewards points for staying at the hotels. These points can be redeemed for a variety of things, including additional stay at the Group's hotels. Many of the hotels feature spas, which can also be used by non-guests. The Oberoi Aviation segment of the group offers two aircraft for charter: a Hawker 850 XP and a King Air C-90A. The planes can be booked with as little as 72 hours notice and fly between locations within India along with a limited international service. In September 2010, the company signed a long term agreement with Lufthansa Airlines to integrate its hotels with Lufthansa's frequent flyer program.

Oberoi Group maintains The Oberoi Centre of Learning and Development (OCLD), which offers a specialized two year course in hospitality management.

FINANCIALS: Sales and profits are in thousands of dollars—add 000 to get the full amount. 2010 Note: Financial information for 2010 was not available for all companies at press time.

		U.S. Stock Ticker:
2010 Sales: $	2010 Profits: $	
2009 Sales: $225,380	2009 Profits: $37,690	Int'l Ticker: 500840 Int'l Exchange: Bombay-BSE
2008 Sales: $270,000	2008 Profits: $47,000	Employees: 12,800
2007 Sales: $	2007 Profits: $	Fiscal Year Ends: 3/31
2006 Sales: $	2006 Profits: $	Parent Company:

SALARIES/BENEFITS:

Pension Plan:	ESOP Stock Plan:	Profit Sharing:	Top Exec. Salary: $	Bonus: $
Savings Plan:	Stock Purch. Plan:		Second Exec. Salary: $	Bonus: $

OTHER THOUGHTS:

Apparent Women Officers or Directors:
Hot Spot for Advancement for Women/Minorities:

LOCATIONS: ("Y" = Yes)

West:	Southwest:	Midwest:	Southeast:	Northeast:	International:
					Y

ODEBRECHT SA

www.odebrecht.com.br

Industry Group Code: 237 Ranks within this company's industry group: Sales: Profits:

Properties:	Financial Services:	Construction/Development:		Investments:	Specialty Services:	Brokerage:
Apartments:	Mortgages:	Commercial Construction:	Y	REIT:	Property Management:	Commercial Sales:
Malls/Shopping:	Title Insurance:	Residential Construction:			Online Services:	Residential Sales:
Offices:	Property Insurance:	Land Development:	Y		Software/IT:	Specialty:
Hotels/Motels:		Support Services:	Y		Consulting:	
Industrial/Warehouses:		Design/Engineering:	Y			
Other:						

TYPES OF BUSINESS:

Engineering & Construction
Environmental Engineering
Real Estate Development
Insurance and Warranties Services
Ethanol and Sugar

BRANDS/DIVISIONS/AFFILIATES:

Construtora Norbeto Odebrecht SA
Odebrecht Oleo e Gas Ldta
Foz do Brazil SA
Odebrecht Realizacoes Imobiliarias SA
Braskem SA
ETH Bioenergia SA
Odebrecht Investimentos em Infraestrutura
Odeprev Odebrecht Previdencia

CONTACTS: *Note: Officers with more than one job title may be intentionally listed here more than once.*

Marcelo Bahia Odebrecht, CEO
Marcelo Bahia Odebrecht, Pres.
Paulo Cesena, Sr. Dir.-Finance
Paulo Lacerda de Melo, VP-Eng. & Construction Oper.
Andre Amaro, VP-Planning & Dev.
Henrique Valladares, CEO-Odebrecht Energia
Marcio Faria, CEO-Odebrecht Engenharia Industrial
Miguel Gradin, CEO-Odebrecht Oil & Gas
Fernando Reis, CEO-Foz do Brazil
Emilio Odebrecht, Chmn.
Euzenando Azevedo, CEO-Odebrecht Venezuela

Phone: 55-71-2105-1111	Fax: 55-71-2105-1112
Toll-Free:	
Address: Av. Luis Viana, 2841 Parelela Edificio Odebrecht, Salvador, 41730-900 Brazil	

GROWTH PLANS/SPECIAL FEATURES:

Odebrecht SA, a Brazilian conglomerate, has operations across a diversified portfolio of industries. These include engineering and construction; oil and gas; real estate development; ethanol and sugar; chemicals and petrochemical; environmental engineering; and support services. The company conducts its operations via its many subsidiaries. Construtora Norbeto Odebrecht, the company's engineering and construction subsidiary, focuses on such projects as highways, thermal electric plants, railroads, airports, steel mills, offshore operation rigs and buildings in Brazil, Venezuela and other international markets. Other businesses in this sector include Odebrecht Energia, which designs, constructs and manages power generation projects; and Odebrecht Engenharia Industrial, which specializes in developing oil and gas, mining, steel mills, petrochemical, fertilizer, metalworking and pulp and paper complexes. Subsidiary Odebrecht Oleo e Gas Ldta is responsible for the company's oil and gas operations, which focus on field exploration, production and services. Through Odebrecht Realizacoes Imobiliarias, it conducts real estate development activities that include residential, corporate, commercial, tourism and mixed use developments. The operations of ETH Bioenergia, managing the ethanol and sugar businesses, include sugarcane cultivation, harvesting, ethanol production and energy cogeneration. Subsidiary Braskem operates in the chemicals and petrochemicals sector, focusing primarily on thermoplastic resins. Foz do Brazil operates in the environmental engineering sector, providing waste and industrial effluent treatment, sanitation services and urban solid waste disposal. Additionally, the company offers support services in the areas of infrastructure investment, insurance, warranties and pension funds. Odebrecht Investimentos em Infraestrutura invests in infrastructure development projects, including energy, transportation and logistics. Odebrecht Administradora e Corretora de Seguros Ltda provides insurance and warranties services that focus on protecting assets and managing risks. Lastly, the company offers pension fund services through its subsidiary Odeprev Odebrecht Previdencia.

FINANCIALS: Sales and profits are in thousands of dollars—add 000 to get the full amount. 2010 Note: Financial information for 2010 was not available for all companies at press time.

2010 Sales: $	2010 Profits: $	U.S. Stock Ticker: Private
2009 Sales: $	2009 Profits: $	Int'l Ticker: Int'l Exchange:
2008 Sales: $	2008 Profits: $	Employees:
2007 Sales: $	2007 Profits: $	Fiscal Year Ends:
2006 Sales: $	2006 Profits: $	Parent Company:

SALARIES/BENEFITS:

Pension Plan:	ESOP Stock Plan:	Profit Sharing:	Top Exec. Salary: $	Bonus: $
Savings Plan:	Stock Purch. Plan:		Second Exec. Salary: $	Bonus: $

OTHER THOUGHTS:

Apparent Women Officers or Directors:
Hot Spot for Advancement for Women/Minorities:

LOCATIONS: ("Y" = Yes)

West:	Southwest:	Midwest:	Southeast:	Northeast:	International:
					Y

OMEGA HEALTHCARE INVESTORS INC   www.omegahealthcare.com

Industry Group Code: 531120 Ranks within this company's industry group: Sales: 53   Profits: 31

Properties:		Financial Services:		Construction/Development:	Investments:		Specialty Services:		Brokerage:
Apartments:		Mortgages:	Y	Commercial Construction:	REIT:	Y	Property Management:	Y	Commercial Sales:
Malls/Shopping:		Title Insurance:		Residential Construction:			Online Services:		Residential Sales:
Offices:		Property Insurance:		Land Development:			Software/IT:		Specialty:
Hotels/Motels:				Support Services:			Consulting:		
Industrial/Warehouses:				Design/Engineering:					
Other:	Y								

TYPES OF BUSINESS:

Real Estate Investment Trust
Health Care Facilities
Long-Term Care Facilities
Lease & Mortgage Financing

BRANDS/DIVISIONS/AFFILIATES:

CONTACTS:
Note: Officers with more than one job title may be intentionally listed here more than once.

C. Taylor Pickett, CEO
Daniel J. Booth, COO
Robert O. Stephenson, CFO
R. Lee Crabill, Jr., Sr. VP-Oper.
Michael D. Ritz, Chief Acct. Officer
Bernard J. Korman, Chmn.

Phone: 410-427-1700	Fax: 410-427-8800
Toll-Free: 866-996-6342	
Address: 200 International Cir., Ste. 3500, Hunt Valley, MD 21030 US	

GROWTH PLANS/SPECIAL FEATURES:

Omega Healthcare Investors, Inc. is a self-administered Real Estate Investment Trust (REIT) investing in healthcare facilities, particularly long-term care facilities located in the U.S. The firm provides lease or mortgage financing to qualified operators of skilled nursing facilities and, to a lesser extent, assisted living facilities, independent living facilities and rehabilitation and acute care facilities. Omega's portfolio of investments is comprised of 400 healthcare facilities (approximately 34,312 licensed beds) located in 35 states and operated by 50 third-party operators. The portfolio includes 371 skilled nursing facilities; 10 assisted living facilities; and five specialty facilities. In addition, the firm maintains fixed rate mortgages on 13 long-term healthcare facilities, as well as one closed skilled nursing facility that is held-for-sale. The company has sought to maintain a diversified investment portfolio in terms of geography and operators, and generally focuses on established, creditworthy, middle-market healthcare operators. Factors considered by Omega in evaluating potential investments include the quality and experience of management; the facility's historical and forecasted cash flow; the construction quality, condition and design of the facility; the geographic area of the facility; the occupancy and demand for similar healthcare facilities in the same or nearby communities; and the payer mix of private, Medicare and Medicaid patients. One of Omega's fundamental investment strategies is to obtain contractual rent escalations under long-term, non-cancelable, triple-net leases and fixed-rate mortgage loans, and to obtain substantial liquidity deposits. Approximately 49% of Omega's properties are managed by the following five companies: Sun Healthcare Group; CommuniCare Health Services; Advocat, Inc.; Airamid Health Management, LLC; and Signature Holding II LLC. In June 2010, Omega acquired (in two transactions) 103 long-term care facilities from CapitalSource, Inc. for approximately $563 million.

FINANCIALS:
Sales and profits are in thousands of dollars—add 000 to get the full amount. 2010 Note: Financial information for 2010 was not available for all companies at press time.

2010 Sales: $258,321	2010 Profits: $58,436	**U.S. Stock Ticker: OHI**
2009 Sales: $197,438	2009 Profits: $82,111	**Int'l Ticker:** Int'l Exchange:
2008 Sales: $193,762	2008 Profits: $78,137	Employees: 19
2007 Sales: $159,558	2007 Profits: $69,374	Fiscal Year Ends: 12/31
2006 Sales: $135,513	2006 Profits: $55,697	Parent Company:

SALARIES/BENEFITS:

Pension Plan:	ESOP Stock Plan:	Profit Sharing:	Top Exec. Salary: $558,000	Bonus: $558,000
Savings Plan: Y	Stock Purch. Plan:		Second Exec. Salary: $344,000	Bonus: $172,000

OTHER THOUGHTS:

Apparent Women Officers or Directors:
Hot Spot for Advancement for Women/Minorities:

LOCATIONS: ("Y" = Yes)

West:	Southwest:	Midwest:	Southeast:	Northeast:	International:
Y	Y	Y	Y	Y	

ORIENT OVERSEAS (INTERNATIONAL) LTD

www.ooilgroup.com

Industry Group Code: 4885 Ranks within this company's industry group: Sales: 1 Profits: 1

Properties:		Financial Services:		Construction/Development:		Investments:		Specialty Services:		Brokerage:	
Apartments:		Mortgages:		Commercial Construction:		REIT:		Property Management:		Commercial Sales:	
Malls/Shopping:		Title Insurance:		Residential Construction:				Online Services:		Residential Sales:	
Offices:	Y	Property Insurance:		Land Development:	Y			Software/IT:		Specialty:	
Hotels/Motels:				Support Services:				Consulting:			
Industrial/Warehouses:	Y			Design/Engineering:							
Other:	Y										

TYPES OF BUSINESS:

Freight Logistics
Deep Sea Shipping
Port & Terminal Operations
Logistics Software & Services
Real Estate Investment
Office Buildings

BRANDS/DIVISIONS/AFFILIATES:

Orient Overseas Container Line, Ltd.
OOCL China Domestic, Ltd.
CargoSmart, Ltd.
OOCL Logistics, Ltd.
Kaohsiung Terminal
Long Beach Container Terminal

CONTACTS: *Note: Officers with more than one job title may be intentionally listed here more than once.*

Chee Chen Tung, CEO
Andy Tung, COO
Chee Chen Tung, Pres.
Kenneth Gilbert Cambie, CFO
Lammy Chee Fun Lee, Corp. Sec.
C. L. Ting, Dir.-Corp. Planning
Bosco Louie, Dir.-Regions Mgmt.
Steve Siu, CEO-CargoSmart
Allan Wong, CEO-OOCL Logistics Ltd.
Chee Chen Tung, Chmn.
Peter Leng, Pres., OOCL USA
Henry Wong, Dir.-Corp. Logistics & Fleet Mgmt.

Phone: 852-2833-3167	Fax: 852-2531-8221
Toll-Free:	
Address: Harbour Center, 25 Harbour Rd., 33rd Fl., Wanchai, Hong Kong, China	

GROWTH PLANS/SPECIAL FEATURES:

Orient Overseas (International) Ltd. (OOIL) is engaged in international container transport and logistics services, port and terminal operation, and property investment. It has more than 280 offices in 55 countries. OOIL's primary subsidiary, Orient Overseas Container Line (OOCL), is an integrated international logistics company offering intermodal transport services worldwide. OOCL has a fleet of 73 ships, four of which are chartered out. It is one of the leading international carriers serving China, through sub-subsidiary OOCL China Domestic, Ltd., which provides a full range of logistics and transportation services throughout the country. OOCL subsidiary CargoSmart, Ltd., uses information and e-commerce to manage the entire cargo process, while its OOCL Logistics, Ltd. subsidiary provides logistics services. OOIL's ports and terminal business operates two private terminals (meaning they are open only to the company and alliance partners): the Kaosiung Terminal in Hong Kong, China and the Long Beach Container Terminal in California. The firm's property investment division holds a 7.9% interest in the Beijing Oriental Plaza and a 100% interest in the Wall Street Plaza. The company has a grand alliance with Hapag-Lloyd, MISC Berhad, P&O Nedlloyd and Nippon Yusen Kaisha, in which they share the same routes for cargos. In addition, the company has strategic alliances with St. Lawrence Co-ordinated Services members; Hapag-Lloyd; Tokyo Senpaku Kaisha Ltd.; and COSCO Container Lines Co., Ltd. The firm recently announced the sale of its Orient Overseas Developments Ltd. (OODL) property development division to CapitaLand China (RE) Holdings Co., Ltd. In February 2011, OOIL's subsidiary, OOCL, launched a new service that operates in the Atlantic and Gulf of Mexico markets.

FINANCIALS: Sales and profits are in thousands of dollars—add 000 to get the full amount. 2010 Note: Financial information for 2010 was not available for all companies at press time.

2010 Sales: $6,033,400	2010 Profits: $1,866,800	**U.S. Stock Ticker:**
2009 Sales: $4,350,200	2009 Profits: $-402,300	**Int'l Ticker: 0316** Int'l Exchange: Hong Kong-HKEX
2008 Sales: $6,545,140	2008 Profits: $275,529	Employees: 7,688
2007 Sales: $5,651,030	2007 Profits: $2,548,402	Fiscal Year Ends: 12/31
2006 Sales: $4,609,751	2006 Profits: $580,603	Parent Company:

SALARIES/BENEFITS:

Pension Plan: Y	ESOP Stock Plan:	Profit Sharing:	Top Exec. Salary: $	Bonus: $
Savings Plan:	Stock Purch. Plan:		Second Exec. Salary: $	Bonus: $

OTHER THOUGHTS:

Apparent Women Officers or Directors: 1
Hot Spot for Advancement for Women/Minorities:

LOCATIONS: ("Y" = Yes)

West:	Southwest:	Midwest:	Southeast:	Northeast:	International:
Y			Y	Y	Y

ORIENT-EXPRESS HOTELS LTD

www.orient-express.com

Industry Group Code: 721110 Ranks within this company's industry group: Sales: 18   Profits: 25

Properties:		Financial Services:		Construction/Development:		Investments:		Specialty Services:		Brokerage:	
Apartments:		Mortgages:		Commercial Construction:	Y	REIT:		Property Management:	Y	Commercial Sales:	
Malls/Shopping:		Title Insurance:		Residential Construction:				Online Services:		Residential Sales:	
Offices:		Property Insurance:		Land Development:	Y			Software/IT:		Specialty:	
Hotels/Motels:	Y			Support Services:				Consulting:			
Industrial/Warehouses:				Design/Engineering:							
Other:	Y										

TYPES OF BUSINESS:

Hotels, Luxury
Tourist Railroads
Cruise Lines
Safari Tours
Restaurants

BRANDS/DIVISIONS/AFFILIATES:

Le Manoir aux Quat'Saisons
Grand Hotel Europe
Copacabana Palace
Le Residence d'Angkor
Eastern & Oriental Express Railway
Royal Scotsman Railway
Inn at Perry Cabin (The)
21 Club

CONTACTS: *Note: Officers with more than one job title may be intentionally listed here more than once.*

Paul M. White, CEO
Filip Boyen, COO/VP
Paul M. White, Pres.
Martin O'Grady, CFO/VP
David C. Williams, VP-Sales & Mktg.
Roger V. Collins, VP-Design & Tech. Svcs.
Edwin S. Hetherington, General Counsel/Sec./VP
Roy Paul, Chief Dev. Officer/VP
Phillip Gesue, VP-Real Estate
Philip Calvert, VP-Legal & Commercial Affairs
Raymond Blanc, VP-Gastronomy
James B. Hurlock, Chmn.
Maurizio Saccani, VP-Italy

Phone: 441-295-2244	**Fax:** 441-292-8666
Toll-Free:	
Address: 22 Victoria St., Hamilton, HM 12 Bermuda	

GROWTH PLANS/SPECIAL FEATURES:

Orient-Express Hotels, Ltd. (OEH) manages and owns complete or partial interests in a portfolio of 50 properties in 24 countries. Its properties include 41 deluxe hotels (with 3,564 individual guestrooms and multi-room suites); one stand-alone restaurant; six tourist trains; and two river or canal cruise businesses. Avoiding chain branding, the company relies on a business model that emphasizes maintaining distinctive properties of cultural, historic or recreational interest in order to provide luxury travel experiences. During 2010, the hotels and restaurants segment generated approximately 78% of revenues, while tourist trains and cruises together accounted for 11%, with property development activities accounting for the remainder. In 2010, approximately 35% of OEH customers came from North America, 45% from Europe, and 20% from elsewhere in the world; approximately 70% of its customers were leisure travelers. The daily room rate for its hotels averaged $405 in 2010. OEH's properties include hotels such as Le Manoir aux Quat'Saisons, a 16th Century manor house in England; Grand Hotel Europe, which occupies an entire city block in St. Petersburg, Russia; The Inn at Perry Cabin, a country inn in St. Michaels, Maryland, dating back to 1812; Copacabana Palace in Rio de Janeiro, Brazil, complete with a casino and a 500-seat theater; three safari camps in Botswana, featuring wildlife viewing from open vehicles or boats; and Le Residence d'Angkor, located in Siem Reap, Cambodia, near the famous Temples of Angkor. The firm's trains include the Venice Simplon-Orient-Express, refurbished in 1920s and '30s decor, traveling between Venice and London; the Royal Scotsman, which visits clan castles, historic battlegrounds and famous Scotch whiskey distilleries in Scotland; and the Eastern & Oriental Express, which travels weekly between Singapore, Kuala Lumpur and Bangkok. The company also owns the historic 21 Club restaurant in New York City; which originated as a Prohibition-era speakeasy.

FINANCIALS: Sales and profits are in thousands of dollars—add 000 to get the full amount. 2010 Note: Financial information for 2010 was not available for all companies at press time.

2010 Sales: $571,942	2010 Profits: $-62,759	**U.S. Stock Ticker:** OEH
2009 Sales: $450,910	2009 Profits: $-68,797	**Int'l Ticker:** Int'l Exchange:
2008 Sales: $494,676	2008 Profits: $-26,551	Employees: 8,400
2007 Sales: $528,956	2007 Profits: $33,642	Fiscal Year Ends: 12/31
2006 Sales: $479,364	2006 Profits: $39,767	Parent Company:

SALARIES/BENEFITS:

Pension Plan:	ESOP Stock Plan:	Profit Sharing:	Top Exec. Salary: $	Bonus: $
Savings Plan:	Stock Purch. Plan:		Second Exec. Salary: $	Bonus: $

OTHER THOUGHTS:

Apparent Women Officers or Directors: 1
Hot Spot for Advancement for Women/Minorities:

LOCATIONS: ("Y" = Yes)

West:	Southwest:	Midwest:	Southeast:	Northeast:	International:
Y				Y	Y

ORIGEN FINANCIAL INC

www.origenfinancial.com

Industry Group Code: 522291 Ranks within this company's industry group: Sales: 2   Profits: 2

Properties:	Financial Services:	Construction/Development:	Investments:	Specialty Services:	Brokerage:
Apartments:	Mortgages:	Commercial Construction:	REIT: Y	Property Management:	Commercial Sales:
Malls/Shopping:	Title Insurance:	Residential Construction:		Online Services:	Residential Sales:
Offices:	Property Insurance:	Land Development:		Software/IT:	Specialty:
Hotels/Motels:		Support Services:		Consulting:	
Industrial/Warehouses:		Design/Engineering:			
Other:					

TYPES OF BUSINESS:

REIT
Managing Manufactured Home Loans

BRANDS/DIVISIONS/AFFILIATES:

Origen Financial, LLC

GROWTH PLANS/SPECIAL FEATURES:

Origen Financial, Inc. is an internally-managed and internally-advised real estate investment trust (REIT) specializing in the manufactured housing business. The company manages a portfolio of approximately $1 billion made up of manufactured housing loans and asset backed securities. Although the company no long engages in its former businesses of originating and servicing loans, it remains focused on the management of its residual interests in its securitized loan portfolios. The firm's operations are carried out by its wholly-owned subsidiary, Origen Financial, LLC.

CONTACTS: *Note: Officers with more than one job title may be intentionally listed here more than once.*

Ronald A. Klein, CEO
W. Anderson Geater, Jr., CFO
Tiffany Thomas, Sr. VP-Human Resources
Paul J. Galaspie, CIO/Sr. VP
W. Anderson Geater, Jr., Sec.
Gina Sheahan, Controller
Mark Landschulz, Exec. VP-Portfolio Mgmt.
Elaine Nesbitt, Head-Portfolio Analysis
Paul A. Halpern, Chmn.

Phone: 248-746-7000	**Fax:** 248-746-7094
Toll-Free:	
Address: 27777 Franklin Rd., Ste. 1700, Southfield, MI 48034 US	

FINANCIALS: Sales and profits are in thousands of dollars—add 000 to get the full amount. 2010 Note: Financial information for 2010 was not available for all companies at press time.

2010 Sales: $71,641	2010 Profits: $-16,594	**U.S. Stock Ticker:** ORGN.PK
2009 Sales: $82,159	2009 Profits: $-12,431	**Int'l Ticker:** Int'l Exchange:
2008 Sales: $	2008 Profits: $-35,364	Employees:
2007 Sales: $26,400	2007 Profits: $-31,767	Fiscal Year Ends: 12/31
2006 Sales: $92,082	2006 Profits: $6,971	Parent Company:

SALARIES/BENEFITS:

Pension Plan:	ESOP Stock Plan:	Profit Sharing:	Top Exec. Salary: $531,058	Bonus: $250,000
Savings Plan:	Stock Purch. Plan:		Second Exec. Salary: $280,096	Bonus: $150,000

OTHER THOUGHTS:

Apparent Women Officers or Directors: 3
Hot Spot for Advancement for Women/Minorities: Y

LOCATIONS: ("Y" = Yes)

West:	Southwest:	Midwest:	Southeast:	Northeast:	International:
		Y			

ORION MARINE GROUP INC

www.orionmarinegroup.com

Industry Group Code: 2389 Ranks within this company's industry group: Sales: 3   Profits: 3

Properties:	Financial Services:	Construction/Development:		Investments:	Specialty Services:	Brokerage:
Apartments:	Mortgages:	Commercial Construction:		REIT:	Property Management:	Commercial Sales:
Malls/Shopping:	Title Insurance:	Residential Construction:			Online Services:	Residential Sales:
Offices:	Property Insurance:	Land Development:			Software/IT:	Specialty:
Hotels/Motels:		Support Services:	Y		Consulting:	
Industrial/Warehouses:		Design/Engineering:	Y			
Other:						

TYPES OF BUSINESS:

Marine Construction & Specialty Services
Dredging Services

BRANDS/DIVISIONS/AFFILIATES:

TW LaQuay Dredging LLC

CONTACTS: *Note: Officers with more than one job title may be intentionally listed here more than once.*

J. Michael Pearson, CEO
J. Michael Pearson, Pres.
Mark R. Stauffer, CFO/Exec. VP
Pete Buchler, General Counsel/VP/Corp. Sec.
Elliott J. Kennedy, Exec. VP-Gulf Coast
James L. Rose, Exec. VP-Atlantic Seaboard & Caribbean
Richard L. Daerr, Jr., Chmn.

Phone: 713-852-6500	Fax: 713-852-6530
Toll-Free:	
Address: 12000 Aerospace, Ste. 300, Houston, TX 77034 US	

GROWTH PLANS/SPECIAL FEATURES:

Orion Marine Group, Inc. is a marine specialty contractor that serves the heavy civil marine infrastructure industry. The firm offers an array of marine construction services on, over and under the water along the Atlantic Seaboard, Canada, the West Coast, the Gulf Coast and in the Caribbean Basin. The company's customers, for which Orion Marine acts as a single-source turnkey solution, include private commercial and industrial enterprises; and federal, state and municipal governments. The firm offers three types of services: marine construction, dredging and specialty services. Its marine construction services include construction of marine transportation facilities, bridges, causeways, marine pipelines and marine environmental structures. Marine transportation facility construction projects include public port facilities; private and special-use Navy terminals; cruise ship port facilities; and recreational use marinas and docks. The firm's bridge and causeway projects include the construction, repair and maintenance of bridges and causeways; and the development of fendering systems in marine environments. Its marine pipeline service projects generally include the installation and removal of underwater buried pipeline transmission lines; installation of pipeline intakes and outfalls for industrial facilities; construction of pipeline outfalls for wastewater and industrial discharges; river crossing and directional drilling; creation of hot taps and tie-ins; and inspection, maintenance and repair services. Orion Marine's dredging services involve removing mud and silt from the channel floor by means of pipeline systems and a mechanical backhoe, crane/bucket or cutter suction dredge. The company's specialty services include demolition; surveying; diving; salvage; towing; and underwater inspection, excavation and repair. In early 2010, the firm acquired specialty dredging services firm T.W. LaQuay Dredging, LLC for $60 million.

The firm offers employees medical, dental vision, life, AD&D and disability insurance; an employee assistance plan; and a 401(k).

FINANCIALS: Sales and profits are in thousands of dollars—add 000 to get the full amount. 2010 Note: Financial information for 2010 was not available for all companies at press time.

2010 Sales: $353,135	2010 Profits: $21,882	**U.S. Stock Ticker: ORN**
2009 Sales: $293,494	2009 Profits: $20,030	**Int'l Ticker:** Int'l Exchange:
2008 Sales: $261,802	2008 Profits: $14,475	Employees: 1,470
2007 Sales: $210,360	2007 Profits: $16,617	Fiscal Year Ends: 12/31
2006 Sales: $	2006 Profits: $	Parent Company:

SALARIES/BENEFITS:

Pension Plan:	ESOP Stock Plan:	Profit Sharing:	Top Exec. Salary: $423,385	Bonus: $621,857
Savings Plan: Y	Stock Purch. Plan:		Second Exec. Salary: $269,520	Bonus: $302,606

OTHER THOUGHTS:

Apparent Women Officers or Directors:
Hot Spot for Advancement for Women/Minorities:

LOCATIONS: ("Y" = Yes)

West:	Southwest:	Midwest:	Southeast:	Northeast:	International:
	Y		Y	Y	

ORLEANS HOMEBUILDERS INC

www.orleanshomes.com

Industry Group Code: 2361 Ranks within this company's industry group: Sales: Profits:

Properties:	Financial Services:	Construction/Development:	Investments:	Specialty Services:	Brokerage:
Apartments:	Mortgages:	Commercial Construction:	REIT:	Property Management:	Commercial Sales:
Malls/Shopping:	Title Insurance:	Residential Construction: Y		Online Services:	Residential Sales: Y
Offices:	Property Insurance:	Land Development: Y		Software/IT:	Specialty:
Hotels/Motels:		Support Services:		Consulting:	
Industrial/Warehouses:		Design/Engineering:			
Other:					

TYPES OF BUSINESS:

Residential Construction
Residential Community Development
Townhouses & Condominiums
Residential Brokerage

BRANDS/DIVISIONS/AFFILIATES:

Orleans Design Center

CONTACTS: *Note: Officers with more than one job title may be intentionally listed here more than once.*

George E. Casey, Jr., CEO

Phone: 215-245-7500	Fax:
Toll-Free:	
Address: 3333 St. Rd., 1 Greenwood Square, Ste. 101, Bensalem, PA 19020 US	

GROWTH PLANS/SPECIAL FEATURES:

Orleans Homebuilders, Inc. and its subsidiaries primarily develop, build and market upper-price range single-family homes, townhouses and condominiums. The company sells homes in eight states and owns or controls approximately 7,299 building lots. The firm divides its business into four regions. The first of these is the Northern region, which includes the Southeastern Pennsylvania; Central and Southern New Jersey and Orange County, New York markets. Second is the firm's Southern region, which includes the Richmond and Tidewater, Virginia and Charlotte, Raleigh and Greensboro, North Carolina markets (some adjacent South Carolina counties are also served). The company's third region is Florida, which includes the Orlando, Palm Coast and Palm Bay markets. The Midwestern region consists entirely of operations in the Chicago area. At its Orleans Design Centers, the company helps prospective homebuyers design and customize their new home, offering choices in trim, moldings, wainscoting, lighting, audio systems, kitchen cabinets and doorknobs, stair rails and windows, among other options. After filing for Chapter 11 bankruptcy protection in March 2010, the firm completed a financial reorganization and emerged from Chapter 11 in February 2011.

FINANCIALS: Sales and profits are in thousands of dollars—add 000 to get the full amount. 2010 Note: Financial information for 2010 was not available for all companies at press time.

2010 Sales: $	2010 Profits: $	U.S. Stock Ticker: Private
2009 Sales: $	2009 Profits: $	Int'l Ticker: Int'l Exchange:
2008 Sales: $583,282	2008 Profits: $-143,413	Employees: 544
2007 Sales: $682,534	2007 Profits: $-66,850	Fiscal Year Ends: 6/30
2006 Sales: $987,193	2006 Profits: $63,041	Parent Company:

SALARIES/BENEFITS:

Pension Plan:	ESOP Stock Plan:	Profit Sharing:	Top Exec. Salary: $	Bonus: $
Savings Plan: Y	Stock Purch. Plan:		Second Exec. Salary: $	Bonus: $

OTHER THOUGHTS:

Apparent Women Officers or Directors:
Hot Spot for Advancement for Women/Minorities:

LOCATIONS: ("Y" = Yes)

West:	Southwest:	Midwest:	Southeast:	Northeast:	International:
		Y	Y	Y	

PACIFIC COAST BUILDING PRODUCTS INC   www.paccoast.com

Industry Group Code: 444130 Ranks within this company's industry group: Sales: Profits:

Properties:	Financial Services:	Construction/Development:		Investments:	Specialty Services:	Brokerage:
Apartments:	Mortgages:	Commercial Construction:		REIT:	Property Management:	Commercial Sales:
Malls/Shopping:	Title Insurance:	Residential Construction:			Online Services:	Residential Sales:
Offices:	Property Insurance:	Land Development:			Software/IT:	Specialty:
Hotels/Motels:		Support Services:	Y		Consulting:	
Industrial/Warehouses:		Design/Engineering:				
Other:						

TYPES OF BUSINESS:

Building Materials-Manufacturing & Distribution
Contracting Services
Transportation Services
Charter Aviation Services

BRANDS/DIVISIONS/AFFILIATES:

Basalite Concrete Products LLC
Epic Plastics, Inc.
Pabco Building Products LLC
Pacific Coast Supply LLC
Transportation Services, Inc.
Pacific Coast Jet Charter, Inc.
Alcal Arcade Contracting, Inc.
Pacific Coast Companies, Inc.

CONTACTS: *Note: Officers with more than one job title may be intentionally listed here more than once.*

David J. Lucchetti, CEO
David J. Lucchetti, Pres.
Darren Morris, CFO
Elaine Keane, Dir.-Mktg.
Hilda Watson, Dir.-Human Resources
James B. Thompson, Chmn.

Phone: 916-631-6500	**Fax:**
Toll-Free:	
Address: 10600 White Rock Rd., Bldg. B, Ste. 100, Rancho Cordova, CA 95670-6032 US	

GROWTH PLANS/SPECIAL FEATURES:

Pacific Coast Building Products, Inc. is a manufacturer and distributor of building materials for residential, commercial and industrial construction on the west coast. The firm operates through its family of companies: Basalite Concrete Products, LLC; PABCO Building Products, LLC; PABCO Clay Products, LLC; Pacific Coast Building Services, Inc; Pacific Coast Supply, LLC; Transportation Services, Inc; Pacific Coast Jet Charter, Inc.; Pacific Coast Companies, Inc.; and PCBP Properties, Inc. Basalite Concrete Products, LLC specializes in wall, roof and block products, and oversees companies such as Blocklite; Columbia Roof Tile; Epic Plastics, Inc.; and Patterson Whittaker Architectural Profiles. PABCO Building Products, LLC manufactures wallboard and asphalt roof shingle products and controls the companies PABCO Gypsum; PABCO Paper; and PABCO Roofing Products. PABCO Clay Products, LLC provides clay veneers and related products, and operates companies such as Gladding McBean; H.C. Muddox; and Interstate Brick. Pacific Coast Building Services offers windows, insulation and related products, and directs companies such as Alcal/Arcade Contracting, Inc.; and Pacific Coast Contracting Specialties, Inc. The divisions under lumber provider Pacific Coast Supply, LLC include Anderson Lumber; Anderson Truss; Diamond Pacific; Pacific Supply; P.C. Wholesale; and Weyrick Pacific. The transportation division operates through Material Transport, which moves products and raw materials to and from the company's subsidiaries; and Pacific Coast Jet Charter, Inc., which operates a Cessna Citation XLS jet that is available for charter to destinations throughout the U.S., Canada and Mexico. The Pacific Coast Companies, Inc. team is in charge of much of the administrative work that corresponds to the family of companies. Finally, the firm's subsidiary, PCBP Properties, Inc. invests and manages a number of properties in the western U.S.

FINANCIALS: Sales and profits are in thousands of dollars—add 000 to get the full amount. 2010 Note: Financial information for 2010 was not available for all companies at press time.

2010 Sales: $	2010 Profits: $	**U.S. Stock Ticker: Private**
2009 Sales: $	2009 Profits: $	**Int'l Ticker:** Int'l Exchange:
2008 Sales: $	2008 Profits: $	Employees:
2007 Sales: $	2007 Profits: $	Fiscal Year Ends: 3/31
2006 Sales: $	2006 Profits: $	Parent Company:

SALARIES/BENEFITS:

Pension Plan:	ESOP Stock Plan:	Profit Sharing:	Top Exec. Salary: $	Bonus: $
Savings Plan: Y	Stock Purch. Plan:		Second Exec. Salary: $	Bonus: $

OTHER THOUGHTS:

Apparent Women Officers or Directors:
Hot Spot for Advancement for Women/Minorities:

LOCATIONS: ("Y" = Yes)

West:	Southwest:	Midwest:	Southeast:	Northeast:	International:
Y					Y

PALM HARBOR HOMES INC   www.palmharbor.com

Industry Group Code: 321991 Ranks within this company's industry group: Sales: 2   Profits: 2

Properties:	Financial Services:		Construction/Development:		Investments:	Specialty Services:	Brokerage:	
Apartments:	Mortgages:	Y	Commercial Construction:		REIT:	Property Management:	Commercial Sales:	
Malls/Shopping:	Title Insurance:		Residential Construction:	Y		Online Services:	Residential Sales:	Y
Offices:	Property Insurance:	Y	Land Development:			Software/IT:	Specialty:	
Hotels/Motels:			Support Services:			Consulting:		
Industrial/Warehouses:			Design/Engineering:					
Other:								

TYPES OF BUSINESS:

Manufactured & Modular Housing
Mortgages
Property & Casualty Insurance

BRANDS/DIVISIONS/AFFILIATES:

Standard Casualty Company
CountryPlace Mortgage, Ltd.
SmartPlus Construction
Masterpiece
Discovery Custom Homes
Windsor Homes
Nationwide Custom Homes, Inc.
River Bend

CONTACTS: *Note: Officers with more than one job title may be intentionally listed here more than once.*

Larry Keener, CEO
Larry Keener, Pres.
Kelly Tacke, CFO/Exec. VP
Joe Kesterson, Pres., Retail
Ron Powell, Pres., Mfg.
Kelly Tacke, Corp. Sec.
Larry Keener, Chmn.

Phone: 972-991-2422	**Fax:** 972-991-5949
Toll-Free: 800-456-8744	
Address: 15303 Dallas Pkwy., Ste. 800, Addison, TX 75001 US	

GROWTH PLANS/SPECIAL FEATURES:

Palm Harbor Homes, Inc. is a U.S. manufacturer and marketer of factory-built and modular homes. The firm markets nationwide through vertically integrated operations encompassing manufactured housing; modular housing; retailing; chattel; and mortgage bank financing and insurance. The company operates nine manufacturing facilities in seven states that sell homes through 55 company-owned retail superstores and approximately 145 independent retail dealers and builders. Subsidiary CountryPlace Mortgage, Ltd. offers chattel and non-conforming land and home mortgages to purchasers of manufactured homes sold by Palm Harbor. In addition, the firm offers property and casualty insurance through subsidiary Standard Casualty Company. Palm Harbor's products include single- and multi-section manufactured homes sold under brand names including Palm Harbor, Masterpiece, Keystone, CountryPlace, River Bend and Windsor Homes. The average retail sales price of the company's manufactured homes is approximately $67,000. The firm also helps customers find an appropriate lot or look for a pre-owned home. Palm Harbor's building system, SmartPlus Construction, uses a process called EnerGmiser, an energy management system that includes added insulation and other efficiency-increasing products. Modular homes are manufactured through subsidiary Nationwide Custom Homes, Inc., principally under the brand name Discovery Custom Homes. Modular offerings include single-story ranch homes, split-levels and two- and three-story homes with an average retail sales price of $166,000. In November 2010, the company filed for Chapter 11 bankruptcy.

The company offers its employees benefits including medical, dental and vision coverage; disability protection; life insurance; a home purchase plan; a down payment assistance plan; tuition reimbursement; a scholarship program; an employee assistance program; a 401(k) plan; and a stock purchase plan.

FINANCIALS: Sales and profits are in thousands of dollars—add 000 to get the full amount. 2010 Note: Financial information for 2010 was not available for all companies at press time.

2010 Sales: $298,371	2010 Profits: $-51,132	**U.S. Stock Ticker:** PHHM
2009 Sales: $409,274	2009 Profits: $-31,995	**Int'l Ticker:** Int'l Exchange:
2008 Sales: $555,096	2008 Profits: $-121,980	Employees:
2007 Sales: $661,247	2007 Profits: $-11,565	Fiscal Year Ends: 3/31
2006 Sales: $710,635	2006 Profits: $11,114	Parent Company:

SALARIES/BENEFITS:

Pension Plan:	ESOP Stock Plan:	Profit Sharing:	Top Exec. Salary: $300,000	Bonus: $240,000
Savings Plan: Y	Stock Purch. Plan: Y		Second Exec. Salary: $170,000	Bonus: $200,000

OTHER THOUGHTS:

Apparent Women Officers or Directors: 1
Hot Spot for Advancement for Women/Minorities:

LOCATIONS: ("Y" = Yes)

West:	Southwest:	Midwest:	Southeast:	Northeast:	International:
Y	Y	Y	Y	Y	

PARKWAY PROPERTIES INC

www.pky.com

Industry Group Code: 531120 Ranks within this company's industry group: Sales: 54   Profits: 50

Properties:		Financial Services:	Construction/Development:	Investments:		Specialty Services:		Brokerage:	
Apartments:		Mortgages:	Commercial Construction:	REIT:	Y	Property Management:	Y	Commercial Sales:	
Malls/Shopping:		Title Insurance:	Residential Construction:			Online Services:		Residential Sales:	
Offices:	Y	Property Insurance:	Land Development:			Software/IT:		Specialty:	
Hotels/Motels:			Support Services:			Consulting:			
Industrial/Warehouses:			Design/Engineering:						
Other:									

TYPES OF BUSINESS:

Real Estate Investment Trust
Office Buildings
Property Management

BRANDS/DIVISIONS/AFFILIATES:

Parkway Realty Services

CONTACTS: *Note: Officers with more than one job title may be intentionally listed here more than once.*

Steven G. Rogers, CEO
William R. Flatt, COO/Exec. VP
Steven G. Rogers, Pres.
Mandy M. Pope, Interim CFO/Exec. VP
W. Randy Lominick, III, VP-IT
Ron W. Coffey, VP-Tech. Svcs.
Mandy M. Pope, Chief Acct. Officer/Exec. VP
James M. Ingram, Chief Investment Officer/Exec. VP
Roy H. Butts, Sr. VP/Treas.
R. Bradley Antici, VP-Investments
Lisa L. Smith, Sr. VP/Senior Asset Mgr.
Leland R. Speed, Chmn.

Phone: 601-948-4091	**Fax:** 601-949-4077
Toll-Free: 800-748-1667	
Address: 188 E. Capitol St., 1 Jackson Pl., Ste. 1000, Jackson, MS 39201 US	

GROWTH PLANS/SPECIAL FEATURES:

Parkway Properties, Inc. is a self-administered real estate investment trust (REIT) specializing in the operation, acquisition, ownership and leasing of office properties, with a focus on Chicago and the southeastern and southwestern U.S. Parkway owns or has interest in 65 office properties located in 11 states, totaling approximately 13.7 million square feet.   Parkway leases its office properties to customers in the banking, insurance, professional services, legal, accounting, consulting, energy, financial services and telecommunications industries.   The company provides investment, administrative, management and maintenance services internally.   Through wholly-owned subsidiary Parkway Realty Services LLC, the company manages and/or leases 1.8 million square feet of rentable space for third-party owners, joint venture interests and fund properties. Parkway is currently attempting to transform itself into an operator-owner rather than an owner-operator in order to leverage its core strength of operating office properties. The company's strategy for achieving this focuses on forming joint ventures; managing its balance sheet; providing public stockholders with higher returns; and recycling assets. In January 2011, the firm acquired the office and retail portion of 3344 Peachtree located in Atlanta, Georgia for $167.3 million.

Parkway offers its employees stock grants; health, vision, life and disability insurance; a 401(k) plan; an employee advocate program; wellness programs and health club benefits; mentoring programs; and monthly company-wide lunches.

FINANCIALS: Sales and profits are in thousands of dollars—add 000 to get the full amount. 2010 Note: Financial information for 2010 was not available for all companies at press time.

2010 Sales: $256,263	2010 Profits: $-2,618	**U.S. Stock Ticker:** PKY
2009 Sales: $264,821	2009 Profits: $-11,603	**Int'l Ticker:** Int'l Exchange:
2008 Sales: $262,165	2008 Profits: $9,274	Employees:
2007 Sales: $234,909	2007 Profits: $19,692	Fiscal Year Ends: 12/31
2006 Sales: $203,218	2006 Profits: $25,682	Parent Company:

SALARIES/BENEFITS:

Pension Plan:	ESOP Stock Plan:	Profit Sharing:	Top Exec. Salary: $544,405	Bonus: $163,322
Savings Plan: Y	Stock Purch. Plan:		Second Exec. Salary: $295,000	Bonus: $73,750

OTHER THOUGHTS:

Apparent Women Officers or Directors: 6
Hot Spot for Advancement for Women/Minorities: Y

LOCATIONS: ("Y" = Yes)

West:	Southwest:	Midwest:	Southeast:	Northeast:	International:
	Y	Y	Y	Y	

PARSONS BRINCKERHOFF INC

www.pbworld.com

Industry Group Code: 237 Ranks within this company's industry group: Sales: Profits:

Properties:	Financial Services:	Construction/Development:		Investments:	Specialty Services:		Brokerage:
Apartments:	Mortgages:	Commercial Construction:	Y	REIT:	Property Management:		Commercial Sales:
Malls/Shopping:	Title Insurance:	Residential Construction:			Online Services:		Residential Sales:
Offices:	Property Insurance:	Land Development:			Software/IT:		Specialty:
Hotels/Motels:		Support Services:			Consulting:	Y	
Industrial/Warehouses:		Design/Engineering:	Y				
Other:							

TYPES OF BUSINESS:

Engineering Services
Planning, Design & Construction
Civic Construction Projects
Commercial Construction
Transportation Consulting
Program Management Services
Telecommunications & Environmental Projects

BRANDS/DIVISIONS/AFFILIATES:

Balfour Beatty PLC
PB Research Library

CONTACTS: *Note: Officers with more than one job title may be intentionally listed here more than once.*

George J. Pierson, CEO
Lisa M. Palumbo, General Counsel
Judy Cooper, Sr. VP/Dir.-Corp. Comm.
Paul Skoutelas, Market Leader-Transit, PB Americas
Gay Knipper, Dir.-National Program Mgmt., PB Americas
Richard A. Schrader, Chmn.

Phone: 212-465-5000	Fax: 212-465-5096
Toll-Free:	
Address: 1 Penn Plz., New York, NY 10119 US	

GROWTH PLANS/SPECIAL FEATURES:

Parsons Brinckerhoff, Inc., a subsidiary of Balfour Beatty PLC, provides engineering, consulting, and management services to local governments and the transportation, energy, and commercial market sectors. The company also offers construction services, program and project management, and facilities management. Parsons Brinckerhoff has taken on projects for clients such as Bangkok Mass Transit System Corporation and the City of Austin, Texas; and its signature works include the design of New York City's first subway and the reconfiguration of the Fort Washington Way interstate connector in Cincinnati. The company also worked with the Delhi Metro Rail Corporation to build a mass transit system designed as an urban transport system to move over 3 million passengers a day. Other relevant projects have included a gas fired power station in Kuwait; a web site and communications plan for lower Manhattan, known as lowermanhatten.info; and designing and engineering the Greater Cairo Metro system. Potential clients can view the company's work through the PB Research Library, a body that showcases and publishes the details of important projects. The firm is organized into three divisions: Americas, International and Facilities. The company is employee-owned with 150 offices worldwide.

FINANCIALS: Sales and profits are in thousands of dollars—add 000 to get the full amount. 2010 Note: Financial information for 2010 was not available for all companies at press time.

2010 Sales: $	2010 Profits: $	**U.S. Stock Ticker: Subsidiary**
2009 Sales: $2,300,000	2009 Profits: $	**Int'l Ticker:** Int'l Exchange:
2008 Sales: $2,343,117	2008 Profits: $73,882	Employees: 13,000
2007 Sales: $1,853,741	2007 Profits: $62,117	Fiscal Year Ends: 10/31
2006 Sales: $1,689,964	2006 Profits: $46,386	Parent Company: BALFOUR BEATTY PLC

SALARIES/BENEFITS:

Pension Plan:	ESOP Stock Plan:	Profit Sharing:	Top Exec. Salary: $	Bonus: $
Savings Plan:	Stock Purch. Plan:		Second Exec. Salary: $	Bonus: $

OTHER THOUGHTS:

Apparent Women Officers or Directors: 3
Hot Spot for Advancement for Women/Minorities: Y

LOCATIONS: ("Y" = Yes)

West:	Southwest:	Midwest:	Southeast:	Northeast:	International:
Y	Y	Y	Y	Y	Y

PCL CONSTRUCTION GROUP INC

www.pcl.com

Industry Group Code: 237 Ranks within this company's industry group: Sales: Profits:

Properties:	Financial Services:	Construction/Development:		Investments:	Specialty Services:	Brokerage:
Apartments:	Mortgages:	Commercial Construction:	Y	REIT:	Property Management:	Commercial Sales:
Malls/Shopping:	Title Insurance:	Residential Construction:			Online Services:	Residential Sales:
Offices:	Property Insurance:	Land Development:			Software/IT:	Specialty:
Hotels/Motels:		Support Services:			Consulting:	
Industrial/Warehouses:		Design/Engineering:	Y			
Other:						

TYPES OF BUSINESS:

Construction
Financial and Accounting Reporting
Development, Support and Project Management
Engineering Services

BRANDS/DIVISIONS/AFFILIATES:

Melloy Industrial Services
Monad Industrial Constructors
PCL Civil Constructors
PCL Industrial Services
PCL Intracon Power
Teton Industrial Construction

CONTACTS: Note: Officers with more than one job title may be intentionally listed here more than once.

Paul Douglas, CEO
Peter Beaupre, COO/Pres., PCL Construction Enterprises, Inc.
Paul Douglas, Pres.
Gordon Panas, CFO
Doug Stollery, Legal Counsel
Brad Nelson, COO/Pres., Canadian Buildings
Gordon Maron, Exec. VP
Peter Stalenhoef, COO/Pres., Heavy Industrial
Ross Grieve, Chmn.
Al Troppmann, Pres., U.S. Buildings

Phone: 780-733-5000	Fax: 780-733-5075
Toll-Free:	
Address: 5410 99 St., Edmonton, AB T6E 3P4 Canada	

GROWTH PLANS/SPECIAL FEATURES:

PCL Construction Group, Inc., founded in 1906, is an employee-owned group of construction companies in 25 locations throughout Canada, the U.S. and the Bahamas, with operations in the buildings, infrastructure and heavy industrial sectors. The firm focuses on three main areas of construction: buildings, infrastructure and heavy industrial. The buildings segment, conducts projects throughout North America and is able to work on an array of projects including commercial; institutional; educational; residential; adaptive reuse, which entails upgrading and converting an existing facility; cultural consideration, including on-site and on-the-job employment and training opportunities; green building; high-tech projects, for meeting cleanliness protocols in the medical, bio-tech and research working environments; and historical preservation, including repair, exterior masonry, renovations combining typical construction methods with scenic construction technology. The infrastructure segment undertakes various civil structure projects including bridges, overpasses, tunnels, interchanges, water treatment facilities, interchanges and light rail transportation projects. The heavy industrial division offers construction assistance to the petrochemical; oil and gas; pulp and paper; mining; and power and generation industries. PCL's building operations include larger projects, such as airports, sports facilities and office towers, and smaller projects, such as renovations, restorations and repairs. Subsidiaries include Melloy Industrial Services; Monad Industrial Constructors; PCL Civil Constructors; PCL Industrial Services; PCL Intracon Power; and Teton Industrial Construction.

Employees of the firm are offered medical, vision and dental insurance; flexible spending accounts; a prescription drug plan; a 401(k); a profit sharing bonus; and an employee assistance programs. Additionally, in 2009, the firm ranked among the top 100 companies to work for according to Fortune Magazine.

FINANCIALS: Sales and profits are in thousands of dollars—add 000 to get the full amount. 2010 Note: Financial information for 2010 was not available for all companies at press time.

2010 Sales: $	2010 Profits: $	**U.S. Stock Ticker: Private**
2009 Sales: $	2009 Profits: $	**Int'l Ticker:** Int'l Exchange:
2008 Sales: $	2008 Profits: $	Employees: 9,989
2007 Sales: $	2007 Profits: $	Fiscal Year Ends:
2006 Sales: $	2006 Profits: $	Parent Company:

SALARIES/BENEFITS:

Pension Plan:	ESOP Stock Plan:	Profit Sharing:	Top Exec. Salary: $	Bonus: $
Savings Plan: Y	Stock Purch. Plan:		Second Exec. Salary: $	Bonus: $

OTHER THOUGHTS:

Apparent Women Officers or Directors:
Hot Spot for Advancement for Women/Minorities:

LOCATIONS: ("Y" = Yes)

West:	Southwest:	Midwest:	Southeast:	Northeast:	International:
Y	Y	Y	Y		Y

PDG REALTY SA EMPREENDIMENTOS E PARTICIPACOES

www.pdgrealty.com.br

Industry Group Code: 5311 Ranks within this company's industry group: Sales: 10   Profits: 15

Properties:	Financial Services:	Construction/Development:		Investments:	Specialty Services:	Brokerage:
Apartments:	Mortgages:	Commercial Construction:		REIT:	Property Management:	Commercial Sales:
Malls/Shopping:	Title Insurance:	Residential Construction:			Online Services:	Residential Sales:
Offices:	Property Insurance:	Land Development:	Y		Software/IT:	Specialty:
Hotels/Motels:		Support Services:			Consulting:	
Industrial/Warehouses:		Design/Engineering:				
Other:						

TYPES OF BUSINESS:
Real Estate Investments

BRANDS/DIVISIONS/AFFILIATES:
TGLT
REP Desenvolvimento Imobiliario S.A.
Goldfarb Incorporacoes e Construcoes S.A

CONTACTS: *Note: Officers with more than one job title may be intentionally listed here more than once.*
Jose Antonio Grabowsky, CEO
Frederico Marinho Carneiro da Cunha, COO
Michel Wurman, CFO
Caue Castello Veiga Innocencio Cardoso, General Counsel
Marcus Vinicius Medeiros Cardoso de Sa, Dir.-Oper.
Michel Wurman, Investor Rel. Officer
Gilberto Sayao da Silva, Chmn.

Phone: 55-21-3504-3800	Fax: 55-21-35043849
Toll-Free:	
Address: 501 Praia de Botafogo, Botafogo, RJ 22250-040 Brazil	

GROWTH PLANS/SPECIAL FEATURES:
PDG Realty SA Empreemdimentos e Participacoes is a Brazilian firm that operates in the real estate industry. The company operates in five segments of the real estate industry: the development of residential projects targeted at income classes ranging from the low middle-income class to the high-income class; the development of residential lots; investments in commercial developments for the generation of rental income; the purchase of commercial and residential units for subsequent resale; and the offering of rendering services as a real estate brokerage and consulting firm. PDG Realty develops real estate projects through investments in its portfolio companies and is involved in co-development real estate projects with several other Brazilian real estate developers. Its portfolio firms include wholly-owned Goldfarb Incorporacoes e Construcoes S.A., which develops residential housing for middle and low middle-income classes in the states of Rio de Janeiro and Sao Paulo; commercial developer REP Real Estate Partners Desenvolvimento Imobiliario S.A. (36.9% owned); wholly-owned CHL, which develops commercial real estate and housing for middle, high-middle, and high-income classes in the state of Rio de Janeiro; residential real estate seller Brasil Brokers (5.47% owned); residential developer Cipasa (15.92% owned). Sao Paulo general real estate developer Lindencorp (15.92% owned); and Argentinian residential building developer TGLT (30% owned).

FINANCIALS: Sales and profits are in thousands of dollars—add 000 to get the full amount. 2010 Note: Financial information for 2010 was not available for all companies at press time.

2010 Sales: $3,338,850	2010 Profits: $504,100	**U.S. Stock Ticker:**
2009 Sales: $1,266,510	2009 Profits: $215,850	**Int'l Ticker: PDGR3** Int'l Exchange: Sao Paulo-SAO
2008 Sales: $786,030	2008 Profits: $116,510	Employees:
2007 Sales: $	2007 Profits: $	Fiscal Year Ends: 12/31
2006 Sales: $	2006 Profits: $	Parent Company:

SALARIES/BENEFITS:

Pension Plan:	ESOP Stock Plan:	Profit Sharing:	Top Exec. Salary: $	Bonus: $
Savings Plan:	Stock Purch. Plan:		Second Exec. Salary: $	Bonus: $

OTHER THOUGHTS:
Apparent Women Officers or Directors:
Hot Spot for Advancement for Women/Minorities:

LOCATIONS: ("Y" = Yes)

West:	Southwest:	Midwest:	Southeast:	Northeast:	International:
					Y

PENNSYLVANIA REIT

www.preit.com

Industry Group Code: 531120 Ranks within this company's industry group: Sales: 38   Profits: 56

Properties:		Financial Services:		Construction/Development:		Investments:		Specialty Services:		Brokerage:	
Apartments:		Mortgages:		Commercial Construction:	Y	REIT:	Y	Property Management:	Y	Commercial Sales:	
Malls/Shopping:	Y	Title Insurance:		Residential Construction:				Online Services:		Residential Sales:	
Offices:		Property Insurance:		Land Development:	Y			Software/IT:		Specialty:	
Hotels/Motels:				Support Services:				Consulting:			
Industrial/Warehouses:				Design/Engineering:							
Other:											

TYPES OF BUSINESS:

Real Estate Investment Trust
Retail Properties
Industrial Properties
Multi-Family Residential Properties
Property Development & Redevelopment

BRANDS/DIVISIONS/AFFILIATES:

PREIT Associates LP
PREIT Services LLC
PREIT RUBIN Inc

CONTACTS: *Note: Officers with more than one job title may be intentionally listed here more than once.*

Ronald Rubin, CEO
Edward A. Glickman, COO
Edward A. Glickman, Pres.
Robert F. McCadden, CFO/Exec. VP
Judith Trias, VP-Retail Mktg.
Judith E. Baker, Sr. VP-Human Resources
Bruce Goldman, General Counsel/Exec. VP/Sec.
Douglas S. Grayson, Exec. VP-Dev.
Nurit Yaron, VP-Investor Rel.
Jonathan Bell, Chief Acct. Officer/Sr. VP
Jeffrey A. Linn, Exec. VP-Acquisitions
Timothy R. Rubin, Exec. VP-Leasing
Joseph F. Coradino, Pres., PREIT Services LLC & PREIT-RUBIN, Inc.
Andrew M. Ioannou, Sr. VP-Capital Markets/Treas.
Ronald Rubin, Chmn.

Phone: 215-875-0700	**Fax:** 215-546-7311
Toll-Free: 866-875-0700	
Address: 200 S. Broad St., Philadelphia, PA 19102 US	

GROWTH PLANS/SPECIAL FEATURES:

Pennsylvania REIT (PREIT) is a fully integrated, self-administered and self-managed real estate investment trust (REIT), whose primary investment focus is on retail shopping malls, strip centers and power centers. It acquires, develops, redevelops and operates properties in the Eastern U.S. The company offers a full complement of real estate capabilities including leasing, acquisition, development, construction, management, property management and marketing. The firm's portfolio currently consists of 49 retail properties in 13 states, of which 38 are shopping malls; eight are strip and power centers; and three are under development. Overall, PREIT controls approximately 33.2 million square feet of rentable property. Prominent tenants of the firm include Gap, Inc.; Foot Locker; J.C. Penney Company, Inc.; Sears; and Limited Brands, Inc. PREIT holds its interests in its portfolio of properties through its operating partnership PREIT Associates, LP, in which the company is the sole general partner, with a 96% controlling interest. The company provides management, leasing and real estate development services through two of its subsidiaries, PREIT Services, LLC and PREIT-RUBIN, Inc. PREIT Services generally develops and manages properties which the firm intends to consolidate for financial reporting purposes. PREIT-RUBIN generally develops and manages properties which the firm does not consolidate for financial reporting purposes, including properties in which the firm owns interests through partnerships with third parties and properties that are owned by third parties in which the firm does not own an interest. In 2010, the firm sold five power centers to Cedar Shopping Centers, Inc. for roughly $134 million and agreed to sell its 50% ownership of two additional power centers to Cedar.

PREIT employees receive benefits including a 401(k) plan; an employee share purchase plan; flexible spending accounts; corporate flex time hours; tuition reimbursement; disability, life and AD&D insurance; and an employee assistance program.

FINANCIALS: Sales and profits are in thousands of dollars—add 000 to get the full amount. 2010 Note: Financial information for 2010 was not available for all companies at press time.

2010 Sales: $455,641	2010 Profits: $-54,363	**U.S. Stock Ticker: PEI**
2009 Sales: $451,306	2009 Profits: $-90,091	**Int'l Ticker:** Int'l Exchange:
2008 Sales: $461,035	2008 Profits: $-16,355	Employees: 705
2007 Sales: $460,590	2007 Profits: $23,120	Fiscal Year Ends: 12/31
2006 Sales: $459,308	2006 Profits: $28,021	Parent Company:

SALARIES/BENEFITS:

Pension Plan:	ESOP Stock Plan:	Profit Sharing:	Top Exec. Salary: $562,648	Bonus: $421,986
Savings Plan: Y	Stock Purch. Plan: Y		Second Exec. Salary: $503,880	Bonus: $327,522

OTHER THOUGHTS:

Apparent Women Officers or Directors: 8
Hot Spot for Advancement for Women/Minorities: Y

LOCATIONS: ("Y" = Yes)

West:	Southwest:	Midwest:	Southeast:	Northeast:	International:
		Y	Y	Y	

PLUM CREEK TIMBER CO INC

www.plumcreek.com

Industry Group Code: 444130 Ranks within this company's industry group: Sales: 1   Profits: 1

Properties:	Financial Services:	Construction/Development:	Investments:	Specialty Services:	Brokerage:
Apartments:	Mortgages:	Commercial Construction:	REIT: Y	Property Management:	Commercial Sales:
Malls/Shopping:	Title Insurance:	Residential Construction:		Online Services:	Residential Sales:
Offices:	Property Insurance:	Land Development: Y		Software/IT:	Specialty: Y
Hotels/Motels:		Support Services:		Consulting:	
Industrial/Warehouses:		Design/Engineering:			
Other: Y					

TYPES OF BUSINESS:

Forestry & Logging
Real Estate Investment Trust
Land Management & Development
Manufactured Timber Products
Specialty Brokerage
Land Investments
Mineral Rights

BRANDS/DIVISIONS/AFFILIATES:

CONTACTS: *Note: Officers with more than one job title may be intentionally listed here more than once.*

Rick R. Holley, CEO
Thomas M. Lindquist, COO/Exec. VP
Rick R. Holley, Pres.
David W. Lambert, CFO/Sr. VP
Barbara L. Crowe, VP-Human Resources
Joan K. Fitzmaurice, VP-IT
Thomas G. Ray, VP-Northwest Resources & Mfg.
James A. Kraft, General Counsel/Sr. VP/Corp. Sec.
Larry D. Neilson, Sr. VP-Bus. Dev.
Joan K. Fitzmaurice, VP-Corp. Comm. & Audit
John B. Hobbs, VP-Investor Rel.
David A. Brown, Chief Acct. Officer/VP
James A. Kilberg, Sr. VP-Real Estate
Thomas M. Reed, VP-Southern Resources
Dan Tucker, VP-Tax
Laura B. Smith, VP/Treas.
John F. Morgan, Sr., Chmn.

Phone: 206-467-3600	Fax: 206-467-3795

Toll-Free: 800-858-5347

Address: 999 3rd Ave., Ste. 4300, Seattle, WA 98104-4096 US

GROWTH PLANS/SPECIAL FEATURES:

Plum Creek Timber Co., Inc. is a real estate investment trust (REIT) that owns, harvests and redevelops timberland. The company is one of the largest private timberland owners in the U.S., with approximately 6.8 million acres in 19 states. Plum Creek's timber assets are well diversified by both geography and by species mix and age distribution. The firm harvests trees and then markets the lumber to the paper and forest products industry and replants and fertilizes the harvested lands. Plum Creek is operated in four divisions: two regional timberland management divisions; a real estate segment; a manufactured products division; and an Other Businesses segment. The Northern Resources segment covers timberlands in Maine, Michigan, Montana, New Hampshire, Oregon, Vermont, Washington, West Virginia and Wisconsin; while the Southern Resources segment covers Alabama, Arkansas, Florida, Georgia, Louisiana, Mississippi, Oklahoma, Texas and the Carolinas. Plum Creek operates six nurseries to provide seedlings for reforestation projects. The real estate division handles the sale and management of higher value lands, sales of non-strategic timberlands and development of certain properties. The manufacturing segment includes two lumber mills, two plywood plants, two medium density fiberboard facilities and two lumber remanufacturing facilities. These operations, located near the firm's Montana timberlands, turn logs into saleable items, including veneer logs, plywood, planks and other materials, which are distributed through a nationwide network of field inventory points. The company's other businesses segment focuses on opportunities related to mineral extraction, natural gas, and communication and transportation rights of way on company lands.

Employees are offered health care coverage; health and dependent daycare funds; savings and retirement benefits; and life and disability protection.

FINANCIALS: Sales and profits are in thousands of dollars—add 000 to get the full amount. 2010 Note: Financial information for 2010 was not available for all companies at press time.

2010 Sales: $1,190,000	2010 Profits: $213,000	**U.S. Stock Ticker: PCL**
2009 Sales: $1,294,000	2009 Profits: $236,000	**Int'l Ticker:** Int'l Exchange:
2008 Sales: $1,614,000	2008 Profits: $233,000	Employees: 1,202
2007 Sales: $1,675,000	2007 Profits: $282,000	Fiscal Year Ends: 12/31
2006 Sales: $1,627,000	2006 Profits: $317,000	Parent Company:

SALARIES/BENEFITS:

Pension Plan:	ESOP Stock Plan:	Profit Sharing: Y	Top Exec. Salary: $830,000	Bonus: $938,108
Savings Plan: Y	Stock Purch. Plan:		Second Exec. Salary: $500,000	Bonus: $462,375

OTHER THOUGHTS:

Apparent Women Officers or Directors: 3
Hot Spot for Advancement for Women/Minorities: Y

LOCATIONS: ("Y" = Yes)

West:	Southwest:	Midwest:	Southeast:	Northeast:	International:
Y	Y	Y	Y	Y	

PMI GROUP INC (THE)

www.pmigroup.com

Industry Group Code: 524126 Ranks within this company's industry group: Sales: 1   Profits: 1

Properties:	Financial Services:		Construction/Development:	Investments:	Specialty Services:	Brokerage:
Apartments:	Mortgages:	Y	Commercial Construction:	REIT:	Property Management:	Commercial Sales:
Malls/Shopping:	Title Insurance:		Residential Construction:		Online Services:	Residential Sales:
Offices:	Property Insurance:		Land Development:		Software/IT:	Specialty:
Hotels/Motels:			Support Services:		Consulting:	
Industrial/Warehouses:			Design/Engineering:			
Other:						

TYPES OF BUSINESS:

Insurance-Financial Guaranty
Mortgage Insurance & Reinsurance
Structured Finance Insurance

BRANDS/DIVISIONS/AFFILIATES:

PMI Mortgage Insurance Co.
PMI Europe
PMI Canada
CMG Mortgage Insurance Company

CONTACTS: *Note: Officers with more than one job title may be intentionally listed here more than once.*

L. Stephen Smith, CEO
Donald P. Lofe, Jr., CFO/Exec. VP
Charles F. Broom, Sr. VP-Human Resources & Organizational Dev.
Donald P. Lofe, Jr., Chief Admin. Officer
Andrew D. Cameron, General Counsel/Exec. VP/Sec.
David Berson, Chief Strategist & Economist/Sr. VP
Thomas H. Jeter, Chief Acct. Officer/Corp. Controller/Sr. VP
Ray D. Chang, Corp. Treas./Sr. VP
Lloyd A. Porter, Chief Risk Officer/Exec. VP
Joanne M. Berkowitz, Chief Insurance Oper. Officer/Exec. VP
David H. Katkov, Chief Bus. Officer/Exec. VP
L. Stephen Smith, Chmn.

Phone: 925-658-7878	Fax: 925-658-6931
Toll-Free: 800-280-4764	
Address: 3003 Oak Rd., Walnut Creek, CA 94597 US	

GROWTH PLANS/SPECIAL FEATURES:

The PMI Group, Inc. provides insurance for residential mortgages. The company operates in three segments: U.S. mortgage insurance operations; international operations; and corporate and other. The U.S. mortgage insurance operations segment, through PMI Mortgage Insurance Co., offers mortgage insurance and loss protection to lenders and investors in the event of borrower default. The company also owns 50% of CMG Mortgage Insurance Company, a joint venture that provides mortgage insurance to credit unions. The international segment consists of PMI Europe and PMI Canada. PMI Europe has since ceased operations to conserve capital, and the firm is in the process of closing PMI Canada. The corporate and other segment consists of corporate debt and expenses of the company. It also focuses on contract underwriting operations and equity in earnings or losses from investments in certain limited partnerships. In July 2010, the company sold its stake in FGIC Corporation.

PMI Group offers its employees medical, dental and vision coverage; life and AD&D insurance; short- and long-term disability; an employee assistance program; domestic partner benefits; business travel insurance; a pension plan; a 401(k) plan; an employee stock purchase plan; flexible spending accounts; college savings plans; a first-time homebuyer program; adoption assistance; and tuition reimbursement.

FINANCIALS: Sales and profits are in thousands of dollars—add 000 to get the full amount. 2010 Note: Financial information for 2010 was not available for all companies at press time.

2010 Sales: $641,118	2010 Profits: $-773,028	**U.S. Stock Ticker: PMI**
2009 Sales: $877,995	2009 Profits: $-659,326	**Int'l Ticker:** Int'l Exchange:
2008 Sales: $814,418	2008 Profits: $-928,508	Employees: 712
2007 Sales: $923,185	2007 Profits: $-915,326	Fiscal Year Ends: 12/31
2006 Sales: $868,344	2006 Profits: $419,651	Parent Company:

SALARIES/BENEFITS:

Pension Plan: Y	ESOP Stock Plan:	Profit Sharing:	Top Exec. Salary: $830,000	Bonus: $1,394,000
Savings Plan: Y	Stock Purch. Plan: Y		Second Exec. Salary: $445,000	Bonus: $573,000

OTHER THOUGHTS:

Apparent Women Officers or Directors: 5
Hot Spot for Advancement for Women/Minorities: Y

LOCATIONS: ("Y" = Yes)

West:	Southwest:	Midwest:	Southeast:	Northeast:	International:
Y	Y	Y	Y	Y	Y

POST PROPERTIES INC   www.postproperties.com

Industry Group Code: 531110 Ranks within this company's industry group: Sales: 13   Profits: 12

Properties:		Financial Services:		Construction/Development:		Investments:		Specialty Services:		Brokerage:	
Apartments:	Y	Mortgages:		Commercial Construction:		REIT:	Y	Property Management:	Y	Commercial Sales:	
Malls/Shopping:		Title Insurance:		Residential Construction:				Online Services:		Residential Sales:	
Offices:		Property Insurance:		Land Development:	Y			Software/IT:		Specialty:	
Hotels/Motels:				Support Services:	Y			Consulting:			
Industrial/Warehouses:				Design/Engineering:	Y						
Other:											

TYPES OF BUSINESS:

Real Estate Investment Trust
Apartment Communities
Landscaping & Design Services
Apartment Management & Development
Corporate Apartments
Condominiums
Retail Space
Preferred Homes

BRANDS/DIVISIONS/AFFILIATES:

Post Apartment Management
Post Investment Group
Post Corporate Services
Post Construction and Property Services

CONTACTS: *Note: Officers with more than one job title may be intentionally listed here more than once.*

David P. Stockert, CEO
David P. Stockert, Pres.
Christopher J. Papa, CFO/Exec. VP
Terri Sherrod, Dir.-Mktg. & Branding
Linda J. Ricklef, Sr. VP-Human Resources
Janet Ham, VP-IT
Sherry W. Cohen, Corp. Sec./Exec. VP
Steve Sadler, VP-Strategic Bus. Svcs.
Arthur J. Quirk, Chief Acct. Officer/Sr. VP
Kevin B. Polston, Sr. VP-Commercial
Kathleen M. Mason, Sr. VP-Taxation
Glen P. Smith, Sr. VP-Legal
S. Jamie Teabo, Exec. VP-Property Mgmt.
Robert C. Goddard, III, Chmn.

Phone: 404-846-5000	Fax: 404-846-6282
Toll-Free:	
Address: 4401 Northside Pkwy., Ste. 800, Atlanta, GA 30327 US	

GROWTH PLANS/SPECIAL FEATURES:

Post Properties, Inc. is a self-administered and self-managed equity real estate investment trust (REIT). The firm owns, develops and manages upscale multifamily apartment communities in Atlanta, Georgia; Dallas, Texas; and the greater Washington, D.C., and Tampa, Florida metropolitan areas. The company owns approximately 20,505 apartment units in 56 apartment communities, including 1,747 units in five communities held in unconsolidated entities and 642 units in two communities currently under construction. Post's major operating divisions include Post Apartment Management; Post Investment Group; Post Corporate Services; and Post Construction and Property Services. Post Apartment Management is responsible for the day-to-day operations of all Post communities and also conducts short-term corporate apartment leasing activities. Post Investment Group handles the company's acquisition, development, rehabilitation, disposition, condominium sales and asset management operations. Post Corporate Services provides all compliance, information systems, human resources, accounting, management reporting, legal, security, personnel recruiting, training/development, risk management and insurance services for Post. The Post Construction and Property Services division oversees all construction and physical asset maintenance activities at each Post community.

Employees are offered benefits including life, disability, auto, homeowners, medical, dental and vision insurance; educational assistance; a 401(k); a stock purchase program; an employee assistance program; a group legal plan; and credit union membership.

FINANCIALS: Sales and profits are in thousands of dollars—add 000 to get the full amount. 2010 Note: Financial information for 2010 was not available for all companies at press time.

2010 Sales: $285,138	2010 Profits: $-6,991	**U.S. Stock Ticker:** PPS
2009 Sales: $276,323	2009 Profits: $-11,489	**Int'l Ticker:** Int'l Exchange:
2008 Sales: $281,940	2008 Profits: $-8,370	Employees: 597
2007 Sales: $277,324	2007 Profits: $182,949	Fiscal Year Ends: 12/31
2006 Sales: $262,324	2006 Profits: $101,469	Parent Company:

SALARIES/BENEFITS:

Pension Plan:	ESOP Stock Plan:	Profit Sharing:	Top Exec. Salary: $420,000	Bonus: $
Savings Plan: Y	Stock Purch. Plan: Y		Second Exec. Salary: $352,000	Bonus: $158,400

OTHER THOUGHTS:

Apparent Women Officers or Directors: 8
Hot Spot for Advancement for Women/Minorities: Y

LOCATIONS: ("Y" = Yes)

West:	Southwest:	Midwest:	Southeast:	Northeast:	International:
	Y		Y	Y	

PRIME GROUP REALTY TRUST

www.pgrt.com

Industry Group Code: 531120 Ranks within this company's industry group: Sales: Profits:

Properties:		Financial Services:	Construction/Development:		Investments:		Specialty Services:		Brokerage:
Apartments:		Mortgages:	Commercial Construction:		REIT:	Y	Property Management:	Y	Commercial Sales:
Malls/Shopping:		Title Insurance:	Residential Construction:				Online Services:		Residential Sales:
Offices:	Y	Property Insurance:	Land Development:	Y			Software/IT:		Specialty:
Hotels/Motels:			Support Services:				Consulting:		
Industrial/Warehouses:	Y		Design/Engineering:						
Other:									

TYPES OF BUSINESS:

Real Estate Investment Trust
Office & Industrial Properties
Land Development
Property Management

BRANDS/DIVISIONS/AFFILIATES:

Lightstone Group LLC
Prime Group Realty Services, Inc.

CONTACTS: *Note: Officers with more than one job title may be intentionally listed here more than once.*

Jeffrey A. Patterson, CEO
Jeffrey A. Patterson, Pres.
James F. Hoffman, General Counsel/Sr. VP/Corp. Sec.
Steven R. Baron, Exec. VP-Office Leasing
Paul G. Del Vecchio, Exec. VP-Capital Markets
Victoria A. Cory, Sr VP-Loan Admin., Real Estate Tax & Due Diligence
George R. Whittemore, Trustee

Phone: 312-917-1300	**Fax:** 312-917-1310
Toll-Free:	
Address: 330 N. Wabash Ave., Ste. 2800, Chicago, IL 60611 US	

GROWTH PLANS/SPECIAL FEATURES:

Prime Group Realty Trust (PGRT), a subsidiary of The Lightstone Group, LLC, is a real estate investment trust (REIT) that owns and operates several office properties in metropolitan Chicago, which contain an aggregate of nearly 3.3 million square feet. It also owns and operates one industrial property in the Chicago metropolitan area and shares interest in an office property joint venture consisting of 101,000 square feet. PGRT provides its own property management, leasing, marketing, acquisition, development, redevelopment and finance services. In addition, the company is the managing and leasing agent for the 1.5 million square foot Citadel Center office building located at 131 South Dearborn Street in Chicago, Illinois. Subsidiary Prime Group Realty Services, Inc. offers property management services to third parties. The REIT also owns a joint venture interest in an office complex in Phoenix, Arizona.

FINANCIALS: Sales and profits are in thousands of dollars—add 000 to get the full amount. 2010 Note: Financial information for 2010 was not available for all companies at press time.

		U.S. Stock Ticker: Subsidiary
2010 Sales: $	2010 Profits: $	
2009 Sales: $	2009 Profits: $	Int'l Ticker: Int'l Exchange:
2008 Sales: $64,840	2008 Profits: $-73,336	Employees:
2007 Sales: $73,174	2007 Profits: $-59,018	Fiscal Year Ends: 12/31
2006 Sales: $	2006 Profits: $	Parent Company: LIGHTSTONE GROUP LLC (THE)

SALARIES/BENEFITS:

Pension Plan:	ESOP Stock Plan:	Profit Sharing:	Top Exec. Salary: $	Bonus: $
Savings Plan:	Stock Purch. Plan:		Second Exec. Salary: $	Bonus: $

OTHER THOUGHTS:

Apparent Women Officers or Directors: 1
Hot Spot for Advancement for Women/Minorities:

LOCATIONS: ("Y" = Yes)

West:	Southwest:	Midwest:	Southeast:	Northeast:	International:
		Y			

PRIME RETAIL INC

www.primeretail.com

Industry Group Code: 531120 Ranks within this company's industry group: Sales: Profits:

Properties:		Financial Services:	Construction/Development:	Investments:		Specialty Services:		Brokerage:
Apartments:		Mortgages:	Commercial Construction:	REIT:	Y	Property Management:	Y	Commercial Sales:
Malls/Shopping:	Y	Title Insurance:	Residential Construction:			Online Services:		Residential Sales:
Offices:		Property Insurance:	Land Development:			Software/IT:		Specialty:
Hotels/Motels:			Support Services:			Consulting:		
Industrial/Warehouses:			Design/Engineering:					
Other:								

TYPES OF BUSINESS:

Real Estate Investment Trust
Shopping & Outlet Centers
Property Management

BRANDS/DIVISIONS/AFFILIATES:

Lightstone Group LLC
Prime Retail, LP
Prime Outlets
Prime Tourism

CONTACTS: *Note: Officers with more than one job title may be intentionally listed here more than once.*

Nicholas G. King, COO
Robert A. Brvenik, Pres.
William G. Ellis, CFO
Karen Fluharty, Sr. VP-Mktg.
Pamela Meadows, Sr. VP-Human Resources
Kelvin Antill, General Counsel/Exec. VP
Bruce Zalaznick, Exec. VP-Real Estate
Lisa H. Kessler, Sr. VP-Leasing Outlet Shopping Centers
Salem LaHood, Sr. VP-Design & Construction
W. Paul Reed, Sr. VP-Construction

Phone: 410-234-0782	Fax:
Toll-Free:	
Address: 217 E. Redwood St., 20 Fl., Baltimore, MD 21202 US	

GROWTH PLANS/SPECIAL FEATURES:

Prime Retail, Inc., owned by Lightstone Group LLC, owns and operates outlet mall and commercial real estate properties. The company is organized as an REIT (Real Estate Investment Trust). The company is divided into three divisions Prime Retail, Prime Outlet and Prime Tourism. The Prime Retail division operates shopping centers across the U.S. The firm's Prime Outlet division is mainly discount-type shopping centers that enable value-oriented shoppers to purchase designer and brand name products directly from manufacturers at discounts. The Prime Tourism division provides services such as, itinerary planning assistance, group reservations, meet and greet services and travel packages. Prime's portfolio consists of 21 properties in 15 states and Puerto Rico, totaling more than 8 million square feet of retail outlets space and 8 million square feet of mall space. Most of these properties are located outside metropolitan areas, and ten of them are standard indoor shopping malls. These outlet centers feature a diversified mix of nationally recognized manufacturers of brand-name merchandise, including 3,000 stores and 450 designer and brand names. Companies currently utilizing Prime Retail's properties include American Eagle Outfitters; Avon; Banana Republic; Barneys New York; Bath & Body Works; Brooks Brothers; Calvin Klein; Disney; DKNY Jeans; Eddie Bauer; Gap; Giorgio Armani; Gucci; GUESS; Lee Wrangler; Saks Fifth Avenue OFF 5th; and Victoria's Secret Outlet. As a fully integrated real estate firm, the company provides accounting, finance, leasing, marketing and management services to its properties. Prime conducts substantially all of its business through operating subsidiary Prime Retail, LP. The company's business strategy includes seeking a tenant mix that represents the biggest and best draws in the outlet industry; operating under the Prime Outlets brand name and using on-site management teams to develop individualized marketing programs; and managing and leasing its properties with in-house personnel, reducing its reliance on third-party service providers and thereby lowering operating expenses.

FINANCIALS: Sales and profits are in thousands of dollars—add 000 to get the full amount. 2010 Note: Financial information for 2010 was not available for all companies at press time.

2010 Sales: $	2010 Profits: $	**U.S. Stock Ticker:** Private
2009 Sales: $	2009 Profits: $	**Int'l Ticker:** Int'l Exchange:
2008 Sales: $	2008 Profits: $	Employees:
2007 Sales: $	2007 Profits: $	Fiscal Year Ends: 12/31
2006 Sales: $	2006 Profits: $	Parent Company: LIGHTSTONE GROUP LLC (THE)

SALARIES/BENEFITS:

Pension Plan:	ESOP Stock Plan:	Profit Sharing:	Top Exec. Salary: $	Bonus: $
Savings Plan:	Stock Purch. Plan:		Second Exec. Salary: $	Bonus: $

OTHER THOUGHTS:

Apparent Women Officers or Directors: 3
Hot Spot for Advancement for Women/Minorities: Y

LOCATIONS: ("Y" = Yes)

West:	Southwest:	Midwest:	Southeast:	Northeast:	International:
Y	Y	Y	Y	Y	

PROLOGIS

www.prologis.com

Industry Group Code: 531120 Ranks within this company's industry group: Sales: 18   Profits: 61

Properties:	Financial Services:	Construction/Development:	Investments:	Specialty Services:		Brokerage:
Apartments:	Mortgages:	Commercial Construction:	REIT: Y	Property Management: Y		Commercial Sales:
Malls/Shopping:	Title Insurance:	Residential Construction:		Online Services:		Residential Sales:
Offices:	Property Insurance:	Land Development: Y		Software/IT: Y		Specialty:
Hotels/Motels:		Support Services: Y		Consulting: Y		
Industrial/Warehouses: Y		Design/Engineering: Y				
Other:						

TYPES OF BUSINESS:

Real Estate Operations
REIT
Property Management
Property Development

BRANDS/DIVISIONS/AFFILIATES:

AMB Property Corporation

CONTACTS: *Note: Officers with more than one job title may be intentionally listed here more than once.*

Walter C. Rakowich, CEO
William E. Sullivan, CFO
Charles E. Sullivan, Chief Admin. Officer
Edward S. Nekritz, General Counsel/Corp. Sec./Head-Global Risk
Gary E. Anderson, Head-Global Oper. & Investment Mgmt.
Larry H. Harmsen, Pres., US & Canada
John R. Rizzo, Chief Sustainability Officer
Mike Yamada, Pres., Japan
Ted R. Antenucci, Pres./Chief Investment Officer
Stephen L. Feinberg, Chmn.
Philip Dunne, Pres., Europe

Phone: 303-567-5000	**Fax:** 303-567-5605
Toll-Free: 800-566-2706	
Address: 4545 Airport Way, Denver, CO 80239 US	

GROWTH PLANS/SPECIAL FEATURES:

ProLogis is a real estate investment trust (REIT) based in Colorado. With more than 2,600 facilities, representing over 435 million square feet owned, managed and under development, the firm is a leading global provider of industrial distribution facilities present in markets throughout Europe, Asia and North America. ProLogis leases its properties to more than 4,400 clients, including manufacturers, retailers, transportation companies, third-party logistics providers and other companies with large-scale distribution needs. The firm manages its business through two operating segments: direct-owned and investment management. The direct-owned segment includes the long-term ownership of industrial and retail properties, as well as industrial properties currently under development, land available for development and land subject to ground leases. Through the division's Global Renewable Energy Group, it manages installations and provides development management services for a portfolio of renewable energy projects. The investment management segment represents the investment management of unconsolidated property funds and certain joint ventures, as well as the properties it owns. It currently manages 11 property investment funds. In November 2010, it sold a North American industrial portfolio to affiliates of Blackstone Real Estate Advisors, as well as minority interests in a hotel property to Hilton Worldwide, Inc. In December 2010, ProLogis agreed to sell of its Catellus retail and mixed-use assets to an affiliate of TPG Capital. In January 2011, the firm signed a merger of equals agreement with AMB Property Corporation. Following the completion of the merger, the combined company will retain the ProLogis name and manage gross assets of $46 billion.

FINANCIALS: Sales and profits are in thousands of dollars—add 000 to get the full amount. 2010 Note: Financial information for 2010 was not available for all companies at press time.

2010 Sales: $909,000	2010 Profits: $-1,270,000	**U.S. Stock Ticker: PLD**
2009 Sales: $1,055,000	2009 Profits: $23,929	**Int'l Ticker:** Int'l Exchange:
2008 Sales: $5,396,000	2008 Profits: $-449,966	Employees: 1,100
2007 Sales: $6,106,471	2007 Profits: $1,057,872	Fiscal Year Ends: 12/31
2006 Sales: $2,446,392	2006 Profits: $874,367	Parent Company:

SALARIES/BENEFITS:

Pension Plan:	ESOP Stock Plan:	Profit Sharing:	Top Exec. Salary: $1,000,000	Bonus: $2,000,000
Savings Plan: Y	Stock Purch. Plan: Y		Second Exec. Salary: $630,000	Bonus: $1,000,500

OTHER THOUGHTS:

Apparent Women Officers or Directors: 2
Hot Spot for Advancement for Women/Minorities:

LOCATIONS: ("Y" = Yes)

West:	Southwest:	Midwest:	Southeast:	Northeast:	International:
Y	Y	Y	Y	Y	Y

PRUDENTIAL REAL ESTATE AFFILIATES INC
www.prudential.com

Industry Group Code: 531210 Ranks within this company's industry group: Sales: Profits:

Properties:	Financial Services:	Construction/Development:	Investments:	Specialty Services:		Brokerage:	
Apartments:	Mortgages:	Commercial Construction:	REIT:	Property Management:		Commercial Sales:	
Malls/Shopping:	Title Insurance:	Residential Construction:		Online Services:	Y	Residential Sales:	Y
Offices:	Property Insurance:	Land Development:		Software/IT:		Specialty:	
Hotels/Motels:		Support Services:		Consulting:			
Industrial/Warehouses:		Design/Engineering:					
Other:							

TYPES OF BUSINESS:
Real Estate Brokerage
Residential Sales
Online Databases & Information

BRANDS/DIVISIONS/AFFILIATES:
Prudential Financial

CONTACTS: *Note: Officers with more than one job title may be intentionally listed here more than once.*
Laurie Keenan, Pres.

Phone: 949-794-7900	Fax: 949-794-7035
Toll-Free:	
Address: 3333 Michelson Dr., Ste. 1000, Irvine, CA 92612-1690 US	

GROWTH PLANS/SPECIAL FEATURES:

Prudential Real Estate Affiliates, Inc. (PREA), a subsidiary of Prudential Financial, is a collection of independently owned and operated franchises engaged in the brokerage of residential real estate throughout every state in the U.S., nine Canadian provinces and Mexico under the Prudential flag. The operations of this group of companies, consisting of more than 2,100 brokerages with more than 48,000 sales associates, are facilitated by an online database. Additionally, 800 affiliated independent commercial brokers make use of the PREA network. The firm's web site offers a search engine for homebuyers that features a home search, a neighborhood search, a brokerage office search and an e-mail registry that updates customers according to their profiles. Homebuyers can also access online guides for buying a home, selling a home and moving. The company also offers an online center for brokers. To its franchisees, PREA offers the well-known and respectable brand name and the symbolic rock of Prudential, as well as educational assistance, advance technology, a referral and relocation program and extensive networking between franchises and Prudential. Through other divisions and affiliates, the firm offers commercial real estate brokerage services, as well as all the financial services involved in buying a home.

FINANCIALS: Sales and profits are in thousands of dollars—add 000 to get the full amount. 2010 Note: Financial information for 2010 was not available for all companies at press time.

2010 Sales: $	2010 Profits: $	U.S. Stock Ticker: Subsidiary
2009 Sales: $	2009 Profits: $	Int'l Ticker: Int'l Exchange:
2008 Sales: $	2008 Profits: $	Employees:
2007 Sales: $	2007 Profits: $	Fiscal Year Ends: 12/31
2006 Sales: $	2006 Profits: $	Parent Company: PRUDENTIAL FINANCIAL INC

SALARIES/BENEFITS:

Pension Plan:	ESOP Stock Plan:	Profit Sharing:	Top Exec. Salary: $	Bonus: $
Savings Plan:	Stock Purch. Plan:		Second Exec. Salary: $	Bonus: $

OTHER THOUGHTS:
Apparent Women Officers or Directors: 2
Hot Spot for Advancement for Women/Minorities:

LOCATIONS: ("Y" = Yes)

West:	Southwest:	Midwest:	Southeast:	Northeast:	International:
Y	Y	Y	Y	Y	Y

Note: Financial information, benefits and other data can change quickly and may vary from those stated here.

PS BUSINESS PARKS INC

www.psbusinessparks.com

Industry Group Code: 531120 Ranks within this company's industry group: Sales: 47   Profits: 23

Properties:		Financial Services:		Construction/Development:		Investments:		Specialty Services:		Brokerage:	
Apartments:		Mortgages:		Commercial Construction:		REIT:	Y	Property Management:	Y	Commercial Sales:	
Malls/Shopping:		Title Insurance:		Residential Construction:				Online Services:		Residential Sales:	
Offices:	Y	Property Insurance:		Land Development:				Software/IT:		Specialty:	
Hotels/Motels:				Support Services:				Consulting:			
Industrial/Warehouses:	Y			Design/Engineering:							
Other:											

TYPES OF BUSINESS:

Real Estate Investment Trust
Industrial Properties
Office Properties
Retail Properties
Business Parks
Property Management

BRANDS/DIVISIONS/AFFILIATES:

PS Business Parks LP
Public Storage Inc
Shady Grove Executive Center
Parklawn Business Park
Tysons Corporate Center
Westpark Business Campus
Austin Flex Portfolio

CONTACTS: Note: Officers with more than one job title may be intentionally listed here more than once.

Joseph D. Russell, Jr., CEO
John W. Petersen, COO/Exec. VP
Joseph D. Russell, Jr., Pres.
Edward Stokx, CFO/Exec. VP
Trenton Groves, Controller/VP
Viola I. Sanchez, VP-Southeast
Robin Mather, VP-Southern California
Maria Hawthorne, Exec. VP-East Coast
Coby Holley, VP-Pacific Northwest
Ronald L. Havner, Jr., Chmn.

Phone: 818-244-8080	Fax: 818-242-0566
Toll-Free:	
Address: 701 Western Ave., Glendale, CA 91201-2397 US	

GROWTH PLANS/SPECIAL FEATURES:

PS Business Parks, Inc. (PSB) is a self-advised and self-managed Real Estate Investment Trust (REIT). It acquires, owns, operates and develops commercial properties, primarily multi-tenant flex, office and industrial space. The company does business primarily through an operating partnership, PS Business Parks LP, in which PSB holds a 77.2% share, with the remainder being held by Public Storage, Inc. As the sole general partner of PS Business Parks LP, PSB maintains complete responsibility and discretion in managing and controlling the operating partnership. The firm's portfolio includes 85 business parks totaling approximately 21.8 million square feet of commercial space located in eight states: Arizona, California, Florida, Maryland, Oregon, Texas, Virginia and Washington. Approximately 13 million square feet of the firm's owned property is classified as flex space. Flex space includes buildings that are configured with a combination of office, assembly, showroom, laboratory, light manufacturing and warehouse space, suitable to a variety of business needs. Approximately 3.9 million square feet of the firm's owned property is classified as industrial space, also suitable for a variety of uses. The remaining 4.9 million square feet consists of low-rise office space. The company also manages approximately 1.4 million rentable square feet on behalf of Public Storage and its affiliated entities. PSB targets properties in select sub-markets located in high-growth areas across the U.S. with above average education and personal income levels, access to critical infrastructure and with universities and major transportation arteries in close proximity. In 2010, PSB acquired a total of five business parks (Westpark Business Campus, Tysons Corporate Center, Parklawn Business Park, Austin Flex Portfolio and Shady Grove Executive Center) located in Maryland, Virginia and Texas, comprising 2.3 million square feet, for roughly $301.7 million.

PSB offers its employees benefits including a 401(k) plan; life and disability insurance; paid vacation; and comprehensive medical and dental coverage.

FINANCIALS: Sales and profits are in thousands of dollars—add 000 to get the full amount. 2010 Note: Financial information for 2010 was not available for all companies at press time.

2010 Sales: $279,089	2010 Profits: $102,022	**U.S. Stock Ticker: PSB**
2009 Sales: $271,655	2009 Profits: $77,178	**Int'l Ticker:** Int'l Exchange:
2008 Sales: $281,843	2008 Profits: $70,044	Employees: 142
2007 Sales: $269,298	2007 Profits: $68,666	Fiscal Year Ends: 12/31
2006 Sales: $242,839	2006 Profits: $64,580	Parent Company:

SALARIES/BENEFITS:

Pension Plan:	ESOP Stock Plan:	Profit Sharing:	Top Exec. Salary: $425,790	Bonus: $340,550
Savings Plan: Y	Stock Purch. Plan:		Second Exec. Salary: $300,790	Bonus: $223,050

OTHER THOUGHTS:

Apparent Women Officers or Directors: 5
Hot Spot for Advancement for Women/Minorities: Y

LOCATIONS: ("Y" = Yes)

West:	Southwest:	Midwest:	Southeast:	Northeast:	International:
Y	Y		Y	Y	

PUBLIC STORAGE INC

www.publicstorage.com

Industry Group Code: 531120 Ranks within this company's industry group: Sales: 9   Profits: 6

Properties:		Financial Services:		Construction/Development:		Investments:		Specialty Services:		Brokerage:	
Apartments:		Mortgages:		Commercial Construction:		REIT:	Y	Property Management:		Commercial Sales:	
Malls/Shopping:		Title Insurance:		Residential Construction:				Online Services:	Y	Residential Sales:	
Offices:		Property Insurance:	Y	Land Development:				Software/IT:		Specialty:	
Hotels/Motels:				Support Services:				Consulting:			
Industrial/Warehouses:	Y			Design/Engineering:							
Other:	Y										

TYPES OF BUSINESS:

Real Estate Investment Trust
Self-Storage Facilities
Commercial Properties
Online Storage Reservations
Transportation Equipment

BRANDS/DIVISIONS/AFFILIATES:

PS Business Parks, Inc.
Shurgard Europe
PS Partners, Ltd.

CONTACTS: *Note: Officers with more than one job title may be intentionally listed here more than once.*

Ronald L. Havner, Jr., CEO
Ronald L. Havner, Jr., Pres./Vice Chmn.
John Reyes, CFO/Sr. VP
Candace N. Krol, Sr. VP-Human Resources
Steven M. Glick, Chief Legal Officer/Sr. VP
David F. Doll, Pres., Real Estate Group
B. Wayne Hughes, Chmn.

Phone: 818-244-8080	Fax: 818-244-9530
Toll-Free: 800-688-8057	
Address: 701 Western Ave., Glendale, CA 91201 US	

GROWTH PLANS/SPECIAL FEATURES:

Public Storage, Inc. is a fully integrated, self-administered and self-managed equity real estate investment trust (REIT) that acquires, develops, owns and operates self-storage facilities primarily used for month-to-month personal and business use. It is one of the largest owners and operators of self-storage space in the U.S. The company operates in three segments: Domestic Self-Storage, Europe Self-Storage and Commercial. The Domestic Self-Storage segment, accounting for 92% of the firm's revenues, consists of the firm's direct and indirect equity interests in 2,048 self-storage facilities, containing approximately 130 million square feet of net rentable space, in 38 states under the Public Storage brand name. The self-storage facilities consist of three to seven buildings containing 350-750 storage spaces, most of which have 25-400 square feet and an interior height of eight to 12 feet. The Europe Self-Storage segment comprises the firm's 49% interest in Shurgard Europe, which owns 188 storage facilities in seven countries in Europe, with 10 million square feet of net rentable space. This segment also manages one facility in the U.K. that is wholly owned by Public Storage. Finally, the Commercial segment includes the company's direct and indirect equity interests in 24 million net rentable square feet of commercial space in 11 states, partially held through its 41% interest in PS Business Parks, Inc., a publicly traded REIT. In April 2010, Public Storage agreed to acquire 30 self-storage facilities in the Los Angeles, California and Chicago, Illinois areas for $189 million.

Employees are offered medical, dental and vision insurance; short- and long-term disability coverage; life insurance; medical care and dependent care spending plans; an employee assistance program; a 401(k) plan; and employee discounts.

FINANCIALS: Sales and profits are in thousands of dollars—add 000 to get the full amount. 2010 Note: Financial information for 2010 was not available for all companies at press time.

2010 Sales: $1,513,324	2010 Profits: $696,114	**U.S. Stock Ticker: PSA**
2009 Sales: $1,487,295	2009 Profits: $790,456	**Int'l Ticker:** Int'l Exchange:
2008 Sales: $1,723,593	2008 Profits: $935,176	Employees: 4,900
2007 Sales: $1,787,202	2007 Profits: $457,535	Fiscal Year Ends: 12/31
2006 Sales: $1,379,066	2006 Profits: $314,026	Parent Company:

SALARIES/BENEFITS:

Pension Plan:	ESOP Stock Plan:	Profit Sharing:	Top Exec. Salary: $1,000,000	Bonus: $1,000,000
Savings Plan: Y	Stock Purch. Plan:		Second Exec. Salary: $600,000	Bonus: $600,000

OTHER THOUGHTS:

Apparent Women Officers or Directors: 2
Hot Spot for Advancement for Women/Minorities:

LOCATIONS: ("Y" = Yes)

West:	Southwest:	Midwest:	Southeast:	Northeast:	International:
Y	Y	Y	Y	Y	

PULTEGROUP INC

www.pulte.com

Industry Group Code: 2361 Ranks within this company's industry group: Sales: 2   Profits: 17

Properties:	Financial Services:		Construction/Development:		Investments:	Specialty Services:	Brokerage:
Apartments:	Mortgages:	Y	Commercial Construction:		REIT:	Property Management:	Commercial Sales:
Malls/Shopping:	Title Insurance:		Residential Construction:	Y		Online Services:	Residential Sales:
Offices:	Property Insurance:		Land Development:	Y		Software/IT:	Specialty:
Hotels/Motels:			Support Services:			Consulting:	
Industrial/Warehouses:			Design/Engineering:				
Other:							

TYPES OF BUSINESS:

Residential Construction
Financial Services
Mortgages
Land Development
Adult Communities

BRANDS/DIVISIONS/AFFILIATES:

DiVosta Homes
Del Webb Corp
Centex Corp
Pulte Mortgage LLC

CONTACTS: *Note: Officers with more than one job title may be intentionally listed here more than once.*

Richard J. Dugas, Jr., CEO
Richard J. Dugas, Jr., Pres.
Roger A. Cregg, CFO/Exec. VP
Deborah W. Meyer, Chief Mktg. Officer/Sr. VP
James R. Ellinghausen, Exec. VP-Human Resources
Jerry R. Batt, CIO/VP
Janice M. Jones, VP-Merch.
Steven M. Cook, General Counsel/Sr. VP/Sec.
Anthony C. Koblinski, VP-Homebuilder Oper.
Steve Schlageter, VP-Strategic Planning
James P. Zeumer, VP-Corp. Comm.
James P. Zeumer, VP-Investor Rel.
Timothy M. Stewart, VP-Finance
Michael J. Schweninger, Controller/VP
Bruce E. Robinson, Treas./VP
Richard J. Dugas, Jr., Chmn.

Phone: 248-647-2750	Fax: 248-433-4598
Toll-Free: 866-785-8325	
Address: 100 Bloomfield Hills Pkwy., Ste. 300, Bloomfield Hills, MI 48304 US	

GROWTH PLANS/SPECIAL FEATURES:

PulteGroup, Inc. is a holding company with subsidiaries in the homebuilding and financial services industries. These subsidiaries include Del Webb Corp.; Pulte Home Corp.; DiVosta Homes; Centex Corp.; and Pulte Mortgage LLC. The firm's business operation consists of two units: homebuilding and financial services. Pulte's core homebuilding business is engaged in the acquisition and development of land, primarily for residential purposes within the U.S. It facilitates the construction of housing on such land targeted for first-time, first and second move-up and active adult home buyers. Pulte builds a wide variety of homes including detached units, townhouses, condominium apartments and duplexes, with varying prices, models, options and lot sizes. Pulte's homebuilding business operates in 67 markets spanning 29 states and the District of Columbia, offering homes in about 800 communities with the average unit selling price of $259,000. Pulte's Homebuilding segments consist of the Atlantic Coast, including Connecticut, Delaware, Georgia, Maryland, Massachusetts, New Jersey, New York, North Carolina, Pennsylvania, Rhode Island, South Carolina, Tennessee and Virginia; the Gulf Coast, including Florida and Texas; the Central zone, including Arizona, Colorado, Illinois, Indiana, Missouri, Michigan, Minnesota, New Mexico and Ohio; and the West Coast, including California, Hawaii, Nevada, Oregon and Washington. The firm's strategy is based on extensive market research that reveals well-defined buying profiles, job demographics and lifestyle choices. Pulte's financial services segment consists principally of mortgage operations conducted through Pulte Mortgage and its subsidiaries. Through its Del Webb brand, the company builds active adult communities.

Employees are offered medical, dental and vision insurance; a 401(k) plan; life and AD&D insurance; business travel accident insurance; short- and long-term disability; a tuition reimbursement plan; an employee assistance program; and time off for volunteering.

FINANCIALS: Sales and profits are in thousands of dollars—add 000 to get the full amount. 2010 Note: Financial information for 2010 was not available for all companies at press time.

2010 Sales: $4,447,627	2010 Profits: $-1,096,729	**U.S. Stock Ticker: PHM**
2009 Sales: $3,966,589	2009 Profits: $-1,182,567	**Int'l Ticker:** Int'l Exchange:
2008 Sales: $6,112,038	2008 Profits: $-1,473,113	Employees: 4,363
2007 Sales: $9,121,730	2007 Profits: $-2,255,755	Fiscal Year Ends: 12/31
2006 Sales: $14,075,248	2006 Profits: $687,471	Parent Company:

SALARIES/BENEFITS:

Pension Plan:	ESOP Stock Plan:	Profit Sharing:	Top Exec. Salary: $1,000,000	Bonus: $500,000
Savings Plan: Y	Stock Purch. Plan:		Second Exec. Salary: $1,000,000	Bonus: $1,799,933

OTHER THOUGHTS:

Apparent Women Officers or Directors: 4
Hot Spot for Advancement for Women/Minorities: Y

LOCATIONS: ("Y" = Yes)

West:	Southwest:	Midwest:	Southeast:	Northeast:	International:
Y	Y	Y	Y	Y	

QMH UK LTD

www.qmh-hotels.com

Industry Group Code: 721110 Ranks within this company's industry group: Sales: Profits:

Properties:		Financial Services:	Construction/Development:	Investments:	Specialty Services:	Brokerage:
Apartments:		Mortgages:	Commercial Construction:	REIT:	Property Management:	Commercial Sales:
Malls/Shopping:		Title Insurance:	Residential Construction:		Online Services:	Residential Sales:
Offices:		Property Insurance:	Land Development:		Software/IT:	Specialty:
Hotels/Motels:	Y		Support Services:		Consulting:	
Industrial/Warehouses:			Design/Engineering:			
Other:	Y					

TYPES OF BUSINESS:

Hotels
Fitness Clubs
Event Planning Services

BRANDS/DIVISIONS/AFFILIATES:

Holiday Inn
Crowne Plaza
Best Western
Club Moativation
Queens Moat Houses plc

CONTACTS: *Note: Officers with more than one job title may be intentionally listed here more than once.*

Richard Moore, Managing Dir.

Phone: 44-1708-730-522	Fax: 44-1708-762-691
Toll-Free:	
Address: Queens Ct., 9-17 Eastern Rd., Romford, Essex RM1 3NG UK	

GROWTH PLANS/SPECIAL FEATURES:

QMH UK Ltd., formerly Queens Moat Houses plc, owns and operates hotels throughout the U.K. In total, it has 18 hotels: 12 Holiday Inns, three Crowne Plaza hotels and three Best Western hotels. QMH also runs 15 Club Moativation health and fitness clubs. The clubs are located on hotel property but make memberships available to anyone, not just hotel guests. All of QMH's hotels offer conference suites that can accommodate groups ranging from 40-800 delegates, as well as providing wireless Internet, a dedicated meeting host and extra rooms for smaller meetings. QMH hotels are all three- or four-star standard. Almost all of the firm's hotels have been awarded Civil Marriage Licenses, allowing couples to utilize the hotel as a dedicated venue for both wedding ceremonies and receptions. Individual hotels offer wedding planning services including table plans, flower arrangements, photographers, catering and entertainment booking. They also provide discounted room rates for wedding guests. The private company is owned by a group of investors that includes Goldman Sachs; Regina Investments Sarl.; and Whitehall 2001 Funds, a real estate private equity fund sponsored and managed by Goldman Sachs affiliates.

FINANCIALS: Sales and profits are in thousands of dollars—add 000 to get the full amount. 2010 Note: Financial information for 2010 was not available for all companies at press time.

2010 Sales: $	2010 Profits: $	U.S. Stock Ticker: Private
2009 Sales: $	2009 Profits: $	Int'l Ticker: Int'l Exchange:
2008 Sales: $	2008 Profits: $	Employees:
2007 Sales: $	2007 Profits: $	Fiscal Year Ends: 12/31
2006 Sales: $	2006 Profits: $	Parent Company:

SALARIES/BENEFITS:

Pension Plan:	ESOP Stock Plan:	Profit Sharing:	Top Exec. Salary: $	Bonus: $
Savings Plan:	Stock Purch. Plan:		Second Exec. Salary: $	Bonus: $

OTHER THOUGHTS:

Apparent Women Officers or Directors: 1
Hot Spot for Advancement for Women/Minorities:

LOCATIONS: ("Y" = Yes)

West:	Southwest:	Midwest:	Southeast:	Northeast:	International:
					Y

RADIAN GROUP INC

www.radian.biz

Industry Group Code: 524126 Ranks within this company's industry group: Sales: 2   Profits: 2

Properties:	Financial Services:		Construction/Development:	Investments:	Specialty Services:		Brokerage:
Apartments:	Mortgages:	Y	Commercial Construction:	REIT:	Property Management:		Commercial Sales:
Malls/Shopping:	Title Insurance:		Residential Construction:		Online Services:	Y	Residential Sales:
Offices:	Property Insurance:		Land Development:		Software/IT:		Specialty:
Hotels/Motels:			Support Services:		Consulting:		
Industrial/Warehouses:			Design/Engineering:				
Other:							

TYPES OF BUSINESS:

Insurance-Financial Guaranty
Mortgage Insurance & Services
Insurance-Related Services
Financial Services
Consumer Asset Services

BRANDS/DIVISIONS/AFFILIATES:

Radian Guaranty, Inc.
Radian Insurance, Inc.
Amerin Guaranty Corp.
Radian Asset Assurance
RAAL
Sherman Financial Services Group LLC
C-BASS

CONTACTS: *Note: Officers with more than one job title may be intentionally listed here more than once.*

S. A. Ibrahim, CEO
C. Robert Quint, CFO/Exec. VP
Richard A. Gillespie, Sr. VP-Mktg.
Lawrence DelGatto, CIO/Exec. VP
Rick Altman, Chief Admin. Officer/Exec. VP
Ted Hoffman, General Counsel/Corp. Sec.
Richard A. Gillespie, Sr. VP-Corp. Comm.
Terri Williams-Perry, Investor Rel.
Cathy Jackson, Controller/Sr. VP
Teresa Bryce, Pres., Radian Guaranty, Inc.
David J. Beidler, Pres., Radian Asset Assurance, Inc.
Robert H. Griffith, COO/Exec. VP-Radian Guaranty, Inc.
H. Scott Theobald, Chief Risk Officer/Exec. VP-Radian Guaranty, Inc.
Herbert Wender, Chmn.

Phone: 215-231-1000	Fax:
Toll-Free: 800-523-1988	
Address: 1601 Market St., Philadelphia, PA 19103 US	

GROWTH PLANS/SPECIAL FEATURES:

Radian Group, Inc. is a global credit enhancement company focused on domestic residential mortgage insurance. The firm operates in three segments: mortgage insurance, financial guaranty and financial services. The mortgage insurance segment provides credit protection for mortgage lenders and other financial services companies on residential mortgage assets, primarily through traditional mortgage insurance. The company provides these products and services through wholly-owned subsidiaries Radian Guaranty, Inc.; Radian Insurance, Inc.; and Amerin Guaranty Corp. The financial guaranty segment insures and reinsures municipal bonds, structured finance transactions and other credit-based risks, and provides synthetic credit protection on various asset classes through credit default swaps. Major industries served by this segment include telecommunications, financial solutions, insurance, retail and utilities. This segment operates primarily through Radian Asset Assurance, a wholly-owned subsidiary of Radian Guaranty, and Radian Asset Assurance's subsidiary RAAL, located in the U.K. The financial services segment consists mainly of the company's 28.7% ownership stake in Sherman Financial Services Group LLC, a consumer asset and servicing firm specializing in credit card and bankruptcy-plan consumer assets. This segment also includes the firm's 46% interest in Credit-Based Asset Servicing and Securitization LLC (C-BASS), a mortgage investment company whose operations are in run-off.

The company offers its employees medical, dental and vision insurance; a 401(k) plan; an employee stock purchase plan; flexible spending accounts; life insurance; a pension plan; short- and long-term disability insurance; tuition reimbursement; charitable matching; and an employee assistance program.

FINANCIALS: Sales and profits are in thousands of dollars—add 000 to get the full amount. 2010 Note: Financial information for 2010 was not available for all companies at press time.

2010 Sales: $417,500	2010 Profits: $-1,805,900	**U.S. Stock Ticker:** RDN
2009 Sales: $1,313,378	2009 Profits: $-147,879	**Int'l Ticker:** Int'l Exchange:
2008 Sales: $1,808,036	2008 Profits: $-410,579	Employees: 767
2007 Sales: $201,051	2007 Profits: $-1,290,299	Fiscal Year Ends: 12/31
2006 Sales: $1,327,946	2006 Profits: $582,172	Parent Company:

SALARIES/BENEFITS:

Pension Plan: Y	ESOP Stock Plan:	Profit Sharing:	Top Exec. Salary: $800,000	Bonus: $630,000
Savings Plan: Y	Stock Purch. Plan: Y		Second Exec. Salary: $400,000	Bonus: $225,000

OTHER THOUGHTS:

Apparent Women Officers or Directors: 3
Hot Spot for Advancement for Women/Minorities: Y

LOCATIONS: ("Y" = Yes)

West:	Southwest:	Midwest:	Southeast:	Northeast:	International:
Y	Y	Y	Y	Y	Y

RAILWORKS CORP

www.railworks.com

Industry Group Code: 237 Ranks within this company's industry group: Sales: Profits:

Properties:	Financial Services:	Construction/Development:		Investments:	Specialty Services:	Brokerage:
Apartments:	Mortgages:	Commercial Construction:	Y	REIT:	Property Management:	Commercial Sales:
Malls/Shopping:	Title Insurance:	Residential Construction:			Online Services:	Residential Sales:
Offices:	Property Insurance:	Land Development:			Software/IT:	Specialty:
Hotels/Motels:		Support Services:	Y		Consulting:	
Industrial/Warehouses:		Design/Engineering:	Y			
Other:						

TYPES OF BUSINESS:

Railroad Construction & Maintenance
Rail Technologies
Electrical & Mechanical Installations
Communications Technologies

BRANDS/DIVISIONS/AFFILIATES:

Railworks Transit, Inc.
Railworks Track Systems, Inc.
RailWorks Signals & Communications, Inc
HSQ Technology
L.K. Comstock & Company, Inc.
PNR Railworks, Inc.
NY Transit
L.K. Comstock National Transit

CONTACTS: *Note: Officers with more than one job title may be intentionally listed here more than once.*

Jeffrey M. Levy, CEO
Jeffrey M. Levy, Pres.
Veronica Lubatkin, CFO/Exec. VP
Harry Z. Glantz, VP-Human Resources
Steven G. Milewicz, General Counsel/Sec./Exec. VP
James R. Hansen, VP-Bus. Dev. Track
Gene Cellini, Sr. VP-Tax
John August, Exec. VP
Michael Holt, Pres., RailWorks Transit, Inc.
Ben D'Alessandro, Pres., L.K. Comstock & Co
Scott Brace, Exec. VP-RailWorks Track Systems

Phone: 212-502-7900	Fax: 212-502-1865
Toll-Free:	
Address: 5 Penn Plz., New York, NY 10001 US	

GROWTH PLANS/SPECIAL FEATURES:

RailWorks Corp. and its network of affiliated companies provide track and transit systems construction and maintenance services for the rail and rail-transit industries in the U.S. and Canada. The firm is owned by Wind Point Partners, a private equity investment firm. The company's business serves a range of railroads, public transit authorities and commuter railroads, as well as private industries. The firm divides its operations into two business units: transit systems and tracks. In total, RailWorks has 11 subsidiaries: HSQ Technology; L.K. Comstock & Company, Inc.; PNR RailWorks, Inc.; PNR Leasing, Ltd.; PNR RailWorks S&C Division; RailWorks Signals & Communications, Inc.; RailWorks Systems, Inc.; RailWorks Track Systems, Inc.; RailWorks Track Systems-Texas, Inc.; NY Transit; and RailWorks Transit, Inc. The transit systems segment handles automatic train controls and systems; traction power systems, including overhead catenary; transit facilities, including general and mechanical contracting; communication systems, including systems that incorporate fiber/Sonet, radio/microwave, cellular and WiFi technology; Supervisory Control and Data Acquisition System (SCADA) and system integration; and rain construction, maintenance and rehabilitation. In addition to these services, the transit systems unit provides design support, construction engineering and installation, testing, start-up and maintenance services for heavy rail, light rail and automated people mover facilities. The track segment designs, builds, manages and supplies railways and railway construction, maintenance and rehabilitation projects. This business involves, in addition to rail and tie installation techniques, the development of signals and crossings, production involving steel and tie gangs, maintenance-of-way services, communication systems, scheduled maintenance work and emergency repairs, which include derailment response.

RailWorks offers its employees medical and dental insurance and a 401(k) plan.

FINANCIALS: Sales and profits are in thousands of dollars—add 000 to get the full amount. 2010 Note: Financial information for 2010 was not available for all companies at press time.

2010 Sales: $	2010 Profits: $	**U.S. Stock Ticker: Private**
2009 Sales: $	2009 Profits: $	**Int'l Ticker:** Int'l Exchange:
2008 Sales: $	2008 Profits: $	Employees:
2007 Sales: $	2007 Profits: $	Fiscal Year Ends: 12/31
2006 Sales: $	2006 Profits: $	Parent Company:

SALARIES/BENEFITS:

Pension Plan:	ESOP Stock Plan:	Profit Sharing:	Top Exec. Salary: $	Bonus: $
Savings Plan: Y	Stock Purch. Plan:		Second Exec. Salary: $	Bonus: $

OTHER THOUGHTS:

Apparent Women Officers or Directors: 2
Hot Spot for Advancement for Women/Minorities:

LOCATIONS: ("Y" = Yes)

West:	Southwest:	Midwest:	Southeast:	Northeast:	International:
Y	Y	Y	Y	Y	Y

RAMADA WORLDWIDE INC

www.ramada.com

Industry Group Code: 721110 Ranks within this company's industry group: Sales: Profits:

Properties:	Financial Services:	Construction/Development:	Investments:	Specialty Services:	Brokerage:
Apartments:	Mortgages:	Commercial Construction:	REIT:	Property Management:	Commercial Sales:
Malls/Shopping:	Title Insurance:	Residential Construction:		Online Services:	Residential Sales:
Offices:	Property Insurance:	Land Development:		Software/IT:	Specialty:
Hotels/Motels: Y		Support Services:		Consulting:	
Industrial/Warehouses:		Design/Engineering:			
Other:					

TYPES OF BUSINESS:
Hotels & Motels

BRANDS/DIVISIONS/AFFILIATES:
Wyndham Worldwide
Ramada Inn
Ramada Plaza Hotel
Ramada Limited
Ramada Hotel & Suites
Ramada Resort
Ramada Hotel & Resorts
Ramada Encore

CONTACTS: *Note: Officers with more than one job title may be intentionally listed here more than once.*
Keith J. Pierce, Pres.
Mark F. Young, Sr. VP-Brand

Phone: 973-428-9700	**Fax:** 605-229-8938
Toll-Free: 800-272-6232	
Address: 1 Sylvan Way, Parsippany, NJ 07054 US	

GROWTH PLANS/SPECIAL FEATURES:
Ramada Worldwide, Inc., a subsidiary of Wyndham Worldwide, is a leading franchisor of hotel and motel properties. The company owns approximately 900 Ramada Limited, Ramada Inn and Ramada Plaza Hotel properties throughout the U.S. and in 45 other countries, and offers discounts for seniors, groups, government employees and AAA and AARP members. The franchise also participates in the Wyndham Rewards program, in which guests can earn rewards points, gift cards or resort vacations by staying in participating hotels. The company's core brand, Ramada, offers room service, bell service, on-site restaurants and cocktail lounges, and full-service meeting facilities. Ramada Limited and Ramada Encore properties offer less expensive rates and limited amenities. Ramada Plaza Hotel properties offer on-site restaurants, lounges and banquet rooms, concierge services and fitness centers. Ramada Resort properties, franchised both domestically and internationally, are designed for leisure travelers on extended stays and offer playgrounds, pools, spas, fitness centers, dining room services and car rental facilities. The franchise's resort properties, principally located outside the U.S. and Canada, include Ramada Hotel & Resorts, which feature oversized rooms, pools, saunas, golf and tennis facilities, restaurants and lounges; and Ramada Hotel & Suites, offering luxury suites, restaurants and meeting and banquet facilities. In December 2010, the firm opened the Ramada Plaza Shenzhen North in Shenzhen, China. In January 2011, the company opened a Ramada Encore in Doha, Qatar.

Wyndham Worldwide and its subsidiaries offer employees a choice of medical, dental and vision plans, flexible spending accounts, adoption reimbursement, business travel accident insurance, an educational assistance program and a 401(k) plan.

FINANCIALS: Sales and profits are in thousands of dollars—add 000 to get the full amount. 2010 Note: Financial information for 2010 was not available for all companies at press time.

2010 Sales: $	2010 Profits: $	**U.S. Stock Ticker: Subsidiary**
2009 Sales: $	2009 Profits: $	**Int'l Ticker:** Int'l Exchange:
2008 Sales: $	2008 Profits: $	Employees:
2007 Sales: $	2007 Profits: $	Fiscal Year Ends: 12/31
2006 Sales: $	2006 Profits: $	Parent Company: WYNDHAM WORLDWIDE

SALARIES/BENEFITS:

Pension Plan:	ESOP Stock Plan:	Profit Sharing:	Top Exec. Salary: $	Bonus: $
Savings Plan: Y	Stock Purch. Plan:		Second Exec. Salary: $	Bonus: $

OTHER THOUGHTS:
Apparent Women Officers or Directors:
Hot Spot for Advancement for Women/Minorities:

LOCATIONS: ("Y" = Yes)

West:	Southwest:	Midwest:	Southeast:	Northeast:	International:
Y	Y	Y	Y	Y	Y

RE/MAX INTERNATIONAL INC

www.remax.com

Industry Group Code: 531210 Ranks within this company's industry group: Sales: Profits:

Properties:	Financial Services:	Construction/Development:	Investments:	Specialty Services:		Brokerage:	
Apartments:	Mortgages:	Commercial Construction:	REIT:	Property Management:		Commercial Sales:	Y
Malls/Shopping:	Title Insurance:	Residential Construction:		Online Services:	Y	Residential Sales:	Y
Offices:	Property Insurance:	Land Development:		Software/IT:		Specialty:	Y
Hotels/Motels:		Support Services:		Consulting:			
Industrial/Warehouses:		Design/Engineering:					
Other:							

TYPES OF BUSINESS:

Real Estate Brokerage
Moving & Relocation Services
Online Database

BRANDS/DIVISIONS/AFFILIATES:

RE/MAX Collection
RE/MAX Commercial Services
E-Loan
CCIMnet

CONTACTS: *Note: Officers with more than one job title may be intentionally listed here more than once.*

Margaret Kelly, CEO
David M.K. Metzger, COO/Exec. VP
Vinnie Tracey, Pres.
David M.K. Metzger, CFO
Mike Reagan, Sr. VP-Brand Mktg.
Pat Lawrence, Sr. VP-Human Resources
Anthony Lopez, VP-IT
Kristi Graning, Sr. VP-Emerging Tech.
Geoff Lewis, Chief Legal Officer/Sr. VP
Gerald Steen, VP-Commercial Bus. Dev.
Kristi Graning, Sr. VP-eBusiness
Shaun White, VP-Corp. Comm.
Kelly Hickey, Controller/VP
Ward Morrison, VP-U.S. Regional Dev.
Tom Kramig, VP-Multi-Media & Education
Abby Lee, VP-Brand Mktg. & Sponsorship
Gary Weil, Asst. General Counsel
Dave Liniger, Chmn.
Larry Oberly, VP-Int'l Dev.

Phone: 303-770-5531	**Fax:** 303-796-3599
Toll-Free:	
Address: 5075 S. Syracuse St., Denver, CO 80237-2712 US	

GROWTH PLANS/SPECIAL FEATURES:

RE/MAX International, Inc. is a real estate brokerage company. Its focus is to aid clients in buying, selling, financing and moving into properties. The firm's network is divided into over 70 regions. These regions can vary in size from a metropolitan area to an entire country. Residential sales make up the majority of the firm's revenue, but it also operates a commercial brokerage division. The firm has a franchised network of approximately 100,000 sales associates operating in more than 65 countries, including Canada, Australia, the U.K. and Mexico, as well as countries in Central and South America, the Caribbean Islands, Europe, the Middle East and southern Africa. The company's commercial properties division gives customers access to the CCIMnet database of commercial properties, which allows clients to find commercial office space, as well as industrial locations, shopping centers, retail-commercial, multi-family, vacant land, hospitality and farm/ranch properties. RE/MAX's commercial associates aid clients in the selling, buying or leasing of their property interests. Through a partnership with E-Loan, the Lending Center on RE/MAX's web site provides customers with access to mortgage information, while realtor.com allows customers to quickly search through its property listings. The RE/MAX Collection program focuses on exclusive properties. Many of the agents that work within this program are Certified Luxury Home Marketing Specialists. All RE/MAX Collection sales associates have additional training concerning the luxury real estate market. RE/MAX uses a hot air balloon as its corporate logo, and it owns it owns the world's largest balloon fleet with over 120 balloons.

FINANCIALS: Sales and profits are in thousands of dollars—add 000 to get the full amount. 2010 Note: Financial information for 2010 was not available for all companies at press time.

2010 Sales: $	2010 Profits: $	**U.S. Stock Ticker: Private**
2009 Sales: $	2009 Profits: $	**Int'l Ticker:** Int'l Exchange:
2008 Sales: $	2008 Profits: $	Employees:
2007 Sales: $	2007 Profits: $	Fiscal Year Ends: 12/31
2006 Sales: $	2006 Profits: $	Parent Company:

SALARIES/BENEFITS:

Pension Plan:	ESOP Stock Plan:	Profit Sharing:	Top Exec. Salary: $	Bonus: $
Savings Plan:	Stock Purch. Plan:		Second Exec. Salary: $	Bonus: $

OTHER THOUGHTS:

Apparent Women Officers or Directors: 8
Hot Spot for Advancement for Women/Minorities: Y

LOCATIONS: ("Y" = Yes)

West:	Southwest:	Midwest:	Southeast:	Northeast:	International:
Y	Y	Y	Y	Y	Y

REALOGY CORPORATION

www.realogy.com

Industry Group Code: 5311 Ranks within this company's industry group: Sales: 6   Profits: 29

Properties:	Financial Services:		Construction/Development:	Investments:	Specialty Services:	Brokerage:	
Apartments:	Mortgages:	Y	Commercial Construction:	REIT:	Property Management:	Commercial Sales:	Y
Malls/Shopping:	Title Insurance:	Y	Residential Construction:		Online Services:	Residential Sales:	Y
Offices:	Property Insurance:		Land Development:		Software/IT:	Specialty:	
Hotels/Motels:			Support Services:		Consulting:		
Industrial/Warehouses:			Design/Engineering:				
Other:							

TYPES OF BUSINESS:

Real Estate Services
Real Estate Brokerages
Settlement Services
Property Financing Services

BRANDS/DIVISIONS/AFFILIATES:

Apollo Management LP
NRT LLC
Realogy Franchise Group
Better Homes and Gardens Real Estate
Century 21 Real Estate Corp
Coldwell Banker Real Estate LLC
ERA
Sotheby's International Realty

CONTACTS: *Note: Officers with more than one job title may be intentionally listed here more than once.*

Richard A. Smith, CEO
Richard A. Smith, Pres.
Anthony E. Hull, CFO/Exec. VP/Treas.
Dave Weaving, Chief Admin. Officer/Exec. VP
Marilyn Wasser, General Counsel/Corp. Sec./Exec. VP
Dea Benson, Chief Acct. Officer/Sr. VP/Controller
Kevin J. Kelleher, CEO/Pres., Cartus Corp.
Alexander E. Perriello III, CEO/Pres., Realogy Franchise Group
Bruce Zipf, CEO/Pres., NRT LLC
Don Casey, CEO/Pres., Title Resource Group LLC
Richard A. Smith, Chmn.

Phone: 973-407-2000	Fax: 973-407-7118
Toll-Free:	
Address: 1 Campus Dr., Parsippany, NJ 07054 US	

GROWTH PLANS/SPECIAL FEATURES:

Realogy Corporation, a subsidiary of Apollo Management, is an integrated provider of real estate and relocation services throughout the U.S., as well as internationally. More specifically, the firm offers a variety of services including real estate franchising, brokerage, relocation and title services. Through the Realogy Franchise Group, the firm operates six brands in the real estate industry: Better Homes and Gardens Real Estate; Century 21 Real Estate LLC; Coldwell Banker; Coldwell Banker Commercial; ERA; and Sotheby's International Realty. Better Homes and Gardens Real Estate is building a new international residential real estate franchise company. Century 21 Real Estate is a residential real estate brokerage franchise with locations in 72 countries around the world. Coldwell Banker is a real estate brokerage franchisor. Coldwell Banker Commercial is a brokerage firm that concentrates on the sale of commercial properties. ERA is a residential brokerage franchisor with locations in over 40 countries. Sotheby's International Realty is a real estate franchise that focuses on luxury properties around the world. Additional Realogy business units include NRT LLC, a leading owner and operator of residential real estate brokerages in over 35 major metropolitan markets of the U.S.; Cartus Corporation, a leading global relocation service provider; and Title Resource Group LLC, a provider of title and settlement services with approximately 375 offices throughout the U.S. Recently, Realogy made a minority equity investment in Century 21 China Real Estate, the master franchisor for its Century 21 brand in China. In March 2011, the company's subsidiary Sotheby's International Realty Affiliates, LLC obtained the rights to expand its business into Australia.

Employees of the firm are offered medical, dental and vision coverage; a 401(k) plan; business travel accident insurance; and flexible spending accounts for dependent care and health care.

FINANCIALS: Sales and profits are in thousands of dollars—add 000 to get the full amount. 2010 Note: Financial information for 2010 was not available for all companies at press time.

2010 Sales: $4,090,000	2010 Profits: $-99,000	U.S. Stock Ticker: Private
2009 Sales: $3,932,000	2009 Profits: $-262,000	Int'l Ticker: Int'l Exchange:
2008 Sales: $4,725,000	2008 Profits: $-1,912,000	Employees: 10,500
2007 Sales: $	2007 Profits: $	Fiscal Year Ends: 12/31
2006 Sales: $	2006 Profits: $	Parent Company: APOLLO MANAGEMENT LP

SALARIES/BENEFITS:

Pension Plan:	ESOP Stock Plan:	Profit Sharing:	Top Exec. Salary: $1,000,000	Bonus: $
Savings Plan: Y	Stock Purch. Plan:		Second Exec. Salary: $525,000	Bonus: $262,500

OTHER THOUGHTS:

Apparent Women Officers or Directors: 4
Hot Spot for Advancement for Women/Minorities: Y

LOCATIONS: ("Y" = Yes)

West:	Southwest:	Midwest:	Southeast:	Northeast:	International:
Y	Y	Y	Y	Y	Y

REALPAGE INC

www.realpage.com

Industry Group Code: 511210H Ranks within this company's industry group: Sales: 1   Profits: 1

Properties:	Financial Services:	Construction/Development:	Investments:	Specialty Services:		Brokerage:
Apartments:	Mortgages:	Commercial Construction:	REIT:	Property Management:		Commercial Sales:
Malls/Shopping:	Title Insurance:	Residential Construction:		Online Services:		Residential Sales:
Offices:	Property Insurance:	Land Development:		Software/IT:	Y	Specialty:
Hotels/Motels:		Support Services:		Consulting:		
Industrial/Warehouses:		Design/Engineering:				
Other:						

TYPES OF BUSINESS:

Online Real Estate Management Services
Customer Service Centers

BRANDS/DIVISIONS/AFFILIATES:

OneSite
CrossFire
YieldStar
MPF Market
Velocity
LeasingDesk
OpsTechnology
Domin-8 Enterprise Solutions LLC

CONTACTS: *Note: Officers with more than one job title may be intentionally listed here more than once.*

Steven Winn, CEO
Jason Lindwall, COO
Dirk Wakeham, Pres.
Timothy J. Barker, CFO
Mark Case, Chief Sales Officer
Jeffrey Roper, Principal Scientist
Norman Denler, CTO
Dean Schmidt, Chief Prod. Officer
Margot Lebenberg, Chief Legal Officer/Exec. VP/Sec.
Timothy J. Barker, Treas.
Andrea Massey, Sr. VP-Mktg.
David Carner, Pres., LeasingDesk
Leslie Turner, Pres., OneSite
William Chaney, Pres., Velocity
Steven Winn, Chmn.

Phone: 972-820-3000	**Fax:** 972-820-3036
Toll-Free: 877-325-7243	
Address: 4000 International Pkwy., Carrollton, TX 75007 US	

GROWTH PLANS/SPECIAL FEATURES:

RealPage, Inc. is a provider of on-demand software services for the rental housing industry. The company's products enable owners and managers of rental property to manage their marketing, pricing, screening, leasing, accounting, purchasing and other property operations. Its systems manage conventional, student, military, senior, commercial, urban and rural housing, as well as tax credit-compliant housing. The firm's primary products include OneSite, CrossFire, MPF Research, YieldStar, Velocity, LeasingDesk and OpsTechnology. OneSite is a centralized product suite that enables users to track leasing, accounting, purchasing and facilities management data. CrossFire provides call center services with a trained professional staff to ensure prompt and informed inquiries about properties. MPF Research specializes in apartment market research, statistics and analysis of the most vital industry trends. YieldStar uses current pricing, revenue and occupancy trends to help a rental manager determine the best price for an individual unit. Velocity is a utility and billing service that consolidates payments, invoicing and submetering to improve records and reduce potential labor costs. LeasingDesk provides automated applicant screening, document management and other similar renting service necessities in a single online setting. OpsTechnology tracks order, procurement and other budget functions in order to provide a complete and transparent spending management system. RealPage also provides professional services such as customer support, technical support, consulting and training services to ease the implementation of its products. In February 2010, the company acquired Domin-8 Enterprise Solutions LLC, a provider of rental property software. In June 2010, the firm acquired eReal Estate Integration, Inc., a developer of customer relations management and market analysis software. In November 2010, RealPage's subsidiary purchased Level One, Inc., which owned the CrossFire customer service center.

FINANCIALS: Sales and profits are in thousands of dollars—add 000 to get the full amount. 2010 Note: Financial information for 2010 was not available for all companies at press time.

2010 Sales: $188,274	2010 Profits: $ 67	**U.S. Stock Ticker: RP**
2009 Sales: $140,902	2009 Profits: $28,429	**Int'l Ticker:** Int'l Exchange:
2008 Sales: $112,568	2008 Profits: $-3,209	Employees: 1,759
2007 Sales: $	2007 Profits: $	Fiscal Year Ends: 12/31
2006 Sales: $	2006 Profits: $	Parent Company:

SALARIES/BENEFITS:

Pension Plan:	ESOP Stock Plan:	Profit Sharing:	Top Exec. Salary: $	Bonus: $
Savings Plan:	Stock Purch. Plan:		Second Exec. Salary: $	Bonus: $

OTHER THOUGHTS:

Apparent Women Officers or Directors: 5
Hot Spot for Advancement for Women/Minorities: Y

LOCATIONS: ("Y" = Yes)

West:	Southwest:	Midwest:	Southeast:	Northeast:	International:
Y	Y			Y	Y

REALTY INCOME CORP

www.realtyincome.com

Industry Group Code: 531120 Ranks within this company's industry group: Sales: 41   Profits: 18

Properties:		Financial Services:		Construction/Development:		Investments:		Specialty Services:		Brokerage:	
Apartments:		Mortgages:		Commercial Construction:	Y	REIT:	Y	Property Management:	Y	Commercial Sales:	
Malls/Shopping:	Y	Title Insurance:		Residential Construction:				Online Services:		Residential Sales:	
Offices:	Y	Property Insurance:		Land Development:				Software/IT:		Specialty:	
Hotels/Motels:				Support Services:				Consulting:			
Industrial/Warehouses:				Design/Engineering:							
Other:											

TYPES OF BUSINESS:

Real Estate Investment Trust
Retail Property
Property Management

BRANDS/DIVISIONS/AFFILIATES:

Crest Net Lease Inc
SuperAmerica

CONTACTS: *Note: Officers with more than one job title may be intentionally listed here more than once.*

Thomas A. Lewis, CEO
Gary M. Malino, COO
Gary M. Malino, Pres.
Paul M. Meurer, CFO/Exec. VP/Treas.
Robert J. Israel, Sr. VP-Research
Michael R. Pfeiffer, General Counsel/Exec. VP/Corp. Sec.
Tere H. Miller, VP-Corp. Comm.
Tere H. Miller, VP-Investor Rel.
Gregory J. Fahey, Controller/VP
Richard G. Collins, Exec. VP-Portfolio Mgmt.
Laura S. King, Sr. VP/Assistant General Counsel/Assistant Sec.
Donald R. Cameron, Chmn.

Phone: 760-741-2111	**Fax:** 760-741-2235
Toll-Free:	
Address: 600 La Terraza Blvd., Escondido, CA 92025-3873 US	

GROWTH PLANS/SPECIAL FEATURES:

Realty Income Corp. (RIC) is a real estate investment trust (REIT). The firm's primary objective is to generate stable monthly cash distributions based on its portfolio of retail properties leased to regional and national chains. The company's portfolio management focus includes contractual rent increases on existing leases; rent increases at the termination of existing leases, when market conditions permit; the re-leasing of vacant properties; and the selective sale of other properties. Of the 2,496 retail properties owned by the company, 2,485 (approximately 99.6%) are single-tenant retail locations; the remaining 11 are multi-tenant, distribution and office properties. RIC leases its properties under long-term, net-lease agreements (usually 15-20 years) that generally require the tenant to pay for maintenance, minimum monthly rents and property operating expenses such as taxes and insurance. The company's acquisition strategy includes a focus on freestanding, commercially-zoned, single-tenant properties, in important retail locations, that can be purchased with the simultaneous execution or assumption of long-term, net-lease agreements, offering both current income and the potential for rent increases. The firm's properties are located in 49 states, are leased to 122 different retail chains in 32 separate industries and have an average of 8,500 square feet of leasable retail space. Additionally, the company's wholly-owned taxable REIT subsidiary, Crest Net Lease, Inc., owns three properties with a total investment value of $3 million, which are currently classified as held for investment. Crest Net Lease primarily engages in the buying and selling of properties, mainly to individual investors involved in tax-deferred exchanges. During 2010, RIC invested a total of $713.5 million in 186 new retail properties located in 14 states and containing over 2.2 million square feet of leasable space. This includes the acquisition of 135 SuperAmerica convenience stores and one support facility for approximately $247.6 million.

FINANCIALS: Sales and profits are in thousands of dollars—add 000 to get the full amount. 2010 Note: Financial information for 2010 was not available for all companies at press time.

2010 Sales: $345,009	2010 Profits: $130,784	**U.S. Stock Ticker: O**
2009 Sales: $325,245	2009 Profits: $131,127	**Int'l Ticker:** Int'l Exchange:
2008 Sales: $325,041	2008 Profits: $131,841	Employees: 79
2007 Sales: $291,483	2007 Profits: $140,409	Fiscal Year Ends: 12/31
2006 Sales: $237,416	2006 Profits: $110,781	Parent Company:

SALARIES/BENEFITS:

Pension Plan:	ESOP Stock Plan:	Profit Sharing:	Top Exec. Salary: $350,000	Bonus: $1,015,000
Savings Plan: Y	Stock Purch. Plan:		Second Exec. Salary: $325,000	Bonus: $480,000

OTHER THOUGHTS:

Apparent Women Officers or Directors: 4
Hot Spot for Advancement for Women/Minorities: Y

LOCATIONS: ("Y" = Yes)

West:	Southwest:	Midwest:	Southeast:	Northeast:	International:
Y	Y	Y	Y	Y	

RED LION HOTELS CORPORATION

www.rdln.com

Industry Group Code: 721110 Ranks within this company's industry group: Sales: 27   Profits: 22

Properties:	Financial Services:	Construction/Development:	Investments:	Specialty Services:	Brokerage:
Apartments:	Mortgages:	Commercial Construction:	REIT:	Property Management:	Commercial Sales:
Malls/Shopping:	Title Insurance:	Residential Construction:		Online Services: Y	Residential Sales:
Offices:	Property Insurance:	Land Development:		Software/IT:	Specialty:
Hotels/Motels: Y		Support Services:		Consulting:	
Industrial/Warehouses:		Design/Engineering:			
Other:					

TYPES OF BUSINESS:

Hotels
Event Ticketing Services
Property Management Services
Entertainment Productions
Guest Loyalty Programs

BRANDS/DIVISIONS/AFFILIATES:

Red Lion Hotels
Red Lion Hotel Oakland International Airport
Red Lion R&R Club
TicketsWest
WestCoast Entertainment
Red Lion Colonial Hotel

CONTACTS: *Note: Officers with more than one job title may be intentionally listed here more than once.*

Jon E. Eliasson, CEO
Jon E. Eliasson, Pres.
Dan R. Jackson, CFO/Exec. VP
Harry G. Sladich, Exec. VP-Sales & Mktg.
Krisann Hatch, Sr. VP-Human Resources
David Barbieri, CIO/Sr. VP
Thomas L. McKeirnan, General Counsel/Sec./Sr. VP
George Schweitzer, Exec. VP/COO-Hotel Oper.
Richard P. Carlson, Sr. VP-Lodging Dev.
Pam Scott, Dir.-Corp. Comm.
Sandi Heffernan, Controller
Kenneth Shore, Regional VP-Hotel Oper.
Jack G. Lucas, VP/Pres., Tickets West
Jason W. Thielbahr, VP-Revenue Mgmt.
Todd S. Thoreson, Regional VP-Hotel Oper.
Donald K. Barbieri, Chmn.
Barry A. Hughes, Sr. VP-Dist. & Mktg.

Phone: 509-459-6100	Fax: 509-325-7324
Toll-Free: 800-733-5466	
Address: 201 W. North River Dr., Ste. 100, Spokane, WA 99201 US	

GROWTH PLANS/SPECIAL FEATURES:

Red Lion Hotels Corporation owns, operates and franchises midscale, full, select and limited service hotels in the western U.S. under the Red Lion Hotels brand. The firm currently holds interests in approximately 44 hotels across eight states and one Canadian province, offering a total of 8,557 rooms and 425,397 square feet of meeting space. Red Lion operates in three segments: hotels, franchise and entertainment. The hotels segment consists of the operations of its 31 company-operated hotels, of which 19 are wholly-owned and 12 are leased. This segment accounts for about 90.9% of total revenue. The franchise segment (2% of revenues) licenses the firm's 13 franchised hotels. To support its hotels, Red Lion provides services in marketing, sales, advertising, guest loyalty programs, revenue management, reservation systems, quality assurance and brand standards. Its guest loyalty program is the Red Lion R&R Club, a point system used by guests to redeem complimentary hotel stays, air miles, car rentals and other entertainment and merchandising incentives. Finally, the entertainment segment (5.6% of revenues), operating through TicketsWest and WestCoast Entertainment, offers ticketing services, ticketing inventory management systems, call center services, promotion services and outlet/electronic channel distribution for event locations. TicketsWest offers tickets for live music, sporting events, family events (such as circuses, expos and fairs) and theater events. The company has also developed an electronic ticketing platform that integrates with its electronic hotel distribution system. In late 2010, Red Lion established three new franchises hotels in California. In January 2011, the firm agreed to sell two hotels in Seattle and Colorado. In February 2011, Red Lion opened Red Lion Hotel Oakland International Airport. In March 2011, the firm agreed to sell Red Lion Colonial Hotel in Montana.

Employees are offered life, medical, dental and vision insurance; a flexible spending plan; an associate travel program; and an assistance program.

FINANCIALS: Sales and profits are in thousands of dollars—add 000 to get the full amount. 2010 Note: Financial information for 2010 was not available for all companies at press time.

2010 Sales: $163,494	2010 Profits: $-8,619	**U.S. Stock Ticker:** RLH
2009 Sales: $165,719	2009 Profits: $-6,664	**Int'l Ticker:** Int'l Exchange:
2008 Sales: $188,208	2008 Profits: $-1,649	Employees: 2,463
2007 Sales: $186,893	2007 Profits: $6,050	Fiscal Year Ends: 12/31
2006 Sales: $170,368	2006 Profits: $- 575	Parent Company:

SALARIES/BENEFITS:

Pension Plan:	ESOP Stock Plan:	Profit Sharing:	Top Exec. Salary: $357,363	Bonus: $
Savings Plan: Y	Stock Purch. Plan: Y		Second Exec. Salary: $208,461	Bonus: $

OTHER THOUGHTS:

Apparent Women Officers or Directors: 3
Hot Spot for Advancement for Women/Minorities: Y

LOCATIONS: ("Y" = Yes)

West:	Southwest:	Midwest:	Southeast:	Northeast:	International:
Y					Y

                                                        Plunkett Research, Ltd.

REGENCY CENTERS CORP

www.regencycenters.com

Industry Group Code: 531120 Ranks within this company's industry group: Sales: 36   Profits: 43

Properties:		Financial Services:	Construction/Development:	Investments:		Specialty Services:		Brokerage:
Apartments:		Mortgages:	Commercial Construction:	REIT:	Y	Property Management:	Y	Commercial Sales:
Malls/Shopping:	Y	Title Insurance:	Residential Construction:			Online Services:		Residential Sales:
Offices:		Property Insurance:	Land Development:			Software/IT:		Specialty:
Hotels/Motels:			Support Services:			Consulting:		
Industrial/Warehouses:			Design/Engineering:					
Other:								

TYPES OF BUSINESS:

Real Estate Investment Trust
Shopping Centers
Property Management

BRANDS/DIVISIONS/AFFILIATES:

Regency Centers, L.P.
Premier Customer Initiative

CONTACTS: *Note: Officers with more than one job title may be intentionally listed here more than once.*

Martin Stein, Jr., CEO
Brian Smith, COO
Brian Smith, Pres.
Bruce Johnson, CFO/Exec. VP
Bonnie Hayflick, Contact-Media
Jim Thompson, Managing Dir.-East
Mac Chandler, Managing Dir.-West
John Delatour, Managing Dir.-Central
Martin Stein, Jr., Chmn.

Phone: 904-598-7000	**Fax:** 904-634-3428
Toll-Free: 800-950-6333	
Address: 1 Independent Dr., Ste. 114, Jacksonville, FL 32202 US	

GROWTH PLANS/SPECIAL FEATURES:

Regency Centers Corp. (REG) is a real estate investment trust (REIT) engaged in the ownership, operation and development of grocery-anchored and community shopping centers located in areas with above-average household incomes and population densities. The firm's operations are conducted primarily through its majority-owned operating partnership, Regency Centers, L.P., of which it owns 99.8%. REG owns and manages 215 shopping centers in 23 states, representing 23.3 million square feet of rentable space, and owns partial interests in 181 shopping centers in 25 states. REG leases space in its shopping centers to grocers, specialty side-shop retailers, restaurants and major retail anchors. The company's largest grocery tenants include Kroger, with 54 stores; Publix, with 56 stores; Safeway, with 59 stores; and Super Valu, with 29 stores. REG has developed a formal partnering process called the Premier Customer Initiative, where the company builds a base of specialty tenants that represent the best operators in their respective merchandising categories. Such connections help stabilize a shopping center's occupancy, reduce re-leasing downtime and tenant turnover and yield higher sustainable rent. The firm also holds a self-funding business model that utilizes center recycling as a key component. In March 2010, the company acquired Providence Commons, a 91,301 square-foot retail center in Charlotte, North Carolina.

Employees are offered medical, dental, vision, life and disability insurance; a 401(k) plan; profit sharing; stock grant awards; wellness programs; and educational assistance.

FINANCIALS: Sales and profits are in thousands of dollars—add 000 to get the full amount. 2010 Note: Financial information for 2010 was not available for all companies at press time.

2010 Sales: $486,806	2010 Profits: $16,199	**U.S. Stock Ticker: REG**
2009 Sales: $488,073	2009 Profits: $-32,743	**Int'l Ticker:** Int'l Exchange:
2008 Sales: $494,934	2008 Profits: $141,521	Employees: 392
2007 Sales: $436,006	2007 Profits: $203,651	Fiscal Year Ends: 12/31
2006 Sales: $404,034	2006 Profits: $218,511	Parent Company:

SALARIES/BENEFITS:

Pension Plan:	ESOP Stock Plan:	Profit Sharing: Y	Top Exec. Salary: $686,000	Bonus: $1,056,000
Savings Plan: Y	Stock Purch. Plan:		Second Exec. Salary: $500,000	Bonus: $733,000

OTHER THOUGHTS:

Apparent Women Officers or Directors: 2
Hot Spot for Advancement for Women/Minorities:

LOCATIONS: ("Y" = Yes)

West:	Southwest:	Midwest:	Southeast:	Northeast:	International:
Y	Y	Y	Y	Y	

REIS INC

www.reis.com

Industry Group Code: 511210J Ranks within this company's industry group: Sales: 1   Profits: 1

Properties:	Financial Services:	Construction/Development:	Investments:	Specialty Services:		Brokerage:
Apartments:	Mortgages:	Commercial Construction:	REIT:	Property Management:	Y	Commercial Sales:
Malls/Shopping:	Title Insurance:	Residential Construction:		Online Services:		Residential Sales:
Offices:	Property Insurance:	Land Development:		Software/IT:	Y	Specialty:
Hotels/Motels:		Support Services:		Consulting:		
Industrial/Warehouses:		Design/Engineering:				
Other:						

TYPES OF BUSINESS:
Real Estate Information & Analytics

BRANDS/DIVISIONS/AFFILIATES:
Reis Services
Reis SE
Reis Value Alert

CONTACTS: *Note: Officers with more than one job title may be intentionally listed here more than once.*
Lloyd Lynford, CEO
Lloyd Lynford, Pres.
Mark P. Cantaluppi, CFO/VP
Jonathan Garfield, Exec. VP
William Sander, COO-Reis Services LLC
Edward Lowenthal, Chmn.

Phone: 212-921-1122	Fax: 212-421-7442
Toll-Free: 800-366-7347	
Address: 530 5th Ave., New York, NY 10036 US	

GROWTH PLANS/SPECIAL FEATURES:

Reis, Inc. is a provider of commercial real estate market information and analytical tools. The company offers these services through its subsidiary, Reis Services. Reis Services maintains a proprietary database that contains detailed information on commercial properties in metropolitan markets and neighborhoods. This database offers information on retail, apartment, office and industrial properties. It currently lists information on 140 retail, 200 apartment, 44 industrial and 132 office metropolitan markets throughout the U.S. The database is utilized by real estate investors, lenders and other professionals that wish to make informed selling, buying and financing decisions. The firm's data is also used by debt and equity investors to assess, quantify and manage the risks of default and loss associated with individual mortgages, properties, portfolios and real estate backed securities. Reis Services' flagship product, Reis SE, provides web-based access to commercial real estate information and analytical tools designed to facilitate debt/equity transactions and ongoing evaluations. Reis SE offers trend and forecast analysis at metropolitan and neighborhood levels; and also provides detailed building-specific information such as vacancy rates, rents, property sales, lease terms, new construction listings and property valuation estimates. The product is designed to meet the needs of banks, developers/builders, property owners, non-bank lenders and equity investors. Reis currently serves roughly 690 companies, most of which have multiple users entitled to access Reis SE. The firm also offers Reis Value Alert, a program that identifies potentially troubled assets; it is especially useful for property and portfolio analysis during recapitalizations and bank consolidations. In early 2010, Reis sold a 235-acre residential development project in Claverack, New York, for roughly $2.75 million. The land included 46 lots and two model homes. In April 2011, the company sold the 119-lot Orchards subdivision located in Connecticut.

FINANCIALS: Sales and profits are in thousands of dollars—add 000 to get the full amount. 2010 Note: Financial information for 2010 was not available for all companies at press time.

2010 Sales: $27,576	2010 Profits: $ 668	**U.S. Stock Ticker: REIS**
2009 Sales: $30,951	2009 Profits: $1,004	**Int'l Ticker:** Int'l Exchange:
2008 Sales: $47,621	2008 Profits: $-7,480	Employees: 142
2007 Sales: $36,367	2007 Profits: $-1,290	Fiscal Year Ends: 12/31
2006 Sales: $	2006 Profits: $	Parent Company:

SALARIES/BENEFITS:

Pension Plan:	ESOP Stock Plan:	Profit Sharing:	Top Exec. Salary: $645,000	Bonus: $168,750
Savings Plan:	Stock Purch. Plan:		Second Exec. Salary: $500,000	Bonus: $168,750

OTHER THOUGHTS:
Apparent Women Officers or Directors:
Hot Spot for Advancement for Women/Minorities:

LOCATIONS: ("Y" = Yes)

West:	Southwest:	Midwest:	Southeast:	Northeast:	International:
				Y	

RELATED GROUP (THE)

www.relatedgroup.com

Industry Group Code: 5311 Ranks within this company's industry group: Sales: Profits:

Properties:		Financial Services:		Construction/Development:		Investments:	Specialty Services:		Brokerage:
Apartments:	Y	Mortgages:	Y	Commercial Construction:	Y	REIT:	Property Management:	Y	Commercial Sales:
Malls/Shopping:	Y	Title Insurance:		Residential Construction:	Y		Online Services:		Residential Sales:
Offices:	Y	Property Insurance:		Land Development:	Y		Software/IT:		Specialty:
Hotels/Motels:				Support Services:	Y		Consulting:		
Industrial/Warehouses:				Design/Engineering:					
Other:	Y								

TYPES OF BUSINESS:

Condominium Construction & Management
Multi-Family Residence Development
Mixed-Use Urban Environments
Financing Services
Property Management
Construction

BRANDS/DIVISIONS/AFFILIATES:

CityPlace
Related Asset Advisors
Related Financial
Related Cervera Realty Services
TRG Management
Fortune Construction Company
Related International
Icon Vallarta

CONTACTS: *Note: Officers with more than one job title may be intentionally listed here more than once.*

Jorge M. Perez, CEO
Matthew J. Allen, COO/Exec. VP
Jeffery Hoyos, Chief Admin. Officer/Sr. VP
Douglas K. Bischoff, General Counsel/Sr. VP
James M. Werbelow, Sr. VP-Construction
Chris Ballard, Principal
Patrick Campbell, VP
Larry Lennon, Pres., TRG Mgmt.
Jorge M. Perez, Chmn.
Carlos Rosso, Exec. VP-Related Int'l

Phone: 305-460-9900	Fax: 305-460-9911
Toll-Free:	
Address: 315 S. Biscayne Blvd., Miami, FL 33131 US	

GROWTH PLANS/SPECIAL FEATURES:

The Related Group is a multi-family real estate development firm and one of the nation's leading builders of luxury condominiums. Since its inception in 1979, it has built and managed over 77,000 residential units throughout its home state of Florida. The Related Group's buildings have signature characteristics, such as very artistic, often decadent designs that are often located in unknown or under-developed neighborhoods, although it has set up some run-of-the-mill country club villas and other smaller scale projects as well. Some of the company's buildings are rental properties. Also in Related Group's portfolio are so-called urban mixed-use environments, which are planned neighborhoods that integrate housing, shopping and entertainment. The company's flagship community, considered to have changed the cityscape forever, is CityPlace in West Palm Beach, Florida. Other major Florida projects include The Plaza on Brickell, Trump Hollywood and St. Regis Resort & Residences. The Group operates various subsidiaries to supplement its chief real estate business, including Related Financial, which offers financing services; Related Cervera Realty Services and TRG Management, which cover sales and property management; Realty Asset Advisors, which offers property management, sales, construction management, leasing and loan workout services; Fortune Construction Company, which serves as the firm's own private contractor; and Related International, which was created to drive the company's $1 billion urbanization project in Mexico. Currently, Related International has one property in Puerto Vallarta: Icon Vallarta, a beachfront luxury condominium featuring three towers, of which two are completed.

The firm offers its employees medical, dental, vision, disability and life insurance; tuition reimbursement; and employee discounts.

FINANCIALS: Sales and profits are in thousands of dollars—add 000 to get the full amount. 2010 Note: Financial information for 2010 was not available for all companies at press time.

2010 Sales: $	2010 Profits: $	U.S. Stock Ticker: Private
2009 Sales: $	2009 Profits: $	Int'l Ticker: Int'l Exchange:
2008 Sales: $	2008 Profits: $	Employees:
2007 Sales: $	2007 Profits: $	Fiscal Year Ends: 12/31
2006 Sales: $1,400,000	2006 Profits: $	Parent Company:

SALARIES/BENEFITS:

Pension Plan:	ESOP Stock Plan:	Profit Sharing:	Top Exec. Salary: $	Bonus: $
Savings Plan: Y	Stock Purch. Plan:		Second Exec. Salary: $	Bonus: $

OTHER THOUGHTS:

Apparent Women Officers or Directors:
Hot Spot for Advancement for Women/Minorities:

LOCATIONS: ("Y" = Yes)

West:	Southwest:	Midwest:	Southeast:	Northeast:	International:
Y			Y		

RESORTQUEST INTERNATIONAL INC   www.resortquest.com

Industry Group Code: 721110 Ranks within this company's industry group: Sales: Profits:

Properties:		Financial Services:		Construction/Development:		Investments:		Specialty Services:		Brokerage:	
Apartments:	Y	Mortgages:		Commercial Construction:		REIT:		Property Management:	Y	Commercial Sales:	
Malls/Shopping:		Title Insurance:		Residential Construction:				Online Services:	Y	Residential Sales:	
Offices:		Property Insurance:		Land Development:				Software/IT:	Y	Specialty:	Y
Hotels/Motels:	Y			Support Services:				Consulting:			
Industrial/Warehouses:				Design/Engineering:							
Other:	Y										

TYPES OF BUSINESS:

Vacation Homes & Condominiums
Property Management Services
Real Estate Sales

BRANDS/DIVISIONS/AFFILIATES:

Leucadia National Corp
Wyndham Exchange & Rentals
Wyndham Worldwide

CONTACTS: *Note: Officers with more than one job title may be intentionally listed here more than once.*

Eileen Erstad, CFO
Cheryl Spezia, VP-Mktg.
Geoff Ballotti, CEO-Pres., Wyndham Exchange & Rentals

Phone: 800-862-4853	Fax:
Toll-Free: 800-467-3529	
Address: 546 Mary Esther Cut-Off NW, Ste. 3, Fort Walton Beach, FL 32548 US	

GROWTH PLANS/SPECIAL FEATURES:

ResortQuest International, Inc. provides vacation condominium and home rental property management services. The firm is a subsidiary of Wyndham Exchange & Rentals, itself a division of travel services giant Wyndham Worldwide. The company markets and provides management services for 6,000 premier beach, golf, ski and tennis destination resort locations. In conjunction with Partner Affiliates in North America and Europe, ResortQuest provides management services to approximately 100,000 vacation rental properties. ResortQuest conducts its business through two divisions: vacation rentals and real estate sales. Vacation rental properties are generally second homes or investment properties owned by individuals who assign ResortQuest the responsibility of managing, marketing and renting their properties. Vacation properties include hotels, lodges, condominiums, town homes, cottages, villas and vacation homes. Properties are located in over 140 locations across the U.S., Canada, Mexico, the Caribbean and Europe. The company offers real estate brokerage services throughout its U.S. resort locations, primarily in Delaware and Florida. This division allows customers to list a home as a ResortQuest property or buy a vacation home. In October 2010, Wyndham Exchange & Rentals acquired ResortQuest from its former parent company, Leucadia National Corp.

The company offers its employees benefits that include health coverage, paid time off and a 401(k) plan.

FINANCIALS: Sales and profits are in thousands of dollars—add 000 to get the full amount. 2010 Note: Financial information for 2010 was not available for all companies at press time.

2010 Sales: $	2010 Profits: $	U.S. Stock Ticker: Subsidiary
2009 Sales: $	2009 Profits: $	Int'l Ticker: Int'l Exchange:
2008 Sales: $	2008 Profits: $	Employees:
2007 Sales: $168,300	2007 Profits: $	Fiscal Year Ends: 12/31
2006 Sales: $	2006 Profits: $	Parent Company: WYNDHAM EXCHANGE & RENTALS

SALARIES/BENEFITS:

Pension Plan:	ESOP Stock Plan:	Profit Sharing:	Top Exec. Salary: $	Bonus: $
Savings Plan: Y	Stock Purch. Plan:		Second Exec. Salary: $	Bonus: $

OTHER THOUGHTS:

Apparent Women Officers or Directors: 2
Hot Spot for Advancement for Women/Minorities:

LOCATIONS: ("Y" = Yes)

West:	Southwest:	Midwest:	Southeast:	Northeast:	International:
Y			Y	Y	Y

REZIDOR HOTEL GROUP AB

www.rezidor.com

Industry Group Code: 721110 Ranks within this company's industry group: Sales: 12   Profits: 21

Properties:		Financial Services:	Construction/Development:	Investments:	Specialty Services:	Brokerage:
Apartments:		Mortgages:	Commercial Construction:	REIT:	Property Management:	Commercial Sales:
Malls/Shopping:		Title Insurance:	Residential Construction:		Online Services:	Residential Sales:
Offices:		Property Insurance:	Land Development:		Software/IT:	Specialty:
Hotels/Motels:	Y		Support Services:		Consulting:	
Industrial/Warehouses:			Design/Engineering:			
Other:						

TYPES OF BUSINESS:

Hotel Management

BRANDS/DIVISIONS/AFFILIATES:

Carlson Hotels Worldwide
Hotel Missoni
Regent
Radisson
Park Inn
Country Inn

CONTACTS: *Note: Officers with more than one job title may be intentionally listed here more than once.*

Kurt Ritter, CEO
Jacques Dubois, COO/Sr. VP
Kurt Ritter, Pres.
Knut Kleiven, CFO/Deputy Pres.
Olivier Jacquin, Sr. VP-Mktg. & Sales
Eugene P.E. Staal, VP-Tech. Dev.
Marianne Ruhngard, General Counsel/Sr. VP/Sec.
Puneet Chhatwal, Chief Dev. Officer/Sr. VP
Urban Jansson, Chmn.
Olivier Jacquin, Sr. VP-Dist.

Phone: 32-2-702-9200	Fax: 32-2-702-9300
Toll-Free:	
Address: Ave. du Bourget 44, Brussels, B-1130 Belgium	

GROWTH PLANS/SPECIAL FEATURES:

Rezidor Hotel Group AB, formerly Rezidor SAS Hospitality, is a hospitality management company that franchises, leases and manages hotel properties. The company currently has over 400 available hotels, with 87,000 rooms in operation or under development. The company's brands include Hotel Missoni, Radisson Blu, Park Inn, Regent and Country Inn; the latter three are operated under a franchise agreement with Carlson Hotels Worldwide. Rezidor's network has grown to its current size, from just 29 hotels 10 years ago, primarily through the Carlson franchise agreement. Radisson Blu is a first-class full-service hotel brand that currently operates almost 240 hotels in Europe, the Middle East and Africa. Park Inn is an up and coming mid-market hotel brand primarily located in Europe, the Middle East and Africa. Country Inn is an international mid-tier lodging chain. Regent is an international brand that offers luxury and high-quality service in its hotels and resorts; the firm operates locations in Germany, Croatia, France, China, Singapore, Taiwan, Maldives and Turks and Caicos, with additional locations under development in Puerto Rico, Thailand, Malaysia, Indonesia, United Arab Emirates and Qatar. Hotel Missoni is the newest member of the Rezidor family, born of a recently signed worldwide licensing agreement with the global fashion brand of the same name. The brand is currently under development in Turkey, Brazil and Oman, with its first openings in Scotland and Kuwait. Rezidor's hotels are primarily located in Western Europe, with additional locations in Scandinavia, Eastern Europe, Russia, Turkey, Malta, Azerbaijan, Kazakhstan, Uzbekistan, Iran, the Arabian Peninsula, Egypt, South Africa and China, among others. The firm actively continues to enlarge its network, with recent additions in Ghana, Sweden, Poland, Russia, Bulgaria and Nigeria.

FINANCIALS: Sales and profits are in thousands of dollars—add 000 to get the full amount. 2010 Note: Financial information for 2010 was not available for all companies at press time.

2010 Sales: $1,153,780	2010 Profits: $-3,670	**U.S. Stock Ticker:**
2009 Sales: $994,460	2009 Profits: $-41,410	**Int'l Ticker: REZT** Int'l Exchange: Stockholm-SSE
2008 Sales: $1,152,460	2008 Profits: $38,330	Employees: 4,947
2007 Sales: $	2007 Profits: $	Fiscal Year Ends: 12/31
2006 Sales: $	2006 Profits: $	Parent Company:

SALARIES/BENEFITS:

Pension Plan:	ESOP Stock Plan:	Profit Sharing:	Top Exec. Salary: $	Bonus: $
Savings Plan:	Stock Purch. Plan:		Second Exec. Salary: $	Bonus: $

OTHER THOUGHTS:

Apparent Women Officers or Directors: 3
Hot Spot for Advancement for Women/Minorities: Y

LOCATIONS: ("Y" = Yes)

West:	Southwest:	Midwest:	Southeast:	Northeast:	International:
					Y

RIO PROPERTIES INC

www.harrahs.com/casinos/rio/hotel-casino/property-home.shtml

Industry Group Code: 721120 Ranks within this company's industry group: Sales: Profits:

Properties:		Financial Services:	Construction/Development:	Investments:	Specialty Services:		Brokerage:
Apartments:		Mortgages:	Commercial Construction:	REIT:	Property Management:	Y	Commercial Sales:
Malls/Shopping:		Title Insurance:	Residential Construction:		Online Services:		Residential Sales:
Offices:		Property Insurance:	Land Development:		Software/IT:		Specialty:
Hotels/Motels:	Y		Support Services:		Consulting:		
Industrial/Warehouses:			Design/Engineering:				
Other:	Y						

TYPES OF BUSINESS:

Hotels & Casinos
Wine Shop
Golf Course

BRANDS/DIVISIONS/AFFILIATES:

Harrah's Entertainment Inc
Rio All-Suite Hotel and Casino
Rio Spa & Salon
Masquerade Village Shops
Rio Secco Golf Club
Carnivale Masquerade Show In The Sky
Lucy Strike Lanes
Gaylord Indian Restaurant

CONTACTS: *Note: Officers with more than one job title may be intentionally listed here more than once.*

Madeleine Weekly, Dir.-Mktg.
Stephen Thayer, VP-Hotel Oper.

Phone: 702-777-7777	Fax: 702-777-7781
Toll-Free: 888-746-7153	
Address: 3700 W. Flamingo Rd., Las Vegas, NV 89103 US	

GROWTH PLANS/SPECIAL FEATURES:

Rio Properties, Inc., a subsidiary of Harrah's Entertainment, Inc., operates the Rio All-Suite Hotel and Casino in Las Vegas, Nevada. Harrah's Entertainment is a diversified U.S. casino company that operates almost 40 establishments under the brand names Harrah's, Caesars, Showboat, Horseshoe, Bally's, Casino Windsor, Flamingo, Imperial Palace and Harveys. The Rio All-Suite Hotel and Casino features over 600 square feet of space for every room as part of its all-suite concept. The suites are equipped with such amenities as a separate dressing area, a couch, a 32-inch TV, a table with chairs, a hairdryer, a refrigerator, an iron, an ironing board and a safe. Rio's hotel additionally features 100,000 square feet of gaming space; such restaurants as Antonio's Italian Ristorante, Café Martorano, Gaylord Indian Restaurant and Carnival World Buffet; the Rio Spa & Salon; the Masquerade Village Shops, with over 60,000 square feet of shops; access to nearby Rio Secco Golf Club; the Carnivale Masquerade Show In The Sky, a free carnival-themed show with suspended floats; and Lucky Strike Lanes bowling alley. Gaming amenities include slot machines, video poker machines, Keno Lounge, a full-service Race & Sports Book and more than 80 table games, including blackjack, craps, baccarat, roulette, Let It Ride, Caribbean Stud Poker and Mini-Baccarat. Rio's Wine Cellar & Tasting Room, a wine bar and retail shop, showcases approximately 50,000 bottles valued at more than $10 million. The company actively markets its services and facilities to both local residents and Las Vegas visitors. Rio believes that its all-suite concept, diverse high-quality dining, easy access and ample parking provide an attractive alternative to the Las Vegas Strip, which is 15 minutes away.

FINANCIALS: Sales and profits are in thousands of dollars—add 000 to get the full amount. 2010 Note: Financial information for 2010 was not available for all companies at press time.

2010 Sales: $	2010 Profits: $	**U.S. Stock Ticker:** Subsidiary
2009 Sales: $	2009 Profits: $	**Int'l Ticker:** Int'l Exchange:
2008 Sales: $	2008 Profits: $	Employees:
2007 Sales: $134,700	2007 Profits: $	Fiscal Year Ends: 12/31
2006 Sales: $	2006 Profits: $	Parent Company: HARRAH'S ENTERTAINMENT INC

SALARIES/BENEFITS:

Pension Plan:	ESOP Stock Plan:	Profit Sharing:	Top Exec. Salary: $	Bonus: $
Savings Plan:	Stock Purch. Plan:		Second Exec. Salary: $	Bonus: $

OTHER THOUGHTS:

Apparent Women Officers or Directors: 2
Hot Spot for Advancement for Women/Minorities:

LOCATIONS: ("Y" = Yes)

West:	Southwest:	Midwest:	Southeast:	Northeast:	International:
Y					

RITZ-CARLTON HOTEL COMPANY LLC (THE)   www.ritzcarlton.com

Industry Group Code: 721110 Ranks within this company's industry group: Sales: Profits:

Properties:		Financial Services:	Construction/Development:	Investments:	Specialty Services:		Brokerage:
Apartments:	Y	Mortgages:	Commercial Construction:	REIT:	Property Management:	Y	Commercial Sales:
Malls/Shopping:		Title Insurance:	Residential Construction:		Online Services:		Residential Sales:
Offices:		Property Insurance:	Land Development:		Software/IT:		Specialty:
Hotels/Motels:	Y		Support Services:		Consulting:		
Industrial/Warehouses:			Design/Engineering:				
Other:	Y						

TYPES OF BUSINESS:

Hotels, Luxury
Condominiums
Golf Courses
Spas
Time Share Units

BRANDS/DIVISIONS/AFFILIATES:

Marriott International Inc
Six Senses
La Prairie
ESPA
Ritz-Carlton Destination Club (The)
Residencies at Ritz-Carlton (The)
Ritz-Carlton Rewards (The)

CONTACTS: *Note: Officers with more than one job title may be intentionally listed here more than once.*

Herve Humler, COO
Herve Humler, Pres.
Peter Cole, CFO
Chris Gabaldon, Chief Sales & Mktg. Officer
Bob Kharazmi, Global Officer-Worldwide Oper.
Vivian A. Deuschl, VP-Public Rel.

Phone: 301-547-4700	Fax: 301-547-4723
Toll-Free:	
Address: 4445 Willard Ave., Ste. 800, Chevy Chase, MD 20815 US	

GROWTH PLANS/SPECIAL FEATURES:

The Ritz-Carlton Hotel Company, LLC, a subsidiary of Marriott International, Inc., is one of the world's best-known luxury hotel chains, operating 74 hotels with 22,044 rooms in 24 countries. The firm also maintains 12 international sales offices in various locations including Chicago, New York, Los Angeles, Dubai, Shanghai, Tokyo and London. In an attempt to cater to an upscale clientele base, full-service luxury spas are offered at most of the company's resorts. Some spas at Ritz-Carlton hotels operate under the brand names Six Senses, La Prairie and ESPA. Besides its hotels, the firm provides vacation properties and residential suites under The Ritz-Carlton Destination Club and The Residencies at Ritz-Carlton. The Ritz-Carlton Destination Club is the firm's time-share ownership unit, offering a flexible alternative to a second home. Membership is currently available in locations such as Aspen, Colorado; St. Thomas, U.S. Virgin Islands; Bachelor Gulch, Colorado; San Francisco, California; Jupiter, Florida; and Kapalua Bay in Maui, Hawaii. The Residencies at Ritz-Carlton offer luxury condominiums and estate homes throughout the U.S. and in Canada, Puerto Rico, Thailand, Israel, the Bahamas and Malaysia.   Ritz-Carlton also markets its 15 luxury golf courses (many designed by leading names in the golf world such as Greg Norman and Jack Nicklaus) and fitness facilities to both local residents and visitors. In September 2010, the firm introduced a frequent guest rewards program, The Ritz-Carlton Rewards.

Employees of the firm are offered benefits that include medical, dental and vision coverage; domestic partner benefits; leave of absence and bereavement leave; a 401(k) plan; a credit union; an employee stock purchase plan; an employee assistance program; educational assistance program; career development programs; uniforms; and employee discounts on hotel rooms, food and retail items.

FINANCIALS: Sales and profits are in thousands of dollars—add 000 to get the full amount. 2010 Note: Financial information for 2010 was not available for all companies at press time.

2010 Sales: $	2010 Profits: $	**U.S. Stock Ticker: Subsidiary**
2009 Sales: $	2009 Profits: $	**Int'l Ticker:** Int'l Exchange:
2008 Sales: $	2008 Profits: $	Employees: 38,000
2007 Sales: $1,576,000	2007 Profits: $72,000	Fiscal Year Ends: 12/31
2006 Sales: $1,423,000	2006 Profits: $	Parent Company: MARRIOTT INTERNATIONAL INC

SALARIES/BENEFITS:

Pension Plan:	ESOP Stock Plan:	Profit Sharing:	Top Exec. Salary: $	Bonus: $
Savings Plan: Y	Stock Purch. Plan: Y		Second Exec. Salary: $	Bonus: $

OTHER THOUGHTS:

Apparent Women Officers or Directors:
Hot Spot for Advancement for Women/Minorities:

LOCATIONS: ("Y" = Yes)

West:	Southwest:	Midwest:	Southeast:	Northeast:	International:
Y	Y	Y	Y	Y	Y

RIVIERA HOLDINGS CORP

www.rivierahotel.com

Industry Group Code: 721120 Ranks within this company's industry group: Sales: 8   Profits: 5

Properties:		Financial Services:	Construction/Development:	Investments:	Specialty Services:		Brokerage:
Apartments:		Mortgages:	Commercial Construction:	REIT:	Property Management:	Y	Commercial Sales:
Malls/Shopping:		Title Insurance:	Residential Construction:		Online Services:	Y	Residential Sales:
Offices:		Property Insurance:	Land Development:		Software/IT:		Specialty:
Hotels/Motels:	Y		Support Services:		Consulting:		
Industrial/Warehouses:	Y		Design/Engineering:				
Other:	Y						

TYPES OF BUSINESS:

Casino Hotel
Casino Management

BRANDS/DIVISIONS/AFFILIATES:

Riviera Hotel and Casino
Black Hawk Casino
Riviera Operating Corporation
Riviera Black Hawk Player's Club

CONTACTS: *Note: Officers with more than one job title may be intentionally listed here more than once.*

Robert A. Vannucci, Co-CEO
Phillip B. Simons, CFO/Co-CEO
Tullio J. Marchionne, General Counsel/Co-CEO/Sec.
Phillip B. Simons, Treas.
Robert A. Vannucci, Pres./COO-Riviera Operating Corp.
Vincent L. DiVito, Chmn.

Phone: 702-734-5110	**Fax:** 702-794-9442
Toll-Free: 800-634-3420	
Address: 2901 Las Vegas Blvd. S., Las Vegas, NV 89109 US	

GROWTH PLANS/SPECIAL FEATURES:

Riviera Holdings Corp., through wholly-owned subsidiary Riviera Operating Corporation (ROC), owns and operates the Riviera Hotel and Casino the Las Vegas Strip. The Riviera opened in 1955 and has a reputation for delivering high-quality, traditional Las Vegas-style gaming, entertainment and other amenities. The casino has approximately 100,000 square feet of gaming space with 900 slot machines and 42 gaming tables, including blackjack, craps, poker and roulette. The hotel has 2,075 guest rooms, including 177 suites, in five towers. It has approximately 160,000 square feet of convention, meeting and banquet space; and four bars and three restaurants. The Riviera also offers live entertainment shows and a race and sports book. Subsidiary Riviera Black Hawk, Inc. owns and operates the Riviera Black Hawk Casino, a limited-stakes casino, in Black Hawk, Colorado. The Black Hawk, located about 40 miles west of Denver, is one of the largest full-service casinos in Colorado, with approximately 750 slot machines and nine live game tables. The firm offers the Riviera Black Hawk Player's Club, rewarding frequent players and collecting data about Club members which the company uses to customize promotions to attract repeat visitors. The company's web site allows travelers to book rooms, buy souvenirs, check Player's Club point balances and make other reservations before a trip. In July 2010, the company filed for Chapter 11 bankruptcy protection.

FINANCIALS: Sales and profits are in thousands of dollars—add 000 to get the full amount. 2010 Note: Financial information for 2010 was not available for all companies at press time.

2010 Sales: $119,156	2010 Profits: $-20,837	**U.S. Stock Ticker: RVHL**
2009 Sales: $134,049	2009 Profits: $-24,859	**Int'l Ticker:** Int'l Exchange:
2008 Sales: $169,760	2008 Profits: $-11,862	Employees: 947
2007 Sales: $205,495	2007 Profits: $-18,258	Fiscal Year Ends: 12/31
2006 Sales: $200,944	2006 Profits: $- 335	Parent Company:

SALARIES/BENEFITS:

Pension Plan:	ESOP Stock Plan: Y	Profit Sharing:	Top Exec. Salary: $400,000	Bonus: $200,000
Savings Plan: Y	Stock Purch. Plan:		Second Exec. Salary: $295,890	Bonus: $

OTHER THOUGHTS:

Apparent Women Officers or Directors:
Hot Spot for Advancement for Women/Minorities:

LOCATIONS: ("Y" = Yes)

West:	Southwest:	Midwest:	Southeast:	Northeast:	International:
Y					

ROSEWOOD HOTELS & RESORTS LLC

www.rosewoodhotels.com

Industry Group Code: 721110 Ranks within this company's industry group: Sales: Profits:

Properties:	Financial Services:	Construction/Development:	Investments:	Specialty Services:	Brokerage:
Apartments:	Mortgages:	Commercial Construction:	REIT:	Property Management:	Commercial Sales:
Malls/Shopping:	Title Insurance:	Residential Construction:		Online Services:	Residential Sales:
Offices:	Property Insurance:	Land Development:		Software/IT:	Specialty:
Hotels/Motels: Y		Support Services:		Consulting:	
Industrial/Warehouses:		Design/Engineering:			
Other:					

TYPES OF BUSINESS:

Hotel & Resort Management
Spas
Private Residences

BRANDS/DIVISIONS/AFFILIATES:

Rosewood Dubai
Rosewood San Miguel de Allende in Mexico
Rosewood Costa Carmel
Rosewood Inn of the Anasazi
San Ysidro Ranch, A Rosewood Resort

CONTACTS: *Note: Officers with more than one job title may be intentionally listed here more than once.*

John M. Scott, CEO
Robert Boulogne, COO
John M. Scott, Pres.
Ralph Aruzza, VP-Sales
Sheri Line, Corp. Dir.-Human Resources
Fred Crespo, VP-IT
George Fong, Sr. VP-Architecture & Design
Susan Aldridge, General Counsel/Sr. VP-Legal
Michael A. Gibb, VP-Oper.
Alex Alt, VP-Dev. & Strategy
Ernest Glidden, Sr. VP-Finance
Katherine Blaisdell, VP-Construction Dev.
Elias Assaly, VP-Oper. Dev.
Gert Kopera, VP-Food & Beverage
Pablo E. Graf, Regional VP/Managing Dir.
Stephen H. Sands, Chmn.
James A. Brackensick, Sr. VP-Purchasing

Phone: 214-880-4200	Fax:
Toll-Free: 888-767-3966	
Address: 500 Crescent Court, Ste. 300, Dallas, TX 75201 US	

GROWTH PLANS/SPECIAL FEATURES:

Rosewood Hotels & Resorts, LLC operates ultra-luxury boutique hotels and resorts worldwide. It has 10 hotels and eight resorts, with over 2,000 rooms, villas and suites, in the U.S., Canada, Mexico, the Caribbean, Saudi Arabia and Japan. It also has various locations under construction, including Rosewood San Miguel de Allende in Mexico (late 2010) and Rosewood Costa Carmel in Costa Rica (2012). Besides constructing its own facilities, Rosewood has acquired existing properties and management contracts, including the Rosewood Inn of the Anasazi in Santa Fe, New Mexico and the San Ysidro Ranch, A Rosewood Resort, located in Santa Barbara, California. Its facilities are generally small, featuring less than 200 accommodations ranging from 350-square-foot rooms to 3,200-square-foot suites. The company uses architecture and decor to attempt to capture the unique history, geography and culture of each hotel or resort location. Services offered at Rosewood facilities can include tennis courts, a courtesy car with 5-mile radius, unpack and packing services, babysitting services, twice-daily housekeeping with nightly turndown service, pools and fitness centers, as well as shops and various dining facilities. Some locations also offer business centers stocked with computers, printers, faxes and copiers. Eight locations also offer spa services, such as exercise training and facilities, facials, aromabaths, hydrotherapy, massages, manicures and pedicures. In addition, three hotels and resorts also feature private residences, which offer owners the same services and amenities as resort guests. The private residences often come fully furnished and feature floor plan inclusions such as full kitchens, fireplaces, private pools and terraces.

FINANCIALS: Sales and profits are in thousands of dollars—add 000 to get the full amount. 2010 Note: Financial information for 2010 was not available for all companies at press time.

2010 Sales: $	2010 Profits: $	U.S. Stock Ticker: Private
2009 Sales: $	2009 Profits: $	Int'l Ticker: Int'l Exchange:
2008 Sales: $	2008 Profits: $	Employees:
2007 Sales: $	2007 Profits: $	Fiscal Year Ends:
2006 Sales: $	2006 Profits: $	Parent Company:

SALARIES/BENEFITS:

Pension Plan:	ESOP Stock Plan:	Profit Sharing:	Top Exec. Salary: $	Bonus: $
Savings Plan:	Stock Purch. Plan:		Second Exec. Salary: $	Bonus: $

OTHER THOUGHTS:

Apparent Women Officers or Directors: 5
Hot Spot for Advancement for Women/Minorities: Y

LOCATIONS: ("Y" = Yes)

West:	Southwest:	Midwest:	Southeast:	Northeast:	International:
Y	Y	Y	Y	Y	Y

ROSSI RESIDENCIAL SA

www.rossiresidencial.com.br

Industry Group Code: 5311 **Ranks within this company's industry group:** Sales: 17   Profits: 18

Properties:	Financial Services:	Construction/Development:		Investments:	Specialty Services:	Brokerage:
Apartments:	Mortgages:	Commercial Construction:	Y	REIT:	Property Management:	Commercial Sales:
Malls/Shopping:	Title Insurance:	Residential Construction:	Y		Online Services:	Residential Sales:
Offices:	Property Insurance:	Land Development:	Y		Software/IT:	Specialty:
Hotels/Motels:		Support Services:			Consulting:	
Industrial/Warehouses:		Design/Engineering:				
Other:						

TYPES OF BUSINESS:

Real Estate Development

BRANDS/DIVISIONS/AFFILIATES:

CONTACTS:
Note: Officers with more than one job title may be intentionally listed here more than once.

Heitor Cantergiani, CEO
Cassio Elias Audi, CFO
Leonardo Nogueira Diniz, Sales Officer
Renato Gamba Rocha Diniz, Mgr.-Eng.
Palmarino Frizzo Neto, Legal Officer
Cassio Elias Audi, Investor Rel. Officer
Edmundo Rossi Cuppoloni, Vice-Chmn.
Joao Rossi Cuppoloni, Chmn.

Phone: 55-11-3759-7516	Fax: 55-11-3759-8547
Toll-Free:	
Address: 5200 Ave. Major Sylvio de Magalhaes Padilha, Fl. 3, Sao Paulo, 05693-000 Brazil	

GROWTH PLANS/SPECIAL FEATURES:

Rossi Residencial SA is a Brazilian holding company involved in real estate and construction. The firm is part of construction, engineering and development conglomerate Grupo Rossi. Rossi Residencial is primarily involved in the construction, development, sale and commercialization of residential and commercial real estate properties. The firm operates in 68 cities located in 14 Brazilian states and the Federal District. Its most important state is Sao Paulo, which accounts for approximately 42% of the company's business. Rossi Residencial has 12 offices located in the cities of Sao Paulo, Rio de Janeiro, Porto Alegre, Curitiba, Vitoria, Salvador, Campinas, Recife, Natal, Fortaleza, Belo Horizonte and Goiania. Approximately 17.9% of the company's income is derived from residential real estate valued at over $306,917; 39.6% is derived from economic housing ($88,520-$98,213); 13.1% from houses valued between $214,817 and $306,916; 18.3% from houses valued between $122,753 and $214,816; 2.8% from residential houses valued between $98,213-$122,752; and 8.3% is derived from commercial real estate. In May 2010, the firm announced a joint venture with GMS Imobiliaria e Construtora. In October 2010, Rossi Residencial launched a real estate joint venture with Toctao Engenhari.

FINANCIALS: Sales and profits are in thousands of dollars—add 000 to get the full amount. 2010 Note: Financial information for 2010 was not available for all companies at press time.

2010 Sales: $1,593,390	2010 Profits: $223,320	**U.S. Stock Ticker:**
2009 Sales: $897,550	2009 Profits: $124,500	**Int'l Ticker:** RSID3 **Int'l Exchange:** Sao Paulo-SAO
2008 Sales: $703,920	2008 Profits: $67,700	Employees:
2007 Sales: $431,510	2007 Profits: $41,960	Fiscal Year Ends: 12/31
2006 Sales: $	2006 Profits: $	Parent Company:

SALARIES/BENEFITS:

Pension Plan:	ESOP Stock Plan: Y	Profit Sharing:	Top Exec. Salary: $	Bonus: $
Savings Plan:	Stock Purch. Plan:		Second Exec. Salary: $	Bonus: $

OTHER THOUGHTS:

Apparent Women Officers or Directors:
Hot Spot for Advancement for Women/Minorities:

LOCATIONS: ("Y" = Yes)

West:	Southwest:	Midwest:	Southeast:	Northeast:	International:
					Y

ROYAL GROUP INC

www.royalbuildingproducts.com

Industry Group Code: 326199 Ranks within this company's industry group: Sales: Profits:

Properties:	Financial Services:	Construction/Development:		Investments:	Specialty Services:	Brokerage:
Apartments:	Mortgages:	Commercial Construction:		REIT:	Property Management:	Commercial Sales:
Malls/Shopping:	Title Insurance:	Residential Construction:			Online Services:	Residential Sales:
Offices:	Property Insurance:	Land Development:			Software/IT:	Specialty:
Hotels/Motels:		Support Services:	Y		Consulting:	
Industrial/Warehouses:		Design/Engineering:				
Other:						

TYPES OF BUSINESS:
Building Materials

BRANDS/DIVISIONS/AFFILIATES:
Georgia Gulf Corporation
Royal Group Technologies Limited

CONTACTS: *Note: Officers with more than one job title may be intentionally listed here more than once.*
Paul D. Carrico, CEO
Paul D. Carrico, Pres.
Gregory Thompson, CFO
Mark O. Badger, VP-Mktg.
Mark O. Badger, VP-Corp. Comm.
Mark J. Orcutt, Exec. VP-Royal Building Prod.
Simon Bates, VP/Gen. Manager-Royal Building Prod.
Mark Fanelli, VP/Gen. Manager-Royal Window & Door Profiles
Shane Short, Gen. Manager-Royal Building Prod.

Phone: 905-850-9700	**Fax:** 905-850-9184
Toll-Free: 800-387-2789	
Address: 91 Royal Gate Blvd., Woodbridge, ON L4H 1X9 Canada	

GROWTH PLANS/SPECIAL FEATURES:
Royal Group, Inc., formerly Royal Group Technologies Limited, manufactures and sells PVC and vinyl construction, improvement and building products. The firm is a subsidiary of Georgia Gulf Corporation, a North American manufacturer and international marketer of commodity chemicals, polymers and durable, custom and other vinyl-based building and home improvement products. Royal Group Inc. operates primarily in Canada and the U.S., and also has international operations in Mexico, Asia, Europe and South America. The majority of Royal's sales come from the U.S. The firm operates through five divisions: Royal Building Products; Royal Mouldings Limited; Royal Outdoor Products; Royal Pipe Systems; and Royal Window and Door Profiles. Royal Building Products offers soffit, shutters, premium vinyl siding, mounts, vents, vinyl/aluminum columns and accessories. Royal Mouldings Limited manufactures decorative polymer and cellular vinyl molding extrusion components and systems. Royal Outdoor Products produces products such as railings, decking systems, columns and fencing. Royal Pipe Systems products include pipes for municipal potable water, sewer systems and storm drains; plumbing pipes; ducts, conduit and other pipes and fittings for electrical construction; and fittings for backwater valves, inspection chambers and controlled settlement joints. Royal Window and Door Profiles utilizes polymer fenestration technologies to produce patio door systems, custom window profiles and window systems.

FINANCIALS: Sales and profits are in thousands of dollars—add 000 to get the full amount. 2010 Note: Financial information for 2010 was not available for all companies at press time.

2010 Sales: $	2010 Profits: $	**U.S. Stock Ticker: Subsidiary**
2009 Sales: $	2009 Profits: $	**Int'l Ticker:** Int'l Exchange:
2008 Sales: $	2008 Profits: $	Employees:
2007 Sales: $1,271,600	2007 Profits: $	Fiscal Year Ends: 12/31
2006 Sales: $	2006 Profits: $	Parent Company: GEORGIA GULF CORPORATION

SALARIES/BENEFITS:

Pension Plan:	ESOP Stock Plan:	Profit Sharing:	Top Exec. Salary: $	Bonus: $
Savings Plan:	Stock Purch. Plan:		Second Exec. Salary: $	Bonus: $

OTHER THOUGHTS:
Apparent Women Officers or Directors:
Hot Spot for Advancement for Women/Minorities:

LOCATIONS: ("Y" = Yes)

West:	Southwest:	Midwest:	Southeast:	Northeast:	International:
Y	Y	Y	Y	Y	Y

RXR REALTY

www.rxrrealty.com

Industry Group Code: 531120 Ranks within this company's industry group: Sales: Profits:

Properties:		Financial Services:	Construction/Development:	Investments:		Specialty Services:	Brokerage:
Apartments:		Mortgages:	Commercial Construction:	REIT:	Y	Property Management:	Commercial Sales:
Malls/Shopping:		Title Insurance:	Residential Construction:			Online Services:	Residential Sales:
Offices:	Y	Property Insurance:	Land Development:			Software/IT:	Specialty:
Hotels/Motels:			Support Services:			Consulting:	
Industrial/Warehouses:	Y		Design/Engineering:				
Other:							

TYPES OF BUSINESS:

Real Estate Investment Trust
Office & Industrial Properties
Commercial Construction & Development
Property Management

BRANDS/DIVISIONS/AFFILIATES:

RexCorp Realty
Tri-State Prime Property
Core Plus Value Enhanced Strategy
Opportunity Fund I
Opportunity Fund II

CONTACTS: *Note: Officers with more than one job title may be intentionally listed here more than once.*

Scott Rechler, CEO
Richard Conniff, Co-COO
Michael Maturo, Pres.
Michael Maturo, CFO
Carol Allen, Sr. VP-Mktg.
Ylisa Kunze, VP-Human Resources
Jason Barnett, General Counsel
Todd Rechler, Co-COO/Pres., RXR Construction & Dev.
Glenn Wasserman, Exec. VP-Strategic Planning, Capital & Markets
Tom Carey, Controller/Exec. VP
Frank Patafio, Sr. Exec. VP/Head-Acquisitions
Jason J. Forte, Sr. VP-Long Island Div.
F.D. Rich, Exec. VP-Special Projects
Scott Rechler, Chmn.

Phone: 516-506-6000	Fax: 516-506-6800
Toll-Free:	
Address: 625 RXR Plz., Uniondale, NY 11556 US	

GROWTH PLANS/SPECIAL FEATURES:

RXR Realty, formerly RexCorp Realty, is a self-administered and self-managed real estate investment trust (REIT) that acquires, owns, develops, constructs, manages and leases office and industrial properties in the New York Tri-State area. The former members of Reckson Associates Realty Corp's management formed the company in recent years after the completion of the original company's acquisition by and merger with SL Green Realty Corp. RXR Realty's primary investment funds include the Tri-State Prime Property Joint Venture, which offers 15 office properties located in Long Island and New Jersey; and Core Plus Value Enhanced Strategy, which includes the Opportunity Fund I, Opportunity Fund II and Value Enhanced Portfolio. The Core Plus portfolios include 48 developed properties in New Jersey, Long Island, Westchester and Connecticut and several active development projects. In total, RXR Realty owns approximately $2.5 billion in class-A properties consisting of a combined 11 million square feet, making the company one of the Tri-State area's leading real estate companies. The company also oversees the Opportunity Fund I and Opportunity Fund II portfolios, which invest in properties and other interests. RXR Realty offers its tenants cross-leasing opportunities to provide enhanced flexibility and the convenience of being able to work with a single owner/manager over multiple spaces. Some of the firm's current tenants include AT&T; Bank of America; Citibank N.A., Del Laboratories, Inc.; Hewlett Packard Company; Merrill Lynch Pierce Fenner; Starbucks Corporation; and Xerox Corporation.

FINANCIALS: Sales and profits are in thousands of dollars—add 000 to get the full amount. 2010 Note: Financial information for 2010 was not available for all companies at press time.

2010 Sales: $	2010 Profits: $	**U.S. Stock Ticker: Private**
2009 Sales: $	2009 Profits: $	**Int'l Ticker:** Int'l Exchange:
2008 Sales: $	2008 Profits: $	Employees:
2007 Sales: $	2007 Profits: $	Fiscal Year Ends: 12/31
2006 Sales: $	2006 Profits: $	Parent Company:

SALARIES/BENEFITS:

Pension Plan:	ESOP Stock Plan:	Profit Sharing:	Top Exec. Salary: $	Bonus: $
Savings Plan:	Stock Purch. Plan:		Second Exec. Salary: $	Bonus: $

OTHER THOUGHTS:

Apparent Women Officers or Directors: 3
Hot Spot for Advancement for Women/Minorities: Y

LOCATIONS: ("Y" = Yes)

West:	Southwest:	Midwest:	Southeast:	Northeast:	International:
				Y	

RYLAND GROUP INC (THE)

www.ryland.com

Industry Group Code: 2361 Ranks within this company's industry group: Sales: 10   Profits: 15

Properties:	Financial Services:		Construction/Development:		Investments:	Specialty Services:	Brokerage:	
Apartments:	Mortgages:	Y	Commercial Construction:		REIT:	Property Management:	Commercial Sales:	
Malls/Shopping:	Title Insurance:	Y	Residential Construction:	Y		Online Services:	Residential Sales:	Y
Offices:	Property Insurance:	Y	Land Development:			Software/IT:	Specialty:	
Hotels/Motels:			Support Services:			Consulting:		
Industrial/Warehouses:			Design/Engineering:	Y				
Other:								

TYPES OF BUSINESS:

Home Building
Mortgages
Title Services
Insurance Brokerage
Escrow Services
Home Brokerage
Homeowners' Warranties

BRANDS/DIVISIONS/AFFILIATES:

Ryland Mortgage Co
Cornerstone Title Co
RH Insurance Company
LPS Holdings Corporation
Columbia National Risk Retention Group Inc

CONTACTS: *Note: Officers with more than one job title may be intentionally listed here more than once.*

Larry T. Nicholson, CEO
Larry T. Nicholson, Pres.
Gordon A. Milne, CFO/Exec. VP
Robert J. Cunnion, III, Sr. VP-Human Resources
Craig McSpadden, CIO/VP
Timothy J. Geckle, General Counsel/Sr. VP/Corp. Sec.
Eric E. Elder, Sr. VP-Corp. Comm.
Drew P. Mackintosh, VP-Investor Rel.
David L. Fristoe, Chief Acct. Officer/Controller/Sr. VP
Peter G. Skelly, Pres., Homebuilding
David A. Brown, Pres., Ryland Mortgage Co.
Rene L. Mentch, VP-Tax
Thomas M. Pearson, VP-Internal Audit
William L. Jews, Chmn.

Phone: 818-223-7500	Fax: 818-223-7667
Toll-Free:	
Address: 24025 Park Sorrento, Ste. 400, Calabasas, CA 91302 US	

GROWTH PLANS/SPECIAL FEATURES:

The Ryland Group, Inc. is one of the largest homebuilding and mortgage finance companies in the U.S. The company has built over 290,000 homes and financed more than 245,000 mortgages since its founding in 1967. The firm's operations span all aspects of the home-buying process from design, construction and sale to mortgage origination, title insurance, escrow and insurance services. The company focuses on marketing single-family homes to entry-level and move-up buyers, as well as to adults seeking retirement housing. Its homes are available in approximately 18 markets in 15 states across the country, which are divided into four broad geographic operating units: including North, Southeast, Texas and West. Moreover, its product line is tailored to local styles and preferences found in each geographic market. The company's prices range from $100,000 to over $450,000, with the average price of a Ryland home closed being roughly $242,000. Although homebuilding represents about 97% of the firm's annual revenue, it is also involved in financial services. Ryland's financial services segment is comprised of Ryland Mortgage Company (RMC); RH Insurance Company; Cornerstone Title Company, which does business as Ryland Title Company; LPS Holdings Corporation and its subsidiaries; and Columbia National Risk Retention Group, Inc. (Columbia). Mortgage financing and related services are provided by RMC and LPS Holdings. RH Insurance Company provides insurance brokerage services to the firm's homebuyers. Cornerstone provides title services and acts as a title insurance agent. Columbia directly insures liability risks, specifically homeowners' warranty coverage, arising in connection with the homebuilding business of the company.

Ryland offers its employees a benefits program including life, AD&D, disability, medical, vision and dental insurance; a 401(k) plan; a stock purchase plan; tuition reimbursement; a mortgage discount program; and paid vacations and holidays.

FINANCIALS: Sales and profits are in thousands of dollars—add 000 to get the full amount. 2010 Note: Financial information for 2010 was not available for all companies at press time.

2010 Sales: $1,063,892	2010 Profits: $-85,139	**U.S. Stock Ticker:** RYL
2009 Sales: $1,283,613	2009 Profits: $-162,474	**Int'l Ticker:** Int'l Exchange:
2008 Sales: $1,976,124	2008 Profits: $-396,585	Employees: 991
2007 Sales: $3,052,000	2007 Profits: $-333,526	Fiscal Year Ends: 12/31
2006 Sales: $4,780,000	2006 Profits: $359,942	Parent Company:

SALARIES/BENEFITS:

Pension Plan:	ESOP Stock Plan:	Profit Sharing:	Top Exec. Salary: $900,000	Bonus: $1,875,000
Savings Plan: Y	Stock Purch. Plan: Y		Second Exec. Salary: $700,000	Bonus: $705,000

OTHER THOUGHTS:

Apparent Women Officers or Directors: 2
Hot Spot for Advancement for Women/Minorities:

LOCATIONS: ("Y" = Yes)

West:	Southwest:	Midwest:	Southeast:	Northeast:	International:
Y	Y	Y	Y	Y	

SAHA PATHANA INTER-HOLDING PCL

www.spi.co.th

Industry Group Code: 5311 Ranks within this company's industry group: Sales: 31   Profits: 24

Properties:		Financial Services:		Construction/Development:		Investments:		Specialty Services:		Brokerage:	
Apartments:		Mortgages:		Commercial Construction:	Y	REIT:		Property Management:		Commercial Sales:	
Malls/Shopping:	Y	Title Insurance:		Residential Construction:				Online Services:		Residential Sales:	
Offices:	Y	Property Insurance:		Land Development:	Y			Software/IT:		Specialty:	
Hotels/Motels:				Support Services:				Consulting:			
Industrial/Warehouses:	Y			Design/Engineering:							
Other:											

TYPES OF BUSINESS:

Industrial Real Estate Holdings

BRANDS/DIVISIONS/AFFILIATES:

Brahma Park
Health Park

CONTACTS: *Note: Officers with more than one job title may be intentionally listed here more than once.*

Boonsithi Chokwatana, Chmn.-Exec. Board
Santi Vilatsakdanont, Pres.
Somchai Puntaprukesa, Mgr.-Finance
Sauwanee Numbenjapol, Mgr.-Human Resources
Anant Soonpan, Mgr.-R&D
Sontaya Tabkhan, Mgr.-Eng. Dept.
Darunee Sooontorntumrong, Mgr.-Project Admin.
Vichai Aramrueng, Mgr.-Legal
Nisa Chindasombatcharoen, Mgr.-Acct.
Tanong Srichit, Exec. VP
Pimsiri Kuansuwan, Mgr.-Bus. Promotion
Tinakorn Bunnag, Mgr.-Land Dev.
Chokchai Aksoranan, Chmn.

Phone: 66-2-293-0030	Fax: 66-2-293-0040
Toll-Free:	
Address: 757/10 Soi Pradoo 1, Sathupradit Rd., Bangkok, 10120 Thailand	

GROWTH PLANS/SPECIAL FEATURES:

Saha Pathana Inter-Holding PCL is a Thailand-based real estate holding and development company investing primarily in industrial parks. The company is currently invested in three industrial parks in Sriracha, Kabinburi and Lamphun. The Sriracha park features a 186 megawatt (MW) power plant; a centralized water treatment plant with a daily capacity of 423,776 cubic feet; a private air field; a trade exhibition center; a 30 million cubic foot water reservoir; and a park. The park located in Kabinburi contains two 50 megavolt ampere (MVA) electrical substations; a centralized waste water treatment plant with a daily capacity of 565,035 cubic feet; a private air field; a 35.3 million cubic foot water reservoir; and an industrial incinerator with a 220 pound per hour capacity. The Lamphun park features two 50 megavolt ampere (MVA) electrical substations; a centralized water treatment plant with a daily capacity of 300,175 cubic feet; a private water supply of 127,133 cubic feet per day; a private air field; a 17.6 million cubic foot water reservoir; a golf driving range; a meeting room; and Brahma Park and Health Park. The company, to a lesser extent, is invested in consumer products, distribution, manufacturing, service and investment firms.

FINANCIALS: Sales and profits are in thousands of dollars—add 000 to get the full amount. 2010 Note: Financial information for 2010 was not available for all companies at press time.

2010 Sales: $101,900	2010 Profits: $34,010	**U.S. Stock Ticker:**
2009 Sales: $93,250	2009 Profits: $31,050	**Int'l Ticker: SPI** Int'l Exchange: Bangkok-BAK
2008 Sales: $86,500	2008 Profits: $28,000	Employees:
2007 Sales: $73,700	2007 Profits: $17,800	Fiscal Year Ends:
2006 Sales: $78,900	2006 Profits: $21,600	Parent Company:

SALARIES/BENEFITS:

Pension Plan:	ESOP Stock Plan:	Profit Sharing:	Top Exec. Salary: $	Bonus: $
Savings Plan:	Stock Purch. Plan:		Second Exec. Salary: $	Bonus: $

OTHER THOUGHTS:

Apparent Women Officers or Directors: 5
Hot Spot for Advancement for Women/Minorities: Y

LOCATIONS: ("Y" = Yes)

West:	Southwest:	Midwest:	Southeast:	Northeast:	International:
					Y

SAMWHAN CORPORATION

www.samwhan.co.kr/sw/english

Industry Group Code: 23 Ranks within this company's industry group: Sales: Profits:

Properties:	Financial Services:	Construction/Development:		Investments:	Specialty Services:	Brokerage:
Apartments:	Mortgages:	Commercial Construction:	Y	REIT:	Property Management:	Commercial Sales:
Malls/Shopping:	Title Insurance:	Residential Construction:	Y		Online Services:	Residential Sales:
Offices:	Property Insurance:	Land Development:			Software/IT:	Specialty:
Hotels/Motels:		Support Services:			Consulting:	
Industrial/Warehouses:		Design/Engineering:				
Other:						

TYPES OF BUSINESS:

Construction
General Importing & Exporting
Precast Concrete

BRANDS/DIVISIONS/AFFILIATES:

Samwhan Camus Co
Samwhan Machinery Co Ltd
Sinmin Mutual Savings Bank
Whoihyun Co Ltd
Woosung Development Co Ltd

CONTACTS: Note: Officers with more than one job title may be intentionally listed here more than once.

Jong Huh, CEO
Jong Huh, Pres.
Sang Tae Choi, Head/Dir.-Construction Bus.
Youn-Kwon Choi, Chmn.

Phone: 82-2-740-2114	Fax: 82-2-742-1849
Toll-Free:	
Address: 98-20 Wooni-dong, Jongno-Gu, Seoul, 110-742 Korea	

GROWTH PLANS/SPECIAL FEATURES:

Samwhan Corporation, established in 1946, is a Korean construction company. It has experience building housing units; commercial buildings; offices; ports and airports; industrial plants; fabrication facilities; power distribution and transmission systems; pipelines and pumping systems; and highways and bridges. More specifically, its projects have included intelligent buildings; resorts and recreational complexes; hospital and medical healthcare facilities; retail complexes, department stores and shopping malls; remodeling and rehabilitation; real estate development; thermal, nuclear and hydraulic power plants; municipal solid waste treatment plants; natural gas pipelines; oil refineries; subways and underground works; dams; and land reclamation. Samwhan offers engineering and consulting services, including feasibility studies; basic and detailed design; and construction management and supervisory services. The firm is also engaged in a general import and export business; and the production and supply of precast concrete. The company has branches in Afghanistan, California, Vietnam, Bangladesh, Japan, Saudi Arabia, Turkey, Russia, Algeria, Libya and the Republic of Yemen. Besides these locations, Samwhan has completed major projects in Afghanistan, Jordan, Papua New Guinea, Guam, Malaysia, Indonesia, Laos and Singapore. It was one of the first Korean contractors to work in Mongolia, and has worked on numerous U.S. military bases in Korea. Samwhan's affiliates include Samwhan Camus Co., which focuses on pre-cast concrete production and construction; Samwhan Machinery Co., Ltd., a manufacturer of materials for metal structures; Sinmin Mutual Savings Bank, a banking and financing company; Whoihyun Co., Ltd., a real estate leasing service; and Woosung Development Co., Ltd., a company involved with land development.

FINANCIALS: Sales and profits are in thousands of dollars—add 000 to get the full amount. 2010 Note: Financial information for 2010 was not available for all companies at press time.

2010 Sales: $	2010 Profits: $	U.S. Stock Ticker:
2009 Sales: $1,055,960	2009 Profits: $-677,720	Int'l Ticker: 000360 Int'l Exchange: Seoul-KRX
2008 Sales: $917,070	2008 Profits: $10,620	Employees:
2007 Sales: $	2007 Profits: $	Fiscal Year Ends:
2006 Sales: $	2006 Profits: $	Parent Company:

SALARIES/BENEFITS:

Pension Plan:	ESOP Stock Plan:	Profit Sharing:	Top Exec. Salary: $	Bonus: $
Savings Plan:	Stock Purch. Plan:		Second Exec. Salary: $	Bonus: $

OTHER THOUGHTS:

Apparent Women Officers or Directors:
Hot Spot for Advancement for Women/Minorities:

LOCATIONS: ("Y" = Yes)

West:	Southwest:	Midwest:	Southeast:	Northeast:	International:
Y					Y

SANDS REGENT

www.sandsregency.com

Industry Group Code: 721120 Ranks within this company's industry group: Sales: Profits:

Properties:		Financial Services:	Construction/Development:	Investments:	Specialty Services:	Brokerage:
Apartments:		Mortgages:	Commercial Construction:	REIT:	Property Management:	Commercial Sales:
Malls/Shopping:		Title Insurance:	Residential Construction:		Online Services:	Residential Sales:
Offices:		Property Insurance:	Land Development:		Software/IT:	Specialty:
Hotels/Motels:	Y		Support Services:		Consulting:	
Industrial/Warehouses:			Design/Engineering:			
Other:	Y					

TYPES OF BUSINESS:

Casino Hotel
Convention Center

BRANDS/DIVISIONS/AFFILIATES:

Herbst Gaming Inc
Sands Regency Casino & Hotel
Terrible's Gold Ranch Casino & RV Resort
Terrible's Rail City Casino

CONTACTS: *Note: Officers with more than one job title may be intentionally listed here more than once.*

David D.Ross, CEO
Ferenc B. Szony, COO
Ferenc B. Szony, Pres.
Donna Lehmann, CFO/Sr. VP
Don Kornstein, Chmn.

Phone: 702-889-7695	Fax: 702-889-7691
Toll-Free:	
Address: 3440 W. Russell Rd., Reno, NV 89118 US	

GROWTH PLANS/SPECIAL FEATURES:

Sands Regent owns and operates casinos and related tourist amenities in Nevada within the Terrible Herbst family of properties. The company portfolio consists of 12 casinos in Northern and Southern Nevada and three casinos in Missouri and Iowa. The company's marquee operation, the Sands Regency Casino and Hotel in downtown Reno, features some 850 hotel rooms and 29,000 square feet of gaming space. While the company derives most of its revenue from its 17 gaming tables, 539 slot machines and sportsbook, it also operates a comedy club, cocktail lounges, a video arcade and a music lounge. Other services include beauty and gift shops; restaurants and fast-food eateries; and a 12,000-square-foot convention and meeting center that accommodates 1,000 people. Some notable properties include: Terrible's Gold Ranch Casino & RV Resort in Verdi, Nevada, 12 miles west of Reno, is the first casino gaming attraction that travelers encounter on Interstate 80 when entering Nevada from California, and the last when leaving. Its facilities include an 8,300-square-foot casino with 235 slot machines, two restaurants, two bars, a California lottery station, an ARCO gas station and a convenience store, as well as a 47-space RV park. Terrible's Rail City Casino in Sparks, Nevada has approximately 16,600 square feet of gaming space and features more than 650 slots, six table games, keno and a sportsbook. It also has a family-style restaurant and a sports bar, with a convenient off-highway location. In addition, the company operations include Terrible Herbst gas stations and convenience stores. Lastly, the firm's operations include installation and operation of slot machines in chain store and street account locations and over 14,000 slot machines in chain stores throughout the state of Nevada. Herbst Gaming, Inc. owns the firm.

FINANCIALS: Sales and profits are in thousands of dollars—add 000 to get the full amount. 2010 Note: Financial information for 2010 was not available for all companies at press time.

2010 Sales: $	2010 Profits: $	**U.S. Stock Ticker: Subsidiary**
2009 Sales: $	2009 Profits: $	**Int'l Ticker:** Int'l Exchange:
2008 Sales: $	2008 Profits: $	Employees:
2007 Sales: $	2007 Profits: $	Fiscal Year Ends: 6/30
2006 Sales: $92,574	2006 Profits: $2,431	Parent Company: HERBST GAMING INC

SALARIES/BENEFITS:

Pension Plan:	ESOP Stock Plan:	Profit Sharing:	Top Exec. Salary: $992,822	Bonus: $
Savings Plan: Y	Stock Purch. Plan:		Second Exec. Salary: $567,211	Bonus: $

OTHER THOUGHTS:

Apparent Women Officers or Directors:
Hot Spot for Advancement for Women/Minorities:

LOCATIONS: ("Y" = Yes)

West:	Southwest:	Midwest:	Southeast:	Northeast:	International:
Y		Y			

SAWYER REALTY HOLDINGS LLC

www.sawyerapts.com

Industry Group Code: 531110 Ranks within this company's industry group: Sales: Profits:

Properties:		Financial Services:	Construction/Development:		Investments:	Specialty Services:		Brokerage:
Apartments:	Y	Mortgages:	Commercial Construction:	Y	REIT:	Property Management:	Y	Commercial Sales:
Malls/Shopping:		Title Insurance:	Residential Construction:	Y		Online Services:		Residential Sales:
Offices:		Property Insurance:	Land Development:	Y		Software/IT:		Specialty:
Hotels/Motels:			Support Services:			Consulting:		
Industrial/Warehouses:			Design/Engineering:					
Other:	Y							

TYPES OF BUSINESS:

Real Estate Investment Trust
Apartment Communities
Property Management

BRANDS/DIVISIONS/AFFILIATES:

Forewinds Hospitality, LLC

CONTACTS:
Note: Officers with more than one job title may be intentionally listed here more than once.

David M. Rosenberg, CEO
Gregg Clickstein, Pres.
Gary J. Gianino, CFO
Tom Rucker, VP-Real Estate Oper., Sawyer Property Mgmt.

Phone: 301-479-1600	Fax: 301-479-1700
Toll-Free:	
Address: 9658 Baltimore Ave., Ste 300, College Park, MD 20740 US	

GROWTH PLANS/SPECIAL FEATURES:

Sawyer Realty Holdings, LLC is a privately held real estate investment and management firm that acquires, maintains and operates undervalued multifamily properties. The company works to add value to its acquisitions through teams of mostly autonomous property specialists across the east coast and throughout the Midwest, and offices in Massachusetts, Maryland and Georgia. Sawyer's multifamily portfolio consists of approximately 39,814 apartment units located inside 137 apartment communities, primarily in Florida and the Southeast, up the East coast into Baltimore, Washington D.C. and New England. Sawyer utilizes real estate as an investment mechanism to enrich all of its stakeholders, including its employees, lenders, suppliers, investors, officers, and principals. In addition to Sawyer's multi-family focus, the company invests in ground up development projects for multifamily, hotel, and commercial projects, which includes the purchase or joint venture of permitted or raw land and acquisition of existing properties for significant redevelopment. Sawyer has also invested in numerous golf course assets through its wholly-owned subsidiary, Forewinds Hospitality, LLC.

Employees of the firm are offered medical, dental, vision and prescription drug plan; flexible spending account for health care and dependent care; long-term and short-term disability; employee assistance program; accidental death, dismemberment and basic life insurance; and a discount program.

FINANCIALS:
Sales and profits are in thousands of dollars—add 000 to get the full amount. 2010 Note: Financial information for 2010 was not available for all companies at press time.

2010 Sales: $	2010 Profits: $	U.S. Stock Ticker: Private
2009 Sales: $	2009 Profits: $	Int'l Ticker: Int'l Exchange:
2008 Sales: $	2008 Profits: $	Employees:
2007 Sales: $	2007 Profits: $	Fiscal Year Ends: 12/31
2006 Sales: $	2006 Profits: $	Parent Company:

SALARIES/BENEFITS:

Pension Plan:	ESOP Stock Plan:	Profit Sharing:	Top Exec. Salary: $	Bonus: $
Savings Plan: Y	Stock Purch. Plan:		Second Exec. Salary: $	Bonus: $

OTHER THOUGHTS:

Apparent Women Officers or Directors:
Hot Spot for Advancement for Women/Minorities:

LOCATIONS: ("Y" = Yes)

West:	Southwest:	Midwest:	Southeast:	Northeast:	International:
				Y	

SCANDIC HOTELS AB

www.scandichotels.com

Industry Group Code: 721110 Ranks within this company's industry group: Sales: 13   Profits: 12

Properties:		Financial Services:	Construction/Development:	Investments:	Specialty Services:	Brokerage:
Apartments:		Mortgages:	Commercial Construction:	REIT:	Property Management:	Commercial Sales:
Malls/Shopping:		Title Insurance:	Residential Construction:		Online Services:	Residential Sales:
Offices:		Property Insurance:	Land Development:		Software/IT:	Specialty:
Hotels/Motels:	Y		Support Services:		Consulting:	
Industrial/Warehouses:			Design/Engineering:			
Other:						

TYPES OF BUSINESS:
Hotels

BRANDS/DIVISIONS/AFFILIATES:
Hotel Rivoli
Hotel Linnea
Hotel Salpaus

CONTACTS: *Note: Officers with more than one job title may be intentionally listed here more than once.*
Anders Ehrling, CEO
Anders Ehrling, Pres.
Gunilla Rudebjer, CFO
Ulrika Kjellstrom Attar, Mgr.-Brand Experience
Roger Olofsson, Sr. VP-Human Resources
Thomas Engelhart, Sr. VP-Commercial Oper.
Martin Creydt, Chief Dev. Officer/Sr. VP
Gunilla Rudebjer, Sr. VP-Finance
Joakim Nilsson, VP
Jens Mathiesen, VP-Denmark
Aarne Hallama, VP-Finland
Svein Arild Steen-Mevold, VP-Norway

Phone: 46-85-17-350-00	Fax: 46-85-17-350-11
Toll-Free:	
Address: Halsingegatan 40, Stockholm, SE-102 33 Sweden	

GROWTH PLANS/SPECIAL FEATURES:
Scandic Hotels AB, which is owned by private equity firm EQT Partners AB, is one of Scandinavia's largest hotel operators. The firm has approximately 160 hotels located in 10 countries: Sweden, Norway, Finland, Denmark, Estonia, Germany, Belgium, Poland, the Netherlands and Lithuania. Every year, Scandic Hotels serve over 8 million guests. Scandic Hotels has a long history of being environmentally conscious, and all of its Swedish hotels carry the Swan eco-label, a certification earned for effort and results toward sustainable practices. Scandic also has partnerships with numerous hotel, travel and entertainment companies to provide more options to its customers. In an effort to simplify services for customers, Scandic Hotels' pricing plan offers two price levels: early and flex. Early means a reduced price reservation without the option to cancel or change, while flex is a higher, flexible reservation price. The company hopes expand and operate a total of 200 hotels within the next few years. In March 2010, the firm agreed to acquire the Finland-based Hotel Rivoli, Hotel Linnea, Hotel Salpaus and a hotel under construction from Next Hotels Finland Oy. In October 2010, the firm opened a three hotels in Bergen, Norway and one in Arvika, Sweden.

FINANCIALS: Sales and profits are in thousands of dollars—add 000 to get the full amount. 2010 Note: Financial information for 2010 was not available for all companies at press time.

2010 Sales: $1,107,670	2010 Profits: $90,750	**U.S. Stock Ticker: Private**
2009 Sales: $838,890	2009 Profits: $78,180	**Int'l Ticker:** Int'l Exchange:
2008 Sales: $982,670	2008 Profits: $143,930	Employees: 6,902
2007 Sales: $	2007 Profits: $	Fiscal Year Ends: 12/31
2006 Sales: $	2006 Profits: $	Parent Company: EQT PARTNERS AB

SALARIES/BENEFITS:

Pension Plan:	ESOP Stock Plan:	Profit Sharing:	Top Exec. Salary: $	Bonus: $
Savings Plan:	Stock Purch. Plan:		Second Exec. Salary: $	Bonus: $

OTHER THOUGHTS:
Apparent Women Officers or Directors: 1
Hot Spot for Advancement for Women/Minorities:

LOCATIONS: ("Y" = Yes)

West:	Southwest:	Midwest:	Southeast:	Northeast:	International:
					Y

SCHUFF INTERNATIONAL INC

www.schuff.com

Industry Group Code: 2389 Ranks within this company's industry group: Sales: 4   Profits: 4

Properties:	Financial Services:	Construction/Development:		Investments:	Specialty Services:		Brokerage:
Apartments:	Mortgages:	Commercial Construction:	Y	REIT:	Property Management:		Commercial Sales:
Malls/Shopping:	Title Insurance:	Residential Construction:			Online Services:		Residential Sales:
Offices:	Property Insurance:	Land Development:			Software/IT:	Y	Specialty:
Hotels/Motels:		Support Services:	Y		Consulting:	Y	
Industrial/Warehouses:		Design/Engineering:	Y				
Other:							

TYPES OF BUSINESS:

Construction Services
Structural Steel Fabrication & Erection
Project Management Services
Design & Engineering Consulting Services
Subcontract Management

BRANDS/DIVISIONS/AFFILIATES:

Schuff Steel Company
Schuff Steel Management Company
Quincy Joist Company
Aitken

CONTACTS: Note: Officers with more than one job title may be intentionally listed here more than once.

Scott A. Schuff, CEO
Scott A. Schuff, Pres.
Michael R. Hill, CFO/VP
Ryan S. Schuff, Pres./CEO-Schuff Steel Company
Robert N. Waldrep, VP
David A. Schuff, Chmn.

Phone: 602-252-7787	Fax: 602-452-4465
Toll-Free: 800-435-8528	
Address: 420 S. 19th Ave., Phoenix, AZ 85009 US	

GROWTH PLANS/SPECIAL FEATURES:

Schuff International, Inc. is a fully integrated steel fabrication and erection company primarily serving the commercial, industrial, public works, healthcare, gaming and hospitality, mixed-use, retail and transportation markets. The firm fabricates and erects structural steel for construction projects such as arenas and stadiums, bridges, casinos and hotels, convention centers, hospitals, power plants, office buildings, parking structures, retail centers, warehouses and distribution facilities. The company is divided into four segments: Schuff Steel Company, Schuff Steel Management Company, Quincy Joist Company and Aitken. Schuff Steel Company, utilizing Design-Build/Design-Assist and building information modeling (BIM) construction methods, offers structural steel design, as well as fabrication and erection. Schuff Steel Company maintains 10 fabrication plants and is divided into five divisions based on geographic region: Pacific Division, Southwest Division, Midwest Division, Gulf Coast Division and Atlantic Division. This segment is headquartered in Phoenix, Arizona. Schuff Steel Management company, headquartered in Mesa, Arizona, specializes in steel subcontract management services. Quincy Joist Company, located in Quincy, Florida, is a manufacturer of open web steel joists, long spans and joist girders used for load bearing members for floors and roofs in commercial and industrial buildings. Aitken, located in Houston, Texas, fabricates and manufactures pressure vessels, flow nozzles and strainers used in the petrochemicals market. Schuff International maintains 13 facilities in California, Arizona, Georgia, Florida, Kansas and Texas.

The company offers employees medical, dental and vision insurance; a 401(k) plan; short- and long-term disability coverage; life and AD&D insurance; and an employee assistance plan.

FINANCIALS: **Sales and profits are in thousands of dollars—add 000 to get the full amount. 2010 Note: Financial information for 2010 was not available for all companies at press time.**

2010 Sales: $287,566	2010 Profits: $1,280	**U.S. Stock Ticker: SHFK**
2009 Sales: $420,871	2009 Profits: $18,951	**Int'l Ticker:** Int'l Exchange:
2008 Sales: $681,629	2008 Profits: $56,315	Employees:
2007 Sales: $736,194	2007 Profits: $59,874	Fiscal Year Ends: 12/31
2006 Sales: $	2006 Profits: $	Parent Company:

SALARIES/BENEFITS:

Pension Plan:	ESOP Stock Plan:	Profit Sharing:	Top Exec. Salary: $	Bonus: $
Savings Plan: Y	Stock Purch. Plan:		Second Exec. Salary: $	Bonus: $

OTHER THOUGHTS:

Apparent Women Officers or Directors:
Hot Spot for Advancement for Women/Minorities:

LOCATIONS: ("Y" = Yes)

West:	Southwest:	Midwest:	Southeast:	Northeast:	International:
Y	Y	Y	Y		

SEKISUI HOUSE LTD

www.sekisuihouse.co.jp

Industry Group Code: 2361 Ranks within this company's industry group: Sales: 1   Profits: 16

Properties:		Financial Services:		Construction/Development:		Investments:	Specialty Services:	Brokerage:	
Apartments:	Y	Mortgages:		Commercial Construction:	Y	REIT:	Property Management:	Commercial Sales:	
Malls/Shopping:		Title Insurance:		Residential Construction:	Y		Online Services:	Residential Sales:	Y
Offices:	Y	Property Insurance:		Land Development:	Y		Software/IT:	Specialty:	
Hotels/Motels:				Support Services:			Consulting:		
Industrial/Warehouses:	Y			Design/Engineering:	Y				
Other:	Y								

TYPES OF BUSINESS:

Residential Construction
Real Estate Sales
Real Estate Leasing
Urban Construction
Garden Design
Pre-fabricated Housing Construction

BRANDS/DIVISIONS/AFFILIATES:

Joint Capital Partners Co., Ltd.
Lend Lease Group
Newland Real Estate Group LLC

CONTACTS: *Note: Officers with more than one job title may be intentionally listed here more than once.*

Isami Wada, CEO
Toshinori Abe, COO
Toshinori Abe, Pres.
Takashi Uchida, Chief Dir.-Sales, Saitama
Mitsugu Iijima, Dir.-Human Resources
Tetsuo Iku, Chief Dir.-Tech.
Kengo Yoshida, Chief Dir.-Prod.
Koji Nakata, Dir.-Legal Affairs
Tsutomu Motomura, Dir.-Bus. Planning
Yoshikazu Takatsuka, Dir.-Sekiwa Construction Reform Bus.
Shiro Inagaki, Sr. Managing Officer
Sumio Wada, Sr. Managing Officer
Naoki Ishii, Dir.-House Bus.
Isami Wada, Chmn.

Phone: 81-6-6440-3111	Fax: 81-6-6440-3369
Toll-Free:	
Address: 1-88 Oyodonaka, 1-Chome, Kita-ku, Osaka, 531-0076 Japan	

GROWTH PLANS/SPECIAL FEATURES:

Sekisui House, Ltd., based in Japan, and its subsidiaries engage primarily in the contract design, construction and leasing of pre-fabricated houses. These residences are built-to-order and include both single- and multi-family houses, condominiums and low-rise apartments. The company is also involved in the construction of urban development projects and the management of recreation facilities, training facilities, restaurants and hotels. Sekisui House manufactures and sells construction materials; purchases and sells materials for reforestation, landscaping and other civil engineering works; and undertakes research, planning, design and consulting business related to regional development, land preparation and environmental improvement. The firm also contracts, executes and supervises civil engineering works; carpentry works; plasterwork; earth, stone and concrete work; roofing; electrical and piping work; tile, brick and blockwork; steel structure and reinforcing; paving; sheet metal and glasswork; painting; waterproofing; interior finishing; furnishing; machinery and tool installation; heating insulation work; telecommunications installation; waterworks; and firefighting equipment construction. In real estate, the company buys and sells properties; manages and appraises real estate; and acts as a broker for property purchase and sale. Sekisui House also engages in the cultivation, purchase and sale of plants and the design and cultivation of gardens. The company has a total of 90 subsidiaries and affiliate companies and 125 sales offices. In February 2010, Sekisui House and Spring Investment Co., Ltd., agreed to jointly acquire asset management firm Joint Capital Partners Co., Ltd., from Joint Corporation. In September 2010, the firm entered a business alliance with Australia-based Lend Lease Group for the development of housing projects in Australia. Also in September, Sekisui House and Newland Real Estate Group LLC formed a joint venture for the acquisition of residential and commercial real estate developments in the U.S. Following the Tohoku Earthquake in Japan in March 2011, the firm halted operations at its Tohoku factory.

FINANCIALS: Sales and profits are in thousands of dollars—add 000 to get the full amount. 2010 Note: Financial information for 2010 was not available for all companies at press time.

2010 Sales: $16,511,100	2010 Profits: $-357,230	**U.S. Stock Ticker: SKHSF**
2009 Sales: $16,083,100	2009 Profits: $122,320	**Int'l Ticker: 1928** Int'l Exchange: Tokyo-TSE
2008 Sales: $15,978,100	2008 Profits: $603,500	Employees:
2007 Sales: $15,961,800	2007 Profits: $626,600	Fiscal Year Ends: 1/31
2006 Sales: $15,018,600	2006 Profits: $430,300	Parent Company:

SALARIES/BENEFITS:

Pension Plan:	ESOP Stock Plan:	Profit Sharing:	Top Exec. Salary: $	Bonus: $
Savings Plan:	Stock Purch. Plan:		Second Exec. Salary: $	Bonus: $

OTHER THOUGHTS:

Apparent Women Officers or Directors:
Hot Spot for Advancement for Women/Minorities:

LOCATIONS: ("Y" = Yes)

West:	Southwest:	Midwest:	Southeast:	Northeast:	International:
					Y

SEMBCORP INDUSTRIES LTD

www.sembcorp.com.sg

Industry Group Code: 237 Ranks within this company's industry group: Sales: 19 Profits: 6

Properties:	Financial Services:	Construction/Development:		Investments:	Specialty Services:	Brokerage:
Apartments:	Mortgages:	Commercial Construction:	Y	REIT:	Property Management:	Commercial Sales:
Malls/Shopping:	Title Insurance:	Residential Construction:			Online Services:	Residential Sales:
Offices:	Property Insurance:	Land Development:			Software/IT:	Specialty:
Hotels/Motels:		Support Services:			Consulting:	
Industrial/Warehouses:		Design/Engineering:				
Other:						

TYPES OF BUSINESS:

Heavy Construction
Marine Construction & Shipbuilding
Utilities Services
Environmental Engineering & Waste Management
Industrial Parks
Internet Service Provider
Floating Oil Production Platforms
Pipelines

BRANDS/DIVISIONS/AFFILIATES:

Sembcorp Marine
Sembcorp Environment
Sembcorp Utilities
Sembcorp Gas
Sembcorp Cogen
Singapore Mint
Singapore Precision Industries
Sembcorp Design and Production

CONTACTS: *Note: Officers with more than one job title may be intentionally listed here more than once.*

Tang Kin Fei, CEO
Tang Kin Fei, Pres.
Koh Chiap Khiong, CFO
Tan Cheng Guan, Exec. VP-Group Bus. & Strategic Dev.
Wong Weng Sun, Pres./CEO-SembCorp Marine
Paul Gavens, Exec. VP-Sembcorp Utilities (U.K.)

Phone: 65-6723-3113	Fax: 65-6822-3254
Toll-Free:	
Address: 30 Hill St., 05-04, Singapore, 179360 Singapore	

GROWTH PLANS/SPECIAL FEATURES:

Sembcorp Industries, Ltd. is one of Singapore's leading utilities and marine groups. The firm's primary businesses include Sembcorp Utilities; Sembcorp Marine; Sembcorp Environment; and Sembcorp Industrial Parks. Sembcorp Utilities provides integrated utilities, energy and water solutions to the chemical and petrochemical industry in Singapore, the U.K. and China. In addition, the firm operates power a desalination plants in Vietnam and the United Arab Emirates (U.A.E.). The firm offers a variety of industrial utilities services including water supply and wastewater treatment; power generation; process stream production and distribution; chemical feedstock; and asset protection. The utility segment's operation has a generation capacity of 5,600 megawatts. Sembcorp Marine has one of the largest ship repair, shipbuilding and ship conversion operations in East Asia. The company offers a full range of marine and offshore engineering solutions including container ships, chemical tankers, production platforms; and converts Floating Production, Storage and Offloading units (FPSO) for the oil and gas industry. Sembcorp Environment provides treatment methods and waste-to-resource technologies to 1.2 million households, 47,000 industrial and commercial customers and government agencies, plus 9,000 healthcare establishments in Singapore, India and Australia. The Sembcorp Industrial Parks segment owns, develops, markets and manages multinational industrial parks predominately located in China, Indonesia and Vietnam. Sembcorp Industries operates numerous subsidiaries including Sembcorp Gas; Sembcorp Cogen; Sembcorp Power; Singapore Mint; SembCorp Design and Production; and Singapore Precision Industries. In January 2010, the firm began construction on a new industrial park in Hai Phong, Vietnam; and Sembcorp Utilities formed 80%-owned joint venture Qinzhou Sembcorp Water Co. (with partner Guangxi Qinzhou Linhai Industrial Investment Co.) to build, own and operate a wastewater treatment facility in Qinzhou Economic Development Zone. In August 2010, through Sembcorp Utilities, Sembcorp increased its ownership of Cascal to roughly 96.43%.

Sembcorp offers employees health benefits; loan/interest subsidies; and bonus and job development programs.

FINANCIALS: Sales and profits are in thousands of dollars—add 000 to get the full amount. 2010 Note: Financial information for 2010 was not available for all companies at press time.

2010 Sales: $6,886,630	2010 Profits: $623,130	**U.S. Stock Ticker: SCRPF**
2009 Sales: $6,870,650	2009 Profits: $490,010	**Int'l Ticker: U96** Int'l Exchange: Singapore-SIN
2008 Sales: $6,548,910	2008 Profits: $482,170	Employees:
2007 Sales: $5,990,000	2007 Profits: $370,000	Fiscal Year Ends: 12/31
2006 Sales: $4,880,000	2006 Profits: $670,000	Parent Company:

SALARIES/BENEFITS:

Pension Plan:	ESOP Stock Plan: Y	Profit Sharing:	Top Exec. Salary: $	Bonus: $1,165,529
Savings Plan:	Stock Purch. Plan:		Second Exec. Salary: $	Bonus: $

OTHER THOUGHTS:

Apparent Women Officers or Directors:
Hot Spot for Advancement for Women/Minorities:

LOCATIONS: ("Y" = Yes)

West:	Southwest:	Midwest:	Southeast:	Northeast:	International:
					Y

SENIOR HOUSING PROPERTIES

www.snhreit.com

Industry Group Code: 531120 Ranks within this company's industry group: Sales: 43   Profits: 21

Properties:		Financial Services:	Construction/Development:	Investments:		Specialty Services:	Brokerage:
Apartments:	Y	Mortgages:	Commercial Construction:	REIT:	Y	Property Management:	Commercial Sales:
Malls/Shopping:		Title Insurance:	Residential Construction:			Online Services:	Residential Sales:
Offices:	Y	Property Insurance:	Land Development:			Software/IT:	Specialty:
Hotels/Motels:			Support Services:			Consulting:	
Industrial/Warehouses:			Design/Engineering:				
Other:	Y						

TYPES OF BUSINESS:

Real Estate Investment Trust
Senior Housing Properties

BRANDS/DIVISIONS/AFFILIATES:

Reit Management and Research LLC

CONTACTS: *Note: Officers with more than one job title may be intentionally listed here more than once.*

David J. Hegarty, COO
David J. Hegarty, Pres.
Richard A. Doyle, CFO
Jennifer B. Clark, Corp. Sec.
Richard A. Doyle, Treas.

Phone: 617-796-8350	Fax: 617-796-8349
Toll-Free:	
Address: 255 Washington St., 2 Newton Pl., Ste. 300, Newton, MA 02458-1634 US	

GROWTH PLANS/SPECIAL FEATURES:

Senior Housing Properties (SHP) is a real estate investment trust (REIT) that invests in properties such as apartments for aged residents, assisted living facilities and nursing homes. SHP owns 320 properties in 36 states and Washington, D.C. The firm's portfolio includes 226 senior living properties, with 26,380 units; two rehabilitation hospitals with 364 licensed beds; 82 medical office, clinic and biotech laboratory buildings, totaling 5.2 million square feet; and 10 wellness centers, with approximately 812,000 square feet of space. The company is managed by Reit Management & Research LLC (RMR), a real estate management company that oversees a large portfolio of publicly owned real estate in the U.S., Puerto Rico and Canada. SHP has no direct employees; activities are conducted by RMR and SHP's trustees/officers. All SHP properties are triple net leased, meaning that each tenant pays rent and is also responsible for expenses including taxes, insurance and maintenance costs. Approximately 87% of the firm's annual rent revenues come from properties where 80% or more of operating revenues are derived from residents who pay from private resources rather than from Medicare or Medicaid. SHP's properties include senior apartments, in which residents care for themselves; independent living properties, which include services such as meals and maid service; assisted living properties, typically offering private units with 24-hour availability of various types of assistance to residents; nursing homes, which generally provide extensive nursing and healthcare services; rehabilitation hospitals, which provide services such as physical therapy, occupational therapy and speech language pathology; and wellness centers, which offer features such as gymnasiums, strength and cardiovascular equipment areas, tennis and racquet sports facilities, pools and spas. Between November 2010 and January 2011, SHP acquired 27 medical office properties in 12 states for $470 million. In March 2011, the company agreed to acquire 20 senior living communities in five states for $304 million.

FINANCIALS: Sales and profits are in thousands of dollars—add 000 to get the full amount. 2010 Note: Financial information for 2010 was not available for all companies at press time.

2010 Sales: $339,009	2010 Profits: $116,485	**U.S. Stock Ticker: SNH**
2009 Sales: $296,777	2009 Profits: $109,715	**Int'l Ticker:** Int'l Exchange:
2008 Sales: $233,210	2008 Profits: $106,511	Employees: 650
2007 Sales: $188,022	2007 Profits: $85,303	Fiscal Year Ends: 12/31
2006 Sales: $179,806	2006 Profits: $66,101	Parent Company:

SALARIES/BENEFITS:

Pension Plan:	ESOP Stock Plan:	Profit Sharing:	Top Exec. Salary: $230,945	Bonus: $
Savings Plan:	Stock Purch. Plan:		Second Exec. Salary: $145,860	Bonus: $

OTHER THOUGHTS:

Apparent Women Officers or Directors: 1
Hot Spot for Advancement for Women/Minorities:

LOCATIONS: ("Y" = Yes)

West:	Southwest:	Midwest:	Southeast:	Northeast:	International:
Y	Y	Y	Y	Y	Y

SERVICEMASTER COMPANY (THE)   www.servicemaster.com

Industry Group Code: 561720 Ranks within this company's industry group: Sales: 1   Profits: 1

Properties:	Financial Services:	Construction/Development:		Investments:	Specialty Services:	Brokerage:
Apartments:	Mortgages:	Commercial Construction:		REIT:	Property Management:	Commercial Sales:
Malls/Shopping:	Title Insurance:	Residential Construction:			Online Services:	Residential Sales:
Offices:	Property Insurance:	Land Development:			Software/IT:	Specialty:
Hotels/Motels:		Support Services:	Y		Consulting:	
Industrial/Warehouses:		Design/Engineering:				
Other:						

TYPES OF BUSINESS:

Lawn Care Services
Landscaping Services
Termite & Pest Control
Home Warranty
Disaster Restoration & Cleaning
Furniture Repair
Home Inspection

BRANDS/DIVISIONS/AFFILIATES:

TrueGreen LawnCare
TrueGreen LandCare
Terminix
American Home Shield
AmeriSpec
Furniture Medic
ServiceMaster Clean
Clayton Dubilier & Rice Inc

CONTACTS: *Note: Officers with more than one job title may be intentionally listed here more than once.*

J. Patrick Spainhour, CEO
Steven J. Martin, CFO/Sr. VP
Jim Kunihiro, Sr. VP-Mktg.
Jed Norden, Sr. VP-Human Resources
Dan J. Marks, CIO
Greer McMullen, General Counsel/Sr. VP
Jim Kunihiro, Sr. VP-Corp. Strategy
Pete Tosches, Sr. VP-Corp. Comm.
Mark Peterson, Treas./Sr. VP
David Martin, Corp. Controller/Sr. VP
Hank Mullany, CEO Elect
Reggie Crenshaw, Sr. VP-Innovation & Process Improvement
Thomas G. Brackett, CEO/Pres., Terminix
George W. Tamke, Chmn.

Phone: 866-348-7672	Fax:
Toll-Free: 888-937-3783	
Address: 860 Ridge Lake Blvd., Memphis, TN 38120 US	

GROWTH PLANS/SPECIAL FEATURES:

The ServiceMaster Company provides various cleaning and maintenance services to residential and commercial customers through a network of approximately 5,500 company-owned or franchised locations. ServiceMaster is divided into nine principal segments: TruGreen; Terminix; TruGreen LandCare; American Home Shield (AHS); ServiceMaster Clean; Merry Maids; Furniture Medic; and AmeriSpec. TruGreen provides lawn care services including lawn care; tree and shrub care; nuisance pest control; and landscaping care. Terminix provides termite and pest control services to over 2,000,000 households worldwide. TruGreen LandCare provides landscaping services through more than 100 locations throughout the U.S. Services include landscape maintenance; golf course management; design and installation; irrigation services; snow and ice management; tree care; sports turf management; and fertilization and weed control. AHS provides home warranty contracts for systems and appliances, administering contracts throughout the U.S. ServiceMaster Clean offers residential cleaning, commercial cleaning and disaster restoration services through 4,500 franchises around the world. Merry Maids offers house cleaning services worldwide through more than 600 global locations. Furniture Medic offers residential and commercial furniture repair and restoration services. Residential services include wood color matching, watermark removal, furniture structural repair and stabilization, refinishing and polishing and cabinet refacing. Commercial services offers wood and furniture repair and restoration services for commercial properties. This segment specializes in lobby and greeting areas repairs, conference rooms, executive suites and restaurants. There are over 300 franchised Furniture Medic locations in the U.S., Canada and Europe. Finally, AmeriSpec offers home inspection services on over 400 internal and external household items in the U.S. and Canada. ServiceMaster is owned by Clayton, Dubilier & Rice, Inc., a private investment company.

FINANCIALS: Sales and profits are in thousands of dollars—add 000 to get the full amount. 2010 Note: Financial information for 2010 was not available for all companies at press time.

2010 Sales: $3,365,902	2010 Profits: $-14,559	**U.S. Stock Ticker: Private**
2009 Sales: $3,240,079	2009 Profits: $13,495	**Int'l Ticker:** Int'l Exchange:
2008 Sales: $3,311,432	2008 Profits: $-126,399	Employees: 30,000
2007 Sales: $3,356,748	2007 Profits: $-42,419	Fiscal Year Ends: 12/31
2006 Sales: $3,322,703	2006 Profits: $169,699	Parent Company: CLAYTON DUBILIER & RICE INC

SALARIES/BENEFITS:

Pension Plan:	ESOP Stock Plan:	Profit Sharing:	Top Exec. Salary: $	Bonus: $
Savings Plan:	Stock Purch. Plan:		Second Exec. Salary: $	Bonus: $

OTHER THOUGHTS:

Apparent Women Officers or Directors:
Hot Spot for Advancement for Women/Minorities:

LOCATIONS: ("Y" = Yes)

West:	Southwest:	Midwest:	Southeast:	Northeast:	International:
Y	Y	Y	Y	Y	Y

SHANGRI-LA ASIA LTD

www.shangri-la.com

Industry Group Code: 721110 Ranks within this company's industry group: Sales: 10   Profits: 6

Properties:		Financial Services:		Construction/Development:	Investments:	Specialty Services:		Brokerage:
Apartments:		Mortgages:		Commercial Construction:	REIT:	Property Management:	Y	Commercial Sales:
Malls/Shopping:		Title Insurance:		Residential Construction:		Online Services:		Residential Sales:
Offices:		Property Insurance:		Land Development:		Software/IT:		Specialty:
Hotels/Motels:	Y			Support Services:		Consulting:		
Industrial/Warehouses:				Design/Engineering:				
Other:	Y							

TYPES OF BUSINESS:

Hotels, Luxury
Property Management
Health Spas
Golf Courses

BRANDS/DIVISIONS/AFFILIATES:

Shangri-La
Rasa
Kerry Hotels
Aberdeen Marina Club
Xili Golf and Country Club
Chi, The Spa at the Shangri-La
Shangri-La Hotel (Malaysia) Berhad
Shangri-La Hotel Public Company Limited

CONTACTS: *Note: Officers with more than one job title may be intentionally listed here more than once.*

Greg Dogan, CEO
Greg Dogan, Pres.
Kent Zhu, Group Dir.-Sales & Mktg.
June Ng, Group Dir.-Human Resources
Anand Rao, CIO
Harold Lee, Group Dir.-Eng.
Nelson Chu, Group Dir.-Planning & Design
Maria Kuhn, Dir.-Corp. Comm.
Vincent Leung, VP-Finance
Peter Leung, Group Dir.-Projects
Jean Michel Offe, Group Dir.-Food & Beverage
Brenden Inns, VP-Brand Comm.
Caroline Cheah, Group Dir.-Rooms
Khoon Ean Kuok, Chmn.

Phone: 852-2599-3000	Fax: 852-2599-3131
Toll-Free:	

Address: 28F, Kerry Ctr., 683 Kings Rd., Quarry Bay, Hong Kong,   China

GROWTH PLANS/SPECIAL FEATURES:

Shangri-La Asia, Ltd., is an investment holding company that owns and manages hotels and resorts, primarily under the Shangri-La, Rasa, Traders Hotels and Kerry Hotels brands. Its portfolio consists of 71 luxury resorts (representing approximately 30,000 rooms) and hotels located in Australia, China, Hong Kong, India, Indonesia, Japan, Malaysia, the Philippines, Singapore, Taiwan, Thailand, Qatar, the United Arab Emirates, Oman, the Fiji Islands, Myanmar, the Republic of Maldives, France, Russia, Turkey, the U.K. and Canada. In addition, the firm's 19 Chi Spa locations, inspired by the Shangri-La legend and located at Shangri-La hotels in 11 countries, feature a variety of treatments and therapies derived from Chinese, Thai and other Asian traditions. The company also manages the Xili Golf and Country Club in Shenzhen; and the Aberdeen Marina Club in Hong Kong. Subsidiaries Shangri-La Hotel (Malaysia) Berhad and Shangri-La Hotel Public Company Limited are engaged in the operation of hotels, beach resorts, golf courses, clubhouses and related facilities in Malaysia and Thailand, respectively. Shangri-La Asia has whole or partial interests in various projects in development, including new hotels in China, Canada, Qatar, the Philippines, Turkey, the U.K., India and Sri Lanka. Recently, the company opened new hotels in Tokyo, Japan; Paris, France; the Philippines; the Republic of Maldives; and various sites in China. In January 2011, the Rasa Sentosa Resort in Singapore was rebranded Shangri-La's Rasa Sentosa Resort, Singapore. In February 2011, the firm opened the Kerry Hotel Pudong in Shanghai, the first of the firm's new Kerry Hotels brand line of five-star hotels.

FINANCIALS: Sales and profits are in thousands of dollars—add 000 to get the full amount. 2010 Note: Financial information for 2010 was not available for all companies at press time.

2010 Sales: $1,575,100	2010 Profits: $287,100	**U.S. Stock Ticker: SHALY**
2009 Sales: $1,230,000	2009 Profits: $255,500	**Int'l Ticker: 0069** Int'l Exchange: Hong Kong-HKEX
2008 Sales: $1,353,300	2008 Profits: $165,900	Employees:
2007 Sales: $1,219,200	2007 Profits: $340,900	Fiscal Year Ends: 12/31
2006 Sales: $1,002,900	2006 Profits: $202,200	Parent Company:

SALARIES/BENEFITS:

Pension Plan:	ESOP Stock Plan:	Profit Sharing:	Top Exec. Salary: $	Bonus: $
Savings Plan:	Stock Purch. Plan:		Second Exec. Salary: $	Bonus: $

OTHER THOUGHTS:

Apparent Women Officers or Directors: 7
Hot Spot for Advancement for Women/Minorities: Y

LOCATIONS: ("Y" = Yes)

West:	Southwest:	Midwest:	Southeast:	Northeast:	International:
Y				Y	Y

SHAW GROUP INC (THE)

www.shawgrp.com

Industry Group Code: 237 Ranks within this company's industry group: Sales: 18   Profits: 23

Properties:	Financial Services:	Construction/Development:		Investments:	Specialty Services:	Brokerage:
Apartments:	Mortgages:	Commercial Construction:		REIT:	Property Management:	Commercial Sales:
Malls/Shopping:	Title Insurance:	Residential Construction:			Online Services:	Residential Sales:
Offices:	Property Insurance:	Land Development:			Software/IT:	Specialty:
Hotels/Motels:		Support Services:			Consulting:	
Industrial/Warehouses:		Design/Engineering:	Y			
Other:						

TYPES OF BUSINESS:

Pipe Manufacturing
Construction & Engineering
Consulting Services
Environmental Services
Facilities Management
Power Plant Construction
Nuclear Power Plant Construction

BRANDS/DIVISIONS/AFFILIATES:

Westinghouse
Shaw Rolta Limited
Coastal Planning & Engineering, Inc.

CONTACTS: *Note: Officers with more than one job title may be intentionally listed here more than once.*

James M. Bernhard, Jr., CEO
Gary P. Graphia, COO/Exec. VP
James M. Bernhard, Jr., Pres.
Brian K. Ferraioli, CFO/Exec. VP
David L. Chapman, Sr., Pres., Fabrication & Mfg. Group
John Donofrio, General Counsel/Exec. VP/Corp. Sec.
Gentry Brann, VP-Corp. Comm.
Gentry Brann, VP-Investor Rel.
Michael J. Kershaw, Chief Acct. Officer/Sr. VP
Clarence L. Ray Jr., CEO-Power Group
Louis J. Pucher, Pres., Energy & Chemicals Group
George P. Bevan, Pres., Environmental & Infrastructure Group
Ron Barnes, Pres., Fossil, Renewables & Nuclear Div.
James M. Bernhard, Jr., Chmn.

Phone: 225-932-2500	Fax: 225-987-3328
Toll-Free:	
Address: 4171 Essen Ln., Baton Rouge, LA 70809 US	

GROWTH PLANS/SPECIAL FEATURES:

The Shaw Group, Inc. is a construction and engineering contractor firm. It is involved in engineering; technology; construction; fabrication; and environmental and industrial services. The company operates in seven segments: power; energy & chemicals (E&C); environmental & infrastructure (E&I); plant services; fabrication & manufacturing (F&M); investment in Westinghouse; and corporate. The power segment provides a range of project-related services, primarily to the global fossil and nuclear power generation industries. The E&C division's offerings include design, engineering, construction, procurement, technology and consulting services, primarily to the oil and gas, refinery, petrochemical and chemical industries. The E&I segment designs and executes remediation solutions involving contaminants in soil, air and water. It also provides project/facilities management for non-environmental construction, watershed restoration, emergency response services, program management and solutions to support and enhance domestic and global land, water and air transportation systems. The maintenance segment performs routine and outage/turnaround maintenance, engineering, construction, recovery and specialty services. The plant services sector' services include fossil/nuclear maintenance and turbine generator repair. The F&M segment supplies fabricated piping systems. Shaw's Investment in Westinghouse division includes its 20% equity interest in Westinghouse, which offers advanced licensing, nuclear plant designs, engineering services, equipment, fuel and other products and services to the international nuclear electric power industry. The corporate segment includes the corporate management and expenses associated with managing the firm. The company's customer base includes multinational oil companies and industrial corporations; regulated utilities; independent and merchant power producers; government agencies; and other equipment manufacturers. In January 2011, Shaw agreed to acquire the additional 50% interest in joint venture Shaw Rolta Limited from partner Rolta India Limited for roughly $23 million. In March 2011, the firm acquired coastal engineering and restoration specialist Coastal Planning & Engineering Inc. for roughly $26 million.

FINANCIALS: Sales and profits are in thousands of dollars—add 000 to get the full amount. 2010 Note: Financial information for 2010 was not available for all companies at press time.

2010 Sales: $7,000,800	2010 Profits: $92,700	**U.S. Stock Ticker: SGR**
2009 Sales: $7,279,690	2009 Profits: $14,995	**Int'l Ticker:** Int'l Exchange:
2008 Sales: $6,998,011	2008 Profits: $140,717	Employees: 27,000
2007 Sales: $5,723,712	2007 Profits: $-19,000	Fiscal Year Ends: 8/31
2006 Sales: $4,775,649	2006 Profits: $50,226	Parent Company:

SALARIES/BENEFITS:

Pension Plan:	ESOP Stock Plan:	Profit Sharing:	Top Exec. Salary: $1,972,768	Bonus: $580,800
Savings Plan: Y	Stock Purch. Plan:		Second Exec. Salary: $853,679	Bonus: $482,933

OTHER THOUGHTS:

Apparent Women Officers or Directors: 1
Hot Spot for Advancement for Women/Minorities:

LOCATIONS: ("Y" = Yes)

West:	Southwest:	Midwest:	Southeast:	Northeast:	International:
Y	Y	Y	Y	Y	Y

SHIMAO PROPERTY HOLDINGS LTD

www.shimaoproperty.com

Industry Group Code: 5311 Ranks within this company's industry group: Sales: 9   Profits: 13

Properties:		Financial Services:		Construction/Development:		Investments:	Specialty Services:	Brokerage:
Apartments:	Y	Mortgages:		Commercial Construction:		REIT:	Property Management:	Commercial Sales:
Malls/Shopping:	Y	Title Insurance:		Residential Construction:			Online Services:	Residential Sales:
Offices:	Y	Property Insurance:		Land Development:	Y		Software/IT:	Specialty:
Hotels/Motels:	Y			Support Services:			Consulting:	
Industrial/Warehouses:				Design/Engineering:				
Other:	Y							

TYPES OF BUSINESS:

Real Estate Holdings & Development

BRANDS/DIVISIONS/AFFILIATES:

Oakwood Residence Beijing
Shanghai Shimao Riviera Garden
Shanghai Shimao International Plaza
Shanghai Le Meridien Sheshan hotel
Wuhan Shimao Splendid River
Shanghai Shimao Real Estate Co., Ltd
Shanghai Shimao International Plaza Co., Ltd
Shimao Manor Real Estate Co., Ltd

CONTACTS: *Note: Officers with more than one job title may be intentionally listed here more than once.*

Wai Man Hui, CFO
Yee Mei Lam, Sec.
Tammy Tam, Investor Rel.
Tammy Tam, Corp. Finance
Sai Tan Hui, Vice Chmn.
Chi Shing Tung, Exec. Dir.
Wing Mau Hui, Chmn.

Phone: 852-2511-9968	**Fax:** 852-2511-0278

Toll-Free:

Address: 1 Harbour Rd., Units 4307-12, 43rd Fl., Hong Kong, China

GROWTH PLANS/SPECIAL FEATURES:

Shimao Property Holdings Ltd., along with its subsidiaries, is engaged in investment holding and develops residential, hotel, office and commercial properties in large cities in China. The company currently has approximately 60 projects under development in over 30 cities. The firm utilizes its Riviera Model, which combines landscape, waterside, gardening and architectural design. Some of its properties include Shanghai Shimao Riviera Garden; Shanghai Shimao International Plaza; the Shanghai Le Meridien Sheshan hotel; Beijing Shimao Olive Garden; Fuzhou Shimao Bund Garden; Wuhan Shimao Splendid River; Nanjing Shimao Rivera New City; The Genesis; and Shanghai Hyatt On The Bund. Subsidiaries of the company that are involved in property development include Shanghai Shimao Real Estate Co., Ltd.; Shanghai Shimao International Plaza Co., Ltd.; and Shanghai Shimao Manor Real Estate Co., Ltd. Subsidiary Shanghai Shimao Jianse Co., Ltd, is focused on investment holding operations. In July 2010, the company acquired the 202 room apartment, Oakwood Residence Beijing from Colony Ambassy Holding Limited.

FINANCIALS: Sales and profits are in thousands of dollars—add 000 to get the full amount. 2010 Note: Financial information for 2010 was not available for all companies at press time.

2010 Sales: $3,345,490	2010 Profits: $717,250	**U.S. Stock Ticker:**
2009 Sales: $2,490,950	2009 Profits: $513,510	**Int'l Ticker: 0813** Int'l Exchange: Hong Kong-HKE
2008 Sales: $1,356,270	2008 Profits: $598,280	Employees: 4,365
2007 Sales: $1,010,840	2007 Profits: $333,190	Fiscal Year Ends:
2006 Sales: $365,600	2006 Profits: $132,760	Parent Company:

SALARIES/BENEFITS:

Pension Plan:	ESOP Stock Plan:	Profit Sharing:	Top Exec. Salary: $	Bonus: $
Savings Plan:	Stock Purch. Plan:		Second Exec. Salary: $	Bonus: $

OTHER THOUGHTS:

Apparent Women Officers or Directors: 3
Hot Spot for Advancement for Women/Minorities: Y

LOCATIONS: ("Y" = Yes)

West:	Southwest:	Midwest:	Southeast:	Northeast:	International:
					Y

SHUN TAK HOLDINGS LIMITED

www.shuntakgroup.com

Industry Group Code: 721110 Ranks within this company's industry group: Sales: 21 Profits: 10

Properties:		Financial Services:		Construction/Development:		Investments:		Specialty Services:		Brokerage:	
Apartments:		Mortgages:		Commercial Construction:	Y	REIT:		Property Management:	Y	Commercial Sales:	
Malls/Shopping:		Title Insurance:		Residential Construction:	Y			Online Services:		Residential Sales:	
Offices:		Property Insurance:		Land Development:				Software/IT:		Specialty:	
Hotels/Motels:	Y			Support Services:				Consulting:			
Industrial/Warehouses:				Design/Engineering:							
Other:											

TYPES OF BUSINESS:

Investment Holding Company
High-Speed Ferry Services
Real Estate Investment
Hotel Management
Casino Management

BRANDS/DIVISIONS/AFFILIATES:

Far East Hydrofoil Co. Ltd.
Shun Tak-China Travel Ship Management Limited
TuboJET
Shun Tak Holdings, Ltd.
Shun Tak Real Estate, Ltd.
Shun Tak Property Management. Ltd.
Shun Tak Macau Services, Ltd.
Clean Living (Macau), Ltd.

CONTACTS: Note: Officers with more than one job title may be intentionally listed here more than once.

Pansy Ho, Managing Dir.
Daisy Ho, CFO/Deputy Managing Dir.
Pansy Ho, Exec. Dir.-Strategic Dev.
Maisy Ho, Exec. Dir.-Planning & Oper., Property Mgmt. Div.
David Shum, Exec. Dir.
Michael Ng, Exec. Dir.
Ambrose So, Exec. Dir.
Stanley Ho, Chmn.

Phone: 852-2859-3111	Fax: 852-2857-7181
Toll-Free:	
Address: Penthouse, 39 Fl. West Tower, 200 Connaught Rd., Hong Kong, China	

GROWTH PLANS/SPECIAL FEATURES:

Shun Tak Holdings Limited is a publicly traded Hong Kong-based conglomerate with core businesses in the transportation, property, hospitality and investment sectors. The transportation segment is operated through the joint venture, Shun Tak-China Travel Ship Management Limited, which is known under the brand name TurboJET. The company's shares ownership of TurboJET with China Travel International Investment Hong Kong Limited. The segment also includes subsidiary Far East Hydrofoil Co. Ltd., which offers 24-hour-a-day passenger ferry service between Hong Kong and Macau. The company operates bus services in Macau and the Guangdong province through joint venture, Shun Tak & CITS Coach (Macao) Limited. Shun Tak's property division develops and invests in property in Hong Kong and Macau. Its major operations include property development and sales, which develops residential, retail and commercial properties through Shun Tak Holdings, Ltd.; property leasing and asset management, through Shun Tak Real Estate Ltd., which markets and leases residential, retail and commercial properties; property management services, through Shun Tak Property Management Ltd., which maintains the company's owned properties; cleaning services, through Shun Tak Macau Services, Ltd.; and laundry services, through Clean Living (Macau), Ltd. Shun Tak's hospitality segment, operated by Shun Tak Hospitality Services Limited, is engaged in hotel and casino management, with a 50% interest in Mandarin Oriental; a 34.9% interest in the Westin Resort Macau; and a 70% interest in the Hong Kong SkyCity Marriott Hotel. The firm's investments segment holds interest in Macau-based casinos, as well as Macau Matters Co. Ltd., which specializes in retail facility operations.

FINANCIALS: Sales and profits are in thousands of dollars—add 000 to get the full amount. 2010 Note: Financial information for 2010 was not available for all companies at press time.

		U.S. Stock Ticker:
2010 Sales: $411,370	2010 Profits: $109,820	Int'l Ticker: 0242 Int'l Exchange: Hong Kong-HKEX
2009 Sales: $429,370	2009 Profits: $370,060	Employees: 2,680
2008 Sales: $561,240	2008 Profits: $14,860	Fiscal Year Ends: 12/31
2007 Sales: $431,400	2007 Profits: $131,800	Parent Company:
2006 Sales: $360,400	2006 Profits: $86,300	

SALARIES/BENEFITS:

Pension Plan:	ESOP Stock Plan:	Profit Sharing:	Top Exec. Salary: $	Bonus: $
Savings Plan:	Stock Purch. Plan:		Second Exec. Salary: $	Bonus: $

OTHER THOUGHTS:

Apparent Women Officers or Directors: 4
Hot Spot for Advancement for Women/Minorities: Y

LOCATIONS: ("Y" = Yes)

West:	Southwest:	Midwest:	Southeast:	Northeast:	International:
					Y

SIEMENS BUILDING TECHNOLOGIES

www.buildingtechnologies.siemens.com

Industry Group Code: 541310 Ranks within this company's industry group: Sales: Profits:

Properties:	Financial Services:	Construction/Development:		Investments:	Specialty Services:	Brokerage:
Apartments:	Mortgages:	Commercial Construction:		REIT:	Property Management:	Commercial Sales:
Malls/Shopping:	Title Insurance:	Residential Construction:			Online Services:	Residential Sales:
Offices:	Property Insurance:	Land Development:			Software/IT:	Specialty:
Hotels/Motels:		Support Services:	Y		Consulting:	
Industrial/Warehouses:		Design/Engineering:				
Other:						

TYPES OF BUSINESS:

Residential & Commercial HVAC Systems

BRANDS/DIVISIONS/AFFILIATES:

Siemens AG

CONTACTS:
Note: Officers with more than one job title may be intentionally listed here more than once.

Johannes Milde, CEO
Heribert Stumpf, CFO
Matthias Rebellius, Head-Fire Safety & Security Prod.
Frank Pedersen, Head-Security Solutions
Hubert Keiber, Head-Building Automation
Stephan Bauer, Head-Control Prod. & Systems
Andreas Matthe, Head-Low Voltage Dist.

Phone: 41-41-724-2424	Fax: 41-41-724-3522
Toll-Free:	
Address: Gubelstrasse 22, Zug, CH-6301 Switzerland	

GROWTH PLANS/SPECIAL FEATURES:

Siemens Building Technologies (SBT) provides products, services and solutions for public, industrial, commercial and residential buildings. Based in Switzerland, SBT is a division of Siemens AG's Industry Sector segment, along with five other divisions: OSRAM, Drive Technologies, Industry Automation, Industry Solutions and Mobility. The division's building specialties include services related to comfort, automation, safety, security and operations. SBT also offers energy solutions aimed at improving buildings' energy costs, reliability and performance while minimizing their impact on the environment. The division operates through five business units: security solutions; building automation; control products and systems; fire safety and security products; and low voltage distribution. Its security solutions unit offers intruder detection, video surveillance and building access control products. The building automation unit offers computerized, distributed control systems that monitor and control a building's mechanical and lighting systems. SBT's control products and systems unit offers includes heating and ventilation controls. The fire safety and security products unit offers fire detectors, protection alarm systems and non-water based fire extinguishers. The low voltage distribution unit, which until recently was part of the Industry Automation division, offers electrical installation equipment for buildings, including low-voltage switchgear, sockets and circuit breakers. SBT operates through approximately 110 branches across the U.S., and maintains operations in 46 other countries on five continents.

FINANCIALS:
Sales and profits are in thousands of dollars—add 000 to get the full amount. 2010 Note: Financial information for 2010 was not available for all companies at press time.

2010 Sales: $	2010 Profits: $	**U.S. Stock Ticker: Subsidiary**
2009 Sales: $	2009 Profits: $	**Int'l Ticker:** Int'l Exchange:
2008 Sales: $	2008 Profits: $	Employees:
2007 Sales: $	2007 Profits: $	Fiscal Year Ends: 9/30
2006 Sales: $	2006 Profits: $	Parent Company: SIEMENS AG

SALARIES/BENEFITS:

Pension Plan:	ESOP Stock Plan:	Profit Sharing:	Top Exec. Salary: $	Bonus: $
Savings Plan:	Stock Purch. Plan:		Second Exec. Salary: $	Bonus: $

OTHER THOUGHTS:

Apparent Women Officers or Directors:
Hot Spot for Advancement for Women/Minorities:

LOCATIONS: ("Y" = Yes)

West:	Southwest:	Midwest:	Southeast:	Northeast:	International:
Y	Y	Y	Y	Y	Y

SIMON PROPERTY GROUP INC

www.simon.com

Industry Group Code: 531120 Ranks within this company's industry group: Sales: 3   Profits: 5

Properties:		Financial Services:		Construction/Development:		Investments:		Specialty Services:		Brokerage:	
Apartments:		Mortgages:		Commercial Construction:	Y	REIT:	Y	Property Management:	Y	Commercial Sales:	
Malls/Shopping:	Y	Title Insurance:		Residential Construction:				Online Services:		Residential Sales:	
Offices:	Y	Property Insurance:		Land Development:				Software/IT:		Specialty:	
Hotels/Motels:				Support Services:				Consulting:	Y		
Industrial/Warehouses:				Design/Engineering:							
Other:											

TYPES OF BUSINESS:

Real Estate Investment Trust
Malls, Shopping & Outlet Centers
Office & Mixed-Use Properties
Real Estate Development
Real Estate Consulting
Marketing Services
Property Management

BRANDS/DIVISIONS/AFFILIATES:

Simon Property Group, L.P.
Chelsea Japan Co., Ltd
Chelsea Premium Outlets
Premium Outlets de Mexico
Shinsegae Chelsea Co., Ltd

CONTACTS: *Note: Officers with more than one job title may be intentionally listed here more than once.*

David Simon, CEO
Richard S. Sokolov, COO
Richard S. Sokolov, Pres.
Stephen E. Sterrett, CFO/Exec. VP
James M. Barkley, General Counsel/Corp. Sec.
Michael E. McCarty, Exec. VP-Dev. Oper.
Steve Broadwater, Chief Acct. Officer/Sr. VP
Gregg M. Goodman, Pres., The Mills
John R. Klein, Pres., Premium Outlet Centers
John Rulli, Exec. VP/Pres., Simon Mgmt. Group
Andrew Juster, Exec.. VP/Treas.
David Simon, Chmn.
Hans C. Mautner, Pres., Int'l Division, Simon Global Limited

Phone: 317-636-1600	Fax: 317-685-7222
Toll-Free:	
Address: 225 W. Washington St., Indianapolis, IN 46204 US	

GROWTH PLANS/SPECIAL FEATURES:

Simon Property Group, Inc. (SPG) is a self-managed real estate investment trust (REIT). It is engaged in owning, managing and developing retail real estate, primarily regional malls, outlet centers and community/lifestyle centers. The company owns all of its real estate properties through Simon Property Group, L.P., a majority-owned subsidiary. The company owns or holds an interest in 338 properties in 41 states. SPG also maintains interests in 45 shopping centers in Europe. The firm's Chelsea Premium Outlets brand, operated through three joint ventures, maintains eight outlet locations in Japan (Chelsea Japan Co., Ltd.); one in Korea (Shinsegae Chelsea Co., Ltd.); and one in Mexico (Premium Outlets de Mexico). SPG's strategy includes aggressively marketing available space and renewing existing leases at higher rents, pursuing acquisitions, developing new properties in major metropolitan areas and expanding and renovating existing properties. Through Simon Brand Ventures, the company develops national, regional and local marketing and media plans for clients.

SPG offers its employees benefits including sick pay, supplemental voluntary programs, flexible spending accounts, educational assistance and a 401(k) plan.

FINANCIALS: Sales and profits are in thousands of dollars—add 000 to get the full amount. 2010 Note: Financial information for 2010 was not available for all companies at press time.

2010 Sales: $3,957,630	2010 Profits: $753,514	**U.S. Stock Ticker: SPG**
2009 Sales: $3,775,216	2009 Profits: $387,262	**Int'l Ticker:** Int'l Exchange:
2008 Sales: $3,783,155	2008 Profits: $599,560	Employees: 5,900
2007 Sales: $3,650,799	2007 Profits: $491,239	Fiscal Year Ends: 12/31
2006 Sales: $3,332,154	2006 Profits: $563,840	Parent Company:

SALARIES/BENEFITS:

Pension Plan:	ESOP Stock Plan:	Profit Sharing:	Top Exec. Salary: $1,038,462	Bonus: $3,000,000
Savings Plan: Y	Stock Purch. Plan:		Second Exec. Salary: $812,077	Bonus: $1,000,000

OTHER THOUGHTS:

Apparent Women Officers or Directors: 1
Hot Spot for Advancement for Women/Minorities:

LOCATIONS: ("Y" = Yes)

West:	Southwest:	Midwest:	Southeast:	Northeast:	International:
Y	Y	Y	Y	Y	Y

SINO LAND COMPANY LIMITED

www.sino.com

Industry Group Code: 5311 Ranks within this company's industry group: Sales: 20   Profits: 11

Properties:		Financial Services:		Construction/Development:		Investments:	Specialty Services:		Brokerage:	
Apartments:	Y	Mortgages:		Commercial Construction:	Y	REIT:	Property Management:	Y	Commercial Sales:	
Malls/Shopping:	Y	Title Insurance:		Residential Construction:	Y		Online Services:		Residential Sales:	Y
Offices:	Y	Property Insurance:		Land Development:	Y		Software/IT:		Specialty:	
Hotels/Motels:	Y			Support Services:	Y		Consulting:			
Industrial/Warehouses:	Y			Design/Engineering:	Y					
Other:	Y									

TYPES OF BUSINESS:

Real Estate Holdings & Development
Commercial & Residential Construction
Property Management Services

BRANDS/DIVISIONS/AFFILIATES:

Fullerton Hotel
Fullerton Bay Hotel
Conrad Hong Kong

CONTACTS: *Note: Officers with more than one job title may be intentionally listed here more than once.*

Thomas Tang Wing Yung, CFO
Ringo Chan Wing Kwong, Exec. VP-Treasury
Sunny Yeung Kwong, Exec. Dir.-Sino Property Svcs.
Robert Ng Chee Siong, Chmn.

Phone: 852-2721-8388	**Fax:** 852-2723-5901
Toll-Free:	

Address: 12th Fl., Tsim Sha Tsui Centre, Salisbury Rd., Hong Kong,   China

GROWTH PLANS/SPECIAL FEATURES:

Sino Land Company Limited, a subsidiary of the Sino Group, is a Hong Kong-based real estate firm whose core business involves the development of property for both sale and investment purposes.   The company holds a property portfolio totaling approximately 40.9 million square feet, consisting of five primary property types: residential, accounting for 64.2% of the firm's portfolio; commercial, accounting for 24.0%; industrial, accounting for 5.2%; car parks, accounting for 3.6%; and hotels, also accounting for 3.0% of the portfolio. Commercial and industrial properties, as well as hotels and car parks, are typically held by the firm as long-term investments to generate recurrent income, while Sino Land generally acquires residential properties with the intention of developing them for resale. The firm aims to acquire residential properties in popular urban areas, with convenient access to various forms of transportation, such as subways and rail lines. Of the company's total holdings, approximately 28.3 million square feet consist of properties currently under development; approximately 11.5 million square feet represent properties held either as investments or for the firm's own use; and approximately 1.1 million square feet are completed properties held for sale. Sino Land also operates a number of hotels, including the Fullterton Hotel and Fullterton Bay Hotel in Singapore, and the Conrad Hotel in Hong Kong. The company is also renovating the One SilverSea property in Hong Kong.

FINANCIALS: Sales and profits are in thousands of dollars—add 000 to get the full amount. 2010 Note: Financial information for 2010 was not available for all companies at press time.

2010 Sales: $990,760	2010 Profits: $784,290	**U.S. Stock Ticker:**
2009 Sales: $1,248,460	2009 Profits: $480,520	**Int'l Ticker: 0083** Int'l Exchange: Hong Kong-HKE
2008 Sales: $812,600	2008 Profits: $1,003,700	Employees: 7,940
2007 Sales: $979,200	2007 Profits: $814,700	Fiscal Year Ends: 6/30
2006 Sales: $1,082,700	2006 Profits: $782,300	Parent Company:

SALARIES/BENEFITS:

Pension Plan:	ESOP Stock Plan:	Profit Sharing:	Top Exec. Salary: $	Bonus: $
Savings Plan:	Stock Purch. Plan:		Second Exec. Salary: $	Bonus: $

OTHER THOUGHTS:

Apparent Women Officers or Directors:
Hot Spot for Advancement for Women/Minorities:

LOCATIONS: ("Y" = Yes)

West:	Southwest:	Midwest:	Southeast:	Northeast:	International:
					Y

SKIDMORE OWINGS & MERRILL LLP

www.som.com

Industry Group Code: 541330 Ranks within this company's industry group: Sales: Profits:

Properties:	Financial Services:	Construction/Development:	Investments:	Specialty Services:		Brokerage:
Apartments:	Mortgages:	Commercial Construction:	REIT:	Property Management:		Commercial Sales:
Malls/Shopping:	Title Insurance:	Residential Construction:		Online Services:		Residential Sales:
Offices:	Property Insurance:	Land Development:		Software/IT:		Specialty:
Hotels/Motels:		Support Services:		Consulting:	Y	
Industrial/Warehouses:		Design/Engineering: Y				
Other:						

TYPES OF BUSINESS:

Architectural & Engineering Services
Urban Design Services
Transportation Planning
Seismic Analysis & Consulting
Environmental Engineering
Digital Design
Graphics
Interior Design

BRANDS/DIVISIONS/AFFILIATES:

CONTACTS: Note: Officers with more than one job title may be intentionally listed here more than once.

Jeffrey J. McCarthy, Managing Partner-Chicago
William F. Baker, Partner-Civil & Structural Eng.
Gene Schnair, Managing Partner-West Coast
Gary P. Haney, Design Partner

Phone: 312-554-9090	Fax: 312-360-4545
Toll-Free: 866-269-2688	
Address: 224 S. Michigan Ave., Ste. 1000, Chicago, IL 60604 US	

GROWTH PLANS/SPECIAL FEATURES:

Skidmore, Owings & Merrill, LLP (SOM) is a leading global leading architecture, urban design, engineering and interior architecture firm. Its services span architectural design and engineering of individual buildings to the master planning and design of entire communities. The firm's projects include corporate offices, banking and financial institutions, government buildings, public and private institutions, health care facilities, religious buildings, airports, recreational and sports facilities, university buildings and residential developments. SOM's graphics group provides branding, corporate identity and graphic design services, with expansive projects for clients including the Bay Area Discovery Museum and Dublin Airport. Additionally, its digital design service provides virtual modeling for potential projects. The SOM Interiors group provides interior design solutions for corporate facilities, educational facilities, retail spaces, performing arts spaces, hotels and residential complexes among others. The company's sustainable designs include extensive uses of natural light and low-impact environmental building systems designed to reduce waste and energy use. SOM's Mechanical and Electrical Engineering Group (MEP Engineering) provides design engineering services for new and existing buildings, such as developing solar heating and cooling for new and existing buildings; modeling energy consumption patterns; forecasting probable operating costs; and developing energy recovery systems. Its urban planning services assist city officials in providing plans for efficient commuting, potable water, adequate housing and related problems. Signature projects include 7 World Trade Center, the Willis Tower (formerly known as the Sears Tower) and the John Hancock Tower. One of the firm's latest projects is 73-story residential Infinity Tower in Dubai, which features a twisting helix shape that gradually rotates 90 degrees while maintaining a consistent structural and architectural floor plate throughout its height.

FINANCIALS: Sales and profits are in thousands of dollars—add 000 to get the full amount. 2010 Note: Financial information for 2010 was not available for all companies at press time.

2010 Sales: $	2010 Profits: $	U.S. Stock Ticker: Private
2009 Sales: $	2009 Profits: $	Int'l Ticker: Int'l Exchange:
2008 Sales: $	2008 Profits: $	Employees:
2007 Sales: $228,000	2007 Profits: $	Fiscal Year Ends: 9/30
2006 Sales: $228,000	2006 Profits: $	Parent Company:

SALARIES/BENEFITS:

Pension Plan:	ESOP Stock Plan:	Profit Sharing:	Top Exec. Salary: $	Bonus: $
Savings Plan:	Stock Purch. Plan:		Second Exec. Salary: $	Bonus: $

OTHER THOUGHTS:

Apparent Women Officers or Directors: 2
Hot Spot for Advancement for Women/Minorities:

LOCATIONS: ("Y" = Yes)

West:	Southwest:	Midwest:	Southeast:	Northeast:	International:
Y		Y		Y	Y

SKYLINE CORPORATION   **www.skylinecorp.com**

Industry Group Code: 332311 Ranks within this company's industry group: Sales: 2   Profits: 2

Properties:	Financial Services:	Construction/Development:		Investments:	Specialty Services:	Brokerage:
Apartments:	Mortgages:	Commercial Construction:		REIT:	Property Management:	Commercial Sales:
Malls/Shopping:	Title Insurance:	Residential Construction:	Y		Online Services:	Residential Sales:
Offices:	Property Insurance:	Land Development:			Software/IT:	Specialty:
Hotels/Motels:		Support Services:	Y		Consulting:	
Industrial/Warehouses:		Design/Engineering:	Y			
Other:						

TYPES OF BUSINESS:

Manufactured Housing
Recreational Vehicles
Prefabricated Metal Buildings & Components

BRANDS/DIVISIONS/AFFILIATES:

Nomad
Shyline Homes
Aljo
Weekender
Hillcrest Homes
Rampage
Trailrider
Wagoneer

CONTACTS: *Note: Officers with more than one job title may be intentionally listed here more than once.*

Thomas G. Deranek, CEO
Jon S. Pilarski, CFO/VP-Finance/Treas.
Terrence M. Decio, VP-Mktg. & Sales
Charles W. Chambliss, VP-Prod. Dev.
Charles W. Chambliss, VP-Eng.
Martin R. Fransted, Sec.
Bruce G. Page, VP-Oper.
Martin R. Fransted, Corp. Controller
Thomas G. Deranek, Chmn.

Phone: 574-294-6521	**Fax:** 574-293-7574
Toll-Free: 800-348-7469	
Address: 2520 By-Pass Rd., P.O. Box 743, Elkhart, IN 46515 US	

GROWTH PLANS/SPECIAL FEATURES:

Skyline Corporation, along with its consolidated subsidiaries, designs, produces and distributes manufactured housing, including single-section, multi-section and modular homes and towable RVs, including travel trailers, fifth wheels and park models. The firm sold 2,008 manufactured homes in 2010. The company also sold 3,100 recreational vehicles in 2010, which are sold under a number of trademarks for travel trailers, fifth wheels and park models. Skyline has 13 manufacturing facilities in 10 states; of which 10 produce housing and 3 produce RVs. The firm's manufactured homes are distributed by approximately 230 independent dealers at 350 locations throughout the U.S., and its RVs are distributed by approximately 150 independent dealers at 180 locations throughout the U.S. The company sells a variety of RVs: Aljo; Aljo Ultra-Lite; Layton; Layton Ultra-Lite; Mountain View; Nomad; Nomad Ultra-Lite; Texan; Wagoneer; Weekender; Trail Rider; and Rampage. The RV market is made up primarily of vacationing middle-income families, retired couples traveling around the country and sports enthusiasts pursuing four-season hobbies. Housing options include Skyline Homes, Hillcrest Homes and Skyline Park Models. Skyline Homes and Hillcrest Homes by Skyline can range from a one bedroom, 400 square foot home to a 5 bedroom, 2,700 square foot multi-sectional modular home, nearly indistinguishable from conventionally built homes, which can be assembled on commercial lots. The Skyline Park Models are meant for temporary use and are commonly used in resort or vacation locations.

FINANCIALS: Sales and profits are in thousands of dollars—add 000 to get the full amount. 2010 Note: Financial information for 2010 was not available for all companies at press time.

2010 Sales: $136,230	2010 Profits: $-28,993	**U.S. Stock Ticker: SKY**
2009 Sales: $166,676	2009 Profits: $-15,434	**Int'l Ticker:** Int'l Exchange:
2008 Sales: $301,765	2008 Profits: $-5,556	Employees: 1,200
2007 Sales: $365,473	2007 Profits: $2,593	Fiscal Year Ends: 5/31
2006 Sales: $508,543	2006 Profits: $14,292	Parent Company:

SALARIES/BENEFITS:

Pension Plan:	ESOP Stock Plan:	Profit Sharing:	Top Exec. Salary: $300,000	Bonus: $
Savings Plan:	Stock Purch. Plan:		Second Exec. Salary: $290,000	Bonus: $

OTHER THOUGHTS:

Apparent Women Officers or Directors:
Hot Spot for Advancement for Women/Minorities:

LOCATIONS: ("Y" = Yes)

West:	Southwest:	Midwest:	Southeast:	Northeast:	International:
Y	Y	Y	Y	Y	

SL GREEN REALTY CORP

www.slgreen.com

Industry Group Code: 531120 Ranks within this company's industry group: Sales: 13   Profits: 10

Properties:		Financial Services:		Construction/Development:		Investments:		Specialty Services:		Brokerage:	
Apartments:	Y	Mortgages:		Commercial Construction:	Y	REIT:	Y	Property Management:	Y	Commercial Sales:	
Malls/Shopping:	Y	Title Insurance:		Residential Construction:				Online Services:		Residential Sales:	
Offices:	Y	Property Insurance:		Land Development:				Software/IT:		Specialty:	
Hotels/Motels:				Support Services:				Consulting:			
Industrial/Warehouses:				Design/Engineering:							
Other:											

TYPES OF BUSINESS:

Real Estate Investment Trust
Commercial Properties
Property Management

BRANDS/DIVISIONS/AFFILIATES:

CONTACTS: *Note: Officers with more than one job title may be intentionally listed here more than once.*

Marc Holliday, CEO
Gregory F. Hughes, COO
Andrew W. Mathias, Pres.
James Mead, CFO
Edward V. Piccinich, Exec. VP-Property Mgmt. & Construction
Andrew S. Levine, Chief Legal Officer
Neil H. Kessner, Exec. VP-Leasing Counsel
Steven M. Durels, Exec. VP/Dir.-Leasing
Isaac Zion, Chief Investment Officer
Stephen L. Green, Chmn.

Phone: 212-594-2700	**Fax:** 212-216-1785
Toll-Free:	
Address: 420 Lexington Ave., New York, NY 10170 US	

GROWTH PLANS/SPECIAL FEATURES:

SL Green Realty Corp. is a self-managed REIT (Real Estate Investment Trust). The firm specializes in property management, acquisitions, financing, development, construction and leasing. The company's portfolio consists of 30 properties in Manhattan, totaling 22.3 million square feet; and 31 properties in the New York Metro area, including Long Island, Brooklyn, Queens, Westchester County, Connecticut and New Jersey, totaling 6.8 million square feet. SL Green's interests in these properties consist of fee ownership of 52 properties, including condominium units; leasehold ownership in six properties; and operating sublease ownership in two properties. Under operating sublease agreements, SL Green is responsible for collecting rent from subtenants and payment of all expenses relating to the property. In addition to commercial properties, SL Green also holds interests in 11 retail properties with approximately 405,362 square feet; four development properties with 465,441 square feet; and three land interests. The company also manages four office properties owned by third-parties and affiliated companies with 1.3 million square feet of rentable space.

FINANCIALS: Sales and profits are in thousands of dollars—add 000 to get the full amount. 2010 Note: Financial information for 2010 was not available for all companies at press time.

2010 Sales: $1,101,246	2010 Profits: $270,826	**U.S. Stock Ticker: SLG**
2009 Sales: $995,847	2009 Profits: $37,669	**Int'l Ticker:**　　Int'l Exchange:
2008 Sales: $1,065,015	2008 Profits: $360,935	Employees: 1,027
2007 Sales: $974,830	2007 Profits: $626,355	Fiscal Year Ends: 12/31
2006 Sales: $469,854	2006 Profits: $220,719	Parent Company:

SALARIES/BENEFITS:

Pension Plan:	ESOP Stock Plan:	Profit Sharing:	Top Exec. Salary: $715,341	Bonus: $4,000,000
Savings Plan: Y	Stock Purch. Plan:		Second Exec. Salary: $600,000	Bonus: $2,500,000

OTHER THOUGHTS:

Apparent Women Officers or Directors:
Hot Spot for Advancement for Women/Minorities:

LOCATIONS: ("Y" = Yes)

West:	Southwest:	Midwest:	Southeast:	Northeast:	International:
				Y	

SOCIETE DES BAINS DE MER ET DU CERCLE DES ETRANGERS A MONACO

en.montecarloresort.com

Industry Group Code: 721120 Ranks within this company's industry group: Sales: Profits:

Properties:		Financial Services:		Construction/Development:		Investments:		Specialty Services:		Brokerage:	
Apartments:		Mortgages:		Commercial Construction:	Y	REIT:		Property Management:	Y	Commercial Sales:	
Malls/Shopping:	Y	Title Insurance:		Residential Construction:				Online Services:		Residential Sales:	
Offices:		Property Insurance:		Land Development:	Y			Software/IT:		Specialty:	
Hotels/Motels:	Y			Support Services:				Consulting:			
Industrial/Warehouses:				Design/Engineering:							
Other:	Y										

TYPES OF BUSINESS:

Hotels
Casinos
Restaurants
Resorts

BRANDS/DIVISIONS/AFFILIATES:

Monte-Carlo SBM
Hotel Hermitage
Hotel de Paris
Monte-Carlo Beach Hotel
Monte-Carlo Bay Hotel & Resort
Les Thermes Marins de Monte-Carlo
Casinos de Monte Carlo
Le Louis XV-Alain Ducasse

CONTACTS: Note: Officers with more than one job title may be intentionally listed here more than once.

Bernard Lambert, Managing Dir.
Luca Allegri, Managing Dir.-Hotels, Spas & Resorts
Jean-Luc Biamonti, Chmn.

Phone: 377-98-06-2000	**Fax:** 377-98-06-5800
Toll-Free:	
Address: Place du Casino, Monaco, 98000 Monaco	

GROWTH PLANS/SPECIAL FEATURES:

Societe Anonyme des Bains de Mer et du Cercle des Etrangers a Monaco (SBM) is a hotel and resort company that manages luxury properties in the Principality of Monaco, located next to France on the Mediterranean coast. It generally refers to all its properties as a single resort: Monte-Carlo SBM. The firm owns and manages four hotels: Hotel Hermitage, with 280 rooms and suites; Hotel de Paris, 182 rooms and suites; Monte-Carlo Beach Hotel, 40 rooms; and Monte-Carlo Bay Hotel & Resort, 334 rooms. Each hotel features luxury accommodations. The Hotel Hermitage and Hotel de Paris directly link to the firm's Les Thermes Marins de Monte-Carlo, one of the most prestigious spas in Europe; the Beach Hotel features an Olympic-sized seawater swimming pool; and the newer, high-tech Bay Hotel & Resort, located on 10 acres of land, features a sand-bottomed lagoon and the Cinq Mondes spa. SBM's five casinos include the legendary Casino de Monte-Carlo, Cafe de Paris Casino, Sun Casino, Bay Casino and Summer Casino. The casinos, some of which require guests to follow a strict dress code, feature a wide variety of European and American table games, as well as slot machines. SBM also offers 35 bars and restaurants, including Le Louis XV-Alain Ducasse, the oldest restaurant in Monaco; 26 conference rooms; an 18-hole golf course; 23 tennis courts; retail outlets; cocktail rooms for up to 1,000 people; an opera company; a live performance arena with regular entertainment; and multiple night clubs. The firm also hosts the annual Grand Prix de Monaco, a Formula One auto race. SBM intertwines all its segments in order to create package deals for its guests.

FINANCIALS: Sales and profits are in thousands of dollars—add 000 to get the full amount. 2010 Note: Financial information for 2010 was not available for all companies at press time.

2010 Sales: $	2010 Profits: $	**U.S. Stock Ticker: Private**
2009 Sales: $	2009 Profits: $	**Int'l Ticker:** Int'l Exchange:
2008 Sales: $	2008 Profits: $	Employees:
2007 Sales: $	2007 Profits: $	Fiscal Year Ends: 3/31
2006 Sales: $	2006 Profits: $	Parent Company:

SALARIES/BENEFITS:

Pension Plan:	ESOP Stock Plan:	Profit Sharing:	Top Exec. Salary: $	Bonus: $
Savings Plan:	Stock Purch. Plan:		Second Exec. Salary: $	Bonus: $

OTHER THOUGHTS:

Apparent Women Officers or Directors:
Hot Spot for Advancement for Women/Minorities:

LOCATIONS: ("Y" = Yes)

West:	Southwest:	Midwest:	Southeast:	Northeast:	International:
					Y

SOL MELIA SA

www.solmelia.com

Industry Group Code: 721110   Ranks within this company's industry group: Sales: 8   Profits: 13

Properties:	Financial Services:	Construction/Development:	Investments:	Specialty Services:	Brokerage:
Apartments:	Mortgages:	Commercial Construction:	REIT:	Property Management: Y	Commercial Sales:
Malls/Shopping:	Title Insurance:	Residential Construction:		Online Services:	Residential Sales:
Offices:	Property Insurance:	Land Development:		Software/IT:	Specialty:
Hotels/Motels: Y		Support Services:		Consulting:	
Industrial/Warehouses:		Design/Engineering:			
Other:					

TYPES OF BUSINESS:

Hotel & Resort Management
Real Estate Development

BRANDS/DIVISIONS/AFFILIATES:

Melia Hotels
TRYP by Wyndham
Sol Hotels
Paradisus Resorts
Hard Rock Hotels
ME
Gran Melia

CONTACTS: *Note: Officers with more than one job title may be intentionally listed here more than once.*

Gabriel Juan Escarrer Jaume, CEO
Luis Del Olmo Pinero, Exec. VP-Mktg.
Fernando De Cevallos Aguaron, Exec. VP-Human Resources
Juan Ignacio Pardo, Sr. VP-Legal, Audit & Corp. Governance
Lourdes Ripoll, VP-Strategic Planning
Onofre Servera Andreu, Exec. VP-Finance
Denis Ebrill, Exec. VP-Sol Melia Vacation Club
Andre Gerandeau, Exec. VP-Hotels
Mark Maurice Hoddinott, Exec. VP-Hospitality Bus. Solutions Unit
Esther Trujillo, VP-Sustainability
Gabriel Escarrer Julia, Chmn.

Phone: 34-97-122-4554	Fax: 34-97-122-44-98
Toll-Free: 888-956-3542	
Address: Gremio Toneleros 24, Palma de Mallorca, 07009 Spain	

GROWTH PLANS/SPECIAL FEATURES:

Sol Melia S.A. is a leading Spanish hotel chain in the city and resort markets. It manages and operates hotels and resorts under management or franchise agreements. Sol Melia operates more than 310 city and resort hotels in 30 countries on four continents. The company has locations throughout Europe, the Americas, the Mediterranean, the Middle East and Asia-Pacific. Its brand names include Melia Hotels, TRYP, Sol Hotels, Paradisus Resorts, Gran Melia, ME, Innside and Sol Melia Vacation Club. Melia hotels are usually in the four- to five-star range, offering luxury accommodations and amenities. The TRYP brand of hotels is designed to appeal to upscale business travelers by providing the latest in technology services and conference facilities within the setting of a scenic resort. The Sol brand is designed for family vacations, while Paradisus Resorts cater to destination-driven resort vacations. The ME brand of luxury hotels, located in urban and resort destinations, integrates contemporary cuisine, design and music. Innside is an upscale German hotel chain featuring modern, minimalist architecture and the latest in communications technology for business travelers. Gran Melia advertises a luxurious red carpet atmosphere, and Sol Melia Vacation Club is a chain of membership resorts offering family villas and condominiums. The firm, through its subsidiaries, is also engaged in real estate activities, primarily the development of new hotels. Sol Melia operates through 30 sales offices in 19 countries. In July 2010, a subsidiary of Wyndham Worldwide, Wyndham Hotel Group, acquired the TRYP brand, rebranding it TYRP by Wyndham. Following the transaction, Wyndham established a license agreement for the current 91 TRYP hotels that will continue to be owned and operated by Sol Melia. In February 2011, the company signed a strategic agreement with China's Jin Jiang International Hotel Company to increase its market share among international Chinese travelers.

FINANCIALS: Sales and profits are in thousands of dollars—add 000 to get the full amount. 2010 Note: Financial information for 2010 was not available for all companies at press time.

2010 Sales: $1,853,750	2010 Profits: $74,260	**U.S. Stock Ticker:**
2009 Sales: $1,532,400	2009 Profits: $50,830	**Int'l Ticker: SOL** Int'l Exchange: Madrid-MCE
2008 Sales: $1,657,000	2008 Profits: $66,330	Employees:
2007 Sales: $1,749,890	2007 Profits: $209,750	Fiscal Year Ends: 12/31
2006 Sales: $1,847,800	2006 Profits: $200,300	Parent Company:

SALARIES/BENEFITS:

Pension Plan:	ESOP Stock Plan:	Profit Sharing:	Top Exec. Salary: $	Bonus: $
Savings Plan:	Stock Purch. Plan:		Second Exec. Salary: $	Bonus: $

OTHER THOUGHTS:

Apparent Women Officers or Directors: 1
Hot Spot for Advancement for Women/Minorities:

LOCATIONS: ("Y" = Yes)

West:	Southwest:	Midwest:	Southeast:	Northeast:	International:
			Y	Y	Y

SONESTA INTERNATIONAL HOTELS CORP   www.sonesta.com

Industry Group Code: 721110 Ranks within this company's industry group: Sales: 28   Profits: 20

Properties:		Financial Services:	Construction/Development:	Investments:	Specialty Services:		Brokerage:
Apartments:		Mortgages:	Commercial Construction:	REIT:	Property Management:	Y	Commercial Sales:
Malls/Shopping:		Title Insurance:	Residential Construction:		Online Services:		Residential Sales:
Offices:		Property Insurance:	Land Development:		Software/IT:		Specialty:
Hotels/Motels:	Y		Support Services:		Consulting:		
Industrial/Warehouses:			Design/Engineering:				
Other:							

TYPES OF BUSINESS:

Hotels
River Cruise Ships
Hotels
Resorts

BRANDS/DIVISIONS/AFFILIATES:

Sonesta Art Collection
Just Us Kids
Sonesta Mikado Hotel
Sonesta Sole
Sonesta Dahabeya

CONTACTS: Note: Officers with more than one job title may be intentionally listed here more than once.

Stephanie Sonnabend, CEO
Stephanie Sonnabend, Pres.
Carol Beggs, VP-Tech.
John J. DePaul, Exec. VP-Dev.
Boy Van Riel, Treas./VP
Kathy Rowe, Exec. VP-Food & Beverages
Jacqueline Sonnabend, Exec. VP
Peter J. Sonnabend, Exec. Chmn.
Felix Madera, Exec. VP-Int'l

Phone: 617-421-5400	Fax: 617-421-5402
Toll-Free: 800-766-3378	
Address: 116 Huntington Ave., Boston, MA 02116 US	

GROWTH PLANS/SPECIAL FEATURES:

Sonesta International Hotels Corp., doing business as Sonesta Collection, specializes in providing upscale accommodation. There are currently 33 Sonesta hotels and resorts, including six Nile cruise ships, totaling 6,471 rooms. The properties are located in Boston, Miami, New Orleans, Orlando, St. Maarten, Brazil, Peru and Egypt. The company has also entered into management agreements to operate new hotels being created in Jaco, Costa Rica; Miami, Florida; and San Carlos, Mexico. In addition, the firm has franchise agreements for two hotels in St. Maarten, one in Brazil, three in Chile, three in Colombia and seven in Peru. Locations feature the Sonesta Art Collection. This group of art consists of more than 7,000 contemporary paintings, sculptures, original prints and tapestries by world-renowned artists, which are placed in public places and guestrooms inside its hotels. Some of the company's resorts also offer Just Us Kids, a complimentary supervised children's program for ages 5-13. Family packages, children's menus, baby-sitting and discounts on a second room add to the appeal for families. Sonesta's strategy is to consolidate assets and position the company for opportunities to expand with more hotels and resorts. The firm intends for its growth to be continuous, but at a pace that will preserve the character that distinguishes each Sonesta property. In late 2010 and early 2011, the firm added two new franchised locations in Columbia and dissolved one franchise location in Brazil.

Employees are offered health and dental insurance; life insurance short- and long-term disability coverage; Sonesta Hotel discounts; educational assistance; and credit union membership.

FINANCIALS: Sales and profits are in thousands of dollars—add 000 to get the full amount. 2010 Note: Financial information for 2010 was not available for all companies at press time.

2010 Sales: $71,544	2010 Profits: $-2,024	**U.S. Stock Ticker: SNSTA**
2009 Sales: $60,458	2009 Profits: $25,277	**Int'l Ticker:** Int'l Exchange:
2008 Sales: $71,552	2008 Profits: $4,080	Employees: 723
2007 Sales: $86,685	2007 Profits: $1,337	Fiscal Year Ends: 12/31
2006 Sales: $98,832	2006 Profits: $-3,523	Parent Company:

SALARIES/BENEFITS:

Pension Plan:	ESOP Stock Plan:	Profit Sharing:	Top Exec. Salary: $414,557	Bonus: $5,541
Savings Plan: Y	Stock Purch. Plan:		Second Exec. Salary: $400,000	Bonus: $

OTHER THOUGHTS:

Apparent Women Officers or Directors: 5
Hot Spot for Advancement for Women/Minorities: Y

LOCATIONS: ("Y" = Yes)

West:	Southwest:	Midwest:	Southeast:	Northeast:	International:
	Y		Y	Y	Y

SOUTHERN ENERGY HOMES INC

www.sehomes.com

Industry Group Code: 321991 Ranks within this company's industry group: Sales: Profits:

Properties:	Financial Services:		Construction/Development:		Investments:	Specialty Services:	Brokerage:
Apartments:	Mortgages:	Y	Commercial Construction:		REIT:	Property Management:	Commercial Sales:
Malls/Shopping:	Title Insurance:		Residential Construction:	Y		Online Services:	Residential Sales:
Offices:	Property Insurance:		Land Development:			Software/IT:	Specialty:
Hotels/Motels:			Support Services:			Consulting:	
Industrial/Warehouses:			Design/Engineering:				
Other:							

TYPES OF BUSINESS:

Manufactured Housing
Home Financing

BRANDS/DIVISIONS/AFFILIATES:

Southern Homes
Southern Energy
Southern Energy of Texas
Southern Estates
Southern Energy Homes Renew Center

GROWTH PLANS/SPECIAL FEATURES:

Southern Energy Homes, Inc. (SE Homes), a subsidiary of Clayton Homes Inc., builds and sells pre-manufactured homes and operates five home manufacturing facilities: four in Alabama and one in Texas. The company offers 200 different floor plans for clients to choose from, ranging from under 1,000 to over 2,500 square foot. SE Homes custom-designs and manufactures homes intended for primary residences in 20 states, primarily in the Southeastern and Southwest U.S., and sold through over 300 independent dealers. The company builds homes in sections at one of its production facilities and then employs independent trucking companies to transport the sections to dealer locations. The firm's homes are marketed under four brand names: Energy Homes, Southern Estates, Southern Homes and Southern Energy of Texas. Additionally, SE Homes sells pre-owned homes through its Southern Energy Homes Renew Center division.

CONTACTS:
Note: Officers with more than one job title may be intentionally listed here more than once.

Keith Holdbrooks, CEO
Keith Holdbrooks, Pres.
James Stariha, CFO
Dan Batchelor, General Counsel/Exec. VP/Corp. Sec.
James Stariha, Treas.

Phone: 256-747-8589	Fax: 256-747-7586
Toll-Free: 866-896-2737	
Address: 144 Corporate Way, Addison, AL 35540 US	

FINANCIALS:
Sales and profits are in thousands of dollars—add 000 to get the full amount. 2010 Note: Financial information for 2010 was not available for all companies at press time.

2010 Sales: $	2010 Profits: $	U.S. Stock Ticker: Subsidiary
2009 Sales: $	2009 Profits: $	Int'l Ticker: Int'l Exchange:
2008 Sales: $	2008 Profits: $	Employees:
2007 Sales: $	2007 Profits: $	Fiscal Year Ends: 12/31
2006 Sales: $	2006 Profits: $	Parent Company: CLAYTON HOMES INC

SALARIES/BENEFITS:

Pension Plan:	ESOP Stock Plan:	Profit Sharing:	Top Exec. Salary: $	Bonus: $
Savings Plan:	Stock Purch. Plan:		Second Exec. Salary: $	Bonus: $

OTHER THOUGHTS:

Apparent Women Officers or Directors:
Hot Spot for Advancement for Women/Minorities:

LOCATIONS: ("Y" = Yes)

West:	Southwest:	Midwest:	Southeast:	Northeast:	International:
	Y	Y	Y	Y	

SOVRAN SELF STORAGE INC

www.unclebobs.com

Industry Group Code: 531120 Ranks within this company's industry group: Sales: 56   Profits: 35

Properties:	Financial Services:	Construction/Development:	Investments:	Specialty Services:	Brokerage:
Apartments:	Mortgages:	Commercial Construction:	REIT: Y	Property Management: Y	Commercial Sales:
Malls/Shopping:	Title Insurance:	Residential Construction:		Online Services:	Residential Sales:
Offices:	Property Insurance:	Land Development:		Software/IT:	Specialty:
Hotels/Motels:		Support Services:		Consulting:	
Industrial/Warehouses:		Design/Engineering:			
Other: Y					

TYPES OF BUSINESS:

Real Estate Investment Trust
Self-Storage Properties
Truck Rental
Moving & Storage Products
Property Management

BRANDS/DIVISIONS/AFFILIATES:

Uncle Bob's Self Storage
Dri-guard
Uncle Bob's Rental Trucks
AllBoxes.com

CONTACTS: *Note: Officers with more than one job title may be intentionally listed here more than once.*

Robert J. Attea, CEO
Kenneth F. Myszka, COO
Kenneth F. Myszka, Pres.
David L. Rogers, CFO/Sec.
Edward Killeen, Exec. VP-Sales
Jennifer Kozub, Dir.-Human Resources
Jeffrey O'Donnell, Dir.-IT
Sandra Herberger, VP-Admin.
Sandra Herberger, VP-Legal Compliance
Edward Killeen, Exec. VP-Oper.
John Rogers, VP-Bus. Dev.
Diane Piegza, VP-Corp. Comm.
Andrew Gregoire, VP-Finance
Kevin Driscoll, Controller
Michael Rogers, VP-Real Estate & Asset Mgmt.
Robert Myszka, VP-Joint Ventures
Jeffrey Myszka, Regional VP
Robert J. Attea, Chmn.

Phone: 716-633-1850	Fax: 716-633-3397
Toll-Free: 800-242-1715	
Address: 6467 Main St., Williamsville, NY 14221 US	

GROWTH PLANS/SPECIAL FEATURES:

Sovran Self Storage, Inc. is a self-administered and self-managed REIT (Real Estate Investment Trust) that acquires, owns and manages self-storage properties. It owns and manages 377 self-storage facilities (including 52 properties that are managed on behalf of two joint ventures) comprising 24.7 million square feet, making it one of the largest self-storage companies in the U.S. Sovran operates its stores under the trade name Uncle Bob's Self Storage, serving over 160,000 customers in 24 states. The states with the largest number of Uncle Bob's stores include Texas, with 90 stores; Florida, 56; New York, 28; Georgia, 23; Ohio, 23; Alabama, 22; Virginia, 18; North Carolina, 18; Louisiana, 14; Massachusetts, 12; and Mississippi, 12. Stores range in size from 23,000-181,000 rentable square feet, with an average size of 65,000 rentable square feet. Sovran's stores typically offer various value-added products and services including the following. Dri-guard, its state-of-the art centrally controlled dehumidification system, is available either singly or paired with the firm's climate controlled storage system. Dri-guard have been used by the Smithsonian, Boeing, Volvo and the U.S. Military, including for the storage of Air Force One and Two. Uncle Bob's Rental Trucks offers moving trucks with 750 cubic feet of storage space on a two-way, local basis only. The firm also sells locks, boxes, tarps and other ancillary items used by its customers, offering these products both at its stores and through its affiliate web site, AllBoxes.com.

Corporate employees are offered health insurance; a 401(k) plan; life insurance; long-term disability; vacation time; personal time; and paid holidays and sick leave. Full-time employees receive a 401(k) plan; life and health insurance; vacation time; and paid holidays and sick leave. Part-time employees receive a 401(k) plan, life insurance and vacations.

FINANCIALS: Sales and profits are in thousands of dollars—add 000 to get the full amount. 2010 Note: Financial information for 2010 was not available for all companies at press time.

2010 Sales: $192,072	2010 Profits: $40,642	U.S. Stock Ticker: SSS
2009 Sales: $191,040	2009 Profits: $19,916	Int'l Ticker: Int'l Exchange:
2008 Sales: $196,286	2008 Profits: $37,399	Employees: 1,027
2007 Sales: $190,013	2007 Profits: $37,958	Fiscal Year Ends: 12/31
2006 Sales: $165,369	2006 Profits: $36,610	Parent Company:

SALARIES/BENEFITS:

Pension Plan:	ESOP Stock Plan:	Profit Sharing:	Top Exec. Salary: $419,000	Bonus: $
Savings Plan: Y	Stock Purch. Plan:		Second Exec. Salary: $408,000	Bonus: $

OTHER THOUGHTS:

Apparent Women Officers or Directors: 6
Hot Spot for Advancement for Women/Minorities: Y

LOCATIONS: ("Y" = Yes)

West:	Southwest:	Midwest:	Southeast:	Northeast:	International:
	Y	Y	Y	Y	

Note: Financial information, benefits and other data can change quickly and may vary from those stated here.

ST JOE COMPANY (THE)
www.joe.com

Industry Group Code: 5311 Ranks within this company's industry group: Sales: 32   Profits: 27

Properties:		Financial Services:		Construction/Development:		Investments:	Specialty Services:		Brokerage:	
Apartments:		Mortgages:		Commercial Construction:		REIT:	Property Management:		Commercial Sales:	
Malls/Shopping:		Title Insurance:		Residential Construction:			Online Services:		Residential Sales:	
Offices:	Y	Property Insurance:		Land Development:	Y		Software/IT:		Specialty:	
Hotels/Motels:				Support Services:			Consulting:			
Industrial/Warehouses:	Y			Design/Engineering:						
Other:	Y									

TYPES OF BUSINESS:
Real Estate Development, Investment & Operations
Residential Communities
Commercial Real Estate Development
Retail, Office & Industrial Properties
Forestry Operations

BRANDS/DIVISIONS/AFFILIATES:
WaterColor
WaterSound Beach
WasterSound West Beach
RiverTown
SummerCamp Beach
RiverCamps
WindMark Beach
SouthWood

CONTACTS:
Note: Officers with more than one job title may be intentionally listed here more than once.
Hugh M. Durden, Acting CEO
Park Brady, COO
William S. McCalmont, CFO/Exec. VP
Bruce R. Berkowitz, Chmn.

Phone: 904-301-4200	Fax: 904-301-4201
Toll-Free: 866-417-7133	
Address: 133 S. WaterSound Pkwy., WaterSound, FL 32413 US	

GROWTH PLANS/SPECIAL FEATURES:
The St. Joe Company, founded in 1936, is a real estate development company with ownership of approximately 574,000 acres primarily in Northwest Florida, approximately 401,800 acres of which are within 15 miles of the Gulf of Mexico coast. St. Joe is engaged in town and resort development; commercial and industrial development; and rural land sales, with significant interests in timber. St. Joe operates through four segments: residential real estate; commercial real estate; rural land sales; and forestry. The residential segment develops large-scale, mixed-use resort, seasonal and primary residential communities including large tracts of land in Northwest Florida and significant Gulf of Mexico beach frontage and waterfront properties. Prominent properties within this category include WaterColor, WaterSound Beach, WaterSound West Beach, RiverCamps, WindMark Beach, SummerCamp Beach, SouthWood and RiverTown. St. Joe's commercial real estate segment develops and sells real estate for commercial purposes primarily in Northwest Florida. The segment provides build-to-suit and ground leases to commercial users and land for commercial and light industrial applications within large and small-scale commerce parks. The rural land sales segment markets undeveloped timberland for rural residential and recreational uses in Northwest Florida. St. Joe's forestry segment manages and harvests its timber holdings. The firm recently underwent a massive restructuring to better deal with the economic downturn. It cut the employee count by 200, shut down its homebuilding operations and outsourced the management of its hotels, marinas and golf courses.

FINANCIALS: Sales and profits are in thousands of dollars—add 000 to get the full amount. 2010 Note: Financial information for 2010 was not available for all companies at press time.

2010 Sales: $99,540	2010 Profits: $-35,864	**U.S. Stock Ticker: JOE**
2009 Sales: $138,257	2009 Profits: $-130,019	**Int'l Ticker:** Int'l Exchange:
2008 Sales: $258,158	2008 Profits: $-35,883	Employees: 118
2007 Sales: $371,551	2007 Profits: $39,207	Fiscal Year Ends: 12/31
2006 Sales: $525,024	2006 Profits: $51,020	Parent Company:

SALARIES/BENEFITS:

Pension Plan: Y	ESOP Stock Plan:	Profit Sharing:	Top Exec. Salary: $726,923	Bonus: $750,000
Savings Plan: Y	Stock Purch. Plan: Y		Second Exec. Salary: $407,789	Bonus: $325,000

OTHER THOUGHTS:
Apparent Women Officers or Directors: 2
Hot Spot for Advancement for Women/Minorities:

LOCATIONS: ("Y" = Yes)

West:	Southwest:	Midwest:	Southeast:	Northeast:	International:
			Y		

STANDARD PACIFIC CORP

www.standardpacifichomes.com

Industry Group Code: 2361 Ranks within this company's industry group: Sales: 14   Profits: 9

Properties:	Financial Services:		Construction/Development:		Investments:	Specialty Services:	Brokerage:
Apartments:	Mortgages:	Y	Commercial Construction:		REIT:	Property Management:	Commercial Sales:
Malls/Shopping:	Title Insurance:	Y	Residential Construction:	Y		Online Services:	Residential Sales:
Offices:	Property Insurance:		Land Development:	Y		Software/IT:	Specialty:
Hotels/Motels:			Support Services:			Consulting:	
Industrial/Warehouses:			Design/Engineering:				
Other:							

TYPES OF BUSINESS:

Residential Construction
Mortgage Financing
Title Services

BRANDS/DIVISIONS/AFFILIATES:

SPH Title, Inc.
Standard Pacific Mortgage, Inc.

CONTACTS: *Note: Officers with more than one job title may be intentionally listed here more than once.*

Kenneth L. Cambell, III, CEO
Scott D. Stowell, COO
Kenneth L. Campbell, III, Pres.
John M. Stephens, CFO/Sr. VP
Wendy Marlett, Chief Mktg. Officer/Exec. VP
John P. Babel, General Counsel/Sr. VP/Corp. Sec.
Elliot Mann, Pres., Carolinas
William Peckman, Pres., Austin
John P. Moroney, Pres., Denver Region
James Palda, Pres., Standard Pacific Mortgage
Ronald R. Foell, Chmn.

Phone: 949-789-1600	Fax: 949-789-1609
Toll-Free:	
Address: 26 Technology Dr., Irvine, CA 92618 US	

GROWTH PLANS/SPECIAL FEATURES:

Standard Pacific Homes Corp. (SPH) is a builder of single-family detached and attached homes. The firm maintains operations in major metropolitan areas in California, Florida, Arizona, Texas, North Carolina, South Carolina, Colorado and Nevada, with California home deliveries accounting for roughly 42% of total deliveries. Single-family detached dwellings account for 80% of deliveries. The company offers a wide variety of products and prices for its homes, which can range in price from $165,000 to $1,000,000 and typically range from 1,500 to 3,500 square feet. The firm currently constructs homes through seven operating divisions, with 133 actively selling projects. SPH typically purchases unimproved or improved land zoned for residential use and employs independent architectural, design, engineering and other third-party consulting firms to assist in project planning and design. SPH supervisory employees are responsible for coordinating and directing subcontractors. The firm also enters into land development and homebuilding joint ventures as a means of accessing lot positions, expanding market opportunities and establishing strategic alliances. In addition to homebuilding operations, SPH provides mortgage financing and title services through subsidiaries and joint ventures such as Standard Pacific Mortgage, Inc. and SPH Title, Inc.

Employees are offered medical, dental, vision, and life insurance; a home purchase discount program; a home mortgage/loan discount program; a college savings plan; work/life programs; paid maternity and military leave; tuition reimbursement programs; health care reimbursement accounts; a dependent care reimbursement program; 401(k) employer contributions; local vendor/supplier discounts; concierge services; and free financial planning/investment advice.

FINANCIALS: Sales and profits are in thousands of dollars—add 000 to get the full amount. 2010 Note: Financial information for 2010 was not available for all companies at press time.

2010 Sales: $912,418	2010 Profits: $-11,724	**U.S. Stock Ticker: SPF**
2009 Sales: $1,166,397	2009 Profits: $-13,786	**Int'l Ticker:** Int'l Exchange:
2008 Sales: $1,535,616	2008 Profits: $-1,233,615	Employees: 775
2007 Sales: $2,905,510	2007 Profits: $-737,380	Fiscal Year Ends: 12/31
2006 Sales: $3,765,336	2006 Profits: $123,693	Parent Company:

SALARIES/BENEFITS:

Pension Plan:	ESOP Stock Plan:	Profit Sharing:	Top Exec. Salary: $750,000	Bonus: $432,000
Savings Plan: Y	Stock Purch. Plan:		Second Exec. Salary: $703,833	Bonus: $615,000

OTHER THOUGHTS:

Apparent Women Officers or Directors: 3
Hot Spot for Advancement for Women/Minorities: Y

LOCATIONS: ("Y" = Yes)

West:	Southwest:	Midwest:	Southeast:	Northeast:	International:
Y	Y		Y	Y	

STARWOOD CAPITAL GROUP GLOBAL LLC www.starwoodcapital.com

Industry Group Code: 721110 Ranks within this company's industry group: Sales: Profits:

Properties:		Financial Services:		Construction/Development:	Investments:		Specialty Services:	Brokerage:
Apartments:	Y	Mortgages:		Commercial Construction:	REIT:	Y	Property Management:	Commercial Sales:
Malls/Shopping:	Y	Title Insurance:		Residential Construction:			Online Services:	Residential Sales:
Offices:	Y	Property Insurance:		Land Development:			Software/IT:	Specialty:
Hotels/Motels:	Y			Support Services:			Consulting:	
Industrial/Warehouses:				Design/Engineering:				
Other:	Y							

TYPES OF BUSINESS:

Real Estate Investments
Energy Investments
Commercial and Residential Development
Industrial Properties
Recreational Properties
Retail Properties
Office Buildings
Golf Courses

BRANDS/DIVISIONS/AFFILIATES:

Starwood Energy Group
Starwood Property Trust Inc
Baccarat Hotels & Resorts
Starwood Real Estate Securities
SH Group
1 Hotels & Resorts
Corus Bank, NA
Andaz Wailea Resort & Residences

CONTACTS: *Note: Officers with more than one job title may be intentionally listed here more than once.*

Barry S. Sternlicht, CEO
Daniel Yih, COO
Jerry C. Silvey, CFO/Exec. VP
Ellis F. Rinaldi, Co-General Counsel/Exec. VP
Jeffrey G. Dishner, Head-Real Estate Acquisitions & Debt Investments
Madison F. Grose, Co-General Counsel/Sr. Managing Dir.
Christopher D. Graham, Managing Dir.-Acquisitions
J. Marc Perrin, Managing Dir.-Acquisitions/Head-Asia
Barry S. Sternlicht, Chmn.
Desmond Taljaard, COO-Europe

Phone: 203-422-7700	Fax: 203-422-7784
Toll-Free:	
Address: 591 W. Putnam Ave., Greenwich, CT 06830 US	

GROWTH PLANS/SPECIAL FEATURES:

Starwood Capital Group Global LLC is a private equity real estate investment firm with approximately $16 billion in assets under management. The company specializes in real estate-related investments on behalf of select private and institutional investor partners. It has invested in a wide range of property types, including multifamily, office, retail, hotel, industrial, residential and commercial land, senior housing, mixed-use and golf property, through equity, preferred equity, mezzanine debt and senior debt capital structures. Starwood operates through a number of subsidiaries and affiliated companies. Subsidiary Starwood Real Estate Securities is a hedge fund designed for global public real estate securities investment. Subsidiary Starwood Energy Group, an energy fund focused on investment in transmission, natural gas, wind and solar power generation facilities in North America. SH Group manages the eco-focused brand 1 Hotels & Resorts, and also holds the license for Baccarat-brand hotels. Subsidiary Starwood Property Trust, Inc., a real estate investment trust (REIT), which originates and invests in commercial mortgage loans and other commercial-related debt investments. Starwood is headquartered in Greenwich, Connecticut, with additional offices in Georgia, California, Washington, D.C., the U.K., Luxembourg, France, India, Japan and Brazil. Recently, the company acquired real estate assets and construction loans owned by Corus Bank, NA. In June 2010, the firm acquired 49.9% of Hersha Hospitality Management. In August 2010, Starwood opened an office Sao Paulo, Brazil. In September 2010, the company sold the Hotel Lutetia to Alrov. Also in September, Starwood invested $150 million in TRI Pointe Homes LLC, a residential construction company based in Southern California. In October 2010, the firm created a joint venture in association with Hyatt Hotels Corporation to develop ocean-front resort Andaz Wailea Resort and Residences in Maui, Hawaii. In January 2011, Starwood acquired a non-performing commercial loan portfolio with a balance of $157 million.

FINANCIALS: Sales and profits are in thousands of dollars—add 000 to get the full amount. 2010 Note: Financial information for 2010 was not available for all companies at press time.

2010 Sales: $	2010 Profits: $	U.S. Stock Ticker: Private
2009 Sales: $	2009 Profits: $	Int'l Ticker: Int'l Exchange:
2008 Sales: $	2008 Profits: $	Employees:
2007 Sales: $	2007 Profits: $	Fiscal Year Ends:
2006 Sales: $	2006 Profits: $	Parent Company:

SALARIES/BENEFITS:

Pension Plan:	ESOP Stock Plan:	Profit Sharing:	Top Exec. Salary: $	Bonus: $
Savings Plan:	Stock Purch. Plan:		Second Exec. Salary: $	Bonus: $

OTHER THOUGHTS:

Apparent Women Officers or Directors: 1
Hot Spot for Advancement for Women/Minorities:

LOCATIONS: ("Y" = Yes)

West:	Southwest:	Midwest:	Southeast:	Northeast:	International:
Y			Y	Y	Y

STARWOOD HOTELS & RESORTS WORLDWIDE INC

www.starwoodhotels.com

Industry Group Code: 721110 Ranks within this company's industry group: Sales: 3 Profits: 2

Properties:		Financial Services:	Construction/Development:	Investments:	Specialty Services:		Brokerage:
Apartments:		Mortgages:	Commercial Construction:	REIT:	Property Management:	Y	Commercial Sales:
Malls/Shopping:		Title Insurance:	Residential Construction:		Online Services:		Residential Sales:
Offices:		Property Insurance:	Land Development:		Software/IT:		Specialty:
Hotels/Motels:	Y		Support Services:		Consulting:		
Industrial/Warehouses:			Design/Engineering:				
Other:							

TYPES OF BUSINESS:

Hotels & Resorts
Financial Services
Hotel Management & Franchising
Spa Services
Online Auction Web Site
Preferred Guest Club

BRANDS/DIVISIONS/AFFILIATES:

Sheraton
W
Four Points
Westin
Le Meridien
St. Regis
Luxury Collection
Aloft

CONTACTS: *Note: Officers with more than one job title may be intentionally listed here more than once.*

Frits van Paasschen, CEO
Frits van Paasschen, Pres.
Vasant M. Prabhu, CFO
Christie Hicks, Sr. VP-Global Sales
Jeffrey M. Cava, Chief Human Resources Officer/Exec. VP
Phil McAveety, Chief Brand Officer/Exec. VP
Kenneth S. Siegel, Chief Admin. Officer
Kenneth S. Siegel, General Counsel
Simon Turner, Pres., Global Dev.
Alan Schnaid, Controller/Sr. VP
Roeland Vos, Pres., EMEA
Denise M. Coll, Pres., North America
Osvaldo V. Librizzi, Pres., Latin America
Matthew E. Avril, Pres., Hotel Group
Bruce W. Duncan, Chmn.
Miguel Ko, Chmn./Pres., APAC

Phone: 914-640-8100	Fax: 914-640-8310
Toll-Free:	
Address: 1111 Westchester Ave., White Plains, NY 10604 US	

GROWTH PLANS/SPECIAL FEATURES:

Starwood Hotels & Resorts Worldwide, Inc. manages the global operation of hotels and resorts, primarily in the luxury and upscale segments of the industry. It owns, leases, manages or franchises approximately 1,041 hotels containing about 308,700 rooms in roughly 100 countries. The company's hotel brand names include St. Regis, The Luxury Collection, W, Westin, Sheraton, Four Points, Le Meridien, Aloft and Element. The firm's earnings are derived mainly from its hotel and leisure operations; the receipt of franchise fees; and the development, ownership and operation of vacation ownership resorts. Additionally, Starwood provides financing to customers who purchase interests in resorts. The firm's frequent guest loyalty program, Starwood Preferred Guest, is unique in the hotel industry for its lack of capacity controls and blackout dates. Starwood's property portfolio includes the St. Regis in New York, New York; The Phoenician in Scottsdale, Arizona; the Hotel Gritti Palace in Venice, Italy; and the St. Regis in Beijing, China. In early 2010, the company sold Bliss, a spa and related product firm, to Steiner Leisure Limited for $100 million. In 2010, Starwood Hotels opened approximately 62 new hotels in locations such as New York, North Carolina, Virginia, Florida, Ohio, Oklahoma, Texas, Arizona, Connecticut, Tennessee, Canada and India. In March 2011, the firm opened a new Westin in Houston, Texas.

The company offers its employees life, disability, medical, dental and vision insurance; a 401(k) plan; an employee stock purchase plan; an employee assistance program; and domestic partner benefits.

FINANCIALS: Sales and profits are in thousands of dollars—add 000 to get the full amount. 2010 Note: Financial information for 2010 was not available for all companies at press time.

2010 Sales: $5,071,000	2010 Profits: $477,000	**U.S. Stock Ticker:** HOT
2009 Sales: $4,696,000	2009 Profits: $73,000	**Int'l Ticker:** Int'l Exchange:
2008 Sales: $5,754,000	2008 Profits: $329,000	Employees: 145,000
2007 Sales: $5,999,000	2007 Profits: $542,000	Fiscal Year Ends: 12/31
2006 Sales: $5,979,000	2006 Profits: $1,043,000	Parent Company:

SALARIES/BENEFITS:

Pension Plan:	ESOP Stock Plan:	Profit Sharing:	Top Exec. Salary: $1,208,333	Bonus: $3,000,000
Savings Plan: Y	Stock Purch. Plan:		Second Exec. Salary: $747,292	Bonus: $902,100

OTHER THOUGHTS:

Apparent Women Officers or Directors: 7
Hot Spot for Advancement for Women/Minorities: Y

LOCATIONS: ("Y" = Yes)

West:	Southwest:	Midwest:	Southeast:	Northeast:	International:
Y	Y	Y	Y	Y	Y

STATION CASINOS INC

www.stationcasinos.com

Industry Group Code: 721120 Ranks within this company's industry group: Sales: Profits:

Properties:		Financial Services:	Construction/Development:	Investments:	Specialty Services:		Brokerage:
Apartments:		Mortgages:	Commercial Construction:	REIT:	Property Management:	Y	Commercial Sales:
Malls/Shopping:		Title Insurance:	Residential Construction:		Online Services:		Residential Sales:
Offices:		Property Insurance:	Land Development:		Software/IT:		Specialty:
Hotels/Motels:	Y		Support Services:		Consulting:		
Industrial/Warehouses:			Design/Engineering:				
Other:	Y						

TYPES OF BUSINESS:

Casino Hotel
Casino Management
Restaurants
Movie Theaters & Entertainment Venues

BRANDS/DIVISIONS/AFFILIATES:

Palace Station Hotel & Casino
Texas Station Gambling Hall & Hotel
Boulder Station Hotel & Casino
Santa Fe Station Hotel & Casino
Barley's Casino & Brewing Company
Sunset Station Hotel & Casino
Fiesta Rancho Casino Hotel
Thunder Valley Casino

CONTACTS: *Note: Officers with more than one job title may be intentionally listed here more than once.*

Frank J. Fertitta, III, CEO
Kevin L. Kelley, COO/Exec. VP
Frank J. Fertitta, III, Pres.
Richard J. Haskins, General Counsel/Exec. VP
Scott M. Nielson, Chief Dev. Officer/Exec. VP
Lori Nelson, Dir.-Corp. Comm.
Thomas M. Friel, Chief Acct. Officer/Treas./Exec. VP
Lorenzo J. Fertitta, Vice Chmn.
Frank J. Fertitta III, Chmn.

Phone: 702-495-3000	**Fax:** 702-495-3530
Toll-Free: 800-634-3101	
Address: 1505 S. Pavilion Ctr. Dr., Las Vegas, NV 89135 US	

GROWTH PLANS/SPECIAL FEATURES:

Station Casinos, Inc. is a gaming and entertainment company concentrated in the Las Vegas area, mainly targeting locals and repeat customers. Its properties include nine major casino and hotel properties and eight smaller casino properties, featuring a total of 4,048 hotel rooms, 2,676 slot machines, 100 gaming tables, 54 restaurants, 112 movie screens and 288 bowling lanes. Other offerings include live entertainment venues, retail outlets, sports betting and convention banquet space. Station's owned and operated casinos include, in Las Vegas, Palace Station Hotel & Casino; Boulder Station Hotel & Casino; Santa Fe Station Hotel & Casino; Red Rock Casino Resort Spa; Wild Wild West Gambling Hall & Hotel; Wildfire Rancho; Texas Station Gambling Hall & Hotel and Fiesta Rancho Casino Hotel. Finally, in Henderson, Nevada, it owns Sunset Station Hotel & Casino; Fiesta Henderson Casino Hotel; Wildfire Boulder; Lake Mead Casino; and Gold Rush Casino. The firm owns 50% of five properties in Henderson: Green Valley Ranch Station Casino; Barley's Casino & Brewing Company; The Greens; Aliante Station Hotel & Casino; and Wildfire Casino & Lanes. It also manages the Thunder Valley Casino in Sacramento, California for the United Auburn Indian Community. Fertitta Colony Partners LLC, comprising two partners, Fertitta Partners LLC and FCP Holding, Inc., privately owns the firm. In recent years, the firm filed for Chapter 11 bankruptcy protection, also announcing that its casinos will continue to operate during the bankruptcy and go through a re-organization. In March 2010, the firm filed a separate reorganization proposal to make an $85.6 million investment to retain stakes in the Red Rock Casino Spa, Palace Station, Boulder Station and Sunset Station. In April 2010, as part of the bankruptcy proceedings, a company was created to hold Station Casino's former assets, including nine casinos plus five joint ventures. The company will sign long-term lease agreements with the new company and continuing operating the casinos.

FINANCIALS: Sales and profits are in thousands of dollars—add 000 to get the full amount. 2010 Note: Financial information for 2010 was not available for all companies at press time.

2010 Sales: $	2010 Profits: $	**U.S. Stock Ticker: Private**
2009 Sales: $	2009 Profits: $	**Int'l Ticker:** Int'l Exchange:
2008 Sales: $	2008 Profits: $	Employees:
2007 Sales: $1,446,995	2007 Profits: $-375,610	Fiscal Year Ends: 12/31
2006 Sales: $1,339,024	2006 Profits: $110,212	Parent Company: FERTITTA COLONY PARTNERS LLC

SALARIES/BENEFITS:

Pension Plan:	ESOP Stock Plan:	Profit Sharing:	Top Exec. Salary: $	Bonus: $
Savings Plan: Y	Stock Purch. Plan:		Second Exec. Salary: $	Bonus: $

OTHER THOUGHTS:

Apparent Women Officers or Directors: 1
Hot Spot for Advancement for Women/Minorities:

LOCATIONS: ("Y" = Yes)

West:	Southwest:	Midwest:	Southeast:	Northeast:	International:
Y	Y				

STERLING CONSTRUCTION COMPANY www.sterlingconstructionco.com

Industry Group Code: 237 Ranks within this company's industry group: Sales: 31   Profits: 26

Properties:	Financial Services:	Construction/Development:		Investments:	Specialty Services:	Brokerage:
Apartments:	Mortgages:	Commercial Construction:	Y	REIT:	Property Management:	Commercial Sales:
Malls/Shopping:	Title Insurance:	Residential Construction:			Online Services:	Residential Sales:
Offices:	Property Insurance:	Land Development:			Software/IT:	Specialty:
Hotels/Motels:		Support Services:	Y		Consulting:	
Industrial/Warehouses:		Design/Engineering:	Y			
Other:						

TYPES OF BUSINESS:

Heavy Construction & Reconstruction, Civil
Transportation & Water Infrastructure
Municipal Construction

BRANDS/DIVISIONS/AFFILIATES:

Texas Sterling Construction LP
Road and Highway Builders LLC
Ralph L Wadsworth Construction Co LLC
Road and Highway Builders, Inc.
Road and Highway Builders of California, Inc.

CONTACTS: *Note: Officers with more than one job title may be intentionally listed here more than once.*

Patrick T. Manning, CEO
Joseph P. Harper, Sr., COO
Joseph P. Harper, Sr., Pres./Treas.
James H. Allen, Jr., CFO/Sr. VP
Roger M. Barzun, General Counsel/Sr. VP/Sec.
Anthony F. Colombo, Exec. VP-Oper.
Brian Manning, Chief Bus. Dev. Officer/Exec. VP
Joseph P. Harper, Jr., Exec. VP-Finance
Elizabeth D. Brumley, Chief Acct. Officer
Patrick T. Manning, Chmn.

Phone: 281-821-9091	Fax: 281-821-2995
Toll-Free:	
Address: 20810 Fernbush Ln., Houston, TX 77073 US	

GROWTH PLANS/SPECIAL FEATURES:

Sterling Construction Company, is a civil construction company that builds and reconstructs water infrastructure and transportation in Nevada and Texas. It operates in the Texas markets of Houston, San Antonio, Dallas/Fort Worth and Austin; and provides services in Utah and Nevada. The firm operates entirely through five subsidiaries: Texas Sterling Construction, LP; Road and Highway Builders, LLC (Nevada); Road and Highway Builders Inc.; Road and Highway Builders of California, Inc.; and Ralph L. Wadsworth Construction Company, LLC (Utah). Sterling Construction's activities include concrete and asphalt paving; concrete slip forming; concrete crushing; concrete batch plant operations; installation of large-diameter water and wastewater distribution systems; bridge construction; and the building of light rail infrastructure. The company provides general contracting services to both public sector and municipal clients, while utilizing its own employees and equipment for activities including excavating, paving, pipe installation and concrete placement. The firm normally purchases its own materials, using subcontractors only for ancillary services. Sterling Construction's largest customer is the Utah Department of Transportation, which accounts for approximately 26.2% of the company's revenues; the Texas Department of Transportation, its second largest customer, represents 20.7% of Sterling Construction's total revenues.

FINANCIALS: Sales and profits are in thousands of dollars—add 000 to get the full amount. 2010 Note: Financial information for 2010 was not available for all companies at press time.

2010 Sales: $459,893	2010 Profits: $26,224	**U.S. Stock Ticker: STRL**
2009 Sales: $390,847	2009 Profits: $23,704	**Int'l Ticker:** Int'l Exchange:
2008 Sales: $415,074	2008 Profits: $18,066	Employees: 1,300
2007 Sales: $306,220	2007 Profits: $14,444	Fiscal Year Ends: 12/31
2006 Sales: $249,348	2006 Profits: $13,320	Parent Company:

SALARIES/BENEFITS:

Pension Plan:	ESOP Stock Plan:	Profit Sharing:	Top Exec. Salary: $365,000	Bonus: $325,000
Savings Plan:	Stock Purch. Plan:		Second Exec. Salary: $365,000	Bonus: $325,000

OTHER THOUGHTS:

Apparent Women Officers or Directors: 1
Hot Spot for Advancement for Women/Minorities:

LOCATIONS: ("Y" = Yes)

West:	Southwest:	Midwest:	Southeast:	Northeast:	International:
Y	Y				

STEWART INFORMATION SERVICES CORP

www.stewart.com

Industry Group Code: 524127 Ranks within this company's industry group: Sales: 3 Profits: 4

Properties:	Financial Services:		Construction/Development:	Investments:	Specialty Services:	Brokerage:
Apartments:	Mortgages:		Commercial Construction:	REIT:	Property Management:	Commercial Sales:
Malls/Shopping:	Title Insurance:	Y	Residential Construction:		Online Services:	Residential Sales:
Offices:	Property Insurance:		Land Development:		Software/IT:	Specialty:
Hotels/Motels:			Support Services:		Consulting:	
Industrial/Warehouses:			Design/Engineering:			
Other:						

TYPES OF BUSINESS:

Title Insurance
Real Estate Information Services & Software

BRANDS/DIVISIONS/AFFILIATES:

Stewart Title Guaranty Co.
Stewart Title Co.
Stewart Lenders Services
Stewart REI Data, Inc.

CONTACTS: *Note: Officers with more than one job title may be intentionally listed here more than once.*

Malcolm S. Morris, Co-CEO
Stewart Morris, Jr., Pres./Co-CEO
Allen Berryman, CFO/Exec. VP
Murshid Khan, CIO
E. Ashley Smith, Chief Legal Officer/Exec. VP
Ted Jones, Dir.-Investor Rel.
Joseph Berryman, Treas./Sec.
Malcolm S. Morris, Chmn./CEO-Stewart Title Guaranty Co.
Matthew S. Morris, Pres., Stewart Professional Svcs.
Stewart Morris, Jr., CEO/Pres., Stewart Title Co.
Michael B. Skalka, Pres., Stewart Title Guaranty Co.
Malcolm S. Morris, Chmn.

Phone: 713-625-8100	Fax: 713-625-4129
Toll-Free: 800-783-9278	
Address: 1980 Post Oak Blvd., Ste. 800, Houston, TX 77056 US	

GROWTH PLANS/SPECIAL FEATURES:

Stewart Information Services Corp. is a real estate information, title insurance and transaction management company. The firm provides title insurance and related information services to the real estate and mortgage industries through more than 8,500 policy-issuing offices and agencies in the U.S. and international markets. Stewart also provides post-closing lender services, automated county clerk land records, property ownership mapping, geographic information systems, property information reports, flood certificates, document preparation, background checks and expertise in tax-deferred exchanges. The company operates in two main segments: title insurance-related services, which includes the functions of searching, examining, closing and insuring the condition of the title to real property; and real estate information (REI), which primarily provides electronic delivery of data, products and services related to real estate. The firm's international division delivers products and services protecting and promoting private land ownership worldwide, through its subsidiaries, business partners and its own offices, in more than 40 countries. Its primary international operations are in Canada, the U.K., Central Europe, Mexico, Central America and Australia. Subsidiaries include Stewart Title Company, which provides real estate title insurance and transaction management; Stewart Title Guaranty Company, the firm's principal underwriter; Stewart Lenders Services, which specializes in loss mitigation for mortgage lenders; and Landata Technologies, Inc., which provides automated government recording and registration services. In July 2010, the company's Stewart Title Guaranty Company subsidiary merged with the Arkansas Title Insurance Company, National Land Title Insurance Company and Stewart Title Insurance Company of Oregon in order to create a more streamlined business.

The firm offers its employees medical, dental and vision insurance; life insurance; short- and long-term disability insurance; flexible spending accounts; a 401(k) plan; a stock purchase plan; a college savings plan; and an educational assistance program.

FINANCIALS: Sales and profits are in thousands of dollars—add 000 to get the full amount. 2010 Note: Financial information for 2010 was not available for all companies at press time.

2010 Sales: $1,672,400	2010 Profits: $-12,582	**U.S. Stock Ticker:** STC
2009 Sales: $1,707,300	2009 Profits: $-50,975	**Int'l Ticker:** Int'l Exchange:
2008 Sales: $1,555,294	2008 Profits: $-247,455	Employees: 5,700
2007 Sales: $2,106,691	2007 Profits: $-40,220	Fiscal Year Ends: 12/31
2006 Sales: $2,471,481	2006 Profits: $43,252	Parent Company:

SALARIES/BENEFITS:

Pension Plan:	ESOP Stock Plan:	Profit Sharing:	Top Exec. Salary: $350,000	Bonus: $175,000
Savings Plan: Y	Stock Purch. Plan: Y		Second Exec. Salary: $300,000	Bonus: $50,000

OTHER THOUGHTS:

Apparent Women Officers or Directors: 2
Hot Spot for Advancement for Women/Minorities:

LOCATIONS: ("Y" = Yes)

West:	Southwest:	Midwest:	Southeast:	Northeast:	International:
Y	Y	Y	Y	Y	Y

STOCK BUILDING SUPPLY INC

www.stockbuildingsupply.com

Industry Group Code: 444130 Ranks within this company's industry group: Sales: Profits:

Properties:	Financial Services:	Construction/Development:	Investments:	Specialty Services:	Brokerage:
Apartments:	Mortgages:	Commercial Construction:	REIT:	Property Management:	Commercial Sales:
Malls/Shopping:	Title Insurance:	Residential Construction:		Online Services:	Residential Sales:
Offices:	Property Insurance:	Land Development:		Software/IT:	Specialty:
Hotels/Motels:		Support Services: Y		Consulting:	
Industrial/Warehouses:		Design/Engineering:			
Other:					

TYPES OF BUSINESS:

Building Materials/Hardware Stores
Design & Installation Services

BRANDS/DIVISIONS/AFFILIATES:

Wolseley plc
Smoot Lumber Co.
Gores Group (The)
Coleman Floor Company
National Home Centers, Inc.
Bison Building Holdings, Inc.

CONTACTS:
Note: Officers with more than one job title may be intentionally listed here more than once.

Joseph Appelmann, CEO
Steve Short, COO/Sr. VP
Joseph Appelmann, Pres.
Jim Major, CFO
Jim Drexinger, Sr. VP-Mktg. & Sourcing
Brian Yeazel, General Counsel/Corp. Sec./Sr. VP
Robin Fastenau, Dir.-Corp. Comm.
Jim Major, Treas./Sr. VP
Nigel Stobart, VP-Sales
Steve Wilson, Dir.-Coleman Floor Bus. Unit
J. Michael Butts, Dir.-Installed Sales
Tim Meyer, Chmn.

Phone: 919-431-1000	Fax:
Toll-Free:	
Address: 8020 Arco Corporate Dr., Raleigh, NC 27617 US	

GROWTH PLANS/SPECIAL FEATURES:

Stock Building Supply, Inc. (SBS) is a supplier of building materials to professional homebuilders and contractors in 12 U.S. states. SBS is a joint venture between the Gores Group and Wolseley plc. The company serves the single- and multi-family residential, repair, remodel and light commercial construction industries. The company divides its products into eight categories: cabinetry and flooring materials, provided in part through its Coleman Floor division; doors, windows and stairs; insulation and drywall products; locks, offered in part through its National Lock Center; lumber, decking and boards; millwork, mouldings and trim, provided in part through subsidiary Smoot Lumber Co.; siding, roofing and exterior features; and wall panels, engineered wood products (EWP), trusses, hangers and connectors. The firm also provides services such as truss design, engineered wood design, blueprint review, custom doors, windows, mouldings and stairs and installation services. In addition, SBS offers construction financing services, including loans and insurance. The company emerged from Chapter 11 bankruptcy, after closing 94 locations, nearly half of its 201 retail outlets. SBS is now 51% owned by the Gores Group; its former parent company, Wolseley plc, controls the remaining 49%. In January 2010, the company sold its Universal Supply Company business to US LBM. In April 2010, SBS sold SBS Commercial Door & Hardware LLC, its commercial door and hardware division; and acquired National Home Centers, Inc., an Arkansas-based building materials supplier. In July 2010, the firm acquired Bison Building Holdings, Inc., based in Houston, Texas.

The company offers its employees life, disability, medical, dental and vision insurance; a 401(k) plan; and flexible spending accounts.

FINANCIALS:
Sales and profits are in thousands of dollars—add 000 to get the full amount. **2010 Note: Financial information for 2010 was not available for all companies at press time.**

2010 Sales: $	2010 Profits: $	**U.S. Stock Ticker: Joint Venture**
2009 Sales: $	2009 Profits: $	**Int'l Ticker:** Int'l Exchange:
2008 Sales: $	2008 Profits: $	Employees:
2007 Sales: $4,600,000	2007 Profits: $	Fiscal Year Ends: 7/31
2006 Sales: $3,300,000	2006 Profits: $	Parent Company:

SALARIES/BENEFITS:

Pension Plan:	ESOP Stock Plan:	Profit Sharing:	Top Exec. Salary: $ Bonus: $
Savings Plan: Y	Stock Purch. Plan:		Second Exec. Salary: $ Bonus: $

OTHER THOUGHTS:

Apparent Women Officers or Directors: 1
Hot Spot for Advancement for Women/Minorities:

LOCATIONS: ("Y" = Yes)

West:	Southwest:	Midwest:	Southeast:	Northeast:	International:
Y	Y	Y	Y	Y	

STRATEGIC HOTELS & RESORTS INC

www.strategichotels.com

Industry Group Code: 721110 Ranks within this company's industry group: Sales: 15   Profits: 28

Properties:	Financial Services:	Construction/Development:	Investments:	Specialty Services:	Brokerage:
Apartments:	Mortgages:	Commercial Construction:	REIT: Y	Property Management: Y	Commercial Sales:
Malls/Shopping:	Title Insurance:	Residential Construction:		Online Services:	Residential Sales:
Offices:	Property Insurance:	Land Development:		Software/IT:	Specialty:
Hotels/Motels: Y		Support Services:		Consulting:	
Industrial/Warehouses:		Design/Engineering:			
Other:					

TYPES OF BUSINESS:

Real Estate Investment Trust
Hotels

BRANDS/DIVISIONS/AFFILIATES:

Westin
InterContinental
Fairmont
Four Seasons
Hyatt
Loews
Marriott
Ritz-Carlton

CONTACTS: *Note: Officers with more than one job title may be intentionally listed here more than once.*

Laurence S. Geller, CEO
Laurence S. Geller, Pres.
Diane M. Morefield, CFO/Exec. VP
Paula C. Maggio, General Counsel/Corp. Sec./Sr. VP
Stephen Briggs, Chief Acct. Officer/Sr. VP
Richard J. Moreau, Exec. VP-Asset Mgmt.
Raymond L. Gellein, Jr., Chmn.

Phone: 312-658-5000	Fax:
Toll-Free:	
Address: 200 W. Madison St., Ste. 1700, Chicago, IL 60606 US	

GROWTH PLANS/SPECIAL FEATURES:

Strategic Hotels & Resorts, Inc. (SHR) is a real estate investment trust (REIT). The firm owns and manages upper upscale and luxury hotels in North America and Europe through its direct and indirect subsidiaries, including SH Funding.   The company owns or leases 15 hotels, comprising 7,954 rooms; owns a 51% interest in affiliates that own two hotels that are asset-managed by SHR; and owns a 34% interest in a joint venture that owns one hotel (for which SHR also acts as asset manager). The company also owns a 31% interest in and acts as asset manager for a joint venture with two third parties that are developing the Four Seasons Residence Club Punta Mita, a luxury vacation home product on property adjacent to its Four Seasons Punta Mita Resort hotel in Mexico. The firm does not operate any of its hotels directly; instead, it employs internationally known hotel management companies to operate them under management contracts or operating leases. The company's existing hotels are operated under the Fairmont, Four Seasons, Hyatt, InterContinental, Loews, Marriott, Ritz-Carlton and Westin brands. The Hotel del Coronado is operated by specialty management company, SHC KSL Partners, LP, in which SHR owns 45% interest. SHR manages properties in Arizona, California, Illinois, Florida and Washington, D.C., as well as worldwide in Mexico, Germany, France and the U.K. In December 2010, the company sold its InterContinental Prague location. In March 2011, the firm acquired the Four Seasons Jackson Hole and Four Seasons Silicon Valley properties from The Woodbridge Company, Ltd.

FINANCIALS: Sales and profits are in thousands of dollars—add 000 to get the full amount. 2010 Note: Financial information for 2010 was not available for all companies at press time.

2010 Sales: $686,293	2010 Profits: $-230,800	U.S. Stock Ticker: BEE
2009 Sales: $655,256	2009 Profits: $-246,433	Int'l Ticker: Int'l Exchange:
2008 Sales: $841,291	2008 Profits: $-317,486	Employees: 39
2007 Sales: $967,552	2007 Profits: $69,158	Fiscal Year Ends: 12/31
2006 Sales: $680,944	2006 Profits: $120,129	Parent Company:

SALARIES/BENEFITS:

Pension Plan:	ESOP Stock Plan:	Profit Sharing:	Top Exec. Salary: $750,000	Bonus: $1,500,000
Savings Plan:	Stock Purch. Plan:		Second Exec. Salary: $325,000	Bonus: $365,625

OTHER THOUGHTS:

Apparent Women Officers or Directors: 2
Hot Spot for Advancement for Women/Minorities:

LOCATIONS: ("Y" = Yes)

West:	Southwest:	Midwest:	Southeast:	Northeast:	International:
Y	Y	Y	Y	Y	Y

STV GROUP INC

www.stvinc.com

Industry Group Code: 541330 Ranks within this company's industry group: Sales: Profits:

Properties:	Financial Services:	Construction/Development:		Investments:	Specialty Services:	Brokerage:
Apartments:	Mortgages:	Commercial Construction:	Y	REIT:	Property Management:	Commercial Sales:
Malls/Shopping:	Title Insurance:	Residential Construction:			Online Services:	Residential Sales:
Offices:	Property Insurance:	Land Development:	Y		Software/IT:	Specialty:
Hotels/Motels:		Support Services:	Y		Consulting:	
Industrial/Warehouses:		Design/Engineering:	Y			
Other:						

TYPES OF BUSINESS:

Architectural & Engineering Services
Construction Management
Infrastructure Design
Defense Systems Engineering
Industrial Process Engineering

BRANDS/DIVISIONS/AFFILIATES:

STV Security Solutions
STV Architects
STV Construction
STV Canada Consulting Inc

CONTACTS: *Note: Officers with more than one job title may be intentionally listed here more than once.*

Dominick M. Servedio, CEO
Milo E. Riverso, Pres.
Peter W. Knipe, CFO
Linda Rosenberg, Sr. VP-Mktg. & Comm.
Patrick M. Austin, Dir.-Human Resources
Ronald Wiseman, CIO/VP
Steve Pressler, Exec. VP/COO-Construction Mgmt. Div.
Debra B. Trace, Mgr.-Corp. Comm., STV Group
Maher Z. Labib, Exec. VP/COO-Buildings & Facilities Div.
William F. Matts, Exec. VP/COO-Transportation & Infrastructure Div.
John A. Agro, Jr., Deputy Dir.-Transportation & Infrastructure Div.
Dominick M. Servedio, Chmn.

Phone: 610-385-8200	Fax: 610-385-8500
Toll-Free:	
Address: 205 W. Welsh Dr., Douglassville, PA 19518 US	

GROWTH PLANS/SPECIAL FEATURES:

STV Group, Inc. is an architectural, engineering, planning, environmental and construction management firm. The firm specializes in constructing airports, highways, bridges, ports, railroad systems and schools, almost all of which are in the U.S.   It operates through three divisions: Construction Management; Buildings/Facilities; and Transportation/Infrastructure.   STV Construction Management undertakes design and building contracts in nearly every field of industry; the firm's personnel oversees construction programs through administrative, inspection and surveillance. The Buildings/Facilities division works directly with architects, to address the safety, practicality, cost and efficiency of its buildings.   STV's Transportation and Infrastructure sector focuses on the management, planning and design of transportation systems and facilities. Specialties of the firm include aviation/transportation architecture, defense systems, and sustainable design. The company's subsidiary, STV Security Solutions Group, Inc., offers security, as well as risk, crisis and emergency management to its clients.   Some of the STV Group's representative projects include the MetroLink in St. Louis, Missouri; the Villanova University Center for Engineering Education and Research; Sprint PCS Environmental Site Assessments in seven states; the Metra Inner Circumferential Rail Study in Chicago, Illinois; Shea Stadium in Queens, New York; and engineering and technical services for the U.S. Naval Air Warfare Center in Patuxent River, Maryland.

Employees are offered health and life insurance; short- and long-term disability benefits; employee assistance program; paid time off; and a credit union membership.

FINANCIALS: Sales and profits are in thousands of dollars—add 000 to get the full amount. 2010 Note: Financial information for 2010 was not available for all companies at press time.

2010 Sales: $	2010 Profits: $	U.S. Stock Ticker: Private	
2009 Sales: $	2009 Profits: $	Int'l Ticker:	Int'l Exchange:
2008 Sales: $250,000	2008 Profits: $	Employees:	
2007 Sales: $205,000	2007 Profits: $	Fiscal Year Ends: 9/30	
2006 Sales: $	2006 Profits: $	Parent Company:	

SALARIES/BENEFITS:

Pension Plan:	ESOP Stock Plan: Y	Profit Sharing:	Top Exec. Salary: $	Bonus: $
Savings Plan: Y	Stock Purch. Plan:		Second Exec. Salary: $	Bonus: $

OTHER THOUGHTS:

Apparent Women Officers or Directors: 3
Hot Spot for Advancement for Women/Minorities: Y

LOCATIONS: ("Y" = Yes)

West:	Southwest:	Midwest:	Southeast:	Northeast:	International:
Y	Y	Y	Y	Y	Y

SUN COMMUNITIES INC

www.suncommunities.com

Industry Group Code: 531120 Ranks within this company's industry group: Sales: 51   Profits: 51

Properties:	Financial Services:	Construction/Development:	Investments:	Specialty Services:	Brokerage:
Apartments:	Mortgages:	Commercial Construction:	REIT: Y	Property Management: Y	Commercial Sales:
Malls/Shopping:	Title Insurance:	Residential Construction:		Online Services:	Residential Sales: Y
Offices:	Property Insurance:	Land Development: Y		Software/IT:	Specialty:
Hotels/Motels:		Support Services:		Consulting:	
Industrial/Warehouses:		Design/Engineering:			
Other: Y					

TYPES OF BUSINESS:

Real Estate Investment Trust
Manufactured Housing Communities
Recreational Vehicle Communities
Manufactured Home Sales
Property Management

BRANDS/DIVISIONS/AFFILIATES:

Sun Home Services, Inc.

CONTACTS: Note: Officers with more than one job title may be intentionally listed here more than once.

Gary A. Shiffman, CEO
John B. McLaren, COO/Exec. VP
Gary A. Shiffman, Pres.
Karen J. Dearing, CFO/Exec. VP
Karen J. Dearing, Sec.
Karen J. Dearing, Treas.
Jonathan M. Colman, Exec. VP
Gary A. Shiffman, Chmn.

Phone: 248-208-2500	Fax: 248-932-3072
Toll-Free:	
Address: 27777 Franklin Rd., Ste. 200, Southfield, MI 48034 US	

GROWTH PLANS/SPECIAL FEATURES:

Sun Communities, Inc. is a self-administered and self-managed Real Estate Investment Trust (REIT) that owns, operates and develops manufactured housing communities concentrated in the midwestern, southern and southeastern U.S. Sun, together with its affiliates and predecessors, has been in the business of acquiring, operating and expanding manufactured housing communities since 1975. The company owns and operates a portfolio of 136 properties in 18 states, including 124 manufactured housing communities; four recreational vehicle (RV) communities; and eight multi-use properties containing both manufactured housing and RV sites. The properties contain a total of 47,572 developed sites, including approximately 47,683 developed manufactured home sites, 3,209 permanent RV sites, 2,032 seasonal recreational vehicle sites and an additional 6,000 manufactured home sites suitable for development. The firm leases individual sites and utility access to customers for the placement of manufactured homes and RVs. Communities may contain improvements similar to other garden-style residential developments, including centralized entrances, paved streets, curbs and gutters and parkways; and often provide of amenities such as a clubhouse, a swimming pool, shuffleboard courts, tennis courts and laundry facilities. Subsidiary Sun Home Services, Inc. markets, sells and leases new and pre-owned manufactured homes for placement in the properties. The firm expands primarily through the acquisition of manufactured housing and RV communities. In its acquisitions, Sun focuses on communities with a minimum of 200 home sites, located near large metropolitan areas; land/lease communities, rather than rental homes; RV communities with more than 50% annual leases; public utilities access; and the potential to expand. Headquartered in Southfield, Michigan, the company also maintains management offices in Texas, Ohio, Indiana and Florida.

Employees of Sun receive medical and prescription coverage; dental and vision plans; life, AD&D and identity theft insurance; a 401(k) plan; an employee assistance program; tuition reimbursement; and health and dependent care reimbursement accounts.

FINANCIALS: Sales and profits are in thousands of dollars—add 000 to get the full amount. 2010 Note: Financial information for 2010 was not available for all companies at press time.

2010 Sales: $263,140	2010 Profits: $-2,883	U.S. Stock Ticker: SUI
2009 Sales: $256,609	2009 Profits: $-6,302	Int'l Ticker: Int'l Exchange:
2008 Sales: $254,291	2008 Profits: $-34,448	Employees: 747
2007 Sales: $235,075	2007 Profits: $-16,643	Fiscal Year Ends: 12/31
2006 Sales: $227,778	2006 Profits: $-24,968	Parent Company:

SALARIES/BENEFITS:

Pension Plan:	ESOP Stock Plan:	Profit Sharing:	Top Exec. Salary: $621,779	Bonus: $340,000
Savings Plan: Y	Stock Purch. Plan:		Second Exec. Salary: $280,696	Bonus: $147,500

OTHER THOUGHTS:

Apparent Women Officers or Directors: 2
Hot Spot for Advancement for Women/Minorities:

LOCATIONS: ("Y" = Yes)

West:	Southwest:	Midwest:	Southeast:	Northeast:	International:
Y	Y	Y	Y	Y	

Note: Financial information, benefits and other data can change quickly and may vary from those stated here.

SUN HUNG KAI PROPERTIES

www.shkp.com.hk

Industry Group Code: 5311 Ranks within this company's industry group: Sales: 5   Profits: 2

Properties:		Financial Services:		Construction/Development:		Investments:	Specialty Services:		Brokerage:	
Apartments:	Y	Mortgages:	Y	Commercial Construction:	Y	REIT:	Property Management:	Y	Commercial Sales:	
Malls/Shopping:	Y	Title Insurance:		Residential Construction:	Y		Online Services:		Residential Sales:	
Offices:	Y	Property Insurance:		Land Development:	Y		Software/IT:	Y	Specialty:	
Hotels/Motels:	Y			Support Services:	Y		Consulting:			
Industrial/Warehouses:	Y			Design/Engineering:	Y					
Other:	Y									

TYPES OF BUSINESS:

Real Estate Operations & Development
Land Development
Engineering Services
Hotels & Shopping Malls
Insurance & Financial Services
Logistics & Transportation
Ocean Port Terminals
Infrastructure

BRANDS/DIVISIONS/AFFILIATES:

Royal Garden
Royal Park Hotel
Royal Plaza Hotel
River Trade Terminal Company Limited
Hoi Kong Container Services Company Limited
Sun Hung Kai Logistics Limited
Hung Kai Finance Company
Honour Finance Company

CONTACTS: *Note: Officers with more than one job title may be intentionally listed here more than once.*

Thomas Kwok Ping-kwong, Co-Managing Dir./Vice Chmn.
Raymond Kwok Ping-luen, Co-Managing Dir./Vice Chmn.
Patrick Chan Kwok-wai, CFO
Chan Kai-ming, Exec. Dir.-Architecture & Eng.
Sandy Yung Sheung-tat, Company Sec.
Kwong Chun, Exec. Dir.
Mike Wong Chik-wing, Exec. Dir.
Thomas Chan Kui-yuen, Exec. Dir.
Kwong Siu-hing, Chmn.

Phone: 852-2827-8111	Fax: 852-2827-2862
Toll-Free:	
Address: Sun Hung Kai Ctr., 30 Harbour Rd., 45th Fl., Hong Kong, China	

GROWTH PLANS/SPECIAL FEATURES:

Sun Hung Kai Properties (SHKP) is one of the largest property developers in Hong Kong. The company's core areas of business include construction, land acquisition and property management; non-core businesses include hotels, insurance and financial services; it also has investments in transportation, infrastructure, logistics, telecommunications and information technology. SHKP's land bank is one of the largest private landholders in Hong Kong, with 27.6 million square feet of completed investment property and 16.6 million square feet of space currently under development. The firm's mainland China land bank has approximately 76.8 million square feet under development and 5.5 million square feet of completed investment properties, with a strategic focus on acquisitions in major cities such as Beijing, Shanghai, Guangzhou and Nanjing. SHKP also owns approximately 50 shopping malls in Hong Kong and five in mainland China. The firm owns four luxury hotels in Hong Kong: the Royal Garden, the Royal View Hotel, the Royal Park Hotel and the Royal Plaza Hotel. It also manages five other Hong Kong hotels, with 10 additional hotels currently under construction.   The company's financial division provides mortgages and related services through Hung Kai Finance Company and Honour Finance Company in support of SHKP's property development activities. SHKP is also active in a number of additional business areas, including bus operations, toll roads, port operations, department stores, broadband telecommunications infrastructure development and IT venture capital investments. In addition, SHKP is involved in air transportation and logistics, with subsidiaries focused on international air cargo consolidation and freight forwarding; airport services such as storage, X-ray scanning, loading and unloading, collection and delivery, palletization and containerization; and aviation services such as aircraft parking, marshalling, towing, fuelling, potable water supply and other turn-around operations. In February 2010, the firm purchased a new residential site in Hong Kong for $432 million.

FINANCIALS: Sales and profits are in thousands of dollars—add 000 to get the full amount. 2010 Note: Financial information for 2010 was not available for all companies at press time.

2010 Sales: $4,262,690	2010 Profits: $3,599,370	**U.S. Stock Ticker: SUHJY**
2009 Sales: $4,411,600	2009 Profits: $1,334,540	**Int'l Ticker: 0016** Int'l Exchange: Hong Kong-HKEX
2008 Sales: $3,154,710	2008 Profits: $2,956,560	Employees: 31,500
2007 Sales: $4,029,200	2007 Profits: $2,759,400	Fiscal Year Ends: 5/31
2006 Sales: $3,327,700	2006 Profits: $2,580,500	Parent Company:

SALARIES/BENEFITS:

Pension Plan:	ESOP Stock Plan:	Profit Sharing:	Top Exec. Salary: $	Bonus: $
Savings Plan:	Stock Purch. Plan:		Second Exec. Salary: $	Bonus: $

OTHER THOUGHTS:

Apparent Women Officers or Directors: 2
Hot Spot for Advancement for Women/Minorities:

LOCATIONS: ("Y" = Yes)

West:	Southwest:	Midwest:	Southeast:	Northeast:	International:
					Y

                                                    Plunkett Research, Ltd.

SUNBURST HOSPITALITY CORPORATION

www.snbhotels.com

Industry Group Code: 721110 Ranks within this company's industry group: Sales: Profits:

Properties:		Financial Services:	Construction/Development:	Investments:	Specialty Services:		Brokerage:	
Apartments:		Mortgages:	Commercial Construction:	REIT:	Property Management:	Y	Commercial Sales:	
Malls/Shopping:		Title Insurance:	Residential Construction:		Online Services:		Residential Sales:	
Offices:		Property Insurance:	Land Development:		Software/IT:		Specialty:	
Hotels/Motels:	Y		Support Services:		Consulting:			
Industrial/Warehouses:	Y		Design/Engineering:					
Other:	Y							

TYPES OF BUSINESS:

Hotels
Hotel Management

BRANDS/DIVISIONS/AFFILIATES:

Comfort Inns & Suites
Holiday Inn Express
Crowne Plaza
Quality Inn
AmeriHost
Sleep Inn
Clarion
Best Western

CONTACTS: *Note: Officers with more than one job title may be intentionally listed here more than once.*

Kevin Hanley, CEO
Kevin Hanley, Pres.
Joe Smith, CFO/VP
Tonia Noonan, VP-Mktg. & Sales
Mark Elbaum, VP-Info. Systems
Pam Williams, Chief Admin. Officer
Pam Williams, General Counsel/Exec. VP
Ned Heiss, VP-Oper.
Chris Milke, VP-Acquisitions & Dev.
Joe Smith, Treas.
Randy Hartig, VP-Construction
Leon Vainikos, Regional General Counsel/VP
Tom Murphy, VP-National Oper.

Phone: 301-592-3800	Fax: 301-592-3830
Toll-Free:	
Address: 10770 Columbia Pike, Ste. 200, Silver Spring, MD 20901-4448 US	

GROWTH PLANS/SPECIAL FEATURES:

Sunburst Hospitality Corporation owns, acquires and manages hotels, a championship golf course and townhomes. The company maintains operations in 16 states: Arkansas; California; Florida; Indiana; Maine; Maryland; Massachusetts; Michigan; New Mexico; New York; North Carolina; Ohio; Pennsylvania; South Carolina; Texas; and Virginia. The firm's hotels are extended-stay, full-service and limited service. On average, Sunburst Hospitality Corp. produces annual revenues of $100 million. Additionally, the company develops residential real estate with current projects in Virginia and Arkansas. Sunburst Hospitality Corp. owns and operates approximately 31 hotels under several brand names including Comfort Inns and Suites; Holiday Inn Express; Crowne Plaza; Quality Inn; Clarion; Sleep Inn; Best Western; and AmeriHost. The company constantly seeks to expand its hotel business through acquisitions. The firm seeks to acquire existing 70-300 room extended-stay, limited-service and full-service hotels, with or without food and beverage.

FINANCIALS: **Sales and profits are in thousands of dollars—add 000 to get the full amount. 2010 Note: Financial information for 2010 was not available for all companies at press time.**

2010 Sales: $	2010 Profits: $	U.S. Stock Ticker: Private
2009 Sales: $	2009 Profits: $	Int'l Ticker: Int'l Exchange:
2008 Sales: $	2008 Profits: $	Employees:
2007 Sales: $84,600	2007 Profits: $	Fiscal Year Ends: 12/31
2006 Sales: $	2006 Profits: $	Parent Company:

SALARIES/BENEFITS:

Pension Plan:	ESOP Stock Plan:	Profit Sharing:	Top Exec. Salary: $	Bonus: $
Savings Plan:	Stock Purch. Plan:		Second Exec. Salary: $	Bonus: $

OTHER THOUGHTS:

Apparent Women Officers or Directors: 2
Hot Spot for Advancement for Women/Minorities:

LOCATIONS: ("Y" = Yes)

West:	Southwest:	Midwest:	Southeast:	Northeast:	International:
Y	Y	Y	Y	Y	

SUNRISE SENIOR LIVING

www.sunriseseniorliving.com

Industry Group Code: 623110 Ranks within this company's industry group: Sales: 3 Profits: 1

Properties:	Financial Services:	Construction/Development:	Investments:	Specialty Services:		Brokerage:
Apartments:	Mortgages:	Commercial Construction:	REIT:	Property Management:	Y	Commercial Sales:
Malls/Shopping:	Title Insurance:	Residential Construction:		Online Services:		Residential Sales:
Offices:	Property Insurance:	Land Development:		Software/IT:		Specialty:
Hotels/Motels:		Support Services:		Consulting:		
Industrial/Warehouses:		Design/Engineering:				
Other: Y						

TYPES OF BUSINESS:

Long-Term Health Care
Assisted Living Centers
Independent Living Centers
Nursing Homes

BRANDS/DIVISIONS/AFFILIATES:

CNL Lifestyle Properties

CONTACTS: *Note: Officers with more than one job title may be intentionally listed here more than once.*

Mark S. Ordan, CEO
Marc Richards, CFO
Kelly Myers, Sr. VP-Sales
Mike Rodis, Sr. VP-Human Resources
Patrick Horne, CIO
Greg Neeb, Chief Admin. Officer
David Haddock, General Counsel/Corp. Sec.
Laura McDuffie, Co-Head/Sr. VP-Oper.
Meghan Lublin, VP-Corp. Comm.
Meghan Lublin, VP-Investor Comm.
Julie A. Pangelinan, Treas.
Karen Rindner, Chief Compliance Officer
Greg Neeb, Chief Investment Officer
Ron Jeanneault, Co-Head/Sr. VP-Oper.
Philip Kroskin, Sr. VP-Asset Mgmt. & Real Estate
Paul J. Klaassen, Chmn.

Phone: 703-273-7500	Fax: 703-744-1601
Toll-Free: 888-434-4648	
Address: 7902 Westpark Dr., McLean, VA 22102 US	

GROWTH PLANS/SPECIAL FEATURES:

Sunrise Senior Living is an international provider of senior living services. The firm operates approximately 277 senior living communities in the U.S., 27 in the U.K. and 15 in Canada, with a resident capacity of approximately 31,200. These 319 communities include 137 that Sunrise owns in unconsolidated ventures; 144 that are owned by third parties; 26 operated under leases; 10 that the company wholly owns; one consolidated venture; and one consolidated as a variable interest entity. Sunrise offers services tailored to the unique needs of each of its residents, typically in apartment-like assisted living environments. Upon move-in, Sunrise assists the resident in developing an individualized service plan, including selection of resident accommodations and the appropriate level of care. Services provided range from basic care, consisting of assistance with activities of daily living; to reminiscence care, which consists of programs and services to help cognitively impaired residents, including residents with Alzheimer's disease. The firm targets sites for development located in major metropolitan areas and their surrounding suburban communities, considering factors such as population, age demographics and estimated level of market demand. In 2010, Sunrise sold all nine of its German facilities, eight of which were sold to GHS Pflegeresidenzen Grundstucks GmbH and Prudential Real Estate Investors for $74.5 million. In late 2010, the company sold its venture interests in nine limited liability companies in the U.S. and two limited partnerships in Canada (a total of 58 communities) to Ventas, Inc. for roughly $41.5 million. In January 2011, the firm established a new joint venture with CNL Lifestyle Properties which is 40% owned by Sunrise Senior Living. The joint venture owns 29 communities managed by the firm.

Sunrise offers employees health, dental, vision, disability and life insurance; flexible spending accounts; a scholarship program; tuition assistance; a meal discount program; and a 401(k).

FINANCIALS: Sales and profits are in thousands of dollars—add 000 to get the full amount. 2010 Note: Financial information for 2010 was not available for all companies at press time.

2010 Sales: $1,406,701	2010 Profits: $100,826	U.S. Stock Ticker: SRZ
2009 Sales: $1,458,760	2009 Profits: $-133,915	Int'l Ticker: Int'l Exchange:
2008 Sales: $1,556,007	2008 Profits: $-439,179	Employees: 31,700
2007 Sales: $1,482,020	2007 Profits: $-70,275	Fiscal Year Ends: 12/31
2006 Sales: $1,628,605	2006 Profits: $15,284	Parent Company:

SALARIES/BENEFITS:

Pension Plan:	ESOP Stock Plan:	Profit Sharing:	Top Exec. Salary: $652,500	Bonus: $4,950,000
Savings Plan: Y	Stock Purch. Plan: Y		Second Exec. Salary: $414,231	Bonus: $675,000

OTHER THOUGHTS:

Apparent Women Officers or Directors: 4
Hot Spot for Advancement for Women/Minorities: Y

LOCATIONS: ("Y" = Yes)

West:	Southwest:	Midwest:	Southeast:	Northeast:	International:
Y	Y	Y	Y	Y	Y

SUNSTONE HOTEL INVESTORS INC   www.sunstonehotels.com

Industry Group Code: 531120 Ranks within this company's industry group: Sales: 26   Profits: 36

Properties:	Financial Services:	Construction/Development:	Investments:	Specialty Services:	Brokerage:
Apartments:	Mortgages:	Commercial Construction:	REIT: Y	Property Management:	Commercial Sales:
Malls/Shopping:	Title Insurance:	Residential Construction:		Online Services: Y	Residential Sales:
Offices:	Property Insurance:	Land Development:		Software/IT:	Specialty:
Hotels/Motels: Y		Support Services:		Consulting:	
Industrial/Warehouses:		Design/Engineering:			
Other:					

TYPES OF BUSINESS:

Real Estate Investment Trust
Hotel Ownership
Online Purchasing Systems

BRANDS/DIVISIONS/AFFILIATES:

Sunstone Hotel TRS Lessee Inc
Sunstone Hotel Properties Inc
Interstate Hotels and Resorts Inc
Strategic Hotels and Resorts Inc
BuyEfficient LLC

CONTACTS: *Note: Officers with more than one job title may be intentionally listed here more than once.*

Kenneth E. Cruse, CEO
Marc A. Hoffman, COO/Exec. VP
Kenneth E. Cruse, Pres.
John V. Arabia, CFO
David Sloan, VP-Legal
John V. Arabia, Exec. VP-Corp. Strategy
Bryan Giglia, Sr. VP-Finance
Lindsay Monge, Sr. VP/Treas.
Denise Hertle, VP-Corp. Acct.
Michael Harvey, VP-Asset Mgmt.
Olivier Kolpin, VP-Tax
Robert A. Alter, Exec. Chmn.

Phone: 949-330-4000	Fax: 949-330-4110
Toll-Free:	
Address: 120 Vantis, Ste. 350, Aliso Viejo, CA 92656 US	

GROWTH PLANS/SPECIAL FEATURES:

Sunstone Hotel Investors, Inc., a REIT (Real Estate Investment Trust), acquires, owns, asset manages and renovates primarily luxury, upper upscale and upscale full service hotels. Sunstone owns 33 hotels with a total of 12,676 rooms, located in 13 U.S. states and Washington, D.C. The firm's portfolio includes 31 upscale or upper upscale hotels, one luxury hotel and one mid-scale hotel. Sunstone also owns a 38% equity interest in the 460-room Doubletree Guest Suites Hotel Times Square in New York. Third-party managers operate the company's hotels through agreements with wholly-owned subsidiary Sunstone Hotel TRS Lessee, Inc. Approximately 13 hotels are operated by Sunstone Hotel Properties Inc., a division of Interstate Hotels and Resorts, Inc. Other hotels are managed as follows: subsidiaries of either Marriott International, Inc. or Marriot Services, Inc. operate 12 of the firm's hotels; and Hyatt Corporation, Fairmont Hotels & Resorts and Hilton Hotels Corp. operate one hotel each. Sunstone specializes in acquiring under-performing properties and developing them into profitable upscale and luxury properties. The firm prefers to acquire major brand properties situated in one of the top 25 U.S. markets, with upscale potential and a location with high barriers to entry. Besides its normal operations, the firm's subsidiary, BuyEfficient, LLC, is an electronic purchasing management platform that helps to simplify procurement and accounting activities.

FINANCIALS: Sales and profits are in thousands of dollars—add 000 to get the full amount. 2010 Note: Financial information for 2010 was not available for all companies at press time.

2010 Sales: $643,090	2010 Profits: $38,542	**U.S. Stock Ticker: SHO**
2009 Sales: $623,857	2009 Profits: $-269,608	**Int'l Ticker:** Int'l Exchange:
2008 Sales: $765,196	2008 Profits: $71,238	Employees: 35
2007 Sales: $866,494	2007 Profits: $123,876	Fiscal Year Ends: 12/31
2006 Sales: $771,219	2006 Profits: $53,237	Parent Company:

SALARIES/BENEFITS:

Pension Plan:	ESOP Stock Plan:	Profit Sharing:	Top Exec. Salary: $637,500	Bonus: $
Savings Plan:	Stock Purch. Plan:		Second Exec. Salary: $342,472	Bonus: $350,000

OTHER THOUGHTS:

Apparent Women Officers or Directors: 2
Hot Spot for Advancement for Women/Minorities:

LOCATIONS: ("Y" = Yes)

West:	Southwest:	Midwest:	Southeast:	Northeast:	International:
Y	Y	Y	Y	Y	

SUPER 8 MOTELS INC

www.super8.com

Industry Group Code: 721110 Ranks within this company's industry group: Sales: Profits:

Properties:	Financial Services:	Construction/Development:	Investments:	Specialty Services:	Brokerage:
Apartments:	Mortgages:	Commercial Construction:	REIT:	Property Management:	Commercial Sales:
Malls/Shopping:	Title Insurance:	Residential Construction:		Online Services: Y	Residential Sales:
Offices:	Property Insurance:	Land Development:		Software/IT:	Specialty:
Hotels/Motels: Y		Support Services:		Consulting:	
Industrial/Warehouses:		Design/Engineering:			
Other:					

TYPES OF BUSINESS:

Hotel Franchising
Economy Motels
Online Reservations & Services

BRANDS/DIVISIONS/AFFILIATES:

Wyndham Worldwide
TripRewards
Guaranteed Best Rate
TripFinder

CONTACTS: *Note: Officers with more than one job title may be intentionally listed here more than once.*

John Valletta, Pres.
Heny Gabay, VP-Mktg.
Jim Darby, VP-Oper.

Phone: 973-428-9700	**Fax:** 973-496-7307
Toll-Free: 800-800-8000	
Address: 1 Sylvan Way, Parsippany, NJ 07054 US	

GROWTH PLANS/SPECIAL FEATURES:

Super 8 Motels, Inc., a subsidiary of Wyndham Worldwide, is one of the world's largest franchised economy lodging chains, with a total of nearly 2,000 motels. The firm offers lodging for the budget traveler, with many rooms below $50 per night. Super 8 motels, which are found in every domestic state besides Hawaii and in every Canadian province, contain an average of 61 single rooms, totaling over 124,000 rooms. The company offers numerous promotions, such as guaranteed best rates, group and corporate rates and AAA and AARP discounts. Super 8 also offers TripFinder packages, which allow guests to construct their custom vacation package including hotel reservation, flight and rental car, as well as hotel package deals organized by the company around Super 8 properties. In addition, the firm is a member of Wyndham Rewards, one of the largest hotel reward programs in the world based on the 6,000 participating hotels. The program allows customers to earn points toward hotel stays, as well as airline miles, gifts, meals and other incentives. Super 8's web site offers customers a wide array of integrated travel resources, including flight tracking, driving directions, street maps, airport maps, destination guides and weather information, in addition to online reservations, location information and special promotional programs. A search feature can automatically find the Super 8 motel and room with the best available rate for a given date in the travel area. The company offers several in-room products and services, including in-room coffee makers, bath amenities and expanded breakfast choices.

FINANCIALS: Sales and profits are in thousands of dollars—add 000 to get the full amount. 2010 Note: Financial information for 2010 was not available for all companies at press time.

2010 Sales: $	2010 Profits: $	**U.S. Stock Ticker: Subsidiary**
2009 Sales: $	2009 Profits: $	**Int'l Ticker:** Int'l Exchange:
2008 Sales: $	2008 Profits: $	Employees:
2007 Sales: $1,335,800	2007 Profits: $	Fiscal Year Ends: 12/31
2006 Sales: $	2006 Profits: $	Parent Company: WYNDHAM WORLDWIDE

SALARIES/BENEFITS:

Pension Plan:	ESOP Stock Plan:	Profit Sharing:	Top Exec. Salary: $	Bonus: $
Savings Plan:	Stock Purch. Plan:		Second Exec. Salary: $	Bonus: $

OTHER THOUGHTS:

Apparent Women Officers or Directors:
Hot Spot for Advancement for Women/Minorities:

LOCATIONS: ("Y" = Yes)

West:	Southwest:	Midwest:	Southeast:	Northeast:	International:
Y	Y	Y	Y	Y	Y

SUPERTEL HOSPITALITY INC

www.supertelinc.com

Industry Group Code: 531120 Ranks within this company's industry group: Sales: 61   Profits: 52

Properties:		Financial Services:		Construction/Development:		Investments:		Specialty Services:		Brokerage:	
Apartments:		Mortgages:		Commercial Construction:		REIT:	Y	Property Management:		Commercial Sales:	
Malls/Shopping:		Title Insurance:		Residential Construction:				Online Services:		Residential Sales:	
Offices:		Property Insurance:		Land Development:				Software/IT:		Specialty:	
Hotels/Motels:	Y			Support Services:				Consulting:			
Industrial/Warehouses:				Design/Engineering:							
Other:											

TYPES OF BUSINESS:

Real Estate Investment Trust
Hotels & Motels

BRANDS/DIVISIONS/AFFILIATES:

Supertel Hospitality REIT Trust
E&P REIT Trust
Supertel Limited Partnership
E&P Financing Limited Partnership
Supertel Hospitality Management, Inc.
TRS Leasing, Inc.
Royco Hotels, Inc.
HLC Hotels, Inc

CONTACTS: *Note: Officers with more than one job title may be intentionally listed here more than once.*

Kelly A. Walters, CEO
Stephen C. Gilbert, COO
Kelly A. Walters, Pres.
Corrine L. Scarpello, CFO
Donavon A. Heimes, Sec.
David L. Walter, Treas./Sr. VP
William C. Latham, Chmn.

Phone: 402-371-2520	**Fax:** 402-371-4229
Toll-Free:	
Address: 309 N. 5th St., Norfolk, NE 68701 US	

GROWTH PLANS/SPECIAL FEATURES:

Supertel Hospitality, Inc. (SHI) is a self-administered REIT (Real Estate Investment Trust) primarily engaged in acquiring and owning hotels. Its portfolio includes 106 limited-service hotels in over 20 states under the following franchise brands: Super 8; Comfort Inn/Comfort Suites; Days Inn; Hampton Inn; Holiday Inn Express; Ramada, Ltd.; Tara Inn; Baymont Inn; Key West Inns; Savannah Suites; Masters Inn; Supertel Inn; Guest House Inn/Guesthouse Inn and Suites; and Sleep Inn. Standard guestroom amenities include high-speed wireless Internet, free local calls, cable TV, including movie channels, and iron and ironing board. Select Supertel properties also have complimentary continental breakfast, pools, suites, conference centers and meeting facilities. Through its two wholly-owned subsidiaries, Supertel Hospitality REIT Trust and E&P REIT Trust, the firm owns a 99% interest in Supertel Limited Partnership and 100% of E&P Financing Limited Partnership. Together, these four firms, along with other subsidiaries and partnerships, own the firm's properties. Those other subsidiaries and partnerships include Supertel Hospitality Management, Inc.; SPPR-BMI Holdings, Inc.; and Solomon's Beacon Inn Limited Partnership. To enter into management agreements with independent contractors, in compliance with the REIT Modernization Act of 1999, Supertel created TRS Leasing, Inc. and its subsidiaries TRS Subsidiary LLC; and SPPR TRS Subsidiary LLC. All SHI hotels are leased to TRS Leasing and are managed by Royco Hotels, Inc. and HLC Hotels, Inc. TRS also holds the firm's furniture, fixtures and equipment.

FINANCIALS: Sales and profits are in thousands of dollars—add 000 to get the full amount. 2010 Note: Financial information for 2010 was not available for all companies at press time.

2010 Sales: $84,114	2010 Profits: $-10,585	**U.S. Stock Ticker: SPPR**
2009 Sales: $81,570	2009 Profits: $-27,395	**Int'l Ticker:** Int'l Exchange:
2008 Sales: $90,996	2008 Profits: $6,656	Employees: 1,664
2007 Sales: $90,084	2007 Profits: $4,078	Fiscal Year Ends: 12/31
2006 Sales: $77,134	2006 Profits: $3,721	Parent Company:

SALARIES/BENEFITS:

Pension Plan:	ESOP Stock Plan:	Profit Sharing:	Top Exec. Salary: $270,000	Bonus: $
Savings Plan:	Stock Purch. Plan:		Second Exec. Salary: $184,807	Bonus: $

OTHER THOUGHTS:

Apparent Women Officers or Directors:
Hot Spot for Advancement for Women/Minorities:

LOCATIONS: ("Y" = Yes)

West:	Southwest:	Midwest:	Southeast:	Northeast:	International:
Y		Y	Y	Y	

SWIRE PACIFIC LTD

www.swirepacific.com

Industry Group Code: 483111 Ranks within this company's industry group: Sales: 1   Profits: 1

Properties:		Financial Services:	Construction/Development:	Investments:	Specialty Services:	Brokerage:
Apartments:	Y	Mortgages:	Commercial Construction:	REIT:	Property Management:	Commercial Sales:
Malls/Shopping:	Y	Title Insurance:	Residential Construction:		Online Services:	Residential Sales:
Offices:	Y	Property Insurance:	Land Development:		Software/IT:	Specialty:
Hotels/Motels:	Y		Support Services:		Consulting:	
Industrial/Warehouses:			Design/Engineering:			
Other:						

TYPES OF BUSINESS:

Deep Sea Shipping
Airlines and Air Freight
International & Regional Airlines
Apparel Retail
Real Estate, Hotels, Commercial Properties
Aircraft Maintenance
Airline Catering Service
Beverage Manufacturing & Distribution

BRANDS/DIVISIONS/AFFILIATES:

Swire Group (The)
Swire Properties, Ltd.
Cathay Pacific Airways, Ltd.
Swire Beverages, Ltd.
Swire Resources, Ltd.
Swire Pacific Offshore Holdings
HUD Group (The)
Hong Kong Dragon Airlines (Dragonair)

CONTACTS: *Note: Officers with more than one job title may be intentionally listed here more than once.*

Peter Alan Kilgour, Exec. Dir.-Group Finance
Yat Hung David Fu, Corp. Sec.
Antony Nigel Tyler, CEO-Cathay Pacific Airways, Ltd.
Geoffrey Leslie Cundle, Exec. Dir.-Beverages Div.
John Bruce Rae-Smith, Exec. Dir.-Swire Pacific Offshore
Christopher D. Pratt, Exec. Chmn.

Phone: 852-2840-8098	**Fax:** 852-2526-9365
Toll-Free:	
Address: 2 Pacific Place, 88 Queensway, 35th Fl., Hong Kong, China	

GROWTH PLANS/SPECIAL FEATURES:

Swire Pacific Ltd. is part of the Swire Group and one of Hong Kong's leading listed companies. It operates several core businesses, organized into five divisions: property; aviation; beverages; marine services; and trading and industrial. Swire Properties, Ltd., a property developer based in Hong Kong, has invested in roughly 17.8 million square feet of real estate. Swire Properties, Inc., its U.S. subsidiary, develops and trades properties in Florida, specifically downtown Miami, including office space, retail space and hotels. The company's aviation holdings include international passenger and freight airline Cathay Pacific Airways, Ltd., with nearly 120 worldwide destinations; Air Hong Kong Ltd.; Cathay Pacific subsidiary, Hong Kong Dragon Airlines (Dragonair), with more than 29 destinations and cargo operations in Asia, Europe, the U.S. and the Middle East; AHK Hong Kong, an all-cargo carrier, and Hong Kong Aircraft Engineering Company, a provider of base and line maintenance at Hong Kong International Airport. Swire Beverages, Ltd., a joint venture between Swire Pacific (owning 87.5%) and The Coca-Cola Company, owns the franchise to manufacture and distribute Coca-Cola products in Hong Kong, Taiwan, 11 U.S. states and seven provinces in China, representing a total franchise population of over 411 million. Swire Beverages is one of The Coca-Cola Company's major international bottlers and works with Coca-Cola on brand development and marketing. The firm's marine services holdings include Swire Pacific Offshore Holdings Ltd., one of the largest offshore energy support fleets in the world, with a fleet of 71 vessels; the HUD Group, which provides ship repair, towage and salvage, mechanical and electrical engineering and steelwork services; and Swire Pacific Ship Management Ltd., a provider of fleet personnel services. Trading and industrial subsidiary Swire Resources acts as the holding company for various retail and wholesale interests in sports and active footwear and apparel, operating more than 180 retail locations in China.

FINANCIALS: Sales and profits are in thousands of dollars—add 000 to get the full amount. 2010 Note: Financial information for 2010 was not available for all companies at press time.

2010 Sales: $3,758,310	2010 Profits: $4,923,220	**U.S. Stock Ticker:** SWRAY
2009 Sales: $3,209,370	2009 Profits: $2,565,380	**Int'l Ticker:** 0019 **Int'l Exchange:** Hong Kong-HKEX
2008 Sales: $3,183,030	2008 Profits: $215,210	Employees: 100,000
2007 Sales: $2,780,860	2007 Profits: $2,589,000	Fiscal Year Ends: 12/31
2006 Sales: $2,445,120	2006 Profits: $1,115,150	Parent Company:

SALARIES/BENEFITS:

Pension Plan:	ESOP Stock Plan:	Profit Sharing:	Top Exec. Salary: $	Bonus: $
Savings Plan:	Stock Purch. Plan:		Second Exec. Salary: $	Bonus: $

OTHER THOUGHTS:

Apparent Women Officers or Directors: 2
Hot Spot for Advancement for Women/Minorities:

LOCATIONS: ("Y" = Yes)

West:	Southwest:	Midwest:	Southeast:	Northeast:	International:
Y	Y	Y		Y	Y

TANGER FACTORY OUTLET CENTERS INC   www.tangeroutlet.com

Industry Group Code: 531120 Ranks within this company's industry group: Sales: 48   Profits: 37

Properties:		Financial Services:	Construction/Development:	Investments:		Specialty Services:		Brokerage:
Apartments:		Mortgages:	Commercial Construction:	REIT:	Y	Property Management:	Y	Commercial Sales:
Malls/Shopping:	Y	Title Insurance:	Residential Construction:			Online Services:		Residential Sales:
Offices:		Property Insurance:	Land Development:			Software/IT:		Specialty:
Hotels/Motels:			Support Services:			Consulting:		
Industrial/Warehouses:			Design/Engineering:					
Other:								

TYPES OF BUSINESS:

Factory Outlet Shopping Centers
Real Estate Investment Trust
Property Management

BRANDS/DIVISIONS/AFFILIATES:

Tanger Outlet Centers
Relax, It's Guaranteed
TangerClub
RioCan Real Estate Investment Trust

CONTACTS: *Note: Officers with more than one job title may be intentionally listed here more than once.*

Steven B. Tanger, CEO
Steven B. Tanger, Pres.
Frank C. Marchisello, Jr., CFO/Exec. VP
Carrie A. Geldner, Sr. VP-Mktg.
Mary Anne Williams, VP-Human Resources
Rick Farrar, VP-IT
Frank C. Marchisello, Jr., Corp. Sec.
Thomas E. Mcdonough, Exec. VP-Oper.
Mona J. Walsh, VP-Corp. Comm.
Virgina R. Summerell, VP-Finance/Treas.
Lisa J. Morrison, Sr. VP-Leasing
James F. Williams, Sr. VP/Controller
Mike Buescher, Dir.-Public Rel.
Jack Africk, Interim Chmn.

Phone: 336-292-3010	Fax: 336-852-2096
Toll-Free:	
Address: 3200 Northline Ave., Ste. 360, Greensboro, NC 27408 US	

GROWTH PLANS/SPECIAL FEATURES:

Tanger Factory Outlet Centers, Inc. (Tanger) is a self-administered and self-managed real estate investment trust (REIT). Through operating subsidiary Tanger Properties Limited Partnership, the company develops, acquires, owns, operates and manages factory outlet shopping centers under the brand name Tanger Outlet Center. The firm owns 31 centers in 22 states with a total gross leasable area of approximately 9.2 million square feet of retail space containing over 2,000 stores (98% occupied). Through unconsolidated joint ventures, Tanger also operates and owns interest in two outlet centers with approximately 948,000 square feet. Tanger Outlet Centers typically incorporate a mix of leading designer and brand name manufacturers, allowing customers to buy discounted products directly from the manufacturer. In addition, frequent shoppers are eligible for TangerClub membership, entitling them to various seasonal discounts, special coupons and fee waivers. The firm also has a money-back, low-price guarantee program called 'Relax, It's Guaranteed,' which gives customers a cash refund equal to the difference in price. The roughly 360 brand names sold at Tanger Outlet Centers include Polo Ralph Lauren, Ann Taylor, GAP, Banana Republic, Old Navy, Juicy, Kate Spade, Saks Fifth Avenue - Off Fifth, Calvin Klein, Lucky Brand Jeans, Reebok, Tommy Hilfiger, Abercrombie & Fitch, Eddie Bauer, Coach Leatherware, Brooks Brothers, BCBG, Michael Kors and Nike. In March 2011, the firm and partner RioCan Real Estate Investment Trust announced plans to build an outlet center in the Toronto area; the companies also hope to build 10-15 outlets over the next 5-7 years.

FINANCIALS: Sales and profits are in thousands of dollars—add 000 to get the full amount. 2010 Note: Financial information for 2010 was not available for all companies at press time.

2010 Sales: $276,303	2010 Profits: $38,244	**U.S. Stock Ticker: SKT**
2009 Sales: $270,595	2009 Profits: $67,495	**Int'l Ticker:** Int'l Exchange:
2008 Sales: $243,793	2008 Profits: $29,718	Employees: 432
2007 Sales: $228,765	2007 Profits: $26,458	Fiscal Year Ends: 12/31
2006 Sales: $210,962	2006 Profits: $37,309	Parent Company:

SALARIES/BENEFITS:

Pension Plan:	ESOP Stock Plan:	Profit Sharing:	Top Exec. Salary: $538,900	Bonus: $931,250
Savings Plan:	Stock Purch. Plan:		Second Exec. Salary: $438,020	Bonus: $652,650

OTHER THOUGHTS:

Apparent Women Officers or Directors: 7
Hot Spot for Advancement for Women/Minorities: Y

LOCATIONS: ("Y" = Yes)

West:	Southwest:	Midwest:	Southeast:	Northeast:	International:
Y	Y	Y	Y	Y	

TAUBMAN CENTERS INC

www.taubman.com

Industry Group Code: 531120 Ranks within this company's industry group: Sales: 25   Profits: 22

Properties:		Financial Services:	Construction/Development:	Investments:		Specialty Services:		Brokerage:
Apartments:		Mortgages:	Commercial Construction:	REIT:	Y	Property Management:	Y	Commercial Sales:
Malls/Shopping:	Y	Title Insurance:	Residential Construction:			Online Services:		Residential Sales:
Offices:		Property Insurance:	Land Development:			Software/IT:		Specialty:
Hotels/Motels:			Support Services:			Consulting:		
Industrial/Warehouses:			Design/Engineering:					
Other:								

TYPES OF BUSINESS:

Real Estate Investment Trust
Malls & Shopping Centers
Property Management

BRANDS/DIVISIONS/AFFILIATES:

Taubman Realty Group Ltd. Partnership (The)
Taubman Company LLC (The)
Taubman Asia

CONTACTS: *Note: Officers with more than one job title may be intentionally listed here more than once.*

Robert S. Taubman, CEO
William S. Taubman, COO
Robert S. Taubman, Pres.
Lisa A. Payne, CFO
Robert R. Reese, Chief Admin. Officer/Sr. VP
Chris B. Heaphy, General Counsel/Sr. VP/Corp. Sec.
Denise Anton, Sr. VP-Center Oper.
Stephen J. Kieras, Sr. VP-Dev.
Karen MacDonald, Dir.-Comm.
Barbara Baker, VP-Investor Rel.
Esther R. Blum, Chief Acct. Officer/Sr. VP/Controller
David T. Weinert, Sr. VP-Leasing
Steven E. Eder, Treas./Sr. VP
Robert S. Taubman, Chmn.
Rene Tremblay, Pres., Taubman Asia

Phone: 248-258-6800	Fax: 248-258-7596
Toll-Free:	

Address: 200 E. Long Lake Rd., Ste. 300, Bloomfield Hills, MI 48304-2324 US

GROWTH PLANS/SPECIAL FEATURES:

Taubman Centers, Inc. is a real estate investment trust (REIT) that owns, develops, acquires and operates regional luxury shopping centers. Headquartered in Michigan with offices in the San Francisco Bay area, Virginia and New York, the company's portfolio includes 23 urban and suburban shopping centers in 10 states, 18 of which are super-regional shopping centers. Taubman Centers owns a majority interest in The Taubman Realty Group Ltd. Partnership, through which all operations are conducted. The Taubman Realty Group Ltd. Partnership also owns certain regional retail shopping center development projects and majority interest in The Taubman Company LLC, which manages the shopping centers and provides other services to the operating partnership. 90% of the firm's revenue comes from national retail chains such as Forever 21, Limited Brands and The Gap. Taubman Asia is the platform for Taubman's expansion into the Asia-Pacific region; it is headquartered in Hong Kong and is engaged in projects that leverage the company's retail planning, design and operational capabilities. In 2010, Taubman Centers' malls averaged $564 in sales per square foot of store space, an amount that is significantly higher than most other mall operators.

The company offers its employees medical, dental, vision, prescription drug and domestic partner benefits; life, AD&D, pet, short-term and long-term disability insurance; flexible spending accounts; and an employee assistance program.

FINANCIALS: Sales and profits are in thousands of dollars—add 000 to get the full amount. 2010 Note: Financial information for 2010 was not available for all companies at press time.

2010 Sales: $654,558	2010 Profits: $102,327	**U.S. Stock Ticker: TCO**	
2009 Sales: $666,104	2009 Profits: $-79,161	**Int'l Ticker:**	Int'l Exchange:
2008 Sales: $671,498	2008 Profits: $-8,052	Employees: 582	
2007 Sales: $626,822	2007 Profits: $116,236	Fiscal Year Ends: 12/31	
2006 Sales: $579,284	2006 Profits: $45,117	Parent Company:	

SALARIES/BENEFITS:

Pension Plan: Y	ESOP Stock Plan:	Profit Sharing:	Top Exec. Salary: $825,000	Bonus: $
Savings Plan: Y	Stock Purch. Plan:		Second Exec. Salary: $677,625	Bonus: $

OTHER THOUGHTS:

Apparent Women Officers or Directors: 5
Hot Spot for Advancement for Women/Minorities: Y

LOCATIONS: ("Y" = Yes)

West:	Southwest:	Midwest:	Southeast:	Northeast:	International:
Y	Y	Y	Y	Y	Y

TDINDUSTRIES

www.tdindustries.com

Industry Group Code: 237 Ranks within this company's industry group: Sales: Profits:

Properties:		Financial Services:	Construction/Development:		Investments:		Specialty Services:	Brokerage:
Apartments:		Mortgages:	Commercial Construction:	Y	REIT:		Property Management:	Commercial Sales:
Malls/Shopping:		Title Insurance:	Residential Construction:	Y			Online Services:	Residential Sales:
Offices:	Y	Property Insurance:	Land Development:	Y			Software/IT:	Specialty:
Hotels/Motels:	Y		Support Services:	Y			Consulting:	
Industrial/Warehouses:	Y		Design/Engineering:	Y				
Other:								

TYPES OF BUSINESS:

Construction
Facilities Services
HVAC

BRANDS/DIVISIONS/AFFILIATES:

Camden Development Inc
Clark Construction Group
Fairfield Development
Gables Residential
Hanover Company (The)
Trammell Crow Residential

CONTACTS: Note: Officers with more than one job title may be intentionally listed here more than once.

Harold MacDowell, CEO
Mike Fitzpatrick, CFO
Maureen Underwood, Sr. VP-People Dept.
Jim Bivins, VP-IT
Jason Cinek, VP-Tech.
L. Steve Canter, Sr. VP-Eng.
L. Steve Canter, Sr. VP-Mfg.
Tim McNew, VP-Fort Worth
Graham T. Moore, Pres., Houston
Bob Richards, Pres., Central Texas
Ed Reeve, Exec. VP-Major Projects
John B. Lowe Jr, Chmn.

Phone: 972-888-9500	Fax: 972-888-9507
Toll-Free:	
Address: 13850 Diplomat Dr., Dallas, TX 75234-8849 US	

GROWTH PLANS/SPECIAL FEATURES:

TDIndustries is a leading facilities service and specialty construction company. The Dallas, Texas-based firm offers construction, installation and operations services for commercial, industrial and institutional buildings in these following industries: education, food service, government, healthcare, historic properties, hotels, multifamily, sports and assembly, pharmaceutical, semiconductor manufacturing and telecom. The company offers its services in these key areas: heating ventilation, air conditioning, electrical, mechanical, millwright, steel fabrication, life safety, facilities management, plumbing, process and high purity piping, life cycle planning, building automation refrigeration and specialty fabrication and installation. The firm provides services in the energy and environment sector, which includes energy audits and energy efficiency modeling of buildings; and the design and construction of LEED (Leadership in Energy and Environmental Design) buildings. Lastly, the company constructs intelligent buildings, which monitors security, controls heating, and air conditioning throughout the property. The firm has construction partnerships with Camden Development, Inc., Clark Construction Group, Fairfield Development, Gables Residential, The Hanover Company and Trammell Crow Residential. Prominent clients include Dallas Cowboys Stadium, the Texas Governor's Mansion and Tyson Foods.

Employees of the firm are offered an employee stock option program. TDIndustries is 100%-owned by its over 900 employees and retirees with no one employee controlling more than 3% of the company's stock. TDIndustries was ranked 37 on FORTUNE magazine's 100 Best Companies to Work For List. The firm has consistently earned placement on the prestigious list since its inception and as a result holds Fortune's All Star distinction, an honor only held by 13 companies.

FINANCIALS: Sales and profits are in thousands of dollars—add 000 to get the full amount. 2010 Note: Financial information for 2010 was not available for all companies at press time.

2010 Sales: $	2010 Profits: $	U.S. Stock Ticker: Private
2009 Sales: $	2009 Profits: $	Int'l Ticker: Int'l Exchange:
2008 Sales: $	2008 Profits: $	Employees: 1,713
2007 Sales: $	2007 Profits: $	Fiscal Year Ends: 12/31
2006 Sales: $	2006 Profits: $	Parent Company:

SALARIES/BENEFITS:

Pension Plan:	ESOP Stock Plan: Y	Profit Sharing:	Top Exec. Salary: $	Bonus: $
Savings Plan:	Stock Purch. Plan:		Second Exec. Salary: $	Bonus: $

OTHER THOUGHTS:

Apparent Women Officers or Directors:
Hot Spot for Advancement for Women/Minorities:

LOCATIONS: ("Y" = Yes)

West:	Southwest:	Midwest:	Southeast:	Northeast:	International:
	Y				

TECHNICAL OLYMPIC USA INC

www.tousa.com

Industry Group Code: 2361 Ranks within this company's industry group: Sales: Profits:

Properties:	Financial Services:		Construction/Development:		Investments:	Specialty Services:	Brokerage:
Apartments:	Mortgages:	Y	Commercial Construction:		REIT:	Property Management:	Commercial Sales:
Malls/Shopping:	Title Insurance:	Y	Residential Construction:	Y		Online Services:	Residential Sales:
Offices:	Property Insurance:	Y	Land Development:			Software/IT:	Specialty:
Hotels/Motels:			Support Services:			Consulting:	
Industrial/Warehouses:			Design/Engineering:				
Other:							

TYPES OF BUSINESS:

Residential Construction
Closing & Settlement Services
Mortgages
Title & Homeowner's Insurance

BRANDS/DIVISIONS/AFFILIATES:

TOUSA Homes Inc
Engle Homes
Newmark Homes
Fedrick, Harris Estate Homes
Trophy Homes
Universal Land Title Inc
Preferred Home Mortgage Company
Alliance Insurance and Information Services

CONTACTS: *Note: Officers with more than one job title may be intentionally listed here more than once.*

Tommy L. McAden, CFO/Exec. VP
George Yeonas, Exec. VP/COO-Homebuilding Oper.
Angie Valdes, Chief Acct. Officer
Peter J. Strawser, Pres., Preferred Home Mortgage Company

Phone: 954-364-4000	Fax: 954-364-4010
Toll-Free:	
Address: 4000 Hollywood Blvd., Ste. 400 N., Hollywood, FL 33021 US	

GROWTH PLANS/SPECIAL FEATURES:

Technical Olympic USA, Inc. (TOUSA) designs, builds and markets detached single-family residences, town homes and condominiums. It builds homes through subsidiary TOUSA Homes, Inc., operating in five states: Texas, Virginia, Colorado, Tennessee and Arizona. TOUSA markets its homes to a diverse group of homebuyers, including first-time, move-up and active-adult homebuyers; buyers who are relocating to a new city or state; and those buying a second or vacation home. Houses are marketed under the brand names Engle Homes in Texas, Colorado, Arizona and Virginia; Fedrick, Harris Estate Homes (a division of Newmark Homes) in Tennessee; and Trophy Homes in Texas. The company also offers complementary financial services, providing mortgage financing, closing and settlement services and offers title, homeowners' and other insurance products. These services are marketed through subsidiaries Preferred Home Mortgage Company, Universal Land Title, Inc. and Alliance Insurance and Information Services. TOUSA selects its target markets based on population growth; projected job and income growth; regional economic conditions; availability of management with local expertise; single-family home permit activity and price; housing inventory and secondary home sales activity, among other criteria. The firm and many of its non-financial services subsidiaries are currently in Chapter 11 bankruptcy. The company is in the process of reorganization with the intent to emerge from Chapter 11.

FINANCIALS: Sales and profits are in thousands of dollars—add 000 to get the full amount. 2010 Note: Financial information for 2010 was not available for all companies at press time.

2010 Sales: $	2010 Profits: $	**U.S. Stock Ticker: TOUSQ**
2009 Sales: $	2009 Profits: $	**Int'l Ticker:** Int'l Exchange:
2008 Sales: $	2008 Profits: $	Employees:
2007 Sales: $2,195,300	2007 Profits: $-1,347,200	Fiscal Year Ends: 12/31
2006 Sales: $2,441,300	2006 Profits: $-201,200	Parent Company:

SALARIES/BENEFITS:

Pension Plan:	ESOP Stock Plan:	Profit Sharing:	Top Exec. Salary: $	Bonus: $
Savings Plan:	Stock Purch. Plan:		Second Exec. Salary: $	Bonus: $

OTHER THOUGHTS:

Apparent Women Officers or Directors: 1
Hot Spot for Advancement for Women/Minorities:

LOCATIONS: ("Y" = Yes)

West:	Southwest:	Midwest:	Southeast:	Northeast:	International:
Y	Y		Y	Y	

THARALDSON ENTERPRISES INC

www.tharaldson.com

Industry Group Code: 721110 Ranks within this company's industry group: Sales: Profits:

Properties:		Financial Services:	Construction/Development:	Investments:	Specialty Services:		Brokerage:
Apartments:		Mortgages:	Commercial Construction:	REIT:	Property Management:	Y	Commercial Sales:
Malls/Shopping:		Title Insurance:	Residential Construction:		Online Services:		Residential Sales:
Offices:		Property Insurance:	Land Development:		Software/IT:		Specialty:
Hotels/Motels:	Y		Support Services:		Consulting:		
Industrial/Warehouses:			Design/Engineering:				
Other:							

TYPES OF BUSINESS:

Hotels
Construction Services
Communications Services
Property Management

BRANDS/DIVISIONS/AFFILIATES:

Tharaldson Property Management, Inc.
Tharaldson Development Company, Inc.
Tharaldson Communications
Tharaldson Motels, Inc.
Room In The Inn Program

CONTACTS: Note: Officers with more than one job title may be intentionally listed here more than once.

Gary Tharaldson, Pres.
Douglas Dobmeier, Sr. VP-Oper.
Richard Larson, Pres., Dev.
Annette Croves, Controller
Charles A. Krumwiede, VP-Oper. & Property Support

Phone: 701-235-1060	Fax: 701-235-0948
Toll-Free:	
Address: 1202 Westrac Dr., Fargo, ND 58103-2344 US	

GROWTH PLANS/SPECIAL FEATURES:

Tharaldson Enterprises, Inc., through Tharaldson Motels, Inc., builds and operates select-service and extended-service hotels across the U.S. The firm's Tharaldson Property Management, Inc. subsidiary is a leading independent hotel property-management company in the U.S., operating over 220 hotels in 30 states. Tharaldson Communications, Inc. provides nationwide telecommunications services to the hospitality industry. Tharaldson Development Company, Inc., one of the largest developers of new hotels in the U.S., has more than 20 hotel projects currently in development. Tharaldson Motels operates properties under brand names including Courtyard, Residence Inn, Fairfield Inn, Springhill Suites and TownePlace Suites by Marriott; Homewood Suites and Hampton Inn by Hilton; Country Inn and Suites; Holiday Inn Express; and Comfort Inn and Suites. Tharaldson properties offer many amenities including cable television; indoor and outdoor pools; complimentary breakfast; free local phone calls; and 24-hour coffee service. In addition, children under 18 stay free. The firm also provides its Room In The Inn Program, which offers free rooms to guests visiting friends or family members in a hospital, nursing home or treatment facility during the Christmas and Thanksgiving seasons. In September 2010, the firm opened a new Residence Inn Lexington - Keeland Airport in Lexington, Kentucky.

Tharaldson offers its employees medical, dental and vision coverage; a 401(k) plan; an employee stock ownership program; lodging discounts; a flexible spending account; training; and an education assistance program.

FINANCIALS: Sales and profits are in thousands of dollars—add 000 to get the full amount. 2010 Note: Financial information for 2010 was not available for all companies at press time.

		U.S. Stock Ticker: Private
2010 Sales: $	2010 Profits: $	
2009 Sales: $	2009 Profits: $	Int'l Ticker: Int'l Exchange:
2008 Sales: $	2008 Profits: $	Employees:
2007 Sales: $312,700	2007 Profits: $	Fiscal Year Ends: 12/31
2006 Sales: $	2006 Profits: $	Parent Company:

SALARIES/BENEFITS:

Pension Plan:	ESOP Stock Plan: Y	Profit Sharing:	Top Exec. Salary: $	Bonus: $
Savings Plan: Y	Stock Purch. Plan:		Second Exec. Salary: $	Bonus: $

OTHER THOUGHTS:

Apparent Women Officers or Directors: 1
Hot Spot for Advancement for Women/Minorities:

LOCATIONS: ("Y" = Yes)

West:	Southwest:	Midwest:	Southeast:	Northeast:	International:
Y	Y	Y	Y	Y	

TOLL BROTHERS INC

www.tollbrothers.com

Industry Group Code: 2361 Ranks within this company's industry group: Sales: 8   Profits: 8

Properties:		Financial Services:		Construction/Development:		Investments:		Specialty Services:		Brokerage:	
Apartments:		Mortgages:	Y	Commercial Construction:		REIT:		Property Management:	Y	Commercial Sales:	
Malls/Shopping:		Title Insurance:		Residential Construction:	Y			Online Services:		Residential Sales:	Y
Offices:		Property Insurance:		Land Development:	Y			Software/IT:		Specialty:	
Hotels/Motels:				Support Services:	Y			Consulting:			
Industrial/Warehouses:				Design/Engineering:	Y						
Other:	Y										

TYPES OF BUSINESS:

Home Building
Mortgages & Insurance
Property Management
Landscaping
Country Club Communities
Golf Courses
Security Monitoring
Lumber Distribution

BRANDS/DIVISIONS/AFFILIATES:

CONTACTS: *Note: Officers with more than one job title may be intentionally listed here more than once.*

Douglas C. Yearley, Jr., CEO
Zvi Barzilay, COO
Zvi Barzilay, Pres.
Martin P. Connor, CFO
Martin P. Connor, Treas.
Robert I. Toll, Chmn.

Phone: 215-938-8000	**Fax:** 215-938-8010
Toll-Free: 800-289-8655	
Address: 250 Gibralter Rd., Horsham, PA 19044 US	

GROWTH PLANS/SPECIAL FEATURES:

Toll Brothers, Inc. designs, builds, markets and arranges financing for single-family detached and attached homes in luxury residential communities. The firm is also involved, both directly and through joint ventures, in building or converting existing rental apartment buildings into high-, mid- and low-rise luxury homes. Toll Brothers markets its services to move-up, empty-nester, active-adult, age-qualified and second-home buyers through its operations in about 20 U.S. states. The company operates in major suburban and urban residential areas including the Philadelphia, Pennsylvania metropolitan area; the Eastern Shore of Maryland and Delaware; central and northern New Jersey; Washington, D.C.; Boston, Massachusetts; Westchester County, New York; Palm Springs, California; the San Francisco Bay area; Phoenix, Arizona; Las Vegas and Reno, Nevada; and Chicago, Illinois, among others. Toll Brothers emphasizes high-quality construction and customer satisfaction. The average base sales price of the company's homes is about $597,600 for detached homes and approximately $469,600 for attached homes. Toll Brothers operates its own land development, architectural, engineering, mortgage, title, landscaping, lumber distribution, house component assembly and manufacturing operations. In addition, the company owns and operates golf courses in conjunction with several of its master planned communities (of which it has 24). Over the past five years, the firm has delivered over 26,062 homes in 549 communities, including approximately 2,642 homes in 265 communities delivered in 2010. In June 2010, Toll Brothers launched Gibralter Capital and Asset Management, a unit that is designed to invest in financially distressed properties.

The company offers its employees medical and dental coverage; a 401(k) plan; short- and long-term disability; educational reimbursement; an employee stock purchase plan; the use of furnished vacation homes; a discount on Toll Brothers homes; and discounts on mortgages, title insurance, home appliances, kitchen cabinets and more.

FINANCIALS: Sales and profits are in thousands of dollars—add 000 to get the full amount. 2010 Note: Financial information for 2010 was not available for all companies at press time.

2010 Sales: $1,494,771	2010 Profits: $-3,374	**U.S. Stock Ticker: TOL**
2009 Sales: $1,755,310	2009 Profits: $-755,825	**Int'l Ticker:** Int'l Exchange:
2008 Sales: $3,148,166	2008 Profits: $-297,810	Employees: 2,117
2007 Sales: $4,635,093	2007 Profits: $35,651	Fiscal Year Ends: 10/31
2006 Sales: $6,123,453	2006 Profits: $687,213	Parent Company:

SALARIES/BENEFITS:

Pension Plan:	ESOP Stock Plan:	Profit Sharing:	Top Exec. Salary: $1,300,000	Bonus: $1,000,000
Savings Plan: Y	Stock Purch. Plan: Y		Second Exec. Salary: $1,017,307	Bonus: $1,000,000

OTHER THOUGHTS:

Apparent Women Officers or Directors:
Hot Spot for Advancement for Women/Minorities:

LOCATIONS: ("Y" = Yes)

West:	Southwest:	Midwest:	Southeast:	Northeast:	International:
Y	Y	Y	Y	Y	

TRACO

www.traco.com

Industry Group Code: 326199 Ranks within this company's industry group: Sales: Profits:

Properties:	Financial Services:	Construction/Development:		Investments:	Specialty Services:	Brokerage:
Apartments:	Mortgages:	Commercial Construction:		REIT:	Property Management:	Commercial Sales:
Malls/Shopping:	Title Insurance:	Residential Construction:			Online Services:	Residential Sales:
Offices:	Property Insurance:	Land Development:			Software/IT:	Specialty:
Hotels/Motels:		Support Services:	Y		Consulting:	
Industrial/Warehouses:		Design/Engineering:				
Other:						

TYPES OF BUSINESS:

Windows & Doors-Manufacturing

BRANDS/DIVISIONS/AFFILIATES:

NRG
Nexgen
Valu
Three Rivers Aluminum Company
ALCOA

CONTACTS: *Note: Officers with more than one job title may be intentionally listed here more than once.*

Robert P. Randall, CEO
Robert P. Randall, Pres.
Fran Stephen, CFO
Robin Randall, VP-Corp. Mktg.

Phone: 724-776-7002	Fax: 724-776-7001
Toll-Free: 800-837-7002	
Address: 71 Progress Ave., Cranberry Township, PA 16066 US	

GROWTH PLANS/SPECIAL FEATURES:

TRACO, formerly Three Rivers Aluminum Company and a subsidiary of Alcoa, Inc., is a designer and manufacturer of custom-made windows and doors primarily for the commercial and residential real estate markets. The firm fashions impact resistant and energy efficient windows and doors, as well as entranceways, skylights sunrooms and curtain walls for buildings in the educational, healthcare, multi-family, office, hotel and government sectors. TRACO's areas of expertise include glass tempering, paint finishing, anodizing, glass insulating and aluminum extruding. The company provides products for new construction projects, as well as historical landmarks. TRACO has serviced notable buildings and structures such as the Empire State Building, the Statue of Liberty, the Waldorf Astoria and the Flat Iron Building in New York, the National Theatre in Washington D.C. and the College of William and Mary in Williamsburg, Virginia. Customers consist primarily of homeowners, general contractors, architects and developers. Commercial product lines include NRG, for aluminum window and door items; Nexgen, for glass and frame insulation; Biscayne Windows and Doors, for aluminum products designed for coastal environments; and Valu products for low-mid rise building applications. The firm sells its products through dealers and distributors nationwide. In August 2010, TRACO was purchased by Alcoa, Inc.

FINANCIALS: Sales and profits are in thousands of dollars—add 000 to get the full amount. 2010 Note: Financial information for 2010 was not available for all companies at press time.

2010 Sales: $	2010 Profits: $	**U.S. Stock Ticker: Subsidiary**
2009 Sales: $	2009 Profits: $	Int'l Ticker: Int'l Exchange:
2008 Sales: $	2008 Profits: $	Employees:
2007 Sales: $	2007 Profits: $	Fiscal Year Ends: 12/31
2006 Sales: $	2006 Profits: $	Parent Company: ALCOA

SALARIES/BENEFITS:

Pension Plan:	ESOP Stock Plan:	Profit Sharing:	Top Exec. Salary: $	Bonus: $
Savings Plan:	Stock Purch. Plan:		Second Exec. Salary: $	Bonus: $

OTHER THOUGHTS:

Apparent Women Officers or Directors: 1
Hot Spot for Advancement for Women/Minorities:

LOCATIONS: ("Y" = Yes)

West:	Southwest:	Midwest:	Southeast:	Northeast:	International:
		Y		Y	

TRAMMELL CROW COMPANY

www.trammellcrow.com

Industry Group Code: 5311 Ranks within this company's industry group: Sales: Profits:

Properties:	Financial Services:	Construction/Development:	Investments:	Specialty Services:		Brokerage:	
Apartments:	Mortgages:	Commercial Construction:	REIT:	Property Management:	Y	Commercial Sales:	Y
Malls/Shopping:	Title Insurance:	Residential Construction:		Online Services:		Residential Sales:	
Offices:	Property Insurance:	Land Development:		Software/IT:		Specialty:	Y
Hotels/Motels:		Support Services: Y		Consulting:	Y		
Industrial/Warehouses:		Design/Engineering: Y					
Other:							

TYPES OF BUSINESS:

Real Estate Development & Investment Services
Building Management
Brokerage Services
Project Management Services
Development Services
Property & Facility Management

BRANDS/DIVISIONS/AFFILIATES:

CB Richard Ellis

CONTACTS: *Note: Officers with more than one job title may be intentionally listed here more than once.*

Robert E. Sulentic, CEO
Chris Kirk, COO
Chris Kirk, General Counsel
John Stirek, Pres., Western Oper.
Chris Roth, Pres., Northeast Oper.
Daniel Queenan, Pres., Central Oper.
Robert E. Sulentic, Chmn.

Phone: 214-863-4101	Fax: 214-863-3138
Toll-Free:	
Address: 2001 Ross Ave., Ste. 3400, Dallas, TX 75201 US	

GROWTH PLANS/SPECIAL FEATURES:

Trammell Crow Company, a subsidiary of CB Richard Ellis, is one of the largest diversified commercial real estate service companies in the world, providing real estate services primarily in North America. The company has offices throughout the U.S., as well as one in Toronto, Canada. Trammel Crow serves the office, industrial, retail, health care, student housing, on-airport distribution and multi-family residential markets by delivering project management and development to both user and investor clients. As the manager of development projects, the firm offers services including the evaluation of project feasibility, budgeting and scheduling; site identification, due diligence and acquisition; cash flow analysis; the procurement of approvals and permits, including zoning and other entitlements; project finance advisory services; coordination of project design and engineering; construction bidding and management; tenant finish coordination; and project close-out and tenant move coordination. Trammell Crow's outsourcing is done on a contractual basis, aiming at long-term and full-service agreements with its clients. In February 2011, the company began construction on the Medical Arts Pavilion at the University Medical Center of Princeton at Plainsboro.

Employee benefits include: medical, dental and vision insurance; educational assistance; life insurance; and long-term disability coverage.

FINANCIALS: Sales and profits are in thousands of dollars—add 000 to get the full amount. 2010 Note: Financial information for 2010 was not available for all companies at press time.

2010 Sales: $	2010 Profits: $	U.S. Stock Ticker: Subsidiary
2009 Sales: $	2009 Profits: $	Int'l Ticker: Int'l Exchange:
2008 Sales: $	2008 Profits: $	Employees:
2007 Sales: $	2007 Profits: $	Fiscal Year Ends: 12/31
2006 Sales: $	2006 Profits: $	Parent Company: CB RICHARD ELLIS GROUP INC (CBRE)

SALARIES/BENEFITS:

Pension Plan:	ESOP Stock Plan:	Profit Sharing:	Top Exec. Salary: $	Bonus: $
Savings Plan: Y	Stock Purch. Plan:		Second Exec. Salary: $	Bonus: $

OTHER THOUGHTS:

Apparent Women Officers or Directors:
Hot Spot for Advancement for Women/Minorities:

LOCATIONS: ("Y" = Yes)

West:	Southwest:	Midwest:	Southeast:	Northeast:	International:
Y	Y	Y	Y	Y	Y

TRANSCONTINENTAL REALTY INVESTORS INC www.transconrealty-invest.com

Industry Group Code: 531120 Ranks within this company's industry group: Sales: 59   Profits: 57

Properties:		Financial Services:	Construction/Development:	Investments:	Specialty Services:		Brokerage:
Apartments:	Y	Mortgages:	Commercial Construction:	REIT:	Property Management:	Y	Commercial Sales:
Malls/Shopping:	Y	Title Insurance:	Residential Construction:		Online Services:		Residential Sales:
Offices:	Y	Property Insurance:	Land Development:		Software/IT:		Specialty:
Hotels/Motels:			Support Services:		Consulting:		
Industrial/Warehouses:	Y		Design/Engineering:				
Other:							

TYPES OF BUSINESS:

Real Estate Investment Trust
Warehouses
Apartments
Office Properties
Retail Properties

BRANDS/DIVISIONS/AFFILIATES:

American Realty Investment
Prime Asset Management
Income Opportunity Realty Investors Inc
South Cochran Corporation
EQK Bridgeview Plaza, Inc.
Transcontinental Brewery, Inc.

CONTACTS: Note: Officers with more than one job title may be intentionally listed here more than once.

Daniel J. Moos, CEO
Daniel J. Moos, Pres.
Gene S. Bertcher, CFO/Exec. VP
Louis J. Corna, General Counsel/Corp. Sec./Exec. VP-Tax
Daeho Kim, Treas.
Henry A. Butler, Chmn.

Phone: 469-522-4200	Fax: 469-522-4299
Toll-Free: 800-400-6407	
Address: 1800 Valley View Ln., 1 Hickory Centre, Ste. 300, Dallas, TX 75234 US	

GROWTH PLANS/SPECIAL FEATURES:

Transcontinental Realty Investors, Inc. (TCI) is an externally advised real estate investment company. The firm specializes in the acquisition, development and ownership of income-producing residential and commercial real estate properties. TCI also acquires land for future development in in-fill or high-growth suburban markets. The company owns approximately 48 residential apartment communities totaling roughly 9,197 units. With regard to commercial property, the firm owns 18 office buildings, three retail centers, and six industrial properties totaling approximately 5.0 million square feet. In addition, TCI owns 6,784 acres of undeveloped and partially developed land and five apartment complexes currently in development. The company produces revenue by managing previously undervalued or underperforming office buildings, apartments, retail centers and warehouses. Day-to-day management of TCI's business is contracted to Prime Asset Management, whose employees serve as company officers. Subsidiaries of American Realty Investment own approximately 82.7% of the company's stock. TCI owns roughly 85.3% interest in Income Opportunity Realty Investors, Inc. In August 2010, the company sold 6.51 acres in Irving, Texas, and Mason Park apartments, located in Katy, Texas. In September 2010, the firm sold Baywalk Apartments, Thornwood Apartments, LLC its interest in South Cochran Corporation, its interest in Transcontinental Brewery, Inc. and its interest in EQK Bridgeview Plaza, Inc. to Warren Road Farm, Inc.

FINANCIALS: Sales and profits are in thousands of dollars—add 000 to get the full amount. 2010 Note: Financial information for 2010 was not available for all companies at press time.

2010 Sales: $129,862	2010 Profits: $-67,098	U.S. Stock Ticker: TCI
2009 Sales: $130,855	2009 Profits: $-79,573	Int'l Ticker: Int'l Exchange:
2008 Sales: $117,623	2008 Profits: $32,209	Employees:
2007 Sales: $123,704	2007 Profits: $11,111	Fiscal Year Ends: 12/31
2006 Sales: $100,591	2006 Profits: $3,506	Parent Company:

SALARIES/BENEFITS:

Pension Plan:	ESOP Stock Plan:	Profit Sharing:	Top Exec. Salary: $	Bonus: $
Savings Plan:	Stock Purch. Plan:		Second Exec. Salary: $	Bonus: $

OTHER THOUGHTS:

Apparent Women Officers or Directors:
Hot Spot for Advancement for Women/Minorities:

LOCATIONS: ("Y" = Yes)

West:	Southwest:	Midwest:	Southeast:	Northeast:	International:
Y	Y	Y	Y	Y	Y

TRANSWESTERN COMMERCIAL SERVICES
www.transwestern.net

Industry Group Code: 5311 Ranks within this company's industry group: Sales: Profits:

Properties:	Financial Services:		Construction/Development:		Investments:	Specialty Services:		Brokerage:	
Apartments:	Mortgages:	Y	Commercial Construction:	Y	REIT:	Property Management:	Y	Commercial Sales:	Y
Malls/Shopping:	Title Insurance:		Residential Construction:	Y		Online Services:		Residential Sales:	
Offices:	Property Insurance:		Land Development:			Software/IT:		Specialty:	
Hotels/Motels:			Support Services:			Consulting:	Y		
Industrial/Warehouses:			Design/Engineering:						
Other:									

TYPES OF BUSINESS:
Real Estate Operations
Property Management
Advisory Services
Development & Research Services
Tenant Representation
Investment & Finance Services

BRANDS/DIVISIONS/AFFILIATES:
Delta Associates

CONTACTS: *Note: Officers with more than one job title may be intentionally listed here more than once.*
Larry P. Heard, CEO
Mark Doran, COO
Larry P. Heard, Pres.
Steve Harding, CFO
Kim Croley, National Dir.-Mktg.
Colleen Dolan, Sr. VP-Human Resources
Eugene Kesselman, CIO
Tom McNearney, Exec. Managing Dir.-Dev. & Investment
Kim Croley, National Dir.-Comm.
Steve Pumper, Exec. Managing Dir.-Investment Svcs.
Robert Duncan, Chmn.

Phone: 713-270-7700	Fax: 713-270-6285
Toll-Free:	
Address: 1900 W. Loop S., Ste. 1300, Houston, TX 77027 US	

GROWTH PLANS/SPECIAL FEATURES:

Transwestern Commercial Services is one of the largest privately held full-service real estate firms in the U.S. The company operates in 25 cities across the U.S. and oversees the leasing and management of more than 900 properties. The firm offers a range of services including agency leasing; development; property and facility management; investment services; tenant advisory; and research. Transwestern's agency leasing services utilize local market knowledge to provide customized marketing plans for each asset being considered by its clients. The development offerings include site analysis and acquisition, construction management and project marketing. Property and facility management services aim at maximizing property values through tenant relations programs, strategic planning, building enhancement and accurate accounting. The company offers its investment services through its Investment Services Group which provides clients with the firm's experience with real estate capital markets and investment banking to improve the financial performance of their assets. The firm's tenant advisory services include strategic planning, needs analysis, market research/analysis, disposition services, document management/negotiation, lease administration and project management. Transwestern's research services, provided by wholly-owned subsidiary Delta Associates, include national economic updates and regional market reports designed for the commercial real estate industry.

The company offers its employees health, dental and vision insurance; a 401(k) plan; flexible spending accounts; life and AD&D insurance; long-term disability insurance; and an employee assistance program.

FINANCIALS: Sales and profits are in thousands of dollars—add 000 to get the full amount. 2010 Note: Financial information for 2010 was not available for all companies at press time.

2010 Sales: $	2010 Profits: $	**U.S. Stock Ticker: Private**
2009 Sales: $	2009 Profits: $	**Int'l Ticker:** Int'l Exchange:
2008 Sales: $	2008 Profits: $	Employees:
2007 Sales: $70,600	2007 Profits: $	Fiscal Year Ends: 12/31
2006 Sales: $	2006 Profits: $	Parent Company:

SALARIES/BENEFITS:

Pension Plan:	ESOP Stock Plan:	Profit Sharing:	Top Exec. Salary: $	Bonus: $
Savings Plan: Y	Stock Purch. Plan:		Second Exec. Salary: $	Bonus: $

OTHER THOUGHTS:
Apparent Women Officers or Directors: 2
Hot Spot for Advancement for Women/Minorities:

LOCATIONS: ("Y" = Yes)

West:	Southwest:	Midwest:	Southeast:	Northeast:	International:
Y	Y	Y	Y	Y	

TRANSWESTERN INVESTMENT CO LLC

www.transinvestco.com

Industry Group Code: 531110 Ranks within this company's industry group: Sales: Profits:

Properties:		Financial Services:	Construction/Development:	Investments:		Specialty Services:	Brokerage:
Apartments:	Y	Mortgages:	Commercial Construction:	REIT:	Y	Property Management:	Commercial Sales:
Malls/Shopping:		Title Insurance:	Residential Construction:			Online Services:	Residential Sales:
Offices:	Y	Property Insurance:	Land Development:			Software/IT:	Specialty:
Hotels/Motels:			Support Services:			Consulting:	
Industrial/Warehouses:	Y		Design/Engineering:				
Other:							

TYPES OF BUSINESS:

Real Estate Investment Trust
Industrial/Flex Properties
Multi-Family Residential Properties
Retail Properties
Mezzanine Loans

BRANDS/DIVISIONS/AFFILIATES:

Transwestern Commercial Services, LLC
Aslan Realty Partners III, LP
Transwestern Mezzanine Realty Partners II, LP
Transwestern Securities Management
Transwestern Realty Finance Partners

CONTACTS: Note: Officers with more than one job title may be intentionally listed here more than once.

Stephen R. Quazzo, CEO/Managing Principal
James A. Fox, CFO
John W. Collins, Controller
Thomas M. McCahill, Principal-Mezzanine Investments
Judy McMahon, Managing Dir.-Mezzanine Investments
Dirk Degenaars, Managing Dir.-Retail Investments
Timothy E. McChesney, Managing Dir.-Asset Mgmt.

Phone: 312-499-1900	Fax: 312-499-1901
Toll-Free:	
Address: 150 N. Wacker Dr., Ste. 800, Chicago, IL 60606 US	

GROWTH PLANS/SPECIAL FEATURES:

Transwestern Investment Co., LLC is a Chicago-based real estate principal investment firm specializing in commercial real estate. Since its founding in 1996, the company has invested in more than 455 properties totaling nearly $11 billion throughout the U.S. through its nine sponsored investment funds. In addition to 42 office properties, the company's portfolio includes nine retail properties totaling in excess of 15 million square feet. Transwestern's other current investments include 12 multi-family complexes totaling 3,600 units and 90 mezzanine loan investments. Currently, the firm is seeking U.S. equity investment opportunities for Aslan Realty Partners IV, LLC, a fully discretionary equity fund that targets office, industrial, and retail investments nationwide. Transwestern also pursues U.S. mezzanine-debt investment opportunities for Transwestern Mezzanine Realty Partners III, LP, a fully discretionary fund; and multifamily investments through Transwestern Multifamily Partners, LLC. The company is affiliated with one of the largest privately-held real estate operating companies in the country, Transwestern Commercial Services, LLC, which specializes in development, tenant advisory, brokerage, leasing, and research for office, industrial, healthcare, retail and multifamily properties. Other subsidiaries include Transwestern Securities Management, which offers public real estate securities and Transwestern Realty Finance Partners, which manages high yield and senior mortgage investment activities. In 2010, the firm was awarded with 2010 Energy Star Sustained Excellence Award from the U.S. Environmental Protection Agency (EPA). This award is to recognize leadership and commitment in operating buildings efficiently by reducing waste and its carbon footprint. In July 2010, Transwestern acquired two multi-family properties in Florida and Colorado totaling 441 units.

FINANCIALS: Sales and profits are in thousands of dollars—add 000 to get the full amount. 2010 Note: Financial information for 2010 was not available for all companies at press time.

2010 Sales: $	2010 Profits: $	U.S. Stock Ticker: Private
2009 Sales: $	2009 Profits: $	Int'l Ticker: Int'l Exchange:
2008 Sales: $	2008 Profits: $	Employees:
2007 Sales: $	2007 Profits: $	Fiscal Year Ends: 12/31
2006 Sales: $	2006 Profits: $	Parent Company:

SALARIES/BENEFITS:

Pension Plan:	ESOP Stock Plan:	Profit Sharing:	Top Exec. Salary: $	Bonus: $
Savings Plan:	Stock Purch. Plan:		Second Exec. Salary: $	Bonus: $

OTHER THOUGHTS:

Apparent Women Officers or Directors: 1
Hot Spot for Advancement for Women/Minorities:

LOCATIONS: ("Y" = Yes)

West:	Southwest:	Midwest:	Southeast:	Northeast:	International:
Y		Y		Y	

TREVI-FINANZIARIA INDUSTRIALE SPA (TREVI GROUP)

www.trevifin.com

Industry Group Code: 541330 Ranks within this company's industry group: Sales: 7   Profits: 6

Properties:	Financial Services:	Construction/Development:		Investments:	Specialty Services:	Brokerage:
Apartments:	Mortgages:	Commercial Construction:	Y	REIT:	Property Management:	Commercial Sales:
Malls/Shopping:	Title Insurance:	Residential Construction:			Online Services:	Residential Sales:
Offices:	Property Insurance:	Land Development:			Software/IT:	Specialty:
Hotels/Motels:		Support Services:	Y		Consulting:	
Industrial/Warehouses:		Design/Engineering:	Y			
Other:						

TYPES OF BUSINESS:

Engineering & Construction Services
Underground Construction Services
Foundation & Drilling Machinery & Services
Wind Farms

BRANDS/DIVISIONS/AFFILIATES:

Trevi Group
TREVI S.p.A.
SOILMEC S.p.A.
DRILLMEC S.p.A.
Trevi Energy S.p.A.

CONTACTS: Note: Officers with more than one job title may be intentionally listed here more than once.

Gianluigi Trevisani, Managing Dir./VP
Daniele Forti, CFO
Stefano Trevisani, Managing Dir.
Cesare Trevisani, Managing Dir.
Davide Trevisani, Chmn.

Phone: 39-05-473-19111	Fax: 39-05-473-19313
Toll-Free:	
Address: 201 via Larga, Cesena, 47023 Italy	

GROWTH PLANS/SPECIAL FEATURES:

Trevi-Finanziaria Industriale S.P.A. (Trevi Group) is a global leader in foundation engineering and drilling and provides project management services supporting related projects around the world. It has branches in over 30 countries and a presence in more than 80. The group operates through five main subsidiaries: Trevi, Petreven, Soilmec, Drillmec and Trevi Energy S.p.A.,   Trevi provides construction services for underground engineering projects, such as special foundations for bridges, railways, dams, industrial systems and tunnels. Petreven is the company's segment in charge of oil drilling. Soilmec manufactures plants and rigs used for foundation engineering.   Drillmec specializes in drilling projects and manufactures hydraulic rigs for oil, geothermal and water drilling. The company, through its subsidiaries, also has operations in well drilling for water research, as well as having completed numerous automated car park projects. Trevi Energy is engaged in the design, development and engineering of offshore wind farms. Trevi Group's strong worldwide presence is illustrated by such past projects as the foundation works for the Third Mainland Bridge of Lagos in Nigeria; the Alicura in Argentina; the Port of Bandar Abbas in Iran; and the Khao dam in Thailand.

FINANCIALS: Sales and profits are in thousands of dollars—add 000 to get the full amount. 2010 Note: Financial information for 2010 was not available for all companies at press time.

		U.S. Stock Ticker:
2010 Sales: $1,318,780	2010 Profits: $67,070	Int'l Ticker: TFI Int'l Exchange: Milan-BI
2009 Sales: $1,366,660	2009 Profits: $111,680	Employees:
2008 Sales: $1,443,130	2008 Profits: $100,830	Fiscal Year Ends: 12/31
2007 Sales: $1,323,600	2007 Profits: $87,600	Parent Company:
2006 Sales: $1,019,100	2006 Profits: $42,000	

SALARIES/BENEFITS:

Pension Plan:	ESOP Stock Plan:	Profit Sharing:	Top Exec. Salary: $	Bonus: $
Savings Plan:	Stock Purch. Plan:		Second Exec. Salary: $	Bonus: $

OTHER THOUGHTS:

Apparent Women Officers or Directors:
Hot Spot for Advancement for Women/Minorities:

LOCATIONS: ("Y" = Yes)

West:	Southwest:	Midwest:	Southeast:	Northeast:	International:
Y	Y		Y	Y	Y

TRINITY LTD

www.trinity.com.au

Industry Group Code: 523920 Ranks within this company's industry group: Sales: Profits:

Properties:		Financial Services:	Construction/Development:	Investments:	Specialty Services:		Brokerage:
Apartments:	Y	Mortgages:	Commercial Construction:	REIT:	Property Management:	Y	Commercial Sales:
Malls/Shopping:	Y	Title Insurance:	Residential Construction:		Online Services:		Residential Sales:
Offices:	Y	Property Insurance:	Land Development:		Software/IT:		Specialty:
Hotels/Motels:			Support Services:		Consulting:		
Industrial/Warehouses:	Y		Design/Engineering:				
Other:							

TYPES OF BUSINESS:

Investment Fund Management
Property Management

BRANDS/DIVISIONS/AFFILIATES:

Trinity Funds Management
Trinity Property Trust
Trinity Opportunistic Property
Trinity Development Trust
Trinity Land Trust

CONTACTS:
Note: Officers with more than one job title may be intentionally listed here more than once.

Craig Bellamy, CEO
Janita Robba, CFO
Janita Robba, Corp. Sec.
Chris Morton, Deputy Chmn.
Brett Heading, Chmn.

Phone: 61-7-3002-4200	**Fax:** 61-7-3002-4201
Toll-Free:	
Address: 88 Creek St. Mezzanine Level, The Tower, Brisbane, QLD 4000 Australia	

GROWTH PLANS/SPECIAL FEATURES:

Trinity Ltd. is a publicly traded Australian property fund management firm. Its core businesses are funds management and direct property investment. Its funds management business, operated by Trinity Funds Management (TFM), manages a portfolio of trusts and funds including Trinity Property Trust (TPT), a direct property fund; Trinity Development Trust (TDT) which makes equity investments in commercial, retail, industrial and residential (non-land) developments; the Trinity Land Trust (TLT), an unlisted, residential land development trust, investing in residential subdivision and master-planned Australian communities; and Trinity Opportunistic Property (TOP) Fund, which invests in a variety of commercial, industrial and residential properties. The company's direct portfolio, the Trinity Stapled Trust (TST) includes retail, commercial and industrial properties. Trinity also provides property services to its investment properties under management by TFM including day-to-day property management; occupant maximization and tenant retention programs; leasing; strategic asset management; capital transactions; and property due diligence. In May 2010, the company sold a 50% interest in Trinity Funds Management Ltd. to Clarence Property Corp. Ltd.

FINANCIALS:
Sales and profits are in thousands of dollars—add 000 to get the full amount. 2010 Note: Financial information for 2010 was not available for all companies at press time.

2010 Sales: $	2010 Profits: $	**U.S. Stock Ticker:**
2009 Sales: $	2009 Profits: $	**Int'l Ticker: TCQ** Int'l Exchange: Sydney-ASX
2008 Sales: $	2008 Profits: $	Employees:
2007 Sales: $	2007 Profits: $	Fiscal Year Ends:
2006 Sales: $	2006 Profits: $	Parent Company:

SALARIES/BENEFITS:

Pension Plan:	ESOP Stock Plan:	Profit Sharing:	Top Exec. Salary: $	Bonus: $
Savings Plan:	Stock Purch. Plan:		Second Exec. Salary: $	Bonus: $

OTHER THOUGHTS:

Apparent Women Officers or Directors:
Hot Spot for Advancement for Women/Minorities:

LOCATIONS: ("Y" = Yes)

West:	Southwest:	Midwest:	Southeast:	Northeast:	International:
					Y

TRIPLE FIVE GROUP

www.triplefive.com

Industry Group Code: 5311 Ranks within this company's industry group: Sales: Profits:

Properties:		Financial Services:		Construction/Development:		Investments:	Specialty Services:		Brokerage:
Apartments:	Y	Mortgages:	Y	Commercial Construction:	Y	REIT:	Property Management:	Y	Commercial Sales:
Malls/Shopping:	Y	Title Insurance:		Residential Construction:			Online Services:		Residential Sales:
Offices:	Y	Property Insurance:		Land Development:	Y		Software/IT:		Specialty:
Hotels/Motels:	Y			Support Services:			Consulting:		
Industrial/Warehouses:				Design/Engineering:					
Other:	Y								

TYPES OF BUSINESS:

Shopping Malls
Hotels
Office Buildings
Mixed-Use Developments
Entertainment Venues & Amusement Parks
Banking
Venture Capital
Oil & Gas Exploration

BRANDS/DIVISIONS/AFFILIATES:

Mall of America
West Edmonton Mall
First Nuclear Corporation
People's Trust
T5 Equity Partners LLC
Xanadu
Wayne Engineering

CONTACTS: *Note: Officers with more than one job title may be intentionally listed here more than once.*

Don Ghermezian, Pres.
Nader Ghermezian, Chmn.

Phone: 780-444-8100	Fax: 780-444-5232
Toll-Free:	
Address: 8882-170 St., Ste. 3000, Edmonton, AB T5T 4M2 Canada	

GROWTH PLANS/SPECIAL FEATURES:

Triple Five Group is a multi-segmented corporation engaged in real estate; resource development and mining; venture capital; hotels; banking; private equity; engineering; manufacturing; and retail operations. Together with its extended group of affiliates, the firm owns major shopping centers and other commercial real estate. It also focuses on planning and development; tourism projects; planned communities; and technology. Its real estate division is one of the most diverse developers in the U.S., with activities that include entertainment venues, amusement parks, commercial real estate and industrial real estate. Triple Five's primary projects include the West Edmonton Mall in Canada and the Mall of America in Bloomington, Minnesota, which are two of the largest mixed-use tourism, retail and entertainment complexes in the world. Subsidiary People's Trust operates throughout Canada and provides investment and lending services, estate and trust asset management and mortgage servicing. Subsidiary T5 Equity Partners LLC provides venture and equity capital investments. The company's Venture Capital group provides funds for development in the wireless, Internet and high technology industries; and through subsidiary First Nuclear Corporation, also active in resource development and exploration within the oil, gas and metallurgical industries and is involved in production, business management and technical aspects of these industries. Subsidiaries of the firm include Maverick Engineering, Inc.; Wayne Engineering; Celonex Pharmaceuticals and DiamondGear. The company has also developed five-star hotel complexes, high-rise office buildings and apartments. In late 2010, Triple Five announced that it will become the new owner-operator of the long-troubled Xanadu Mall, a 2.3 million square foot retail and entertainment complex in Meadowlands, New Jersey that was originally scheduled to open in 2007 but faced financial problems. Triple Five hopes to open the complex by 2014. Triple Five attracts 60 million visitors yearly to its two existing supermalls.

FINANCIALS: Sales and profits are in thousands of dollars—add 000 to get the full amount. 2010 Note: Financial information for 2010 was not available for all companies at press time.

2010 Sales: $	2010 Profits: $	**U.S. Stock Ticker: Private**	
2009 Sales: $	2009 Profits: $	**Int'l Ticker:** Int'l Exchange:	
2008 Sales: $	2008 Profits: $	Employees:	
2007 Sales: $	2007 Profits: $	Fiscal Year Ends: 7/31	
2006 Sales: $	2006 Profits: $	Parent Company:	

SALARIES/BENEFITS:

Pension Plan:	ESOP Stock Plan:	Profit Sharing:	Top Exec. Salary: $	Bonus: $
Savings Plan:	Stock Purch. Plan:		Second Exec. Salary: $	Bonus: $

OTHER THOUGHTS:

Apparent Women Officers or Directors: 1
Hot Spot for Advancement for Women/Minorities:

LOCATIONS: ("Y" = Yes)

West:	Southwest:	Midwest:	Southeast:	Northeast:	International:
Y	Y	Y	Y	Y	Y

TRT HOLDINGS

www.omnihotels.com

Industry Group Code: 721110 Ranks within this company's industry group: Sales: Profits:

Properties:		Financial Services:	Construction/Development:	Investments:	Specialty Services:		Brokerage:
Apartments:		Mortgages:	Commercial Construction:	REIT:	Property Management:	Y	Commercial Sales:
Malls/Shopping:		Title Insurance:	Residential Construction:		Online Services:	Y	Residential Sales:
Offices:		Property Insurance:	Land Development:		Software/IT:		Specialty:
Hotels/Motels:	Y		Support Services:		Consulting:		
Industrial/Warehouses:	Y		Design/Engineering:				
Other:	Y						

TYPES OF BUSINESS:

Hotels
Gymnasiums
Oil & Gas Exploration

BRANDS/DIVISIONS/AFFILIATES:

Omni Hotels
Executive Service Plan
Select Guest
Omni Express
Omni Kids
Select Guest Gold
Gold's Gym International
Tana Exploration Company

CONTACTS: *Note: Officers with more than one job title may be intentionally listed here more than once.*

Robert B. Rowling, CEO
James D. Caldwell, Pres.
James D. Caldwell, CEO-Omni Hotels & Resorts
Michael J. Deitemeyer, Pres., Omni Hotels & Resorts
Joy Rothschild, Sr. VP-Human Resources, Omni Hotels & Resorts
Jeff Smith, VP-Oper., Omni Hotels & Resorts
Robert B. Rowling, Chmn.

Phone: 972-730-6664	**Fax:** 972-871-5665
Toll-Free: 800-843-6664	
Address: 420 Decker Dr., Ste. 200, Irving, TX 75062-3952 US	

GROWTH PLANS/SPECIAL FEATURES:

TRT Holdings owns and franchises the Omni Hotel chain. Omni Hotels offer luxury and first-class accommodations at 45 locations across North America, totaling roughly 15,000 rooms. The company owns or manages 43 of the properties and franchises two. A typical Omni Hotel has over 300 rooms, and it offers amenities such as marble bathrooms, voicemail, modem connections, high-speed Internet access, gourmet dining, fitness centers; 24-hour and online room service; valet ordering, baggage retrieval and housekeeping, among other services. The firm's specialty programs operate at all locations and include the Executive Service Plan, designed to aid corporate travelers; and the Select Guest and Select Guest Gold customer loyalty programs, whereby members are rewarded on business and other types of stays, including most government, leisure and group discounts. The hotel chain caters primarily to corporate business and upscale leisure travelers. The Omni is part of The Global Hotel Alliance (GHA), which consists of 13 prominent hotel brands in more than 48 countries. Additionally, TRT owns Gold's Gym International, a franchiser of more than 600 fitness centers in 29 countries. Apart from these operations, the company holds stakes in businesses involved in oil and gas exploration (the Tana Exploration Company), as well as retail chains in Mexico and other real estate investments. In early 2010, the firm launched a new brand of upscale hotels called Mokara Hotel and Spa.

Employees receive tuition reimbursement; relocation allowances; a flexible spending account; short-term and long-term disability; discounted associate room rates; and medical, dental, life and disability insurance.

FINANCIALS: Sales and profits are in thousands of dollars—add 000 to get the full amount. 2010 Note: Financial information for 2010 was not available for all companies at press time.

2010 Sales: $	2010 Profits: $	**U.S. Stock Ticker: Private**
2009 Sales: $	2009 Profits: $	**Int'l Ticker:** Int'l Exchange:
2008 Sales: $	2008 Profits: $	Employees:
2007 Sales: $404,000	2007 Profits: $	Fiscal Year Ends: 12/31
2006 Sales: $	2006 Profits: $	Parent Company:

SALARIES/BENEFITS:

Pension Plan:	ESOP Stock Plan:	Profit Sharing:	Top Exec. Salary: $	Bonus: $
Savings Plan: Y	Stock Purch. Plan:		Second Exec. Salary: $	Bonus: $

OTHER THOUGHTS:

Apparent Women Officers or Directors: 1
Hot Spot for Advancement for Women/Minorities:

LOCATIONS: ("Y" = Yes)

West:	Southwest:	Midwest:	Southeast:	Northeast:	International:
Y	Y	Y	Y	Y	Y

TRUE HOME VALUE INC

www.thv.com

Industry Group Code: 444130 Ranks within this company's industry group: Sales: Profits:

Properties:	Financial Services:	Construction/Development:		Investments:	Specialty Services:	Brokerage:
Apartments:	Mortgages:	Commercial Construction:		REIT:	Property Management:	Commercial Sales:
Malls/Shopping:	Title Insurance:	Residential Construction:	Y		Online Services:	Residential Sales:
Offices:	Property Insurance:	Land Development:			Software/IT:	Specialty:
Hotels/Motels:		Support Services:	Y		Consulting:	
Industrial/Warehouses:		Design/Engineering:	Y			
Other:						

TYPES OF BUSINESS:

Building Materials
Door & Window Assemblies
Retail & Installation
Roofing & Siding Materials
Coatings

BRANDS/DIVISIONS/AFFILIATES:

Thermal Line Windows, Inc.
Leingang Home Center
Primax Home Center
Rolox Home Center
Thomas Home Center
ThermoView Industries, Inc.
THV, Inc.

CONTACTS: *Note: Officers with more than one job title may be intentionally listed here more than once.*

Phone: 502-968-2020	Fax: 502-968-7798
Toll-Free: 800-669-2020	
Address: 5611 Fern Valley Rd., Louisville, KY 40228 US	

GROWTH PLANS/SPECIAL FEATURES:

True Home Value, Inc., or THV, (formerly ThermoView Industries, Inc.) is one of the largest full-service national home improvement companies in the U.S. It designs, manufactures, sells and installs custom vinyl replacement for residential and retail commercial customers. These customers reside primarily in the Midwestern U.S. The company sells and installs thermal replacement windows, doors, textured coatings, vinyl siding, patio decks, patio enclosures, cabinet refacings, bathroom and kitchen remodeling products and residential roofing. THV operates in approximately 16 states under the retail trade names Primax Home Center; Leingang Home Center; Thomas Home Center; and Rolox Home Center. The firm's primary business is in the replacement window market. THV has a single manufacturing subsidiary, Thermal Line Windows, Inc. in Mandan, ND, which produces one of its three lines of replacement windows; the other two lines are manufactured in Toledo, Ohio and Saltsburg, Pennsylvania by unaffiliated third parties. Its windows use high-technology glass that allows sunlight in while keeping damaging ultraviolet rays out. THV offers a 50-year non-prorated glass and window warranty as well as a 25% fuel savings pledge in writing on all its window products. The firm offers custom-made insulated steel doors with a wood grain finish in over 30 different styles and more than 100 color combinations, as well as several variations of sliding glass doors. The company's primary goal is to become a national leader in the home improvement and replacement window industry by building a network of sales and installation subsidiaries.

FINANCIALS: Sales and profits are in thousands of dollars—add 000 to get the full amount. 2010 Note: Financial information for 2010 was not available for all companies at press time.

2010 Sales: $	2010 Profits: $	**U.S. Stock Ticker: Private**
2009 Sales: $	2009 Profits: $	**Int'l Ticker:** Int'l Exchange:
2008 Sales: $	2008 Profits: $	Employees:
2007 Sales: $	2007 Profits: $	Fiscal Year Ends: 12/31
2006 Sales: $	2006 Profits: $	Parent Company:

SALARIES/BENEFITS:

Pension Plan:	ESOP Stock Plan:	Profit Sharing:	Top Exec. Salary: $	Bonus: $
Savings Plan:	Stock Purch. Plan:		Second Exec. Salary: $	Bonus: $

OTHER THOUGHTS:

Apparent Women Officers or Directors:
Hot Spot for Advancement for Women/Minorities:

LOCATIONS: ("Y" = Yes)

West:	Southwest:	Midwest:	Southeast:	Northeast:	International:
	Y	Y	Y	Y	

TRUMP ENTERTAINMENT RESORTS INC
www.trumpcasinos.com

Industry Group Code: 721120 Ranks within this company's industry group: Sales: 7 Profits: 6

Properties:	Financial Services:	Construction/Development:	Investments:	Specialty Services:	Brokerage:
Apartments:	Mortgages:	Commercial Construction:	REIT:	Property Management:	Commercial Sales:
Malls/Shopping:	Title Insurance:	Residential Construction:		Online Services:	Residential Sales:
Offices:	Property Insurance:	Land Development:		Software/IT:	Specialty:
Hotels/Motels: Y		Support Services:		Consulting:	
Industrial/Warehouses:		Design/Engineering:			
Other: Y					

TYPES OF BUSINESS:

Casino Hotels
Casino Management

BRANDS/DIVISIONS/AFFILIATES:

Trump Taj Mahal Casino Resort
Trump Plaza Hotel & Casino
Trump Marina Hotel Casino
Xanadu Theater

CONTACTS: *Note: Officers with more than one job title may be intentionally listed here more than once.*

Robert F. Griffin, CEO
David R. Hughes, CFO/Exec. VP
Robert M. Pickus, Chief Admin. Officer
Robert M. Pickus, General Counsel/Sec.
Marc Lasry, Chmn.

Phone: 609-449-5866	Fax: 609-449-6586
Toll-Free: 800-777-1177	
Address: 15 S. Pennsylvania Ave., Atlantic City, NJ 08401 US	

GROWTH PLANS/SPECIAL FEATURES:

Trump Entertainment Resorts, Inc. (TER) operates three casino properties, all in Atlantic City: Trump Taj Mahal Casino Resort; Trump Plaza Hotel and Casino; and Trump Marina Hotel and Casino. Trump Taj Mahal, located on Atlantic City's Boardwalk, features the 782-room Chairman Tower, which includes 66 suites and 8 penthouse suites. The Taj Mahal also houses 1,228 hotel rooms, which include 243 suites and 7 penthouse suites; 16 dining locations; five cocktail lounges; and 143,000 square feet of ballroom, meeting room and pre-function area space. Its casino facilities include 162,000 square feet of gaming space with approximately 204 gaming tables, 2,996 slot machines and 12,500 square feet dedicated to Asian gaming favorites, as well as the Xanadu Theater, a 20,000 square foot entertainment complex with seating capacity for 1,200. Trump Plaza, also on the Boardwalk, features 906 hotel rooms and 87,000 square feet of casino space for 1,808 slot machines and 71 gaming tables. Additional amenities include 18,000 square feet of conference space, a 750-seat cabaret theater, 11 dining locations and two cocktail lounges. Trump Marina, in Atlantic City's Marina District, offers a 27-story hotel with 728 guest rooms and 79,000 square feet of gaming space for 1,815 slot machines, 71 gaming tables 30,500 square feet of convention, ballroom and meeting space. In July 2010, the firm completed a financial restructuring process and emerged from bankruptcy. In February 2011, the firm agreed to sell the Trump Marina Hotel and Casino to Landry's, Inc.

Employees of TER receive an employee assistance program; health benefits; tuition reimbursement; a 401(k) plan; a free employee cafeteria; and a credit union.

FINANCIALS: Sales and profits are in thousands of dollars—add 000 to get the full amount. 2010 Note: Financial information for 2010 was not available for all companies at press time.

2010 Sales: $710,570	2010 Profits: $-60,804	**U.S. Stock Ticker: TRMP**
2009 Sales: $792,149	2009 Profits: $-533,938	**Int'l Ticker:** Int'l Exchange:
2008 Sales: $908,008	2008 Profits: $-232,203	Employees: 5,500
2007 Sales: $988,235	2007 Profits: $-188,681	Fiscal Year Ends: 12/31
2006 Sales: $1,007,775	2006 Profits: $-18,507	Parent Company:

SALARIES/BENEFITS:

Pension Plan:	ESOP Stock Plan:	Profit Sharing:	Top Exec. Salary: $	Bonus: $
Savings Plan: Y	Stock Purch. Plan:		Second Exec. Salary: $	Bonus: $

OTHER THOUGHTS:

Apparent Women Officers or Directors:
Hot Spot for Advancement for Women/Minorities:

LOCATIONS: ("Y" = Yes)

West:	Southwest:	Midwest:	Southeast:	Northeast:	International:
				Y	

TRUMP ORGANIZATION (THE)   www.trump.com

Industry Group Code: 5311 Ranks within this company's industry group: Sales: Profits:

Properties:		Financial Services:		Construction/Development:		Investments:	Specialty Services:		Brokerage:	
Apartments:	Y	Mortgages:		Commercial Construction:	Y	REIT:	Property Management:	Y	Commercial Sales:	Y
Malls/Shopping:	Y	Title Insurance:		Residential Construction:	Y		Online Services:		Residential Sales:	Y
Offices:	Y	Property Insurance:		Land Development:	Y		Software/IT:		Specialty:	
Hotels/Motels:	Y			Support Services:			Consulting:			
Industrial/Warehouses:				Design/Engineering:						
Other:	Y									

TYPES OF BUSINESS:

Real Estate Investment, Development & Operations
Property Management
Residential & Commercial Brokerage
Hotel, Casino & Resort Management
Golf Courses

BRANDS/DIVISIONS/AFFILIATES:

Miss Teen USA
Trump Sales and Leasing
Trump International Hotel & Tower
Trump Golf
Trump Productions LLC
Miss Universe
Miss USA
Trump Home

CONTACTS: *Note: Officers with more than one job title may be intentionally listed here more than once.*

Matthew F. Calamari, COO/Exec. VP
Donald J. Trump, Pres.
Allen Weisselberg, CFO/Exec. VP
Donald Trump, Jr., Exec. VP-Dev. & Acquisitions
Ivanka Trump, Exec. VP-Dev. & Acquisitions
Eric Trump, Exec. VP-Dev. & Acquisitions
Cathy Hoffman Glosser, Exec. VP-Global Licensing
Donald J. Trump, Chmn.

Phone: 212-832-2000	**Fax:** 212-935-0141
Toll-Free:	
Address: 725 5th Ave., New York, NY 10022-2519 US	

GROWTH PLANS/SPECIAL FEATURES:

The Trump Organization is a global firm active in luxury real estate development, sales and marketing, as well as entertainment and brand licensing activities. The company's portfolio includes residential, commercial, hotel and golf properties, with over 70 projects current and in development. The Trump real estate portfolio includes a number of well-known buildings, such as Trump International Hotel & Tower in Manhattan and the Taj Mahal casino in Atlantic City, New Jersey. Trump Sales and Leasing is the firm's residential brokerage division, which purchases, sells or leases luxury real estate. The luxury Trump International Hotel & Tower, itself a redevelopment of Gulf and Western's landmark Manhattan office building, is a mixed-use residential and hotel property re-designated as One Central Park West. Additional Trump International Hotel & Tower locations recently opened in Chicago, Illinois, and Waikiki, Hawaii, with development begun on sites in Toronto, Canada; Dubai, United Arab Emirates; Punta Pacifica, Panama; New Orleans, Louisiana; and Fort Lauderdale, Florida. Trump Golf is the developer and operator of 12 premium golf clubs in New York, New Jersey, Washington, D.C., California, Florida, Scotland, Puerto Rico and the Caribbean. In addition, The Trump Organization owns the rights to 50% of the Miss USA, Miss Teen USA and Miss Universe beauty pageants, while subsidiary Trump Productions LLC oversees television programming such as The Apprentice on NBC. The company also has several licensing ventures, such as a partnership with Drinks Americas for the production and marketing of Trump Super Premium Vodka. In April 2010, the firm and Serta introduced the Trump Home Luxury mattress series. In September 2010, the company partnered with Hallmark Collectibles, Inc. to offer bedding products under the Trump Home brand name. In February 2011, The Trump Organization partnered with Kassatex to develop a bath collection also to be sold under the brand name Trump Home.

FINANCIALS: Sales and profits are in thousands of dollars—add 000 to get the full amount. 2010 Note: Financial information for 2010 was not available for all companies at press time.

2010 Sales: $	2010 Profits: $	**U.S. Stock Ticker:** Private
2009 Sales: $	2009 Profits: $	**Int'l Ticker:** Int'l Exchange:
2008 Sales: $	2008 Profits: $	Employees: 22,000
2007 Sales: $10,700,000	2007 Profits: $	Fiscal Year Ends: 12/31
2006 Sales: $	2006 Profits: $	Parent Company:

SALARIES/BENEFITS:

Pension Plan:	ESOP Stock Plan:	Profit Sharing:	Top Exec. Salary: $	Bonus: $
Savings Plan:	Stock Purch. Plan:		Second Exec. Salary: $	Bonus: $

OTHER THOUGHTS:

Apparent Women Officers or Directors: 2
Hot Spot for Advancement for Women/Minorities:

LOCATIONS: ("Y" = Yes)

West:	Southwest:	Midwest:	Southeast:	Northeast:	International:
Y		Y	Y	Y	Y

TUTOR PERINI CORPORATION

www.tutorperini.com

Industry Group Code: 237 Ranks within this company's industry group: Sales: 23   Profits: 21

Properties:	Financial Services:	Construction/Development:		Investments:	Specialty Services:		Brokerage:
Apartments:	Mortgages:	Commercial Construction:	Y	REIT:	Property Management:		Commercial Sales:
Malls/Shopping:	Title Insurance:	Residential Construction:	Y		Online Services:		Residential Sales:
Offices:	Property Insurance:	Land Development:			Software/IT:		Specialty:
Hotels/Motels:		Support Services:	Y		Consulting:	Y	
Industrial/Warehouses:		Design/Engineering:	Y				
Other:							

TYPES OF BUSINESS:

Construction Services
Hospitality & Casino Construction
Construction Management Services
Civic & Infrastructure Construction
Design Services

BRANDS/DIVISIONS/AFFILIATES:

Perini Building Company
James A. Cummings, Inc.
Rudolph and Sletten, Inc.
Perini Civil Construction
Cherry Hill Construction, Inc.
Tutor-Saliba Corporation
Keating Building Corporation
Perini Corporation

CONTACTS: *Note: Officers with more than one job title may be intentionally listed here more than once.*

Ronald N. Tutor, CEO
Robert Band, Pres.
Kenneth R. Burk, CFO/Exec. VP
William B. Sparks, Corp. Sec./Clerk/Exec. VP
William B. Sparks, Treas./Exec. VP
Robert Band, Pres./CEO-Mgmt. Svcs.
Mark Caspers, Exec. VP/CEO-Building Group
James A. Frost, Exec. VP/CEO-Civil Group
Craig W. Shaw, Pres./CEO-Perini Building Company, Inc.
Ronald N. Tutor, Chmn.

Phone: 818-362-8391	Fax: 818-367-5379
Toll-Free:	
Address: 15901 Olden St., Sylmar, CA 91342 US	

GROWTH PLANS/SPECIAL FEATURES:

Tutor Perini Corporation and its subsidiaries provide general contracting, construction management and design-build services worldwide. It operates in three segments: building, civil and management services. The building segment is comprised of Perini Building Company; James A. Cummings, Inc.; Rudolph and Sletten, Inc.; Keating Building Company; Desert Plumbing & Heating Company, Inc.; and Powerco Electric Corporation. This segment focuses on large, complex projects in the hospitality and gaming, transportation, healthcare, municipal offices, sports and entertainment, education, correctional facilities, biotech, pharmaceutical, industrial and high-tech markets. The civil segment is comprised of Tutor Perini Civil Construction, Tutor-Saliba Corporation and Cherry Hill Construction, Inc. The segment focuses on public works construction, including the new construction, repair, replacement and reconstruction of public infrastructure such as highways, bridges, mass transit systems and wastewater treatment facilities. The company's customers primarily award contracts through the public competitive bid, in which price is the major determining factor; or through a request for proposals, where contracts are awarded based on a combination of technical capability and price. The management services segment, comprised of Perini Management Services, Inc. and Black Construction's operation in Guam, provides diversified construction, design-build and maintenance services to the U.S. military and government agencies, as well as surety companies and multi-national corporations domestically and overseas. In January 2011, the firm acquired Fisk Electric Company.

Employees are offered life, disability, accident, medical and dental insurance; a 401(k) plan; medical and dependent care spending accounts; educational assistance; and an employee assistance program.

FINANCIALS: Sales and profits are in thousands of dollars—add 000 to get the full amount. 2010 Note: Financial information for 2010 was not available for all companies at press time.

2010 Sales: $3,199,210	2010 Profits: $103,500	**U.S. Stock Ticker: TPC**
2009 Sales: $5,151,966	2009 Profits: $137,061	**Int'l Ticker:** Int'l Exchange:
2008 Sales: $5,660,286	2008 Profits: $-75,140	Employees: 3,538
2007 Sales: $4,628,358	2007 Profits: $97,114	Fiscal Year Ends: 12/31
2006 Sales: $3,042,839	2006 Profits: $41,536	Parent Company:

SALARIES/BENEFITS:

Pension Plan:	ESOP Stock Plan:	Profit Sharing:	Top Exec. Salary: $1,500,000	Bonus: $2,544,870
Savings Plan: Y	Stock Purch. Plan:		Second Exec. Salary: $612,500	Bonus: $593,800

OTHER THOUGHTS:

Apparent Women Officers or Directors: 1
Hot Spot for Advancement for Women/Minorities:

LOCATIONS: ("Y" = Yes)

West:	Southwest:	Midwest:	Southeast:	Northeast:	International:
Y			Y	Y	Y

UDR INC

www.udr.com

Industry Group Code: 531110 Ranks within this company's industry group: Sales: 4   Profits: 16

Properties:		Financial Services:		Construction/Development:		Investments:		Specialty Services:		Brokerage:	
Apartments:	Y	Mortgages:		Commercial Construction:		REIT:	Y	Property Management:	Y	Commercial Sales:	
Malls/Shopping:		Title Insurance:		Residential Construction:	Y			Online Services:		Residential Sales:	
Offices:		Property Insurance:		Land Development:	Y			Software/IT:		Specialty:	
Hotels/Motels:				Support Services:				Consulting:			
Industrial/Warehouses:				Design/Engineering:							
Other:	Y										

TYPES OF BUSINESS:

Real Estate Investment Trust
Apartment Communities

BRANDS/DIVISIONS/AFFILIATES:

Heritage Communities LP
United Dominion Realty LP
RE3

CONTACTS: *Note: Officers with more than one job title may be intentionally listed here more than once.*

Thomas W. Toomey, CEO
Thomas W. Toomey, Pres.
David L. Messenger, CFO/Sr. VP
Steven H. Taraborelli, VP/Dir.-Mktg. & Sales
Katie Miles-Ley, Sr. VP-Human Resources
Cameron A. Etezadi, CIO
Jerry A. Davis, Sr. VP-Property Oper.
Mark M. Culwell Jr., Sr. VP-Dev.
H. Andrew Cantor, VP-Investor Rel.
William T. O'Shields, III, Treas./VP
Matthew T. Akin, Sr. VP-Acquisitions & Dispositions
Richard A. Giannotti, Exec. VP-Redevelopment
Warren L. Troupe, Sr. Exec. VP
S. Douglas Walker, Sr. VP-Transactions
James D. Klingbeil, Chmn.

Phone: 720-283-6120	Fax: 720-283-2451
Toll-Free:	
Address: 1745 Shea Center Dr., Ste. 200, Highlands Ranch, CO 80129 US	

GROWTH PLANS/SPECIAL FEATURES:

UDR, Inc. is a self-administered real estate investment trust (REIT) that owns, acquires, renovates, develops and manages multifamily apartment communities nationwide. UDR's property portfolio includes 172 communities located in 23 markets in 10 U.S. states and Washington, D.C. The firm currently owns 48,553 completed apartment homes and maintains an ownership interest in 9,891 apartment units (37 communities) through joint ventures. United's subsidiaries include two operating partnerships: Heritage Communities L.P. and United Dominion Realty L.P. Another subsidiary, RE3, provides development, land entitlement and short-term hold investment services. UDR's upgrade and rehabilitation programs enable it to raise rents and attract residents with higher levels of disposable income who are more likely to accept the transfer of expenses, such as water and sewer costs, from the landlord to the resident. It focuses on the middle-market segment of the apartment market, generally renters-by-necessity, including young professionals, blue-collar families, single-parent households, singles, immigrants and families renting while waiting to purchase a home. The company believes this renting-by-necessity population provides the highest profit potential in terms of rent growth, stability of occupancy and investment opportunities. In the future, UDR will continue to emphasize aggressive lease management, improved expense control, increased resident retention efforts and the realignment of employee incentive plans tied to its bottom line performance. In September 2010, UDR agreed to acquire a pre-sale venture in Massachusetts and five communities in California, Maryland and Massachusetts for roughly $455.1 million. In November 2010, the firm acquired The Hanover Company's interest in a joint venture with MetLife that owns 26 communities (5,748 homes). In March 2011, the company agreed to acquire a 493-unit community in New York City from Witkoff Group for $260.8 million.

UDR offers its employees benefits including life, disability, medical, dental and vision coverage; a 401(k) plan; a stock purchase plan; educational assistance; and apartment discounts.

FINANCIALS: Sales and profits are in thousands of dollars—add 000 to get the full amount. 2010 Note: Financial information for 2010 was not available for all companies at press time.

2010 Sales: $632,249	2010 Profits: $-112,362	U.S. Stock Ticker: UDR
2009 Sales: $600,702	2009 Profits: $-95,858	Int'l Ticker: Int'l Exchange:
2008 Sales: $561,073	2008 Profits: $688,708	Employees: 1,363
2007 Sales: $501,618	2007 Profits: $198,958	Fiscal Year Ends: 12/31
2006 Sales: $467,511	2006 Profits: $128,605	Parent Company:

SALARIES/BENEFITS:

Pension Plan:	ESOP Stock Plan:	Profit Sharing:	Top Exec. Salary: $500,000	Bonus: $1,336,000
Savings Plan: Y	Stock Purch. Plan: Y		Second Exec. Salary: $450,000	Bonus: $850,000

OTHER THOUGHTS:

Apparent Women Officers or Directors: 9
Hot Spot for Advancement for Women/Minorities: Y

LOCATIONS: ("Y" = Yes)

West:	Southwest:	Midwest:	Southeast:	Northeast:	International:
Y	Y		Y	Y	

UNIBAIL-RODAMCO

www.unibail.com

Industry Group Code: 531120 Ranks within this company's industry group: Sales: 7   Profits: 1

Properties:		Financial Services:		Construction/Development:	Investments:	Specialty Services:	Brokerage:
Apartments:		Mortgages:		Commercial Construction:	REIT:	Property Management:	Commercial Sales:
Malls/Shopping:	Y	Title Insurance:		Residential Construction:		Online Services:	Residential Sales:
Offices:	Y	Property Insurance:		Land Development:		Software/IT:	Specialty:
Hotels/Motels:				Support Services:		Consulting:	
Industrial/Warehouses:				Design/Engineering:			
Other:	Y						

TYPES OF BUSINESS:

Commercial Property Investment Company
Office Buildings
Shopping Center Real Estate
Convention Center Real Estate

BRANDS/DIVISIONS/AFFILIATES:

comexposium
Viparis

CONTACTS: *Note: Officers with more than one job title may be intentionally listed here more than once.*

Guillaume Poitrinal, CEO
Michel Dessolain, COO
Peter van Rossum, CFO
Catherine Pourre, Chief Resources Officer
Jaap L. Tonckens, General Counsel
Jaap L. Tonkcens, Chief Investment Officer
Guillaume Poitrinal, Chmn.

Phone: 33-1-53-43-74-37	Fax:
Toll-Free:	
Address: 7 Place du Chancelier Adenauer, Paris, Cedex 16, CS 31622-75722 France	

GROWTH PLANS/SPECIAL FEATURES:

Unibail-Rodamco, formed by the July 2007 merger of Rodamco Europe NV and Unibail Holdings SA, is a Paris-based commercial property investment company that spans across 11 European countries. It operates within three business sectors: offices; shopping centers; and exhibition and convention complexes. The firm's office portfolio is comprised of office buildings, mainly located in the Paris central business district and its western outskirts. This segment has a portfolio of 17 office buildings and is focused on large buildings mostly over 10,000 square meters, which have been refurbished and equipped with advanced technical installations. Four more buildings are under development in Paris. Unibail's portfolio of 88 shopping centers is almost exclusively made up of very large shopping centers. The exhibition and convention centers segment is divided into two companies, VIPARIS and Comexposium, which are jointly owned by the company and the Paris Chamber of Commerce and Industry. This segment consists of 10 venues, are located in Paris and its western outskirts, and spread over 360,000 square meters. The firm's roughly $8 billion development pipeline is divided into segments that include 35% offices, 7% office extension and renovation, 34% retail and 24% retail extension and renovation. In July 2010, the company acquired the Simon Ivanhoe portfolio, which controls seven shopping centers in France and Poland, from the Simon Property group.

FINANCIALS: Sales and profits are in thousands of dollars—add 000 to get the full amount. 2010 Note: Financial information for 2010 was not available for all companies at press time.

2010 Sales: $2,224,290	2010 Profits: $3,242,400	U.S. Stock Ticker:
2009 Sales: $1,942,350	2009 Profits: $-1,958,090	Int'l Ticker: UL Int'l Exchange: Paris-Euronext
2008 Sales: $1,893,300	2008 Profits: $-1,484,300	Employees: 1,616
2007 Sales: $1,180,900	2007 Profits: $1,256,600	Fiscal Year Ends:
2006 Sales: $869,000	2006 Profits: $2,845,900	Parent Company:

SALARIES/BENEFITS:

Pension Plan:	ESOP Stock Plan:	Profit Sharing:	Top Exec. Salary: $	Bonus: $
Savings Plan:	Stock Purch. Plan:		Second Exec. Salary: $	Bonus: $

OTHER THOUGHTS:

Apparent Women Officers or Directors: 1
Hot Spot for Advancement for Women/Minorities:

LOCATIONS: ("Y" = Yes)

West:	Southwest:	Midwest:	Southeast:	Northeast:	International:
					Y

UNITECH LIMITED

www.unitechgroup.com

Industry Group Code: 5311 Ranks within this company's industry group: Sales: 23   Profits: 20

Properties:		Financial Services:		Construction/Development:		Investments:		Specialty Services:		Brokerage:	
Apartments:	Y	Mortgages:		Commercial Construction:	Y	REIT:		Property Management:	Y	Commercial Sales:	
Malls/Shopping:	Y	Title Insurance:		Residential Construction:	Y			Online Services:		Residential Sales:	
Offices:	Y	Property Insurance:		Land Development:				Software/IT:		Specialty:	
Hotels/Motels:	Y			Support Services:				Consulting:			
Industrial/Warehouses:	Y			Design/Engineering:							
Other:											

TYPES OF BUSINESS:

Real Estate Development
Construction and Civil Engineering Services
Telecommunications

BRANDS/DIVISIONS/AFFILIATES:

Uninor Cellular Services
Unitech Infra Limited
Unitech Corporate Parks Plc

CONTACTS: *Note: Officers with more than one job title may be intentionally listed here more than once.*

Sanjay Chandra, Joint Managing Dir.
Manoj Popli, CFO
Deepak Jain, Sec./Compliance Officer
Ajay Chandra, Joint Managing Dir.
Ramesh Chandra, Chmn.

Phone: 91-11-4166-4040	**Fax:** 91-11-2685-7338
Toll-Free:	
Address: 6, Community Centre, New Delhi, 110 017 India	

GROWTH PLANS/SPECIAL FEATURES:

Unitech Limited is an India-based real estate development and construction firm. The company's operations are organized into five segments: Residential, Commercial, Retail & Leisure, Construction and Wireless. The residential segment includes housing units in such areas as Bangalore, Mumbai, Gurgaon, Mohali, Noida, Lucknow, and Kolkata. The commercial segment, operating through Unitech Corporate Parks Plc, includes office complexes and business parks in Kolkata, Gurgaon and Noida. The retail & leisure category includes an amusement park, hotel and shopping centers in Noida, as well as shopping malls in Gurgaon. The construction segment is focused on various industrial and residential construction projects, including highways, transmission lines and overseas turnkey projects. Completed projects in the construction category include exhaust chimneys at power plants in various parts of India, steel and cement plant construction projects, a 305-room hotel in New Delhi, a multi-purpose indoor stadium in Madras and a residential apartment complex in Gurgaon, as well as various highway construction and expansion projects. The wireless segment operates through Uninor Cellular Services, a joint venture with Norwegian mobile communications group Telenor. The firm owns 32.75% interest in the venture. Uninor Cellular Services, with over 5 million subscribers, currently offers mobile telephony services in Uttaranchal, Bihar, Orissa, Tamil Nadu, Karnataka, Kerala and Andhra Pradesh, India. Unitech maintains business offices in Gurgaon, Agra, Bangalore, Chennai, Hyderabad, Kochi, Lucknow and Mumbai. In April 2010, the firm demerged its infrastructure construction business into a separate entity, Unitech Infra Limited. Unitech Infra will be responsible for general construction activities and transmission tower manufacturing; development of hotels, amusement parks and industrial and logistics parks; and facilities and property management services. It will also control Unitech's interest in Uninor Cellular.

FINANCIALS: Sales and profits are in thousands of dollars—add 000 to get the full amount. 2010 Note: Financial information for 2010 was not available for all companies at press time.

2010 Sales: $673,260	2010 Profits: $150,730	**U.S. Stock Ticker:**	
2009 Sales: $747,730	2009 Profits: $269,820	**Int'l Ticker: 507878**	Int'l Exchange: Bombay-BSE
2008 Sales: $844,600	2008 Profits: $327,730	Employees: 1,109	
2007 Sales: $668,580	2007 Profits: $257,740	Fiscal Year Ends: 3/31	
2006 Sales: $185,770	2006 Profits: $16,690	Parent Company:	

SALARIES/BENEFITS:

Pension Plan:	ESOP Stock Plan:	Profit Sharing:	Top Exec. Salary: $	Bonus: $
Savings Plan:	Stock Purch. Plan:		Second Exec. Salary: $	Bonus: $

OTHER THOUGHTS:

Apparent Women Officers or Directors:
Hot Spot for Advancement for Women/Minorities:

LOCATIONS: ("Y" = Yes)

West:	Southwest:	Midwest:	Southeast:	Northeast:	International:
					Y

URS CORPORATION

www.urscorp.com

Industry Group Code: 541330   Ranks within this company's industry group: Sales: 1   Profits: 1

Properties:	Financial Services:	Construction/Development:		Investments:	Specialty Services:	Brokerage:
Apartments:	Mortgages:	Commercial Construction:		REIT:	Property Management:	Commercial Sales:
Malls/Shopping:	Title Insurance:	Residential Construction:			Online Services:	Residential Sales:
Offices:	Property Insurance:	Land Development:			Software/IT:	Specialty:
Hotels/Motels:		Support Services:	Y		Consulting:	
Industrial/Warehouses:		Design/Engineering:	Y			
Other:						

TYPES OF BUSINESS:

Engineering Design Services
Systems Engineering & Technical Assistance
Operations & Maintenance Services
Construction

BRANDS/DIVISIONS/AFFILIATES:

Infrastructure & Environment
Federal Services
Energy & Construction

CONTACTS: *Note: Officers with more than one job title may be intentionally listed here more than once.*

Martin M. Koffel, CEO
Martin M. Koffel, Pres.
H. Thomas Hicks, CFO/VP-Finance
Joseph Masters, General Counsel/Sec.
Thomas W. Bishop, VP-Strategy/Sr. VP-Construction Svcs.
Susan B. Kilgannon, VP-Comm.
Reed N. Brimhall, Chief Acct. Officer/Controller/VP
Thomas H. Zarges, Pres., Energy & Construction
Gary V. Jandegian, VP/Pres., Infrastructure & Environment
Randall A. Wotring, VP/Pres., Federal
Martin M. Koffel, Chmn.

Phone: 415-774-2700	Fax: 415-398-1905
Toll-Free:	
Address: 600 Montgomery St., Fl. 26, San Francisco, CA 94111 US	

GROWTH PLANS/SPECIAL FEATURES:

URS Corporation is a worldwide engineering design services firm and a U.S. federal government contractor for systems engineering, technical assistance, operations and maintenance services. The company focuses primarily on providing fee-based professional and technical services in the engineering and construction services and defense markets. The firm operates in three divisions: Infrastructure & Environment, Federal Services and Energy & Construction. The Infrastructure & Environment division provides professional planning and design; program management; construction management; and operations and maintenance services to various government agencies and departments in the U.S. and internationally, as well as to private industry clients. The Federal Services division provides planning; systems engineering and technical assistance; operations and maintenance; and program management services to various U.S. governmental agencies, including the Departments of Defense and Homeland Security. The Energy and Construction division builds transportation infrastructure, including airports, mass transit systems and tolls roads. The unit also performs intricate tasks such as nuclear waste disposal, mining, engineering and facility management. The company has a network of offices and job sites across the U.S. and in more than 30 foreign countries in the Americas, Europe, the Middle East and Asia-Pacific.

URS offers its employees medical, vision and dental insurance; short- and long-term insurance; life and AD&D insurance; an employee assistance program; flexible spending accounts; and tuition reimbursement.

FINANCIALS: Sales and profits are in thousands of dollars—add 000 to get the full amount. 2010 Note: Financial information for 2010 was not available for all companies at press time.

2010 Sales: $9,177,051	2010 Profits: $287,889	**U.S. Stock Ticker:** URS
2009 Sales: $9,249,088	2009 Profits: $269,120	**Int'l Ticker:** Int'l Exchange:
2008 Sales: $10,086,289	2008 Profits: $219,791	Employees: 47,000
2007 Sales: $5,383,007	2007 Profits: $132,243	Fiscal Year Ends: 12/31
2006 Sales: $4,222,869	2006 Profits: $113,012	Parent Company:

SALARIES/BENEFITS:

Pension Plan: Y	ESOP Stock Plan:	Profit Sharing:	Top Exec. Salary: $1,000,002	Bonus: $2,500,004
Savings Plan: Y	Stock Purch. Plan: Y		Second Exec. Salary: $700,000	Bonus: $961,568

OTHER THOUGHTS:

Apparent Women Officers or Directors: 2
Hot Spot for Advancement for Women/Minorities:

LOCATIONS: ("Y" = Yes)

West:	Southwest:	Midwest:	Southeast:	Northeast:	International:
Y	Y	Y	Y	Y	Y

VENTAS INC

www.ventasreit.com

Industry Group Code: 531120 Ranks within this company's industry group: Sales: 16   Profits: 11

Properties:	Financial Services:	Construction/Development:	Investments:	Specialty Services:	Brokerage:
Apartments:	Mortgages:	Commercial Construction:	REIT: Y	Property Management:	Commercial Sales:
Malls/Shopping:	Title Insurance:	Residential Construction:		Online Services:	Residential Sales:
Offices:	Property Insurance:	Land Development:		Software/IT:	Specialty:
Hotels/Motels:		Support Services:		Consulting:	
Industrial/Warehouses:		Design/Engineering:			
Other: Y					

TYPES OF BUSINESS:

Real Estate Investment Trust
Hospitals
Senior Housing Properties
Medical Office Buildings
Skilled Nursing Facilities

BRANDS/DIVISIONS/AFFILIATES:

Ventas Realty LP
Nationwide Health Properties Inc
PSLT OP LP
Lillibridge Healthcare Services, Inc.
Atria Senior Living Group

CONTACTS: *Note: Officers with more than one job title may be intentionally listed here more than once.*

Debra A. Cafaro, CEO
Raymond Lewis, Pres.
Richard A. Schweinhart, CFO/Exec. VP
Julie M. Dreixler, Sr. VP-Human Resources
T. Richard Riney, Chief Admin. Officer/Exec. VP
T. Richard Riney, General Counsel/Corp. Sec.
Todd W. Lillibridge, Exec. VP-Medical Property Oper.
David J. Smith, VP-Investor Rel.
Robert J. Brehl, Chief Acct. Officer/Controller
Raymond Lewis, Pres./CEO-Lillibridge Healthcare Svcs.
Timothy A. Doman, Sr. VP-Asset Mgmt.
Brian K. Wood, Sr. VP-Tax
Kristen M. Benson, VP/Senior Securities Counsel
Debra A. Cafaro, Chmn.

Phone: 312-660-3800	**Fax:** 312-660-3850
Toll-Free:	
Address: 111 S. Wacker Dr., Ste. 4800, Chicago, IL 60606 US	

GROWTH PLANS/SPECIAL FEATURES:

Ventas, Inc. is a health care real estate investment trust (REIT) with a geographically diverse portfolio of health care facilities. This portfolio consists of 40 hospitals, 187 skilled nursing facilities, 135 medical office buildings and 240 senior housing facilities in 43 states and two Canadian provinces. The company is the sole owner of 538 of these assets, holds a majority interest in six and between 5% and 20% interest in the remaining 58 properties. The company leases its facilities to health care operating companies under triple-net or absolute-net leases. Kindred Healthcare, Inc. and its subsidiaries lease Ventas' nursing facilities and some of its hospitals; Brookdale Living Communities, Inc., is the company's other major customers. The firm's business strategy includes three primary objectives: diversifying its portfolio of properties; maintaining a strong balance sheet and liquidity; and increasing its earnings. In July 2010, Ventas acquired Lillibridge Healthcare Services, Inc. In October 2010, the firm agreed to acquire Atria Senior Living Group for roughly $3.1 billion. In December 2010, Ventas acquired 58 senior living facilities from Sunrise Senior Living, Inc. for $186 million; and Lillibridge Healthcare Services acquired five medical office buildings (225,000 square feet) for $36.6 million. In March 2011, the company agreed to acquire Nationwide Health Properties, Inc. in a deal worth $7.4 billion.

FINANCIALS: Sales and profits are in thousands of dollars—add 000 to get the full amount. 2010 Note: Financial information for 2010 was not available for all companies at press time.

2010 Sales: $1,016,867	2010 Profits: $246,729	**U.S. Stock Ticker:** VTR
2009 Sales: $931,575	2009 Profits: $266,495	**Int'l Ticker:** Int'l Exchange:
2008 Sales: $919,145	2008 Profits: $222,603	Employees: 263
2007 Sales: $746,697	2007 Profits: $273,681	Fiscal Year Ends: 12/31
2006 Sales: $397,951	2006 Profits: $131,430	Parent Company:

SALARIES/BENEFITS:

Pension Plan:	ESOP Stock Plan:	Profit Sharing:	Top Exec. Salary: $652,000	Bonus: $2,013,865
Savings Plan:	Stock Purch. Plan:		Second Exec. Salary: $407,000	Bonus: $854,700

OTHER THOUGHTS:

Apparent Women Officers or Directors: 4
Hot Spot for Advancement for Women/Minorities: Y

LOCATIONS: ("Y" = Yes)

West:	Southwest:	Midwest:	Southeast:	Northeast:	International:
Y	Y	Y	Y	Y	

VINCI

www.vinci.com

Industry Group Code: 237 Ranks within this company's industry group: Sales: 1   Profits: 2

Properties:	Financial Services:	Construction/Development:		Investments:	Specialty Services:		Brokerage:
Apartments:	Mortgages:	Commercial Construction:	Y	REIT:	Property Management:	Y	Commercial Sales:
Malls/Shopping:	Title Insurance:	Residential Construction:			Online Services:		Residential Sales:
Offices:	Property Insurance:	Land Development:	Y		Software/IT:	Y	Specialty:
Hotels/Motels:		Support Services:	Y		Consulting:		
Industrial/Warehouses:		Design/Engineering:	Y				
Other:							

TYPES OF BUSINESS:

Heavy Construction
Infrastructure Management
Information & Energy Technologies
Commercial Construction
Engineering Services
Highway Construction
Airport Management & Support Services
Power Transmission Services

BRANDS/DIVISIONS/AFFILIATES:

VINCI Concessions
VINCI Energies
Eurovia
VINCI Construction
Taylor Woodrow Construction
Autoroutes Du Sud De La France (ASF)
Haymills Property Solutions
Freyssinet

CONTACTS: Note: Officers with more than one job title may be intentionally listed here more than once.

Xavier Huillard, CEO
Christian Labeyrie, CFO/Exec. VP
Franck Mougin, Exec. VP-Human Resources
Richard Francioli, CEO-Construction
Patrick Richard, Dir.-Legal Affairs/Sec.
Jean-Luc Pommier, VP-Bus. Dev.
Pierre Duprat, Dir.-Corp. Comm.
Jean-Yves le Brouster, CEO-VINCI Energies
Louis-Roch Burgard, CEO-VINCI Concessions
Jacques Tavernier, CEO-Eurovia
Yves-Thibault de Silguy, Chmn.

Phone: 33-1-47-16-3500	Fax: 33-1-47-51-9102
Toll-Free:	
Address: 1 Cours Ferdinand-de-Lesseps, Rueil-Malmaison, 92851 France	

GROWTH PLANS/SPECIAL FEATURES:

VINCI, one of the largest companies operating in construction and related services worldwide, consists of four major divisions: VINCI Concessions, VINCI Energies, Eurovia and VINCI Construction. VINCI Concessions is engaged in the design, turnkey construction, financing and operation of facilities, as well as outsourced infrastructure management. Its comprehensive approach is applied to major public facilities such as the Stade de France stadium near Paris, as well as to the operation of various motorways, car parks and airports. The overall Concessions business line accounts for approximately 25% of company revenues. VINCI Energies is a leading European producer of information and energy technologies for infrastructure, industry, the service sector and telecommunications. It operates through several brands in Europe, including Actemium, offering energy services to industry; Axians, offering voice-data-image communication services; Citeos, specializing in urban lighting; Graniou, supporting telecommunications infrastructure; Omexom, specializing in high-voltage power; and Opteor, offering industrial and services maintenance. The Energies business line accounts for approximately 15% of company revenues. Eurovia is a leading European company in the road industry and in recycled materials, operating in roadworks, materials production, environment-related activities and services. It accounts for approximately 25% of company revenues. VINCI Construction, representing roughly 45% of overall company revenues, is an industry leader in building, civil engineering, hydraulics and facilities management. The division is composed of three main components: Mainland France; Local Markets outside mainland France; and Worldwide activities, including major structures, specialized civil engineering and dredging. VINCI is engaged in a design-build project for a causeway between Qatar and Bahrain, which will be among the world's longest bridges. In October 2010, Freysinnet, a subsidiary of VINCI construction was awarded the contract to design, manufacture and install the stay cable of the Russky Island Bridge in Russia, which will feature the longest cable-stayed span in the world.

FINANCIALS: Sales and profits are in thousands of dollars—add 000 to get the full amount. 2010 Note: Financial information for 2010 was not available for all companies at press time.

2010 Sales: $47,566,100	2010 Profits: $2,484,410	**U.S. Stock Ticker:**
2009 Sales: $44,101,500	2009 Profits: $2,168,390	**Int'l Ticker: DG** Int'l Exchange: Paris-Euronext
2008 Sales: $42,717,900	2008 Profits: $2,003,070	Employees:
2007 Sales: $33,820,000	2007 Profits: $1,680,000	Fiscal Year Ends: 12/31
2006 Sales: $35,200,919	2006 Profits: $	Parent Company:

SALARIES/BENEFITS:

Pension Plan:	ESOP Stock Plan:	Profit Sharing:	Top Exec. Salary: $	Bonus: $
Savings Plan:	Stock Purch. Plan:		Second Exec. Salary: $	Bonus: $

OTHER THOUGHTS:

Apparent Women Officers or Directors:
Hot Spot for Advancement for Women/Minorities:

LOCATIONS: ("Y" = Yes)

West:	Southwest:	Midwest:	Southeast:	Northeast:	International:
Y	Y	Y	Y	Y	Y

VORNADO REALTY TRUST

www.vno.com

Industry Group Code: 531120 Ranks within this company's industry group: Sales: 5 Profits: 7

Properties:		Financial Services:	Construction/Development:	Investments:		Specialty Services:	Brokerage:
Apartments:		Mortgages:	Commercial Construction:	REIT:	Y	Property Management:	Commercial Sales:
Malls/Shopping:	Y	Title Insurance:	Residential Construction:			Online Services:	Residential Sales:
Offices:	Y	Property Insurance:	Land Development:			Software/IT:	Specialty:
Hotels/Motels:	Y		Support Services:			Consulting:	
Industrial/Warehouses:	Y		Design/Engineering:				
Other:	Y						

TYPES OF BUSINESS:

Real Estate Investment Trust
Office Properties
Retail Properties
Toys
Merchandise

BRANDS/DIVISIONS/AFFILIATES:

Merchandise Mart
Toys-R-Us Inc
Alexander's
Hotel Pennsylvania
Vornado Retail Portfolio
LNR Property Corporation
J.C. Penney Company Inc

CONTACTS: *Note: Officers with more than one job title may be intentionally listed here more than once.*

Michael D. Fascitelli, CEO
Michael D. Fascitelli, Pres.
Joseph Macnow, CFO
Joseph Macnow, Exec. VP-Admin.
Joseph Macnow, Exec. VP-Finance
David R. Greenbaum, Pres., New York Office Div.
Christopher Kennedy, Pres., Merch. Mart Div.
Micheal J. Franco, Exec. VP/Co-Head-Acquisitions & Capital Markets
Wendy Silverstein, Exec. VP/Co-Head-Acquisitions & Capital Markets
Steven Roth, Chmn.

Phone: 212-894-7000	Fax: 201-587-0600
Toll-Free:	
Address: 888 7th Ave., New York, NY 10019 US	

GROWTH PLANS/SPECIAL FEATURES:

Vornado Realty Trust, which conducts its business through 93.2%-owned Vornado Realty L.P., is a fully integrated real estate investment trust (REIT). It is one of the largest property owners in New York City, primarily in Manhattan. The firm has four different platforms: office, retail, merchandise mart and toys. The office portfolio is made up of 111 wholly- or partially-owned office properties (40.3 million square feet) in the New York City metropolitan area; Washington, D.C.; northern Virginia; and San Francisco. The Vornado Retail Portfolio controls and/or manages 161properties (25.6 million square feet) in 21 states, Puerto Rico and Washington, D.C. The Merchandise Mart division includes six properties in four states and Washington, D.C., with 6.9 million square feet of showroom and office space. The toys division holds a 32.7% interest in Toys-R-Us, Inc., which owns and/or operates approximately 1,589 stores worldwide. Vornado's additional properties include the Hotel Pennsylvania in Manhattan, containing 1 million square feet with 1,700 rooms and 400,000 square feet of retail and office space; a 32.4% interest in Alexander's, which owns seven properties in the greater New York metropolitan area; and 9.9% ownership of J.C. Penney Company, Inc. In July 2010, the firm acquired 26.2% interest in commercial mortgage loan provider LNR Property Corporation. In October 2010, Vornado sold 45% interest in a Washington, D.C., property to The Canada Pension Plan Investment Board (the firm retains the remaining 55% interest). In January 2011, the company agreed to sell two office buildings in Washington, D.C., totaling 319,000 square feet for roughly $107 million.

FINANCIALS: Sales and profits are in thousands of dollars—add 000 to get the full amount. 2010 Note: Financial information for 2010 was not available for all companies at press time.

2010 Sales: $2,779,727	2010 Profits: $647,883	**U.S. Stock Ticker: VNO**
2009 Sales: $2,696,692	2009 Profits: $160,169	**Int'l Ticker:** Int'l Exchange:
2008 Sales: $2,697,051	2008 Profits: $395,043	Employees: 4,780
2007 Sales: $2,405,243	2007 Profits: $607,833	Fiscal Year Ends: 12/31
2006 Sales: $1,909,100	2006 Profits: $560,140	Parent Company:

SALARIES/BENEFITS:

Pension Plan:	ESOP Stock Plan:	Profit Sharing:	Top Exec. Salary: $1,000,000	Bonus: $750,000
Savings Plan:	Stock Purch. Plan:		Second Exec. Salary: $1,000,000	Bonus: $750,000

OTHER THOUGHTS:

Apparent Women Officers or Directors: 2
Hot Spot for Advancement for Women/Minorities:

LOCATIONS: ("Y" = Yes)

West:	Southwest:	Midwest:	Southeast:	Northeast:	International:
Y	Y	Y	Y	Y	Y

WASHINGTON REAL ESTATE INVESTMENT TRUST www.writ.com

Industry Group Code: 531110 Ranks within this company's industry group: Sales: 12 Profits: 8

Properties:		Financial Services:	Construction/Development:	Investments:		Specialty Services:	Brokerage:
Apartments:	Y	Mortgages:	Commercial Construction:	REIT:	Y	Property Management:	Commercial Sales:
Malls/Shopping:	Y	Title Insurance:	Residential Construction:			Online Services:	Residential Sales:
Offices:	Y	Property Insurance:	Land Development:			Software/IT:	Specialty:
Hotels/Motels:			Support Services:			Consulting:	
Industrial/Warehouses:	Y		Design/Engineering:				
Other:							

TYPES OF BUSINESS:

Real Estate Investment Trust
Office Buildings
Industrial Properties
Retail Properties
Apartments
Medical Office Buildings

BRANDS/DIVISIONS/AFFILIATES:

Ridges (The)
Ammendale I
Ammendale II

CONTACTS: *Note: Officers with more than one job title may be intentionally listed here more than once.*

George F. McKenzie, CEO
George F. McKenzie, Pres.
William T. Camp, CFO/Exec. VP
Laura M. Franklin, Exec. VP-Admin.
Thomas C. Morey, General Counsel/Sr. VP
Laura M. Franklin, Exec. VP-Acct.
Michael Paukstitus, Sr. VP-Real Estate
Thomas L. Regnell, Sr. VP
Laura M. Franklin, Corp. Sec.
James B. Cederdahl, Managing Dir.-Property Mgmt.
Edmund B. Cronin, Jr., Chmn.

Phone: 301-984-9400	**Fax:** 301-984-9610
Toll-Free: 800-565-9748	
Address: 6110 Executive Blvd., Ste. 800, Rockville, MD 20852 US	

GROWTH PLANS/SPECIAL FEATURES:

Washington Real Estate Investment Trust (WRIT) is a self-administered, self-managed, equity real estate investment trust (REIT) that owns and develops income-producing real properties in the greater Washington, D.C./Baltimore region. Its portfolio contains general purpose office buildings, medical office buildings, industrial/flex properties, multifamily buildings and retail centers. WRIT owns 85 properties (approximately 10.7 million square feet of commercial space and 2,540 residential units) consisting of 25 general purpose office properties; 16 industrial/flex properties and land held for development; 15 retail centers; 18 medical office properties; and 11 multifamily properties. Its principal objective is to invest in high quality properties in prime locations, then proactively manage, lease and develop ongoing capital improvement programs to improve their economic performance. In June 2010, WRIT acquired two new four-story Class A office buildings (roughly 271,000 square feet) in Quantico Corporate Center in Virginia for approximately $68 million. In December 2010, the firm acquired a 214,281 square foot Class A shopping center in Gateway Overlook in for roughly $88.35 million; sold The Ridges office building for $27.5 million; and sold Ammendale I and II and Amvax industrial buildings for $23 million. All of these properties are located in Maryland. In January 2011, the company acquired 12-story, 184,135 square foot office building 1140 Connecticut Avenue, NW in Washington, D.C., for roughly $80.25 million; and agreed to acquire 8-story, 130,434 square foot office building 1227 25th Street, NW, also in Washington, D.C., for $47 million.

The company offers its employees medical, dental and vision insurance; a 401(k) plan; tuition reimbursement; short- and long-term disability; flexible spending accounts; an annual incentive bonus program; an employee assistance program; and an in-house fitness center.

FINANCIALS: Sales and profits are in thousands of dollars—add 000 to get the full amount. 2010 Note: Financial information for 2010 was not available for all companies at press time.

2010 Sales: $297,977	2010 Profits: $37,559	**U.S. Stock Ticker: WRE**
2009 Sales: $298,161	2009 Profits: $40,948	**Int'l Ticker:** Int'l Exchange:
2008 Sales: $268,709	2008 Profits: $27,082	Employees: 293
2007 Sales: $248,899	2007 Profits: $57,451	Fiscal Year Ends: 12/31
2006 Sales: $205,940	2006 Profits: $38,661	Parent Company:

SALARIES/BENEFITS:

Pension Plan:	ESOP Stock Plan:	Profit Sharing:	Top Exec. Salary: $405,521	Bonus: $466,735
Savings Plan: Y	Stock Purch. Plan:		Second Exec. Salary: $320,925	Bonus: $284,729

OTHER THOUGHTS:

Apparent Women Officers or Directors: 2
Hot Spot for Advancement for Women/Minorities:

LOCATIONS: ("Y" = Yes)

West:	Southwest:	Midwest:	Southeast:	Northeast:	International:
				Y	

WATSON LAND COMPANY

www.watsonlandcompany.com

Industry Group Code: 5311 Ranks within this company's industry group: Sales: Profits:

Properties:		Financial Services:		Construction/Development:		Investments:		Specialty Services:		Brokerage:	
Apartments:		Mortgages:		Commercial Construction:	Y	REIT:		Property Management:	Y	Commercial Sales:	
Malls/Shopping:		Title Insurance:		Residential Construction:				Online Services:		Residential Sales:	
Offices:	Y	Property Insurance:		Land Development:	Y			Software/IT:		Specialty:	
Hotels/Motels:				Support Services:	Y			Consulting:			
Industrial/Warehouses:	Y			Design/Engineering:	Y						
Other:											

TYPES OF BUSINESS:

Office & Industrial Properties
Land Development
Commercial Construction
Property Management
Building Maintenance & Operations

BRANDS/DIVISIONS/AFFILIATES:

Heritage Customer Service Program
Legacy Building Series

CONTACTS: *Note: Officers with more than one job title may be intentionally listed here more than once.*

Bruce A. Choate, CEO
Bruce A. Choate, Pres.
Roger von Ting, CFO
Lance P. Ryan, VP-Mktg. & Leasing
Bradley D. Frazier, General Counsel/Corp. Sec.
Kirk R. Johnson, Exec. VP-Real Estate Oper.
Craig B. Halverson, VP-Acquisitions
Pilar M. Hoyos, VP-Public Affairs
Jeffrey R. Jennison, VP-Real Estate Asset Mgmt.
Christopher L. Trujillo, VP-Construction
Robert W. Huston, Chmn.

Phone: 310-952-6400	Fax: 310-522-8788
Toll-Free:	
Address: 22010 S. Wilmington Ave., Ste. 400, Carson, CA 90745 US	

GROWTH PLANS/SPECIAL FEATURES:

Watson Land Company is a private REIT (Real Estate Investment Trust) that develops, owns and manages industrial properties in Southern California including the Los Angeles area. It is one of the largest developers of industrial centers in Los Angeles County, having planned more than 1,000 acres of industrial and commercial property in addition to owning and managing approximately 14 million square feet of industrial, office and technology buildings and business centers. Watson specializes in building master-planned facilities for warehousing, distribution, assembly and manufacturing. It also builds office buildings and multi-tenant business centers that serve as corporate headquarters; administrative and general offices; and computer operations, data processing, technology and service-related centers. Watson's Heritage Customer Service Program offers clients a unique lease structure through which Watson assumes and manages the maintenance and operating functions typically performed by the customer. The Heritage program is tailored to the client and can include roofing, yard, lighting, painting and HVAC maintenance repair and replacement services. Watson's Legacy Building Series consists of build-to-suit industrial buildings and corporate headquarters for clients such as Mercedes-Benz, Kmart, NEC Logistics, TRW, McDonnell Douglas and Honda. Watson has also completed the incorporation of several master-planned business centers into a General Purpose Zone Site as part of Foreign Trade Zone (FTZ) 202, sponsored by the Port of Los Angeles. FTZ status is intended to provide approved customers enhanced cost savings and operating benefits to maximize efficiency. In addition, the company has land holdings available for development in the Inland Empire region of California. Other notable customers have included Boeing; BP West Coast Products; DHL; Hansen's; Hitachi Transport; Target Logistics; The Pasha Group; Union Pacific Railroad; the United States Postal Service; and Whirlpool.

FINANCIALS: Sales and profits are in thousands of dollars—add 000 to get the full amount. 2010 Note: Financial information for 2010 was not available for all companies at press time.

2010 Sales: $	2010 Profits: $	U.S. Stock Ticker: Private
2009 Sales: $	2009 Profits: $	Int'l Ticker: Int'l Exchange:
2008 Sales: $	2008 Profits: $	Employees:
2007 Sales: $	2007 Profits: $	Fiscal Year Ends: 12/31
2006 Sales: $	2006 Profits: $	Parent Company:

SALARIES/BENEFITS:

Pension Plan:	ESOP Stock Plan:	Profit Sharing:	Top Exec. Salary: $	Bonus: $
Savings Plan:	Stock Purch. Plan:		Second Exec. Salary: $	Bonus: $

OTHER THOUGHTS:

Apparent Women Officers or Directors:
Hot Spot for Advancement for Women/Minorities:

LOCATIONS: ("Y" = Yes)

West:	Southwest:	Midwest:	Southeast:	Northeast:	International:
Y					

WCI COMMUNITIES INC

www.wcicommunities.com

Industry Group Code: 2361 Ranks within this company's industry group: Sales: Profits:

Properties:		Financial Services:		Construction/Development:		Investments:	Specialty Services:		Brokerage:	
Apartments:	Y	Mortgages:	Y	Commercial Construction:	Y	REIT:	Property Management:	Y	Commercial Sales:	
Malls/Shopping:		Title Insurance:	Y	Residential Construction:	Y		Online Services:		Residential Sales:	Y
Offices:		Property Insurance:		Land Development:	Y		Software/IT:		Specialty:	
Hotels/Motels:				Support Services:	Y		Consulting:			
Industrial/Warehouses:				Design/Engineering:	Y					
Other:	Y									

TYPES OF BUSINESS:

Homebuilding
Country Club Management
Title Insurance
Design & Engineering Services
Residential Brokerage
Land Development
Mortgages

BRANDS/DIVISIONS/AFFILIATES:

Prudential Florida WCI Realty
WCI Amenities
Florida Title & Guarantee

CONTACTS: Note: Officers with more than one job title may be intentionally listed here more than once.

David L. Fry, CEO
David L. Fry, Pres.
Russel Devendorf, CFO/Sr. VP
Vivien N. Hastings, General Counsel/Sr. VP
Tim Oak, Sr. VP-Homebuilding Oper.
Douglas L. Schwartz, Sr. VP-Community Oper.
Rei L. Mesa, CEO/Pres., Prudential Florida Real Estate Svcs.

Phone: 239-498-8200	Fax: 239-498-8338
Toll-Free: 800-924-4005	
Address: 24301 Walden Ctr. Dr., Ste. 300, Bonita Springs, FL 34134 US	

GROWTH PLANS/SPECIAL FEATURES:

WCI Communities, Inc. (WCI) is a designer, builder and seller of traditional and luxury high-rise homes, which are typically part of master planned communities. WCI has locations in Florida, Connecticut New Jersey and New York. The company's community and mid-rise and high-rise tower (known as Sky Homes) locations contain homes ranging in price from around $100,000 to under $1 million. WCI communities offer a wide array of world-class amenities including hotel services, boating, river clubs, marinas, championship golf courses, tennis complexes, fine dining, concierge services, nature trails, spas and fitness studios. The company's Prudential Florida WCI Realty division operates its mortgage and title business; Florida Title & Guarantee underwrites its policies on behalf of large national title insurers. The firm's amenities division, WCI Amenities, operates many of the clubhouses, golf courses, restaurants and marinas within WCI communities. WCI recently filed for Chapter 11 bankruptcy protection and later emerged as a private company.

WCI offers its employees medical and dental coverage; a vision reimbursement plan; life and AD&D insurance; flexible spending accounts; short- and long-term disability; and discounts for Dell computers, Sprint Wireless, dry cleaners, hotel accommodations and more.

FINANCIALS: Sales and profits are in thousands of dollars—add 000 to get the full amount. 2010 Note: Financial information for 2010 was not available for all companies at press time.

2010 Sales: $	2010 Profits: $	U.S. Stock Ticker: Private
2009 Sales: $	2009 Profits: $	Int'l Ticker: Int'l Exchange:
2008 Sales: $556,077	2008 Profits: $-936,796	Employees: 1,450
2007 Sales: $936,376	2007 Profits: $-578,531	Fiscal Year Ends: 12/31
2006 Sales: $2,044,585	2006 Profits: $9,014	Parent Company:

SALARIES/BENEFITS:

Pension Plan:	ESOP Stock Plan:	Profit Sharing:	Top Exec. Salary: $	Bonus: $
Savings Plan: Y	Stock Purch. Plan:		Second Exec. Salary: $	Bonus: $

OTHER THOUGHTS:

Apparent Women Officers or Directors: 2
Hot Spot for Advancement for Women/Minorities:

LOCATIONS: ("Y" = Yes)

West:	Southwest:	Midwest:	Southeast:	Northeast:	International:
			Y	Y	

WEINGARTEN REALTY INVESTORS   www.weingarten.com

Industry Group Code: 531120 Ranks within this company's industry group: Sales: 33   Profits: 33

Properties:		Financial Services:		Construction/Development:		Investments:		Specialty Services:		Brokerage:	
Apartments:		Mortgages:		Commercial Construction:	Y	REIT:	Y	Property Management:	Y	Commercial Sales:	
Malls/Shopping:	Y	Title Insurance:		Residential Construction:				Online Services:		Residential Sales:	
Offices:	Y	Property Insurance:		Land Development:	Y			Software/IT:		Specialty:	
Hotels/Motels:				Support Services:				Consulting:			
Industrial/Warehouses:	Y			Design/Engineering:							
Other:											

TYPES OF BUSINESS:

Real Estate Investment Trust
Industrial & Office Properties
Shopping Centers
Commercial Construction
Property Management

BRANDS/DIVISIONS/AFFILIATES:

CONTACTS: *Note: Officers with more than one job title may be intentionally listed here more than once.*

Andrew M. Alexander, CEO
Johnny Hendrix, COO/Exec. VP
Andrew M. Alexander, Pres.
Stephen C. Richter, CFO/Exec. VP
Michael Townsell, VP-Human Resources
Lee Pearson, CIO/VP
Jeffrey A. Tucker, General Counsel/Sr. VP
Robert Smith, Sr. VP-Dev.
Kristin Gandy, Dir.-Investor Rel.
Joe D. Shafer, Chief Acct. Officer/Sr. VP
Patricia A. Bender, Exec. VP-Leasing
Bill Goeke, Sr. VP-Property Mgmt.
Gary Greenberg, Sr. VP-Capital Markets
M. Candace DuFour, Sr. VP-Acquisitions/Corp. Sec.
Stanford Alexander, Chmn.

Phone: 713-886-6000	**Fax:** 713-886-6049
Toll-Free:	
Address: 2600 Citadel Plaza Dr., Houston, TX 77292-4133 US	

GROWTH PLANS/SPECIAL FEATURES:

Weingarten Realty Investors, a Real Estate Investment Trust (REIT), primarily owns and develops neighborhood and community shopping centers, as well as industrial properties. It owns or operates under long-term leases, directly and through interests in joint ventures or partnerships, a total of 383 income-producing properties and nine properties in various stages of construction and development. The firm's portfolio, totaling roughly 71.5 million square feet, includes 312 neighborhood and community shopping centers, accounting for 89% of Weingarten's revenues; 77 industrial properties, representing 9.4%; and three other properties, representing 1.6% of revenues.   33.4% of Weingarten's income is derived from properties located in the Houston metropolitan area and other parts of Texas; in all, its properties are divided between 23 states, including retail properties in 22 states and industrial properties in six states. The company's operating strategy consists of intensive hands-on management with a focus on long-term ownership. When acquiring properties, it attempts to accumulate enough to establish a regional office, enabling the company to obtain in-depth knowledge of the market from a leasing perspective and to have easy access to the property and tenants from a management standpoint.   Weingarten's criteria for retail acquisition includes an anchored community, neighborhood or power shopping center; over 100,000 square feet; multiple tenants, including an existing anchor store or accommodations for one; properties that can be leased-up, re-merchandised or renovated; a trade area with a minimum population of 50,000; and a location at a major intersection of two thoroughfares.   The firm's criterion for industrial acquisition includes bulk warehouses, office/warehouse or service center/flex buildings; and good location within first- and second-tier markets.   In November 2010, the firm acquired two retail properties, one in Colorado and one in Texas, totaling 630,000 square feet.

Weingarten offers its employees benefits including medical, dental, life and disability insurance; a 401(k); and education reimbursement.

FINANCIALS: Sales and profits are in thousands of dollars—add 000 to get the full amount. 2010 Note: Financial information for 2010 was not available for all companies at press time.

2010 Sales: $554,667	2010 Profits: $51,238	**U.S. Stock Ticker: WRI**	
2009 Sales: $571,988	2009 Profits: $175,276	**Int'l Ticker:** Int'l Exchange:	
2008 Sales: $592,647	2008 Profits: $154,595	Employees:	
2007 Sales: $561,200	2007 Profits: $240,338	Fiscal Year Ends: 12/31	
2006 Sales: $523,424	2006 Profits: $305,010	Parent Company:	

SALARIES/BENEFITS:

Pension Plan: Y	ESOP Stock Plan:	Profit Sharing:	Top Exec. Salary: $700,000	Bonus: $650,000
Savings Plan: Y	Stock Purch. Plan:		Second Exec. Salary: $675,000	Bonus: $450,000

OTHER THOUGHTS:

Apparent Women Officers or Directors: 5
Hot Spot for Advancement for Women/Minorities: Y

LOCATIONS: ("Y" = Yes)

West:	Southwest:	Midwest:	Southeast:	Northeast:	International:
Y	Y		Y	Y	

WELLS REAL ESTATE FUNDS INC

www.wellsref.com

Industry Group Code: 531120　Ranks within this company's industry group: Sales:　Profits:

Properties:	Financial Services:	Construction/Development:		Investments:		Specialty Services:		Brokerage:
Apartments:	Mortgages:	Commercial Construction:	Y	REIT:	Y	Property Management:	Y	Commercial Sales:
Malls/Shopping:	Title Insurance:	Residential Construction:				Online Services:		Residential Sales:
Offices: Y	Property Insurance:	Land Development:				Software/IT:		Specialty:
Hotels/Motels:		Support Services:				Consulting:		
Industrial/Warehouses: Y		Design/Engineering:						
Other:								

TYPES OF BUSINESS:

Real Estate Investment Trust
Office & Industrial Properties
Property Management
Construction Management

BRANDS/DIVISIONS/AFFILIATES:

Wells REIT II
Wells S&P REIT Index Mutual Fund
Wells Capital
Wells Limited Partnership Program
Wells Timberland

CONTACTS: *Note: Officers with more than one job title may be intentionally listed here more than once.*

Leo F. Wells, III, Pres.
Robert M. McCullough, CFO
Michael Dobbs, Chief Mktg. Officer
Rebecca Padgett, Chief People Officer
Thomas Brittelle, CIO
Steve Franklin, Chief-New Bus. Dev.
Kevin Race, Chief-Financial Strategy
Jess Jarratt, Pres., Wells Timberland Mgmt. Organization
Don Henry, Chief Real Estate Officer
Doug Williams, Prod. Chief Financial Officer
Doug Buce, Chief Learning Officer

Phone: 770-449-7800	Fax: 770-243-8199
Toll-Free: 800-448-1010	
Address: 6200 The Corners Pkwy., Norcross, GA 30092-3365 US	

GROWTH PLANS/SPECIAL FEATURES:

Wells Real Estate Funds, Inc. is a national real estate investment management firm that purchases corporate and industrial property. It leases its holdings on a long-term basis to tenants with a net worth of at least $100 million. The company offers two chief investment products: the Wells REIT II (closed to new investors), a private real estate investment trust that owns 90 office buildings; and the Wells S&P REIT Index Mutual Fund, a REIT tracking fund based on the S&P REIT Composite Index. In total, Wells manages more than $11 billion in assets for over 250,000 investors nationwide. The firm generally maintains a conservative investment strategy that focuses on acquiring and managing high-quality properties. Part of its strategy is leasing only to credit-worthy tenants; securing leases with major clients before acquiring a property; and using net leases in which the tenant pays all cost of taxes, insurance and maintenance. The firm maintains a diversified portfolio consisting of various geographic regions, tenants, industries and staggered lease terms. Complementing the investment business, property acquisitions and leasing, Wells also oversees property management, construction, and tenant relations. Wells Limited Partnerships is a wholly-owned subsidiary of the company, for the purpose of acquiring, developing, owning, operating, leasing, and managing income-producing commercial properties for investment purposes. Wells Capital manages investment assets for its clients. Wells Timberland is the firm's nature resource division, which maintains and distributes timber. Wells Timberland also may lease timberland to others for recreational and extraction purposes. The timberland properties are located in Georgia and Alabama.

FINANCIALS: Sales and profits are in thousands of dollars—add 000 to get the full amount. 2010 Note: Financial information for 2010 was not available for all companies at press time.

2010 Sales: $	2010 Profits: $	U.S. Stock Ticker: Private
2009 Sales: $	2009 Profits: $	Int'l Ticker:　Int'l Exchange:
2008 Sales: $	2008 Profits: $	Employees:
2007 Sales: $	2007 Profits: $	Fiscal Year Ends: 12/31
2006 Sales: $	2006 Profits: $	Parent Company:

SALARIES/BENEFITS:

Pension Plan:	ESOP Stock Plan:	Profit Sharing:	Top Exec. Salary: $	Bonus: $
Savings Plan:	Stock Purch. Plan:		Second Exec. Salary: $	Bonus: $

OTHER THOUGHTS:

Apparent Women Officers or Directors: 1
Hot Spot for Advancement for Women/Minorities:

LOCATIONS: ("Y" = Yes)

West:	Southwest:	Midwest:	Southeast:	Northeast:	International:
Y	Y	Y	Y	Y	

WESTFIELD GROUP (THE)   www.westfield.com

Industry Group Code: 531120 Ranks within this company's industry group: Sales: 2   Profits: 4

Properties:		Financial Services:	Construction/Development:		Investments:	Specialty Services:		Brokerage:
Apartments:		Mortgages:	Commercial Construction:	Y	REIT:	Property Management:	Y	Commercial Sales:
Malls/Shopping:	Y	Title Insurance:	Residential Construction:			Online Services:		Residential Sales:
Offices:		Property Insurance:	Land Development:	Y		Software/IT:		Specialty:
Hotels/Motels:			Support Services:	Y		Consulting:		
Industrial/Warehouses:			Design/Engineering:	Y				
Other:								

TYPES OF BUSINESS:

Real Estate Operations
Shopping Centers
Design & Construction
Asset Management
Property Management
Leasing
Marketing

BRANDS/DIVISIONS/AFFILIATES:

CONTACTS: *Note: Officers with more than one job title may be intentionally listed here more than once.*

Steven M. Lowy, Co-Managing Dir.
Peter Allen, CFO
Gerhard Karba, CIO
Simon Tuxen, General Counsel/Corp. Sec.
Mark Ryan, Dir.-Corp. Affairs
Mark Bloom, Deputy CFO
Peter S. Lowy, Co-Managing Dir./Managing Dir.-US
Eamonn Cunningham, Chief Risk Officer
Mark Ryan, Dir.-Corp. Affairs
Frank P. Lowy, Chmn.
Michael Gutman, Managing Dir.-U.K. & Europe

Phone: 61-02-9358-7000	**Fax:** 61-02-9358-7079
Toll-Free:	
Address: 100 William St., Westfield Towers, Sydney, NSW 2011 Australia	

GROWTH PLANS/SPECIAL FEATURES:

The Westfield Group is an internally managed retail property group based in Sydney, Australia with other offices throughout Australia, New Zealand, the U.K. and the U.S. The company is currently one of the largest retail property groups in the world by equity market capitalization as well as a leading entity on the Australian Stock Exchange. It has investment interests in 119 shopping centers in four countries. The firm divides its services into the following three categories: property management, marketing and leasing; property development, design and construction; and funds/asset management. The property management, marketing and leasing division handles day-to-day management and marketing duties for the company's properties. The firm's property development, design and construction segment oversees building development duties, which usually involves coordinating with a shopping center's anchor clients to satisfy their requirements. The funds/asset management division invests or coordinates investments in strategic companies or properties. In August 2010, the group and Costco announced a deal to build three new shopping centers in California, Florida and Maryland.

FINANCIALS: Sales and profits are in thousands of dollars—add 000 to get the full amount. 2010 Note: Financial information for 2010 was not available for all companies at press time.

		U.S. Stock Ticker:
2010 Sales: $3,967,570	2010 Profits: $1,214,880	Int'l Ticker: WDC Int'l Exchange: Sydney-ASX
2009 Sales: $4,506,080	2009 Profits: $-499,260	Employees:
2008 Sales: $4,797,050	2008 Profits: $-2,395,520	Fiscal Year Ends: 6/30
2007 Sales: $3,019,800	2007 Profits: $2,474,800	Parent Company:
2006 Sales: $2,739,000	2006 Profits: $4,019,800	

SALARIES/BENEFITS:

Pension Plan:	ESOP Stock Plan:	Profit Sharing:	Top Exec. Salary: $	Bonus: $
Savings Plan:	Stock Purch. Plan:		Second Exec. Salary: $	Bonus: $

OTHER THOUGHTS:

Apparent Women Officers or Directors: 7
Hot Spot for Advancement for Women/Minorities: Y

LOCATIONS: ("Y" = Yes)

West:	Southwest:	Midwest:	Southeast:	Northeast:	International:
Y		Y	Y	Y	Y

WHARF (HOLDINGS) LIMITED, THE

www.wharfholdings.com

Industry Group Code: 5311 Ranks within this company's industry group: Sales: Profits:

Properties:		Financial Services:	Construction/Development:		Investments:	Specialty Services:	Brokerage:
Apartments:	Y	Mortgages:	Commercial Construction:	Y	REIT:	Property Management:	Commercial Sales:
Malls/Shopping:	Y	Title Insurance:	Residential Construction:	Y		Online Services:	Residential Sales:
Offices:	Y	Property Insurance:	Land Development:	Y		Software/IT:	Specialty:
Hotels/Motels:	Y		Support Services:			Consulting:	
Industrial/Warehouses:			Design/Engineering:				
Other:	Y						

TYPES OF BUSINESS:

Real Estate Holdings & Development

BRANDS/DIVISIONS/AFFILIATES:

Modern Terminals Limited
i-Cable Communications Limited
Wharf T&T
Marco Polo Hongkong Hotel
Star Ferry (The)
Plaza Hollywood

CONTACTS: *Note: Officers with more than one job title may be intentionally listed here more than once.*

Paul Yiu Cheung Tsui, CFO/Exec. Dir.
T Y Ng, Exec. Dir.
Stephen Tin Hoi Ng, Deputy Chmn./Managing Dir.
Doreen Yuk Fong Lee, Exec. Dir.
Peter Kwong Ching Woo, Chmn.

Phone: 852-2118-8118	Fax: 852-2118-8018
Toll-Free:	
Address: 16th Fl., Ocean Centre, Canton Rd., Hong Kong, China	

GROWTH PLANS/SPECIAL FEATURES:

The Wharf (Holdings) Limited is a Hong Kong-based real estate investment holding firm. The company's two core properties, both located in Hong Kong, are Harbour City and Times Square. Harbour City, located in the commercial center of Tsim Sha Tsui, is Wharf Holding's flagship property, typically generating 58% of the company's annual rental income. With roughly 700 shops, the center encompasses approximately 8.4 million total square feet of commercial space consisting of offices, retail stores, serviced apartments, clubs, hotels and parking facilities. The Times Square property, located in the Causeway Bay commercial district of northern Hong Kong, encompasses approximately 900,000 square feet of retail space and over 1 million square feet of office space. Other Hong Kong properties include Plaza Hollywood, a retail center totaling over 562,000 square feet, as well as a number of upscale residential properties. In addition to its Hong Kong investments, Wharf Holding has been expanding its activities in Mainland China in recent years, having acquired a land bank there totaling approximately 95 million square feet, primarily in or near metropolitan areas such as Beijing, Shanghai, Chongqing, Wuhan, Dalian, Chengdu, Suzhou, Wuxi, Hangzhou, Nanjing and Changzhou. The firm currently operates three investment properties in Beijing, Shanghai and Chongqing under its Times Square brand. The company also holds a 67.6% share in Modern Terminals Limited, a provider of container terminal services in the South China region since 1969. Modern Terminals is currently engaged in developing new container terminal locations in the Pearl River Delta and Yangtze River Delta areas, in addition to other projects along the coast of China. Additional subsidiaries include i-Cable Communications Limited, a telecommunications firm; Wharf T&T, a fixed line operator; and The Star Ferry, a cross-harbor ferry service.

FINANCIALS: Sales and profits are in thousands of dollars—add 000 to get the full amount. 2010 Note: Financial information for 2010 was not available for all companies at press time.

2010 Sales: $	2010 Profits: $	U.S. Stock Ticker: Subsidiary
2009 Sales: $	2009 Profits: $	Int'l Ticker: Int'l Exchange:
2008 Sales: $	2008 Profits: $	Employees:
2007 Sales: $	2007 Profits: $	Fiscal Year Ends:
2006 Sales: $	2006 Profits: $	Parent Company: WHEELOCK AND COMPANY LIMITED

SALARIES/BENEFITS:

Pension Plan:	ESOP Stock Plan:	Profit Sharing:	Top Exec. Salary: $	Bonus: $
Savings Plan:	Stock Purch. Plan:		Second Exec. Salary: $	Bonus: $

OTHER THOUGHTS:

Apparent Women Officers or Directors: 1
Hot Spot for Advancement for Women/Minorities:

LOCATIONS: ("Y" = Yes)

West:	Southwest:	Midwest:	Southeast:	Northeast:	International:
					Y

WHEELOCK AND COMPANY LIMITED

www.wheelockcompany.com

Industry Group Code: 5311 Ranks within this company's industry group: Sales: 12   Profits: 4

Properties:		Financial Services:		Construction/Development:		Investments:	Specialty Services:	Brokerage:
Apartments:	Y	Mortgages:		Commercial Construction:		REIT:	Property Management:	Commercial Sales:
Malls/Shopping:	Y	Title Insurance:		Residential Construction:			Online Services:	Residential Sales:
Offices:	Y	Property Insurance:		Land Development:	Y		Software/IT:	Specialty:
Hotels/Motels:	Y			Support Services:			Consulting:	
Industrial/Warehouses:				Design/Engineering:				
Other:	Y							

TYPES OF BUSINESS:

Real Estate Holdings & Development

BRANDS/DIVISIONS/AFFILIATES:

Wharf (Holdings) Limited (The)
Wheelock Properties Limited
Harbour City
Times Square in Hong Kong
Harbour Centre Development Ltd
i-CABLE Communications

CONTACTS: *Note: Officers with more than one job title may be intentionally listed here more than once.*

Paul Y. C. Tsui, Exec. Dir.
Paul Y. C. Tsui, CFO
Peter K.C. Woo, Chmn.

Phone: 852-2118-2118	Fax: 852-2118-2018
Toll-Free:	
Address: Wheelock House 20 Pedder St., 23rd Fl., Hong Kong, China	

GROWTH PLANS/SPECIAL FEATURES:

Wheelock and Company Limited (Wheelock & Co), founded in 1857, is an investment holding company based in Hong Kong, with services offered in China and Singapore. The firm operates through two main subsidiaries: The Wharf (Holdings) Limited (Wharf), and Wheelock Properties Limited. Wharf, with consolidated assets of $22.4 billion, focuses on property and infrastructure in Hong Kong and China. Its properties include Harbour City and Times Square in Hong Kong, which offer retail and commercial real estate space. These properties account for half of the subsidiary's total assets. Wharf's group of companies includes Harbour Centre Development, Ltd., a real estate property investor and developer, and i-CABLE Communications, a telecommunications company. Wharf also has over 100 million square feet of investment properties and developable land in China. It is currently developing container terminals in the Pearl River Delta and the Yangtze River Delta and other projects along China's coast. Wheelock & Co has a 50% interest in Wharf Holdings. Wheelock Properties Limited's primary business is property with a land bank of 1.2 million square feet in Hong Kong. It aims to increase its development opportunities in China, having already acquired two sites in the Guangdong province. Wheelock Properties, which is a wholly-owned subsidiary of Wheelock & Co. currently holds approximately 5.55 million square feet in China, and maintains offices in Singapore and Hong Kong. In July 2010, the firm took Wheelock Properties private for $889 million.

FINANCIALS: Sales and profits are in thousands of dollars—add 000 to get the full amount. 2010 Note: Financial information for 2010 was not available for all companies at press time.

2010 Sales: $3,112,860	2010 Profits: $2,599,070	**U.S. Stock Ticker:**
2009 Sales: $2,441,730	2009 Profits: $1,240,510	**Int'l Ticker: 0020** Int'l Exchange: Hong Kong-HKE
2008 Sales: $2,913,850	2008 Profits: $1,219,710	Employees: 13,800
2007 Sales: $2,311,550	2007 Profits: $1,345,510	Fiscal Year Ends: 12/31
2006 Sales: $	2006 Profits: $	Parent Company:

SALARIES/BENEFITS:

Pension Plan:	ESOP Stock Plan:	Profit Sharing:	Top Exec. Salary: $	Bonus: $
Savings Plan:	Stock Purch. Plan:		Second Exec. Salary: $	Bonus: $

OTHER THOUGHTS:

Apparent Women Officers or Directors:
Hot Spot for Advancement for Women/Minorities:

LOCATIONS: ("Y" = Yes)

West:	Southwest:	Midwest:	Southeast:	Northeast:	International:
					Y

WILLIAM LYON HOMES INC

www.lyonhomes.com

Industry Group Code: 2361 Ranks within this company's industry group: Sales: Profits:

Properties:	Financial Services:		Construction/Development:		Investments:	Specialty Services:	Brokerage:	
Apartments:	Mortgages:	Y	Commercial Construction:		REIT:	Property Management:	Commercial Sales:	
Malls/Shopping:	Title Insurance:	Y	Residential Construction:	Y		Online Services:	Residential Sales:	Y
Offices:	Property Insurance:		Land Development:	Y		Software/IT:	Specialty:	
Hotels/Motels:			Support Services:			Consulting:		
Industrial/Warehouses:			Design/Engineering:	Y				
Other:								

TYPES OF BUSINESS:

Residential Construction
Land Development
Home Sales
Home Financing
Home Design
Title Reinsurance

BRANDS/DIVISIONS/AFFILIATES:

William Lyon Mortgage
Duxford Escrow
Duxford Title Reinsurace Company

CONTACTS:
Note: Officers with more than one job title may be intentionally listed here more than once.

William Lyon, Sr., CEO
William H. Lyon, Jr., COO
William H. Lyon, Jr., Pres.
Colin T. Severn, CFO/VP
Maureen L. Singer, VP-Human Resources
Colin T. Severn, Corp. Sec.
Richard S. Robinson, Sr. VP-Finance
Cynthia E. Hardgrave, VP-Tax & Internal Audit
Mary J. Connelly, Sr. VP/Pres., Nevada Div.
W. Thomas Hickox, Sr. VP/Pres., Arizona Div.
Brian W. Doyle, VP/Pres., Southern California Div.
William Lyon, Sr., Chmn.

Phone: 949-833-3600	Fax: 949-476-2178
Toll-Free:	
Address: 4490 Von Karman Ave., Newport Beach, CA 92660 US	

GROWTH PLANS/SPECIAL FEATURES:

William Lyon Homes, Inc. and its subsidiaries design, construct and sell single-family detached and attached homes in California, Arizona and Nevada. The company has four homebuilding operations, which are geographically divided into Southern California, Northern California, Arizona and Nevada and include both wholly-owned projects and projects being developed in unconsolidated joint ventures. The majority of the firm's home closings occur in California. William Lyon markets its homes through about 20 sales locations; its homes range in price from $99,000 to $1,200,000. The company offers a wide range of homes, primarily emphasizing sales to the entry-level and move-up homebuyer markets.   Since its founding in 1956 as a company that provided homes for military families, William Lyon and its joint ventures have sold over 100,000 homes. Subsidiaries William Lyon Mortgage, Duxford Escrow and Duxford Title Reinsurance Company provide home financing loans, title reinsurance and financial assistance to William Lyon customers. In the near future, the company expects to temporarily suspend all development, sales and marketing activities at 10 of its actively-selling projects which are in the early stages of development.

FINANCIALS:
Sales and profits are in thousands of dollars—add 000 to get the full amount. 2010 Note: Financial information for 2010 was not available for all companies at press time.

2010 Sales: $	2010 Profits: $	U.S. Stock Ticker: Private
2009 Sales: $309,243	2009 Profits: $-20,525	Int'l Ticker: Int'l Exchange:
2008 Sales: $526,078	2008 Profits: $-111,638	Employees:
2007 Sales: $1,105,357	2007 Profits: $-349,408	Fiscal Year Ends: 12/31
2006 Sales: $	2006 Profits: $	Parent Company:

SALARIES/BENEFITS:

Pension Plan:	ESOP Stock Plan:	Profit Sharing:	Top Exec. Salary: $	Bonus: $
Savings Plan:	Stock Purch. Plan:		Second Exec. Salary: $	Bonus: $

OTHER THOUGHTS:

Apparent Women Officers or Directors: 3
Hot Spot for Advancement for Women/Minorities: Y

LOCATIONS: ("Y" = Yes)

West:	Southwest:	Midwest:	Southeast:	Northeast:	International:
Y	Y				

WOLSELEY PLC

www.wolseley.com

Industry Group Code: 4233 Ranks within this company's industry group: Sales: 1   Profits: 3

Properties:	Financial Services:	Construction/Development:		Investments:	Specialty Services:	Brokerage:
Apartments:	Mortgages:	Commercial Construction:		REIT:	Property Management:	Commercial Sales:
Malls/Shopping:	Title Insurance:	Residential Construction:			Online Services:	Residential Sales:
Offices:	Property Insurance:	Land Development:			Software/IT:	Specialty:
Hotels/Motels:		Support Services:	Y		Consulting:	
Industrial/Warehouses:		Design/Engineering:				
Other:						

TYPES OF BUSINESS:

Building Materials Wholesale Distribution
Plumbing & Heating Products Distribution

BRANDS/DIVISIONS/AFFILIATES:

Ferguson Enterprises Inc
Wolseley Canada
Reseau Pro
Panofrance
Cerland
Brosette Batiment
Tobler
Wasco-Kopex

CONTACTS: *Note: Officers with more than one job title may be intentionally listed here more than once.*

Ian K. Meakins, CEO
John Martin, CFO
Richard Shoylekov, General Counsel/Group Company Sec.
Gareth Davis, Chmn.
Frank W. Roach, CEO-North America

Phone: 41-41-723-22-30	**Fax:** 41-41-723-22-31
Toll-Free:	
Address: Grafenauweg 10, Zug, CH-6301 Switzerland	

GROWTH PLANS/SPECIAL FEATURES:

Wolseley plc is one of the world's largest distributors of residential construction materials, including plumbing, building and heating equipment. It operates over 4,100 branches in 25 countries across Europe and North America, dividing its business into six geographic divisions: the U.S.; Canada; U.K.; Nordic; France; and Central and Eastern Europe. Its U.S. subsidiary, Ferguson Enterprises, Inc., operates 1,241 locations and primarily sells equipment such as heating, ventilation and air conditioning (HVAC) supplies; pipes, valves, hydrants and other plumbing supplies; and fire protection systems. Ferguson and Wolseley have integrated their operations, but maintain separate brands. Wolseley's U.S. building materials distribution segment is one of the largest wholesalers and retailers of lumber and building materials to professional contractors in the U.S.   This segment supplies lumber and building materials, including value-added pre-assembled components such as roof and floor trusses and wall panels and floor systems, doors, windows and staircases, to house builders and professional contractors. The company's Canadian operations function similarly to its U.S. businesses. The firm's primary U.K. operations include plumbing and heating parts; construction materials; pipe and climate products; and other businesses involved in interior walls, electrical materials and bathroom products. Wolseley's Nordic operations primarily provide building materials to the Danish, Swedish, Norwegian and Finnish markets.   Its French segment businesses include Reseau Pro, a distributor of building materials; Panofrance, a provider of timber and interior wood products; Softwood, a marketer of processed wood; Cerland, which specializes in garden furniture; and Brosette Batiment, a provider of plumbing and HVAC materials. The company's Central and Eastern Europe division operates Tobler, OAG, Wasco-Kopex and Manzardo, which are Swiss, Austrian, Dutch and Italian providers of plumbing and HVAC materials, respectively. Altogether, the European countries host about 2,700 of the firm's branches. In August 2010, the firm sold its Brandon Hire Limited business to Rutland Partners.

FINANCIALS: Sales and profits are in thousands of dollars—add 000 to get the full amount. 2010 Note: Financial information for 2010 was not available for all companies at press time.

2010 Sales: $22,003,900	2010 Profits: $-566,640	**U.S. Stock Ticker:**
2009 Sales: $23,382,600	2009 Profits: $-189,930	**Int'l Ticker: WOS** Int'l Exchange: London-LSE
2008 Sales: $24,071,500	2008 Profits: $437,820	Employees: 47,000
2007 Sales: $23,594,400	2007 Profits: $1,095,280	Fiscal Year Ends: 7/31
2006 Sales: $26,384,800	2006 Profits: $950,400	Parent Company:

SALARIES/BENEFITS:

Pension Plan:	ESOP Stock Plan:	Profit Sharing:	Top Exec. Salary: $	Bonus: $
Savings Plan:	Stock Purch. Plan:		Second Exec. Salary: $	Bonus: $

OTHER THOUGHTS:

Apparent Women Officers or Directors:
Hot Spot for Advancement for Women/Minorities:

LOCATIONS: ("Y" = Yes)

West:	Southwest:	Midwest:	Southeast:	Northeast:	International:
Y	Y	Y	Y	Y	Y

WORLDMARK BY WYNDHAM INC

www.worldmarktheclub.com

Industry Group Code: 561599 Ranks within this company's industry group: Sales: Profits:

Properties:		Financial Services:	Construction/Development:	Investments:	Specialty Services:		Brokerage:
Apartments:		Mortgages:	Commercial Construction:	REIT:	Property Management:	Y	Commercial Sales:
Malls/Shopping:		Title Insurance:	Residential Construction:		Online Services:		Residential Sales:
Offices:		Property Insurance:	Land Development:		Software/IT:		Specialty:
Hotels/Motels:	Y		Support Services:		Consulting:		
Industrial/Warehouses:			Design/Engineering:				
Other:	Y						

TYPES OF BUSINESS:

Timeshare Resorts
Property Management

BRANDS/DIVISIONS/AFFILIATES:

Wyndham Worldwide
Wyndham Vacation Ownership
WorldMark, The Club
Resort Condominiums International

CONTACTS: *Note: Officers with more than one job title may be intentionally listed here more than once.*

Franz S. Hanning, Pres./CEO-Wyndham Vacation Ownership

Phone: 425-498-2500	Fax: 425-498-3050
Toll-Free:	
Address: 9805 Willows Rd., Redmond, WA 98052 US	

GROWTH PLANS/SPECIAL FEATURES:

WorldMark by Wyndham, Inc. (formerly Trendwest Resorts, Inc.), a wholly-owned subsidiary of Wyndham Worldwide, develops and markets the vacation ownership program WorldMark, The Club. It is one of the three brands operated by Wyndham Vacation Ownership, another subsidiary of Wyndham Worldwide. Unlike traditional timeshare owners, who have access to a specific time at a specific place, WorldMark member-owners purchase annually-renewed credits, which can be spent like currency to reserve vacations in WorldMark resorts. Among other this, this gives member-owners flexibility over vacation dates and locations. The firm operates more than 60 WorldMark resorts mostly in the U.S., with additional locations in Canada, Mexico, the Caribbean and the South Pacific. Most of the resorts are designed to be a short drive away from major metropolitan areas, and the remaining resorts are in exotic locations, such as those in Hawaii and Fiji. Resorts are often located near golf courses, beaches, sightseeing locations, hiking trails, romantic getaways, shopping centers, skiing slopes or family-friendly entertainment. A typical resort room includes a stocked kitchen; laundry facilities; television and video player; stereo; fireplace; private deck with access to swimming pools; indoor and outdoor spas; exercise rooms; arcade games; and sports facilities. Its WorldMark, The Club program has over 270,000 member-owners. The firm also operates a vacation exchange partnership with Resort Condominiums International (RCI), one of the largest vacation ownership companies in the world. This partnership grants WorldMark, The Club member-owners access to thousands of resorts worldwide, for an exchange fee.

Employees of Wyndham Vacation Ownership receive medical, dental and vision plans; a 401(k) plan; long- and short-term disability benefits; an educational assistance plan; adoption assistance; domestic partner benefits; paid time off; an employee assistance program; and discounts on various products and services, including hotels.

FINANCIALS: Sales and profits are in thousands of dollars—add 000 to get the full amount. 2010 Note: Financial information for 2010 was not available for all companies at press time.

2010 Sales: $	2010 Profits: $	**U.S. Stock Ticker: Subsidiary**
2009 Sales: $	2009 Profits: $	**Int'l Ticker:** Int'l Exchange:
2008 Sales: $	2008 Profits: $	Employees:
2007 Sales: $	2007 Profits: $	Fiscal Year Ends: 12/31
2006 Sales: $	2006 Profits: $	Parent Company: WYNDHAM WORLDWIDE

SALARIES/BENEFITS:

Pension Plan:	ESOP Stock Plan:	Profit Sharing:	Top Exec. Salary: $	Bonus: $
Savings Plan: Y	Stock Purch. Plan:		Second Exec. Salary: $	Bonus: $

OTHER THOUGHTS:

Apparent Women Officers or Directors:
Hot Spot for Advancement for Women/Minorities:

LOCATIONS: ("Y" = Yes)

West:	Southwest:	Midwest:	Southeast:	Northeast:	International:
Y	Y	Y	Y		Y

WP CAREY & CO LLC

www.wpcarey.com

Industry Group Code: 5311 Ranks within this company's industry group: Sales: 28   Profits: 21

Properties:		Financial Services:	Construction/Development:	Investments:		Specialty Services:		Brokerage:	
Apartments:		Mortgages:	Commercial Construction:	REIT:	Y	Property Management:	Y	Commercial Sales:	Y
Malls/Shopping:		Title Insurance:	Residential Construction:			Online Services:		Residential Sales:	
Offices:	Y	Property Insurance:	Land Development:			Software/IT:		Specialty:	
Hotels/Motels:			Support Services:			Consulting:			
Industrial/Warehouses:	Y		Design/Engineering:						
Other:									

TYPES OF BUSINESS:

Real Estate Operations
Commercial Properties
Property Management & Leasing
Real Estate Financing
Commercial Construction
Commercial Brokerage

BRANDS/DIVISIONS/AFFILIATES:

Corporate Property Associates 14 Inc
Corporate Property Associates 15 Inc
Corporate Property Associates 16-Global Inc
Corporate Property Associates 17-Global Inc

CONTACTS:
Note: Officers with more than one job title may be intentionally listed here more than once.
Trevor Bond, CEO
Thomas E. Zacharias, COO
Trevor Bond, Pres.
Mark J. DeCesaris, CFO
Paul Marcotrigiano, Chief Legal Officer
Susan C. Hyde, Dir.-Investor Rel./Corp. Sec.
Thomas Ridings, Chief Acct. Officer
John D. Miller, Chief Investment Officer
Christopher Franklin, Exec. Dir.
Jiwei Yuan, Exec. Dir.
Anne Coolidge Taylor, Managing Dir.
William P. Carey, Chmn.
H. Cabot Lodge, III, Head-European Investments

Phone: 212-492-1100	Fax: 212-492-8922
Toll-Free: 800-972-2739	
Address: 50 Rockefeller Plz., New York, NY 10020 US	

GROWTH PLANS/SPECIAL FEATURES:

W.P. Carey & Co., LLC is a real estate advisory and investment company that invests primarily in commercial properties that are each triple-net leased to single corporate tenants, domestically and internationally. Founded in 1973, the company is one of the world's largest publicly traded limited liability companies; it has nearly $10 billion in assets, owning approximately 880 commercial and industrial facilities in 15 countries, mainly in Europe and the U.S. The company operates in two segments: investment management, which generates approximately 70% of the firm's revenue; and real estate ownership, 30%. The investment management segment, operating mainly through various subsidiaries, consists primarily of advising REITs (Real Estate Investment Trusts) that it sponsors, including Corporate Property Associates 14 Incorporated (CPA 14, Inc.), CPA 15, Inc., CPA 16-Global, Inc. and CPA 17-Global, Inc., which it collectively refers to as the CPA REITs. The firm provides various services to the CPA REITs, including day-to-day management, transaction related services and asset management. The real estate ownership segment typically acquires a property and leases it back to the tenant company (referred to as sale-leaseback) on a triple-net long-term basis, meaning the tenant company bears the responsibility for maintaining the premises, insuring the building and paying real estate taxes, among other operating costs. As a result, the tenant company preserves operational control of the property and benefits from the immediate access to capital, which can be used to improve its balance sheet, fund future growth or reduce debt. Most of the firm's real estate acquisitions in recent years have been done on behalf of the CPA REITs. In May 2010, W.P. Carey acquired a 106-suite select service hotel located in Hillsboro, Oregon; and acquired (through CPA 17) two office facilities in Tampa, Florida, from Brookfield Real Estate Opportunity Group. In December 2010, CPA 14 agreed to merge into CPA 16.

FINANCIALS:
Sales and profits are in thousands of dollars—add 000 to get the full amount. 2010 Note: Financial information for 2010 was not available for all companies at press time.

2010 Sales: $273,910	2010 Profits: $73,972	**U.S. Stock Ticker:** WPC	
2009 Sales: $232,350	2009 Profits: $69,023	**Int'l Ticker:**	Int'l Exchange:
2008 Sales: $234,700	2008 Profits: $78,047	Employees:	
2007 Sales: $257,956	2007 Profits: $79,252	Fiscal Year Ends: 12/31	
2006 Sales: $267,487	2006 Profits: $86,303	Parent Company:	

SALARIES/BENEFITS:

Pension Plan:	ESOP Stock Plan:	Profit Sharing: Y	Top Exec. Salary: $600,000	Bonus: $985,000
Savings Plan: Y	Stock Purch. Plan:		Second Exec. Salary: $300,000	Bonus: $880,000

OTHER THOUGHTS:

Apparent Women Officers or Directors: 4
Hot Spot for Advancement for Women/Minorities: Y

LOCATIONS: ("Y" = Yes)

West:	Southwest:	Midwest:	Southeast:	Northeast:	International:
Y	Y			Y	Y

WS ATKINS PLC

www.atkinsglobal.com

Industry Group Code: 541330 Ranks within this company's industry group: Sales: 6   Profits: 3

Properties:	Financial Services:	Construction/Development:		Investments:	Specialty Services:		Brokerage:
Apartments:	Mortgages:	Commercial Construction:		REIT:	Property Management:		Commercial Sales:
Malls/Shopping:	Title Insurance:	Residential Construction:			Online Services:		Residential Sales:
Offices:	Property Insurance:	Land Development:			Software/IT:		Specialty:
Hotels/Motels:		Support Services:	Y		Consulting:	Y	
Industrial/Warehouses:		Design/Engineering:	Y				
Other:							

TYPES OF BUSINESS:

Engineering Services-Building Design
Infrastructure & Transportation Engineering
Consulting
Technology Support Services

BRANDS/DIVISIONS/AFFILIATES:

Gimsing & Madsen A/S

CONTACTS: *Note: Officers with more than one job title may be intentionally listed here more than once.*

Keith Clarke, CEO
Heath Drewett, Dir.-Finance
Alun Griffiths, Dir.-Human Resources
Sara Lipscombe, Dir.-Comm
Richard Barrett, Managing Dir.-Middle East
Richard Hall, Managing Dir.-Faithful & Gould
Neil Thomas, Managing Dir.-Highways & Transportation
Allan Cook, Chmn.
Samson Sin, Managing Dir.-Atkins China

Phone: 44-372-726-140	Fax: 44-372-740-055
Toll-Free:	
Address: Woodcote Grove, Ashley Rd., Epsom, Surrey KT18 5BW UK	

GROWTH PLANS/SPECIAL FEATURES:

WS Atkins plc, an engineering consultancy company, plans, designs and enables delivery of complex infrastructure and buildings, primarily in the U.K. It has six primary business segments: Design and Engineering Solutions; Highways and Transportation; Rail; Middle East, China and Europe; Management and Project Services; and Asset Management. The Design and Engineering Solutions segment operates in the following areas: water, nuclear, defense, environment, oil/gas, urban development, buildings, communications, aerospace, education and other. The Highways and Transportation segment is involved in designing new roads; developing intelligent transport systems; transport planning; road improvements; integrated road network management; and road maintenance management. The Rail segment offers electrification, civil and signaling engineering services, as well as strategic planning, systems integration, asset management and safety specialist services. The Middle East, China and Europe segment offers engineering, design and project management services for infrastructure including transportation and buildings. Project and cost management consultancy subsidiary Faithful & Gould, Inc. operates in both the Middle East and China and Management and Project Services segments. The Management and Project Services segment mainly offers IT and management consultancy, as well as cost, project and program management services. Lastly, the Asset Management segment manages property for private and public sector clients. Atkins has over 200 offices in approximately 27 countries and ongoing projects in more than 80. In November 2010, the company acquired bridge and structural design consultancy group Gimsing & Madsen A/S. In March 2011, the firm acquired RWE npower's Bellshill Technical Services division's Technical Services Scotland consultancy and technical support group.

FINANCIALS: Sales and profits are in thousands of dollars—add 000 to get the full amount. 2010 Note: Financial information for 2010 was not available for all companies at press time.

2010 Sales: $2,314,280	2010 Profits: $181,490	**U.S. Stock Ticker:**
2009 Sales: $2,287,330	2009 Profits: $129,500	**Int'l Ticker: ATK** Int'l Exchange: London-LSE
2008 Sales: $2,076,210	2008 Profits: $148,360	Employees: 17,026
2007 Sales: $1,840,040	2007 Profits: $-85,010	Fiscal Year Ends: 3/31
2006 Sales: $2,150,000	2006 Profits: $113,800	Parent Company:

SALARIES/BENEFITS:

Pension Plan:	ESOP Stock Plan:	Profit Sharing:	Top Exec. Salary: $	Bonus: $345,327
Savings Plan:	Stock Purch. Plan:		Second Exec. Salary: $	Bonus: $

OTHER THOUGHTS:

Apparent Women Officers or Directors: 4
Hot Spot for Advancement for Women/Minorities: Y

LOCATIONS: ("Y" = Yes)

West:	Southwest:	Midwest:	Southeast:	Northeast:	International:
Y	Y	Y	Y	Y	Y

WYNDHAM VACATION OWNERSHIP

www.wyndhamworldwide.com/about/wyndham_vacation_ownership.cfm

Industry Group Code: 561599 Ranks within this company's industry group: Sales: Profits:

Properties:	Financial Services:	Construction/Development:	Investments:	Specialty Services:	Brokerage:
Apartments:	Mortgages:	Commercial Construction:	REIT:	Property Management:	Commercial Sales:
Malls/Shopping:	Title Insurance:	Residential Construction:		Online Services:	Residential Sales:
Offices:	Property Insurance:	Land Development:		Software/IT:	Specialty: Y
Hotels/Motels: Y		Support Services:		Consulting:	
Industrial/Warehouses:		Design/Engineering:			
Other: Y					

TYPES OF BUSINESS:

Resorts
Timeshare Resorts
Property Management

BRANDS/DIVISIONS/AFFILIATES:

Wyndham Worldwide
Wyndham Vacation Resorts
Fairfield Resorts Inc.

CONTACTS: *Note: Officers with more than one job title may be intentionally listed here more than once.*

Franz S. Hanning, CEO
Franz S. Hanning, Pres.
Mike Hug, CFO
Jeff Myers, Chief Sales & Mktg. Officer/Exec. VP
Adam Schwartz, Sr. VP-Corp. Rel.
Mike Hug, Exec. VP-Finance
Mark Johnson, Sr. VP-Consumer Finance
Gary Byrd, Exec. VP-Hospitality Svcs.
Geoff Richards, Exec. VP-Global Sales & Mktg. Oper.

Phone: 407-370-5200	**Fax:** 407-370-5143
Toll-Free: 800-251-8736	
Address: 8427 SouthPark Cir., Orlando, FL 32819 US	

GROWTH PLANS/SPECIAL FEATURES:

Wyndham Vacation Ownership (WVO), a subsidiary of Wyndham Worldwide Corp., is one of the world's leading time share companies. The firm markets point-based vacation ownership through the brands Wyndham Vacation Resorts and Trendwest. WVO primarily operates through Wyndham Vacation Resorts (WVR), formerly Fairfield Resorts, Inc. Through WVR, it markets, sells and finances vacation ownership interests and develops vacation ownership resorts. Additionally, WVR provides property management services to property owners' associations. The firm maintains over 160 resort properties, as well as over 20,500 individual vacation ownership units and more than 814,000 owners of vacation ownership interests across the U.S., Canada, Mexico, the Caribbean and the South Pacific. Domestic locations can be found in every region of the U.S., including Texas, California, Florida and Massachusetts. WVR's units are fully furnished, and many include washers/dryers, whirlpool spas, fireplaces and VCRs. The company offers travel discounts and other member specials to all vacation ownership members. In 2010, WVR opened new properties in Orlando, Florida and Myrtle Beach, South Carolina; and added inventory at existing properties in Orlando, Florida.

Through Wyndham Worldwide Corp., the company offers employees a variety of benefits including medical and life insurance; short- and long-term disability; a 401(k); an employee stock purchase program; adoption assistance; educational assistance; and discounts.

FINANCIALS: Sales and profits are in thousands of dollars—add 000 to get the full amount. 2010 Note: Financial information for 2010 was not available for all companies at press time.

2010 Sales: $	2010 Profits: $	U.S. Stock Ticker: Subsidiary
2009 Sales: $	2009 Profits: $	Int'l Ticker: Int'l Exchange:
2008 Sales: $	2008 Profits: $	Employees:
2007 Sales: $	2007 Profits: $	Fiscal Year Ends: 12/31
2006 Sales: $	2006 Profits: $	Parent Company: WYNDHAM WORLDWIDE

SALARIES/BENEFITS:

Pension Plan:	ESOP Stock Plan:	Profit Sharing:	Top Exec. Salary: $	Bonus: $
Savings Plan: Y	Stock Purch. Plan: Y		Second Exec. Salary: $	Bonus: $

OTHER THOUGHTS:

Apparent Women Officers or Directors:
Hot Spot for Advancement for Women/Minorities:

LOCATIONS: ("Y" = Yes)

West:	Southwest:	Midwest:	Southeast:	Northeast:	International:
Y	Y	Y	Y	Y	Y

WYNDHAM WORLDWIDE

www.wyndhamworldwide.com

Industry Group Code: 721110 Ranks within this company's industry group: Sales: 4   Profits: 5

Properties:	Financial Services:	Construction/Development:	Investments:	Specialty Services:	Brokerage:
Apartments:	Mortgages:	Commercial Construction:	REIT:	Property Management: Y	Commercial Sales:
Malls/Shopping:	Title Insurance:	Residential Construction:		Online Services:	Residential Sales:
Offices:	Property Insurance:	Land Development:		Software/IT:	Specialty:
Hotels/Motels: Y		Support Services:		Consulting:	
Industrial/Warehouses:		Design/Engineering:			
Other: Y					

TYPES OF BUSINESS:

Hotels, Motels & Resorts
Property Management
Hotel Development
Vacation Property Exchange and Rental
Timeshare Resorts
Franchising
Vacation Ownership

BRANDS/DIVISIONS/AFFILIATES:

Hoseasons
Wingate Inns
Ramada
Days Inn
Tryp
Howard Johnson
AmeriHost
Trendwest

CONTACTS: Note: Officers with more than one job title may be intentionally listed here more than once.

Stephen P. Holmes, CEO
Thomas G. Conforti, CFO/Exec. VP
Betsy O'Rourke, Sr. VP-Mktg.
Mary R. Falvey, Chief Human Resources Officer/Exec. VP
Scott G. McLester, General Counsel/Exec. VP
Betsy O'Rourke, Sr. VP-Comm.
Nicola Rossi, Sr. VP/Chief Acct. Officer
Franz S. Hanning, Pres./CEO-Wyndham Vacation Ownership
Eric A. Danziger, Pres./CEO-Wyndham Hotel Group
Geoff Ballotti, Pres./CEO-Wyndham Exchange & Rentals
Tom Anderson, Exec. VP/Chief Real Estate Dev. Officer
Stephen P. Holmes, Chmn.

Phone: 973-753-6000	Fax:
Toll-Free:	
Address: 22 Sylvan Way, Parsippany, NJ 07054 US	

GROWTH PLANS/SPECIAL FEATURES:

Wyndham Worldwide (WW) is a hospitality company offering individual consumers and business customers an array of hospitality products and services, as well as various accommodation alternatives and price ranges through its portfolio of world-renowned brands. The company encompasses over 7,210 hotels representing over 612,700 rooms on six continents and more than 900 hotels representing 102,700 rooms in development. Wyndham Hotel Group offers the TripRewards loyalty program. Group RCI, the firm's vacation exchange business, offers its 3.8 million members access for specified periods to over 4,000 vacation properties in 100 countries around the world. WW also offers Wyndham Vacation Ownership, which includes marketing and sales of vacation ownership interests, consumer financing in conjunction with the purchase of vacation ownership interests, property management services to property owners' associations and development and acquisition of vacation ownership resorts. Wyndham Vacation has over 160 vacation ownership resorts in U.S., Canada, Mexico, the Caribbean and the South Pacific that represent over 814,000 owners of vacation ownership interests. WW's extensive portfolio of brands includes Wyndham Hotels and Resorts; Ramada; Days Inn; Super 8; Wyndham Rewards; Wingate by Wyndham; Microtel; RCI; The Registry Collection; Endless Vacation Rentals; Landal GreenParks; Cottages4You; Novasol; Wyndham Vacation Resorts; and WorldMark by Wyndham. In March 2010, WW announced that its Registry Collection program welcomed 24 new resort destinations, increasing its total number of properties to 175. In 2010, the firm acquired four hotel brands: Tryp, ResortQuest, James Villa Holidays and Hoseasons.

Employees are offerd business travel accident, long-term disability, life, personal accident, medical, dental and vision insurance; flexible spending accounts; a 401(k) plan; an educational assistance program; an employee assistance program; adoption reimbursement; flexible work arrangements; and travel discounts.

FINANCIALS: Sales and profits are in thousands of dollars—add 000 to get the full amount. 2010 Note: Financial information for 2010 was not available for all companies at press time.

2010 Sales: $3,851,000	2010 Profits: $379,000	**U.S. Stock Ticker: WYN**
2009 Sales: $3,750,000	2009 Profits: $293,000	**Int'l Ticker:** Int'l Exchange:
2008 Sales: $4,281,000	2008 Profits: $-1,074,000	Employees: 26,400
2007 Sales: $4,360,000	2007 Profits: $403,000	Fiscal Year Ends: 12/31
2006 Sales: $3,842,000	2006 Profits: $287,000	Parent Company:

SALARIES/BENEFITS:

Pension Plan:	ESOP Stock Plan:	Profit Sharing:	Top Exec. Salary: $1,085,011	Bonus: $2,712,528
Savings Plan: Y	Stock Purch. Plan:		Second Exec. Salary: $606,008	Bonus: $825,000

OTHER THOUGHTS:

Apparent Women Officers or Directors: 4
Hot Spot for Advancement for Women/Minorities: Y

LOCATIONS: ("Y" = Yes)

West:	Southwest:	Midwest:	Southeast:	Northeast:	International:
Y	Y	Y	Y	Y	Y

WYNN RESORTS LIMITED

www.wynnresorts.com

Industry Group Code: 721120 Ranks within this company's industry group: Sales: 4   Profits: 3

Properties:	Financial Services:	Construction/Development:	Investments:	Specialty Services:	Brokerage:
Apartments:	Mortgages:	Commercial Construction:	REIT:	Property Management:	Commercial Sales:
Malls/Shopping:	Title Insurance:	Residential Construction:		Online Services:	Residential Sales:
Offices:	Property Insurance:	Land Development:		Software/IT:	Specialty:
Hotels/Motels: Y		Support Services:		Consulting:	
Industrial/Warehouses:		Design/Engineering:			
Other: Y					

TYPES OF BUSINESS:

Hotel Casinos

BRANDS/DIVISIONS/AFFILIATES:

Wynn Las Vegas, LLC
Wynn Resorts (Macau), S.A.
Encore Suites at Wynn Las Vegas
Encore Suites at Wynn Macau
PokerStarsWynn.com

CONTACTS: *Note: Officers with more than one job title may be intentionally listed here more than once.*

Stephen A. Wynn, CEO
Marc D. Schorr, COO
Matt Maddox, CFO
Linda Chen, Pres., Wynn Int'l Mktg., Ltd.
John Strzemp, Chief Admin. Officer/Exec. VP
Kim Sinatra, General Counsel/Sec./Sr. VP
Matt Maddox, Treas.
Marilyn W. Spiegel, Pres., Wynn Las Vegas, LLC
Maurice Wooden, COO-Wynn Las Vegas, LLC
Scott Peterson, Sr. VP/CFO-Wynn Las Vegas, LLC
Stephen A. Wynn, Chmn.
Ian M. Coughlan, Pres., Wynn Resorts (Macau), S.A.

Phone: 702-770-7555	Fax:
Toll-Free:	
Address: 3131 Las Vegas Blvd. S., Las Vegas, NV 89109 US	

GROWTH PLANS/SPECIAL FEATURES:

Wynn Resorts Limited is a developer, owner and operator of destination casino resorts. It owns and operates two destination casino resorts: The Wynn Las Vegas on the Strip in Las Vegas, Nevada, which includes Encore at Wynn Las Vegas; and the Wynn Macau in the Macau Special Administrative Region of China. Wynn Las Vegas offers 2,716 rooms and suites. The 111,000-square-foot casino features 147 table games, a baccarat salon, private VIP gaming rooms, a poker room, 1,842 slot machines, and a race and sports book. The resort's 22 food and beverage outlets feature five fine dining restaurants. Other amenities include two nightclubs; a spa and salon; a Ferrari and Maserati automobile dealership; wedding chapels; an 18-hole golf course; 223,000 square feet of meeting space; and a 74,000 square foot retail promenade featuring boutiques from Alexander McQueen, Cartier, Chanel, and Louis Vuitton. Wynn Las Vegas also has a showroom which features Le Reve, a water-based theatrical production. The Encore at Wynn Las Vegas features 2,034 suites, a 76,000 square feet casino with 95 table games, a baccarat salon, 778 slot machines and a sports book. It also features 13 food and beverage outlets; two night clubs; a spa and salon; meeting space; and 27,000 square feet of upscale retail outlets. The Wynn Macau features 595 hotel rooms and suites; 410 table games, 935 slot machines; a poker room; six restaurants; a spa and salon; lounges; meeting facilities; and 48,000 square feet of retail space. The company's newest hotel, the Encore at Wynn Macau, features 410 luxury suites; four villas; approximately 34,000 square feet of casino gaming space, including a sky casino, containing 60 table games and 80 slot machines; two restaurants; a luxury spa; and retail brands Chanel, Piaget and Cartier. In March 2011, Wynn Resorts and PokerStars agreed to launch Internet poker site PokerStarsWynn.com.

FINANCIALS: Sales and profits are in thousands of dollars—add 000 to get the full amount. 2010 Note: Financial information for 2010 was not available for all companies at press time.

2010 Sales: $4,184,698	2010 Profits: $160,127	**U.S. Stock Ticker: WYNN**
2009 Sales: $3,045,611	2009 Profits: $20,654	**Int'l Ticker:** Int'l Exchange:
2008 Sales: $2,987,324	2008 Profits: $210,479	Employees: 16,405
2007 Sales: $2,687,519	2007 Profits: $196,336	Fiscal Year Ends: 12/31
2006 Sales: $1,432,257	2006 Profits: $628,728	Parent Company:

SALARIES/BENEFITS:

Pension Plan:	ESOP Stock Plan:	Profit Sharing:	Top Exec. Salary: $2,953,125	Bonus: $4,062,500
Savings Plan: Y	Stock Purch. Plan:		Second Exec. Salary: $1,817,308	Bonus: $2,000,000

OTHER THOUGHTS:

Apparent Women Officers or Directors: 5
Hot Spot for Advancement for Women/Minorities: Y

LOCATIONS: ("Y" = Yes)

West:	Southwest:	Midwest:	Southeast:	Northeast:	International:
Y					Y

XANTERRA PARKS AND RESORTS

www.xanterra.com

Industry Group Code: 721110 Ranks within this company's industry group: Sales: Profits:

Properties:	Financial Services:	Construction/Development:	Investments:	Specialty Services:	Brokerage:
Apartments:	Mortgages:	Commercial Construction:	REIT:	Property Management:	Commercial Sales:
Malls/Shopping:	Title Insurance:	Residential Construction:		Online Services:	Residential Sales:
Offices:	Property Insurance:	Land Development:		Software/IT:	Specialty:
Hotels/Motels: Y		Support Services:		Consulting:	
Industrial/Warehouses:		Design/Engineering:			
Other:					

TYPES OF BUSINESS:

Hotel & Restaurant Management
Conference Center Management

BRANDS/DIVISIONS/AFFILIATES:

Anshutz Company (The)
Xanterra South Rim LLC
Grand Canyon Railway Hotel, LLC

CONTACTS: *Note: Officers with more than one job title may be intentionally listed here more than once.*

Andrew N. Todd, CEO
Andrew N. Todd, Pres.
Michael F. Welch, CFO/VP-Finance
Dave M. Hartvigsen, VP-Mktg. & Sales
Kate A. Longenecker, VP-Human Resources
John W. Wimmer, CIO
Richard Rabinoff, Dir.-Hospitality Tech.
Susan J. Jessup, Dir.-Retail Merch.
Kirk H. Anderson, General Counsel/VP
Susan Jessup, Dir.-Oper.
Robert T. Tow, VP-Bus. Dev.
Lonnie S. Clark, Controller
Stephen W. Tedder, VP-National Parks
Hans Desai, VP-State Parks & Resorts
Chris R. Lane, VP-Environmental Affairs
Bill J. Bub, VP-Retail
Rebecca L. Ritter, Dir.-Purchasing

Phone: 303-600-3400	Fax: 303-600-3600
Toll-Free:	
Address: 6312 South Fiddlers Green Cir., Ste. 600N, Greenwood Village, CO 80111 US	

GROWTH PLANS/SPECIAL FEATURES:

Xanterra Parks and Resorts is a parks concessions management company operating in national parks and state parks across the U.S. The company operates hotels, including the world-famous Old Faithful Inn in Yellowstone National Park and the El Tovar in Grand Canyon National Park; 68 restaurants; and gift shops in some of the U.S.'s most popular parks, including Yellowstone, Zion, Crater Lake, Death Valley, Rocky Mountain and Petrified Forest National Parks. Additionally, the company operates conference facilities, premium golf courses, tennis courts and spa amenities. Outside of its national park operations, Xanterra offers services at Mount Rushmore National Memorial and nine Ohio state parks. Other operations of the firm include resorts in Napa Valley and Death Valley, California; Grand Canyon National Park through affiliate Xanterra South Rim, LLC; and the Grand Canyon Railway in Williams, Arizona, via affiliate Grand Canyon Railway Hotel, LLC. The firm is owned by The Anschutz Company.

The firm offers a number of seasonal employment opportunities for both U.S. citizens and foreign nationals.

FINANCIALS: Sales and profits are in thousands of dollars—add 000 to get the full amount. 2010 Note: Financial information for 2010 was not available for all companies at press time.

2010 Sales: $	2010 Profits: $	U.S. Stock Ticker: Subsidiary
2009 Sales: $	2009 Profits: $	Int'l Ticker: Int'l Exchange:
2008 Sales: $	2008 Profits: $	Employees:
2007 Sales: $	2007 Profits: $	Fiscal Year Ends:
2006 Sales: $	2006 Profits: $	Parent Company: ANSCHUTZ COMPANY (THE)

SALARIES/BENEFITS:

Pension Plan:	ESOP Stock Plan:	Profit Sharing:	Top Exec. Salary: $	Bonus: $
Savings Plan:	Stock Purch. Plan:		Second Exec. Salary: $	Bonus: $

OTHER THOUGHTS:

Apparent Women Officers or Directors: 5
Hot Spot for Advancement for Women/Minorities: Y

LOCATIONS: ("Y" = Yes)

West:	Southwest:	Midwest:	Southeast:	Northeast:	International:
Y	Y	Y			

YIT CORPORATION

www.yitgroup.com

Industry Group Code: 23 Ranks within this company's industry group: Sales: 2   Profits: 2

Properties:	Financial Services:	Construction/Development:		Investments:	Specialty Services:	Brokerage:
Apartments:	Mortgages:	Commercial Construction:	Y	REIT:	Property Management:	Commercial Sales:
Malls/Shopping:	Title Insurance:	Residential Construction:	Y		Online Services:	Residential Sales:
Offices:	Property Insurance:	Land Development:			Software/IT:	Specialty:
Hotels/Motels:		Support Services:	Y		Consulting:	
Industrial/Warehouses:		Design/Engineering:	Y			
Other:						

TYPES OF BUSINESS:

Development of Living Environments
Building Systems
Construction Services
Industrial Services
Network Services

BRANDS/DIVISIONS/AFFILIATES:

YIT Construction Ltd
YIT Industrial and Network Services Ltd
YIT Building Systems Ltd
Carl Christensen Co
Caverion GmbH
Reding AS
NNE Pharmaplan AB
Johnson Controls Systems & Services AB

CONTACTS: *Note: Officers with more than one job title may be intentionally listed here more than once.*

Juhani Pitkakoski, CEO
Juhani Pitkakoski, Pres.
Timo Lehtinen, CFO
Antero Saarilahti, Sr. VP-Human Resources
Antero Saarilahti, Sr. VP-Admin.
Antero Saarilahti, Corp. Sec.
Sakari Toikkanen, Sr. VP-Bus. Dev.
Pekka Frantti, Pres., YIT Industrial & Network Svcs. Ltd.
Tero Kiviniemi, Pres., YIT Construction Svcs.
Arne Malonaes, Head-Building Svcs., Northern Europe
Karl-Walter Schuster, Head-Building Svcs., Central Europe
Henrik Ehrnrooth, Chmn.

Phone: 358-20-433-111	Fax: 358-20-433-3700
Toll-Free:	
Address: PO Box 36, Panuntie 11, Helsinki, 00621 Finland	

GROWTH PLANS/SPECIAL FEATURES:

YIT Corporation is a Helsinki-based company whose mission is to build, develop and maintain a good living environment for people.   The firm, which operates as a group of companies, offers technical infrastructure investment and upkeep services for the property, construction, industry and telecommunications sectors. In all sectors of operations, YIT Group's services cover the entire lifecycle of its projects. The firm's main market areas are the Nordic countries, Central Europe, the Baltic countries and Russia.   YIT's operations are divided into three business segments: Building and Industrial Systems, which accounted for 60% of 2010 revenues; Construction Services Finland, which accounted for 28%; and International Construction Services, accounting for 12%. Building and Industrial Systems offers technical building systems, infrastructure upgrading, building maintenance, industrial piping, tanks and pulp towers, access-control systems, industrial maintenance, and energy-efficiency services. The Construction Services segments are primarily focused on the construction of residential, commercial and industrial properties, as well as the provision of civil engineering, water and environmental services. YIT's strategy for building an international presence is to bolster its construction services in the Baltic countries and Russia, building system services in the Nordic and Baltic countries as well as industrial and data network services in its entire market area.   In July 2010, the company acquired Carl Christensen Co., a Danish heat, water and sanitation systems developer. In September 2010, the firm took control of the operations of Caverion GmbH, a building system services company based in Central Europe.   In October 2010, YIT acquired Reding AS, a Slovakia-based construction company.   In January 2011, the company obtained the clean room contracting operations services of NNE Pharmaplan AB. In March 2011, the firm announced plans to acquire Johnson Controls Systems & Services AB, a Swedish commercial refrigeration firm.

FINANCIALS: Sales and profits are in thousands of dollars—add 000 to get the full amount. 2010 Note: Financial information for 2010 was not available for all companies at press time.

2010 Sales: $5,701,910	2010 Profits: $339,570	**U.S. Stock Ticker:**
2009 Sales: $4,608,410	2009 Profits: $89,110	**Int'l Ticker: YTY1V** Int'l Exchange: Helsinki-Euronext
2008 Sales: $5,245,600	2008 Profits: $176,800	Employees: 25,832
2007 Sales: $4,931,900	2007 Profits: $299,100	Fiscal Year Ends:
2006 Sales: $4,373,400	2006 Profits: $227,400	Parent Company:

SALARIES/BENEFITS:

Pension Plan:	ESOP Stock Plan:	Profit Sharing:	Top Exec. Salary: $	Bonus: $
Savings Plan:	Stock Purch. Plan:		Second Exec. Salary: $	Bonus: $

OTHER THOUGHTS:

Apparent Women Officers or Directors:
Hot Spot for Advancement for Women/Minorities:

LOCATIONS: ("Y" = Yes)

West:	Southwest:	Midwest:	Southeast:	Northeast:	International:
					Y

ZIPREALTY INC   www.ziprealty.com

Industry Group Code: 531210 Ranks within this company's industry group: Sales: 3   Profits: 2

Properties:	Financial Services:	Construction/Development:	Investments:	Specialty Services:		Brokerage:	
Apartments:	Mortgages:	Commercial Construction:	REIT:	Property Management:		Commercial Sales:	
Malls/Shopping:	Title Insurance:	Residential Construction:		Online Services:	Y	Residential Sales:	Y
Offices:	Property Insurance:	Land Development:		Software/IT:		Specialty:	
Hotels/Motels:		Support Services:		Consulting:			
Industrial/Warehouses:		Design/Engineering:					
Other:							

TYPES OF BUSINESS:

Real Estate Brokerage

BRANDS/DIVISIONS/AFFILIATES:

ZipAgent Platform

CONTACTS: *Note: Officers with more than one job title may be intentionally listed here more than once.*

Lanny Baker, CEO
Lanny Baker, Pres.
David A. Rector, CFO/Sr. VP
Robert Yakominich, Sr. VP-Sales
Joan Burke, VP-Human Resources
Joe Trifoglio, CIO/VP
Genevieve Combes, Sr. VP-Tech.
Samantha Harnett, General Counsel/VP/Corp. Sec.
Stefan Peterson, VP-Oper.
Genevieve Combes, Exec. VP-Oper. Strategy
David A. Rector, Chief Acct. Officer/Controller
Donald F. Wood, Chmn.

Phone: 510-735-2600	**Fax:** 510-735-2850
Toll-Free: 800-225-5947	
Address: 2000 Powell St., Ste. 300, Emeryville, CA 94608 US	

GROWTH PLANS/SPECIAL FEATURES:

ZipRealty, Inc. is a full-service residential real estate brokerage firm that utilizes the Internet, proprietary technology, local agents and efficient business processes to provide home buyers and sellers with the appropriate tools for the home-buying process. The company employs a client-centric approach, a sophisticated web site and a proprietary business management technology platform. The firm operates in 23 markets and employs over 2,500 independent sales agents. ZipRealty's web site provides users with direct access to more than 60 comprehensive local Multiple Listing Services (MLS), home listings data, asking prices, home layouts and other features. The company also provides further information such as neighborhood attributes, school district information, comparable home sales data, maps and driving directions. The firm attracts users to its web site through a number of marketing channels, including online advertising, word-of-mouth and traditional media advertisements. The proprietary ZipAgent Platform, or ZAP, automatically matches registered users with local agents who market and provide the company's comprehensive real estate brokerage services, including showing properties to buyers and listing and marketing properties on behalf of its sellers, as well as negotiating, advisory, transaction processing and closing services. The firm has about than 2.5 active registered users and has closed over 100,000 real estate transactions. In January 2011, the company announced restructuring plans which entail ceasing operations in 11 markets and cutting about 25% of its sales and administrative staff.

FINANCIALS: Sales and profits are in thousands of dollars—add 000 to get the full amount. 2010 Note: Financial information for 2010 was not available for all companies at press time.

2010 Sales: $118,696	2010 Profits: $-15,550	**U.S. Stock Ticker:** ZIPR
2009 Sales: $123,130	2009 Profits: $-12,892	**Int'l Ticker:** Int'l Exchange:
2008 Sales: $107,450	2008 Profits: $-13,342	Employees: 3,346
2007 Sales: $103,862	2007 Profits: $-14,884	Fiscal Year Ends: 12/31
2006 Sales: $95,387	2006 Profits: $-20,594	Parent Company:

SALARIES/BENEFITS:

Pension Plan:	ESOP Stock Plan:	Profit Sharing:	Top Exec. Salary: $379,167	Bonus: $122,345
Savings Plan:	Stock Purch. Plan:		Second Exec. Salary: $300,000	Bonus: $61,200

OTHER THOUGHTS:

Apparent Women Officers or Directors: 5
Hot Spot for Advancement for Women/Minorities: Y

LOCATIONS: ("Y" = Yes)

West:	Southwest:	Midwest:	Southeast:	Northeast:	International:
Y	Y	Y	Y	Y	

ADDITIONAL INDEXES

Contents:

INDEX OF FIRMS NOTED AS HOT SPOTS FOR ADVANCEMENT FOR WOMEN & MINORITIES

PARSONS BRINCKERHOFF INC
PENNSYLVANIA REIT
PLUM CREEK TIMBER CO INC
PMI GROUP INC (THE)
POST PROPERTIES INC
PRIME RETAIL INC
PS BUSINESS PARKS INC
PULTEGROUP INC
RADIAN GROUP INC
RE/MAX INTERNATIONAL INC
REALOGY CORPORATION
REALPAGE INC
REALTY INCOME CORP
RED LION HOTELS CORPORATION
REZIDOR HOTEL GROUP AB
ROSEWOOD HOTELS & RESORTS LLC
RXR REALTY
SAHA PATHANA INTER-HOLDING PCL
SHANGRI-LA ASIA LTD
SHIMAO PROPERTY HOLDINGS LTD
SHUN TAK HOLDINGS LIMITED
SONESTA INTERNATIONAL HOTELS CORP
SOVRAN SELF STORAGE INC
STANDARD PACIFIC CORP
STARWOOD HOTELS & RESORTS WORLDWIDE
INC
STV GROUP INC
SUNRISE SENIOR LIVING
TANGER FACTORY OUTLET CENTERS INC
TAUBMAN CENTERS INC
UDR INC
VENTAS INC
WEINGARTEN REALTY INVESTORS
WESTFIELD GROUP (THE)
WILLIAM LYON HOMES INC
WP CAREY & CO LLC
WS ATKINS PLC
WYNDHAM WORLDWIDE
WYNN RESORTS LIMITED
XANTERRA PARKS AND RESORTS
ZIPREALTY INC

INDEX OF SUBSIDIARIES, BRAND NAMES AND AFFILIATIONS

Brand or subsidiary, followed by the name of the related corporation

INDEX OF SUBSIDIARIES, BRAND NAMES AND AFFILIATIONS, CONT.

INDEX OF SUBSIDIARIES, BRAND NAMES AND AFFILIATIONS, CONT.

INDEX OF SUBSIDIARIES, BRAND NAMES AND AFFILIATIONS, CONT.

INDEX OF SUBSIDIARIES, BRAND NAMES AND AFFILIATIONS, CONT.

INDEX OF SUBSIDIARIES, BRAND NAMES AND AFFILIATIONS, CONT.

INDEX OF SUBSIDIARIES, BRAND NAMES AND AFFILIATIONS, CONT.

INDEX OF SUBSIDIARIES, BRAND NAMES AND AFFILIATIONS, CONT.

INDEX OF SUBSIDIARIES, BRAND NAMES AND AFFILIATIONS, CONT.

INDEX OF SUBSIDIARIES, BRAND NAMES AND AFFILIATIONS, CONT.

INDEX OF SUBSIDIARIES, BRAND NAMES AND AFFILIATIONS, CONT.

Furniture Medic; **SERVICEMASTER COMPANY (THE)**
G&I VI Investment South Florida Portfolio, LLC; **EQUITY ONE INC**
Gables Advantage Home Mortgage Program; **GABLES RESIDENTIAL TRUST**
Gables Corporate Accommodations; **GABLES RESIDENTIAL TRUST**
Gables Realty, LP; **GABLES RESIDENTIAL TRUST**
Gables Residential; **TDINDUSTRIES**
Gafisa Vendas; **GAFISA SA**
Gale Construction Company; **MACK-CALI REALTY CORP**
Garco Building Systems; **NCI BUILDING SYSTEMS INC**
Garden Treasures; **LOWE'S COMPANIES INC**
Gaylord Indian Restaurant; **RIO PROPERTIES INC**
Gaylord National Resort & Convention Center; **GAYLORD ENTERTAINMENT CO**
Gaylord Opryland Resort & Convention Center; **GAYLORD ENTERTAINMENT CO**
Gaylord Palms Resort & Convention Center; **GAYLORD ENTERTAINMENT CO**
Gaylord Springs Golf Links; **GAYLORD ENTERTAINMENT CO**
Gaylord Texan Resort & Convention Center; **GAYLORD ENTERTAINMENT CO**
Gaysorn; **HONGKONG LAND HOLDINGS LTD**
GE Capital; **GENERAL ELECTRIC CO (GE)**
GE Capital Aviation Services; **GENERAL ELECTRIC CO (GE)**
GE Energy Infrastructure; **GENERAL ELECTRIC CO (GE)**
GE Healthcare; **GENERAL ELECTRIC CO (GE)**
GE Money; **GE CAPITAL**
GE Real Estate; **ARDEN REALTY INC**
GE Technology Infrastructure; **GENERAL ELECTRIC CO (GE)**
General Electric; **GE CAPITAL**
General Electric Co (GE); **GE CAPITAL REAL ESTATE**
General Growth Properties Inc; **GENERAL GROWTH PROPERTIES INC**
General Jackson Showboat; **GAYLORD ENTERTAINMENT CO**
General Motors Building; **BOSTON PROPERTIES INC**
Genesis Homes; **CHAMPION ENTERPRISES INC**
Geocisa; **GRUPO ACS**
Georgia Gulf Corporation; **ROYAL GROUP INC**
Georgia-Pacific Corp; **FAIRMONT HOMES INC**
GetSmart.com; **LENDINGTREE LLC**
GGP Inc; **GENERAL GROWTH PROPERTIES INC**
GIFTS Software, Inc.; **FIDELITY NATIONAL INFORMATION SERVICES INC**
Gimsing & Madsen A/S; **WS ATKINS PLC**

Glacier; **HOME DEPOT INC**
GMAC Inc; **ALLY FINANCIAL INC**
GMAC Mortgage Corporation; **DITECH.COM**
GO House; **CHAMPION ENTERPRISES INC**
Goff Capital, Inc; **CRESCENT REAL ESTATE EQUITIES LP**
Gold Coast Hotel and Casino; **BOYD GAMING CORP**
Golden Ruler (The); **CENTURY 21 REAL ESTATE LLC**
Golden Tulip Hotels; **GOLDEN TULIP HOSPITALITY GROUP**
Golden Tulip Resort; **GOLDEN TULIP HOSPITALITY GROUP**
Goldfarb Incorporacoes e Construcoes S.A; **PDG REALTY SA EMPREENDIMENTOS E PARTICIPACOES**
Goldman Sachs Group; **AMERICAN CASINO & ENTERTAINMENT PROPERTIES INC**
Gold's Gym International; **TRT HOLDINGS**
Goldston Engineering, Inc.; **CH2M HILL COMPANIES LTD**
Goodstein Management; **FIRSTSERVICE CORPORATION**
Gores Group (The); **STOCK BUILDING SUPPLY INC**
Government Properties Income Trust; **COMMONWEALTH REIT**
G-Prop (Holdings) Limited; **CHINESE ESTATES HOLDINGS LTD**
GradeDec; **HDR INC**
Gran Melia; **SOL MELIA SA**
Grand Canyon Railway Hotel, LLC; **XANTERRA PARKS AND RESORTS**
Grand Gateway 66; **HANG LUNG PROPERTIES LIMITED**
Grand Hotel Europe; **ORIENT-EXPRESS HOTELS LTD**
Grand Hyatt; **HYATT HOTELS CORPORATION**
Grand Ole Opry; **GAYLORD ENTERTAINMENT CO**
Grand Reserve Collection; **DOMINION HOMES INC**
Grande Jolly Srl; **NH HOTELES SA**
Granite Construction Northeast Inc; **GRANITE CONSTRUCTION INC**
Granite Construction Supply; **GRANITE CONSTRUCTION INC**
Granite Land Company; **GRANITE CONSTRUCTION INC**
Granite Northwest Inc; **GRANITE CONSTRUCTION INC**
Grecam S.A.S.; **COSTAR GROUP INC**
GRI-EQY I LLC; **EQUITY ONE INC**
Group Aecon Quebec Ltee.; **AECON GROUP INC**
Grubb & Ellis Apartment REIT, Inc.; **GRUBB & ELLIS CO**
Grubb & Ellis Co; **GRUBB & ELLIS REALTY INVESTORS LLC**

INDEX OF SUBSIDIARIES, BRAND NAMES AND AFFILIATIONS, CONT.

INDEX OF SUBSIDIARIES, BRAND NAMES AND AFFILIATIONS, CONT.

INDEX OF SUBSIDIARIES, BRAND NAMES AND AFFILIATIONS, CONT.

Hypo Real Estate Capital Corp.; **HYPO REAL ESTATE HOLDING AG (HYPO BANK)**
Hypo Real Estate Capital India Corp. Private Ltd.; **HYPO REAL ESTATE HOLDING AG (HYPO BANK)**
Hypo Real Estate Capital Japan Corporation; **HYPO REAL ESTATE HOLDING AG (HYPO BANK)**
Hypo Real Estate Transactions S.A.S.; **HYPO REAL ESTATE HOLDING AG (HYPO BANK)**
Hyundai Corporation; **HYUNDAI ELEVATOR CO LTD**
Hyundai Engineering Co., Ltd.; **HYUNDAI ENGINEERING & CONSTRUCTION COMPANY LTD**
Ibis; **ACCOR NORTH AMERICA**
ICA Fluor; **EMPRESAS ICA SA DE CV**
i-CABLE Communications; **WHEELOCK AND COMPANY LIMITED**
i-Cable Communications Limited; **WHARF (HOLDINGS) LIMITED, THE**
Icon Vallarta; **RELATED GROUP (THE)**
IDI Investment Management; **INDUSTRIAL DEVELOPMENTS INTERNATIONAL INC**
IGLI SpA; **IMPREGILO SPA**
IMH Assets Corp.; **IMPAC MORTGAGE HOLDINGS INC**
Impac Commercial Capital Corporation; **IMPAC MORTGAGE HOLDINGS INC**
Impac Funding Corporation; **IMPAC MORTGAGE HOLDINGS INC**
Impac Secured Assets Corp.; **IMPAC MORTGAGE HOLDINGS INC**
Impac Warehouse Lending Group Inc.; **IMPAC MORTGAGE HOLDINGS INC**
Income Opportunity Realty Investors Inc; **TRANSCONTINENTAL REALTY INVESTORS INC**
Independent Living Program; **ATRIA SENIOR LIVING GROUP**
Indian Hotels Company Ltd. (The); **INDIAN HOTELS COMPANY LIMITED (THE)**
Indianapolis Marriott Downtown; **LASALLE HOTEL PROPERTIES**
IndiTravel Private Limited; **INDIAN HOTELS COMPANY LIMITED (THE)**
Industrial Design and Construction; **CH2M HILL COMPANIES LTD**
Industrial Income Trust; **DIVIDEND CAPITAL GROUP LLC**
Industrial Water Treatment Processes; **LAYNE CHRISTENSEN COMPANY**
Infrastructure & Environment; **URS CORPORATION**
ING Clarion; **GABLES RESIDENTIAL TRUST**
Inland American Industrial Management LLC; **INLAND AMERICAN REAL ESTATE TRUST INC**
Inland American Lodging Corporation; **INLAND AMERICAN REAL ESTATE TRUST INC**
Inland American Office Management LLC; **INLAND AMERICAN REAL ESTATE TRUST INC**
Inland American Orchard Hotels, Inc; **INLAND AMERICAN REAL ESTATE TRUST INC**
Inland American Retail Management LLC; **INLAND AMERICAN REAL ESTATE TRUST INC**
Inland American Urban Hotels, Inc; **INLAND AMERICAN REAL ESTATE TRUST INC**
Inland American Winston Hotels, Inc; **INLAND AMERICAN REAL ESTATE TRUST INC**
Inland Real Estate Group of Companies Inc (The); **INLAND AMERICAN REAL ESTATE TRUST INC**
Inland Real Estate Group of Companies Inc (The); **INLAND REAL ESTATE CORPORATION**
Inn at Perry Cabin (The); **ORIENT-EXPRESS HOTELS LTD**
Innovative Senior Care; **BROOKDALE SENIOR LIVING INC**
Innovative Steam Technologies, Inc.; **AECON GROUP INC**
Insight Equity Holdings LLC; **MEADOW VALLEY CORPORATION**
Insitu Envirotech (S.E. Asia) Pte Ltd.; **INSITUFORM TECHNOLOGIES**
Insituform Blue; **INSITUFORM TECHNOLOGIES**
Insituform CIPP Process; **INSITUFORM TECHNOLOGIES**
Integrated Real Estate Service Corporation; **IMPAC MORTGAGE HOLDINGS INC**
InterContinental; **STRATEGIC HOTELS & RESORTS INC**
InterContinental Hotels and Resorts; **INTERCONTINENTAL HOTELS GROUP PLC**
Intermountain Slurry Seal Inc; **GRANITE CONSTRUCTION INC**
International Hardwood Resource; **ANDERSON-TULLY LUMBER COMPANY**
International Housing Solutions; **MUNICIPAL MORTGAGE & EQUITY**
Interstate China Hotels & Resorts; **INTERSTATE HOTELS & RESORTS INC**
Interstate Hotels and Resorts Inc; **SUNSTONE HOTEL INVESTORS INC**
Intevras Technologies, LLC; **LAYNE CHRISTENSEN COMPANY**
Investment Management Program; **HCP INC**
Investors Capital Management Company; **INVESTORS TITLE COMPANY**
Investors Title Accommodation Corporation (ITAC); **INVESTORS TITLE COMPANY**
Investors Title Exchange Corporation (ITEC); **INVESTORS TITLE COMPANY**
Investors Title Insurance Company (ITIC); **INVESTORS TITLE COMPANY**

INDEX OF SUBSIDIARIES, BRAND NAMES AND AFFILIATIONS, CONT.

INDEX OF SUBSIDIARIES, BRAND NAMES AND AFFILIATIONS, CONT.

INDEX OF SUBSIDIARIES, BRAND NAMES AND AFFILIATIONS, CONT.

INDEX OF SUBSIDIARIES, BRAND NAMES AND AFFILIATIONS, CONT.

INDEX OF SUBSIDIARIES, BRAND NAMES AND AFFILIATIONS, CONT.

INDEX OF SUBSIDIARIES, BRAND NAMES AND AFFILIATIONS, CONT.

INDEX OF SUBSIDIARIES, BRAND NAMES AND AFFILIATIONS, CONT.

INDEX OF SUBSIDIARIES, BRAND NAMES AND AFFILIATIONS, CONT.

INDEX OF SUBSIDIARIES, BRAND NAMES AND AFFILIATIONS, CONT.

INDEX OF SUBSIDIARIES, BRAND NAMES AND AFFILIATIONS, CONT.

INDEX OF SUBSIDIARIES, BRAND NAMES AND AFFILIATIONS, CONT.

INDEX OF SUBSIDIARIES, BRAND NAMES AND AFFILIATIONS, CONT.

INDEX OF SUBSIDIARIES, BRAND NAMES AND AFFILIATIONS, CONT.

INDEX OF SUBSIDIARIES, BRAND NAMES AND AFFILIATIONS, CONT.